T0189289

Lecture Notes in Computer Science　　10393

Commenced Publication in 1973
Founding and Former Series Editors:
Gerhard Goos, Juris Hartmanis, and Jan van Leeuwen

More information about this series at http://www.springer.com/series/7407

Shadi Ibrahim · Kim-Kwang Raymond Choo
Zheng Yan · Witold Pedrycz (Eds.)

Algorithms and Architectures for Parallel Processing

17th International Conference, ICA3PP 2017
Helsinki, Finland, August 21–23, 2017
Proceedings

 Springer

Editors
Shadi Ibrahim
Inria
Rennes
France

Zheng Yan
Aalto University
Espoo
Finland

Kim-Kwang Raymond Choo
University of Texas at San Antonio
San Antonio, TX
USA

Witold Pedrycz
University of Alberta
Edmonton, AB
Canada

ISSN 0302-9743   ISSN 1611-3349   (electronic)
Lecture Notes in Computer Science
ISBN 978-3-319-65481-2   ISBN 978-3-319-65482-9   (eBook)
DOI 10.1007/978-3-319-65482-9

Library of Congress Control Number: 2017948181

LNCS Sublibrary: SL1 – Theoretical Computer Science and General Issues

Printed on acid-free paper

This Springer imprint is published by Springer Nature
The registered company is Springer International Publishing AG
The registered company address is: Gewerbestrasse 11, 6330 Cham, Switzerland

Preface

Welcome to the proceedings of the 17th International Conference on Algorithms and Architectures for Parallel Processing (ICA3PP 2017), held in Helsinki, Finland, during August 21–23, 2017. ICA3PP 2017 was hosted by Aalto University and co-hosted by Xidian University, ISN – State Key Laboratory of Integrated Services Networks of Xidian University, Federation of Finnish Learned Societies, TEKES – the Finnish Funding Agency for Innovation, and the National 111 Project on Mobile Internet Security of China (Xidian University). The conference would not have been possible without the support of the hosts, Nokia for their Gold Patron support, the research community, and many other stakeholders.

ICA3PP 2017 was in its 17th year, which started out as a conference devoted to research on algorithms and architectures for parallel processing. Previous iterations of this conference include ICA3PP 2016 (Granada, Spain, December 2016), ICA3PP 2015 (Zhangjiajie, China, November 2015), ICA3PP 2014 (Dalian, China, August 2014), ICA3PP 2013 (Vietri sul Mare, Italy, December 2013), ICA3PP 2012 (Fukuoka, Japan, September 2012), ICA3PP 2011 (Melbourne, Australia, October 2011), ICA3PP 2010 (Busan, Korea, May 2010), ICA3PP 2009 (Taipei, Taiwan, June 2009), ICA3PP 2008 (Cyprus, June 2008), ICA3PP 2007 (Hangzhou, China, June 2007), ICA3PP 2005 (Melbourne, Australia, October 2005), ICA3PP 2002 (Beijing, China, October 2002), ICA3PP 2000 (Hong Kong, China, December 2000), ICA3PP 1997 (Melbourne, Australia, December 1997), ICA3PP 1996 (Singapore, June 1996), and ICA3PP 1995 (Brisbane, Australia, April 1995).

ICA3PP is now recognized as a mainstream event covering the many dimensions of parallel algorithms and architectures, encompassing fundamental theoretical approaches, practical experimental projects, and commercial/industry applications. As computing systems and applications permeate every aspect of our daily life, the role of computing systems and the underlying components (e.g., applications) will be increasingly critical in ensuring the stability of our society. This conference provides a forum for academics and practitioners from different countries and (sub) disciplines to exchange ideas for improving the efficiency, performance, reliability, security, and interoperability of computing systems and applications.

This year, the conference received 93 submissions. Each submission was reviewed by three or more experts in the relevant areas for each paper, on the basis of their significance, novelty, technical quality, presentation, and practical impact. After an intense post-review discussion by the Program Committee, 25 papers were selected for presentation at the conference and included in this Springer volume (i.e., acceptance rate of 26.8%). In addition to the regular paper presentations, the program of the conference included eight keynote speeches from, esteemed scholars in the area, namely: Prof. Elisa Bertino, Purdue University, USA; Prof. Francisco Herrera, University of Granada, Spain; Dr. Anand Prasad, NEC Corporation, Japan; Prof. Laurence T. Yang, St. Francis Xavier University, Canada; Prof. Shiwen Mao,

Auburn University, Auburn AL, USA; Prof. Jinjun Chen, Swinburne University of Technology, Australia; Mr. Tatu Ylönen, SSH Communications Security, USA and Lauri Oksanen, Vice President of Research and Technology, Nokia Bell Labs, Finland. We were extremely honored to have them as the conference keynote speakers.

The ICA3PP 2017 program also included four workshops, namely: the 4th International Workshop on Data, Text, Web, and Social Network Mining (DTWSM 2017), the 5th International Workshop on Parallelism in Bioinformatics (PBio 2017), the First International Workshop on Distributed Autonomous Computing in Smart City (DACSC 2017), and the Second International Workshop on Ultrascale Computing for Early Researchers (UCER 2017). We would like to express our sincere appreciation to the workshop chairs: Prof. Jun Liu, Prof. Zheng Yan, Dr. Miguel A. Vega-Rodríguez, Dr. José M. Granado-Criado, Dr. Alvaro Rubio-Largo, Dr. Sergio Santander-Jiménez, Prof. Wendong Wang, Dr. Yan Chen, Prof. Riku Jäntti, Dr. Yu Xiao, Prof. Jesus Carretero, Prof. Pedro Alonso, Dr. Juan Durillo, and Dr. Fabrizio Marozzo.

ICA3PP 2017 was also made possible by the behind-the-scene effort of selfless individuals and organizations who volunteered their time and energy to ensure the success of this conference. We would like to acknowledge the track chairs of the conference for their hard and excellent work in organizing the Program Committee. We are grateful to all Program Committee members for their great efforts in reading, reviewing, discussing, and finally selecting the papers. We also thank all external reviewers for assisting the Program Committee in their particular areas of expertise.

We also thank the honorary chair, Prof. Xinbo Gao, Xidian University, China, for his support in the conference organization. We would like to emphasize our gratitude to the general chairs, Prof. Zheng Yan, Prof. Witold Pedrycz, and Prof. Geoffrey Fox; and the program chairs, Dr. Shadi Ibrahim, Prof. Kim-Kwang Raymond Choo, and Prof. Florin Pop, for their generous support and leadership that ensured the success of the conference. We also appreciate Miss Wenxiu Ding's assistance with the conference organization. Thanks also go to the: panel chair, Yan Zhang; publicity chair, Prof. Raimo Kantola; Steering Committee, Prof. Yang Xiang, Prof. Weijia Jia, Prof. Yi Pan, Prof. Laurence T. Yang, and Prof. Wanlei Zhou; Web chairs, Mr. Mingjun Wang and Mr. Mohsin Muhammad.

Lastly, the conference would not have been possible without the contributing authors and all conference attendees, as well as the staff at Springer, who assisted in producing the conference proceedings, and the developers and maintainers of EasyChair.

August 2017   Shadi Ibrahim
                                                  Kim-Kwang Raymond Choo
                                                             Zheng Yan
                                                          Witold Pedrycz

ICA3PP 2017 Organization

Honorary Chair

Xinbo Gao   Xidian University, China

General Chairs

Zheng Yan   Xidian University, China
Witold Pedrycz   Alberta University, Canada
Geoffrey Fox   Indiana University, USA

Program Chairs

Shadi Ibrahim   Inria, France
Kim-Kwang Raymond   University of Texas at San Antonio, USA
  Choo
Florin Pop   University Politehnica of Bucharest, Romania

Panel Chair

Yan Zhang   University of Oslo, Norway

Workshop Chairs

Jun Liu   Xi'an Jiaotong University, China
KP Lam   Keele University, UK

Publication Chair

Peng Zhang   Zalando, Finland

Publicity Chair

Wenxiu Ding   Xidian University, China

Local and Finance Chair

Raimo Kantola   Aalto University, Finland

Steering Committee

Yang Xiang   Deakin University, Australia (Chair)
Weijia Jia   Shanghai Jiaotong University, China
Yi Pan   Georgia State University, USA
Laurence T. Yang   St. Francis Xavier University, Canada
Wanlei Zhou   Deakin University, Australia

Web Chairs

Mingjun Wang   Xidian University, China
Mohsin Muhammad   Aalto University, Finland

Track Chairs

Guillaume Aupy   Inria, France
Jing Chen   Wuhan University, China
Gene Cooperman   Northeastern University, USA
Marc Frîncu   West University of Timisoara, Romania
Javier Garcia-Blas   University Carlos III of Madrid, Spain
Julian Kunkel   German Climate Computing Center, Germany
Laurent Lefèvre   Inria, France
Haikun Liu   Huazhong University of Science and Technology,
                       China
Ting Liu   Xi'an Jiaotong University, China
Yining Liu   Guilin University of Electronic Technology, China
Anne-Cécile Orgerie CNRS, France
Zhonghong Ou   BUPT, China
Etienne Rivière   Université de Neuchâtel, Switzerland
Domenico Talia   University of Calabria, Italy
Xueyan Tang   Nanyang Technological University, Singapore
Tomoaki Tsumura   Nagoya Institute of Technology, Japan
Yu Xiao   Aalto University, Finland
Yanjiang Yang   Huawei Research Center, Singapore

Technical Program Committee

Marco Aldinucci   University of Torino, Italy
Cosimo Anglano   Universitá del Piemonte Orientale, Italy
Kapil Arya   Mesosphere Inc., USA
Marcos Assuncao   Inria - ENS Lyon, France
Man Ho Au   Hong Kong Polytechnic University, SAR China
Joonsang Baek   Khalifa University of Science, Technology and
                       Research, UAE
Jorge Barbosa   FEUP, Portugal
Anirban Basu   KDDI Research, Japan

Leonardo Bautista-Gomez	Barcelona Supercomputing Center, Spain
Sourav Bhattacharya	Nokia Bell Labs, Ireland
Vicente Blanco	La Laguna University, Spain
Javier Garcia Blas	Carlos III University, Spain
Thomas Bönisch	High Performance Computing Center Stuttgart, Germany
George Bosilca	University of Tennessee, USA
Pascal Bouvry	University of Luxembourg, Luxembourg
Andre Brinkmann	Johannes Gutenberg-Universität Mainz, Germany
Lei Bu	Nanjing University, China
Massimo Cafaro	University of Salento, Italy
Philip Carns	Argonne National Laboratory, USA
Alexandra Carpen-Amarie	Vienna University of Technology, Austria
Eugenio Cesario	ICAR-CNR, Italy
Wei Chang	Saint Joseph's university, USA
Jerry H. Chang	National Center for High-performance Computing, Taiwan
Jinfu Chen	Jiangsu University, China
Min Chen	Huazhong University of Science and Technology, China
Taolue Chen	Middlesex University London, UK
Wei Chen	Institute of Software Chinese Academy of Sciences, China
Yu Chen	State University of New York - Binghamton, USA
Feng Chen	Louisiana State University, USA
Yueqiang Cheng	Acetti Software Inc., USA
Houssem Chihoub	Grenoble Institute of Technology (Grenoble INP), France
Johanne Cohen	LRI-CNRS, France
Gene Cooperman	Northeastern University, USA
Jose Alfredo Ferreira Costa	Federal University - UFRN, Brazil
Raphaël Couturier	University Bourgogne Franche-Comté, France
Felix Cuadrado	Queen Mary University of London, UK
Bogusław Cyganek	AGH University of Science and Technology, Poland
Gregoire Danoy	University of Luxembourg, Luxembourg
Frederic Desprez	Inria, France
Aaron Yi Ding	Technical University of Munich, Germany
Matthieu Dorier	Argonne National Laboratory, USA
Yucong Duan	Hainan University, China
Fanny Dufossé	Inria, France
Avgoustinos Filippoupolitis	University of Greenwich, UK
Holger Fröning	University of Heidelberg, Germany
Ana Gainaru	Mellanox Inc., USA
Paolo Gasti	New York Institute of Technology, USA
Stéphane Genaud	Inria, France
Vladimir Getov	University of Westminster, UK

Olivier Gluck	Université de Lyon, France
Jing Gong	KTH Royal Institute of Technology, Sweden
Daniel Grosu	Wayne State University, USA
Amina Guermouche	Telecom Sud-Paris, France
Yanfei Guo	Argonne National Laboratory, USA
Jeff Hammond	Intel, USA
Jinguang Han	Nanjing University of Finance and Economics, China
Junwei Han	Northwestern Polytechnical University, China
Houcine Hassan	Universitat Politecnica de Valencia, Spain
Daojing He	East China Normal University, China
Weimin He	University of Wisconsin-Stevens Point, USA
Judith Hill	Oak Ridge National Laboratory, USA
Liting Hu	Florida International University, USA
Zhiyi Huang	University of Otago, New Zealand
Yasuaki Ito	Hiroshima University, Japan
Mathias Jacquelin	Lawrence Berkeley National Laboratory, USA
Shouling Ji	Zhejiang University, China
Rongrong Ji	Xiamen University, China
Yu Jiang	University of Illinois at Urbana-Champaign, USA
Krzysztof Kaczmarski	Warsaw University of Technology, Poland
Helen Karatza	Aristotle University of Thessaloniki, Greece
Gabor Kecskemeti	Liverpool John Moores University, UK
Michael Kluge	ZIH - TU Dresden, Germany
Sokol Kosta	Aalborg University, Denmark
Dieter Kranzlmüller	Ludwig-Maximilians-Universität München, Germany
Atsushi Kubota	Hiroshima City University, Japan
Michael Kuhn	University of Hamburg, Germany
Pierre Kuonen	University of Applied Sciences of Western Switzerland, Switzerland
Sebastien Lafond	Åbo Akademi University, Finland
Junzuo Lai	Jinan University, China
Algirdas Lančinskas	Vilnius University, Lithuania
Ken Laskey	The MITRE Corporation (McLean, VA), USA
Artur Lasoń	AGH University of Science and Technology, Poland
Che-Rung Lee	National Tsing Hua University, Taiwan
Arnaud Legrand	CNRS, France
Peng Li	The University of Aizu, Japan
Chuanyou Li	Nanyang Technological University, Singapore
Dingding Li	South China Normal University, China
Guoqiang Li	Shanghai Jiao Tong University, China
Kaitai Liang	Manchester Metropolitan University, UK
Ruixuan Li	Huazhong University of Science and Technology, China
Yusen Li	Nankai University, China
Meiyu Liang	Beijing University of Posts and Telecommunications, China

Fang-Pang Lin	National Center for High-Performance Computing, Taiwan
Zhen Ling	Southeast University, China
Joseph Liu	Monash University, USA
Wu Liu	Beijing University of Posts and Telecommunications, China
Jaime Lloret	Universidad Politécnica de Valencia, Spain
Jay Lofstead	Sandia National Laboratories, USA
Jiqiang Lu	Institute for Infocomm Research, Singapore
Haibing Lu	Santa Clara University, USA
Xiaoqiang Lu	Chinese Academy of Sciences, China
Amit Majumdar	University of California San Diego - San Diego Supercomputer Center, USA
Manolis Marazakis	Institute of Computer Science - FORTH, Greece
Stefano Markidis	KTH Royal Institute of Technology, Sweden
Weizhi Meng	Technical University of Denmark, Denmark
Qiguang Miao	Xidian University, China
Sonia Ben Mokhtar	CNRS, France
Sébastien Monnet	University Savoie Mont Blanc, France
Raffaele Montella	University of Naples Parthenope and Computation Institute, Italy
Miguel Cárdenas Montes	CIEMAT, Spain
Sai Narasimhamurthy	Seagate, UK
Pablo Neira Ayuso	Universidad de Sevilla, Spain
Esmond Ng	Lawrence Berkeley National Laboratory, USA
Edith C.H. Ngai	Uppsala University, Sweden
Bogdan Nicolae	Huawei Research Germany, Germany
Petteri Nurmi	University of Helsinki, Finland
Kazuhiko Ohno	Mie University, Japan
Shaoliang Peng	National University of Defense Technology, China
Yanwei Pang	Tianji University, China
Swann Perarnau	Argonne National Laboratory, USA
Hector Perez	Universidad de Cantabria, Spain
Maria S. Perez	Universidad Politecnica de Madrid, Spain
Dana Petcu	West University of Timisoara, Romania
Riccardo Petrolo	Rice University, USA
Florin Pop	University Politehnica of Bucharest, Romania
Radu Prodan	University of Innsbruck, Austria
Lingjun Pu	Nankai University, China
Ying Qian	East China Normal University, China
Ioan Raicu	Illinois Institute of Technology, USA
Weixiong Rao	Tongji University, China
Thomas Rauber	University of Bayreuth, Germany
Seungmin (Charlie) Rho	Sungkyul University, Korea
Suzanne Rivoire	Sonoma State University, USA
Ivan Rodero	Rutgers - The State University of New Jersey, USA

Gabriel Rodríguez	Universidade da Coruña, Spain
Paul Roe	QUT, Australia
Romain Rouvoy	University of Lille/Inria/IUF, France
Françoise Sailhan	CNAM, France
Sherif Sakr	The University of New South Wales, Australia
Bertie Schmidt	University of Mainz, Germany
Manu Shantharam	San Diego Supercomputer Center, USA
Jun Shao	Zhejiang Gongshang University, China
Pieter Simoens	Ghent University - imec, Belgium
Ben Smyth	Huawei, France
Patricia Stolf	IRIT, France
John Stone	University of Illinois at Urbana-Champaign, USA
Aaron Striegel	University of Notre Dame, USA
Chunhua Su	Osaka University, Japan
Hari Subramoni	The Ohio State University, USA
Hongyang Sun	Vanderbilt University, USA
Frederic Suter	CNRS, France
Shanjiang Tang	Tianjin University, China
Dan Tao	Beijing Jiaotong University, China
Zhenzhou Tian	Xi'an University of Posts and Telecommunications, China
Jerry Trahan	Louisiana State University, Baton Rouge, USA
Paolo Trunfio	DEIS, University of Calabria, Italy
Yuichi Tsujita	RIKEN AICS, Japan
Radu Tudoran	HUAWEI ERC, Germany
Geoffroy Vallee	ORNL, USA
Sebastien Varrette	University of Luxembourg, Luxembourg
Vladimir Vlassov	Royal Institute of Technology (KTH), Sweden
Chongjun Wang	Nanjing University, China
Haijun Wang	Chinese Academy of Sciences, China
Li Wang	Beijing University of Posts and Telecommunications, China
Liang Wang	University of Cambridge, UK
Ren Wang	Intel Corp, USA
Wendong Wang	Beijing University of Posts and Telecommunications, China
Yipeng Wang	Intel labs, USA
Yunsheng Wang	Kettering University, USA
Zeke Wang	National University of Singapore, Singapore
Zheng Wei	Northwest Polytechnic University, China
Roman Wyrzykowski	Czestochowa University of Technology, Poland
Yinglong Xia	Huawei Research America, USA
Xiaolan Xie	Guilin University of Technology, China
Quanqing Xu	Data Storage Institute - A*STAR, Singapore
Wei Xu	Tsinghua University, China
Ramin Yahyapour	GWDG - University of Göttingen, Germany

Hayato Yamaki	University of Electro-Communications, Japan
Da Yan	The University of Alabama at Birmingham, USA
Shoumeng Yan	Intel, China
Qiliang Yang	PLA University of Science and Technology, China
Qing Yang	Montana State University, USA
Wun-She Yap	Universiti Tunku Abdul Rahman, Malaysia
Peter Yoon	Trinity College, USA
Masato Yoshimi	University of Electro-Communications, Japan
Yong Yu	Shaanxi Normal University, China
Yue Yu	National University of Defense Technology, China
Quan Yuan	University of Texas-Permian Basin, USA
Tsz Hon Yuen	Huawei Singapore, Singapore
Haitao Zhang	Lanzhou University, China
Tao Zhang	Harbin Engineering University, China
Xinpeng Zhang	Shanghai University, China
Zhaoxiang Zhang	Chinese Academy of Sciences, China
Dong Zhao	Beijing University of Posts and Telecommunications, China
Yunhui Zheng	IBM T.J. Watson Research Center, USA
Jianlong Zhong	GRAPHSQL Inc., USA
Amelie Chi Zhou	Inria, France
Anfu Zhou	Beijing University of Posts and Telecommunications, China

External Reviewers

Yutong Ai	Xiang Ling
Mohamad Al Hajj Hassan	Ximeng Liu
Abbas Arghavani	Roland Mathà
Tayebeh Bahreini	Gabriele Mencagli
Fu Cai	Maxime Meyer
Jin Cao	Claudia Misale
Daniele De Sensi	Nader Mohamed
Mathieu Faverge	Pablo Neira
Laleh Ghalami	Kazumasa Omote
Tobias Guggemos	Tien-Dat Phan
Cheng Guo	Nicholas Rodofile
Ye Guodong	Nishant Saurabh
Jinguang Han	Dong Su
Matthias Hauck	Cong Tian
Xiaoying Jia	Wufeng Tian
Yichen Jia	Zheng Wang
Rubao Lee	Zhe Xia

Tao Xiang	Pengfei Zhang
Xiaolan Xie	Xiaojian Zhang
Jianxin Xue	Xinpeng Zhang
Anjia Yang	Zijian Zhang
Chung-Huang Yang	Jieyi Zhao
Orcun Yildiz	Amelie Chi Zhou
Xie Yong	

DTWSM2017 Organization

Workshop Organizers

Jun Liu	Xi'an Jiaotong University, China
Zheng Yan	Xidian University, China/Aalto University, Finland

Technical Program Committee

Ari Visa	Tampere University of Technology, Finland
Bifan Wei	Xi'an Jiaotong University, China
Garimella Rama Murthy	The International Institute of Information Technology, Hyderabad (IIIT-H), India
Haifei Max Li	Union University, USA
Hao Chen	Xi'an Jiaotong University, China
Jiang Zheng	ABB US Corporate Research Center, USA
József Mezei	Åbo Akademi University, Finland
Qingtang Liu	Central China Normal University, China
Susanna Pirttikangas	University of Oulu, Finland
Tianrui Li	Southwest Jiaotong University, China
Wei Zhang	Amazon Inc., USA
Weizhan Zhang	Xi'an Jiaotong University, China
Xia Sun	Northwest University, China
Xiaohua Tony Hu	Drexel University, USA
Ye Tian	China Internet Network Information Center (CNNIC), China
Yoan Miche	Nokia Inc., Finland
Zhe Guo	Huawei Inc., China

PBio 2017 Organization

Workshop Organizers

Miguel A. Vega-Rodríguez	University of Extremadura, Spain
José M. Granado-Criado	University of Extremadura, Spain
Alvaro Rubio-Largo	University Nova of Lisbon, Portugal
Sergio Santander-Jiménez	University of Extremadura, Spain

Technical Program Committee

Antonio Gómez-Iglesias	Texas Advanced Computing Center, USA
Beatriz Paniagua	Kitware, USA
César Gómez-Martín	University of Extremadura, Spain
David L. González-Álvarez	University of Extremadura, Spain
Francisco Prieto-Castrillo	MIT (Massachusetts Institute of Technology), USA
María Arsuaga-Ríos	CERN, Switzerland
María Botón-Fernández	Institute Suarez de Figueroa, Spain
Marisa da Silva Maximiano	Polytechnic Institute of Leiria, Portugal
Miguel Cárdenas-Montes	CIEMAT, Spain
Sónia M. Almeida-Luz	Polytechnic Institute of Leiria, Portugal
Víctor Berrocal-Plaza	AOIFES, Spain

DACSC 2017 Organization

Workshop Organizers

Wendong Wang	Beijing University of Posts and Telecommunications, China
Yan Chen	Beijing University of Posts and Telecommunications, China
Riku Jäntti	Aalto University, Finland
Yu Xiao	Aalto University, Finland

Technical Program Committee

Edith C.H. Ngai	Uppsala University, Sweden
Hengshu Zhu	Baidu, China
Jiujun Cheng	Tongji University, China
Sigg Stephan	Aalto University, Finland
Themistoklis Charalambous	Aalto University, Finland
Xiangyang Gong	Beijing University of Posts and Telecommunications, China
Yang Chen	Fudan University, China
Yannan Hu	IBM, China
Ye Tian	Beijing University of Posts and Telecommunications, China
Yong Li	Tsinghua University, China

UCER 2017 Organization

Workshop Organizers

Jesus Carretero	University Carlos III of Madrid, Spain
Pedro Alonso	UP Valencia, Spain
Juan Durillo	University of Innsbruck, Austria
Fabrizio Marozzo	University of Calabria, Italy

Technical Program Committee

Eugenio Cesario	ICAR-CNR, Italy
Biagio Cosenza	TU Berlin, Germany
Grégoire Danoy	University of Luxembourg, Luxembourg
Manuel F. Dolz	University Carlos III of Madrid, Spain
Gábor Kecskeméti	Liverpool John Moores University, UK
Daniele Lezzi	BSC, Spain
Hugo Daniel Meyer	BSC, Spain
Sergio Nesmachnow	Universidad de la Republica, Uruguay
José Ranilla	University of Oviedo, Spain
Juan Antonio Rico	University of Extremadura, Spain
Krzysztof Rojek	Czestochowa University of Technology, Poland

Contents

Parallel and Distributed Architectures

Workload Type-Aware Scheduling on big.LITTLE Platforms   3
  Simon Holmbacka and Jörg Keller

Pipelining Computation and Optimization Strategies for Scaling
GROMACS on the Sunway Many-Core Processor 18
  Yang Yu, Hong An, Junshi Chen, Weihao Liang, Qingqing Xu,
  and Yong Chen

Exploring FPGA-GPU Heterogeneous Architecture for ADAS:
Towards Performance and Energy 33
  Xiebing Wang, Linlin Liu, Kai Huang, and Alois Knoll

Software Systems and Programming Models

Hzmem: New Huge Page Allocator with Main Memory Compression 51
  Guoxi Li, Wenzhi Chen, Kui Su, Zhongyong Lu, and Zonghui Wang

An FPGA-Based Real-Time Moving Object Tracking Approach 65
  Wenjie Chen, Yangyang Ma, Zhilei Chai, Mingsong Chen,
  and Daojing He

Automatic Acceleration of Stencil Codes in Android Devices 81
  Sergio Afonso, Alejandro Acosta, and Francisco Almeida

Distributed and Network-based Computing

Optimizing Concurrent Evacuation Transfers for Geo-Distributed
Datacenters in SDN. 99
  Xiaole Li, Hua Wang, Shanwen Yi, Xibo Yao, Fangjin Zhu,
  and Linbo Zhai

Energy-Balanced and Depth-Controlled Routing Protocol for Underwater
Wireless Sensor Networks 115
  Hao Qin, Zhiyong Zhang, Rui Wang, Xiaojun Cai, and Zhiping Jia

On the Energy Efficiency of Sleeping and Rate Adaptation
for Network Devices 132
  Timothée Haudebourg and Anne-Cécile Orgerie

Big Data and its Applications

Private and Efficient Set Intersection Protocol for Big Data Analytics   149
  Zakaria Gheid and Yacine Challal

A Topology-Aware Framework for Graph Traversals.   165
  Jia Meng, Liang Cao, and Huashan Yu

Adaptive Traffic Signal Control with Network-Wide Coordination   180
  Yong Chen, Juncheng Yao, Chunjiang He, Hanhua Chen, and Hai Jin

Parallel and Distributed Algorithms

A Novel Parallel Dual-Character String Matching Algorithm on Graphical
Processing Units.   197
  Chung-Yu Liao and Cheng-Hung Lin

Distributed Nonnegative Matrix Factorization with HALS
Algorithm on MapReduce   211
  Rafał Zdunek and Krzysztof Fonal

Applications of Parallel and Distributed Computing

GPU-Accelerated Block-Max Query Processing   225
  *Haibing Huang, Mingming Ren, Yue Zhao, Rebecca J. Stones,
  Rui Zhang, Gang Wang, and Xiaoguang Liu*

KD-Tree and HEALPix-Based Distributed Cone Search Indexing System
for Multi-Band Astronomical Catalogs.   239
  *Chen Li, Ce Yu, Jian Xiao, Xiaoteng Hu, Hao Fu, Kun Li,
  and Yanyan Huang*

An Out-of-Core Branch and Bound Method for Solving the 0-1 Knapsack
Problem on a GPU   254
  *Jingcheng Shen, Kentaro Shigeoka, Fumihiko Ino,
  and Kenichi Hagihara*

The Curve Boundary Design and Performance Analysis for DGM
Based on OpenFOAM.   268
  *Yongquan Feng, Xinhai Xu, Yuhua Tang, Liyang Xu,
  and Yongjun Zhang*

Service Dependability and Security in Distributed and Parallel Systems

Leakage-Resilient Password-Based Authenticated Key Exchange.   285
  Ou Ruan, Mingwu Zhang, and Jing Chen

Secure Encrypted Data Deduplication with Ownership Proof
and User Revocation   297
   Wenxiu Ding, Zheng Yan, and Robert H. Deng

Optimally Selecting the Timing of Zero-Day Attack via Spatial
Evolutionary Game   313
   Yanwei Sun, Lihua Yin, Yunchuan Guo, Fenghua Li, and Binxing Fang

Performance Modeling and Evaluation

Performance Analysis of a Ternary Optical Computer Based
on M/M/1 Queueing System.   331
   XianChao Wang, Sulan Zhang, Mian Zhang, Jia Zhao,
   and Xiangyang Niu

Efficient Computation Offloading for Various Tasks of Multiple Users in
Mobile Edge Clouds   345
   Weiyu Liu, Xiangming Wen, Zhaoming Lu, Luning Liu, and Xin Chen

A CNN-Based Supermarket Auto-Counting System.   359
   Zhonghong Ou, Changwei Lin, Meina Song, and Haihong E

Research and Implementation of Question Classification Model
in Q&A System   372
   Haihong E, Yingxi Hu, Meina Song, Zhonghong Ou, and Xinrui Wang

**The 4th International Workshop on Data, Text, Web, and Social
Network Mining (DTWSM 2017)**

An Android Malware Detection System Based on Behavior
Comparison Analysis.   387
   Jing Tao, Yan Zhang, Pengfei Cao, Zheng Wang, and Qiqi Zhao

Stream-Based Live Probabilistic Topic Computing and Matching   397
   Kun Ma, Ziqiang Yu, Ke Ji, and Bo Yang

Experiment for Analysing the Impact of Financial Events on Twitter.   407
   Ana Fernández-Vilas, Lewis Evans, Majdi Owda,
   Rebeca P. Díaz Redondo, and Keeley Crockett

APK-DFS: An Automatic Interaction System Based on Depth-First-Search
for APK.   420
   Jing Tao, Qiqi Zhao, Pengfei Cao, Zheng Wang, and Yan Zhang

Optimized Data Layout for Spatio-temporal Data in Time
Domain Astronomy   431
    Jie Yan, Ce Yu, Chao Sun, Zhaohui Shang, Yi Hu, Jinghua Feng,
    Jizhou Sun, and Jian Xiao

Cloud Multimedia Files Assured Deletion Based on Bit Stream
Transformation with Chaos Sequence   441
    Wenbin Yao, Yijie Chen, and Dongbin Wang

Interval Merging Binary Tree   452
    István Finta, Lóránt Farkas, Sándor Szénási, and Szabolcs Sergyán

Mining Suspicious Tax Evasion Groups in a Corporate
Governance Network   465
    Wenda Wei, Zheng Yan, Jianfei Ruan, Qinghua Zheng, and Bo Dong

PerRec: A Permission Configuration Recommender System
for Mobile Apps   476
    Yanxiao Cheng and Zheng Yan

The 5th International Workshop on Parallelism in Bioinformatics (PBio 2017)

A Resource Manager for Maximizing the Performance of Bioinformatics
Workflows in Shared Clusters.   489
    Ferran Badosa, César Acevedo, Antonio Espinosa, Gonzalo Vera,
    and Ana Ripoll

Massively Parallel Sequence Alignment with BLAST Through Work
Distribution Implemented Using PCJ Library   503
    Marek Nowicki, Davit Bzhalava, and Piotr Bała

On the Use of Binary Trees for DNA Hydroxymethylation Analysis   513
    César González, Mariano Pérez, Juan M. Orduña, Javier Chaves,
    and Ana-Bárbara García

Parallel Multi-objective Optimization for High-Order Epistasis Detection   523
    Daniel Gallego-Sánchez, José M. Granado-Criado,
    Sergio Santander-Jiménez, Álvaro Rubio-Largo,
    and Miguel A. Vega-Rodríguez

Configuring Concurrent Computation of Phylogenetic Partial Likelihoods:
Accelerating Analyses Using the BEAGLE Library   533
    Daniel L. Ayres and Michael P. Cummings

Accelerating FaST-LMM for Epistasis Tests.   548
    Héctor Martínez, Sergio Barrachina, Maribel Castillo,
    Enrique S. Quintana-Ortí, Jordi Rambla De Argila, Xavier Farré,
    and Arcadi Navarro

Pipelined Multi-FPGA Genomic Data Clustering.   558
  Rick Wertenbroek, Enrico Petraglio, and Yann Thoma

First Experiences Accelerating Smith-Waterman on Intel's Knights
Landing Processor.   569
  Enzo Rucci, Carlos Garcia, Guillermo Botella, Armando De Giusti,
  Marcelo Naiouf, and Manuel Prieto-Matias

Power-Performance Evaluation of Parallel Multi-objective EEG Feature
Selection on CPU-GPU Platforms   580
  Juan José Escobar, Julio Ortega, Antonio Francisco Díaz,
  Jesús González, and Miguel Damas

Using Spark and GraphX to Parallelize Large-Scale Simulations
of Bacterial Populations over Host Contact Networks   591
  Andreia Sofia Teixeira, Pedro T. Monteiro, João A. Carriço,
  Francisco C. Santos, and Alexandre P. Francisco

PPCAS: Implementation of a Probabilistic Pairwise Model for
Consistency-Based Multiple Alignment in Apache Spark   601
  Jordi Lladós, Fernando Guirado, and Fernando Cores

Accelerating Exhaustive Pairwise Metagenomic Comparisons   611
  Esteban Pérez-Wohlfeil, Oscar Torreno, and Oswaldo Trelles

**The First International Workshop on Distributed Autonomous
Computing in Smart City (DACSC 2017)**

The Impact of International Inter-City Investment on Enterprises
Performance: Pluralistic Interpretation of Geographical Death   623
  Yanghao Zhan, Yan Chen, and Ruirui Zhai

Energy Efficient Manycast Routing, Modulation Level and Spectrum
Assignment in Elastic Optical Networks for Smart City Applications.   633
  Xiao Luo, Xue Chen, and Lei Wang

An Advanced Random Forest Algorithm Targeting the Big Data with
Redundant Features   642
  Ying Zhang, Bin Song, Yue Zhang, and Sijia Chen

En-Eye: A Cooperative Video Fusion Framework for Traffic Safety in
Intelligent Transportation Systems.   652
  Tianhao Wu and Lin Zhang

Comparing Electricity Consumer Categories Based on Load Pattern
Clustering with Their Natural Types   658
  Zigui Jiang, Rongheng Lin, Fangchun Yang, Zhihan Liu,
  and Qiqi Zhang

When Clutter Reduction Meets Machine Learning for People Counting
Using IR-UWB Radar   668
  Xiuzhu Yang and Lin Zhang

Fine-Grained Infer $PM_{2.5}$ Using Images from Crowdsourcing   678
  Shuai Li, Teng Xi, Xirong Que, and Wendong Wang

Security/Reliability-Aware Relay Selection with Connection Duration
Constraints for Vehicular Networks   687
  Zhenyu Liu and Lin Zhang

Smart City Environmental Perception from Ambient Cellular Signals   695
  Isha Singh and Stephan Sigg

A Multi-task Oriented Selection Strategy for Efficient Cooperation of
Collocated Mobile Devices.   705
  Hui Gao, Jun Feng, Ruidong Wang, and Wendong Wang

Research on Properties of Nodes Distribution on Internet of Vehicles   715
  Cheng Jiujun, Shang Zheng, Mi Hao, Cheng Cheng,
  and Huang Zhenhua

Application of Batch and Stream Collaborative Computing in Urban
Traffic Data Processing   725
  Tao Zhang and Shuai Zhao

ESD-WSN: An Efficient SDN-Based Wireless Sensor Network
Architecture for IoT Applications   735
  Zhiwei Zhang, Zhiyong Zhang, Rui Wang, Zhiping Jia, Haijun Lei,
  and Xiaojun Cai

**The 2nd International Workshop on Ultrascale Computing for Early
Researchers (UCER 2017)**

Probabilistic-Based Selection of Alternate Implementations for
Heterogeneous Platforms   749
  Javier Fernández, Andrés Sánchez Cuadrado, David del Rio Astorga,
  Manuel F. Dolz, and J. Daniel García

Accelerating Processing of Scale-Free Graphs
on Massively-Parallel Architectures   759
  Mikhail Chernoskutov

A Hybrid Parallel Search Algorithm for Solving Combinatorial
Optimization Problems on Multicore Clusters   766
  Victoria Sanz, Armando De Giusti, and Marcelo Naiouf

Concurrent Treaps.   776
  Praveen Alapati, Swamy Saranam, and Madhu Mutyam

Survey on Energy-Saving Technologies for Disk-Based Storage Systems. . . .   791
  *Ce Yu, Jianmei Wang, Chao Sun, Xiaoxiao Lu, Jian Xiao,
  and Jizhou Sun*

The Open Community Runtime on the Intel Knights Landing Architecture   801
  Jiri Dokulil, Siegfried Benkner, and Jakub Yaghob

High-Performance Graphics in Racket with DirectX   814
  Antoine Bossard

Author Index   827

Parallel and Distributed Architectures

Workload Type-Aware Scheduling on big.LITTLE Platforms

Simon Holmbacka[1,2](✉) and Jörg Keller[2](✉)

[1] Faculty of Science and Engineering, Åbo Akademi University, Turku, Finland
sholmbac@abo.fi
[2] Faculty of Mathematics and Computer Science, FernUniversität in Hagen,
Hagen, Germany
joerg.keller@fernuni-hagen.de

Abstract. Optimizing energy efficiency in execution strategies has traditionally been heavily influenced by hardware mechanisms such as frequency scaling and core sleep states. With such facilities, the system can be scaled dynamically and on-demand to trade power dissipation for clock speed or parallelism. Determining the most efficient execution configuration has been described in much related work, but few efforts have been put on including the workload type into the calculation. The type of the workload affects both the performance and the power of the processor, and is especially important when considering heterogeneous systems like the big.LITTLE, since different cores handle the workload with different efficiency. In this paper, we demonstrate the influence of the workload type when choosing an optimal execution strategy on a big.LITTLE platform. We implement schedulers capable of including workload type, and we provide a runtime system capable of executing the schedules on a real-world platform. Results demonstrate that including workload types into the scheduler saves between 7.1% and 31.3% of energy in our best/worst corner case studies, a result that should be considered in future implementations of big.LITTLE schedulers.

1 Introduction

The debate about energy efficiency in computer systems is a phenomenon of argumentation related to execution strategies in all sizes of platforms from desktop- to cloud-, mobile- and IoT systems. Different strategies in executing the workload will affect the power dissipation and the performance of the processor, and it will hence affect the energy consumption. It is therefore of essence to find the most important parameters for making intelligent execution choices using scheduling and resource allocation.

Indeed, the primary driver in the debate around execution time vs. power dissipation has been clock frequency scaling. High or low clock frequency will consume different amounts of energy because of a difference in the execution time and power dissipation, which the application causes. This has led to the discussion about whether an application should execute fastly [2,16] (Race-to-Idle) to save execution time at the cost of increased power, or execute slowly [1,7,13,22] to save power at the cost of increased execution time.

© Springer International Publishing AG 2017
S. Ibrahim et al. (Eds.): ICA3PP 2017, LNCS 10393, pp. 3–17, 2017.
DOI: 10.1007/978-3-319-65482-9_1

While the debate focuses mostly on the hardware, less focus has been on tracing the causes of the power dissipation and the performance to the software executing on the hardware. In fact, different types of software utilize the hardware microarchitecture differently, thus giving cause to a varying power dissipation [23]. In modern heterogeneous multi-core systems, a new parameter is included in this energy optimization: the core type. Both core types are completely binary compatible, but the microarchitectures differ. The big core is equipped with out-of-order execution, deep pipelines and advanced instruction level parallelism, while the LITTLE core is in-order, has short pipelines and has very limited instruction level parallelism. Because the core types execute the workload in different ways, it leads to situations where applications execute at different relative performance levels depending on *how well* the core type is able to execute the stream of dispatched instructions. Different instructions and instruction sequences will stress different engines inside the processor, and hence the power dissipation and the performance is directly dependent on the dispatched instruction stream and the core type.

Although progress has been made in determining the significant parameters for efficient execution, the **workload type** has not, to our best knowledge, been included in the execution on big.LITTLE systems. The official reference is the Global Task Scheduling (GTS)[1] support for the ARM big.LITTLE devices. Using this scheduler, "High performance threads" are scheduled to the big cores and "Low performance threads" are scheduled to LITTLE cores based on the workload activity of the threads. The current implementation uses a fixed parameter SCHED_CAPACITY_SCALE to set the relative performance difference between a big and a LITTLE core. It currently relies on a fixed constant; e.g. a big core is 2x faster than a LITTLE. Even though this is an early attempt of categorizing workload type to a core type, the practical results are poor. In other words, the scheduler often schedules a thread on *the wrong core*. This results not only in poor energy efficiency, but also in poor performance of the applications and poor user experience.

In this paper, we include the workload type when finding the most energy efficient execution, rather than performance, using an off-the-shelf big.LITTLE platform. We evaluate a worst case, an average case and a best case scenario and we demonstrate the energy savings when taking workload types into account.

2   Related Work

Much related work has been presented on energy efficient execution, and the primary findings are tunables like clock frequency, multi-cores and scheduling. The work presented in both [2,16] argues for a Race-to-Idle (RTI) algorithm to reduce energy consumption in real-time systems. The power model is directly created by integrating the power values of a single-core CPU into a system simulator. Rather than a predictable real-time system, our work focus on general

---

[1] https://developer.arm.com/technologies/big-little.

applications, and modern general purpose multi-core systems with more complex power characteristics. We also account for different types of workloads that exercise parts of the CPU differently, and hence influence the power dissipation and the execution schedule significantly. In a similar way, workload consolidation in cloud systems [3] implicitly promote RTI, since packing jobs requires fewer servers, and the unused servers can be shut down. This work also ignored the workload type, and the difference in power and performance it gives cause to.

In other systems [12,15,21], an intermediate clock frequency was considered optimal for energy efficiency. Again, the work in [15] compared RTI to several algorithms capable of adapting the clock frequency of the CPU according to what was predicted to be optimal. The schedulers were implemented in SystemC, and the power values were extracted from an existing Intel processor. The authors did not further discuss the impact of the hardware platform and its capability to pipeline instructions, which is one of the most important factors when choosing execution strategy in heterogeneous systems. Further, the authors in [1] presented several task mapping strategies on a multi-core system running in the SIMICS simulator. Mapping strategies included algorithms to keep over-used cores idle in order to even out the mean time to failure because of aging. In this work, different workload patterns were used, but not in the context of having different power characteristics or different performance. Little attention was put on the platform executing the tasks and pre-mature conclusions regarding the energy model were drawn as a results from the experiments. In our work, we acknowledge the impact of the power dissipation characteristics using different core types and all experimental results are generated from real hardware rather than from simulators.

Scheduling of multi-core systems has been covered in other work, and an important aspect affecting the execution has been the level of software scalability based on the selected processor [11]. Trading clock frequency for parallelism has also been a technique to increase the efficiency [10] of computer systems since the power invested in driving several cores usually is less than the power saved by lower their clock frequency. The work in [11] presented a power manager capable of spotting parallel paths in a program, and scale the clock frequency on a multi-core ARM platform to obtain sufficient QoS from an application. The results were, however, valid only for similar types of platforms with the same type of power dissipation characteristics. More focus was put on the hardware platform in [13]. The authors compared execution strategies using two server platforms, one desktop platform and one mobile ARM platform. Further discussions regarding the power dissipation caused by hardware influence on the software or the measurement methods were not made, nor were motivations for creating a power- or energy model made in the work.

Thermal dissipation was considered as a significant factor for choosing execution strategy in [8]. Hot and cold ambient temperature was used for investigating the effect on load consolidation or fair mapping. Similarly to this work, we consider the impact of the ambient temperature by creating the power models based on real execution. We furthermore include the effect of the workload types on the ambient temperature and the related power dissipation.

The authors in [25] use Heartbeats to identify performance characteristics of the big and the LITTLE to optimize scheduling decisions. This includes a profiling stage of the application to measure the relative speed-up between the cores. In contrast, our work aims to identify the power and performance offline so no overhead is required to identify the application. Other work included workload types [19, 26, 27] on homogeneous HPC systems, and the focus has been put on high CPU vs. high I/O loads. On big.LITTLE systems, the authors in [6] presented a scheduler, which included knowledge about co-running applications and performance degradation. The work in [23] showed how the energy consumption on a big.LITTLE system was affected by the workload applied on the processor, but the presented work was more of an analysis than a discussion into what causes the power dissipation. On a more fundamental level, we focus on how the very microarchitecture is able to efficiently dispatch the workload onto the execution stages in the processor, and how this information can be exploited to determine the most energy efficient execution.

3   Power Breakdown

The power dissipation of the CPU is the single most important parameter when determining the efficiency of the execution. Dynamic power is being dissipated whenever the CPU is performing operations, but not otherwise. The dynamic power dissipation P_d is linearly dependent on the clock frequency and quadratically on the core voltage as $P_d = f \cdot V_{dd}^2$. As the core cannot operate on arbitrarily low voltage levels when the clock frequency is increased, the core voltage must be dynamically adjusted as the clock frequency is increased. This often leads to a cubic increase in dynamic power as a function of clock frequency. Moreover, the static power caused by transistor leakage is becoming more and more dominant as the transistors shrink in size [14]. The static power is always present even if a processor is not executing any workload; this means that the processor is wasting energy always when being connected to a power source. The static power is dependent on the temperature because of the increased leakage current [8], therefore it is also dependent on the voltage and clock frequency, which affect the temperature. The relation between leakage current and temperature is found in [14]. Therefore the optimal balance between using dynamic power for setting the clock frequency and the static power present as long as the platform is powered should be found.

4   Influence of Workload Type

Software is broken down into CPU instructions that exercise parts of the CPU when being executed. First and foremost, the type of workload impacts on which part of the microarchitecture is stressed – this in turn impacts on the power dissipation because a different amount of transistors are used depending on the type of instruction being executed. For example an ALU operation dissipates a different amount of power than a memory operation because they use very different parts of the CPU. The microarchitecture also influences the power dissipation because of its capabilities to pipeline the stream of instructions, potentially using instruction level parallelism or out-of-order execution. Power models usually omit this fact [4,5,20,24], and rely on the assumption that software is a monolith that dissipates a single amount of power independently of what parts of the CPU are being exercised.

We therefore investigated the impact of the workload itself on the power dissipation by selecting six different benchmarks from the stress-ng suite[2]. These benchmarks were chosen because they were designed to stress different parts of the processor. The chosen benchmarks were: ackermann, cdouble, fibonacci, float, callfunc and fnv1a compiled with the default build flags on an ARM device. The complete instruction sequence was then traced by a gdb script[3], and the instructions were categorized based on their functionality as seen in Fig. 1.

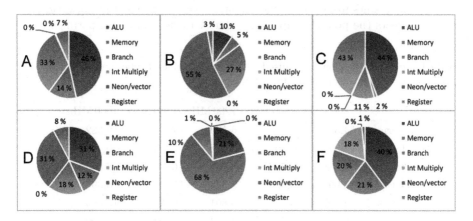

Fig. 1. Instruction break-down of all six benchmarks. A: ackermann B: cdouble C: fibonacci D: float E: callfunc F: fnv1a

We categorized the instructions into 6 categories: *ALU* (Arithmetic-logic operations), *Memory* (off-chip memory operations), *Branch* (Conditional- and non-conditional branches), *Int multiply* (Integer multiplication/divisions), *SIMD* (All single instruction multiple data operations), *Register* (Load/Store instructions using CPU registers). As seen in the figure, the ackermann benchmark consists of a relatively even balance between ALU, memory and branch instructions, cdouble contains mostly SIMD instructions, fibonacci uses many ALU instructions and register operations (mostly the mov instruction). float contains a balanced amount of all instruction types except the integer multiplications, while callfunc uses mostly memory instructions to the external memory. Finally, fnv1a contains a balanced amount of instructions but it uses integer multiplications rather than SIMD instructions.

---

[2] http://kernel.ubuntu.com/~cking/stress-ng/.
[3] https://git.it.abo.fi/simon.holmbacka/GDBInstructionScanner/.

The average power dissipation was measured for all benchmarks using an Odroid-XU4 board with the Exynos 5422 SoC. The board contains four ARM Cortex-A7 cores and four Cortex-A15 cores. Four benchmark threads were executed in all experiments, and the threads were mapped to the Cortex-A15 cores. For each benchmark, the clock frequency was scaled from 800 MHz to 1600 MHz in steps of 200 MHz. An external Raspberry Pi device was used to measure and log the power of the complete board with a sampling interval of 10 ms. Table 1 shows the average power dissipation from the benchmarks as a function of clock frequency. It is clear that some workloads cause significantly higher power dissipation than others. For example the `callfunc` workload is causing up to 13 W of power dissipation using the highest clock frequency while executing `fnv1a`, barely 8 W of power is being dissipated. From the table we can see that the increase in power dissipation is not equally fast for all tasks, hence highlighting the need for including workload specific power-awareness in the scheduler. By studying the results from these experiments, we confirm that the workload type executed affects the power dissipation – almost by 40% in this experiment.

Table 1. Power dissipation [W] caused by different workload types on an Exynos 5422 board using different clock frequency settings

	800 MHz	1000 MHz	1200 MHz	1400 MHz	1600 MHz
ackermann	4.354	5.206	6.190	7.931	10.382
cdouble	3.968	5.492	6.038	7.643	10.403
fibonacci	3.588	4.753	5.168	6.274	8.886
float	3.995	5.526	5.913	7.687	10.393
callfunc	4.697	6.193	6.801	9.201	13.369
fnv1a	3.415	4.588	4.734	5.880	8.009

5   Type Based Schedule Optimization

The hypothesis in this paper is that types of workload will affect the energy efficiency if included in the scheduling. We have shown in Sect. 4 that types of workload indeed affect the power dissipation significantly, and in this section we investigate the benefits of workload type-aware scheduling. Since energy consumption is dependent on the execution time as well as the power, we measure both values for each workload on each core type. We then create schedules using an optimizer with different levels of accuracy in terms of power and performance awareness, and we execute the resulting schedule on real hardware.

5.1   Workload Types

Rather than using complex benchmark kernels, we chose to evaluate workload types consisting of mostly one type of instruction in order to cover the extreme case for power and performance difference between the types. Four simple benchmark kernels shown in Table 2 were extracted from the epEBench suite[4]. These benchmarks consist of a small kernel which is looped over a given number of iterations, after which the thread is terminated. We also included a generic matrix multiplication benchmark without any code optimization implemented as a fifth benchmark. All benchmarks were compiled with the -O0 flag using gcc on the ARM device.

Table 2. Benchmark kernels with different workload type

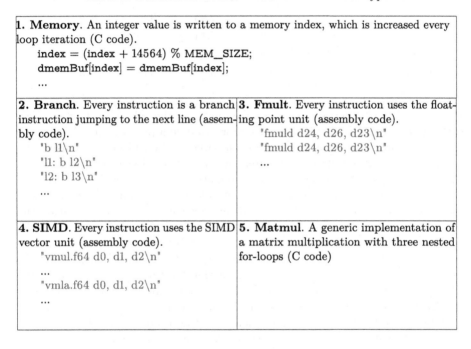

1. Memory. An integer value is written to a memory index, which is increased every loop iteration (C code).		

index = (index + 14564) % MEM_SIZE;
dmemBuf[index] = dmemBuf[index];
...		

2. Branch. Every instruction is a branch instruction jumping to the next line (assembly code). "b l1\n" "l1: b l2\n" "l2: b l3\n" ...	**3. Fmult**. Every instruction uses the floating point unit (assembly code). "fmuld d24, d26, d23\n" "fmuld d24, d26, d23\n" ...	
4. SIMD. Every instruction uses the SIMD vector unit (assembly code). "vmul.f64 d0, d1, d2\n" ... "vmla.f64 d0, d1, d2\n" ...	**5. Matmul**. A generic implementation of a matrix multiplication with three nested for-loops (C code)	

Power consumption. The power dissipation was measured for all benchmarks on the Odroid-XU4 device using 1 to 4 available cores and clock frequencies 600 MHz to 1600 MHz on the big A15 core and clock frequencies 600 MHz to 1400 MHz on the LITTLE A7 core. The power was measured with an external power meter, and hence no performance overhead was introduced. The performance was simply measured by the timestamps for executing a set of instructions so no additional code was inserted in the benchmark kernel. The results from the SIMD (4) benchmark is shown in Table 3, and the results from all the other benchmarks are found at https://zenodo.org/record/290651 due to space limitations.

---

[4] https://gitlab.com/MuellerRobert/epEBench.

Table 3. Power dissipation [W] caused by the SIMD workload type on an Odroid-XU4 board using different clock frequency settings and number of cores

big	600 MHz	800 MHz	1000 MHz	1200 MHz	1400 MHz	1600 MHz
1 core	2.81	2.99	3.28	3.44	3.91	5.38
2 cores	3.15	3.45	3.96	4.39	5.21	7.57
3 cores	3.50	3.91	4.71	5.29	6.55	10.00
4 core	3.81	4.27	5.62	6.09	8.21	12.40
LITTLE	600 MHz	800 MHz	1000 MHz	1200 MHz	1400 MHz	1600 MHz
1 core	2.71	2.77	2.88	2.95	3.01	n/a
2 core	2.77	2.87	2.95	3.14	3.21	n/a
3 core	2.83	2.99	3.07	3.32	3.43	n/a
4 core	2.89	3.07	3.17	3.51	3.65	n/a

Performance. The performance was measured as the relative execution time with respect to the LITTLE core type. For example a performance value of 0.5 on the big core indicates a 2x speedup compared to the LITTLE core using the same clock frequency. It was measured by executing a fixed number of loops, while calculating the elapsed time for completing all loop iterations. Both core types were operating at a clock frequency of 1000 MHz and one thread was used for each experiment. The performance (execution time) of executing the kernels was normalized to the performance of the LITTLE A7 core, and the relative performance of the big A15 is shown in Table 4. As seen in the table, the performance of the A15 core is usually higher due to its out-of-order execution, its deep pipeline and more advanced instruction level parallelism. For example when executing SIMD instructions, the A15 core is more than 3.5x faster than the A7 core because of its 10 stage SIMD pipeline and two completely parallel SIMD engines. On the other hand, when executing branch instructions, the A7 is seemingly faster because the A15 cannot use any of its deep pipelines as every instruction is a branch.

Table 4. Relative performance of the A7 and A15 core executing various benchmark kernels (Lower is better)

	Memory	Branch	Fmult	SIMD	Matmul
Cortex-A15	0.676	1.376	0.264	0.277	0.746
Cortex-A7	1.0	1.0	1.0	1.0	1.0

5.2   Schedule Generation

Clearly, the type of workload executed on the processor affects both the power dissipation of the core and the performance of the application depending on the core type used. To determine the impact of the execution strategy, we implemented a scheduler capable of including workload type when optimizing the runtime. Including the workload type means creating a power and performance model for each workload type, and selecting the relevant power and performance model when calculating the energy consumption for a schedule. Using an ignorant scheduler, the power and performance values of a task is the average value of all task types, i.e. all task types "look" the same to the ignorant scheduler.

We consider 4 scheduler variants each with different levels of accuracy with regard to the workload type:

(1) **Completely ignorant.** This scheduler ignores both task specific power and performance values. The scheduler considers average power and performance values over all task types used.
(2) **Power-aware.** This scheduler considers task specific power values but ignores performance values.
(3) **Performance-aware.** This scheduler considers task specific performance values but ignores power values.
(4) **Power-performance-aware.** This scheduler considers task specific power and performance values. It is hence the most accurate schedule compared to the real-world execution by definition.

All of the four schedulers always select the clock frequency and the core type which results in the lowest energy consumption based on the performance and the power information available.

6 Evaluation

Our evaluation was aimed at showing how much energy can be saved by using increased levels of awareness in the scheduler compared to an ignorant scheduler.

6.1 Case Studies

We selected two important corner cases using static schedulers and furthermore two average cases using dynamic schedulers with all task types. The corner cases are intended to represent the best and worst cases as power and performance values are taken into account or ignored.

Corner case 1. Based on the results in Sect. 5, we chose to include four tasks of type Branch and four tasks of type SIMD. These were chosen because: (1) Branch has the worst performance on the big, but also the lowest power dissipation on the big. This indicates that Branch is poorly utilizing the big microarchitecture. (2) SIMD has the highest power dissipation on the big and a very high performance on the big. This indicates that SIMD is utilizing the big microarchitecture well.

To schedule sets of tasks of different task types onto a heterogeneous multicore machine, we first perform bin packing-based distributions of each set for 1 to p cores, if there are p cores per core type. Then we proceed similarly to [9]:

we enumerate all possible mappings, and among the feasible mappings, i.e. those where the predicted runtime is smaller than the deadline, we choose the one where the prediction for energy consumption is lowest. In other words, the optimizer performs an exhaustive search and the optimum is hence guaranteed.

Corner case 2. The second corner case was choosing four tasks of type `Memory` and four tasks of type `Matmul`. These types were chosen because both types obtain a performance close to the average performance, and the power dissipation is close to the average power dissipation of all task types. The mapping is performed using the same optimization method as in Corner case 1.

RM CFS case. A multi-core Rate-Monotonic (RM) Completely-Fair (CF) scheduler was implemented[5] in the SimSo[6] framework. The scheduler supported the declaration of workload types and the level of Power/Performance awareness when deciding a schedule. The RM scheduler is a dynamic scheduler using the following rules:

- Schedule the task on the core with the cheapest cost (Power*Performance).
- Use as much parallelism as possible within the core type.
- The priority is determined by the task period (shorter period = higher priority).
- A core is over-utilized if the utilization $U > n \cdot (2^{1/n} - 1)$ where n is the total number of tasks scheduled on the core, according to [17].

EDF CFS case. A multi-core Earliest-Deadline-First (EDF) Completely-Fair (CF) scheduler was also implemented (See footnote 5) in the SimSo framework. The scheduler supported the declaration of workload types and the level of Power/Performance awareness when deciding a schedule similarly to the RM scheduler. The EDF scheduler is a dynamic scheduler using the following rules:

- Schedule the task on the core with the cheapest cost (Power*Performance).
- Use as much parallelism as possible within the core type.
- The priority is determined by the deadline (earlier deadline = higher priority).
- A core is over-utilized if the utilization $U > 1$, according to [18].

Hence, Corner case 1 represents the worst case deviation between an ignorant scheduler and a P&P-aware scheduler and Corner case 2 represents the best case. The RM CFS case and the EDF CFS case represent a more realistic average case by using many types of workloads and popular dynamic scheduling methods.

6.2 Experimental Results

Corner case 1 and 2 was fed to the optimizer for all four types of awareness levels (defined in Sect. 5). The mapping order is decided by the order of which the tasks

---

[5] https://zenodo.org/record/290651.
[6] http://projects.laas.fr/simso/.

are sent to the optimizer. Since the ignorant scheduler is unable to distinguish between task types, the tasks are mapped first to the big core since it is deemed to be more efficient based on the average power and performance values. As the big core is fully utilized, the remaining tasks are mapped to the LITTLE cores. The schedule determined by the optimizer was then fully replicated on real hardware using our runtime framework[7]. The two later cases are using a dynamic scheduler rather than the optimizer. This means that the scheduling algorithms will determine the mapping during runtime. The resulting dynamic schedule was also replicated on our runtime framework.

Table 5 shows the results as two parts: the first part is the model created by the optimizer of the dynamic scheduler upon which scheduling decisions are being made. The second part is the energy measurements data from real hardware execution. Gantt charts of all tasks and schedules are externally available (See footnote 5).

Table 5. Energy consumption model/data [J] for various schedulers with various levels of awareness on an Exynos 5422 board.

Model	Corner case 1	Corner case 2	RM CFS	EDF CFS
(1) Completely ignorant	161.50	161.50	423.03	475.67
(2) Power-aware	186.62	203.85	470.71	525.85
(3) Performance-aware	145.77	202.27	405.25	455.15
(4) P&P-aware	145.92	164.71	391.44	462.25
Data	Corner case 1	Corner case 2	RM CFS	EDF CFS
(1) Completely ignorant	206.15	173.41	475.99	638.64
(2) Power-aware	206.15	161.08	514.94	596.43
(3) Performance-aware	141.71	161.08	409.46	496.28
(4) P&P-aware	141.71	161.08	409.46	496.28
Energy savings (1) vs. (4)	**31.3%**	**7.1%**	**14.0%**	**23.3%**

Corner case 1. Since the ignorant scheduler (1) is unable to distinguish between the task types, `Branch` tasks are being scheduled on the big core and `SIMD` tasks are being scheduled on the LITTLE cores. This is the worst possible mapping for all task types and the difference in energy consumption between (1) and (4) is significant both for the model and for the data. The model in (1) predicts a lower energy consumption than what is measured because (1) cannot accurately predict the execution time nor the power. By mapping the extreme case tasks on the *wrong* core, the execution time is significantly extended, and the real energy consumption is higher than the model predicts. This is clearly visible as the energy consumption for the performance-aware scheduler is lower than the power-aware scheduler. On the other hand, by including power and performance

---

[7] https://git.it.abo.fi/simon.holmbacka/SchedulingTemplate.git.

into the model, the scheduler is not only able to map the tasks onto the *correct* cores, but the model is also able to predict the outcome more accurately. The PP-aware and the performance-aware scheduler has an equal energy consumption in practice because the real schedule is identical. This is because including only the performance parameter (in these cases) is enough to predict the optimal schedule. The results from the extreme corner case shows that a maximum of 31.3% can be saved by using workload type-aware scheduling.

Corner case 2. The second case is a best case study for using an ignorant scheduler (1), because the power and the performance of the workload types (`Memory` and `Matmul`) are close to the average case which the ignorant scheduler is based upon. As seen in Table 5, the model is more accurately able to predict the energy consumption than in Corner case 1. This is because the average power and performance is an approximation fairly close to the measured data. Nevertheless, the P&P-aware scheduler (4) still outperforms (1, 2, 3) because of the slight additional accuracy. The results from the best case corner case shows that a 7.1% of energy can be saved by using workload type-aware scheduling.

RM CFS. In the use case of the dynamic RM CF scheduler, a larger set of tasks (See footnote 5) were used and a mixture of all five task types were furthermore included. The accuracy of the model is fairly high for all four scheduler types, but the energy consumption of the P&P-aware scheduler is clearly lower than (1) and (2). In all use cases, the Performance-aware scheduler (3) achieves an identical energy consumption as (4). This is because the schedule created predicted based on only the performance model is identical to the schedule created predicted both based on power and performance. It suggests that the link between workload performance and energy consumption is stronger than between power dissipation and energy consumption for the chosen workloads executing on the chosen platform.

EDF CFS. The energy savings are even larger when comparing (1) to (4) using the EDF scheduler, because a slightly larger task set was used (See footnote 5). Since the scheduler more often is capable of mapping right-task-to-right-core, the difference is larger. In both the EDF case and in the RM case, the prediction for (1) is much lower than the actual energy consumption. This is because an ignorant scheduler assumes that the tasks are mapped on the *right* core, and the execution time of the tasks are hence assumed to be shorter than the actual execution time. This means that not only is a P&P-aware scheduler desired to decrease the energy consumption, it is also needed for accurate model prediction.

7   Conclusions

Workload type has previously been omitted in most research work on energy efficient execution to our best knowledge. Schedule and runtime optimizations have been done purely based on hardware parameters such as clock frequency or core number, and the software has been considered mainly a naïve "user" of the CPU. This paper has demonstrated that the workload type is an important factor for determining the execution strategy on big.LITTLE platforms. We have evaluated the workload type based on the most fundamental building blocks – the instruction stream. We have shown that both the power dissipation and the performance of the software is highly dependent on the type of the instructions in the stream. Our conclusions are that workload type should be a parameter in big.LITTLE schedulers rather than relying on indirect metrics such as the workload level, as currently used.

Although not part of this paper, to apply this discovery in practice our future work includes how to analyze and monitor applications to determine the instruction stream of applications. With a given instruction stream, methods such as neural networks can be used to categorize the instruction stream and a core type "Fitness" of an application can hence be determined. Then use this knowledge in the scheduler of for example the Linux kernel to make workload-aware scheduling decisions.

References

1. Allred, J.M., Roy, S., Chakraborty, K.: Long term sustainability of differentially reliable systems in the dark silicon era. In: 2013 IEEE 31st International Conference on Computer Design (ICCD), pp. 70–77, October 2013
2. Awan, M.A., Petters, S.M.: Enhanced race-to-halt: a leakage-aware energy management approach for dynamic priority systems. In: 2011 23rd Euromicro Conference on Real-Time Systems, pp. 92–101, July 2011
3. Chen, K., Lenhardt, J., Schiffmann, W.: Improving energy efficiency of web servers by using a load distribution algorithm and shutting down idle nodes. In: 2015 15th IEEE/ACM International Symposium on Cluster, Cloud and Grid Computing (CCGrid), pp. 745–748, May 2015
4. Cho, S., Melhem, R.: On the interplay of parallelization, program performance, and energy consumption. IEEE Trans. Parallel Distrib. Syst. **21**(3), 342–353 (2010)
5. Cupertino, L., Da Costa, G., Pierson, J.M.: Towards a generic power estimator. Comput. Sci. - Res. Dev. **30**(2), 1–9 (2014). http://dx.doi.org/10.1007/s00450-014-0264-x
6. Fan, X., Sui, Y., Xue, J.: Contention-aware scheduling for asymmetric multicore processors. In: 2015 IEEE 21st International Conference on Parallel and Distributed Systems (ICPADS), pp. 742–751, December 2015
7. Fu, C., Li, M., Xue, C.J.: Race to idle or not: balancing the memory sleep time with dvs for energy minimization. In: 2015 Design, Automation Test in Europe Conference Exhibition (DATE), pp. 13–18, March 2015
8. Hällis, F., Holmbacka, S., Lund, W., Slotte, R., Lafond, S., Lilius, J.: Thermal influence on the energy efficiency of workload consolidation in many-core architecture. In: Bolla, R., Davoli, F., Tran-Gia, P., Anh, T.T. (eds.) Proceedings of the 24th Tyrrhenian International Workshop on Digital Communications, pp. 1–6. IEEE (2013)
9. Holmbacka, S., Keller, J., Eitschberger, P., Lilius, J.: Accurate energy modeling for many-core static schedules with streaming applications. Microprocess. Microsyst. **43**(C), 14–25 (2016)

10. Holmbacka, S., Nogues, E., Pelcat, M., Lafond, S., Menard, D., Lilius, J.: Energy-awareness and performance management with parallel dataflow applications. J. Sig. Process. Syst., 1–16 (2015). http://dx.doi.org/10.1007/s11265-015-1059-4

11. Holmbacka, S., Nogues, E., Pelcat, M., Lafond, S., Lilius, J.: Energy efficiency and performance management of parallel dataflow applications. In: Pinzari, A., Morawiec, A. (eds.) The 2014 Conference on Design & Architectures for Signal & Image Processing, pp. 1–8. ECDI Electronic Chips & Systems Design Initiative (2014)

12. Jejurikar, R., Gupta, R.: Procrastination scheduling in fixed priority real-time systems. In: Proceedings of the 2004 ACM SIGPLAN/SIGBED Conference on Languages, Compilers, and Tools for Embedded Systems, LCTES 2004, NY, USA, pp. 57–66 (2004). http://doi.acm.org/10.1145/997163.997173

13. Kim, D.H.K., Imes, C., Hoffmann, H.: Racing and pacing to idle: theoretical and empirical analysis of energy optimization heuristics. In: 2015 IEEE 3rd International Conference on Cyber-Physical Systems, Networks, and Applications (CPSNA), pp. 78–85, August 2015

14. Kim, N., Austin, T., Baauw, D., Mudge, T., Flautner, K., Hu, J., Irwin, M., Kandemir, M., Narayanan, V.: Leakage current: Moore's law meets static power. Computer 36(12), 68–75 (2003)

15. Kluge, F., Uhrig, S., Mische, J., Satzger, B., Ungerer, T.: Dynamic workload prediction for soft real-time applications. In: 2010 IEEE 10th International Conference on Computer and Information Technology (CIT), pp. 1841–1848, June 2010

16. Lee, Y.H., Reddy, K.P., Krishna, C.M.: Scheduling techniques for reducing leakage power in hard real-time systems. In: Proceedings of the 15th Euromicro Conference on Real-Time Systems, pp. 105–112, July 2003

17. Liu, C.L., Layland, J.W.: Scheduling algorithms for multiprogramming in a hard-real-time environment. J. ACM 20(1), 46–61 (1973). http://doi.acm.org/10.1145/321738.321743

18. Liu, J.W.S.: Real-Time Systems, 1st edn. Prentice Hall PTR, Upper Saddle River (2000)

19. Lucanin, D., Pietri, I., Holmbacka, S., Brandic, I., Lilius, J., Sakellariou, R.: Performance-based pricing in multi-core geo-distributed cloud computing. IEEE Trans. Cloud Comput. PP(99), 1 (2016)

20. Mesa-Martinez, F.J., Ardestani, E.K., Renau, J.: Characterizing processor thermal behavior. SIGPLAN Not. 45(3), 193–204 (2010). http://doi.acm.org/10.1145/1735971.1736043

21. Niu, L., Quan, G.: Reducing both dynamic and leakage energy consumption for hard real-time systems. In: Proceedings of the 2004 International Conference on Compilers, Architecture, and Synthesis for Embedded Systems, CASES 2004, NY, USA, pp. 140–148 (2004). http://doi.acm.org/10.1145/1023833.1023854

22. Rountree, B., Lownenthal, D.K., de Supinski, B.R., Schulz, M., Freeh, V.W., Bletsch, T.: Adagio: making DVS practical for complex HPC applications. In: Proceedings of the 23rd International Conference on Supercomputing, ICS 2009, NY, USA, pp. 460–469 (2009). http://doi.acm.org/10.1145/1542275.1542340

23. Seo, W., Im, D., Choi, J., Huh, J.: Big or little: a study of mobile interactive applications on an asymmetric multi-core platform. In: 2015 IEEE International Symposium on Workload Characterization, pp. 1–11, October 2015

24. Shen, H., Lu, J., Qiu, Q.: Learning based DVFS for simultaneous temperature, performance and energy management. In: 2012 13th International Symposium on Quality Electronic Design (ISQED), pp. 747–754, March 2012

25. Sozzo, E.D., Durelli, G.C., Trainiti, E.M.G., Miele, A., Santambrogio, M.D., Bolchini, C.: Workload-aware power optimization strategy for asymmetric multiprocessors. In: 2016 Design, Automation Test in Europe Conference Exhibition (DATE), pp. 531–534, March 2016
26. Spiliopoulos, V., Kaxiras, S., Keramidas, G.: Green governors: a framework for continuously adaptive DVFS. In: 2011 International Green Computing Conference and Workshops, pp. 1–8, July 2011
27. Tiwari, N., Bellur, U., Sarkar, S., Indrawan, M.: CPU frequency tuning to improve energy efficiency of mapreduce systems. In: 2016 IEEE 22nd International Conference on Parallel and Distributed Systems (ICPADS), pp. 1015–1022, December 2016

Pipelining Computation and Optimization Strategies for Scaling GROMACS on the Sunway Many-Core Processor

Yang Yu[1(✉)], Hong An[1(✉)], Junshi Chen[1], Weihao Liang[1], Qingqing Xu[1], and Yong Chen[2]

[1] University of Science and Technology of China, Hefei, Anhui, China
{yy130611,cjuns,lwh,tsqua}@mail.ustc.edu.cn,
han@ustc.edu.cn
[2] Department of Computer Science, Texas Tech University, Lubbock, TX, USA
yong.chen@ttu.edu

Abstract. The increasing gap between plentiful computing elements and limited memory bandwidth makes it increasingly difficult and sometimes even infeasible for HPC community to port more applications onto many-core processor architectures. The Sunway many-core processor SW26010 used to build the Sunway TaihuLight System contains a total of 260 heterogeneous cores. All these cores can be divided into 4 core groups (CGs). Each CG includes a Management Processing Element (MPE) core and 64 Computing Processing Elements (CPEs) cores. In this paper, we refactor an important molecular dynamics (MD) application GROMACS on the Sunway Taihulight system. By rewriting the compute-intensive kernel of GROMACS, we exploit a suitable parallelism for CPE cluster and implement pipelining computation between MPE and CPE cluster. Optimization strategies including the efficient use of scratchpad, the software-emulated cache and a hybrid parallel algorithm are adopted to solve the challenging memory bandwidth limitation. When comparing the refactored version using MPE and 64 CPEs with the original ported version using only MPE, we achieve a 16x speedup for the compute-intensive kernel. For simulating a molecule with 3 million atoms, we currently have managed to scale to 798,720 cores. Moreover, we analyze the adaptability of our mapping and optimization strategies for solving the memory bandwidth limitation when refactoring a real-world application on the Sunway heterogeneous many-core processor system.

Keywords: Sunway TaihuLight system · GROMACS · Parallel model · Performance optimization · Bandwidth competition · Adaptability

1 Introduction

The Sunway TaihuLight System, developed by the National Research Center of Parallel Computer Engineering and Technology (NRCPC) of China, with a Linpack score of 93 petaflops, captured the number-one spot on the latest Top 500 list of supercomputers released at the conference SC16. As the only 100-PFLOPS system in the world, it

© Springer International Publishing AG 2017
S. Ibrahim et al. (Eds.): ICA3PP 2017, LNCS 10393, pp. 18–32, 2017.
DOI: 10.1007/978-3-319-65482-9_2

contains about ten million heterogeneous cores in total. 40,960 computing nodes, each of which has an extremely high peak performance of 3 TFLOPS. However, given the specific heterogeneous many-core architecture, it is challenging to utilize such plentiful computing resource effectively to achieve high performance.

Molecular Dynamics (MD) simulation [1] plays an important role in theoretical studies of biomolecular systems. The fundamental algorithm includes computing the interactions between particles and updating the coordinates and velocities via Newton's second law [2] in finite time. GROMACS is a widely-used software package for MD simulation. It is computationally intensive but highly efficient at calculating the nonbonded interactions. In recent years, several research efforts have focused on refactoring GROMACS for heterogeneous system architectures and analyzing its scalability. Typical examples include refactoring GROMACS for the Cell processor [3] and to GPU accelerators [4]. Recently, a study focusing on the challenges for exascale simulation [5] was performed by the official GROMACS developers.

The main contributions of this paper are as follows.

- We exploit a suitable parallelism to refactor GROMACS onto the Sunway Taihu-Light System. By adopting a task-level pipeline, we solve the load imbalance and data dependency problems that were exposed during parallelization of the compute-intensive kernel without introducing additional execution time.
- We introduce effective optimization strategies to reuse data and reduce memory-access delays, thus solving the challenging bandwidth limitation problem on the Sunway TaihuLight System. A detailed analysis is presented concerning the implementation and benefits of each optimization strategy.
- We compare the refactored GROMACS code using both MPE and CPE clusters to the serial official GROMACS code on MPE. We achieve up to a 16x speed improvement for the main compute-intensive kernel.
- We discuss the adaptability of our parallel model and optimization strategies that are not only suitable for GROMACS but also potentially apply to other HPC applications and benchmarks as they are refactored onto the Sunway heterogeneous many-core architecture.

2 The Sunway TaihuLight System

2.1 Overview

As the fastest supercomputer in the world, The Sunway TaihuLight System [8] has a theoretical peak performance of 125.4 PFLOPS. The full system adopts a multilevel tree topology composed of 40 cabinets, each of which contains 4 supernodes. Every super-node contains 256 nodes, each of which has 260 heterogeneous cores and 32 GB of main memory. In total, this system includes 10,649,600 heterogeneous cores and 1.31 PB of main memory.

The software environment includes a customized 64-bit Linux operating system and compiler components that support C/C++ and Fortran. In addition, a targeted thread library called Athread and some other parallel programming libraries, including MPI and OpenACC, are also provided.

2.2 The SW26010 Processor

The processor chip of the Sunway Taihulight System is the SW26010, manufactured by the Shanghai High Performance IC Design Center, running at a frequency of 1.45 GHz. The SW26010 is composed of four core groups (CGs) which are connected via the network on chip (NoC). Each CG includes one management processing element (MPE), one computing processing element (CPE) cluster, and one memory controller (MC). The MPE—a 64-bit RISC core with 256-bit vector instructions—includes a 32 KB L1 instruction cache, a 32 KB L1 data cache and a 256 KB L2 cache. The CPE cluster contains 64 CPEs which are integrated in an 8 × 8 mesh structure. Each CPE includes a 16 KB L1 instruction cache and a 64 KB Scratch Pad Memory (SPM), and also supports 256-bit vectorization. Each CG has its own memory space, which can be accessed by the MPE and the CPE cluster through the MC (Fig. 1).

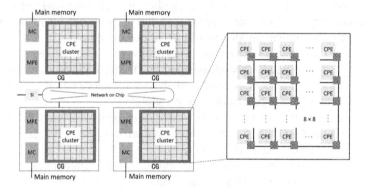

Fig. 1. The general architecture of the SW26010 processor

Some features of the SW26010 chip that serve as the prerequisites of our optimization strategies should be explained. In one core group, the MPE can continue to run after offloading compute tasks to the CPE cluster. Unlike commercial hardware accelerators like Xeon phi and Graphic Processing Unit, the CPE cluster has no shared memory. Each CPE can access main memory and its own SPM. Continuous data blocks in the main memory can be transferred to the SPM efficiently by Direct Memory Access (DMA). Given the limited size and the low access latency of the SPM, like an L1 cache, it can be configured as a software-emulated cache for data reuse or as a read-only buffer for resident data. Moreover, data transmission is supported among the CPEs in one CPE cluster. Each CPE can transfer data at the register level to the other CPEs located in the same row or column. This capability is significant in fostering cooperative computing and CPE synchronization.

3 GROMACS

3.1 Application Introduction

As one of the mainstream MD applications, the GROMACS package has been substantially optimized from the MD algorithm and computing platform aspects. It supports all the usual algorithms of modern molecular-dynamics implementations and employs efficient parallel models for different task-granularity levels [6, 7]. Both single-and double-precision floating point operations are supported in GROMACS. However, GROMACS has not yet provided effective support on unique many-core architectures such as the Sunway architecture. As a baseline, we adopted the official GROMACS 5.0.3 release, which supports coarse-grained parallelism using interfaces such as MPI and OpenMP and fined-grained parallelism for use with platforms such as Compute Unified Device Architecture (CUDA) and Single Instruction Multiple Data (SIMD).

The entire simulation work can be divided into two procedures: calculating interactions between atoms and updating spatial information. The interactions consist of both bonded forces between bonded atoms and nonbonded forces such as electrostatic and Van der Waals forces. The spatial information consists of coordinates and velocities. Through numerous iterations of these two procedures, GROMACS can simulate the physical motions of molecules in finite time. In addition to these two procedures, the software calculates some other molecular features such as temperature and energy. It can output the results of all the calculations to files.

3.2 The Nonbonded Kernel

Calculating the nonbonded interactions is the most time-consuming part of GROMACS; consuming more than eighty-five percent of the total simulation time. Several dozen modules, distinguished by different methods for calculating electrostatic and Van der Waals forces, are integrated in the nonbonded kernel. We chose this kernel as the target for execution on the CPEs. The code framework of this hotspot can be simplified into the two nested loops shown in Algorithm 1.

Algorithm 1 The nonbonded kernel
1: **for** every atomic cluster i in the pair list
2:      data preprocessing
3:      **for** every atomic cluster j in i's neighbor list
4:          calculate nonbonded forces between i and j
5:          update force array via accumulate
6:      **end for**
7: **end for**

The inner loop body that calculates the nonbonded forces will be executed numerous times in this kernel. Figure 2 shows the data-access feature requirements and the execution order of the inner loop body in a molecule with 17,089 atoms. The X-axis indicates the atomic cluster id of each outer iteration, and the Y-axis indicates the atomic cluster id in the neighbor list required by the given outer iteration. Each point represents the interaction between two atomic clusters. Given that the data of atomic cluster are stored in id sequence, the coordinates of each point correspond to the data required by the two atomic clusters during one execution of the inner loop body. Therefore, the distribution of the scattered points in Fig. 2 reflects the memory-access behavior of the nonbonded kernel to some degree. We notice that adjacent atomic clusters are accessed in adjacent outer iterations or inner iterations and almost all the data of each atomic cluster are reused several times during the full iterative process. These two features inspire us to focus on data locality and reuse, which are the key factors affecting the design of our optimization strategies.

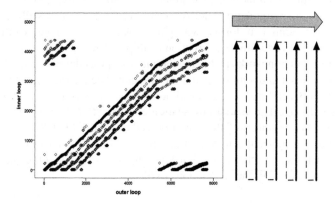

Fig. 2. The memory-access requirements and execution order of the inner loop body in the nonbonded kernel

4   Refactoring GROMACS for the Sunway System

The MPE can be used as a general-purpose CPU. To begin, we refactor the official GROMACS 5.0.3 code for the Sunway system with all the CPEs inoperative. This procedure is similar to compilation and installation on a commercial server running a Linux OS. Then, we use the CPEs to accelerate the nonbonded kernel.

4.1   Parallelization Using CPEs

Considering the task granularity, we choose to split the outer loop for parallelization. This partition of tasks leads to two deficiencies. First, the neighbor lists of different atomic clusters potentially have common members, which causes concurrency problem when writing data. Second, the neighbor lists of the different atomic clusters vary in length, which usually leads to load imbalances among the CPEs. Two methods are proposed to solve these two problems. Before initializing the CPE threads, the computing tasks should be partitioned evenly. The results must be stored redundantly and updated serially after the 64 CPE threads complete. However, implementing these two methods would necessarily increase the execution time. Thus, we introduce the targeted pipeline strategy, shown in Fig. 3. The three components in our pipeline are as follows.

- *Task partitioning:* By accumulating the neighbor lists in the serial outer iterations until their lengths reach a finite threshold, this component specifies the computing task for each CPE thread. The total length and iteration id of each task are recorded when accessing the data array of atomic cluster and allocating the result array.
- *Calculating:* This component is responsible for the main computing load of the nonbonded kernel according to the given task. It is also responsible for recording intermediate outputs to the newly allocated result array in the form of index and value.
- *Data updating:* This component use the intermediate results obtained from different CPE threads to update the force array serially, which avoids concurrency problem of writing data.

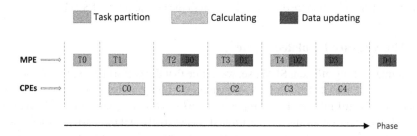

Fig. 3. A pipeline with three components: *task partitioning*, *calculating* and *data updating*

These three components are dispatched in phases. In each phase, the *task partitioning* component and the *data updating* component are executed serially on the MPE, and the *calculating* component is executed on the CPEs in parallel. The computing tasks are partitioned evenly in the *task partitioning* component, and the force array is updated serially in the *data updating* component. The execution time of the *task partitioning* component and the *data updating* component are almost entirely hidden. In summary, we handle the load imbalance and data dependency problems successfully without introducing additional execution time. Moreover, the *task partitioning* component is useful for data reuse, as will be explained in Sect. 4.3.

4.2 The Efficient Use of SPM

By introducing the pipeline strategy, we solve the above problems without increasing the time overhead. However, the memory bandwidth competition among 64 CPEs is extremely intense because of the frequent main-memory accesses. Consequently, the execution time of the nonbonded kernel running on the CPEs is much longer than running on the MPE. Therefore, we consider moving the repeatedly accessed data on SPM to reduce the main-memory access frequency of each CPE thread. The SPM is a 64 KB memory that is not large enough to completely store the data required by the nonbonded kernel. For example, storing three-dimensional coordinates for 10,000 atoms in single-precision floating point form requires at least 120 KB of memory. Therefore, to use the SPM efficiently, we need to analyze the data-access characteristics in the nonbonded kernel and evaluate the advantages that could accrue from transferring data into the SPM in different ways.

In our work, we move some frequently reused data such as the constants and small arrays into the SPM, which serve as resident data until the CPE threads finish. For large arrays such as the coordinate and force arrays, we choose to transfer the data that are useful for the current iteration to the SPM and then replace them during the next iteration to avoid address-space overflow. Therefore, we just have to transfer several small data blocks into the SPM in each iteration instead of buffering all these large arrays. All these data movements mentioned above are implemented through DMA. By doing this, we make almost all the required data available as either resident or temporary data in the local SPM. Each CPE can fetch most of its data from the local SPM instead of the main memory, which reduces the main memory access frequency. Consequently, the execution time of the nonbonded kernel is shortened obviously through the efficient use of SPM.

4.3   The Software-Emulated Cache

After implementing efficient SPM use, we notice that the performance of the nonbonded kernel is still dominated by the data-transmission time, indicating that the bandwidth competition is still intense. In the pipeline's *task partitioning* component described in Sect. 4.1, the outer iterations are partitioned successively and the intrinsic data features are maintained. Therefore, we can capitalize on the locality and reuse of the atomic clusters analyzed above to further reduce the frequency of main-memory accesses. Moreover, the SPM is not that limited after efficient use described in Sect. 4.2 and there is still some free memory space in the SPM. To implement more intensive data reuse, it is necessary to design a software-emulated cache.

In our work, we implement a cache with a software-controlled cache size and cache line size. Continuous data block can be prefetched in a cache line and we adopt a FIFO algorithm as a cache replacement policy. Considering the memory-access behavior revealed in Fig. 2, we exchange the outer loop and inner loop for a new iterative sequence to utilize data locality sufficiently. As shown in Fig. 4, the reuse distance of some atomic cluster data is shortened and adjacent atomic cluster data can be accessed in adjacent loop iterations. This means that the prefetched data are more likely to be used before replacement, which is highly beneficial for the cache hit rate. We then set various cache sizes to discover the most suitable value for optimal performance. Moreover, we implement an output buffer to store intermediate results. Some intermediate results can be accumulated in the local SPM instead of in the main memory. By doing this, we further decrease the main-memory access frequency.

As shown in Fig. 5, the cache size is determined by the number of atomic clusters it contains. A larger cache size always leads to a higher cache hit rate and a longer execution time for maintaining the cache mechanism. When the overhead of maintaining a large cache eclipses the benefits gained by the high hit rate, the performance of the nonbonded kernel will decline. We obtain the maximum performance when the cache is set to contain thirty atomic cluster, which yields a sixty-percent cache hit rate, saving approximately sixty

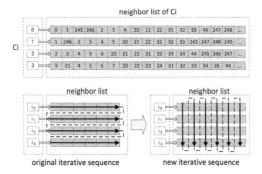

Fig. 4. Alteration of the iterative sequence according to the locality of memory access

percent of the data transmissions in the nonbonded kernel. By implementing the software-emulated cache, we exploit the data locality and reuse that are implicit in the memory-access behavior, achieving a noticeable performance improvement.

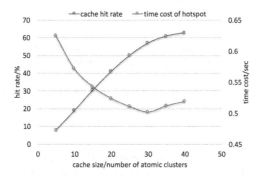

Fig. 5. The influence of cache size on execution time and hit rate. The best performance is achieved with a soft-emulated cache where 30 atomic clusters can be stored

4.4 A Hybrid Parallel Algorithm for Computing and Scheduling

The strategies presented in Sects. 4.2 and 4.3 speed up the nonbonded kernel by decreasing the main-memory access frequency. However, the bandwidth competition introduced by 64 CPE threads is still intense; consequently, the performance improvement achieved by using 64 CPE threads is no better than that from using only 32 CPE threads. Given this result, the other 32 CPE threads can be freed from the main computing load to act as helpers, performing data-transmission tasks and supportive computations. Our strategies are illustrated below.

We divide the 64 CPEs into two blocks: 32 CPEs for computing and 32 CPEs for scheduling. As shown in Fig. 6, one computing CPE thread collaborates with one scheduling CPE thread to undertake the tasks that is previously assigned to one CPE thread. The scheduling CPE thread is responsible for maintaining a software-emulated cache and transmitting required data to the corresponding computing CPE thread at the register level after scheduling. The scheduling process includes a query algorithm that finds all the reusable records in the given data through array traversal—regardless of the data locality. The computing CPE thread is responsible for the main computing load of the nonbonded kernel after receiving the required data and for updating the intermediate results in the output buffer before sending them to main memory. Moreover, data transmitted earlier will always be received earlier, which guarantees the sequence of the cooperation operations between the computing thread and scheduling thread.

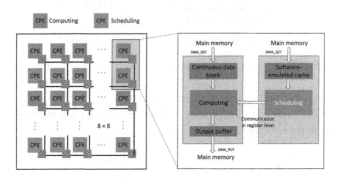

Fig. 6. A logical mapping of the hybrid parallel algorithm between a scheduling CPE and a computing CPE. The arrowheads indicate the data transmission directions

This approach mitigates the bandwidth competition by halving the number of threads attempting to access main memory. The cooperation between the computing thread and scheduling thread can be regarded as a two-level pipeline. One level includes the transmission of the required data from main memory and a scheduling algorithm; the other level includes computing the nonbonded kernel and sending the intermediate results to main memory. As a computing thread executes one iteration, the data required for the next iteration is prepared by the corresponding scheduling thread in parallel. By doing this, the required data have already been transmitted into local registers when the computing thread begins to execute a new iteration. The execution time of data-transmission, the software-emulated cache and the query algorithm in the scheduling thread are effectively hidden by the computing thread.

5   Results and Analysis

In this section, we provide data showing the performance of the nonbonded kernel after implementing our parallel model and optimization strategies on the Sunway TaihuLight System. We adopt a membrane protein sample with 70,960 atoms as the benchmark for the single CG performance test. This simulation spans 2,000 time steps. Moreover, we test the scalability and parallel efficiency using a large benchmark with 3 million atoms.

5.1   Single CG Performance

In Table 1, the parallel model and optimization strategies are combined into five configurations. The specific data illustrate the speedup contribution by each strategy appear in Fig. 7. In Config 1, the data required for the CPE task have to be fetched from main memory frequently which leads to extremely intense bandwidth competition. consequently, the execution time of the pipeline framework is much longer than the baseline. The efficient use of SPM in Config 2 utilizes explicit data reuse based on the code structure, which significantly reduces the main-memory access frequency. In contrast, the software-emulated cache in Config 3 capitalizes on the implicit data reuse of the nonbonded kernel, which is hidden in the data-access feature. A high cache hit rate leads to substantial reductions in main-memory accesses. After implementing the strategies described above, the bandwidth competition is still intense; the performance achieved by 64 CPEs is no better than that of 32 CPEs. Therefore, we choose to use 32 CPEs as assistant cores. These 32 CPEs analyze data reuse to lower main memory access and feed data to the 32 computing CPEs. By doing this, we manage to exploit the computing power of the 32 computing CPEs efficiently and achieve higher performance.

Table 1. Different configurations using different optimization strategies

Name	Description
Baseline	Execution of serial GROMACS code on MPE
Config 1	Parallelization of the nonbonded kernel using the pipeline strategy on an MPE + 64CPEs
Config 2	Config 1 + The efficient use of SPM
Config 3	Config 2 + The software-emulated cache
Config 4	Config 3 + Hybrid parallelism among CPEs

In Fig. 7, the hotspot refers to the Algorithm 1—the nonbonded kernel that we use 64 CPEs to accelerate. After implementing our parallel model and optimization

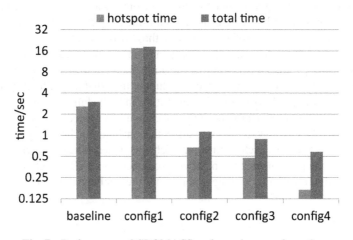

Fig. 7. Performance of GROMACS under various configurations

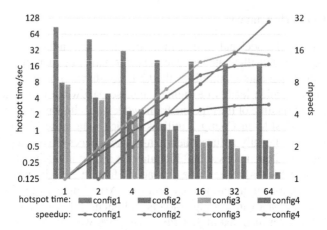

Fig. 8. The execution time and speedup of the nonbonded kernel using different numbers of CPEs in different configs;

strategies, the execution time of the nonbonded kernel decreases from 2.56 s to 0.16 s, which means that our 64-CPE implementation achieves a 16X speedup compared to the baseline. Specifically, through efficient use of the SPM, we achieve a 26.62X speedup compared to Config 1. A software-emulated cache tuned for a sixty-percent hit rate speeds up the nonbonded kernel by 1.41X compared to Config 2. Introducing the cooperative computing among the CPEs brings about a 2.83X speedup compared to Config 3. After that, the overall time of our optimized code in config 4 has a 5x speedup compared to the baseline due to the restriction of Amdahl's law. Given that further optimizations of the main compute kernel could bring only limited speedup of the overall time, we plan to focus on parallelizing other computational functions in future work.

The execution time and speed improvement for each configuration obtained by increasing the number of CPEs are shown in Fig. 8. In Config 1, the bandwidth competition is extremely intense; consequently, we cannot obtain an obvious speedup in hotspot performance using more than 8 CPEs. In Config 2 and Config 3, the bandwidth competition is mitigated by decreasing the main-memory access frequency. Obvious performance improvements can be achieved in these two configs when we use no more than 32 CPEs and the performance decreases in Config 3 when we use 64 CPEs due to the saturation of parallelism. Owing to the implementation of a software-emulated cache, the performance in Config 3 is always higher than that in Config 2. In Config 4, we always halve the number of CPEs for computing and scheduling no matter how many CPEs are used. A higher performance can be achieved compared to Config 3 when we use more than 32 CPEs. Overall, we solve the challenging bandwidth-constrained problem on the Sunway architecture and achieve a near-linear growth in hotspot performance, which means that the bandwidth competition is effectively mitigated and data-transmission operations no longer dominates the nonbonded kernel.

5.2   Strong Scaling

We test the scalability and parallel efficiency of our code using a large benchmark with 3 million atoms. Each node of the Sunway TaihuLight System includes 4 core groups, with 260 heterogeneous cores in total. Each core group corresponds to one process, which means that a task undertaken by one core in the Intel architecture is undertaken by 65 heterogeneous cores in the Sunway architecture. In this way, scalability is significantly improved. Thus far, GROMACS on the Sunway TaihuLight System has been scaled to 798,720 heterogeneous cores.

Simulation performance and parallel efficiency are shown below. In general, GROMACS, when executed on MPEs and CPEs, has higher performance than using only MPEs at any scale. In small node scale (1, 2, 4, 8 nodes), 5x speedup can be achieved. In large node scale (3072 nodes), roughly 2.5x speedup can be achieved. Although the total execution time when using MPE + CPEs is better, the parallel efficiency using MPE + CPEs saturates faster than that using only MPE. In view of this behavior, we think that higher performance on single node always increases the portion of communication among nodes and therefore leads to the faster saturation in parallel efficiency (Fig. 9).

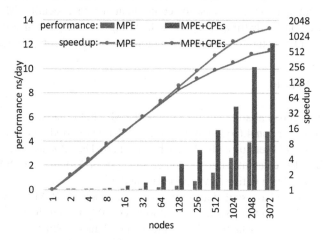

Fig. 9. Performance and parallel efficiency of GROMACS in strong scaling test. We demonstrate both the results for running on only MPE and the results for running on MPE + CPEs.

5.3   Analysis

In this paper, we present a parallel pipeline model to solve data dependency and load imbalance problems without increasing the execution time. This pipeline, which can be considered as cooperative computing, is implemented based on parallelism between the MPE and the CPE clusters. This approach is efficient not only in the Sunway architecture but also for other master-slave architectures such as the "Xeon CPU + Xeon Phi" combination. Given the 8 GB of shared memory and the high bandwidth of the Xeon Phi [9], our pipeline can be extended to multi-level configurations based on the requirements, and the main computing load can be distributed over multiple levels, instead of concentrating the computing component implementation as is done in this case on the Sunway architecture.

Among our optimization strategies, the efficient use of SPM serves as a conventional optimization step for the memory bandwidth limitation. Many works on application optimization on the Sunway TaihuLight System adopt this strategy to handle bandwidth competition, which always leads to high performance improvements. However, this approach is not enough for some applications which requires high memory bandwidth, such as GROMACS. Even after this optimization step, bandwidth competition might still be intense. To address this situation, we introduce the strategies of the software-emulated cache and cooperative computing among the CPEs, which are the main innovation points in this paper. The hit rate of the software cache is based on the locality of memory access. For the memory-access feature of GROMACS, optimal performance is achieved with a sixty-percent hit rate. This strategy is suitable for applications with good data locality. Using the hybrid parallel algorithm among CPEs, the bandwidth competition is mitigated by using 32 CPEs solely to access memory. We actualize a scheduling algorithm that schedules CPEs for data reuse regardless of locality. This strategy is widely suitable for applications with good data reuse and—unlike the strategy of software-emulated cache—it has no requirement for data locality. Moreover, the computing load can be distributed by the scheduling CPEs to best use the available computing power under the condition of maintaining the original computation sequence.

6 Related Work

GROMACS is a classical software package in the MD field that supports multi-level parallelism. From version 4.6 onward, GROMACS has supported efficient GPU acceleration [6]. In the GPU version code, the nonbonded kernel is offloaded to a GPU device; meanwhile, the CPU calculates bonded forces and lattices. Moreover, GROMACS can be executed on MIC in a native and symmetric model.

In recent years, we have started to see projects that refactor GROMACS for heterogeneous many-core architectures such as refactoring GROMACS on the Cell architecture [3]. The Cell processor contains 1 Power Processor Element (PPE) and 8 Synergistic Processing Elements (SPE) and the memory bandwidth seemed not to be a bottleneck in their optimization procedure. Compared to their work, we explore the new challenge—the memory bandwidth limitation when using much more on-chip computing elements to accelerate GROMACS and gave multiple optimization steps to overcome this challenge. Moreover, we use a different way to solve the data dependencies. When compared to other MD packages such as AMBER [10], NAMD [11], CHARMM [12] and LAMMPS [13], GROMACS has good support for the x86 vector instruction sets. By grouping 4 or 8 atoms into one cluster, the nonbonded kernel is quite suitable for execution in the SIMD model [6]. The current scalability is not very ideal compared to NAMD. Using the same benchmark, NAMD can scale to more computing nodes. An extremely large benchmark is needed for possible utilization of the entire computing nodes on the Sunway TaihuLight System.

Before our work on the Sunway Taihulight architecture, the idea of using multiple cores in a heterogeneous way has already been applied in some other multiple/many core architectures. A technique named Speculative Precomputation aiming to improve single-thread performance on a multi-threaded architecture was explored in Jamison D. Collins et al.'s work [14]. This technique utilized otherwise idle hardware thread contexts to execute speculative threads on behalf of the non-speculative thread. These speculative threads attempted to trigger future cache miss events far enough in advance of access by the non-speculative thread that the memory miss latency was avoided entirely. Besides, Daniele Buono et al. [15] investigated message-passing supports on many-core architecture (notably Intel Xeon Phi). In their work, part of threads were used to execute support activities like point-to-point communications so as to overlap communications with calculation. Moreover, the idea of exploiting register-to-register communications between cores has also be used in Daniele Buono's another work [16]. In this work, efficient run-time mechanisms for inter-thread synchronization/communication were developed for fine-grained parallelism on network processors.

7 Conclusions and Future Work

GROMACS is a typical scientific application for high performance computing. It is highly optimized to use fined-grained parallelism such as SIMD and SIMT and exhibits irregular data-access features in hotspots. These characteristics form large challenges when migrating applications to the Sunway TaihuLight System architecture. In this paper, we present an up-to-date parallel pipeline model and several optimization strategies, including efficient use of the SPM, a software-emulated cache, a hybrid parallel algorithm among CPEs to remove the bottlenecks in the source code and to better utilize the hardware architecture in the parallelization procedure. All these strategies play well for solving the challenging bandwidth-constrained problem on the Sunway architecture. In one CG, we achieve a 16X speed improvement in the nonbonded kernel using 64 CPEs. The performance and scalability of this simulation are also significantly improved in strong scaling tests.

To further discuss the adaptability, we also plan to undertake the task of refactoring GROMACS for the Xeon Phi using an offload model. Furthermore, the performance of GROMACS on the Sunway TaihuLight System has the potential to be improved through further vectorization.

References

1. Allen, M.: Introduction to molecular dynamics simulation. Comput. Soft Matter-From Synthet. Polym. Prot. **23**, 1–28 (2004)
2. Haile, J.M.: Molecular Dynamics Simulation: Elementary Methods. Wiley, New York (1992)
3. Olivier, S., Prins, J., Derby, J., Vu, K.: Porting the gromacs molecular dynamics code to the cell processor. In: 21st International Parallel and Distributed Processing Symposium, pp. 1–8. IEEE, California (2007)

4. Elsen, E., Houston, M., Vishal, V., Darve, E., Hanrahan, P., Pande, V.S.: N-Body simulation on GPUs. In: Proceedings of the 2006 ACM/IEEE Conference on Supercomputing, p. 188. ACM, New York (2006)
5. Páll, S., Abraham, M.J., Kutzner, C., Hess, B., Lindahl, E.: Tackling exascale software challenges in molecular dynamics simulations with GROMACS. In: Markidis, S., Laure, E. (eds.) EASC 2014. LNCS, vol. 8759, pp. 3–27. Springer, Cham (2015). doi: 10.1007/978-3-319-15976-8_1
6. Abraham, M.J., Murtola, T., Schulz, R., Páll, S., Smith, J.C., Hess, B., Lindahl, E.: Gromacs: high performance molecular simulations through multi-level parallelism from laptops to supercomputers. SoftwareX 1, 19–25 (2015)
7. Hess, B., Kutzner, C., van der Spoel, D., Lindahl, E.: GROMACS 4: algorithms for highly efficient, load-balanced, and scalable molecular simulation. J. Chem. Theory Comput. 4(3), 435–447 (2008)
8. Fu, H., Liao, J., Yang, J., Wang, L., Song, Z., Huang, X., Zhao, W.: The Sunway TaihuLight supercomputer: system and applications. Sci. China Inf. Sci. 59(7), 1–16 (2016)
9. Chrysos, G.: Intel® Xeon Phi™ coprocessor-the architecture. Intel Whitepaper (2014)
10. Pearlman, D., Case, D., Caldwell, J., Ross, W., Cheatham III, T., DeBolt, S., Ferguson, D., Seibel, G., Kollman, P.: AMBER, a package of computer programs for applying molecular mechanics, normal mode analysis, molecular dynamics and free energy calculations to simulate the structural and energetic properties of molecules. Comput. Phys. Commun. 91, 1–41 (1995)
11. Nelson, M.T., Humphrey, W., Gursoy, A., Dalke, A., Kale, L.V., Skeel, R.D., Schulten, K.: NAMD: a parallel, object oriented molecular dynamics program. Int. J. High Perform. Comput. Appl. 10(4), 251–268 (1996)
12. Brooks, B.R., Bruccoleri, R.E., Olafson, B.D., States, D.J., Swaminathan, S., Karplus, M.: CHARMM—a program for macromolecular energy, minimization, and dynamics calculations. J. Comput. Chem. 4(2), 187–217 (1983)
13. Plimpton, S., Crozier, P., Thompson, A.: LAMMPS-Large-Scale Atomic/Molecular Massively Parallel Simulator, vol. 18. Sandia National Laboratories (2007)
14. Collins, J.D., Wang, H., Tullsen, D.M., Hughes, C., Lee, Y.F., Lavery, D., Shen, J.P.: Speculative precomputation: long-range prefetching of delinquent loads. In: 28th Annual International Symposium on Computer Architecture, pp. 14–25. ACM, Göteborg (2001)
15. Buono, D., De Matteis, T., Mencagli, G., Vanneschi, M.: Optimizing message-passing on multicore architectures using hardware multi-threading. In: 22nd Euromicro International Conference on Parallel, Distributed and Network-Based Processing, pp. 262–270. IEEE, Torino (2014)
16. Buono, D., Mencagli, G.: Run-time mechanisms for fine-grained parallelism on network processors: the tilepro64 experience. In: International Conference on High Performance Computing Simulation, pp. 55–64. IEEE, Bologna (2014)

Exploring FPGA-GPU Heterogeneous Architecture for ADAS: Towards Performance and Energy

Xiebing Wang[1(✉)], Linlin Liu[2], Kai Huang[2], and Alois Knoll[1]

[1] Technische Universität München, 85748 Garching bei München, Germany
{wangxie,knoll}@in.tum.de
[2] Sun Yat-sen University, Guangzhou 510275, People's Republic of China
liull28@mail2.sysu.edu.cn, huangk36@mail.sysu.edu.cn

Abstract. This paper investigates the feasibility of using heterogeneous computing for future advanced driver assistance systems (ADAS) applications. In particular, we take lane detection algorithm (LDA) as a test case. The algorithm is customized into FPGA-GPU heterogeneous implementations which can be executed in either workload constant or balanced scheme. Then the heterogeneous executions are evaluated in view of performance and energy consumption, and further compared with the single-accelerator run. Experiments show that the heterogeneous execution alleviates both the performance and energy bottlenecks caused when only using a single accelerator. Moreover, compared with the single FPGA execution, the workload balance scheme increases the performance by 236.9% and 42.9% on our two tested platforms respectively, while ensuring the low energy cost.

Keywords: Advanced Driver Assistance Systems (ADAS) · OpenCL · FPGA · GPU

1 Introduction

For the automotive industry, advanced driver assistance systems (ADAS) are born to take full advantage of massive multi-sensor information so as to improve in-car and on-road safety. However, the input database space for ADAS applications is so large that it poses a big challenge for software developers to design both real-time and highly efficient algorithms. For these applications, time constraint and reliability guarantee are vital, due to the critical personal and property safety.

To flatten the real-time bound, commercial-off-the-shelf (COTS) hardware accelerators are used to precipitously shorten the execution time of the on-vehicle applications. For instance, since 2014 Nvidia has launched Jetson series [14] for GPU-accelerated parallel processing in the mobile embedded system market. Nevertheless, together with the high performance benefited from GPU also comes the inevitable significant energy consumption. Meanwhile, due to the low energy

© Springer International Publishing AG 2017
S. Ibrahim et al. (Eds.): ICA3PP 2017, LNCS 10393, pp. 33–48, 2017.
DOI: 10.1007/978-3-319-65482-9_3

cost, FPGA as another mainstream accelerator, is widely used in integrated embedded systems.

Aiming at high performance computing (HPC) applications in embedded systems, heterogeneous computing emerges as it leverages different accelerators, such as FPGAs and GPUs, to strengthen the advantages of the individual counterpart. Moreover, this type of reconfigurable computing framework is very compatible with portable platforms because of its high flexibility and scalability. From 2008, open computing language (OpenCL) arises and turns out to be an ideal heterogeneous programming framework as it enables to scale computations among CPUs, GPUs and FPGAs without changing the source code. However, the performance portability on different COTS components cannot be guaranteed due to the diverse OpenCL implementations by respective board vendors. Moreover, to our best knowledge, it is still unknown to what extent the heterogeneous context could be used for the automotive applications.

This paper uses typical lane detection as case study to probe the feasibility of using FPGA-GPU heterogenous architecture for ADAS applications. Lane detection algorithm (LDA) is a well-tested technique and commonly used on conventional electronic control units (ECUs) to assist better driving. We adopted the algorithms developed by [10]. In [10], the authors proposed a particle-filter based algorithm that can detect and track on-road lane markings real-timely. However, the algorithm was only tested in view of performance, while using a single FPGA or GPU. We customized this algorithm into a data-level parallel program to enable its execution in heterogeneous context. Afterwards the program was deployed and executed on two heterogeneous platforms which were equipped with different COTS hardware accelerators. Furthermore, based on the workload constant scenario, we developed a lightweight workload balance scheme that could dynamically identify and adjust the workloads on FPGA and GPU. Experiments showed that the heterogeneous execution resolved both the performance and energy bottlenecks caused when only using a single FPGA or GPU. The workload balance scheme could further reduce the time cost to a large extent, while ensuring the low energy cost. Besides, the proposed scheme can robustly adjust and stabilize the workload according to the computation capacity of each computation device. The main contribution of this paper lies in:

- We use a real-life LDA as the test case and propose a time and energy efficient heterogeneous implementation of this widely-used automotive application.
- Based on the heterogeneous design, we give a lightweight workload balance scheme that can increase the performance by 236.9% and 42.9% on our two test platforms respectively, while ensuring the low energy cost. What's more, the scheme can robustly adjust the workload in diverse road scenarios, based on the computation capacity of each accelerator in use.
- Taking real-life road scenarios as input, we conduct a series of experiments on two heterogeneous platforms, on which different pairs of FPGA and GPU are equipped. Experimental results demonstrate the necessity of utilizing FPGA-GPU combined heterogeneous architecture for future ADAS.

The rest of this paper is organized as follows: Sect. 2 is related work and Sect. 3 overviews the procedure of the tested LDA. Section 4 presents the heterogeneous design and the workload balance scheme. Section 5 gives experimental analysis and Sect. 6 concludes the paper.

2 Related Work

Lots of previous research has compared the performance of using FPGA and GPU in different areas, like deep learning [13], information security [5] and image processing [3,6,7]. These studies present the distinct characteristics that FPGA and GPU show in their computing competence. Generally, FPGA is adept at floating-point arithmetic operations and GPU shows better performance on matrix manipulations. Due to these features, researchers attempt to explore heterogenous architecture to accelerate scientific computing applications. Authors in [1] proposed a heterogenous FPGA-GPU-CPU platform for a sport real-time locating system. The platform is task-level parallel as FPGA is used for data acquisition and GPU is mainly for object tracking. In their design, FPGA is used more as a data gathering processor than a computation accelerating device. Similarly, authors in [12] used the combined FPGA-GPU architecture to perform cardiac physiological optical mapping. In this system, the FPGA is responsible for camera data capture and the GPU mainly disposes fast fourier transform (FFT), inverse fast fourier transform (IFFT) and filtering operations.

Among the aforementioned research, GPU always handles the major computation workload and the performance of FPGA and GPU cannot be directly compared since the task granularity on each device is apparently different.

Several other research is also emerging to compare the performance of FPGA and GPU in the field of real-time processing. Authors in [7] presented a systematic approach to compare FPGA and GPU with five case study algorithms. Their work focused on the algorithmic, data and hardware characteristics of the applications and finally gave a throughput performance of the target devices. In [8], the authors used the roofline model [16] to identify the appropriate accelerator for candidate applications and then performed the comparison based on a pedestrian recognition application called fastHOG. Their work concentrated on the task distribution between different accelerators. Both of the studies in [7,8] do not involve the energy evaluation. Authors in [15] gave a thorough comparison of FPGA and GPU for computer vision algorithms, using a case study of threaded isle detection. Their evaluations are rather comprehensive, including performance, hardware cost, power efficiency and integratability. However, their work cannot reveal the impact of OpenCL on FPGA and GPU, since the algorithms are individually implemented using different programming languages. The most related work to this paper is [4]. In [4], pedestrian detection applications are implemented on a heterogeneous FPGA-GPU-CPU platform and then the authors compared the power, speed and accuracy of several different scenarios, where either FPGA, GPU or both are used for the computation. The difference to our work is that they also used the task-level parallelism like [1] and [12], among the accelerators.

Different to all the work mentioned above, we adopt the data-level parallelism for FPGA and GPU devices so that their performance characteristics can be directly and intuitively compared. Thereupon the heterogeneous designs are evaluated in consideration of time and energy consumption to demonstrate the advantage of using heterogeneous architecture for ADAS applications.

3   Particle-Filter Based LDA

3.1   Algorithm Overview

This section briefly describes the naive design of the LDA and the procedure is shown in Fig. 1. The algorithm mainly consists of three modules (the slash boxes in Fig. 1), namely *pre-processing*, *lane detection* and *lane tracking*. The algorithm analyzes the video stream captured by a moving vehicle and attempts to extract the exact positions of the lane markings highlighted in the output stream.

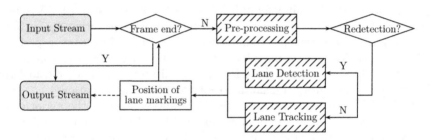

Fig. 1. Flow chart of LDA.

Pre-processing module includes four steps successively applied to the original image. First a region of interest (ROI) is cropped from the raw image and only this ROI is further processed. Then the ROI is transformed into grayscale space where each pixel reflects the intensity of the pixel in original image. After grayscaling, the edges of the lane markings are slightly obvious since they are substantially brighter than the streets and roads around. To enhance this contrast of pixel intensity, a Sobel filter is applied to the grayscaled image to detect pixel variations and extract edges. Finally, a threshold is used to tune the intensity of all pixels in the image to avoid noise influence.

Lane detection module generates a set of *candidate lines* via assigning random values from a normal distribution to form the candidate line set. For each candidate line, a weight is calculated to reveal how close the line is located to the real lane. Given this weight set, the line with the highest weight is chosen as the *best line* and certain number of candidate lines are reserved as *good lines*, which would be further used in the *lane tracking* module.

Lane tracking module adopts a particle filter to predict the positions of the lane markings, using both the ROI of the current frame and the *best line* and *good lines* of the previous frame. The particle filter consists of three steps:

1. The *prediction update* step amends previous *good lines* with a normal distribution $N(\mu, \sigma^2)$, with mean $\mu = 0$ and standard deviation $\sigma > 0$. $\mu = 0$ means no shift is expected in optimal case, while $\sigma > 0$ reveals a deviation in real scenarios. The updated lines are seen as prior probability distribution of the lane markings in current frame.
2. The *importance weight update* step recalculates the weights of the particles via Gaussian function

$$\omega_i = \frac{1}{\sigma_f \sqrt{2\pi}} e^{-(X_i - \mu_f)^2 / 2\sigma_f^2}, i = 1, 2, \cdots, N \qquad (1)$$

where N is the particle number, μ_f indicates the *best line* in previous frame and σ_f expresses the noise that accounts for a possible error in case the position of the lane marking does not change within two frames. Then the importance weight of each particle is normalized to obtain the updated weight

$$\omega_i^{updated} = \frac{\omega_i}{\sum_{i=1}^{N} \omega_i}. \qquad (2)$$

3. Based on the importance weights, the *resampling* step selects particles from the newly updated set to prevent a degeneration of the particle set.

Finally the redetection checking step verifies whether the detected positions reasonably conform to the physical properties of the lane markings. If not, additional detection step is triggered to seek the lane markings again. The criteria of redetection is as follows: (i) Lane markings do not cross. (ii) There exists a minimum distance between each two detected lane markings. This value is adjustable and can be small when lots of lanes have to be detected. (iii) There should be a minimum percentage of the lane marking within the ROI. This parameter is flexible and can be user-defined.

3.2   Initial Design

In the basic version, each of the modules depicted in Sect. 3.1 is programmed as an OpenCL kernel which will be executed on the hardware accelerator. For simplicity, KERNEL_PRE, KERNEL_LD and KERNEL_PF are used as their individual kernel names. Note that both lane detection and tracking require normally distributed random numbers to process their following tasks. Hence these numbers should be generated by a random number generator. Therefore another kernel called KERNEL_RNG is required. With above four kernels, the flow chart in Fig. 1 is abstracted as the pseudo-code shown in Algorithm 1, where the red lines (lines 2, 4, 6, 9 in Algorithm 1) represent the kernel tasks.

4   Heterogeneous Design

4.1   Data-Level Parallelism

The heterogeneous version of the application tries to distribute the kernel tasks among different accelerators. From Algorithm 1 it is seen that for each input

---

Algorithm 1. LDA (basic version)

Input: raw camera-captured video stream
Output: video stream with lanes marked
 1: initialization
 2: random number generation //KERNEL_RNG
 3: **while** not the end frame **do**
 4:    ROI image pre-processing //KERNEL_PRE
 5:    **if** redetection **then**
 6:       lane detection //KERNEL_LD
 7:       *candidate line* generation
 8:    **else**
 9:       lane tracking //KERNEL_PF
10:       *good line* resampling
11:    **end if**
12:    *best line* extraction and mark lanes in current frame
13: **end while**

---

video stream, random number generation (KERNEL_RNG) is run only once and the other three kernels are executed repeatedly inner the frame loop. For this reason, KERNEL_RNG can be performed on every accelerator since its time cost is rather small, while the other kernels should be scattered across the accelerators as they are the main tasks.

Meanwhile, it is worth noting that two layers of data dependencies exist here: (i) both the executions of KERNEL_LD and KERNEL_PF use the output of KERNEL_RNG and KERNEL_PRE, and (ii) if the current frame is the first tracking frame, then it will need the detected positions of lane markings in the previous frame, in this case the execution of KERNEL_PF relies on the output of KERNEL_LD. Consequently, task-level parallelism for these three kernels is not desirable as it requires the indirect Device→Host→Device data transfer, which is considerably time-consuming due to the lack of state-of-the-art commercial direct FPGA-GPU data communication mechanism.

From the above, data-level parallelism of the basic LDA is used for the heterogeneous context and Fig. 2 gives the overall processing procedure. In general, the host utilizes an installable client driver (ICD) loader to coordinate the tasks executing on FPGA and GPU. When invoking OpenCL API functions, the program runtime passes kernel parameters to the ICD loader and then the ICD loader calls FPGA- and GPU-specific functions with *fpga-* and *gpu-*specific parameters respectively.

The host side is responsible for (i) kernel parameters initialization and raw image I/O when the program begins, and (ii) result collection, weight updating and line resampling during the frame loop. On each hardware accelerator, the ROI of the image is preprocessed and then the detection kernel (KERNEL_LD) samples a set of *candidate lines* and calculates their intensity weights individually. As shown in Fig. 2, KERNEL_LD processes n lines on the FPGA and m lines on the GPU, and subsequently returns the intensity weights to the host. On the host,

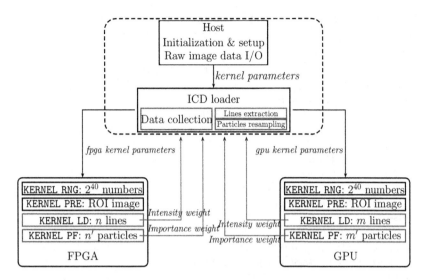

Fig. 2. Execution of LDA in heterogeneous context overview. Red and blue items are distributed tasks on the FPGA and GPU. The italic items show the transfer of parameters. (Color figure online)

after extracting a series of *good lines* and one *best line*, the lane detection operation outputs the position of the lane markings as the form of *best line*. Similarly for lane tracking kernel (KERNEL_PF), a group of particles are extracted from the output data of KERNEL_LD. Again these particles are scattered and processed on the two accelerators. Here n' and m' particles are respectively disposed on the FPGA and GPU. When the importance weights of the particles are finished calculating, they are returned back to the host side and new particles are resampled based on the aggregated results to step into the new iteration.

4.2 Workload Balance

To get the optimal execution, the workload of KERNEL_LD and KERNEL_PF on GPU and FPGA needs to be dynamically assigned since GPU and FPGA show distinct computation capacities in consideration of different types of data manipulations. This is especially important when the application is intended to be scaled across different platforms, where different FPGA and GPU boards are used. Since time and energy costs are two of the most important indicators when monitoring ADAS applications, this paper gives a time optimization based workload balance scheme for the heterogeneous LDA and the energy cost is afterwards investigated.

Algorithm 2 briefs the workload balance scheme. Here *funcRNG*, *funcPRE*, *funcLD* and *funcPF* are corresponding kernel functions, from which the timing information can be profiled. The details of function *funcAdjustWL* are shown in Algorithm 3. Assume that the input is the initial task load for FPGA and GPU devices (i.e., m, n, m', n' in Fig. 2), and the output is the time-optimal executions

---

Algorithm 2. Workload balance scheme

Input: m, n, m', n'
Output: t_{kernel}
 1: $t_{rng_f} \leftarrow funcRNG(m + n)$, $t_{rng_g} \leftarrow funcRNG(m + n)$
 2: $t_{kernel} \leftarrow max(t_{rng_f}, t_{rng_g})$
 3: **while** not the end frame **do**
 4:    $t_{pre_g} \leftarrow funcPRE(m)$, $t_{pre_f} \leftarrow funcPRE(n)$
 5:    $t_{pre} \leftarrow t_{pre_f} + t_{pre_g}$
 6:    $t_{kernel} \leftarrow t_{kernel} + t_{pre}$
 7:    **if** redetection **then**
 8:        $t_{ld_g} \leftarrow funcLD(m)$, $t_{ld_f} \leftarrow funcLD(n)$
 9:        $t_{kernel} \leftarrow t_{kernel} + max(t_{ld_f}, t_{ld_g})$
10:        $m, n \leftarrow funcAdjustWL(t_{ld_f}, t_{ld_g}, m, n)$
11:    **else**
12:        $t_{pf_g} \leftarrow funcPF(m')$, $t_{pf_f} \leftarrow funcPF(n')$
13:        $t_{kernel} \leftarrow t_{kernel} + max(t_{pf_f}, t_{pf_g})$
14:        $m', n' \leftarrow funcAdjustWL(t_{pf_f}, t_{pf_g}, m', n')$
15:    **end if**
16: **end while**

Algorithm 3. Function $funcAdjustWL$ in Algorithm 2

Input: t_f, t_g, W_f, W_g
Output: W_f, W_g
 1: $c_f \leftarrow \frac{W_f}{t_f}$, $c_g \leftarrow \frac{W_g}{t_g}$
 2: $W_f \leftarrow \frac{c_f}{c_f+c_g}(W_f + W_g)$, $W_g \leftarrow \frac{c_g}{c_f+c_g}(W_f + W_g)$

---

of the program (indicated as kernel execution time t_{kernel}). The idea is that the workload for a device should be proportional to its computation capacity, i.e., its throughput. Hence, after each frame is processed complete, the kernel execution time on each device is recorded (lines 1, 4, 8, 12 in Algorithm 2) and the throughput is calculated. Then the total work load is re-assigned based on the current throughputs of the computing devices (lines 10, 14 in Algorithm 2). This scheme assumes that for each frame, the execution times of KERNEL_LD and KERNEL_PF are proportional to their current task load.

4.3   Performance and Energy Evaluation

In our context, totally four scenarios are involved, namely, single FPGA execution (*singleFPGA*), single GPU execution (*singleGPU*), work-load-constant (*heteroConstant*) and work-load-balanced (*heteroBalanced*) heterogeneous execution. In work-load-constant scenario, the whole task is partitioned in advance and then fed to FPGA and GPU devices. Thus the task proportions on FPGA and GPU are always constant. While in work-load-balanced scenario, with given partitioned task, the workload balance scheme tunes the task proportions on FPGA and GPU during the processing of each frame.

To reveal the tradeoffs between these situations, we record the execution time of all the four implementations to evaluate their real-time performance over the energy cost. In order to calculate the energy cost, we construct the runtime environment where both FPGA and GPU cards are working in full load mode, so that the peak power consumption can be reached. To fulfill this, we use extremely large computation task load since the particle filter is highly scalable and consequently the larger the particle number is, the more the computation task load would be. During the evaluation, the execution time of each run is measured to calculate the real-time performance. We use the same power estimation method as [9] and Altera PowerPlay power analyzer [11] is used to estimate the power consumption of running each OpenCL kernel on FPGA. As for the power estimation of GPU and CPU, we use data from official specifications of the COTS components.

5 Experiment and Analysis

5.1 Experimental Setup

The applications are run in two different heterogeneous contexts listed in Table 1. Both platforms contain one FPGA and one GPU board. For contrast, they are equipped with two groups of boards which show rather different computation capacities. Platform #1 is deployed with a Terasic Arria 10 FPGA and an AMD W7100 GPU, while a Nallatech pcie385n FPGA and an Nvidia Quadro K600 are used on platform #2. Note that the computation capacities of the FPGA and GPU boards on each platform are rather different. AMD W7100 presents an obviously superior performance than Arria 10, while Nallatech pcie385n and Quadro K600 have comparable computing capacities. The purpose of this is to demonstrate the robustness of our applications in heterogeneous contexts where accelerators have unbalanced computation competence.

Table 1. Detailed specification of the hardware platforms

Platform	#1		#2	
Host CPU	Intel Xeon E31225 @ 3.10 GHz		Intel Core 2 Quad Q9300 @ 2.50 GHz	
Thermal Design Power	95 W		95 W	
Device	FPGA	GPU	FPGA	GPU
Model	Terasic Arria 10	AMD W7100	Nallatech 385	Quadro K600
Architecture	Arria 10 AX	FirePro	Stratix V GS	Kepler GK
OpenCL SDK version	Intel FPGA SDK 16.0	AMD APP SDK 3.0	Intel FPGA SDK 13.1	CUDA 8.0
Peak GFLOPS	1366	3379.2	294.7	336.4
Peak board power (W)	95	150	25	40

To demonstrate the high availability of using the tested LDA for real-life driving conditions, we use video streams from different data sets with different scenarios. The detailed information of these videos is listed in Table 2, of which cordova1, cordova2, washington1 and washington2 are from Caltech lanes dataset [2], while the others are self-recorded. These videos are captured in different resolutions and the frame numbers have a great range from 232 (washington2) to 4992 (night_land_car). Moreover, these videos represent various road situations including in day and night, with heavy traffic, with blurred and broken lines, in street and highway, in urban and rural areas, etc. The purpose of this is to obtain as actual results as possible.

Table 2. Detailed information of the test videos

Videos	Name	Total frames	Resolution	Scenario
1	cordova1	250	640×480	bus view
2	cordova2	406	640×480	blur lane
3	washington1	337	640×480	street shade
4	washington2	**232**	640×480	blur lane
5	street	3056	640×480	street road
6	day_highway	1718	640×480	high way
7	Frontfacingobstacle	4601	480×360	crossing lane
8	HighSpeedDrivingShort	1871	1920×1080	high way
9	clip2	1289	640×360	rural
10	clip4	899	640×360	dark
11	night_land_car	**4992**	640×480	night
12	night_traffic	2654	640×480	heavy traffic
13	oli_4	2287	480×320	broken lane
14	night_4	2799	640×480	night highway
15	night_brokenlanes	1897	640×480	broken lane
16	Weilerhemmen	4944	640×480	light disturbance

During the experiments each video is run 10 times per platform and the overall results are collected and averaged. To construct the large task load, we use rather large numbers of particles to iterate over each generation of the line sets. In details, during each run we use 2^{12} *good lines* and 2^{13} *candidate lines* to detect 2 *best lines*. As for the heterogeneous executions, the initial task proportion on FPGA is set as the range from 1% to 99% and the rest part is executed on GPU. When using the workload balance scheme, an initial task proportion is given and afterwards both the task proportions of FPGA and GPU are recorded frame by frame to present the real-time work load distribution.

Note that for *singleFPGA* and *singleGPU* scenarios, the task proportions on FPGA are constant 100% and 0%, respectively. Hence the results of *singleFPGA* and *singleGPU* are used as reference for evaluating the heterogenous executions.

5.2   Results and Analysis

Workload Balance Scheme. The objective of the workload balance scheme is to minimize the kernel execution time (t_{kernel} in Algorithm 2). To validate the correctness and robustness of this scheme, (i) the kernel execution times of the four designs are recorded and (ii) during the *heteroBalanced* run, the real-time task rates on both FPGA and GPU devices are monitored. Figure 3 summarizes the experimental results. Due to the page limit, Fig. 3(c) and (d) only show the real-time task rates of washington2 and night_land_car as they are the two videos with the smallest and largest frame numbers.

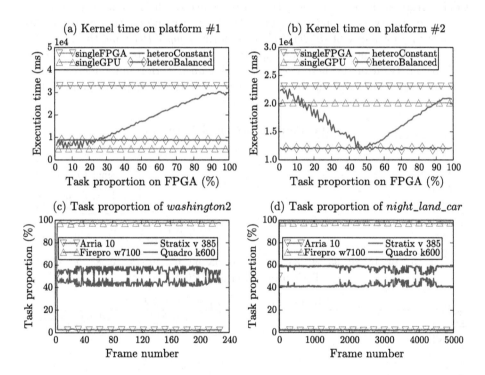

Fig. 3. Validity and robust test results of the workload balance scheme.

Figure 3(a) and (b) indicate that when compared with *singleFPGA*, both of the *heteroConstant* and *heteroBalanced* implementations can shorten the kernel execution time to a large degree. The kernel time cost of *heteroBalanced* is 26.94% and 51.96% of *singleFPGA*, 177.76% and 59.49% of *singleGPU* on platform #1 and #2, respectively. It's seen that the time costs of the heterogeneous executions on platform #1 are larger than the *singleGPU* case. This is because the time cost of *singleFPGA* is an order of magnitude larger than that of *singleGPU*. Therefore simply shifting the task a little from GPU to FPGA would incur considerable latency. As can be oberserved, on both platforms the kernel execution time of *heteroConstant* always surpasses *heteroBalanced*, which verifies the validity of the workload balance scheme. In Fig. 3(c) and (d), it is seen that the real-time task proportions of both videos converge within 5 frames and then keep relatively constant with minor fluctuations. What's more, the workload balance scheme can identify the optimal task distributions on FPGA and GPU, regardless of the input video. To be specific, the optimal task rates on the FPGA of platform #1 and #2 are around 2% and 41%, respectively. This demonstrates the robustness of the workload balance scheme.

Performance. Figure 4 depicts the performance of the four implementations running on the two test platforms. From the figure we observe that on both platforms the performance of *singleGPU* outperforms *singleFPGA* and this is reasonable due to the lower computation capacity of FPGA (refer to the peak GFLOPS in Table 1). Both of the heterogeneous runs gain a performance increase than *singleFPGA*, which without doubt benefits from the high performance GPU.

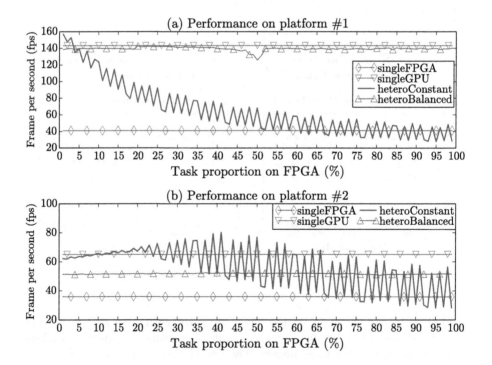

Fig. 4. Performance results overview.

The *heteroConstant* execution displays a considerable fluctuation. This is because when gradually increasing the task rate, due to the OpenCL specification, the task load on FPGA shows a discrete step change, which greatly influences the CPU↔FPGA data transfer latency since direct memory access (DMA) requires data alignment of the transmitted data. Intuitively, the performance declines when more and more tasks are shifted to FPGA. As for *heteroBalanced* scenario, the performance turns out very stable since the task load is dynamically allocated and the heterogeneous execution would rapidly converges to equilibrium after several frames, which is verified in Sect. 5.2. Moreover, on platform #1 the balanced run could achieve a comparative performance over the *singleGPU* run.

On the whole, using heterogeneous architecture improves the performance when compared with the *singleFPGA* lower bound. The workload balance scheme reconciles the heterogeneous system and during all task rates, *heteroBalanced* increases the performance by 236.9% and 42.9% on platform #1 and #2 respectively, when compared with *singleFPGA*.

Energy. Figure 5 shows the overall energy cost for the four different designs. Figure 5(a) and (b) present the energy cost of the overall system, while Fig. 5(c) and (d) give the results of the accelerator energy consumption.

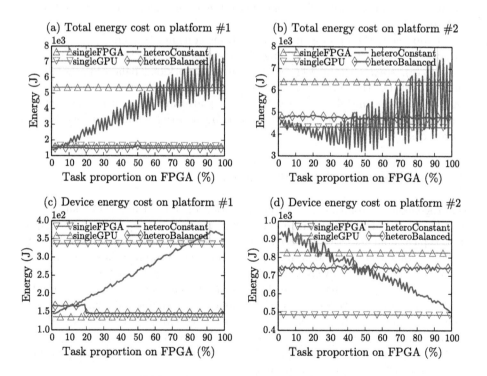

Fig. 5. Energy consumption overview.

As indicated by Fig. 5(a) and (b), the system energy is much larger when using a single FPGA, compared with the energy cost of *singleGPU*. This is mainly because the overall execution time of *singleFPGA* is much longer than *singleGPU*, which poses a huge increment of the CPU energy cost. However, on both platforms our heterogeneous designs are able to consume almost as less energy as *singleGPU*. The *heteroBalanced* implementation utilizes the least energy on platform #1 and increases the energy by only 10.98% when compared with *singleGPU* on platform #2.

With regards to the on-device energy cost (Fig. 5(c) and (d)), the two platforms exhibit different features. On platform #1, using a single GPU costs the least device energy and we owe this to the huge speedup of the AMD W7100 card. The energy cost of FPGA is not able to outperform the GPU because the low-power advantage of FPGA over GPU simply cannot compensate for the far-behind performance gap. As the consequence, the device energy increases linearly when tasks are migrated on FPGA, which is clearly observed via the *heteroConstant* curve. Nevertheless, the *heteroBalanced* design commendably suppresses the energy cost, as it manages to identify the power-performance tradeoff of FPGA and GPU and subsequently always distributes more task load on GPU. As for platform #2, the performance gap between Stratix V 385 and Quadro K600 is much narrower and in this case FPGA fully displays its low-power characteristic, when comparing the result of the *singleFPGA* and *singleGPU* curves. Compared with the *singleGPU* upper bound, *heteroConstant* reduces the energy cost to 89.49%.

In summary, the heterogeneous executions consume less energy, when compared with the most-energy-cost single accelerator (i.e., *singleFPGA* in Fig. 5(a), (b) and (c), *singleGPU* in Fig. 5(d)). Using the workload balanced scheme not only "smoothes" the heterogeneous execution, but also shortens the energy cost regardless of the initial task rates. On both platforms, when using the heterogeneous architecture, the performance can be boosted while ensuring the low energy cost.

6 Conclusion and Future Work

Heterogeneous computing is a promising solution for future ADAS since it is able to regulate the performance and energy tradeoff in the system. This paper used typical lane detection as case study to probe the feasibility of using FPGA-GPU combined heterogenous architecture for ADAS applications. The performance and energy costs were carefully evaluated among the heterogeneous and single-accelerator executions. We demonstrated that the heterogeneous implementations could solve both the performance and energy bottlenecks caused when only using a single accelerator. Moreover, the proposed workload balance scheme can further boost the performance, while ensuring the low energy cost.

Our future work is to use more ADAS applications to verify the pros and cons of the heterogeneous computing.

Acknowledgments. This work is supported in part by the scholarship from China Scholarship Council (CSC) under the Grant No. 201506270152.

References

1. Alawieh, M., Kasparek, M., Franke, N., Hupfer, J.: A high performance FPGA-GPU-CPU platform for a real-time locating system. In: 23rd European Signal Processing Conference (EUSIPCO), pp. 1576–1580. IEEE (2015)
2. Aly, M.: Caltech lanes. http://www.vision.caltech.edu/malaa/datasets/caltech-lanes. Accessed 10 Mar 2017
3. Asano, S., Maruyama, T., Yamaguchi, Y.: Performance comparison of FPGa, GPU and CPU in image processing. In: 19th International Conference on Field Programmable Logic and Applications (FPL), pp. 126–131. IEEE (2009)
4. Blair, C., Robertson, N.M., Hume, D.: Characterizing a heterogeneous system for person detection in video using histograms of oriented gradients: power versus speed versus accuracy. IEEE J. Emerg. Sel. Top. Circ. Syst. **3**(2), 236–247 (2013)
5. Che, S., Li, J., Sheaffer, J.W., Skadron, K., Lach, J.: Accelerating compute-intensive applications with GPUs and FPGAs. In: Proceedings of the 6th IEEE Symposium on Application Specific Processors (SASP), pp. 101–107. IEEE (2008)
6. Chen, D., Singh, D.: Fractal video compression in OpenCL: an evaluation of CPUs, GPUs, and FPGAs as acceleration platforms. In: 18th Asia and South Pacific Design Automation Conference (ASP-DAC), pp. 297–304. IEEE (2013)
7. Cope, B., Cheung, P.Y., Luk, W., Howes, L.: Performance comparison of graphics processors to reconfigurable logic: a case study. IEEE Trans. Comput. **59**(4), 433–448 (2010)
8. Da Silva, B., Braeken, A., D'Hollander, E.H., Touhafi, A., Cornelis, J.G., Lemeire, J.: Comparing and combining GPU and FPGA accelerators in an image processing context. In: 23rd International Conference on Field Programmable Logic and Applications (FPL), pp. 1–4. IEEE (2013)
9. Fowers, J., Brown, G., Cooke, P., Stitt, G.: A performance and energy comparison of FPGAs, GPUs, and multicores for sliding-window applications. In: Proceedings of the ACM/SIGDA International Symposium on Field Programmable Gate Arrays (FPGA), pp. 47–56. ACM (2012)
10. Huang, K., Hu, B., Botsch, J., Madduri, N., Knoll, A.: A scalable lane detection algorithm on COTSs with OpenCL. In: Design, Automation & Test in Europe Conference & Exhibition (DATE), pp. 229–232. IEEE (2016)
11. Intel: Powerplay early power estimators and power analyzer. https://www.altera.com/support/support-resources/operation-and-testing/power/pow-powerplay.html. Accessed 10 Mar 2017
12. Meng, P., Jacobsen, M., Kastner, R.: FPGA-GPU-CPU heterogenous architecture for real-time cardiac physiological optical mapping. In: International Conference on Field-Programmable Technology (ICFPT), pp. 37–42. IEEE (2012)
13. Nurvitadhi, E., Sheffield, D., Sim, J., Mishra, A., Venkatesh, G., Marr, D.: Accelerating binarized neural networks: comparison of FPGA, CPU, GPU, and ASIC. In: International Conference on Field-Programmable Technology (ICFPT), pp. 37–42. IEEE (2016)
14. Nvidia: Nvidia® jetson™: the embedded platform for autonomous everything. http://www.nvidia.com/object/embedded-systems-dev-kits-modules.html. Accessed 10 Mar 2017

15. Struyf, L., De Beugher, S., Van Uytsel, D.H., Kanters, F., Goedemé, T.: The battle of the giants: a case study of GPU vs FPGA optimisation for real-time image processing. In: Proceedings of the 4th International Conference on Pervasive and Embedded Computing and Communication Systems (PECCS), vol. 1, pp. 112–119. VISIGRAPP (2014)
16. Williams, S., Waterman, A., Patterson, D.: Roofline: an insightful visual performance model for multicore architectures. Commun. ACM **52**(4), 65–76 (2009)

Software Systems and Programming Models

Hzmem: New Huge Page Allocator with Main Memory Compression

Guoxi Li$^{(\boxtimes)}$, Wenzhi Chen, Kui Su, Zhongyong Lu, and Zonghui Wang

College of Computer Science, Zhejiang University, Hangzhou 310027, China
{guoxili,chenwz,sukuias12,lzy6032,zhwang}@zju.edu.cn

Abstract. Today, applications that require large memory footprint prevail in cloud computing fields from both industry and academia. They impose great stress on the memory management of operating system, spend quite a substantial proportion of time dealing with TLB misses and excessively reduce consolidation ratio in term of server consolidation and virtualization. There are two methods to address these problems: main memory compression and large page support. However, to the best of our knowledge, there is no existing practical research on combination of these two methods since the combination in commodity operating system requires lots of low-level design modifications.

We propose a new memory management framework that is decoupled and flexible for easy developments and is able to run simultaneously with the original memory management. On top of the new framework, we implement Hzmem, a completely new large page memory management redesign with features of main memory compression to address the aforementioned problems once for all but requires only minor modifications to the other subsystems of the underlying operating system. Our method achieves competitive performance compared with native large page support, increases effective memory size and impacts little on other subsystems of operating system.

Keywords: Large page · Main memory compression · Linux

1 Introduction

Nowadays, with more and more applying of cloud computing both in business area and research community, workloads are very likely to consume more memory than a single physical machine can offer. These memory-hungry workloads often require large memory footprint but show poor temporal locality [2,6,13]. They often involve relational databases, key-value stores and huge gateway machines handling huge routing data.

All above workloads require memory overcommitment to fulfill tasks in such situations. One kind of memory overcommitment like swapping can swap out memory presumably not to be used in the recent future onto disks. However, disk accesses are far slower than memory accesses, bringing lots of overheads. Thus developers and researchers resort to another practical memory overcommitment

© Springer International Publishing AG 2017
S. Ibrahim et al. (Eds.): ICA3PP 2017, LNCS 10393, pp. 51–64, 2017.
DOI: 10.1007/978-3-319-65482-9_4

technique—main memory compression. Main memory compression compresses memory and stores compressed data in reserved memory regions, enormously increasing effective memory size and avoiding disk access latencies.

In the meantime, traditional physical memory management with granularity of constant size lacks its meaningfulness and efficiency. Current commodity operating systems, like Linux and FreeBSD, have introduced their own large page (memory page size larger than base page) supports. They are not self-contained mechanisms, but are heavily dependent on the traditional memory management on base pages.

We consider such problems in the context of modern commodity operating system like Linux, but the ideas are not specific to the Linux. Currently, the Linux `hugepage` (Linux terms for large page) mechanism demands 4 KB base pages from the famous `Buddy System` and merges them to form a larger size (2 MB on x86-64 platforms), which is complicated and time-consuming. Since hugepage mechanism stems from traditional base page managements, frequent and heavy `hugepage` allocations would fail in most cases due to the lack of enough physically continuous memory especially after a long time of running. Moreover, `hugepage` in Linux does not support main memory compression and it is difficult to add main memory compression feature since that needs heavy modifications to low level design of memory management which brings considerable effort.

Therefore, it has motivated us to redesign a completely new memory management framework that is decoupled and flexible for convenient development. Based on the new memory management framework, we implement Hzmem that includes a self-contained hugepage allocator which is decoupled from the normal page allocator in the environment of frequent and heavy hugepage allocations and easily equips the new hugepage allocator with main memory compression feature. It achieves competitive performance over native large page supports, increases effective memory size and impacts little on other subsystems of operating system.

Hzmem's benefits are (1) the new hugepage allocator has competitive performance compared with native hugepage implementations; (2) performance isolation, which means new allocator brings no or little performance punishment to other parts of system utilizing normal physical memory management; (3) increasing effective memory capacity, which increases consolidation ratio and improves performance when applications require memory beyond the capacity.

2   Related Work

We briefly discuss some works related to our work.

Memory mangement architecture: Recently, with trends of workloads using memory quite differently from the time when memory management was designed, lots of researches [2, 3, 7, 9] are focused on modern memory management.

Basu et al. [2] propose mapping part of a process's virtual memory address with *Direct Segment*, removing TLB miss penalty. *Direct Segment* maps a contiguous virtual memory directly to a contiguous physical memory using simple hardware requirements. However, *Direct Segment* needs both software and hardware supports, making it not suitable for commodity hardware.

Clements et al. [3] propose a new virtual memory system design called RadixVM that removes serial operations on virtual memory and enables fully concurrent operations by ensuring non-overlapping memory regions. RadixVM need so many modifications to a commodity operating system that it is only implemented on a Unix-like teaching operating system.

Huang et al. [9] conduct a comprehensive and quantitative survey on the development of the Linux memory management over five years (2009–2015). The study shows the changes and bugs are highly centralized around the key functionalities, like memory allocator and page fault handler.

These studies give many insights and lessons that modifications to commodity operating system's key functionalities are very challenging and our work manages to avoid the challenges by using a decoupled and flexible framework.

Huge page support: Navarro et al. [12] implement OS support for large pages in FreeBSD. They focus on reservation-based allocation and fragmentation control. Hzmem is built on a decoupled and flexible memory framework which is detached from the normal base page allocator. Therefore, fragmentations of base pages impact little on Hzmem.

Kwon et al. [10] propose Ingens, a framework for transparent huge page support through tracking utilization and access frequency of memory pages. In contrast to Ingens, Hzmem's focused on adding main memory compression feature in order to increase effective memory size and improve consolidation ratio in terms of server consolidation and virtualization.

Main memory compression: Ekman et al. [5] propose a main memory compression framework that eliminates performance losses by exploiting simple and yet effective compression scheme, a highly-efficient compressed data locating and a hierarchical memory layout. Pekhimenko et al. [14] propose *Linearly Compressed Pages* (LCP) that avoids the performance degradation problem without requiring costly or energy-inefficient hardware. Like these two work, Hzmem also makes optimizations on zeroed pages yet with no need of any hardware modifications.

Tuduce et al. [15] propose a main memory compression solution that adapts the allocation of real memory between uncompressed and compressed pages. It allows to shrink or grow the size of the compressed area without user involvement and it is implemented in Linux over commodity hardware. In contrast to this work, Hzmem is focused on the compression of large pages and stores the compressed data in base pages. This will lead to negligible wasting space at a percentage of no more than $1/512$.

3   Motivation

Most modern commodity operating systems support large pages. For example, Linux allows applications to use specific API (it is called `hugetlbfs` in Linux) to allocate memory based on large pages (`hugepage` in Linux). These large pages are allocated from memory pools that are preserved in advance by administrators. Moreover, these memory pools are in turn allocated from Linux `Buddy System`.

What leads to this lengthy detour on implementation of large page memory management? It is that the memory management design in Linux inherently bases on the fact that the page size is constant (4 KB in Linux). Linux uses the macro `PAGE_SIZE` to represent this base page size, which is used throughout almost all the Linux subsystems, like virtual memory management, physical memory management, I/O subsystem, page reclaiming, etc. For example, I/O subsystem assumes a fixed page size as 4 KB and this goes well with the 4 KB block size that is multiples of a sector size. As for large page support, it is around in Linux since 2003 [4] when it has been long after Linux was designed and developed and some assumptions of design cannot be modified easily.

Consequently, Linux resigns itself to adding large page feature upon the base page memory management though overheads and maintainability problems will be caused. For example, a large page is treated as 512 contiguous base pages in an aligned 2 MB region and still uses the same page descriptors (`struct page` in Linux which holds meta informations for one page). However the page descriptors for large pages are page descriptors for base pages linked together as `compound pages` with heads in linked lists holding useful information, which is a great waste of memory space. As one of the most used data structures in kernel, the page descriptor in Linux has to meet requirements from many subsystems and thus this largely increases its size. Since there are so many page descriptors that a single byte increase will lay much stress on kernel memory use.

Linux has already had supports for main memory compression like `zram`, `zswap` and `zcache`, but currently these supports are highly dependent on page reclaiming subsystem. Page reclaiming subsystem is an important part in Linux which also assumes a fixed page size. It mainly contains two reclaiming procedures that are (1) writing back pages that are backed up by files and (2) swapping out pages that are not backed up by any persistent storage devices. Both these two processes involve the aforementioned I/O subsystems that also assume a fixed page size. For example, `zram` treats itself as a block device that is used as destination for swapping.

Equipping large page support with data compression feature based on these compression techniques will cost non-trivial efforts to modify Linux and even question some assumptions Linux has long held. Moreover, large page supported through `hugetlbfs` has no backing up storage devices and there is no need for swapping or writing back to persistent storage devices. Thus it is not practical to enhance Linux with data compression feature using current compression supports and may bring instability to Linux base code. Therefore, in order to meet our requirements, we need to redesign the physical memory management.

4   Architecture and Implementation

We implement Hzmem based on the decoupled and flexible memory management framework with a completely new hugepage allocator, a feature of main

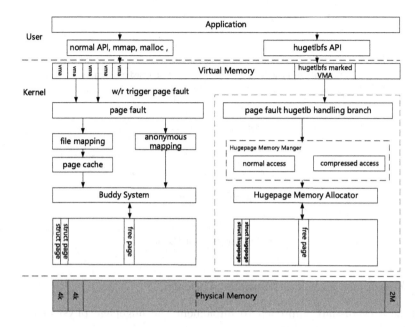

Fig. 1. Architecture of decoupled and flexible memory management framework

memory compression and `hugetlbfs` API compatibility. The decoupled and flexible memory management framework is shown in Fig. 1. The new framework contains a placeholder for a physical memory manager that can be implemented according to academic or industrial requirements and run with the original one at the same time, thus making it decoupled and flexible. Figure 1 only takes Hzmem for example in that placeholder. Applications in user space using normal API or `hugetlbfs` API to create virtual memories which will be translated into different physical memories managed by different manager respectively. Hzmem contains four components: physical hugepage memory management, page fault handler for hugepages, page reclaiming for compressing hugepages and hugepage compression data management. Figure 2 shows workflow among four components. A daemon in page reclaiming module checks allocated huge pages in every NUMA node, selects the cold ones and invokes compression interfaces in compression data management. It also changes the page table accordingly, which makes it possible to retrieve the compressed huge pages. When an application accesses the compressed data, a page fault is triggered. The page handler identifies the compressed huge page, invokes decompression interfaces and restores the page table entries. Finally the application can resume and access the data. In a word, page reclaiming and page fault handling work in reverse ways. Their cooperation makes the framework function properly.

We implement 4148 lines of C code (LoC). It runs over Linux with kernel 3.10, functioning simultaneously well with the original Linux memory management subsystem.

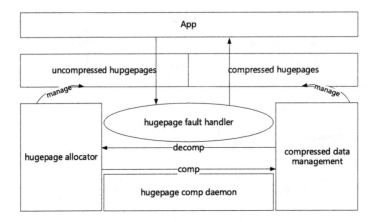

Fig. 2. Workflow of Hzmem

4.1 Hugepage Physical Memory Allocator

We take a clean-slate approach to implement the hugepage physical memory allocator from the ground up.

New Page Descriptors. The new memory management is specialized for 2 MB huge pages in x86-64 architecture (currently we do not support 1 GB large pages) and only used by user level applications through `hugetlbfs` API. In the new framework, we drop the original method or workaround that combines 512 contiguous page descriptors into a compound page descriptor for a huge page. Instead, we use customized page descriptors specific only to huge pages that are simple and without any "compound" and space-wasting problems. This will significantly save memory space used for storing page descriptors since both the number and the size are decreasing. For example, a modern commodity server with memory capacity of over 256 GB using the new page descriptors can save several GBs which is 1%-2% percent of the memory and the situation worsens when larger memory available.

Without any need of concerns on other subsystems, our new page descriptor `struct hugepage` only deals with the specific use cases for huge pages used through `hugetlbfs` by use level applications. This makes the new descriptor deprive itself of the fields of structure related to `slab`, `compound page`, etc., which is very suitable for use cases where memory is under severe pressure that it is resigned to main memory compression.

Free and Allocated Page Management. With large memory capacity, each node in NUMA system can reach tens of GBs. To maintain such large memory, one node cannot be managed like that of Linux: except the first node, a node contains only one zone called `ZONE_NORMAL`. In our memory management framework, memory of one node is divided into several sections according to its size. Currently, we set size of one section to be 4 GB heuristically. It enables us manage memory in a smaller granularity and achieve better scalability and parallelism.

In Linux `Buddy System`, the highest order of contiguous memory is 10. It is contiguous memory of up to 4 MB that Linux is designed to manage. A huge page is 2 MB of order 9 that is almost the highest. Therefore, maintaining free huge pages in higher order will not bring much benefits and thus we keep free huge pages in a linked list in each section one by one. It deprives us of splitting and coalescing neighboring memory, thus accelerating allocation and deallocation speed.

During allocation, the allocator moves one free huge page from the free list into a new linked list called `lru list`. Every node has two `lru lists` that are used for holding allocated pages: one active list for hot pages and the other for cold pages, which makes it convenient for page reclaiming described in Sect. 4.3. During deallocation, the allocator can get information of node and section from the new page descriptor which helps put the huge page back to the proper free list.

Initialization. Our hugepage physical memory allocator should be initialized at the same time of other unmodified memory management subsystems like `Buddy System`.

First, we reserve a range of contiguous physical memories that are to be detached from the management from `Buddy System`. After operating system finishes booting, we have (1) `Buddy System` manage memory of base pages mainly for kernel memory and user level applications' sections of base pages; (2) the new hugepage physical memory allocator manage the reserved memory for huge pages that are used by applications through `hugetlbfs` API.

We make minor modifications to Linux code base. We add hooks to the architecture-specific memory detect during booting and mark a range of memories as reserved, making them invisible to `Buddy System`.

Finally, as is ignored by operating system, we set up the direct mapping for the specific range of memories on our own, making it convenient to access the memory without triggering page faults in kernel mode.

4.2   Page Fault Handler

A page fault is called "soft" page fault when it merely allocates a new page and sets up a new page table entry, without reading contents from backing physical store devices like disks. Huge pages are not backed up by persistent storage. Therefore, what we focus on is the soft page faults triggered by huge pages.

A user level application allocates huge pages from our new memory management through compatible `hugetlbfs` API. After mounting `hugetlbfs` filesystem, creating a file at the `mount` point and calling `mmap` system call on the file, an application is able to take advantage of our new huge page memory management by accessing the mapped memory. It is the `mmap` system call that marks the range of virtual memory as "MAP_HUGETLB" which enables us identify what needs to be allocated through the new hugepage memory allocator in page fault handler.

We replace the old hugepage code path in page fault handler with our new code path based on the new hugepage memory allocator. Since the page fault related to huge pages is the soft page fault and has the feature of compression, there are two situations:

1. Normal page fault case where the physical page is accessed for the first time. Since the huge page fault is a soft page fault, the page fault handler just allocates a zeroed huge page from the new hugepage physical memory allocator.
2. Page fault case where the physical page is protection violation. It is either a shared page that can be retrieved from page cache or a compressed page that can be decompressed and reclaimed from the compression data mangement subsystem described in Sect. 4.4.

4.3 Page Reclaiming

Page reclaiming monitors and identifies the allocated huge pages as cold or hot pages. Cold pages are isolated to be ready for reclaiming. In every node of operating system, there is one daemon called `hp_kscannerd` that does periodical checks on the usage of huge pages. We take lessons from Linux `Buddy System` that every node has a watermark indicating whether the memory usage of the node is under pressure. If the number of free huge pages is below the watermark, the daemon on the corresponding node wakes up and starts reclaiming pages identified as cold through compressing interface of compression data management described in Sect. 4.4 and changes the page table entries accordingly.

We use the second chance algorithm taken from original Linux page reclaiming mechanism to identify an allocated page as cold or hot. There are two states involved in page descriptor: active and referenced in the page descriptor; and one state in page table: page accessed bit in page table entry. Referenced state indicates whether the page is accessed and active state indicates whether the page is in active list. Whenever the physical page is accessed the bit in page table entry is set by hardware without any operating system interferences. Software is responsible for clearing the bit periodically and setting referenced state accordingly in page descriptors. The waked daemon scans `lru lists` and checks the referenced state to determine whether the page should be reclaimed: (1) only two consecutive referenced state sets or clears can cause the page to be transferred between the active list and the inactive list; (2) the pages in inactive list are ready for reclaiming.

4.4 Hugepage Compression Data Management

Hugepage compression data management participates in controls of compression/decompression and compressed data management. It is the lowest level part as it provides compression/decompression interfaces for other parts to invoke. It is also important part as the speed of compression/decompression and efficiency of compressed data management impact greatly on performance of the whole system.

Compression Algorithms. There are various kinds of lossless data compression algorithms. We choose LZO and LZ4 algorithms (the insight of choosing is out of scope of this paper). LZO algorithm appears since Linux kernel 3.10 and LZ4 algorithm since Kernel 3.15. We port both algorithms to our system. LZO is better than LZ4 in compression ratio and compressing speed, but LZ4 is better in decompressing [16] which we believe more important in memory management framework.

Optimization on Zeroed Huge Pages. As mentioned before, when first accessed, the allocator just allocates zeroed huge pages, which account for substantial proportions of memory. When zeroed huge pages get compressed, they still occupy a good amount of memory. Thus, we optimize zeroed huge page compression through setting its size to 0 in compressed data region. This optimization, we believe, will achieve good improvements both in space and time when zeored huge pages are pervasive.

Compressed Data Management. Compressed data cannot be stored in memory backed up by huge pages. Since one compressed huge page is usually smaller than 2 MB, storing in huge page memory will waste a lot of space and make it difficult to manage the compressed data. The new allocator runs simultaneously with the `Buddy System`, which means there are two memory management mechanisms taking charge of memory of different granularities in one machine. Taking advantage of this, we split the compressed data and store them in multiples of 4 KB blocks in physical memory space backed up by base pages.

In Linux we use the mature `vmalloc` to allocate memory from base pages. There are two reasons: (1) simple, robust and virtual space for `vmalloc` is large enough in x86-64 architecture; (2) one compressed huge page will at most waste 1/512 space which is small and acceptable. Thus we create a red black tree and use the `hugetlbfs` file along with index of huge pages as key for retrieving when decompressing is triggered in page fault handler.

5   Evaluation

We evaluate Hzmem using a variety of user applications and benchmarks, comparing against the performance of Linux's `hugetlbfs` support which is state-of-the-art. Experiments are performed on one machine with 16 Intel Xeon E7520 1.87 GHz CPUs and 64 GB memory. We use Linux 3.10 and Centos 7 for the host environment and use 4 KB for base pages and 2 MB for large pages.

We first use SPEC CPU2006 [8] and STREAM [11] benchmarks to evaluate overheads and throughput of Hzmem when compression is disabled. Then we use datasets from Yelp Dataset Challenge [1] to measure effective memory increasing introduced by Hzmem when compression is enabled. Finally we conduct a series of benchmarks to test the new page fault overhead in order to show performance isolations guaranteed by Hzmem. We use consistent parameters for hot and cold pages detecting: watermark is 80% and detecting period is 10 s.

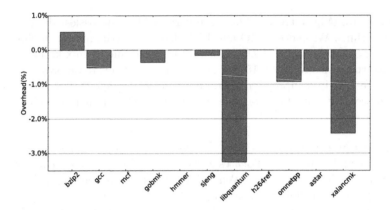

Fig. 3. Overhead of Hzmem relative to unmodified Linux

5.1 Overheads of Hzmem

Figure 3 shows the overheads introduced by Hzmem from SPEC CPU2006 benchmarks. To evaluate the overall overheads of Hzmem physical memory management, we utilize `hugectl` from `libhugetlbfs` to run the benchmarks. `libhugetlbfs` is a set of user tools making use of Linux `hugetlbfs`, which requires only re-linking binaries without modifications to source codes. `Hugectl` can remap the text and data segments of programs into memories backed up by large pages and hook `libc` memory allocation functions `malloc` with mappings of large pages.

From the results, we can find that Hzmem slows down 3.25% in the worst case and 0.7% in average. The performance loss is mainly from the extra code path dealing with decompression/compression. Hzmem is not showing advantage but achieving comparative performance when memory is not under pressure.

5.2 Throughputs of Hzmem

Table 1 shows the throughput of Hzmem using STREAM benchmark against unmodified Linux. STREAM is a synthetic memory bandwidth benchmark that measures the performance of four long vector operations: Copy, Scale, Add, and Triad. We configure STREAM to use different array sizes. From the results, we see that in small sizes from 10 million to 40 million the throughput is almost the same with the difference lower than 1%. On the contrary, with size from 80 million on, the difference gets larger. Hzmem has 7% larger throughput than unmodified Linux in the best case and 5% in average.

The reason is that Hzmem is based on our decoupled and flexible memory framework which uses new page descriptor for each large page without splitting or coalescing neighboring memory. When memory is under pressure and fragmented after long running, unmodified Linux tends to split or coalesce tremendous amounts of memory to meet large page memory allocation from user applications, thus bringing overheads and reducing throughput.

Table 1. Throughput (MB/s) of benchmark **STREAM** when different sizes are applied.

Size(m)	COPY		SCALE		ADD		TRIAD	
	Hzmem	Unmod	Hzmem	Unmod	Hzmem	Unmod	Hzmem	Unmod
10	3035.7	3043.0	2594.3	2595.8	3244.0	3226.5	2930.7	2928.4
20	2318.0	2321.6	1970.0	1968.6	2298.3	2278.1	1839.0	1838.9
30	2315.5	2317.7	1973.2	1970.6	2395.9	2397.8	2214.7	2216.7
40	2319.0	2325.0	1972.2	1976.0	2294.5	2295.7	1825.9	1829.9
80	2503.4	2324.0	2131.7	1978.2	2440.6	2299.9	1956.0	1828.2
100	2383.6	2324.2	2029.5	1978.1	2327.5	2278.8	1875.9	1836.7

5.3 Effective Memory Increasing

By compressing large pages, Hzmem makes larger effective memory available to applications and avoids disk accesses or being killed due to OOM killer. Effective memory size increasing by compressing is dependent on the compression ratio. We measure an average compression ratio of 0.23 tested on dataset of Yelp Dataset using LZ4 algorithm. To evaluate the actual effective memory increasing introduced by Hzmem, we configure the same size of large memory in advance both in Hzmem and unmodified Linux. We run an application that keeps allocating memory using hugetlbfs API and writing memory until it fails. The largest memory it can obtain is the effective memory size.

Figure 4 shows effective memory increasing introduced by Hzmem against unmodified Linux using hugetlbfs API in different large memory size configurations in advance. We can see that unmodified Linux cannot increase effective memory size at all and the largest size available is the same as configured in advance. Hzmem can increase the effective memory size by 4465% but the gap is narrowing as the memory size configured in advance gets larger. This stems from the fact that Hzmem stores the compressed data in base page space.

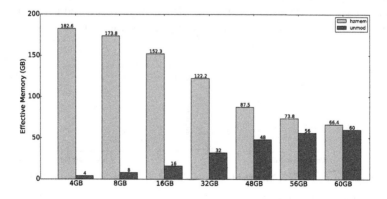

Fig. 4. Effective memory of Hzmem relative to unmodified Linux

The smaller large page memory size is configured in advance the larger base page space can be used to store the compressed data from large page space. However, data compressing brings overheads and trade off between effective memory size and performance should be taken into consideration by system administrators.

5.4   Overhead of Page Fault and Performance Isolation

Page faults in Hzmem involve data decompressing and lie in critical path of memory accesses. Thus performance of the new page fault handler of large pages is important. To evaluate the performance of the new page fault handling, we run an application that stresses heavily on the page faults. It first uses `hugetlbfs` API to allocate certain amounts of large pages and writes pages to trigger page faults. The amounts of large page to be allocated from user applications are divided into two groups dependent on whether beyond size of large pages configured in advance: non-overcommitted and overcommitted. To eliminate overheads of data compressing from page reclaiming, we configure size of large pages to be 4 GB in advance and let the application sleep for 30 s in the case of overcommitted and we subtract this period of time from running time for fairness when evaluating throughput. Another reason why we let the application sleep is that it can make the allocated pages as cold as possible, which stresses more heavily on the new page fault handler.

Figure 5a shows throughput of page faults stress test against unmodified Linux when not overcommitted. We can see that Hzmem has larger throughput than unmodified Linux but the difference is not larger than 9 MB/s, which means 4% in the best case.

Figure 5b shows throughput of page faults stress test against unmodified Linux when overcommitted. Since 4 GB of large pages are configured in advance, when allocating not over 4 GB the throughput are almost the same. When allocating over 4 GB large pages, the throughput of unmodified Linux becomes zero since it cannot increase effective memory size. However, when over 4 GB throughput of Hzmem are decreasing no more than 27%, which is apparently quite better than swapping involved in disk accesses which are much slower.

In the meantime, we also measure the CPU utilization caused by compressing daemons: 16.6% in the worst case and 11.0% in average. In our case, we have

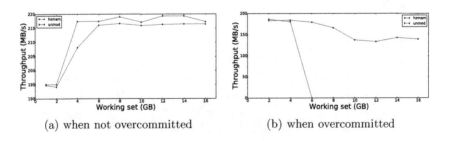

(a) when not overcommitted   (b) when overcommitted

Fig. 5. Throughput of page fault stress test

compressing daemons work on two nodes. If more daemons operate on more nodes, compressing overhead will be amortized and become much smaller on each CPU.

6   Conclusion

With trends towards running workloads that require big-memory, large page support and main memory compression are the techniques that developers often rely on to improve performance. However, applying the two techniques is beyond a matter of engineering. Combination of the two techniques is related to the low level design modifications and considerable effort. This motivates us to propose a completely new memory management framework that is decoupled and flexible for easy development and able to run simultaneously with the original memory manager. On top of the new memory management framework, Hzmem is large page memory management redesign with compression features independent from the base page memory management. It achieves competitive performance with native large page supports, increases effective memory size and impacts little on other subsystems of operating system.

Acknowledgments. Many thanks to members of ARC Lab of Zhejiang University for their constructive comments and helps during the project. We would like to thank the anonymous reviewers for their feedbacks. This research is funded by National Key Technologies R&D Program of Ministry of Science and Technology of the People's Republic of China under Grant NO. 2016YFB0800201.

References

1. Yelp Dataset Challenge. https://www.yelp.com/dataset_challenge/
2. Basu, A., Gandhi, J., Chang, J., Hill, M.D., Swift, M.M.: Efficient virtual memory for big memory servers. In: Proceedings of the International Symposium on Computer Architecture, pp. 237–248 (2013)
3. Clements, A.T., Kaashoek, M.F., Zeldovich, N.: RadixVM: scalable address spaces for multithreaded applications. In: EuroSys, pp. 211–224 (2013)
4. Corbet, J.: Huge pages part 1 (Introduction) (2010). https://lwn.net/Articles/374424/
5. Ekman, M., Stenstrom, P.: A robust main-memory compression scheme. In: Proceedings of the International Symposium on Computer Architecture 00(C), pp. 74–85 (2005)
6. Ferdman, M., Adileh, A., Kocberber, O., Volos, S., Alisafaee, M., Jevdjic, D., Kaynak, C., Popescu, A.D., Ailamaki, A., Falsafi, B.: Clearing the clouds: a study of emerging scale-out workloads on modern hardware. ACM SIGPLAN Not. **47**, 37–48 (2012). ACM
7. Gerber, S., Zellweger, G., Achermann, R., Kourtis, K., Roscoe, T., Milojicic, D.: Not your parents' physical address space. In: HotOS (2015)
8. Henning, J.L.: Spec cpu2006 benchmark descriptions. ACM SIGARCH Comput. Archit. News **34**(4), 1–17 (2006)

9. Huang, J., Qureshi, M.K., Schwan, K.: An evolutionary study of linux memory management for fun and profit methodology. In: Review-ATC 2016 (2016)
10. Kwon, Y., Yu, H., Peter, S., Rossbach, C.J., Witchel, E.: Coordinated and efficient huge page management with ingens. In: 12th USENIX Symposium on Operating Systems Design and Implementation (OSDI 2016), pp. 705–721 (2016)
11. McCalpin: STREAM benchmark (2002). http://www.cs.virginia.edu/stream/
12. Navarro, J., Iyer, S., Druschel, P., Cox, A.: Practical, transparent operating system support for superpages. ACM SIGOPS Oper. Syst. Rev. **36**, 89 (2002)
13. Ousterhout, J., Agrawal, P., Erickson, D., Kozyrakis, C., Leverich, J., Mazières, D., Mitra, S., Narayanan, A., Ongaro, D., Parulkar, G., et al.: The case for RAMCloud. Commun. ACM **54**(7), 121–130 (2011)
14. Pekhimenko, G., Mowry, T.C., Mutlu, O.: Linearly compressed pages: a low-complexity, low-latency main memory compression framework. In: MICRO-46 Proceedings of the 46th Annual IEEE/ACM International Symposium on Microarchitecture (MICRO), p. 489 (2013)
15. Tuduce, I.C., Gross, T.R.: Adaptive main memory compression. In: USENIX Annual Technical Conference, General Track, pp. 237–250 (2005)
16. Zaitsev, P., Tkachenko, V.: Evaluating Database Compression Methods: Update (2016). https://www.percona.com/blog/2016/04/13/evaluating-database-compression-methods-update/

An FPGA-Based Real-Time Moving Object Tracking Approach

Wenjie Chen[1,2], Yangyang Ma[1], Zhilei Chai[3,4(✉)], Mingsong Chen[1,2],
and Daojing He[2]

[1] MoE Engineering Research Center for Software/Hardware Co-Design,
East China Normal University, Shanghai, China
wjchen@sei.ecnu.edu.cn
[2] Shanghai Key Laboratory of Trustworthy Computing, Shanghai, China
[3] State Key Laboratory of Mathematical Engineering and Advanced Computing,
Wuxi 214125, China
[4] School of IoT Engineering, Jiangnan University, Wuxi, China
zlchai@jiangnan.edu.cn

Abstract. Due to high complexity on matching computation, real-time object tracking is generally a very challenging task for practical applications. This paper proposes a new algorithm for moving object tracking, which improves the traditional KLT algorithm by using the motion information for feature points selection to avoid the irrelevant feature points residing in the background area. Moreover, this paper designs the hardware architecture of the FPGA part to accelerate the computation by optimizing the inherent parallelism of the algorithm. The proposed algorithm is able to significantly reduce the computation time. Experimental results show that our algorithm implemented in an FPGA-SoC (Zynq 7020, 667 MHz) requires only 0.030 s to handle a VGA resolution frame, which is suitable for real-time tracking. This achieves up to 30× performance improvement compared with the desktop PC (i3, 3.4 GHz), or 370× compared with the ARM (Cortex-A8, 1 GHz). The experiment also shows that our approach consumes less energy significantly than PC and ARM for the same workload, which indicates that it is suitable for energy-critical system.

Keywords: FPGA · Object tracking · KLT · MKLT · ZYNQ

1 Introduction

With the rapid progress on emerging industries such as driverless car, robotics, UAV(unmanned aerial vehicle), object detection and tracking technology becomes more and more important. It is widely applied in real-life applications, such as visual surveillance [9], traffic detection (e.g., traffic accident detection [14], vehicle detection [2], and pedestrian detection [11]) and human gesture recognition [13]. Essentially, object tracking is to robustly estimate the motion

© Springer International Publishing AG 2017
S. Ibrahim et al. (Eds.): ICA3PP 2017, LNCS 10393, pp. 65–80, 2017.
DOI: 10.1007/978-3-319-65482-9_5

state (e.g., location, orientation, size) of a target object in each frame of an input image sequence [6].

Up to now, many object tracking approaches have been developed, such as PF (*Particle Filter*) [15], MS (*Mean Shift*) [4], and KLT (*Kanade-Lucas-Tomasi*) [8,19]. KLT is faster than traditional techniques for examining far fewer potential matches between the images, because that only some special points (feature points) are used for matching. *Shi-Tomasi corners* [18] are selected as feature points used in KLT. In this paper, we use KLT as the basis of our algorithm.

"Real time" is an inherent requirement for image tracking applications. However, KLT still require a large amount of computation due to the high complexity of the feature descriptor. Fortunately, the parallel acceleration techniques, such as Multi-core, GPU (*Graphics Processing Unit*) and FPGA (*Field-Programmable Gate Array*), have rapidly developed in industry.

The emerging technology of "FPGA-SoC" give us more supports. An FPGA-SoC is a chip encapsulated both FPGA and a processor (such as an ARM core). Liu et al. [7] proposed a moving object detection system based on FPGA-Soc (ZYNQ 7000). Sajjanar et al. [17] and Rohilla et al. [16] reported the similar work independently with ZYNQ 7020. All these three systems use "*background subtraction*" as the object detection algorithm. Background subtraction is very fast on object detection for fixed camera, since only subtraction operation are invoke for each pixel. However, background subtraction is often not quite robust in real environments, where reflections, rain or illumination change breaks up the static background hypothesis.

In this paper, we also propose an object tracking system with an FPGA-SoC (ZYNQ 7020). But our system is based on KLT, which tracks the obvious feature points only. Therefore, it is immune for small change in background. What's more, each feature point's movement (moving direction and velocity) can be visualized. Our contributions are: (1) improve the traditional KLT algorithm by exploiting the moving information to avoid selecting the inferior feature points that are on the static background; (2) design the hardware architecture of the FPGA part to accelerate the computation by optimizing the inherent parallelism of the algorithm; and (3) develop this system with a high-level language (C language) instead of HDL (*Hardware Description Language*, such as VHDL, Verilog), which can further improve flexibility, scalability and portability.

For the sake of comparison and evaluation, the algorithm is also implemented on a normal desktop PC and on an independent ARM system. The experimental results show that our algorithm implemented on the FPGA-SoC takes only 0.030 s to capture the moving object and visualize it for two sequential frames of an image with a resolution of 640 × 480. It is approximately 34 times faster than the normal PC and 370 times faster than the ARM system.

The remainder of this paper is organized as follows. Section 2 introduces the basic conception of feature points and KLT algorithm and proposes our improvement on KLT algorithm. Section 3 proposes the hardware architecture for our parallel optimization technique to improve computational performance on an FPGA. Section 4 describes the implementation and the experimental results, and Sect. 5 concludes this paper.

2   Methodology

In this section, we briefly review the conception of feature points and the feature points based object tracking algorithm, i.e., the KLT algorithm. Then, by analyzing the deficiency of KLT for moving object tracking, we propose our improvement.

2.1   Feature Points

Feature points (*a.k.a. interest points*) are the key points on object detection and tracking. Typical features include *corners* (interest points), *edges* (curves), *blobs* (regions of interest points) and *ridges*. Feature detection is the method to calculate abstractions of image information and decide whether there is an image feature around each pixel of the image. Since a majority of computer vision algorithms start from features detection, the performance of feature detectors is essential to the entire algorithm.

Corners and edges are frequently used as feature points for object detection and tracking. Edges are points where there is a boundary (or an edge) between two image regions. And corner is the intersection of two edges. Harris *et al.* [5] took **corners** as the regions in the image with large variation in intensity in all the directions.

Let $E(x, y)$ be the difference in intensity for a displacement of (u, v) in all directions:

$$E(x, y) = \sum_{u,v} w(u, v) \left[I(x + u, y + v) - I(u, v) \right]^2 \tag{1}$$

where $I(x, y)$ is the intensity of point (x, y), and $w(u, v)$ is the weighted window. To detect feature points, the basic idea is to maximize this $E(x, y)$. After Taylor Expansion to Eq. (1), we get

$$E(x, y) \approx \begin{bmatrix} x & y \end{bmatrix} M \begin{bmatrix} x \\ y \end{bmatrix} \tag{2}$$

where

$$M = \sum_{u,v} w(u, v) \begin{bmatrix} I_x I_x, & I_x I_y \\ I_x I_y, & I_y I_y \end{bmatrix}. \tag{3}$$

Here, I_x and I_y are image derivatives in x and y directions respectively.

An interest point (includes corner and edge) is characterized by a large variation of E, in all directions of the vector (x, y). By analyzing the eigenvalues of M, this characterization can be expressed in the following way: M should have two large eigenvalues (λ_1 and λ_2) for an interest point, where the eigenvalues (λ) can be computed by

$$\lambda = (\sum_{u,v} I_x^2 + \sum_{u,v} I_y^2 \pm \sqrt{(\sum_{u,v} I_x^2 - \sum_{u,v} I_y^2)^2 + 4 * (I_x * I_y)^2})/2 \tag{4}$$

In [18], Shi and Tomasi proposed the following conditions to decide the feature points (corners and edges) for object tracking.

$$\begin{cases} max(\lambda_1, \lambda_2) < \lambda_{th0} & \Rightarrow flat \\ \lambda_1 < \lambda_{th0} \ and \ \lambda_2 > \lambda_{th1} \ or \ \lambda_2 < \lambda_{th0} \ and \ \lambda_1 > \lambda_{th1} & \Rightarrow edge \\ min(\lambda_1, \lambda_2) > \lambda_{th1} & \Rightarrow corner \end{cases} \quad (5)$$

where λ_{th0} and λ_{th1} is the low threshold and the high threshold respectively that could be set by user.

2.2 The KLT Approach

Object tracking is an special image registration problem between two sequential image frames. The KLT algorithm utilizes spatial intensity information to search for the position that yields the best match. it is based on the following three assumptions.

1. **Intensity conservation.** The intensity of the special point keeps unchanged after a small time period, i.e., $I(x + dx, y + dy, t + dt) = I(x, y, t)$.
2. **Limited displacement.** The displacement for a small time period is limited, i.e., $dt < \epsilon_t \Rightarrow d^2x + d^2y < \epsilon_d$, where ϵ_t and ϵ_d are limited values.
3. **Approximate neighbor.** In a small neighborhood of the target point, all points have similar motion direction and speed. It is called a *"window"*.

Let I, J denote the two sequential image frames. Each point $\mathbf{x}(x, y)$ in window W moves through the same displacement $\mathbf{d}(dx, dy)$ from I to J. Then, the request of KLT algorithm is: Given I, J, find the best reasonable $\mathbf{d}(dx, dy)$ to satisfy the above three assumptions. It can also be expressed as to find a solution to minimize the dissimilarity:

$$\epsilon(\mathbf{d}) = \epsilon(dx, dy) = \sum_{x=u_x-w_x}^{u_x+w_x} \sum_{y=u_y-w_y}^{u_y+w_y} (J(x + dx, y + dy) - I(x, y))^2. \quad (6)$$

or, it can be expressed as the integral format:

$$\epsilon = \iint_W [J(\mathbf{x} + \mathbf{d}/2) - I(\mathbf{x} - \mathbf{d}/2)]^2 w(\mathbf{x}) d\mathbf{x} \quad (7)$$

here ϵ means the difference between image I and J on the window W. W is the window with a radius of $w/2$ and centered in $(\mathbf{x} - \mathbf{d}/2)$ for I and $(\mathbf{x} + \mathbf{d}/2)$ for J accordingly.

To minimize ϵ, let $\frac{\partial \epsilon}{\partial \mathbf{d}} = 0$. Finally, it could be deduced to:

$$\mathbf{Zd} = \mathbf{e} \quad (8)$$

where $\mathbf{Z}$ is a 2×2 matrix, and $\mathbf{e}$ is a 2×1 vector:

$$\mathbf{Z} = \iint_W \mathbf{g}(\mathbf{x})\mathbf{g}^T(\mathbf{x})w(\mathbf{x})d\mathbf{x} \quad (9)$$

$$\mathbf{e} = \iint_W [I(\mathbf{x}) - J(\mathbf{x})]\mathbf{g}(\mathbf{x})w(\mathbf{x})d\mathbf{x} \tag{10}$$

where

$$\mathbf{g} = [\frac{\partial}{\partial x}(\frac{I+J}{2}) \quad \frac{\partial}{\partial y}(\frac{I+J}{2})]^T. \tag{11}$$

Then,

$$\mathbf{d} = \mathbf{Z}^{-1} \cdot \mathbf{e}, \text{ if } \mathbf{Z} \text{ is invertible} \tag{12}$$

For feature points, the condition that $\mathbf{Z}$ is invertible is satisfied. Then we get $\mathbf{d}$, the best match of two feature points between two images. It is faster than traditional techniques because it examines feature points only, which are far fewer potential matches between the images.

2.3   The KLT Procedure and Its Deficiency

At first, the feature points (KLT use Shi-Tomasi corners) are selected in the initial frame. (The number of feature points is set by user.) Then, these feature points will be tracked in the next frame. If some feature points cannot be found in the next frame (lost), they should be discarded and new feature points will be re-selected by returning to the previous frame. For large displacement point tracking, the image pyramid operation is involved. Unfortunately, these operations bring feedbacks or loops, which result in destruction of the pipeline. These will decrease the performance and the efficiency of the algorithm when implemented on an FPGA.

Let us consider the problem of moving object detection on a static background. Many Shi-Tomasi corners fall on the background rather than on the object. As an example shown in Fig. 1, for the first detected four Shi-Tomasi corners (points marked in red), three points ('A', 'B', and 'C') fall on the background, and only one point ('D') falls on the moving object ("the pedestrians"). Therefore, when we perform the object tracking, the three feature points with no movement should be replaced.

2.4   Our Improvement of KLT–MKLT

New approach to select feature points. KLT selects the corner feature points following Eqs. 3, 4, and 5. During the procedure, no motion information is involved. Therefore, the corner points can be located in the static background as well as in the moving object, which leads to the aforementioned problems.

In this paper, we improve the KLT algorithm by introducing the motion information into the feature matrix to filter out the static corner points. This improved algorithm is named *motion-enhanced KLT(MKLT)*. The feature matrix is illustrated in Eq. 13.

$$F = \begin{bmatrix} \sum_W (I_{x1}+I_{x2})^2, & \sum_W (I_{x1}+I_{x2})(I_{y1}+I_{y2}), & \sum_W (I_{x1}+I_{x2})(I_{t1}-I_{t2}) \\ \sum_W (I_{x1}+I_{x2})(I_{y1}+I_{y2}), & \sum_W (I_{y1}+I_{y2})^2, & \sum_W (I_{y1}+I_{y2})(I_{t1}-I_{t2}) \end{bmatrix} \tag{13}$$

Fig. 1. An example of Shi-Tomasi corners using KLT. Source image: [12]. (Color figure online)

I_{x1}, I_{x2} means the horizontal gradient; I_{y1}, I_{y2} means the vertical gradient; and I_{t1}, I_{t2} refers to the intensity of two continuous frames.

In the case of a fixed-camera scene, let M_{xx}, M_{xy}, M_{yy}, M_1, and M_2 denote the larger values and μ_1 and μ_2 denote the smaller values. The feature matrix can be classified into 4 categories by the point status (static/moving) and the background type (weak/strong texture region).

As shown in Eq. 14, only the moving points on the strong texture region have larger elements. Therefore, we distinguish the moving points with a strong texture from other points.

$$F \rightarrow \begin{cases} \begin{bmatrix} 0 & 0 & 0 \\ 0 & 0 & 0 \end{bmatrix}, \text{static points on weak texture region} \\[2em] \begin{bmatrix} 0 & 0 & \mu_1 \\ 0 & 0 & \mu_2 \end{bmatrix}, \text{moving points on weak texture region} \\[2em] \begin{bmatrix} M_{xx} & M_{xy} & 0 \\ M_{xy} & M_{yy} & 0 \end{bmatrix}, \text{corner points} \\[2em] \begin{bmatrix} M_{xx} & M_{xy} & M_1 \\ M_{xy} & M_{yy} & M_2 \end{bmatrix}, \text{moving points on strong texture region} \end{cases} \quad (14)$$

An overview of MKLT. In the traditional KLT algorithm, multi-layer pyramid operations are introduced to calculate the image motion tensor iteratively from coarse to fine. These operations cause FPGA to access DDR memory during each iteration. Frequent access to DDR extends the computing time. Moreover, iterative operations decrease the efficiency of the pipeline. In some cases, we are not concerned with real-time tracking on a specific target but concerned with

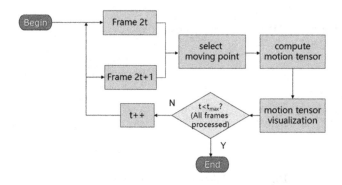

Fig. 2. An Overview of our MKLT algorithm

whether any moving object appears in the target scene. In this situation, we can omit the multi-layer pyramid operation and iterations.

Figure 2 presents an overview of the MKLT procedure. The objective is to find the moving points between two adjacent frames, calculate the motion tensor of these points, and mark the moving velocity and direction. In the traditional KLT algorithm, the points in Frame0 are tracked in Frame1, the points in Frame1 are tracked in Frame2, and so on. However, in MKLT, points in even frames are tracked in odd frames, but points in odd frames will not be tracked in even frames. For example, points in Frame0 are tracked in Frame1 and points in Frame2 are tracked in Frame3, but points in Frame1 will not be tracked in Frame2. The advantage of this scheme is that when the hardware accesses the image data, the starting addresses of all the odd frames are the same, and it is the same as the even frames.

3   Hardware Design of MKLT

3.1   Workflow of MKLT

As shown in Fig. 2, MKLT object tracking is a circular procedure. For each iteration between two frames, there are four stages, as shown in Fig. 3.

- **S1: smoothing**. This stage is to smooth the image sequence to reduce the image noise and external influence. Generally, this stage is realized by convolution.
- **S2: gradient calculation**. This is to calculate the gradient of the image that has been smoothed. The gradient includes 3 dimensions: the horizontal gradient (I_x), the vertical gradient (I_y) and the time gradient (I_t).
- **S3: motion tensor calculation**. This stage calculates the cumulative accumulation of the gradient in the rectangular feature window. This accumulating operation can be perform row by row first and then column by column, which is suitable for the pipeline.
- **S4: visualization**. The motion tensors are visualized using the *Munsell color system* [1] according to the moving velocity and direction.

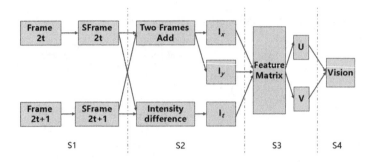

Fig. 3. Workflow of an iteration of MKLT

3.2   Parallelism Analysis

Similar with the parallelism analysis we have discussed in [3], there are three types of parallelism in MKLT work flow. We can exploit these parallelism features for parallel optimization in FPGA.

- **Task parallelism.** As shown in Fig. 3, data dependency exists in the operations of adjacent stages. The result of one stage is used as the input for the next stage. Thus, operations belonging to different stages have to compute one after the other. Fortunately, multiple operations belonging to the same stage can be computed independently. As shown in Fig. 3, smoothing of two input images ($Frame_{2t}$ and $Frame_{2t+1}$) can be processed simultaneously to obtain two smoothed images ($SFrame_{2t}$ and $SFrame_{2t+1}$), respectively. Furthermore, the first derivatives (I_x, I_y) are computed based on the average of the two smoothed images (($SFrame_{2t} + SFrame_{2t+1}$)/2). I_t can be computed by ($SFrame_{2t}$ - $SFrame_{2t+1}$). All of the derivatives can be computed independently and simultaneously. Finally, the Feature matrix can also be computed simultaneously. Thus, it is straightforward to accelerate operations within each stage by computing them as parallel tasks.
- **Data parallelism.** The operations of the first three stages can be mapped to the convolution calculation, and the convolution is separable, which contains a typical type of data parallelism.
- **Pipeline parallelism.** Although data dependency exists in different stages, as mentioned above, and operations in different stages have to be computed one after the other, it is not necessary to wait for all results from the previous stages to be available to start the next stages. For each stage, only the pixels of the beginning rows and columns should be available to start the operation. Thus, when suitable hardware is available, all stages of MKLT can work simultaneously in a pipeline fashion.

3.3   Hardware Architecture Design for MKLT

As mentioned above, we choose a separable kernel for the convolution, i.e., we calculate the horizontal and vertical convolution separately. Then, the hardware for image smoothing (S1) and gradient calculation (S2) can be implemented as the hardware of horizontal and vertical convolution. To calculate the motion tensor, it is necessary to construct the feature matrix. The feature matrix computation involves the square of the horizontal gradient, the product value of the horizontal gradient and vertical gradient, and the accumulation of the vertical gradient on the detection window. Therefore, the computation can be transformed as the accumulation on rows and columns sequentially. It is similar with the convolution operation.

Hardware Design for Horizontal Convolution. As shown in Fig. 4(a), assume that the kernel length is 5; then, in the window, 5 pixel data (P1, P2, P3, P4, and P5) will pass into the Line buffer sequentially. After P5 enters, the convolution will be calculated as the new value of middle pixel P3 (P3'). i.e.,

$$Pixel\_OUT = Pixel(P3') = \sum_{i=1}^{5} P_i * K_i \tag{15}$$

Hardware design for vertical convolution. There is a difference between vertical convolution and horizontal convolution. In the vertical convolution, the data enter row by row. So multiple line buffers are needed to temporarily store the data. As the example shown in Fig. 4(b) (with a kernel length of 3), only when the input data fill the first column of the third row (P31), the calculation of the vertical convolution of P21 (the middle point of the first column) can be started.

$$Pixel\_OUT = Pixel(P'_{21}) = \sum_{i=1}^{3} P_{i1} * K_i \tag{16}$$

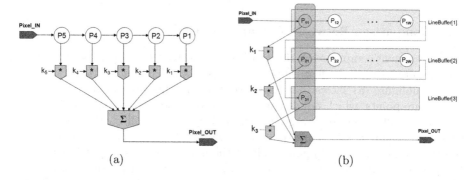

(a)   (b)

Fig. 4. (a) Data path of horizontal convolution. (b) Data path of vertical convolution.

Data Path and Hardware Architecture of MKLT. After analyzing the flow chart of the hardware module, the hardware data path diagram for the entire MKLT algorithm can be constructed as shown in Fig. 5.

There are four stages in this data path, corresponding to the workflow of Fig. 3. In S1, horizonal and vertical convolution are used consequently for smoothing. In S2, horizonal and vertical convolution are used independently for horizonal and vertical gradient computation. Horizonal and vertical accumulation are used for feature matrix in S3. Then in S4, motion vector visualization are called.

4   Evaluation

4.1   Implementation

In this paper, we implement the MKLT in *"Flyx"*, which is a *ZYNQ*-based board for the further computer vision research made by our team [10]. Figure 6(a) shows the picture of Flyx. The camera board with dual CMOS cameras are connected to the main board via a GigE Vision interface.

ZYNQ integrates an ARM-based application processor (PS part) and FPGA (PL part) in a single chip. We use Xilinx Vivado HLS [20] as the development tools. The MKLT is realized as a customized IP module that resides in the PL part. As shown in Fig. 6(b), it was connected to the PS part and other necessary modules. In addition to the input image data and output data, there are several control signals, such as *ap_start* to start the MKLT-IP, *ap_done* to indicate completion of the work, and so on.

For the sake of fair comparison between different resolutions, the images are not captured from cameras, but read from the files stored in the SD card. The file-reading time is not counted in the experiments. All the images are from the pedestrian data set of PETS2009 [12]. All test images have standard VGA resolution (640×480).

4.2   Comparison Between KLT and MKLT

The experiment compares the effect of MKLT and KLT on moving object detection. Figure 7 shows the feature points selected by KLT and by MKLT respectively. Subfigure (a) shows that KLT selects many Shi-Tomasi corner points as the feature points, which fall on the static background. In contrast, as shown in (b), almost all of the feature points selected by MKLT fall on the pedestrian, which are moving points. The experimental results show that for the first selected 100 feature points, only 75 points fall on the moving objects for KLT, while all 100 points for MKLT. This results demonstrate that MKLT can separate the moving points from the static points with different feature values.

Figure 8 shows the result of MKLT for 3 samples. The left two columns are the original sequential frames, and the third column show the result of the visualized motion tensor (u, v), which indicates the moving direction and displacement

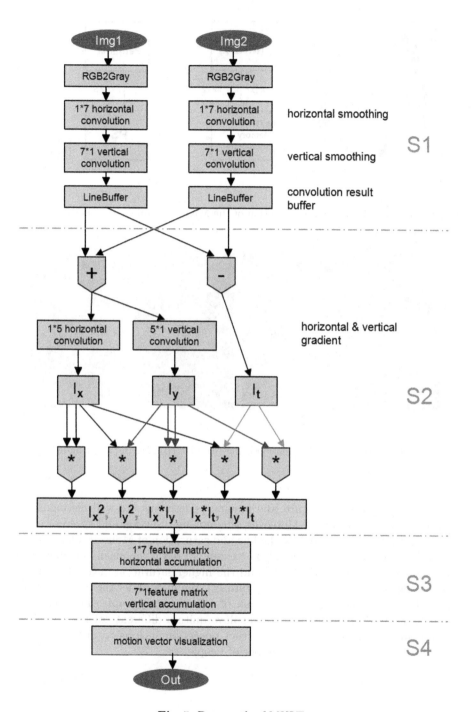

Fig. 5. Data path of MKLT

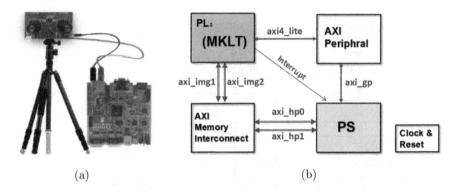

(a)   (b)

Fig. 6. (a) Flyx. (b) The interconnection of the MKLT module with other modules in the Zynq

(a)   (b)

Fig. 7. Feature points (in red) selection using (a) KLT (b) MKLT (Color figure online)

of every pixel. From the figure, the moving pedestrians are well distinguished from the static background. Moreover, the moving direction and speed of every pedestrian are well indicated by the hue and saturation of Munsell color system, as the last subfigure (j) indicated. For example, red color means moving right and cyan color means moving left, and the higher saturation means the higher moving speed. Remarkably, in subfigure (g), the man under the arrow is going right, that is, in the opposite direction of all the other people. This situation could be noticed obviously since it displays quite a different color with others in subfigure (i). This is useful for further operation such as to distinguish the suspicious person from a large number of people.

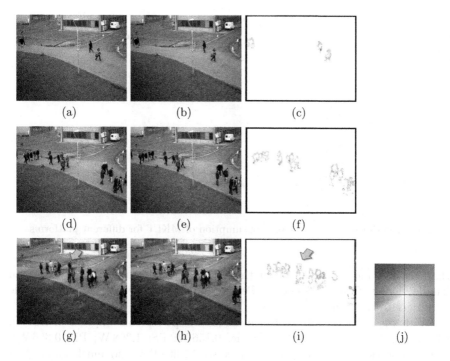

Fig. 8. Moving object detection using MKLT (Color figure online)

4.3 Performance and Energy Consumption Comparison

To evaluate the acceleration effect of FPGA, the MKLT algorithm was implemented on an FPGA, PC and ARM. Table 1 lists the configuration of each platform.

Table 1. Configurations of platforms

	PC	Flyx	ARM
Chip type	Intel Core i3-3240	*FPGA*: xc7z020clg4841 *ARM*: dual Cortex-A9	Samsung S5PV210, Cortex-A8
Frequency	3.40 GHz	667 MHz	1 GHz
Memory	4 GB	512 MB	512 MB
IDE	VS2012	Vivado HLS	Vim
OS	Windows 7	Linux 3.0.8	Linux 3.0.8

Figure 9 compares the performance (run-time per frame), power and energy consumption per frame. The experimental results show that The FPGA takes only 0.030 s to compute and visualize, and it is approximately 34 times faster

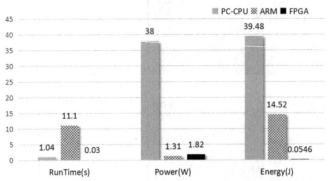

Fig. 9. Performance and energy consumption of MKLT for different platforms

than the PC and 370 times faster than the ARM. In other words, FPGA can handle video with 30 FPS (Frame Per Second), which means that it is suitable for object tracking in real time.

With the Vivado tool, we can evaluate the power consumption of ZYNQ, which is 1.82 W totally. (device static: 0.156 W; PS: 1.308 W; PL: 0.356 W). This is a little higher than ARM processor (1.308 W), and much lower than PC-CPU (38 W) However, since FPGA is much more faster than ARM and PC-CPU, the energy consumed per frame (0.0546 J) is quite less than both ARM (14.5188 J) and PC-CPU (39.482 J). In other words, the FPGA have the best energy efficiency.

5   Conclusion

In this paper, we proposed a FPGA-based approach to optimize the computation of the object tracking algorithm. The proposed algorithm improves the KLT algorithm by using the motion information of the feature points. Moreover, we designed a FPGA-based hardware architecture that can efficiently exploit the advantages of the heterogeneous architecture of FPGA while fully exploiting the parallelism of the algorithm. Experimental results show that our approach can drastically improve the performance and energy efficiency.

Acknowledgments. This paper is supported by the National High Technology Research and Development Program of China (2015AA015304), Natural Science Foundation of China (61672230), the Shanghai Natural Science Foundation (15ZR1410000) and the Open Project Program of the State Key Laboratory of Mathematical Engineering and Advanced Computing.

References

1. Baker, S., Scharstein, D., Lewis, J.P., Roth, S., Black, M.J., Szeliski, R.: A database and evaluation methodology for optical flow. Int. J. Comput. Vision **92**(1), 1–31 (2011)
2. Cao, L., Ji, R., Wang, C., Li, J.: Towards domain adaptive vehicle detection in satellite image by supervised super-resolution transfer. In: 30th AAAI Conference on Artificial Intelligence, pp. 1138–1144 (2016)
3. Chen, W., Wang, Z., Wu, Q., Liang, J., Chai, Z.: Implementing dense optical flow computation on a heterogeneous FPGA SOC in C. ACM Trans. Architect. Code Optim. (TACO) **13**(3), 25:1–25:25 (2016)
4. Comaniciu, D., Meer, P.: Mean shift: a robust approach toward feature space analysis. IEEE Trans. Pattern Anal. Mach. Intell. **24**(5), 603–619 (2002)
5. Harris, C., Stephens, M.: A combined corner and edge detector. In: Alvey Vision Conference, vol. 15, p. 50. Citeseer (1988)
6. Li, X., Hu, W., Shen, C., Zhang, Z., Dick, A., Hengel, A.V.D.: A survey of appearance models in visual object tracking. ACM Trans. Intell. Syst. Technol. (TIST) **4**(4), 58–105 (2013)
7. Liu, W., Chen, H., Ma, L.: Moving object detection and tracking based on ZYNQ FPGA and ARM SOC. In: IET International Radar Conference, pp. 1–4, October 2015
8. Lucas, B.D., Kanade, T.: An iterative image registration technique with an application to stereo vision. IJCAI **81**, 674–679 (1981)
9. Ojha, S., Sakhare, S.: Image processing techniques for object tracking in video surveillance-a survey. In: International Conference on Pervasive Computing (ICPC), pp. 1–6. IEEE (2015)
10. OpenHEC: Flyx   (2017).   http://www.iopenhec.com/#/hardware/0000201606070000000000002. Retrieved 6 Jan 2017
11. Paisitkriangkrai, S., Shen, C., van den Hengel, A.: Pedestrian detection with spatially pooled features and structured ensemble learning. IEEE Trans. Pattern Anal. Mach. Intell. **38**(6), 1243–1257 (2016)
12. PETS2009: Pets 2009 benchmark data (2009). http://www.cvg.reading.ac.uk/PETS2009/. Retrieved 6 Jan 2017
13. Rautaray, S.S., Agrawal, A.: Vision based hand gesture recognition for human computer interaction: a survey. Artif. Intell. Rev. **43**(1), 1–54 (2015)
14. Ren, J., Chen, Y., Xin, L., Shi, J., Li, B., Liu, Y.: Detecting and positioning of traffic incidents via video-based analysis of traffic states in a road segment. IET Intel. Transport Syst. **10**(6), 428–437 (2016)
15. Ristic, B., Arulampalam, S., Gordon, N.: Beyond the kalman filter-particle filters for tracking applications. IEEE Trans. Aerosp. Electron. Syst. **19**(7), 37–38 (2004)
16. Rohilla, R., Raj, A., Kejriwal, S., Kapoor, R.: FPGA accelerated abandoned object detection. In: 2016 International Conference on Computational Techniques in Information and Communication Technologies (ICCTICT), pp. 302–306 (2016)
17. Sajjanar, S., Mankani, S.K., Dongrekar, P.R., Kumar, N.S., Mohana, Aradhya, H.V.R.: Implementation of real time moving object detection and tracking on FPGA for video surveillance applications. In: IEEE Distributed Computing, VLSI, Electrical Circuits and Robotics (DISCOVER), pp. 289–295 (2016)

18. Shi, J., Tomasi, C.: Good features to track. In: Proceedings of the CVPR 1994, pp. 593–600. IEEE (1994)
19. Tomasi, C., Kanade, T.: Shape and motion from image streams under orthography: a factorization method. Int. J. Comput. Vision **9**(2), 137–154 (1992)
20. Vivado: Vivado design suite - hlx editions (2015). http://www.xilinx.com/products/design-tools/vivado/. Retrieved 6 Jan 2017

Automatic Acceleration of Stencil Codes in Android Devices

Sergio Afonso$^{(\boxtimes)}$, Alejandro Acosta, and Francisco Almeida

Universidad de La Laguna, San Cristóbal de La Laguna, Spain
{safonsof,aacostad,falmeida}@ull.es

Abstract. The increase of performance in handheld devices due to their widespread adoption has required the integration of several distinct kinds of processor in a single chip. These technologies have turned current Systems on Chip into heterogeneous platforms. Stencil codes are a family of algorithms that appear in many relevant scientific and image processing codes. In order to improve the performance of these algorithms in heterogeneous platforms, the usage of accelerators is very important but, for a mobile applications developer, the development cost is very high. We propose a methodology, based in our framework Paralldroid, for automatically generating accelerated implementations of several well-known representative stencil codes. The performance of these codes has also been measured in order to demonstrate how Paralldroid is able to accelerate code without extensive or complex modifications. Results show great performance improvements for few code modifications.

Keywords: Android · OpenCL · Stencil code · Source-to-source translation · Parallelizing compiler · Renderscript

1 Introduction

The architecture of embedded systems has seen a revolution in recent years transforming it from low-power and low-performance specific purpose hardware to current Systems on Chip (SoC). These new architectures provide very high performance whilst maintaining a low level of power consumption, and have been the basis of the new era of mobile computing. Conceptually, modern SoCs are heterogeneous platforms where one or more multi-core CPUs, a Graphics Processing Unit (GPU) and possibly Digital Signal Processors (DSP) share access to a unified memory system.

Although different vendors develop these platforms, the vast majority are currently based on ARM technology. Some of the best known such platforms are Qualcomm Snapdragon [13], Samsung Exynos [15], Apple Ax [9] and NVIDIA Tegra [10]. Nevertheless, we can find alternatives, such as Intel Atom [8], not based on ARM. The heterogeneity present between platforms and processors makes difficult to write code that performs well in all cases. Because of this reason, it is generally a good idea to find ways to automate code optimization

© Springer International Publishing AG 2017
S. Ibrahim et al. (Eds.): ICA3PP 2017, LNCS 10393, pp. 81–95, 2017.
DOI: 10.1007/978-3-319-65482-9_6

so that developers can focus on the business logic of applications instead. This has the potential of improving performance across a wider variety of platforms and improving their programmability, reducing development costs.

Stencil codes are involved in many important applications, partly because very efficient methods exist for numerically solving partial differential equations using stencil codes [17]. Several scientific simulations and image and video processing algorithms are based on stencil codes, so methods for improving their performance have already been worked on by many authors [7,16,20]. Furthermore, implementing complex image processing methods that run in real time is becoming increasingly more important especially for mobile and embedded applications. As the need for performance in stencil codes and the difficulties associated to developing efficient code for heterogeneous platforms are clear, we consider that an automated tool to reduce the cost of developing such high performance applications would be a very important step forward.

One such tool that has been developed for the purpose of simplifying writing highly efficient stencil codes is PATUS [5]. This is an auto-tuning framework that is able to generate code for stencils from an specification of the stencil operation and a description of the parallelization and optimization methods to apply. However, PATUS still requires the application programmer to know about code optimization techniques and about the hardware that will execute the application. This is often not the case for general purpose mobile applications developers. In addition, it requires the usage of a domain specific language (DSL) for writing stencil kernels that is not easy to integrate in a Java application developed by an Android programmer.

Alternatively, we propose using Paralldroid [1–3] so that we can reduce the development cost at the expense of some overhead due to the increased level of abstraction. However, because it is a source-to-source compiler, it allows more experienced developers to use it to generate a first implementation that they can tweak and improve afterwards. This significantly reduces development time. Mint [18] is also a source-to-source translator capable of generating high performance parallel CUDA code for NVIDIA GPUs from standard C code with annotations. Although it is similar to Paralldroid in this regard, the only notable Android platform that supports CUDA is NVIDIA Tegra. Moreover, as annotations are still applied to C code, it requires some extra work to be executed by a Java application, making it less suitable for Android development. Most OpenACC implementations, such as PGI's [12] or Cray's [6], are not designed to be used in this context. They are targeted towards other type of hardware, and other OpenACC compilers like accULL [14], which can generate OpenCL code, still need native code as input.

As a contribution of this paper we propose a methodology for the rapid prototyping and acceleration of sequential stencils in Android, based on a generic tool named Paralldroid. This methodology allows for the automatic generation of Renderscript and OpenCL codes. In this regard, we also contribute by characterizing the performance of the Renderscript and OpenCL codes generated for various different stencil patterns. This performance is characterized in terms of several parameters such as the input size and computational load per element. We analyzed strengths and weaknesses inherent to each programming model, and determined features of an algorithm that make it run better using one language or the other. The stencil examples used for testing are widely representative of patterns appearing in many scientific and multimedia applications. We conclude that Paralldroid is a useful tool to accelerate stencils, since the development time is significantly reduced and it also provides different backend options. Generated code could indeed be manually optimized if required, but results show that, in many cases, it provides similar performance to handwritten code.

This paper is structured as follows: In Sect. 2 we give an overview of the features of Paralldroid that allow us to accelerate stencil codes, Sect. 3 introduces the general definition of a stencil code and describe the set of examples that we have implemented in order to validate our methodology. We describe the new methodology that allows a developer to accelerate stencil codes in Android using Paralldroid in Sect. 4. In Sect. 5 we show and discuss the results we obtained on different platforms, and we finish with conclusions and future work in Sect. 6.

2   Paralldroid

Paralldroid is a development framework designed to simplify the development of parallel applications on the Android platform. It achieves this by defining a set of high-level Java annotations, which provide the information it needs in order to be able to generate accelerated code. Paralldroid introduces a new stage in the compilation process, in which the annotated Java code written by the developer gets translated into one of the target languages of Paralldroid. The goal of Paralldroid is to also unify the different development models there are on Android (Java, Renderscript and C/C++), so the set of target languages were selected according to this. The integration of Paralldroid in the Android development model is shown in Fig. 1. The target languages Paralldroid can generate are:

- **Renderscript:** It is a programming language designed for computationally intensive tasks in Android. Based on C, it allows to define Single Program Multiple Data (SPMD) tasks and runs code asynchronously. Renderscript supports CPU code execution and GPU acceleration. However, the device where the code is run cannot be controlled by the programmer, but only by the Android runtime. It provides a high level way to accelerate code, but it still requires the mobile developer to learn a new language and introduces the need to maintain multiple source files for a single class.
- **Native C:** It is possible to run native code from an Android application by using the Java Native Interface (JNI) and the Android Native Development Kit (NDK). Many algorithms can benefit from running natively, due to the reduced overhead as opposed to running managed code. However, this option is not recommended for performance, but for accessing third-party native libraries in the device and for reusing code instead. Calling native code from

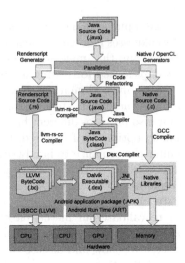

Fig. 1. Paralldroid development model

Java sometimes improves performance, but it always results in a higher program complexity.

– **OpenCL:** It is a well known standard for cross-platform access to accelerator devices. It provides a mechanism for parallel programming and a low-level API for communicating data and handling the different computing devices present in the hardware platform. A typical OpenCL application has code running in the host processor and computing kernels running on accelerator devices (multicore CPUs, GPUs, DSPs...). Unlike Renderscript, the amount of platforms that support OpenCL is very extensive. However, as it is a low level interface over the hardware, it usually increases development cost considerably. If the hardware architecture is taken into account, it can be made to produce very highly optimized code, but this is a very difficult task considering how heterogeneous the SoC market is in this regard.

In order to allow transparent execution of generated code, Paralldroid needs to also generate Java code. While maintaining the interface of the original Java classes, the translated classes are modified in order to forward the execution to the generated code. They also synchronize the memory in the Java and target contexts, hiding this complexity to the caller code. This allows different Paralldroid-generated classes to interoperate seamlessly.

One main advantage of using Paralldroid is that it allows quick testing of the various parallelism options in Android. Some algorithms, or code sections, may be better suited to running on Renderscript while others may benefit from lower level access to the hardware through OpenCL, or it might be interesting to have multiple implementations for different devices. As OpenCL is not officially supported in Android, but available in many mainstream platforms, it would be necessary to provide a fallback implementation for devices that do not support it. Furthermore, because the Paralldroid code generation is an independent preliminary compiler stage, an expert developer could improve the generated code without having to implement it in full.

3   Stencil Codes

The class of algorithms commonly known as stencil codes have very important applications, and tend to become important bottlenecks for many scientific applications. Their most important feature is that a stencil has an n-dimensional grid with an element per cell that must be computed according to the values of neighbor elements. The shape of the neighborhood is called the stencil, and its size and shape are usually fixed on each problem. Many stencil codes are iterative, so they are applied repeatedly over the complete mesh, in which case the value of each element depends on the values of the neighborhood of that element on the previous iteration.

The most commonly used stencil shapes are those based on a Von Neumann neighborhood or a Moore neighborhood [11]. The Von Neumann neighborhood contains the element at hand and its direct neighbors in the cardinal directions, although it can be generalized to contain all elements within a Manhattan distance of r. The Moore neighborhood, on the other hand, also includes diagonally adjacent elements, hence being defined as the set of elements within a maximum Chebyshev distance of r. Graphical representations of these are shown in Fig. 2.

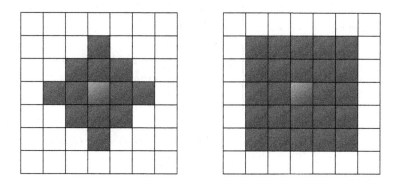

Fig. 2. 2D Von Neumann and Moore neighborhoods with a range of 2

It is clear that stencil codes are easily parallelizable, because the calculation of each element is independent of every other, as long as there are two separate buffers for reading and writing the mesh. However, the memory access patterns imposed by the stencil can be problematic regarding memory locality and coalescing. These problems are especially important because stencil codes are very frequently memory bound, and these traits are detrimental towards memory access performance in modern CPU and GPU architectures.

In order to evaluate the suitability of our proposal for automatic acceleration of stencils, we have implemented several stencil codes that are widely representative of stencils appearing in scientific applications. These codes are the Heat and Poisson equations, the Gaussian Blur, the Discrete Laplacian and a Pattern Thinning algorithm.

The main features of these stencils are summarized in Table 1. In that table, we use the notation $u_{i,j}^k$ to refer to the value of the input cell located in the row i and the column j, on the time step k. We can use this notation because we discretize space as well as time in these examples. On the examples for which the concept of time is not relevant, k is to be interpreted as an iteration index. The Discrete Laplacian stencil is applied to an image only once, so its equation in Table 1 indicates how each output pixel is calculated from the inputs, and it is not iteratively executed. The Pattern Thinning and Gaussian Blur stencils, on the other hand, have to run repeatedly and they both have one equation for even and odd iterations. The Pattern Thinning stencil will run until there are no

Table 1. Stencil examples

Algorithm	Stencil equation	Shape
Discrete Laplacian	$u_{i,j}^{k+1} = u_{i-1,j}^k + u_{i,j-1}^k + u_{i+1,j}^k + u_{i,j+1}^k - 4u_{i,j}^k$	
Pattern Thinning	$u_{i,j}^{k+1} = \begin{cases} 0, & \text{if } u_{i,j}^k = 0 \\ 0, & \text{if } A(i,j) = 1 \wedge 2 \le B(i,j) \le 6 \wedge \\ & u_{i-1,j}^k u_{i,j+1}^k u_{i+1,j}^k = 0 \wedge \\ & u_{i,j+1}^k u_{i+1,j}^k u_{i,j-1}^k = 0 \\ 1, & \text{otherwise} \end{cases}$ $u_{i,j}^{k+1} = \begin{cases} 0, & \text{if } u_{i,j}^k = 0 \\ 0, & \text{if } A(i,j) = 1 \wedge 2 \le B(i,j) \le 6 \wedge \\ & u_{i-1,j}^k u_{i,j+1}^k u_{i,j-1}^k = 0 \wedge \\ & u_{i-1,j}^k u_{i+1,j}^k u_{i,j-1}^k = 0 \\ 1, & \text{otherwise} \end{cases}$	
Gaussian Blur	$u_{i,j}^{k+1} = u_{i,j-2}^k \, G(0) + u_{i,j-1}^k \, G(1) + u_{i,j}^k \, G(2) + u_{i,j+1}^k \, G(3) + u_{i,j+2}^k \, G(4)$ $u_{i,j}^{k+1} = u_{i-2,j}^k \, G(0) + u_{i-1,j}^k \, G(1) + u_{i,j}^k \, G(2) + u_{i+1,j}^k \, G(3) + u_{i+2,j}^k \, G(4)$	
2D Heat equation	$u_{i,j}^{k+1} = \dfrac{1}{4} \left(u_{i-1,j}^k + u_{i,j-1}^k + u_{i+1,j}^k + u_{i,j+1}^k \right)$	
2D Poisson equation	$u_{i,j}^{k+1} = \dfrac{1}{4} \left(u_{i-1,j}^k + u_{i,j-1}^k + u_{i+1,j}^k + u_{i,j+1}^k + \dfrac{\rho(i,j)h^2}{\varepsilon_0} \right)$	

further modifications to the inputs, but the Gaussian Blur algorithm will only apply each stencil once.

In the Pattern Thinning stencil equations, $A(i, j)$ is the amount of times the sequence 01, representing a white pixel followed by a black one, is found among the neighbors of the current pixel whilst going through them in clockwise order. $B(i, j)$ is the amount of black neighbor pixels. In the Gaussian Blur stencil equations we use $G(x)$ to refer to the value of the gaussian function in the position x, normalized inside the range $[0, 4]$ so that the sum of all values is equal to 1. In the Poisson equation, we use h to refer to the width and height of each cell, $\rho(i, j)$ is the charge density function of the input material and ε_0 is the vacuum permittivity.

4   Methodology

With our approach, the development workflow of a mobile applications developer is slightly modified. In Fig. 3, this new workflow is outlined. Firstly, the developer identifies the stencil to accelerate. Once this is done, it is necessary to adapt the class to the limitations of the tool, which are roughly the impossibility of creating new objects anywhere outside of the constructor and using complex objects inside of the class to translate. Adapting the original Java class should not be a very complex task because it is possible to create another class responsible for preparing the input and output data or acting as a simpler interface between the

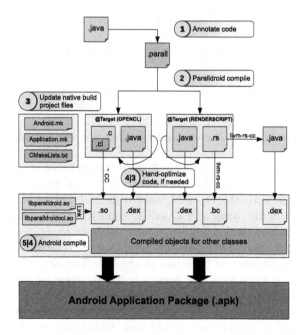

Fig. 3. Stencil development methodology

accelerated algorithm and the rest of the application. If a section of code is known to be compute-intensive and eligible for parallelization beforehand, the easiest approach would be to directly design the application with these constraints in mind.

When the code is expressed in a simpler form supported by Paralldroid, the next step is to annotate this Java class so that the compiler knows the required memory synchronizations and parallel methods to generate in order to offload execution to Renderscript or OpenCL, as well as the target language to use. Then, the Paralldroid compiler is run on the whole project. It will find all classes having @Target annotations and it will try to translate them. The original files are preserved, so that they can be iteratively improved until the generated code is correct. An example implementation of an stencil can be seen in Listing 1.1.

```
1  @Target(OPENCL)
2  public class DiscreteLaplacian {
3    @Map(TO) private int width;
4    @Map(TO) private int height;
5
6    public DiscreteLaplacian (Activity act, int width, int height) {
7        this.width = width;
8        this.height = height;
9    }
10
11   @Parallel
12   public void run (@Map(TO) Bitmap srcPxs, @NumThreads @Map(FROM) Bitmap outPxs,
13                    @Index int x, @Index int y) {
14       int current = srcPxs.getPixel(x, y);
15       int neighbourN = y > 0? srcPxs.getPixel(x, y - 1) : current;
16       int neighbourE = x < (width - 1)? srcPxs.getPixel(x + 1, y) : current;
17       int neighbourS = y < (height - 1)? srcPxs.getPixel(x, y + 1) : current;
18       int neighbourW = x > 0? srcPxs.getPixel(x - 1, y) : current;
19
20       // Assume input is already in grayscale format, so all channels have the same value
21       int output = Color.red(neighbourN) + Color.red(neighbourE) + Color.red(neighbourS)+
22                    Color.red(neighbourW) - 4 * Color.red(current);
23
24       if (output < 0) output = 0;
25       outPxs.setPixel(x, y, Color.argb(255, output, output, output));
26   }
27 }
```

Listing 1.1. Discrete Laplacian stencil in Paralldroid

For each translated class with OpenCL as the target language, the Paralldroid compiler will generate a Java file intended to be the interface to the generated code, and a C file with the OpenCL host code and JNI code that allow the interaction between the Java and OpenCL contexts. In that file there is the source code of the kernels that implement the methods annotated as @Parallel in the original Java class. That code is compiled at runtime in the target device the first time an instance of the class is created. The first time an OpenCL version of a class is generated, the developer has to integrate it into the native build scripts (ndk-build or CMake, for example) so that it gets compiled into a shared library and included in the application package. These libraries have to be linked to the Paralldroid runtime libraries, which have to also be manually included in the application together with its associated header files.

For Renderscript, the process is simpler. The Android compilers and tools will automatically process new Renderscript source files and generate wrapper classes as part of the build process. These classes are used by Paralldroid's own generated classes in order to transparently offload the execution to the Renderscript runtime.

Triggering an application build using the Android development tools would be all left to do in order to get the whole application, using the accelerated code, in a package that can be installed and run in an Android device. If performance was still not sufficient, the developer could then revise the Paralldroid implementation or try another supported target language and generate again and profile the application. If, however, this developer knows about these languages and performance optimization techniques, and needs more performance, they could modify the generated code as much as needed. This is much faster to do than starting the implementation from scratch, especially in OpenCL. This methodology has the added advantage of allowing to quickly test the behavior of each implementation before spending time optimizing the code by hand.

5   Computational Results

5.1   Hardware Testbed

The two devices we used as testbed platform, represent two of the major SoC architectures that are most widely used in modern handheld devices, which are Qualcomm Snapdragon and Samsung Exynos. Therefore, the results we obtained are applicable to a large portion of devices currently in use.

- **Sony Xperia Z (SXZ):** Based on a Qualcomm APQ8064 Snapdragon S4 Pro SoC with a Quad-core Krait CPU @ 1.5 GHz and an Adreno 320 GPU with 4 OpenCL compute units and 2 GB of shared RAM. Its GPU supports OpenCL 1.1 embedded profile. Its OpenCL driver reports 32 KB of cache memory and 8 KB of local memory.
- **Odroid-XU3 (XU3):** Based on a Samsung Exynos 5422 Octa SoC with dual ARM CPUs (Cortex-A15 @ 2 GHz and Cortex-A7 @ 1.3 GHz) and a 6-core ARM Mali-T628 MP6 GPU with 2 GB of shared RAM. Its GPU supports OpenCL 1.1 full profile and it reports 128 KB of cache memory and 32 KB of local memory.

5.2   Testing Methodology

We have implemented several versions of the stencil codes mentioned in Table 1. For each stencil, we have implemented a reference serial Java version and another one annotated using Paralldroid directives. We have automatically generated Renderscript and OpenCL implementations from the annotated Java class using Paralldroid, and we have used these implementations as a starting point for manually developing optimized Renderscript and OpenCL versions. We have restricted our optimizations to these that maintain the same interface as the original Java code (i.e. the inputs come from the Java context and the outputs have to be transferred back to it). This way the results demonstrate the gap that exists between automatically generated code and its handwritten counterpart in equal conditions.

Each stencil has been applied to different inputs varying in size and complexity. For the image processing stencils, we have used different image standard sizes ranging from VGA (640×480) to UHD (3840×2160). For the Heat and Poisson equations we used smaller input sizes, ranging from 32×32 to 256×256, but we also varied the number of iterations computed. Sizes were chosen in order to prevent the Android operating system from killing the application and to run in a reasonable time.

In order to avoid thermal throttling that would skew results favoring sooner executions, each stencil code was executed separately, as well as each of its implementations. Running very demanding GPU workloads for extended periods of time would very often make the operating system kill the application or even completely freeze the device. Each of the executions was repeated several times and averaged to reduce the impact of other processes and the garbage collector running at the same time. There was also a single warm-up run before measuring execution times in order to get the average behaviour and not be affected by one-off overheads.

Both the generated and handwritten OpenCL codes use the first available GPU device found in the platform, so in the case of the Odroid-XU3, which features $4 + 2$ GPU cores reported as different devices, we only use four of the six. Using all of the GPU cores would need code similar to what would be needed for multi-GPU systems and tackling load balancing problems that are still not considered. On the other hand, Renderscript execution cannot be set to run in a specific processor, but it is the driver that selects the most suitable one.

5.3   Benchmarks

Each of our performance illustrations show the speedup we obtain for every stencil code and input parameter in each device, in relation to the reference Java sequential implementation. Because of that, we can obtain in many cases superlinear speedups, which happens due to the overhead of running Java serial code. Hence, this situations are not unusual in the figures we are presenting and are not to be taken into special consideration.

As a guide to interpreting the figures, there are four columns representing the speedup of each implementation of the stencil code that refer to each device. The implementations labelled *SXZ*, which go first, were obtained in the Sony Xperia Z, and the implementations labelled *XU3* relate to the Odroid-XU3. The first two columns of each set of four are OpenCL implementations, and the second two are Renderscript implementations. Of these two columns, the first is generated and the second is handwritten.

For the discrete Laplacian stencil, we obtained speedups of up to almost 5x. These are shown in Fig. 4(a). In this case, we observe that Renderscript implementations perform better than OpenCL implementations, and that the

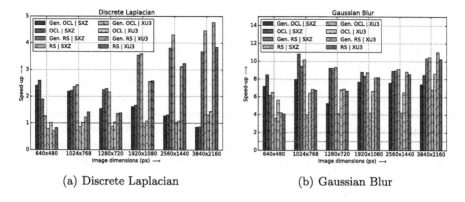

(a) Discrete Laplacian   (b) Gaussian Blur

Fig. 4. Discrete Laplacian and Gaussian Blur speedups

speedups are not very high. It is only on the smallest image size that we obtain better results using OpenCL. There is also a very noticeable trend on the SXZ device that shows how performance of OpenCL code degrades as the image size increases. This behaviour seems counter-intuitive, but by taking a closer look at the OpenCL execution trace, we observe that this problem is due to the overhead of copying images between the native and OpenCL contexts. If we consider this when interpreting the results for the smallest image size we realize that this overhead is the reason why OpenCL kernels are running slower than Renderscript's. Conversely, Renderscript performance improves as the image dimensions increase, implying it does not suffer from this problem.

The only way these platforms allow to allocate shared memory between CPU and GPU in OpenCL is by using the CL_MEM_ALLOC_HOST_PTR flag when creating an OpenCL buffer, and then mapping and unmapping the memory to and from the host in order to use its content in the CPU or the GPU. The problem that prevents us from being able to allocate memory this way is that memory has already been allocated by the Java context, and we can only try to pin it for access from native code. Even the possibility of accessing a Java array from native code without copying it is not guaranteed. The OpenCL 1.1 specification considers the case of host-allocated memory and provides the CL_MEM_USE_HOST_PTR flag to allow using this memory as an OpenCL memory buffer in unified memory architectures. However, in platforms like the ones we are analyzing, this still triggers a memory copy operation [4]. However, in Renderscript creating an allocation from a Bitmap and using it in a kernel can avoid memory copies.

The effect of this situation is less visible on the XU3, which experiences very low OpenCL performance in this application. Possibly the reason why we do not observe an even further reduction of OpenCL performance when increasing the image size in this case is a higher computation to memory copy time ratio, either because of faster memory speeds or slower relative GPU execution of kernels.

For the Gaussian Blur stencil, we have obtained speedups of up to 11x for generated code, which are better overall than any other stencil we tried in this work. These are shown in Fig. 4(b). In this ocassion the performance difference between Renderscript and OpenCL executions is much smaller, though Renderscript performs better on average. The memory copy overhead of OpenCL tipped the scales on favor of Renderscript.

Hand coded optimizations to the Renderscript code were only effective on the SXZ, and even reduced the performance of the generated code on the XU3. Even on the SXZ, the performance improvements were minimal. In this case, hand coded optimizations to the kernels did not have any real effect on performance. On the other hand, the handwritten OpenCL code is a substantial improvement over the generated code, but also required a considerable amount of extra work.

The runtime of the Pattern Thinning algorithm we have implemented [19] is dependent on the size of the image and on the complexity of the pattern we want to process. For this reason, we present two figures in Fig. 5. Figure 5(a) contains the results for a simple text in an image, and Fig. 5(b) contains the results for a more complex image of a fingerprint. We obtained speedups of up to about 10x for this stencil, while the generated code reached an almost 8x speedup.

In this example we observe how increasing the amount of processing to be made on each image also increases the obtained speedup. This is clear by comparing the two figures, showing that when the image is more complex the speedups are better. On the XU3, it takes much larger images until OpenCL is faster than Renderscript code, due to the greater performance achieved by the CPU on smaller images and the smaller overhead of processing larger images by avoiding memory copies. In the SXZ, Renderscript obtained similar speedups to the Laplacian stencil, which unlike all other implementations did not benefit from the increased computation to memory ratio.

It is interesting to note how much faster is OpenCL execution in the SXZ, even when it is dealing with expensive memory copies from host to device and vice versa. This gives us a hint of the possibilities that this programming model could provide when removed the software limitations that currently prevent from making use of the unified memory architecture we have in current SoCs.

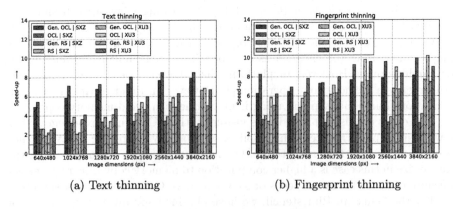

(a) Text thinning   (b) Fingerprint thinning

Fig. 5. Pattern Thinning speedups

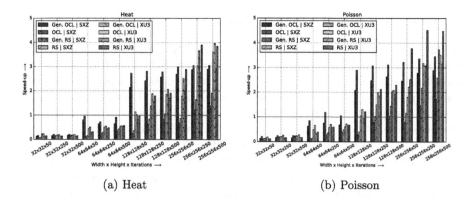

(a) Heat   (b) Poisson

Fig. 6. Heat and Poisson speedups

The Heat and Poisson equations are very similar, so they have achieved similar speedups (Fig. 6). However, speedups in the case of the Poisson equation are slightly higher due to the few extra operations that it requires. In this case we observed how the overhead of setting up parallel execution made it perform worse than Java for sizes smaller than 128×128. Smaller sizes require too low computation time to finish for offloading to be effective.

In the SXZ tests, there is a noticeable improvement when using OpenCL over Renderscript. In the case of Renderscript, it barely improves Java performance when running on the largest problems, especially for the Heat equation. This drop in performance compared to the other algorithms we tried is due to the parameter types used. Input and output are not Bitmaps, but arrays, so copying them from and to the Java context cannot be avoided. This fact, and the low processing done for each element, cause this drop in performance. In the XU3, the effect is smaller because of the higher performance of its CPU in comparison to its GPU. This gets clearer as the problem size is increased. We notice that increasing the number of computed iterations or steps has not as much of an impact on performance as the increase of the problem size has. This was expected, since iterations run sequentially unlike the elements inside the input matrix.

In Android, if a Java application needs some part of the code to be accelerated, the main alternatives are Renderscript and OpenCL. Due to differences in the hardware features they can make use of when interacting with the Java context, each of the programming models provides the best performance in different situations. In our stencil codes we have observed that the stencils that get better improvements from OpenCL execution are those that require a significant amount of processing per item, use Bitmaps of smaller sizes or work with regular arrays. Renderscript is better suited to image processing due to its ability to avoid memory copies, but since it tends to produce slower code, when the amount of processing to be done for each pixel is high enough, OpenCL is able to compensate for the memory transfer overhead. On the other hand, it is possible to run Renderscript on every Android device, and it would always be possible to resort to it if an OpenCL driver was not found.

6   Conclusion and Future Work

We have presented a methodology to automatically accelerate stencil codes on the Android platform. It takes advantage of current SoC architectures that feature GPUs and multicore processors. Our approach involves using a general purpose source-to-source translation framework (Paralldroid), specifically designed to allow easy parallelization of Android Java applications, to obtain implementations of several stencil codes in the OpenCL and Renderscript languages.

We validated our approach with five different stencil codes representing a wide range of stencil patterns, and running them in two devices based on different SoCs. Results show, in most of the cases, improvements of the generated code over a hand optimized Java version of each stencil, both in Renderscript and OpenCL. The generated code appeared slower for some of the smaller problem sizes, which happened for handwritten code as well. Handwritten versions of the code performed better than the generated versions, but the difference in performance is negligible if compared to the difference in development time.

Software limitations regarding memory sharing between the CPU and accelerators on the Android platform lead to the best programming model for accelerating each algorithm to be a different one. We observed that, in current versions, it is not possible to share a memory buffer between an OpenCL device and the Java application, even if we are working in a unified memory system. OpenCL would perform better than Renderscript without these memory sharing limitations in the vast majority of situations. This situation makes the ability of automatically generating both OpenCL and Renderscript very useful, because it allows developers to quickly determine the best performing implementation language for an algorithm in Android.

Simpler stencil codes do not perform as well as the more complex ones in Paralldroid-generated implementations, due to the overhead of offloading to accelerator devices and launching threads. Optimization techniques such as tiling could be integrated into Paralldroid for these cases. Further testing should be done to measure the energy impact and memory footprint of the generated code.

Acknowledgement. This work was supported by the EC (ERDF), the NESUS IC1315 COST Action, the Spanish Ministry of Economy, Industry and Competitiveness through the TIN2016-78919-R project, and the CAPAP-H network.

References

1. Acosta, A., Almeida, F.: Parallel implementations of the particle filter algorithm for android mobile devices. In: 2015 23rd Euromicro International Conference on Parallel, Distributed, and Network-Based Processing, pp. 244–247, March 2015
2. Acosta, A., Afonso, S., Almeida, F.: Extending paralldroid with object oriented annotations. Parallel Comput. **57**, 25–36 (2016). http://www.sciencedirect.com/science/article/pii/S0167819116300126
3. Acosta, A., Almeida, F.: Towards a unified heterogeneous development model in android. In: Eleventh International Workshop HeteroPar 2013: Algorithms, Models and Tools for Parallel Computing on Heterogeneous Platforms (2013)

4. ARM: ARM®Mali™ GPU OpenCL developer guide. http://malideveloper.arm. com/documentation/developer-guides/arm-guide-opencl/
5. Christen, M., Schenk, O., Burkhart, H.: Patus: a code generation and autotuning framework for parallel iterative stencil computations on modern microarchitectures. In: 2011 IEEE International Parallel & Distributed Processing Symposium (IPDPS), pp. 676–687. IEEE (2011)
6. Cray Inc.: Cray®XC™ series software environment. http://www.cray.com/sites/ default/files/resources/CrayXC40_SoftwareEnvironment.pdf
7. Datta, K., Murphy, M., Volkov, V., Williams, S., Carter, J., Oliker, L., Patterson, D., Shalf, J., Yelick, K.: Stencil computation optimization and auto-tuning on state-of-the-art multicore architectures. In: Proceedings of the 2008 ACM/IEEE Conference on Supercomputing, SC 2008, pp. 4:1–4:12. IEEE Press, Piscataway (2008). http://dl.acm.org/citation.cfm?id=1413370.1413375
8. Intel: Intel® Atom™ Processor for Smartphone and Tablet. https://ark.intel.com/ products/family/70095/Intel-Atom-Processor-for-Smartphone-and-Tablet
9. Notebook Check: Apple A10 Fusion. https://www.notebookcheck.net/ Apple-A10-Fusion-SoC.173824.0.html
10. NVIDIA: Tegra mobile processors: Tegra 2, Tegra 3 and Tegra 4. http://www. nvidia.com/object/tegra-superchip.html
11. Packard, N.H., Wolfram, S.: Two-dimensional cellular automata. J. Stat. Phys. **38**(5), 901–946 (1985). http://dx.doi.org/10.1007/BF01010423
12. PGI: PGI Accelerator compilers with OpenACC directives. https://www.pgroup. com/resources/accel.htm
13. Qualcomm: Snapdragon mobile processors. http://www.qualcomm.com/ snapdragon
14. Reyes, R., López-Rodríguez, I., Fumero, J.J., Sande, F.: accULL: an OpenACC implementation with CUDA and OpenCL support. In: Kaklamanis, C., Papatheodorou, T., Spirakis, P.G. (eds.) Euro-Par 2012. LNCS, vol. 7484, pp. 871–882. Springer, Heidelberg (2012). doi:10.1007/978-3-642-32820-6_86
15. Samsung: Exynos mobile processors. http://www.samsung.com/global/business/ semiconductor/minisite/Exynos/
16. Shimokawabe, T., Aoki, T., Onodera, N.: High-productivity framework for large-scale GPU/CPU stencil applications. Procedia Comput. Sci. **80**, 1646–1657 (2016). http://www.sciencedirect.com/science/article/pii/S1877050916309863
17. Smith, G.D.: Numerical Solution of Partial Differential Equations: Finite Difference Methods. Oxford University Press, New York (1985)
18. Unat, D., Cai, X., Baden, S.B.: Mint: realizing cuda performance in 3d stencil methods with annotated c. In: Proceedings of the International Conference on Supercomputing, pp. 214–224. ACM (2011)
19. Zhang, T., Suen, C.Y.: A fast parallel algorithm for thinning digital patterns. Commun. ACM **27**(3), 236–239 (1984)
20. Zhang, Y., Mueller, F.: Auto-generation and auto-tuning of 3d stencil codes on GPU clusters. In: Proceedings of the Tenth International Symposium on Code Generation and Optimization, CGO 2012, NY, USA, pp. 155–164 (2012). http:// doi.acm.org/10.1145/2259016.2259037

Distributed and Network-based Computing

Optimizing Concurrent Evacuation Transfers for Geo-Distributed Datacenters in SDN

Xiaole Li[1], Hua Wang[1(✉)], Shanwen Yi[1], Xibo Yao[1], Fangjin Zhu[1], and Linbo Zhai[1,2]

[1] School of Computer Science and Technology, Shandong University, Jinan 250101, China
leo0539@163.com, wanghua@sdu.edu.cn
[2] School of Information Science and Engineering, Shandong Normal University, Jinan 250014, China

Abstract. Disaster evacuation assigns bulk endangered data to geographically distributed datacenters out of disaster zone within acceptable duration. However, previous works overlooked the bandwidth allocation proportion problem and multi-path routing problem for multiple concurrent evacuation transfers (especially with shared links). Therefore they could not guarantee full utilization of network transmission capability in disaster evacuation. In this paper, with flexible traffic scheduling in the Software Defined Network scenarios, we propose a new optimal bandwidth proportion allocation strategy for concurrent evacuation transfers. To maximize disaster evacuation capability, we formulate the bandwidth allocation problem as a new Bandwidth-Proportion-Constrained Multi-Commodity Flow (BPC-MCF) problem. To obtain optimal solution for practical networks of large scale, we propose a Bandwidth-Proportion-Aware Ant Colony Optimization (BPA-ACO) algorithm to achieve maximum evacuation flow matching data amount proportion of concurrent evacuation transfers. We introduce available evacuation capability, bandwidth proportion offset and link sharing degree to guide optimal solution searching. We adjust bandwidth proportion by rearranging flows in shared links and alternate paths. Through extensive simulations we demonstrate that our algorithm has better performance with less total evacuation time and higher network utilization.

Keywords: Disaster evacuation · Concurrent evacuation transfers · Bandwidth-Proportion-Constrained · Bandwidth-Proportion-Aware · Software Defined Network

1 Introduction

Due to the increasing demand of cloud services, more and more large enterprises such as Google, Amazon and Microsoft, use multiple geographically distributed (geo-distributed) datacenters to improve the end-to-end service performance [1]. Meanwhile, datacenters consisting of massive amount of content are vulnerable to various disasters. For example, in 2008, the Great Sichuan earthquake in China disrupted over 60 enterprise datacenters [2]; in 2012, cascading failures caused by

© Springer International Publishing AG 2017
S. Ibrahim et al. (Eds.): ICA3PP 2017, LNCS 10393, pp. 99–114, 2017.
DOI: 10.1007/978-3-319-65482-9_7

Hurricane Sandy damaged many datacenters and communication services in the Northeastern US [3].

And fortunately, uninterruptible power supplies (UPSs) and power generators still can keep servers and network devices operational for tens of minutes [4], maintaining Internet connectivity after disasters. In that case, disaster evacuation means that endangered data should be transferred from the datacenters in disaster zones to other datacenters in safe zones within evacuation deadline (e.g., before the depletion of UPSs). So it is crucial to minimize total evacuation time of concurrent bulk data transfers by optimal bandwidth allocation with limited available network resources.

Ultimately, how to evacuate endangered data efficiently with maximum utilization of limited residual bandwidth is actually a typical traffic engineering problem for concurrent evacuation transfers. The disaster-aware bulk transfer problem among geo-distributed datacenters has attracted more and more attentions [2, 5–7]. Previous works mainly focused on data distribution and priority control problems, such as providing largest data-transfer throughput for disaster backup pairs one by one [2], fair load distribution among destination datacenters in case of disaster [5], selection of optimal single path with least delay for every evacuation transfer one by one [6], and reasonable evacuation order with maximum benefit for prioritized data [7].

However, we notice that the research on bandwidth allocation and routing selection in data transmission process is still not sufficient. On the one hand, because traditional network paradigm can hardly support flow splitting of arbitrary proportions, specified bandwidth amount cannot be flexibly allocated for concurrent transfers according to their data amount. So previous works had to schedule the transmission order or bandwidth allocation order for evacuation transfers one by one to reduce total evacuation time [2, 5–7]. But there is a strong possibility that this evacuation pattern will cause transmission capability underutilization and some available links lying idle. This will result in more evacuation time than concurrent characterized bandwidth customization pattern, especially with shared links. On the other hand, based on single-path routing that is usually used in most traditional networks, previous works mainly searched for a single shortest path [2] or least-delay path [6] for every evacuation transfer one by one to reduce completion time or maximize total network flow in evacuation transmission. Although single-path routing is simple, obviously this will cause some available paths lying idle in evacuation process. Multi-path routing provides more residual bandwidth and has higher network transmission capacity utilization [8]. (Due to space limitation here, we will illustrate the benefit of bandwidth proportion allocation and multi-path routing by an example at the beginning of Sect. 2.) It is necessary to add bandwidth proportion constraint (BPC) into concurrent transfer optimization with multi-path routing for more efficient disaster evacuation solution.

Furthermore, to properly solve the two traffic engineering problems above, we still need a new network paradigm supporting flexible flow splitting and multi-path routing for better traffic control and management. Fortunately, the Software Defined Network (SDN) matches our requirement well. SDN is becoming leading technology behind many traffic engineering solutions both for backbone network and datacenter network [9]. Many large enterprises such as Google and Microsoft have used SDN to interconnect their geo-distributed datacenters due to the ease, efficiency and flexibility in performing traffic engineering functions, expecting its architecture to result in better network capacity utilization and improve delay and loss performance [10].

In this paper, we investigate concurrent evacuation transfer optimization problem in the SDN scenarios. Different from previous works, we control bandwidth allocation proportion for multiple concurrent transfers to maximize network evacuation capability. Especially, we allow evacuation transmission via multiple routing paths instead of single path, meaning that each evacuation transfer can be routed through multiple paths to improve network utilization. Our objective is to propose an optimal bandwidth allocation strategy for multiple concurrent evacuation transfers to achieve full use of network transmission capability. Our contributions are as follows:

- We propose a new idea of scheduling bandwidth proportion for concurrent evacuation transfers from data amount proportion's perspective in SDN to achieve more efficient use of network transmission capability for disaster evacuation.
- We add BPC into Multi-Commodity Flow (MCF) problem, and propose a new Bandwidth-Proportion-Constrained Multi-Commodity Flow (BPC-MCF) problem to maximize feasible traffic for concurrent evacuation transfers with multi-path routing.
- We design a Bandwidth-Proportion-Aware Ant Colony Optimization (BPA-ACO) algorithm to solve the BPC-MCF problem. We introduce available evacuation capability, bandwidth proportion offset and link sharing degree to guide optimal solution searching. We adjust bandwidth proportion by rearranging flows in shared links and alternate paths.
- By extensive simulations, our algorithm achieves good performance in terms of reducing total evacuation time and achieving higher network utilization compared with the state-of-the-art algorithms.

The rest of the paper is organized as follows. In Sect. 2, we give a high-level overview of disaster evacuation process, and formulate the problem of maximizing total evacuation traffic with BPC. In Sect. 3, we design BPA-ACO algorithm to solve the BPC-MCF problem. In Sect. 4, we evaluate the performance of our solution through extensive simulations. At last, we draw our conclusion in Sect. 5.

2 Problem Formulation

As mentioned in Sect. 1, we notice that none of existing works jointly considered bandwidth allocation proportion problem and multi-path routing problem for concurrent evacuation transfers. But the two factors significantly affects data transmission efficiency in the disaster evacuation scenarios, and we illustrate this by an example.

We assume that there are two evacuation transfers et_1 and et_2 to destination datacenter dc_1 or dc_2 respectively. Considering data integrity and limited storage, the data in the same evacuation transfer can be evacuated to only one datacenter. Here we suppose that et_1 and et_2 own different data amounts (200 GB for et_1 and 100 GB for et_2) and different importance factors (et_2's is higher than et_1's). Previous works scheduled transmission order of evacuation transfers according to data amount [2, 7] or

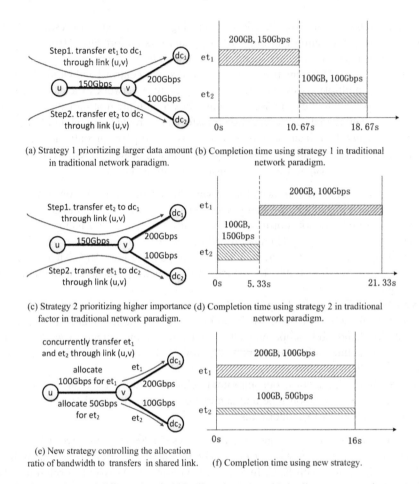

(a) Strategy 1 prioritizing larger data amount in traditional network paradigm.

(b) Completion time using strategy 1 in traditional network paradigm.

(c) Strategy 2 prioritizing higher importance factor in traditional network paradigm.

(d) Completion time using strategy 2 in traditional network paradigm.

(e) New strategy controlling the allocation ratio of bandwidth to transfers in shared link.

(f) Completion time using new strategy.

Fig. 1. Comparison of different bandwidth allocation strategies in disaster evacuation scenarios.

importance factor [6]. As in Fig. 1(a) and (c), we can obtain two bandwidth allocation strategies in traditional network paradigm.

In traditional network paradigm, bandwidth allocation for multiple evacuation transfers in shared links is preemptive. In Fig. 1(b), et_1 obtains whole bandwidth available (150 Gbps) in shared link (u, v) and evacuates 200 GB data to destination dc_1 spending 10.67 s, and then et_2 evacuates 100 GB data to destination dc_2 spending 8 s, so the total evacuation time is 18.67 s. In Fig. 1(d), et_2 obtains whole bandwidth available (150 Gbps) in shared link (u, v) and evacuates 100 GB data to destination dc_1 spending 5.33 s, and then et_1 evacuates 200 GB data to destination dc_2 spending 16 s, so the total evacuation time is 21.33 s. In both cases, although the evacuation with larger data amount or higher importance factor is completed firstly, the total evacuation completion time is not the shortest because the bandwidth in shared link (u, v) has not yet been fully utilized during the whole evacuation process, especially in step 2 of Fig. 1(a) and (c).

Fortunately we can do better if we control allocation proportion of bandwidth to et_1 and et_2 in shared link (u, v) according to the proportion of their data amount as shown in Fig. 1(e). In that case, we transfer et_1 and et_2 concurrently. We allocate bandwidth in (u, v) according to data amount in evacuation transfers respectively. So et_1 obtains 100 Gbps bandwidth while et_2 obtains 50 Gbps bandwidth in (u, v), and they evacuate data concurrently to destination dc_1 or dc_2 respectively. As shown in Fig. 1(f), the two evacuation transfers will be completed at the same time using 16 s. We omit the case of data transmission for et_1 to dc_2 and et_2 to dc_1, because the evacuation time in that case is equal to the result in Fig. 1(f). As shown above, by scheduling bandwidth proportion for concurrent evacuation transfers from data amount proportion's perspective, we can make full use of network transmission capacity and consequently obtain more efficient evacuation solution, meaning shorter total evacuation completion time or more data to be evacuated in limited time.

As a result, we add BPC into the MCF problem for more efficient disaster evacuation solution. Because SDN can arbitrarily split traffic across multiple paths and is highly flexible for routing optimization purposes, we will investigate such concurrent evacuation transfer optimization problem in the SDN scenarios. On the other hand, compared with single-path routing, multi-path routing provides more residual bandwidth and has higher network transmission capacity utilization, so we allow evacuation transmission via multiple routing paths.

2.1 Topology Description

In the disaster evacuation process among geo-distributed datacenters, we evacuate bulk data from endangered datacenters in disaster zones to destination datacenters in safe zones by multiple transfers concurrently. Because of no alternate network dedicated to evacuation, we can only make use of residual network bandwidth.

Our network topology includes datacenters and links. We consider routing problems on a network with a symmetric directed graph $G = (V, E)$, where V is node set, and E is link set. We denote the link from node u to node v as (u, v). We assume that each link (u, v) has a maximum capacity $c(u, v)$ and the total traffic amount through it cannot exceed this limit. In [6], they divided endangered data to be multiple evacuated contents. Hence we use a transfer to denote the transmission of a content. We define $ET = \{et_1, et_2, \ldots, et_n\}$ as the set of evacuation transfers. We also denote et_i by a source-sink pair $<s_i, d_i>$. Note that the d_i means an evacuation destination rather than a datacenter, because multiple different destinations may be in the same one datacenter. Considering data integrity, the data in the same evacuation transfer can be evacuated to only one datacenter while a datacenter can receive data from multiple evacuation transfers if its storage space is enough. Due to space limitations in this paper, we omit the construction process of et_i which allocates the evacuated data sets to destination datacenters with enough available storage resource, and we mainly aim at bandwidth allocation for multiple concurrent transfers via multi-path routing. We use dm_i to denote the data amount of et_i. We define $\alpha_i = dm_i \left/ \sum_{i=1}^{n} dm_i \right.$ as the proportion of data amount for et_i in total data amount for all evacuation transfers. We define $b_i = am_i/dl_i$ as the lower bound of total bandwidth allocated to et_i for successfully completing evacuation within deadline dl_i.

Some notations used in this paper are listed in Table 1.

Table 1. Parameters and variables.

Notation	Description
p	a path for data evacuation in the network
P_i	the set of the paths for et_i
$f(p)$	the flow in path p
x_{uv}^p	$= 1$ if the link (u, v) belongs to path p $= 0$ otherwise
f_{uv}	the flow in link (u, v)
f_{uv}^i	the flow that can be allocated to et_i in link (u, v)
p_i^t	the path for et_i in the tth iteration
$path_i^t$	the set of candidate paths for et_i after the tth iteration

2.2 Mathematical Model

We formulate the BPC-MCF problem as follows:

Maximize:

$$\sum_{i=1}^{n} \sum_{p \in Pi} f(p) \tag{1}$$

Subject to:

$$\sum_{i=1}^{n} \sum_{p \in Pi} x_{uv}^p f(p) \leq c(u, v), \forall (u, v) \in E, x_{uv}^p \in \{0, 1\} \tag{2}$$

$$\sum_{v \in V} f_{uv}^i - \sum_{v \in V} f_{vu}^i = \begin{cases} -\sum_{p \in P_i} f(P) & u = d_i \\ 0 & otherwise \\ \sum_{p \in P_i} f(P) & u = s_i \end{cases} \tag{3}$$

$$\left| \left(\left(\sum_{p \in Pi} f(p) \right) \Big/ \left(\sum_{i=1}^{n} \sum_{p \in Pi} f(p) \right) \right) - \alpha i \right| \leq \sigma, \forall i \in N \tag{4}$$

$$\sum_{p \in = P_i} f(p) \geq b_i, \forall i \in N \tag{5}$$

$$f(p) \geq 0, \forall p \in P_i, i \in N \tag{6}$$

The objective function is to maximize the sum of the available network flows. For all evacuation pairs, we calculate total amount of flows in the set of paths for them.

Link capacity constraint (2) ensures that total traffic through link (u, v) should not exceed maximum capacity. Flow conservation constraint (3) means that for each flow, the input traffic equals to the output traffic at any intermediate node on the paths to destinations. To achieving more efficient use of bandwidth, for all $i \in N$, the proportion of the bandwidth allocated to et_i in total bandwidth allocated to all evacuation transfers should be as close as possible to α_i. So flow proportion constraint (4) ensures that the proportion of total flows for et_i in the sum of evacuation flows should be as close as possible to α_i. The σ is a very small non negative decimal. Flow constraint (5) ensures that total flows for et_i must be greater than or equal to b_i so as to guarantee the transmission completion of every et_i. The constraint (6) denotes that the flow value should be positive.

It is noticed that whether we can find optimal solution is of great significance in the disaster evacuation scenarios. Because the solution quality determines the evacuation efficiency to avoid disaster loss. Owing to computational impracticality of exact algorithms to produce optimal solutions for practical networks of large scale, we consider ant colony optimization (ACO) [11]. In ACO, solution component is associated with pheromone trail. Artificial ants probabilistically add solution component to partial solution until they generate a completely feasible solution. During these iterations, pheromone values are dynamically updated based on the information derived from some high quality solutions to force the search to concentrate on regions containing high quality solutions in solution space. ACO is widely used to solve discrete optimization problems and is effective method to solve MCF problem [12]. In next section, we design BPA-ACO algorithm for scheduling multiple concurrent evacuation transfers with flow splitting and multi-path routing to solve the BPC-MCF problem.

3 Algorithm Design

To solve the BPC-MCF problem, we propose a BPA-ACO algorithm to achieve maximum evacuation flow matching data amount proportion of concurrent evacuation transfers. We introduce available evacuation capability, bandwidth proportion offset and link sharing degree to guide optimal solution searching. We adjust bandwidth proportion by rearranging flows in shared links and alternate paths.

3.1 Basic Idea

The main process of BPA-ACO algorithm can be divided into four stages. At first, we reorder evacuation transfers in descending order of the value equaling to b_i minus the current total bandwidth of et_i. The evacuation transfer with the widest gap between its owning bandwidth and its lower bound should be severed with the highest priority. And then in every iteration, for every et_i, an ant searches path following a probabilistic model. If the ant finds a path p_i^t, then we add it to $path_i^t$. If every et_i has flow path(s), then the proportion of the bandwidth allocated to et_i in the total bandwidth allocated to all evacuation transfers should be as close as possible to α_i by adjusting bandwidth proportion. Based on experience and experiments, we set $\sigma = 0.012$. Next we check whether the solution satisfies lower bound constraint in (5). If not, we continue to increase bandwidth allocation by another path searching round. When there is a better solution with larger total feasible flow than best-so-far solution, we replace best-so-far solution with the better one. At last, we update the pheromone and the algorithm runs multiple iterations until the termination condition is met.

3.2 Transition Probability

While constructing evacuation path, an ant moves from current node u to next node until it reaches destination. The choice of next node v depends on pheromone intensity $\tau_{uv}(t)$ and heuristic information $\eta_{uv}(t)$ in (u, v). The transition probability is:

$$R_{uv}(t) = \frac{(\tau_{uv}(t))^\beta \cdot (\eta_{uv}(t))^\gamma}{\sum\limits_{w \in N(u)} (\tau_{uw}(t))^\beta \cdot (\eta_{uw}(t))^\gamma} \tag{7}$$

The β and γ express the influence of pheromone trail and heuristic factors in transition probability respectively, and $N(u)$ defines the neighborhood set of node u.

3.3 Pheromone Trail and Heuristic Information

During multiple iterations, pheromone values are dynamically updated based on the information derived from some high-quality solutions. In BPA-ACO algorithm, after each iteration, the pheromones are updated as follows:

$$\tau_{uv}(t+1) = \rho\tau_{uv}(t) + (1-\rho)(\Delta\tau(t)^{lb} + \Delta\tau(t)^{gb}) \tag{8}$$

ρ represents evaporating parameter to control the evaporating speed of pheromone. $\Delta\tau(t)^{lb}$ and $\Delta\tau(t)^{gb}$ denote pheromone increment calculated by the evaluation value of current best solution and best-so-far solution respectively:

$$\Delta\tau(t)^{lb} = \kappa^{lb} \cdot f(t)^{lb} \tag{9}$$

$$\Delta\tau(t)^{gb} = \kappa^{gb} \cdot f(t)^{gb} \tag{10}$$

κ^{lb} and κ^{gb} are coefficients to control pheromone increment related to current best solution evaluation value $f(t)^{lb}$ and best-so-far solution evaluation value $f(t)^{gb}$.

$$f(t)^{lb} = x_{uv}^{cu} \cdot \left(\lambda \cdot \frac{cu\_aec}{up\_aec} + \frac{\mu}{\delta(t)+1} \right) \tag{11}$$

$$x_{uv}^{cu} = \begin{cases} 1 & \text{if link } (u,v) \text{ belongs to the path(s) for } cu\_aec \\ 0 & \text{otherwise} \end{cases} \tag{12}$$

$$f(t)^{gb} = y_{uv}^{bsf} \cdot \left(\lambda \cdot \frac{bsf\_aec}{up\_aec} + \frac{\mu}{\varepsilon(t)+1} \right) \tag{13}$$

$$y_{uv}^{bsf} = \begin{cases} 1 & \text{if link } (u,v) \text{ belongs to the path(s) for } bsf\_aec \\ 0 & \text{otherwise} \end{cases} \tag{14}$$

$$up\_aec = \min\{\sum_{i=1}^{n}\sum_{u\in V} c(s_i, u), \sum_{i=1}^{n}\sum_{v\in V} c(v, d_i)\} \tag{15}$$

cu_aec and *bsf_aec* denote available evacuation capability in current best solution and best-so-far solution respectively. For a solution, available evacuation capability is defined as the sum of available flows in all evacuation paths. Under the precondition of satisfying bandwidth proportion constraint, the strategy with larger available evacuation capability realizes more efficient evacuation. *up_aec* represents upper bound of maximum evacuation traffic and is greater than or equals to available evacuation capability in all solutions. λ and μ express influence of available evacuation capability and bandwidth proportion offset on evaluation values respectively.

$$\delta(t) = \sqrt{\frac{1}{n}\sum_{i=1}^{n}\left(\frac{cu\_et_i}{cu\_aec} - \alpha i\right)^2} \tag{16}$$

$$\varepsilon(t) = \sqrt{\frac{1}{n}\sum_{i=1}^{n}\left(\frac{cu\_et_i}{bsf\_aec} - \alpha i\right)^2} \tag{17}$$

cu_et_i denotes the bandwidth allocated to et_i in the tth iteration. We compute the difference between the ratio of cu_et_i to cu_aec and α_i, and then use $\delta(t)$ and $\varepsilon(t)$ to denote bandwidth proportion offset of et_i in current best solution and best-so-far solution. Obviously smaller bandwidth proportion offset means more reasonable bandwidth allocation for et_i and the strategy with it can realize more efficient evacuation under the precondition of owning the same available evacuation capability.

On the other hand, heuristic information presents the desirability to transfer data through the link in a path to destination. Heuristic information $\eta_{uv}(t)$ is as follows:

$$\eta_{uv}(t) = \omega \cdot c_{uv}^i \cdot (\phi(t)+1)^\psi \tag{18}$$

$$\phi(t) = \sum_{i=1}^{n} z_{uv}^{ti} \tag{19}$$

$$z_{uv}^{ti} = \begin{cases} 1 & \text{if link } (u, v) \text{ belongs to the path(s) for } et_i \text{ in the } tth \\ & \text{iteration} \\ 0 & \text{otherwise} \end{cases} \qquad (20)$$

For et_i, heuristic information in link (u, v) depends on residual bandwidth capacity c_{uv}^i in link (u, v) and sharing degree of link (u, v). ω is used to adjust the value of $\eta_{uv}(t)$. Sharing degree $\phi(t)$ of link (u, v) is calculated by the number of evacuation transfers in (19). If $\phi(t)$ is larger, link (u, v) is shared by more evacuation transfers. So it can provide larger scope to adjust bandwidth allocation in algorithm implementation. Therefore, the proportion of total flows for et_i in total flows for evacuation would be closer to α_i. ψ is a coefficient to weigh the relative importance of $\phi(t)$.

3.4　Bandwidth Proportion Adjustment Rules

In bandwidth allocation process for concurrent evacuation transfers, there is a strong possibility that the bandwidth allocation proportion for et_i does not meet α_i in a solution. But as shown in the example of Sect. 2, bandwidth allocation according to data amount of evacuation transfers is a critical factor to maximize network evacuation capability and improve evacuation efficiency. So it is necessary to modify the solution by bandwidth proportion adjustment if bandwidth proportion offset exceeds σ. In this paper, we adjust bandwidth proportion by rearranging flows in shared links and alternate paths. Due to space limit here, we only describe the rules as follows:

- rearranging flows in shared links. In the links shared by multiple evacuation transfers, we adjust bandwidth allocation proportion according to their data amount.
- rearranging flows in alternate paths. If $et_j's$ destination d_j is an intermediate node of a certain path for et_i, we can abandon this $et_i's$ path, construct a new path with destination d_j and use it to allocate more bandwidth for et_j if necessary.

We use the two rules above to adjust bandwidth allocation proportion of multiple evacuation transfers if necessary. The adjustment process terminates if the convergence condition is satisfied, for example that the bandwidth proportion offset is less than σ or the number of adjustment iterations reaches a specified value.

3.5   Algorithm Implementation

The pseudo code of BPA-ACO algorithm is as follows:

BPA-ACO algorithm for solving BPC-MCF

Input: $G(V,E)$, $c(u,v)$, ET .

Output: evacuation solutions.

1. Set parameters, initialize pheromone trails, transition probability, etc.
2. **while** termination condition not met **do**
3.   **for** j =1 to m (the number of ants) **do**
4.   Reorder ET in descending order based on the value equaling to b_i minus the current total bandwidth of et_i
5.   **for** i =1 to n (the number of evacuation transfers) **do**
6.   **while** not reach destination **do**
7.   Calculate heuristic information according to (18)
8.   Select next node according to (7)
9.   **if** reach destination **do**
10.   Add p_i^t to $path_i^t$
11.   Update network $G(V,E)$
12.   **end if**
13.   **if** next node not exist **do**
14.   Break
15.   **end while**
16.   **end for**
17.   **if** every et_i has flow path(s) **do**
18.   Adjust bandwidth allocation proportion according to (4)
19.   Update network $G(V,E)$
20.   **end if**
21.   **end for**
22.   Obtain $path^t = \{path_1^t, path_2^t, ..., path_n^t\}$ and compute cu_aec according to (11)
23.   **if** not satisfy lower bound constraint in (5) **do**
24.   Goto 3
25.   **if** find a better solution **do**
26.   Update bsf_aec according to (13)
27.   Update pheromone according to (8)
28. **end while**

In BPA-ACO algorithm, path set construction for every et_i may be solved by multiple ants. For every evacuation transfers, at most m paths are generated, so the time complexity of this algorithm is approximately $O(nm|V|)$. Through extensive simulations, we get reasonable values of simulation parameters. We let the initial intensity of pheromone $\tau_0 = 7$ and set $\rho = 0.3$, $\kappa^{lb} = 0.4$, $\kappa^{gb} = 0.6$, $\lambda = 7$, $\mu = 5$, $\omega = 0.03$, $\psi = 0.5$, $\beta = 0.8$, $\gamma = 0.4$ on the basis of experience and experiment.

4 Performance Evaluation

4.1 Environment and Configuration

BPA-ACO algorithm is written with C++ in Visual Studio 2015, and runs on a machine equipped with Inter Core i7 8-Core processors and 8.00 GB RAM. We compare BPA-ACO algorithm with two representative algorithms suitable for disaster evacuation in [2, 6] on the same platform aiming at transmission process. In [2], we choose OneStep-MDF algorithm. OneStep-MDF algorithm handles the backup pair with the most data to be backed up first one after another and chooses the destination that can provide the largest data-transfer throughput for it. To make it more suitable for disaster evacuation, we release the constraint about one to one correspondence between source datacenter and destination datacenter. So we call the modified algorithm as Modified-OneStep-MDF (M-OS-MDF) algorithm. In [6], they proposed a rapid data evacuation (RDE) heuristic algorithm through least-delay path not considering multi-path routing. Here we also choose RDE algorithm for comparison.

We perform our experiments over two types of network topologies.

- The Waxman model [13]: Here we set the amount of data for evacuation as 1 PB and the number of evacuation transfers as 50.
- The US-Backbone topology [6]: As in Fig. 2, it has 24 nodes and 10 datacenters. The nodes with thick black circles represent datacenter nodes. We consider areas covered by the red shade including datacenters at nodes 9 and 12 as disaster zone to evacuate data. We set the size of contents ranges from 2 TB to 25 TB.

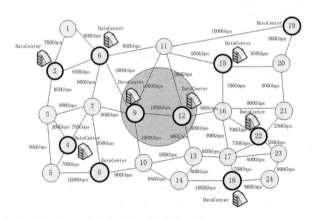

Fig. 2. US-Backbone topology with disaster zone.

4.2 Evacuation Time Comparison

(1) Comparison in Waxman model: Fig. 3 represents comparison of evacuation time with increase of node (including intermediate nodes, application datacenters and endangered datacenters) number. As node number increases, the gaps between evacuation times become larger. RDE algorithm searches a single least-delay path

while other available paths lying idle. M-OS-MDF algorithm allows multiple paths for every evacuation transfer one by one, so evacuation time decreases much faster. But it does not consider bandwidth allocation proportion problem to make full use of network transmission capability. With multi-path routing, BPA-ACO algorithm schedules multiple concurrent transfers from entire topology according to proportion of data amount in evacuation transfers, so it performs better than others obviously.

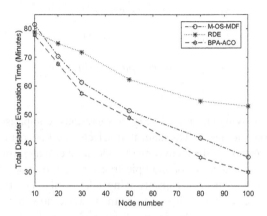

Fig. 3. Comparison of evacuation time with the increase of node number.

(2) Comparison in US-Backbone topology: Fig. 4 represents comparison of evacuation time with the increase of data amount. The evacuation time of RDE algorithm grows faster than others and ultimately exceeds 70 min. M-OS-MDF algorithm has better performance because it searches maximum flow to transfer data through multiple available paths for every evacuation transfer one by one. BPA-ACO algorithm performs even better by scheduling bandwidth allocation according to proportion of data amount in evacuation transfers and spends less than 60 min ultimately.

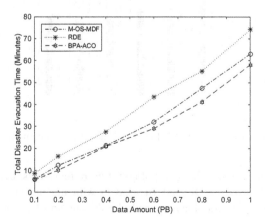

Fig. 4. Comparison of evacuation time with the increase of data amount.

4.3   Network Utilization Comparison

To compute network utilization, we first compute maximum network flow called MaxFlow from endangered datacenters to other datacenters in safe zone. And then, we run M-OS-MDF, RDE and BPA-ACO algorithm respectively to get their throughput as $Throughput_{MDF}$, $Throughput_{RDE}$ and $Throughput_{BPA}$. The Normalized Throughput (NT) [8] for M-OS-MDF, RDE and BPA-ACO are defined as follows:

$$NT_{MDF} = Throughput_{MDF}/MaxFlow \tag{21}$$

$$NT_{RDE} = Throughput_{RDE}/MaxFlow \tag{22}$$

$$NT_{BPA} = Throughput_{BPA}/MaxFlow \tag{23}$$

(1) Comparison in Waxman model: Fig. 5 represents comparison of NTs with increase of node number. RDE algorithm selects one best path for every evacuation transfer. Although the increasing of node number may raise the possibility of better single path selection for multiple transfers one by one, there will still be more and more transmission capacity lying idle. So its NT gradually decreases. M-OS-MDF algorithm searches maximum network flow for every evacuation transfer sequentially, so its NT keeps steady and rises slightly. BPA-ACO algorithm further considers proportion of data amount in concurrent evacuation transfers avoiding transmission capacity lying idle, so its NT is even higher than others.

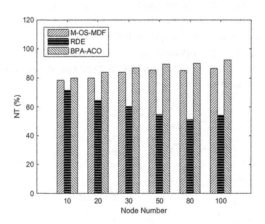

Fig. 5. Comparison of NT with the increase of node number.

(2) Comparison in US-Backbone topology: Fig. 6 represents comparison of NT between M-OS-MDF, RDE and BPA-ACO with the increase of data amount. Because the network topology is fixed, the fluctuation of NT is relatively small.

But the gap between their NT still can be observed. RDE algorithm uses single path. Although its NT will be improved with increase number of evacuation transfers, the average value is still relatively low, ranging from 48.69% to 64.07%. M-OS-MDF algorithm obtains relatively higher NT because it searches maximum network flow through multi-routing, ranging from 78.80% to 82.23%. BPA-ACO obtains even higher NT, ranging from 81.04% to 86.24% by more reasonable allocation strategy according to data amount in concurrent evacuation transfers.

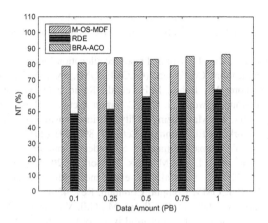

Fig. 6. Comparison of NT with the increase of data amount.

5   Conclusion

Nowadays, datacenters holding massive services and data are faced to increasing risks. To reduce loss in disasters, efficient evacuation requires appropriate allocation strategy of residual network bandwidth for multiple concurrent evacuation transfers. Hence, in the SDN scenarios with traffic scheduling, we propose an optimal bandwidth proportion allocation strategy for multiple concurrent evacuation transfers according to proportion of their transmission data amount via multi-path routing and then design a BPA-ACO algorithm to realize it. Through extensive simulations, we demonstrate that our algorithm has better performance with less total evacuation time and higher network utilization compared with state-of-the-art algorithms.

Acknowledgment. The study is supported by the National Natural Science Foundation of China (NSFC No. 61672323), the Natural Science Foundation of Shandong Province (Grant No. ZR2015FM008, BS2015DX003), and the Fundamental Research Funds of Shandong University (Grant No. 2017JC043).

References

1. Greenberg, A., Hamilton, J., Maltz, D., Patel, P.: The cost of a cloud: research problems in datacenter networks. ACM SIGCOMM Comput. Commun. Rev. **39**, 68–73 (2009)
2. Yao, J., Lu, P., Gong, L., Zhu, Z.: On fast and coordinated data backup in geo-distributed optical inter-datacenter networks. J. Lightwave Technol. **33**, 3005–3015 (2015)
3. Henderson, N.: Noise filter: Hurricane Sandy floods NYC data center, impacts hosts, colocation providers. http://www.thewhir.com/web-hosting-news/noise-filter-hurricane-sandy-floods-nyc-data-center-impacts-hosts
4. Guerrero, J.M., Vasquez, J.C., Matas, J., Castilla, M.: Control strategy for flexible microgrid based on parallel line-interactive UPS systems. IEEE Trans. Industr. Electron. **56**, 726–736 (2009)
5. Bianco, A., Giraudo, L., Hay, D.: Optimal resource allocation for disaster recovery. In: IEEE Global Telecommunications Conference (GLOBECOM), pp. 1–5 (2010)
6. Ferdousi, S., Tornatore, M., Habib, M.F., et al.: Rapid data evacuation for large-scale disasters in optical cloud networks. J. Opt. Commun. Netw. **7**, B163–B172 (2015)
7. Lu, P., Ling, Q., Zhu, Z.: Maximizing utility of time-constrained emergency backup in inter-datacenter networks. IEEE Commun. Lett. **20**, 890–893 (2016)
8. Cho, S., Elhourani, T., Ramasubramanian, S.: Independent directed acyclic graphs for resilient multipath routing. IEEE/ACM Trans. Networking **20**, 153–162 (2012)
9. Jain, S., Kumar, A., Mandal, S., et al.: B4: experience with a globally-deployed software defined wan. ACM SIGCOMM Comput. Commun. Rev. **43**(4), 3–14 (2013)
10. Hong, C.Y., Kandula, S., Mahajan, R., Zhang, M., Gill, V., Nanduri, M., Wattenhofer, R.: Achieving high utilization with software-driven WAN. In: ACM SIGCOMM 2013 Conference, pp. 15–26 (2013)
11. Dorigo, M., Stützle, T.: Handbook of Metaheuristics. Springer, USA (2010)
12. Masri, H., Krichen, S., Guitouni, A.: An ant colony optimization metaheuristic for solving bi-objective multi-sources multicommodity communication flow problem. In: 4th IFIP Wireless and Mobile Networking Conference (WMNC), pp. 1–8 (2011)
13. Naldi, M.: Connectivity of Waxman topology models. Comput. Commun. **29**, 24–31 (2005)

Energy-Balanced and Depth-Controlled Routing Protocol for Underwater Wireless Sensor Networks

Hao Qin, Zhiyong Zhang, Rui Wang, Xiaojun Cai, and Zhiping Jia[✉]

School of Computer Science and Technology, Shandong University, Jinan, China
jzp@sdu.edu.cn

Abstract. As the ocean exploration becomes more and more popular, the Underwater Wireless Sensor Network (UWSN) has recently received extensively attentions. In UWSN, a large number of nodes are deployed at different depths, which means once deployed, it will be difficult to replace or recharge due to the complex underwater environment. Therefore, improving the lifetime of the UWSN network is one of critical issue to be studied. Since the sensor nodes are distributed at different depths, the energy of the nodes near to the horizontal plane which have more data to forward will be exhausted more quickly. The unbalanced energy consumption leads to a decline in network lifetime. To address this problem, we propose an Energy-Balanced and Depth-Controlled Routing Protocol for Underwater Wireless Sensor Networks in this paper. The proposed protocol replaces the low-energy nodes with the high-energy nodes by adjusting their depths to achieve balanced energy consumption among the whole network. Experimental results show our scheme effectively improves the lifetime of the whole network.

1 Introduction

In recent years, UWSN has gained increasing popularity in both academia and industry area because people are interested in exploring the vast underwater environment. UWSN has a large number of applications such as tactical surveillance, seismic monitoring, assisted navigations, pollution monitoring and many more scientific based applications [1,2,17].

Although there are many routing protocols that are proposed for terrestrial Wireless Sensor Networks (WSNs), these existing routing protocols may not be suitable for underwater environment [3,18]. Radio signals have rapid attenuation in the water, which means UWSN has to use acoustic channels for communication. In the harsh underwater environment, the acoustic signals have unique characteristics such as long propagation delay (five orders of magnitudes slower than radio), high signal to noise ratio, low bandwidth etc. So designing routing protocol for UWSNs is very challenging [4].

In UWSN, the sensor nodes have limited battery power and replacing the batteries of all the nodes is very expensive and difficult. Hence, improving the network lifetime is one of the most important issues. In UWSN, the sensor nodes are distributed at different depths and have different number of data to forward.

© Springer International Publishing AG 2017
S. Ibrahim et al. (Eds.): ICA3PP 2017, LNCS 10393, pp. 115–131, 2017.
DOI: 10.1007/978-3-319-65482-9_8

There is a problem that each node has different energy consumption. Due to the unbalanced energy consumption, some nodes with high load die earlier than other nodes, which influences the lifetime of UWSN. Therefore, the energy consumption balance among the sensor nodes is one major method to improve the network lifetime.

Some protocols are proposed to address this issue (e.g. EEDBR [6]). Although these protocols consider balancing the energy consumption and prolonging the network lifetime, they don't consider the energy balance between the nodes near the sink nodes and the nodes far from the sink nodes. The nodes close to the sink nodes have unbalanced load and forward more packets than the nodes far from the sink nodes. This results that the nodes close to the sink nodes die earlier. Due to the unbalanced energy consumption, the nodes far from the sink still have energy to work when the overall network is dead.

To address this problem, we propose Energy-Balanced and Depth-Controlled Routing Protocol (EBDCR) to improve the network lifetime. In EBDCR, we replace the low-energy nodes near the sink nodes by the high-energy nodes far from the sink nodes through depth adjustment. We decline the low-energy nodes and float up the high-energy nodes to make the high-energy nodes closer to the sink nodes. Doing like this, we ensure the nodes now near the sink nodes have more energy to forward data. Hence, the lifetime of the network can be prolonged.

The major contributions of this paper can be summarized as follows:

– We propose a strategy to prolong the lifetime of the network through depth adjustment. We decline the low-energy nodes and float up the high-energy nodes to achieve the balance of the energy consumption between the nodes near the sink nodes and the nodes far from the sink nodes.
– We put forward an algorithm to identify the time when the nodes should be replaced. And then we determine a strategy to ensure the data transmission thereby improving the network lifetime.

The remainder of this paper is organized as follows. Section 2 describes the related work. The proposed protocol is presented in Sect. 3. In Sect. 4, we present simulations results that we have conducted in order to evaluate the proposed protocol. Finally, Sect. 5 concludes this paper.

2   Related Work

Recently, a number of routing protocols have been proposed for UWSNs. In this section, we present some related routing protocols as follows.

In [7], the authors propose the VBF routing protocol which uses the distance between the node and the routing vector to determine whether it should forwards the data packet. The forwarding process of VBF can be seen as to build a routing pipe between the source node and the destination node so that packets are delivered through the nodes in the pipe. Moreover, VBF uses a self-adaption algorithm in order to reduce the number of forwarding nodes and conserve energy. In [19], CVBF divides all nodes into the number of predefined clusters, and selects one node at the top of each cluster as a virtual sink. The rest of nodes transmit the data packets to their respective cluster virtual sink following the methodology of VBF routing protocol. The cluster virtual sink node forwards the aggregated data to the main sink node deployed on water surface through single-hop mechanism.

In Depth-based routing (DBR) protocol [4], the decision of forwarding the packet is based on the node depth and the depth of the previous sender. If the node can forward the packet, it will wait a holding time. During the holding time, the node discards the packet when it receives the same packet. For efficient energy consumption, EEDBR [6] computes holding time on the bases of residual energy of sensor nodes to enhance the network lifetime. And in [15], DSEEDBR provides enhanced network lifetime along with delay sensitivity to EEDBR by implementing Delay-Sensitive Holding time (DSH_t) and adaptive variations in d_{th} for sensor nodes. AMCTD [13] encourages the deployment of courier nodes and devises efficient weight functions to increase the stability period of the network.

Depth-Controlled Routing protocol (DCR) [5] adjusts the depths of some nodes in order to organize the network topology and forward data when the problem of communication void arises. DCR provides a centralized algorithm to identify the nodes which are disconnected and the nodes which are the void nodes, and then calculates the new depths of these nodes to improve both the network connectivity and rate data delivery.

Amara et al. [14] propose DEADS to improve reliability and efficiency. In DEADS, the authors propose DS (the Dominating Set) based cooperative routing algorithm with sink mobility. They discuss two mobility pattern of mobile sink: elliptical mobility pattern and linear mobility pattern. And DEADS works in three phases: neighbor selection, DS and CC set formation, and threshold based data sensing and routing.

In [16], EBECRP avoids depth base routing and uses mobile sinks to balance load on all nodes. It uses the concept of clustering to reduce multi hoping which results in more energy consumption. The selected Cluster Heads (CHs) collect data from one hope neighbor nodes to reduce global communication into locally compressed communication.

These routing protocols don't consider the energy balance between the nodes near the sink nodes and the nodes far from the sink nodes. Hence, the nodes near the sink nodes will die earlier because they have more data to forward. Inspired by the idea of adjusting the depth to improve the network connectivity and forwarding data, which is proposed in DCR [5], we propose Energy-Balanced and Depth-Controlled Routing Protocol (EBDCR) to improve the network lifetime by adjusting the depth of the sensor nodes.

3 Energy-Balanced and Depth-Controlled Routing Protocol

In this section, we present our Energy-Balanced and Depth-Controlled Routing Protocol in detail. Firstly we introduce the network architecture of EDBCR.

Secondly, we explain the phases of network initialization and data forwarding. And then we introduce our node replacement strategy to prolong the lifetime of the network and explain how our algorithm identifies which nodes should be replaced and which nodes can replace the low-energy nodes. At the end of the algorithm, we calculate their respective new depths and adjust them to new depths to continue forwarding data thereby prolonging the network lifetime.

3.1 Network Architecture

As shown in Fig. 1, UWSN consists of one or more sink nodes and lots of sensor nodes. The sink nodes are deployed on the surface of water with the help of the floating buoy or the anchor. The sink nodes are equipped with both acoustic and radio (e.g., Wi-Fi or Satellites) transceivers. These sink nodes use acoustic modem for communication with the sensor nodes to receive the data packets, while they can communicate with each other by radio links to forward the data packets collected from sensor nodes to the onshore data center or the research ship. We assume that all the sink nodes have enough energy because they can exchange the batteries expediently or they can utilize solar energy. So we don't consider the energy consumption of the sink nodes.

The sensor nodes are deployed underwater from the top to the bottom of the deployment region. They are equipped with a variety of sensors to sense the surrounding environment and they use acoustic modem to send the collected data towards the sink nodes. In this communication, the sensor node sends the data packet to its neighbor node which is selected as next-hop and then this neighbor node repeats this step. So the data packet is delivered to one of the sink nodes by multi-hops. Because the radio communication is much faster than

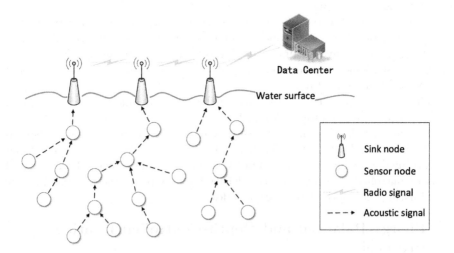

Fig. 1. Architecture of UWSN.

the acoustic communication, we assume that a packet is delivered successfully as long as it is received by one of the sink nodes.

In addition, all the sensor nodes can be fixed at a specific depth by the anchor, and we can adjust their depths by adjusting the length of the anchor chain (using winch-based module) [5]. We assume each sensor node has unique ID and has the same communication range which defined as R.

In this paper, we denote the sink node as S_i and the sensor nodes as N_i. The residual energy of the sensor node N_i is defined as E_i.

3.2   Network Initialization Phase

After the deployment of all the nodes, the network initialization phase begins. At first, all of the sink nodes obtain their locations by means of a positioning system like GPS. The coordinate of the sink node S_i is defined as $(X_{s_i}, Y_{s_i}, Z_{s_i})$. And then the sensor nodes use the AUV aided localization system [8] and the on-board pressure sensor to obtain their respective locations. During the AUV aided localization, the AUV broadcasts the locations of all the sink nodes which have been sent to the AUV before the localization. So each sensor node has its own coordinate denoted as (X_i, Y_i, Z_i) and all coordinates of the sink nodes. And then each sensor node uses the Algorithm 1 to calculate the Euclidean distance between itself and its nearest sink node. We define this distance as Ds. After that, the sensor node broadcasts its self-information packet to its neighbors periodically. The information packet contains the ID, coordinate, residual energy, and Ds. The format of the information packet is shown in Fig. 2a.

Algorithm 1. Ds Calculation

1: (X_i, Y_i, Z_i) the coordinate of the sensor node N_i
2: $(X_{s_i}, Y_{s_i}, Z_{s_i})$ the coordinate of the sink node S_i
3: $Ds = infinite$
4: **for all** sink node S_i **do**
5:     $D_{s_i} = \sqrt{(X_i - X_{s_i})^2 + (Y_i - Y_{s_i})^2 + (Z_i - Z_{s_i})^2}$
6:     **if** $D_{s_i} < Ds$ **then**
7:         $Ds = D_{s_i}$
8:     **end if**
9: **end for**
10: **return** Ds

When the sensor node receives the information packet from one of its neighbors, it compares its Ds with the neighbor's Ds. If the neighbor's Ds is smaller, it means that this neighbor is closer to the sink nodes than the sensor node, and the sensor node can forward the data packets to this neighbor to deliver the packets to the sink nodes. The sensor node will record this neighbor's information (such as ID, coordinate, residual energy) into the forwarding node candidate list. The format of the forwarding node candidate list is shown as Table 1. At the last of

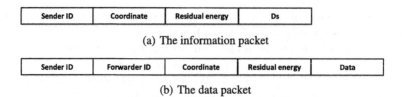

(a) The information packet

(b) The data packet

Fig. 2. The format of packet

this phase, the sensor node sorts the forwarding node candidate list and selects the neighbor node which has smallest Ds from the forwarding node candidate list as the forwarding node(the next-hop node).

Table 1. The forwarding node candidate list.

Node ID	Coordinate	Ds	Residual energy (J)
1	$(10, 5, 7)$	7	90
18	$(10, 15, 27)$	30	80

3.3   Data Forwarding Phase

After network initialization, all the sensor nodes sense the surrounding environment and collect data of interest from the environment. Then it comes to data forwarding phase and sensor nodes start to send data packets. In network initialization phase, each sensor node uses greedy forwarding strategy to select the neighbor node which has smallest Ds from the forwarding node candidate list as the forwarding node (the next-hop node). After that, in order to balance the energy consumption of the neighbor nodes in the forwarding node candidate list, each sensor node periodically checks the residual energy of the neighbor nodes in the forwarding node candidate list and selects the node which has largest residual energy as its forwarding node. When the sensor node needs to send a data packet towards sink nodes, it just sends the packet to its forwarding node. The forwarding node (the next-hop node) receives the data packet and sends to its forwarding node. Finally the data packet will be delivered to one of the sink nodes by multi-hops.

As shown in Fig. 2b, the data packet includes five parts: sender ID, forwarder ID, sender's coordinate, sender's residual energy and the data. When a sensor node sends a data packet, all its neighbors can receive the packet in UWSN. In order to avoid redundant packets and save energy, the sensor node checks the forwarder ID when it receives a packet. If its ID is same with the forwarder ID, it will forward this packet. At the same time, the sensor node adds the sender's information into the child node list. The format of the child node candidate list is shown as Table 2. The sender ID, coordinate and the residual energy can obtain

Table 2. The child node candidate list.

Sender ID	Coordinate	P_s	Residual energy (J)
3	$(12, 20, 7)$	7	90
10	$(10, 15, 27)$	10	80

from the data packet directly. And the packet flow sent by the sender (defined as P_s) can be obtained by counting the number of packets received from the sender per unit time.

3.4 Node Replacement Strategy and Algorithm

Because during data forwarding phase each sensor node needs to send its collected data and the data that its child nodes send to it, the sensor nodes close to the sink nodes have more load than other sensor nodes far from the sink nodes. So the sensor nodes close to the sink nodes die earlier, which results that the sensor nodes far from the sink nodes still have energy to work when the network is dead. In order to overcome this problem and make full use of these residual energy to prolong the lifetime of the network, we propose our node replacement strategy.

The main idea of our proposed node replacement strategy is using the high-energy nodes which are far from the sink nodes to replace the low-energy nodes which are close to the sink nodes. Because each sensor node is equipped with the anchor and the length of the anchor chain can be adjusted, we can adjust the depths of the sensor nodes to achieve the node replacement. As shown in Fig. 3, the node replacement means that one sensor node (named B) replaces the function of another sensor node (named A) through depth adjustment. In other words, the child nodes of node A can send the data packets to node B, and then node B can forward these data packets to node A's forwarding node.

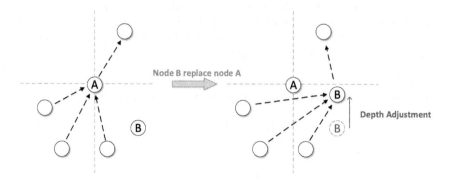

Fig. 3. The node replacement.

The node replacement strategy is divided into the following steps:

1. One of the sensor nodes meets node replacement condition which means its energy consumption is larger than a defined threshold.
2. The sensor node selects one of its child nodes that have more energy as the replacement node.
3. The replacement node adjusts its depth to replace the function of the sensor node. At the same time the sensor node adjusts its depth to replace the function of the replacement node.

Because the sink nodes are deployed on the water surface, the low-depth sensor nodes have more energy consumption than the high-depth sensor nodes. Through the node replacement, we decline the low-energy nodes and float up the high-energy nodes. So the high-energy nodes currently are closer to the sink nodes and forward more data packets than the low-energy nodes, this achieves the balance of the energy consumption between the nodes close to the sink nodes and the nodes far from the sink nodes. Hence, the lifetime of the network can be prolonged.

Node Replacement Condition. Since each sensor node is deployed at different locations and has different number of child nodes, each sensor node has different load. So each sensor node has different residual energy as time increases. In order to balance the energy of each sensor node quickly, the node replacement condition should meet the following requirements:

1. In the similar depth, the sensor node which has low energy should be replaced earlier than the node which has high energy.
2. In the similar depth, the sensor node which has large packet flow should be replaced earlier than the node which has small packet flow.
3. Since the sensor node which has high depth has fewer load, the energy consumption of high-depth sensor node is slow. If the node replacement condition is independent of the location of sensor node, the node with high depth will be replaced slower than the node with low depth. In order to balance the energy between the high-depth sensor nodes and the low-depth sensor nodes effectively and quickly, the sensor node with high depth should be replaced earlier than the node with low depth.

Therefore, the node replacement condition is that the energy consumption of the sensor node N_i is larger than threshold T_i. T_i is calculated as follows:

$$T_i = \frac{1}{x \cdot L_i} \cdot E_i \tag{1}$$

$$L_i = \lceil \frac{Ds}{R} \rceil \tag{2}$$

E_i is current residual energy of node N_i when T_i is calculated. Once the sensor node N_i adjusts its depth, T_i should be updated. x is a pre-defined positive constant and L_i is the ideal minimum number of hops for node N_i sending data to sink nodes. (L_i represents how far the node is from sink nodes.) It can be seen that the farther away from the sink nodes (the larger Ds), the larger L_i will be. So when two sensor nodes have same E_i and packet flow, the node with higher depth has smaller T_i, causing replacement earlier.

For example, we set $x = 2$, the sensor node A has $100\,J$ initial energy, and its $Ds < R$. so $L_A = Ds/R = 1$ and its threshold $T_A = 1/(2*1)*100\,J = 50\,J$. So when node A consumes $50\,J$ of energy, it selects one of its child nodes as the replacement node and adjusts to new depth. After node replacement, we assume that the sensor node A consumes $10\,J$ to adjust depth and its new $Ds \in (R, 2R)$. E_i is the current residual energy which is $50\,J - 10\,J = 40\,J$ and now its threshold $T_A' = 1/(2*2)*40\,J = 10\,J$. Hence, the next replacement of node A occurs when it consumes $10\,J$.

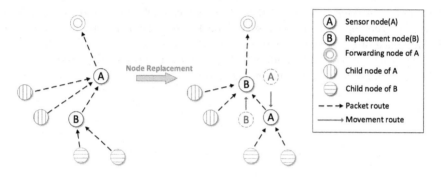

Fig. 4. The node replacement between node A and node B.

Replacement Node Selection. When the sensor node meets its node replacement condition, this means the energy consumption is large enough and the sensor node should select one of its child nodes as replacement node. Then the sensor node and the replacement node replace each other. As shown in Fig. 4, the node B is the replacement node of the node A. The sensor node A drops to an appropriate depth in order to receive the data packets from the child nodes of the replacement node B and forward them to the replacement node B. The replacement node B floats up to receive the data packets from the sensor node A's child nodes (except the replacement node B) and the data packets from the sensor node A. And then the replacement node B forwards them to the sensor node A's forwarding node.

Due to only the depth of the sensor node can be adjusted and the sensor nodes are different in horizontal position, it is difficult for the sensor node to find a child node which can reach the sensor node's position. When a child node is selected as the replacement node and adjusts its depth to replace the function of the sensor node, it is possible that some child nodes of the sensor node cannot communicate with the replacement node (the distance between the replacement node and the child node is larger R). As shown in Fig. 5, node F is the forwarding node of node A, node B,C,D are child nodes of A and node E,F are child nodes of B. The node communication radius is R. When node A selects node B as the replacement node, node B floats up to replace the function of node A. But node D is so far from node B that node B cannot communicate with node D. Similarly, the sensor node A needs drop to an appropriate depth to forward the data packets from the child nodes of node B to node B, but node A doesn't guarantee to communicate with all of node B's child nodes (node A cannot communicate with node E). After node replacement, node B only receives the packets from node A's child nodes which can communicate with node B and the packets that node A forwards. And the packets that node A forwards are from the child nodes of B that can communicate with A. Therefore, the number of packets forwarded by node B after the replacement is not more than the number of the packets forwarded by node A before the replacement. We define the number of packets forwarded by the replacement node (node B) per unit time after the replacement as reserved packet flow (P_r). In order to minimize the influence of node replacement on the other parts of the network, we should consider selecting the child node which can make the reserved packet flow (P_r) as large as possible as the replacement node.

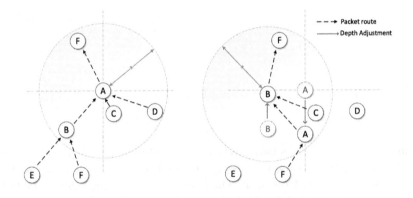

Fig. 5. The communication problem after node replacement.

In order to calculate the (P_r), the sensor node needs to know the information of its child nodes' child nodes, such as the coordinate and the packet flow (P_s). At the beginning of node selection, the sensor node sends request packet to all its child nodes and child nodes send the information recorded in their child node lists to the sensor node. After that the sensor node calculates the (P_r) of all child nodes which have more energy than it. Then it selects the replacement node according to the P_r and the residual energy. And during the calculation, the new depths of the sensor node and the replacement node are also calculated.

The Replacement Node Selection Algorithm: The notations used in our replacement node selection are shown in Table 3. As illustrated in Algorithm 2,

Algorithm 2. Replacement node selection.

1: **for all** $c \in Child(n)$ **do**
2:     **if** $E(c) > E(n)$ **then**
3:         $P_r(c) = P_c(c)$
4:         $D(c) \leftarrow S(c, f) \leftarrow \left\{ z \,\middle|\, \sqrt{(X_f - X_c)^2 + (Y_f - Y_c)^2 + (Z_f - z)^2} \leq R \right\}$
5:         sort $Child(n)$ according the nodes' packet flow in descending order.
6:         **for all** $k \in Child(n) - \{c\}$ **do**
7:             $S(c, k) \leftarrow \left\{ z \,\middle|\, \sqrt{(X_k - X_c)^2 + (Y_k - Y_c)^2 + (Z_k - z)^2} \leq R \right\}$
8:             **if** $D(c) \cap S(c, k) \neq \emptyset$ **then**
9:                 $D(c) \leftarrow D(c) \cap S(c, k)$
10:                $P_r(c) = P_r(c) + P_s(k)$
11:            **end if**
12:        **end for**
13:        $Z'_c = z \quad (min|z - Z_c| \quad and \quad z \in D(c))$
14:        $P_r(n) = P_c(n)$
15:        $D(n) \leftarrow S(n, c') \leftarrow \left\{ z \,\middle|\, \sqrt{(X_c - X_n)^2 + (Y_c - Y_n)^2 + (Z'_c - z)^2} \leq R \right\}$
16:        sort $Child(c)$ according the nodes' packet flow in descending order.
17:        **for all** $j \in Child(c)$ **do**
18:            $S(n, j) \leftarrow \left\{ z \,\middle|\, \sqrt{(X_j - X_n)^2 + (Y_j - Y_n)^2 + (Z_j - z)^2} \leq R \right\}$
19:            **if** $D(n) \cap S(n, j) \neq \emptyset$ **then**
20:                $D(n) \leftarrow D(n) \cap S(n, j)$
21:                $P_r(n) = P_r(n) + P_s(j)$
22:            **end if**
23:        **end for**
24:        $Z'_n = z \quad (min|z - Z_n| \quad and \quad z \in D(n))$
25:        $P_r(c) = P_r(c) + P_r(n)$
26:        $E'(c) = E(c) - |Zc - Zc'| \cdot E_a$
27:        $E'(n) = E(n) - |Zn - Zn'| \cdot E_a$
28:        **if** $E'(c) > E(n)$ and $\frac{E'(n)}{P_r(n) \cdot E_f} \geq \frac{E(n)}{P_s(n) \cdot E_f}$ **then**
29:            add c into $Candidates$
30:        **end if**
31:    **end if**
32: **end for**
33: select the child node whose P_r is largest as the replacement node from $Candidates$.

the sensor node n checks each its child node at first (line 1). If its child node c has smaller energy than node n, node n will check next child node because node c reduces the network lifetime if it replaces node n. Otherwise, node n initializes the P_r of node c as its created packet flow ($P_c(c)$) and calculates the depth range (defined as $S(c, f)$ for convenience) where node c can communicate directly with the forwarding node f of node n. Simultaneously, the optimal depth range of node c (defined as $D(c)$) is initialized as $S(c, f)$ (lines 3–4). Then node n sorts its child nodes according the nodes' packet flow P_s (in descending order) (line 5), it checks each one (defined as k for convenience) in the set of node n's child nodes in descending order and calculates the depth range (defined as $S(c, k)$ for

Table 3. Notations in replacement node selection.

Notation	Definition
$Child(i)$	the set of child nodes of sensor node i
f	the forwarding node of the sensor node
$E(i)$	the energy of sensor node i
E_a	the energy consumption of adjusting depth per meter
E_f	the energy consumption of forwarding per packet
$D(i)$	the optimal depth range of node i
$S(i,j)$	the depth range of node i in which node i can communicate directly with j
$P_r(i)$	the reserved packet flow of sensor node i
$P_s(i)$	the packet flow sent by the sensor node i before the node replacement
$P_c(i)$	the packet flow created by the sensor node i
$Z'(i)$	the new depth of node i
(X_i, Y_i, Z_i)	the coordinate of sensor node i
$Candidates$	The set of candidate replacement nodes

convenience) where node c can communicate with the node k (line 6). If the range $D(c)$ and $S(c,k)$ have an intersection, it means that node c can forward the packets from node k to the forwarding node of node n. Then the range $D(c)$ and the P_r of node c are updated (lines 8–11). After traversing all child nodes of node n except node c, $D(c)$ is the proper range where node c can forward the packets from node n's child nodes as more as possible. Then the new depth of node c is determined which minimizes the node c moving distance (line 13). According to the new depth of node c, node n calculates the optimal depth range for itself where node n forwards the packets from node c's child nodes to node c as more as possible (lines 14–23). The new depth of node n is determined (line 24) and the P_r of node c is updated (line 25). And then the residual energy that node n and node c have after replacement can be calculated (lines 26–27). If the residual energy of node c after replacement is larger than the energy of node n before the replacement and the lifetime of node n is prolonged through the replacement, node n adds node c into the set of $Candidates$ (lines 28–30). At last, node n selects the child node whose P_r is largest as the replacement node from $Candidates$.

Depth Adjustment. After the replacement node is selected, the sensor node (named A for easy explanation) broadcasts the new depth of the replacement node (named B for easy explanation) and the ID of the replacement node B. Each child node except the replacement node B checks whether the replacement node B can communicate with it at the new depth. If the replacement node B can forward the packets sent from the child node, the child node will use the replacement node B as its new forwarding node and delete the original forwarding node (node A) from the forwarding node candidate list. Otherwise, the child node will delete the original forwarding node (node A) from the forwarding node candidate list and then it will select the neighbor node which has largest residual energy from the forwarding node candidate list as its new forwarding node. Similarly, the replacement node B broadcasts the new depth of the sensor node A to its child nodes. The replacement node B's child nodes select their new forwarding nodes according whether they can communicate with the sensor node A.

After that, the sensor node A and the replacement node B adjust to their new depths. They update their forwarding node, coordinate, residual energy and Ds, and they broadcast their information (ID, coordinate, residual energy and Ds) to their new neighbors. Then they continue to work to forward packets and the network lifetime can be prolonged.

4   Experiments

4.1   Experimental Setup

In this section, we evaluate the performance of our proposed protocol EBDCR and compare it with DCR [5] and EEDBR [6]. We perform the simulations using Network Simulator (NS-2) [9]. In order to simulate the impairment of acoustic communication we use Aqua-Sim. Aqua-Sim is developed on NS-2 and can effectively simulate acoustic signal attenuation and packet collisions in underwater sensor networks [10]. In our simulations, sensor nodes are randomly deployed in a 1500 m × 1500 m × 1500 m 3-D area. One or multiple sink nodes are deployed at the water surface, and we assume that all the sink nodes are stationary once deployed. All the sensor nodes have same communication range of 250 m, data rate of 50 Kbps, and CSMA MAC protocol, as in [11]. The packet generation rate for each sensor node is one packet per second. We consider that the data packet has size of 50 bytes, as [4]. Because the values of consumption in idling mode for all nodes are same, we don't consider the idling mode consumption for simplicity. The values of consumption in sending and receiving mode are 2 W and 0.1 W, respectively. And each node has initial energy of 60 WHr and consumes 15 J/m through vertical movement [12]. And the variable x in Formula 1 is set as 2. Simulation parameters are given in Table 4.

We used the following metrics for evaluating the performance of our proposed routing protocol:

- Network lifetime: The network lifetime is the time when the first node dies in the network because of the energy exhaustion.
- Average end-to-end delay: The average end-to-end delay is the average delay for the delivered packets.
- Average energy consumption: The average energy consumption is the energy consumption for every delivered packet.

4.2   Experimental Results

In Fig. 6a, b and c, the number of sink nodes is set as 9. We first compare the network lifetime of three schemes with different number of sensor nodes.

Table 4. Simulation parameters.

Parameter	Value
Network size	$1500\,\mathrm{m} \times 1500\,\mathrm{m} \times 1500\,\mathrm{m}$
Communication range	$250\,\mathrm{m}$
Data rate	$50\,\mathrm{Kbps}$
Data packet size	$50\,\mathrm{bytes}$
Initial energy	$60\,\mathrm{WHr}$
Transmission power	$2\,\mathrm{W}$
Reception power	$0.1\,\mathrm{W}$
Idle power	$10\,\mathrm{mW}$
Vertical movement consumption	$15\,\mathrm{J/m}$

The result is shown as Fig. 6a. In DCR, each node forwards the packets to its neighbor which has smallest Ds all the time, it results that this neighbor will die earlier than the other neighbor nodes. So the lifetime of DCR is the smallest in three schemes. In EEDBR, each node selects the node with high residual energy in its neighbor as next forwarder and balances the energy consumption between its neighbors. Simulation shows that the lifetime of EEDBR is 50% higher than the lifetime of DCR. Our proposed EBDCR not only considers the balance of energy between each node's neighbors, but also balance the energy consumption between the nodes that have different depths. Hence, compared by the EEDBR, the lifetime of EBDCR is extended by 10% to 20%. And as the number of sensor nodes increases, the lifetime of three schemes decrease a little because the load of nodes near the sink nodes increases.

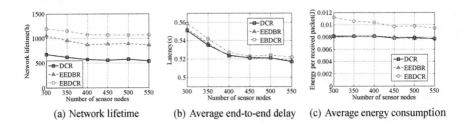

(a) Network lifetime   (b) Average end-to-end delay   (c) Average energy consumption

Fig. 6. Results with 9 sink nodes

Figure 6b shows the average end-to-end delay for all delivered packets with different number of sensor nodes. DCR and EEDBR have almost the same latency because the data packets are transmitted immediately when it arrives in a sensor node. The latency of our scheme increases by 1% to 2%. This is because the node replacement will affect the delivery of the data packets which are sent from the replaced node, the replacement node and their child nodes.

Furthermore, all the delays in three schemes decrease due to sensor nodes have greater selection to forward data as the number of nodes increases.

The energy consumption per delivered packet with different number of sensor nodes is shown in Fig. 6c. Because DCR and EEDBR don't adjust the depths of all sensor nodes, their energy consumption per delivered packet is almost same. In our scheme, sensor nodes need to adjust their depths to balance the energy. The energy consumption per delivered packet increases by 20% to 30%. Although our scheme needs a part of the energy to adjust, we take full advantage of the energy of the sensor nodes far from the sink nodes, thereby prolonging the network lifetime.

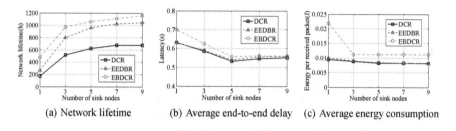

(a) Network lifetime   (b) Average end-to-end delay   (c) Average energy consumption

Fig. 7. Results with 300 sensor nodes

In Fig. 7a, b and c, the number of sensor nodes is set as 300. Figure 7a shows the lifetime with different number of sink nodes. As the number of sink nodes increases, the number of sensor nodes which can communicate with sink nodes directly increases. So the lifetime of three schemes also increases, and our scheme performs better than DCR and EEDBR. The average end-to-end delay with different number of sink nodes is shown in Fig. 7b. The fewer sink nodes we have, the more load the sensor nodes near the sink nodes have, the more data packets will be influenced when the nodes near the sink nodes are involved in node replacement. Hence, the latency of our scheme increases by 10% compared to DCR and EEDBR when the number of sink nodes is 1. As the sink nodes increase, the difference between our scheme and other two schemes decreases. Finally, we compare the energy consumption with different number of sink nodes in Fig. 7c. The sensor nodes near the sink nodes have more load when there is only one sink node. This caused that the sensor nodes around the sink node will be involved in node replacement more frequently. So the energy consumption per delivered packet in our scheme is higher. The difference between our scheme and other two schemes decreases as the sink nodes increase.

5   Conclusion

In this paper, we propose EBDCR, an energy-balanced and depth-controlled routing protocol for UWSN. In order to balance the energy consumption between the nodes near the sink nodes and the nodes far from the sink nodes, we decline the low-energy nodes and float up the high-energy nodes through the node replacement strategy we proposed. Moreover, we provide an algorithm to select a appropriate node to replace the node which has low energy. After that, we adjust them to their new depths to continue working. Finally, the experimental results demonstrate that our proposed routing protocol effectively prolongs the network lifetime.

Acknowledgement. This research is sponsored by National Key R&D Program of China No. 2017YFB0902602, the State Key Program of National Natural Science Foundation of China No. 61533011, Shandong Provincial Natural Science Foundation under Grant No. ZR2015FM001 and the Fundamental Research Funds of Shandong University No. 2015JC030.

References

1. Akyildiz, I.F., Pompili, D., Melodia, T.: Underwater acoustic sensor networks: research challenges. Ad Hoc Netw. **3**(3), 257–279 (2005)
2. Partan, J., Kurose, J., Levine, B.N.: A survey of practical issues in underwater networks. In: The Workshop on Underwater Networks, WUWNET 2006, Los Angeles, CA, USA, September, pp. 17–24. DBLP (2006)
3. Davis, A., Chang, H.: Underwater wireless sensor networks. In: Oceans, pp. 1–5. IEEE (2012)
4. Yan, H., Shi, Z.J., Cui, J.-H.: DBR: depth-based routing for underwater sensor networks. In: Das, A., Pung, H.K., Lee, F.B.S., Wong, L.W.C. (eds.) NETWORKING 2008. LNCS, vol. 4982, pp. 72–86. Springer, Heidelberg (2008). doi:10.1007/978-3-540-79549-0_7
5. Coutinho, R.W.L., Vieira, L.F.M., Loureiro, A.A.F.: DCR: depth-controlled routing protocol for underwater sensor networks. In: Proceedings - International Symposium on Computers and Communications, pp. 000453–000458 (2013)
6. Wahid, A., Lee, S., Jeong, H.-J., Kim, D.: EEDBR: energy-efficient depth-based routing protocol for underwater wireless sensor networks. In: Kim, T., Adeli, H., Robles, R.J., Balitanas, M. (eds.) AST 2011. CCIS, vol. 195, pp. 223–234. Springer, Heidelberg (2011). doi:10.1007/978-3-642-24267-0_27
7. Xie, P., Cui, J.-H., Lao, L.: VBF: vector-based forwarding protocol for underwater sensor networks. In: Boavida, F., Plagemann, T., Stiller, B., Westphal, C., Monteiro, E. (eds.) NETWORKING 2006. LNCS, vol. 3976, pp. 1216–1221. Springer, Heidelberg (2006). doi:10.1007/11753810_111
8. Erol, M., Vieira, L.F.M., Gerla, M.: AUV-aided localization for underwater sensor networks. In: International Conference on Wireless Algorithms, Systems and Applications, pp. 44–54. IEEE Xplore (2007)
9. The ns mannual. http://www.isi.edu/nsnam/ns/doc/index.html
10. Xie, P., Zhou, Z., Peng, Z., Yan, H.: Aqua-Sim: an NS-2 based simulator for underwater sensor networks, pp. 1–7. IEEE (2009)
11. Lee, U., Wang, P., Noh, Y., Vieira, L.F.M., Gerla, M., Cui, J.H.: Pressure routing for underwater sensor networks. In: Conference on Information Communications, pp. 1676–1684. IEEE Press (2016)

12. O'Rourke, M., Basha, E., Detweiler, C.: Multi-modal communications in underwater sensor networks using depth adjustment. In: ACM International Conference on Underwater Networks and Systems, pp. 1–5. ACM (2012)
13. Jafri, M.R., Ahmed, S., Javaid, N., Ahmad, Z., Qureshi, R.J.: AMCTD: adaptive mobility of courier nodes in threshold-optimized DBR protocol for underwater wireless sensor networks. Int. J. Distrib. Sens. Netw. **2**, 218–222 (2014)
14. Umar, A., Javaid, N., Ahmad, A., et al.: DEADS: depth and energy aware dominating set based algorithm for cooperative routing along with sink mobility in underwater WSNs. Sensors **15**(6), 14458–14486 (2015)
15. Javaid, N., Jafri, M.R., Ahmed, S., et al.: Delay-sensitive routing schemes for underwater acoustic sensor networks. Int. J. Distr. Sensor Netw. **11**, 532676 (2015)
16. Majid, A., Azam, I., Waheed, A., et al.: An energy efficient and balanced energy consumption cluster based routing protocol for underwater wireless sensor networks. J. Intell. Rob. Syst. **27**(4), 324–333 (2016)
17. Ahmed, M., Salleh, M., Channa, M.I.: Routing protocols based on node mobility for Underwater Wireless Sensor Network (UWSN): a survey. J. Netw. Comput. Appl. **78**, 242–252 (2016)
18. Li, N., Martínez, J.F., Chaus, J.M.M., Eckert, M.: A survey on underwater acoustic sensor network routing protocols. Sensors **16**(3), 414 (2016)
19. Ibrahim, D.M., Eltobely, T.E., Fahmy, M.M., et al.: Enhancing the vector-based forwarding routing protocol for underwater wireless sensor networks: a clustering approach. In: The Tenth International Conference on Wireless and Mobile Communications, ICWMC 2014, pp. 98–104 (2014)

On the Energy Efficiency of Sleeping and Rate Adaptation for Network Devices

Timothée Haudebourg[1] and Anne-Cécile Orgerie[2(✉)]

[1] ENS Rennes - University of Rennes 1, Rennes, France
timothee.haudebourg@ens-rennes.fr
[2] CNRS - IRISA, Rennes, France
anne-cecile.orgerie@irisa.fr

Abstract. The ever-growing appetite of Internet applications for network resources has led to an unprecedented electricity bill for these telecommunication infrastructures. Several techniques have been developed to improve the energy consumption of network devices. As their utilization highly varies over time, the two main techniques for saving energy, namely sleeping and rate adaptation, exploits the lower workload periods to either put to sleep some hardware elements or adapt the network rate to the actual traffic level. In this paper, we compare two emblematic approaches of these energy-efficient techniques: Low Power Idle and Adaptive Link Rate. Our simulation-based study quantifies the reachable energy savings of these two approaches depending on the traffic characteristics. We show that, with little impact on the Quality of Service and consequent energy savings, Low Power Idle has a clear advantage. On the contrary, ALR is almost always consuming more than LPI and can reach unacceptable QoS levels. We also show that they can be combined to achieve better energy-efficiency, but at the cost of important QoS degradation.

Keywords: Energy efficiency · Wired networks · Sleeping · Adaptive Link Rate · Low Power Idle

1 Introduction

Information and Communications Technologies (ICT) currently consume around 5% of global electricity with one third of this consumption that is imputed to communication networks [19]. The multiplication of end-user devices leads to a rapid growth of the traffic. A recent study made by Cisco estimates that annual global IP traffic will pass the zettabyte threshold by the end of 2016 [13]. This ever-growing appetite of Internet applications for network resources has led to an unprecedented electricity bill for these telecommunication infrastructures.

Yet, it has been shown that network infrastructures are not used at their full capacity and present high redundancy for fault-tolerance and security purposes [11,22,25]. Moreover, network devices such as routers and switches are power-hungry even when they are little or not used [7,16,23]. The energy consumption of networks is not only incurred by powering networking equipment

© Springer International Publishing AG 2017
S. Ibrahim et al. (Eds.): ICA3PP 2017, LNCS 10393, pp. 132–146, 2017.
DOI: 10.1007/978-3-319-65482-9_9

(routers, switches, links, hubs, etc.), but also by end-hosts that demand high availability and full-time connectivity even if the network is not used [18].

The ideal power-proportionality has still not been reached by device manufacturers [4]. These observations have led to the proposition of various solutions to save energy in wired networks. Approaches found in literature can be categorized into two categories, both exploiting the lower charge periods to either put to sleep some hardware elements (sleeping) or adapt the network rate to the actual traffic level (rate adaptation).

The emblematic sleeping solution proposes a standardized Low Power Idle (LPI) mode [12] (norm IEEE 802.3az). The basic idea of this Energy-Efficient Ethernet (EEE) standard consists in sending packets as fast as possible and entering a low-power idle state when there is no data to transmit. The first network devices implementing this capability have appeared on mass market in 2013. Packet coalescing can be used to improve LPI performances at the cost of a slight latency increase [9,14].

As for rate adaptation, the most famous implementation is Adaptive Link Rate (ALR) which has been proposed in 2005 [16–18]. It follows the idea of the Dynamic Voltage Frequency Scaling (DVFS) for CPUs adapted to the network device port rates. When full speed is not needed, a lower rate is negotiated between the network ports sharing a common link, thus incurring less power consumption [5]. Two buffer thresholds are employed to decide when to switch to a lower or a higher rate. Several policies have been proposed to adjust these buffer threshold with the aim of reducing oscillations between rates [5,17].

While these two techniques pursue a common goal, they adopt radically different approaches. Moreover, while LPI is standardized and deployed for several years, ALR is still looking for a viable implementation resolving its oscillation issues. One can wonder which approach can provide the larger energy savings, at what cost for the Quality-of-Service, and whether they can be combined for a better result or not. The only study comparing both approaches that can be found in literature proposes a theoretical comparison based on models of sleeping and rate adaptation general techniques [20]. In particular, as this study was published in 2008, before the adoption of IEEE 802.3az, the employed sleeping model is using values differing by an order of magnitude from the one implemented in Low Power Idle (for the switching time for instance). This study does not try to combine both approaches.

In this paper, we propose a simulation-based comparison relying on an implementation of the two existing protocols (LPI and ALR) under various traffic conditions, and we provide a quantified study of both approaches separately and combined. This evaluation of the practical implementations of the two main energy-efficient techniques found in literature – namely sleeping and rate adaptation – quantifies the impacts of both techniques combined and separately, on energy consumption and quality of service (QoS).

Contrarily to previous work, we show that LPI has a clear advantage in terms of energy savings compared to ALR, and an even larger advantage on QoS for most of the traffic scenarios. Our results also indicate that combining both protocols, LPI and ALR, reduces the energy saving dependence to packet coalescing. But, at the same time, it hugely impacts QoS, thus making LPI alone more suitable.

Section 2 introduces the context, shows the different solutions proposed in literature and presents a comparative study of these solutions. Section 3 describes our experimentation conditions. The validation simulations are conducted using our ECOFEN module implemented within the ns3 network simulator. Simulation results are provided in Sect. 4 along with considerations on how to improve these solutions. Section 5 concludes and presents future work.

2   State of the Art

Internet traffic presents a high dynamicity and variability [11,22]. Typically, the Amsterdam Internet Exchange point [2] handles three times more traffic during its peak periods than during its low periods on a daily basis. This fluctuation leads to infrastructure over-provisioning and energy waste for QoS purpose. Indeed, networks usually stay fully operational at any time even during low periods.

2.1   Rate Adaptation: Adaptive Link Rate (ALR)

ALR exploits low-traffic periods to downgrade the negotiated link rate and to save energy [16]. Practically, for backward compatibility reasons, 10 Gbps ports can operate at 1 Gbps, 100 Mbps or 10 Mbps, and consume less under lower rates. For instance, a port operating at 1 Gbps consumes 9 times more power than when operating at 100 Mbps [29]. However, switching between rates can be costly in terms of time and energy. For instance, switching from 100 Mbps to 10 Mbps requires 575.8 ms and consumes 0.8 W on average, while the port consumes 0.4 W at 100 Mbps and 0.1 W at 10 Mbps [29].

ALR [5] is relying on a MAC handshake protocol to negotiate the rate between the ports sharing the same link and requires the physical layers of both ports to be resynchronized [18]. This process explains the lengthy switching times. The policy for switching between rates is based on a dual threshold on the buffer occupancy: a lower threshold and an upper one [17]. When the upper threshold is reached, ALR initiates a switching to an upper rate, and symmetrically, when the buffer occupancy goes under the lower threshold, ALR switches to a lower rate. These two thresholds have to be carefully tuned in order to avoid oscillations [17].

2.2   Sleeping: Low Power Idle (LPI)

LPI also relies on low-traffic periods to save energy, but with a different approach: it puts the device in a low-power mode at the Ethernet physical layer level when there is no traffic for a short period of time. A refresh signal is then sent periodically to avoid renegotiating link parameters when coming back to normal

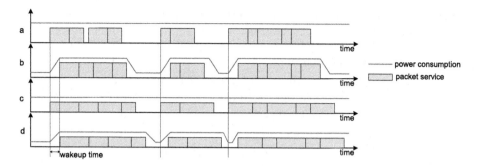

Fig. 1. Packet service times and power consumption in the following cases: (a) no power-aware optimizations, (b) sleeping, (c) rate adaptation, (d) sleeping and rate adaptation (from [8]).

mode [12]. Typically, the energy consumption when the device is in low power mode can be as low as 10% that of the active mode [12].

As stated in the IEEE 802.3az standard, the length of the transitions to and from the LPI mode are not negligible and these transitions also consume energy [1]. For instance, according to the standard [1], from 100 Mbps it takes 200 μs to go to LPI mode, and 30 μs to wake up, while the transmission time for a 1500 byte frame is 120 μs. These values are three orders of magnitude lower than the rate switching times of ALR. In order to increase LPI energy savings, coalescing strategies have been developed to buffer incoming packets and to send them in burst, thus increasing sleeping duration [9]. A typical coalescing strategy consists of combining a timer and a buffer size threshold to trigger the sending burst [12].

Figure 1 summarizes the different options for using sleeping and rate adaptation techniques and the corresponding impact on power consumption.

3   Experimentation Conditions

We evaluate the energy savings-QoS trade-off achieved by ALR, LPI, and ALR and LPI combined, and the impact of traffic characteristics on this trade-off. For comparing sleeping and rate adaptation techniques, we have implemented ALR and LPI protocols within the network simulator ns3 [21]. For the simulations, a single link between two nodes is considered with a 100 Mbps bandwidth and a latency of 5 ms. The injected traffic is described in the next section.

3.1   Energy Consumption

The energy consumption for the network devices has been computed using the models provided in [24]. These models include per-byte and per-packet energy costs for Ethernet ports as measured on real hardware [28].

Table 1. Time and power costs per network port utilized for the simulations

Category	State	Time (s)	Power (W)
Idle consumption	100 Mbps	-	0.4
ALR	10 Mbps → 100 Mbps	72.4×10^{-3}	0.8
	100 Mbps → 10 Mbps	574.8×10^{-3}	0.8
	at 10 Mbps	-	0.1
LPI	Time to awake T_w	30×10^{-6}	0.8
	Time to sleep T_s	200×10^{-6}	0.8
	in LPI mode	-	0.04

Concerning the energy consumption of ALR and LPI operations (switching), we have used real measurements from the literature: [26] for LPI (made on a RTL8111E Realtek NIC implementing draft 3.2 of the LPI standard) and [29] for ALR (using a Xilinx Virtex-II Pro NetFPGA). Concerning ALR, we have used the dual threshold policy described in [17]. For LPI, we have implemented the coalescing strategy with a fixed timer as described in [12]. Table 1 summarizes the main time and power costs per network port as utilized in our simulations for ALR and LPI.

3.2 Traffic Characteristics

Our experiments target a quantification of the energy consumption and the QoS parameters (latency and jitter) of ALR and LPI over a single link connecting two nodes. A single flow is injected from one node to the other one. We vary three main characteristics of this flow:

- α_d: the flow density, the ratio of sent bits per second over the link capacity. From the buffer threshold policy analysis, this utility ratio seems to be the main parameter influencing ALR.
- α_r: the flow regularity, it characterizes the delay variance between each sent packet. This parameter characterizes the time gap between consecutive packets, and thus may influence the ability of both approaches to save energy.
- α_c: the flow coalescence, the probability of packets to be sent by bursts. As explained in the description of LPI, coalescence can greatly help LPI to reach larger energy savings.

Each parameter is normalized (belongs to $[0, 1]$). Then, flows are generated according to these parameters as follows. The density parameter α_d allows to compute the mean delay between each packet: $T_{delay} = \frac{P_{size}}{C_{link} \times \alpha_d}$.

With C_{link} the link capacity and P_{size} the packet size. The regularity parameter α_r determines the random variable Y used to define the delay between two consecutive packets. Following previous traffic studies [6,15], we set: $Y = \alpha_r \times T_{delay} + (1 - \alpha_r) \times X$.

With X a random variable following an exponential law of parameter $\lambda = \frac{1}{T_{delay}}$. When α_r goes to 1, this guarantees that the density parameter is respected, without having a perfectly (non realistic) regular flow. Finally, the coalescing parameter α_c determines the probability for a packet to be delayed and sent with the next one (if the next one is also delayed, they are both sent with the packet after the next one, and so on).

The graphs presented in this paper result from more than 30,000 simulations overall (with varying the three parameters). The link capacity is set to 100 Mbps for simulation duration constraints (a 1 Gbps link produces much longer simulations). ALR can reduce this rate to 10 Mbps if the utility ratio is under 0.1 following its buffer threshold policy. For each given triplet $(\alpha_d, \alpha_r, \alpha_c)$, the same flow is simulated with ALR, LPI, and ALR and LPI combined (thanks to the deterministic pseudo-random generator of ns3). The simulation is also run without any energy saving techniques to norm the energy consumption results of the different experiments (i.e. the 100% in energy on the graphs represents this scenario). We observe that the energy consumption of the two ports without energy saving techniques is independent from the three parameters $(\alpha_d, \alpha_r, \alpha_c)$. Then the same experiments are repeated with a different seed for the random variables. Each point on the figures is thus the average value of 10 different runs.

4   Energy Savings and Performance Degradation of Sleeping and Rate Adaptation Techniques

4.1   Energy Consumption

Figure 2 shows the energy consumption of the two connected ports with ALR as a function of the coalescence parameter α_c and the density parameter α_d. The energy is shown in percentage of the consumption without energy saving technique. As expected, energy savings occur only below 10% of link utilization (i.e. $\alpha_d < 0.1$). The observed results for energy saved are similar to those observed in literature [3,29].

In the best case, when the utilization is really low (α_d close to 0), the overall energy consumption reduces to 25%. Unfortunately, such a low bandwidth utilization is not frequent in all kinds of network. While it can often happen in access networks, it rarely occurs in core networks for instance. It can also be observed that, for beneficial traffic for ALR (traffic below 10% of link capacity), packet coalescence increases the energy savings by less than 10%.

Figure 3 presents the same experiment using LPI instead of ALR. As expected, the energy consumption in this case highly depends on the packet coalescence: it diminishes with the coalescence increase. These results are in line with previous estimations from the literature [12,14]. This coalescence can be reached either by traffic engineering at the application level or by utilizing coalescing buffers within the ports.

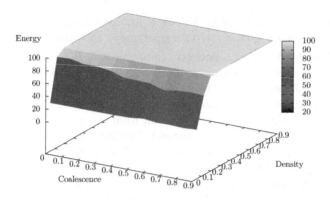

Fig. 2. Energy consumption when using ALR

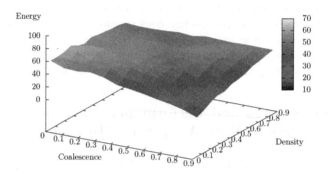

Fig. 3. Energy consumption when using LPI

Similarly to ALR, LPI is sensitive to the link utilization. The lower α_d is, the higher energy savings are. In the worst scenario for LPI, it can still reach 40% of energy savings, and 80% in the best case.

In both cases ALR and LPI, we observe that the flow regularity has low impact on energy consumption, although it slightly improves the savings when the flow is less regular (α_r small). More generally, it appears that, from a pure energy saving point of view, LPI behaves better than ALR in most of the cases. Only under 10% of utilization and without packet coalescence, ALR allows for slightly greater energy savings than LPI. However, as shown in [29], with ALR, the link has to stay several seconds in the lower rate to amortize the switching energy cost.

Concerning ALR, it would probably perform better if more rates were available from a hardware point of view, as it is the case for the CPU frequencies and DVFS (Dynamic Voltage Frequency Scaling) [27]. However, the availability of these rates in current network ports results from a side effect of the heterogeneity and backward compatibility principle that is essential in today's networks.

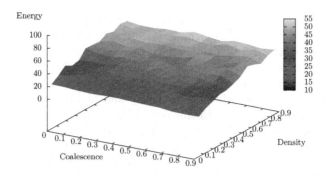

Fig. 4. Energy consumption while combining ALR and LPI

Indeed, the lower frequencies of a network port are used if the port of the corresponding device to which it is connected is not able to operate at this speed. Introducing intermediate rates without any compatibility requirement coming from previous Ethernet norms will need an important standardization effort from the manufacturers to offer identical rates for all new devices. Furthermore, it would need a thorough analysis on real hardware to measure the potential energy-related benefits of new rates.

Figure 4 shows the results with ALR and LPI combined. Although, higher energy savings are reached (more than 80%), the dependency to packet coalescence (parameter α_c) has disappeared. In this scenario, savings are bigger on average than the LPI-only case and packets coalescence is not useful any more. Indeed, when switching to lower rates, ALR increases per-packet transmission time and thus, naturally coalesces packets.

These experiments allow us to confirm that our implementations behave according to the literature for the ALR and LPI alone scenarios. Combining both approaches, we have found original results not previously studied in related work. Moreover, from a technical point of view, combining ALR and LPI required the design of a new algorithm to prioritize actions done by the two protocols. For instance, when the link utilization is low, if we use ALR first, idle periods are reduced because the rate is lower, and thus, LPI switches to low power mode for smaller periods although it could lead to better savings than ALR.

4.2   Quality of Service

In the three scenarios (ALR, LPI and ALR+LPI), the energy-efficient protocols are impacting the packet delivery, and thus the QoS experienced by the users. These impacts concern:

- the bandwidth, when ALR is reducing the link rate;
- the latency, when LPI is in low power mode (this adds the time to wake up the port), or when ALR is reducing the link rate;
- the jitter, when using packet coalescence to improve LPI performances for instance.

Here we will quantify these impacts on the QoS for the experiments performed in the previous section. For the simulations, the link latency was set to 5 ms (typical LAN network). For LPI alone, the measured latency increase is negligible in most cases. Indeed, the time parameters of LPI (T_s, T_r and T_w) are in the order of microseconds, and thus have little impact on the end-to-end packet latency. In the worst case, which is for heavy and highly irregular traffic, the latency does not exceed 6.5 ms. In this case, LPI has more chances to switch to low power mode while receiving new packets. The port needs then to completely switch to low power mode before waking up and sending the packets.

Fig. 5 shows the latency (in milliseconds) induced by ALR depending on flow density and flow regularity. In the worst case, when ALR is energy-efficient (link utilization under 10% = $\alpha_d \approx 0.1$), the latency can go up to almost 50 ms, against 5 ms usually. This result comes from ALR which reduces the link rate, and this automatically increases the reception delays. The jitter is particularly high when the link utilization is around 10% because this is when ALR tends to oscillate between high and low rate, thus inducing substantial oscillations on the latency. Under this threshold, latency is stabilized around 50 ms, and over this threshold, it is stabilized around 5 ms, thus keeping the jitter stable in these two regions.

In ALR and LPI cases, this QoS degradation comes from the switching times between states (rates for ALR and sleep/aware for LPI). ALR, with its switching time three orders of magnitude higher than LPI, performs poorly in comparison. Moreover, while LPI's switching times depends mostly on hardware, ALR's switching times result mainly from network protocol costs (physical layer resynchronization) [29]. Switching times are thus more complex to reduce for ALR than for LPI.

If the combined use of ALR and LPI seems promising in terms or energy savings, its effects on QoS are less pleasing. Figure 6 shows the QoS provided when combining ALR and LPI. When flow density is small, latency and jitter

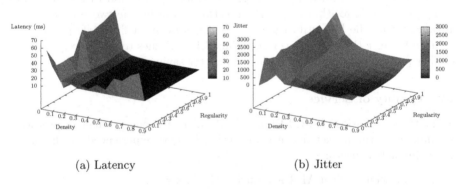

(a) Latency   (b) Jitter

Fig. 5. Latency and jitter with ALR

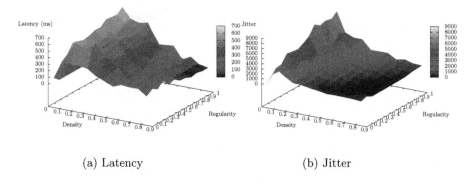

(a) Latency   (b) Jitter

Fig. 6. Latency and jitter with ALR and LPI combined

are high. The worst case is still around $\alpha_d = 0.1$, but the latency is ten times worse than in the case of ALR alone, while the latency is three times worse. ALR rate adaptation mechanisms are even less reactive when combined with sleeping periods due to LPI switching to low power mode. On a small network, such a poor QoS is not bearable for latency-critical applications like voice over IP. On a larger network, latency may accumulate at each device and results could even be worse from a QoS point of view.

4.3   Heterogeneous Network

Our second scenario considers a realistic network based on the description of an Italian Internet Service Provider (ISP) given in [10]. This scenario aims at evaluating the performances of ALR and LPI on an heterogeneous network, where links do not present the same throughput. While the authors of [10] consider switching off entire nodes (i.e. routers or switches), here, we only act on the links and associated ports through ALR and LPI. Our approach is thus less disruptive and easier to apply in practice (no re-routing protocol needed). As we do not consider switching off entire network nodes, in the following experiments, we do not take into account the static energy consumption of these devices (it remains the same values for all the experiments).

The original network is hierarchical and presented in [10]; it consists of 8 core nodes, 52 backbone nodes, 52 metro nodes and 260 feeders. Due to long simulation duration and for symmetry reasons, we accurately simulate only a quarter of this network, the rest is aggregated into several nodes. The simulated network is presented in Fig. 7.

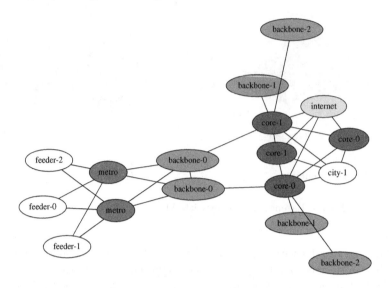

Fig. 7. Simulated representative section of the ISP network

The network has a hierarchical design, it is composed of:

- *core nodes*: they are connected among themselves through 50 Gbps links, each link being redundant for failure protection. They represent points of presence in a major city (4 core nodes per city). The second city is aggregated in one node called *city-1* in our scenario.
- *backbone nodes*: they are connected to the core nodes through 20 Gbps links, each backbone node being connected to two different core nodes. They are spread across the city.
- *metro nodes*: they are connected to two backbone nodes each through 20 Gbps links.
- *feeders*: they are connected to metro nodes through 10 Gbps links. They are responsible for bringing connectivity to the DSLAMs to which users are connected, so each feeder aggregates traffic from users in the same neighborhood or small town.
- *Internet node*: two central core nodes are connected to an Internet node by means of a 100 Gbps link, representing the gateway to access the Internet and the other networks (like an Internet exchange point).

In this scenario, only feeders and the Internet nodes are able to generate traffic, the other nodes only route the traffic. On Fig. 7, the nodes aggregating the traffic from nodes of the original network design presented in [10] are *backbone-1*, *backbone-2*, *core-0*, *core-1* and *city-1*. For simulation reasons also, we have divided all the link throughputs by 1,000; so the smaller links have a 10 Mbps bandwidth instead of a 10 Gbps. Our experiment simulates one hour of real traffic, and in spite of our simplifications for reducing the simulation duration, it still lasts more than 40 h on average (for 1 simulated hour).

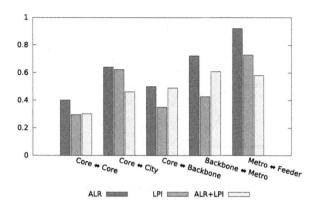

Fig. 8. Energy consumption ratio between the different energy saving options and the case where no energy saving technique is applied

Connections are distributed according to a normal law centered on 30 min, in order to show a peak of use in the middle of the simulation. Hence, the behaviors of ALR and LPI can be studied under different traffic loads. For a realistic traffic distribution, we consider that 70% of the connections are between the Internet node (outside the ISP) and one of the feeders, and 30% are between two feeders of the ISP [10].

In an heterogeneous network, ALR and LPI may present different behavior depending on the considered network part. Figure 8 compares the energy consumed by the different network parts during the simulation with ALR, LPI and ALR+LPI combined. The energy is expressed as the ratio between the considered consumption and the network consumption without any energy saving method (represented by 1).

One can see that the largest energy savings are realized on the most consuming links: at the core of the network between core nodes. For these devices, whatever the considered techniques, it leads to at least 60% of the energy saved compared to no energy reduction technique. However, unlike in the first scenario, LPI allows for the largest energy savings among the 3 considered options. Combining ALR and LPI allows for better energy savings at the edge of the networks for links between metro nodes and feeders. In this case, ALR+LPI can save up to 40% of the energy on average, against 25% with LPI only and 5% with ALR only.

Although overall energy savings are smaller on edge links, they are largely more numerous than core links. Indeed, considering the entire original network presented in [10], one can estimate that the energy consumed by the network ports at the edge (feeders) represent 36% of the overall energy consumed by all the ports of the network. One should notice that this value is different from the one presented in [10] as we only consider the dynamic energy consumption of the network devices (consumption of the ports) which are the only elements on which one can act when not considering to switch off entire devices (contrary to

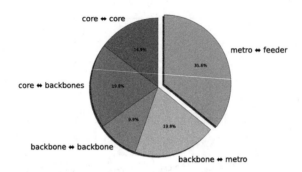

Fig. 9. Energy consumption of the network ports by category of network

what is done in [10]). Figure 9 presents the energy consumption proportion for the network ports by network category.

The largest energy consumption part resides in the network between the metro network and the feeders. For this part, the ALR+LPI option reaches the lowest energy consumption. Yet, as outlined by the first scenario, ALR and ALR+LPI are leading to unacceptable QoS degradation that make them unsuitable for users. In this scenario, we consider only ISP point of view: residential and access networks (last mile) are not taken into account in the overall picture.

5   Conclusion

In this article, we provide a quantified comparison of ALR and LPI, two protocols implementing the two main energy-efficient approaches of the literature. This simulation-based study has been conducted in terms of energy savings and QoS. It appears that in the majority of the cases, LPI allows for more savings than ALR, independently from the network topology. Indeed, the limited number of available rates for current network ports (10 Mbps, 100 Mbps, 1 Gbps, 10 Gbps) constrains the energy efficiency of ALR to operate only under 10% of link usage. However, under this 10% limit, some rare cases show better savings for ALR than for LPI, in particular when the coalescence of the traffic is low.

The previous literature study comparing these two generic approaches was notably more to the benefit of rate adaptation than sleeping [20]. This study from 2008 was considering much higher switching costs for sleeping technique than the one achieved in practice with LPI, and switching costs between states (rates for rate adaptation and sleep/awake for sleeping) constitute the most influencing factor on energy savings and QoS.

This study also shows that combining LPI and ALR provides better energy savings than with LPI only. In particular, combining ALR with LPI would reduce the impact of coalescing on the reached energy savings. However, these energy savings come at the cost of significantly higher latency and jitter which are not acceptable for end-users. LPI alone would then be a more suitable option to save energy while keeping expected QoS levels. Consequently, with the current state-of-the-art hardware, ALR should stop being considered as a suitable solution by the community. Our future work include exploring future hardware architecture achieving a relative low static power dissipation compared to the dynamic part, and studying from which ratio ALR would start to be more beneficial.

Acknowledgments. Experiments presented in this paper were carried out using the Grid'5000 experimental test-bed, being developed under the Inria ALADDIN development action with support from CNRS, RENATER and several Universities as well as other funding bodies (see https://www.grid5000.fr).

The authors would like to thank the reviewers for their valuable comments.

References

1. IEEE Standard for Information technology- Local and metropolitan area networks-Specific requirements- Part 3: CSMA/CD Access Method and Physical Layer Specifications Amendment 5: Media Access Control Parameters, Physical Layers, and Management Parameters for Energy-Efficient Ethernet. IEEE Std 802.3az-2010 (Amendment to IEEE Std 802.3-2008), pp. 1–302, October 2010
2. Amsterdam internet exchange. https://ams-ix.net/technical/statistics. Accessed October 2016
3. Anand, H., Reardon, C., Subramaniyan, R., George, A.: Ethernet adaptive link rate (ALR): analysis of a MAC handshake protocol. In: 31st IEEE Conference on Local Computer Networks, pp. 533–534 (2006)
4. Barroso, L., Holzle, U.: The case for energy-proportional computing. Computer **40**(12), 33–37 (2007)
5. Bennett, M., Christensen, K., Nordman, B.: Improving The Energy Efficiency Of Ethernet: Adaptive Link Rate Proposal. Ethernet Alliance White Paper (2006)
6. Benson, T., Akella, A., Maltz, D.: Network traffic characteristics of data centers in the wild. In: Conference on Internet measurement (IMC), pp. 267–280 (2010)
7. Bolla, R., Bruschi, R., Christensen, K., Cucchietti, F., Davoli, F., Singh, S.: The potential impact of green technologies in next generation wireline networks - is there room for energy savings optimization? IEEE Commun. **49**(8), 80–86 (2011)
8. Bolla, R., Bruschi, R., Davoli, F., Cucchietti, F.: Energy efficiency in the future internet: a survey of existing approaches and trends in energy-aware fixed network infrastructures. IEEE Commun. Surv. Tutor. **13**(2), 223–244 (2011)
9. Chatzipapas, A., Mancuso, V.: Measurement-based coalescing control for 802.3az. In: IFIP Networking Conference (Networking) and Workshops, pp. 270–278 (2016)
10. Chiaraviglio, L., Mellia, M., Neri, F.: Energy-aware backbone networks: a case study. In: IEEE International Conference on Communications (ICC) Workshops, pp. 1–5 (2009)
11. Christensen, K., Gunaratne, C., Nordman, B., George, A.: The next frontier for communications networks: power management. Comput. Commun. **27**(18), 1758–1770 (2004)
12. Christensen, K., Reviriego, P., Nordman, B., Bennett, M., Mostowfi, M., Maestro, J.: IEEE 802.3az: the road to energy efficient ethernet. IEEE Commun. Mag. **48**(11), 50–56 (2010)
13. The zettabyte era: trends and analysis. Technical report, Cisco (2016)

14. De La Oliva, A., Hernández, T.R.V., Guerri, J.C., Hernández, J.A., Reviriego, P.: Performance analysis of energy efficient ethernet on video streaming servers. Comput. Netw. **57**(3), 599–608 (2013)

15. Ersoz, D., Yousif, M., Das, C.: Characterizing network traffic in a cluster-based, multi-tier data center. In: International Conference on Distributed Computing Systems (ICDCS) (2007)

16. Gunaratne, C., Christensen, K., Nordman, B.: Managing energy consumption costs in desktop PCs and LAN switches with proxying, split TCP connections, and scaling of link speed. Int. J. Netw. Manage. **15**(5), 297–310 (2005)

17. Gunaratne, C., Christensen, K., Suen, S.: Ethernet adaptative link rate (ALR): analysis of a buffer threshold policy. In: IEEE Global Telecommunications Conference (GLOBECOM 2006), pp. 1–6 (2006)

18. Gunaratne, C., Christensen, K., Nordman, B., Suen, S.: Reducing the energy consumption of ethernet with adaptive link rate (ALR). IEEE Trans. Comput. **57**(4), 448–461 (2008)

19. Impact of ICT on the energy consumption around the world. Technical report. National Academy of Technologies of France (2014)

20. Nedevschi, S., Popa, L., Iannaccone, G., Ratnasamy, S., Wetherall, D.: Reducing network energy consumption via sleeping and rate-adaptation. In: USENIX Symposim on Network Systems Design & Implementation (NSDI), pp. 323–336 (2008)

21. ns3 network simulator. http://www.nsnam.org

22. Odlyzko, A.: Data networks are lightly utilized, and will stay that way. Rev. Netw. Econ. **2**, 210–237 (2003)

23. Orgerie, A.C., Dias de Assunção, M., Lefèvre, L.: A survey on techniques for improving the energy efficiency of large-scale distributed systems. ACM Comput. Surv. **46**(4), 47 (2014)

24. Orgerie, A.C., Lefèvre, L., Guérin-Lassous, I., Lopez Pacheco, D.: ECOFEN: an end-to-end energy cost model and simulator for evaluating power consumption in large-scale networks. In: SustaInet: Workshop on Sustainable Internet and Internet for Sustainability (2011)

25. Patel-Predd, P.: Energy-efficient ethernet: ethernet connections waste lots of watts. It need not be so. IEEE Spectr. Mag. **45**(5), 13 (2008)

26. Reviriego, P., Christensen, K., Rabanillo, J., Maestro, J.: An initial evaluation of energy efficient ethernet. IEEE Commun. Lett. **15**(5), 578–580 (2011)

27. Shang, L., Peh, L.S., Jha, N.: Dynamic voltage scaling with links for power optimization of interconnection networks. In: International Symposium on High-Performance Computer Architecture (HPCA) (2003)

28. Sivaraman, V., Vishwanath, A., Zhao, Z., Russell, C.: Profiling per-packet and per-byte energy consumption in the NetFPGA Gigabit router. In: IEEE INFOCOM Workshops, pp. 331–336 (2011)

29. Zhang, B., Sabhanatarajan, K., Gordon-Ross, A., George, A.: Real-time performance analysis of adaptive link rate. In: IEEE Conference on Local Computer Networks (LCN), pp. 282–288 (2008)

Big Data and its Applications

Private and Efficient Set Intersection Protocol for Big Data Analytics

Zakaria Gheid[1(✉)] and Yacine Challal[1,2,3]

[1] Laboratoire des Méthodes de Conception des Systèmes,
Ecole Nationale Supérieure d'informatique, Algiers, Algeria
{z_gheid,y_challal}@esi.dz
[2] Centre de Recherche sur l'Information Scientifique et Technique, Algiers, Algeria
[3] Université de Technologie de Compiègne,
Heudiasyc UMR CNRS 7253, Compiègne Cedex, France

Abstract. Private Set Intersection (PSI) is a fundamental multi-party computation primitive used to secure many political, commercial, and social applications. PSI allows mistrustful parties to compute the intersection of their private sets without leaking additional information. PSI protocols have been largely proposed for both the semi-honest and the malicious settings. Nevertheless, the semi-honest setting does not suffice in many realistic scenarios and security in the malicious setting is built upon cryptographic schemes, which require hard assumptions and induce a high computational cost. In this work, we propose a novel two-party PSI protocol secure under the mixed model, where the server may be semi-honest and the client may be malicious. We build our protocol upon matrix algebra without using any cryptographic schemes or non-standard assumptions and we provide simulation-based security proof. Our protocol achieves a linear asymptotic complexity of $O(k_v + k_c)$ for communications and server computations, where k_v and k_c are sizes of the server and the client sets. Besides, we compare empirical performance of our solution to the insecure hashing solution used in practice. Experimental results reveal the efficiency and the scalability of our new PSI protocol, which makes it adequate for Big Data analytics.

Keywords: Multi-party computation · Private set intersection · Big Data Analytics

1 Introduction

Private set intersection (PSI) protocol allows a client and a server to jointly compute the intersection of their private input sets without leaking any additional information. The client should only learn the intersection and the server should learn nothing. PSI functionality is a core building-block for a variety of privacy-preserving Big Data applications such as relationship path discovery in social networks [1], online recommendation systems [2], medical studies of human genomes [3], suspects detection by government agencies [4] and other applications [5,6].

© Springer International Publishing AG 2017
S. Ibrahim et al. (Eds.): ICA3PP 2017, LNCS 10393, pp. 149–164, 2017.
DOI: 10.1007/978-3-319-65482-9_10

As a very active research field, PSI problem has been largely studied and several protocols have been proposed for both the semi-honest setting (meaning that the adversary follows the protocol specifications) and the malicious setting (meaning that the adversary may deviate arbitrarily from the protocol) [6,7]. However, there has been a poor adoption of PSI protocols in real applications due to several reasons [7]. The semi-honest assumption provides weak security guarantees and does not suffice for many realistic scenarios [8]. On the other hand, PSI protocols that are secure against malicious adversaries achieve an excessive overhead in communication and computation costs [7]. This is mainly due to the strong assumptions that require to be satisfied.

Recently, there has been a great interest in improving the efficiency of malicious-resistant PSI protocols [6,9,10]. Several works [5,11] have achieved linear communication and computation complexities under non-standard security models as the Oracle [12] and the Common Reference String [13] models. Other works [6] proposed efficient PSI protocols with linear cost under the standard model, but relying heavily on strong security assumptions and Homomorphic public key cryptosystems [14]. Despite an efficient asymptotic complexity, homomorphic encryption induces a high computational overhead and so, does not meet Big Data requirements [15].

Our Contribution. Facing the need for more efficient PSI schemes under realistic security models, we propose a novel PSI protocol that is secure under the mixed model of adversaries [16], where the client may be corrupted by a malicious adversary and the server may be corrupted by a semi-honest adversary. This model is more realistic than semi-honest one, since server entities are mostly governed by laws requiring data privacy and security. We give a simulation-based security proof for both cases where the client is corrupted and where the server is corrupted. We build our protocol only upon matrix algebra without any cryptographic scheme to cope with Big Data requirements in terms of computation efficiency. We achieve a linear complexity in communication and server computation costs, thereby, we provide a better support for a high velocity stream and a high server set volume. We confirm the efficiency of our protocol through experimental evaluations.

In Sect. 2, we provide a short survey on literature works in PSI field and we discuss them. Section 3 is devoted to preliminaries and standard notations used throughout this work. In Sect. 4, we present our methodology to build a novel PSI protocol and we describe its design. In Sect. 5, we give a simulation-based security proof using Real/Ideal paradigm [17]. In Sect. 6, we analyse asymptotic complexities of communications and computations involved in our protocol. Then, we make experimental performance evaluations in Sect. 7 and we end up this work by a final conclusion.

2   Related Work

Private set intersection (PSI) problem is a fundamental functionality that has been largely studied due to its important applications. In this section, we review important PSI protocols working in the standard (plain) model, where security is based only on complexity assumptions.

Assume a client (C) and a server (V) having private sets X and Y of sizes k_c and k_v respectively. Two main approaches were used to solve PSI(X,Y), namely Oblivious Polynomial Evaluation (OPE) [18] and Oblivious Pseudo-Random Functions (OPRF) evaluation [19].

OPE Based-PSI. In this approach, C defines a polynomial $P(.)$ such that $P(x) = 0$ for each $x \in X$, and sends to V homomorphic encryptions of the coefficients of $P(.)$. Then, V computes the encryption of $(r.P(y)+y)$ for each $y \in Y$, using homomorphic properties of the encryption system and a fresh random r. Finally, C decrypts the received cyphertexts and gets either elements of the intersection (if plaintexts match an element of X) or random values. Following this approach, Freedman et al. [2] proposed two PSI protocols for semi-honest and mixed models using balanced allocations. They incur linear communications and linear client computations besides quadratic server computations that can be reduced to $O(k_c + k_v \log \log k_c)$. Kissner and Song [20] proposed two OPE-based protocols for semi-honest and malicious settings. The former incurs a quadratic complexity and the latter relies on expensive generic zero knowledge proofs to achieve correctness [5,10]. Later, Dachman-Soled et al. [21] proposed a PSI protocol based on [20]. Their construction incurs communication of $O(k_v.k^2 \log^2 k_c + k.k_c)$ and computation of $O(k_v.k_c.k \log k_c + k_v.k^2 \log^2 k_c)$, where k is a security parameter. Recently, [6] proposed a more efficient OPE-based PSI protocol for malicious settings. Their protocol incurs $O(k_v + k_c)$ communications and implies $O(k_c + k_v \log \log k_c)$ computations under the strong Decisional Diffie-Hellman assumption (strong DDH).

OPRF-Based PSI. They rely on a secure computation of a pseudo random function (PRF) $f_k(x)$ on key (k) introduced by the server (V) and input (x) introduced by the client (C), such that C should only learn $f_k(x)$, whereas V should not learn x. PSI functionality was implemented using OPRF as follows: V defines a random key (k) for a PRF $f_k(.)$ and computes the set $f_{ky} = \{f_k(y) : y \in Y\}$. Then, V and C executes an OPRF protocol where V inputs $f_k(.)$ and C inputs the set X and gets the set $f_{kx} = \{f_k(x) : x \in X\}$. At the end, V sends the set f_{ky} to C that evaluates $f_{kx} \cap f_{ky}$. OPRF was used by Hazay and Lindell [22] to develop a maliciously-secure protocol with simulation-proof for one corruption case (the client only). Besides, they proposed another PSI protocol secure under the covert model of adversaries, which is a non-standard model between semi-honest and malicious [21]. Their protocols incur $O(k_v.p(n) + k_c)$ communications and computations, where elements of the sets are taken from $\{0,1\}^{p(n)}$. Jarecki and Liu [11] improved the protocol of [22] to propose a more efficient PSI protocol secure in the presence of both malicious parties in the Common Reference String Model [13]. Their protocol incurs $O(k_v + k_c)$ communication and computation costs, but it requires a trusted third party for a safe RSA generation [5]. Later, Hazay and Nissim [9] improved the work of [2] for malicious settings. Their protocol incurs $O(k_v + k_c)$ communications and $O(k_c + k_v \log \log k_c)$ computations, but it is fairly complicated and uses both

OPE and OPRF approaches [6]. Recently, [6] introduced more efficient OPRF-based PSI protocols with $O(k_v + k_c)$ costs under the strong-DDH assumption and $O((k_v + k_c) \log (k_v + k_c))$ communication and computation costs under the DDH assumption.

In this work, we propose a novel PSI protocol approach based on matrix representation of the private sets. We use efficient matrix algebra without any cryptographic operations and we provide security under the mixed model of adversaries. Our protocol incurs $O(k_v + k_c)$ communication and server computation costs while maintaining fairness. We provide a detailed discussion about efficiency of our work in Sects. 6.2 and 7.2.

3 Preliminaries

In this section, we present preliminaries and standard security notations used in this work. More specific notations will be described later.

3.1 Private Set Intersection

In what follows, we give a formal definition of the Private Set Intersection (PSI) computation. Let C and V denote respectively a client and a server. A private set intersection (PSI) scheme is a two-party computation protocol between C and V, where C holds a set of private inputs of size k_c, drawn from some domain of size n, and V holds a set of private inputs of size k_v drawn from the same domain. At the end of the protocol, C should learn which specific inputs are shared by both C and V, whereas, V should learn nothing. Let $X = \{x_1, ..., x_{kc}\}$ and $Y = \{y_1, ..., y_{kv}\}$ denote respectively C's and V's sets of inputs, then, C learns $PSI(X, Y) = X \cap Y \longmapsto \{x_i \mid \exists j : x_i = y_j\}$. This is a branch of multi-party computation (MPC) problems [23].

3.2 Multi-Party Computation

Let us consider a set of participants that want to jointly compute the value of a public function f relying on their private data. Let $P_1,...,P_n$ denote the participants and $v_1,...,v_n$ their private data respectively. We call Multi-Party Computation (MPC) model the running process of $f(v_1, ..., v_n)$. Let Π denote a multi-party protocol executed by n participants $(P_1,...,P_n)$ in order to evaluate the function f. Let v denote the set of inputs $(v_1, ..., v_n)$ and sec denote the set of security parameters.

Notation 1. *Let $view_E^\Pi (w, sec)_i$ denote the set of messages received by the party $P_{i \in \{1,...,n\}}$ along with its inputs and outputs during the execution E of Π on the set of inputs w and security parameters sec.*

Notation 2. *Let $out_E^\Pi (w, sec)_i$ denote the output of the party $P_{i \in \{1,...,n\}}$ by the execution E of the protocol Π on the set of inputs w and security parameters* *sec. Let out_E^{Π} (v,sec) denote the global output of all collaborating parties from the same execution of Π, where*

$$out_E^{\Pi}(w, sec) = \cup_{i=1}^{n} out_E^{\Pi}(w, sec)_i \qquad (1)$$

In next section, we introduce a novel MPC protocol for private set intersection. Later, we will use these MPC notations to prove the security of our proposal.

3.3   Privacy Threat Model

In MPC protocols, the possible security threat raising from a corrupted party that participates to the execution of the protocol can be classified according to the corrupting adversary's model.

Passive Model (Semi-honest). In this model, the corrupted parties are supposed following the protocol's specifications, yet they are allowed to analyse all information gathered during the execution of the protocol.

Active Model (Malicious). In this model, the corrupted parties may randomly deviate from the protocol specifications. The two common behaviors in such a model are (a) aborting the protocol untimely or (b) injecting fake inputs.

Mixed Model. This is an extension of the above assumed behavioral models, in which the adversary can either corrupt some parties actively, and other parties passively. Thus, allowing each party to behave according to its corruption model (active or passive).

4   A Novel Private and Efficient Set Intersection Protocol

In this section, we present our novel private set intersection protocol and we describe its design.

4.1   Overview and Motivation

In many real-world applications, set intersection functionality is secured across hash-based schemes, in which, they use a commutative one-way hash function to encrypt all items [24]. Each party encrypts its items with its own key, then, each set is passed to the other party to be encrypted. Since, encryption is commutative, encrypted values will be equal if and only if the original values were the same. This hash-based scheme is very efficient, but provides weak security guarantees if the input domain is not large or does not have a high entropy [7]. One party could run a brute force attack by applying all items that can be in the input domain to the hash function and compare the results to the received hashes.

In this work, we introduce a novel matrix model that is secure against such brute force attacks. To do this, we represent the private input sets as row-matrices (each matrix corresponds to a private set and each row within it corresponds to an element in the set). Then, each party obfuscates its matrix by performing a product with a random matrix chosen independently from the input domain. Next, each party sends its resultant matrix to the other party to be multiplied by the other random matrix. Since, matrix product is not commutative, which is required for the correctness of the scheme, the two parties will interchange the side of the matrix product (left multiplication and right multiplication). At the end, the two resultant matrices will be checked for rows equality as each row corresponds to an original element in the set.

4.2   Notational Conventions

In this work, we use a special typographical style to denote matrix tools that we use to build our proposal. The used notational conventions are as follows.

- We represent matrices by capital letters in bold with one-underline, e.g. $\underline{\mathbf{M}}$.
- The set of all m-by-n matrices is denoted $\mathbb{M}(m, n)$.
- Elements of matrix are indexed between brackets, e.g. $\underline{\mathbf{M}}[2, 5]$. An asterisk is used to refer to a whole row or column, e.g. $\underline{\mathbf{M}}[1, *]$.
- The multiplication operator between two matrices is denoted $\otimes$.

4.3   Protocol Design

To introduce our novel private set intersection protocol (Π-SI), we consider a client denoted C and a server denoted V having respectively $X = \{x_1, ..., x_k\}$ and $Y = \{y_1, ..., y_k\}$ sets of private data and want to securely get the intersection between their sets (Sect. 3.1). Assume for $1 \leq i \leq k$ and $1 \leq j \leq k$: x_i and y_j $\in \mathbb{R}^n$. Let $\underline{\mathbf{M1}}$ and $\underline{\mathbf{M2}}$ denote random invertible matrices used by C and V respectively to obfuscate their sets, where $\underline{\mathbf{M1}} \in \mathbb{M}(k, k)$ and $\underline{\mathbf{M2}} \in \mathbb{M}(n, n)$. Let $\underline{\mathbf{MX}}$ and $\underline{\mathbf{MY}}$ denote the private sets X and Y respectively, represented as row matrices, where $\underline{\mathbf{MX}} \in \mathbb{M}(k, n)$ and $\underline{\mathbf{MY}} \in \mathbb{M}(k, n)$. Without loss of generality, we consider the case where the sets X and Y have the same size (k) and we present the detail of Π-SI protocol in Algorithm 1. Later, we describe the more general case.

4.4   Generalization

In a more general case, we consider the client (C) having k_c elements and the server (V) having k_v elements. Then, V can simply creates several matrices $\underline{\mathbf{MY}}_i \in \mathbb{M}(k, n)$, where $i > 1$ (Instruction b. Algorithm 1) and distributes its k_v elements on them. Thus, V will repeat instruction 6 for each $\underline{\mathbf{MY}}_i$ and will send $\bigcup_{i>1} \underline{\mathbf{MY}}_i$ instead of $\underline{\mathbf{MY}}$ during instruction 7. At the reception, C will perform instruction 8 and instruction 9 for each received $\underline{\mathbf{MY}}_i$.

ALGORITHM 1 (Π-SI): A Private and Efficient Set Intersection Protocol

INPUT. C's input is a set X = {x1, . . ., xk}, V's input is a set Y = {y1, . . ., yk }. The elements in the input sets are taken from a domain of size n.

REQUIRE. 0 < k < n (where k is the size of the sets)

PRE-PROCESSING.

  a. "C" Creates MX ∈ $\mathbb{M}$ (k,n) with X's elements put as rows
  b. "V" Creates MY ∈ $\mathbb{M}$ (k,n) with Y's elements put as rows

STEP1. "C" performs the following
  1. Generates a random invertible M1 ∈ $\mathbb{M}$ (k,k)
  2. Computes M1X = M1 ⊗ MX
  3. Sends M1X to "V"

$$\xrightarrow{\text{M1X}}$$

STEP2. "V" performs the following
  4. Generates a random invertible M2 ∈ $\mathbb{M}$ (n,n)
  5. Computes M1X2 = M1X ⊗ M2
  6. Computes MY2 = MY ⊗ M2
  7. Sends M1X2 and MY2 to "C"

$$\xleftarrow{\text{M1X2, MY2}}$$

STEP3. "C" performs the following
  8. Computes M1Y2 = M1 ⊗ MY2
  9. Compares M1X2[i,*] and M1Y2[j,*] such that for any (1≤i≤k) and (1≤j≤k), if M1X2[i,*]= M1Y2[j,*], then, MX[i,*]= MY[j,*]. Therefore, adds the row MX[i,*] to the set Ψ (defined as an empty set).

OUTPUT. "C" returns Ψ that contains all items of the intersection

5 Security Analysis

In this section, we present a simulation-based security proof for our protocol using the Real/Ideal model [17].

5.1 Real/Ideal Model

Let Π denote a multi-party protocol executed by m participants $(P_1,...,P_m)$ in order to evaluate a function f. Let B denote the class of adversary that may corrupt participants in Π. Let R and D denote respectively the real and the ideal executions of Π on the set of inputs w and the set of security parameters sec.

During a **real execution** (R) we consider the presence of an adversary denoted A that behaves according to the class B while corrupting a set of participants $P_{i(1 \leq i \leq m)}$. At the end of R, uncorrupted parties output whatever was specified in Π and the corrupted P_i outputs any random functions of their $view_R^\Pi(w,sec)_i$.

During an **ideal execution** (D) we consider the presence of a trusted incorruptible party denoted T, which receives the set of inputs w from all participants in order to evaluate the function f in the presence of an adversary denoted S. We assume S corrupts the same P_i as the correspondent adversary A of real execution, and behaves according to the same class B before sending inputs to T. By the end of D, uncorrupted participants output what was received from T and the corrupted P_i output any random functions of their $view_D^\Pi(w,sec)_i$.

Definition 1. *Let Π and f be as above. We consider Π a secure multi-party protocol if for any real adversary A having a class B and attacks the protocol Π during its execution on the set of inputs w and the set of security parameters sec, there exists an adversary S in the ideal execution having the same class B and that can emulate any effect achieved by A. Let $\overset{d}{\equiv}$ denote the distribution equality. We formalize the definition of a secure multi-party protocol Π as follows*

$$\{out_R^\Pi(w, sec)\} \overset{d}{\equiv} \{out_D^\Pi(w, sec)\} \tag{2}$$

5.2   Security Proof

In what follows, we give security simulations of Π-SI protocol using Real/Ideal paradigm. The allowed behavioural class of adversary is the mixed one (Sect. 3.3), where the client (C) is actively corrupted and the server (V) is passively corrupted.

Let A, S and T denote respectively a real adversary, an ideal adversary and a trusted third party, where A and S have the same class. Let Π denote the Π-SI protocol (Algorithm 1), w denote the set of inputs $\{\mathbf{MX}, \mathbf{MY}\}$, sec denote security parameters that will be presented below and $PSI(X,Y)$ denote the private set intersection between X and Y, which are the private sets of C and V respectively. For simplicity, we give a simulation for the specific case where the sets X and Y have the same size (k). Next, we show how to generalize the proof.

Theorem 1. *Given a set of security parameters (sec) defined as $sec = \{(n, k) \in \mathbb{N}^2 : 0 < k < n\}$. Under these conditions, the protocol Π-SI defined in Algorithm 1 is a secure multi-party protocol against an active corruption of C.*

Proof. Assume C is actively corrupted by A. Then, it can only inject fake inputs $(\mathbf{MX})$ since aborting the protocol untimely will have no meaning. Assume C sends a fake **MX**. In this case, S can emulate A by just handling the fake **MX** and sends it to T, which performs the required computation and sends back $PSI(X, Y)$ to C. Thereby, completing the simulation. At the end, the views of C in Ideal and Real executions will be as follows

$$view_D^{\Pi}(w, sec)_C = \{\underline{\mathbf{MX}}, PSI(X, Y)\} \tag{3}$$

$$view_R^{\Pi}(w, sec)_C = \{\underline{\mathbf{MX}}, \underline{\mathbf{M1X2}}, \underline{\mathbf{MY2}}, PSI(X, Y)\} \tag{4}$$

Otherwise, $\underline{\mathbf{M1X2}} = \underline{\mathbf{M1X}} \otimes \underline{\mathbf{M2}}$, where $\underline{\mathbf{M1X}} \in \mathbb{M}(k, n)$ and $\underline{\mathbf{M2}} \in \mathbb{M}(n, n)$. According to security parameters (sec), we have $k < n$. This, preserves well the privacy of $\underline{\mathbf{M2}}$. Thereby, $\underline{\mathbf{M1X2}}$ that contains $(k \times n)$ equations opposite to $(n \times n)$ unknowns for C, will not involve meaningful information for it and can be reduced from its view. Likewise, $\underline{\mathbf{MY2}} = \underline{\mathbf{MY}} \otimes \underline{\mathbf{M2}}$, where $\underline{\mathbf{MY}} \in \mathbb{M}(k, n)$ and $\underline{\mathbf{M2}} \in \mathbb{M}(n, n)$. Then, $\underline{\mathbf{MY2}}$ will contain $(k \times n)$ equations opposite to $((k \times n) + (n \times n))$ unknowns for C, which does not involve meaningful information for it and can be so, reduced from its view. After these reductions, the view of C in real execution could be described as follows

$$view_R^{\Pi}(w, sec)_C = \{\underline{\mathbf{MX}}, PSI(X, Y)\} \tag{5}$$

Thus, relying on (3) and (5) we get

$$\{out_R^{\Pi}(w, sec)_C\} \overset{d}{\equiv} \{out_D^{\Pi}(w, sec)_C\} \tag{6}$$

On the other hand, the uncorrupted V can not be affected by the corruption of C since V does not require any output in real execution. Thus, T will simply not send it any output during ideal execution. This, means that

$$\{out_R^{\Pi}(w, sec)_V\} \overset{d}{\equiv} \{out_D^{\Pi}(w, sec)_V\} \tag{7}$$

Through (6) and (7), we proved by simulation that all effects achieved by a real active adversary corrupting C can also be achieved in an ideal execution. Then, Π-SI is a secure multi-party protocol against active corruption of C (Definition 1).

Theorem 2. *Given a set of security parameters (sec) defined as $sec = \{(n, k) \in \mathbb{N}^2 : 0 < k < n\}$. Under these conditions, the protocol Π-SI defined in Algorithm 1 is a secure multi-party protocol against a passive corruption of V.*

Proof. Assume V is passively corrupted. In this case, V should follow the specification of the protocol Π-SI, yet, it is allowed to analyse all data gathered during the execution. Then, S will just handle V's input and sends it to T, which performs the required computation and sends $PSI(X, Y)$ to C while sending nothing to V. Thereby, completing the simulation. At the end, the views of V in Ideal and Real executions will be as follows

$$view_D^{\Pi}(w, sec)_V = \{\underline{\mathbf{MY}}\} \tag{8}$$

$$view_R^{\Pi}(w, sec)_V = \{\underline{\mathbf{MY}}, \underline{\mathbf{M1X}}\} \tag{9}$$

Moreover, $\underline{\mathbf{M1X}} = \underline{\mathbf{M1}} \otimes \underline{\mathbf{MX}}$, where, $\underline{\mathbf{M1}} \in \mathbb{M}(k,k)$ and $\underline{\mathbf{MX}} \in \mathbb{M}(k,n)$. Then, since we defined $0 < k$ as security parameter (sec), we get $(k \times n) < ((k \times n) + (k \times k))$. Thus, $\underline{\mathbf{M1X}}$ that contains $(k \times n)$ equations opposite to $((k \times n) + (k \times k))$ unknowns for V, will not involve meaningful information for it and can be so, reduced from its view. After reduction, we obtain

$$view_R^\Pi(w, sec)_V = \{\underline{\mathbf{MY}}\} \tag{10}$$

Thus, relying on (8) and (10) we get

$$\{out_R^\Pi(w, sec)_V\} \stackrel{d}{\equiv} \{out_D^\Pi(w, sec)_V\} \tag{11}$$

On the other hand, the uncorrupted C outputs what was received from T in ideal execution, which is $PSI(X, Y)$ according to the simulation given above and outputs what was specified int the protocol Π-SI in real execution, which is $PSI(X, Y)$ (Algorithm 1, Output section). Then, we have

$$\{out_R^\Pi(w, sec)_C\} \stackrel{d}{\equiv} \{out_D^\Pi(w, sec)_C\} \tag{12}$$

Through (11) and (12) we proved by simulation that all effects achieved by a real passive adversary corrupting V can also be achieved in an ideal execution. Then, Π-SI is a secure multi-party protocol against passive corruption of V (Definition 1).

Corollary 1. *Given a set of security parameters (sec) defined as $sec = \{(n, k) \in \mathbb{N}^2 : 0 < k < n\}$. Under these conditions, the protocol Π-SI defined in Algorithm 1 is a secure multi-party protocol in the mixed model of adversary, where C is actively corrupted and V is passively corrupted.*

Proof. Corollary 1 relies heavily on the Theorems 1 and 2 proved above, while considering separately the case when the client (C) is corrupted and the case when the server (V) is corrupted. We assume that if both parties are corrupted we are not required to provide security guarantees.

Note 1. To generalize the proof (Sect. 4.4), assume the client (C) has k_c elements and the server (V) has k_v elements. This, will affect the view of C in real execution when it is corrupted (Eq. (4)), which will be defined as follows

$$view_R^\Pi(w, sec)_C = \{\underline{\mathbf{MX}}, \underline{\mathbf{M1X2}}, \bigcup_{i>1} \underline{\mathbf{MY}}_i \mathbf{2}, PSI(X, Y)\} \tag{13}$$

Where $\underline{\mathbf{MY}}_i\mathbf{2} = \underline{\mathbf{MY}}_i \otimes \underline{\mathbf{M2}}$ for $i > 1$. According to security parameters (sec), $\underline{\mathbf{M2}}$ is unknown for C (Proof Theorem 1), then, each $\underline{\mathbf{MY}}_i$ remains private and does not involve meaningful information for C and can be so, reduced from its view. Likewise, $\underline{\mathbf{M1X2}}$ can be reduced from the view of C in Real execution (Proof Theorem 1). Thus, Theorem 1 remains valid in the general case. On the other hand, the views of V when it is corrupted will be augmented with $\bigcup_{i>1} \underline{\mathbf{MY}}_i$ instead of $\underline{\mathbf{MY}}$. However, this will affect the views of V in both ideal and real executions. Thus, Theorem 2 remains valid in the general case.

6 Complexity Analysis

In this section, we analyse asymptotic complexities of communications and computations involved in our protocol (Π-SI: Algorithm 1, Sect. 4.3). We make comparison with existing protocols and we highlight our improvements.

6.1 Analysis

Let C and V denote a client and a server and k_c and k_v denote respectively the number of elements in their sets (General case, Sect. 4.4), where each element is assumed to be in $\mathbb{R}^n$. As off-line operations do not affect significantly the running time, we do not consider complexities of random matrices generation (Algorithm 1: Instruction1, Instruction4).

In step 1, getting **M1X** requires $O(k_c^2 n)$ computations and sending **M1X** costs $O(k_c n)$. In step 2, the server (V) performs $O(k_c n^2)$ operations to get **M1X2**, then, it performs at most $((k_v/k_c) + 1)\ O(k_c n^2)$ to get the set $\bigcup_{i>1} \mathbf{MY}_i\mathbf{2}$. This, results in $O((k_v + k_c)n^2)$. Moreover, sending **M1X2** costs $O(k_c n)$ and sending $\bigcup_{i>1} \mathbf{MY}_i\mathbf{2}$ is bounded by $O((k_v + k_c)n)$. In step 3, C should compute $\mathbf{M1Y}_i\mathbf{2}$ for each $\mathbf{MY}_i\mathbf{2}$ received ($i > 1$), which requires at most $O((k_v.k_c)n)$.

As a the length of elements (n) is assumed to be fixed for each application, we can reduce the complexities formulas to get a communication cost of $O(k_v + k_c)$, a server computation cost of $O(k_v + k_c)$ and a client computation cost of $O(k_v.k_c)$.

6.2 Discussion

In communication cost, we have achieved a linear complexity of $O(k_v + k_c)$. As far as we know, this is the most efficient complexity achieved by protocols working under standard assumptions and secure against malicious clients. The client computation cost is quadratic, bounded by $O(k_v.k_c)$, which is the minimum required for the native set intersection verification. Moreover, our protocol brings a significant improvement on the server side computations, costing a linear complexity of $O(k_v + k_c)$ without requiring any hard or non-standard assumption. This efficient cost will ensure the scalability of our protocol for multi-client contexts. To the best of our knowledge, the most efficient set intersection protocol, which is secure against malicious client and that reached $O(k_v + k_c)$ computations on the server side without requiring non-standard assumption is [6]. The latter protocol is proven to be secure under the strong Decisional Diffie-Hellman assumption. In contrast, our protocol does not require any cryptographic assumption, which makes it more practical.

7 Empirical Evaluation

In this section, we evaluate the computational performance of our proposed Π-SI protocol and we make comparison with the efficient and insecure hashing scheme used in practice.

7.1 Experimental Environment and Scenarios

In order to prove the efficiency of Π-SI protocol in practical scenarios, we evaluate the computational time required by a server (V) and a client (C) while executing Π-SI protocol in a real environment. We make two experiments denoted E_1 and E_2 to simulate respectively the case of equal and unequal dataset sizes. Let k_v and k_c denote the sizes of the set of V and the set of C respectively, where each element within a set is assumed to be in $\mathbb{R}^n$. Let $mult$ and add denote one multiplication and one addition respectively. We evaluate the computational costs involved in Π-SI protocol (Algorithm 1) as follows

$$Cost_V^{(\Pi-SI)} = n^2(k_v + k_c)\ mult\ + n(n-1)(k_v + kc)\ add$$

$$Cost_C^{(\Pi-SI)} = nk_c(k_v + 2k_c)\ mult\ + n(k_c - 1)(k_v + 2k_c)\ add$$

For more realistic results, we compare the performance of our solution to the hashing PSI scheme used in practice. We chose a simple and efficient commutative hash function H, such as $H_k(x) = x^k\ mod\ p$, where k is a 32-bit security parameter and p is a 32-bit random prime. Let exp and mod denote respectively one exponentiation and one modulo. We evaluate the hashing scheme as follows

$$Cost_V^{(hashing)} = Cost_C^{(hashing)} = n(k_v + k_c)\ exp + n(k_v + k_c)\ mod$$

We make evaluations on the same elements using a custom simulator built in Python and an Intel i5-2557M CPU running at 1.70 GHz and having a 4 GB of RAM.

7.2 Results and Discussion

E_1 **Expriment.** In E_1, we evaluated the running time of Π-SI and hashing protocols over server and client sets having equal sizes ($k_v = k_c$). We varied the size of the sets in the range $\{2^6, 2^7, 2^8, 2^9, 2^{10}\}$ of elements belonging to $\mathbb{R}^n$ ($n = 2^7$) and we sketch results in Table 1 and Fig. 1. Regarding server computation cost, Π-SI protocol has a short efficiency distance ($0.x$ s) lower than the hashing scheme for small sets ($2^6, 2^7$). Then, Π-SI execution revealed a slower increasing rate than the hashing scheme, which makes its more efficient for big sets

Table 1. E_1. Running time of Π-SI and the insecure hash solution over equal set sizes (set elements $\in \mathbb{R}^n, n = 2^7$)

k_v ($k_c = k_v$)		2^6	2^7	2^8	2^9	2^{10}
Server computation cost(s)	**Π-SI**	0.72	1.33	2.62	5.38	**10.77**
	Hashing	0.50	1.28	2.76	5.64	11.40
Client computation cost(s)	**Π-SI**	0.50	2.06	8.04	32.53	129.35
	Hashing	0.50	1.28	2.76	5.64	11.40

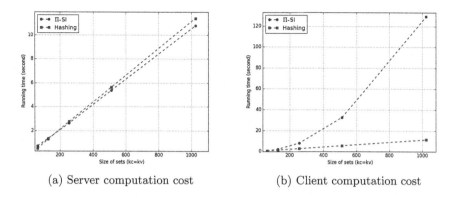

(a) Server computation cost   (b) Client computation cost

Fig. 1. Running time of Π-SI and the insecure hash solution over equal set sizes (set elements $\in \mathbb{R}^n$, $n = 2^7$)

Table 2. E_2. Running time of Π-SI and the insecure hash solution over unequal set sizes (set elements $\in \mathbb{R}^n$, $n = 2^7$)

k_v ($k_c = 2^6$)		2^6	2^7	2^8	2^9	2^{10}
Server computation cost(s)	Π-**SI**	0.72	1.01	1.67	3.03	**5.70**
	Hashing	0.50	0.97	1.72	3.18	6.08
Client computation cost(s)	Π-**SI**	0.50	0.69	1.01	1.69	**3.04**
	Hashing	0.50	0.97	1.72	3.18	6.08

(2^8,2^9). This efficient increasing rate presented by Π-SI is due to the use of efficient arithmetic operations (addition, multiplication) compared to the expensive operations involved in the hashing solution (modulo, exponentiation). Regarding the client computation cost, the hashing solution outperforms Π-SI with at most one order of magnitude ($\times 10$), which is very efficient compared to existing solutions [7].

E_2 Expriment. In E_2, we simulated the case of unequal set sizes, which is more realistic. For this, we fixed the size of the client set to $k_c = 2^6$ elements of $\mathbb{R}^n$ ($n = 2^7$) and we varied the size of the server sets in the range $\{2^6, 2^7, 2^8, 2^9, 2^{10}\}$. Results presented in Table 2 and Fig. 2 reveal a very efficient level of Π-SI that outperforms the hashing solution on the server side for big sets (2^8,2^9). Regarding the client computational cost, Π-SI presented a slow increasing rate that makes it more efficient than the hashing solution. This efficiency presented by Π-SI on the client side contrary to E_1 is due to the linear dependability of the client computational cost on the server set size. These results, confirm the adequacy of Π-SI protocol to be implemented on servers having Big Data sets.

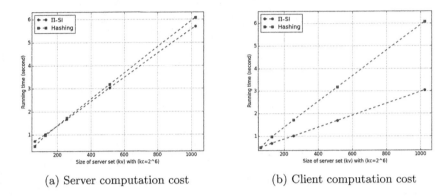

(a) Server computation cost   (b) Client computation cost

Fig. 2. Running time of Π-SI and the insecure hash solution over unequal set sizes with $(k_c = 2^6)$ and (set elements $\in \mathbb{R}^n$, $n = 2^7$)

8   Conclusion

In this paper, we have proposed a novel two-party Private Set Intersection protocol named (Π-SI). We have built this protocol upon efficient matrix algebra without any cryptographic scheme to cope with Big Data sets. Through security analysis conducted with the standard Real/Ideal paradigm, we have proved the privacy protection ensured by (Π-SI) against a semi-honest server and a malicious client. Asymptotic analysis has revealed linear complexities for both communications and server computations. Across empirical evaluations performed on large Data sets, we have confirmed the efficiency level provided by (Π-SI) protocol compared to the insecure hashing solution used in real applications.

References

1. Mezzour, G., Perrig, A., Gligor, V., Papadimitratos, P.: Privacy-preserving relationship path discovery in social networks. In: Garay, J.A., Miyaji, A., Otsuka, A. (eds.) CANS 2009. LNCS, vol. 5888, pp. 189–208. Springer, Heidelberg (2009). doi:10.1007/978-3-642-10433-6_13

2. Freedman, M.J., Nissim, K., Pinkas, B.: Efficient private matching and set intersection. In: Cachin, C., Camenisch, J.L. (eds.) EUROCRYPT 2004. LNCS, vol. 3027, pp. 1–19. Springer, Heidelberg (2004). doi:10.1007/978-3-540-24676-3_1

3. Baldi, P., Baronio, R., De Cristofaro, E., Gasti, P., Tsudik, G.: Countering gattaca: efficient and secure testing of fully-sequenced human genomes. In: Proceedings of the 18th ACM Conference on Computer and Communications Security, CCS 2011, pp. 691–702. ACM, New York (2011)

4. Fischlin, M., Pinkas, B., Sadeghi, A.-R., Schneider, T., Visconti, I.: Secure set intersection with untrusted hardware tokens. In: Kiayias, A. (ed.) CT-RSA 2011. LNCS, vol. 6558, pp. 1–16. Springer, Heidelberg (2011). doi:10.1007/978-3-642-19074-2_1

5. Cristofaro, E., Kim, J., Tsudik, G.: Linear-complexity private set intersection protocols secure in malicious model. In: Abe, M. (ed.) ASIACRYPT 2010. LNCS, vol. 6477, pp. 213–231. Springer, Heidelberg (2010). doi:10.1007/978-3-642-17373-8_13

6. Hazay, C.: Oblivious polynomial evaluation and secure set-intersection from algebraic PRFs. In: Dodis, Y., Nielsen, J.B. (eds.) TCC 2015. LNCS, vol. 9015, pp. 90–120. Springer, Heidelberg (2015). doi:10.1007/978-3-662-46497-7_4

7. Pinkas, B., Schneider, T., Zohner, M.: Scalable private set intersection based on OT extension (2016)

8. Aumann, Y., Lindell, Y.: Security against covert adversaries: efficient protocols for realistic adversaries. J. Cryptol. **23**(2), 281–343 (2010)

9. Hazay, C., Nissim, K.: Efficient set operations in the presence of malicious adversaries. J. Cryptol. **25**(3), 383–433 (2012)

10. Hazay, C., Venkitasubramaniam, M.: Scalable multi-party private set-intersection. In: Fehr, S. (ed.) PKC 2017. LNCS, vol. 10174, pp. 175–203. Springer, Heidelberg (2017). doi:10.1007/978-3-662-54365-8_8

11. Jarecki, S., Liu, X.: Efficient oblivious pseudorandom function with applications to adaptive OT and secure computation of set intersection. In: Reingold, O. (ed.) TCC 2009. LNCS, vol. 5444, pp. 577–594. Springer, Heidelberg (2009). doi:10.1007/978-3-642-00457-5_34

12. Bellare, M., Rogaway, P.: Random oracles are practical: a paradigm for designing efficient protocols. In: Proceedings of the 1st ACM Conference on Computer and Communications Security, CCS 1993, pp. 62–73. ACM, New York (1993)

13. Canetti, R., Fischlin, M.: Universally composable commitments. In: Kilian, J. (ed.) CRYPTO 2001. LNCS, vol. 2139, pp. 19–40. Springer, Heidelberg (2001). doi:10.1007/3-540-44647-8_2

14. Paillier, P.: Public-key cryptosystems based on composite degree residuosity classes. In: Stern, J. (ed.) EUROCRYPT 1999. LNCS, vol. 1592, pp. 223–238. Springer, Heidelberg (1999). doi:10.1007/3-540-48910-X_16

15. Lu, R., Zhu, H., Liu, X., Liu, J.K., Shao, J.: Toward efficient and privacy-preserving computing in big data era. IEEE Network **28**(4), 46–50 (2014)

16. Ishai, Y., Kushilevitz, E., Lindell, Y., Petrank, E.: On combining privacy with guaranteed output delivery in secure multiparty computation. In: Dwork, C. (ed.) CRYPTO 2006. LNCS, vol. 4117, pp. 483–500. Springer, Heidelberg (2006). doi:10.1007/11818175_29

17. Canetti, R.: Security and composition of multiparty cryptographic protocols. J. Cryptol. **13**(1), 143–202 (2000)

18. Naor, M., Pinkas, B.: Oblivious transfer and polynomial evaluation. In: Proceedings of the Thirty-first Annual ACM Symposium on Theory of Computing, STOC 1999, pp. 245–254. ACM, New York (1999)

19. Freedman, M.J., Ishai, Y., Pinkas, B., Reingold, O.: Keyword search and oblivious pseudorandom functions. In: Kilian, J. (ed.) TCC 2005. LNCS, vol. 3378, pp. 303–324. Springer, Heidelberg (2005). doi:10.1007/978-3-540-30576-7_17

20. Kissner, L., Song, D.: Privacy-preserving set operations. In: Shoup, V. (ed.) CRYPTO 2005. LNCS, vol. 3621, pp. 241–257. Springer, Heidelberg (2005). doi:10.1007/11535218_15

21. Dachman-Soled, D., Malkin, T., Raykova, M., Yung, M.: Efficient robust private set intersection. In: Abdalla, M., Pointcheval, D., Fouque, P.-A., Vergnaud, D. (eds.) ACNS 2009. LNCS, vol. 5536, pp. 125–142. Springer, Heidelberg (2009). doi:10.1007/978-3-642-01957-9_8

22. Hazay, C., Lindell, Y.: Efficient protocols for set intersection and pattern matching with security against malicious and covert adversaries. J. Cryptol. **23**(3), 422–456 (2010)
23. Lindell, Y., Pinkas, B.: Secure multiparty computation for privacy-preserving data mining. J. Priv. Confid. **1**(1), 5 (2009)
24. Vaidya, J., Clifton, C.: Secure set intersection cardinality with application to association rule mining. J. Comput. Secur. **13**(4), 593–622 (2005)

A Topology-Aware Framework for Graph Traversals

Jia Meng, Liang Cao, and Huashan Yu[✉]

School of Electronics Engineering and Computer Science, Peking University,
Beijing 100871, China
{mengjiajia,1300012902,yuhs}@pku.edu.cn

Abstract. Computation on a large-scale graph is to propagate and update the vertex values systematically. Efficient graph computing depends on techniques compatible with the algorithm's value propagating pattern. Graph traversing is a value propagating pattern used by representative graph applications. This paper presents an efficient value propagating framework for large-scale graph traversing applications. By partitioning the input graph based on the topology, it allows values for different source vertices to be propagated together, so as to reduce value propagating overhead. A locality-based vertex partitioning strategy is proposed to improve locality on processors. To improve parallel efficiency of graph traversals, a novel task scheduling mechanism has been devised. The mechanism allows the framework to improve load balance without loss of locality. A prototype for the framework has been implemented. On four large real graphs and a synthetic graph, the work was evaluated with two typical graph applications. By comparing with the owner-computing rule, experimental results show that this work has an overall speedup from 1.28 to 2.67. The speedup to Ligra is more than 5 in most cases.

Keywords: Graph traversing · Graph partitioning · Computation decomposing · Dynamic scheduling · Work stealing

1 Introduction

In the domain of data and network science, information is often linked to form large-scale graphs that may consist of billions of edges. Such a connected data tends to be scale-free that the degree distribution follows a power law, and its effective diameter is also low. The Computation on a connected data is vertex-centric and data-driven. During the computation, values of the vertices are propagated along the edges concurrently, according to value propagating pattern specified by the graph algorithm. For example, breadth-first search (BFS) specifies that every vertex can receive at most one propagated value; and PageRank [3] specifies that a vertex should propagate its newly updated value to every outgoing neighbor. On every vertex, the local value is updated according to the received data, and the new value is propagated in turn except the local value has gotten stable.

Although graph computing technology has been studied extensively in recent years [5, 7, 8, 9–13, 15, 17–21], efficiently processing large-scale graphs remains a grand challenge, due to three factors. First, the computation involves value propagations along billions of edges, resulting in that a large amount of data is accessed randomly and

© Springer International Publishing AG 2017
S. Ibrahim et al. (Eds.): ICA3PP 2017, LNCS 10393, pp. 165–179, 2017.
DOI: 10.1007/978-3-319-65482-9_11

intensively. The locality optimizing strategies vary from one application to another. Second, a vertex and its neighbors are to be updated in an order compatible with the value propagating trace. The parallelism often varies from time to time during the computation. Third, the workload on each vertex depends heavily on both the algorithm's propagating pattern and the input graph's degree distribution. The load balancing strategies are algorithm sensitive and data sensitive. To meet the performance requirements of most large-scale graph applications, a feasible solution is to develop techniques specialized for typical propagating patterns. Each technique optimizes one pattern exhaustively, and enables a class of applications to achieve acceptable performance for most input graphs.

Graph traversing is a typical vertex value propagating pattern. It is used by representative graph applications like BFS, connected-component detection [16], graph-diameter estimation [1, 2, 4, 6, 14], and etc. According to this pattern, values are only allowed to be propagated from visited vertices to those yet unvisited, and a vertex is marked as visited immediately after it has received a propagated value. A graph traversing algorithm starts by propagating values from some source vertex, which is initially marked as visited. Every vertex can receive data from at most one neighbor. The overall value propagating trace is a traversing tree, which covers all vertices reachable from the source. Vertices on the tree are updated systematically. There is often more than one source vertex in applications like connected-component detection and graph-diameter estimation. Different sources can be processed in any order.

This paper presents a parallel graph traversing framework that improves application efficiency with topology-adaptive techniques. The framework elaborately divides vertices of the input graph into a relatively small number of vertex blocks, according to the graph topology and memory distribution of these vertices. Every block is a task scheduling unit during the computation, and is ready for task assignment when at least one of its vertices is ready to be updated. A double-queue task scheduling mechanism has been devised to process these blocks concurrently. This mechanism enables a processor to dynamically select tasks according to both distances from the accessed data and sizes of the tasks, so as to improve both load balance and locality. Furthermore, two strategies are exploited to improve value propagating efficiency. One is to allow every subgraph to select the most appropriate value propagating mechanism. Another is to enable different vertex sources to share value propagating overheads by propagating values simultaneously for these sources. We have implemented a prototype for this framework, and evaluated it with both real and synthetic graphs.

2 Problem Statement and Analysis

In this work, a graph traversing application is represented as a quadruple $<V, E, S, f>$, where V is the input graph's vertex set and E is its edge set, $S \subseteq V$ is the source vertex set, and f is the function updating values on every vertex. The graph$<V, E>$ is either directed or undirected. Every edge in E serves as a channel with unlimited bandwidth for exchanging data between the two connected vertices. If $<V, E>$ is undirected, the channels are bidirectional; otherwise, the channels are unidirectional. It always costs one time unit for an edge to transfer data from its original vertex to the terminal. Every vertex in V has an initial value, and computes a new value for every received value with f. When a vertex receives multiple values at the same time, it processes these values independently and simultaneously. On every vertex, the time cost by f to process the received values is ignored. The application is to propagate every source's value on the graph non-cyclically. On the propagating trace, every vertex will use f to replace the received value with a new one before it is propagated further. Every vertex is allowed to receive at most one value for every source. When multiple values for the same source arrive at the same time, the vertex selects one value randomly.

Obviously, the value-propagating trace for every $s \in S$ is a BFS tree rooted from s on the graph <V, E>. The value-propagating trees for different sources are independent. The application is to construct the value-propagating for every $s \in S$, and perform the required value update with f on every reached vertex. Therefore, this application model covers any graph-traversing applications based on BFS.

For the graph traversing application <V, E, S, f>, the complexity mainly originates from the intensive and random accesses to the edges and vertices. This section first analyzes the chances for the application to reduce the amount of data accesses. The issues of data access efficiency are discussed later. To be convenient, the following terms are defined.

- **Dot**. A dot is a vertex that has no neighbors, and hence is not reachable by other vertices.
- **Terminal**. If <V, E> is undirected, a terminal is a vertex that has only one neighbor. If <V, E> is directed, a terminal is a vertex that has only either outgoing neighbors or ingoing neighbors.
- **Linear segment**. A linear segment is a path from vertex $v_s \in V$ to $v_e \in V$, where: (a) either v_s or v_e is a terminal; (b) except v_s and v_e, other vertices have exactly two neighbors.
- **Linear path**. A linear path is a path from vertex $v_s \in V$ to $v_e \in V$, where: (a) neither v_s nor v_e is a terminal; (b) both v_s and v_e have more than two neighbors, and other vertices have exactly two neighbors.
- **Netlike graph**. Given a graph <V, E>, its netlike graph consists of all linear paths on it, and is denoted as NG(V, E). A vertex on NG(V, E) is called as a hub vertex when it is also on some linear segments.

2.1 Complexity Analysis

Given a source $s \in S$, the traversing tree often consists of a large amount of vertices, and is constructed by systematically propagating values from previously visited vertices. Initially, s is the only vertex on the traversing tree. The traversing tree is then extended iteratively by propagating values along edges outgoing from its vertices to those unvisited. The newly added vertices are found with either the pushing- or pulling-mechanism. If the pulling-mechanism is selected, every unvisited vertex is a candidate for visiting next, and its ingoing neighbors are inspected one after another. When an ingoing neighbor is found to be visited, the neighbor's value is fetched back and the rest neighbors are ignored. If the pushing-mechanism is selected, candidates for visiting next are limited to outgoing neighbors of the visited vertices. For every visited vertex, its outgoing neighbors are inspected in some order, and its value is sent to the unvisited ones. Therefore, it is very complex to construct the traversing tree, due to the intensive edge accesses and random vertex accesses.

It is possible for different sources to propagate values together, so as to share the propagating overhead caused by edge accesses and vertex inspections. Let $vg(s_1, s_2)$ be a subgraph where every vertex is reachable to both $s_1 \in S$ and $s_2 \in S$. On $vg(s_1, s_2)$, if it is compatible with the value propagating pattern to start value propagating from the same vertex for both s_1 and s_2, then these two sources can share the same value propagating trace on $vg(s_1, s_2)$. For example, let $vg(s_1, s_2)$ be a linear segment that is reachable to both s_1 and s_2, then s_1 and s_2 must share the same value propagating trace on $vg(s_1, s_2)$. In a typical social network graph like Twitter and Friendster, the linear segments cover more than 15% vertices. When s_1 and s_2 reach NG(V, E) via the same hub vertex, they also can share the same value propagating trace on NG(V, E).

2.2   Efficiency Analysis

As discussed in Sect. 2.1, constructing the traversing trees for different sources simultaneously can make chances for reducing complexity of applications. In this case, values for different sources may reach a vertex via different edges concurrently; and every vertex needs a vector to indicate its visiting statuses. The vector's i-th element designates whether current vertex has been visited from the i-th source. A vertex is said to be active when it is still unvisited for at least one source vertex. A vertex $v \in V$ is de-noted as a frontier when there is at least one source $s \in S$ that: (a) v has been visited by s; (b) it is not sure whether v's every outgoing neighbor has been visited by s.

Given a graph traversing algorithm, its computation on the linear segments is relatively simple. Without loss of generality, we can assume that there is at most one frontier on every linear segment. Hence, the vertex to be updated next is always the frontier's outgoing neighbor. However, the computation on NG(V, E) is much more complex, since every active vertex is a candidate for updating next and the update may require more than one frontier's value. To maximize the parallelism, the computation is divided into a sequence of supersteps. For two reasons, the pulling-mechanism is selected to propagate values from frontiers to their active neighbors. One is that most active vertices on a super-step are to be updated, since the input graph tends to be scale free and neighbors of a few frontiers often cover most vertices. Another is that the pushing-mechanism requires writing to a vertex's neighbors frequently and randomly.

To improve efficiency for the computation on NG(V, E), two key issues are to be addressed for each super-step. One is load balance. Different active vertices can be independently processed. On every active vertex, the computation is to inspect its ingoing neighbors and update local value with these included in current frontiers. Hence the workload on an active vertex tends to be proportional to its degree. Another key issue is locality. The active vertices on each super-step are random, and number of active vertices varies greatly from one super-step to another. The value-propagating efficiency will be significantly cut down if neighbors of a large amount of active vertices are randomly accessed.

3   A Topology-Aware Value-Propagating Framework

This section presents a topology-aware framework to propagate values for graph traversals. We assume that a computer consists of n computing nodes, and each node has m processors and a local memory. The distance from a processor to its local memory is shorter than that to any remote memory. The input graph's vertices are equally divided into n blocks. Each block and edges associated with these vertices are saved in one computing node. It is also assumed that a vertex can buffer an initial value and all the updates on it. When the initial value is propagated, the buffered updates are to be propagated together.

Given a graph traversing application $<V, E, S, f>$, the framework schedules its computation on different vertices carefully with three strategies. The first strategy is to partition the input graph's edges according to the graph topology. It enables the framework to reduce edge accesses by selecting value propagating mechanism for every subgraph independently. It also enables the framework to find the chances for sharing value propagating overhead between different source vertices. The second strategy is to partition the input graph's vertices according to both their memory distribution and graph topology. This strategy enables the framework to efficiently filter out vertices that are unreachable to current frontiers, and to improve locality on each processor. The third strategy is to schedule computation partitions greedily and dynamically. The framework carefully selects a processor for every computation partition, according to both every processor's workload and the partition's data accessing efficiency on different processors.

Before the application starts its graph traversals, the framework first partitions the input graph's edges, resulting in a netlike graph and a set of linear segments. Then it partitions the vertex block on each computing node into a relatively small number of vertex chunks. With these subgraphs and chunks, the framework partitions the computation into three kinds of tasks. Every source on some linear segment represents a type-I task, which is to traverse on the linear segment from the source. Every chunk and current frontiers represents a type-II task, which is to (a) propagate values along edges outgoing from current frontiers to the chunk and (b) update the chunk's vertices with the propagated values. Every updated hub vertex and a linear segment outgoing from the hub represents a type-III task, which is to propagate the hub's new value on the linear segment.

By concurrently executing the computations on different subgraphs, the framework constructs the traversing trees for different source vertices simultaneously. At the beginning, every type-I task is assigned to a processor and is executed independently. The framework will not propagate values on the netlike graph, until all type-I tasks have been completed. Value propagating procedure on the netlike graph is divided into a sequence of super-steps. The computation on each super-step is partitioned into a set of type-II tasks. These type-II tasks are greedily scheduled to improve both data accessing efficiency on each processors and load balance between different processors. After computation on the netlike graph has been completed, the type-III tasks are scheduled to be executed on different processors concurrently.

To reduce edge accesses in constructing the traversing trees, the framework independently selects propagating mechanism for every subgraph. If the subgraph is a linear segment, the pushing mechanism is selected; otherwise, the pulling mechanism is selected.

3.1   A Topology-Based Edge Partitioning Strategy

By partitioning the input graph's edges according to the graph topology, our graph traversing framework partitions the input graph into dots, linear segments and a net-like graph. Dots are ignorable, since they are always unreachable. Based on the net-like graph

---

Algorithm 1. The three-phased graph traversing algorithm.

Phase I

$\emptyset \Rightarrow ihub(S);$

for every $s \in S$ that is on some linear segment $ls(s)$ **do**
    propagate value of s on ls(s);
    if v is the hub vertex of ls(s) and is visited **then**
        $\{v\} \cup ihub(S) \Rightarrow ihub(S);$
    end if
end do

Phase II

$\emptyset \Rightarrow ohub(S);$
$\emptyset \Rightarrow$ next frontier;
$ihub(S) \cup \{s \in S : s$ is on $NG(V, E)\} \Rightarrow$ frontier;
$\{v : v$ is on $NG(V, E)\} \Rightarrow$ active vertices;
while neither active vertices nor frontiers is null **do**
    for every $v \in$ active vertices **do**
        find_and_update(v) $\Rightarrow$ flag;
        if flag is true **then**
            $\{v\} \cup$ next frontier $\Rightarrow$ next frontier;
            if v is a hub vertex **then**
                $\{v\} \cup ohub(S) \Rightarrow ohub(S);$
            end if
        end if
        if v has been reached by every s $\in$ S **then**
            active vertices $- \{v\} \Rightarrow$ active vertices;
        end if
    end for
end while

Phase III

for every linear segment $ls(v)$ that is reachable from $v \in ohub(S)$ **do**
    propagate value of v on ls(v);
end do

---

and linear segments, computation on the input graph can be described with a three-phased algorithm. The algorithm constructs the traversing trees for different source vertices simultaneously, and enables different sources to share value propagating overhead automatically.

Algorithm 1 is the three-phased algorithm. The first phase of the three-phased algorithm is to propagate values on linear segments with the pushing mechanism. Computation of this phase is decomposed into a set of independent type-I tasks. Every task processes one source that is on some linear segment, and creates the source's value propagating trace on the linear segment. If a hub vertex is visited by some type-I task, then the hub is included in $ihub(S)$. The second phase is to propagate values on NG(V, E) with the pulling mechanism, consisting of a sequence of super-steps. Sources on NG(V, E) and vertices in $ihub(S)$ are the first super-step's frontiers. On each super-step, every active vertex independently tries to update its value by finding its ingoing neighbors from current frontiers and comparing its visiting status with those found. A vertex is a frontier of the next super-step when its value is updated. If a hub vertex is updated, then the hub is included in $ohub(S)$. The last phase is to propagate values on linear segments outgoing from hub vertices in $ohub(S)$. The computation consists of a set of independent type-III tasks. For every line segment that is reachable to $h_v \in ohub(S)$, a type-III task is executed. The task propagates value of h_v on the line segment, using the pushing mechanism.

3.2   A Locality-Based Vertex Partitioning Strategy

This strategy aims at improving locality on each processor when vertex values are propagated with the pulling-mechanism. The vertices on each computing node are partitioned into a relatively small number of vertex chunks carefully, according to both their memory distribution and graph topology. Every chunk consists of a set of vertices that are continuously saved. It can be used to represent a type-II task, which is to propagate values from current frontiers to vertices included the chunk. And the task's workload is estimated with the graph's topology information. Different chunks can be processed concurrently to make use of parallel processors.

We estimate the workload on vertex v with Eq. (1), where c_s is a constant denoting the overhead for inspecting the vertex's visiting status, c_e is a constant denoting the overhead for inspecting one ingoing neighbor. If the input graph is undirected, $ideg(v)$ is the vertex's degree; otherwise, $ideg(v)$ is either the ingoing degree or outgoing degree, depending on the value propagating direction. When there are enough chunks with carefully selected upper bound workload, dynamic task scheduling mechanism can be used to improve load balance without loss of locality.

$$\text{workload}(v) = c_s + ideg(v) \times c_e \tag{1}$$

In our topology-aware framework, the pulling-mechanism is used on the netlike graph only. When all vertices in a chunk are outside of the netlike graph, the chunk is denoted as a *vacancy*, and can be filtered out for computation on the netlike graph. To enable this kind of vertex filtering and to make full use of parallel processors, the framework divides vertices on every computing node into about $m \times \alpha$ non-vacancy chunks independently, where m is processor number of the computing node and α is an experimental constant. Let niv be the number of local vertices that are outside of the netlike graph. We first search the vacancies, and each one must consist of at least $niv \div (m \times \alpha)$ vertices. These vacancies divide the rest vertices into a set of initial non-vacancy chunks. Let twb be the total workload of these initial non-vacancy chunks. Each initial non-vacancy chunk is further divided into a minimum of chunks, where each one's workload should be no more than $twb \div (m \times \alpha)$.

3.3   A Double-Queue Task Scheduling Strategy

As discussed above, computation on the netlike graph is divided into a sequence of super-steps, and each super-step consists of a set of independent type-II tasks. Every type-II task processes one non-vacancy chunk. To improve each super-step's parallel efficiency, we have devised a two-level queue to schedule its tasks dynamically. This task scheduling mechanism synthesizes three typical task scheduling techniques. The first is the owner-computing rule, aiming at improving locality on processors. The second is the dynamic task scheduling technique, aiming at improving load balance between processors in a computing node. The last is the work stealing technique, aiming at improving load balance between computing nodes.

Our topology-aware framework maintains two queues on every computing node. Let cpn be a computing node, **tque**(cpn) and **dque**(cpn) denote these two local queues separately. The **tque**(cpn) consists of non-vacancy vertex chunks local to cpn. It automatically computes average workload of these chunks, and sorts them according to both their workloads and memory addresses. A chunk is denoted as heavy if its workload is greater than the average; otherwise, it is denoted as light. A heavy chunk is in front of any light chunk, so as to enable load balance between processors. Chunks of the same kind are further sorted according to their memory addresses, so as to improve locality on processors. Every element in **dque**(cpn) represents one computing node. It sorts the elements according distances from local processors to the corresponding computing nodes. Local memory of **dque**(cpn)[i] is not farer way from cpn's local processors than that of **dque**(cpn)[$i + 1$].

When a super-step is executed, each computing node schedules tasks in its local **tque** independently, and complex tasks are first assigned to processors. Different tasks are executed concurrently. When a processor is free, it submits first submits a task apply to **dque**(cpn)[0], attempting to get a task from **tque**(cpn). If the processor fails in getting tasks from **dque**(cpn)[i], it then submits task applies to **dque**(cpn)[$i + 1$], trying to steal tasks from the remote computing node specified by **dque**(cpn)[$i + 1$].

4   Implementation

We have developed a prototype with C/C++ for the topology-aware value propagating framework. The prototype is for NUMA architecture and uses Pthreads to execute parallel computations. The prototype consists of an edge slicer, a vertex slicer and a value propagator (Fig. 1). The edge slicer partitions a graph's edges according to the topology, and divides the graph into a netlike graph and a set of linear segments. The vertex slicer partitions a graph's vertices according to both their memory distribution and graph topology. One each computing node, it divides the local vertices into a set of vacancies and non-vacancy chunks. The vertex slicer sets α required by the locality-based computation decomposing mechanism to be 16. The value propagator automatically propagates values on a graph traversing application's input graph, and calls its vertex updating function to compute new vertex values. The value propagator can perform graph traversals simultaneously for a list of source vertices.

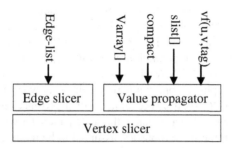

Fig. 1. Prototype of the topology-aware value propagating framework.

In a large-scale graph traversing application $<V, E, S, f>$, the framework is initialized by providing the input graph's edge list to the edge slicer. The application then can call the value propagator to perform graph traversals for a list of sources. It is required to provide four arguments to the value propagator: **slist[]**, **compact**, **varray[]**, and **vf**(u, v, tag). "**slist[]**" is the list of sources, and its length cannot be more then 64. "**varray[]**" is an array for storing the input graph's vertex values. If "**compact**" is true, **varray**[i] is the value of the i-th vertex; otherwise, "**varray[]**" saves 64 elements for every vertex, **varray**[$i*64 + j$] is the j-th element of the i-th vertex. "**vf**(u, v, tag)" is the vertex updating function, which is called by the framework to update value on the v-th vertex when value of the u-th vertex is propagated to the v-th vertex. If "**compact**" is true, "tag" is always zero when "**vf**(u, v, tag)" is called; otherwise, it is a bitmap to indicate which elements are to be updated on the v-th vertex. If there are more than 64 sources in S, the application is required to divide its sources into groups. Each group contains at most 64 sources, and requires one call to the value propagator.

In the prototype, the input graph is represented as a vertex list and an adjacent list. In the vertex list, every element represents one vertex, and includes a type flag, a triplet (*offset, ideg, odeg*), and a visiting status vector. The type flag is to distinguish between dots, terminals, hub vertices, vertices on the path between a terminal and the hub vertex, and the netlike graph's vertices except the hub vertices. The vertex saves identifiers of its neighbors in the adjacent list; and the triplet (*offset, ideg, odeg*) describes addresses of these identifiers in the adjacent list, where *offset* is the first identifier's address, *ideg* is number of its ingoing neighbors and *odeg* is number of its outgoing neighbors. If the input graph is undirected, then *ideg* and *odeg* are equal. The visiting status vector consists of 64 bits, where the i-th bit denotes whether the vertex has been visited by the source specified by "**slist**[i]".

When the framework is initialized with the input graph's edge list, the edge slicer and vertex slicer cooperate automatically to initialize the vertex list and the adjacent list. When the value propagator is called, it first resets the visiting status vector of every vertex, then automatically propagates values on the input graph and calls the vertex updating function to update values in "varray[]".

5 Experimental Evaluation

This section presents the experimental results for various real-world and synthetic graphs. The platform for the experiments is a Dell R820 server. The server has 4 Intel(R) Xeon(R) E5-4640 CPUs and 256 GB memory. Each CPU has 8 physical cores sharing 20 M LLC, and can support 16 parallel threads with hyper-thread. In the experiments, the server is configured as a NUMA with 4 nodes.

We used four real graphs and one synthetic graph, as shown in Table 1. The synthetic graph is denoted as Kro_26_16. It was generated with the Kronecker model implemented in Graph500. When the graph was created, the scale parameter was set to be 26 and the edge-factor was 16. All the five graphs are assumed to be undirected. For each graph, we have also counted the vertices and edges of its netlike graph, denoted as NG's vertices and NG's edges respectively.

Table 1. Graphs used in the experiments.

	Vertices	Edges	NG's vertices	NG's edges
wikipedia	27,154,800	601,038,301	4,751,326	4,680,898
com-friendster	65,608,368	1,806,067,136	13,867,424	13,867,424
socfb-konect	59,216,216	92,522,017	20,959,355	54,348,978
twitter_rv	61,578,416	1,468,365,182	39,724,449	1,465,994,803
Kro_26_16	67,108,862	1,073,741,824	42,663,341	8,345,041

We developed two typical applications to evaluate the prototype and these three strategies presented in Sect. 3. One application is to estimate diameter of the input graph, requiring that every vertex saves one value to indicate its longest distance to other vertices. Another is to construct the BFS trees for a set of source vertices, requiring that every vertex saves one value for each source vertex. For each application, we have tested performance of five versions independently. One version is provided by the Ligra [15]. We denote it as the Ligra version. This version is implemented with OpenMP. It divides the input graph's vertices into equal chunks, and schedules these chunks dynamically to balance workload between processors. Other four versions were self-developed.

- **OCL version**. This version uses the owner-computing rule to partition the computation. Every computing node equally divides its local vertices into 16 chunks, and every chunk is statically assigned to one processor. When the application is executed, every processor propagates values from current frontiers to its chunk with the pulling mechanism, and updates these vertices accordingly.

- **EP version**. This version enhances the OCL version with the topology-based edge partitioning strategy. The input graph is partitioned into a netlike graph and a set of linear segments. Accordingly, computation on the input graph is divided into three phases. The first phase is to execute type-I tasks, and the last phase to execute type-III tasks. In the second phase, computation on the netlike graph is executed just as the OCL version does.
- **VP version**. This version enhances the EP version with the locality-based vertex partitioning strategy. It decomposes computation on the input graph into type-II tasks, and schedules these tasks dynamically. However, tasks in **tque**(cpn) can be assigned only to local processors of the computing node cpn.
- **ST version**. This version enhances the VP version with the work stealing technique. After all tasks in **tque**(cpn) have been assigned, it allows processors on the computing node cpn to steal tasks from other computing node.

On each graph, we randomly selected 192 vertices as the source vertices. Every implementation was repeated 10 times to traverse from these 192 source vertices on the input graph. The average time cost is the experimental result of the implementation for the input graph. We failed to run the Ligra versions of these two applications on soc-friendster, because this graph is too large for Ligra.

5.1 Experimental Results for Estimating Graph Diameter

In this experiment, every implementation equally divides the 192 source vertices into 3 groups, the traversing trees for all 64 sources of the same group are constructed simultaneously. Table 2 is the time costs of different versions, where the time unit is second.

Table 2. Time costs for estimating diameters of different graphs.

	Socfb	Web-wiki	KRO_26_16	Twitter_rv	Soc-friendster
Ligra	9.63	44.79	55.8	140.79	–
OCL	5.64	17.88	16.11	42.3	88.17
EP	5.34	15.63	12.93	31.8	82.65
VP	5.01	11.64	10.68	27.81	84.45
ST	4.38	8.34	10.38	18.57	69.45

Although the Ligra version exploits the dynamic scheduling technique to balance workload, the OCL version has achieved significant better performance for all the first four graphs. On twitter_rv, speedup of the OCL version to the Ligra version is up to 3.46. The performance improvement tends to increase as the input graph's size increases. This results show that the performance bottleneck for most graph traversals is data accessing efficiency instead of load balance.

We evaluate the strategies presented in Sect. 3 with speedups to the OCL version. Figure 2(a) illustrates the results. Our topology-aware framework has achieved an overall speedup from 1.28 to 2.28. The edge partitioning strategy and work stealing strategy are effective for all the five graphs. The locality-based vertex partitioning strategy is ineffective for the synthetic graph. This is because that the OCL version partitions computation almost equally between processors of the same computing node. We believe this case only occurs by chance. Result of the ST version shows that the owner-computing rule cannot balance workload between computing nodes.

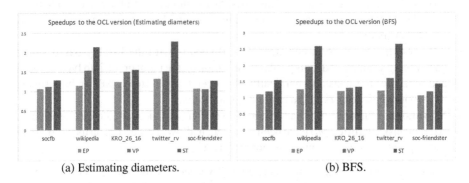

(a) Estimating diameters.   (b) BFS.

Fig. 2. Speedups to the OCL version.

5.2 Experimental Results for BFS

In this experiment, the Ligra BFS can process only one source vertex every time. To process 192 sources for every input graph, we have inserted a loop in the source code. Each of the four self-developed versions equally divides the 192 source vertices into 3 groups, the traversing trees for all 64 sources of the same group are constructed simultaneously. Table 3 is the time costs of different versions, where the time unit is second.

Table 3. Time costs for BFS of different graphs.

	Socfb	Web-wiki	KRO_26_16	Twitter_rv	Soc-friendster
Ligra	75.6	126.99	96	307.71	–
OCL	13.8	53.1	29.76	118.29	225.21
EP	12.51	42	24.87	97.41	211.89
VP	11.64	27.21	22.74	73.62	189.15
ST	8.91	20.52	22.47	44.34	156.78

The OCL version's performance is significantly better than that of the Ligra version, due to two factors. One is that Ligra version's locality is too poor, as shown in the previous subsection. Another is that the OCL version constructs 64 BFS trees simultaneously, resulting that value propagating overhead are shared between different sources.

We evaluate the strategies presented in Sect. 3 with speedups to the OCL version. Figure 2(b) illustrates the results. Our topology-aware framework has achieved an overall speedup from 1.32 to 2.67. All the three strategies are effective for all the five graphs.

6   Related Work

In recent years, many graph processing frameworks have been developed, including Pregel [11], Pregel+ [19], Giraph [5], Giraph++ [17], GraphLab [9], GraphX [18], and PowerGraph [7]. Although these systems are general enough to support different kinds of graph algorithms, there is no single system that has superior performance in all cases, two phenomena widely exists [10, 12]. One is that a general framework often shows different performance for different graph algorithms. Another is that an application's performance also often varies on different graphs. These phenomena are among the motivations behind this paper's work.

Data accessing efficiency and load balance are two key factors that hinder performance of graph applications, and are widely studied. Pregel introduced the message combining mechanism to reduce data-exchanging overhead between machines. Pre-gel+ introduced the vertex mirroring mechanism to reduce accesses to remote data. These two works give us beneficial hints for sharing value propagating overhead be-tween different sources. The difference is that our work focuses on data exchanging between vertices instead of machines. In GPS [13], the authors developed the large adjacency-list partitioning schema and dynamic repartitioning scheme to improve load balance. However, these two schemas often sacrifice locality, and in turn de-creases the performance, as shown by the Ligra's results in this paper. Giraph uses the multithreading method to maximize resource utilization. Experiments results in [20] disclose that sequential remote accesses can be faster than random local accesses. Our work exploits the vertex partitioning strategy to reduce random accesses, and improves load balance with the double-queue task scheduling strategy.

Different graph partitioning techniques have also been proposed to partition graph computation. PowerGraph has proposed the vertex-cut partitioning technique to improve load balance between tasks. GraphLego [21] replaces the traditional vertex-centric or edge-centric graph partitioning with a 3D cube model, so as to partition graph at the granularity of subgraphs. In [8], a graph transformation is proposed to reduce a large input graph into a small graph, so as to decompose computation on the original input graph. Our work combines the edge partitioning strategy and vertex partitioning strategy to partition graph computation.

7   Conclusion

Graph traversing is a value propagating pattern used by representative graph applications. This paper presents an efficient value propagating framework for large-scale graph traversing applications. It enables a graph computation to be partitioned according to both topology of the input graph and memory distribution of the graph's vertices. In this work, we propose to partition graph computation by combining edge partitioning and vertex partitioning. The proposed edge partitioning strategy is beneficial to reduce value propagating overhead. The proposed vertex partitioning strategy is beneficial to improve locality on each processor. To balance workload between processors and improve data accessing efficiency, a greedy task scheduling strategy was devised. We have developed a prototype for the topology-aware graph traversing framework. The prototype was evaluated with two typical graph applications and five graphs. The experimental results show that this prototype has obvious better performance than Ligra. We also have evaluated the effectiveness of the strategies presented in this paper. Comparing with the owner-computing rule, the framework presented in this paper has an overall speedup from 1.28 to 2.67.

Acknowledgements. This work was supported by the National Key Research and Development Program of China (2016YFB0201900), and the National High Technology Research and Development Program ("863" Program) of China (Grant No. 2015AA015305).

References

1. Aingworth, D., Chekuri, C., Motwani, R.: Fast estimation of diameter and shortest paths (without matrix multiplication). SIAM J. Comput. **28**(4), 1167–1181 (1996)
2. Borassi, M., Crescenzi, P., Habib, M., Kosters, W.A., Marino, A., Takes, F.W.: Fast diameter and radius bfs-based computation in (weakly connected) real-world graphs. Theor. Comput. Sci. **586**(C), 59–80 (2015)
3. Brin, S., Page, L.: The anatomy of a large-scale hypertextual Web search engine. Comput. Netw. ISDN Syst. **30**(1–7), 107–117 (1998)
4. Chechik, S., Larkin, D.H., Roditty, L., Schoenebeck, G., Tarjan, R.E., Williams, V.V.: Better approximation algorithms for the graph diameter. In: Proceedings of the twenty-fifth annual ACM-SIAM symposium on Discrete algorithms, pp. 1041–1052. Society for Industrial and Applied Mathematics, Philadelphia (2014)
5. Ching, A., Edunov, S., Kabiljo, M., Logothetis, D., Muthukrishnan, S.: One trillion edges: Graph processing at facebook-scale. Proc. VLDB Endow. **8**(12), 1804–1815 (2015)
6. Crescenzi, P., Grossi, R., Lanzi, L., Marino, A.: On computing the diameter of real-world directed (weighted) graphs. In: Klasing, R. (ed.) SEA 2012. LNCS, vol. 7276, pp. 99–110. Springer, Heidelberg (2012). doi:10.1007/978-3-642-30850-5_10
7. Gonzalez, J.E., Low, Y., Gu, H., Bickson, D., Guestrin, C.: PowerGraph: distributed graph-parallel computation on natural graphs. In: Proceedings of the 10th USENIX Conference on Operating Systems Design and Implementation, pp. 17–30. USENIX Association, Berkeley (2012)
8. Kusum, A., Vora, K., Gupta, R., Neamtiu, I.: Efficient processing of large graphs via input reduction. In: Proceedings of the 25th ACM International Symposium on High-Performance Parallel and Distributed Computing, pp. 245–257. ACM, New York (2016)
9. Low, Y., Bickson, D., Gonzalez, J., Guestrin, C., Kyrola, A., Hellerstein, J.M.: Distributed graphlab: A framework for machine learning and data mining in the cloud. Proc. VLDB Endow. **5**(8), 716–727 (2012)
10. Lu, Y., Cheng, J., Yan, D., Wu, H.: Large-scale distributed graph computing systems: an experimental evaluation. Proc. VLDB Endow. **8**(3), 281–292 (2014)
11. Malewicz, G., Austern, M.H., Bik, A.J.C., Dehnert, J.C., Horn, I., Leiser, N., Czajkowski, G.: Pregel: a system for large-scale graph processing. In: Proceedings of the 2010 ACM SIGMOD International Conference on Management of Data, pp. 135–146. ACM, New York (2010)

12. Nai, L., Xia, Y., Tanase, I.G., Kim, H., Lin, C.Y.: GraphBIG: understanding graph computing in the context of industrial solutions. In: Proceedings of the International Conference for High Performance Computing, Networking, Storage and Analysis, p. 69. ACM, New York (2015)
13. Salihoglu, S., Widom, J.: GPS: A graph processing system. In: Proceedings of the 25th International Conference on Scientific and Statistical Database Management, p. 22. ACM, New York (2013)
14. Shun, J.: An evaluation of parallel eccentricity estimation algorithms on undirected real-world graphs. In: Proceedings of the 21st ACM SIGKDD International Conference on Knowledge Discovery and Data Mining, pp. 1095–1104. ACM, New York (2015)
15. Shun, J., Blelloch, G.E.: Ligra: A lightweight graph processing framework for shared memory. ACM Sigplan Not. **48**(8), 135–146 (2013)
16. Skeina, B.S.: The Algorithm Design Manual, 2nd edn. Springer, Heidelbergz (2008)
17. Tian, Y., Balmin, A., Corsten, S.A., Tatikonda, S., Mcpherson, J.: From think like a vertex to think like a graph. Proc. VLDB Endow. **7**(3), 193–204 (2013)
18. Xin, R.S., Gonzalez, J.E., Franklin, M.J., Stoica, I.: GraphX: a resilient distributed graph system on Spark. In: First International Workshop on Graph Data Management Experiences and Systems, p. 2. ACM, New York (2013)
19. Yan, D., Cheng, J., Lu, Y., Ng, W.: Effective techniques for message reduction and load balancing in distributed graph computation. In: Proceedings of the 24th International Conference on World Wide Web, pp. 1307–1317. ACM, New York (2015)
20. Zhang, K., Chen, R., Chen, H.: NUMA-aware graph-structured analytics. In: Proceedings of the 20th ACM SIGPLAN Symposium on Principles and Practice of Parallel Programming, pp. 183–193. ACM, New York (2015)
21. Zhou, Y., Liu, L., Lee, K., Pu, C., Zhang, Q.: Fast iterative graph computation with resource aware graph parallel abstractions. In: Proceedings of the 24th ACM International Symposium on High-Performance Parallel and Distributed Computing, pp. 179–190. ACM, New York (2015)

Adaptive Traffic Signal Control
with Network-Wide Coordination

Yong Chen[1,2], Juncheng Yao[1(✉)], Chunjiang He[2], Hanhua Chen[1], and Hai Jin[1]

[1] Big Data Technology and System Lab,
Services Computing Technology and System Lab,
Cluster and Grid Computing Lab,
School of Computer Science and Technology,
Huazhong University of Science and Technology, Wuhan 430074, China
{yaojc,chen,hjin}@hust.edu.cn
[2] China Electric Power Research Institute, Beijing 100192, China
{ychen,cjhe}@epri.sgcc.com.cn

Abstract. Today, Traffic congestion has become an increasingly serious problem. Efficient *adaptive traffic signal control* (ATSC) is a challenging issue in the road network. The existing *multi-agent reinforcement learning* (MARL) schemes do not have satisfactory performance due to the difficulty of coordination between agents and the delay consequence of reward function. In this paper, we present an novel adaptive traffic signal control scheme in the urban road network based on MARL. In the scheme, we adopt a delay time estimation model with network-wide coordination to estimate the total delay time of vehicles for each road link, and control traffic signals adaptively based on the estimated delay time with traffic flow data. We conduct comprehensive simulations using large-scale data collected from real world systems to evaluate the performance of our design, especially under heavy traffic pressure. The results show that our scheme can significantly alleviate the road congestion as well as improving the road network throughput and reducing the vehicles delay time.

Keywords: Network-wide coordination · Multi-agent systems · Traffic signal control · Delay time estimation · Reinforcement learning

1 Introduction

Urban road traffic congestion has generated many inconveniences to people's lives. It not only increases the travel cost, but also adversely affects the urban air environment. With continuous increase in the number of vehicles, the problem is becoming increasingly more serious. There are many causes of urban traffic congestion, among which, unreasonable traffic signal control is one of the major issues. As a fixed signal timing plan, traffic signal control tends to cause low traffic efficiency since it is difficult to stipulate effective control policy according to traffic flow variations.

© Springer International Publishing AG 2017
S. Ibrahim et al. (Eds.): ICA3PP 2017, LNCS 10393, pp. 180–194, 2017.
DOI: 10.1007/978-3-319-65482-9_12

By using the *adaptive traffic signal control* (ATSC) scheme, we can control traffic signals dynamically based on real-time traffic flow data to achieve a specific objective. In order to reduce traffic congestion, we generally minimize the total delay time of all vehicles in the network as the optimization target. By adopting dynamic programming approach, the optimal control strategy can be realized in stable condition at a single intersection. However, as the number of intersections increases, the state space will become extremely large, which will cause this scheme to fall into the predicament of computational complexity. Function approximation method can be used to estimate the delay time of each state for dynamic programming, but it is difficult to estimate the total delay time accurately, and the parameters are also difficult to train. Heuristic optimization models can be used to optimize traffic signal control in a straightforward manner, but these schemes often require a long training process. Moreover, it will affect the adaptability in real control. Reinforcement learning is an efficient way to solve the ATSC problem. *Multi-agent reinforcement learning* (MARL) uses many agents to control traffic signals for each intersection. The agents control traffic signals for each intersection separately, but how to implement efficient coordination between agents is a big challenge. The actual delay time of vehicles is hard to obtain immediately. This will lead to the delayed consequence of reward value. How to estimate the state reward function accurately for each action is another challenge.

In this paper, we present an adaptive traffic signal control scheme based on MARL. We implement a delay time estimation model with network-wide coordination between agents. We estimate the delay time of vehicles in each road link first, and then amend the delay time in accordance with the daily flow fluctuating prediction. Through traffic flow network iteration, we estimate vehicles' delay time in the road network. With this delay time estimation method, we can train a state action reward function for MARL model. Thus, the traffic controllers can select control policy to minimize the reward function efficiently. Through network-wide coordination between agents [1], the local flow information can be delivered to the entire road network. Thus, the agents could simultaneously control congestion situation. We conduct comprehensive simulations to evaluate the performance of our design, especially under heavy traffic pressure. The results show that the average link delay can be reduced by 36% under heavy traffic. Our scheme can alleviate severe road congestion, improve the road network throughput, and significantly reduce delay time of vehicles.

The rest of this paper consists of the following sections. Section 2 describes related work. Section 3 describes the scheme of delay time estimation model in details. Section 4 describes the experiment with simulated urban traffic data. Section 5 summarizes the work.

2   Related Work

A direct way to solve the traffic signal control problem is to use a dynamic programming approach. Dynamic programming explores the reward value for each control strategy in stable condition. Excessive system state can lead to high complexity, which will make the algorithm impractical. In order to simplify the state complexity, Yin et al. [2] divide the state of a single intersection into several classes. They solve the optimal control problem efficiently through decomposition of Markov decision process method. Yin et al. [3] use a fair strategy to stabilize the length of the waiting queue. Li et al. [4] present a signal control method based on adaptive dynamic programming. Dynamic programming methods work well in a single intersection. However, as the number of intersections increases, the system states will also increase significantly, causing this method to fall into the predicament of computational complexity. Cai et al. [5] present an adaptive traffic signal control scheme by using approximate dynamic programming. Yin et al. [6, 7] estimate the delay time of each state with the function approximation method for dynamic programming. However, it is difficult to accurately estimate the total delay time, while the parameters of value function are also difficult to train.

Heuristic optimization models can be used to optimize traffic signal control in a straightforward manner. Vallati et al. [8] try to quickly solve the traffic congestion problem caused by accidents by using heuristic forward search method. Kwatirayo et al. [9] use a heuristic algorithm to control the traffic signal in accordance with the system state of the last time period. These schemes cannot achieve ideal results due to strict conditional constraints. Renfrew et al. [10] heuristically control traffic signal with an ant colony algorithm. Oliveira et al. [11] observe the environment of traffic network by using multiple neural networks [12,13], and then make decisions to control traffic signals. The convergence speed of this method is slow, and the adaptability will be affected in real control.

Reinforcement learning is an efficient approach to solve the ATSC problem. The Q-Learning schemes can be used to solve the traffic control problem at single intersection after a quick training process. But as the number of intersections increases, such a method with single agent will face the state space explosion. Multi-agent reinforcement learning can be used to address this situation [14–16]. However, the coordination between agents is difficult to control. Wiering [17] try to solve the traffic control problem with a multi-agent reinforcement learning method. Arel et al. [18] let each agent make decision to reduce the time cost locally. However, it is difficult to reach the global optimum since there is no interaction between each agent. Kuyer et al. [19] use MARL to control traffic signal through coordination between neighboring agents. Prashanth et al. [20] try a function approximation and policy iteration method for multi-agent reinforcement learning method. Tantawy et al. [21] apply an adaptive traffic signal controller method in downtown Toronto, and they try to coordinate controllers in an integrated network with multi-agent reinforcement learning. Xie et al. [22,23] try to control the traffic flow in Pittsburg with a schedule-driven method from the microscopic view. These methods also involve certain difficulties [24,25]. For example, it is difficult to use the reward function to obtain result immediately due to the delayed consequences. It is also difficult for multiple agents to achieve coordinated control.

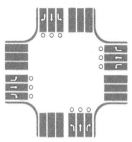

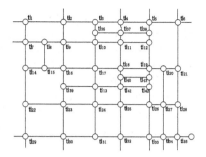

Fig. 1. An example intersection   **Fig. 2.** 43-intersection traffic network

3   Methodology

3.1   Problem Description

In this paper, we aim to realize optimal control of traffic signals in an urban area. In order to address this issue, the optimization target is to minimize the total delay time of all vehicles moving in the urban area. Specifically, a road network is composed of many road links, while each intersection is connected with four incoming links and four outgoing links. Figure 1 shows an example of intersection. Each road link has three directions: leftward, rightward, and forward. The signal controller (agent) controls four incoming links at each intersection, indicating the permit of vehicles in three directions for each incoming link. Figure 2 shows a 43-intersection traffic network. When the controller allows vehicles to pass in a specific direction, the vehicles could go through the intersection toward corresponding outgoing links respectively. We set a slot time for signal control. The signal controller at each intersection needs to make a decision for 12 signals in total during each slot time. We calculate the delay time penalty $p(l,t)$ as the number of vehicles in incoming link l which cannot leave the link during each slot time t. The optimization target of all vehicles passed through the area is $\sum_{t \in T} \sum_{l \in L} p(l,t)$, where T is the number of time slots set in a day; L denotes the links set in the road network.

The traffic signals at each intersection are generally controlled by a signal timing plan. The timing plan changes the roads permit according to a fixed phase schedule, and ensures that vehicles in different directions at the intersection have equal opportunities to pass through the intersection. Due to the uneven distribution of traffic flow within the whole road network and the different traffic flow during different time periods, some busy intersections have a higher probability of congestion.

ATSC can be used to control traffic signals dynamically based on real-time traffic flow data. In this way, it can achieve a certain objective. It is an efficient way to alleviate traffic congestion by changing traffic signals according to the fluctuations of traffic flow. We can get real-time traffic flow data from sensors deployed in the road network. The data includes traffic flow in each road link and the vehicle passing rate at each intersection. We assume that the maximum passing rate at each intersection is a fixed value, the distribution of traffic flow is subject to a certain fluctuating law, and the local traffic flow could be partially changed by the traffic signal controllers. Under the assumption, the problem is how to control each traffic signal so that the total delay time for all vehicles passing through the area can be minimized.

3.2 The MARL Approach

Reinforcement learning is a learning process in which a single agent interacts with the environment to find the maximum long-term reward. The environment is generally stationary and modeled as a Markov decision process. A tuple $\langle S, A, T, R \rangle$ can be used to represent this learning process, where S is the state set of the agent; A is the action set; $T(s, a, s')$ is the transition function which represents the transition probability of the agent from state s to a new state s' under action a; $R(s, a, s')$ is the reward function of different transitions. When an agent needs to make an action, the agent checks its optimal policy in the current state with a Q-value which represents the expected long-term reward for the state-action pair (s, a). Agent learns from the value function to make an action, and continues to explore the value function during its interaction with the environment. The Q-values are updated according to the following equation in Q-learning method, where α is the learning rate which controls how many Q-values are updated at each time step t, γ is the discount factor controlling how the agent regards future rewards, r_t is the immediate reward.

$$Q_{t+1}(s_t, a_t) = Q_t(s_t, a_t) + \alpha(r_t + \gamma Q_{max_a}(s_{t+1}, a) - Q_t(s_t, a_t)) \quad (1)$$

MARL uses multiple agents to control complex systems, and each agent interacts with the environment and tries to learn policies to optimize the target value. In terms of ATSC issues, each agent controls signals at each intersection independently. The traffic flow data around an intersection is the agent's state. The control schedule made by an agent at some time slot is the agent's action. The state transition is the probability distribution of the state transitioning to the next state under this action. The reward is the total expected waiting time.

MARL can simplify the problem by improving the computational efficiency through distributed agents. However, this method has the following defects: (1) The immediate short-term reward of the agent is not representative due to the delayed consequences; the target optimization object is the total delay time; and the agents that only care about local reward may affect reward during other time period and the surrounding agents, thereby affecting the global optimization target. (2) Since each agent can only observe the surrounding environment, agents cannot make an accurate prediction of reward value. (3) The environment is constantly changing. It is hard to flexibly respond to unexpected situations; while fluctuating flow over time is not considered.

Table 1. Notations in delay estimation model

Notation	Description
$Inflow(i, l, t)$	In flow number of vehicles for agent i in link l at time slot t
$Outflow(i, l, t)$	Out flow number of vehicles for agent i in link l at time slot t
$InR(i, l, t)$	In flow rate of vehicles for agent i in link l at time slot t
$OutR(i, l, t)$	Out flow rate of vehicles for agent i in link l at time slot t
$Qlen(i, l, t_0)$	Current queue length for agent i in link l
$IncR(i, l, t)$	Increase rate of vehicles for agent i in link l at time slot t
$FlowEst(i, l, t)$	Estimated traffic flow for each agent i in link l
$Flucflow(i, l, t)$	Fluctuating flow for each agent i in link l at time slot t
$FlowEstFluc(i, l, t)$	Estimated traffic flow with fluctuation for each agent i in link l at time slot t
$turnL(i, l, t)$	Left turn vehicle number for agent i in link l at time slot t
$turnR(i, l, t)$	Right turn vehicle number for agent i in link l at time slot t
$turnS(i, l, t)$	Straight going vehicle number for agent i in link l at time slot t
$TpL(i, l, t)$	Estimated turn left probability of vehicles for agent i in link l at time slot t
$TpR(i, l, t)$	Estimated turn right probability of vehicles for agent i in link l at time slot t
$TpS(i, l, t)$	Estimated straight going probability of vehicles for agent i in link l at time slot t
$LDest(i, l, t)$	Estimated local delay time for agent i in link l at time slot t
$GDest(i, l, t)$	Estimated global delay time for agent i in link l at time slot t

3.3   Delay Estimation Model

Through analysis of historical traffic flow, we find that the traffic congestion of a few road links has seriously affected the efficiency of entire road network. The effect of coordination control for nearby traffic signals is not obvious. Coordination between agents in a large area can alleviate congestion effectively. By controlling the traffic signal through network-wide coordination, it can change the distribution of traffic flow at busy intersections. Thus changing the flow distribution of the traffic in the network makes it possible to alleviate the congestion situation in the network.

The main idea of our adaptive traffic signal control method is to control traffic signals in the network-wide area in a coordinative way and use a delay estimation model to help agents get an accurate reward function. The model estimates the expected global delay time for each road link with the flow iterative propagation. The global reward function can guide vehicles out of a busy road and make efficient use of each road, and then, it can also reduce traffic of busy road to avoid congestion. By combining it with the fluctuating flow prediction method, we can determine the expected delay time more accurately. These value functions can help agents find the optimal action efficiently.

The delay estimation model needs to estimate the total delay time for a vehicle in each road link from the time it enters the road link until it leaves the entire area. In this method, it first updates the vehicle outflow speed and inflow speed at each road link. Then it calculates the expected delay time of vehicles in corresponding road link, and estimates the probability of vehicles at current link entering the next outgoing links through the moving average method. The global delay time of vehicles in current road link is estimated by iteratively updating the global delay time in the network. Table 1 shows the notations in this section.

Algorithm 1. Traffic Flow Estimate

Input: $Inflow(i, l, t)$, $Outflow(i, l, t)$, $Qlen(i, l, t)$ at current time slot t
Output: $FlowEst(i, l, t)$
1 **for** *each agent i* **do**
2   **for** *each ingoing link l* **do**
3        $InR(i, l, t) \leftarrow \alpha InR(i, l, t - 1) + (1 - \alpha)Inflow(i, l, t)$
4        $OutR(i, l, t) \leftarrow \alpha OutR(i, l, t - 1) + (1 - \alpha)Outflow(i, l, t)$
5        $FlowEst(i, l, t) \leftarrow Qlen(i, l, t) + (InR(i, l, t) - OutR(i, l, t))d$

6 **return** $FlowEst(i, l, t)$

Algorithm 1 estimates the traffic flow in each road link for time slots in the future. Agents need to observe the number of inflow vehicles and outflow vehicles for the links around each intersection, and then update the inflow rate and outflow rate with the moving average of recent data. The future flow of vehicles for each road link is estimated in the end. In the algorithm, α is the moving average update constant of inflow and outflow rate; while d is the delay time of this estimation. The algorithm will be invoked for each decision time slot first.

The actual distribution of vehicle flow has a high correlation with the historical traffic flow distribution. Since the actual traffic flow will be affected by the traffic fluctuations, there will be a difference between the estimated traffic flow and actual traffic flow, which will result in deviation in the estimation of delay time. In order to avoid these deviations, we design a method of traffic flow

---

Algorithm 2. Traffic Flow Estimate Amend

Input: $Histflow(i, l, t)$, $FlowEst(i, l, t)$ at current time slot t
Output: $FlowEstFluc(i, l, t)$
1 **for** *each agent i* **do**
2   **for** *each ingoing link l* **do**
3        $Flucflow(i, l, t) \leftarrow 1/|N_{rec}| \sum_{t \in T_{rec}} Histflow(i, l, t)$
4        $Flucflow(i, l, t) \leftarrow \sum_{t \in T_a} (Flow(i, l, t)/Flucflow(i, l, t))Flucflow(i, l, t)$
5        $FlowEstFluc(i, l, t) \leftarrow \alpha FlowEst(i, l, t) + (1 - \alpha)Flucflow(i, l, t)$

6 **return** $FlowEstFluc(i, l, t)$

---

estimation amend based on the fluctuation of historic traffic flow growth. This method divides the historical data into different classes according to the date feature (e.g., workday and holiday), and amends the estimated link flow data by using the historical data with similar features.

Algorithm 2 amends the traffic flow with historic flow fluctuation. The fluctuating flow is updated with the average similar link flow in similar days first. N_{rec} is the number of similar records; T_{rec} is the record time set. After getting the fluctuating flow volume, we adjust the fluctuating flow to fit the current traffic pressure. T_a is the time set for average fitting. Finally, the average of estimated traffic flow and fluctuating flow is used as the final value of estimated traffic flow. α is the average parameter. This algorithm will be invoked for each decision time slot after the traffic flow estimation.

Algorithm 3 estimates the vehicles' accumulative delay time for each link. Agents need to observe the outflow rate and the number of vehicles turning left, turning left, and going straight forward respectively in the current time slot. Then, efforts will be made to estimate the probabilities of turning left, turning right, and going straight forward based on the moving average of recent data. Agents will estimate the local delay time of vehicles that have entered each road link. Finally, agents in this network will estimate the global delay time through iterative value update until the global delay time converges. The agent will receive the value of global delay time of surrounding outgoing links from the neighboring agents, then update the global delay time by ingoing links around

---

Algorithm 3. Accumulate Delay Time Estimate

Input: $Outflow(i, l, t)$, $turnL(i, l, t)$, $turnR(i, l, t)$, $turnS(i, l, t)$ at current time slot t

Output: $GDest(i, l, t)$

1 **for** *each agent i* **do**
2   **for** *each ingoing link l* **do**
3   /* Update turning probability for outgoing links: */
4   **if** $Outflow(i, l, t) > 0$ **then**
5     $TpL(i, l, t) \leftarrow \alpha TpL(t-1, l) + (1-\alpha)turnL(i, l, t)/Outflow(i, l, t)$
6     $TpR(i, l, t) \leftarrow \alpha TpR(t-1, l) + (1-\alpha)turnR(i, l, t)/Outflow(i, l, t)$
7     $TpS(i, l, t) \leftarrow \alpha TpS(t-1, l) + (1-\alpha)turnS(i, l, t)/Outflow(i, l, t)$
8   /* Update estimated local delay time: */
9    $LDest(i, l, t) \leftarrow FlowEstFluc(i, l, t)/OutR(i, l, t)$

10 /* Update estimated global delay time iteratively until convergence: */
11 **while** $\|\Delta GDest(i, l, t)\| > \epsilon$ **do**
12   **for** *each agent i* **do**
13   **for** *each ingoing link l* **do**
14     $GDest(i, l, t) \leftarrow LDest(i, l, t) + TpL(i, l, t)GDest(i, l_l, t) +$
    $TpR(i, l, t)GDest(i, l_r, t) + TpS(i, l, t)GDest(i, l_s, t)$

15 **return** $GDest(i, l, t)$

---

the agent and send the value to neighboring agents in the end. This algorithm will be invoked for each time slot before agents make decisions. The iterative value update process is similar to solving a linear system of equations iteratively. Since traffic flow only changes slightly during one slot time, the estimated global delay time variables will converge quickly during the iteration.

Through the above method, we can see that agents will estimate the traffic flow and local delay time by ingoing links to corresponding intersection based on local observation. Then, agents will estimate the accumulative delay time through iterative propagation between agents. After obtaining the total delay time for each link of the vehicle until it leaves the entire area, we can use the optimization method to set the control status of each traffic signal in a real-time manner. The optimization method is based on each intersection as an agent. Among the four directions of road at each intersection, three directions (leftward, rightward, and forward) of each road are controlled by the agent of this intersection. The control method is to enumerate all the traffic signal plans that meet the traffic rules of the intersection and calculate the total expected delay time of vehicles in the four routes under the scheme, and the shortest total expected delay time will be selected as the target scheme. Otherwise, we can treat the value of the accumulative delay time as a state value, and train the reinforcement model with other states which the agents can observe. We try to add agents' last action state and neighboring agents' last action state. The model performance will benefit from more information used by us.

In this model, the vehicles' delay time is estimated in a real-time manner. The agents can estimate the global total delay time for each road link under different actions. Agents will choose the action that can minimize the estimated total delay time. This method is very adaptive to traffic congestion. When road congestion occurs, the agent will quickly respond by increasing vehicles' flow out time in the congested link, and try to alleviate congestion. The iteration between agents can quickly propagate the estimated delay time of the congested link to surrounding agents, and the surrounding agents will minimize traffic flow to the congested road link according to estimated delay time and guide traffic flow to other paths. Since this method considers the influence of traffic trends, it can predict the tendency of periodic traffic flow, and control the traffic of road susceptible to congestion ahead of peak period to achieve minimum total delay time during the whole day.

4   Experiment

We evaluate the proposed scheme with traffic flow simulation with real flow data. In the evaluation, we use the traffic flow data in Nanming District of Guiyang City. Figure 3 shows the road map of this area. There are 43 intersections with 155 road links in this area. We set the schedule slot time to 30 s. The control time is from 6 a.m. to 8 p.m. There are 1,680 time slots in a day. Agents will make a control decision in each time slot.

We collect the traffic flow data from sensors deployed in each road links. The average amount of data records is 3.045 million each day. We can get traffic

Fig. 3. Road map of nanming district

Table 2. Average queue length comparison between models

	Avg. queue length @200 flow rate (veh)	Avg. queue length @400 flow rate (veh)	Avg. queue length @600 flow rate (veh)
MARL with local info	12.7	35.7	79.3
MARL with neighbors info	12.1	32.8	72.1
Delay estimation heuristic search	14.4	29.1	52.3
Delay estimation MARL	12.9	25.3	48.9
Delay estimation MARL with flow amend	13.1	23.1	45.8

flow data for each road link in each slot time with these data records. The performance is verified by simulating the distribution of vehicles in the historical traffic environment. Figure 4 shows a historical traffic flow data for one day in this area. From this chart, we can see the traffic pressure is varying over time. Predicting flow trends in advance can help traffic control during the peak periods.

We employ the MARL model with local information and the MARL model with additional neighboring information for the comparison of this experiment. The agents in the MARL model with local information can only get the link's flow data around the corresponding intersection. The agents in the MARL model with additional neighboring information can get both action states of its neighboring agents and the flow information. In the MARL model with local information, there is no coordination between the agents. In the MARL model with additional neighboring information, there is coordination between adjacent agents. Three models are tested in the experiment, and these models all use network-wide coordination for delay time estimation. The first model uses the estimated delay value as the reward function, and selects the optimal control policy heuristically.

Table 3. Average link delay comparison between models

	Avg. link delay @200 flow rate (sec)	Avg. link delay @400 flow rate (sec)	Avg. link delay @600 flow rate (sec)
MARL with local info	36.3	119.1	297.3
MARL with neighbors info	34.5	109.2	270.3
Delay estimation heuristic search	41.1	96.9	195.9
Delay estimation MARL	36.6	84.3	183.3
Delay estimation MARL with flow amend	37.5	76.8	171.9

The second model utilizes MARL with delay time estimation for agents training. The additional states include the local information and the information of neighboring agents. The traffic flow estimation amend is not implemented in this model. The last model uses MARL with delay time estimation, where the traffic flow amend is implemented with the flow fluctuation effect.

The comparison of the average queue length between models is shown in Table 2. The comparison of average link delay of vehicles which have entered this link between models is shown in Table 3. The average link delay represents the average delay time of the vehicles in each road link. We test the models at different flow rates in the road network. When the network traffic flow is at a low level, the difference between these models is not obvious. As the network traffic flow increase the congestion occurred in the road network, the advantage of delay estimation model becomes quite obvious. Compared with the MARL model with neighboring information, the delay estimation of the MARL model with flow amendment can reduce the average link delay time by 36% under high traffic pressure. In the experiment, since the traffic flow in the network is relatively stable, the network iteration between agents requires only a few rounds to converge in the delay estimation model.

We employ the throughput observation at different flow rate. The inflow rate of the network increases from zero to 600 vehicles per minute. Figure 5 shows the result of throughput at different flow rates. The results show that the delay estimation model will increase the network throughput in advance to alleviate congestion. Compared with the MARL model with neighboring information, the delay estimation of MARL model with flow amend can increase throughput by 52% under heavy traffic flow.

In order to demonstrate the performance of the method in controlling traffic congestion, a road link with high traffic pressure is chosen to observe the queue length variation when these models are employed respectively. We start to observe when there is no traffic in the road network. Then, we inject the traffic flow into

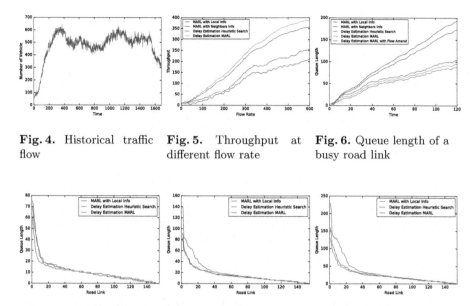

Fig. 4. Historical traffic flow

Fig. 5. Throughput at different flow rate

Fig. 6. Queue length of a busy road link

Fig. 7. Queue length distribution @ 200 flow rate

Fig. 8. Queue length distribution @ 400 flow rate

Fig. 9. Queue length distribution @ 600 flow rate

the network at a rate of 600 vehicles per minute, and observe the change of waiting queue length in 5 models in a busy road link. Figure 6 shows the queue length variation in a busy road link during the rushing hours when these models are employed. We can see that as the traffic pressure increases, our method is very effective for the control of stranded vehicle number. Compared with the MARL model with neighboring information, the delay estimation of MARL model with flow amend can reduce the queen length by 54% in a busy road link.

To reveal the queue length distribution under different flow rates, we intercept the same time slot into the road network of each model. Figures 7, 8 and 9 show the sorted queue length distribution, respectively. From this experiment, we can see our delay estimation model can significantly reduce the queue length in road links with heavy traffic.

5   Conclusion

In this paper, we propose an MARL-based scheme to address the ATSC problem. We design an adaptive traffic signal control method based on th network-wide coordination. By designing a delay estimation model with network-wide coordination, our scheme offers an accurate reward function for each agent's decision making. This reward function takes all agents' reward and feature delayed consequences into consideration, and uses the overall reward to determine the actions of agents to the maximum extent to guarantee the global reward optimization.

In addition, we adopt a forward-looking traffic flow amend measure to ensure the accuracy of delay prediction. With this model, we can enable agents to find a near optimal action model to address the ATSC problem. Experimental results with large-scale real data show the advantages of our design, especially under heavy traffic pressure. The result shows that our scheme can effectively alleviate the traffic congestion, improve the road network throughput, and significantly reduce the vehicle delay time. The results also show that our scheme can be realized conveniently by self-organizing network and extended easily with guaranteed efficiency.

Acknowledgements. This research is supported in part by the National Key Research and Development Program of China under grant No. 2016QY02D0202, NSFC under grants Nos. 61370233, 61422202, Foundation for the Author of National Excellent Doctoral Dissertation of PR China under grant No. 201345, and Research Fund of Guangdong Province under grant No. 2015B010131001.

References

1. Chen, J., Yuan, Q., Du, R., Wu, J.: Mucar: A greedy multi-flow-based coding-aware routing in wireless networks. In: Proceedings of the 12th Annual IEEE International Conference on Sensing, Communication, and Networking (SECON), Seattle, USA, 22–25 June, pp. 310–318 (2015)
2. Yin, B., Dridi, M., El Moudni, A.: Traffic control model and algorithm based on decomposition of mdp. In: Proceedings of the 2014 International Conference on Control, Decision and Information Technologies (CoDIT), Metz, France, 3–5 November, pp. 78–89. IEEE (2014)
3. Yin, B., Dridi, M., El Moudni, A.: Markov decision process for traffic control at an isolated intersection. In: Proceedings of the 2013 IEEE 25th International Conference on Tools with Artificial Intelligence (ICTAI), Washington DC, USA, 4–6 November, pp. 789–794. IEEE (2013)
4. Li, T., Zhao, D., Yi, J.: Adaptive dynamic programming for multi-intersections traffic signal intelligent control. In: Proceedings of the 2008 11th International IEEE Conference on Intelligent Transportation Systems (ITSC), Beijing, China, 12–15 October. pp. 286–291. IEEE (2008)
5. Cai, C., Wong, C.K., Heydecker, B.G.: Adaptive traffic signal control using approximate dynamic programming. Transport. Res. Part C: Emerg. Technol. **17**(5), 456–474 (2009)
6. Yin, B., Dridi, M., El Moudni, A.: Adaptive traffic signal control for multi-intersection based on microscopic model. In: Proceedings of the 2015 IEEE 27th International Conference on Tools with Artificial Intelligence (ICTAI), Vietri sul Mare, Italy, 9–11 November, pp. 49–55. IEEE (2015)
7. Yin, B., Dridi, M., El Moudni, A.: Approximate dynamic programming with recursive least-squares temporal difference learning for adaptive traffic signal control. In: Proceedings of the 2015 54th IEEE Conference on Decision and Control (CDC), Osaka, Japan, 15–18 December, pp. 3463–3468. IEEE (2015)
8. Vallati, M., Magazzeni, D., De Schutter, B., Chrpa, L., McCluskey, T.L.: Efficient macroscopic urban traffic models for reducing congestion: a pddl+ planning approach. In: Proceedings of the 2016 30th Conference on Artificial Intelligence (AAAI), Phoenix, Arizona USA, 12–17 February, pp. 3188–3194. AAAI (2016)

9. Kwatirayo, S., Almhana, J., Liu, Z., Siblini, J.: Optimizing road intersection traffic flow using stochastic and heuristic algorithms. In: Proceedings of the 2014 IEEE International Conference on Communications (ICC), Sydney, Australia, 10–14 June, pp. 586–591. IEEE (2014)
10. Renfrew, D., Yu, X.H.: Traffic signal optimization using ant colony algorithm. In: Proceedings of the 2012 International Joint Conference on Neural Networks (IJCNN), Brisbane, Australia, 10–15 June, pp. 1–7. IEEE (2012)
11. De Oliveira, M.B., Neto, A.D.A.: Optimization of traffic lights timing based on multiple neural networks. In: Proceedings of the 2013 IEEE 25th International Conference on Tools with Artificial Intelligence (ICTAI), Washington DC, USA, 4–6 November, pp. 825–832. IEEE (2013)
12. Ezugwu, A.E., Frîncu, M., Adewumi, A.O., Buhari, S.M., Junaidu, S.B.: Neural network-based multi-agent approach for scheduling in distributed systems. Concurr. Comput. Prac. Exper. **29**(1), e3887 (2017)
13. Cai, Y., Ji, R., Li, S.: Dynamic programming based optimized product quantization for approximate nearest neighbor search. Neurocomputing **217**, 110–118 (2016)
14. Mannion, P., Duggan, J., Howley, E.: An experimental review of reinforcement learning algorithms for adaptive traffic signal control. In: McCluskey, T.L., Kotsialos, A., Müller, J.P., Klügl, F., Rana, O., Schumann, R. (eds.) Autonomic Road Transport Support Systems. AS, pp. 47–66. Springer, Cham (2016). doi:10.1007/978-3-319-25808-9_4
15. Bazzan, A.L.C.: Opportunities for multiagent systems and multiagent reinforcement learning in traffic control. Auton. Agents Multi-Agent Syst. **18**(3), 342–375 (2009)
16. Xu, L.H., Xia, X.H., Luo, Q.: The study of reinforcement learning for traffic self-adaptive control under multiagent markov game environment. Math. Prob. Eng. **2013**, 10p (2013). Article ID 962869
17. Wiering, M.: Multi-agent reinforcement learning for traffic light control. In: Proceedings of the 17th International Conference on Machine Learning (ICML), Stanford, USA, 29 June–2 July, JMLR.org, pp. 1151–1158 (2000)
18. Arel, I., Liu, C., Urbanik, T., Kohls, A.G.: Reinforcement learning-based multi-agent system for network traffic signal control. IET Intell. Transp. Syst. **4**(2), 128–135 (2010)
19. Kuyer, L., Whiteson, S., Bakker, B., Vlassis, N.: Multiagent reinforcement learning for urban traffic control using coordination graphs. In: Daelemans, W., Goethals, B., Morik, K. (eds.) ECML PKDD 2008. LNCS, vol. 5211, pp. 656–671. Springer, Heidelberg (2008). doi:10.1007/978-3-540-87479-9_61
20. Prashanth, L.A., Bhatnagar, S.: Reinforcement learning with average cost for adaptive control of traffic lights at intersections. In: Proceedings of the 2011 14th International IEEE Conference on Intelligent Transportation Systems (ITSC), Washington, DC, USA, 5–7 October, pp. 1640–1645. IEEE (2011)
21. El-Tantawy, S., Abdulhai, B., Abdelgawad, H.: Multiagent reinforcement learning for integrated network of adaptive traffic signal controllers (marlin-atsc): methodology and large-scale application on downtown toronto. IEEE Trans. Intell. Transp. Syst. **14**(3), 1140–1150 (2013)
22. Xie, X.F., Smith, S.F., Barlow, G.J.: Schedule-driven coordination for real-time traffic network control. In: Proceedings of the International Conference on Automated Planning and Scheduling (ICAPS), Atibaia, Brazil, 25–19 June. AAAI (2012)

23. Smith, S.F., Barlow, G.J., Xie, X.F., Rubinstein, Z.B.: Smart urban signal networks: Initial application of the surtrac adaptive traffic signal control system. In: Proceedings of the International Conference on Automated Planning and Scheduling (ICAPS), Rome, Italy, 10–14 June. AAAI (2013)
24. Jia, S.Y., Wang, G.H., Zhang, Y., Zhang, L.: Resolution and parameters estimations for multiple maneuvering targets. Sci. Chin. Inf. Sci. **57**(8), 1–13 (2014)
25. Tong, S., Li, Y.: Robust adaptive fuzzy backstepping output feedback tracking control for nonlinear system with dynamic uncertainties. Sci. Chin. Inf. Sci. **53**(2), 307–324 (2010)

Parallel and Distributed Algorithms

A Novel Parallel Dual-Character String Matching Algorithm on Graphical Processing Units

Chung-Yu Liao and Cheng-Hung Lin[✉]

Deptartment of Electrical Engineering, National Taiwan Normal University,
162, Section 1, Heping E. Rd., Taipei city 106, Taiwan
cbsghost@gmail.com, brucelin@ntnu.edu.tw

Abstract. Aho-Corasick algorithm has been widely used in network intrusion detection system to inspect network packets against thousands of attack patterns. To improve the performance of network intrusion detection systems, many variations of Aho-Corasick algorithm are proposed to accelerate multiple string matching on GPUs or dedicated hardware. One of the proposed variations is to increase the number of characters that are processed per cycle. However, increasing the number of characters processed per cycle will encounter two major problems. The first problem is the input alignment problem while the second problem is the large increase of memory required for storing the state transition table. The two problems cause the multi-character approach become less feasible. In this paper, we propose a novel parallel dual-character string matching algorithm on graphical processing units. In order to solve the two major problems, the proposed algorithm presents a new state machine to solve the input alignment problem, and compresses the state transition table using perfect hashing to solve the memory explosion problem. The experimental results show that the proposed algorithm is superior to the state-of-the-art approaches in terms of performance and memory requirements.

Keywords: Aho-Corasick algorithm · Multiple string matching · Graphical processing units · Perfect hashing

1 Introduction

Aho-Corasick algorithm has been widely used in network intrusion detection system to inspect network packets against thousands of attack patterns. To improve the performance of network intrusion detection systems, many hardware and software variations of Aho-Corasick algorithm are proposed to accelerate multiple string matching on GPUs or dedicated hardware. Among the proposed approaches, a specific class of multi-character approaches [1,3,5,6,8–12,19] are proposed to improve performance by increasing the number of characters processed in a cycle. However, the multi-character approach encounters two major problems. The first problem is called input alignment problem while

© Springer International Publishing AG 2017
S. Ibrahim et al. (Eds.): ICA3PP 2017, LNCS 10393, pp. 197–210, 2017.
DOI: 10.1007/978-3-319-65482-9_13

the second problem is the large increase in the width of the state transition table which causes memory explosion. These two problems make the multi-character approach become less feasible. The input alignment problem indicates that when a pattern does not appear in even positions, it will be missed. Consider to match the three patterns, "hey", "ho", and "error", Fig. 1 shows the trie built by Aho-Corasick algorithm. In order to process two characters in a cycle, we can simply merge two adjacent transitions to form a new state machine as shown in Fig. 2 where "?" denotes any character. And then, we can traverse the new state machine by reading two characters at a time. Given an input string "xheyho", the dual-character sequences of "xh", "ey", and "ho" are read to traverse the new state machine. We find that only the pattern "ho" is found and the pattern "hey" is missed because "hey" is divided into two blocks. The problem is so-called "input alignment problem." To solve the input alignment problem, we can read two more characters from odd positions. Consider the same input string, the dual-character sequences from the second position is "he", "yh", "o?", and then the pattern "hey" can be found. However, reading two characters from odd positions will encounter another problem which is so-called data structure alignment [18]. Data structure alignment is the way data is arranged and accessed in computer memory. Modern computers access a memory address in fixed sized chunks (e.g. one byte, two bytes, four bytes, or larger). Reading an input string from an odd address violates data structure alignment, which generates an alignment fault and degrades system performance.

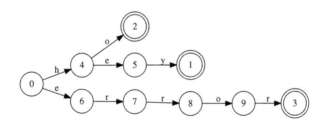

Fig. 1. A single-character finite state machine

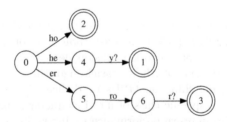

Fig. 2. A dual-character finite state machine

On the other hand, the memory required to store the state transition table for multi-character approaches will be significantly increased. The state transition table of a single-character method contains 256 columns for storing the next status information for each ASCII alphabet. Instead, the state transition table of a dual-character approach will need 65,536 columns for storing the next state information for each pair of ASCII alphabets. In contrast, the state transition table of a four-character approach will need 4,294,967,296 (4G) columns to store the next state information for each group of four ASCII alphabets. The memory explosion makes four-character approaches become not feasible and impractical. In the middle of a single character and a four-character method, a dual-character method becomes more feasible for implementation.

In this paper, we propose a novel parallel dual-character string matching algorithm on graphical processing units. The proposed algorithm presents a new state machine to solve the input alignment problem, and compresses the state transition table using perfect hashing to solve the memory explosion problem. The experimental results show that the proposed algorithm is superior to the state-of-the-art approaches in terms of performance and memory requirements.

2   Related Works

In this section, we first review the traditional Aho-Corasick algorithm, which is a well-known algorithm for parallel matching multiple patterns. And then, we will review the Parallel Failureless Aho-Corasick (PFAC) algorithm, a highly parallel extension of the Aho-Corasick algorithm. Finally, we will introduce a perfect hashing algorithm which is suitable for compressing a state transition table.

2.1   Review of Aho-Corasick Algorithm

The Aho-Corasick algorithm [2] has been widely used to match multiple patterns. The Aho-Corasick algorithm compiles multiple string patterns into a single state machine. By traversing the state machine, the Aho-Corasick algorithm can search multiple string patterns in parallel. For example, Fig. 3 shows an Aho-Corasick state machine for matching "hey", "ho", and "error" patterns. In Fig. 3, the solid lines indicate valid transitions, and the dashed lines indicate failure transitions. The circle nodes indicate internal states, and the double circle nodes indicate final states. In each state, the Aho-Corasick algorithm will check whether there is a valid transition for an input character. If so, it will switch to the next state pointed by the valid transition. Otherwise, it will switch to the next state pointed by a failure transition and check again whether the input character has a valid transition. Whenever a final state is reached, a string pattern is matched. In Fig. 3, states 1, 2, and 3 are the final states of the patterns "hey", "ho", and "error".

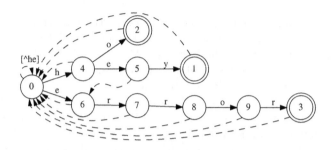

Fig. 3. Traditional Aho-Corasick state machine with failure transitions

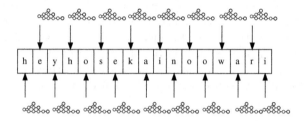

Fig. 4. The parallelization of PFAC

2.2   Review of Parallel Failureless Aho-Corasick Algorithm

The Parallel Failureless Aho-Corasick (PFAC) algorithm [14], the highly parallel extension of the Aho-Corasick algorithm provides high performance for string matching on SIMD platforms, especially on GPUs. Figure 4 shows the parallelization of the PFAC algorithm which allocates each position a thread to traverse a specific PFAC state machine. The PFAC state machine removes all failure transitions as well as the loop-back transitions in the initial state. In other words, a PFAC thread only concerns whether any pattern is matched from its starting address. As long as there is no valid transition for an input character, the thread will terminate immediately. A pattern ID will be recorded if its final state is reached. In Fig. 4, all threads terminate quickly except the 1st and 4th thread, which match the pattern "hey" and "ho", respectively.

2.3   Review of Perfect Hashing Algorithm

Reducing the size of a state transition table has always been a critical issue [4,13]. The original state transition table is a 2-dimensional sparse array. Compression can reduce the memory requirements for storing a state transition table and improve the hit rate of hardware cache, but increase the complexity of looking up state transitions. A perfect hashing algorithm [13] is adopted to compress a sparse state transition table with less overhead when retrieving the next state information of a state transition. The perfect hashing algorithm starts with a 2-dimensional table. Figure 5(a) shows an example where nine keys are first

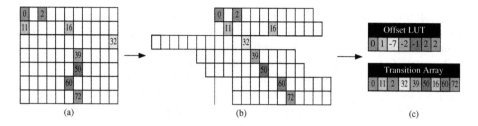

Fig. 5. Transition table compression using perfect hashing

placed in a 2-dimensional table in order. In Fig. 5(a), different colors are used to distinguish the keys on different rows. In the second step, each row is prioritized by the number of keys that are owned. In the third step, depending on the precedence of rows, each row moves left and right until no two keys are located in the same column, as shown in Fig. 5(b). The offset of each row is recorded in a table called Offset LUT. Finally, the 2-dimensional table is compressed into a one-dimensional hash table called Transition Array, as shown in Fig. 5(c). Compared with the original 2-dimensional table which has 77 elements (7 rows and 11 columns), the compressed hash table has only one row of 9 elements, 88% of memory is reduced.

There are only four steps to query whether an input key exists in this hash table. The first step is to get the row and column where the key exists in the original 2-dimensional table. The second step is to get the row offset of the key by looking up the Offset LUT. The third step is to calculate the position of the key in the one-dimensional hash table. Finally, the input key is compared with the key stored in the hash table. If they are the same, the input key is a valid key. Otherwise, the input key is not the real key. In our application, a key represents a valid transition.

3 Parallel Dual-Character String Matching Algorithm

In this section, we propose a dual-character string matching algorithm to improve the throughput of string matching. The dual-character state machine, matching kernel, and trie compression are described as follows.

3.1 Dual-Character State Machine

We start our idea by modifying the PFAC algorithm to process two characters in a cycle. We choose to deal with two characters in a cycle because the growth of a dual-character state transition table is within a reasonable range. As we have mentioned, a dual-character state transition table need 65,536 columns to store the next state information for each pair of ASCII alphabets. In other words, each state needs 256K (65536 * 4) bytes to store next state information. On the other hand, processing four characters in a cycle will need 4,294,967,296

(4G) columns to store the next state information for each group of four ASCII alphabets. The storage of the state transition table causes the processing of four or more characters to become infeasible and impractical.

Instead of storing state transition table on commodity memory, many hardware approaches such as FPGA, ASIC and TCAM [1,3,5,6,8–10,12,19] are proposed to lookup state transition. In so far as the authors are aware, this paper proposes the first software-based algorithm for processing two characters in a cycle on GPUs and using perfect hashing to compress state transition table. Figure 2 begins the basic idea of the proposed dual-character string matching algorithm [11]. If two consecutive input characters match the two characters on a transition, the state machine moves to the next state pointed by the transition, otherwise it moves to the trap state and terminates the processing of the thread.

A major problem with the dual-character algorithm is the input alignment problem. As shown in Fig. 6, the pattern "ho" appears in an odd position marked with red. Reading two characters every time by striding two characters will miss this pattern. To solve the input alignment problem, a simple solution is to read two characters every time by striding one character. However, as we have mentioned before, striding one character will encounter data structure alignment problem. Data structure alignment problem indicates that unaligned memory accesses will degrade system performance because the hardware has to read two consecutive blocks of memory and mask out irrelevant bytes. [10] proposes a variable-stride multi-pattern matching algorithm. However, variable-stride sizes can cause memory accesses to not satisfy the principle of data structure alignment and significantly degrade the performance of memory accesses. For modern single instruction multiple data (SIMD) computer systems, fixed-stride sizes would be more appropriate than variable-stride sizes for multi-character string matching approaches.

To solve the input alignment problem and satisfy the principle of data structure alignment, our idea is that if we can deal with the input alignment problem at the initial state, we can further process by reading two characters and then striding two characters without unaligned data accesses. In other words, we can solve the problem by separating the transitions of initial state into two routes. As shown in Fig. 7, we create another route to final states by introducing a new transition in the initial state. The new transition contains a meta-character "?" in the beginning which denotes any character. In other words, we insert a "don't care" character in front of a pattern so that we can find the pattern that occurs in the odd position. In addition, the dual-character algorithm has to deal with the string patterns whose length is not a multiple of 2. For the patterns of odd

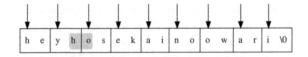

Fig. 6. The pattern "ho" in the odd position will be missed

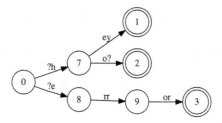

Fig. 7. Insert a "don't care" character in front of a pattern

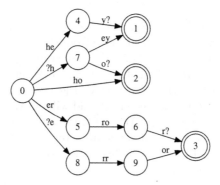

Fig. 8. The combined dual-character finite state machine

length, we also insert a "don't care" character in the end of the pattern. Finally, the two state machines in Figs. 2 and 7 can be merged together to form a new state machine. As shown in Fig. 8, each pattern has two different routes to its final state. Using the new state machine, the memory accesses are always aligned to the addresses of multiple of 2. We would like to mention that compared with the one-character state machine, the cost of the dual-character state machine is very low. In this example, the total number of transitions increases slightly, while the number of states remains the same.

Figure 9 shows the parallelization of the proposed dual-character string matching algorithm which allocates every two characters a thread to traverse the dual-character state machine. Each thread processes two characters in a cycle and then strides two characters. In the initial state, every thread traverses the dual-character state machine via two paths by the two-character sequence from its starting position. Because each thread traverses two paths of the dual-character trie, we can find patterns occurring at any position. Moreover, since each thread is only responsible for matching patterns from its starting position and next position, the thread terminates when no valid transition exists. When a final state is reached, the state value (pattern ID) is recorded and the thread terminates. For example in Fig. 9, the first thread processes the two-character sequence, "he, yh, os, ...". In the initial state, the first thread will activate state

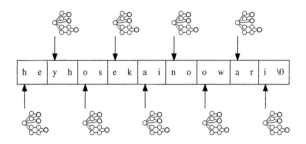

Fig. 9. The parallelization of DCSM

4 and state 8 because the dual-character "he" matches "he" and "?e", respectively. And then, the first thread will move from state 4 to state 1 because the next dual-character "yh" matches "y?". Because state 1 is the final state of the pattern "hey", the first thread finds the pattern "hey" at the first position. On the other hand, the second thread processes the two-character sequence, "yh, os, ek...". In the initial state, the second thread will activate state 7 because the dual-character "yh" matches "?h". And then, the second thread will move from state 7 to state 2 because the next dual-character "os" matches "o?". Because state 2 is the final state of the pattern "ho", the second thread finds the pattern "ho" at the third position.

3.2   Trie Compression

Traditionally, the state transition table of the dual-character transition trie is stored in a two-dimensional array where each row represents a state and each column represents a pair of characters in a transition. In other words, each row requires $65{,}536$ (256^2) columns to store the next state information, which results in a huge memory requirement. Because the state transition table of the dual-character transition trie is very sparse, we propose to use perfect hashing to compress the state transition table into a one-dimensional table. Experimental results show that perfect hashing significantly reduces the size of the state transition table, small enough to fit into the cache of processing units. When the size of the compressed state transition table is small enough to fit into cached memory, the performance is significantly improved.

4   Experimental Results

In this section, the proposed dual-character string matching (DCSM) algorithm is compared with the parallel AC and PFAC. Experiments are conducted on an Intel-based workstation. We evaluate the proposed DCSM, parallel AC, and PFAC algorithms on various devices, including an Intel Xeon E5-1620 CPU (4 cores operating at 3.60 GHz, with 2 hardware threads each core), an Intel Xeon Phi 3120P MIC device (56 cores operating at 1.10 GHz, with 4 hardware threads

Table 1. Comparison of existing algorithms with our proposed method

	Parallel AC	PFAC	DCSM
Time complexity	$O(N + ms)$	$O(mN)$	$O(mN/2)$
Space complexity	$O(256 * S)$	$O(256 * S)$	$O(256^2 * S)$
Load imbalance	Low	High	High
Performance variation	Low	High	Median

each core), and an NVIDIA GeForce GTX Titan X GPU (Maxwell GM200, 24 stream processors operating at 1.08 GHz). A variety of SIMD methods are adopted to accelerate the algorithms written by OpenMP [17], OpenCL [16], and CUDA [15]. The Clang-3.8 [7] and CUDA-8.0's NVCC are used for compilation.

Table 1 shows the differences in parallel AC, PFAC, and the proposed dual-character string matching (DCSM) algorithm for time complexity, space complexity, load imbalance, and performance variation. In Table 1, N represents the length of the input string, m represents the longest pattern length, S represents the number of states, and s represents the number of segments. Compared to the PFAC algorithm, the proposed DCSM has 50% of time complexity. Before using perfect hashing to compress state transition table, the proposed algorithm has more space complexity than other algorithms.

In order to evaluate the performance and the effect of load imbalance, we generate different kind of input stings and patterns. The input string file is a 256 MB text file with duplicated text. The pattern file contains only one pattern with different amount of "b". For example, given an input string "AbAbAbAb..." and a pattern "b", each thread will find the pattern "b", so the average match length per thread is 1. On the other hand, given an input string "AbbAbbAbbAbb..." and a pattern "bb", each thread will find the pattern "bb", so the average match length per thread is 2.

Table 2 shows the throughput of the five string matching algorithms performed on Intel Xeon E5-1620 CPU. The AC and PFAC are performed using single thread while AC-OMP, PFAC-OMP, and DCSM-OCL are performed using multiple threads on a multi-core CPU. The first column shows the average matched string length. Each data is the average of 32 experiments performed.

Figure 10 shows the throughput of each algorithm in terms of average matched string length. The proposed DCSM algorithm is superior to the traditional AC algorithm, but worse than the PFAC algorithm. The possible reason is that the cache hardware is more suitable for the PFAC algorithm than our proposed algorithm.

Table 3 shows the throughput of string matching algorithms running on dedicated SIMD hardware. In order to reduce the memory access time, it is best to put patterns into shared memory of GPUs. We find that manually cache string patterns into shared memory will lead to additional time consuming. The automatic global cache function works relatively well. Moreover, the new Opt-In L1 cache method introduced in compute capability 5.2 of NVIDIA's GPUs cache

Table 2. Thoughput of string matching algorithms on CPU (Gbps)

Len	AC	PFAC	AC-OMP	PFAC-OMP	DCSM-OCL
0	3.003265	6.461977	3.109569	17.599781	6.241063
1	1.944218	4.121960	2.098434	7.629187	7.430604
2	1.747764	3.384988	1.912033	7.619888	4.888151
3	1.596871	2.835836	1.718806	7.628115	4.196878
4	1.467276	2.389326	1.523695	7.316531	3.896687
5	1.369525	1.973989	1.359593	6.544737	3.379701
6	1.271533	1.685289	1.222860	5.862118	3.281834
7	1.183336	1.290091	1.109950	5.306875	2.874439
8	1.119125	1.276692	1.012377	4.829496	2.826690
9	1.052028	1.129413	0.931223	4.308836	2.494296
10	0.991375	1.012270	0.862948	4.013759	2.427218
11	0.940956	0.905610	0.802917	3.742073	2.185619
12	0.889874	0.829753	0.750737	3.520241	2.147560
13	0.847851	0.758642	0.665933	3.339794	1.945141
14	0.806011	0.698257	0.633191	3.165751	1.880892
15	0.766781	0.644466	0.597062	2.892655	1.723106
16	0.730333	0.598859	0.568756	2.575769	1.649733
17	0.696826	0.557244	0.514232	2.475240	1.524064
18	0.664104	0.522199	0.497940	2.378750	1.498077
19	0.588959	0.489555	0.460690	2.235594	1.391194
20	0.560490	0.458940	0.444000	2.067800	1.364938
21	0.536560	0.426624	0.429269	1.987974	1.275266
22	0.484535	0.403728	0.400936	1.842082	1.240864
23	0.453467	0.380238	0.390517	1.799058	1.162725
24	0.418239	0.361198	0.376786	1.763723	1.164886
25	0.414786	0.344072	0.345002	1.706004	1.083368
26	0.384740	0.327696	0.353840	1.653063	1.084081
27	0.364139	0.316330	0.329335	1.608079	1.015276
28	0.343706	0.293329	0.311075	1.555089	1.015196
29	0.330598	0.278171	0.297853	1.507681	0.961770
30	0.320936	0.264541	0.285636	1.454268	0.960174
31	0.309753	0.253609	0.262843	1.401605	0.911594

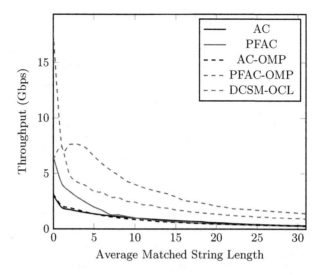

Fig. 10. Throughput of string matching algorithms on CPU (Gbps)

Table 3. Thoughput of string matching algorithms on CPU (Gbps)

Len	(MIC)DCSM-OCL	(GPU)PFAC-CUDA	(GPU)DCSM-CUDA
0	21.441349	628.870897	319.769612
1	27.029806	461.863151	340.382600
2	12.599209	280.428175	214.278467
3	12.954708	207.998002	188.814390
4	8.477064	164.863106	158.220112
5	8.601811	137.101213	144.809349
6	6.669896	118.474421	127.003311
7	6.827178	103.901415	118.563154
8	5.488810	92.104392	106.338814
9	5.542212	82.715548	100.244526
10	4.680273	75.271303	91.624524
11	4.710292	69.047148	86.720623
12	4.078782	63.640013	80.195513
13	4.098180	58.958746	76.820802
14	3.605530	55.032578	71.649087
15	3.645438	51.528281	68.924011
16	3.249860	48.347110	64.861113
17	3.250740	45.716155	62.816724

(*continued*)

Table 3. (*continued*)

Len	(MIC)DCSM-OCL	(GPU)PFAC-CUDA	(GPU)DCSM-CUDA
18	2.965682	43.381114	59.370970
19	2.948099	41.211043	57.654006
20	2.725243	39.231509	54.639669
21	2.694917	37.266576	53.142429
22	2.515006	35.660377	50.581263
23	2.485380	34.137180	49.345691
24	2.335990	32.768088	47.079678
25	2.300857	31.493322	45.966321
26	2.179472	30.319198	44.039056
27	2.146681	29.256904	43.078256
28	2.040959	28.337732	41.405870
29	2.011340	27.226866	40.540811
30	1.922978	26.320876	38.961908
31	1.891966	25.488163	38.263773

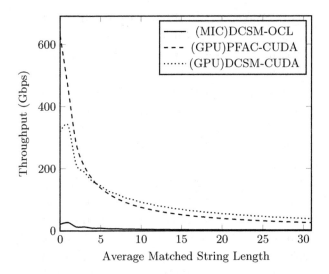

Fig. 11. Throughput of string matching algorithms on accelerators (Gbps)

the global memory of patterns to the L1 cache, the same area as the texture memory. Each data in this table is the average of 256 experiments performed.

Figure 11 shows the throughput of each algorithm performed on dedicated SIMD hardware including MIC and GPU. When the average matched string length is greater than 5, the proposed DCSM algorithm is superior to PFAC.

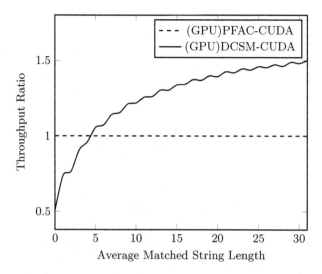

Fig. 12. Performance comparison with PFAC

Figure 12 shows the improvement rate of our proposed algorithm relative to the PFAC algorithm on GPUs. Our proposed algorithm is about 50% more efficient than the PFAC algorithm when the average matched length is 31.

5   Conclusion

In this paper, we have proposed a novel parallel dual-character string matching algorithm to accelerate exact string matching on GPUs. We also have discussed several optimization techniques for the proposed algorithm performed on variable SIMD devices, including CPU, MIC, and GPU. The experimental results show that the proposed algorithm is superior to the state-of-the-art PFAC algorithm on GPUs.

References

1. AbuHmed, T., Mohaisen, A., Nyang, D.: A survey on deep packet inspection for intrusion detection systems. CoRR abs/0803.0037 (2008)
2. Aho, A.V., Corasick, M.J.: Efficient string matching: An aid to bibliographic search. Commun. ACM **18**(6), 333–340 (1975)
3. Alicherry, M., Muthuprasanna, M., Kumar, V.: High speed pattern matching for network ids/ips. In: Proceedings of the 2006 IEEE International Conference on Network Protocols, pp. 187–196 (2006)
4. Bremler-Barr, A., Hay, D., Koral, Y.: CompactDFA: Generic state machine compression for scalable pattern matching. In: 2010 Proceedings of IEEE INFOCOM, pp. 1–9 (2010)

5. Chang, Y.K., Chang, C.R., Su, C.C.: The cost effective pre-processing based nfa pattern matching architecture for nids. In: 2010 24th IEEE International Conference on Advanced Information Networking and Applications, pp. 385–391 (2010)
6. Chen, C.C., Wang, S.D.: An efficient multicharacter transition string-matching engine based on the aho-corasick algorithm. ACM Trans. Archit. Code Optim. **10**(4), 25:1–25:2 (2013)
7. Clang: A C language family frontend for LLVM. https://clang.llvm.org/ (April 2017)
8. Dharmapurikar, S., Lockwood, J.W.: Fast and scalable pattern matching for network intrusion detection systems. IEEE J. Select. Areas Commun. **24**(10), 1781–1792 (2006)
9. Dharmapurikar, S., Lockwood, J.: Fast and scalable pattern matching for content filtering. In: Proceedings of the 2005 ACM Symposium on Architecture for Networking and Communications Systems ANCS 2005, NY, USA. pp. 183–192. ACM, New York (2005)
10. Hua, N., Song, H., Lakshman, T.V.: Variable-stride multi-pattern matching for scalable deep packet inspection. IEEE INFOCOM **2009**, 415–423 (2009)
11. Jiang, W., Yang, Y.H.E., Prasanna, V.K.: Scalable multi-pipeline architecture for high performance multi-pattern string matching. In: 2010 IEEE International Symposium on Parallel Distributed Processing (IPDPS), pp. 1–12 (2010)
12. Kim, J., i. Choi, S.: High speed pattern matching for deep packet inspection. In: 2009 9th International Symposium on Communications and Information Technology, pp. 1310–1315 (2009)
13. Lin, C.H., Li, J.C., Liu, C.H., Chang, S.C.: Perfect hashing based parallel algorithms for multiple string matching on graphic processing units. IEEE Trans. Parallel Distrib. Syst. **99**, 1 (2017)
14. Lin, C.H., Liu, C.H., Chien, L.S., Chang, S.C.: Accelerating pattern matching using a novel parallel algorithm on gpus. IEEE Trans. Comput. **62**(10), 1906–1916 (2013)
15. NVIDIA: CUDA Zone (2016). https://developer.nvidia.com/cuda-zone
16. OpenCL - The open standard for parallel programming of heterogeneous systems (2017). https://www.khronos.org/opencl/
17. The OpenMP API specification for parallel programming (2016). http://www.openmp.org/
18. Wikipedia: Data structure alignment (2017). https://en.wikipedia.org/wiki/Data_structure_alignment
19. Yamagaki, N., Sidhu, R., Kamiya, S.: High-speed regular expression matching engine using multi-character nfa. In: 2008 International Conference on Field Programmable Logic and Applications, pp. 131–136 (2008)

Distributed Nonnegative Matrix Factorization with HALS Algorithm on MapReduce

Rafał Zdunek$^{(\boxtimes)}$ and Krzysztof Fonal

Department of Electronics, Wroclaw University of Science and Technology,
Wybrzeze Wyspianskiego 27, 50-370 Wroclaw, Poland
rafal.zdunek@pwr.edu.pl, krzysiekfonal@gmail.com

Abstract. Nonnegative Matrix Factorization (NMF) is a commonly used method in machine learning and data analysis for feature extraction and dimensionality reduction of nonnegative data. Recently, we observe its increasing popularity in processing massive data, and advances in developing various distributed algorithms for NMF. In the paper, we propose a computational strategy for implementation of the Hierarchical Alternating Least Squares (HALS) algorithm using the MapReduce programming paradigm. Due to this approach, the scalable HALS NMF, which can be implemented on parallel and distributed computer architectures, is obtained. The scalability and efficiency of the proposed algorithm is confirmed in the numerical experiments, performed on large-scale synthetic and recommendation system datasets.

Keywords: Distributed nonnegative matrix factorization · Large-scale NMF · HALS algorithm · Mapreduce paradigm · Recommendation systems

1 Introduction

Nonnegative Matrix Factorization (NMF) [1] is an unsupervised method for extracting a latent structure from an input matrix that contains only nonnegative entries. The basic model of NMF assumes an approximate decomposition of an input nonnegative matrix into lower-rank nonnegative factors. Lee and Seung [2] considerably popularized NMF by proposing simple multiplicative algorithms for updating the factors. Since then, thousands of research papers on NMF and its applications have been published. Nowadays, many computational strategies exist for updating the factors in various NMF models.

Most of the existing algorithms are intended for a single node implementation, assuming that the whole data matrix is uploaded to the RAM memory. However, in the era of big data, this assumption cannot be often satisfied, which motivates the need for developing distributed versions of computational algorithms. Recently, many research papers have reported a potential of NMF for processing massive data, especially a large volume data. It mostly results from flexibility of many NMF algorithms for partitioning computational problems and processing block-wise updates using the MapReduce programming paradigm.

© Springer International Publishing AG 2017
S. Ibrahim et al. (Eds.): ICA3PP 2017, LNCS 10393, pp. 211–222, 2017.
DOI: 10.1007/978-3-319-65482-9_14

MapReduce is a programming model for applications that aim to perform distributed and parallel processing of large datasets on commodity hardware units. It consists of two procedures: Map and Reduce. The former is invoked on the input data to break down it into so-called tuples (key/value pairs). Then, the shuffle step redistributes the output data from the mapping function according to their output keys. The data with the same output key is usually processed by the same node (server). The latter combines the data tuples from the nodes into a smaller set of tuples, and finally writes the output, usually to the Hadoop Distributed File System (HDFS). Due to the distributed and parallel nature of the MapReduce model, many numerical algorithms can be implemented very efficiently.

Many attempts have been made to implement NMF algorithms on distributed computer architectures. Liu *et al.* [3] faced up the scalability problem of multiplicative algorithms for NMF. They analyzed how to partition the data and arrange the computation using the MapReduce paradigm to factorize very large matrices that contain more than 4 billion nonzero entries. Unfortunately, multiplicative algorithms suffer from terrible slow convergence. Hence, there is a need to develop other distributed NMF algorithms which are more faster. The MapReduce paradigm has been also used in the work [4] to scale up convex NMF [5]. This model of NMF is very useful for solving clustering problems, and the proposed algorithm was able to factorize matrices with 600 million nonzero entries. However, this work should be also regarded as an extension of multiplicative algorithms, which is not profitable due to convergence reasons. Another approach to distributed NMF is presented by Yin *et al.* in the paper [6], where the input matrix is split into blocks that are used for updating the corresponding blocks of the latent factors. The partitioning is performed by the mapping procedure and the reduction step unifies the partial results. The block-wise updates can be applied to any decomposable objective function but the discussed algorithms are only derived for the Euclidean function, and the distributed updating rules are formulated on the basis of multiplicative rules. Hence, this algorithm cannot converge fast. The MapReduce paradigm has also been used in the paper [7] for implementing the standard multiplicative NMF algorithms [2] in the computational cloud. The proposed approach has been applied for extracting the latent components from the STRING dataset that contains biological data represented by a $1,349,909 \times 1,349,909$ matrix. In the literature, we can find more examples of using the MapReduce paradigm for scaling up various matrix factorization methods, e.g. see [8,9].

For many computational problems, the condition number depends on their size, e.g. for a matrix with normally distributed entries, the condition number grows asymptotically to $\log n$ if $n \to \infty$ (size). Hence, the gradient descent algorithms need more iterations to reach a given error threshold if n increases. The rate of convergence for a given iterative solver plays a very important role, especially if a computational task is very large. To face up this problem in multiplicative algorithms, many other updating rules were proposed for NMF [1]. One of them is the Hierarchical Alternating Least Squares (HALS) algorithm that was first proposed by Cichocki *et al.* [10], and then considerably improved by Cichocki and Phan [11]. Many independent researches [12–16] confirmed its high efficiency for solving various NMF problems and its very fast convergence.

In this paper, we further extend the HALS algorithm to the distributed implementation with the MapReduce paradigm. Despite the HALS belongs to a family of block-coordinate descent algorithms, its most computationally involving operations can be implemented using the BLAS-3 routines (matrix-matrix multiplications). The coordinate descent updates, which must be implemented with at most BLAS-2 (matrix-vector multiplications), are swept only through the latent components. Thus, the operations with the BLAS-2 do not require large computational complexity since the number of latent components is usually much lower than the number od samples or attributes. Our concept of applying the MapReduce paradigm to the HALS concerns partitioning the most computationally involving tasks in the HALS into chunks, which are computed with the BLAS-3. Obviously, the BLAS-2 routines are also used for each chunks of data but these computations can be easily performed.

The paper is organized as follows: Sect. 2 discusses the standard HALS algorithm implemented on a single node. The distributed HALS NMF is presented in Sect. 3. The experiments carried out for large-scale matrices are described in Sect. 4. Finally, the conclusions are drawn in Sect. 5.

2   Single Node HALS Algorithm

The basic model of NMF assumes an approximate decomposition of the nonnegative input matrix $\boldsymbol{Y} = [y_{it}] \in \mathbb{R}_+^{I \times T}$ into the lower-rank nonnegative matrices $\boldsymbol{A} = [a_{ij}] \in \mathbb{R}_+^{I \times J}$ and $\boldsymbol{X} = [x_{jt}] \in \mathbb{R}_+^{J \times T}$, given the lower rank J, and possibly some prior knowledge on the matrices $\boldsymbol{A}$ or $\boldsymbol{X}$. Usually: $J << \min\{I, T\}$. Thus: $\boldsymbol{Y} \cong \boldsymbol{A}\boldsymbol{X} \in \mathbb{R}_+^{I \times T}$.

The factors $\boldsymbol{A}$ and $\boldsymbol{X}$ are typically estimated from $\boldsymbol{Y}$ by using the following alternating optimization scheme: **For** $s = 1, 2, \ldots,$ **do:**

$$\boldsymbol{X}^{(s)} = \arg \min_{\boldsymbol{X} \geq 0} \Psi(\boldsymbol{Y} || \boldsymbol{A}^{(s-1)} \boldsymbol{X}) \,, \tag{1}$$

$$\boldsymbol{A}^{(s)} = \arg \min_{\boldsymbol{A} \geq 0} \Psi(\boldsymbol{Y} || \boldsymbol{A} \boldsymbol{X}^{(s)}) \,, \tag{2}$$

where $\Psi(\boldsymbol{Y} || \boldsymbol{A}\boldsymbol{X})$ is an assumed objective function that measures dissimilarity between the observed data in $\boldsymbol{Y}$ and the model $\boldsymbol{A}\boldsymbol{X}$. The matrices $\boldsymbol{A}^{(0)}$ and $\boldsymbol{X}^{(0)}$ are the initial guesses.

The optimization problems in (1) and (2) can be solved with many solvers. A survey of such methods can be found in [1,17]. The HALS [10,11] performs block-coordinate descent updates. For approximating the problem (1) in the s-th iterative step, the j-th row vector $\underline{\boldsymbol{x}}_j$ of $\boldsymbol{X}$ is updated by solving the subproblem:

$$\underline{\boldsymbol{x}}_j^{(s)} = \arg \min_{\underline{\boldsymbol{x}} \in \Omega_X^{(j)} \subset \mathbb{R}_+^T} \Psi\left(\boldsymbol{A}^{(s-1)}, \left[\underline{\boldsymbol{x}}_1^{(s)}; \ldots; \underline{\boldsymbol{x}}_{j-1}^{(s)}; \underline{\boldsymbol{x}}; \underline{\boldsymbol{x}}_{j+1}^{(s-1)}; \ldots; \underline{\boldsymbol{x}}_J^{(s-1)}\right]\right), \tag{3}$$

where $\Omega_X^{(j)} = \{x_{j1}, \ldots, x_{jT}\}$, $j = 1, \ldots, J$, and $\boldsymbol{X}^{(s)} = [\boldsymbol{x}_1^{(s)}; \ldots; \boldsymbol{x}_J^{(s)}] \in \mathbb{R}_+^{J \times T}$.

The objective function Ψ can take various forms. The HALS-based algorithms for minimizing the α- and β-divergences can be found in [1]. Without loss of generality, the distributed HALS will be presented for the squared Euclidean function which is optimal for Gaussian noise. Assuming $\Psi(\boldsymbol{A}, \boldsymbol{X}) = \frac{1}{2} \| \boldsymbol{Y} - \sum_{j=1}^{J} \boldsymbol{a}_j \boldsymbol{x}_j \|_F^2$, and performing some straightforward algebraic computations [1], the HALS rule for updating $\boldsymbol{X}$ is given by:

$$\boldsymbol{x}_j \leftarrow \left[\boldsymbol{x}_j + \frac{[\boldsymbol{A}^T \boldsymbol{Y}]_{j,*} - [\boldsymbol{A}^T \boldsymbol{A}]_{j,*} \boldsymbol{X}}{[\boldsymbol{A}^T \boldsymbol{A}]_{jj}} \right]_+ , \tag{4}$$

where $[\boldsymbol{C}]_{j,*}$ stands for the j-th row vector of the matrix $\boldsymbol{C}$, and $[\xi]_+ = \max\{0, \xi\}$ projects ξ onto the set of nonnegative numbers.

Algorithm 1. HALS

Input : $\boldsymbol{A} \in \mathbb{R}_+^{I \times J}$, $\boldsymbol{Y} \in \mathbb{R}_+^{I \times T}$, $\boldsymbol{X}^{(0)} \in \mathbb{R}_+^{J \times T}$, k_{max} - maximum number of iterations,

Output: $\boldsymbol{X}$ - estimated factor

1 Initialization: $\boldsymbol{C}^{(X)} = \boldsymbol{A}^T \boldsymbol{Y}$, $\boldsymbol{B}^{(X)} = \boldsymbol{A}^T \boldsymbol{A}$;

2 **for** $k = 0, 1, \ldots, k_{max}$ **do**

3 $\quad$ **for** $j = 1, \ldots, J$ **do**

4 $\quad\quad$ $\boldsymbol{x}_j^{(k+1)} = \left[\boldsymbol{x}_j^{(k)} + \frac{\boldsymbol{c}_j^{(X)} - \boldsymbol{b}_j^{(X)} \boldsymbol{X}^{(k)}}{b_{jj}^{(X)}} \right]_+$; $\qquad$ // Projected updates

---

The pseudo-code for implementation of the rule (4) is shown in Algorithm 1. It contains two loops **for** - the outer for sweeping the iterations, and the inner for sweeping over the block-coordinates, where the block is regarded as the set of variables in the vector $\boldsymbol{x}_j = [x_{j1}, \ldots, x_{jT}]$. Note that due to the precomputation of the matrices $\boldsymbol{C}^{(X)} \in \mathbb{R}_+^{J \times T}$ and $\boldsymbol{B}^{(X)} \in \mathbb{R}_+^{J \times J}$ in the step 1, the computational complexity for the inner-loop computations is only $O(JT)$. Thus, when the inner loop is completed, the complexity is $O(J^2 T)$. The computations in the inner loop are performed only with the BLAS-2 routine, but this is not a problem because their complexity is low under the assumption $J << T$. The most computationally involving tasks are performed in the step 1, which hopefully can be implemented according to the BLAS-3 routines. The matrices $\boldsymbol{C}^{(X)}$ and $\boldsymbol{B}^{(X)}$ need $O(IJT)$ and $O(IJ^2)$, respectively. Hence, the overall time complexity for updating $\boldsymbol{X}$ can be estimated as $O(J^2 T k_{max}) + O(IJ^2) + O(IJT)$. Assuming $J << T$ and $k_{max} \approx J$, the roughly approximated time complexity for these updates amounts to $O(IJT)$.

To solve the problem (2), the squared Euclidean distance is minimized with respect to $\boldsymbol{A}$ using the similar numerical approach, which leads to the update rule:

$$a_j \leftarrow \left[a_j + \frac{c_j^{(A)} - A b_j^{(A)}}{b_{jj}^{(A)}} \right]_+ , \tag{5}$$

where $C^{(A)} = [c_1^{(A)}, \dots, c_J^{(A)}] = Y X^T \in \mathbb{R}_+^{I \times J}$ and $B^{(A)} = [b_{ij}^{(A)}] = X X^T \in \mathbb{R}_+^{J \times J}$. In this case, we also need the inner loop **for** for sweeping the column vectors in A. Thus, under the same assumption as above, the time complexity for updating A can also be roughly estimated as $O(IJT)$.

3   Distributed HALS Algorithm

The update rules (4) and (5) can be easily implemented in many computational environments and run on a single-node computational machine, i.e. under the assumption that the whole matrix Y can be uploaded to the shared memory. If so, A and X can also be shared easily among the cores of CPU, and $C^{(X)}$ can be calculated in parallel on different cores by partitioning the corresponding columns of Y. Similarly, the parallel calculation of $C^{(A)}$ requires partitioning of Y along their rows.

The matrix Y, which has only one dimension large (I or T), belongs to a class of tall-and-skinny matrices, and for it the geometric algorithms based on the MapReduce paradigm have been proposed by Benson *et al.* [18]. Unfortunately, when Y is large, in the sense that both I and T are large, neither the geometric algorithms nor the parallelization of computations are sufficient. To tackle this problem, the computations should be distributed across many nodes in a distributed cluster. For this case, the updating rules (4) and (5) must be modified. We assume that the matrix Y can be divided into blocks which can be distributed across the nodes. Let $Y = [Y_{mn}]$ be composed of the blocks $Y_{mn} \in \mathbb{R}_+^{I_m \times T_n}$, where $\sum_{m=1}^{M} I_m = I$ and $\sum_{n=1}^{N} T_n = T$, for $m = 1, \dots, M$, $n = 1, \dots, N$. Since $J << \min\{I, T\}$, X is partitioned only along the columns, i.e. $X = [X_1, \dots, X_N]$, where $\forall n : X_n \in \mathbb{R}_+^{J \times T_n}$. Similarly, A is divided into row-blocks, i.e. $A = [A_1; \dots; A_M]$ with $A_m \in \mathbb{R}_+^{I_m \times J}$. Considering the above partitioning, $C^{(X)}$ and $B^{(X)}$ in Algorithm 1 can be computed as follows:

$$C^{(X)} = \sum_{m=1}^{M} C_m^{(X)}, \text{ where } C_m^{(X)} = A_m^T Y_m, \tag{6}$$

$$B^{(X)} = \sum_{m=1}^{M} B_m^{(X)} \quad \text{and} \quad B_m^{(X)} = A_m^T A_m. \tag{7}$$

For updating the matrix A, $C^{(A)}$ and $B^{(A)}$ have the forms:

$$C^{(A)} = \sum_{n=1}^{N} C_n^{(A)}, \text{ where } C_n^{(A)} = [C_{1n}^{(A)}; \dots; C_{Mn}^{(A)}] \text{ and } C_{mn}^{(A)} = Y_{mn} X_n^T, \tag{8}$$

$$\boldsymbol{B}^{(A)} = \sum_{n=1}^{N} \boldsymbol{B}_n^{(A)} \quad \text{and} \quad \boldsymbol{B}_n^{(A)} = \boldsymbol{X}_n \boldsymbol{X}_n^T. \tag{9}$$

The above block-partitioning approach determines a fully distributed HALS algorithm. However, in this paper we present its MapReduce implementation, assuming that $\boldsymbol{A}$ and $\boldsymbol{X}$ are kept in the shared memory. If so, the blocks $\boldsymbol{B}_m^{(X)}$ and $\boldsymbol{B}_n^{(A)}$ can be computed in parallel across the cores, where each $\boldsymbol{B}_m^{(X)}$ or $\boldsymbol{B}_n^{(A)}$ is computed by one thread. In our approach, we assume that only the matrices $\boldsymbol{C}^{(X)}$ and $\boldsymbol{C}^{(A)}$ require distributed computations. Moreover, we assume that the data are read in chunks that are blocks of rows in the matrix $\boldsymbol{Y}$. This way of reading is motivated by the *datastore* function in Matlab 2016a. It creates chunks specified by a given number of rows from a textual file (e.g. csv-file) or specified by a collection of other files (such as mat-files or image-files). Considering the above notation, one chunk of data is denoted by $\boldsymbol{Y}_m = [\boldsymbol{Y}_{m1}, \dots, \boldsymbol{Y}_{mN}] \in \mathbb{R}_+^{I_m \times T}$. Because of the characteristics of *datastore* chunks, the computation of (8) is a little bit more complex than its counterpart (6) but it will be explained later.

The computation of $\boldsymbol{C}^{(X)}$ requires one MapReduce job. According to (6), the mapper simply creates $< m, \boldsymbol{Y}_m >$ - the key-value pair that refers to the m-th chunk. The reducer calculates $\boldsymbol{C}_m^{(X)}$ and then the summation is performed over m. To calculate $\boldsymbol{C}^{(X)}$ the following MapReduce operations are needed:

- **Map**: Map $< m, \boldsymbol{Y}_m >$ on m such that tuples with the same m are shuffled to the same machine in the form of $< m, \{\boldsymbol{Y}_m, \boldsymbol{A}\} >$,
- **Reduce I**: Take $< m, \{\boldsymbol{Y}_m, \boldsymbol{A}\} >$ and emit $< m, \boldsymbol{C}_m^{(X)} >$,
- **Reduce II**: Sum $< m, \boldsymbol{C}_m^{(X)} >$ over m.

The reducer gets the chunks ordered as key values and multiplies every chunk with the counterpart row-chunk from $\boldsymbol{A}$. Each key contains a single value which is the whole row-chunk of $\boldsymbol{Y}$. The output datastore from the step **Reduce I** contains a *KeyValueDatastore* object, hence the second mapping (in Matlab) is not necessary. The second reducer performs the summation over the values in the output object. Note that the chunks $\{\boldsymbol{Y}_m\}$ and the blocks $\{\boldsymbol{A}_m\}$ are disordered in the same way, but the sum of matrices is commutative, and hence it does not affect the matrix $\boldsymbol{C}^{(X)}$.

To compute $\boldsymbol{C}^{(A)}$ we also need one MapReduce job, however, it is more difficult because our chunks are still the same blocks $\{\boldsymbol{Y}_m\}$. Since the updating $\boldsymbol{C}^{(A)}$ requires the summation over n but the chunks are read over m, the mapper is different than the previous one. Here, the mapper produces multiple key-value pairs per a single block as it splits the block with n partitions. In consequence, the mapper generates a m-length list of values per key. Because of the fact that the MapReduce paradigm does not ensure the ordering in the list of values (it has usually different order than it was added), we need to keep a label with every value (block of rows) which refers to m-block it was taken from. The reducer calculates $\boldsymbol{C}_{mn}^{(A)}$ for every item in the list of n-th key, filling the proper part of

$C_n^{(A)}$ thanks to the label. The MapReduce-based operations needed to compute $C^{(A)}$ can be listed as follows:

- **Map**: Map $< m, n, \boldsymbol{Y}_{mn} >$ on n such that tuples with the same n are shuffled to the same machine in the form of $< n, \{m, \boldsymbol{Y}_{mn}, \boldsymbol{X}\}, \forall m \in \{1, \ldots, M\} >$,
- **Reduce I**: Take $< n, \{m, \boldsymbol{Y}_{mn}, \boldsymbol{X}\}, \forall m \in \{1, \ldots, M\} >$ and emit $< n, \boldsymbol{C}_n^{(A)} >$ by calculating $C_{mn}^{(A)}$ and filling it to $C_n^{(A)}$ according to the m-label.
- **Reduce II**: Sum $< n, \boldsymbol{C}_n^{(A)} >$ over n.

The MapReduce paradigm is not only used for computing the matrices $\boldsymbol{C}^{(A)}$ and $\boldsymbol{C}^{(X)}$. The alternating iterations, indexed by s in (1) and (2), are terminated according to the stopping criterion based on the residual error. The normalized residual error is given by:

$$r_s = \frac{|| \boldsymbol{Y} - \boldsymbol{A}^{(s)} \boldsymbol{X}^{(s)} ||_F}{|| \boldsymbol{Y} ||_F}. \tag{10}$$

Both the nominator and the denominator involve the operations on large matrices, and hence must be computed using the distributed approach. The MapReduce operations for computing the nominator in (10) are given by the steps:

- **Map**: Map $< m, \boldsymbol{Y}_m >$ on m such that tuples with the same m are shuffled to the same machine in the form of $< m, \{\boldsymbol{Y}_m, \boldsymbol{A}, \boldsymbol{X}\} >$,
- **Reduce I**: Take $< m, \{\boldsymbol{Y}_m, \boldsymbol{A}, \boldsymbol{X}\} >$
  and emit $\langle 'KeyName', \{\tilde{r}_m = || \boldsymbol{Y}_m - \boldsymbol{A}_m \boldsymbol{X} ||_F^2\}\rangle$,
- **Reduce II**: Take $<' KeyName', \{\tilde{r}_m\}, \forall m \in \{1, \ldots, M\} >$
  and emit $\tilde{r} = \sum_m \tilde{r}_m$.

The denominator in (10) needs the following steps:

- **Map**: Map $< m, \boldsymbol{Y}_m >$ on m such that tuples with the same m are shuffled to the same machine in the form of $< m, \{\boldsymbol{Y}_m\} >$,
- **Reduce I**: Take $< m, \{\boldsymbol{Y}_m\} >$ and emit $\langle 'KeyName', \{\hat{r}_m = || \boldsymbol{Y}_m ||_F^2\}\rangle$,
- **Reduce II**: Take $<' KeyName', \{\hat{r}_m\}, \forall m \in \{1, \ldots, M\} >$
  and emit $\hat{r} = \sum_m \hat{r}_m$.

Finally $r = \sqrt{\frac{\tilde{r}}{\hat{r}}}$ in each iterative step s. The final version of the Distributed (D-HALS) is given by Algorithm 2. The functions $\mathrm{MR}(D_s, \ldots)$ are executed with the MapReduce paradigm using the datastore D_s and the other respective arguments.

Algorithm 2. D-HALS

Input : $\boldsymbol{Y} \in \mathbb{R}_+^{I \times T}$, s_{max} - maximum number of alternating iterations, k_{max} - maximum number of inner iterations.

Output: $\boldsymbol{A}$, $\boldsymbol{X}$ - estimated factors

1 Initialization: $\boldsymbol{A}^{(0)}$, $\boldsymbol{X}^{(0)}$;
2 Create the datastore D_s from $\boldsymbol{Y}$;
3 **for** $s = 0, 1, \ldots, s_{max}$ **do**
4   Compute: $\boldsymbol{C}^{(A)} = \mathrm{MR}(D_s, \boldsymbol{X})$ with (8); $\boldsymbol{B}^{(A)}$ with (9) ;   `// Update for A`
5   **for** $k = 0, 1, \ldots, k_{max}$ **do**
6      $\boldsymbol{G}^{(A)} = \boldsymbol{A}\boldsymbol{B}^{(A)} - \boldsymbol{C}^{(A)}$;   `// Gradient of the objective w.r.t. A`
7   **if** *Stopping criterion based on $\boldsymbol{G}^{(A)}$ is satisfied,* **then**
8   break
9   **for** $j = 1, \ldots, J$ **do**
10   Update $\boldsymbol{a}_j$ with the rule (5);
11   Compute: $\boldsymbol{C}^{(X)} = \mathrm{MR}(D_s, \boldsymbol{A})$ with (6); $\boldsymbol{B}^{(X)}$ with (7) ;   `// Update for X`
12   **for** $k = 0, 1, \ldots, k_{max}$ **do**
13      $\boldsymbol{G}^{(X)} = \boldsymbol{B}^{(X)}\boldsymbol{X} - \boldsymbol{C}^{(X)}$;   `// Gradient of the objective w.r.t. X`
14   **if** *Stopping criterion based on $\boldsymbol{G}^{(X)}$ is satisfied,* **then**
15   break
16   **for** $j = 1, \ldots, J$ **do**
17   Update $\underline{\boldsymbol{x}}_j$ with the rule (4);
18   Compute the residual error: $r = \mathrm{MR}(D_s, \boldsymbol{A}, \boldsymbol{X})$ with (10);
19   **if** *r satisfies a given stopping criterion,* **then**
20   break

---

4   Experiments

The D-HALS algorithm has been tested on the following datasets:

– **Benchmark I**: The matrix $\boldsymbol{Y} \in \mathbb{R}_+^{I \times T}$ is generated synthetically from the factor matrices: $\boldsymbol{A} = [a_{ij}] \in \mathbb{R}_+^{I \times J}$ and $\boldsymbol{X} = [x_{jt}] \in \mathbb{R}_+^{J \times T}$, where $a_{ij} = \max\{0, \hat{a}_{ij}\}$, $x_{jt} = \max\{0, \hat{x}_{jt}\}$ and $\forall i, j, t : \hat{a}_{ij}, \hat{x}_{jt} \sim \mathcal{N}(0, 1)$. The algorithm is tested for various sizes of $\boldsymbol{Y}$: (A) $I = 10^3$, $T = 10^4$; (B) $I = T = 10^4$; (C) $I = 10^4$, $T = 10^5$; (D) $I = T = 10^5$. In each case, we set $J = 10$, and for this value the matrix $\boldsymbol{Y}$ is nearly fully dense, despite $\boldsymbol{A}$ and $\boldsymbol{X}$ have nearly 50% zero-entries. Thus, the chunks are represented in double-precision floating-point, and the number of entries being processed for each case amounts to: (A) 10^7, (B) 10^8, (C) 10^9, (D) 10^{10}. For the cases A-C, the data are split into 10 chunks along the rows, and due to the shared memory limit this number was increased to 100 for the dataset D.

- **Benchmark II**: The matrix Y is created from the dataset (ml-latest) issued by MovieLens[1] [19]. It contains 5-star rating and free-text tagging activity from a movie recommendation service. We used the dataset that has 22884377 ratings and 586994 tag applications across 33670 movies, evaluated by 247753 users within the period from January 09, 1995 to January 29, 2016. Thus $Y \in \mathbb{R}_+^{247753 \times 33670}$ is a sparse matrix, containing about 27.43% nonzero entries. The number of chunks amounts to 10.

The aim of the numerical experiments is to show that the D-HALS is scalable, and its performance increases with the size of the datasets that are generated from the same distributions (as in benchmark I). The benchmark II is used to demonstrate usefulness of the D-HALS in processing real data from a movie recommendation system.

The D-HALS is coded in Matlab 2016a according to the MapReduce paradigm (the *mapreduce* function accessible since Matlab R2014a). Using the Parallel Computing Toolbox or MATLAB Distributed Computing Server, it can be executed using parallel pool on the specified cluster, including the Hadoop cluster. In this paper, we present the results mainly obtained with the parallel pool of 8 workers, run on the workstation equipped with CPU Intel i7-6700, 3.4 GHz, 32 GB RAM, 500 GB SSD disk. The selected computations have been also run in PBS queues on the distributed cluster server in Wroclaw Center for Networking and Supercomputing (WCSS)[2]. The proposed algorithm can be run on any multi-node cluster, and we will use another publicly available computational servers for larger-scale computations in the near future.

Due to the intrinsic ambiguities of the NMF model, statistical validation of NMF algorithms requires to use the Monte Carlo (MC) scheme. We assumed 30 MC runs of the algorithm for each dataset from the benchmark I, where in each run new factors A and X and their initial approximations are generated. In each alternating iteration (step s in Algorithm 2), the normalized residual error is calculated, and the iterations are terminated when the normalized difference in the residual error between consecutive iterations drops below the threshold 10^{-5}. The inner iterations (steps k) and the other parameters are set similarly as in the Lin's Projected Gradient (LPG) algorithm [20].

For each MC run, the ratio of the runtime to the number of performed iterations is measured. The averaged runtime/iteration is plotted in Fig. 1(a) for all the datasets in the benchmark I. The whiskers determine the Standard Deviation (STD). For comparison, the dataset A was also computed in the WCSS using 24 cores (ncpus) and 24 GB RAM (mem). The runtime/iteration ratio amounts to 3.836 s. Regarding the ratio of 3.08 s obtained for the workstation (and other limitations in WCSS), the remaining computations were restricted only to the workstation.

The performance of the D-HALS is also evaluated with the Signal-to-Interference Ratio (SIR) [1] between the estimates and the true factors. Figure 1(b) illustrates the averaged SIR-values and the STD-ranges for each

---

[1] https://grouplens.org/datasets/movielens/.
[2] https://www.wcss.pl/en/.

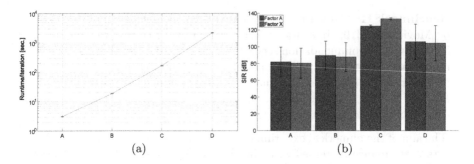

(a)   (b)

Fig. 1. MC simulations: (a) runtime per iteration [in seconds]; (b) SIR-values [dB], obtained for the synthetic data – benchmark I with various sizes: (A) $I = 10^3$, $T = 10^4$; (B) $I = T = 10^4$; (C) $I = 10^4$, $T = 10^5$; (D) $I = T = 10^5$. The whiskers (in both figures) denote the standard deviation.

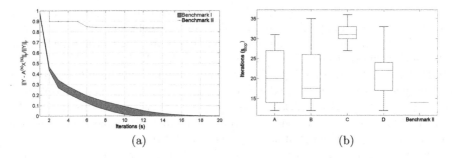

(a)   (b)

Fig. 2. MC simulations: (a) normalized residual error plots versus iterations with the marked STD area (in green); (b) boxplots of truncated alternating iterations over MC runs. Benchmarks I (with A-D sizes) and II. (Color figure online)

problem. The normalized residual errors versus alternating steps are presented in Fig. 2(a) for both benchmarks. The green patch highlights the region determined by the standard deviation of all 120 curves (30 by 4). The red line represents the residual error obtained for the benchmark II. Figure 2(b) illustrates the box plots of the performed alternating iterations for each dataset. The D-HALS applied to the benchmark II stopped after 14 alternating iterations, decreasing the residual error monotonically to the value 0.8373. The runtime per one iteration amounts to 696 s.

For comparison, the benchmark II was also factorized with the ALS algorithm from the MLib library in the Apache Spark. For this case, RMSE is equal to 0.92 if the regularization parameter is set optimally to 0.1 [21].

5   Conclusions

In this paper, we extended the HALS-based NMF algorithm to the distributed version by partitioning the computational tasks according to the MapReduce paradigm. The results presented in Fig. 1(a) clearly demonstrate that the proposed D-HALS is linearly scalable and can be applied to factorize a data matrix of any size, provided that the factors A and X are kept in the shared memory. This condition will be relaxed in the further extensions. The performance expressed in terms of the SIR measure slightly increases with the size of the analyzed problem at the constant rank of factorization, which is intuitively justified – see Fig. 1(b). For the case D, the number of chunks raised tenfold with respect to the previous cases, and this might account for the slightly lower performance. Figure 2(a) shows that in each analyzed case the residual error diminishes monotonically. Surprisingly, larger problems do not necessary involve more iterations to reach a given threshold for stagnation of the residual error. As presented in Fig. 2(b) for all the tested problems, the threshold occurs within less than 36 iterations. The number of performed iterations varies in the range [12, 36]. For the benchmark II, the algorithm stopped after 14 iterations, and the behavior of the residual error suggests that a larger number of iterations does not improve the fitting of the model to the data. The similar behavior was also observed with the ALS algorithm in the Apache Spark. The stagnation of the residual error is obvious since an exact nonnegative factorization of the data in benchmark II does not exist. The aim is to find the best fitting of a low-rank model to the large-scale nonnegative data. Better fitting requires to change the rank of factorization.

Summing up, the proposed algorithm is experimentally demonstrated to be linearly scalable, if the estimated factors can be kept in the shared memory. In the future works, the D-HALS will be applied to process larger and real data on powerful multi-node clusters, and the linear scalability will be proved analytically.

Acknowledgment. This work was supported by the grant 2015/17/B/ST6/01865 funded by National Science Center (NCN) in Poland. Some calculations have been carried out in Wroclaw Centre for Networking and Supercomputing, grant no. 127.

References

1. Cichocki, A., Zdunek, R., Phan, A.H., Amari, S.I.: Nonnegative Matrix and Tensor Factorizations: Applications to Exploratory Multi-way Data Analysis and Blind Source Separation. Wiley, Hoboken (2009)
2. Lee, D.D., Seung, H.S.: Algorithms for nonnegative matrix factorization. In: Advances in Neural Information Processing, NIPS, vol. 13, pp. 556–562. MIT Press (2001)
3. Liu, C., Yang, H.c., Fan, J., He, L.W., Wang, Y.M.: Distributed nonnegative matrix factorization for web-scale dyadic data analysis on MapReduce. In: Proc. 19th International Conference on World Wide Web (WWW 2010), pp. 681–690. ACM, New York, NY, USA (2010)
4. Sun, Z., Li, T., Rishe, N.: Large-scale matrix factorization using MapReduce. In: ICDM Workshops, pp. 1242–1248. IEEE Computer Society (2010)
5. Ding, C., Li, T., Jordan, M.I.: Convex and semi-nonnegative matrix factorizations. IEEE Trans. Pattern Anal. Mach. Intell. **32**(1), 45–55 (2010)

6. Yin, J., Gao, L., Zhang, Z.M.: Scalable nonnegative matrix factorization with block-wise updates. In: Calders, T., Esposito, F., Hüllermeier, E., Meo, R. (eds.) ECML PKDD 2014. LNCS, vol. 8726, pp. 337–352. Springer, Heidelberg (2014). doi:10.1007/978-3-662-44845-8_22

7. Liao, R., Zhang, Y., Guan, J., Zhou, S.: CloudNMF: A MapReduce implementation of nonnegative matrix factorization for large-scale biological datasets. Genomics, Proteomics and Bioinform. 12(1), 48–51 (2014)

8. Schelter, S., Boden, C., Schenck, M., Alexandrov, A., Markl, V.: Distributed matrix factorization with MapReduce using a series of broadcast-joins. In: ACM Conference on Recommender Systems (RecSys) (2013)

9. Tan, W., Cao, L., Fong, L.L.: Faster and cheaper: Parallelizing large-scale matrix factorization on GPUs. CoRR abs/1603.03820 (2016)

10. Cichocki, A., Zdunek, R., Amari, S.: Hierarchical ALS algorithms for nonnegative matrix and 3D tensor factorization. In: Davies, M.E., James, C.J., Abdallah, S.A., Plumbley, M.D. (eds.) ICA 2007. LNCS, vol. 4666, pp. 169–176. Springer, Heidelberg (2007). doi:10.1007/978-3-540-74494-8_22

11. Cichocki, A., Phan, A.H.: Fast local algorithms for large scale nonnegative matrix and tensor factorizations. IEICE Trans. Fund. Electron. Commun. Comput. Sci. E92–A(3), 708–721 (2009)

12. Han, L., Neumann, M., Prasad, U.: Alternating projected Barzilai-Borwein methods for nonnegative matrix factorization. Electron. Trans. Numer. Anal. 36, 54–82 (2009–2010)

13. Kim, J., Park, H.: Fast nonnegative matrix factorization: An active-set-like method and comparisons. SIAM J. Sci. Comput. 33(6), 3261–3281 (2011)

14. Gillis, N., Glineur, F.: Accelerated multiplicative updates and hierarchical ALS algorithms for nonnegative matrix factorization. Neural Comput. 24(4), 1085–1105 (2012)

15. Chen, W., Guillaume, M.: HALS-based NMF with flexible constraints for hyperspectral unmixing. EURASIP J. Adv. Sig. Proc. 54, 1–14 (2012)

16. Laudadio, T., Sava, C., Anca, R., Sima, D.M., Wright, A.J., Heerschap, A., Mastronardi, N., Van Huffel, S.: Hierarchical non-negative matrix factorization applied to three-dimensional 3T MRSI data for automatic tissue characterization of the prostate. NMR Biomed. 29(6), 751–758 (2016)

17. Wang, Y.X., Zhang, Y.J.: Nonnegative matrix factorization: A comprehensive review. IEEE Trans. on Knowl. Data Eng. 25(6), 1336–1353 (2013)

18. Benson, A.R., Lee, J.D., Rajwa, B., Gleich, D.F.: Scalable methods for nonnegative matrix factorizations of near-separable tall-and-skinny matrices. In: Proceedings of Neural Information Processing Systems, pp. 945–953(2014)

19. Harper, F.M., Konstan, J.A.: The movielens datasets: History and context. ACM Trans. Interact. Intell. Syst. 5(4), 19:1–19:19 (2015)

20. Lin, C.J.: Projected gradient methods for non-negative matrix factorization. Neural Comput. 19(10), 2756–2779 (2007)

21. Buksak, D.: Implementation of nonnegative matrix factorization algorithms in apache spark framework. Master's thesis, Wroclaw University of Science and Technology Supervised by Dr. R. Zdunek (2016)

Applications of Parallel and Distributed Computing

GPU-Accelerated Block-Max Query Processing

Haibing Huang, Mingming Ren[(✉)], Yue Zhao, Rebecca J. Stones, Rui Zhang,
Gang Wang, and Xiaoguang Liu

Nankai-Baidu Joint Lab, College of Computer and Control Engineering,
Nankai University, Tianjin 300350, China
{hbhuang,renmingming,zhaoy,rebecca.stones82,zhangruiann,
wgzwp,liuxg}@nbjl.nankai.edu.cn

Abstract. In this paper, we propose a method for parallel top-k query processing on GPU(s). We employ a novel partitioning strategy which splits the posting lists according to document ID numbers. Individual GPU threads simultaneously perform top-k query processing within their allocated subsets of posting lists, the results of the query are merged to give the final top-k results. We further design a CPU-GPU cooperative query processing method, where a majority of queries involving shorter posting lists are processed on the GPU side. We experiment with AND, OR, WAND, and Block-Max WAND (BMW) queries, with experimental results showing a promising improvement in query throughput, particularly in the case of BMW queries.

Keywords: Information retrieval · GPU · Index partition · Query assignment

1 Introduction

Search engines face a large number of queries from users. To provide high query throughput and response time, current commercial search engines use large clusters consisting of thousands of nodes. Each node is responsible for processing a subset of the whole posting data. Distributing the workload over a large number of nodes facilitates the timely return of top-k results to users. In this paper, we design a GPU-accelerated query processing method, where the workload is distributed over GPU threads (and even the CPU).

In many domains, we see applications of graphics processing units (GPUs) extending from their original purpose (graphics processing) into a wide range of general-purpose applications, primarily for the single goal of making software run faster. GPU programming requires carefully balancing workloads, data transfers, and utilizing the GPU's memory hierarchy, and programs are typically custom built for an application.

Several GPU-based query processing techniques have been proposed previously (see Sect. 2.5 for a review). The research presented here takes three new directions: (a) we design a method which can subdivide the task of generating the top-k results for a single query among threads, (b) we address several query processing strategies, such as WAND [3] and block-max WAND (BMW) [6] (WAND queries

© Springer International Publishing AG 2017
S. Ibrahim et al. (Eds.): ICA3PP 2017, LNCS 10393, pp. 225–238, 2017.
DOI: 10.1007/978-3-319-65482-9_15

for block-max indexes), and (c) we extend the proposed method to utilize both the CPU and GPU for query processing. In addition, previous work has typically assumed that the inverted index can be fully loaded into the GPU memory, which is unrealistic for large indexes, which we do not assume here.

The remainder of this paper proceeds as follow: Sect. 2 gives the background and related research of the information retrieval and parallel query processing. Section 3 presents our method of GPU-based and CPU-GPU cooperation algorithm. Section 4 presents the experimental results of our method. Finally, Sect. 5 concludes and discusses future work.

2   Background and Related Work

2.1   Block-Max Index

Documents are assigned *docID* numbers $0, 1, \ldots, N - 1$, where N is the number of indexed documents. A term t has a corresponding *posting list*, denoted

$$\ell(t) = \langle s_t; (d_0, f_0), (d_1, f_1), \ldots, (d_{s_t-1}, f_{s_t-1}) \rangle \tag{1}$$

which lists the documents $d_0, d_1, \ldots, d_{s_t-1}$ containing the term t. The posting list has *length* s_t and the number of occurrences of term t in document d_i is denoted $f_i = f(t, d_i)$. We assume $d_0 < d_1 < \cdots < d_{s-1}$. Posting lists belong to a large index known as the *inverted index*.

The differences between consecutive docIDs in a posting list are referred to as *d*-gaps, and are numerically much smaller than the raw docID values. As such, *d*-gaps are typically used in place of the raw docIDs to reduce the inverted index size with effective compression method.

The inverted index is usually stored in a compressed form to significantly reduce its size. At the same time, its contents need to be readily accessible to allow fast query processing. Many inverted index compression techniques having been proposed [17] balancing these goals. In this paper we use *NewPFD* [15] to compress the posting lists and corresponding frequency lists with a block size of 64 (although the proposed method could use other compression techniques).

Ding and Suel [6] proposed a *block-max index* data structure, where posting lists are partitioned into *blocks* comprising, say, 64 docIDs (corresponding to the 64 docIDs in the *NewPFD* blocks). The docIDs and their frequencies are stored in a compressed format, and are stored along with the least and greatest docIDs and the maximum "impact score" (essentially, the maximum contribution to the top-k ranking). In this way, every *NewPFD* block can be decompressed separately, and the top-k results can be computed with early termination. This was shown to be an effective technique for improving the performance of WAND query processing. In this paper, we borrow aspects of this index method.

2.2   Query Processing

In query processing, for documents relevant to a query, we compute a *score*, and those with the highest score are considered the most relevant. To this end, we traverse all of the relevant posting lists (those with terms in the query) from beginning to end. For index traversal, we use a *Document-At-A-Time* (DAAT) approach, where each list has a pointer that points to the "current" docID, which moves forward to identify the docIDs which are common among the relevant posting lists for conjunctive query. The document scores are computed while traversing the lists, and we can use min-heap data structure to store the top-k results.

The DAAT approach can work well for conjunctive (AND) and disjunctive (OR) query processing [3], and WAND [3] and BMW [6] can also be implemented using the DAAT approach. The WAND and BMW algorithm can avoid fully evaluating the score of all documents in the posting list of each term belonging to a given query, a smart pointer movement technique is used to skip many documents that would be evaluated by an exhaustive algorithm. In this paper, we will take these four kind query processing strategies into consideration.

2.3 Scoring

Ranking functions are used to give a numerical score for a document d and a query q. BM25 [9] is a well-known ranking function, which varies with both d and q (and two parameters $a \geq 0$ and $b \in [0,1]$), given by

$$\text{BM25}_{a,b}(d,q) := \sum_{t \in q} w_t(q)\, \text{IR}_{a,b}(d,t) \tag{2}$$

where

$$\text{IR}_{a,b}(d,t) = \frac{(1+a)f(d,t)}{a\big(1+b(l_d-1)\big) + f(d,t)} \tag{3}$$

where l_d is the length of document d divided by the average document length, $f(d,t)$ is the number of occurrences of t in document d, and the *inverse document frequency weight* is defined as

$$w_t(q) = \log \frac{N - s_t + 0.5}{s_t + 0.5} \tag{4}$$

where N is the number of the documents in the collection and s_t is the number of documents containing term t (which is included in the posting list (1)).

During query processing, we use DAAT approach to iterate through the relevant posting lists, retaining the top-k highest scoring documents, the top-k results are returned to the user finally.

2.4 GPUs

Modern GPUs have a massively parallel architecture consisting of thousands of cores. NVIDIA brand GPUs support *Compute Unified Device Architecture* (CUDA) [8], where threads are organized into *thread blocks* and *thread blocks* are organized into *Grid*. A GPU computation is performed by invoking a *kernel* which is executed by a *grid* of thread blocks.

GPUs have their own memory, which is organized into a hierarchy, and the GPU memory is usually far smaller than the (CPU side) system memory. The relevant GPU memories for this paper are: (a) *Global memory*, the largest but the slowest GPU memory, and is accessible to all the GPU threads. Data transferred from the CPU to the GPU goes into the global memory. (b) *Shared memory*, which is much faster than the global memory, but is much smaller, and is only accessible to the threads in the corresponding thread block. (c) *Registers*, the fastest but the most scarce memory resource. Each multiprocessor has a set of registers partitioned among the warps (which partition thread blocks). Overall, registers are unique to a thread, shared memory is unique to a block, and global memory exist across all blocks.

Efficient GPU programming requires careful consideration of (a) GPU memory usage, (b) CPU-GPU transfers, (c) workload distribution. and (d) parallel algorithm.

2.5   Related Work

GPUs have been widely utilized in general-purpose application. Zhang *et al.* [18] proposed an effective algorithm which can parallelize DNN training on multiple GPU cards in a single computing server. Fang *et al.* [7] proposed a in-memory GPU algorithms, which support three common database operations. Agrawal [1] utilized data parallel accelerators and a software architecture, Rhythm, to address throughput and efficiency demands of future server workloads.

To speed up the query processing, there are many previous papers that focus on how to efficient parallel query processing. Rojas *et al.* [10] proposed the parallelization the Block-Max WAND algorithm using two-level ranking on distributed search engine. Ding *et al.* [4] achieved good performance using specialized mechanisms for executing batch queries. Tatikonda *et al.* [12] achieved more than five times reduction average query processing time by exploiting parallelism at the finest-level of granularity in on an eight-core system.

There are also several previous papers that focus on GPU-based query processing. Ding *et al.* [5] presented a general architecture for GPU-based query processing and proposed a parallel lists intersection algorithm with the GPU, but queries are dispatched to CPU or GPU one by one, incurring a impractical transfer overhead. Wu *et al.* [14] presented a GPU-based lists intersection framework in which queries are first grouped into batches, and then processed in parallel on the GPU using their proposed PARA algorithm. Zhang *et al.* [16] proposed a Bloom filter batched algorithm for intersection aiming at reducing the number of memory accesses for each GPU thread. Ao *et al.* [2] proposed linear regression and hash segmentation algorithms for GPU-based lists intersection (a component of query processing), which was up to around 23 times faster using a NVIDIA GTX480.

However, previous GPU-based query processing methods have some limitations:

– Methods have been restricted to conjunctive (AND) query processing.
– The total inverted index is typically assumed to be residing in the GPU global memory, which might be assuming an unrealistic GPU memory size on current hardware for large indexes.

In this paper, we do not assume the whole inverted index resides in the GPU memory. To cope with this, we batch transfer the user queries together with the relevant posting lists not residing in the GPU memory. Another major aspect of this paper is also incorporating OR, WAND, and BMW strategies for query processing.

3   The Proposed Method

3.1   Overview

Figure 1 illustrates the proposed GPU-based query processing framework.

The entire inverted index is assumed to reside in the (CPU-side) system memory. In the case that the index's size actually exceeds the CPU memory capacity, some queries will require disk access to be processed. Without modifying the inverted index compression method, this will be unavoidable and an essentially constant overhead (i.e., will not substantially vary with the design of the GPU query processing method). and we assume user queries are continuously incoming rapidly enough to allow them to be batched and transferred jointly to the GPU. The queries will be added to the current batch along with any required posting list not residing in the GPU list cache. Once the batch size reaches a certain threshold, or the number of queries in the batch reaches the maximum value that can be processed, the batch is transferred to the GPU global memory.

The GPU global memory space contains two main parts: a *list cache*, which contains a portion of the whole inverted index, and a *buffer space*, which contains the batches. The posting lists residing in the list cache is determined by some

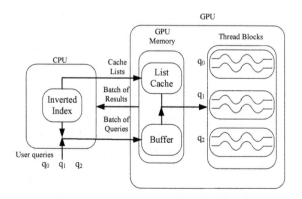

Fig. 1. The workflow of GPU-based query processing.

Algorithm 1. The proposed GPU-based query processing algorithm

Input: a batch of queries Q
Output: top-k results for each query in Q
1: Transfer Q to the GPU buffer space
2: **for** thread block $b_{id} \in \{0, 1, \ldots, (|Q| - 1)\}$ **do**
3:     **for each** thread $t_{id} \in \{0, 1, \ldots, P - 1\}$ **do**
4:         Compute local top-k results by using a query processing strategy.
5:     **end for**
6:     Synchronize threads for thread block b_{id}
7:     Merge local top-k results for thread block b_{id}
8: **end for**
9: Transfer every thread block top-k results to CPU

admission policy (described in Sect. 4.1). A hash table is maintained on the CPU side to record which posting lists in the GPU list cache.

Algorithm 1 shows our proposed GPU-based query processing algorithm. The algorithm assigns a thread block the task of generating the top-k results for a single user query. An individual thread within a thread block generates the local top-k results on its assigned subset of the docIDs. Specifically, the set of docIDs $\{0, 1, \ldots, N-1\}$ is partitioned into d-sized ($d = \lceil N/P \rceil$) intervals $\{0, 1, \ldots, d-1\}$, $\{d, d+1, \ldots, 2d-1\}$, and so on, with each thread being assigned to work on one part, and we have P threads in every thread block. In our experiments, we will test a range of P-values.

Figure 2 shows a toy example of the inverted index partition strategy. The four threads T0, T1, T2, and T3 are responsible for processing the subsets of three compressed block-max posting lists respectively. Thread T0, for example, is responsible for the subsets of posting lists in first left dashed box, i.e., the docIDs interval $\{0, \ldots, 999\}$.

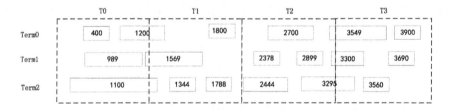

Fig. 2. A toy example of the document-based index partition strategy. Threads T0, T1, T2, and T3 are responsible for their assigned subsets of three compressed block-max posting lists. The number in the solid box shows the max docID in corresponding compressed a NewPFD block. The subsets are indicated by a dashed boundary and each subset's docIDs interval is 1000 in this example. For term Term0, thread T0 is responsible for the whole first NewPFD block and first part of the second NewPFD block. Thread T1 is responsible for second part of the second NewPFD block and the whole third NewPFD block, and so on.

After the posting lists are partitioned for each thread, the threads perform query processing on their assigned sub-posting lists and compute the *local top-k results*. Before computing the merge operation in a thread block, a synchronization barrier is needed. Once all of the local top-k results are obtained, the threads in a thread block merge every thread's local top-k results to compute the thread block top-k results. we select insert sort method to complete the merge operation. Once the thread block top-k results for the whole batch of queries has been computed, they are transferred to the CPU as a batch, and the final results can be displayed to the users.

3.2 CPU-GPU Cooperative Version

Algorithm 1, by itself, would result in a large amount of CPU idle time. To avoid this, we propose a CPU-GPU cooperative algorithm, which is a modified version of the proposed GPU query processing method. Essentially, some queries are processed on the CPU side and the other queries would be transferred to the GPU for query processing.

Before we introduce the CPU-GPU cooperative algorithm, we first do some experiments about the relation between the queries' posting length and query processing time about our GPU algorithm. Figure 3 shows the average query processing time for different queries' posting block number S with AND, OR, WAND, and BMW queries (both with $P = 64$ threads per thread block and top-$K = 10$, other parameters have similar results). We can see that CPU algorithm

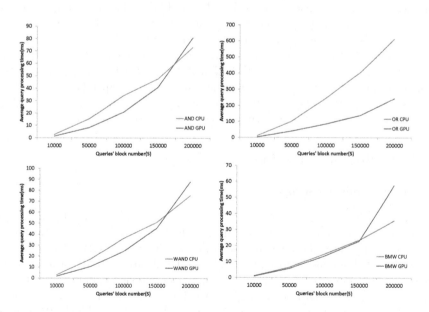

Fig. 3. The average query processing time on different queries' block number S (horizontal axis) on CPU and GPU for AND, OR, WAND, and BMW queries.

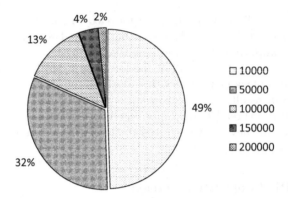

Fig. 4. The proportion of the queries' posting lists block number in TREC 2009 query set.

is more effective than GPU algorithm when query block number S increases (except for OR queries).

The reason is that: as the document-based index partition is a simple partitioning method and the distribution of docIDs is clustered, long posting lists result in imbalanced lengths of sub-posting lists. A thread responsible for processing longer sub-posting lists will spend a greater amount of time than other threads, which will be idle because of the synchronization step.

Therefore, we propose a *length-based distribution* (LBD) method to determine which queries to distribute to the CPU and GPU. From the Fig. 4, we can find that short posting lists queries (queries's posting lists block number less 50000) take up the majority of the query set, approximately 81%. The GPU will be responsible for processing queries involving short posting lists, comprising a majority of the queries. and the CPU will be responsible for processing the smaller number of queries containing longer posting lists. Specifically, the GPU processes the queries whose relevant posting lists have fewer than S *NewPFD* blocks in total, and we will experiment with varying the threshold S.

4   Experimental Testing

4.1   Experimental Setup

For our experiments, we use the TREC GOV2 [13] data set which consists of about 25 million documents crawled from web sites in the .gov domain during early 2004. The index data is composed of approximately 12 GB inverted index, another 12 GB frequency information index and a file about 97 MB storing document sizes. The docIDs are assigned according to the lexicographic order of their URLs [11]. We use *NewPFD* to compress the index and also store a array about the greatest docIDs and the maximum "impact score" of each block. We choose the *RREC 2009* query set, which contains 32,255 queries, as our test query set. We carry out our experiments on a 2.60 GHz Intel(R) Xeon(R) E5-2630 CPU with 64 GB of memory and a NVIDIA GeForce GTX Titan graphics card with 6 GB global memory. The gcc version is 4.4.6, and the nvcc version is 6.5.12.

For the parameters in the ranking function BM25, we set $a = 1.2$ and $b = 0.75$. These parameters may affect the quality of the final top-k ranking, but will not significantly affect the throughput and response time of our method. We experiment with top-$k = 10$ unless we have special statement.

For the GPU list cache policy, we calculate that the number of the short lists (posting length 1,...,64) takes up the majority of the whole compression lists; approximately 97.45% in GOV2 data set. As long lists need more transfer time and there are fewer long lists. Therefore we put the lists with more than 1 *NewPFD* block in the GPU list cache memory as our (static) cache policy.

4.2   Query Processing Time

Table 1 shows the average query processing time of the proposed GPU query parallel processing method (the non-cooperative version) as the number of threads GPU thread block and top-K vary (i.e., the P-value and top-K), for AND, OR, WAND and BMW query processing strategies. For comparison, we also include CPU a thread results in the bottom of Table 1.

We see that the GPU method results in improved query processing times for every query type, AND, OR, WAND, and BMW, with a average query processing time drop of up to 54.68%, 55.31%, 51.15%, and 50.11%, respectively (all when $P = 64$ and top-$K = 10$). We attribute this modest improvement to workload imbalance: the processing of long posting lists is time-consuming, resulting in long synchronization waiting times. The proposed CPU-GPU cooperative version aims to reduce this problem, by performing query processing on queries involving

Table 1. The comparison between average query processing time (ms) for the GPU as the number of threads per GPU thread block and top-K vary with the CPU a thread, for the AND, OR, WAND, and BMW queries. Values in bold show the best result in corresponding row.

P	AND			OR			WAND			BMW		
	Top1	Top10	Top20	Top1	Top10	Top20	Top1	Top10	Top20	Top1	Top10	Top20
32	8.07	8.08	8.14	45.57	45.88	45.97	8.29	10.22	11.18	3.54	4.90	6.49
64	**5.78**	**5.81**	**5.86**	30.26	30.32	30.37	**5.97**	**7.45**	**8.23**	**2.69**	**4.47**	**5.21**
128	6.06	6.08	6.13	**29.48**	**29.53**	**29.57**	6.19	7.86	8.73	2.96	**4.47**	**5.21**
256	7.53	7.56	7.61	34.38	34.42	34.49	7.55	8.97	9.65	4.14	6.51	7.60
320	9.33	9.35	9.39	39.86	39.91	39.95	9.24	11.71	13.03	4.91	7.51	8.71
512	12.24	12.28	12.36	49.02	49.08	49.21	12.05	15.23	16.93	6.17	9.14	10.53
CPU	12.70	12.82	12.93	65.77	66.08	66.15	15.11	15.25	15.34	8.82	8.96	9.03

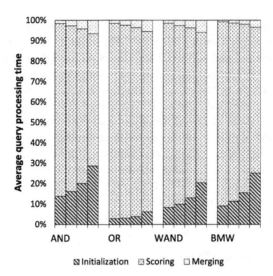

Fig. 5. The proportion of the average query processing time for the three stages in GPU-based query processing. We include measurements for $P \in \{32, 64, 128, 256\}$ threads per thread block, and for AND, OR, WAND, and BMW queries.

long posting lists on the CPU. and $P = 64$ threads per thread block is almost always the best P-value among those tested except for OR queries. In addition, average query processing time increases as top-K increases for every query type and different threads per thread block.

In the proposed GPU-based query processing algorithm, the query processing time splits into three major stages: (a) *Initialization*: The GPU threads identify which docIDs in posting lists belong to its assigned docID range, along with other initialization tasks; (b) *Scoring*: Traversing the posting lists to calculate the top-k results with the different strategies (AND, OR, WAND, and BMW); and (c) *Merging*: Going from the local top-k results to the final top-k results. Figure 5 plots the proportion of the average query processing time of these three stages, computed using 1000 random user queries. We see (a) the top-k scoring takes up most of the GPU query processing time and (b) the proportion of time spent on scoring decreases as P increases, while the proportion of initialization and merging time increases as P increases. This can explain the unimodal behavior seen in Table 1.

4.3 CPU-GPU Cooperative Version

We compare the performance of the proposed LBD method (introduced in Sect. 3.2) with the GPU and CPU-only methods, and with a *simple distribution* (SD) method, which randomly allocates half of the queries to CPU and the

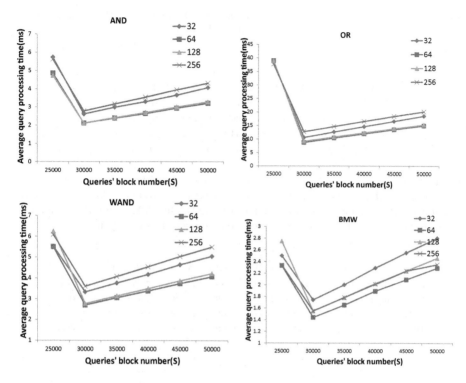

Fig. 6. The average query processing time for different threshold S (horizontal axis) in LBD. We include measurements for $P \in \{32, 64, 128, 256\}$ threads per thread block, and for AND, OR, WAND, and BMW queries.

other half to GPU. In order to achieve the best query processing throughput with our LBD method, we carry out the experiments by varying the threshold S. Figure 6 shows the average query processing time with different threshold S for AND, OR, WAND, and BMW queries. We see that (a) threshold $S = 30000$ results in the best performance among those tested in every case, and (b) $P = 64$ threads per thread block is almost always the best P-value among those tested.

Table 2 tabulates the average query processing time of SD and LBD, with a varying number of threads per thread block P (all when top-$K = 10$), and for AND, OR, WAND, and BMW queries. We list the best results among the tested threshold value (S) as the LDB results. We see (a) that LBD outperforms SD in every case, and (b) LBD algorithm shows a greater improvement in query processing time, particularly in the case of BMW queries.

4.4 Extensions

In this section we give some extensions of our GPU-based algorithm. we will test our algorithm on multi-GPUs cluster. In the experiment setting, we distribute

Table 2. Average query processing time (ms) for LBD and SD, and the difference Δ as a percentage of the SD time. Values in bold highlight the best observed average query processing time.

Method	32			64			128			256		
	SD	LBD	Δ	SD	LBD	Δ	SD	LBD	Δ	SD	LBD	Δ
AND	5.36	2.61	51.31%	4.2	**2.11**	49.76%	4.03	2.12	47.39%	5.22	2.78	46.74%
OR	23.2	10.6	54.31%	17.54	**8.76**	50.06%	16.87	9.19	45.52%	20.8	12.71	38.89%
WAND	6.32	3.33	47.31%	4.85	**2.69**	44.54%	4.84	2.77	42.77%	6.15	3.6	41.46%
BMW	3.79	1.74	54.09%	3.82	**1.44**	62.30%	3.85	1.55	59.74%	4.19	1.77	57.76%

Table 3. Average query processing time (ms) of the GPU-based algorithm on four GPUs and one GPU as the number of threads per GPU thread block, and the difference Δ as a percentage on one GPU time, and for the AND, OR, WAND and BMW queries. Values in bold highlight the best observed average query processing time.

Method	64			128			256		
	1 GPU	4 GPU	Δ	1 GPU	4 GPU	Δ	1 GPU	4 GPU	Δ
AND	5.81	1.51	74.01%	6.08	**1.38**	77.30%	7.56	1.65	78.17%
OR	30.32	5.67	81.30%	29.53	**5.38**	81.78%	34.42	6.50	81.12%
WAND	7.45	1.75	76.51%	7.86	**1.63**	79.26%	8.97	1.98	77.93%
BMW	4.47	0.94	78.97%	4.47	**0.93**	79.19%	6.51	1.12	82.80%

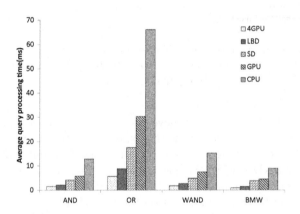

Fig. 7. The comparison between average query processing time (ms) for GPU-only, CPU-GPU cooperative (LBD and SD) and multi-GPUs (4 GPUs) ($P = 64$ and top-$K = 10$) with the CPU time. and for AND, OR, WAND, and BMW queries.

query batches across four GPUs. Table 3 tabulates the average query processing time of the one GPU and four GPUs algorithm as the number of threads GPU thread block (all top-$K = 10$). Interestingly, $P = 128$ threads per thread block is the best P-value among those tested.

Figure 7 compares the average query processing time for the two CPU-GPU cooperative query processing methods (LBD and SD, both with $P = 64$

threads per thread block) along with the GPU non-cooperative, 4 GPUs (all when $P = 64$) and CPU-only query processing methods. We see that utilizing a GPU and multi-GPUs for query processing can result in performance improvements for AND, OR, WAND, and BMW queries. Of the inspected methods, the LBD CPU-GPU cooperative method minimized query processing time, particularly in the case of BMW queries.

5   Conclusion and Future Work

In this paper, we propose two GPU-based query processing methods: one where the GPU performs parallel query processing for queries, and a CPU-GPU cooperative version where queries are simultaneously processed by both the CPU and GPU. We further develop a method for deciding which queries are processed by the CPU and GPU based on the lengths of the posting lists relevant to a query. In addition, we also evaluate the parallel query processing algorithm on multi-GPUs. Experiments indicate the CPU-GPU cooperative version results in around a 84% drop in average query processing time on one GPU and the multi-GPUs results can achieve 89% drop in average processing time.

We make the following suggestions on how to build upon this work:

- The GPU list cache policy could be optimized for the LBD method, e.g., by designing a dynamic caching algorithm which determines which posting lists are more likely to be needed by the GPU.
- We have not incorporated early termination in this work, which would reduce the time spent on top-k ranking. We have also not incorporated CPU-side parallelism in this work, which could allow the CPU to process a heavier workload.

Acknowledgment. This work is partially supported by NSF of China (grant numbers: 61373018, 61602266 11550110491), Science and Technology Development Plan of Tianjin (17JCYBJC15300, 16JCYBJC41900) and the Fundamental Research Funds for the Central Universities (Grant number: 65141020).

References

1. Agrawal, S.R., Pistol, V., Pang, V., Tran, J., Tarjan, D., Lebeck, A.R.: Rhythm: harnessing data parallel hardware for server workloads. In: Proceedings of ASPLOS, pp. 19–84 (2014)
2. Ao, N., Zhang, F., Wu, D., Stones, D.S., Wang, G., Liu, X., Liu, J., Lin, S.: Efficient parallel lists intersection and index compression algorithms using graphics processing units. Proc. VLDB Endow. **4**, 470–481 (2011)
3. Broder, A.Z., Carmel, D., Herscovici, M., Soffer, A., Zien, J.Y.: Efficient query evaluation using a two-level retrieval process. In: Proceedings of CIKM, pp. 426–434 (2003)
4. Ding, S., Attenberg, J., Baeza-Yates, R., Suel, T.: Batch query processing for web search engines. In: Proceedings of WSDM, pp. 137–146 (2011)

5. Ding, S., He, J., Yan, H., Suel, T.: Using graphics processors for high performance IR query processing. In: Proceedings of WWW, pp. 421–430 (2009)
6. Ding, S., Suel, T.: Faster top-k document retrieval using block-max indexes. In: Proceedings of SIGIR, pp. 993–1002 (2011)
7. Fang, R., He, B., Lu, M., Yang, K., Govindaraju, N.K., Luo, Q., Sander, P.V.: GPUQP: query co-processing using graphics processors. In: Proceedings of SIG-MOD, pp. 1061–1063 (2007)
8. NVIDIA: NVIDIA CUDA C programming guide (2015)
9. Robertson, S.E., Walker, S., Jones, S., Hancock-Beaulieu, M.M., Gatford, M.: Okapi at TREC-3, p. 109. NIST Special Publication, Gaithersburg (1995)
10. Rojas, O., Gil-Costa, V., Marin, M.: Efficient parallel block-max WAND algorithm. In: Wolf, F., Mohr, B., Mey, D. (eds.) Euro-Par 2013. LNCS, vol. 8097, pp. 394–405. Springer, Heidelberg (2013). doi:10.1007/978-3-642-40047-6_41
11. Silvestri, F.: Sorting out the document identifier assignment problem. In: Amati, G., Carpineto, C., Romano, G. (eds.) ECIR 2007. LNCS, vol. 4425, pp. 101–112. Springer, Heidelberg (2007). doi:10.1007/978-3-540-71496-5_12
12. Tatikonda, S., Cambazoglu, B.B., Junqueira, F.P.: Posting list intersection on multicore architectures. In: Proceeding of the 34th International ACM SIGIR Conference on Research and Development in Information Retrieval, SIGIR 2011, Beijing, China, pp. 963–972, 25–29 July 2011
13. Voorhees, E.M.: Overview of TREC 2003. In: Proceedings of TREC, pp. 1–13 (2003)
14. Wu, D., Zhang, F., Ao, N., Wang, G., Liu, X., Liu, J.: Efficient lists intersection by CPU-GPU cooperative computing. In: Proceedings of IPDPSW, pp. 1–8 (2010)
15. Yan, H., Ding, S., Suel, T.: Inverted index compression and query processing with optimized document ordering. In: Proceedings of WWW, pp. 401–410 (2009)
16. Zhang, F., Wu, D., Ao, N., Wang, G., Liu, X., Liu, J.: Fast lists intersection with bloom filter using graphics processing units. In: Proceedings of SAC, pp. 825–826 (2011)
17. Zhang, J., Long, X., Suel, T.: Performance of compressed inverted list caching in search engines. In: Proceedings of WWW, pp. 387–396 (2008)
18. Zhang, S., Zhang, C., You, Z., Zheng, R., Xu, B.: Asynchronous stochastic gradient descent for DNN training. In: IEEE International Conference on Acoustics, Speech and Signal Processing, ICASSP 2013, Vancouver, BC, Canada, pp. 6660–6663, 26–31 May 2013

KD-Tree and HEALPix-Based Distributed Cone Search Indexing System for Multi-Band Astronomical Catalogs

Chen Li[1], Ce Yu[1(✉)], Jian Xiao[1], Xiaoteng Hu[1], Hao Fu[1], Kun Li[1],
and Yanyan Huang[2]

[1] School of Computer Science and Technology,
Tianjin University, Tianjin 300350, China
{tju_lichen,yuce,xiaojian,xiaotenghu,haofu,likun30901}@tju.edu.cn
[2] Service Center for Information Security and Technology, Hebei University
of Technology, Tianjin 300130, China
huangyy@hebut.edu.cn

Abstract. An increasing number of telescopes are being built to provide multi-band data of celestial objects, which is indispensable to astronomical research. The amount of collected observation data, however, have put tremendous pressure on computing systems. Moreover, with the development of the observation equipment, the number of astronomical catalogs that telescopes generated per day keeps increasing rapidly. In this paper, we propose a distributed cone search indexing system (DCSIS) for Multi-Band Astronomical Catalogs among multi-band astronomical catalogs to solve this problem. Major contributions of DCSIS include defining new meta file format for astronomical catalogs, achieving scalability and parallelism for cone search, and the ability to flexibly add data to index system. Evaluations are performed on the Tianhe-1A supercomputer to showcase DCSIS' scalability for large scale deployment, the results of which show that DCSIS reduce the response time of Multi-band cone search into a tolerant range.

Keywords: Astronomical catalogs · Cone search · Distributed query system · HEALPix · Protobuf · KD-tree

1 Introduction

Multi-band observation data refers to the data about the same object obtained by telescopes of different bands (e.g. optical telescope, radio telescope, etc.). Varied astronomical features of a celestial object can be observed by telescopes of different bands. Figure 1(a) [1] shows the images of the Crab Nebula observed in 6 distinct bands.

No matter which band of observation apparatus it is, the astronomical catalog is the standard file recording all the corresponding information in tabular form. In other words, observation data of different bands associated with each other by astronomical catalogs.

© Springer International Publishing AG 2017
S. Ibrahim et al. (Eds.): ICA3PP 2017, LNCS 10393, pp. 239–253, 2017.
DOI: 10.1007/978-3-319-65482-9_16

Astronomical research requires all related records among the entire existing astronomical catalogs. With the development of virtual observatory (VO), more and more astronomical data has been uploaded to VO servers [5]. VO faces the problem of how to let astronomers get the required data from certain catalogs online in real time.

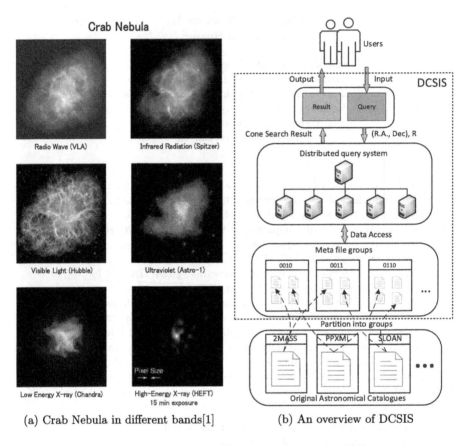

(a) Crab Nebula in different bands[1]   (b) An overview of DCSIS

Fig. 1. Background and the architecture of DCSIS

As telescopes keep producing huge amount of data, especially the telescopes like Five hundred meters Aperture Spherical Radio Telescope (FAST) in Guizhou China [19], the online service quality of VO might has difficulties to guaranteed. Investigation shows that FAST will take 3 TB storage space each day. The performance of VO might be affected due to the massive increasing data.

For astronomers, an efficient indexing service is needed to find related records from massive astronomical catalogs.

However, the features of massive astronomical data complicate this goal.

Data Integrity. Data integrity requires the completeness of all the observed ever produced. The massive spatial data push astronomical data centers to scale storage volume from terabyte (TB) to petabyte (PB) and force engineers to find an efficient way to guarantee the speed of response.

Cone Search. Cone search is a special search method in the field of astronomy and requires more calculations than ordinary search. It describes sky position and an angular distance, defining a cone on the sky. The response returns a list of astronomical sources from the catalog whose positions lie within the cone [14]. Because each catalog contains millions even billions of records, the amount of calculation could be very alarming if we were to do cone search among all existing catalogs.

Scalability. Because of the incremental data that all the telescopes produced each day, a distributed system with excellent scalability is needed.

In this paper, DCSIS (**D**istributed **C**one **S**earch **I**ndexing **S**ystem), is proposed to solve the problems listed above.

The architecture of DCSIS is shown as Fig. 1(b).

The major contributions of DCSIS can be summarized as follows.

Define a new meta file format for astronomical catalogs. We divide the astronomical catalogs and build KD-tree [8] for every partition to define a new meta file format of DCSIS. It reduce the time complexity of cone search from $O(N)$ to $O(\log(N))$. The meta file is also designed to handle boundary problem.

Design a parallel system with great scalability for cone search. We design a distributed query system whose compute nodes and storage nodes are separated to handle cone search request. When query coming, compute nodes load corresponding related meta files from storage nodes and execute cone search operation, then gather all results and return to users.

Flexibly add incremental data into index system. For incoming observation records, DCSIS transfers them into meta files and sort them with existing data together. When total data size reach the limit of storage system, the system can extend storage capability. The computing capability can be scaled to keep the response time unchanged.

Tianhe-1A [20] supercomputer is used as the evaluation environment. The astronomical catalogs like 2MASS, PPMXL, SDSS acquired from National Astronomical Observatories of the Chinese Academy of Sciences (NAOC) as the data set.

Evaluation result shows that DCSIS have great scalability and shorter response time compared to other databases.

The rest of the paper is organized as follows: Sect. 2 gives background and related work that motivated our work. The design of the DCSIS is present in Sect. 3. Section 4 describes experimentally evaluation of DCSIS. We conclude and discuss future work in Sect. 5.

2   Related Work

Cone search among multi-band astronomical catalogs is generally the first step of celestial object study, such as supernova discovery or drawing lighting curve.

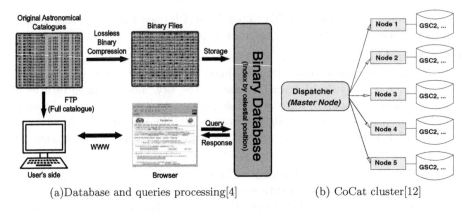

(a)Database and queries processing[4]   (b) CoCat cluster[12]

Fig. 2. Construction of VizieR

However, getting the complete result is difficult because of the large amount of multi-band catalogs.

A naive method is using relative database management system (RDBMS) [3,17]. But RDBMS meets its bottleneck when handle massive data. For instance, the observing data from Antarctic astronomy project of NAOC is stored in RDBMS which employed in VO servers. It takes up to 6.11 s doing cone search in a single astronomical catalog containing 13 million records. Consider there are a plenty of catalogs, its performance is not satisfactory for the need of astronomers.

Besides, RDBMS shows very poor performances especially in the updating phase: the addition of a new catalog can be required up to 4.6 millions times which perform dramatically slow.

There are a number of method that can handle massive scientific data. NoSQL is one of the most popular methods used to deal with such problem but it has high storage cost. HIVE, which is distributed SQL-like interface querying data based on Hadoop [16], and SciDB [2,15,18], which is designed to work on multi-dimensional scientific data, both need to import raw data files into file system. That means both methods would effectively require at least doubling the storage space. What's worse, astronomical data are no exception to the 20/80 rule (i.e. 80% of the queries focuses only on 20% of the data), which makes it even less cost-efficient to duplicate the entire data [7].

The mainstream approach for astronomers to do cone search is using VizieR [13]. VizieR, the most used cone search service involving multi-band astronomical catalogs, utilize indexing to find celestial targets. Users can upload parameters of cone search by browser and receive result online.

VizieR divides all catalogs into two categories: standard and large [12]. The standard catalogs with up to a few millon records are managed by a standard relational DBMS. The large catalog is defined as having more than 10^7 rows.

As shown in Fig. 2(a), those very large catalogs are compressed into binary files losslessly and consist of the index. Besides, Fig. 2(a) also present the ordinary astronomical research work flow that astronomers utilize VizieR to find which catalogs contain the records they interested and then download the original catalogs. When querying such a large catalog, a dedicated program handles the request, extracts and decodes the matching data, and sends its output back to VizieR [4].

In fact, astronomers need to access all catalogs involving the interested position. VizieR creates an inverted index in order to search complete result for astronomers [9]. The key of index is sky coverage ID and value is the catalogs that obtain data in corresponding block. VizieR find the index of the coordinate that users input and then look successively into the corresponding value finding all related catalogs [11].

Moreover, to reduce the response time, VizieR designs a Co-Cat (Co-processor Catalog, Fig. 2(b)) project to parallelize the VizieR [12]. Co-Cat put replication of all data on each node. The master node gather the results from slave nodes and response it to users.

VizieR, though widely used, still possesses a number of deficiencies, and improvements can be made to increase its query efficiency.

(1) Due to the two catalog categories, VizieR is obliged to handle cone search query in two method. What's more, relative DBMS has negative impact on scalability of the system.
(2) VizieR has to load and handle whole involved catalogs during every single query. That's inefficient because the involved data is actually a very small part of the whole (80/20 rule).
(3) Co-Cat put replication of all data on each node which is space-wasting.

By reference of VizieR, we propose our DCSIS. Our approach has some similar parts to VizieR and some optimization has been done in order to increase storage efficiency, reduce response time and improve scalability.

3   Proposed Distributed Cone Search Indexing System

The design of DCSIS is present in this section. The basic idea can be demonstrated by the three contributions of DCSIS that mentioned above.

3.1   Define a New Meta File Format for Astronomical Catalogs

Cone search needs 3 inputs: right ascension (R.A.), denoted by T_{ra}, declination (Dec), denoted by T_{dec}, and radius, denoted by R. It will find all the celestial objects that satisfy following formula:

$$(S_{ra} - T_{ra})^2 + (S_{dec} - T_{dec})^2 \leq R^2 \tag{1}$$

where S_{ra} and S_{dec} denote the set of celestial object's coordinate records from all existing astronomical catalogs. The time complexity is O(N) while using exhaustive search.

If we let M_E be the average number of records in a single catalog and *Total* denotes the number of catalogs we have, the time complexity of cone search among all catalogs is as followed:

$$Total \times O(M_E) \tag{2}$$

There are millions even billions of records in each existing catalog so that exhaustive search isn't appropriate because the time complexity is outrageous. To tackle this problem, a new meta file that fit for cone search is defined in DCSIS to reduce computational complexity. One of the favorable features is that astronomical catalogs are static after published. That's to say, there is no update or modification in any published catalogs. What's more, catalogs are independent for each catalog maps only one astronomical observation. The process of building meta files for a single catalog is demonstrated as followed.

Step 1: Divide Astronomical Catalogs into Blocks. First of all, R.A and Dec are extracted from original catalog and combined a temporary file. Then, we divided the whole sky into a mesh and every block in the mesh has its own ID so that every record in the temporary file has an ID of sky block that it belongs to. The records with the same block ID are put together and combined into new files. So the temporary file has been split into many smaller partition files.

Step 2: Control the File Size Within a Certain Range. For M_E is increasing day by day, the scalability must be considered. Thus, a distributed query system is set up to reduce response time. As we will demonstrate in the following section, the complete time of a single query depends on the most time-consuming task. The size of all partition files must be kept at about the same level (the reason why we don't make blocks as small as possible will be addressed in **Step 3**) ensuring that there is no obstacle affecting response time of each search. Thus, adaptive mesh refinement (AMR) is applied to control the partition file size within a certain range. Here is our AMR strategy:

(1) If the size of a sky block exceeded a certain threshold, divide it into 4 sub-blocks;
(2) If the total size of 4 sub-blocks less than threshold, combine them into a whole;
(3) Do (1) and (2) until all blocks needn't to be changed.

The most appropriate size of the certain threshold will be discussed in Sect. 4.

Step 3: Adding Redundancy into Partition File. Redundant data is added into every partition file to solve boundary problem. As the Fig. 3(a) shows, if we want to find all objects around circular area in a certain block whose center is very close to the block boundary, the target that located in the adjoining block might be missed. It's a common and inevitable problem in cross-matching and

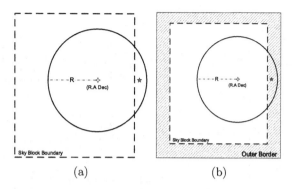

Fig. 3. Boundary problem and "outer border"

cone search. Therefore, "outer border" is added in each partition file to ensure the completeness of the query results.

As Fig. 3(b) shown, the "outer border" consists of the data from eight neighboring blocks in different directions and the breadth of it must larger than cone search radius.

If the breadth of "outer border" is fixed, the proportion of redundancy data would increase when using smaller blocks. That's why the blocks can't be as small as possible.

Step 4: Build KD-tree for Partition File. K-dimensional tree (KD-tree) is a data structure which can organize points in a k-dimensional space by spatial-partition [8]. It is useful in searching by multidimensional keys and finding K nearest neighbours. The time complexity using KD-tree to search is log(N). KD-tree is applied in building meta files because it is consistent with the need of cone search. We take all (R.A., Dec) in partition files as coordinate of points and build KD-tree for every partition file.

Step 5: Serialization. Our last step is serializing KD-tree into binary files because KD-tree is just a type of data structure stored in memory. The produced binary files are saved in disks for data persistence. Those binary files are the final meta files of DCSIS. The whole process of generating meta file for a single catalog is shown in Fig. 4.

All existing catalogs are processed from **Step 1** to **Step 5**. Thus, the time complexity of cone search on all existing catalogs is as followed:

$$Total \times O(log(\frac{M_E}{p} + M_{red})) \qquad (3)$$

where p denotes the average number of partition files for a single catalog and M_{red} denotes the redundancy of each partition. When M_{red} is as small as possible, (3) is much less than (2).

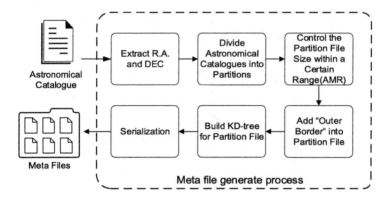

Fig. 4. Process of generating meta files

So far, we have already reduced time complexity of cone search from O(N) to O(log(N)). When query coming, DCSIS will load corresponding meta files into memory and do cone search.

3.2 Design a Distributed Query System for Cone Search

Though meta file has good performance on time complexity of cone search, it can just be processed by only one thread or node since KD-tree must be read from the root. But we can still parallelize cone search query by partitioning the whole task since each cone search query involves a number of catalogs. Each process load meta files and return result.

The complete time of doing cone search in serial can be defined as:

$$T_{serial} + T_{para} \tag{4}$$

where T_{serial} denotes the time of the part that can't be paralleled. and T_{para} denotes the time of the part which can be paralleled. So if we run cone search in parallel, the overall completion time $T_{overall}$ can be defined as:

$$T_{overall} = T_{serial} + \frac{T_{para}}{M} \tag{5}$$

where M denotes the number of threads or nodes in parallel system.

The process time of each meta file is almost the same since the meta file size is controlled. Thus, let $t_{process}$ represent it,

$$T_{para} = t_{process} * n_k \tag{6}$$

$$T_{overall} = T_{serial} + \frac{t_{process} * n_k}{M} \tag{7}$$

where n_k denoted the number of meta files that involved in a single cone search. The makespan decided by the maximal of $t_{process}$. Thus, The makespan could be

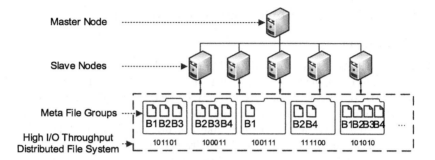

Fig. 5. The architecture of distributed query system in DCSIS

minimized if M is maximized and the maximal of $t_{process}$ is minimized. That's why we must control the meta file size.

In order to maximize M, in other words, utilize as many threads or nodes as possible, a parallel querying system whose architecture is shown in Fig. 5 is designed, of which compute nodes and storage nodes are separated and connected via a infinite-band network. It's composed by master node, slave nodes and storage nodes with high I/O throughput distributed file system. In this kind of file system, slave nodes can access any of meta files and benefit the workload balance for different query.

What's more, in order to make slave nodes find related indexing easily, the meta files in file system are sorted by sky block ID and consist of many meta file groups.

When a cone search query comes:

(1) Master node broadcast the input to the slave nodes.
(2) Every slave node start to search corresponding meta file groups finding a related meta file which is not be found by other slave nodes.
(3) Then the slave node do cone search on the meta file and return result to master node.
(4) Do (2)(3) until there is no related meta file can be found.
(5) Master node gather all results from slave nodes and send it to users.

Compared to CoCat, the distributed query system we design can make better use of storage resource without replication of the data. By sharing the whole storage nodes, we can take advantage of the compute nodes as much as possible and maximize M.

3.3   Flexibly Add Incremental Data into Index System

When new astronomical catalogs comes, they will be processed step by step like Sect. 3.1. The new meta files will be put in storage nodes with other existing meta data generated before. Due to the compute nodes and storage nodes are separated, when total data size reach the limit of storage system, the system can extend storage capability and the computing capability can be scaled accordingly to keep the response time in range.

4   Implement and Performance Evaluation

4.1   Implement

HEALPix. HEALPix is acronym for Hierarchical Equal Area isoLatitude Pixe-
lation of a sphere [10] developed by NASA. It is a typical virtual spatial-indexing
function partitioning the whole sky into a recursive quad-tree pixel sub-blocks,
which establishes a index of sky coverage blocks, and each block has an unique
ID by their coordinate and hierarchy, like Fig. 6(a). It is utilized to partition
the astronomical catalogs. Each block partitioned by HEALPix is divided into
4 sub-blocks, which means only the additional 2-bit-length code need be added
to the end of the father block's number. Since HEALPix is a hierarchical mesh,
we apply it on AMR.

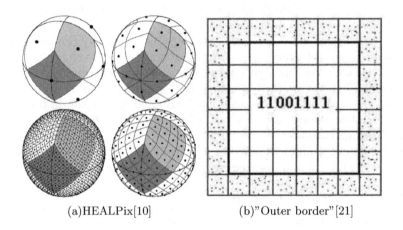

(a)HEALPix[10]   (b)"Outer border"[21]

Fig. 6. HEALPix and "outer border"

As far as we know, the common radius of cone search is 15–20. We partition
the eight neighboring blocks on the level 13 using HEALPix C facility, since 13
is the maximum level of the C HEALPix. More importantly, the breadth of the
level-13 blocks is slightly larger than 20 arcsec. All level-13 blocks next to border
are picked up and combine them into "outer border" like Fig. 6(b) [21].

Protocol Buffer. Protobuf is an open-source tool developed by Google [6]. It's
a method of serializing structured data into binary format which is compact,
forward- and backward-compatible. And we take advantage of it to serialize
meta files.

4.2   Evaluation Results

With the help of NAOC, the widely-used astronomical data like 2MASS,
PPMXL, SDSS, USNOB2 and other truthful astronomical catalogs are as the
dataset. The details of dataset are shown in Table 1.

Table 1. The file size of DCSIS data set

Name of catalogs	2MASS	PPMXL	SDSS	USNOB2
Num of records	470,992,971	910,469,430	134,269,975	305,391,856
Original file size (GB)	200.2	198.2	253.4	39.1

Building Time and Storage Effect of the Different Meta File Sizes.
First of all, we evaluate the building time and storage efficiency in various meta
file size. Our test PC is equipped with an Intel i7-4970 CPU (4 cores@3.6 GHz),
16 GB of RAM, and two HDDs, one (1 TB) for the Ubuntu operating system,
the other (3 TB) for storing the data set. The files which contain from 1 million
to 15 million records are extracted from 2MASS. We transfer them into meta
files and compared the building time and file size with each other.

Table 2. Evaluation of indexing building time

Num of records (Million)	1	3	5	7	9	11	13	15
Original file size (GB)	0.422	1.275	2.128	2.973	3.524	4.676	5.526	6.375
Meta file size (MB)	27.1	83.4	141.8	191.8	242.7	308.7	358.7	408.7
Rates(%)	6.27	6.38	6.50	6.30	6.73	6.44	6.30	6.26
Building time (s)	0.914	2.960	5.318	7.368	10.386	12.299	14.166	16.016

From Table 2, we can see that the "Rates", which means the ratio of meta
file size to original file, are similar in different amount of data records. As we can
see from the results, the meta file building time, in principle, increases linearly
as the data set grows. This is due to the meta file building process having a
time complexity of $O(n)$. Building meta file for 6 GB of a astronomical catalog
takes about 16 s, which, considering that the meta file building is just a one-time
thing, is pretty acceptable in real life usage.

Consider the redundancy data would increase when using smaller block and
the IO increase when using larger block, we choose 7 million as our file size
threshold in AMR.

Response Time of Cone Search Query. Table 3 shows the response time of
cone search query on a single meta file. Through the comparison with the correct
results from VizieR, the query results returned in our evaluation are credible.

The time of locating corresponding meta files can be ignored since all the
meta files are sorted by sky block IDs in our storage system. Therefore, the
response time consists of two parts: meta file loading time, whose time complexity
is $O(N)$, and query time, whose time complexity is $O(logN)$.

From Table 3 we can see that the response time can form a linear curve.
That's because the consuming time of loading meta files is far greater than

Table 3. Response time of different meta file size

Num of records (Million)	1	3	5	7	9	11	13	15
File loading time (s)	0.154	0.462	0.763	1.092	1.419	1.695	2.027	2.316
Query time (ms)	0.008	0.008	0.009	0.009	0.009	0.009	0.010	0.011
Response time (s)	0.154	0.462	0.764	1.092	1.419	1.695	2.028	2.317

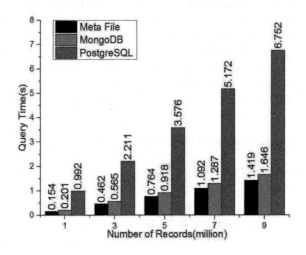

Fig. 7. Query time comparison between different databases

which of query time. Due to the time complexity, the query time is pretty short and almost keep unchanged when number of records increasing.

Besides, our approach has compared with the other two query methods: MongoDB and PostgreSQL on query time. The records in indexing are put into different databases whose query time are present in Fig. 7. When doing cone search on the same dataset, our approach consumes the shortest time compared with other methods and shows the excellent performance. It is worth mentioning that MongoDB and PostgreSQL take about 5 min and 2 h loading a single indexing with 1 million records. Compared to the building time of meta file, it is extremely slow.

Scalability. DCSIS is deployed on Tianhe-1A supercomputer for evaluate the scalability. Tianhe-1A supercomputer equipped with 256 compute nodes, 8 I/O nodes, 8 TB memory capacity and 96 TB storage capacity. The communication bandwidth of Tianhe-1A is 40 Gbps. The number of processes we set in Tianhe-1A are 1, 2, 4, 8, 16, 32, 64 and 128.

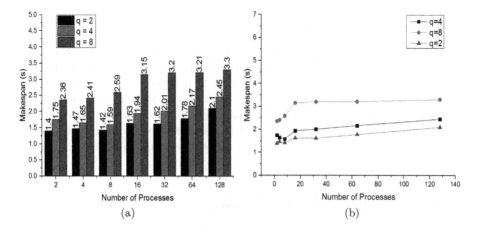

Fig. 8. Makespan of DCSIS in different process workload

To expand data scale, we add noise into 4 truthful catalogs which mentioned before and create 1200 different astronomical catalogs which totally contain about 70 billion records. These experimental catalogs are processed into meta files and threw into the Lustre of Tianhe-1A, which can handle very high concurrent IO requests efficiently. The dataset of meta files we use is expanded up to 10 TB and the related original astronomical catalogs is up to 200 TB.

The scalability of our method is tested by executing cone search query on different amount of datasets with different number of processes. Based on the evaluation result before, the AMR threshold is set to 7 million to allow for best performance.

DCSIS showed excellent both on weak scalability and strong scalability.

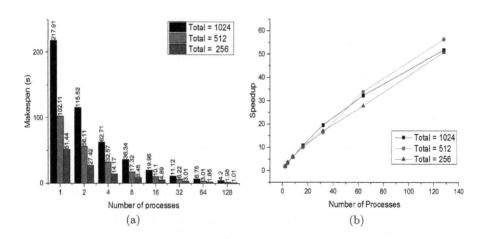

Fig. 9. Makespan and speedup of DCSIS in different amount of data set

From Fig. 8 we can see that, when q fixed, the makespan almost remains unchanged. Here q means the Ratio of the total number of files and the number of processes, or can be realized as the workload of each process. In our evaluation environment, a single node has 12 processors. Thus, when we test DCSIS in more than 12 processes, the communication and I/O increase. That's why when we use 2, 4 and 8 processes, the makespan is a bit shorter than 16, 32, 64 and 128.

The *Total* in Fig. 9 denotes the total number of catalogs in the data set. The speedup shown in Fig. 9(b) increases linearly as the number of processes grows. That's because there is a few communication between processes when doing cone search and the workload of every process keep balanced.

5   Conclusion and Future Work

In this paper, DCSIS, KD-tree and Protobuf-Based distributed cone search indexing System for multi-band astronomical catalogs is presented. DCSIS defines a new meta file format for cone search indexing about astronomical catalogs, do cone search in parallel and handle the incremental astronomical data.

Evaluation results shows that DCSIS perform well on scalability. The method of the meta file definition, distributed query system design are presented, whose experimental results has corroborated the theory and testified that our method have reduced the time complexity of cone search.

Generally speaking, the three contributions of DCSIS fix the problem that how to unify astronomical catalogs into a query system since catalogs is the common description of astronomical observation in any band.

For future work, distributed meta file building process, meta files storage with fault-tolerant as well as the optimization of response time in high concurrency might bring new interesting challenges to DCSIS.

Acknowledgements. This work is supported by the Joint Research Fund in Astronomy (U1531111) under cooperative agreement between the National Natural Science Foundation of China (NSFC) and Chinese Academy of Sciences (CAS), the National Natural Science Foundation of China (11573019, 61602336). Special thanks goes to Mr. Zhi Hong for providing writing assistance for the paper.

References

1. Crab nebula messier 1. http://www.constellation-guide.com/crab-nebula-messier-1/
2. Brown, P.G.: Overview of sciDB: large scale array storage, processing and analysis. In: ACM SIGMOD International Conference on Management of Data, pp. 963–968 (2010)
3. Chilingarian, I., Bartunov, O., Richter, J., Sigaev, T.: PostgreSQL: the suitable DBMS solution for astronomy and astrophysics, vol. 314, p. 225 (2004)
4. Derriere, S., Ochsenbein, F., Egret, D.: On-line access to very large catalogues. In: Astronomical Data Analysis Software and Systems IX, vol. 216, p. 235 (2000)

5. Djorgovski, S.G., Williams, R.: Virtual observatory: From concept to implementation. Computer Science (2005)
6. Google: Google protocol buffers homepage. https://developers.google.com/protocol-buffers/
7. Hong, Z., Yu, C., Xia, R., Xiao, J., Wang, J., Sun, J., Cui, C.: AQUAdex: a highly efficient indexing and retrieving method for astronomical big data of time series images. In: Wang, G., Zomaya, A., Perez, G.M., Li, K. (eds.) ICA3PP 2015. LNCS, vol. 9529, pp. 92–105. Springer, Cham (2015). doi:10.1007/978-3-319-27122-4_7
8. Hu, L., Nooshabadi, S., Ahmadi, M.: Massively parallel KD-tree construction and nearest neighbor search algorithms. In: IEEE International Symposium on Circuits and Systems, pp. 2752–2755 (2015)
9. Landais, G., Ochsenbein, F.: The new version of the vizier catalogue service. Mod. Lang. Notes **461**(3), 383 (2012)
10. NASA: Jet propulsion laboratory healpix homepage. http://healpix.jpl.nasa.gov/
11. Ochsenbein, F.: The vizier system for accessing astronomical data. vol. 145, p. 387 (1998)
12. Ochsenbein, F., Derriere, S., Nicaisse, S., Schaaff, A.: Clustering the large vizier catalogues, the cocat experience. vol. 314, p. 58 (2004)
13. Ochsenbein, F., Bauer, P., Marcout, J.: Astronomy and astrophysics the vizier database of astronomical catalogues (2000)
14. Plante, R., Williams, R., Hanisch, R., Szalay, A.: Simple cone search version 1.03 (2008)
15. Planthaber, G., Stonebraker, M., Frew, J.: EarthDB: scalable analysis of MODIS data using sciDB. In: ACM Sigspatial International Workshop on Analytics for Big Geospatial Data, pp. 11–19 (2012)
16. Richter, S., Schuh, S., Dittrich, J.: Towards zero-overhead static and adaptive indexing in hadoop. VLDB J. **23**(3), 469–494 (2014)
17. Smareglia, R., Laurino, O., Knapic, C.: VODance: VO data access layer service creation made easy. vol. 442, p. 575 (2011)
18. Stonebraker, M., Brown, P., Poliakov, A., Raman, S.: The architecture of sciDB. In: Bayard Cushing, J., French, J., Bowers, S. (eds.) SSDBM 2011. LNCS, vol. 6809, pp. 1–16. Springer, Heidelberg (2011). doi:10.1007/978-3-642-22351-8_1
19. Xinhua: Xinhua insight: Installation complete on world's largest radio telescope. http://news.xinhuanet.com/english/2016-07/03/c_135485389.htm
20. Yang, X.J., Liao, X.K., Lu, K., Hu, Q.F., Song, J.Q., Su, J.S.: The TianHe-1A supercomputer: its hardware and software. J. Comput. Sci. Technol. **26**(3), 344–351 (2011)
21. Zhao, Q., Sun, J., Yu, C., Xiao, J., Cui, C., Zhang, X.: Improved parallel processing function for high-performance large-scale astronomical cross-matching. Trans. Tianjin Univ. **17**(1), 62–67 (2011)

An Out-of-Core Branch and Bound Method for Solving the 0-1 Knapsack Problem on a GPU

Jingcheng Shen[1]([✉]), Kentaro Shigeoka[2], Fumihiko Ino[1], and Kenichi Hagihara[1]

[1] Graduate School of Information Science and Technology, Osaka University,
1-5 Yamadaoka, Suita, Osaka 565-0871, Japan
jc-shen@ist.osaka-u.ac.jp
[2] Hitachi High-Technologies Corporation, 14-24-1 Nishishinjuku,
Minato-ku, Tokyo 105-8717, Japan

Abstract. In this paper, we propose an out-of-core branch and bound (B&B) method for solving the 0–1 knapsack problem on a graphics processing unit (GPU). Given a large problem that produces many subproblems, the proposed method dynamically swaps subproblems out to CPU memory. We adopt two strategies to realize this swapping-out procedure with minimum amount of CPU-GPU data transfer. The first strategy is a GPU-based stream compaction strategy that reduces the sparseness of arrays. The second strategy is a double buffering strategy that hides the data transfer overhead by overlapping data transfer with GPU-based B&B operations. Experimental results show that the proposed method can store 33.7 times more subproblems than the previous method, solving twice more instances on the GPU. As for the stream compaction strategy, an input-output separated scheme runs 13.1% faster than an input-output unified scheme.

Keywords: Out-of-core computation · Branch and bound · Knapsack · GPU

1 Introduction

The 0-1 knapsack problem [1], a combinatorial optimization problem, appears in a wide range of fields such as manufacturing, logistics, and finance. Given n (≥ 1) items, each with its profit and weight, the problem is to determine which item should be included in a knapsack such that the total weight is not beyond capacity c and the total profit is as large as possible:

$$\text{maximize} \quad \sum_{i=1}^{n} p_i x_i$$
$$\text{subject to} \quad \sum_{i=1}^{n} w_i x_i \leq c, \ i \in \{1, 2, \ldots, n\},$$

where p_i and w_i are the profit and weight of the i-th item, respectively, and $x_i \in \{0, 1\}$ is the binary decision variable that decides if the i-th item will be

© Springer International Publishing AG 2017
S. Ibrahim et al. (Eds.): ICA3PP 2017, LNCS 10393, pp. 254–267, 2017.
DOI: 10.1007/978-3-319-65482-9_17

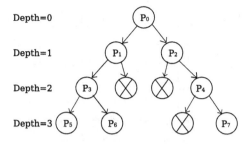

Fig. 1. A search tree of B&B approach. In this figure, node P_i refers to the i-th subproblem. Especially, the root P_0 refers to the original problem. Pruned subproblems (i.e., passive subproblems) are marked with "X."

included or not: $x_i = 1$ if included and $x_i = 0$ otherwise. The B&B [2] approach, a widely-known scheme for obtaining optimal solutions for NP-hard combinatorial optimization problems, is the most common way to effectively find the optimal solutions of knapsack problems [1]. This iterative scheme reduces the search space by using upper and lower bounds updated every time iterations continue. Each iteration consists of branching, bounding, and pruning operations. The branching operation decomposes a problem into multiple small subproblems. The bounding operation then computes the lower and upper bounds for each subproblem. Finally, the pruning operation discards unpromising (passive) subproblems whose upper bounds are smaller than the best solution found so far. The remained promising (active) subproblems proceed to the next iteration to further apply these three operations. The outline of B&B approach is shown in Fig. 1.

Many B&B approaches successfully solved knapsack problems by exploiting data parallelism using various parallel machines such as single-instruction multiple-data (SIMD) machines [3], cluster systems [4], computational grids [5,6], and graphics processing units (GPUs) [7–10]. Among these parallel machines, the GPU [11] is a powerful accelerator device for not only graphics applications but also compute- and memory-intensive applications [12,13]. However, the capacity of GPU memory, 12 GB for example, is relatively small as compared to that of CPU memory. Furthermore, previous GPU-based methods use the GPU memory to manage subproblems, so that these methods fail to solve large problems that rapidly consume GPU memory due to splitting subproblems.

Therefore, in this paper, we present an out-of-core B&B method for solving large 0-1 knapsack problems that exhaust the GPU memory due to many subproblems to be investigated. Our out-of-core method relaxes the limitation of problem size (i.e., maximum number of subproblems) from the capacity of GPU memory to that of CPU memory. To solve a large problem, our method buffers the data of subproblems in the CPU memory rather than the GPU memory. However, such a CPU-centric subproblem management scheme increases the CPU-GPU data transfer that impairs the performance of GPU acceleration. For the purpose of alleviating this side effect, we integrate two optimization

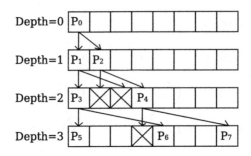

Fig. 2. An array-based subproblem management scheme. Pruned subproblems (i.e., passive subproblems) marked with "X" make the array sparse as the depth of the search tree increases.

strategies into our method: (1) a stream compaction strategy accelerated on the GPU completely and (2) a double buffering strategy required for efficient pipelining. Stream compaction here is an important process that converts sparse arrays into dense arrays for reducing the data to be transferred as well as achieving full utilization of massive GPU cores. In order to find an efficient scheme for the stream compaction strategy, we compare a separated scheme with a unified scheme. The separated scheme differentiates an output array from the input array to store the compacted data. On the contrary, the unified scheme uses a single array for both input and output. As such, the unified scheme allows the GPU to simultaneously process 1.5–2 times more subproblems than the separated scheme. As for the double buffering strategy, it hides the data transfer overhead by overlapping data transfer with GPU-based B&B operations.

Following this introduction, Sect. 2 presents related studies of this paper. Section 3 then summarizes GPU-based B&B methods. Section 4 describes our method and Sect. 5 shows experimental results. Finally, Sect. 6 comprises conclusion and future work.

2   Related Work

Boukedjar *et al.* [8] presented a B&B approach that solves the 0-1 knapsack problem on a GPU. Their method managed subproblems in the GPU memory with arrays standing for subproblems. Their method describes a subproblem with several attributes such as the upper and the lower bounds of profit, and currently obtained profit and weight. They prepared an array for each of those attributes. However, those arrays may get sparse after B&B operations (Fig. 2), because elements representing passive subproblems will never be referred again. The sparseness wastes the GPU memory with useless data and harms the locality of reference. Therefore, they integrated a CPU-based compaction strategy into their method for reducing the sparseness. The basic idea for their compaction strategy is to exchange passive elements and active elements with a quicksort-wise scheme, so that all the active subproblems are stored continuously in the front of the array. Because this is a CPU-based sequential operation, their method transfers all attributes from the GPU memory to the CPU memory every time the compaction proceeds. Therefore, CPU-GPU data transfer remains as a performance bottleneck.

To reduce the amount of data transfer between the CPU and GPU, Lalami *et al.* [9] presented an extension of [8] by restricting transferred data to a single attribute: label data (i.e., label array), where a label shows whether an element is active (*label* = 1) or passive (*label* = 0). They focused on the data access pattern required for compaction. That is, any attribute array generates the same pattern as those generated by other attribute arrays. As such, they computed the pattern on the CPU, according to the label data, and reused that information to carry out stream compaction for every attribute array on the GPU. This extension successfully doubled the performance compared to the baseline method [8]. However, it is still inevitable to transfer data between the GPU and the CPU every time the stream compaction proceeds. Moreover, their method can solve larger problems if subproblems are managed in the CPU memory.

Carneiro *et al.* [14] presented a GPU-accelerated B&B approach that uses a hybrid scheme of breadth first search and depth first search to solve the symmetric traveling salesman problem. Their method initially performs breadth first search on the CPU to generate many initial subproblems to be examined in parallel. After that, the method switches to depth first search that processes B&B operations on the GPU. However, similar to [8], the stream compaction strategy was not integrated into this approach.

3   B&B Approach for Solving Knapsack Problem

The branching operation of the B&B approach is to divide one n-variable (item) problem into two $(n-1)$-variable subproblems. These two subproblems respectively stand for the two cases of decision for the i-th item, where $1 \leq i \leq n$. For an n-item knapsack problem, from the first item to the last item, we iteratively divide one problem into two subproblems with a breadth-first search scheme.

On the other hand, the bounding operation is to reduce the search space by judging each subproblem whether it is possible to get an optimal solution or not. For this purpose, the bounding operation computes the upper and the lower bounds for every existing subproblem. A subproblem whose upper bound is smaller than the best (i.e., biggest) lower bound is passive and must be deleted from the search space. In the following discussion, we assume that items are sorted according to decreasing profit per ratio. This assumption facilitates lower bound computation mentioned below. Let k be the index of the current item to be examined for decision. Let also I_v be the set of items picked for a subproblem, i.e., a vertex v in the search tree. The weight and profit of vertex v, W_v and P_v, respectively, then can be computed as follows:

$$W_v = \sum\nolimits_{i \in I_v} w_i, \tag{1}$$

$$P_v = \sum\nolimits_{i \in I_v} \tag{2}$$

A vertex v can be described as a tuple $(W_v, P_v, U_v, L_v, S_v)$, where U_v and L_v represent an upper and lower bounds of the vertex, respectively, and S_v is the slack variable [9] for the vertex such that

$$\sum_{i=k+1}^{S_v-1} w_i \le c - w_v < \sum_{i=k+1}^{S_v} w_i. \qquad (3)$$

That is, the slack variable S_v is determined by picking all items after the k-th item as long as the knapsack can. Using the slack variable, the residual capacity r of the knapsack is given by:

$$r = c - W_v - \sum_{i=k+1}^{S_v-1} w_i. \qquad (4)$$

A lower bound L_v can be obtained by picking the abovementioned items (i.e., from $k+1$ to $S_v - 1$) and others in a greedy manner:

$$L_v = P_v + \sum_{i=k+1}^{S_v-1} p_i + \sum_{i=k+1}^{n} p_i x_i, \qquad (5)$$

where $x_i = 1$ if $w_i \le r - \sum_{j=S_v+1}^{i-1} w_j x_j$. With respect to an upper bound U_v, on the other hand, we adopt the Dantzig bound [15] that can be given by:

$$U_v = P_v + \sum_{i=k+1}^{S_v-1} p_i + \lfloor rP_{S_v}/W_{S_v} \rfloor. \qquad (6)$$

4   Proposed Method

The proposed method deploys a CPU-centric subproblem management scheme that exploits the large capacity of the CPU memory to relax the limitation of problem size. However, this out-of-core method can increase the amount of CPU-GPU data transfer, so that we integrate two strategies into our method to mitigate this side effect. The first strategy is a stream compaction strategy that proceeds on GPU completely. As such, it eliminates the data transfer for the pattern computation and increases the parallelism of the pattern computation, compared to [9]. The second strategy is a double buffering strategy that pipelines a series of operations. The strategy hides the overhead of CPU-GPU data transfer by overlapping the GPU-based B&B operations with the CPU-GPU data transfer.

4.1   CPU-Centric Subproblem Management

For an efficient CPU-centric subproblem management, the data structure that stores subproblems must satisfy two requirements.

(1) The data structure must be accessed randomly by a GPU thread with $\mathcal{O}(1)$ time.
(2) The data structure stores subproblems continuously without fragmentation in order to improve the efficiency of direct memory access (DMA) required for CPU-GPU data transfer.

To satisfy requirement (1), we choose arrays as a buffer for storing subproblems in the CPU memory. To satisfy requirement (2), we organize the buffer in a circular manner with two pointers: pointer *head* pointed to the first subproblem in the buffer and pointer *tail* pointed to the position behind the last subproblem in the buffer. For every iteration, we transfer a series of subproblems that begin with the subproblems pointed by head from the CPU memory to the GPU memory in order to process GPU-based B&B operations. On the other hand, when we predict that the GPU memory will be exhausted after the next branching operation, we transfer the subproblems from the GPU memory to the CPU memory, stored from the position pointed by tail. Every time a data transfer operation proceeds, the position of head or tail (according to the operation) is updated by an increment of the amount of transferred data. Furthermore, the circular manner means that if we reach the last position of the buffer during transferring data, we turn to its first position again. However, in this occasion, we must call the data transferring function once more, because of the change of the baseline address.

These transfer and computation jobs proceed iteratively until all the subproblems are finished, meaning that decision of the last item, i.e., x_n, is done for every subproblem. Moreover, the proposed method either prunes a finished subproblem if it is judged as passive, or set aside the finished subproblem if it is judged as active currently. In no case does the proposed method branch a finished subproblem.

4.2 Stream Compaction Strategy

To avoid extra CPU-GPU data transfer when computing the data access pattern required for compaction, we adopt a stream compaction strategy that proceeds on the GPU completely. Our stream compaction strategy computes the data access pattern on the GPU instead of the CPU. Moreover, we compare two stream compaction variations, a separated scheme and a unified scheme. The separated scheme requires that the input array (i.e., the array to be compacted) is separated from the output array. As such, the separated scheme consumes more GPU memory than the unified scheme. However, the separated scheme is cogent and it avoids any preprocess. On the other hand, the unified scheme compacts the input array within itself, instead of using a separated output array. Therefore, given that we adopt a double buffering strategy, the buffer size of the unified scheme is 1.5 times bigger than that of the separated scheme. However, the unified scheme requires a preprocess phase for compaction, which incurs an extra overhead. The details of both schemes are presented below.

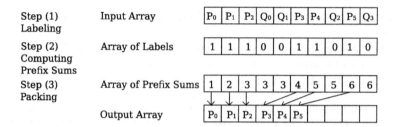

Fig. 3. An overview of the separated stream compaction scheme. In this figure, P_i refers to an active subproblem while Q_i refers to a passive subproblem. In step (1), we associate active and passive subproblems with 1 and 0, respectively. In step (2), we then apply the computation of prefix sums to the array of labels, in order to obtain the array of prefix sums that indicates where to move the active subproblems (i.e., the data access pattern). Finally, in step (3), we contiguously pack the active subproblems into the output array according to the array of prefix sums.

Separated Scheme. The separated stream compaction is a filtering process. The elements that meet the requirements will be selected from the input array, and then be packed into the output array. Generally, the compaction process is done in three steps (Fig. 3): (1) preparation of the array of labels, (2) computation of prefix sums, and (3) packing procedure. We use the thrust library [16] to implement prefix sums computation.

Unified Scheme. The unified scheme overwrites the input array by immediately moving some active elements onto passive elements (Fig. 4). The general idea is to calculate the number of active elements n_a that is used as a border index. We can predict that all active elements will be stored in the first n_a elements of the input array after compaction. Thus, we only need to move the active elements stored after the border index onto the passive elements stored before the border index. The unified scheme requires preparation of the array of labels, computation of prefix sums, and packing procedure, the same as the separated scheme. Besides, the unified requires a preprocess phase before the packing procedure. This preprocess phase consists of two steps:

(1) The unified scheme computes the number of active elements (n_a) that is used as the border index.
(2) The unified scheme associates active elements with passive elements by calculating the order number of every active element stored after the border index and the order number of every passive element stored before the border index. For instance, the i-th active element stored after the border index is associated with the i-th passive element stored before the border index. By doing so, the unified scheme prepares a lookup table for looking up the destinations where the active elements should be moved.

Algorithm 1 describes the lookup table preparation procedure.

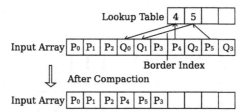

Fig. 4. An overview of the unified stream compaction scheme based on a lookup table.

Algorithm 1. Preparation for a lookup table.

Input: (1)*Labels*, the array of labels and (2) *Sums*, the array of prefix sums
Output: *Table*, the lookup table
1 $i := threadID$
2 **if** $n_a \leq i$ **then**
3   **return**
4 **end if**
5 $l := Labels[i]$
6 **if** $l = 0$ **then**
7      $passive\_order\_number := i - Sums[i]$
8      $Table[passive\_order\_number] := i$
9 **end if**

4.3 Double Buffering Strategy

In order to hide the overhead of CPU-GPU data transfer, we realize a double buffering strategy that overlaps the CPU-GPU data transfer with GPU-based B&B operations using two CUDA streams (Fig. 5). A CUDA stream here is a sequence of operations that execute in issue-order on the GPU [17]. The data transfer proceeds on a stream using buffer A while the GPU-based B&B operations proceed on the other stream using buffer B. When operations on both streams complete, the strategy exchanges the references of buffer A and buffer B (i.e., pointer A and pointer B in Fig. 5), and then proceeds to the next iteration of this overlapped transfer and computation procedure until finishing processing all subproblems left in the circular buffer. However, before the next iteration, the strategy must synchronize both streams to ensure operations of the current iteration have finished. We carry out synchronization to prevent both streams from simultaneous data transfer, lest the circular buffer is inconsistent.

Besides, we appropriately use two execution modes according to the number of subproblems managed on the CPU. If the circular buffer lacks sufficient subproblems to fully exploit the massive parallelism on the GPU, we only use CPU to process the branching, bounding, and pruning operations. We use GPU to process the operations otherwise. We experimentally determined 24, 576 as the threshold number of subproblems that triggers changing the execution mode. The threshold number may vary under different environments.

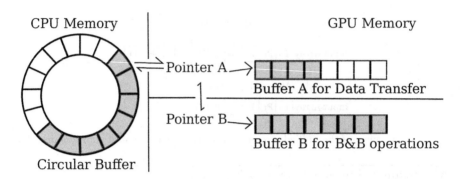

Fig. 5. An overview of the double buffering strategy, which overlaps the CPU-GPU data transfer with GPU-based B&B operations using two CUDA streams.

5   Experimental Results

We conducted experiments to evaluate the proposed method in terms of the problem size and the execution time. We used Lalami's method [9] as a comparable method. Both the proposed method and the previous method are honestly implemented with the same optimization techniques. As for the stream compaction strategy, we compared the separated scheme with the unified scheme in terms of the performance. For datasets, we used a suite of benchmarking datasets [18,19] shown in Table 1. We used strongly correlated instances with up to $n = 1000$ items, where the weight of each item mainly determines its profit. Such instances can be efficiently parallelized because of enormous combinations of items that may be an optimal solution, and therefore, represent the most difficult problems. We generated 20 different instances for each n.

Table 2 shows the specifications of two experimental machines. We prepared two machines equipped with different capacities of GPU memory: 2 GB and 12 GB for machines 1 and 2, respectively. These capacities were relatively small for the datasets, which consumed at most 20 GB of memory space. Both machines ran on the Ubuntu 14.04 with CUDA 7.5 [20]. Besides, the version of thrust library [16] was 1.8.3.

Table 1. Experimental datasets.

Parameter	Value
p_i: profit of the i-th item	$w_i + 1000 + \text{random}(-20, 20)$
w_i: weight of the i-th item	$\text{random}(1, 10000)$
c: knapsack capacity	$\sum_{i=1}^{n} w_i * 100/1001$

Table 2. Specification of experimental machines.

	Machine 1	Machine 2
CPU	Intel Core i7-6700	Intel Xeon E5-2660 v3
CPU memory capacity	32 GB	64 GB
GPU	GeForce GTX 680 Kepler	GeForce GTX Titan X Pascal
GPU memory capacity	2 GB	12 GB
GPU driver version	375.39	352.39
PCIe Controller	gen3 ×16	gen3 ×16

5.1   Robustness Against the Increase of Problem Size

We prepared ten classes of instances, varying from 100 items to 1000 items. We generated 20 different instances for each class. In this experiment, we allocated an array of 20 GB for the circular buffer. On the other hand, two arrays of total 2 GB were used for processing B&B and stream compaction operations on the GPU. As shown in Fig. 6, our CPU memory subproblem management scheme successfully solved more instances, demonstrating more robustness against the increase of problem size. This robustness is noticeable especially for the "properly" large instances, varying from 400 items to 700 items. However, there was no significant difference for the instances of more than 700 items because sharply increasing subproblems beat the capacity of CPU memory, resulting in a memory exhaustion. Moreover, we can conclude that our out-of-core method solved 33.7 times more subproblems than the previous in-core method. For example, our method successfully stored 845, 940, 791 subproblems at a time, whereas the number of subproblems was limited by 25, 096, 462 in the previous method.

5.2   Performance Comparison

For each instance class, from the instances which can be solved by both methods, we selected a representative one to compare the execution time of the two methods. For example, presuming that in the 700-item instance class there were three instances which can be solved by both methods, we first computed the average execution time of the three instances processed by the previous method. We then selected the instance whose execution time was nearest to the average execution time (Fig. 7). Obviously, the instances that can be solved by both methods did not produce so many subproblems that exhaust the GPU memory, thus, there is no extra data transfer for swapping-out operations. Our method achieved a higher performance because our stream compaction strategy (with the separated scheme) was completely processed on the GPU in parallel. As presented in Sect. 2, the previous stream compaction strategy computed data access pattern on the CPU, sequentially instead of in parallel, and it required to transfer the array of label between the CPU and GPU. Therefore, our stream compaction strategy ran 4.5 times faster than the previous strategy, shortening the total execution time by 26% on average.

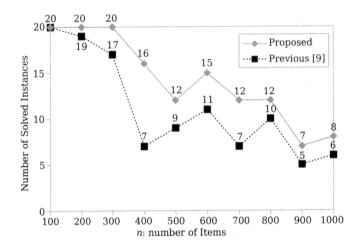

Fig. 6. Comparison of the numbers of instances solved by the proposed method and the previous method [9].

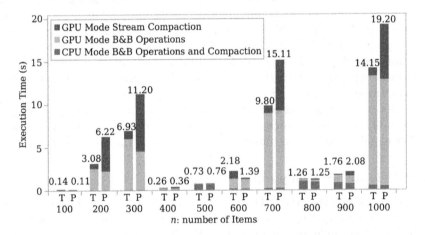

Fig. 7. Comparison and breakdown of execution time with different number of items. In this figure, the notations "T" and "P" refer to this work and previous work [9], respectively.

5.3 Comparison of Separated and Unified Schemes

In this experiment, we allocated 1 GB (i.e., half) of GPU memory because the experimental machine 1 had only 2 GB GPU memory. Thus, we thought the efficiency of GPU memory usage would be more important. As for the CPU memory, the same amount (20 GB) was used for execution. We compared the execution time of both schemes by selecting a representative instance for each instance class in the same manner described in Sect. 5.2. As we mentioned above, the buffer size of the unified scheme is 1.5 times larger than that of the separated

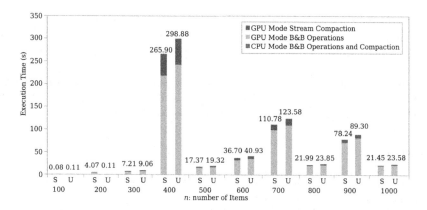

Fig. 8. Comparison and breakdown of execution time with different number of items. In this figure, the notations "S" and "U" refer to the separated and unified schemes, respectively.

scheme. Consequently, the unified scheme allowed 26.2 million subproblems to be processed at a time on the GPU, while the separated scheme allowed 17.4 million subproblems (Fig. 8).

According to the result, the execution time of GPU-based B&B operations (that are overlapped with data transfer) of the separated scheme was 12.3% shorter than that of the unified scheme. The execution time of stream compation of the separated scheme was 19.6% shorter than that of the unified scheme. Totally, the separated scheme was 13.1% faster than the unified scheme. We therefore concluded that the separated scheme is better than the unified scheme from the aspect of performance.

6   Conclusion

In this paper, we presented a GPU-accelerated, out-of-core B&B method for solving the 0-1 knapsack problem. The maximum problem size depends on the capacity of the CPU memory rather than that of the GPU memory. To realize this relaxation, our method buffers active subproblems in the CPU memory instead of the GPU memory. Because such a CPU-centric management scheme can suffer from increased amount of data transfer between the CPU and GPU, our method minimizes the data transfer overhead by a stream compaction strategy and hides the minimized overhead by a double buffering strategy that overlaps data transfer with GPU-based B&B operations.

In our experiments, we found that our out-of-core method stored 33.7 times more subproblems at a time, solving twice more problems than a previous in-core method. We also found that our completely CPU-based compaction strategy was 4.5 times faster than the previous compaction strategy. Moreover, we determined that the separated scheme was better because the separated scheme ran 13.1% faster than the unified scheme.

Our future work includes investigation of more sophisticated ways to traverse the search tree, e.g., dynamically choosing breadth first search and depth first search, which improves robustness against rapidly growing subproblems.

Acknowledgments. This study was supported in part by the Japan Society for the Promotion of Science KAKENHI Grant Numbers 15H01687, 16H02801 and 15K12008. We are also grateful to the anonymous reviewers for their valuable comments.

References

1. Martello, S., Toth, P.: Knapsack Problems: Algorithms and Computer Implementations. Wiley, Chichester (1990)
2. Land, A.H., Doig, A.G.: An automatic method of solving discrete programming problems. Econometrica **28**(3), 497–520 (1960)
3. Lin, J., Storer, J.A.: Processor-efficient hypercube algorithms for the knapsack problem. J. Parallel Distrib. Comput. **13**(3), 332–337 (1991)
4. Eckstein, J., Phillips, C.A., Hart, W.E.: PICO: an object-oriented framework for parallel branch and bound. Stud. Comput. Math. **8**, 219–265 (2001)
5. Goux, J.-P., Kulkarni, S., Yoder, M., Linderoth, J.: Master-worker: an enabling framework for applications on the computational grid. Cluster Comput. **4**(1), 63–70 (2001)
6. Tanaka, Y., Sato, M., Hirano, M., Nakada, H., Sekiguchi, S.: Performance evaluation of a firewall-compliant Globus-based wide-area cluster system. In: Proceedings of HPDC 2000, pp. 121–128 (2000)
7. Boyer, V., Baz, D.E., Elkihel, M.: Solving knapsack problems on GPU. Comput. Oper. Res. **39**(1), 42–47 (2012)
8. Boukedjar, A., Lalami, M.E., El-Baz, D.: Parallel branch and bound on a CPU-GPU system. In: Proceedings of PDP 2012, pp. 392–398 (2012)
9. Lalami, M.E., El-Baz, D.: GPU implementation of the branch, bound method for knapsack problems. In: Proceedings of IPDPSW 2012, pp. 1769–1777 (2012)
10. Pedemonte, M., Alba, E., Luna, F.: Towards the design of systolic genetic search. In: Proceedings of IPDPSW 2012, pp. 1778–1786 (2012)
11. Luebke, D., Humphreys, G.: How GPUs work. Computer **40**(2), 96–100 (2007)
12. Ino, F., Munekawa, Y., Hagihara, K.: Sequence homology search using fine grained cycle sharing of idle GPUs. IEEE Trans. Parallel Distrib. Syst. **23**(4), 751–759 (2012)
13. Mitani, Y., Ino, F., Hagihara, K.: Parallelizing exact and approximate string matching via inclusive scan on a GPU. IEEE Trans. Parallel Distrib. Syst. **28**, 1989–2002 (2017)
14. Carneiro, T., Muritiba, A.E., Negreiros, M., de Campos, G.A.L.: A new parallel schema for branch-and-bound algorithms using GPGPU. In: Proceedings of SBAC-PAD 2011, pp. 41–47 (2011)
15. Dantzig, G.B.: Discrete variable extremum problems. Oper. Res. **5**(2), 266–277 (1957)
16. Bell, N., Hoberock, J.: Thrust: A Productivity-Oriented Library for CUDA. Morgan Kaufmann, San Mateo (2011). Chap. 26. http://thrust.github.io/
17. Rennich, S.: CUDA C/C++ Streams and Concurrency, Nvidia GTC express (2011). http://on-demand.gputechconf.com/gtc-express/2011/presentations/StreamsAndConcurrencyWebinar.pdf

18. Martello, S., Pisinger, D., Toth, P.: New trends in exact algorithms for the 0-1 knapsack problem. Eur. J. Oper. Res. **123**(2), 325–332 (2000)
19. Martello, S., Pisinger, D., Toth, P.: Dynamic Programming and Tight Bounds for the 0-1 Knapsack Problem, Datalogisk Institut København: DIKU-Rapport, Datalogisk Institut, Københavns Universitet (1997)
20. CUDA Toolkit Documentation: Nvidia (2017). http://docs.nvidia.com/cuda/index.html

The Curve Boundary Design and Performance Analysis for DGM Based on OpenFOAM

Yongquan Feng, Xinhai Xu$^{(\boxtimes)}$, Yuhua Tang, Liyang Xu, and Yongjun Zhang

State Key Laboratory of High Performance, Computing College of Computer,
National University of Defense Technology, Changsha, China
yqfeng0418@163.com, {xuxinhai,xuliyang08,yjzhang}@nudt.edu.cn,
yhtang62@163.com

Abstract. OpenFOAM is a widely used numerical simulation software, and Discontinuous Galerkin method (DGM), a high-order numerical method, has been developed on OpenFOAM. In order to obtain meaningful numerical simulations, curve boundary is needed, but it has not been implemented on OpenFOAM. In this paper, based on *codeStream* function of original OpenFOAM, we design and implement curve boundary interface with reference to the interface of original OpenFOAM, so that users can use C++ code to describe curve boundary. Furthermore, in order to move the high-order points on the linear boundary to the curve boundary, we propose an algorithm to move each high-order point to a specific position on the curve, where the normal of this position passes through the origin point. Experimental results based on the flow around a cylinder show that curve boundary is needed by DGM numerical simulation, and DGM high-order simulation is much more efficient than DGM low-order. Typically, when the error of drag coefficient is about 0.03, the DGM high-order can save 89.6% time cost and 83.0% memory cost.

Keywords: Curve boundary · OpenFOAM · DGM · High-order

1 Introduction

Computational Fluid Dynamics (CFD) is a branch of fluid mechanics that uses numerical simulation to solve and analyse problems that involve fluid flows. With the development of computer technology, it is widely used in many research domains, such as automotive industry and aerospace field [1]. There are a variety of CFD softwares, including some famous commercial softwares (Fluent, CFX, etc.), and some open-source softwares (OpenFOAM, deal.II, etc.) [15]. Typically, OpenFOAM is a open-source C++ toolbox for flexible engineering simulation in CFD [14], whose numerical method is based on Finite Volume Method (FVM) [20]. It has good expansibility that supports users to develop their own solvers. Moreover, parallelization is well implemented in OpenFOAM, thus large-scale problems are supported in OpenFOAM. Due to these advantage, OpenFOAM

© Springer International Publishing AG 2017
S. Ibrahim et al. (Eds.): ICA3PP 2017, LNCS 10393, pp. 268–282, 2017.
DOI: 10.1007/978-3-319-65482-9_18

has become the major research tool for CFD academia and industry, such as properties of fluid analysis [5,10,11], coastal engineering simulation [13].

For large-scale simulations, such as the wind tunnel, computational cost has become a key problem. There are several factors that affect the amount of calculation, including grid size, numerical method, parallel algorithm, computer architecture and so on. Wang [21] suggests that, at a same precision, high-order method requires fewer grid cells than low-order method so high-order method becomes the research hotspot of CFD. However, the current CFD numerical simulation softwares mostly use low-order methods to perform numerical discretization, like Fluent, OpenFOAM, and so on. Typically, DGM is a famous high-order finite element method with high stability and accuracy [4]. Therefore, to conduct high-order numerical simulations, our group have coupled DGM into OpenFOAM.

[6–8] suggest that for a numerical simulation with curved geometry, if a high-order method is used, the computational grid must be generated with curved boundaries as well. However, original OpenFOAM does not support the curve boundary. In addition, Bassi [2,3] demonstrated that the curve boundary of grid had an effect on the accuracy of DGM. But, the existing analysis of this effect is qualitative and non-quantitative. Therefore, the first question considered in this paper is how to develop the original OpenFOAM platform to support curve boundary, in order to make DGM discretization more accurate. Furthermore, after the platform supports curve boundary, whether the cost of the high-order DGM numerical discretization is less than low-order DGM discretization at the same precision. This paper studies the above two questions, and the main contributions of this paper are summarized below:

- Based on *codeStream* function on original OpenFOAM, we design and implement the curve boundary interface in *boundary* configure file, which is consistent with the architecture of OpenFOAM. Users can describe curve boundary with C++ code in curve boundary interface.
- In order to move the high-order points on original OpenFOAM geometric mesh boundary to curve boundary with a specific rule, we propose an algorithm to move each high-order point to a specific position on the curve, where the normal of this position passes through the origin point, thus high-order numerical discretization requirements of DGM could be met on the mesh of OpenFOAM.
- The effect of the curve boundary on DGM high-order numerical simulation is verified on the benchmark of flow around a cylinder. Our results show that DGM high-order simulation is much more efficient than DGM low-order. Typically, when the error of drag coefficient is about 0.03, compared to the DGM low-order numerical simulation, the DGM high-order can save 89.6% time cost and 83.0% memory cost.

The rest of the paper is organized as follows. Section 2 reviews the background and related work. Section 3 presents the process of design and implementation of curve boundary on OpenFOAM. Section 4 describes our evaluation methodology and demonstrates the performance superiority of DGM high-order numerical simulation with curve boundary by experiments. Section 5 conclude the paper.

2   Background

2.1   Original OpenFOAM and DGM

By using numerical methods, the theoretical models in hydromechanics are discretized into linear equations which can be solved by computer. The basis of numerical discretization is the geometric mesh which is obtained by dividing the computational domain of the theoretical model into cells. The geometric mesh of original OpenFOAM not only contains the topology of the grid, but also retains the properties of the domain boundary through a configuration file named *boundary*. Figure 1 shows the process of dividing a circular computational domain into 6 cells on the original OpenFOAM. From the left figure, we can acquire that the boundary of this domain consists of two part, UP and $DOWN$, UP for the upper semicircle boundary, and $DOWN$ for the other half. The result of the division is shown in the right figure. Since only the coordinate information of the cell vertices is preserved, the topology of the geometric mesh is shown by solid line. The *boundary* file of this geometric mesh is shown in Fig. 2, where there are three keywords for each mesh boundary:

- **type**: represents the type of mesh boundary. The original OpenFOAM supports multiple boundary types and assigns different boundaries with different properties. In Fig. 2, *wall* is one of boundary types on the original Open-FOAM.
- **nFaces & startFace**: **nFaces** is the number of faces, and **startFace** is the start index of faces belonging to this boundary. Both of them can describe the component of boundary. For example, as shown in Fig. 1, UP consists of three faces, numbered 0, 1 and 2, so that **nFaces** and **startFace** are 3 and 0.

From Figs. 1 and 2, it is clear that the original OpenFOAM does not hold the information of circular boundary so that it can not support curve boundary, as mentioned earlier.

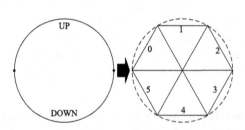

Fig. 1. Circle domain 6 equal division

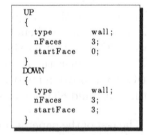

Fig. 2. Content in *boundary* file

DGM was firstly introduced by Reed and Hill in 1973 for solving the Neutron transport equation [17]. As a high-order finite element method, it obtains a higher accuracy by fitting the flow fields with higher order polynomial in the grid cell. According to the basic theory of solving polynomial, the higher order of polynomial, the more nodes are needed. Thus, more nodes are required by DGM high-order numerical discretization, so that the mesh for DGM high-order numerical discretization needs to insert points within the cells of original OpenFOAM geometry mesh. The process developing DGM on OpenFOAM can be described by Fig. 3.

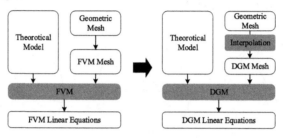

Fig. 3. DGM on OpenFOAM

2.2 Simulation Accuracy and Discretization Error

By using numerical methods, CFD can obtain the approximate solution to the theoretical model, and in this process, the difference between the linear equations and the theoretical model is termed discretization error, which is the main factor affecting the accuracy of numerical simulation. The exact solution to theoretical model can be expressed by Eq. 1:

$$f_{exact} = f_k + DE_k. \tag{1}$$

where f_{exact} is the exact solution to the theoretical model, f_k is a discrete solution on mesh level k, and DE_k is the corresponding discretization error. According to [18], Eq. 1 can be rewritten as:

$$f_k = f_{exact} + g_1 h_k + g_2 h_k^2 + g_3 h_k^3 + O(h_k^4). \tag{2}$$

where g_i is the ith-order error term coefficient and h_k is some measure of the grid spacing on mesh k. When the second-order method is used, the coefficient g_1 is 0, then Eq. 2 can be written as:

$$f_k = f_{exact} + O(h_k^2). \tag{3}$$

Therefore, we can obtain the relationship between the simulation accuracy and the discrete order of numerical method:

$$A_k = DE_k = O(h_k^n). \tag{4}$$

where A_k is the simulation accuracy on mesh level k and n is the discretization order. Wang [21] points out that high-order methods are those $n \geq 3$.

3 Design and Implementation of Curve Boundary

3.1 DGM Discretization and Curve Boundary Requirement

The numerical method of the original OpenFOAM, FVM, is low-order, and only the cell vertex information is used in the numerical simulation, so that original OpenFOAM can only reduce the loss of the computational domain by generating finer cells. Dividing the circular domain into 6 cells, 12 cells, and 24 cells are shown in Fig. 4 respectively, and it is clear that the larger the number of cells, the less the loss of the computational domain.

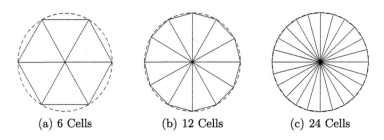

(a) 6 Cells   (b) 12 Cells   (c) 24 Cells

Fig. 4. Circle domain mesh generation

DGM has the advantage of obtaining higher accuracy on coarse-grained grid cells by using high-order numerical simulation which requires to insert nodes within cells, which are named high-order points in this paper. Figure 5 indicates the result of inserting high-order points on a grid cell when DGM perform third-order numerical discretization. There is curve boundary belonging to this cell, indicated by a dashed line. Figure 5(a) illustrates the result based on the geometric mesh of original OpenFOAM. When DGM discretizes the theoretical model, it is required that, after discretization, the residuals of the theoretical model and the basis functions of finite element methods have to be orthogonal, that is to say, the integration of the product of the two on each cell is 0 (Eq. 5) [12]. However, if we insert high-order points as Fig. 5(a), the loss of the computational domain will not reduce, and the situation shown in Fig. 5(b) is expected. Therefore, curve boundary is required by DGM high-order numerical discretization.

$$\int_{D^k} (R_h(\boldsymbol{x}, t)) \psi_n(\boldsymbol{x}) dx = 0, 1 \leq n \leq N_p \tag{5}$$

where D^k is the area of the kth cell, $\boldsymbol{x}$ contains the coordinate information for all points in this cell, t is time, R_h is the residual caused by discretization, ψ_n is the basis function of DGM, and N_p is the number of nodes in kth cell.

The principle of curve boundary is to ensure high-order points locate on the actual boundary of the computational domain, so the following functions are required:

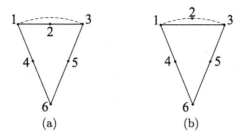

Fig. 5. The process of interpolating high-order points

- Firstly, a interface is required for user to describe the curved geometry. As indicated earlier, the original OpenFOAM geometric mesh loses the information of curve boundary, so that DGM, which is developed on OpenFOAM, can not acquire it, and high-order points can not locate on the actual boundary of the computational domain. Therefore, we need to design and implement the curve boundary interface, by reference to the interface of the geometric mesh on original OpenFOAM, to hold curve boundary information;
- Secondly, it is necessary to move the high-order points on the geometric mesh boundary of original OpenFOAM to curve boundary according to a specific rule. According to [12], the high-order points of DGM have the properties of the Legendre-Gauss-Lobatto (LGL) integral points. The influence on it needs to be minimized, which is produced by moving. So we need to design and implement a rule of moving high-order points.

3.2 Design and Implementation of Curve Boundary Interface

Original OpenFOAM supports multiple boundary types and assigns a type for every boundary by a configuration file named *boundary*. We can add a new boundary type on original OpenFOAM to make it support curve boundary function. The curve boundary interface is designed by reference to the boundary type interfaces of original OpenFOAM in *boundary* configure file, and we need to add the curve boundary information into the curve boundary interface. According to [9], original OpenFOAM allows users to write C++ code in configuration files, and through a function called *codeStream*, the code will be compiled so that it can be executed in the numerical simulation process. Therefore, we can use C++ code to describe curve boundary.

Figure 6 illustrates the result of splitting circular computational domain with curve boundary. Compared to geometric mesh of original OpenFOAM, the content of configuration file *boundary* has changed, and Fig. 7 shows new interface of *UP* boundary. **type** is turned into *arc* which is the type name of curve boundary, and **nFaces** and **startFace** are kept unchanged. There are four more keywords:

- **name** & **code**: **name** is the name of the code in UP. **code** is the code which is used to describe curve boundary, and its style is standardized by *codeStream* function.
- **u_Range** & **v_Range**: The curve boundary is described with parametric equations using C++ code, and the parameters are u and v. These two keywords are used to define the range of them.

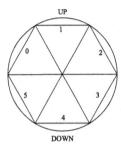

```
UP
{
    type         arc;
    nFaces       3;
    startFace    0;
    name         codeup;
    u_Range      (-0.5  0.5);
    v_Range      (0  0);
    code
    #{
        sin(pi*u),
        cos(pi*u),
        v
    #};
}
```

Fig. 6. Curve boundary mesh generation   **Fig. 7.** Curve boundary interface

3.3   Design and Implementation of Moving Rule

In order to reduce the influence on the LGL property of high-order points, we design the moving rule as follow: For a high-order point P, we choose a point P' on the curve boundary, whose normal passes P, and replace P with P'. Figure 8 illustrates the process to find P' for P. For P_1, first, the endpoint of the curve face is selected as the initial point P_0', and we can get the unit normal vector $\overrightarrow{n_0}$ of P_0' according to the parametric equations of curve boundary. Then, the cross product of $\overrightarrow{n_0}$ and $\overrightarrow{P_1 P_0'}$ can be achieved, and we can correct P_0' to get the new point P_1' on curve boundary according to the cross product. Finally, repeat the process of correction until the cross product less than a threshold value which is preset by us, and replace P_1 with P_n'. From the point of view of performance optimization, P_n' can be the initial point in process of moving P_2. The whole process can be described abstractly by Algorithm 1.

By adding curve boundary interface and the function of moving high-order points on OpenFOAM, where our research group has developed DGM, the platform can support curve boundary for DGM numerical discretization (Fig. 9).

4   Experiment and Analysis

4.1   Platform and Test Cases

The numerical simulation platform of this experiment is OpenFOAM4.0 where our research group has developed DGM, so it can support high-order numerical simulation. As introduced above, we have added curve boundary on it.

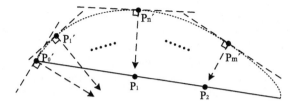

Fig. 8. High-order points moving process

Algorithm 1. High-order Points Moving Algorithm
___

1: Get curved boundary faces **faces**;
2: Get curved boundary equations;
3: Set threshold **threshold**;
4: **for all face** in **faces do**
5:    Get initial point P';
6:    Get high-order points **highOrderPoints** of **face**;
7:    **for all** P in **highOrderPoints do**
8:       Initial $\overrightarrow{res} = \overrightarrow{0}$;
9:       **repeat**
10:          Correct P' according to $| \overrightarrow{res} |$;
11:          Calculate unit normal vector $\overrightarrow{n}$ of P';
12:          Calculate $\overrightarrow{res} = \overrightarrow{n} \times \overrightarrow{PP'}$;
13:       **until** $| \overrightarrow{res} | < threshold$
14:       Mapping P to P';
15:    **end for**
16: **end for**
___

First, we select the 2-dimensional vortex problem to verify the correctness of DGM on our platform. The computational domain of this case does not contain the curve boundary (Fig. 10(a)), and there is a exact solution to this problem:

$$
\begin{cases}
u = -\sin(2\pi y) \exp -\nu 4\pi^2 t, \\
v = \sin(2\pi x) \exp -\nu 4\pi^2 t, \\
p = -\cos(2\pi x) \cos(2\pi y) \exp -\nu 8\pi^2 t.
\end{cases}
\tag{6}
$$

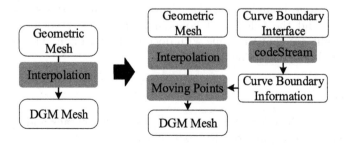

Fig. 9. DGM mesh generation

where u and v are the velocity components in x and y directions, p is the pressure, nu is viscosity coefficient which is equal to 10^{-2} in this case, and t is time. We apply the incompressible Navier-Stokes equations to solving the problem, and the computational domain and its boundary are shown in Fig. 10(a). For *inlet*, the value velocity is equal to the exact solution, and the gradient of pressure is 0. For outlet, the gradient of velocity is equal to the gradient of the exact solution, and the value of the pressure is equal to the exact solution. The incompressible Navier-Stokes equations are discretized on Fig. 10(b), (c) and (d). Figure 10(c) is obtained by cut each cell into quarters in Fig. 10(b), and by cutting each cell into quarters in Fig. 10(c), we can get the geometric mesh shown in Fig. 10(d). Therefore, if we measure the cell edge length of geometric mesh in Fig. 10(b) with h, then $h/2$ for Fig. 10(c) and $h/4$ for Fig. 10(d).

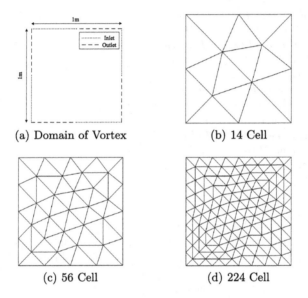

(a) Domain of Vortex   (b) 14 Cell

(c) 56 Cell   (d) 224 Cell

Fig. 10. Vortex domain and grid

Then, the flow around a cylinder in 2-dimension is selected to verify the effect of the curve boundary on the accuracy and the performance of DGM. The pressure and the velocity of boundary, the viscosity coefficient and the simulation time are kept the same with document [16]. Figure 11 illustrates the computational domain of this problem.

4.2 Methodology

In order to verify the effect of curve boundary on the accuracy and performance of DGM numerical simulation, the experiments of this paper are divided into three parts.

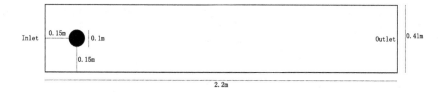

Fig. 11. Domain of flow around a cylinder

- First, through the vortex problem numerical simulation, we can complete the correctness verification of DGM on our platform, thus excluding the influence of DGM on curve boundary. The correctness of DGM can be verified by comparing the convergence order of the simulation error with discretization order. According to [19], we can calculate the convergence order of numerical simulation based on the maximum point error of pressure on Fig. 10(b), (c) and (d).
- Then, to demonstrate the effect of curve boundary on DGM, we simulate the flow around a cylinder under the condition of using curve boundary and linear boundary, and compare the simulation error of them. The geometric mesh of this part is shown in Fig. 12. In this experiment, we select the maximum value of drag coefficient C_d and the maximum value of lift coefficient C_l as the evaluation index, that is to say, the simulation error is expressed by the error of Cd and Cl.
- Finally, to compare the performance of high-order method and low-order method, the problem of flow around a cylinder is numerically simulated with high-order DGM using curve boundary and the low-order DGM (the discretization order is 2) using linear boundary, and after that, we count the time cost and the memory cost of simulation. In order to save the time of experiment, the relevant performance statistics are obtained by simulating the physical process lasting for 0.1 s. According to [21], high-order numerical simulation has less geometric mesh cells than the low-order. Thus, 460 cells grid and $1840(460 * 4^1)$ grid are selected as the geometric mesh of high-order numerical simulation, and $7360(460 * 4^2)$ cells, $29440(460 * 4^3)$ cells, $117760(460 * 4^4)$ cells for the low-order. All the grids above have similar topology to 460 cells grid.

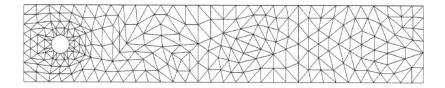

Fig. 12. 460 Cells grid for flow around a cylinder

However, it should be noted that there is no exact solution to the flow around a cylinder. By reference to [22] we select the data from [16] as the exact value of C_d and C_l, which is $C_d = 2.950921575$, $C_l = 0.47795$.

4.3 Experimental Results and Analysis

Table 1 details the result of the vortex problem. The convergence order is basically consistent with [12], So the correctness of DGM on our platform can be proved.

Table 1. Vortex pressure field error

Order	h	0.5h	0.25h	Convergence order
2	8.41058E−01	1.23537E−01	2.45985E−02	2.5478
3	1.31690E−01	2.23336E−02	4.57408E−03	2.4238
4	7.72596E−02	2.94520E−03	1.75313E−04	4.3918
5	5.66944E−03	6.16050E−04	1.38162E−05	4.3404
6	9.10737E−03	3.51222E−05	6.38626E−07	6.8999

Figure 13 shows the exact value from [16] and the simulation result of C_d and C_l. It is clear that the test results using the curve boundary tend to approach the exact value with the increase of the preset order, and the result using non-curve boundary grid tends to a value different from the exact one. When $order \geq 9$, the error of C_d is maintained at 0.04, and the error of C_l maintained at 0.01. Therefore, it is clear that the numerical discretization of high-order method needs curve boundary.

Figure 14 shows the result of flow around a cylinder using high-order DGM. Figure 14(a) and (b) illustrate the relationship between the error of C_d, C_l and

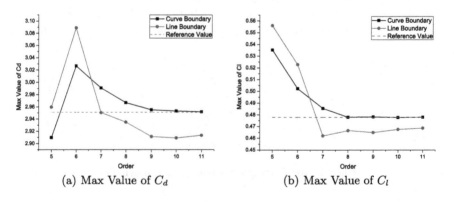

(a) Max Value of C_d (b) Max Value of C_l

Fig. 13. Test result of 460 cells grid

the discretization order, and it can be figure out that the more cells, the high accuracy, and the larger the discretization order, the high accuracy. Figure 14(c) and (d) show the relationship between the time cost, memory cost and the discretization order, which indicates that the higher the number of grids, the higher the time and memory cost. Moreover, if the number of cell is fixed, the time cost and the memory cost increase exponentially with the increase of the discretization order.

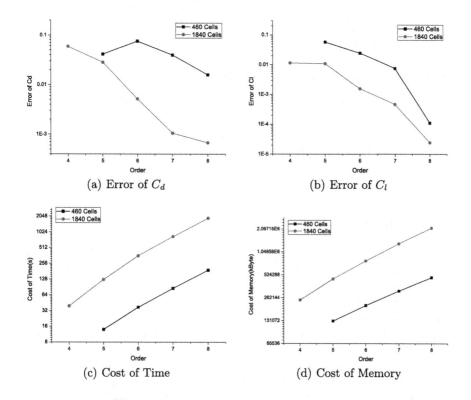

(a) Error of C_d (b) Error of C_l

(c) Cost of Time   (d) Cost of Memory

Fig. 14. High-order numerical simulation result

According to the above, the error of C_d and the error of C_l have the same trend. Due to limited by the length of paper, we only show the experimental result based on the error of C_d. Figure 15 describes the relationship between simulation cost and the error of C_d. From Fig. 15(a) and (b), it is clear that the time and memory cost of the high-order DGM are much less than the low-order DGM, under the same test error premise. When the error of C_d is about 0.03, compared to the DGM low-order numerical simulation, the DGM high-order can save 89.6% time cost and 83.0% memory cost (shown as Table 2). For this problem, on 460 cells grid and 1840 cells grid, the cost of DGM high-order numerical simulation is basically the same, in order to achieve the same accuracy.

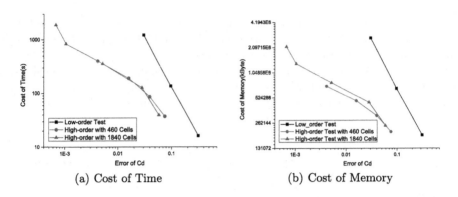

(a) Cost of Time   (b) Cost of Memory

Fig. 15. Cost of high-order numerical simulation and low-order numerical simulation

Table 2. Cost when error of C_d is about 0.03

Type	C_d Error	Memory cost	Time cost
High-order	2.82206E−2	463228 KB	125.96 s
Low-order	3.03178E−2	2720016 KB	1209.16 s

5   Conclusion

High-order methods can deliver higher accuracy with lower cost than low-order methods, and they have received much attention of CFD researchers. DGM is a locally conservative, stable and high-order accurate method, which has brought it into the mainstream high-order methods of CFD. Our research group has developed DGM on OpenFOAM. However, the conclusion that the curve boundary has effect on the numerical simulation of DGM has be proposed, but the platform of OpenFOAM with DGM can not support curve boundary.

This paper analyses the process of inserting high-order points of DGM numerical discretization based on the original OpenFOAM geometric mesh, and designs and implements the curve boundary on OpenFOAM with DGM. The effect of the curve boundary on DGM is verified by experiments, and we conclude that curve boundary is needed by high-order numerical simulation, and linear boundary lead to a fixed error. Furthermore, compared to low-order DGM numerical simulations, high-order DGM numerical simulations with curve boundary are much more efficient, that is to say, under the same precision, the latter cost much less.

Acknowledgments. The authors would like to thank the National Key Research and Development Program of China (No. 2016YFB0201301), Science Challenge Project (No. JCKY2016212A502) and the open fund from the State Key Laboratory of High Performance Computing (Grant No. 201503-01 and 201503-02).

References

1. Anderson, J.D., Wendt, J.: Computational Fluid Dynamics, vol. 206. Springer, Heidelberg (1995)
2. Bassi, F., Rebay, S.: Accurate 2D Euler computations by means of a high order discontinuous finite element method. In: Deshpande, S.M., Desai, S.S., Narasimha, R. (eds.) Fourteenth International Conference on Numerical Methods in Fluid Dynamics, pp. 234–240. Springer, Heidelberg (1995)
3. Bassi, F., Rebay, S.: High-order accurate discontinuous finite element solution of the 2D Euler equations. J. Comput. Phys. **138**(2), 251–285 (1997)
4. Cockburn, B.: Discontinuous Galerkin methods. ZAMM-J. Appl. Math. Mech./Z. Angew. Math. Mech. **83**(11), 731–754 (2003)
5. Favero, J., Secchi, A., Cardozo, N., Jasak, H.: Viscoelastic flow analysis using the software openfoam and differential constitutive equations. J. Nonnewton. Fluid Mech. **165**(23), 1625–1636 (2010)
6. Gao, H., Wang, Z., Liu, Y.: A study of curved boundary representations for 2D high order Euler solvers. J. Sci. Comput. **44**(3), 323–336 (2010)
7. Gordon, W.J., Hall, C.A.: Construction of curvilinear co-ordinate systems and applications to mesh generation. Int. J. Numer. Methods Eng. **7**(4), 461–477 (1973)
8. Gordon, W.J., Hall, C.A.: Transfinite element methods: blending-function interpolation over arbitrary curved element domains. Numer. Math. **21**(2), 109–129 (1973)
9. Greenshields, C.J.: Openfoam user guide. Version 3(1), OpenFOAM Foundation Ltd. (2015)
10. Guo, X.W., Yang, W.J., Xu, X.H., Cao, Y., Yang, X.J.: Non-equilibrium steady states of entangled polymer mixtures under shear flow. Adv. Mech. Eng. **7**(6), 1687814015591923 (2015)
11. Guo, X.W., Zou, S., Yang, X., Yuan, X.F., Wang, M.: Interface instabilities and chaotic rheological responses in binary polymer mixtures under shear flow. RSC Adv. **4**(105), 61167–61177 (2014)
12. Hesthaven, J.S., Warburton, T.: Nodal Discontinuous Galerkin Methods: Algorithms, Analysis, and Applications. Springer Science & Business Media, New York (2007)
13. Higuera, P., Lara, J.L., Losada, I.J.: Simulating coastal engineering processes with openfoam®. Coast. Eng. **71**, 119–134 (2013)
14. Jasak, H., Jemcov, A., Tukovic, Z., et al.: OpenFOAM: a C++ library for complex physics simulations. In: International Workshop on Coupled Methods in Numerical Dynamics, vol. 1000, pp. 1–20. IUC Dubrovnik, Croatia (2007)
15. Jian-hua, Z.: Review of commercial CFD software. J. Hebei Univ. Sci. Technol. **2**, 160–165 (2005)
16. John, V.: Reference values for drag and lift of a two-dimensional time-dependent flow around a cylinder. Int. J. Numer. Methods Fluids **44**(7), 777–788 (2004)
17. Reed, W.H., Hill, T.: Triangular mesh methods for the neutron transport equation. Los Alamos Report LA-UR-73-479 (1973)
18. Roy, C.J.: Grid convergence error analysis for mixed-order numerical schemes. AIAA J. **41**(4), 595–604 (2003)
19. Slater, J.W.: Examining spatial (grid) convergence. Public tutorial on CFD verification and validation, NASA Glenn Research Centre, MS 86 (2006)
20. Versteeg, H.K., Malalasekera, W.: An Introduction to Computational Fluid Dynamics: The Finite Volume Method. Pearson Education, New York (2007)

21. Wang, Z.J., Fidkowski, K., Abgrall, R., Bassi, F., Caraeni, D., Cary, A., Deconinck, H., Hartmann, R., Hillewaert, K., Huynh, H.T., et al.: High-order CFD methods: current status and perspective. Int. J. Numer. Methods Fluids **72**(8), 811–845 (2013)
22. Yano, M., Darmofal, D.L.: Case C1.3: Flow over the NACA 0012 airfoil: Subsonic inviscid, transonic inviscid, and subsonic laminar flows. In: First international workshop on high-order CFD methods (2012)

Service Dependability and Security in Distributed and Parallel Systems

Leakage-Resilient Password-Based Authenticated Key Exchange

Ou Ruan[1]([⊠]), Mingwu Zhang[1], and Jing Chen[2]

[1] School of Computer Science, Hubei University of Technology, Wuhan, China
ruanou@163.com
[2] School of Computer Science, Wuhan University, Wuhan, China

Abstract. Password-based authenticated key exchange (PAKE) protocols are among the most practically cryptographic primitives, where no additional device is required, but just a short human-memorable password. There are lots of works for PAKE protocols. All these protocols were proven secure in the traditional model, but could be completely insecure in the presence of side-channel attacks. In many practical applications such as Internet of Things, PAKE systems are very vulnerable to side-channel attacks, where a very small leakage may be completely exposed the whole password. Therefore, it is very important to model and design the leakage-resilient (LR) PAKE protocols. However, there is no prior work for modelling and constructing LR PAKE protocols. In this paper, we first formalize the LR eCK security model for PAKE, and then propose a continuous after-the-fact LR eCK-secure PAKE protocol based on key derivation function, leakage-resilient storage (LRS) and leakage-resilient refreshing of LRS, and show a formal security proof in the standard model.

Keywords: Leakage-Resilience · Password-based Authenticated Key Exchange · Side-channel attacks · Internet of Things

1 Introduction

With the development of Internet of Things (IoT), the fourth industrial revolution is coming, known as Industrie 4.0 factories, traditional industries will evolve into smart factories, intelligent productions. Intelligent system of the industrial control involves many smart control terminals (nodes), which communicate and cooperate with others to accomplish the production tasks. In order to ensure the security of productions, security mechanisms must be taken to protest these terminals and their communication. Secure communication between terminals, first of all, will need to generate a common cryptographically strong session key. In order to satisfy this demand, the authenticated key exchange (AKE) protocols were introduced. Among AKEs, the password-based authenticated key exchange (PAKE) protocols are most widely used, since no additional device is required, but just a human-memorable password for authenticating the parties. There are lots of works to model and design PAKE protocols. For a brief reviews, please refer to related works of traditional PAKE.

Computations or communications of the smart terminals will emit signals known as "side channels" such as electromagnetic emissions, power consumption. A majority of

© Springer International Publishing AG 2017
S. Ibrahim et al. (Eds.): ICA3PP 2017, LNCS 10393, pp. 285–296, 2017.
DOI: 10.1007/978-3-319-65482-9_19

these IoT terminals are exposed to the public outside, and an attacker can overcome the security protecting by measuring these signals, which are called side-channel attacks [1]. Because of the cost control, side-channel attacks are not considered in the hardware design of these terminals. Thus, in order to ensure communication security and data privacy of the smart terminals, the secure protocols such as PAKE not only should be employed, but also the measures to resist side-channel attacks must be taken. Therefore, it is very important to model and design the leakage-resilient (LR) PAKE protocols. However, there has no prior work for modelling and constructing LR PAKE protocols.

In this paper, we first formalize the LR eCK security model for PAKE, and then propose a LR PAKE protocol based on key derivation function (KDF) [2], leakage-resilient storage (LRS) [3] and leakage-resilient refreshing of LRSl. We consider a more strong security model, λ-continuous after-the-fact (AF) LR (CAFLR) eCK security model, and formally prove the security of the proposed protocol in the standard mode. In the CAFLR model, the leakages are continuous and are allowed after the adversary chooses the test session, and the overall leakage amount could be arbitrarily large, but for each protocol instance the amount of leakage is bounded by λ.

Overview of our construction. We first map the short shared secret password pw to a random element s of a group G with a large order using a one-way collision-free hash function H, and then encode s using a LRS scheme; this approach can resist the leakage attacks to the shared secret password. However, how to use the encodings of the shared password to accomplish authentication and generate a secure session key, become a big challenge. We find a good solution to this challenge by combining Diffie-Hellman key exchange and Dziembowski-Faust (DF) [4] LRS (DF-LRS) scheme appropriately. The important observations are as follows: (1) Two primitives can share a common group G with a big prime order p; (2) In DF-LRS scheme, $(g^{s_L})^{s_R} = g^{s_L \cdot s_R} = g^s$ since $s = s_L \cdot s_R$, where g is a generator of G, s denotes the secret mapping element, and (s_L, s_R) represents two encodings of s using DF-LRS scheme; (3) there has an efficient leakage-resilient refreshing protocol for DF-LRS scheme, and we could refresh two encodings of s after using them in the end of the protocol, thus our construction is secure against continuous leakage attacks.

The rest of this paper is organized as follows. Section 2 addresses related works. Section 3 describes the CAFLR eCK security model of PAKE. Section 4 presents the proposed protocol and analyzes the provable security and the performance comparison. Finally, Sect. 5 concludes the paper and discusses the future works.

2   Related Works

Traditional PAKE. Bellovin *et al.* [5] first showed a PAKE protocol, but its security was not formally treated. In 2000, Bellare *et al.* [6] and MacKenzie *et al.* [7] proposed the provably secure PAKE protocols in the random oracle (RO) model. Byun *et al.* [8] and Mohammad *et al.* [9] showed some improvements and generalizations to PAKE protocols in the RO model. Goldreich *et al.* [10] first designed a PAKE protocol in the standard model, and Katz *et al.* [11] designed an efficient PAKE protocol with a proof of security based on the decisional Diffie-Hellman (DDH) assumption. Then, [12–14] gave some different efficient constructions for PAKE protocols in the standard model. Ruan et al. [15] gave a formal security definition of explicit PAKE, which is a mutual PAKE protocol with mutual key confirmation. Yi et al. [16] presented a two-server PAKE protocol, where two servers cooperate to authenticate the client without knowing the password of the client. Recently, Islam et al. [17], Amin et al. [18] and Lu [19] proposed the provably secure three-party/multi-party PAKE protocols; Nam et al. [20] and Guo et al. [21] designed the provably secure group PAKE protocol.

Leakage-Resilient AKE. Moriyama and Okamoto [22] first proposed the formal λ-LR security model of authenticated key exchange (AKE) protocols in the eCK security model [23], where λ is a leakage parameter. The eCK security model is an extension of the CK security model [24], where the adversary is much stronger than the CK model and could access either the long-term secret key or the ephemeral secret randomness of the test session. They presented a two-pass λ-LR eCK-secure AKE protocol based on hash proof system and gave a formal proof in the standard model. There has a central limitation in the MO model, in which the leakages are only allowed before the adversary chooses the test session and gets the challenge. Leakage which happens after the adversary gets the challenge is called AF leakage. In 2014, Alawatugoda et al. [25] first presented an AFLR CK security model, and constructed a CAFLR AKE protocol using existing LR public key encryption system. In 2015, Alawatugoda et al. [26] proposed an AFLR eCK security model for AKE protocols, and Alawatugoda et al. [26] presented the first bounded AFLR (BAFLR) eCK-secure AKE protocols and Alawatugoda et al. [27] gave the first concrete construction of CAFLR eCK-secure AKE protocol. In 2016, Chen et al. [28] introduced a strong AFLR eCK security model, named challenge-dependent LR eCK (CLR-eCK) model, which not only captured leakage attacks on long-term secret private key, but also considered leakage of ephemeral secret randomness. Based on smooth projective hash functions and pseudo-random functions, they constructed a one-round CLR-eCK secure AKE protocol. In 2017, Ruan et al. [29] first proposed a ID-based LR AKE protocol based on leakage-smooth ID-based hash proof system, and gave a bounded AFLR eCK-secure proof in the standard model. Recently, Toorani [30] showed that Alawatugoda et al.'s AKE protocol [25] was vulnerable to ephemeral key compromise impersonation (KCI) attack; Yang et al. [31] also indicated that Alawatugoda et al.'s AKE protocol [26] was insecure by presenting a KCI attack and that their proofs of Case 2 (the adversary is active) were incorrectly reduced to DDH assumption, and then they improved their constructions and gave formal proofs in the RO model under Gap Diffie-Hellman (GDH) assumption; Chakaraborty et al. [32] showed the proofs of Chen et al.'s AKE protocol [28] had the same problem as [26] and reproved it in the RO model under GDH assumption.

It is very surprising that there has no prior work for LR PAKE protocols. In this paper, we first propose a λ-CAFLR PAKE protocol and formally prove its security in the standard model.

3 The λ-CAFLR eCK Security Model for PAKE

This section formalizes the λ-CAFLR eCK security model for PAKE by extending the eCK security PAKE model and following the OCL model. We assume that leakage occurs only in computations associated with the long-term shared secret password pw. In the λ-CAFLR eCK security model an adversary A can continuously obtain arbitrarily large amount of leakage of the secret password, but for each protocol instance the amount of leakage is bounded by λ. In each instance, A can adaptively choose arbitrary PPT leakage functions $f = (f_1, \ldots, f_n)$ to obtain leakage of pw, and the total leakage amount is bounded by λ, i.e., $\sum |f_i(pw)| \leq \lambda$. After issuing a **Send** query with an adaptive leakage function chosen by A, A will be given a normal protocol message generated according to the protocol specifications and the leakage of the long-term secret password.

Notation: Assume $s \xleftarrow{\$} S$ represent that s is a random value chosen uniformly from a finite set S, κ denote a system security parameter, and λ is a leakage parameter.

3.1 Adversarial Powers

Let U, V identify two parties, the term "principal" represent a party involved into a protocol instance, and the term "session" denote a protocol instance with principals. Each principal may have multiple sessions that maybe run concurrently. We denote the sth session at the owner principal U interacting with the intended partner principal V as the oracle $\Pi_{U,V}^s$, and denote the principal who activates a session as the initiator of the session, and the principal who responds to the initiator as the responder.

The adversary A is a PPT algorithm that controls all communications over the whole network and interacts with a set of oracles. In fact, A can do anything as he wants. The following queries model the capabilities of the adversary A.

Send (U, V, s, m, f) query: A can run the protocol by this query, and can also activate a new protocol instance as an initiator by using this query with blank m and f. After issuing this **Send** query in the sth session with a protocol message m and a leakage function f, A will be given a normal protocol message and the leakage $f(pw)$ of the long-term password, which are produced by the oracle $\Pi_{U,V}^s$ based on the protocol specifications and f.

RevealSessionKey (U, V, s) query: $\Pi_{U,V}^s$ sends the sth session key to A. This query models A's ability to compromise certain session key.

RevealEphemeralKey (U, V, s) query: $\Pi_{U,V}^s$ sends the sth session ephemeral keys to A. This query models A's ability to compromise certain ephemeral keys.

RevealPassword () query: Any one of the principal U and V sends their long-term shared secret password pw to A. This query models A's ability to get the principals' shared password.

Test (U, s)* query:** After receiving a ***Test query, the challenger picks a random bit $b \xleftarrow{\$} (0, 1)$, if $b = 1$ then ***A*** is given the actual session key, while a random session key is sent to ***A***. This query is used to formalize the security notion of a PAKE protocol, and could be activated only once across all sessions.

3.2   λ-CAFLR eCK Security Model

In the λ-CAFLR eCK security model, the overall leakage size of the secret password for each instance are bounded by the leakage parameter λ, *i.e.*, $\sum |f_i(pw)| \leq \lambda$.

Definition 3.1 [Partner sessions in λ-CAFLR eCK security model]. Two oracles $\Pi_{U,V}^{s}$ and $\Pi_{U',V'}^{s'}$ are called partners if the followings hold:

(1) Both $\Pi_{U,V}^{s}$ and $\Pi_{U',V'}^{s'}$ have generated session keys;
(2) Messages sent from $\Pi_{U,V}^{s}$ are same as messages received by $\Pi_{U',V'}^{s'}$;
(3) Messages sent from $\Pi_{U',V'}^{s'}$ are same as messages received by $\Pi_{U,V}^{s}$;
(4) $U = V'$ and $V = U'$;
(5) Exactly one of U and V is the initiator and the other is the responder

Correctness of a PAKE protocol means that two partner oracles generate same session keys.

Definition 3.2 [λ-CAFLR-eCK-freshness]. Let $f = (f_1, \ldots, f_n)$ be n arbitrary PPT leakage functions for an instance of the protocol chosen by the adversary. An oracle $\Pi_{U,V}^{s}$ is λ-CAFLR-eCK-fresh if the followings hold:

(1) The oracle $\Pi_{U,V}^{s}$ or its partner, $\Pi_{V,U}^{s'}$ (if it exists) has not been queried a ***RevealSessionKey***.
(2) If the partner $\Pi_{V,U}^{s'}$ exists, none of the following combinations has been queried:
     (a) ***RevealPassword*()** and ***RevealEphemeralKey*(U, V, s)**.
     (b) ***RevealPassword*()** and ***RevealEphemeralKey*(V, U, s')**.
(3) If the partner $\Pi_{V,U}^{s'}$ does not exist, A could not ask the ***RevealPassword*()** query.
(4) For all ***Send*(.,U, ., .,fᵢ)** queries, $\sum |f_i(pw)| \leq \lambda$.
(5) For all ***Send*(.,V, ., .,fᵢ)** queries, $\sum |f_i(pw)| \leq \lambda$.

3.3   Security Game and Security Definition

This section formalizes the security definition of the λ-CAFLR eCK model.

Definition 3.3 [λ-CAFLR eCK security game]. Security definition of the λ-CAFLR eCK model is captured by the following distinguishing game, which the protocol challenger C runs with a PPT adversary A:

(1) **A** queries any of **Send**, **RevealSessionKey**, **RevealEphemeralKey** and **RevealPassword** to any oracle as he wants.

(2) **A** selects a λ-CAFLR-eCK-fresh oracle and issues a **Test** query. After receiving a **Test** query, **C** picks a random bit $b \xleftarrow{\$} (0, 1)$, if $b = 1$ then sends the actual session key to **A**, while a random session key is sent to **A**.

(3) **A** continues querying **Send**, **RevealSessionKey**, **RevealEphemeralKey** and **RevealPassword**. All these queries should not violate the λ-CAFLR-eCK-freshness of the test session.

(4) At last **A** outputs a bit $b' \in (0, 1)$. **A** wins if $b' = b$.

Definition 3.4 [λ-CAFLR eCK security]. λ-CAFLR eCK security means that

$$Adv_{PAKE}^{\lambda-CAFLR\ eCK} = |\Pr[b' = b] - 1/2| = N_S/N + \varepsilon(\kappa),$$

where $Adv_{PAKE}^{\lambda-CAFLR\ eCK}$ is the advantage of **A** in winning the λ-CAFLR eCK distinguishing game in Definition 4.3, N_S represents the number of sessions on a principal, N denotes the size of the password dictionary, and $\varepsilon(\kappa)$ is a negligible function. In other words, a PAKE protocol is λ-CAFLR eCK-secure if there doesn't exist any PPT adversary **A** that can win the above distinguishing game with an advantage more than N_S/N.

Note: In PAKE protocols, the on-line dictionary attack is unavoidable, and N_S/N represents the success probability of the on-line dictionary attack. But this attack can be limited by some kind of strategy, for example, continuous attempts will not be allowed after a certain number of failed attempts to a password.

4 A New λ-CAFLR eCK-Secure PAKE Protocol

This section gives our proposed λ-CAFLR eCK-secure PAKE protocol and its formal security proof in the standard model.

4.1 Dziembowski-Faust(DF) LRS Scheme

DF-LRS Scheme [4] is a LRS that efficiently stores a secret value $s \in (Z_p^*)^m$ with any $m \in \mathbb{N}$, where p is a large prime.

Encode: Pick $s_L \xleftarrow{\$} (Z_p^*)^n \backslash \{(0^n)\}$ at random and compute $s_R \in (Z_p^*)^{n \times m}$ such that $s_L \times s_R = s$, where $n \in \mathbb{N}$, then output (s_L, s_R).

Decode: Output $s_L \times s_R$.

Lemma 4.1 [4]. The above Definition 3.7 is a λ-secure LRS scheme if $20\ m < n$, where $\lambda = (0.3\ n\log p, 0.3\ n\log p)$.

Lemma 4.2 [4]. If $\Phi_{Z_p^*}^{n,m}$ is a λ-secure DF-LRS scheme and $m/3 \leq n \wedge n \geq 16$, there has a $(\lambda/2, \lambda)$-secure leakage-resilient refreshing $Refresh_{Z_p^*}^{n,m}$ for $\Phi_{Z_p^*}^{n,m}$.

4.2 The Proposed Protocol:

Figure 1 shows the proposed protocol, which includes the following two stages:

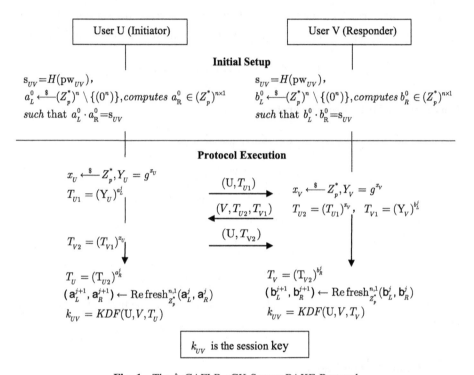

Fig. 1. The λ-CAFLR eCK-Secure PAKE Protocol

The Initial Setup stage. User U and V first map the shared secret password to a random element of the group G, $s_{UV} = H(pw_{UV})$. We assume that this computation is executed in secret and leakage attacks aren't allowed. Then, U runs a λ-secure DF-LRS scheme $\Phi_{Z_p^*}^{n,1}$, picks $a_L^0 \xleftarrow{\$} (Z_p^*)^n \setminus \{(0^n)\}$ at random and generates $a_R^0 \in (Z_p^*)^{n \times 1}$ such that $a_L^0 \cdot a_R^0 = s_{UV}$, and V also chooses $b_L^0 \xleftarrow{\$} (Z_p^*)^n \setminus \{(0^n)\}$ at random and computes $b_R^0 \in (Z_p^*)^{n \times 1}$ such that $b_L^0 \cdot b_R^0 = s_{UV}$.

The Protocol Execution stage: Step 1. User U chooses a number $x_U \xleftarrow{\$} Z_p^*$ at random, computes $Y_U = g^{x_U}$, $T_{U1} = (Y_U)^{a_L^j}$, and then sends (U, T_{U1}) to user V.

Step 2. After receiving the messages (U, T_{U1}), V picks a random number $x_V \xleftarrow{\$} Z_p^*$, computes $Y_V = g^{x_V}, T_{U2} = (T_{U1})^{x_V}$ and $T_{V1} = (Y_V)^{b_L^j}$, then sends (V, T_{U2}, T_{V1}) to U.

Step 3. After receiving the messages (V, T_{U2}, T_{V1}), U computes $T_{V2} = (T_{V1})^{x_U}$ and sends it to V. Finally, U generates the session key k_{UV} by computing $T_U = (T_{U2})^{a_R^j}$ and $k_{UV} = KDF(U, V, T_U)$, and refresh the store pieces with $(a_L^{j+1}, a_R^{j+1}) \leftarrow \text{Refresh}_{Z_p^*}^{n,1} (a_L^j, a_R^j)$.

Step 4. After receiving the messages (U, T_{V2}), V generates the session key k_{UV} by computing $T_V = (T_{V2})^{b_R^j}$ and $k_{UV} = KDF(U, V, T_V)$, and refresh the store pieces with

$$(b_L^{j+1}, b_R^{j+1}) \leftarrow \text{Refresh}_{Z_p^*}^{n,1} (b_L^j, b_R^j)$$

Correctness of the proposed protocol: Since,

$$
\begin{aligned}
T_U = (T_{U2})^{a_R^j} &= (((g^{x_U})^{a_L^j})^{x_V})^{a_R^j} \\
&= (((g^{x_U})^{x_V})^{a_L^j})^{a_R^j} = ((g^{x_U})^{x_V})^{a_L^j \cdot a_R^j} \\
&= ((g^{x_U})^{x_V})^{s_{UV}} = (((g^{x_U})^{x_V})^{b_L^j})^{b_R^j} \\
&= (((g^{x_V})^{b_L^j})^{x_U})^{b_R^j} \\
&= (((Y_V)^{b_L^j})^{x_U})^{b_R^j} \\
&= (T_{V2})^{b_R^j} = T_V
\end{aligned}
$$

We get $KDF(U, V, T_U) = KDF(U, V, T_V)$. Thus, the correctness of the proposed protocol holds.

4.3 Mutual Authentication

If parties want to make sure that the other is his/her intended partner and the partner has actually computed the session key, then mutual authentication can be incorporated into AKE protocol. To add mutual authentication to our scheme, we can use $KDF(U, V, k_{UV})$ as an additional authenticator structure, where $k_{UV} = KDF(U, V, T_V)$. After generating the session key, parties compute an authenticator Auth = $KDF(U, V, k_{UV})$, and send Auth to the other who verifies whether the received authenticator Auth is equal to $KDF(U, V, k_{UV})$. This authenticator transformation for mutual authentication preserves the indistinguishability security of the original proto-col. Thus, we do not consider a security of mutual authentication in the paper.

4.4   Security Proof

This section formally proves the security of the proposed protocol in the standard model.

Theorem 4.1. The proposed PAKE protocol is λ-CAFLR eCK-secure, if the DDH assumption is hold, the leakage-resilient refreshing of LRS is $(\lambda, 2\lambda)$-secure and the KDF is secure with a uniformly random key material. Let $Adv_{\text{PAKE}}^{\lambda-CAFLR\ eCK}$ denote the advantage of a PPT adversary A against λ-CAFLR eCK-security of the proposed protocol, there has:

$$Adv_{\text{PAKE}}^{\lambda-CAFLR\ eCK} \leq N_S/N + N_P^2 N_S^2 (Adv_{DDH} + Adv_{Refresh-LRS} + Adv_{KDF})$$

where $Adv_{DDH}, Adv_{KDF}, Adv_{Refresh-LRS}$ are advantages of A against the security of DDH problem, KDF and leakage-resilient refreshing of LRS, respectively, and N_P denotes the number of protocol principals, N_S represents the number of sessions on a principal, N is the size of the password dictionary.

Proof. Due to the space limitation, we just describe the proof sketch here. The full security proof will be given in the full paper. The proof can be split into the following two main cases.

Case 1 A partner session to the test session exists. In this case, (1) A may ask a *RevealPassword* query, or (2) A may ask *RevealEphemeralKey* query. In this **Case 1.1**, the adversary A can get principals' long-term shared secret password pw_{UV} by the *RevealPassword* query, and learns $s_{UV}=H(pw_{UV})$, thus leakage attacks don't need to be considered. In order not to violate the λ-CAFLR-eCK-freshness of the test session, A could not get any principals' ephemeral keys (x_U, x_V) to the **Test** session. Thus, A could not learn the **Test** session key because he could not get $T_U=((g^{x_U})^{x_V})^{s_{UV}}$. In this **Case 1.2**, the adversary A can get (x_U, x_V), but not pw_{UV} and $s_{UV}=H(pw_{UV})$. And A could not get $(a_L^i, a_R^i, b_L^i, b_R^i)$ from the security of λ-LRS and leakage-resilient refreshing of LRS. Thus A could not learn the **Test** session key.

Case 2 A partner session to the test session does not exist. In this case, A is an active adversary who could run the protocol with the owner of the test session by masquerading as the intended partner principal. Therefore, A is not allowed to get the principals' long-term shared password by asking a *RevealPassword* query. But, A can learn two parties' session ephemeral keys (x_U, x_V) by asking the *RevealEphemeralKey* queries. This case is similar to Case 1.2 except for the followings: A could execute online password guessing attacks whose probability of success is $\frac{N_S}{N}$. □

4.5   Security and Performance Comparison

We analyze the security and performance of our protocol by comparing with other representative AKE protocols. The comparison between our protocol and others is shown in Table 1, where Exp is modular exponentiation. From Table 1, we should note that: (1) our new protocol is the first protocol for LR PAKE; (2) our new protocol is the first AFLR eCK-secure AKE protocol in the standard model, while [23] did not allowed leakage attacks, [22] only addressed the leakage that happens before the test session was selected by the adversary, [25] just gave the proof in the CK security model, and [26–28] only proved the security in the RO model; (3) our protocol is more efficient than other LR AKE protocols [22, 25–28].

Table 1. Security and Efficiency comparison of AKE protocols

Scheme	[23]	[22]	[25]	[26]	[27]	[28]	Ours
Security model	eCK	eCK	CK	eCK	eCK	eCK	eCK
Leakage Feature	None	RLM	CLM	RLM	CLM	RLM	**CLM**
After-the-fact	Yes	No	Yes	Yes	Yes	Yes	**Yes**
Proof model	RO	Standard	Standard	RO	RO	RO	**Standard**
Key Infrastructure	PKI	PKI	PKI	PKI	PKI	PKI	**PW-based**
Rounds	2	2	1	2	1	1	**2**
Computations	8Exp	16Exp	20Exp	24Exp	12Exp	16Exp	**8Exp**

5   Conclusion and Future Works

In this paper, we first formalize the LR eCK security model for PAKE and propose a LR PAKE protocol. We consider a more strong security model, λ-CAFLR eCK security model, and formally prove the security of the proposed protocol in the standard mode. Our future works include: and 1) extending our result to the group setting; 2) considering a strong security model that not only captures leakage attacks on long-term secret password but also considers leakage of ephemeral secret randomness.

Acknowledgement. The work was supported by the Educational Commission of Hubei Province of China (No. D20151401) and the Green Industry Technology Leading Project of Hubei University of Technology (No. ZZTS2017006).

References

1. Chen, C.S., Wang, T., Tian, J.: Improving timing attack on RSA-CRT via error detection and correction strategy. Inf. Sci. **232**, 464–474 (2013)
2. Krawczyk, H.: On extract-then-expand key derivation functions and an HMAC based KDF (2008). http://webee.technion.ac.il/ ~ hugo/kdf/kdf.pdf
3. Davì, F., Dziembowski, S., Venturi, D.: Leakage-resilient storage. In: Garay, J.A., Prisco, R. (eds.) SCN 2010. LNCS, vol. 6280, pp. 121–137. Springer, Heidelberg (2010). doi:10.1007/978-3-642-15317-4_9
4. Dziembowski, S., Faust, S.: Leakage-resilient cryptography from the inner-product extractor. In: Lee, D.H., Wang, X.Y., (eds.) Asiacrypt 2011, Seoul, South Korea, pp. 702–721 (2011)
5. Bellovin, S.M., Merritt, M.: Encrypted key exchange: password-based protocols secure against dictionary attacks. In: Proceedings of IEEE Symposium on Security & Privacy, Oakland, California pp. 72–84. IEEE Computer Society Press (1992)

6. Bellare, M., Pointcheval, D., Rogaway, P.: Authenticated key exchange secure against dictionary attacks. In: Preneel, B., (ed.) Proceedings of EUROCRYPT 2000, Bruges, Belgium, pp. 139–155 (2000)
7. MacKenzie, P.D., Patel, S., Swaminathan, R.: Password-authenticated key exchange based on RSA. In: Okamoto, T. (ed.) ASIACRYPT 2000. LNCS, vol. 1976, pp. 599–613. Springer, Heidelberg (2000). doi:10.1007/3-540-44448-3_46
8. Byun, J.W., Lee, D.H., Lim, J.I.: EC2C-PAKA: an efficient client-to-client password-authenticated key agreement. Inf. Sci. **177**(19), 3995–4013 (2007)
9. Mohammad, S.F., Mahmoud, A.: An efficient client–client password-based authentication scheme with provable security. J. Supercomput. **70**(2), 1002–1022 (2014)
10. Goldreich, O., Lindell, Y.: Session-key generation using human passwords only. J. Cryptol. **19**(3), 241–340 (2006)
11. Katz, J., Ostrovsky, R., Yung, M.: Efficient and secure authenticated key exchange using weak passwords. J. ACM **57**(1), 78–116 (2009)
12. Katz, J., MacKenzie, P.D., Taban, G., Gligor, V.D.: Two-server password-only authenticated key exchange. J. Comput. Syst. Sci. **78**(2), 651–669 (2012)
13. Canetti, R., Dachman-Soled, D., Vaikuntanathan, V., Wee, H.: Efficient password authenticated key exchange via oblivious transfer. In: Fischlin, M., Buchmann, J., Manulis, M. (eds.) PKC 2012. LNCS, vol. 7293, pp. 449–466. Springer, Heidelberg (2012). doi:10.1007/978-3-642-30057-8_27
14. Goyal, V.: Positive results for concurrently secure computation in the plain model. In: 53rd Annual Symposium on Foundations of Computer Science (FOCS), New Brunswick, NJ, USA, pp. 41–50. IEEE Computer Society (2012)
15. Ruan, O., Kumar, N., He, D.B., Lee, J.H.: Efficient provably secure password-based explicit authenticated key agreement. Pervasive Mob. Comput. **24**(12), 50–60 (2015)
16. Yi, X., Rao, F.Y., Tari, Z., Hao, F.: ID2S password-authenticated key exchange protocols. IEEE Trans. Comput. **2016**, 1–14 (2016)
17. Islam, S.H.: Design and analysis of a three party password-based authenticated key exchange protocol using extended chaotic maps. Inf. Sci. **312**(C), 104–130 (2015)
18. Amin, R., Biswas, G.P.: Cryptanalysis and design of a three-party authenticated key exchange protocol using smart card. Arab. J. Forence Eng. **40**(11), 1–15 (2015)
19. Lu, C.F.: Multi-party password-authenticated key exchange scheme with privacy preservation for mobile environment. Ksii Trans. Internet Inf. Syst. **9**(12), 5135–5149 (2015)
20. Nam, J., Paik, J., Kim, J., Lee, Y., Won, D.: Server-aided password-authenticated key exchange: from 3-party to group. In: Smith, M.J., Salvendy, G. (eds.) Human Interface 2011. LNCS, vol. 6771, pp. 339–348. Springer, Heidelberg (2012). doi:10.1007/978-3-642-21793-7
21. Guo, C., Zhang, Z., Zhu, L., Tan, Y.A., Yang, Z.: Scalable protocol for cross-domain group password-based authenticated key exchange. Front. Comput. Sci. **9**(1), 157–169 (2014)
22. Moriyama, D., Okamoto, T.: Leakage resilient eCK-secure key exchange protocol without random oracles. In: Cheung,B., Hui, L., (eds.) ASIACCS 2011, Hong Kong, China, pp. 441–447 (2011)
23. LaMacchia, B.A., Lauter, K., Mityagin, A.: Stronger security of authenticated key exchange. In: Susilo, W., Liu, J.K., Mu, Y. (eds.) ProvSec 2007. LNCS, vol. 4784, pp. 1–16. Springer, Heidelberg (2007). doi:10.1007/978-3-540-75670-5_1
24. Canetti, R., Krawczyk, H.: Analysis of key-exchange protocols and their use for building secure channels. In: Pfitzmann, B. (ed.) EUROCRYPT 2001. LNCS, vol. 2045, pp. 453–474. Springer, Heidelberg (2001). doi:10.1007/3-540-44987-6_28
25. Alawatugoda, J., Boyd, C., Stebila, D.: Continuous after-the-fact leakage-resilient key exchange. In: Susilo, W., Mu, Y. (eds.) ACISP 2014. LNCS, vol. 8544, pp. 258–273. Springer, Cham (2014). doi:10.1007/978-3-319-08344-5_17

26. Alawatugoda, J., Stebila, D., Boyd, C.: Modelling after-the-fact leakage for key exchange. In: Moriai, S., Jaeger, T., Sakurai, K., (eds.) ASIACCS 2014, Kyoto, Japan, 207–216 (2014)

27. Alawatugoda, J., Stebila, D., Boyd, C.: Continuous after-the-fact leakage-resilient eCK-secure key exchange. In: Groth, J. (ed.) IMACC 2015. LNCS, vol. 9496, pp. 277–294. Springer, Cham (2015). doi:10.1007/978-3-319-27239-9_17

28. Chen, R., Mu, Y., Yang, G., Susilo, W., Guo, F.C.: Strongly leakage-resilient authenticated key exchange. In: Sako, K. (ed.) CT-RSA 2016. LNCS, vol. 9610, pp. 19–36. Springer, Cham (2016). doi:10.1007/978-3-319-29485-8_2

29. Ruan, O., Zhang, Y.Y., Zhang, M.W., Zhou, J., Harn, L.: After-the-fact leakage-resilient identity-based authenticated key exchange. IEEE Syst. J. (2017). doi:10.1109/JSYST.2017.2685524

30. Toorani, M.: On continuous after-the-fact leakage-resilient key exchange. In: Pimentel (ed.) Proceedings of the Second Workshop on Cryptography and Security in Computing Systems, Amsterdam, Netherlands, pp. 31–35 (2015)

31. Yang, Z., Li, S.Q.: On security analysis of an after-the-fact leakage resilient key exchange protocol. Inf. Process. Lett. **116**(1), 33–40 (2016)

32. Chakraborty, S., Paul, G., Rangan, C.P.: Flaw in the Security Analysis of Leakage-resilient Authenticated Key Exchange Protocol from CT-RSA 2016 and Restoring the Security Proof (2016). http://eprint.iacr.org/2016/862.pdf

Secure Encrypted Data Deduplication
with Ownership Proof and User Revocation

Wenxiu Ding[1], Zheng Yan[1,2(✉)], and Robert H. Deng[3]

[1] State Key Lab of Integrated Services Networks,
School of Cyber Engineering, Xidian University, Xi'an, China
wenxiuding_1989@126.com, zyan@xidian.edu.cn
[2] Department of Communications and Networking,
Aalto University, Espoo, Finland
[3] School of Information Systems,
Singapore Management University, Singapore, Singapore
robertdeng@edu.smu.sg

Abstract. Cloud storage as one of the most important cloud services enables cloud users to save more data without enlarging its own storage. In order to eliminate repeated data and improve the utilization of storage, deduplication is employed to cloud storage. Due to the concern about data security and user privacy, encryption is introduced, but incurs new challenge to cloud data deduplication. Existing work cannot achieve flexible access control and user revocation. Moreover, few of them can support efficient ownership proof, especially public verifiability of ownership. In this paper, we propose a secure encrypted data deduplication scheme with effective ownership proof and user revocation. We evaluate its performance and prove its security. The simulation results show that our scheme is efficient and effective for potential practical employment.

Keywords: Deduplication · User revocation · Homomorphic encryption · Proxy re-encryption

1 Introduction

Cloud computing provides seemingly unlimited resources as services to cloud users by rearranging various resources. Cloud storage as one of the most popular cloud services enables cloud users to store tremendous amount of data in the cloud, which may exceed their own storage spaces.

In order to improve the storage services, deduplication has become an important technique in cloud storage. Data deduplication can help eliminate multiple copies of same files and improve the utilization of storage. It has proved to achieve high cost savings, such as reducing up to 68% storage for standard file systems [1]. The savings can be passed back to cloud users in many ways, such as reducing storage cost. Thus, efficient deduplication is extremely desired by both cloud service providers and cloud users. Though data deduplication brings many benefits, it also faces some challenges.

© Springer International Publishing AG 2017
S. Ibrahim et al. (Eds.): ICA3PP 2017, LNCS 10393, pp. 297–312, 2017.
DOI: 10.1007/978-3-319-65482-9_20

First, cloud storage and deduplication management incurs the concern about data privacy and user privacy [2]. Cloud users would lose the full control over their out-sourced personal data, which even may be disclosed by the dishonest cloud service providers. Thus encryption as a popular method is introduced to solve this problem [3]. But the same file encrypted with different encryption schemes would result in different ciphertexts, which makes it difficult to check duplication and conduct deduplication. Second, how to share the duplicated data flexibly to authorized data holders is an issue [4]. Duplicated data would not be stored again, but it should guarantee the access right of data holders. Third, data deletion by users complicates the deduplication management. If some data holders delete their stored data, their access to the data should be completely prevented even when they still hold the previous key for obtaining the data. Thus, deduplication management should support user revocation. Fourth, how to guarantee the ownership proof of data holders is an open issue [5]. In order to reduce the communication cost and computation cost caused by duplicated data upload, file tag is always employed for duplication check. But it is vulnerable to forgery attack and difficult to guarantee the ownership.

In order to solve the above problems, this paper presents a flexible encrypted data deduplication scheme under the cooperation of an Authorized Party (AP) and a cloud service provider (CSP). First, we propose an Additive Homomorphic Re-Encryption (AHRE) algorithm. In our deduplication scheme, uploaded file is encrypted with symmetric encryption while the symmetric key is encrypted with AHRE. It can efficiently update the ciphertexts and revoke those data holders who delete their data at the cloud. Moreover, we propose a scheme to prove the ownership without complicated interactions between data holders and CSP or AP, which can support flexible public verifiability. Different from existing work [6, 7], our scheme can effectively deal with encrypted data deduplication with revocation at the cloud without involvement of data owners or data holders. Specifically, the contributions of this paper are:

- We construct an additive homomorphic re-encryption algorithm, which supports re-encryption and additive homomorphic computation. It lays the basic foundation of our proposed scheme for encrypted data deduplication with effective ownership proof and user revocation.
- We integrate data deduplication with flexible access control based on AHRE, which results in a secure and efficient encrypted data deduplication.
- We design an encrypted data update and user revocation protocol to enhance data security. It can refresh the stored data at any time and support the data holder revocation when it deletes the data. In addition, the above operations do not need any involvement of data holders.
- We design an efficient ownership proof scheme, which does not incur complicated interaction between data holders and CSP and can support public verifiability.
- We prove the security and justify the performance of our scheme through analysis and implementation.

The rest of this paper is organized as follows. Section 2 gives a brief overview of related work. System model and security model are introduced in Sect. 3, followed by the detailed design of proposed schemes in Sect. 4. In Sect. 5, security analysis and performance evaluation are given. Finally, we conclude the paper in the last section.

2 Related Work

Cloud storage service providers such as Dropbox [8], Google Drive [9], Mozy [10], perform deduplication to save space by eliminating redundancy in cloud storage and optimizing its utilization. In order to preserve the privacy of data holders, encryption is employed. However, storage savings through deduplication are totally lost if clients conventionally encrypt their data. This is because the encrypted data are saved as different contents by applying different keys, which complicates the deduplication. For example, DeDu [11] - a deduplication system is unable to handle encrypted data.

Encrypted Data Deduplication
Convergent Encryption (CE) as the most prominent manifestation of Message Locked Encryption (MLE) was introduced [12, 13]. In CE, a user employs the hash code of data as the key to encrypt the data, which results in $E_{H(m)}(m)$. Any user with the same data can generate the same ciphertext, thus realizing deduplication. However, CE suffers from offline brute-force dictionary attacks. Moreover, it is hard to support user revocation. Bellare et al. proposed DupLESS to resist the above-mentioned brute-force attacks [14] by introducing a Key Server. But it still cannot control data access of other data users in a flexible way. Wen et al. [15] constructed a session-key-based convergent key management scheme and a convergent key sharing scheme to overcome the problem caused by frequently changed ownership and data blocks. But this work requests all data owners communicate with each other to manage their session key. Liu et al. proposed a secure cross-user deduplication scheme that supports client-side encryption without requiring any additional independent servers by applying a password authenticated key exchange protocol [16]. But this scheme requests that the data owner is always online for data ownership check and deduplication. Thus this approach cannot handle the situation that the data owner is not available, which is very common in practice.

In another work [17], attribute-based encryption (ABE) is applied to realize deduplicated data access control managed by data owners. But it needs the data owners to be online and incurs much computation cost to them. In our previous work [18, 19], we proposed deduplication schemes based on proxy re-encryption (PRE). But the ciphertext update needs the data holders to download the stored file from the cloud and then encrypt it, which incurs higher communication cost and computation overhead. Liu et al. proposed a policy-based deduplication proxy scheme [20], but they did not consider data deletion. Another work [21] even proposed to forfeit deduplication to reduce chunk fragmentation by container capping. But all of the above work does not consider user revocation management. Though the work [7] proposed to solve the deduplication with user revocation, it complicates the key management of Attribute-Based Encryption (ABE) especially during user revocation. Hur et al. proposed a novel server-side deduplication scheme for encrypted data [6]. It allows a cloud server to control access to outsourced data even when data ownership changes dynamically by exploiting randomized convergent encryption and secure ownership group key distribution. This scheme prevents data leakage from revoked users. But it needs all users to upload their encrypted files and data owners should be online for user revocation, which is not efficient.

Data Ownership Verification

Halevi et al. introduced a practical implementation of Proofs of Ownership (PoW) for deduplication [22]. They proposed to use Merkle tree on the pre-processed data to generate verification information. When challenging a prover, a verifier randomly chooses several leaves of the tree and obtains the corresponding sibling-paths of all these leaves. Only when all paths are valid, will the verifier accept the proof. Pietro et al. [23] chose the projection of a file onto some randomly selected bit-positions as proof to realize the PoW. But both schemes above do not consider data privacy. Ng et al. [24] also applied Merkle tree to manage the deduplication of encrypted data. The value of each leaf node is generated from several data blocks, while only one leaf is considered in each interactive proof protocol. Thus, it needs to execute the protocol multiple times to enhance its correctness, which causes high computation overhead.

Yang et al. proposed an efficient scheme to check the ownership [25]. A data holder only needs to access partial and dynamical portions of an original file to generate the proof of possession. In addition, the data holder has no need to upload the file, which can reduce communication and computation costs. In our previous work [19], Elliptic Curve Cryptography (ECC) is employed to verify data ownership by challenging data holders. The scheme presented in this paper simplifies this procedure, which can support public verifiability of ownership when data holders are offline.

3   Problem Statements

3.1   System Model and Security Model

Our proposed scheme mainly consists of four types of entities as shown in Fig. 1:

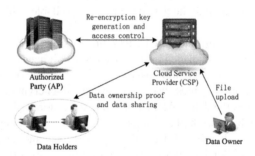

Fig. 1. System model

(1) Cloud Service Provider (CSP) is in charge of data storage and duplication check. CSP is curious about user data, but it follows designed protocols strictly in order to gain commercial benefits from providing storage service to its consumers or users.

(2) Authorized Party (AP) is responsible for access policy check, re-encryption key generation, and user revocation by cooperating with the CSP. It would never collude with the CSP and is fully trusted. AP cannot access the data stored at the CSP.

(3) Data owner is the cloud service consumer and the first data uploder. It encrypts an original file and uploads it to the CSP. The CSP generates one file tag based on the proof message of the data owner.

(4) Data holders are subsequent uploaders, who do not need to encrypt the file but need to pass ownership check in order to obtain the access right of the stored file. If one user deletes its file at the CSP, AP and CSP should revoke its privilege on the file.

We further assume that communication channels among system entities are secure and each system entity can be authenticated based on a unique identifer.

3.2 Preliminary and Notations

Preliminary

A simplified variant scheme [26]: Given two large primes p and q, then $n = p * q$. Let g and h be two elements of maximal order in $\mathbb{G}$, where $\mathbb{G}$ is the cyclic group of quadratic residues modulo n^2.

Key Generation: The public parameters are n, g and $h = g^x \bmod n^2$ by randomly choosing a secret value $x \in [1, ord(\mathbb{G})]$.

Encryption (Enc): Given a message $m \in \mathbb{Z}_n$, random number r is chosen in $\mathbb{Z}_n^*$. The ciphertext is computed as $[m]_h = (T, T') = \{h^r(1 + m * n), g^r\} \, (mod \, n^2)$.

Decryption (Dec): Knowing x, m can be obtained as follows: $m = L(T/(T')^x mod \, n^2)$, where $L(u) = (u - 1)/n$.

Notations

Table 1 summarizes the notations used throughout the paper.

Table 1. System notations

Symbols	Description
g	The system generator that is public
n	The system parameter
$[m]$	The ciphertext of data m
$\mathcal{L}(*)$	The bit length of input data
$H()$	The hash function
$e(;)$	The bilinear pairing: $G_1 \times G_1 \rightarrow G_T$
v	The generator in G_1
$(sk_{AP}, pk_{AP}) = (b, v^b)$	The key pair of AP
$(sk_{CSP}, pk_{CSP}) = (a, v^a)$	The key pair of CSP
$(sk_i, pk_i) = (u_j, v^{u_j})$	The key pair of user j
$uKey$	The updating key for ciphertext refresh
$rk_{i \rightarrow j}$	The re-encryption key from user i to user j
$E_k()$	The symmetric encryption under symmetric key k
PrM	The proof message generated by data uploaders

4 Algorithm and Scheme Design

In this section, we first combine PRE and homomorphic encryption to obtain a newly designed AHRE algorithm. Then we propose some schemes to support flexible duplicated data management based on AHRE.

4.1 Additive Homomorphic Re-Encryption (AHRE)

AHRE lays the technical foundation of deduplication, which can support homomorphic processing and re-encryption computation. Its detailed design is described below.

System Setup: Let p, q be two large primes. Due to the property of safe primes, there exist two primes p' and q' that satisfy that $p = 2p' + 1$, $q = 2q' + 1$. We compute $n = p * q$ and choose generator g with order $\lambda = 2p'q'$, which can be chosen by selecting a random number $z \in \mathbb{Z}_{n^2}^*$ and computing $g = -z^{2n}$. The value λ can be used for decryption, but we choose to conceal it and protect it from all parties. In addition, the system chooses two groups G_1 and G_T of a prime order with bilinear map e: $G_1 \times G_1 \rightarrow G_T$. The system parameters are random generators $v \in G_1$ and $Z = e(v, v) \in G_T$. A cryptographic hash function: H: $\{0, 1\}^* \rightarrow Z_n$ is also applied.

Key Generation *(KGen)*: The CSP and the AP generates their key pairs: $(sk_{CSP}, pk_{CSP}) = (a, v^a)$ and $(sk_{AP}, pk_{AP}) = (b, v^b)$ respectively. User j generates key pair (u_j, v^{u_j}).

Encryption *(Enc)*: Any users upload their data to CSP for storage and deduplication management. User i chooses two random values r_1 and r_2, and then encrypts its raw data m with public keys pk_{AP}. The ciphertext of data m is denoted as: $[m] = \{C_1, C_2, C_3\} = \{(1 + m * n)g^{H(Z^{r_1}) * r_2} \bmod n^2, g^{r_2} \bmod n^2, pk_{AP}^{r_1}\}$.

Re-Encryption Key Generation *(RKGen)*: The AP wants to delegate user j by publishing re-encryption key $rk_{AP \rightarrow j} = v^{u_j/b}$.

Re-Encryption *(ReEnc)*: The CSP computes $C_3' = e(pk_{AP}^{r_1}, rk_{AP \rightarrow j}) = Z^{r_1 * u_j}$, and sets $C_2' = C_2$ and $C_1' = C_1$. Finally, the CSP forwards $\{C_1', C_2', C_3'\}$ to user j.

Decryption *(Dec)*: Upon receiving the encrypted data, user j can directly decrypt it to obtain the original data: (1) compute $C_3'' = H((C_3')^{1/u_j}) = H(Z^{r_1})$; (2) decrypt to obtain the raw data $m = L(C_1/(C_2')^{C_3''} \bmod n^2)$ where $L(u) = (u - 1)/n$.

Moreover, it can also support ciphertext refresh and additive homomorphism.

Updating Key Issue *(UKI)*: In case that the CSP wants to update the ciphertext $[m]$, AP can generate an auxiliary parameter for the CSP: $uKey = g^{H(Z^{r_1})} = g^{H(e(v^{1/b}, pk_{AP}^{r_1}))} \bmod n^2$.

Ciphertext Refresh *(CipR)*: The CSP can update the ciphertext with its own secret key and $uKey$ by: (1) choose random r_3 and compute $\overline{C}_1 = C_1 * uKey^{r_3} \bmod n^2$; (2) compute $\overline{C}_2 = C_2' * g^{r_3} \bmod n^2$; (3) $\overline{C}_3 = C_3$.

Additive Homomorphism (AH)**:** With the updating key, the CSP can achieve additive homomorphic operation over the ciphertext $[m]$. It simply chooses another data m' and computes $\widetilde{C}_1 = (1 + m' * n) * C_1 \bmod n^2$. Finally, it directly calls *CipR* to update $\left\{\widetilde{C}_1, C_2, C_3\right\}$. As a result, we get the ciphertext of $(m' + m)$.

4.2   Ownership Check

In order to support deduplication, we first present an ownership proof scheme in Fig. 2. If U1 wants to upload its file m, then it generates a proof message $PrM_1 = pk_{CSP}^{H(m)/u_1}$ and forwards it to CSP. Upon receiving the message, the CSP first computes a file tag with the public key of uploader U1: $e(PrM_1, pk_{u_1}) = Z^{a*H(m)}$. It then checks if this tag has been stored. If yes, it means that the corresponding file has been kept and the CSP only needs to record U1 as a data holder. Otherwise, it informs U1 to upload the file. The details will be presented in the next section.

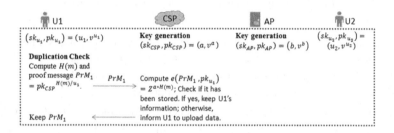

Fig. 2. The procedure of ownership check

Specially, the ownership proof can realize public verifiability. AP or any data owner can check the legality of data holders based on proof message and file tag. The ownership check is also applied during re-encryption key generation executed by AP, which can help prevent the collusion of CSP with unauthorized cloud users.

4.3   Data Deduplication Management

We suppose that data holder U1 stores file m at the CSP and later U2 wants to store the same file. If U2 wants to save the same data to the CSP, then the CSP will cooperate with the AP to enable U2 to access file m without uploading file. Figure 3 illustrates a brief protocol of encrypted data deduplication and data retrieve based on the AHRE. The details are presented below (system setup refers to Sect. 4.1):

Step 1 - Original Data Upload: Data holder U1 wants to store file m at the CSP. It follows the ownership check above and sends proof message PrM_1 to CSP. Upon receiving PrM_1, the CSP first computes file tag $Z^{a*H(m)}$ and checks if this file has been stored. If not, the CSP informs U1 to upload its file and related files to CSP for storage.

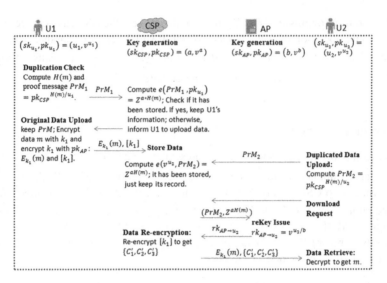

Fig. 3. The procedure of data deduplication management

U1 as the first data uploader should encrypt its file with k_1 using symmetric key encryption, call *Enc* to encrypt k_1. The data package $\{E_{k_1}(m),\ [k_1] = \{C_1, C_2, C_3\}, Z^{a*H(m)}\}$ is kept by the CSP for data storage and duplication check.

When U2 wants to upload the same file, it follows:

Step 2 - Duplicated Data Upload: U2 also generates proof message $PrM_2 = pk_{CSP}^{H(m)/u_2}$ based on its own secret key, while the CSP finds that $e(v^{u_2}, PrM_2) = Z^{a*H(m)}$ has been stored. The CSP directly informs U2 that the data has been stored.

Step 3 - Download Request: The data holder (such as U2) sends its request for accessing file m to the CSP. The CSP contacts the AP for re-encryption key generation.

Step 4 - Re-encryption Key Issue: AP checks the legality of data holders through public verifiability. If it does not pass the check, it rejects to provide the re-encryption key; Otherwise, AP calls *RKGen* to generate a re-encryption key for authorized data holder U2: $rk_{AP \to u_2} = v^{u_2/b}$. Notably, the failed cases of ownership check can be broadcasted, which will obviously reduce the reputation of CSP and its benefits.

Step 5 - Data Re-Encryption: CSP calls *ReEnc* using $rk_{AP \to u_2}$ to encrypt $[k_1]$ to generate new key ciphertext for U2: $\{C'_1, C'_2, C'_3\}$. Then data packet $\{C'_1, C'_2, C'_3\}$ and $E_{k_1}(m)$ are sent back to data holder U2.

Step 6 - Data Retrieve: Upon receiving data packet, U2 decrypts $\{C'_1, C'_2, C'_3\}$ first to get the symmetric key k_1 and then performs decryption to gain the original file m.

4.4   Encrypted Data Update

In some cases, the data holders or owners would like to update the stored data periodically to enhance data security. But in most of existing schemes, the data holders always need to download the file and use new keys to encrypt the original file, which is time-consuming and causes high communication cost. In order to solve this problem, we propose the following scheme to update encrypted data without user interaction.

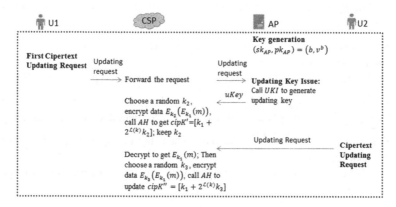

Fig. 4. Procedure of encrypted data updating

The ciphertext update request may occur in two cases (See Fig. 4) and lead to different operating procedures, which are presented as follows:

Scheme 1 - First ciphertext update request: In this case, it is the first update initiated by the CSP or data holders over the stored data $\{E_{k_1}(m), [k_1] = \{C_1, C_2, C_3\}\}$.

The CSP randomly chooses key k_2 to further encrypt the ciphertext of file m. In order to optimize the management of keys, we concatenate two keys in a secure way. The CSP first scales k_2 by $2^{\mathcal{L}(k)}$ where $\mathcal{L}(k)$ is the largest length of symmetric keys, and calls AH to get the ciphertext of $(k_1 + 2^{\mathcal{L}(k)}k_2)$. It keeps the packet $\{E_{k_2}(E_{k_1}(m)),$ $cipK' = [k_1 + 2^{\mathcal{L}(k)}k_2]\}$ and keeps k_2 secret in its storage.

Scheme 2 - Follow-up update request: In this case, the ciphertext update is requested after first ciphertext update request, which is over the ciphertext $\{E_{k_2}(E_{k_1}(m)), cipK' = [k_1 + 2^{\mathcal{L}(k)}k_2]\}$. The CSP follows the steps below:

(a) Use k_2 to decrypt the ciphertext $E_{k_2}(E_{k_1}(m))$;

(b) Choose a random number k_3, and compute $(n - 2^{\mathcal{L}(k)}k_2 + 2^{\mathcal{L}(k)}k_3)$;

(c) Call AH to get the ciphertext of $(k_1 + 2^{\mathcal{L}(k)}k_3)$: $cipK'' = [k_1 + 2^{\mathcal{L}(k)}k_3]$;

(d) Update its stored packet with $\{E_{k_3}(E_{k_1}(m)), [k_1 + 2^{\mathcal{L}(k)}k_3], k_3\}$.

4.5   User Revocation Management

If use i deletes their storage in the cloud, the ciphertext update as described above is not secure enough since it cannot prevent the access of user i if it has kept some previously secret keys. Thus, we further design a secure scheme to really block the access from these revoked users.

Similar to the ciphertext update, the user revocation also falls into two types:

Scheme 3 – Revocation before ciphertext update (See Fig. 5): Some user deletes its storage of file m without any update on its ciphertext $E_{k_1}(m)$. In this case, this revocation can be completed through the following steps:

(a) CSP chooses a random number r_3, and calls AH to get $cipK = [k_1 + r_3]$; finally, $cipK$ is sent to AP;

(b) The AP decrypts $cipK$ to get $(k_1 + r_3)$, calls Enc to encrypt $(k_1 + r_3)$ with newly chosen randoms to get $cipK' = [k_1 + r_3] = \{(1 + (k_1 + r_3) * n)g^{H(Z'_1)*r'_2} \bmod n^2,\ g^{r'_2} \bmod n^2,\ Y^{r'_1}\}$; in addition, it calls UKI to generate a new updating key $uKey' = g^{H(e(v^{1/y}, Y^{r'_1}))} = g^{H(Z'_1)} \bmod n^2$. Then, the data packet $\{cipK', uKey'\}$ is sent back to the CSP.

(c) The CSP directly updates its ciphertext with a new symmetric key k_4 to get the new packet $\{E_{k_4}(E_{k_1}(m)),\ [k_1 + 2^{\mathcal{L}(k)}k_4]\}$.

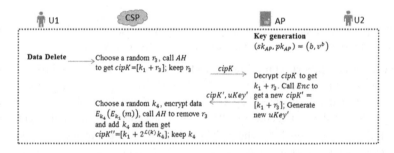

Fig. 5. Procedure of user revocation caused by user deletion

Scheme 4 – Revocation after ciphertext update: In some cases, data holder deletes its storage after ciphertext update. Hence, the CSP executes user revocation over ciphertext $\{E_{k_2}(E_{k_1}(m)),\ [k_1 + 2^{\mathcal{L}(k)}k_2]\}$.

(a) The CSP chooses a random r_4; then it calls AH to get $cipK = [k_1 + r_4 + 2^{\mathcal{L}(k)}k_2]$; finally, $cipK$ is sent to AP.

b) Similar to the step b) above, the AP chooses random numbers r'_1 and r'_2, and then get $\{cipK' = [k_1 + r_4 + 2^{\mathcal{L}(k)}k_2]\,,uKey'\}$.

(c) Upon receiving the data packet, the CSP decrypts $E_{k_2}(E_{k_1}(m))$ with k_2 and chooses random key k_5 to get $E_{k_5}(E_{k_1}(m))$; then it calls AH to remove r_4 and update k_2 with k_5 to get a new ciphertext key $cipK'' = [k_1 + 2^{\mathcal{L}(k)}k_5]$. It updates its storage with new ciphertexts $\{E_{k_5}(E_{k_1}(m)), [k_1 + 2^{\mathcal{L}(k)}k_5]\}$.

Through the schemes above, CSP finally block unauthorized users' access without the need of the intervention of data holders or data owner.

5 Security Analysis and Performance Evaluation

5.1 Security Analysis

Our scheme provides a secure approach to realize the deduplication management. The security of the proposed scheme is guaranteed by the security of the AHRE algorithm. Thus, we mainly concentrate on the security proof of AHRE and the ownership check.

Assumptions

Definition 5.1. Discrete Logarithm (DL) Problem: Given $g \in G$ and $y = g^x$ ($x \in Z_q^*$), it is hard to get x.

Definition 5.2. Computational Diffie-Hellman (CDH) Problem: Given a group G and group element v, and v^x and v^y, it is hard to compute the value of v^{xy}.

Proposition 1. If the CDH problem holds, then it is hard for adversaries to pass the ownership proof without the original file even when it colludes with CSP.

Proof. We prove it by contraction. For this purpose, we assume that the adversary can pass the ownership proof without the real file. Our goal then is to use $\mathcal{A}$ to construct an algorithm to solve the CDH problem.

Given the challenge public parameters $(v, Z, e(;))$, the adversary $\mathcal{A}$ can construct its own key pair (u_A, v^{u_A}). If it colludes with CSP, then the adversary can further get $pk_{CSP}^{H(m)/u_1}$, $v^{H(m)/u_1}$ and $Z^{H(m)}$ of real data holder u_1 from CSP. The adversary can compute to get its own proof message $pk_{CSP}^{H(m)/u_A} = v^{aH(m)/u_A}$ on the $pk_{CSP}^{H(m)/u_1} = v^{aH(m)/u_1}$ and v^{u_1}. The adversary can generate real proof message $v^{aH(m)/u_A}$, and easily gain $v^{aH(m)}$ with its own secret key.

Here, we set $v^x = v^{aH(m)/u_1}$ and $v^y = v^{u_1}$, thus it means the adversary gets $v^{xy} = v^{aH(m)}$ and breaks the problem of CDH. Hence, our ownership proof is secure and can guarantee that only real data holders can pass the proof. In addition, anyone can verify the ownership of data holders with proof message and file tag.

Proposition 2. If the DL problem holds in group G_1 and the CDH problem holds in group $Z_{n^2}^*$, then the AHRE is secure.

Proof. Given the AHRE ciphertext of data m under the secret key of CSP: $[m] = \{C_1, C_2, C_3\} = \{(1 + m * n)g^{H(Z^{r_1}) * r_2} \bmod n^2, g^{r_2} \bmod n^2, pk_{AP}^{r_1}\}$, the adversary $\mathcal{A}$ would like to obtain the original data m.

Due to the difficulty of DL problem, it is hard to get v^{r_1} from $pk_{AP}^{r_1} = v^{b*r_1}$. Hence, the adversary cannot obtain the value of $H(Z^{r_1})$. In the update process, the updating key $g^{H(Z^{r_1})}$ is issued to CSP. If the adversary colludes with CSP, it can get packet

$(\{C_1, C_2, C_3\} = \{(1 + m * n)g^{H(Z^{r_1})*r_2} \bmod n^2, g^{r_2} \bmod n^2, pk_{AP}^{r_1}\}, g^{H(Z^{r_1})})$. But due to CDH problem, the adversary cannot get $g^{H(Z^{r_1})*r_2}$ from the packet and cannot obtain the original data.

Proposition 3. The cooperation of CSP and AP without collusion guarantees that only eligible data holders can access the original file m and the file can be deduplicated securely.

Proof. The adversary has no way to obtain the original file m even when it colludes with CSP as it is always in an encrypted form. The file m is encrypted with symmetric encryption (such as AES) while the symmetric key is encrypted with AHRE. Owing to the security of AHRE, the symmetric key is protected and unauthorized users cannot get it. Moreover, original data confidentiality is guaranteed by symmetric encryption. Hence, only the authorized users can decrypt ciphertext of keys to further obtain the original file.

The ownership proof helps check the legality of cloud users without reducing the confidentiality of original data. The re-encryption key issue further transforms the ciphertext under the secret key of AP to another one under the secret key of authenticated data holders. It helps control the access to the ciphertext. In addition, the ciphertext of original file is kept by the CSP, thus the AP can only control the ciphertext of symmetric key.

In the ciphertext update, a random number is introduced to mask the original symmetric key, which can make sure neither CSP nor AP can get the symmetric key.

5.2   Computation Complexity

The proposed scheme involves four kinds of system roles: data owner, CSP, AP, and data holder. To present the computation complexity in details, we adopt AES and AHRE. As the encryption over the uploaded data is unavoidable, we neglect the symmetric encryption. Due to the limitation of paper length, we analyze the complexity of deduplication presented in Sect. 4.3 as below:

Data Owner: It needs to do one hash, one modular exponentiation in duplication check, and two modular exponentiations and two exponentiations over group G_1 or G_T to upload its data to the CSP. Thus, its computation complexity is $\mathcal{O}(1)$.

CSP: CSP performs one pairing to compute the file tag for duplication check and one pairing for re-encryption with regard to each data holder's data upload. Thus, its computation complexity is $O(N)$, where N is the number of data holders.

AP: It conducts one pairing for duplication check and one exponentiation over group G_1 for re-encryption key generation. Thus, its computation complexity is $\mathcal{O}(N)$.

Data Holder: It also needs one modular exponentiation in duplication check. In order to get the data, it should do one exponentiation over G_T, one hash and one modular exponentiation. Thus, its computation complexity is $\mathcal{O}(1)$.

Besides the computation above, they all need to generate one key pair for themselves, which involves one exponentiation over G_1. Table 2 lists the computation of all entities. We also compare it with our previous work [18, 19]. We can observe that our scheme incurs a little higher computation cost during data upload and data retrieval process but enables more functionalities, such as public verifiability and user revocation. In addition, it simplifies ownership challenge and reduces the communication costs caused by ciphertext update or user revocations. In our scheme, CSP and AP only need to exchange the ciphertexts of keys. The ciphertext of original file is always kept and updated by CSP without any involvement of data owners or data holders, which saves the communication cost, especially for multimedia data.

Table 2. Computation complexity of each entity by comparing with previous work [18, 19]

Entity	Algorithm	Computations [our scheme]	Computations [19]	Computations [18]
Data owner	Setup	1 * Exp	1 * PointMulti + 1 * Exp	1 * ModInv + 1 * ModExp
	Data upload	2 * Ex + 2 * ModExp	2 * ModExp + 1 * PointMulti	3 * ModExp
Csp	Re-encryption	1 * Pair	1 * Pair	1 * Pair
	Duplication check	1 * Pair	–	–
Data holder	System setup	1 * Exp	1 * PointMulti + 1 * ModExp	1 * ModInv + 1 * ModExp
	Duplication check	1 * ModExp	2 * ModExp + 1 * PointMulti	–
	Data upload	–	–	3 * ModExp
	Data retrieval	1 * Exp + 1 * Hash + 1 * ModExp	1 * ModExp	1 * ModExp
AP	System setup	1 * Exp	1 * ModExp	1 * ModExp
	Ownership check and rekey generation	1 * Exp + 1 * Pairing	2 * ModExp + 2 * PointMulti	1 * ModExp

Notes: Pair: Bilinear Pairing; Exp: Exponentiation in G_1 or G_T; ModInv: Modular Inversion; ModExp: Modular Exponentiation; N: Number of data holders; PointMulti: Point multiplication in ECC

5.3 Performance Analysis

System Setting

In this section, we further implemented the proposed schemes and tested their performances to check with our theoretic analysis and prove its correctness. The evaluations are performed on a laptop with Intel Core i5-3337U CPU 1.8 GHz and 8 GB RAM with Java Paring-Based Cryptography library (jPBC). To achieve better accuracy, we tested each algorithm 1000 times and reported the average value of all testing results. We choose AES as the symmetric key encryption. Unless particularly specified, some parameters in our tests are set as default values: (1) $\mathcal{L}(n) = 1024$ bits; (2) bilinear pairing parameters generator - TYPE A; (3) length of random numbers – 500 bits; (4) length of symmetric key – $\mathcal{L}(k) = 128$ bits.

Performance of AHRE

As AHRE is applied to encrypt symmetric key, we only evaluate its performance over data with $\mathcal{L}(m) = 128$ bits. The computation time of each algorithm in AHRE is presented in Table 3. Through tests, one pairing in jPBC library can be computed in approximately 10.1 milliseconds (ms). From the simulation results, we can observe that the encryption is a little time-consuming but the decryption is very efficient, which is acceptable for cloud users as they only need to execute it once. Moreover, if the cloud users are subsequent data holders, they do not need to execute encryption.

Table 3. The computation time of each algorithm in AHRE (Unit: ms)

Algorithm	System Setup	KGen	Enc	RKGen	ReEnc	Dec	UKI	CipR	AH	Pairing
Time	89.81	13.04	38.82	13.9	10.01	4.08	25.5	13.46	14.02	10.1

Performance of Our Proposed Schemes

In this experiment, we test the performance of our proposed schemes by testing their simulation time over different size of original files: 10 MB, 30 MB and 50 MB. As some basic operations are similar to the operations of AHRE and are not affected by the size of files, we only present the computation time varying with the size of original file, which is shown in Table 4.

Table 4. The computation time of some operations in deduplication schemes (Unit: ms)

Operation			Time		
			File size: 10 MB	File size: 30 MB	File size: 50 MB
Data upload (User)			82.1	317.9	618.1
Decryption before update or revocation (User)			55.78	300.7	589.7
Update	Scheme 1 (CSP)		62.2	298.1	581.8
	Scheme 2 (CSP)		117.6	619.4	1210.1
Revocation	Scheme 3	Step 1 (CSP)	13.7	13.8	13.8
		Step 2 (AP)	80.5	82.5	78.7
		Step 3 (CSP)	67.6	314.7	591.3
	Scheme 4	Step 1 (CSP)	13.6	14.0	12.3
		Step 2 (AP)	79.8	82.7	76.6
		Step 3 (CSP)	124.9	600.7	1202.0
Decryption after update or revocation (User)			104.8	608.7	1182.9

We can observe that the ciphertext update and user revocation almost double the decryption time of users. But it does not involve the data holders in the two operations. In most of existing schemes, the data holders need to download the outsourced file, decrypt the ciphertext and then re-encrypt them, which is not efficient, especially for large files, such as multimedia data. Though revocation and update introduce much computation overhead, they are almost undertaken by the CSP, which is acceptable for a cloud service provider.

6   Conclusion

Data deduplication helps improving the utilization of cloud storage and in turn helps reducing the storage cost of cloud users. In this paper, we proposed a flexible data deduplication scheme with effective ownership proof and user revocation. Our scheme can flexibly support outsourced data update and data sharing among data holders. Moreover, it can support public verifiability of ownership and user revocation without intervention of data owners, which greatly enhances cloud data security and effectively reduces the communication cost caused by ciphertext update, especially significant for large files. Extensive performance analysis and test shows that our scheme is secure and efficient. Although our scheme incurs a little higher computation cost than some existing work, it can provide advanced features. In future work, we will optimize our design and study privacy-preserving and verifiable data deduplication.

Acknowledgment. This work is sponsored by the National Key Research and Development Program of China (grant 2016YFB0800700), the NSFC (grants 61672410 and U1536202), the Project Supported by Natural Science Basic Research Plan in Shaanxi Province of China (Program No. 2016ZDJC-06), the 111 project (grants B08038 and B16037), and Academy of Finland (Grant No. 308087).

References

1. Meyer, D.T., Bolosky, W.J.: A study of practical deduplication. ACM Trans. Storage **7**(4), 1–20 (2012)
2. Ali, M., Dhamotharan, R., Khan, E., Khan, S.U., Vasilakos, A.V., Li, K., Zomaya, A.Y.: SeDaSC: secure data sharing in clouds. IEEE Syst. J. **99**, 1–10 (2015)
3. Liu, C., Yang, C., Zhang, X.Y., Chen, J.J.: External integrity verification for outsourced big data in cloud and IoT: a big picture. Future Gener. Comput. Syst. **49**, 58–67 (2015)
4. Puzio, P., Molva, R., Onen, M., Loureiro, S.: ClouDedup: secure deduplication with encrypted data for cloud storage. In: Proceedings of IEEE 5th International Conference on Cloud Computing Technology and Science, pp. 363–370. IEEE (2013)
5. Mulazzani, M., Schrittwieser, S., Leithner, M., Huber, M.: Dark clouds on the horizon: using cloud storage as attack vector and online slack space. In: Proceedings of USENIX Security Symposium, p. 5 (2011)
6. Hur, J., Koo, D., Shin, Y., Kang, K.: Secure data deduplication with dynamic ownership management in cloud storage. IEEE Trans. Knowl. Data Eng. **28**(11), 3113–3125 (2016)
7. Kwon, H., Hahn, C., Kim, D., Hur, J.: Secure deduplication for multimedia data with user revocation in cloud storage. Multimedia Tools Appl. **76**(4), 5889–5903 (2017)
8. Dropbox: A file-storage and sharing service. http://www.dropbox.com/
9. Google Drive. http://drive.google.com
10. Mozy, Mozy: a file-storage and sharing service. http://mozy.com/
11. Sun, Z., Shen, J., Yong, J.M.: DeDu: building a deduplication storage system over cloud computing. In: IEEE International Conference on Computer Supported Cooperative Work in Design, pp. 348–355. IEEE (2014)

12. Wallace, G., Douglis, F., Qian, H.W., Shilane, P., Smaldone, S., Chamness, M., Hsu, W.: Characteristics of backup workloads in production systems. In: Proceedings of USENIX Conference on File and Storage Technologies, p. 500 (2012)
13. Wilcox, Z.O.: Convergent encryption reconsidered (2011). http://www.mail-archive.com/cryptography@metzdowd.com/msg08949.html
14. Bellare, M., Keelveedhi, S., Ristenpart, T.: DupLESS: server aided encryption for deduplicated storage. In: Proceedings of 22nd USENIX Conference on Security, pp. 179–194 (2013)
15. Wen, M., Ota, K., Li, H., Lei, J.S., Gu, C.H., Su, Z.: Secure data deduplication with reliable key management for dynamic updates in CPSS. IEEE Trans. Comput. Soc. Syst. 2(4), 137–147 (2015)
16. Liu, J., Asokan, N., Pinkas, B.: Secure deduplication of encrypted data without additional independent servers. In: Proceedings of the 22nd ACM SIGSAC Conference on Computer and Communications Security, pp. 874–885. ACM (2015)
17. Yan, Z., Wang, M.J., Li, Y.X., Vasilakos, A.V.: Encrypted data management with deduplication in cloud computing. IEEE Cloud Comput. 3(2), 28–35 (2016)
18. Yan, Z., Ding, W., Zhu, H.: A scheme to manage encrypted data storage with deduplication in cloud. In: Wang, G., Zomaya, A., Perez, G.M., Li, K. (eds.) ICA3PP 2015. LNCS, vol. 9530, pp. 547–561. Springer, Cham (2015). doi:10.1007/978-3-319-27137-8_40
19. Yan, Z., Ding, W.X., Yu, X.X., Zhu, H.Q., Deng, R.H.: Deduplication on encrypted big data in cloud. IEEE Trans. Big Data 2(2), 138–150 (2016)
20. Liu, C., Liu, X., Wan, L.: Policy-based de-duplication in secure cloud storage. In: Yuan, Y., Wu, X., Lu, Y. (eds.) ISCTCS 2012. CCIS, vol. 320, pp. 250–262. Springer, Heidelberg (2013). doi:10.1007/978-3-642-35795-4_32
21. Lillibridge, M., Eshghi, K., Bhagwat, D.: Improving restore speed for backup systems that use inline chunk-based deduplication. In: Proceedings of USENIX Conference on File and Storae Technologies, pp. 183–198 (2013)
22. Halevi, S., Harnik, D., Pinkas, B., Shulman-Peleg, A.: Proofs of ownership in remote storage systems. In: Proceedings of the 18th ACM conference on Computer and communications security, pp. 491–500. ACM (2011)
23. Pietro, R.D., Sorniotti, A.: Boosting efficiency and security in proof of ownership for deduplication. In: Proceedings of the 7th ACM Symposium on Information, Computer and Communications Security, pp. 81–82. ACM (2012)
24. Ng, W.K., Wen, Y., Zhu, H.: Private data deduplication protocols in cloud storage. In: Proceedings of the 27th Annual ACM Symposium on Applied Computing, pp. 441–446. ACM (2012)
25. Yang, C., Ren, J., Ma, J.F.: Provable ownership of file in de-duplication cloud storage. In: IEEE Global Communications Conference, pp. 695–700. IEEE (2013)
26. Bresson, E., Catalano, D., Pointcheval, D.: A simple public-key cryptosystem with a double trapdoor decryption mechanism and its applications. In: Laih, C.-S. (ed.) ASIACRYPT 2003. LNCS, vol. 2894, pp. 37–54. Springer, Heidelberg (2003). doi:10.1007/978-3-540-40061-5_3

Optimally Selecting the Timing of Zero-Day Attack via Spatial Evolutionary Game

Yanwei Sun[1,2], Lihua Yin[1], Yunchuan Guo[1(✉)], Fenghua Li[1,2],
and Binxing Fang[3]

[1] State Key Laboratory of Information Security,
Institute of Information Engineering, Chinese Academy of Sciences, Beijing, China
`guoyunchuan@iie.ac.cn`
[2] School of Cyberspace Security, University of Chinese Academy of Sciences,
Beijing, China
[3] Electronic Information Engineering Research Institute,
University of Electronic Science and Technology of China, Dongguan, China

Abstract. Zero-day attacks pose a serious threat to the government agencies and companies. To get better protection of the internet infrastructure, it is very important for the defenders to analyze the behavior of attackers who exploit the zero-day vulnerabilities and predict their attack timing. For attackers, when to exploit the zero-day vulnerability means a tough tradeoff between profit and risk: If the attackers exploit too soon, they may get limited profits; too late, they may suffer the higher risk of being found before the attack. To help defenders make a better prediction, this paper computes the optimal timing from the perspective of attackers. We use an evolutionary game to estimate the risk of being found and then chooses the optimal timing based on the risk and profit. In detail, we design a learning strategy to deal with individual differences among multi-attackers, and use spatial structure to model the evolutionary process. The experiment results show the efficiency of this approach.

Keywords: Zero-day attack · Optimal timing · Evolutionary game

1 Introduction

1.1 Background

Zero-day attacks against government agencies and companies are increasing at an alarming rate. In 2016, 10822 vulnerabilities were found in China, and 2203 of them were zero-day vulnerabilities[1], which may cause serious consequences. According to *The Hacker News*, hackers exploited the zero-day vulnerability to attack Bangladesh's central bank in 2016 and stole over \$80 million from the Federal Reserve Bank[2]. Because of the serious consequence of zero-day attack, it

This work was supported by the National Key R&D Program of China (No. 2016YFB0800702), and NSFC General Projects (No. 61672515).

[1] http://www.cert.org.cn/publish/main/upload/File/2016CNVDannual1.pdf.
[2] http://thehackernews.com/2016/03/bank-hacking-malware.html.

© Springer International Publishing AG 2017
S. Ibrahim et al. (Eds.): ICA3PP 2017, LNCS 10393, pp. 313–327, 2017.
DOI: 10.1007/978-3-319-65482-9_21

is very important for the defenders to analyze the zero-day attack behavior from the perspective of attackers to reasonably allocate their limited *defense* resource and relieve the attack. In recent years, many approaches have been proposed to analyze attacker behaviors. However, these approaches mainly focus on the relationship between exploits and system vulnerabilities [17], the attacker preference and skill set [3]; yet few of them have analyzed attack timing. Obviously, if a defender can accurately predict the timing that attackers exploit zero day vulnerability, (s)he can allocate his/her defense resource more efficiently to prevent the attack.

1.2   Motivation

Axelrod *et al.* [6] formulated the zero-day attack as a long-term process. They claimed that the use of the zero-day exploits this time might make it unavailable for use later. This revealed that the long-term profit should be a higher priority than any one-time attacking income to the attacker. But the research only considered the behavior of the attacker but ignored that of the defender, so the final result had low accuracy. This motivated us to rethink the predication model of attack timing from the perspective of the attack-defense game.

Most of existing game-based approaches used in behavior analysis assume that all attackers are adequately rational [18]. That is, they make their strategic choice on a wholly rationally determined evaluation of probable outcomes. However, in practice, attackers who use the zero-day vulnerabilities do not know completely information about the attacked target systems before initiating an attack and even during the attack. This means that the adequate rationality assumption is not realistic enough in modeling the behaviors of attackers who exploit the zero-day vulnerability. On the contrary, evolutionary game, based on the hypothesis of bounded rationality is more efficient than the other game models when applied to analyze attack-defense behavior [19]. So in this paper, the evolutionary game is used to select the optimal attack timing of the attacker who exploits zero-day vulnerabilities.

1.3   Challenge

The main challenges of optimally selecting the timing of zero-day attack are summarized as follows:

- *Proper modeling of the long-term process of zero-day attacks.* As mentioned above, zero-day attack is a long-term process. The zero-day exploit (also called cyber resources) will always be available unless the vulnerability is fixed by the defender. As the process goes on, the attacker needs to make a tradeoff between risk and profit for each time point: if the vulnerability is exploited, the attacker may get some profit but the risk of being noticed may also increase. On the contrary, if the zero-day vulnerability is exploited too late or not exploited, there is also a chance for the defender to fix it, leave no chances for the attacker. So the first challenge is how to model this process properly.

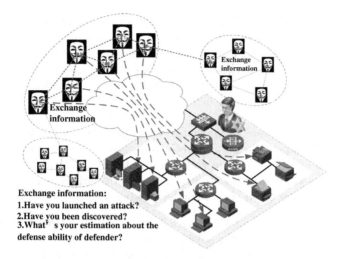

Fig. 1. Multi-attackers vs. a certain company

- *Proper modeling of the information sharing mechanism among multiple attackers.* Many hackers think that all the information should be free, so they will form a unique "black ecosystem" to share information more effectively. According to the director of Baidu security laboratory[3], the information sharing mechanism of black ecosystem is much better than that of white ecosystem. To get a better understanding of the process, attackers will exchange their views about the defender. So the second challenge is how to model the information sharing mechanism properly among multiple attackers.
- *Precise evaluating the profit for each game.* During the process, the attacker is most concerned about the long-term profit rather than the one-time attacking income. The long-term profit highly depends on the duration of the process, however the duration is difficult to be estimated if the attacker knows little about the defender. So the third challenge is how to evaluate the profit precisely.

1.4 Contribution

To solve those challenges, this paper analyzes the attack-defense scenario (shown in Fig. 1) between multiple attackers and a single defender. Our main contributions are as follows.

- *We use evolutionary game to model the zero-day attacks.* We consider the problem from the perspective of the attack-defense game. At the beginning of the game, attackers know little about the defender. But with the game process, their understandings become more and more accurate due to their observation and information sharing, so this is an evolutionary process.
- *We design a new learning strategy to model the information sharing mechanism.* The most common learning strategy in evolutionary game is to simply

---

[3] Baidu is the predominant search engine in China.

imitate the strategy of the neighbor who has the highest payoffs. But this is not fitted in our scenario, because different attackers have different zero-day exploits. Individual difference will lead to the fact that the optimal timing for some certain attackers may not suitable for other attackers. So a new learning strategy is designed to model the information sharing mechanism. By doing so, the attackers could get a better understanding of the defense capability of the defender.

- *We specify and compute all the factors that affect the payoffs.* We first specify all the factors that affect the payoffs and discuss the relationship between factors and payoffs. Then we compute the factors and the payoffs to help attackers to decide whether to attack or not for each time point. By doing this, the attackers could get a relatively better reward for the whole game.

The rest of the paper is organized as follows. Section 2 introduces the related works. Section 3 introduces our solution. Section 4 discusses the details about the players' payoffs. Section 5 reports experimental results, and Sect. 6 gives the conclusions.

2   Related Work

2.1   Zero-Day Attack Protection

To protect against the zero-day attack, a lot of researches have focused on detecting [5,14] and evaluating [22,23] the zero-day vulnerabilities. To identify the unknown files, Acasarala et al. [5] introduced the class-matching approach. Mishra et al. [14] proposed a hybrid solution which used the concept of CSS matching and URI matching to defend against zero-day phishing attacks. To evaluate the robustness of networks, Wang et al. [23] proposed two complementary diversity metrics and Wang et al. [22] conducted the evaluation process based on how many zero-day vulnerabilities are required to compromise a network asset.

Another way of protection is analyzing the attacker behavior. Ekelhart et al. [10] developed a simulation-driven approach which took attack strategies and attacker behavior into consideration. Al et al. [1] used the time delay neural network which embedded the temporal behavior of the attacks to maximize the recognition rate of network. Mitshell et al. [15] proposed a specification-based IDS which could adapt to different types of attackers such as reckless, random, and opportunistic ones. In this way, it could get a higher detection accuracy. Allodi et al. first pointed out that not all the vulnerabilities were equally exploited by the attacker [2], and then focused on the choice of attackers [3]. By validating the actual 'traces' attackers leave on real systems, they claimed that the real attacker would not be as powerful as we thought and would not exploit every vulnerability. The attackers would strategically choose the busy periods and some certain vulnerabilities while the efforts of security professionals are diffused across many vulnerabilities [16,17]. Based on this observation, Dumitrace et al. [9] proposed a novel metrics that enabled a more accurate assessment of the risk of cyber-attacks. Bozorgi *et al.* [8] used machine learning method with high dimensional feature vectors input to predict the vulnerability which was most likely to be exploited by the attacker. All these analyses, however, have been carried out from the perspective of defenders, ignoring the information sharing mechanism among attackers where the mechanism is the most important part during the attack and can guide attackers to changer their strategies dynamically.

2.2   The Use of Evolutionary Game Against Cyber-Security

Realizing the importance of information sharing, lots of researchers have used evolutionary game approaches to improve network security. Tosh *et al.* [21] used non-cooperative information sharing game for participants to protect against the cyber-attacks. The participation costs were considered and dynamic cost adjustment were proposed to help to Cyber-security Information Exchange framework to increase information sharing as well as its own revenue. Guo *et al.* [11] proposed a general defense mechanism against various routing attacks on DTNs. They used evolutionary game theory to promote nodes to cooperate with each other and demonstrated the ESS of the game. That is, when a few nodes change their strategies, the whole system can return to the original stable status. Ruan *et al.* [19] first proposed a new authentication protocol in crowdsensing networks and then used evolutionary game theory to formulate the attack-defense model. The model could alleviate the defense cost and achieve security assurance by means of setting the parameters in the new protocol. In wireless sensor networks, to make an optimal tradeoff between maximizing the secrecy rate of a sensor node and minimizing power consumed for data transmission, Jiang *et al.* [12] used evolutionary game to help the sensor node to adaptively select the power level. However, all of these researches have considered the problem from the defender's perspective, ignoring the fact that the attackers could also benefit from cooperation.

3   Computing Defender's Protecting Ability via Evolutionary Game

Before introducing the evolutionary game model, a brief discussion about the differences between general cyber-attack and zero-day attack is given as follows. According to the stealth features of zero-day exploit, most of the software and the security products cannot detect the existence of threat [7]. So, the first difference is that the attackers with zero-day exploits can get the one-time attacking income as long as they launch an attack and regardless of whether the target is protected or not. Second, as mentioned above, attackers using zero-day exploits are more concerned about the long-term profit, and they have to make sure if the resource will be invalid after this attack. Therefore, the key points to the entire game process are the attacker's actions and the defense capability of the defender, i.e. whether the defender could discover and recove the vulnerability in time before (after) the attack happens. What's more, the attackers' decisions are closely related to the defense capability. For example, if the attacker believes that the defender is sensitive enough to the attack, he will not attack until the one-time attacking income is worth the risk. On the contrary, if the attacker thinks that the defender has a strong capability of discovering the vulnerability even if nothing happens, the attacker will choose to attack as soon as possible. So in this section, we will explain the evolutionary game model from the perspective of the attacker, to show how to get an exact assessment of the defense capability and then make a proper decision.

3.1   Problem Description

In order to make a precise assessment of the defense capability, the attacker needs to play a number of games and revise the assessment time by time according to each result. But this is not practical for a single attacker, for the game is likely to be terminated after several attacking attempts. Therefore, it is important to learn from the surrounding attackers, observe the state of neighbors and exchange information with each other. On the one hand, to a great extent, it avoids the risk of being discovered to a great extent; on the other hand, it helps them to understand the real defense capability quickly and precisely. Therefore, we use the evolutionary game model to analyze this problem. It should be noted that due to space constraints and for the purpose of simplifying the model, this article mainly discusses about the parameters and the learning strategy of attackers, and simplifies the discussion of the defender. Before discussing the model, some notations should be introduced.

Because this is a long-term process, an explanation about the *time point* is necessary. The notation t represents the time point, and we assume that one time point equals to a short period required for a one-time attack. At the beginning of each time point, a new sub-game starts and the attacker should decide whether to attack at this time point or not.

In terms of the zero-day vulnerability, which is called cyber resource from the perspective of the attacker, we use notation L to represent the lifecycle of certain vulnerability. Different vulnerabilities have different lifecycles. For example, compared with buffer overflow and executable code, other vulnerabilities such as PHP vulnerability or SQL injection often have longer lifecycles [20]. During the lifecycle, the related process of vulnerabilities are generally divided into several key stages [4], including being discovered, being used, being disclosed, being repaired, etc. Risk levels are also different at different stages. So we define threats coefficient $TA(t)$ to characterize the vulnerability threat level at different stages where $t \in [0, L]$. For example, $TA(t)$ equals to 1 when the vulnerability are not disclosed and reduces to 0.2 when the patches of certain vulnerability are provided. Along with the threats coefficient $TA(t)$, we also define the gain function of time $g(t)$ to represent the one-time attacking income that the attacker can get when he attacks the target at the certain time point t. $G(t)$ is determined by both the resource itself and the target, in this paper, it is assumed that the $g(t)$ is preset and known to the attacker and defender.

As to the defender, $P_D(t)$ denotes the protection probability at time point t, and P_a denotes the passive-defense capability, indicating the probability of discovering the vulnerability after being attacked. P_b denotes the initiative-defense capability, indicating the probability of discovering the vulnerability without being attacked. If notation A is used to indicate that the vulnerability is found by the defender, notation B is used to indicate that the resource is used by the attacker; notation C is used to indicate that the defender decides to protect, then $P_a = \{A|BC\}$ and $P_b = \{A|\overline{B}C\}$ can be concluded. P_a and P_b are both fixed values which are known to the defender and unknown to the attackers during the game process. In addition, it should be noted that P_a is bigger than P_b in most cases. That is, the vulnerability is much more likely to be discovered by defender after being attacked compared with the situation where nothing happens. In this paper, P_a and P_b are preset and known to the defender but unknown to the attacker.

For each attacker, $P_A(t)$ denotes the attack probability. Both $P_A(t)$ and $P_D(t)$ are determined by the payoffs of the attacker and the defender at time point t. We use $P_a(t)$ and $P_b(t)$ to represent the attacker's assessment of P_a and P_b at time point t respectively. As the game goes on, the attacker will revise these two assessments by observing the state of other neighbors and exchanging information with each other.

3.2   Game Formulation

Participants: It is assumed that the game is between multiple attackers and a single defender. Each attacker owns a kind of particular resource, set $AT = \{1, 2, \ldots, n\}$ is used to denote the multiple attackers. The defender may protect multiple targets at the same time. Each attacker chooses a certain target for which the resource is applicable to start the game. We assume that all the targets share the same P_a and P_b, because they are protected by the same defender.

Strategy set: General analysis is conducted, which means the network is not specific but abstract [13], and the strategy set of attacker is $SA = \{$attack, not attack$\}$, meanwhile the set of defender is $SD = \{$protect, not protect$\}$.

Payoff: For any attacker $i \in AT$, at any time point $t \in [0, L]$, the payoff of the sub-game consists of three parts: the attacking cost denoted as C_a^i, the one-time attacking income $g_i(t)$ and the long-term profit expectancy from time point t to the end of the lifecycle, denoted as $E_i(t)$. The specific parameter settings are discussed in next section. For the defender, the loss also includes two parts, the cost of protecting denoted as C_d, and the loss caused by the attack. In order to reduce the complexity of this model, it is assumed that the attacking loss equals to the negative of the attacker's attacking revenue.

The total number of attackers: During the whole process of the game, the total number of attackers n will change from time to time. So $n(t)$ is used to represent the total number at time point t. There are three main aspects that will influence the number: First, at the beginning of time point t, $n_{new}(t)$ is used to denote the newly discovered resource. Second, at the end of time point t, $n_{exp}(t)$ is used to denote the number of expired resource. Third, according to the defense capability, some of the resource are randomly eliminated at the end of time point t, the number is notated as $n_{dis}(t)$. Then the total number of attackers at time point $t + 1$ is: $n(t + 1) = n(t) + n_{new}(t) - n_{dis}(t) - n_{exp}(t)$

Game rules: For each attacker-target pair, given the payoffs, both attacker and defender will make their decisions by calculating the Nash equilibrium. At the end of time point, the attacker revises the assessment by observing the state of other neighbors and exchanging information with each other in order to recalculate the payoffs for next time point.

Learning strategy: The most common learning strategy in evolutionary game is imitating the neighbor's strategy which has the highest payoffs after comparing with all the surrounding neighbors. However, as mentioned above, $g_i(t)$ may be various so that it is not likely that two different attackers share the same optimal timing. Therefore, in this model, the learning strategy is to revise the assessment of $P_a(t)$ and $P_b(t)$ by observing the state of other neighbors instead of imitating their strategies directly.

Evolutionary stable strategy: In this model, the stability of the evolution refers to the stability of revising the parameters $P_a(t)$ and $P_b(t)$, which means when the game become stable, the assessment of $P_a(t)$ and $P_b(t)$ of each attacker will not fluctuate dramatically when new attackers join in. In other words, the assessment will converge to an exact value after several times of corrections.

Assessment update rule: The update rule includes the following main steps.

- *Initializing the assessment randomly at the beginning of the game.* The initial assessments are random because the attacker knows little about the defender.
- *Calculating the observed result of P_a and P_b.* At the end of the time point t, the attacker observes his neighbors and counts the numbers of them (1) who had attacked this time and been discovered and (2) who hadn't attacked this time and been discovered, and then calculates the observed result of P_a and P_b.
- *Combining the observed result, neighbors' assessment with his previous assessment to be his new assessment.* When combining these three results, the *reference value difference* should be considered. For the neighbor who has survived longer, its assessment has a higher reference value. What's more, at the beginning of the game, the observed result plays an important role. However, as the game goes on, this importance diminished. Because the observed samples, i.e. attacker's neighbors, are limited, so that the observed result has a strong randomness.

Some new parameters and notations are introduced as follows. Let P_{aD} denote the probability of the attacker being eliminated after attack, so $P_{aD} = P_a \times P_D$. Similarly, P_{bD} is used to denote the probability of being eliminated without attack, so $P_{bD} = P_b \times P_D$. For any attacker $i \in AT$ at the end of time point $t \in [0, L_i]$, $P_a^i(t)$ and $P_b^i(t)$ represent the attacker's assessment of P_a and P_b,

$P_a^i(0)$ and $P_b^i(0)$ are the initial estimates. We use $s = \{s_1^t, s_2^t, \ldots, s_{k_t}^t\}$ to denote the neighbors' strategy, and $f = \{f_1^t, f_2^t, \ldots, f_{k_t}^t\}$ to denote whether these neighbors are found by the defender or not, where k_t is the total number of neighbors of i, $s_j^t \in Sa$, $f_j^t \in 0, 1$. AD is used to denote the neighbors who had attacked this time and had been found, so $AD = \{j | s_j^t = 1 \wedge f_j^t = 1, j \in [0, k_t]\}$. ND is used to denote the neighbors who were not attacked and had been found, so $ND = \{j | s_j^t = 0 \wedge f_j^t = 1, j \in [0, k_t]\}$. $P_D^t(j)$ is used to denote the P_D calculated by neighbor j. Let P_{obaD}^t denote the observed value of P_{aD}, so $P_{obaD}^t(i) = \frac{|AD|}{\sum s_j^t}$, let P_{obbD}^t denote the observed value of P_{bD} so $P_{obbD}^t(i) = \frac{|ND|}{k - \sum s_j^t}$. Thus the updating rules for revising the parameters $P_a(t)$ and $P_b(t)$ are as follows:

$$P_a(t+1) = \begin{cases} \dfrac{(\sum_{j=1}^{k_t} P_a^t(j)P_D^t(j)t_j + P_a^t(i)P_D^t(i)t + \frac{|AD|}{s_j^t})(k_t+1)}{(\sum_{j=1}^{k_t} t_j + t + 1)(\sum_{j=1}^{k_t} P_D^t(j) + P_D^t(i))} & t+1 \le \frac{L}{2} \\[4mm] \dfrac{(\sum_{j=1}^{k_t} P_a^t(j)P_D^t(j)t_j + P_a^t(i)P_D^t(i)t)(k_t+1)}{(\sum_{j=1}^{k_t} t_j + t)(\sum_{j=1}^{k_t} P_D^t(j) + P_D^t(i))} & t+1 > \frac{L}{2} \end{cases} \quad (1)$$

$$P_b(t+1) = \begin{cases} \dfrac{(\sum_{j=1}^{k_t} P_b^t(j)P_D^t(j)t_j + P_b^t(i)P_D^t(i)t + \frac{|AD|}{s_j^t})(k_t+1)}{(\sum_{j=1}^{k_t} t_j + t + 1)(\sum_{j=1}^{k_t} P_D^t(j) + P_D^t(i))} & t+1 \le \frac{L}{2} \\[4mm] \dfrac{(\sum_{j=1}^{k_t} P_b^t(j)P_D^t(j)t_j + P_b^t(i)P_D^t(i)t)(k_t+1)}{(\sum_{j=1}^{k_t} t_j + t)(\sum_{j=1}^{k_t} P_D^t(j) + P_D^t(i))} & t+1 > \frac{L}{2} \end{cases} \quad (2)$$

4   Specification of Player's Pay-off

As mentioned in Sect. 3, the pay-off consists of three parts. As the long-term profit expectancy is the main focus, it is assumed that the attacking cost is a fixed value and $g(t)$ is known to the attacker.

For the certain attacker, we use $E(t)$ to represent the profit expectancy from time t to the end of the lifecycle, so $E(t) = \sum_{\sigma=t}^{L} P_A(\sigma)g'(\sigma)TA(\sigma)$ where $g'(\sigma) = max\{g(\sigma) - C_a, 0\}$ and $\sigma \in [t, L]$. So, there is a need to compute all the $P_A(\sigma)$ for $\sigma = t, t+1, \ldots, L$. If notation Q is used to indicate that the resource is still available at time point σ and notation R is used to indicate that the attacker will choose to attack, then $P_A(\sigma) = P(Q) * P(R)$. So we have

$$P_A(\sigma) = [P_A(\sigma - 1) * (1 - P_a) + (1 - P_A(\sigma - 1)) * (1 - P_b)] * P_A(t-1) \quad (3)$$

$P_A(\sigma - 1) * (1 - P_a)$ means that the attacker has attacked last time but has not been discovered, $(1 - P_A(\sigma - 1)) * (1 - P_b)$ means that the attacker has not attacked last time and has not been discovered. For simplify the computation, it is assumed that the defender will always been protected when calculating $P_A(\sigma)$. And $P_A(t-1)$ used in (4) is an approximate value. Because the exact value of $P(Y)$ which is determined by calculating the Nash equilibrium of the sub-game at time point σ could not be known, the probability $P_A(t-1)$ is used instead. According to the above recursive formula, we can get:

$$P_A(\sigma) = [P_A(t-1) + \frac{(1-P_b)*P_A(t-1)}{(P_b-P_a)*P_A(t-1)-1}][(P_b-P_a)*P_A(t-1)]^{t-1} - \frac{(1-P_b)*P_A(t-1)}{(P_b-P_a)*P_A(t-1)-1} \quad (4)$$

The payoffs matrix can be as follow (Table 1):

Table 1. Payoff in the multi-player evolutionary game.

	Protect	Not protect
Attack	$G_A^D, -G_A^D - C_d$	$G_A^{ND}, -G_A^{ND}$
Not attack	$G_{NA}^D, -G_{NA}^D - C_d$	$G_{NA}^{ND}, -G_{NA}^{ND}$

where:

$$G_A^D = g(t) - C_a + (1 - P_A)E(t+1) \tag{5}$$

$$G_{NA}^D = (1 - P_b)E(t+1) \tag{6}$$

$$G_A^{ND} = g(t) - C_a + E(t+1) \tag{7}$$

$$G_{NA}^{ND} = E(t+1) \tag{8}$$

Here's a brief discussion of the game's Nash equilibrium, also the optimal timing selection guidelines:

1. At some time t, when $g(t) - C_a \leq 0$ and $C_d < P_b E(t+1)$, attacker will not attack but the defender will protect. When $g(t) - C_a \leq 0$ and $C_d > P_b E(t+1)$, attacker will not attack and the defender will not protect.
   Because $g(t) - C_a \leq 0$ and $P_a > P_b$, so $G_A^{ND} < G_{NA}^{ND}$, the best choice for attackers is not attack whatever the defending choice is. But in terms of the defenders, if $C_d < P_b E(t+1)$, that means there is some probability of discovering the vulnerability by expending a little defending cost, so the defender will defend. But if the cost is high, i.e. $C_d > P_b E(t+1)$, the defender will not defend.
2. At some time t, when $g(t) - C_a > (P_a - P_b)E(t+1)$ and $C_d < P_a E(t+1)$, attacker will attack and the defender will protect. When $g(t) - C_a > (P_a - P_b)E(t+1)$ and $C_d \geq P_a E(t+1)$, attacker will attack and the defender will not protect.
3. At some time t, when $0 < g(t) - C_a \leq (P_a - P_b)E(t+1)$ and $C_d \geq P_a E(t+1)$, the defender will not protect and the attacker will attack.
4. At some time t, when $0 < g(t) - C_a \leq (P_a - P_b)E(t+1)$ and $C_d < P_b E(t+1)$, the defender will protect and the attacker will not attack.
5. At some time t, when $0 < g(t) - C_a \leq (P_a - P_b)E(t+1)$ and $P_b E(t+1) < C_d < P_a E(t+1)$, there is no pure Nash equilibrium, but only mixed Nash equilibrium, that is, the attacker will attack with the probability of $\frac{C_d - P_b E(t+1)}{(P_a - P_b)E(t+1)}$, and the defender will defend with the probability of $\frac{g(t) - C_a}{(P_a - P_b)E(t+1)}$.

We use X to denote the probability of attack for the attacker, and Y to denote the probability of defend. So the expected utility function of the attacker is:

$$U_A = X[YG_A^D + (1-Y)G_A^{ND}] + (1-X)[YG_{NA}^D + (1-Y)G_{NA}^{ND}] \quad (9)$$

$$U_D = Y[X(-G_A^D - C_d) + (1-X)(-G_{NA}^D - C_d)] + (1-Y)[X(-G_A^{ND}) + (1-X)(-G_{NA}^{ND})] \quad (10)$$

Differentiated the above-mentioned function:

$$\frac{\partial U_A}{\partial X} = [YG_A^D + (1-Y)G_A^{ND}] - [YG_{NA}^D + (1-Y)G_{NA}^{ND}] \quad (11)$$

Let $\frac{\partial U_A}{\partial X} = 0$, we get:

$$Y = \frac{G_{NA}^{ND} - G_A^{ND}}{G_A^D + G_{NA}^{ND} - G_A^{ND} - G_{NA}^D} = \frac{g(t) - C_a}{(P_a - P_b)E(t+1)} \quad (12)$$

Similarly,

$$X = \frac{G_{NA}^D - G_{NA}^{ND} + C_d}{-G_A^D - G_{NA}^{ND} + G_A^{ND} + G_{NA}^D} = \frac{C_d - P_b E(t+1)}{(P_a - P_b)E(t+1)} \quad (13)$$

5   Experiment

The effectiveness of the proposed evolutionary games by synthetic data set has been evaluated. All experiments are conducted on a Windows7 system with Intel Core i7-6700 3.4 GHz CPUs and 8G memory.

Exp. 1: Numbers of attackers. The experiment is carried out to observe the total number of attackers. Ten types of gain functions with various monotonicity and codomain are used.

The lifecycle of each resource is assumed to be 20 (each round represents 1), and the total number of attackers at the beginning is 12000, distributed at a $200 * 100$ matrix. The numbers of new found resource can be regarded as a statistic process obeying Poisson distribution. Different P_a and P_b are picked to see whether the population could stay stable with different number of newly found resource. Figure 2 shows the total number of attackers when the average of newly found resource equals 500, 1000, 1500 and 2000. We can see all of them can stay stable though the amplitudes are a little bit large. It can be found that when P_b equals 0.1 (notated as the black line and blue line), the number is greater than those when P_b equals 0.2 (the red line and pink line) whatever the P_a is. However, the difference of P_a doesn't have a major impact on the change of the total number. That is reasonable because during the whole evolution process, the probability of attack is much less than the probability of waiting. So the impact of P_a is much less.

Exp. 2: Convergence of estimations of P_a and P_b. The convergence of estimations of P_a and P_b is observed. The same configuration with Exp. 1 is used. In addition, we assume the initial estimate of P_a and P_b are random, and the real $P_a = 80\%$

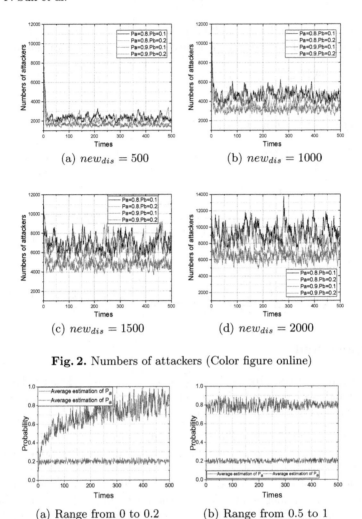

Fig. 2. Numbers of attackers (Color figure online)

Fig. 3. Convergence of estimations of P_a and P_b, where the range of initial estimations of P_a in (a) is from 0 to 0.2 and in (b) is from 0.5 to 1. P_b is random in (a) and (b). (Color figure online)

and $P_b = 20\%$. Figure 3 shows the average value of estimations of P_a and P_b. It can be seen that the convergence of P_b is fast, while the convergence of P_a is a little bit slow when the initial estimation of P_a is small. That is reasonable because most of the attacker will not attack most of the time, and the large base set makes the observation quite valuable. So the convergence of P_b is fast. The amplitudes of P_a are both quite large. There are two reasons accounting for this: First, because only a few attackers choose to attack, so the base set is quite small, which will lead to the uncertainty of estimation. Second, both numbers

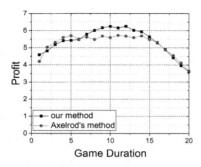

Fig. 4. The average profit of the attacker.

of eliminated attackers and the new comers are large and that will affect the average value of P_a.

Exp. 3: The average profit of the attacker. The last experiment is about profit comparison. This method is compared with the method introduced in [6]. The same configuration with Exp. 2 is used. In addition, same with the assumption in [6], it is assumed that there is an equal chance of the stakes, which will be 1, 2, 3, 4, 5, or 6. All the estimations of P_a and P_b are initiated randomly, and in this method, the estimation will be revised during the game and will not change in Axelrod's method. For each attacker, when his game is over (he has been discovered or the resource has been expired), the duration of the game and the overall profits of this attacker will be recorded, and the average of overall profit of the attackers whose games have the same duration will be calculated. The result (shown in Fig. 4) shows that with this method, there is a significant improvement for the attackers whose game duration ranges from five to fifteen.

6   Conclusion

This paper focuses on computing the optimal timing for launching a zero-day attack. The evolutionary game is used to model this long-term process. In detail, the fact that attackers will cooperate and share information with each other to get a better understanding about the target has been considered. A new learning strategy is designed to model this information sharing mechanism. After assessing the defense capability, the attacker will make a tradeoff between risk and profit by computing the Nash equilibrium. Spatial structure is used to model the evolutionary process. The results show that attackers can make a reasonable estimation about the defense capability and get a relatively higher profit.

References

1. Al-Jarrah, O., Arafat, A.: Network intrusion detection system using attack behavior classification. In: 2014 5th International Conference on Information and Communication Systems (ICICS), pp. 1–6. IEEE (2014)
2. Allodi, L., Massacci, F.: Comparing vulnerability severity and exploits using case-control studies. ACM Trans. Inf. Syst. Secur. (TISSEC) **17**(1), 1 (2014)
3. Allodi, L., Massacci, F., Williams, J.M.: The work-averse cyber attacker model: theory and evidence from two million attack signatures, 27 June 2017. https://ssrn.com/abstract=2862299
4. Arbaugh, W.A., Fithen, W.L., McHugh, J.: Windows of vulnerability: a case study analysis. Computer **33**(12), 52–59 (2000)
5. Avasarala, B.R., Day, J.C., Steiner, D., et al.: System and method for automated machine-learning, zero-day malware detection, US Patent 9,292,688, 22 March 2016
6. Axelrod, R., Iliev, R.: Timing of cyber conflict. Proc. Natl. Acad. Sci. **111**(4), 1298–1303 (2014)
7. Bilge, L., Dumitras, T.: Before we knew it: an empirical study of zero-day attacks in the real world. In: Proceedings of the 2012 ACM Conference on Computer and Communications Security, pp. 833–844. ACM (2012)
8. Bozorgi, M., Saul, L.K., Savage, S., Voelker, G.M.: Beyond heuristics: learning to classify vulnerabilities and predict exploits. In: Proceedings of the 16th ACM SIGKDD International Conference on Knowledge Discovery and Data Mining, pp. 105–114. ACM (2010)
9. Dumitraş, T.: Understanding the vulnerability lifecycle for risk assessment and defense against sophisticated cyber attacks. In: Jajodia, S., Shakarian, P., Subrahmanian, V.S., Swarup, V., Wang, C. (eds.) Cyber Warfare, vol. 56, pp. 265–285. Springer, Cham (2015). doi:10.1007/978-3-319-14039-1_13
10. Ekelhart, A., Kiesling, E., Grill, B., Strauss, C., Stummer, C.: Integrating attacker behavior in it security analysis: a discrete-event simulation approach. Inf. Technol. Manage. **16**(3), 221–233 (2015)
11. Guo, H., Wang, X., Cheng, H., Huang, M.: A routing defense mechanism using evolutionary game theory for delay tolerant networks. Appl. Soft Comput. **38**, 469–476 (2016)
12. Jiang, G., Shen, S., Hu, K., Huang, L., Li, H., Han, R.: Evolutionary game-based secrecy rate adaptation in wireless sensor networks. Int. J. Distrib. Sens. Netw. **11**(3), 975454:1–975454:13 (2015)
13. Liang, X., Xiao, Y., et al.: Game theory for network security. IEEE Commun. Surv. Tutor. **15**(1), 472–486 (2013)
14. Mishra, A., Gupta, B.: Hybrid solution to detect and filter zero-day phishing attacks. In: Proceedings of the Second International Conference on Emerging Research in Computing, Information, Communication and Applications, pp. 373–379 (2014)
15. Mitchell, R., Chen, R.: Adaptive intrusion detection of malicious unmanned air vehicles using behavior rule specifications. IEEE Trans. Syst. Man Cybern. Syst. **44**(5), 593–604 (2014)
16. Mitra, S., Ransbotham, S.: Information disclosure and the diffusion of information security attacks. Inf. Syst. Res. **26**(3), 565–584 (2015)
17. Nayak, K., Marino, D., Efstathopoulos, P., Dumitraş, T.: Some vulnerabilities are different than others. In: Stavrou, A., Bos, H., Portokalidis, G. (eds.) RAID 2014. LNCS, vol. 8688, pp. 426–446. Springer, Cham (2014). doi:10.1007/978-3-319-11379-1_21

18. Niyato, D., Wang, P., Kim, D.I., Han, Z., Xiao, L.: Game theoretic modeling of jamming attack in wireless powered communication networks. In: 2015 IEEE International Conference on Communications (ICC), pp. 6018–6023. IEEE (2015)

19. Ruan, N., Gao, L., Zhu, H., Jia, W., Li, X., Hu, Q.: Toward optimal dos-resistant authentication in crowdsensing networks via evolutionary game. In: 2016 IEEE 36th International Conference on Distributed Computing Systems (ICDCS), pp. 364–373. IEEE (2016)

20. Shahzad, M., Shafiq, M.Z., Liu, A.X.: A large scale exploratory analysis of software vulnerability life cycles. In: Proceedings of the 34th International Conference on Software Engineering, pp. 771–781. IEEE Press (2012)

21. Tosh, D., Sengupta, S., Kamhoua, C., Kwiat, K., Martin, A.: An evolutionary game-theoretic framework for cyber-threat information sharing. In: 2015 IEEE International Conference on Communications (ICC), pp. 7341–7346. IEEE (2015)

22. Wang, L., Jajodia, S., Singhal, A., Cheng, P., Noel, S.: k-zero day safety: a network security metric for measuring the risk of unknown vulnerabilities. IEEE Trans. Depend. Secur. Comput. **11**(1), 30–44 (2014)

23. Wang, L., Zhang, M., Jajodia, S., Singhal, A., Albanese, M.: Modeling network diversity for evaluating the robustness of networks against zero-day attacks. In: Kutyłowski, M., Vaidya, J. (eds.) ESORICS 2014. LNCS, vol. 8713, pp. 494–511. Springer, Cham (2014). doi:10.1007/978-3-319-11212-1_28

Performance Modeling and Evaluation

Performance Analysis of a Ternary Optical Computer Based on M/M/1 Queueing System

XianChao Wang[1(✉)], Sulan Zhang[2], Mian Zhang[3], Jia Zhao[1], and Xiangyang Niu[3]

[1] School of Computer and Information Engineering, Fuyang Normal University,
Fuyang 236037, China
wxcdx@126.com
[2] School of Computer Engineering and Science, Shanghai University,
Shanghai 200444, China
[3] School of Mathematics and Statistics, Fuyang Normal University,
Fuyang 236037, China

Abstract. A Ternary Optical Computer (TOC), a dynamically reconfigurable computing platform, has attracted more and more attentions. However, Quality of Service (QoS) is a crucial factor for its commercial success. This paper presents a service model for TOC based on first-come-first-service strategy, the M/M/1 queueing system and tandem queueing. And it uses the mean response time to analyze and evaluate the performance of TOC. Moreover, this paper shows the influence of various metrics on the response time by simulating the model. The results demonstrate that the computation and network transmission speed are the bottlenecks of system response time. Therefore, the proposed model is good for designing the task management system of TOC.

Keywords: M/M/1 queueing system · Ternary Optical Computer · Task scheduling · Response time · Tandem queue

1 Introduction

The speed of high-performance electronic computers is increasingly limited not only by processing power but also by the bandwidth and number of the interconnections and by data access rate. On the other side, optics can offer interesting solutions to alleviate these limitations on account of its three-dimensional inter-connection capabilities and inherent parallelism. Therefore, more and more attentions have been paid to optical computing, an emerging technology. A multitude of significant advances have been obtained in the development of optical computing hardware [1–7], including Ternary Optical Computer (TOC), during the past decades.

The architecture and principle of TOC was proposed by Jin in 2003 [6, 7]. Many significant achievements have been obtained in hardware and software of TOC [8–22]. For example, Jin et al. put forward the lane theory of parallel through carry to solve the carry problem of adder [8]; Yan et al. proposed the Decrease-Radix Design Principle (DRDP) to construct reconfigurable optical processors [9]. Wang, Song, Shen and Peng et al. designed and implemented carry-free addition [10–13] on TOC in several different

© Springer International Publishing AG 2017
S. Ibrahim et al. (Eds.): ICA3PP 2017, LNCS 10393, pp. 331–344, 2017.
DOI: 10.1007/978-3-319-65482-9_22

ways based on Modified Signed-Digit (MSD) number system, and Wang implemented vector-matrix multiplication [10] on the basis of MSD addition. Wang et al. designed the modular architecture of TOC task management system and implemented it [14–17], and proposed task scheduling algorithm [16] and processor allocation algorithms [16, 18] which were suitable for TOC. These achievements promoted the development of TOC from theory to practice.

In particular, DRDP makes the processors of TOC dynamically reconfigurable, and the reconfiguration has been implemented by use of different ways [20–22]. In other words, TOC can bitwise reconfigure different optical processors according to customer demands, which increases the flexibility of computing. At the same time, TOC has much more data-bits than electronic computers on account of the parallelism of optical computing. As a consequence, TOC, a novel computing paradigm, can provide services with high-performance, scalability and security.

TOC has captured many researchers' attentions because of its pleasurable features and many achievements. However, there are a lot of problems to solve before it comes into real services. Currently, the research on system performance of TOC is wanted. Hence, the paper will investigate the service performance of TOC based on M/M/1 queueing system in order to deliver guaranteed QoS. The main contribution of this paper consists of a service QoS model for TOC, a computation model of response time based on queueing system and experiments showing favorable results.

The remainder of the paper is organized as follows. Section 2 briefs the related work. Section 3 presents our modeling proposal to guarantee QoS for customer tasks based on tandem M/M/1 queueing system. Simulation experimentation illustrating a perfect behavior of the proposed model is presented in Sect. 4. Finally, Sect. 5 outlines the main conclusions and future work.

2   Related Work

2.1   Task Management System of Ternary Optical Computer

Figure 1 shows the computing paradigm of TOC. Server is a single access node for the computing services of the customers being served in the model. Tasks can be submitted through Network to Server by Client. After finish computing, Server transmits the results to the corresponding Client.

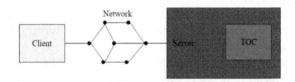

Fig. 1. Computing paradigm of TOC.

The task management system architecture of TOC is shown in Fig. 2. It consists of the following modules, Request Accepting Module (RAM), Data PreProcessing Module

(DPPM), Task Scheduling Module (TSM), Processor Allocating Module (PAM), Processor Reconfiguring Module (PRM), Optical Computing Module (OCM) including encoder and optical processor, Decoding Module (DM) and Result Transmitting Module (RTM). Meanwhile, TOC, which executes the optical computing, is mainly comprised of PRM, OCM and DM.

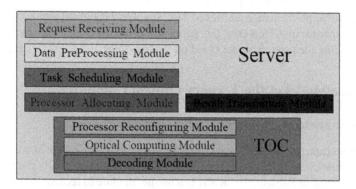

Fig. 2. Modular architecture of TOC task management system.

The functions of these modules are as follows. RAM is responsible for accepting operation-requests, i.e. tasks submitted in communication internal code (CIC) [16] by customer clients. DPPM calculates the task priorities, transforms operands from CIC into control internal code, and inserts them into a queue to schedule according to their priorities. TSM schedules the tasks in the queue according to a scheduling strategy and send the operands to TOC. PAM looks up the reconfigurable codes [22] for different operations (Supposing that there are no more than 15 kinds of two-input trivalued logic operations in a task), allocates the optical processor resource for the scheduled tasks and their various operations in accordance with allocation-by-demand algorithm [16] and sends the reconfigurable codes and the allocation result to TOC. PRM reconfigures the optical processors for various operations in parallel after receiving the information from PAM. The encoder of OCM generates the optical signals (no intensity light, horizontal polarized light, and vertical polarized light) according to the control internal codes of operands, and the optical processors carry out the optical computing. DM decodes the operation results and sends them to RTM. Finally, RTM feeds the results in communication internal code back to the right client. In short, all of the modules work harmoniously to implement computing services for the customers.

2.2 Brief Introduction to Queueing System

Queueing theory, an important branch of stochastic operations research, was constructed by Erlang in 1909 [23]. Now it has been widely used in communication [23–25], transportation [26], inventory [27], task scheduling [28, 29], resource allocation [30–32], cloud computing [32–35] and many other areas, highlighting its powerful vitality.

Researchers have investigated the performance of cloud computing based on various queueing systems in recent years. For instance, Khazaei obtained some important performance metrics such as task blocking probability and total waiting time by using interactive continuous time Markov chain [29]. Vilaplana studied a cloud computing QoS (i.e. response time) in an open Jackson networks based on M/M/1 queueing system and obtained the system bottleneck [32].

Similarly, the performance metrics of TOC involve throughput, resource utilization and mean response time. However, this paper will primarily explore the mean response time by building the service model based on tandem M/M/1 queueing system.

3   Service Model of the Ternary Optical Computer

3.1   Service Model of the Ternary Optical Computer

In this subsection, we propose a service model for TOC based on M/M/1 queueing system and first come first service (FCFS) strategy to analyze the response time.

As mentioned in Subsect. 2.1, RAM is a unique module to receive the tasks sent by the customer clients. To reduce transmission data, the operands in every operation are sent to RAM not in ASCII but in CIC. Each couple of operands are stored with four binary bits in CIC [16]. In other words, each byte can store two couples of operands. The tasks will queue to be accepted after arriving since various customers can concurrently submit them. Therefore, the RAM can be represented by an M/M/1 queueing system.

In this paper, a bit two-input trivalued logic operation is looked upon as a counting unit for computation. Suppose that the arrival of n tasks follows the exponential distribution with parameter λ, the mean computation of these tasks is μ, the mean transmission speed of network is ω. Thus, the mean transmission data and mean transmission time are $\mu/2$ and $\mu/2\omega$, respectively, and the number of tasks received by RAM per unit of time is $2\omega/\mu$. In other word, the service of RAM follows the exponential distribution with parameter $2\omega/\mu$.

Suppose that the rate of data preprocessing is τ. Similarly, DPPM can be also modeled by an M/M/1 queueing system, and its service follows the exponential distribution with parameter τ/μ.

The timing scheduling strategy was proposed for the tasks of TOC [16]. RSM can simultaneously schedule several tasks for the optical processor to compute. However, we shall use another simpler scheduling strategy. In the strategy, the first task is scheduled immediately when it arrives, and RSM will once again schedule tasks in task queue after the optical processors finishes the being serviced ones. The scheduling strategy is called scheduling strategy after (the being serviced tasks) being finished. For simplicity, this paper assumes that RSM schedules a task at a time. Obviously, the assumption increases the times of scheduling and the ones of reconfiguring in some degree.

As mentioned in Subsect. 2.1, PAM allocates the optical processors for every operation of the scheduled tasks to guarantee that all operations can be finished simultaneously, obtains the reconfigurable codes of optical processors. And then it sends the allocation result and reconfigurable codes to TOC and PRM, respectively. Obviously, the time PRM spends on allocating optical processors for a task hardly changes. Therefore, we can suppose that the allocation time is a constant.

PRM reconfigures optical processors as soon as it receives the information sent by PAM. For a given optical processors, the time spent on reconfiguring them is a constant since the reconfiguration is independent and parallel.

In the TOC module, the encoder of OCM transforms the operands into optical signals according to their control internal codes. The optical processors implement the transformation between optical signals, i.e. optical computing after the reconfiguration is over. And the decoder changes the optical signals i.e. computation results into electronic signals and transmits them to RTM. Apparently, the computing time is relevant to the computation μ and the speed of optical computing δ.

It can be seen that there is a task queue, shown in Fig. 3, before RSM to schedule from RSM to DM. In other words, the course from scheduling to decoding can be likewise manifested by an M/M/1 queueing system.

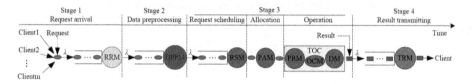

Fig. 3. Task queueing model on TOC.

The operation results of tasks may have to wait in a queue before being transmitted by RTM to the right clients because the optical computing speed of TOC is much greater than the transmission speed of networks. Consequently, RTM can be also described by an M/M/1 queueing system. The transmission data in communication internal code is $\mu/4$ because a couple of operands generate an operation results. Thus, the service of RTM follows the exponential distribution with parameter $4\omega/\mu$.

It can be easily seen that all of these modules constitute a 4-stage queueing system shown in Fig. 3. In the queue, Stage 1, Stage 2 and Stage 4 are made up of RAM, DPPM and TRM, respectively. However, Stage 3 is made up of RSM, PAM, PRM, OCM and DM modules, and divided into three sub-stages, request scheduling, processor allocation and optical computing. The four stages are cascaded into a tandem M/M/1 queueing system.

Meanwhile, the mean response time T of n tasks can be obtained in the following formula:

$$T = T_{RA} + T_{DPP} + T_{RS} + T_{RT} \tag{1}$$

Where T_{RA} is the mean time RAM spends on receiving these tasks, T_{DPP} is the mean time DPPM spend on data preprocessing, T_{RS} is the mean time spent from task scheduling to decoding and T_{RT} is the mean time RTM spends on transmitting the results to the right clients.

3.2   Obtaining T_{RA}

As discussed above, RAM can be modeled by an M/M/1 queueing system. According to [36, 37], the mean response time T_{RA} of RAM is defined as

$$T_{RA} = \frac{1}{\dfrac{2\omega}{\mu} - \lambda} = \frac{\mu}{2\omega - \lambda\mu} \qquad (2)$$

Where λ is the number of arrival tasks per unit of time, i.e. arrival rate of tasks, μ is the mean computation of these tasks and ω is the mean speed of receiving them.

3.3   Obtaining T_{DPP}

The arrival rate of the tasks is also λ when they reach DPPM, according to [36]. Similarly, the mean response time of DPPM is defined by the following formula:

$$T_{DPP} = \frac{1}{\dfrac{\tau}{\mu} - \lambda} = \frac{\mu}{\tau - \lambda\mu} \qquad (3)$$

Where τ is the speed of data preprocessing.

3.4   Obtaining T_{RS}

During scheduling, RSM sends the operands in control internal code of the scheduled task to TOC and deletes it from the queue. And then, PAM allocates the optical processors, PRM reconfigures the optical processors, OCM executes optical computing and DM decodes the operation results. Therefore, the combination of these five modules can be modeled by an M/M/1 queueing system. In other words, T_{RS} consists of not only scheduling time but also allocating processor time, reconfiguring processor time, computing time and decoding time.

As mentioned in Subsect. 3.1, both allocating processor time and reconfiguring processor time are constants. In particular, the processor reconfiguring module is peculiar to TOC according to the DRDP. The reconfiguration increases the flexibility of computing, but it also increases system overhead. Consequently, we shall not ignore the two constants in order to show an analysis of how PAM and PRM influence system performance, especially response time T.

As mentioned in Subsect. 3.1, OCM executes optical computing after TOC receiving the operands and PRM accomplishes the optical processor reconfiguration, and then DM decodes the computation results. As a consequence, the computation speed of TOC is the less between OCM speed and DM speed.

According to the analysis above, we assume that the mean transmission speed from RSM to TOC is φ, allocating processor time is a constant C_1, reconfiguring time is another constant C_2, and the computation speed of TOC is δ. Thus, the service rate π of Stage 3 in Fig. 3 is defined by the following formula.

$$\pi = \frac{1}{\dfrac{\mu}{\varphi} + C_1 + C_2 + \dfrac{\mu}{\delta}} = \frac{\varphi\delta}{\mu(\varphi + \delta) + \varphi\delta(C_1 + C_2)} \tag{4}$$

Similarly, T_{RS} is defined as:

$$T_{RS} = \frac{1}{\pi - \lambda} \tag{5}$$

3.5   Obtaining T_{RT}

RTM transmits the operation results to relevant clients after receiving them. As discussed above, T_{RT} is similarly obtained by the following formula.

$$T_{RT} = \frac{1}{\dfrac{4\omega}{\mu} - \lambda} = \frac{\mu}{4\omega - \lambda\mu} \tag{6}$$

Response time T is obtained by the following formula (7), based on tandem M/M/1 queueing system, after formulas (2), (3), (5) and (6) are substituted into (1).

$$T = \mu\left(\frac{1}{2\omega - \lambda\mu} + \frac{1}{\tau - \lambda\mu} + \frac{1}{4\omega - \lambda\mu}\right) + \frac{1}{\pi - \lambda} \tag{7}$$

4   Simulation

The following section illustrates an analysis of how the response time T is influenced by modifying some parameters presented in the model. Our purpose is to testify whether the proposed model behaves as expected when a range of metrics and system configurations are tested.

4.1   System Metrics

The model will be implemented on Matlab R2010b platform. The metrics in the simulation are described as follows.

- Arrival rate λ of tasks. It is the average number of operation requests, i.e. tasks reaching the system per unit of time and $1/\lambda$ is the mean inter-arrival time. We shall show how the response time T is affected by changing the metric λ. It can be easily seen that T is an increasing function of arrival rate λ according to formula (7).
- Computation μ. Here the computation is referred to the two-input trivalued logic operation in operation requests though the carry-free addition and vector-matrix multiplication have been implemented on TOC. The reason is that other operations can be implemented with different two-input trivalued logic operations and only two-input trivalued logic operations can be submitted by costumer clients in the current

task management system. Consequently, computation is referred to the mean couple number of operands. As discussed in Subsect. 2.1, the operands are stored in CIC. Thus, MB can be looked upon as the unit of computation, and the mean transmission data from costumer clients to server and from server to right clients are $\mu/2$ and $\mu/4$, respectively.

- Transmission speed ω of networks. The transmission speed of WAN is very different from the one of LAN. Meanwhile, there are much more potential customers in WAN than those in LAN. We shall implement the model simulation by use of the transmission speed ω (MB per second) of WAN.
- Speed τ of data preprocessing. As mentioned in Subsect. 2.1, DPPM mainly transforms operands from CIC into control internal code. Thus, τ is relevant to the server speed, reaching G (in bytes per second) magnitude.
- Transmission speed φ from server to TOC. The Server is connected with TOC by cable to achieve the communication between them. Therefore, φ (in MB per second) is the transmission speed of LAN.
- Computing speed δ of TOC. Now computing speed of TOC is restricted in the rotating light speed of liquid crystal and the decoding speed of decoder. However, the computing speed still reaches G (in bytes per second) magnitude because of its parallelism.

4.2 Response Time

In order to demonstrate an analysis of how the response time T is influenced by arrival rate λ, we simulate the tandem queueing model with the average number of tasks reaching the system per hour. Thus, the service rate of RAM is equal to 7200 ω/μ. In other words, the module can deal with 7200 ω/μ tasks per hour.

Let $\rho = \max\{\lambda\mu/(3600 * 2\omega), \lambda\mu/3600\tau, \lambda\mu/3600\varphi, \lambda\mu/3600\delta\}$, then ρ is determined by the minimum of ω, τ, φ and δ. Generally speaking, ω is the minimum of them. The system will reach the equilibrium state when $\rho < 1$.

As we expected, Fig. 4 shows how the response time T is affected by increasing the arrival rate from 1 to 60 when the queueing system reaches the equilibrium state and the metrics μ, ω, τ, φ, δ, C_1 and C_2 are equal to 100 MB, 5 MB/s, 2 GB/s, 50 MB/s, 1 GB/s, 0.01 s and 0.01 s, respectively. It can be seen that the response time is about 32 s when λ is equal to 1. However, the response time T is not doubled and redoubled but approximately linearly increased with the increase of arrival rate λ. The reason is that the modules work in parallel when there are multi-tasks in the system though each task undergoes the four stages in the queueing model which is cascaded with four M/M/1 queueing systems.

According to formula (7), response time T not only is an increasing function of arrival rate λ but also is an increasing function of computation μ. The change of response time is shown in Fig. 5 when μ is increased from 100 to 250 and the other parameters are fixed.

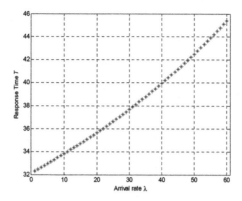

Fig. 4. Response time T of the queueing model in function of λ.

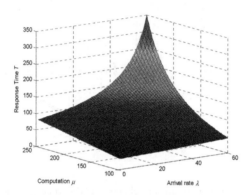

Fig. 5. Response time T in functions of λ and μ.

4.3 System Bottlenecks

Response time T shown in Fig. 6(a) and (b) changes significantly compared with Fig. 4 when computation μ is equal to 100 MB and transmission speed ω of WAN is equal to 10 MB/s while the other metrics are unchanged. However, response time shown in Fig. 6(c) and (d) hardly changes when the other parameters, such as δ and τ are changed. Therefore, computation μ and transmission speed ω of WAN are bottlenecks of the queueing system, i.e. TOC computing platform. The reason is that the magnitudes of the parameters are different. δ and τ are in G magnitude but μ and ω are in M magnitude. Thus, slight increase of ω will make response time T reduce distinctly while large increase of δ and τ hardly makes response time reduce, shown in Fig. 6. In addition, it can be seen from Fig. 6(d) that response time doesn't change remarkably even though δ, C_1 and C_2 synchronously and greatly improve.

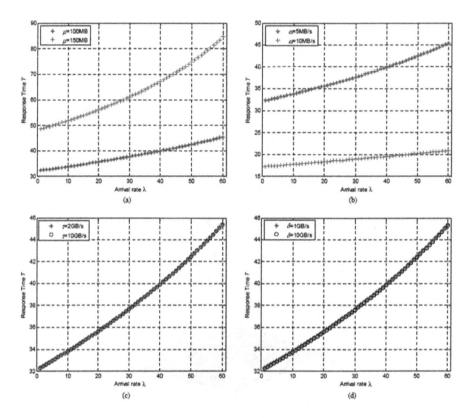

Fig. 6. Response time T when parameters change (a) different computation μ, (b) different transmission speed ω of WAN, (c) different data preprocessing rate τ, (d) different optical computing rate δ.

According to the analysis above, decreasing transmission time can reduce the response time and improve system efficiency. Obviously, there are several approaches, such as increasing the number of RAM, improving the transmission speed of WAN, and decreasing the transmission data, to reduce transmission time. RAM can be modeled by an M/M/c queueing system when several RAM modules are used to receive the costumer tasks (This will be discussed in another paper). Improving the transmission speed of WAN by a large margin needs novel technologies and equipment. In other words, it is arduous to substantially improve the transmission speed in the existing network environment. On the other hand, as mentioned above, the operations achieved on TOC are basically two-input trivalued logic operations and the operands are stored and transmitted in CIC which can decrease the transmission data in some degree. However, input of the mathematical operators and operands in routine will reduce substantially the transmission data and improve the response time. Therefore, to make the costumers use TOC like electronic computer, we should expedite the investigation of TOC task management system.

Figure 6(b) shows that improving the transmission speed of WAN can reduce greatly the response time. In order to illustrate a further analysis of how the response time T is affected by the transmission speed ω of WAN, we present the change tendency, shown in Fig. 7, of response time when ω varies from 1 to 15 and the other metrics are fixed, compared with Fig. 4. Meanwhile, the response time reduced sharply with the increase of ω when $1 \leq \omega \leq 7$. However, the response time further reduced with the further increase of ω, but the decreasing amplitude is small.

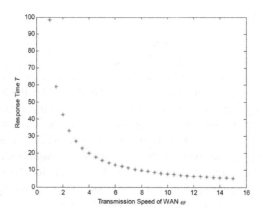

Fig. 7. Response time T in function of transmission speed ω.

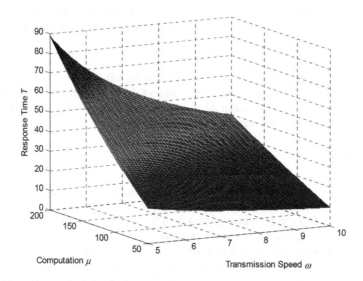

Fig. 8. Response time T in functions of transmission speed ω and computation μ, given arrival rate $\lambda = 30$.

Figure 8 shows that the change of response time T in functions of computation μ and transmission speed ω of WAN given arrival rate $\lambda = 30$. As we imagine, the response time increased with the increase of μ and the decrease of ω.

The simulation results demonstrate that the proposed model not only represents the service of TOC but also reveals the law that the parameters affect the response time. Moreover, the model can provide the solutions to improve system efficiency.

5   Conclusions

This paper proposed a service model for analyzing and exploring the performance of TOC based on M/M/1 queueing system. After discussing in details the modules composed of TOC task management system and their functions, it designed and modeled not only several independent modules, such as RAM, DPPM and RTM, but also the combination of several modules by the use of M/M/1 queueing system, linked them in series, and obtained the formula of the mean response time. Simulation results illustrated that the response time increased with the increase of arrival rate, computation, and with the decrease of transmission speed of WAN. Moreover, computation and transmission speed of WAN are the bottleneck of the system. We can conclude that our model is very beneficial for improving the QoS of TOC, especially the response time, guaranteeing the contract between the costumers and TOC service providers.

In future, we plan to investigate other issues, such as resource utilization and throughput capacity, of the service performance of TOC. In addition, we shall redesign the architecture of task management system and remodel the system based on other queueing systems. Our final purpose is to enable TOC to own much higher QoS and to satisfy the servicing need of many areas.

Acknowledgements. This work was supported by the by the NSFC (No. 61672006), Key Project of Science Research in Colleges and Universities of Anhui Province (No. KJ2015A191, KJ2015A182). And the authors thanked the reviewers for their helpful comments, remarks, and suggestions, which led to improvements of the paper.

References

1. Heinz, R.A., Artman, J.O., Lee, S.H.: Matrix multiplication by optical methods. Appl. Opt. **9**(9), 2161–2168 (1970)
2. Mosca, E.P., Griffin, R.D., Pursel, F.P., Lee, J.N.: Acoustooptical matrix-vector product processor: implementation issues. Appl. Opt. **28**(18), 3843–3851 (1989)
3. Ellett, S.A., Walkup, J.F., Krile, T.F.: Error-correction coding for accuracy enhancement in optical matrix-vector multipliers. Appl. Opt. **31**(26), 5642–5653 (1992)
4. Goodman, J.W., Dias, A.R., Woody, L.M.: Fully parallel, high-speed incoherent optical method for performing discrete Fourier transforms. Opt. Lett. **2**(1), 1–3 (1978)
5. Paquot, Y., Schroder, J., Eggleton, B.J.: Reconfigurable linear combination of phase-and-amplitude coded optical signals. Opt. Express **22**(3), 2609–2619 (2014)
6. Jin, Y., He, H.C., Lü, Y.T.: Ternary optical computer principle. Sci. Chin. Ser. F **46**(2), 145–150 (2003)

7. Jin, Y., He, H.C., Lü, Y.T.: Ternary optical computer architecture. Phys. Scr. **59**(T118), 98–101 (2005)
8. Jin, Y., He, H.C., Ai, L.R.: Lane of parallel through carry in ternary optical adder. Sci. Chin. Ser. F **48**(1), 107–116 (2005)
9. Yan, J.Y., Jin, Y., Zuo, K.Z.: Decrease-radix design principle for carrying/borrowing free multi-valued and application in ternary optical computer. Sci. Chin. Ser. F **51**(10), 1415–1426 (2008)
10. Wang, X.C., Peng, J.J., Li, M., Shen, Z.Y., Ouyang, S.: Carry-free vector-matrix multiplication on a dynamically reconfigurable optical platform. Appl. Opt. **49**(12), 2352–2362 (2010)
11. Song, K., Yan, L.P.: Design and implementation of the one-step MSD adder of optical computer. Appl. Opt. **51**(7), 917–926 (2012)
12. Peng, J.J., Shen, R., Jin, Y., Shen, Y.F., Luo, S.: Design and implementation of modified signed-digit adder. IEEE Trans. Comput. **63**(5), 1134–1143 (2014)
13. Shen, Y.F., Pan, L.: Principle of a one-step MSD adder for a ternary optical computer. Sci. Chin. Ser. F **57**(1), 012107 (2014)
14. Wang, X.C., Peng, J.J., Ouyang, S.: Control method for the optical components of a dynamically reconfigurable optical platform. Appl. Opt. **50**(5), 662–670 (2011)
15. Song, K., Jin, Y.: Overall plan and design of the task management system of ternary optical computer. J. Shanghai Univ. **15**(5), 467–472 (2011)
16. Wang, X.C., Yao, Y.F., Wang, C.S., Sun, W.W., Wang, K.Z.: Architecture of the monitor system in ternary optical computer. Adv. Mater. Res. **616–618**, 2158–2161 (2013)
17. Yan, L.P., Song, K.: Communication mechanism of the monitor system of the ternary optical computer. Int. J. Digit. Content Technol. Appl. **5**(11), 283–289 (2011)
18. Wang, X.C., Yao, Y.F., Wang, C.S., Sun, W.W., Wang, K.Z.: Processor allocation of a ternary optical computer. Adv. Sci. Lett. **19**(6), 1714–1717 (2013)
19. Wang, X.C., Yao, Y.F., Wang, C.S., Wang, K.Z.: Dynamic data-bit allocation of a ternary optical computer. Appl. Mech. Mater. **109**, 181–186 (2012)
20. Shen, Z.Y., Wu, L.L.: Reconfigurable optical logic unit with a terahertz optical asymmetric demultiplexer and electro-optic switches. Appl. Opt. **47**(21), 3737–3742 (2008)
21. Shen, Z.Y., Wu, L.L., Yan, J.R.: The reconfigurable module of ternary optical computer. Optik **124**(13), 1415–1419 (2013)
22. Wang, H.J., Song, K.: Simulative method for the optical processor reconfiguration on a dynamically reconfigurable optical platform. Appl. Opt. **51**(2), 167–175 (2012)
23. Erlang, A.K.: The theory of probabilities and telephone conversations. Nyt Tidsskrift for Matematik B **20**, 33–39 (1909)
24. Panlop, Z., Anthony, B., James, B., Peter, D., Zahir, T.: Queuing theory applications to communication systems: control of traffic flows and load balancing. In: Pham, H. (ed.) Springer Handbook of Engineering Statistics. Springer, London (2006). doi: 10.1007/978-1-84628-288-1_52
25. Van, D.N.M.: On the arrival theorem for communication networks. Compu. Netw. ISDN Syst. **25**(10), 1135–2013 (1993)
26. Anokye, M., Abdul-Aziz, A.R., Annin, K., Oduro, F.T.: Application of queuing theory to vehicular traffic at signalized intersection in Kumasi-Ashanti region, Ghana. Am. Int. J. Contemp. Res. **3**, 23–29 (2013)
27. Liu, L.M., Liu, X.M., Yao, D.D.: Analysis and optimization of a multistage inventory-queue system. Manage. Sci. **50**, 365–380 (2004)
28. Mor, H.-B.: Scheduling: SRPT and Fairness, Performance Modeling and Design of Computer Systems. Cambridge University Press, Cambridge (2013)

29. Khazaei, H., Misic, J., Misic, V.B.: A Fine-grained performance model of cloud computing centers. IEEE Trans. Parallel Distrib. **24**(11), 2138–2147 (2013)
30. Murugesan, R., Elango, C., Kannan, S.: Resource allocation in cloud computing with M/G/s-queuing system. Int. J. Adv. Res. Comput. Sci. Softw. Eng. **4**(9), 443–447 (2014)
31. Li, B.F., Wang, D.H.: Configuration issues of cashier staff in supermarket based on queuing theory. In: Zhu, R., Zhang, Y., Liu, B., Liu, C. (eds.) ICICA 2010. CCIS, vol. 106, pp. 334–340. Springer, Heidelberg (2010). doi:10.1007/978-3-642-16339-5_44
32. Vilaplana, J., Solsona, F., Teixidó, I., Mateo, J., Abella, F., Rius, J.: A queuing theory model for cloud computing. J. Supercomput. **69**(1), 492–507 (2014)
33. Mary, N.A.B., Saravanan, K.: Performance factors of cloud computing data centers using [(M/G/1): (∞/GDmodel)] queuing systems. Int. J. Grid Comput. Appl. **4**(1), 1–9 (2013)
34. Sandeep, K.S.: Dynamic resource provisioning in cloud based on queuing model. Int. J. Cloud Comput. Serv. Sci. **2**(4), 314–320 (2013)
35. Oumellal, F., Hanini, M., Haqiq, A.: MMPP/G/m/m+r queuing system model to analytically evaluate cloud computing center performances. Br. J. Math. Comput. Sci. **4**(10), 1301–1317 (2014)
36. Gross, D., Shortie, J.F., Thompson, J.M., Harris, C.M.: Fundamentals of Queuing Theory, 4th edn. Wiley, Hoboken (2008)
37. Kleinrock, L.: Queuing Systems: Theory, vol. 1. Wikey-Interscience, New York (1975)

Efficient Computation Offloading for Various Tasks of Multiple Users in Mobile Edge Clouds

Weiyu Liu$^{(\boxtimes)}$, Xiangming Wen, Zhaoming Lu, Luning Liu, and Xin Chen

Beijing Laboratory of Advanced Information Networks, Beijing, China
`wyliu@bupt.edu.cn`

Abstract. Mobile edge clouds (MEC) is a novel paradigm to augment computation capabilities of mobile devices for resource-scarce applications. This paper first investigates the computation offloading decision making problem among mobile users and leverages the variability in types of tasks, capabilities of mobile devices and user preferences. As it is NP-hard to compute an optimal solution, this paper transforms the problem into a system utility maximization problem. This paper formulates the system utility maximization problem as a resource allocation offloading mechanism (RAOM) for achieving efficient computation offloading. This paper then designs a resource allocation offloading algorithm that can maximize system utility within the constraints of system bandwidth and maximum instructions per second allowed in edge clouds and quantifies its efficiency ratio over the optimal solutions in terms of two vital performance metrics. This paper further extends the study to the scenario of multi-user computation offloading in the wireless interference model. Numerical results demonstrate that the extension is worthwhile and the proposed mechanism RAOM achieves efficient computation offloading performance either with interference or without interference.

Keywords: Edge cloud · Mobile edge computing · Multi-user offloading · Resource allocation · Various tasks

1 Introduction

As mobile devices are gaining enormous popularity, resource-intensive mobile applications, such as natural language processing, face recognition, augmented reality and interactive gaming, are increasingly emerging [8]. Nevertheless, mobile devices are always restricted in processing capacity and battery, so that many applications cannot be run in such devices. The conflict between increasing demand of resource-intensive applications and resource-limited devices becomes a bottleneck for providing satisfactory quality of service (QoS) [9].

Mobile cloud computing (MCC) is conceived as a promising method of addressing the above challenges. By offloading part of the tasks through wireless access to the resource-abundant cloud infrastructure, such as Amazon EC2 and Microsoft Azure [4], MCC can enhance the functionalities of mobile devices for resource-scarce applications. However, an obvious drawback of MCC is that

© Springer International Publishing AG 2017
S. Ibrahim et al. (Eds.): ICA3PP 2017, LNCS 10393, pp. 345–358, 2017.
DOI: 10.1007/978-3-319-65482-9_23

mobile devices always go through long delay for data exchange with the cloud infrastructure, which would hurt the interaction as humans are sensitive to delay and jitter. To take care of this problem, the cloudlet based MCC was proposed as a promising solution [14]. Unlike depending on remote cloud infrastructure, it is through one-hop WiFi wireless access that efficiency is promoted by reducing latency, which is realized by offloading computation tasks to computing servers nearby. However, the cloudlet based MCC has two obvious drawbacks: (1) indoor environments are always neglected by the cloudlet based MCC owing to limited coverage of WiFi networks; (2) owing to space constraint, the cloudlet based MCC can not guarantee QoS of users as the cloudlet has no alternative but to use computing servers with small/medium computation resources [4].

To take care of these problems, authors in [2,6,11] proposed mobile edge clouds (MEC), a novel solution to supplement the cloudlet based MCC. As described in Fig. 1, at the edge of access networks, MEC leverages the physical proximity to mobile devices to augment the capabilities of mobile devices for resource-scarce applications. Under this circumstance, fiber transmission from the wireless base-station to the resource-abundant cloud infrastructure deployed by telecom operators can meet the demand for fast interaction.

However, the task of developing a reliable and comprehensive MEC system remains challenging. A key challenge is the communication from the mobile devices to the MEC server incurs extra overhead, which are latency fluctuation and extra energy cost. Another critical factor is bandwidth and computing resources are limited, if too many mobile users offload computation tasks to the cloud simultaneously, the cloud may not accommodate all of users and guarantee users' QoE (Quality of Experience). Hence how to achieve an efficient computation offloading coordination among mobile devices becomes an issue. This paper computes offloading utility of each user and picks only part of them for offloading. Owing to the constraint of limited bandwidth and computing resources, the total bandwidth and computing resources of picked users could not be more than that of the system. This paper designs an efficient offloading algorithm considering to maximize the system utility with varying number of users, under the constraint of limited bandwidth and computing resources. This paper formulates the issue as a resource allocation offloading problem solved by offloading qualification judgement (described in Sect. 4.1) and resource allocation offloading mechanism (described in Sect. 4.2), which transforms the NP-hardness issue into a polynomial problem.

The rest of the paper is organized as follows. This paper first discusses the related work in Sect. 2 and introduces the system model in Sect. 3. This paper then proposes the resource allocation offloading problem and develops the resource allocation offloading mechanism in Sects. 4 and 5, respectively. This paper further extends the study to the case under the wireless contention model and presents the numerical results in Sect. 6. The conclusion is in Sect. 7.

2   Related Work

Single-user computation offloading has been proposed in many previous work (e.g., [7,12,16]). Rudenko *et al.* in [12] investigated that computation offloading can significantly reduce energy consumption. Xian *et al.* in [16] demonstrated a suspension scheme where mobile devices' energy efficiency increase by computation offloading. Huang *et al.* in [7] developed an efficient majorization policy for mobile computing by dynamic offloading to minimize the energy consumption.

A few works have addressed the centralized decision making of offloading tasks from mobile devices to the cloud in a multi users context [13]. Lyu *et al.* in [8] jointly optimized the offloading decision and resource utilization, formulated the problem as a system utility maximization problem and solved the problem by a centralized heuristic genetic algorithm. The previous work in [8] determined the number of users who eventually can be offloaded first (i.e., the system bandwidth 20 MHz, UE (User Equipment) bandwidth 1 MHz, 20 MHz divided by 1 MHz is equal to 20) and let users participate in the selection of offloading algorithm process then. Given the fact that UE bandwidth is varied owing to the varied cloud computing service contract subscribed by the user i from the telecom operator and hence the number of users who eventually can be offloaded can not be determined before the selection of offloading algorithm process, this paper studies the generalized multi-user computation offloading problem in a multi-service and multi-bandwidth of UE setting, which results in significant differences in analysis with [8]. For example, this paper derives the input data size of the face recognition application and processing the English main page of Wikipedia (different services corresponding to different occupied bandwidth), which is not true for the single-service case. This paper carries out the user selection of offloading algorithm process first, unnecessary to determine the number of users who eventually can be offloaded before the selection. This paper also investigates the issue of maximum system utility, which is solved by a resource allocation offloading mechanism and sharply reduces the complexity compared with the previous work in [8].

3   System Model

A multi-service MEC scenario is shown in Fig. 1. This paper considers a LTE (Long Term Evolution) wireless base-station which serves N mobile users (e.g. tablets, laptops and smartphones) in its range and connects to an edge cloud. This paper denotes by $Q \triangleq \{i : 1, 2, ..., N\}$ the set of all the users, and by $y_i \in \{0, 1\}$ whether each user offloads or not (0 indicates no offloading and 1 indicates offloading). This paper also denotes by $Y \triangleq \{i | y_i = 1\}$ the set of all the offloading users. Service, users' occupied bandwidth and computation capability assigned to each user are varied.

Each mobile user i has a computation task $\Gamma_i \triangleq (w_i, d_i)$ [3,4,8,9]: the total CPU cycles w_i to accomplish the task and the size of computation input data d_i (bit) to transfer the input parameters and program codes from local to the edge

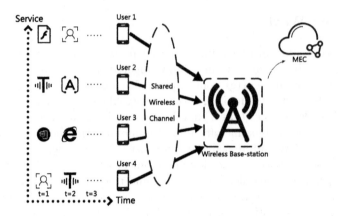

Fig. 1. Multi-service offloading scenario

cloud. A mobile device i can apply the means in [5,17] to obtain the information of w_i and d_i.

Each computation task can be either executed locally or remotely in the edge cloud. Since task completion time and energy consumption are the key influencing factors for both the users' quality of experience and offloading decision-making, this paper next investigates them in local and remote contexts.

3.1 Local Execution

For the local execution approach, a mobile device user i executes its computation task Γ_i locally on the mobile device. Task completion time T_i^l by local computing is given as:

$$T_i^l = \frac{w_i}{f_i^l} \tag{1}$$

where f_i^l is local computation capability (i.e., CPU cycles per second) of mobile user i. Energy consumption of mobile user i E_i^l can be written as:

$$E_i^l = P_i^l \cdot T_i^l = \alpha \cdot (f_i^l)^\beta \cdot \frac{w_i}{f_i^l} = \alpha \cdot (f_i^l)^{\beta-1} \cdot w_i \tag{2}$$

where P_i^l is the CPU power consumption, $\alpha = 10^{-11}$ and $\beta = 2$. α and β can be obtained by the measurement method in [3,4].

3.2 Remote Execution

For the remote execution approach, a mobile device user i will offload its computation task Γ_i to the cloud in proximity deployed by telecom operator via wireless access and the cloud will execute the computation task on behalf of the mobile device user.

For the computation offloading, a mobile user i would incur the extra overhead in terms of time and energy for transmitting the computation input data to the cloud via wireless access.

It is known that the intra-cell interface is alleviated greatly in LTE networks for the uplink transmission. Accordingly, the uplink data rate of user i can be written as:

$$R_i = B_i \cdot \log_2(1 + \frac{p_i H_i}{\omega_0}) \tag{3}$$

where B_i (Hz) denotes the occupied bandwidth of user i and is related with task service type. The primary motivation of relating occupied bandwidth with service is that the running applications of mobile devices are quite different. B (Hz) denotes the system bandwidth, p_i is transmission power of user i and ω_0 denotes the background noise power. H_i is the channel gain (related to pathloss, Rayleigh fading and lognormal shadowing standard deviation) from the user i to the LTE base-station.

T_i^r, the total task completion time of remote execution for user i, consists of two parts:

$$T_i^r = T_i^t + T_i^e = \frac{d_i}{B_i \log_2(1 + \frac{p_i H_i}{\omega_0})} + \frac{w_i}{f_i^r} \tag{4}$$

where T_i^t and T_i^e are transmission time and remote execution time, respectively.

It is supposed that the time for remote edge cloud to send the results back to the mobile device could be neglected [7]. This is because the size of computation results is also much smaller than that of input data in general. So the transmission energy of mobile user i for offloading the input data of size d_i can be computed as

$$E_i^r = p_i \cdot T_i^t = p_i \cdot \frac{d_i}{B_i \log_2(1 + \frac{p_i H_i}{\omega_0})} \tag{5}$$

3.3 Offloading Utility Function

For user i, task completion time and energy consumption can be obtained as:

$$T_i = y_i \cdot T_i^r + (1 - y_i)T_i^l \tag{6}$$

$$E_i = y_i \cdot E_i^r + (1 - y_i)E_i^l \tag{7}$$

We define an offloading utility function of user i as [8]:

$$u_i = \lambda_i^t \frac{T_i^l - T_i}{T_i^l} + \lambda_i^e \frac{E_i^l - E_i}{E_i^l} = y_i(\lambda_i^t \frac{T_i^l - T_i^r}{T_i^l} + \lambda_i^e \frac{E_i^l - E_i^r}{E_i^l}) \tag{8}$$

Note that the utility function characterizes the improvement in quality of experience compared with executing locally. To provide flexibility in capturing users' preferences on task completion time and energy consumption, this paper defines:

$$\lambda_i^t, \lambda_i^e \in [0, 1], \lambda_i^t + \lambda_i^e = 1 \tag{9}$$

where λ_i^t is users' preference on time for task completion and λ_i^e is user' preference on task energy consumption. In practice the proper preferences which capture users' valuations on task completion time and energy consumption can be determined by applying the multi-attribute utility method in the multiple criteria decision making theory [15].

This paper formulates the system utility maximization problem as follows:

$$
\begin{aligned}
&\max \sum_{i=1}^{|Q|} u_i(B_i, f_i^r, y_i) \\
&\quad s.t. \quad C1 : y_i = \{0, 1\}, \forall i \in Q \\
&P : \qquad\quad C2 : B_i > 0, \forall i \in Q \\
&\qquad\qquad\quad C3 : f_i^r > 0, \forall i \in Q
\end{aligned}
\tag{10}
$$

where B_i denotes the occupied bandwidth, f_i^r represents the computation capability (i.e., CPU cycles per second) assigned to user i and y_i denotes the offloading decision, respectively. B_i and f_i^r are determined according to the cloud computing service contract subscribed by the mobile user i from the telecom operator. Q denotes the set of all the users. Constraint C1 states that a task can be either executed locally or offloaded. According to Constraint C2, the occupied bandwidth must be positive. Constraint C3 ensures that the computation capability assigned to users must be positive.

The optimal offloading decision can be obtained by enumerating and comparing the whole possible offloading decisions. However, it is NP-hard. Thence, this paper decomposes the system utility maximization problem into offloading qualification judgement (described in Sect. 4.1) and resource allocation offloading mechanism (described in Sect. 4.2).

4   Resource Allocation Offloading Problem

4.1   Offloading Qualification Judgement

Users in Q transmit the pilot signal to the wireless base-station, and receive the information of assigned computation capability and occupied bandwidth according to the cloud computing service contract subscribed by the mobile users from the telecom operator.

Judgement 1. Users can calculate u_i according to the Eq. (8). If $u_i > 0$, user i obtains qualification to participate in the process of Algorithm 1 and $i \in Y$. If $u_i \leq 0$, user i loses offloading qualification and $i \in \{Q \backslash Y\}$. Since the system utility is the sum of user utilities, if $u_i \leq 0$, user i has a negative impact on the system utility, and also has a negative impact on its own QoE of remote execution. Hence, it loses qualification to participate in the process of Algorithm 1 naturally.

The set Y whose users own qualification to participate in the process of Algorithm 1 can be obtained. Then all users in Y send offloading requests to the edge cloud. After the edge cloud receives all requests, it judges whether the first user offloads the task or not. As long as the communication and computation resources are both adequate, the first user is permitted to offload. Then the utility value of the first user and the current maximum system utility can be calculated.

4.2 Resource Allocation Offloading Problem

For the second user, if the communication and computation resources remain both adequate, $G[B_{norm}][F_{norm}]$ and $G[B_{norm} - B_{1\_norm}][F_{norm} - f^r_{1\_norm}] + u_2$ should be compared, which indicates the maximum system utility when the first user offloads under the constraints of bandwidth B and the maximum instructions F per second allowed at the remote edge cloud, and indicates the maximum system utility of the first user and the second user, respectively. If $G[B_{norm}][F_{norm}]$ is greater, the second user is prevented offloading. If $G[B_{norm} - B_{1\_norm}][F_{norm} - f^r_{1\_norm}] + u_2$ is greater, the second user is permitted to offload.

If the user j executes the task locally, the system utility is $G[B_{norm}][F_{norm}]$. If the user j offloads the task, the system utility is $G[B_{norm} - B_{j\_norm}][F_{norm} - f^r_{j\_norm}] + u_j$. Then the comparison procedure repeats until all users in Y are decided to be offloaded or not. The problem L is transformed as:

$$\max \sum_{i=1}^{|Y|} u_i(B_i, f^r_i, y_i)$$
$$s.t. \quad C1 : y_i = \{0, 1\}, \forall i \in Y$$
$$C2 : B_i > 0, \forall i \in Y \qquad (11)$$
$$L : \quad C3 : \sum_{i \in Z} B_i \le B$$
$$C4 : f^r_i > 0, \forall i \in Y$$
$$C5 : \sum_{i \in Z} f^r_i \le F$$

where B_i, f^r_i, y_i, Q, Constraint C1, constraint C2 and constraint C4 are the same as those in the problem P. Constraint C3 ensures that the total occupied bandwidths of users are less than the system bandwidth B. Constraint C5 guarantees that the total computation capability assigned are less than the maximum instructions per second allowed at the remote edge cloud, denoted as F. Z represents the set of all the users who eventually offload the task to the wireless base-station (i.e. Y is the input of Algorithm 1 and Z is the output of Algorithm 1, $Z \subset Y$).

5   Resource Allocation Offloading Mechanism

In Algorithm 1, B_{remain} and F_{remain} denotes current remaining channel bandwidth and remaining computation capability, respectively. B_{norm} is the unit-normalized symbol of B and F_{norm} is the unit-normalized symbol of F. (i.e., B is set to 20 MHz, thence B_{norm} is 20. F is set to 20 GHz, thence F_{norm} is 20.) The primary motivation of using unit-normalized symbol is the application

---

Algorithm 1. Resource Allocation Offloading Mechanism (RAOM)

Stage I (Judgement 1): at each user i

1: **if** $u_i \leq 0$ **then**

2:   lose the offloading qualification

3: **else**

4:   send an offloading request to the edge cloud

5: **end if**

Stage II: the edge cloud judge whether the first user offload the task or not

6: wait until all the requests are received

7: **for** $index\_F = F_{norm} : -1 : 0$

8:   **for** $index\_B = B_{norm} : -1 : 0$

9:     **if** $B_{|Y|} < B_{remain}$ && $f_{|Y|}^r < F_{remain}$

10:       $G(index\_B, index\_F) = u_{|Y|}$

11:     **else**

12:       $G(index\_B, index\_F) = 0$

13:     **end if**

14:   **end**

15: **end**

Stage III: the edge cloud, repeat Stage II, judge
          whether the latter user offload the task or not

16: **for** $index\_B = B_{norm} : -1 : 0$

17:   **for** $index\_F = F_{norm} : -1 : 0$

18:     $G[B_{norm}][F_{norm}] = \max\{G[B_{norm}][F_{norm}], G[B_{norm} - B_{i\_norm}][F_{norm} - f_{i\_norm}^r] + u_i\}$

19:   **end**

20: **end**

Stage IV: the edge cloud find out the users who offload the task

21: determine the users whose task should be offloaded by the value of G

22: the edge cloud send the offloading decision to the mobile users who have sent
    an offloading request to notice them whether their task can be offloaded or not

---

convenience in Algorithm 1. $|Y|$ denotes the user number of set Y, and 1,2,...,$|Y|$ are the serial numbers of users in set Y, $index\_|Y| \in \{1, 2, ..., |Y|\}$.

The time complexity of Algorithm 1 is $O(N \cdot B_{norm} \cdot F_{norm})$ and the space complexity of Algorithm 1 is $O(B_{norm} \cdot F_{norm})$. Note that the loop $index\_B = B_{norm} : -1 : 0$ has to be inverse order rather than $index\_B = 1 : 1 : B_{norm} + 1$. The loop $index\_F = F_{norm} : -1 : 0$ has to be inverse order rather than $index\_F = 1 : 1 : F_{norm} + 1$. The step length is set to -1, which guarantees that the space complexity is $O(B_{norm} \cdot F_{norm})$ rather than $O(N \cdot B_{norm} \cdot F_{norm})$.

6   Numerical Results

6.1   Comparison of System Utility and Task Completion Time

In this section, this paper evaluates the proposed resource allocation offloading mechanism by numerical studies. This paper adopts the face recognition in [4,8] and the workload of processing the English main page of Wikipedia in [10].

Table 1. Simulation parameters

Parameters	Values
LTE base-station radius r	500 m
System bandwidth B	60 MHz
Maximum instructions allowed at edge cloud F	60 GHz
Input data size of face recognition d_1	420 KB
Input data size of wikipedia d_2	125 B
Number of CPU cycles of face recognition w_1	1000 MCycles
Number of CPU cycles of wikipedia w_2	737500 Cycles
Occupied bandwidth of face recognition	3 MHz
Occupied bandwidth of wikipedia	1 MHz
Assigned computation capability	1 GHz–3 GHz
Noise power ω_0	−174 dBm/Hz
Rayleigh fading	20 dB
Lognormal shadowing standard deviation	10 dB
Pathloss from mobile device to LTE BS	$128.1 + 37.5\log_{10}(r)$
Maximum transmission power of mobile device p_i	23 dBm
Local CPU computation capability f_i^l	0.5 GHz–1.5 GHz
Users preference on task completion time λ_i^t	0–1
Users preference on task energy consumption λ_i^e	$1 - \lambda_i^t$

For comparing the performances, this paper also considers other four algorithms as follows:

(1) Enumeration algorithm (EA): All 2^N offloading decisions are enumerated and compared to find the optimal one.
(2) Joint optimization without offloading qualification judgement (JWOJ): All users participate in the selection of RAOM directly rather than participate in Judgement 1 before the selection.
(3) Simulated Annealing Algorithm (SAA): Firstly, it is assumed that all users offload and a group of initial solution can be gotten. Then a new decision is generated, updating the number of offloading users and the maximum system utility. If the new utility is greater than the previous one, the new decision will be adopted. As a heuristic algorithm, SA employs initial temperature and cooling factor to control iterations. When temperature drops to the designated value, iteration stops and the maximum system utility at this time is the final result.
(4) 0-1 Linear Programing (LP): The optimal object is maximum system utility. Meanwhile, the total occupied bandwidths are less than the system channel bandwidth and the total computation capability assigned are less than the maximum instructions per second allowed at the remote edge cloud.

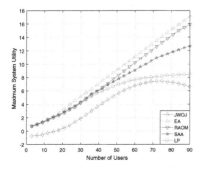

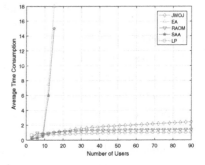

Fig. 2. Comparison of system utility   **Fig. 3.** Comparison of task time

Figure 2 demonstrates a comparison of maximum system utility achieved by JWOJ, EA, RAOM, SAA and LP. JWOJ performs much worse than RAOM as no Judgement 1 implements: Users whose $u_i \leq 0$ also participate in offloading, causing the system utility decreases. RAOM performs very close to the optimal solution computed by EA. Its performance remains within 10% of the optimal. Comparing RAOM, SAA and LP, when number of users is less than 40, three algorithms have similar performance. As number of users increases, RAOM has a more thorough and superior resource allocation mechanism than the other two algorithms and achieves better computation offloading performance when number of users is greater than 40.

Figure 3 reflects a QoS comparison for the users, which is the comparison of task completion time realized by JWOJ, EA, RAOM, SAA and LP. When number of users is less than 16, the time consumption of JWOJ is slightly shorter than RAOM as JWOJ involves no Judgement 1. When number of users is greater than 16, the drawback of involving no Judgement 1 becomes visible. The time consumption of JWOJ is much longer than RAOM as too many users who do not satisfy Judgement 1 ($u_i \leq 0$) also participate in offloading. RAOM can achieve up-to 99% time consumption reduction over with SAA and EA while the system utility of RAOM remains outside 20% of SAA and within 10% of the optimal computed by EA. Although the task completion time realized by LP is shorter than that of RAOM, the system utility realized by LP in Fig. 2 is much less than those of the optimal and RAOM. For users, RAOM brings better user experience of offloading than the other four algorithms, which means shorter time and higher efficiency. Figure 4 further illustrates how RAOM significantly reduces users' task completion time.

Figure 4 shows a distribution of 90 users' task completion time realized by RAOM. In this random simulation, 38 users whose completion time is close to 0 are offloaded users. The remaining 52 users are not picked by RAOM and execute their tasks locally. In this case, RAOM properly chooses 38 users to be offloaded and help them save a lot of time (from around 2.5 to around 0).

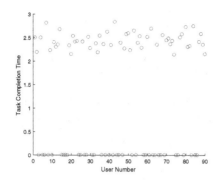

Fig. 4. Distribution of task completion time

6.2   Extension to Wirelessinterference Model

In the previous sections above, this paper mainly focuses on exploring the computation offloading problem under the model as given in Fig. 1, which consists of a LTE macro wireless base-station and N mobile users in its range. In order to be more accordant with practical circumstances, this paper extends the study to the wireless interference between the macro base-station and small base-stations. In this case, the number of simulated users should increase synchronously.

Hotspot is an appropriate model to simulate the topology of the whole system as shown in Fig. 5. The hotspot graph starts with 4 seed points. 6 small cells and approximate 60 users distribute randomly besides each seed point. A macro cell is set up in the center of the area, in charge of the area which can not be covered by small cells. By applying hotspot model, mobile users can distribute more intensively so as to be more accordant with practical circumstances.

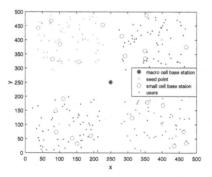

Fig. 5. Wireless interference model

As interference among users in the same small cell and between different small cells can be eliminated by receiving ends, this paper only considers interference between the macro cell and small cells. Based on Eq. (3), the modified uplink data rate of user R_{i_n} can be written as:

$$R_{i_n} = B_{i_n} \cdot \log_2(1 + \frac{p_{i_n} H_{i_n}}{I_{i_n} + \omega_0}) \tag{12}$$

n, k denotes the serial number of small cells. i, j denotes the serial number of users. I_{i_n} denotes the total interference from other cells:

$$I_{i_n} = \sum_{j_K \in I, k \neq n} p_{j_k} H_{j_k} \tag{13}$$

According to the 3GPP specification [1], the bandwidth of each small cell is set to 10 MHz and the bandwidth of the macro cell is set to 20 MHz. The scenario area is 500 m * 500 m. The other communication and computation parameters used in the simulations are summarized in Table 1.

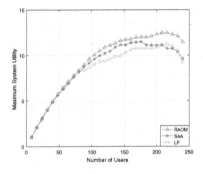

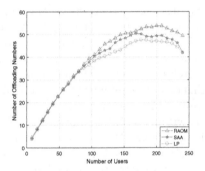

Fig. 6. Comparison of system utility   **Fig. 7.** Comparison of offloading users

Figure 6 depicts maximum system utility changes with number of users when considering interference between the macro cell and small cells. Compared with Fig. 2, the curve trend is totally different, testifying the interference is too serious to be ignored and the model extension is worthwhile. When number of users is less than 80, three algorithms have similar performance. As number of users increases, the effect of interference on system utility becomes appreciable. RAOM has superior interference immunity than the other two algorithms and achieves efficient computation offloading performance when number of users is greater than 80 (Fig. 7).

As shown in Fig. 8, when preference coefficient on task energy consumption in the range of 0.35 to 0.55 and 0.65 to 1, the maximum system utility realized by RAOM is slightly greater than the other two algorithms. The superior range occupies 55% of the whole range. As shown in Figs. 8 and 9, RAOM is also the most sensitive algorithm as its curve slope has the most obvious change as the preference coefficient changes, which has more adaptability to different users' preferences in practice.

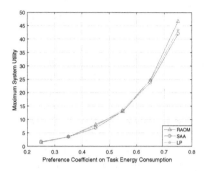

Fig. 8. Sensitivity of system utility

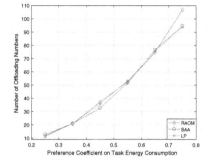

Fig. 9. Sensitivity of offloading users

7   Conclusion

This paper proposes a resource allocation offloading mechanism for the computation offloading decision making problem among multiple mobile users for mobile edge clouds. This paper formulates the problem as a system utility maximization problem, designs a resource allocation offloading mechanism that can maximize system utility within the constraints of system bandwidth and maximum instructions per second allowed in edge clouds and also quantifies its efficiency ratio over the optimal solutions in terms of two vital performance metrics. This paper further extends the study to the scenario of multi-user computation offloading in the wireless interference model. Numerical results demonstrate that the extension is worthwhile and the proposed mechanism RAOM achieves efficient computation offloading performance either with interference or without interference.

References

1. EUTR Access: Further advancements for E-UTRA physical layer aspects. Technical report, 3GPP TR 36.814 (2010)
2. Barbarossa, S., Sardellitti, S., Di Lorenzo, P.: Joint allocation of computation and communication resources in multiuser mobile cloud computing. In: 2013 IEEE 14th Workshop on Signal Processing Advances in Wireless Communications (SPAWC), pp. 26–30. IEEE (2013)
3. Chen, X.: Decentralized computation offloading game for mobile cloud computing. IEEE Trans. Parallel Distrib. Syst. **26**(4), 974–983 (2015)
4. Chen, X., Jiao, L., Li, W., Fu, X.: Efficient multi-user computation offloading for mobile-edge cloud computing. IEEE/ACM Trans. Netw. **24**, 2795–2808 (2015)
5. Cuervo, E., Balasubramanian, A., Cho, D.K., Wolman, A., Saroiu, S., Chandra, R., Bahl, P.: MAUI: making smartphones last longer with code offload. In: Proceedings of the 8th International Conference on Mobile Systems, Applications, and Services, pp. 49–62. ACM (2010)
6. Drolia, U., Martins, R., Tan, J., Chheda, A., Sanghavi, M., Gandhi, R., Narasimhan, P.: The case for mobile edge-clouds. In: 2013 IEEE 10th International Conference on Ubiquitous Intelligence and Computing and 10th International Conference on Autonomic and Trusted Computing (UIC/ATC), pp. 209–215. IEEE (2013)

7. Huang, D., Wang, P., Niyato, D.: A dynamic offloading algorithm for mobile computing. IEEE Trans. Wirel. Commun. **11**(6), 1991–1995 (2012)
8. Lyu, X., Tian, H., Zhang, P., Sengul, C.: Multi-user joint task offloading and resources optimization in proximate clouds. IEEE Trans. Veh. Technol. (2016)
9. Mao, Y., Zhang, J., Letaief, K.B.: Dynamic computation offloading for mobile-edge computing with energy harvesting devices. IEEE J. Sel. Areas Commun. **34**, 3590–3605 (2016)
10. Miettinen, A.P., Nurminen, J.K.: Energy efficiency of mobile clients in cloud computing. HotCloud **10**, 4 (2010)
11. Patel, M., Naughton, B., Chan, C., Sprecher, N., Abeta, S., Neal, A., et al.: Mobile-edge computing introductory technical white paper. White Paper, Mobile-Edge Computing (MEC) Industry Initiative (2014)
12. Rudenko, A., Reiher, P., Popek, G.J., Kuenning, G.H.: Saving portable computer battery power through remote process execution. ACM SIGMOBILE Mob. Comput. Commun. Rev. **2**(1), 19–26 (1998)
13. Sardellitti, S., Scutari, G., Barbarossa, S.: Joint optimization of radio and computational resources for multicell mobile-edge computing. IEEE Trans. Sig. Inf. Process. Netw. **1**(2), 89–103 (2015)
14. Satyanarayanan, M., Bahl, P., Caceres, R., Davies, N.: The case for VM-based cloudlets in mobile computing. IEEE Pervasive Comput. **8**(4) (2009)
15. Wallenius, J., Dyer, J.S., Fishburn, P.C., Steuer, R.E., Zionts, S., Deb, K.: Multiple criteria decision making, multiattribute utility theory: recent accomplishments and what lies ahead. Manage. Sci. **54**(7), 1336–1349 (2008)
16. Xian, C., Lu, Y.H., Li, Z.: Adaptive computation offloading for energy conservation on battery-powered systems. In: 2007 International Conference on Parallel and Distributed Systems, vol. 2, pp. 1–8. IEEE (2007)
17. Yang, L., Cao, J., Yuan, Y., Li, T., Han, A., Chan, A.: A framework for partitioning and execution of data stream applications in mobile cloud computing. ACM SIGMETRICS Perform. Eval. Rev. **40**(4), 23–32 (2013)

A CNN-Based Supermarket
Auto-Counting System

Zhonghong Ou$^{(\boxtimes)}$, Changwei Lin, Meina Song, and Haihong E

Beijing University of Posts and Telecommunications, Beijing, China
{zhonghong.ou,linchangwei,mnsong,ehaihong}@bupt.edu.cn

Abstract. Deep learning has made significant breakthrough in the past decade. In certain application domain, its detection accuracy has surpassed human being in the same task, e.g., voice recognition and object detection. Various novel applications has been developed and achieved good performance by leveraging the latest advances in deep learning. In this paper, we propose to utilize deep learning based technique, specifically, Convolutional Neural Network (CNN), to develop an auto-counting system for supermarket scenario. Given a picture, the system can automatically detect the specified categories of goods (e.g., Head & Shoulders bottles) and their respective numbers. To improve detection accuracy of the system, we propose to combine hard example mining and multi-scale feature extraction to the Faster R-CNN framework. Experimental results demonstrate the efficacy of the proposed system. Specifically, our system achieves an mAP of 92.1%, which is better than the state-of-the-art, and the response time is about 250 ms per image, including all steps on a GTX 1080 GPU.

Keywords: Auto-counting system · Deep learning · Convolutional Neural Network

1 Introduction

Deep learning based techniques have experienced significant development in the past decade. From the milestone paper published by Hinton et al. [8] in 2006 in Science, deep learning has made breakthrough in many domains. In 2009, deep learning was introduced to solve the problem of voice recognition. In 2010, the voice recognition accuracy was improved by more than 20%, which is more than the accumulative total in the past few years. In machine vision domain, in the 2012 ImageNet Large Scale Visual Recognition Challenge (ILSVRC) [22], Hinton et al. utilized Convolutional Neural Network (CNN) to classify images and decreased the top-5 classification error rate to 15.3%. It improved the state-of-the-art (with 26.2% error rate) by more than 10%. Moreover, deep learning based techniques have been used in other domains as well, e.g., text understanding, activity recognition, and medical image processing, and achieved significant better performance than conventional approaches.

© Springer International Publishing AG 2017
S. Ibrahim et al. (Eds.): ICA3PP 2017, LNCS 10393, pp. 359–371, 2017.
DOI: 10.1007/978-3-319-65482-9_24

On the other hand, a number of deep learning based frameworks and libraries have been made publicly available. For example, Google open sourced Tensor-Flow [12], a software library for numerical computation using data flow graphs. Berkeley also open sourced Caffe [4], a deep learning framework which supports good expression, speed, and modularity. There are also a number of other frameworks which are publicly available, e.g., Torch [31], Theano [28], Keras [18], and CNTK [5], just to name a few. These open source deep learning libraries and frameworks have made deep learning techniques readily accessible to many other domains than computer science. A lot of novel applications have been developed based on the frameworks mentioned above. For example, Esteva et al. [6] utilized Google Inception v3 architecture, which is a model contained in TensorFlow, to detect skin cancers from pictures, and achieved comparable and even slightly better detection accuracy than board-certified dermatologists. Put it in another way, deep learning based techniques have become a tool to enable application scenarios in many domains.

Fig. 1. Output of the proposed system. Rectangles label the products that are of interests to the system. Different color stands for different product category.

In this paper, we propose to utilize CNN to develop an auto-counting system for supermarket scenarios. The system takes an picture as input, and then outputs the different categories and the respective number of each category contained in the picture. Figure 1 illustrates one example of the output of the proposed system. The system can be used in various scenarios, e.g., auto-counting products on supermarket shelves, or estimating the number of goods in storage. We use Caffe [4] to train the model and encapsulate it into our system module as the core recognition component. The clients gain recognition results from the server through HTTP requests and carry out analysis and rendering. We implement the system on both CPU and GPU based machines, and conduct well-defined experiments to evaluate its performance.

To summarise, we make the following key contributions in this paper:

1. We propose to utilize CNN to develop an auto-counting system for supermarket scenarios;
2. We propose a new object detection method which combines hard example mining and multi-scale feature extraction into the Faster R-CNN framework, and acquire better performance than Faster R-CNN;
3. We implement the proposed system on both CPU and GPU based machines; experimental results demonstrate efficacy of the system. Specifically, our system achieves a mAP of 92.1%, which is better than Faster R-CNN, and the response time is around 250 ms per image, including all steps on a GTX 1080 GPU.

2   Background

In this section, we describe background information that are necessary to understand the architecture of our system. Specifically, we present existing object proposal and detection techniques, especially deep learning based approaches. We first describe Faster R-CNN in Sect. 2.1, then present the techniques to resolve hard example mining in Sect. 2.2, and introduce multi-scale feature maps for object detection in Sect. 2.3.

2.1   Faster R-CNN

In the past few years, a number of object detection techniques have been proposed. Typical examples include R-CNN [10], Fast R-CNN [9] and Faster R-CNN [21]. Faster R-CNN was proposed by Ren et al. [21], and is mainly based on the R-CNN and Fast-RCNN framework. As shown in Fig. 2, the Faster R-CNN architecture consists of three steps: (1) CNN feature extraction; (2) region proposal; and 3) object classification and fine-grained bounding box regression (bbox reg in Fig. 2). As an improvement, Faster R-CNN introduced a novel Region Proposal Networks (RPN) for region proposal with higher accuracy and faster speed. RPN, regarded as the highlight of Faster R-CNN, generates proposals with a deep convolutional network and shares full-image convolutional features with Fast R-CNN. The unified network of Faster R-CNN gains better performance both in speed and accuracy.

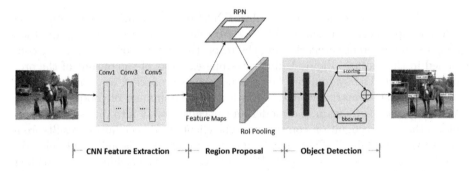

Fig. 2. Architecture of faster R-CNN.

2.2 Hard Example Mining

There are a few recent studies [20, 24, 25, 34] that select hard examples for training deep networks. Shrivastava et al. [24] proposed a novel bootstrapping technique called online hard example mining (OHEM) for training state-of-the-art CNN-based detection models. The algorithm is a simple modification to Stochastic Gradient Descent (SGD) in which training examples are sampled according to a non-uniform, non-stationary distribution that depends on the current loss of each example under consideration. The method takes advantage of detection-specific problem structure in which each SGD mini-batch consists of only one or two images, but thousands of candidate examples. The candidate examples are subsampled according to a distribution that favors diverse, high loss instances. Gradient computation (back propagation) is still efficient because it only uses a small subset of all candidates. Applying OHEM to the standard Fast R-CNN detection method has shown a consistent and significant boost in mean average precision compared to the baseline training algorithm.

2.3 Multi-scale Feature Maps for Object Detection

The popular CNN-based detection method such as Faster R-CNN extracts features only from the last convolution layer for region proposal and object classification. Deep feature maps are highly semantic. Nevertheless, they still struggle in small-size object detection and precise localization, mainly due to the coarseness of its feature maps. A number of recent approaches improve detection by aggregating feature maps from multiple layers and then compressing them into a uniform space before making the prediction. Multi-scale feature maps well incorporate deep but highly semantic, intermediate but really complementary, and shallow but naturally high-resolution features of the image, thus are helpful to both generate proposals and detect objects. Representatives include Hypercolumns [13], HyperNet [16], ParseNet [19], and ION [3].

3   Design and Implementation

In this section, we present the auto-counting system, which combines hard example mining and multi-scale feature extraction to the Faster R-CNN framework. We first introduce the training details in Sect. 3.1, and then present the design and implementation of the system in Sect. 3.2.

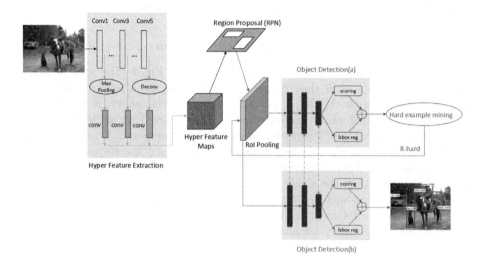

Fig. 3. Structure of our model. (Color figure online)

3.1   Training Model

The structure of our model is illustrated in Fig. 3. We simultaneously add hard example mining and hyper feature extraction method to the Faster R-CNN baseline structure. We implement both methods using the Caffe framework. The two improvements made in the model are described briefly as follows:

The implementation of hard example mining is composed of two copies of the detection network: (1) detection network (a), which allocates memory only for forward pass of all Region of Interest (RoI); (2) standard detection network (b), which allocates memory for both forward and backward passes. It is notable that detection network (a) and (b) share parameters. For an SGD iteration, given the feature maps, detection network (a) performs a forward pass and computes loss for all input RoIs (green arrows); then the hard RoI sampling module selects hard examples (R-hard) by ranking loss and inputs them to detection network (b) (red arrows). This network computes forward and backward passes only for R-hard, and accumulates the gradients and passes them to the front convolution network.

The implementation of hyper feature extraction combines feature maps from multiple layers. Because of subsampling and pooling operations in CNN, these feature maps from multiple layers are not at the same resolution. To combine multi-level maps at the same resolution, we carry out different sampling strategies for different layers. We add a max pooling layer on the lower layer to carry out subsampling. For higher layers, we add a deconvolutional operation (`Deconv`) to conduct upsampling. A convolutional layer (`Conv`) is applied to each sampled result. The `Conv` operation not only extracts more semantic features but also compresses them into a uniform space. Finally, we can acquire the hyper feature maps and apply them to the subsequent detection modules.

3.2   Design and Implementation of Our System

The overall architecture of our system is shown in Fig. 4. The system takes an picture as input, and then passes it to the recognition server through an HTTP request. In the HTTP response returned by the server, a list of parameters are contained where instances of the objects are detected in the image. The parameters contain 4 aspects, consisting of class name, location coordinates, corresponding classification confidence score, and the response time on the recognition server as a reference. Note that this problem is distinct from and more challenging than the simple classification problem, which decides whether an input image contains an instance of the specific object class or not. The additional location information of the detection task is useful for the counting problem, and is necessary for image rendering for better display.

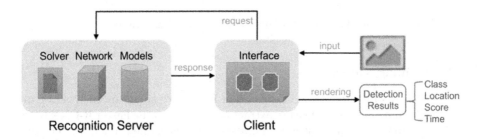

Fig. 4. Overall architecture of our proposed system.

4   Performance Evaluation

In this section, we evaluate performance of our system. We first present the dataset used in Sect. 4.1, then describe the evaluation metrics in Sect. 4.2, and finally, present the experimental results in Sect. 4.3.

4.1   Datasets

To test detection performance, we first used the standard PASCAL VOC 2007 detection benchmarks [15] to validate our method. PASCAL VOC 2007 dataset covers 20 categories, 9,963 images in total containing 24,640 annotated objects. Then, in order to detect goods on supermarket shelves, we collected 500 goods pictures mainly belonging to shampoo category from different supermarket, and labeled 4 subcategories with class name (hfs-qsqysmall, hfs-qsqybig, hfs-ysblsmall, hfs-ysblbig) and location coordinates. It is notable that the class name with "small" suffix indicates the object has smaller size in actual compared with the class name with "big" suffix. `hfs` is the Chinese acronym of the shampoo brand, i.e., Heads & Shoulders, which we used to test our system; `qsqy` and `ysbl` stands for different subcategory. In total, our shampoo dataset consists of 500 images containing 5306 object instances. The dataset is divided into training set and testing set, containing 400 images and 100 images, respectively.

4.2   Evaluation Metrics

We use `recall`, `precision` and `mAP` as the evaluation metrics of our proposed method.

`Recall` is defined as the proportion of all positive examples ranked above a given rank. The detailed calculation is listed in Eq. 1.

$$Recall = \frac{TruePositive}{TruePositive + FalseNegative} \qquad (1)$$

`Precision` is defined as the proportion of all examples above that rank which are from the positive class. The detailed calculation is listed in Eq. 2.

$$Precision = \frac{TruePositive}{TruePositive + FalsePositive} \qquad (2)$$

The terms *positive* and *negative* refer to the classifier's prediction, and the terms *true* and *false* refer to whether that prediction corresponds to the external judgment.

Average Precision (AP) summarises the shape of the precision/recall curve, and is defined as the mean precision at a set of eleven equally spaced recall levels [0, 0.1, ..., 1]:

$$AP = \frac{1}{11} \sum_{r \in \{0,0.1,\cdots,1\}} P_{interp}(r) \qquad (3)$$

The precision at each recall level **r** is interpolated by taking the maximum precision measured for a method for which the corresponding recall exceeds **r**:

$$P_{interp}(r) = \max_{\tilde{r}:\tilde{r} \geq r} p(\tilde{r}) \qquad (4)$$

mean Average Precision (mAP) is the mean value of AP of all N classes, representing the overall result.

$$mAP = \frac{1}{N} \sum_{i}^{N} AP_i \qquad (5)$$

4.3 Results

PASCAL VOC 2007 Data Set. We first compare our proposed scheme, as shown in Fig. 3, with Faster R-CNN for generic object detection on PASCAL VOC 2007. Detailed results are listed in Table 1. The performance is measured by the AP of each category and the mAP of the 20 categories contained in the PASCAL VOC 2007 dataset. Both methods start from the same pre-trained VGG16 [32] network and use bounding box regression, ensuring consistency of test procedures by the same parameters with Intersection over Union (IoU = 0.5).

From Table 1, we can see that the overall trend is that our approach outperforms Faster R-CNN in every category. However, the exact outperformance ranges from category to category. For example, for the bike category, our approach outperforms Faster R-CNN by 1.8%; while for the plant category, the improvement of our approach reaches 14.7%. Overall, faster R-CNN achieves a mAP of **69.9%**, while our method achieves a mAP of **75.0%**, which is 5.1 points higher than the former.

As we have shown above, the improvement of our method is mainly because of the benefits from multi-scale feature maps and hard example mining. The extraction of multi-scale feature can acquire both detailed texture feature and highly semantic feature, which is useful for small-size object detection and precise location. On this basis, the hard example mining method, which selects better samples as the negative samples, further optimizes the region proposal and classification quality. Consequently, the use of both multi-scale feature extraction and hard example mining improves detection accuracy significantly.

Moreover, reasonable resolution of multi-scale feature maps makes for better object localization, especially when the object size is small. For objects of small size, our detection network outperforms Faster R-CNN by a significant margin, as shown in dotted circles in Table 1. For the bottle category, our approach achieves an AP of 60.2%, which is 10.3 points improvement than Faster R-CNN; while for the plant category, our method improves AP by 14.7 points (53.8% − 39.1% = 14.7%), compared with Faster R-CNN.

Table 1. Results on PASCAL VOC 2007 test set (with IoU = 0.5). Dotted circles stand for small-object detection results.

Method	mAP	arco	bike	bird	boat	bottle	bus	car	cat	chair	cow
Faster R-CNN	69.9	70.0	80.6	70.1	57.8	49.9	78.2	80.4	82.0	52.2	75.3
Ours	**75.0**	**73.6**	**82.4**	**75.1**	**63.3**	**60.2**	**80.2**	**83.3**	**85.6**	**59.3**	**77.2**

Method		table	dog	horse	mbike	person	plant	sheep	sofa	train	tv
Faster R-CNN		67.2	80.3	79.8	75.0	76.3	39.1	68.3	67.3	81.1	67.6
Ours		**74.5**	**84.8**	**86.5**	**78.4**	**80.9**	**53.8**	**70.4**	**73.2**	**83.2**	**74.6**

Shampoo Data Set. Then, we train both Faster R-CNN baseline network and our improvement network through the newly collected dataset, as described in Sect. 4.1. Recall results are illustrated in Fig. 5, while precision results are demonstrated in Fig. 6. `Conf_thresh` value shown on the x-axis stands for the confidence threshold. Through the two figures, we can see that recall decreases as the `conf_thresh` increases, while precision increases along with `conf_thresh`. On the other hand, it is obvious that detection results of the objects with small size (`hfs-qsqysmall`, `hfs-ysblsmall`) are worse than the objects with large size (`hfs-qsqybig`, `hfs-ysblbig`), including both recall and precision. If the camera is far away from the shelves which leads to smaller size of the objects in the picture, the detection result will be worse.

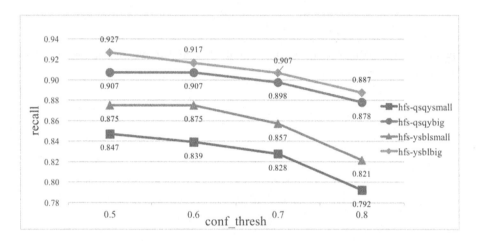

Fig. 5. Recall along with confidence threshold (`conf_thresh`) on the shampoo data set.

The AP results of our system compared with Faster R-CNN are illustrated in Fig. 7. From the figure, it is clear that our method acquires better AP than Faster R-CNN on each class. Especially, the detection result of small size objects of our approach is comparable to that of large objects from Faster R-CNN. Finally, our method on the new shampoo dataset achieves a `mAP` of 92.1%, while Faster R-CNN achieves a `mAP` of 85.8%. The running time for obtaining results is about 250 ms per image, including all steps on a GTX 1080 GPU. Figure 8 illustrates some detection results of our system on the shampoo dataset, which demonstrates that our system can successfully detect the objects of interest.

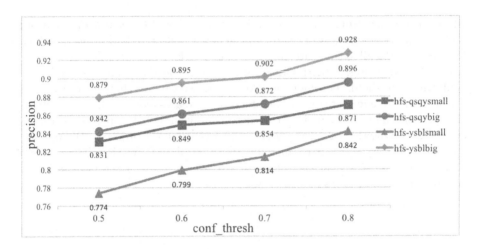

Fig. 6. Precision along with confidence threshold (`conf_thresh`) on the shampoo data set.

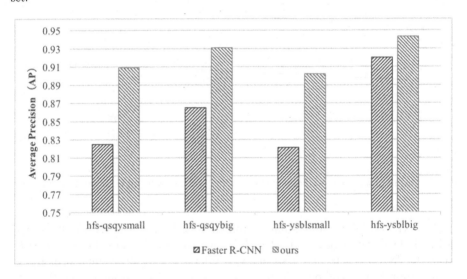

Fig. 7. `Average Precision (AP)` along with confidence threshold on the shampoo data set.

5   Related Work

CNN-based object detection. In the past few years, significant improvement has been made in object detection. Inspired by the successful application of deep CNN to ImageNet classification [22], the R-CNN [10] and OverFeat [23] detectors have been proposed with good results on PASCAL VOC [15] and ImageNet detection task. OverFeat is based on the sliding-window detection method, which is presumably the most intuitive and oldest search method for

Fig. 8. Selected examples of object detection results on the shampoo data set using our system, illustrating that our system can successfully detect the objects of interest.

detection. R-CNN [10], in contrast, uses region proposals, a method that was made popular by the selective search algorithm [32]. Since R-CNN, there has been rapid progress in region-based detection network, including SPPnet [14], Fast R-CNN [9], and Faster R-CNN [21].

Object detection application cases. There have been many practical usage scenarios of CNN-based object detection to deal with different problems such as face detection [7,15,17], pedestrian detection [29,30,35], vehicle detection [33,36], traffic-sign detection [26,27,37], fruit detection [1,2] and part detection [11]. Nevertheless, to the best of our knowledge, there has not been any object detection application to solve goods detection for supermarket auto-counting scenario. Thus, the study conducted in this paper is necessary and well-motivated.

6   Conclusion

We presented object detection method using hard example mining and multi-scale feature extraction based on Faster R-CNN in this paper, and applied it to the practical scenario of goods detection for supermarket auto-counting scenario. Our system can help calculate the occupancy of various categories of goods on the shelves automatically by using pictures, which can reduce the operating costs of the wholesale industry and promote the wholesale decision making. By combining hard example mining and multi-scale feature extraction to the Faster R-CNN framework, our system improved the state-of-the-art in terms of detection accuracy. Moreover, our system can return response within a reasonable time frame. Thus, it is of practical value for realistic scenarios. In the future, we will extend our system to cover panoramic pictures, and improve response time further.

References

1. Bargoti, S., Underwood, J.: Deep fruit detection in orchards. arXiv preprint arXiv:1610.03677 (2016)
2. Bargoti, S., Underwood, J.P.: Image segmentation for fruit detection and yield estimation in apple orchards. J. Field Robot. arXiv preprint arXiv:1610.08120 (2017)
3. Bell, S., Lawrence Zitnick, C., Bala, K., Girshick, R.: Inside-outside net: detecting objects in context with skip pooling and recurrent neural networks. In: Proceedings of the IEEE Conference on Computer Vision and Pattern Recognition, pp. 2874–2883 (2016)
4. Caffe (2017). http://caffe.berkeleyvision.org/. Accessed 13 Apr 2017
5. CNTK (2017). https://github.com/Microsoft/CNTK/. Accessed 13 Apr 2017
6. Esteva, A., Kuprel, B., Novoa, R.A., Ko, J., Swetter, S.M., Blau, H.M., Thrun, S.: Dermatologist-level classification of skin cancer with deep neural networks. Nature **542**, 115–118 (2017)
7. Farfade, S.S., Saberian, M.J., Li, L.J.: Multi-view face detection using deep convolutional neural networks. In: Proceedings of the 5th ACM on International Conference on Multimedia Retrieval, pp. 643–650. ACM (2015)
8. Hinton, G.E., Salakhutdinov, R.R.: Reducing the dimensionality of data with neural networks. Science **313**(5786), 504–507 (2006)
9. Girshick, R.: Fast R-CNN. In: Proceedings of the IEEE International Conference on Computer Vision, pp. 1440–1448 (2015)
10. Girshick, R., Donahue, J., Darrell, T., Malik, J.: Rich feature hierarchies for accurate object detection and semantic segmentation. In: Proceedings of the IEEE Conference on computer Vision and Pattern Recognition, pp. 580–587 (2014)
11. Gonzalez-Garcia, A., Modolo, D., Ferrari, V.: Objects as context for part detection. arXiv preprint arXiv:1703.09529 (2017)
12. TensorFlow (2017). https://www.tensorflow.org/. Accessed 13 Apr 2017
13. Hariharan, B., Arbeláez, P., Girshick, R., Malik, J.: Hypercolumns for object segmentation and fine-grained localization. In: Proceedings of the IEEE Conference on Computer Vision and Pattern Recognition, pp. 447–456 (2015)
14. He, K., Zhang, X., Ren, S., Sun, J.: Spatial pyramid pooling in deep convolutional networks for visual recognition. In: Fleet, D., Pajdla, T., Schiele, B., Tuytelaars, T. (eds.) ECCV 2014. LNCS, vol. 8691, pp. 346–361. Springer, Cham (2014). doi:10.1007/978-3-319-10578-9_23
15. Hu, P., Ramanan, D.: Finding tiny faces. arXiv preprint arXiv:1612.04402 (2016)
16. Hwang, K., Ghosh, J.: Hypernet: a communication-efficient architecture for constructing massively parallel computers. IEEE Trans. Comput. **100**(12), 1450–1466 (1987)
17. Kalinovskii, I., Spitsyn, V.: Compact convolutional neural network cascade for face detection. arXiv preprint arXiv:1508.01292 (2015)
18. Keras (2017). https://github.com/fchollet/keras/. Accessed 13 Apr 2017
19. Liu, W., Rabinovich, A., Berg, A.C.: ParseNet: looking wider to see better. arXiv preprint arXiv:1506.04579 (2015)
20. Loshchilov, I., Hutter, F.: Online batch selection for faster training of neural networks. arXiv preprint arXiv:1511.06343 (2015)
21. Ren, S., He, K., Girshick, R., Sun, J.: Faster R-CNN: towards real-time object detection with region proposal networks. In: Advances in Neural Information Processing Systems, pp. 91–99 (2015)

22. Russakovsky, O., Deng, J., Su, H., Krause, J., Satheesh, S., Ma, S., Huang, Z., Karpathy, A., Khosla, A., Bernstein, M., Berg, A.C., Fei-Fei, L.: Imagenet large scale visual recognition challenge. Int. J. Comput. Vis. **115**(3), 211–252 (2015). http://dx.doi.org/10.1007/s11263-015-0816-y
23. Sermanet, P., Eigen, D., Zhang, X., Mathieu, M., Fergus, R., LeCun, Y.: Overfeat: integrated recognition, localization and detection using convolutional networks. arXiv preprint arXiv:1312.6229 (2013)
24. Shrivastava, A., Gupta, A., Girshick, R.: Training region-based object detectors with online hard example mining. In: Proceedings of the IEEE Conference on Computer Vision and Pattern Recognition, pp. 761–769 (2016)
25. Simo-Serra, E., Trulls, E., Ferraz, L., Kokkinos, I., Moreno-Noguer, F.: Fracking deep convolutional image descriptors. arXiv preprint arXiv:1412.6537 (2014)
26. Song, M., Zhonghong, O., Castellanos, E., Ylipiha, T., Kämäräinen, T., Siekkinen, M., Ylä-Jääski, A., Hui, P.: Exploring vision-based techniques for outdoor positioning systems: a feasibility study. IEEE Trans. Mob. Comput. (2017)
27. Song, M., Ou, Z., E, H., Song, J., Zhao, X.: Vision-based positioning system. J. Chin. Univ. Posts Telecommun. **23**(5), 88–96 (2016)
28. Theano (2017). http://deeplearning.net/software/theano/. Accessed 13 Apr 2017
29. Tian, Y., Luo, P., Wang, X., Tang, X.: Deep learning strong parts for pedestrian detection. In: Proceedings of the IEEE International Conference on Computer Vision, pp. 1904–1912 (2015)
30. Tian, Y., Luo, P., Wang, X., Tang, X.: Pedestrian detection aided by deep learning semantic tasks. In: Proceedings of the IEEE Conference on Computer Vision and Pattern Recognition, pp. 5079–5087 (2015)
31. Torch (2017). http://torch.ch/. Accessed 13 Apr 2017
32. Uijlings, J.R., Van De Sande, K.E., Gevers, T., Smeulders, A.W.: Selective search for object recognition. Int. J. Comput. Vis. **104**(2), 154–171 (2013)
33. Wang, L., Lu, Y., Wang, H., Zheng, Y., Ye, H., Xue, X.: Evolving boxes for fast vehicle detection. arXiv preprint arXiv:1702.00254 (2017)
34. Wang, X., Gupta, A.: Unsupervised learning of visual representations using videos. In: Proceedings of the IEEE International Conference on Computer Vision, pp. 2794–2802 (2015)
35. Zhang, L., Lin, L., Liang, X., He, K.: Is Faster R-CNN doing well for pedestrian detection? In: Leibe, B., Matas, J., Sebe, N., Welling, M. (eds.) ECCV 2016. LNCS, vol. 9906, pp. 443–457. Springer, Cham (2016). doi:10.1007/978-3-319-46475-6_28
36. Zhou, Y., Liu, L., Shao, L., Mellor, M.: DAVE: a unified framework for fast vehicle detection and annotation. In: Leibe, B., Matas, J., Sebe, N., Welling, M. (eds.) ECCV 2016. LNCS, vol. 9906, pp. 278–293. Springer, Cham (2016). doi:10.1007/978-3-319-46475-6_18
37. Zhu, Z., Liang, D., Zhang, S., Huang, X., Li, B., Hu, S.: Traffic-sign detection and classification in the wild. In: Proceedings of the IEEE Conference on Computer Vision and Pattern Recognition, pp. 2110–2118 (2016)

Research and Implementation of Question Classification Model in Q&A System

Haihong E[✉], Yingxi Hu, Meina Song, Zhonghong Ou, and Xinrui Wang

Beijing University of Posts and Telecommunications, Beijing 100876, China
{ehaihong,mnsong,zhonghong.ou}@bupt.edu.cn,
huyingxi.cn@gmail.com, w19941025110@gmail.com

Abstract. Question classification is the core of the question-and-answer (Q&A) sys-tem. This paper intends to use the method of deep learning to explore the ques-tion classification model in Q&A systems, the aim of which is to improve the accu-racy of question classification.

The characteristics of natural language questions, such as the use of short texts and basic grammar, were well considered. Subsequently, we want to fully extract the features of questions by using the following methods: multi-channel inputs, multi-granularity convolution kernels, and direct connection with high-speed channels. By combining the three methods, this paper proposes the multi-channel and Bidirec-tional long-and short-term memory and multi- granularity convolution neural net-work (MC–BLSTM–MGCNN) model to fully extract the features from interrogative sentences, both in time and spatial domains.

To verify the validity of the model, this paper experimented with the TREC [1] classification standard dataset. Results achieved 96.6% accuracy, which is superior to the highest existing industry benchmark (96.1%). In addition, this paper used the complete TREC dataset to innovate further, and results obtained 98% accuracy, which greatly improved the classification.

Keywords: Q&A system · Question classification · Deep learning · Convolution neural network · Long- and short-term memory network

1 Introduction

The Q&A system is currently a popular research topic in the field of natural language processing. A Q&A system is divided into three parts: problem analysis, information retrieval, and answer extraction. Problem analysis highlights the importance of problem classification, as its performance will directly affect the accuracy of subsequent answer-extraction protocols. Question classification is highly significant to the Q&A system based on these two aspects: (1) reduced candidate choice of space and (2) for different types of questions, a follow-up process implies different strategies. Therefore, an intelligent Q&A system requires a highly accurate question classification model.

Early models on question classification adopted the rule-based matching method [2–6], which requires the manual development and establishment of multiple rules. In recent years, methods on question classification mainly aimed at formulating lexical, syntactic, semantic,

© Springer International Publishing AG 2017
S. Ibrahim et al. (Eds.): ICA3PP 2017, LNCS 10393, pp. 372–384, 2017.
DOI: 10.1007/978-3-319-65482-9_25

and related extraction strategies, after which machine learning methods are employed to classify a problem. However, in this method, the accuracy of the results depended on the characteristics and quality of extraction; that is, the richer the characteristics being extracted, the higher the classification accuracy. Consequently, scholars have adopted deep learning [7–18]. The deep learning model adopts the recurrence neural network (RNN) and convolution neural network (CNN) for question classification. RNN is widely used in the field of natural language processing. Meanwhile, CNN is increasingly being applied to natural language processing because of its outstanding performance in image processing. CNN can also extract information in spatial domain, and many experiments have verified the contribution of CNN to natural language processing.

Nonetheless, existing models on question classification are still constrained by low accuracy, so this paper intends to use the method of deep learning to explore the question classification model in Q&A systems, the aim of which is to improve the accuracy of question classification.

2   Related Work

The goal of question classification is to assign a category label to each natural language question to represent the type of final answer desired by the question. A text search conference in 1999 led to the evaluation of automatic Q&A systems. Subsequently, an increasing number of scholars have contributed to the field of question classification. Accordingly, several scholars have conducted considerable research on problem classification.

Question classification is divided into two categories: (1) traditional question classification; (2) question classification based on deep learning. Regardless of the categories, most studies use the TREC standard question classification dataset, which will be described in Sect. 4.1.

This section introduces the present application of the two aforementioned question classification categories.

2.1   Traditional Question Classification Methods

Zhang et al. [2] extracted the characteristics of word frequency and part of speech, and classified the problem by improving the Bayesian model. Based on the basic characteristics of word frequency, Wen et al. [3] used syntactic structures to extract main words and questions, such that words and their subsidiary components are classified according to their characteristics. Sun et al. [4] used the knowledge network as a semantic resource to extract classification characteristics. Silva et al. [5] used feature combinations to classify the problem using linear kernels (i.e., linear SVM). Li et al. [6] proposed to combine parts of speech and bag-of-words to the syntactic-dependent tree method to calculate the value of kernel functions and explore the structure of the question. The abovementioned methods mainly express a question in terms of its characteristics. Combining the characteristics—although it may lead to subjectivity—and accommodation of language diversity can make the proposed question classification model more accurate compared with feature extraction method, but this endeavor is more expensive.

Traditional machine-learning process uses fixed-length data, that is, in the length of the interrogative sentence, should be fixed, otherwise it will lead to loss of information, and this type of research method does not consider the data field information (i.e., classifier), as any dissonance will lead to performance degradation. Feature extraction in the machine-learning model also requires manual extraction. Human error is rather expected; hence, this method is costly in terms of human and material resources.

2.2 Deep Learning Question Classification Methods

Sauer et al. [7] used the improved recursive automatic coding model to deal with problems on semantic synthesis and emotional analysis. Cui et al. [8] explored the depth of neural networks to learn the thematic expressions of statistical machine-translation disambiguation. Nal et al. [9] explored sentence structures and proposed dynamic CNN for semantic sentence modeling. Li et al. [10] used multi-column CNN method to deal with knowledge-based Q&A system problems. Zhang et al. [11] used the convolution depth belief network to study the vocabulary characteristics and sentence levels of the relation classification of words-between-words. For the classification of questions, the present study uses deep learning to acquire the initiative to learn the syntactic and semantic features implied in a sentence [12] and deploy deep analysis of the problem structure. Irosy et al. [13] proposed the DRNN model to achieve temporal and structural deep reproduction. Lei et al. [14] proposed a neural network based on tensor products for question classification to fuse nonlinear characteristics. Iyyer et al. [15] proposed a question classification model based on the syntactic-independent deep-average network for the embedding layers, considering that syntactic functions require additional training time and is costlier in terms of computational resources compared with using the disordered combinatorial function. Tai et al. [16] proposed the tree–LSTM question classification model based on the syntactic nature of combined words and phrases. Li et al. [17] proposed a model to combine the CNN and LSTM networks, considering that CNN can better tap stylistic features while LSTM can better represent the semantic meaning of word sequences. Moreover, Fang et al. [18] compared the performance of CNN with multiple LSTM and multi-convolution kernels for problem classification; their findings showed that CNN and bidirectional LSTM (BLSTM) achieved the best performance.

In summary, studies on classification using the deep learning method mainly focused on improving and integrating CNN and cyclic neural networks. Previous studies also focused on the features of text sequence, nonlinear extraction, and grammatical structures. However, results from previous works are only applicable for sentence-level or text-level classification tasks, and these can limit short-text question classification in the Q&A scenes. The aforementioned models were also independent and did not combine scene and model features that could filter and integrate multiple models. Previous models could still be improved.

In this paper, the short-text questioning classification task in Q&A system is modeled, and the characteristics of multiple models are integrated to improve the classification accuracy.

3 MC-BLSTM-MGCNN Neural Network Question Classification Model

In this chapter, we introduce the MC–BLSTM–MGCNN model. Short texts and grammars may be missing in the questions of the Q&A system. Hence, this paper adopts multi-channel input, multi-granularity convolution, and high-speed channel direct connection to anticipate these missing elements. Neural network and CNN are combined to extract and characterize the features by their time and spatial dimensions. The model can then be explored in terms of characteristics and structure.

3.1 Characteristics

Multi-channel Input. Traditional neural networks use the single-channel word-embedding layer as input, which can be divided as trained embedding layer and non-trained embedding layer. The first training embedding layer is modified during model training to better express scene semantics. However, at present, we cannot quantitatively analyze the performance of this change. The change may also encounter excessive modification and cause larger semantic deviations. Furthermore, the single-embedding layer in the random discarding layer could lose most of its value, thereby affecting subsequent calculation. The second non-trained embedding layer directly uses the trained word vector as input. In the process of model training, the embedding layer is not optimized automatically by the input data, and thus, it is not fully adapted to the task scene. Similarly, the single-embedding layer (i.e., through the discarding layer) could further lose information, and this could also affect subsequent calculation.

In this paper, we use the dual-channel embedding layer as input. The embedding layer may or may not be a trained parameter to balance the original semantic information and dynamically modify semantic information.

Multi-granularity Convolution. Most traditional models use a single granularity convolution kernel where only the feature extraction of the sentence information is carried out on a single granularity; however, this brings problems if the feature extraction of the question is insufficient. Considering the short-text characteristic of a natural language question, information needs to be fully excavated by the user input (i.e., in short text) to obtain accurate semantics. Therefore, this paper intends to use the multi-granularity convolution kernel to extract multi-range features. The approach also combines the characteristics of time-dimension information to the output of long- and short-term memory (i.e., BLSTM) network to extract the range of related information. The feature of different time range is extracted, and the question information is extracted completely in its space and time dimension.

High-Speed Way. In the neural network, the random discarding layer and the pooling layer are added for model performance, and the features are abstracted gradually. This task is required by the extraction characteristics and data dimensionality to prevent over-fitting in the model. However, layer integration can also cause some loss of information (original data). In the case of short texts, the full use of original information becomes particularly important. Therefore, this paper adds high-speed channel to achieve the following: first, the original embedding-layer information is directly connected to the BLSTM output, and second, the same layer is added as input to the CNN layer, but without affecting the embedding-layer output to prevent over-fitting. Hence, the full use of original information is ensured, and information loss is reduced (Fig. 1).

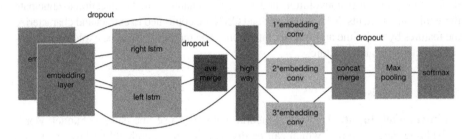

Fig. 1. The architecture of MC-BLSTM-MGCNN model

3.2 Architecture

Multi-channel Input. In this paper, we use the dual-channel embedding layers as the input of the subsequent network (i.e., BLSTM). By setting the embedding layer to dual channel, we can increase the weight of the embedding layer in the high-speed channel layer. At the same time, by changing the parameter value, the model can be trained. Equilibrium dynamic change and primitive word vector representation of the semantic information can further control the optimization model.

BLSTM. The key to the RNN model lies in the connection of the previous information to the current task. LSTM, a type of RNN, can learn long-term dependency information. In a given input sequence, the LSTM unit is in chronological order and generally includes the following steps: decision to discard the information (Eq. 1) for the output between the value of zero and one; updating of information (Eqs. 2 and 3); updating of hidden state (Eq. 4); and output information (Eqs. 5 and 6).

$$f_t = \sigma\left(W_f \cdot \left[h_{t-1}, x_t\right] + b_f\right) \tag{1}$$

$$i_t = \sigma\left(W_i \cdot \left[h_{t-1}, x_t\right] + b_i\right) \tag{2}$$

$$\tilde{C}_t = tanh\left(W_c \cdot \left[h_{t-1}, x_t\right] + b_c\right) \tag{3}$$

$$C_t = f_t * C_{t-1} + i_t * \tilde{C}_t \tag{4}$$

$$O_t = \sigma\left(W_o\left[h_{t-1}, x_t\right] + b_o\right) \tag{5}$$

$$h_t = o_t * tanh\left(C_t\right) \tag{6}$$

Taking into account the continuity of the natural language problem, this paper models the questionnaires in their time dimension using the two LSTM networks, and then adds the user questions into the two networks (i.e., one is in the forward direction, the other is in the reverse time order). To complete the text information, we obtain the output of all hidden nodes at each point in time in the LSTM network and connect them for averaging. Equation 7 shows that the output of the hidden nodes is in the forward direction of t, indicating the output of the hidden nodes in the reverse direction of t, and the average output of each node at the same time node forms a two-dimensional tensor (i.e., input of subsequent network).

$$h_t = \frac{\overrightarrow{h_t} + \overleftarrow{h_t}}{2} \tag{7}$$

Multi-granularity. The input of the convolution layer is considered as the two-dimensional tensor output of the BLSTM network that contains time-dimension and hidden-node information at each time point. Hence, the short-text version of the question refers to the particle size of the two-dimensional tensor for different ranges of convolution (i.e., text extraction features). The volume of the convolution kernel in this paper is different from those in image processing tasks, as the lengths of convolution kernels are usually consistent with word vector dimensions. To confirm the optimal value, this paper experimented with convolution kernel size and convolution kernel category. Experimental results showed consistency in convolution kernel length and word vector. Convolution kernel width is set to three to achieve the best classification accuracy. Subsequently, this paper selected a single-granularity convolution kernel with the following sizes: (1, embedding dims), (2, embedding dims), and (3, embedding dims).

Maximum Pooling. Compression extraction is adopted to simplify the calculation of the feature graph and the computational complexity of the network. The model also adopted the commonly used two-dimensional maximum pooling operation. Compared with other pooling operations, maximum pooling provides better robustness. Maximum pooling also integrates feature points in a small neighborhood of tensors to obtain new features. More particularly, in a two-dimensional pool, the pooling operation will be applied to various places of tensor (Eq. 8).

$$P_{i,j} = down\left(O_{i:i+P_1,\, j:j+P_2}\right) \tag{8}$$

This approach represents the specific and simultaneous operation of the two-dimensional pool. The pooled output is shown in Eq. 9.

$$h^* = \left[P_{1,1},\, P_{1,1+p_2},\, \cdots,\, P_{\left(1+\left\lfloor 1-k+\frac{1}{P_1}-1\right\rfloor \cdot p_1\right),\, 1 + \left(d^w - d + 1/p_2 - 1\right)\cdot p_2} \right] \tag{9}$$

Softmax. The last layer of this model is the softmax layer (Eqs. 10 and 11), which uses the output of the hidden layer as input to predict the problem category to which the S-question belongs. The classifier performs probability analysis on the question and determines the matching degree of each category. Outputs with the highest probability are inputted to the final prediction category.

This paper also uses categorical cross-entropy for the loss function (Eq. 12), where m is the number of classification types, as defined in the L2 regularization of ultra-parameters. The model is further optimized by the Adadelta objective function.

$$\hat{p}(y|s) = softmax\left(W^{(s)}h^* + b^{(s)}\right) \tag{10}$$

$$\hat{y} = arg\ \max_{y} \hat{p}(y|s) \tag{11}$$

$$J(\theta) = -\frac{1}{m}\sum_{i=1}^{m} t_i log(y_i) + \sigma\|\theta\|_F^2 \tag{12}$$

4   Experiment

4.1   Dataset

The present study uses the standard question classification dataset in the academic community, particularly the TREC dataset (Li and Roth 2002) [1]. Hence, this paper intends to make experiment with this dataset for comparing with existing models.

The dataset divides the question into six categories (abbreviations, descriptions, entities, people, locations, and numbers) and classified by training sets and test sets (Table 1). The training set consists of five text documents, while the testing set contains one text document. To the best of our knowledge, most scholars train models by using only the fifth TREC document [9, 11–14], and none of the studies in the literature review show the effect of the model using the complete training set. Therefore, this paper divides the dataset into standard and complete datasets: (1) Standard datasets, including 5,432 training sets and 500 test sets. (2) Complete dataset, including 15,432 training set and 500 test sets.

Table 1. Files in TREC dataset.

	Number	Standard dataset	Complete dataset
Train file			
Train file 1	1000		√
Train file 2	2000		√
Train file 3	3000		√
Train file 4	4000		√
Train file 5	5432	√	√
Test file			
Test file	500	√	√

Both standard and complete training sets were used for the experiment. At the outset, it is easy to compare and verify the validity of the present model with existing models. Therefore, the training set was expanded to improve model accuracy and model performance.

4.2   Environment

The hardware support for this experiment comes from the NVIDIA GPU – GTX1080, and we use python programming language to achieve our model with the Tensorflow deep learning framework.

4.3   Word Vector

Word2vec is a word-vector training tool launched by Google in 2013. The software is based on a given corpus, and the optimized training model can quickly and effectively express a word in its vector form. Its word vector library contains a large number of datasets for training use, and the software continues to form complete words for scholars. Thus, this article uses Google's Word2vec for the word vector library of the proposed model.

4.4   Hyper-parameter Setting

In this paper, 10% of the training set was selected as the verification set, while the remaining 90% was used as is (i.e., training set). Model parameters were optimized according to the accuracy of the verification set. The model effect was verified according to the accuracy of the test set. The settings for selecting the optimal super parameters are shown in Table 2.

Table 2.   Optimal settings of hyper-parameter

Hyper parameter	Hyper parameter setting
Batch size	32
Word vector dimension	300
Number of Embedding layer	2
Embedding layer trainable	Both false
MaxPooling of embedding layer	0.5
Number of hidden units in BLSTM layer	300
MaxPooling of BLSTM	0.2
Optimizer	Adadelta
L2 regularizer	0.02
MaxPooling in dense layer	0.4

4.5   Experiment Result

Result. In this paper, we use the common TREC dataset to test model validity. Table 3 compares the accuracy of existing models with those for the proposed model. The model achieved 96.6% accuracy for the TREC standard dataset, which implies that the model in the present study is superior to the existing model in terms of accuracy.

Table 3. Compares the accuracy of existing models with those for the proposed model

Network	Model	TREC accuracy (%)
CNN	DCNN (2014) [19]	93.0
	CNN-non-static (2014) [20]	93.6
	CNN-MC (2014) [20]	92
	TBCNN (2015) [21]	96
	CNN-Ana (2015) [22]	91.37
RNN	BLSTM (2016) [23]	93
	BSLTM-Att (2016) [23]	93.8
	BLSTM-2DPooling (2016) [23]	94.8
Others	Combine-skip (2015) [24]	92.2
	AdaSent (2015) [25]	92.4
	C-LSTM (2015) [26]	94.6
	DSCNN (2016) [27]	95.4
	BLSTM-2DCNN (2016) [23]	96.1
Our	MC-BLSTM-MSCNN	**96.6**

Effect of Embedding Layers. To explore the effect of word-embedding layers on the model, this paper experimented with single-, double-layer, trained-, and non-trained embedding layers (Table 4). When the embedding layer is set to non-trainable, results are generally better for training. More specifically, the best effect is achieved with dual non-trainable embedding layers.

Table 4. Compares the accuracy of different embedding layers

Embedding layer	Single-	Double-(both not-trainable)	Double-
Trainable	95.6%	96%	96%
Not-trainable	96.2%		96.6%

Effect of Convolution Kernel Number. To explore the effect of the number of convolution on the model, the number of convolution was set to 1, 2, 3, and 4. Figure 2 shows that the best results were achieved when convolution number was set to 3.

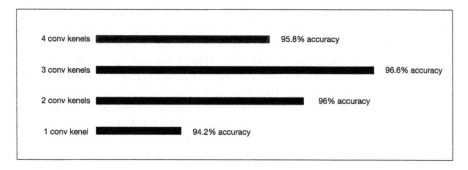

Fig. 2. Compares the accuracy of different number of kernels

Effect of Highway. To explore the effect of high-speed channel on the model, high-speed channels were used to integrate the double-embedding layer and bi-directional LSTM output, and the output to the convolution layer. The model directly forwards the bi-directional LSTM output as the input of the convolution layer. The accuracy of the model, which is without high-speed way is 90.8, and the accuracy of the high-speed way is 96.6%, which is higher than the accuracy of model without high-speed way.

Effect of Training Set Size. Both standard and complete TREC datasets were used to verify the performance of the model. The standard dataset can be used to experiment and compare with the existing model to show the effectiveness of the model. Moreover, the complete dataset can be used to experiment with the standard dataset of this comparison and effectively explain the observation that the larger training dataset of the model leads to better effects which accuracy is up to 98%. Experimental results further show that using the complete dataset, the proposed model can be better trained for accuracy and performance, unlike the existing model that uses the standard dataset.

4.6 Discussion

In the prior research, the most competitive works are TBCNN [22] and BLSTM-2DCNN [24]. TBCNN model only uses CNN to achieve a very good accuracy, the model splits the word embedding layer into different region sizes, each of which has two filters. And the max pooling is performed over the generated feature maps which finally send into the softmax layer. And the BLSTM+2DCNN model stacks the LSTM layer over the convolution layer, which can fuse the time information and spatial information at the same time, and the experiment shows that the model is better than the former in terms of accuracy. However, the previous work about this question do not make use of the short text information well. And the model in our paper can increase the accuracy by adding the multi-granularity convolution kernel, multi-channel input and high-speed way, which has a high signification to improve the understanding of other short-text problems.

An analysis of the experimental results showed that independent models could not fully exploit information in short text for natural language processing, hence the need to integrate various models and features. Information loss should also be minimized. Natural language processing can use both BLSTM and CNN networks, as the aim should be to better integrate two information and improve model performance. BLTSM networks can extract features in space–time domain. CNN networks can extract information in spatial domain and superimpose this onto network order and convolution kernel size. However, CNN texts must have the same length as the BLSTM output in order for the information of the time dimension to be entered into spatial dimension for further abstraction. A high-speed channel direct-connection module is also required by short texts for maximum use of information; it also does not compromise model performance with over-fitting. To the best of our knowledge, several scholars have used the standard dataset to train models. By contrast, the innovative method presented by the current study uses both standard and complete datasets (i.e., the former is used for comparison with existing model; the latter is used to quantitatively show the effect of dataset size on the model performance). Multiple datasets further improve model accuracy and provide additional reference for future research and model construction.

5   Conclusion

Many natural language processing tasks can be attributed to text classification, and question classification as a text classification is being studied extensively. This paper focuses on the application of depth learning to the question classification model. To overcome some challenges (i.e., lack of short text and grammar of user questions), this paper proposes a model by adopting the LSTM neural network for (1) single- or dual-channel input, (2) single or multi-granularity convolution kernel, and (3) with or without high-speed channel. Direct analysis and other factors on the use of control variable method for a number of experiments and the optimal model and its parameter settings were explored. Finally, the experimental results show that the accuracy of this method is 96.6%, which is better than the existing best model. The method in the present study also does not need to develop cumbersome characteristic rules. However, the results of this paper is not sufficient to optimize the parameters, such as no test, convolution, and whole connection layers.

References

1. Li, X., Roth, D.: Learning question classifiers. In: Proceedings of the 19th International Conference on Computational Linguistics, vol. 1, pp. 1–7. Association for Computational Linguistics (2002)
2. Zhang, Y., Liu, T., et al.: Modified Bayesian model based question classification. J. Chin. Inf. Process. **19**(2), 100–105 (2005). (in Chinese)
3. Wen, X., Zhang, Y., et al.: Syntactic structure parsing based chinese question classification. J. Chin. Inf. Process. **20**(2), 33–39 (2006)

4. Sun, J.G., Cai, D.F., et al.: How Net based Chinese question automatic classification. J. Chin. Inf. Process. **21**(1), 90–95 (2007). (in Chinese)

5. Silva, J., Coheur, L., et al.: From symbolic to sub-symbolic information in question classification. Artif. Intell. Rev. **35**(2), 137–154 (2011)

6. Liu, L., Yu, Z., et al.: Chinese question classification based on question property kernel. J. Mach. Learn. Cybern. **5**(5), 713–720 (2014)

7. Socher, R., Pennington, J., et al.: Semi-supervised recursive auto encoders for predicting sentiment distributions. In: Proceedings of the Empirical Methods in Natural Language Conference, pp. 151–161. Association for Computational Linguistics (2011)

8. Cui, L., Zhang, D., et al.: Learning topic representation for SMT with neural networks. In: Proceedings of the 52nd Annual Meeting, pp. 133–143. Association for Computational Linguistics (2014)

9. Blunsom, P., Grefenstette, E., et al.: A convolutional neural network for modelling sentences. In: Proceedings of the 52nd Annual Meeting, pp. 655–665. Association for Computational Linguistics (2014)

10. Dong, L., Wei, F., et al.: Question answering over freebase with multi-column convolutional neural networks. In: Proceedings of the 53rd Annual Meeting of the Association for Computational Linguistics and the 7th International Joint Conference on Natural Language Processing, pp. 260–269 (2015)

11. Zhang, D., Wang, D.: Relation classification via recurrent neural network. J. Comput. Sci. Process. (2015)

12. Kim, Y.: Convolutional neural networks for sentence classification. In: Proceedings of the Empirical Methods in Natural Language, pp. 1746–1751 (2014)

13. Irsoy, O., Cardie, C.: Deep recursive neural networks for compositionality in language. J. Adv. Neural Inf. Process. Syst. 2096–2104 (2014)

14. Lei, T., Barzilay, R., et al.: Molding CNNs for text: non-linear, non-consecutive convolutions. J. Indiana Univ. Math. Process. **58**(3), 1151–1186 (2015)

15. Iyyer, M., Manjunatha, V., et al.: Deep unordered composition rivals syntactic methods for text classification. In: Proceedings of the Annual Meeting of the Association for Computational Linguistics (2015)

16. Tai, K.S., Socher, R., et al.: Improved semantic representations from tree-structured long short-term memory networks. In: Proceedings of the Annual Meeting of the Association for Computational Linguistics (2015)

17. Graves, A.: Generating sequences with recurrent neural networks. J. Comput. Sci. (2014)

18. Fang, I.-T.: Deep learning for query semantic domains classification (2016). http://cs224d.standford.edu/reports_2016.html

19. Kalchbrenner, N., Grefenstette, E., et al.: A convolutional neural network for modelling sentences. arXiv preprint arXiv:1404.2188 (2014)

20. Kim, Y.: Convolutional neural networks for sentence classification. arXiv preprint arXiv:1408.5882 (2014)

21. Mou, L., Peng, H., et al.: Discriminative neural sentence modeling by tree-based convolution. arXiv preprint arXiv:1504.01106 (2015)

22. Zhang, Y., Wallace, B.: A sensitivity analysis of convolutional neural networks for sentence classification. arXiv preprint arXiv:1510.03820 (2015)

23. Zhou, P., Qi, Z.Y., et al.: Text classification improved by integrating bidirectional LSTM with two-dimensional max pooling. arXiv preprint arXiv:1611.06639 (2016)

24. Kiros, R., Zhu, Y.K., et al.: Skip-thought vectors. In: Advances in Neural Information Processing Systems, pp. 3295–3302 (2015)

25. Zhao, H., Lu, Z.D., et al.: Self-adaptive hierarchical sentence model. arXiv preprint arXiv: 1504.05070 (2015)
26. Zhou, C., Sum, C., et al.: A C-LSTM neural network for text classification. J. Comput. Sci. 1(4), 39–44 (2015)
27. Zhang, R., Lee, H., et al.: Dependency sensitive convolutional neural networks for modeling sentences and documents. In: Proceedings of NAACL-HLT, pp. 1512–1521 (2016)

The 4th International Workshop on Data, Text, Web, and Social Network Mining (DTWSM 2017)

An Android Malware Detection System Based on Behavior Comparison Analysis

Jing Tao[✉], Yan Zhang, Pengfei Cao, Zheng Wang, and Qiqi Zhao

Ministry of Education Key Lab for Intelligent Networks and Network Security,
Xi'an Jiaotong University, Xi'an 710049, China
jtao@mail.xjtu.edu.cn

Abstract. At present, Android malwares become more and more subtle and intelligent, after their invasion, they often detect whether the running environment is a real environment, to decide whether to perform their malicious behavior. Therefore, malware tend to execute different behavior when running in different environments. Benign applications will perform the same functions in different environments, their behaviors have a strong consistency. Based on this basic idea, we design an Android malware detection method based on behavior comparison analysis. First, design and development a number of specific different running environments, and then execute application in these environments. With the same event input, record and compare the behaviors of this application, calculate the difference, determine whether it is malicious. Under the guidance of this thought, we design and development the Android malware detection system EmuProtect. We evaluate EmuProtect system from the aspects of accuracy and validity, the results show that this system can effectively detect Android malicious applications.

Keywords: Android malware detection · Android application behavior model · Behavior analysis

1 Introduction

In recent years, with the rapid development of mobile smart devices, mobile devices such as smart phones and tablet computers are increasingly involved in all aspects of people's daily life. According to the survey results of Kantar Worldpanel ComTech, as of the first quarter of 2016, the market share of Android operation system in US, Europe and china have been a significant growth compared to the same period last year.

As the Android system has the characteristics of openness and the huge number of users, it has become more and more malicious code author's main target. Apps can gather environment information while running process, similarly, malware can change their behaviors according to the change of external running environment. Such as checking the IMEI (International Mobile Equipment Identification) of the device, if the IMEI of the current device is found to be the same as the preset value in the emulator, the malicious behavior is not executed and thus the detection is evaded.

With the improvement of malicious application developers' anti-detection awareness, malware will become more intelligent and more hidden, according to the operating

S. Ibrahim et al. (Eds.): ICA3PP 2017, LNCS 10393, pp. 387–396, 2017.
DOI: 10.1007/978-3-319-65482-9_26

environment feature automatically change and hide their behavior. There is an urgent need for a detection method for malicious applications whose behavior changes with the environment, and can effectively detect various behaviors of malicious applications.

In response to the above questions, this paper designs an abstract model for analyzing the behavior of Android applications to support the analysis of application behavior. On this basis, we proposed a malware detection method using comparative analysis of application behavior in different operating environments. With this method, the EmuProtect system is designed and implemented.

We have proved that this method can generate different operating environment, capture the difference of the behavior of the app in different environments, and effectively determine the malicious app.

Our work makes the following contributions:

We design an abstract model to analyze the behavior of Android applications. This abstract model supports the comparative analysis of application behavior.

We propose a method of judging the consistency of application behavior. By comparing the behavioral differences between applications in different operating environments, this method can analyze the consistency of application behavior under different operating environments. On this basis, determine the malicious nature of the malware.

We prove the validity and accuracy of the proposed method. After a series of experiments, we proved the effectiveness of the method.

2   Related Works

Based on the research of attacker's point view, Boris [1] proposed a variety of methods to detect the underlying APIs of the operating environment, such as the communication channel of VMWare tools. Raffetseder [2] found a series methods to detect system emulator, their approach si to take advantage of various features of the emulation runtime framework, such as the limitations of simulating CPU execution, instruction length limitations, and runtime relative performance comparisons. Paleari et al. [3] proposed a method for automating the generation of special code segments which, when run, can produce different results depending on the operating environment, thereby enabling the identification of the current environment. Timothy [4] introduced a series emulation environment detection methods specifically for Android, which can find the characteristics of emulation environment, such as checking return values of the system APIs, static fields and analyzing runtime performance. Petsas [11] systematically classified methods for detecting emulated operating environments and selected some of the typical features to test some of the publicly available malware detection tools, found that the vast majority of analyze tools [7, 8, 12, 13] did not attach enough importance to the confrontation of environment detection. Timing [5] design a method to automatically generate static characteristics for Android to distinguish the emulation environment, these features are mainly specific content of system files, system APIs and system properties.

3   Background and Thread Model

This section begins with an introduction to the background knowledge of the operating environment detection of Android platform, and then presents the threat model that is being addressed in this study.

Traditional operation system such as Windows and Linux are user-centric, believe that the user is not credible, mostly thinking isolation between resources of different users. Android defaults assume that the application is not credible, which means that expect system applications, other applications that user installed are not credible. Under such constraints, if an application attempts to determine whether it is running in an emulated environment, only a limited amount of information can be obtained from the exterior of isolation sandbox can be used by it. In order to avoid detection of malware detection system, malware will check some environment features which are easy to implement and effective.

As shown in Fig. 1, applications can check the value of Build.BORAD static variable with only one line Java code, if it is equal to the default value of Android emulator.

```
public static boolean isEmulator()
{
  return (Build.MODEL.equalsIgnoreCase("sdk")) ||
         (Build.MODEL.equalsIgnoreCase("google_sdk"));
}
```

Fig. 1. A method to check operating environment.

According to what has been discussed above, we set the threat model in this paper as Android malware that can analyze the information of operating environment to perform different behavior in different environment.

4   Android Application Behavior Model

Android is an event-based response system, in which the behavior of an application's entire lifecycle can be viewed as a series of responses to various events occurring in the system. Which means that the Android application itself is a response system of exterior operating environment.

This feature of Android applications can abstract its behavior model as follows:

An Android application P runs in the environment E and given the input event I, then the set of behavior it displays in the process of running is BP. That is, application P runs in environemtn Ei and Ej with same input event I, the sets of behaviors if Bp(Ei, I) and BP(Ej, I).

All the behavior in the behavior set BP that the application exhibits, can be divided into three categories according to conditions of occurrence, the sensitive behavior α influenced by the external environment, the non-sensitive behavior β influenced by the external environment and the behavior γ that not influenced by the external environment. The behavior of application can be redefined to the following form:

$$Bp(E, I) = \alpha(E, I) + \beta(E, I) + \gamma(E, I) \tag{1}$$

The behavior contained in $\alpha(E, I)$ is the sensitive behavior that hides or occurs that changes in the operating environment, such as making a phone call, sending messages, reading privacy data, etc. The behavior contained in $\beta(E, I)$ is the non-sensitive behavior that is hidden as the environment changes, such as file operation, accessing to system information. The behavior contained in $\gamma(E, I)$ is all behavior independent of the operating environment. These behavior is only affected by the input events and do not change regardless of the operating environment.

5 EmuProtect Detection System

This paper presents a new malicious code detection method, that is, by changing the operating environment features to generate different environment, then run applications in these different operating environment with same input events, analyze the difference between each behaviors in different environment, and thus determine the malicious. In this method, we design and development the Android malware detection system EmuProtect.

EmuProtect system architecture shown in Fig. 2, mainly composed of five modules.

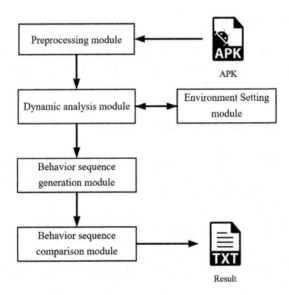

Fig. 2. EmuProtect detection system architecture.

6   System Implementation

6.1   Dynamic Analysis and Application Behavior Triggering Technique

EmuProtect system dynamic analysis module uses sandbox technology to analyze Android application.

The most sensitive behavior of malware is triggered by registering a broadcast receiver that receives specific system events in the system, and these system events are able to reflect the system status, with a certain regularity, such as the system boot complete broadcast, the user interactive broadcast, network status change broadcast, etc. Therefore, after the emulator is booted, application is installed and the operating environment features are set, the detection system need to start the application and input a series of system events to trigger the application's response behavior.

Because the malware can start a service, which runs in the background and execute sensitive behavior secretly, and will not start an activity in the foreground, the behavior trigger method cannot rely entirely on the UI trigger technology to achieve goals. Most of the system events that trigger application behavior are related to user behavior, as shown in Table 1.

Table 1.   Trigger event content.

Event name	Broadcast name or telnet command	Content
tBootComplete	BOOT_COMPLETED	System boot complete
tLockScreen	SCREEN_OFF	Screen lock
tUnLock	USER_PRESENT	Screen unlock
tReceiveSMS	sms send	Receive SMS
tSendSMS	SENDTO	Send SMS
tCall	CALL	Dial call
tACCall	gsm call/accept	Receive call
tLocatioin	geo fix	Geographical change

6.2   Operating Environment Feature Setting Technique

In the case of the emulator's default settings, the features of emulation environment are static and obvious regularity, so if the features are not disguised, the application can obtain the information and compare it with some known values in order to determine whether it is running in an emulation environment.

According to the treat model set in this paper, the features that can be used to determine operating environment can be divided into three levels: the Android framework layer, the Linux kernel layer and the emulator environment layer. The main features in each layer are shown in Table 2.

Table 2. Java layer emulation environment detection methods

Method level	Feature class
Android framework level	Device status information/device hardware information/ system properties/simulation event/ ...
Linux kernel level	Hardware driver/device profile/shell property command
Emulator level	CPU info

Dynamic analysis module runs the application for the first and second round in default emulator environment without any camouflage, the third round in the environment that set the features of the Android framework layer, the fourth in the environment that set the features of the Linux kernel layer, the fifth in the environment that set the features of the emulator environment layer, and the sixth round in the environment that set all of the features of the three layers.

The ability to dynamically modify all of the features of the camouflage is based on the modification of Android source code.

6.3   Behavior Record Generation and Comparison Technique

When an application is running in an operating environment, the external input events will lead to the corresponding response of it. These behavior can be recorded by generating its system API call sequence during the application is running. All the recording information output in the Android log system, the module filter and extract these records with logcat tool, and then save it in file.

When comparing two behavior records obtained by an application in different operating environment, the behavior record comparison module calculates the similarity of the system API call sequences between the corresponding threads in two records according to the thread numbers. Here we use the edit distance between records to measure the similarity between them, get a real number between 0 to 1 as a measure of similarity, the greater the similarity, the more similar of the two records. After calculating the similarity between each thread pair, according to the proportion of the API call sequence of each thread in the whole behavior record, these individual similarities are summed up as an overall similarity C.

Other behavior records are calculated similarity with the two reference objects, the average of the two similarity is the final similarity C' of each round. If the ratio of C' to C0 is less than a threshold t, that is

$$C'/C0 < t \tag{2}$$

It is considered that there is a difference between the behavior of this round and the reference objects in the original environment. By adjusting the threshold t, we can adjust the discrimination of this detection system.

After processing the records in last four rounds of an application as above, we can determine whether or not there is some difference between these records and the reference objects. And combined with the behavior classification statistics result S, determine whether the application has hidden sensitive behavior.

7   Evaluation

Three experiments were conducted to evaluate the effectiveness of the EmuProtect detection system.

In each experiment, we ran each of the application to detected in six rounds, recording their behavior information in every operating systems as described in the previous chapter. The effectiveness of the EmuProtect system was evaluated by analyzing the results of the detection results of different types of applications in three experiments.

7.1   Experiment I

To compare the behavior exhibited by an application when it is run in different environments, the input system events need to be consistent. Because if there is a difference in the input information, that will inevitably lead to differences in the application's behavior. The ability to accurately repeat the input events is the basis for comparing the behavior of the application. In the first experiment, we tested applications that did not have environment detection behavior, in order to evaluate the accuracy of the EmuProtect system's repetitive entry of system events.

The data set used in this experiment is 400 popular apps in 10 categories from the Google Play and 50 malware samples.

The Fig. 3 shows the detection data for some of three categories of applications. Each application in the figure shows four data, the first column on the left is the similarity reference C0 between the two reference objects, the other three columns is the value of C'/C0 in the third, fourth and fifth rounds.

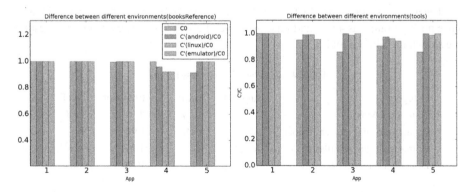

Fig. 3.   Similarity comparison results of books Reference and tools categories

7.2   Experiment II

In the second experiment, we verified the ability of the system to detect malware that detect environment while runtime. Due to the limited number of malware that have been discovered to detect operating environments, there are currently only a few types of environment detection method used by malware in the real world. In order to fully validate EmuProtect's detection capabilities, the applications being tested in this experiment are repackaged and injected several kinds of code that detect the emulating environments. The original malware in this experiment is AndroidXBot malicious code family. Table 3 shows the environment detection method we injected to the malware and their test results.

Table 3.   Samples and test results

Category	Record length	Result
XBot + IMEI	101	Success
Xbot + MAC	102	Success
Xbot + Build.DEVICE	98	Success
Xbot + drivers	101	Success
Xbot + qemud	102	Success
Xbot + ro.kernel.qemu	101	Success

7.3   Experiment III

In this experiment, we tested the ability of EmuProtect system to detect malware in the real world that hide malicious behavior in specific environments.

We used a calibrated standard test data set as the ground truth, which contains four types of application samples: normal application without anti-emulator behavior (class A, 30), malware without anti-emulator behavior (class B, 51), real world malware with anti-emulator behavior (class C, 21), repackaged malware with anti-emulator behavior (class D, 10).

The data set was detected by EmuProtect. The overall detection accuracy was 90.3%, false positive rate was 4.9%, and false negative rate was 9.7%. The detailed test results are shown in Tables 4 and 5.

Table 4.   Standard data set test results

Category	Android	Linux	Emulator	Total
A: normal APP	0	3.3%	0	3.3%
B: malware (not anti-emulator)	3.9%	1.9%	1.9%	8%
C: malware (anti-emulator)	76.2%	4.7%	4.7%	85.6%
D: malware repackaged	60%	30%	10%	100%

Table 5. False positive and false negative

Index	A	B	C	D
False positive	3.3%	8%	–	–
False negative	–	–	14.2%	0

From the experiment results, we can see that most of anti-emulator method used by malware are against the features of the Android framework layer, relatively, the anti-emulator behavior of other two layers accounted for a smaller proportion. Experiment results show that EmuProtect system can effectively detect the behavior difference of malware in different operating environments, determine the anti-emulator behavior targeting on each layer, and maintain high accuracy and low false positive rate.

8 Discussion

Chapter 6 introduces the key techniques and the advantages of the system, but the system still has some limitations, the following are the limitations of the system and the future work of about this detection method.

(1) The detection system proposed in this paper has some expansion, mainly in two aspects. First, in the emulation of the operating environment architecture, we can add more emulation environment, not only limited to the use of QEMU-based ARM architecture. Second, in the environment camouflage features, this currently only deal with some of the features of three layers above, we can add more features in the future.

(2) Because many applications have network operation, and network behavior can also been as a kind of input event of external environment and affect application behavior. This kind of network behavior is not under control in our system for now.

Based on the limitations of current dynamic analysis methods in hiding malicious behavior problems, this paper designs an abstract model for Android application behavior analysis. On the basis, we present a method to detect malware based on comparing the behavior of application in different operating environments and systematically implements it. The system complements the lack of existing methods of detecting anti-emulator malware problem from the defender's perspective. Finally, this paper validates the effectiveness and accuracy of the system to detect malware and its hidden behavior through experiments. The experiment results show that the system is running properly and can achieve the intended design goals.

References

1. Lau, B., Svajcer, V.: Measuring virtual machine detection in malware using DSD tracer. J. Comput. Virol. **6**(3), 181–195 (2008)
2. Raffetseder, T., Kruegel, C., Kirda, E.: Detecting System Emulators. In: Garay, J.A., Lenstra, A.K., Mambo, M., Peralta, R. (eds.) ISC 2007. LNCS, vol. 4779, pp. 1–18. Springer, Heidelberg (2007). doi:10.1007/978-3-540-75496-1_1

3. Paleari, R., Martignoni, L., Roglia, G., Bruschi, D.: A fistful of red-pills: how to automatically generate procedures to detect CPU emulators. In: The 3rd USENIX Conference on Offensive Technologies (WOOT 2009), Berkeley, CA, USA (2009)
4. Vidas, T., Christin, N.: Evading android runtime analysis via sandbox detection. In: Proceedings of the 9th ACM Symposium on Information, Computer and Communications Security (ASIA CCS 2014), Kyoto Garden Palace, Kyoto, Japan, pp. 447–458 (2014)
5. Jing, Y., Zhao, Z., Ahn, G., Hu, H.: Morpheus: automatically generating heuristics to detect android emulators. In: Annual Computer Security Applications Conference (ACSAC 2014), New Orleans, Louisiana, USA, pp. 216–225 (2014)
6. Neuner, S., Veen, V.V.D., Lindorfer, M., et al.: Enter Sandbox: Android sandbox comparison. In: Proceedings of the IEEE Mobile Security Technologies workshop (MoST), San Jose, California, USA (2014)
7. Tam, K., Khan, S., Fattori, A., Cavallaro, L.: CopperDroid: automatic reconstruction of Android Malware behaviors. In: The Network and Distributed System Security Symposium (NDSS), San Diego, California, USA, pp. 8–11 (2015)
8. Spreitzenbarth, M., Freiling, F., Echtler, F., Schreck, T., et al.: Mobile-Sandbox: having a deeper look into Android applications. In: ACM Symposium on Applied Computing (SAC), New York, NY, USA, pp. 1808–1815 (2013)
9. Gajrani, J., Sarswat, J., Tripathi, M., et al.: A robust dynamic analysis system preventing SandBox detection by Android malware. In: Proceedings of the 8th International Conference on Security of Information and Networks (SIN 2015), New York, NY, USA, pp. 290–295 (2015)
10. Tal, G., Keith, A., Andrew, W., and Jason, F.: Compatibility is not transparency: VMM detection myths and realities. In: Proceedings of the 11th USENIX Workshop on Hot Topics in Operating Systems (HOTOS 2007), Berkeley, California, USA, pp. 6:1–6:6 (2007)
11. Petsas, T., Voyatzis, G., Athanasopoulos, E., Polychronakis, M., Ioannidis, S.: Rage against the virtual machine: hindering dynamic analysis of Android malware. In: Proceedings of the Seventh European Workshop on System Security (EuroSec 2014), Amsterdam, Netherlands, pp. 5:1–5:6 (2014)
12. Enck, W., Gilbert, P., Chun, B., et al.: TaintDroid: an information-flow tracking system for realtime privacy monitoring on smartphones. ACM Trans. Comput. Syst. (TOCS) 32(2), 5 (2014)
13. Yan, L., Yin, H.: Droidscope: seamlessly reconstructing the OS and Dalvik semantic views for dynamic android malware analysis. In: Proceedings of the 21st USENIX Security Symposium, Berkeley, California, USA, p. 29 (2012)
14. Dhilung, K., Giovanni, V., Christopher, K.: BareCloud: bare-metal analysis-based evasive malware detection. In: 23rd USENIX Security Symposium (USENIX Security 2014), San Diego, California, USA, pp. 287–301 (2014)
15. Simone, M., Christopher, K. et al.: BareDroid: large-scale analysis of Android apps on real devices. In: Annual Computer Security Applications Conference (ACSAC 2015), Los Angeles, California, USA (2015)

Stream-Based Live Probabilistic Topic Computing and Matching

Kun Ma$^{(\boxtimes)}$, Ziqiang Yu, Ke Ji, and Bo Yang

Shandong Provincial Key Laboratory of Network Based Intelligent Computing,
University of Jinan, Jinan 250022, China
{ise_mak,ise_yuzq,ise_jik,yangbo}@ujn.edu.cn

Abstract. Public opinion monitoring refers to real-time first story detection (FSD) on a particular Internet news event. It play an important part in finding news propagation tendency. Current opinion monitoring methods are related to text matching. However, it has some limitations such as latent and hidden topic discovery and incorrect relevance ranking of matching results on large-scale data. In this paper, we propose one improved solution to live public opinion monitoring: stream-based live probabilistic topic computing and matching. Our method attempts to address the disadvantages such as semantic matching and low efficiency on timely big data. Topic real-time computing with stream processing paradigm and topic matching with query-time document and field boosting are proposed to make substantial improvements. Finally, our experimental evaluation on topic computing and matching using crawled historical Netease news records shows the high effectiveness and efficiency of the proposed approach.

Keywords: Public opinion · Public sentiment · Topic computing · Topic matching · Probabilistic topic model · Stream computing · Stream processing · Mapreduce

1 Introduction

1.1 Background

Public opinion, by definition, refers to individual views and attitudes on a particular news event from Internet news media, forum, Twitter, and WeChat. With the explosive growth of social media, automatic opinion analysis and monitoring on media data has provided critical decision making in various fields [7]. However, traditional public opinion monitoring systems are usually based on text matching without latent topic, and the relevance ranking of the matching results is not always correct.

To overcome the lack of real-time monitoring of opinion monitoring systems, this paper has proposed a new stream-based live probabilistic topic computing and matching method. The innovations of this method come in topic real-time computing with stream processing paradigm and query-time topic matching with

© Springer International Publishing AG 2017
S. Ibrahim et al. (Eds.): ICA3PP 2017, LNCS 10393, pp. 397–406, 2017.
DOI: 10.1007/978-3-319-65482-9_27

document and field boosting. Topic real-time computing with stream processing paradigm. In our public opinion monitoring solutions, stream processing framework with proposed topology and its processing elements can speed up the inference processing in real time, which powers extremely low-latency velocities and accelerates the batch parallel computing. The core role of stream processing replies rather on in-memory computing than high-volume storage. Topic matching with query-time document and field boosting. Compared with existing index-time boosting, we use query-time boosting with popularity (document boosting) and query coordination (field boosting) instead. For document boosting, a new field *rowboosting* is to store the row boosting value to formulate *function_score* query. For field boosting, each news record has different fields with different weights for matching.

The remainder of the paper is organized as follows. The related work of public opinion monitoring is discussed in Sect. 2. Section 3 gives the improved version of live public opinion monitoring, which is called stream-based live probabilistic topic computing and matching. This method firstly crawls the timely news, and then puts the data in the full-text searching engine and messaging middleware at the same time. Deduplication, pagerank, and sentiment analysis are processed in the messaging middleware. Finally, topic estimation with MapReduce, topic inference with stream processing paradigm, and topic matching with document boosting are proposed. Section 4 gives the experimental evaluation for our live public opinion monitoring, and compares it with the existing approaches. Brief conclusions are outlined in the last section.

2   Related Work

The first method is content matching. Ubiquitous content matching is to seek to maximize the overall relevance of the matched content. There are a lot of content matching algorithms [6]. In the popular TF-IDF scheme [14], a basic vocabulary of words is chosen for each document in the corpus, an inverse document frequency count is to measure the number of occurrences of a word in the entire corpus. Using TF-IDF, Apache Lucene scoring evolves from underlying Vector Space Model (VSM) of Information Retrieval to implementation [10]. There are some distributed parallel content matching methods [8,9]. Elasticsearch [4] and Apache Solr [12] are distributed RESTful search engines using Lucene storage. GreedyMR and StackMR algorithms were proposed to produce high-quality solutions to content matching on large datasets using MapReduce paradigm [2]. The second method is semantic matching. Since the synonyms convey the same meaning with different words, content matching might not get the correct result. So, similar features clustering, as a method of semantic matching, is used to group the synonyms which express the same features under the same feature group. The semi-supervised EM algorithm is a method to solve the problem by considering two soft constraints based on sharing of words and the lexical similarity [15]. Although several methods have been proposed to extract product features from comment texts, limited work has been done on clustering of similar features [16], especially in the field of public opinion monitoring. A new neural network architecture was presented to embed multi-relational graphs into a flexible continuous vector space [1]. This method can be applied to perform semantic matching. The goal is to learn to assign a structured meaning representation to almost any sentence of free text, demonstrating that it can scale up to tens of thousands of nodes and thousands of types of relation. A semantic graph was built to label columns with scale and timestamp information, and compute semantic matches between columns even when the same numeric attribute [17]. A novel deep relevance matching model (DRMM) for ad-hoc retrieval was proposed to employ a joint deep architecture at the query term level for relevance matching [3]. This model includes a feed forward matching and a term gating network using matching histogram mapping. word2vec [11] provides the efficient deep learning method to implement the continuous bag-of-words (CBOW) and skip-gram architectures for computing the vector representations of words in the high-dimensional vector space and calculate the cosine distances between words. The CBOW architecture predicts the current contextual word, and the skip-gram predicts surrounding words given the current word. That is to say that word2vec tool can find the semantic relationships between words in the document. Therefore, it can be used for semantic matching.

3 Stream-Based Live Probabilistic Topic Computing and Matching

3.1 Architecture

Figure 1 shows the architecture of stream-based live probabilistic topic computing and matching, which is composed of collector layer, topic acquisition layer, messaging layer, and topic alert layer. The collector layer is the same as simple probabilistic topic computing and matching. In the topic acquisition layer, we improve the LDA topic acquisition with MapReduce-based batch processing framework. In the messaging layer, we use publish-subscribe messaging rethought to deduplicate, cache, evaluate pagerank and sentiment of the new timely media data from the spiders. This messaging middleware can handle hundreds of megabytes of reads and writes per second from thousands of clients without downtime. Streams of news records are partitioned and spread over a cluster of nodes. Compared with the topic alert layer of simple probabilistic topic computing and matching, we propose stream-based LDA framework to infer the topics of the new data, and propose a new topic matching method where the ranking of matching result is based on the combination of key probability, pagerank, and sentiment boosting. Some new improvements are real-time processing with stream-based paradigm and new ranking method with field and document boost.

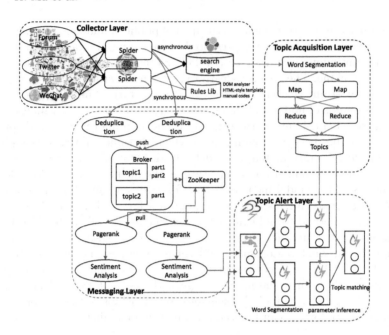

Fig. 1. Architecture of stream-based live probabilistic topic computing and matching.

3.2 Method

Pagerank and Sentiment Analysis. The crawled news record is from the web HTML pages, we use Google pagerank to determine the news record's relevance and importance. Generally, it is more concerning if the pagerank of the news record is higher. When the spiders crawl the web pages, it takes the pagerank of the page as the pagerank of the news record. In the same news site or news aggregator site, all the news pages are linked together to calculate pagerank. PageRank is an eigenvector-based algorithm to measure the importance of news entries. The score for a given vertex may be thought of as the fraction of time spent 'visiting' that vertex in a random walk over the vertices. PageRank modifies this random walk by adding to the model a probability (specified as α) of jumping to any vertex. We take 0.15 for α. Besides, the sentiment score is another factor to determine the importance of the news record. Generally, it is more concerning if it is a very positive or negative news. We implement recursive deep sentiment model [13] to compute the sentiment score of the crawled news data, which is related to the average sentiment score of several segmented sentences based on sentence length. Logic behind it is that longer sentences should carry more weight than shorter ones. The overall average sentiment score is denoted as $avgSentiment = \sum sentiPerSent * sentLength/textLength$, where $avgSentiment$ is the average sentiment score, $sentiPerSent$ is the sentiment per sentence, $sentLength$ is the sentence length, and $textLength$ is the text length.

Each crawled news record has different significance degrees, we propose an indexing-based row boosting method using page rank and sentiment score, denoted as $rowboosting = duplication * avgSentiment * pagerank$, where $rowboosting$ is the indexing-based row boosting, $duplication$ is duplicated times of this record, and $pagerank$ is the pagerank of this record. To avoid index rebuilding using index-time boosting, $rowboosting$ is taken as a separate field to be stored in the indexing.

Topic Inference with Stream Processing Paradigm. Topic inference consumes real-time crawled news, and produces topics per news. It seemed like an ideal use case for stream processing which can scale up the work by adding more resources. Compared with simple probabilistic topic computing and matching, we propose stream-based topic inference in the topic alert layer. The topic alert layer of Fig. 1 shows the network topology containing the whole application logic. Spouts are the entry point of the topic inference and are responsible for reading data from the messaging layer. Bolts on the other hand are the logical units of the topic inference and can perform word segmentation, parameter inference, and topic matching using running functions, filtering, aggregations and joins of streams.

Topic Matching with Query-Time Document Boosting. Compared with simple probabilistic topic computing and matching, we make the improvement of score boosting of ranking matching result. Generally, the topic matching determines which news records match, while the similarity determines how to assign scores to the matching records. As per LDA algorithm, a news record is represented with several topics with different probabilities. The news record we are sorting can be considered as a document, and the topics per document can be considered as the fields. This is important because two documents with the exact same content, but one having the content in two fields and the other in one field may return different scores for the same query due to length normalization. To match the keywords with the existing news data, we propose document and field boosting to match the keywords with topics per document.

Since index-time boosting is combined with the field-length norm, we use query-time boosting with popularity (document boosting) and query coordination (field boosting) instead. For each news record, a new field $rowboosting$ is to store the row boosting value. At search time, we can use the $function\_score$ query with the $field\_value\_factor$ function to combine the number of $rowboosting$ with the full-text relevance score. The $function_score$ query wraps the main query and the function we would like to apply. First, the main query is executed. Then, the $field_value_factor$ function is applied to every document matching the main query. Every document must have a number in the $rowboosting$ field for the $function_score$ to work.

Topic Matching with Query-Time Field Boosting. With LDA algorithm, each news record has several fields with different probabilities. As for matching, different fields have different significance degree. To increase the weight of the field, we add a boost value, and the value depends on the probability of this field. Boosts with higher value has more impact on the topic matching. $probability_i$ is mapped into the interval between 0 and 1 using Min-Max normalization, denoted as $fieldboosting_i = (probability_i - probability_{min})/(probability_{max} - probability_{min})$, where $probability_i$ is the field probability, $probability_{min}$ and $probability_{max}$ is the minimum and maximum of field probability.

4   Experiment Results

4.1   Experiment Setup

For our experiments, we use the same input dataset obtained from the Netease News, which is a Chinese news syndication websites to several mainstream Internet news sites in China. To monitor the public opinions that lead to a set of topics, we include historical 352, 971 Netease news records captured from 1st June 2016 to 30th December 2016 as the training data, and include some new 9, 624 Netease news records captured from 1st 2017 to 10th 2017 as the test data.

To evaluate topic computing and matching, we set up 4 developing and testing environments: standalone, MapReduce-based, Message Passing Interface (MPI)-based, and stream-based environment. Standalone machine has an Intel Xeon(R) E5-2620 @2.00 GHz CPU and 24 GB memory, and runs a 64-bit CentOS Linux OS with a Java 1.8 64-bit server JVM. Intel Xeon(R) E5-2620 has 6 cores with 12 threads. MPI-based environment is a standardized and portable message-passing system on a wide variety of parallel computing architectures. Since we do not have enough hardware resources, we use virtualization technology to simulate distributed MapReduce-based and stream-based environment. We adopt Hadoop 2.7.3 to implement the MapReduce framework. In order to maximize the parallelism and make full use of the resources, we made the following changes to the default Hadoop configuration: we set the block size of the DFS of Hadoop to 256 MB, allocate 1 GB to each Hadoop daemon and 1 GB virtual memory to each map and reduce task, and disable speculative execution feature. The ratio of map and reduce tasks per job is set 2:1, which is the default configuration of Hadoop. We adopt Apache Storm 0.10.2 to implement the stream topology.

4.2   Topic Computing

In this section, we compare serial topic computing, PLDA+, MapReduce-based topic computing, and stream-base topic computing. We adopt the 4 environments described in Sect. 4.1. We have made PLDA+ on different sizes of processors from 2 to 12. We have made MapReduced-based topic computing on 2 Hadoop instances with 6 CPU cores and 24 GB memory. The capability of this Hadoop instances are to run at most 12 map and 6 reduce tasks in parallel. The stream topology has 2 computing instances, and each instance has a 6-core CPU and 24 GB memory. The capability of this stream cluster is to run at most 12 groups. We accept the same training and test data described in Sect. 4.1.

We calculate the execution time of topic computing, and observe the speedup. Speedup is defined as the ratio of the serial runtime of the best sequential algorithm for solving a problem, to the time taken by the parallel algorithm to solve the same problem on p tasks. $S_p = \frac{T_{serial}}{T_p}$ is used to compute the speedup of PLDA+, where S_p is the speedup with p processors, and T_{serial} means the execution time of serial topic computing. $S_{m=2r=p} = \frac{T_{serial}}{T_{m=2r=p}}$ is used to compute the speedup of MapReduce-based topic, where $S_{m=2r=p}$ is the speedup with p map and $p/2$ reduce tasks, $T_{m=2r=p}$ means the execution time with p map and $p/2$ reduce tasks, and T_{serial} means the execution time of serial topic computing. $S_{stream\ computing\ with\ p\ groups} = \frac{T_{serial}}{T_{stream\ computing\ with\ p\ groups}}$ is used to compute the speedup of stream-base topic computing, where $S_{stream\ computing\ with\ p\ groups}$ is the speedup of stream-based topic inference with p groups, $T_{stream\ computing\ with\ p\ groups}$ means the execution time of stream-based topic inference with p groups, and T_{serial} means the execution time of serial topic inference.

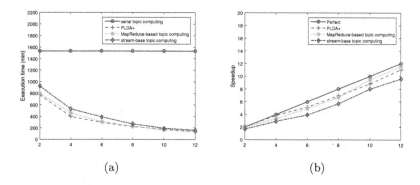

Fig. 2. Execution time and speedup of topic estimation of the training news records.

The first experiment involves topic estimation of the training news records. All programs share the same training and test data as described in Sect. 4.1. The serial topic estimation creates several topics using simple probabilistic topic computing. PLDA+ comes from this implementation [5]. MapReduce-based and stream topic estimation program performs the same operations as the sequential code using MapReduce framework shown in Fig. 1. With the same LDA parameters and 500 iterations, these methods will achieve the same level of accuracy. Figure 2(a) shows the average execution time of topic estimation, and Fig. 2(b) shows the speedup as a measure of scalability. The average execution time and speedup are important because it shows whether the parallel implementation is an improvement. Serial topic estimation is baseline. For PLDA+, axis x means the number of processors. For MapReduce-based topic computing, axis x means the number of map tasks. For stream-based topic computing, axis x means the number of groups in the stream topology. In each case, we report the average execution time of 500 iterations. PLDA+ is nearly linear speedup. To sum up, axis x means processor/map task/group in stream topology. Figure 2(a) and (b) highlights two points of topic inference. First, the parallel method such as PLDA+, MapReduce-based, and stream-based work well. Improvement of MapReduce-based computing was dramatic until 10 map tasks. The best solution of topic estimation is MapReduce-based topic estimation.

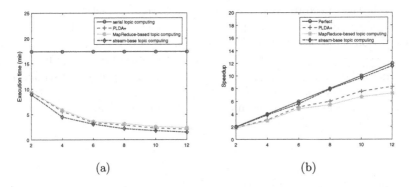

Fig. 3. Execution time and speedup of topic inference of the test news records.

The second experiment involves topic inference of the test news records. Figure 3(a) shows the average execution time of topic inference, and Fig. 3(b) shows the speedup as a measure of scalability. Axis x is the same as the first experiment. It highlights two points. Compared with MapReduce-based topic computing, stream-based topic computing has nearly linear speedup. The execution time of stream-based topic computing is slightly faster than other methods. This improvement of the computation is caused by the stream-based topology and parallel grouping strategy. This result can be explained. First, a MapReduce runtime system introduces overhead due to job startup, communication, and sorting. Additional overhead is incurred by MapReduce's inter-particle messages. Second, stream processing has no startup issue due to continuous work. Without repeated startup of topic computing jobs, stream-based topic computing is better in inferring small amount of real-time crawled news records.

4.3   Topic Matching

Next, we compare our query-time boosting with index-time boosting. Index-time boosting has two limitations. First, index-time boosting will reindex all documents, and it will has serious performance issue with large frequent data. Second, index-time boosting reduces the resolution of the field length normalization factor leading to lower quality relevance calculations.

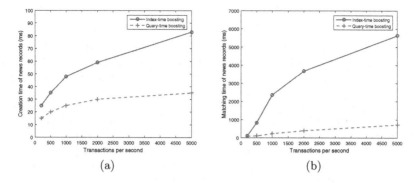

Fig. 4. Average creation and matching time of with different transactions per second.

Figure 4(a) shows the average creation time of a timely news record with different transactions per second using query-time and index-time boosting respectively. Since the frequent changes will rebuild the index using index-time boosting, index maintenance issue become the bottleneck of the creation. Thus, index-time boosting is worse than query-time boosting. The creation time of index-time boosting rose sharply in the case of high transactions per second. Figure 4(b) shows the average matching time of historical 352, 971 Netease news records with different write transactions using query-time and index-time boosting respectively. With high write transactions, the matching time of index-time boosting is serious affected due to the indexes rebuilding. It indicates that the query-time boosting is better than index-time boosting.

5 Conclusions

In this paper, we have introduced stream-based public opinion monitoring approach with adaptive probabilistic topic model. Innovations highlights two points: topic real-time computing with stream processing paradigm and topic matching with query-time document and field boosting. Probabilistic topic computing and matching addressed latent and hidden topic discovery, and stream-based live probabilistic topic computing and matching addressed timely monitoring on big data and relevance ranking of matching results.

Acknowledgments. This work was supported by the Science and Technology Program of University of Jinan (XKY1734), the Open Project Joint Funding of Information Science and Engineering School of Linyi University and Discipline Team of Intelligent Logistics and Information Engineering (LDXX2017KF155), the Shandong Provincial Natural Science Foundation (ZR201702170261), the Shandong Provincial Key R&D Program (2015GGX106007 & 2016ZDJS01A12), and the Project of Shandong Province Higher Educational Science and Technology Program (J16LN13).

References

1. Bordes, A., Glorot, X., Weston, J., Bengio, Y.: A semantic matching energy function for learning with multi-relational data. Mach. Learn. **94**(2), 233–259 (2014)
2. De Francisci Morales, G., Gionis, A., Sozio, M.: Social content matching in mapreduce. Proc. VLDB Endow. **4**(7), 460–469 (2011)
3. Guo, J., Fan, Y., Ai, Q., Croft, W.B.: A deep relevance matching model for ad-hoc retrieval. In: Proceedings of the 25th ACM International on Conference on Information and Knowledge Management, pp. 55–64. ACM (2016)
4. Kononenko, O., Baysal, O., Holmes, R., Godfrey, M.W.: Mining modern repositories with elasticsearch. In: Proceedings of the 11th Working Conference on Mining Software Repositories, pp. 328–331. ACM (2014)
5. Liu, Z., Zhang, Y., Chang, E.Y., Sun, M.: PLDA+: parallel latent dirichlet allocation with data placement and pipeline processing. ACM Trans. Intell. Syst. Technol. (TIST) **2**(3), 26 (2011)
6. Ma, K., Dong, F., Yang, B.: Large-scale schema-free data deduplication approach with adaptive sliding window using mapreduce. Comput. J. **58**(11), 3187–3201 (2015)
7. Ma, K., Tang, Z., Zhong, J., Yang, B.: LPSMon: a stream-based live public sentiment monitoring system. Lect. Notes Comput. Sci. **9659**, 534–536 (2016)
8. Ma, K., Yang, B.: Stream-based live data replication approach of in-memory cache. Concurrency Comput. Pract. Exp. **29**(11), 1–9 (2017)
9. Ma, K., Yang, B., Yang, Z., Yu, Z.: Segment access-aware dynamic semantic cache in cloud computing environment. J. Parallel Distrib. Comput., 1–10 (2017)
10. McCandless, M., Hatcher, E., Gospodnetic, O.: Lucene in Action: Covers Apache Lucene 3.0. Manning Publications Co., Cherry Hill (2010)
11. Mikolov, T., Yih, W.T., Zweig, G.: Linguistic regularities in continuous space word representations. In: HLT-NAACL, vol. 13, pp. 746–751 (2013)
12. Shahi, D.: Apache solr: an introduction. In: Shahi, D. (ed.) Apache Solr, pp. 1–9. Springer, Heidelberg (2015)
13. Socher, R., Perelygin, A., Wu, J.Y., Chuang, J., Manning, C.D., Ng, A.Y., Potts, C.: Recursive deep models for semantic compositionality over a sentiment treebank. In: Proceedings of the Conference on Empirical Methods in Natural Language Processing (EMNLP), vol. 1631, p. 1642. Citeseer (2013)
14. Wu, H.C., Luk, R.W.P., Wong, K.F., Kwok, K.L.: Interpreting TF-IDF term weights as making relevance decisions. ACM Trans. Inf. Syst. (TOIS) **26**(3), 13 (2008)
15. Zhai, Z., Xu, H., Kang, B., Jia, P.: Exploiting effective features for Chinese sentiment classification. Expert Syst. Appl. **38**(8), 9139–9146 (2011)
16. Zhang, D., Xu, H., Su, Z., Xu, Y.: Chinese comments sentiment classification based on word2vec and SVM perf. Expert Syst. Appl. **42**(4), 1857–1863 (2015)
17. Zhang, M., Chakrabarti, K.: InfoGather+: semantic matching and annotation of numeric and time-varying attributes in web tables. In: Proceedings of the 2013 ACM SIGMOD International Conference on Management of Data, pp. 145–156. ACM (2013)

Experiment for Analysing the Impact of Financial Events on Twitter

Ana Fernández-Vilas[1]([⊠]) [iD], Lewis Evans[2], Majdi Owda[2],
Rebeca P. Díaz Redondo[1], and Keeley Crockett[2]

[1] Information & Computing Laboratory, AtlantTIC Research Centre,
University of Vigo, 36310 Vigo, Spain
{avilas, rebeca}@det.uvigo.es
[2] School of Computing, Mathematics and Digital Technology, Manchester
Metropolitan University, Manchester M1 5GD, UK
{L.Evans, m.owda, k.crockett}@mmu.ac.uk

Abstract. Twitter, as the heart of publicly accessible Social Media, is one of the currently used platforms to share financial information and is a valuable source of information for different roles in the financial market. For all these roles, the quality analysis of Twitter as a source of financial information is essential to take decisions. The work in this paper is aligned with the ongoing work of the authors to a solution for irregularity monitoring in the financial market by harnessing data in online social media. To do so, the permeability of a variety of social media data feeders to financial irregularities should be analysed. That is the case of the experiment in this paper by putting the focus on Twitter microblogging platform and checking if this general purpose social media is permeable to a specific financial event. For this, we detail the analysis of Twitter permeability to a specific event in the past few months: the announcement about the merge of Tesco and Booker to create a UK's Leading Food Business on the 27th January 2017. Both companies Tesco PLC and Booking Group PLC are listed in the main market of LSE (London Stock Exchange). Our findings provide promising evidences to address the problem of real-time detection of irregularities in the financial market via Twitter according to the volume (as a sign of the importance of the irregularity) and to other features (as signs of the potential origin causing the irregularity).

Keywords: Twitter · Stock market · Financial irregularities · Permeability

1 Introduction

As the heart of publicly accessible Social Media, Twitter has become a vital source for open source intelligence in natural disasters, politics, consumers' opinion, etc. Also, Twitter is one of the currently used platforms to share financial information from businesses, brokers, news agencies or through individual investors tweets. As Twitter usage to share financial information is definitely increasing [1]; it is important to stress that, according to [2], stock microblogs exhibit three distinct characteristics above stock message boards: (i) Twitter's public timeline may capture the natural market conversation more accurately and reflect up to date developments; (ii) Twitter

© Springer International Publishing AG 2017
S. Ibrahim et al. (Eds.): ICA3PP 2017, LNCS 10393, pp. 407–419, 2017.
DOI: 10.1007/978-3-319-65482-9_28

reflects a more ticker-like live conversation which allows micro-bloggers to be exposed to the most recent information of all stocks and does not require users to actively enter the forum for a particular stock; and (iii) micro-bloggers have a strong incentive to publish valuable information to maintain reputation (increase mentions, the rate of retweets, and their followership), meanwhile financial bloggers can be indifferent to their reputation in the forum. Providing sensing, harvesting and analysing methods and tools of such information could be very useful for many stakeholders such as businesses and individuals making decisions to invest, stock market analysts and law enforcement agencies.

Our medium-term objective is a collaboration project among the University of Vigo and the Manchester Metropolitan University to deploy an architecture for real-time monitoring of irregularities in the stock market. That architecture will apply data mining and fusion technologies from a pool of social feeders related with the stock market. In order to design the architecture, the permeability of the different feeders should be analysed, that means, to what extent a specific financial information feeder is permeable to fraudulent and common irregularities in the financial market. That is the case of the experiment in this paper by putting the focus on Twitter microblogging platform.

This paper states the following research question: Is Twitter permeable to specific actions ion the financial market? We hypothesize that Twittersphere, the total universe of Twitter users and their habits, is permeable towards relevant actions in the financial market and that the impact of this permeability can be measure according to (1) the disturbance of Twitter behaviour in terms of volume, tweets features and geographical distribution; and (2) the rapidness of this permeable layer between the financial market and the social media (Twitter in our experiment). Showing that a general purpose social media is permeable to financial-specific events is the first step to consider Twitter as a relevant feeder for taking decisions regarding the financial market and event fraudulent activities in that market. For this, we detail the analysis of Twitter permeability to a specific event in the past few months: the announcement about the merger of Tesco PLC (hereinafter Tesco) and Booker Group PLC (hereinafter Booker) to create UK's Leading Food Business on the 27th January 2017. Both companies Tesco PLC and Booking Group PLC are listed in the main market of LSE (London Stock Exchange).

This paper is structured as follows. Section 2 introduces the Twitter efforts to accommodate financial information in a general-purpose microblogging platform as well as related work in the area of the use of Twitter data for financial analysis where researchers capture data by using the APIs provided by Twitter, which are discussed in Sect. 2.1 along with the selection of Twitter features we consider during our experiment. Section 3 describes the scenario, the extraction strategy and the resulting datasets for the experiment, which aims to analyse permeability for the Tesco & Booker merger. After cleaning the data and conducting the analysis, the paper reports the impact of the merger on 27th January 2017 in terms of tweets volume and features (Sect. 4), in terms of geographical distribution (Sect. 5) and in terms of its rapidness to react to the action (Sect. 6). Finally, Sect. 7 discusses our findings and introduces our ongoing work in the study of permeability of Twitter to financial events.

2 Twitter and Financial Information

It is fair to say that it was Twitter that popularised the term hashtag as well as its # symbol to index keywords or topics so that people can easily follow topics they are interested in. Also, in 2012 Twitter unveiled a new clicking & tracking feature for stock symbols (known as Cashtags). Cashtags are stock market symbols that can be included in tweets and when preceded with a dollar sign (for example $VOD in regards to Vodafone) become clickable. [3] reported an exploratory analysis of public tweets in English, extracted via Firehose, which should contain at least one Cashtag from NASDAQ or NYSE. The analysis concludes that the use of Cashtag is higher in the technologic sector, which seems to be related with the technological profile of most of the Twitter users; and the top 10 Twitter accounts according to the usage of cash-tags are companies or news agencies (i.e. automatic or semi-automatic Twitter accounts). The analysis also highlights the existence of relevant information behind the co-occurrence of Cashtags (revealing main competitors of companies) and the co-occurrence of Cashtags with Hashtags (allowing to group companies into clusters). Some other works research on the possible connections between Twitter information and market performance, that is the predictive value of information gathered form social media [2, 4]. Most of these works, based on the twitter data volume, also apply some sentiment analysis technique in order to distinguish the polarity of the impact [5–8].

2.1 Twitter Mining

There are three different ways to catch Twitter data: Search API, Streaming API and Firehose. The Twitter Search API provides the endpoints to recover tweets that were published in the previous two weeks, with the possibility of filtering according to several criteria. On the other hand, Twitter Streaming API returns 1% of the tweets that match some search parameters in real time. Finally, Twitter Firehose provide access to 100% of the tweets, but it is not a free-access API. Twitter APIs are constructed around four main "objects": Tweets, Users, Entities (hashtags, URLs, mentions and media in a tweet) and Places. Then, users construct API queries (combining object fields and query operators) to retrieve information posted from specific users, containing a particular combination of keywords, including particular entities, etc. With regard to this work, the experiment does not include the analysis of the spreading perspective of information on Twitter so we select the following features (existing in both Search and Streaming APIs under different field names) for the analysis, all of them accessible from a Tweet object:

- Content perspective: the status update (`Tweet:text`) and the entities (`Tweet:entities`), specifically `hashtags` (including cashtags) and `urls`.
- Context perspective: the post time of the status update (`Tweet:created_at`) and, if available, also the place (`Tweet:coordinates`; `Tweet:place:bounding_box`).
- Social Perspective: User (`Tweet:user`, specifically the field `verified`).

There are highly relevant differences between the Searching API and the Streaming API, time direction being the most apparent and functionally-impacting one. Search API goes back in time meanwhile Streaming API goes forward. Moreover, there are other differences related to mainly the format and the rate limit rules. Regarding their extracting capacity, Twitter forums contain plenty of discussion about this issue which has not ever made enough clear from Twitter officially.

3   The Experiment and the Data

As mentioned, the aim of this experiment is analysing the permeability of Twitter to the occurrence of specific events in the day to day of financial market. For that, we perceive TESCO on Twitter with the pair (cashtag, keyword), that is ($TSCO, "tesco"), representing the financial perspective of TESCO on Twitter ($TSCO) and general references to TESCO on Twitter ("tesco"). According to this representation, we respond to our research question. Our hypothesis is that Twitter (although not a specific financial forum) is permeable to financial events and this permeability can be analysed by monitoring the name of companies as a keyword ("tesco" in this case) and the Cashtag of the company ($TSCO). Also, we hypothesize that the permeability and the impact is not alike in the two perspectives. Meanwhile the cashtag is invariably linked to financial news of a company, the general content, or 'Tesco' content, have some completely different dynamics which is generally driven by company decisions, marketing campaigns, consumer opinions, etc. Presumably, financial events should have a bigger impact on cashtag tweets (according to volume and features) than on tweets containing the keyword 'Tesco'. Nevertheless, this presumably different behaviour should be inspected. Taking this merge action as our first experiment to a general measure of permeability, while taking into account that we are reporting a single event, we analyse the impact of this financial event on Twitter $cashtag-content and on Twitter keyword-content related with the company, separately. The impact on both data sources ($TSCO and 'tesco') is measured in terms of Twitter volume (Sect. 4), in terms of geographical distribution (Sect. 5) and in terms to their response to the announcement by the RNS (Regulatory News Service) of LSE[1] (Sect. 6).

3.1   Data Extraction

We prepared the experiment according to the following extraction strategy for the query ($TSCO, "tesco"). Once we selected the event, we used the Search API to recover the information backwards before the announcement on 27th of January 7:00 a.m. and the streaming API to recover information forwards. The aim of streaming data just after the announcement was to visualize the impact of the announcement and analyse the time Tesco Twitter behaviour returns to a regular pattern. The results of the combination of the search and streaming results is shown in Fig. 1. Once the behaviour becomes stable,

---

[1] http://www.londonstockexchange.com/exchange/news/market-news/market-news-home.html.

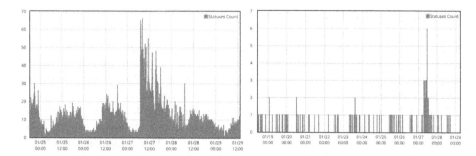

Fig. 1. Total Twitter volume for 'tesco' (left) and $TSCO (right) by merging (without duplicates) the retrieved data from queries to Search API (backwards) and Steaming API (backwards).

we used the Search API again to obtain a regular dataset as a reference for the experiment.

Clearly, the Twitter Search API is not appropriate for continuous analytical monitoring and as a data source to taking decisions in real time. It is not intended and does not fully support the repeated constant searches that would be required to deliver 100% coverage. However, the experiment in this paper is limited to one individual company, 2 keywords and timelines in the scale of weeks. In such conditions, Search API provide a better coverage than de Streaming API (1% according to the Twitter official information) if we use the superior filtering characteristics of the Search API. Nevertheless, as the Search API has a limit on the number of returning Tweets, to get the whole data, we repeatedly ask Twitter for the most recent results backwards by windowing the searches according to the publication date and merging results according to the post Id. Apart from that, the Search API guarantees a fair comparison according to the volume of data, in any manner we should compare Search results with Streaming results. According to that, and to give response to the research questions, we use Search API queries to cover the time periods in Table 1.

Table 1. Time Periods (UK Time) extracted with the Search API.

Name/Period	'Tesco'		$TSCO	
	Total	Per/hour	Total	Per/hour
Pre-announcement 25th Jan 00:00–27th Jan 06:59	11,817	214.85	12	0.218
Post-announcement 27th Jan 07:00–29th Jan 23:59	25,547	393.03	91	1.400
Regular 2-weeks-after 8th Feb 00:00–10th Feb 06:59	13,417	243.94	26	0.473
Regular 2-weeks-after 10th Feb 07:00–12th Feb 23:59	20,012	307.88	22	0.338

4 Impact on Twitter Volume

In this section, we detail the impact of the event by analysing the variation in the number of tweets (volume) with respect to the regular behaviour, which provides a quantitative measure of Twitter permeability to the Tesco & Booker merger. During this part of the analysis some irregularities appeared which uncovered an inconsistency in the named scheme of tickers in Twitter. In particular, to our knowledge, Twitter has not promoted the specific distinction among markets so that the uniqueness of ticker symbols inside a market disappear in the Twittersphere. That is the case of $TSCO cashtag which corresponds to 'Tesco PLC' in LSE and to 'Tractor Supply Company' in NASDAQ (National Association of Securities Dealers Automated Quotation), the second stock exchange in USA. So, the returned results to a $TSCO query include tweets related to Tesco Plc and also to Tractor Supply Company. If cashtags are the Twitter vehicle to aggregate and allow the spreading of financial information about companies, some kind of market prefix should be used, specially in the times when companies are becoming increasingly global.

Figure 2 shows the temporal series in a tweets-per-hour (TPH) scale. Although it is quite obvious that the number of TPH in 'tesco' dataset is up several orders of magnitude higher than those of $TSCO dataset, the peak behaviour is more acute in the $TSCO one. As it is shown in Table 2, considering the hourly volume of 'tesco' dataset on the 27th January, there are not outliers during the day, with a peak value of 2,057 tweets in the sample from 8:00 to 9:00. Nevertheless, there are 3 outliers in the $TSCO dataset: samples 8:00–9:00, 9:00–10:00 and 12:00–13:00, corresponding to the time just after the announcement and lunch time in the UK, the latter being consistent with previous studies about social timing, i.e. [9].

Apart from the peak comparison, we also inspected the potential disturbances on other dataset features before and after the announcement, also comparing these dates with the regular behaviour 2 weeks later (see Table 3). We highlight the invariability on the number of verified users either along all the periods and along the two datasets. Secondly, the percentage of tweets which contain URL are significantly higher in the $TSCO dataset with respect to the 'tesco' one, which is a result of the professional and financial orientation of the $TSCO data as a channel to spread facts and news rather than opinions and sentiments. Finally, the retweeting activity is higher in the announcement periods (pre- and post-) compared to the regular periods in both datasets. The increase of retweeting is, by nature, linked to the need or desire of spreading a piece of content but, the reason behind may be different as, in fact, it is in our case study: retweeting in the 'tesco' keyword dataset is mainly related with a Tesco campaign for wining a voucher, meanwhile retweeting in $TSCO data is mainly linked to spreading the information about the merge (post-announcement) and about other financial news.

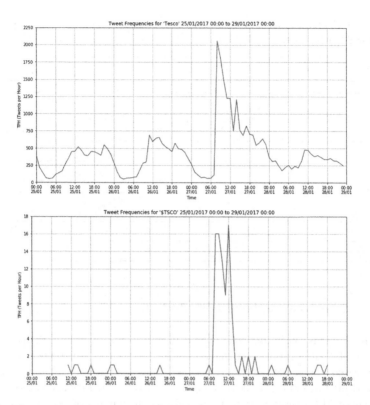

Fig. 2. Time series of the 'tesco' and $TSCO dataset from 25th January to 29th January

Table 2. Peak behaviour on the 27th January for 'tesco' and $TSCO.

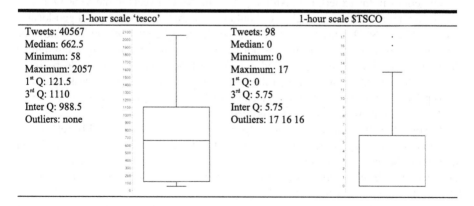

1-hour scale 'tesco'	1-hour scale $TSCO
Tweets: 40567	Tweets: 98
Median: 662.5	Median: 0
Minimum: 58	Minimum: 0
Maximum: 2057	Maximum: 17
1st Q: 121.5	1st Q: 0
3rd Q: 1110	3rd Q: 5.75
Inter Q: 988.5	Inter Q: 5.75
Outliers: none	Outliers: 17 16 16

Table 3. Variability of features in 'tesco' and $TSCO datasets (Green bars correspond to the variation in the 'tesco' dataset and blue bars correspond to the variation in the $TSCO dataset).

Periods	Pre-Announcement (25th-27th Jan 06:55) TUESDAY-WEDNESDAY-THURSDAY				Post-Announcement (27th 07:00-29 Jan) FRIDAY- SATURDAY-SUNDAY			
Counting & percentages	"tesco"	%	STSCO	%	"tesco"	%	STSCO	%
Tweets	17,154		8		25,547		91	
Tweets per hour	311.89		0.15		393.03		1.40	
Tweets from verified users	2,560	14.92%	0	0.00%	2,696	10.55%	2	2.20%
Tweets with URL	5,383	31.38%	6	75.00%	12,367	48.41%	64	70.33%
Tweets being RT	7,522	43.85%	0	0.00%	8,070	31.59%	18	19.78%
Different users	12,141	43.85%	7	0.00%	15,757	31.59%	47	19.78%
Different erified users	155	1.28%	0	0.00%	336	1.32%	2	4.26%
Periods	2 Weeks after (7th - 9th Feb 06:55) TUESDAY-WEDNESDAY-THURSDAY				2 weeks after (10th 07:00 - 12th Feb) FRIDAY-SATURDAY-SUNDAY			
Counting & percentages	"tesco"	%	STSCO	%	"tesco"	%	STSCO	%
Total Tweets	16,878		23		20,011	100.00%	22	
Tweets per hour	306.87		0.42		307.86		0.34	
Tweets from verified users	2,364	14.01%	0	0.00%	2,650	13.24%	0	0.00%
Tweets with URL	4,980	29.51%	19	82.61%	6,971	34.84%	19	86.36%
Tweets being RT	6,530	38.69%	3	13.04%	5,676	28.36%	5	22.73%
Different users	10,749	38.69%	10	13.04%	11,374	28.36%	13	59.09%
Different verified users	164	0.97%	0	0.00%	150	0.75%	0	0.00%

5   Impact on Geographical Distribution

Although Twitter is one of the most used data source in data mining, the geo-location component of Twitter is not comparable to other data sources which we can refer to as Location-based social networks. In fact, according to [10], the geo-located tweets returned by the Streaming API cover up to the 90% of the geo-located tweets extracted from Firehose API. However, [10] also reveals that the number of geo-located tweets is low, being only a 1.45% of the tweets obtained from Firehose API and 3.17% of the tweets obtained from Streaming API. The total percentage of geo-located tweets for the 'tesco' dataset is consistent with this previous study [10], with a percentage of 4.3% for all the periods in the experiment. Although the number of tweets in the $TSCO dataset may be not representative enough, we should remark that the percentage of geo-located tweets in the $TSCO dataset is almost 0%, 1 tweet out of a total of 199, so bellow the 4.3% in 'tesco' dataset. Also, there is not variability of those percentages throughout the periods considered (pre- post- and regular). Although these data should be interpreted with caution, we may consider the possibility of accessing from a desktop device or corporate mobile in the case of financial professionals (supposedly devices without location feature or whit this feature disabled).

Beyond the percentage of geo-located tweets that the Twitter APIs return, the variation of the geographical distribution of the tweets due to the financial event deserves to be analysed. Figure 3 shows this distribution and, apparently, there is not much variation if we compare post-announcement with the regular period for the same days of the week.

A deeper inspection of the tweets per country in Table 4 confirms that most of tweets come from the countries where Tesco deploy its main business either under Tesco trademark or thorough subsidiary local companies. Apart from UK and Republic of Ireland, the main retail locations of Tesco PLC all over the world are the Czech Republic, Hungary, Poland, Slovakia, Turkey, Malaysia and Thailand.

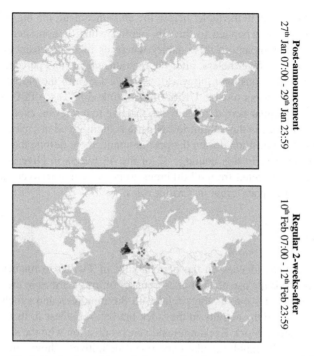

Fig. 3. Geographical distribution of 'tesco' dataset after the announcement and during a regular period.

Table 4. Geographical distribution of tweets in 'tesco' dataset

Pre-Announcement			Post-Announcement		
Country	**Geolocated Tweets**	**%**	**Country**	**Geolocated Tweets**	**%**
UK	443	61.27%	UK	585	51.32%
Malysia	196	27.11%	Malysia	341	29.91%
Thailand	53	7.33%	Thailand	125	10.96%
			Nigeria	42	3.68%
			Ireland	15	1.32%
Rest of the wor	31	4.29%		32	2.81%
TOTAL	723		**TOTAL**	1140	
2 Weeks after (8th - 10th Feb)			**2 weeks after (10th- 12th Feb)**		
Country	**Geolocated Tweets**	**%**	**Country**	**Geolocated Tweets**	**%**
UK	333	58.12%	UK	503	55.76%
Malysia	162	28.27%	Malysia	242	26.83%
Thailand	33	5.76%	Thailand	100	11.09%
Ireland	18	3.14%	Ireland	22	2.44%
	27	4.71%		35	3.88%
TOTAL	573		**TOTAL**	902	

According to the results in the table, before the announcement, the bigger contribution to Twitter volume corresponded to the UK market which is consistent with the historical roots of the company in this country where its retailing business is fully integrated in the society. Nevertheless, after the announcement, this percentage decreases in favour of other locations over the world, which is a sign of the global impact of the action so that twitter users outside UK are not so linked to Tesco PLC main business campaigns during regular period but they are reactive to a relevant event related with a company with presence in their countries. Nigeria is highlighted in Table 4 as a country with a definitely high position during the post-announcement despite the fact that Tesco does not have business in this country. 42 of the 43 tweets in Nigeria has the same content but they are tweeted from 42 different users, not being retweets, so that it may be a violation of the spam terms in Twitter rules.

6 Rapidness

Although our analysis focuses on the permeability of Twitter to financial events our long-term objective is the use of Twitter as a sensor of irregularities in the stock market. So, this section includes our findings related to the rapidness and synchronization of Twitter as a channel to the activity in the stock market: rapidness in its response to the RNSs of LSE (London Stock Exchange) and synchronization with the share prices also in LSE. Regarding the rapidness, the experiment definitively shows the good characteristics of Twitter. The first tweet referring to the RNS was at 7:03 a.m. on 27th, just 3 min before the RNS announcement about the Tesco and Booker merge. Beyond the very first tweet, it is remarkable the rapidness of the peak response to the

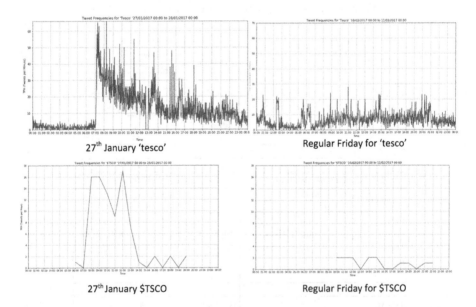

27th January 'tesco'

Regular Friday for 'tesco'

27th January $TSCO

Regular Friday for $TSCO

Fig. 4. Time series at hour scale on the 27th January in comparison with a regular Friday.

announcement in both datasets, so that the 27th Twitter time series ('tesco' and $TSCO) can be considered abnormal time series when a regular Friday is taken as a reference. We highlight that the peak starts form 7:00 to 8:00 both in the #TSCO and $TSCO dataset (see Fig. 4).

Regarding the synchronization with the share prices at LSE (Fig. 5), it is fair to mention that although the share prices were abnormally low the day before the announcement, we haven't found any reference to a potential Tesco & Booker merger in tweets before the announcement in our dataset, neither by manual inspection of Twitter Web Site.

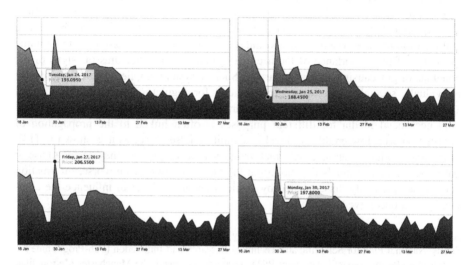

Fig. 5. Main observational points in the evolution of the Tesco PLC share price (16th January to 27th March 2017)

7 Discussion

This paper inspects the permeability of Twitter to financial events in order to provide evidences which allows Twitter to be used as social sensor for the financial and stock market. Bearing in mind that this a single experiment for a single financial event and also that the event was fully covered by traditional social media, we can conclude that the event in the financial market invaded the Twittersphere on the 27th January, just after the RNS announcement at 7:00, and that the behaviour of ($TSCO, "tesco") was altered in comparison with the regular behaviour around the company involved in the financial event. Nevertheless, the experiment had a little success in predicting the irregularity, that is, identifying some rumour or sign of the announcement. Even considering that the experiment was not deployed over the whole Firehose Twitter data, uncovering rumours before the announcement turns definitively into a hard task if the human spreading of rumours is not mimic inside Twitter, that means, if the rumour is not there. At this respect, and according to [11], social media data can only be generalized to human behaviour if social media provides a representative description of human activity. Twitter is a social media which, at least, exhibit some demographic bias. Moreover, Twitter may be providing a skewed representation of their content. Although well-known rumour detection algorithms [12, 13] can be applied to Twitter, an alternative approach can be the fusion of financial information from different data sources in a way that we can mitigate the inevitable bias in a single source, and, at the same time, combine their weaknesses and strengthens in a proper representation of the real financial activity.

Meanwhile this paper analyses the quantitative and objective permeability of a financial event on Twitter, our ongoing work has conducted and initial analysis the qualitative characteristics of that permeability: in terms of topic modelling and information provenance, but also considering the polarity of twitter financial information. The experiment in this paper provides promising results to address our final objective: a real-time monitoring system which would detect irregularities according to the volume (as a sign of the importance of the irregularity) and to other features (as signs of the potential origin causing the irregularity). Such a system implies prime benefits for individuals, specially uninformed traders, and for regulatory and low enforcement agencies as a sign which may trigger further actions. Unfortunately, the need to influence social media for different purposes is often linked to the propagation of information with low credibility level or definitely false. Also, as it is shown in [14], firms strategically disseminate information in social media, that is, they decide to use or not to use certain channels depending on the piece of news. Even worse, information may be automatically disseminated by artificial agents in order to influence the community in a deceptive way.

Acknowledgement. This work was funded by Spanish Ministry of Education Culture and Sports, National Plan for Scientific and Technical Research and Innovation (Sub-Programme for Mobility) under the research stay grant PRIX16/00368. We thank the Manchester Metropolitan University (School of Computing Mathematics and Digital Technology) for its support during the research stay. This work is also partially funded by the Spanish Ministry of Economy and Competitiveness under the National Science Program (TEC2014-54335-C4-3-R).

References

1. Cazzoli, L., Sharma. R., Treccani, M., Lillo, F.A.: Large scale study to understand the relation between Twitter and financial market. In: Third European Network Intelligence Conference (2016)
2. Sprenger, T.O., Tumasjan, A., Sandner, P.G., Welpe, I.M.: Tweets and trades: the information content of stock microblogs. In: European Financial Management, vol. 20, pp. 926–957 (2014)
3. Hentschel, M., Alonso, O.: Follow the money: a study of cashtags on Twitter. First Monday **19**(8) (2014)
4. Ruiz, E.J., Hristidis, V., Castillo, C., Gionis, A., Jaimes, A.: Correlating financial time series with microblogging activity. In: Proceedings of the Fifth ACM International Conference on Web Search and Data Mining (2012)

5. Oliveira, N., Cortez, P., Areal, N.: The impact of microblogging data for stock market prediction: using Twitter to predict returns, volatility, trading volume and survey sentiment indices. Expert Syst. Appl. **73**, 125–144 (2017)
6. Liew, J.K.S., Budavári, T.: Do Tweet Sentiments Still Predict the Stock Market? SSRN (2016)
7. Rajesh, N., Gandy, L.: CashTagNN: using sentiment of tweets with CashTags to predict stock market prices. In: 11th International Conference on Intelligent Systems: Theories and Applications (2016)
8. Cortez, P., Oliveira, N., Ferreira, J.P.: Measuring user influence in financial microblogs: experiments using stocktwits data. In: Proceedings of the 6th International Conference on Web Intelligence, Mining and Semantics, WIMS 2016 (2016)
9. Adnan, M., Leak, A., Loingley, P.: A geocomputational analysis of Twitter activity around different world cities. Geo-Spatial Inf. Sci. **17**(3), 145–152 (2014)
10. Morstatter, F., Pfeffer, J., Liu, H., Carley, K.M.: Is the sample good enough? Comparing data from twitter's streaming API with Twitter's firehose. In: Proceedings of the 7th International Conference on Weblogs and Social Media, ICWSM 2013 (2013)
11. Liu, H., Morstatter, F., Tang, J., Zafarani, R.: The good, the bad, and the ugly: uncovering novel research opportunities in social media mining. Int. J. Data Sci. Anal. **1**(3–4), 137–143 (2016)
12. Vosoughi, S.: Automatic Detection and Verification of Rumors on Twitter. Massachusetts Institute of Technology (2015)
13. Tafti, A., Zotti, R., Jank, W.: Real-time diffusion of information on Twitter and the financial markets. PLoS ONE **11**(8) (2016)
14. Jung, M.J., Naughton, J.P., Tahoun, A., Clare, A.W.: Do Firms Strategically Disseminate? Evidence from Corporate Use of Social Media. SSRN (2016)

APK-DFS: An Automatic Interaction System Based on Depth-First-Search for APK

Jing Tao[✉], Qiqi Zhao, Pengfei Cao, Zheng Wang, and Yan Zhang

Ministry of Education Key Lab for Intelligent Networks and Network Security,
Xi'an Jiaotong University, Xi'an 710049, China
jtao@mail.xjtu.edu.cn

Abstract. Android is paid more and more attention by many mobile phone manufacturers and software vendors. Due to defects of the Android and the huge potential economic benefits, there are more and more malicious codes. The majority of malicious applications will exhibit malicious behavior only if they interact with users. However, there is not a mature solution to traverse APKs automatically currently. By studying and analyzing the framework of Android system, we design and implement a system called APK-DFS which can traverse APKs automatically. This system can extract and recognize views in UI pages, and interact with these views via depth-first-search algorithm layer by layer; it establishes a UI storage stack and a UI trash can; it can also generate strings with specified format for views which require text input. We evaluate the system by testing it with APKs downloaded from Android markets. The results show that APK-DFS can simulate real users to trigger views in APKs effectively. For APK-DFS, in 30 min the average of effective trigger rate is 91%, and the average number of views that can be triggered in 50 events is 32.58. Compared with Monkey and PUMA, APK-DFS is the best one.

Keywords: Android · Automatically trigger · Traverse all views · Interaction of UI · Depth first search

1 Introduction

In recent years, the market share of smart phones has risen rapidly. With the promotion of Android mobile phones, the number of APKs is also increasing. However, due to the defects of Android and the huge potential economic benefits, there are more and more malicious applications. The majority of malicious applications will exhibit malicious behavior only if they interact with users. By installing APKs in simulator, simulating users to interact with the APKs, we can witness the malicious acts, and do safety inspection of APKs before using them. Now, there are some tools that can interact with APKs automatically, such as Monkey, PUMA [2] and Dynodroid [3].

Monkey is an automated testing tool that comes with the Android system and can generate a specified number of random events, including keystroke entry, touch screen operations, gesture input, and so on. But it just generates random events, it can't generate events as users need. In those random events, there are some repeated events which will

© Springer International Publishing AG 2017
S. Ibrahim et al. (Eds.): ICA3PP 2017, LNCS 10393, pp. 420–430, 2017.
DOI: 10.1007/978-3-319-65482-9_29

trigger the same view, and some of the events are not needed in some UI pages, but there is no way to avoid them in Monkey.

Shuai et al. proposed to separate two tasks which are analyzing the UI pages and exploring the execution logic of the application, so that the trigger strategy is defined after analyzing the APK. They implemented the PUMA system [2]. But PUMA ignores views which need users to input text into; some applications has advertisements when started, and PUMA will get the advertising page, then exit without recognizing any useful views, so it cannot trigger any useful views in the applications.

Aravind et al. proposed to use the "observe - select – execute" cycle for automatic trigger and they implemented Dynodroid system [3]. First, it observes events related to the current page of the APK, next it selects one of these events, then it executes the event, and repeats the process. When getting the events, it needs a collection of registered callback functions and a collection of overridden methods which need to be analyzed in the source code. In Dynodroid system, the Android SDK source code is modified to obtain the information of events, but this needs to modify the Android source code and is not compatible with different Android versions.

In a word, these tools proposed in the existing researches can trigger APKs automatically with good results in some aspects, but there are still some problems. Aiming at solving these problems, we designs an APK interactive system named APK-DFS.

The contributions of this paper are as follows:

(1) **We design and implement an automatic interaction system based on Depth-First-Search for APK named APK-DFS.** The APK-DFS system uses the depth first search algorithm to extract, identify and traverse UI views layer by layer, and interacts with views that need to be clicked and input text in. It also records the views that have been triggered, avoids triggering the same views repeatedly, and performs a more complete traversal of all the UI views in APKs.
(2) **We design a method to construct fingerprints for UI pages and record information of UI pages in a UI storage stack and a UI trash can.** APK-DFS distinguishes different UI pages through the fingerprint information of different UI pages. It records the UI states in traversal process, establishes UI storage stack to store related information, and establishes UI trash can to record UI pages that have been visited.
(3) **The effectiveness of the APK-DFS is verified by experiments on APKs from Android markets.** We use APK-DFS, Monkey and PUMA to trigger APKs from Android markets, and the results show that APK-DFS is the best one.

2   The Framework of APK-DFS

APK-DFS is used to start APKs and trigger all views that can interact with users in APKs automatically. The whole system can be divided into three modules: APK analysis preprocess module, APK automatic installation and startup module, and APK automation interaction module. The framework of the system is shown in Fig. 1.

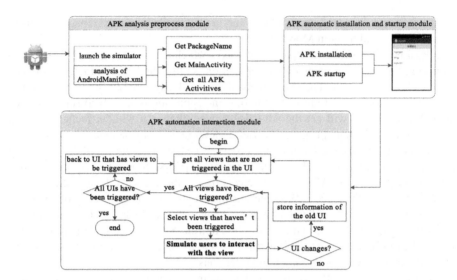

Fig. 1. The framework of the system

APK analysis preprocess module includes two parts which are launch the simulator and analysis of AndroidManifest.xml. Launch the simulator provides a runtime environment for APK-DFS to simulate users for automatic triggering; analysis of Android-Manifest.xml file provides the PackageName, MainActivity and all valid Activity classes of the APK, which provide reference information to judge whether an Activity belongs to the APK, so as to avoid wasting time in useless UI pages.

The APK automatic installation and startup module is divided into APK installation and APK startup. After getting the position of APK to be tested, we can install it onto the simulator through "adb install" command, and then start the APK according to the PackageName and MainActivity by using "adb shell am start" command.

The APK automation interaction module is the main part of the system, which simulates the interaction between users and views in UI pages by the depth first search traversal algorithm. It is described in Sect. 3.

3　Design and Implementation of Automated Interaction

3.1　Automatic Interaction Process

The process of automated interaction is shown in Fig. 1. The steps are as follows:

(1) Get the UI page and all views that are not triggered in the UI page.
(2) Judge whether all views in the current UI page have been triggered, if so, enter (4), else enter (3).
(3) Select a view that hasn't been triggered before, and simulate users to interact with the view according to the class of the view, then judge whether UI changes, if so

save the original UI information and interact with the new UI page, back to (1), else trigger the original UI page, back to (2).

(4) Judge whether all UI pages in the APK have been triggered, if so, the interaction is ended, else go back to the UI page that has views to be triggered, then back to (1).

3.2 Depth First Search Traversal Algorithm

The APK-DFS system is based on "layer" to implement the depth first search traversal (DFS) algorithm, which is the key to the system. The layer refers to different UI pages. In the system, each UI page belongs to and only belongs to a certain layer. When APK starts, the initial UI page is the 1st layer, such as 1-1 in Fig. 2. If a new UI page emerges after triggering a view in the first layer, it belongs to the 2nd layer, such as 2-1, 2-2 and 2-3 in Fig. 2. The new UI pages which have never emerged after triggering the views in the 2nd layer belong to the 3rd layer, such as 3-1 in Fig. 2, and so on. After triggering the views in n layer, new UI pages belong to the n + 1 layer. If a UI belongs to k (0 < k <= m) layer which has already emerged after triggering a view of the m layer, the layer to which the UI belongs will not change, it belongs to k layer. In the 2-3, clicking the "registration" will show 2-2, but 2-2 has already emerged in the 2nd level, so 2-2 belongs to the 2nd layer instead of the 3rd layer.

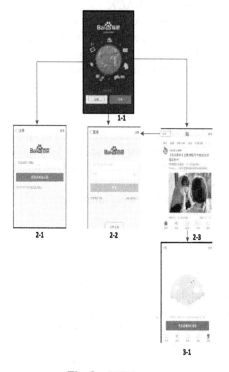

algorithm 1: depth first search traversal algorithm

```
installApk;
startApk;
dump the first UI;
push the first UI into UIstack;
WHILE UIstack != null DO
    UIn = UIstack.pop ;
    toUIn ;
    get all views in the UIn as viewlist;
    FOR each view in viewlist DO
        interactWithView;
        dump the UIn+1;
        IF UIn+1 != UIn && UIn+1 not in
UItrash
            push UIn into UIstack;
            push n+1UI into UIstack;
            CONTINUE WHILE;
        END IF
    END FOR
    push UIn into the UItrash;
END WHILE
```

Fig. 2. APK layers

APK-DFS's main interactive traversal algorithm is depth first search traversal (DFS) algorithm, the detailed design of the which is as follows

(1) The DFS method is used when traversing an APK. First, start the application. When traversing a UI page, get all the interactive views of the UI page, then traverse all views one by one. After triggering a view in the n layer, UI page changes, then the new UI belongs to n + 1 layer. Then store the old UI page information, and traverse the new UI page. When finish traversing the n + 1 page, go back to the n page to traverse the remaining views. The depth first traversal algorithm is described in algorithm 1.
Regard "Baidu Tieba" APK as an example in Fig. 2. It launched the "Baidu Tieba" firstly, and in the initial 1-1 page, there are three interactive UI views which are "login", "registered" and "look". When clicking "login", page changes, and new page 2-1 emerges, so the information of the 1-1 is stored, and then it traverse the 2-1 UI. After finishing triggering the views in 2-1, go back to the 1-1 to trigger other views.

(2) In the traversal process, if you go through all views of a UI page in layer n + 1, then find the click path in this page to reach the n layer page, and go back to the n layer page. In Fig. 2, if you want to go back to 2-3 after 3-1 traversal, you can reach 2-3 directly by clicking "home page". If the n + 1 layer page is fully traversed and there is no path to the n layer pages, click the backspace key BACK.

(3) If you don't go back to the n layer pages after clicking BACK, but to an m ($0 < m < n$) layer page, then click the appropriate button in the page, until you reach the page of layer n. As shown in Fig. 2, after clicking BACK in 3-1, it isn't back to the target page 2-3, but back to 1-1, then click the "random look" in 1-1 to reach 2-3.

3.3 UI Page Fingerprint

Judging whether UI pages are the same one requires a standard, and APK-DFS uniquely identifies UI pages by building fingerprints for them. The fingerprint of a UI page is composed by all views with different attributes in the UI, so before building the fingerprint of a UI, we need to build fingerprints of views with its attributes.

The fingerprint information of a view consists of the following attributes:

(1) class of the view, such as RadioButton, TextView;
(2) coordinate information of the view;
(3) the size of the view;
(4) the class name of the Activity where the view is located.

The string is spliced by above information, and the fixed length string, which is the fingerprint of the view, is obtained by using Hash algorithm. Then the string obtained by using Hash algorithm in fingerprints of all views is the fingerprint of the UI page.

According to whether the fingerprints of two UI pages are the same, we can judge whether the they are the same and the method is as follows:

(1) If the Activity class names of the two UI pages are different, they are different UI pages, else enter (2);

(2) If the numbers of views in the two UI pages are different, they are different UI pages, else enter (3);

(3) If the fingerprints of the two UI pages are inconsistent, they are different UI pages, otherwise they are the same UI page.

3.4 UI Storage Stack and UI Trash Can

To ensure that all UI pages that you can get are completely traversed in sequence, APK-DFS constructs a UI storage stack for UI pages, as shown in Fig. 3. When an APK is triggered automatically, there is a UI storage stack that stores all the UI pages that emerged and the views in which haven't been triggered. When a UI page is being traversed, if there is a new UI page emerging, then the old UI page information is stored, and the old UI page is pushed into the UI storage stack, then traverse views in the new UI page. When all of the UI pages in the stack on one UI page have been traversed, the stack pops up this UI page and traverses the views that have not yet been triggered. If all views have already been triggered, then mark the UI page as "completed traversal" and no longer push it into the stack.

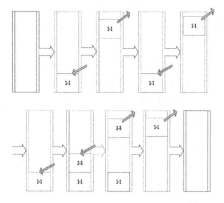

Fig. 3. UI storage stack

Those UI pages marked as "completed traversal" may emerge later in the process of interaction. In order to avoid repeated traverse, APK-DFS constructs a UI trash can to store information of those pages that have been triggered. When the system is running, if there is a new UI page, and the page is in the UI trash can, there is no need to traverse it, so leave from it directly, otherwise traverse it as needed.

Take "Baidu Tieba" APK as an example, as shown in Fig. 3, which is the change process of the UI storage stack corresponding to Fig. 2. The initial UI page stack is empty. In the traversal of 1-1, the new page 2-1 emerges, it will push 1-1 into the stack, then traverse 2-1. When finish traversing 2-1, pop the 1-1, and continue to traverse the 1-1. When 2-2 emerges, put 1-1 into the stack. After traversing the 2-2, pop 1-1, continue to traverse 1-1. 2-3 emerges, put 1-1 into the stack, then traverse the 2-3. 3-1 emerges, put 2-3 into the stack, too, traverse 3-1. After the traversal of 3-1, pop 2-3. After the traversal of 2-3, pop 1-1 stack.

3.5   User Operation Simulation

APK-DFS mainly simulates the interaction on views that are clickable and need text to input. Through the simulation of these two types of operation, it can interact with most of the views. Clickable views include Button, RadioButton, ImageView, TextView, CheckBox, and so on. APK-DFS uses the AndroidViewClient [10], an open source tool to obtain UI page information and performs click operations.

Text input boxes are usually required to enter text with specified format, such as "username", "password", the format is usually indicated in the text property of the view. APK-DFS automatically generates strings that conform to the format requirements. The string types and formatting requirements that can be generated are shown in Table 1. In the system, first of all, extract all views that need to input text according to the class of them, then generate string automatically according to the text property of the views, then trigger other views. Many views in the UI pages need text input before they are triggered. Inputting valid strings automatically can trigger more pages.

Table 1.   The string format generated automatically

String type	String format
Mailbox	Ended with @xx.com. The mailbox name is a combination of 5–9 letters and digit numbers
Mobile phone number	A combination of 11 digit numbers at the beginning of 1
Verification code	A combination of 6 digit numbers
Username	A combination of 4–9 characters, special characters and numbers
Password	A combination of 4–9 characters, special characters and numbers
Others	A combination of 1–20 characters, special characters and numbers

4   Experiments and Results

4.1   Experimental Results

In order to validate the effectiveness of APK-DFS system, we choose Monkey and PUMA to compare. Monkey is an automated testing tool that comes with Android system. It uses socket communication and can generate random click events, touch screen, gestures and other types of events. PUMA is a tool that identifies UIs in APK dynamically, and identifies various views in the page to trigger automatically.

The APKs used in the experiment are downloaded from the Android markets, including many frequently used APKs such as Renren and Baidu Tieba. The total number is 100. In experiments, APK-DFS, Monkey and PUMA are used to automatically trigger APKs. By counting the number of views that are effectively triggered by each tool, the results of various tools triggering APK are compared.

The 1st experiment, set the trigger time of APKs to be 30 min, then count the total number of generated events(TN) and the number of events that can effectively trigger views(EN), then calculate the effective trigger rate, the formula of which is:

$$\text{effective trigger rate} = \frac{EN}{TN}$$

The experimental results of monkey, PUMA and APK-DFS are shown in Figs. 4, 5 and 6. The abscissa is the serial number of APK, and the ordinate is the effective trigger rate. Lines in Figs. 4, 5 and 6 are average numbers. According to the experimental results, the maximum value of monkey effective trigger rate is 26%, the minimum is 0%, the average is 14%. We can see from Fig. 4 that triggering views by monkey, each APK's effective trigger rate remains at a low level, and the automatic trigger result is poor; the maximum value of effective rate of PUMA is 100%, the minimum is 0%, and the average is 29.93%. We can see from Fig. 5, the PUMA trigger results are not stable that many APKs' trigger ratio being 0%. The results are not very good; the maximum value of APK-DFS system effective trigger rate is 91%, the minimum is 0%, and the average is 59%. As shown in Fig. 6, a small number of APKs' trigger rate is 0%, but the number of those APKs is little. Overall, the results of APK-DFS are more stable and better than that of PUMA and APK-DFS.

The 2nd experiment, setting the number of events that each APK can trigger to be 50, and counting the number of views that are effectively triggered after each APK triggers 50 events automatically. The experimental results of monkey, PUMA and APK-DFS are shown in Figs. 7, 8 and 9. The abscissa is the serial number of APK, and the ordinate is the number of views that are effective triggered. Lines in Figs. 7, 8 and 9 are the average numbers. The number of views triggered effectively by monkey maintains in low level; there is a large gap for numbers of views triggered by different APKs when use PUMA, and the number of views triggered for many APKs is 0. The trigger results are not stable. The numbers of views APK-DFS triggered are relatively stable, the numbers of most of the APKs are near the average number 32.58, so its automatically trigger results are the best.

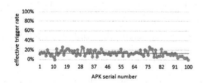

Fig. 4. Monkey results of the 1st experiment   **Fig. 5.** PUMA results of the 1st experiment

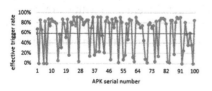
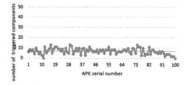

Fig. 6. APK-DFS results of the 1st experiment   **Fig. 7.** Monkey results of the 2nd experiment

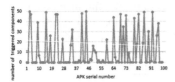

Fig. 8. PUMA results of the 2nd experiment   **Fig. 9.** APK-DFS results of the 2nd experiment

4.2 Result Analysis

The number of views that Monkey effectively triggers is less due to the random events which include a large number of repeated events and invalid events, such as various sliding events, which rarely trigger views. The APK-DFS takes class of each view, generates effective events that can trigger views, and records the trigger states of each view to avoid generating events that trigger the same view repeatedly.

When PUMA triggers, many APKs end automatic triggering process shortly after the start, and can't trigger views in APKs. This is because when APK starts, the ad page first appears, and PUMA identifies the ad page, without identifying the active views. Without triggering any views, it ends the trigger process. Most of these ad pages need to be slid to skip, and PUMA doesn't deal with them effectively. When APK starts running, APK-DFS can simulate users' sliding action to avoid advertising, then entering the main page and triggering the active view. But for the views requiring users to input text, PUMA can't input string as needed, so that PUMA can't trigger some views, while APK-DFS can generate strings in accordance with the demand and trigger more views. In APK-DFS, some APKs stop soon after starting, because the ad page at these APK starts requires more sophisticated user actions to skip.

In a word, the features of APK-DFS are as follows:

(1) Avoid triggering views repeatedly. APK-DFS takes a layered approach, defining each of the UI pages as a layer, and traversing all the views based on the layers. For views in each layer, it can conduct a comprehensive interactive traverse, and views have been triggered in the running process of the system won't be triggered again, so it can reduce time consumption used by triggering the same views repeatedly. APK-DFS enables more comprehensive triggering of views in APKs, exposing more malicious behavior hidden behind views (Tables 2 and 3).
(2) Strings of the corresponding format is generated according to the need of the text input boxes. APK-DFS can generate the corresponding string format according to the text property of a text input box to meet the need of the majority of the text input boxes, thereby triggering more pages, simulate the interaction with more views.
(3) It can avoid the influence of initial advertisement pages. At APK startup, the ad pages can be skipped by simulating sliding operation, so that it can enter main page and trigger more views.

Table 2. Effective trigger rate of the 1st experiment

Tools	Maximum value	Minimum value	Average value
Monkey	26%	0%	14%
PUMA	100%	0%	29.93%
APK-DFS	100%	0%	91%

Table 3. Effectively triggered views of the 2nd experiment

Tools	Maximum value	Minimum value	Average value
Monkey	14	0	6.95
PUMA	50	0	10.73
APK-DFS	50	0	32.58

5 Summary

In order to test APKs and expose malicious behaviors, we design and implement an automatic interaction system based on DFS for APKs named APK-DFS. APK-DFS is based on layer and uses the depth first search traversal algorithm to traverse all views in APKs. For different UI pages, it builds fingerprints to distinguish them. It establishes UI storage stack to store information of UI pages that need to visit, and builds UI trash can to store UI pages that have been traversed. It can generate strings according to string format requirements. When the system is running, it automatically installs and starts APK, and traverses the UI page automatically in APK. By comparing with Monkey and PUMA, we can see that APK-DFS triggers APKs better.

There are still some problems: APK-DFS can't recognize views developed by developers; because of the verification code mechanism, it can't simulate the registration operation. To resolve these problems, we will conduct further research from these aspects: (1) Use other methods to obtain UI page information, and further analyze the page information about custom views. (2) Analyze the verification mechanism of verification code, simulate verification of mailbox, mobile phone, etc., so as to bypass these steps and jump to the next page directly. In the future, we will search relevant papers about these methods, and learn related technologies to perfect our system.

References

1. Domenico, A., Anna, R.F., Porfirio, T., Bryan, D.T., Atif, M.: MobiGUITAR–A tool for automated model based testing of mobile apps. IEEE Softw. **32**(5), 53–59 (2014)
2. Shuai, H., Bin L., Suman, N., William, G.J.H., Ramesh, G.: PUMA: Programmable UI-automation for large-scale dynamic analysis of mobile apps. In: 12th Annual International Conference on Mobile Systems, Applications, and Services, pp. 204–217 (2014)
3. Aravind, M., Rohan, T., Mayur, N.: Dynodroid: An input generation system for android apps. In: 9th Joint Meeting on Foundations of Software Engineering, pp. 422–434 (2013)

4. Peng, W., Bin, L., Wei, Y., Jingzhe, L., Wenchang, S.: Automatic android GUI traversal with high coverage. In: International Conference on Communication Systems and Network Technologies, pp. 1161–1166 (2014)
5. Wontae, C., George, N., Koushik, S.: Guided GUI testing of android apps with minimal restart and approximate learning. ACM Sigplan Not. **48**(10), 623–640 (2013)
6. Vaibhav, R., Yan, C., William, E.: AppsPlayground: Automatic Security Analysis of Smartphone Applications. In: Third ACM Conference on Data and Application Security and Privacy, pp. 209–220 (2013)
7. Tanzirul, A., Iulian, N.: Targeted and depth-first exploration for systematic testing of android apps. Acm Sigplan Not. **48**(10), 641–660 (2013)
8. Hsiang-Lin, W., Chia-Hui, L., Tzong-Han, H., Cheng-Zen, Y.: PATS: A parallel GUI testing framework for android applications. In: Computer Software amd Applications Conference, pp. 210–215 (2015)
9. Wei, Y., Mukul, R.P., Tao, X.: A grey-box approach for automated GUI-model generation of mobile applications. In: International Conference on Fundamental Approaches to Software Engineering, pp. 250–265 (2013)
10. AndroidViewClient. https://github.com/dtmilano/AndroidViewClient accessed 1 Feb 2017

Optimized Data Layout for Spatio-temporal Data in Time Domain Astronomy

Jie Yan[1], Ce Yu[1(✉)], Chao Sun[1], Zhaohui Shang[2], Yi Hu[2], Jinghua Feng[3],
Jizhou Sun[1], and Jian Xiao[1]

[1] School of Computer Science and Technology, Tianjin University,
Tianjin 300350, China
{jerryan,yuce,sch,jzsun,xiaojian}@tju.edu.cn
[2] National Astronomical Observatories, CAS, Beijing 100000, China
zshang@gmail.com, huyi.naoc@gmail.com
[3] National Supercomputer Center in Tianjin, Tianjin 300457, China
fengjh@nscc-tj.gov.cn

Abstract. Spatio-temporal data is a common data-type in astronomy, and layouts for this data are generally to improve the performance. However, restricted by Antarctic environmental conditions, the energy consumption of the storage system is the most pivotal problem. Traditional storage layout consumes a lot of energy for request execution. In this paper, a new storage layout for the astronomical observation data on Antarctic Dome A is designed, which divides the disk array by the observant sky coverage, stores data according to the space while the traditional storage method stores data chronologically. Then we use the tree-like structure to store the popular data and use the redundant mode to store the cold data. In simulated experiments, this storage layout is applied on the Antarctic storage system, and the average number of disks that needs to be opened at request can be reduced from 23.88 to 2.74, greatly reducing the energy consumption of the request.

Keywords: Data layout · Storage · Disk array · Energy efficient · Time domain astronomy · Spatio-temporal data

1 Introduction

Time domain research is an important branch of astronomy which puts emphasis on how astronomical objects change with time. For the analysis of time domain astronomy, a massive volume of data from astronomical observation is indispensable. China has established a series of telescopes for astronomical observations in Antarctic, namely by Antarctic Schmidt Telescopes (AST3) [8]. The AST3 is a trio of 50-cm optical telescopes installed on Dome A, which is the highest place in Antarctica with the lowest temperature reaching about $-80\,°C$. In Antarctica, the power supply is extremely limited. While the generation and the storage of the massive data of the telescope is highly energy-consuming, and a large part of the power will be used to maintain the operating of the disk. Therefore an

© Springer International Publishing AG 2017
S. Ibrahim et al. (Eds.): ICA3PP 2017, LNCS 10393, pp. 431–440, 2017.
DOI: 10.1007/978-3-319-65482-9_30

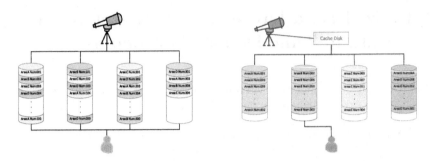

Fig. 1. Traditional layout   **Fig. 2.** Optimized layout (request the grey area)

array of disks is used to store it which usually only keeps the disk being used running and closes other disks to reduce the energy consumption.

The traditional method to store astronomical observation data is to store in chronological order. As shown in Fig. 1. After one disk is filled of data, it will be closed and the disk management system will wake up an other disk to continue. It will cut down on electricity when saving data. However, when scientists want to find the data that they are interested in, they usually search in spatial order. Due to the inconsistent order organization, the system has to access all the disks to find the target data, which will cost too much time and power to both wake up all the disk. It is also very contradictory to the idea of saving energy by shutting down more disks. So it is necessary to change the data storage layout and reduce the number of disks which will be waken up when someone requesting the data. Only thus can the power supply support the observation system longer. In this article, we propose an optimized layout for spatio-temporal data storage which is based on the demand of Time domain astronomy. As shown in Fig. 2. Unlike the traditional data layout which stores data in the order that they are produced, we divide the disk array by the sky coverage and design a partition model for the data. In this model, each piece of sky coverage corresponds to one or more disks and each disk only saves data from the corresponding sky coverage. In order to reduce the number of disks being opened during the storage stage, a cache disk is used to store the data generated by the telescope. Whenever the cache disk is full of data, the largest part of data from the same sky coverage will be transferred to the specified disk. Compared with the old method, the power consumption of this data layout will increase a little. But the number of disks being opened at each request will be significantly reduced. Experiments show that in the AST3 simulation environment, the power consumption in the request stage is reduced about 57.6%, The average number of disks that have been opened during each request drop from 23.88 to 2.74, and the waiting time is also reduced about 26.15%.

The rest of the paper is organized as follows. Section 2 presents the background and the related works. Section 3 presents the model of the data layout.

In Sect. 4, we evaluate the performance of the optimized layout. We conclude and discuss future work in Sect. 5.

2 Related Work

We can not ignored the energy consumption of the storage system in data center. This is also true for data processing of Antarctic astronomical observations. Disk is very important for the storage system. There are many energy-saving plan for the disk. S. W. Son [9] and Hai Huang [4] have tried to use the head positioning to optimize the movement, by changing the storage on the disk and reducing the power consumption of the head positioning. There are also many plans for disk management systems, such as power-aware prefetching schemes [10], multi-speed settings [3], power-aware cache management strategies [13]. But taking the extreme conditions in the Antarctic into consideration, the disk which not in use will be shut down instead of entering standby model. Almost all of the above methods can not solve this problem. However, Yuan [12] using a special storage system for the Antarctic disk matrix management. In this system, the system will shut down the disk which not running. But this system can not solve the problem of data layout.

Lu [6] introduce a family of energy-efficient disk layouts that generalize the data mirroring of a conventional RAID1 system. The scheme called DiskGroup distributes the workload between the primary disks and secondary disks based on the characteristics of the workload. But in Antarctic, the power supply is not enough to support any backup, the data is simply save on the storage system. The same problem also exist in Lius theory [5].

Moreover, Reddy R. [1] proposed a data layout for power efficient archival storage systems. They present a two-tier architecture for active archives comprising of online and offline disks, and provide an accessaware intelligent data layout mechanism to bring power efficiency. However, the time domain astronomys data is peculiar, it contains both time and space attributes, and uses a completely different order when it is generated and read. Although there are some researches for optimizing the spatio-temporal data [2], they mainly scheduling the operations to optimize the performance, rather than focus on energy saving.

For the Antarctic astronomical data layout, it should consider the following characteristics:

1. Use a disk array to store data and shut down the disk when it is not in use.
2. The spatio-temporal data will be generated in chronological order, while the request will search for all the data of a part of the sky coverage.
3. The key purpose of this paper is to reduce power consumption, and then consider the performance of the request.

This is the main consideration of data layout model.

3 Design

Our storage layout model has three parts. The first part is called the partitioned layout. It is used to divide the sky coverage. In second part, the layout of the partition accessed frequently by the search request is adjusted. The binary tree layout is used to adjusted the layout. In the last part, we handle the layout of non-popular data called redundant layout. The first part of the layout is the most basic and indispensable section and the other two parts can be used independently according to the requirement. When build the model, we assume that the image size of the generated stage and the search request stage is the same.

3.1 Partitioned Layout

Table 1 shows the parameters of the astronomical observation. To simplify the calculation, we assume that the maximum observing range of the telescope is a rectangle which has length L and width W. The size of the telescope observation image is called the field of view. It has length l' and width w'. After the interval of observation t, the total time of the observation D, and m, the size of the data for each time, are determined. the total size of data N can be calculate as:

$$N = m \times \frac{D}{t} \tag{1}$$

Assuming that the observed data is uniform, the entire observation areas should be divided equally. Since we have already known N and V, it is clear that the number of required disks can be estimate. Besides, the biggest problem of partitioning is that the scope of the request may span multiple divided regions. That's to say, the storage system may need to open multiple disks instead of only one to read the data. So it is necessary to make the request regions as less as possible. For each divided region, we want to minimize the proportion of the

Table 1. Parameters of the astronomical observation

Parameter	Description (Unit)
l' w'	The length and width of the field of view
L W	The length and width of observation area
m	Image's size (MB)
t	The interval at which the image is generated (second)
D	The total time of observation (second)
N	The total size of data (MB)
V	Disk capacity (MB)

cross-query area in total area. If we assume that each region has length l and width w after the partition, the probability of image that will span multiple regions is:

$$\frac{l \times w' + l' \times w - l' \times w'}{l \times w} \qquad (2)$$

Considering S, the total area for each region has been determined, let w in the molecule be $\frac{S}{l}$ and transferred the denominator $l \times w$ to S. S is a constant, then take the derivative of (2) with respect to l:

$$\frac{w' - l' \times S \times l^{-2}}{S} \qquad (3)$$

Let (3) equal to zero and get the limit value: $l = \sqrt{\frac{S \times l'}{w'}}$ $w = \sqrt{\frac{S \times w'}{l'}}$

We can see that when the ratio between l and w equal to the ratio between l' and w', the probability of image that will span multiple regions will be reduced to the minimum. So when partitioning the sky coverage, we try to ensure that each region's proportion between length and width is closed to $\frac{l'}{w'}$. At this point, we can list the following equation:

$$l' \times p_1 \times x = L \qquad (4)$$

$$w' \times p_2 \times y = W \qquad (5)$$

$$x \times y = \frac{N}{V} \times k \qquad (6)$$

where p_1 and p_2 are the expansion ratio, and x and y mean the number of regions in the row and column respectively. It is expected that p_1 and p_2 are as close as possible. k means the magnification.

To solve the above equation, we assume that p_1 equal to p_2. After solving the equation, the condition that x and y must be integers has been considered, and p_1 and p_2 will be adjusted according to x and y to obtain the final result. The following figure is a partitioned layout diagram:

Fig. 3. Result of partitioned layout

In the observation stage, a cache disk is needed. Firstly, The data will be saved to the cache disk until it is full. Then the data from the most populated areas will be migrated from the cache disk to the partitioned disk. In this way, the frequency of disk opening will be reduced when observing.

3.2 Binary Tree Layout

In Sect. 3.1, we assumed that the whole data of the sky coverage is hypodispersion. However, it is obviously impossible in the actual situation. In fact, a single region may involved with multiple disks. In Sect. 3.2, we try to divide this region and change its layout to the binary tree layout.

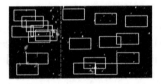   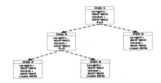

Fig. 4. Divide a region into two parts   **Fig. 5.** Binary tree layout for a region

Figures 4 and 5 shows an example of the binary tree layout. When the current writing disk is full, the data will write into anther spare disk. At this moment, the region will also be re-layout and divided into two sub-regions. It can be chosen to be divided by either horizontal or vertical line. Figure 4 chooses the vertical way. The split line divide the region into two parts. Each one of which would have the same size of data. After that, two spare disks will be waken up and each disk will be responsible for a new region. The previous data are still stored on the old disk.

Figure 5 shows that by the storage structure changes from chain to tree in the binary tree layout.

3.3 Redundant Layout

In this subsection, we will focus on the cold region. Normally, cold region refers to the sky coverage which contains a few astronomical celestial so that the data from single cold region mostly store in a single disk. This disk is not full usually. Therefore we can change the layout of those regions to make a backup for some data on the border like Fig. 6.

The condition that one image belongs to a region is that the upper-left vertex of the image is in this region. However, when responding a request, any images having overlapping areas with the request image should be submitted to the user. If the upper-left part of a request image belongs to the shadow part, the request may need data from the light blue region. We put data which from the light blue region and the shadow border on the same disk, and the request of this region will no longer need to open the white area's disks.

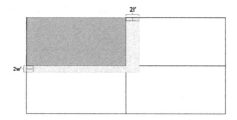

Fig. 6. Redundant layout

4   Simulation Results Analysis

In this section, the performance of traditional layout and optimized layout are compared under the simulated system. After evaluating performance in simulated environment, the optimized layout will deployed in real astronomical system. AST3 telescope is chosen as our simulation dataset.

4.1   Simulation Parameter Settings

AST3 telescope has two observation modes, sky survey mode and asteroid mode. When observing in the asteroid mode, AST3 will fixed on a specific location on the sky and stored separately. It isn't discussed in this paper. For the former one, the dataset should include stored data and requested data. According to the real specific observation plan, some locations in the sky coverage will be visited more times. However, the data layout become non-sense if every request involved all the observation result for the density of the data. Eventually when generating the dataset, we randomly selected two areas as the popular region. The popular region included half of the observed data. The remaining areas occupy the other half together. Similarly, each request has a probability of 50% to access the popular region, and others will be decided randomly.

The basic parameters of the AST3 telescope are shown in Table 2.

Table 2. parameters of AST3

Parameter	Value	Description
l' w'	1.5 3	The length and width of the field of view
L W	360 50	The length and width of observation area
m	120	Image's size (MB)
t	120	The interval at which the image is generated (second)
D	25920000	The total time of observation (second)
N	25920000	The total size of data (MB)
S	1000000	Disk capacity (MB)

Table 3. Parameters of seagate ST2000DM001

Value	Description (Unit)
0.75	Standby mode power (W)
5.4	Idle mode power (W)
8	Active mode power (W)
54	The energy consumed from idle mode to standby mode (J)
300	The energy consumed from standby mode to active mode (J)
10	Time from idle mode to standby mode (second)
10	Time from standby mode to active mode (second)
120	Average read/write speed (MB/s)

ST2000DM001 [7] is selected as the disks of the storage system, and the parameters of the disk shows in Table 3.

In the Antarctic observation system, the disk will be completely powered off after idling for a long time. We set this as 30 s. On the other hand, to reduce the power consuming of the storage system, the total number of disks is limited. In the simulation, the total number set as 64 and the total capacity twice than the size of data. In fact some of disks are not used at all, they are set for the KDUST [11].

Finally, due to the feature of the Antarctic storage system, we do not consider the competition between requests. That's to say, all requests are handled individually. There is no concurrency or contextual. The code of the simulator can be fetched at: https://github.com/muxiaokui/PE/tree/data.

4.2   Non-uniform Data Model

In this model, we will discuss C (short for Chronological), P (short for partitioned), PB (short for Partitioned & Binary Tree) and PBR (short for Partitioned & Binary Tree & Redundancy) layout, four different layouts performance.

First shown the result of the partition by the partitioned layout. Divided the observation area into $20 \times 2 = 40$ regions. The length and width of each region are 20 and 25 Considered the original area has length 360 and width 50, the result is aim to the field of views length 1.5 and width 3.

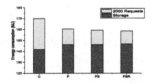

Fig. 7. Total consumption of storage system

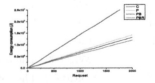

Fig. 8. Request energy consumption

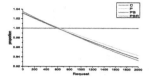 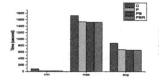 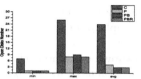

Fig. 9. Ratio of Consumption   **Fig. 10.** Time for request   **Fig. 11.** Open disks number

Figures 7 and 8 shown that the power consuming is increased from about 3.17% to 3.50% in the storage stage, but decreased from about 49.82% to 57.82% after the 2000th request.

The excellent performance of PBR can be seen in Fig. 9. After the 375th request, PBR is better than P in all respects. And PBR takes more 228 times request to surpass the C. When the number of request is beyond 655 times, PBR is the best layout in this data model. While 600 requests are easy to reach in any data center, PBR demonstrates to be the most efficient layout.

We can see that the average time of accessing reduces slightly and each layout spend more time on reading data, which indicates that the inference we are concerned about in the stage of data proved that if the data is too concentrated, it will lose the meaning of the layout.

Figure 11 shows the worth of our work is valuable in reducing energy consumption. The number of open disks declines significantly. No matter it is maximum, minimum or average, the new layout's open disk number is less than half of old method's number. In short, the optimized data layout can reduce up to 88.53% of the number of open disks.

5   Conclusion and Future Work

In this paper, a new storage layout model include partitioned layout, binary tree layout and redundant layout is designed for astronomical observation. Because of the environmental conditions, especially the strict limit of electricity, the data storage system should be energy efficient. Since partitioned layout used to store the data which generated by telescope according to the space, less disks are opened to get data than before. The binary tree layout reduced the energy consumption of the popular data and the redundant layout reduced the consumption of cold data. This layout model is evaluated on TB data level simulator storage systems, and the results show that the energy consumption reduces about 49.81% to 57.61% when requesting compared with the original layout, and decrease the number of open disks from 23.88 to 2.74.

This storage layout is also expected to play a significant role in KDUST which the observation data size will be larger than petabyte (PB) level. We will test whether it can be use to manage the data of KDUST. In addition, the layout model can be optimized further, such as the strategy of the cache disk's data migration, and the way to schedule the request sequence. In this paper the layout is simply presented practical application will be our main work in the future.

Acknowledgments. This work is supported by the National Natural Science Foundation of China (11573019, 61602336), the Joint Research Fund in Astronomy (U1531111) under cooperative agreement between the National Natural Science Foundation of China (NSFC) and Chinese Academy of Sciences (CAS).

References

1. Basak, J., Basak, J., Basak, J., Katz, R.: Data layout for power efficient archival storage systems. In: The Workshop on Power-Aware Computing and Systems, pp. 16–20 (2015)
2. Gong, Z., Lakshminarasimhan, S., Jenkins, J., Kolla, H., Ethier, S., Chen, J., Ross, R., Klasky, S., Samatova, N.F.: Multi-level layout optimization for efficient spatio-temporal queries on isabela-compressed data. In: Parallel & Distributed Processing Symposium, pp. 873–884 (2012)
3. Gurumurthi, S., Sivasubramaniam, A., Kandemir, M., Franke, H.: DRPM: dynamic speed control for power management in server class disks. ACM SIGARCH Comput. Archit. News **31**(2), 169–181 (2003)
4. Huang, H., Hung, W., Kang, G.S.: Fs2: dynamic data replication in free disk space for improving disk performance and energy consumption. In: Twentieth ACM Symposium on Operating Systems Principles, pp. 263–276 (2005)
5. Liu, J., Zheng, J., Li, Y., Sun, Z., Wang, W., Yuan, T.: Hybrid s-raid: an energy-efficient data layout for sequential data storage. J. Comput. Res. Dev. **50**(1), 37–48 (2013)
6. Lu, L., Varman, P., Wang, J.: Diskgroup: energy efficient disk layout for raid1 systems. In: International Conference on Networking, Architecture, and Storage, pp. 233–242 (2007)
7. Seagate: Desktop HDD product manual. http://www.seagate.com/wwwcontent/product-content/barracuda-fam/desktop-hdd/barracuda-7200-14/enus/docs/100686584p.pdf
8. Shang, Z., Hu, K., Hu, Y., Li, J., Li, J., Liu, Q., Ma, B., Quinn, J.L., Sun, J., Wang, L.: Operation, control, and data system for Antarctic survey telescope (ast3). In: Observatory Operations Strategies Processes & Systems IV. Proceedings of the SPIE, vol. 8448(8), p. 26 (2012)
9. Son, S.W., Chen, G., Kandemir, M.: Disk layout optimization for reducing energy consumption. In: International Conference on Supercomputing, pp. 274–283 (2005)
10. Son, S.W., Kandemir, M.: Energy-aware data prefetching for multi-speed disks. In: Conference on Computing Frontiers, Ischia, Italy, pp. 105–114, May 2006
11. K.D.U.S. Telescope: Kdust. http://en.wikipedia.org/wiki/Kunlun_Dark_Universe_Survey_Telescope
12. Yuan, Z., Yu, C., Sun, J., Xiao, J., Wang, J., Shang, Z., Hu, Y.: An energy efficient storage system for astronomical observation data on dome A. In: Wang, G., Zomaya, A., Perez, G.M., Li, K. (eds.) ICA3PP 2015. LNCS, vol. 9531, pp. 33–46. Springer, Cham (2015). doi:10.1007/978-3-319-27140-8_3
13. Zhu, Q., David, F.M., Devaraj, C.F., Li, Z., Zhou, Y., Cao, P.: Reducing energy consumption of disk storage using power-aware cache management. In: International Symposium on High PERFORMANCE Computer Architecture, p. 118 (2004)

Cloud Multimedia Files Assured Deletion Based on Bit Stream Transformation with Chaos Sequence

Wenbin Yao[1], Yijie Chen[1(✉)], and Dongbin Wang[2]

[1] Beijing Key Laboratory of Intelligent Telecommunications Software and Multimedia, Beijing University of Posts and Telecommunications, No.10, Xitucheng Road, Beijing 100876, China
yijie8899@126.com

[2] National Engineering Laboratory for Mobile Network Security, School of Computer Science, Beijing University of Posts and Telecommunications, No. 10, Xitucheng Road, Beijing 100876, China

Abstract. As more and more data is outsourced to the cloud, data owners lose direct control of their data. When clients delete their data, it is important to prevent illegal users from visiting the deleted or backup data. The mainstream method of this problem is to encrypt the data in advance, and then protect the decryption key without being sent to unauthorized users. However, if we remain the full encrypted data in the cloud, once the decryption key is stolen by attackers, the data is unsafe. Especially, it is important to protect the privacy of cloud pictures, videos and other multimedia files which contain plenty of private information. In this paper, a new scheme named ADBST is presented for cloud multimedia files. In this method, the bit stream of multimedia files will be transformed into a new one by using logistic chaotic mapping before being encrypted in order to make the cloud file be different from the original file. It can even ensure the security of files on the condition of missing the encryption key. Moreover, this scheme does not bring other third parties in order to reduce the risk of data leakage. Compared with other schemes on the same condition, it only brings little time costs in the acceptable range.

Keywords: Cloud multimedia files · Assured deletion · Logistic chaotic mapping · Bit stream transformation

1 Introduction

With the development of cloud storage technology, an increasing number of people or companies try to reduce the cost of computing by outsourcing their data to the storage server. Cloud storage reduces data management costs. However, it causes some problems for information security. Because data owners lose control of the outsourced data, data security becomes a major concern while users consume the cloud storage. When a data owner pretends to delete the data, he expects that his data becomes permanently inaccessible once he makes the request.

Data assured deletion is one of those security concerns, because data owners cannot make sure whether a cloud service provider (CSP) has deleted the data upon their

© Springer International Publishing AG 2017
S. Ibrahim et al. (Eds.): ICA3PP 2017, LNCS 10393, pp. 441–451, 2017.
DOI: 10.1007/978-3-319-65482-9_31

deletion request. With the arrival of the whole media era, more and more information is transmitted in the form of multimedia. Multimedia files often contain a lot of important information or personal privacy. So, it is necessary to realize the assured deletion of cloud multimedia files.

In order to protect the data from malicious visits by illegal users, data owners usually encrypt the data before it is delivered to CSP. The encryption key will be protected by data owner himself. Although the data has been stored by CSP, there also exist some potential risks. For instance, in order to improve the reliability of service, CSP might have many data backups and put them into different servers. On this condition, if the data is overdue and the data owner orders CSP to delete his data, CSP might not delete all of the data or the backups absolutely. Once the attacker takes both the encryption key and the encrypted file data which has not been deleted from CSP through violent attacks, the confidentiality of the data will be destroyed. When the data owner deletes the data, he can not be sure that the deleted data will never resurface in the future if CSP does not perform the actual data removal. This is what this paper will really discuss about.

In the following part, we present several previous solutions in order to solve the problem of data assured deletion. The scheme in [1] designed a file assured deletion system which can make it impossible to recover the encrypted file by destroying the encryption key at the right time. But it only put forward a conception model without implementation and its theoretical model is not very persuasive. In a cloud environment, the ownership of the data and the management right are divided. In order to protect data security, data has to be encrypted before being outsourced to the cloud. To some degree, this idea makes the problem of data assured deletion transformed into another problem, that is, how to delete the encryption key. However, this method exists the risk that the attacker might get the encryption key by cryptanalysis or brute force. The scheme in [2] pointed out another method based on strategy. The main point is that the file was encrypted by a data encryption key at first, and then, the data encryption key was encrypted by a control key related to strategy. Finally, in that paper the deletion of the control key equals to the deletion of the file. However, the control key used in [2] is managed by a third party, that is, a centralized management which exists potential safety hazard that the trustless key manager might delete or give away the control keys. Compared with centralized management for secret keys, distributed management gains higher security. E.g. the Vanish system in [3] distributed secret keys into Distributed Hash Tables (DHT) randomly after threshold cryptographic process. When privileged time is up, the secret keys will be deleted by DHT. Although the scheme in [3] has realized the destruction of mail servers and mail courtesy copies, attackers can also get the secret keys by sniffing attack or leap attack.

Furthermore, [4] indicated that if the scheme only destroyed the encryption key without the encrypted data, there exist potential safety hazards which might make the encrypted data attacked by analysis of cryptography or brute force. In its scheme, they distributed both the encryption key and part of the encrypted data into DHT. The cipher text which is stored on the servers is incomplete, so the traditional cryptanalysis attacks will fail. Even though, this method has prevented some attacks mentioned above, someone can also decode the encrypted data if he has gained the secret key before and make some backups. In a word, the scheme in [4] can not guarantee backward security, and it will also increase the communication overhead of the network.

Next, [5] pointed out another scheme which divided the original encrypted data into sampling data and remaining data. Then, they delivered the remaining data to the cloud, which makes the trustless CSP unable to obtain the total encrypted data. The disadvantage in [5] is that it introduces the third party which is supposed to be trustworthy to keep the sampling data. However, that premise is too idealistic. As it is mentioned in [6], if we can not fully trust the cloud service provider, shouldn't we place the same benefit of doubt on any other third-party? If the government has a court order to force the cloud and the third party to surrender the data and the keys of a company under investigation, no matter how hard the data owner tries to delete its data, it will be useless [7, 8].

To reduce the risk of data breaches, we propose ADBST (data assured deletion based on bit stream transformation with chaos sequence), which not only allows the encryption key to be stolen but also does not need the management or storage from any other third party. As for this paper, the object of assured deletion is cloud multimedia file, which can make the process much simple and convenient. For multimedia file, it will be destroyed even if there is a very small change to the bit stream of its source file. In our ADBST, we firstly do some transformation for the multimedia file before it is encrypted and uploaded to the cloud. The algorithm of transformation guarantees the randomness of data extraction based on logistic chaotic mapping. When the data is required to be deleted, the only thing should do is to delete the random sequences which is used to be the location number of transformation. Without the location number, the transformation can not be recovered by anyone. Moreover, we do not need any other third party. The transformed multimedia file is different from the original one. What we do next is to encrypt the changed file into a corresponding encrypted one. Then, we upload the encrypted file to the cloud. It makes the data on the cloud not the encrypted file of the original one but the changed one. These process can ensure that the deleted data will not be visited anymore even if the cloud data and the decryption key have been both stolen by attacker.

2   Security Assumptions and Threat Model

2.1   Security Assumptions

In this paper, a model with three main entities is provided: data owner, cloud service provider (CSP) and data user.

Data owner is not only responsible for multimedia file's transformation and recovery, but also responsible for the changed data's encryption. And it will keep the algorithm of file change and recovery. The random sequences which are generated by logistic chaotic mapping are stored by data owner too.

Cloud service provider is responsible for the storage of encrypted data. But CSP is untrusted. It will do the operation for the data storage loyally, but at the same time, it is curious about the sensitive data and expects to get the sensitive information.

Data user is responsible for the decryption for the unreal encrypted file.

The process of file access for data user is shown in Fig. 1.

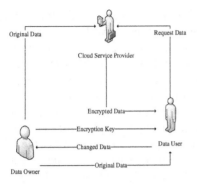

Fig. 1. Data access for data user

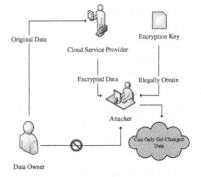

Fig. 2. Data access for attacker

2.2 Threat Model

According to the security assumptions above, several conditions are defined as follows:

CSP is untrusted. It will give away the encrypted file to others or some malicious users. What stored in CSP is not secure. The action of attackers is not real time but a kind of subsequent conduct. So the attacker will not know which the useful data is before the data has been visited.

Data user is believable. It won't keep either the original data or transmit after using. The process of data access for attacker is shown in Fig. 2.

3   System Design

Our security goal is to achieve data assured deletion even if the encryption key has been gotten by the attacker. Three assumptions are made for this approach. First, the encryption operation is secure, on the condition that it is impossible for the attacker to recover the encrypted data without the decryption key. Second, although the attacker can decrypt the cloud encrypted data into the corresponding one, it is impossible for them to get the unchanged original one without the recovery of bit stream transformation. Third, data user will not back up the original data after visiting because of the heavy storage cost.

In our design, what is kept on the cloud is not the original encrypted data. The scheme is based on the condition that if the encryption key should be leaked in active and passive situation by attacker, the data can also be safe. Moreover, our design only contains data owner and data user without any other third party to do some transfer or storage work.

We firstly do some transformation for the bit stream of the multimedia file before it is encrypted and uploaded to the cloud. We create an algorithm to do the transformation work and the algorithm and transformation information are only kept by data owner. The algorithm guarantees the randomness of data extraction based on logistic chaotic mapping. Choosing proper parameter value, the logistic mapping can come into chaotic state. When the data is required to be deleted, the only thing should do is to delete the random sequences which is used to be the location number of transformation. Without the location number, the transformation can not be recovered by anyone.

To formalize, we now revise our notations as follows. Let $\{M\}$ be the original data. Let n be the total number of the original data blocks. Let $\{M_i\}$ be the original data block with a unique identifier $i(1 \le i \le n)$ for each one. Let l be the total bit number of each block. Let q be the bit number of extracting bits for each block. Let $\{S_i\}(1 \le S_i \le l)$ be the position number for each data block. Let $\{K_i\}$ be the changed data block. Let m be the number of changed data blocks. Let $\{C_i\}$ be the encrypted data block. Let k be the encryption key. Let Round() be the function of rounding to the nearest integer. Let Trans() be the function of bit stream transformation. Let Com() be the function of data combination.

In this paper, the original data will be firstly segmented into n data blocks $\{M_i\}$. Next, the original data blocks will be transformed into new ones $\{K_i\}$ according to the position numbers $\{S_i\}$. The detail transformation will be explained in the following parts.

3.1 Logistic Chaotic Mapping

In order to make every data block has its own transformation way, it is necessary to use logistic chaotic mapping to generate chaos sequence. It is precisely the random sequences made the transformation more secure. According to the traditional definition, the expression of logistic chaotic mapping is (1):

$$X_{i+1} = f(X_i) = \mu X_i(1 - X_i) \tag{1}$$

In this formula: $X_i \in [0, 1]$ is the state of logistic mapping. From the definition of Chaos Sequence, we can know that when the parameter of logistic mapping $\mu \in [3.5699456, 4]$, logistic mapping will come into chaotic state [9].

There are n irregular numbers which are generated by logistic mapping. In this design, we choose $\mu = 4$ because of that state is the whole chaotic state. As $X_i \in [0, 1]$, it has to been done a mapping relation between X_i and S_i. It is shown in (2).

$$S_i = Round(X_i * l) \tag{2}$$

There is another characteristic for logistic chaotic mapping. It is such a sensitive system that the tiny difference of initial value will lead to great changes of the results. So, different files will be chosen different X_0 in order to ensure the security of each file. When the input variable X_0 is chosen to be 0.200001, 0.200010 and 0.200100, the responding outputs are 0.013014, 0.025865, 0.832657. Especially, when the iterations come to the last time, the difference of input is one ten thousandth, the one output result is 64 times of the other. From this result, it is impossible for attacker to guess the next transformation position without the chaos sequence. The following content will describe the calculation of X_0. Firstly, each file will be done hash summary calculations. Then, the hash value will be changed into a number range from 0 to 1. Finally, the generated number will be X_0.

$$X_0 = Change[Hash(file)] \tag{3}$$

As every file has its own X_0, every file has its own $\{S_i\}$. There is no possibility for anyone to guess another file's transformation rules according to the existed one. This is the key procedure to ensure the security of deleted data.

3.2 Original Data Transformation

In order to protect the confidentiality of the data, before the data owner begin to encrypt the original data, we firstly extract it. Based on the idea mentioned above, we do some transformation for the original data before it has been encrypted and uploaded to the cloud. The algorithm of this process and a small fraction of the extracted data are both kept by data owner. Anyone who does not get either the algorithm of the extracting process or the small fraction of the data can not get the real full original data. This is the key point for our design to guarantee the security of the cloud data for multimedia files. The sketch of bit stream transformation is shown in Fig. 3.

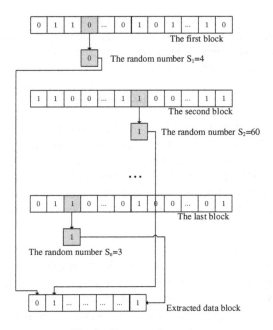

Fig. 3. Data transformation

Firstly, we segment the bit stream of the original data, and the length of each block is set to be l bits. Secondly, we randomly generate n positive integer $\{S_i\}$. Thirdly, we take out the data in the position of S_i in the blocks. Finally, we arrange the taken out data in order to the last position of the entire data bit stream.

$$K_i = Trans(M_i, S_i) \tag{4}$$

Our algorithm ensures double randomness. We firstly divide the original data into several data blocks. The purpose of this step is to avoid random data concentrating in a near location. This is one part of the randomness which can help the bit data to be completely disrupted. The other is that we use logistic chaotic mapping to generate the numbers on behalf of extraction location in different data blocks. It makes the extracting process more irregular. We call the very small part of the extraction data *extracted data block*, the other blocks *changed data blocks*. After transformation, we will generate two important things. The one is extracted data, the other is the location information of data transformation. They will both be kept by data owner only without sending to anyone else.

3.3 Data Encryption, Recovery and Assured Deletion

Each extracted original data block $\{K_i\}$ will be encrypted into encrypted data block $\{C_i\}$ by the encryption key k. We encrypt the changed data blocks by using the symmetric cryptography named AES. Then, encrypted data blocks are created.

$$C_i = E_k(S_i) \tag{5}$$

After data encryption, the new encrypted data will be uploaded to the cloud. It can be decrypted by the encryption key.

$$S_i = D_k(C_i) \tag{6}$$

After data decryption, we can get the changed encrypted data blocks $\{S_i\}$. They can be changed into $\{M_i\}$ by using the function of Com().

$$M_i = Com(K_i, S_i) \tag{7}$$

When data owner wants to delete the data, the only thing he should do is to delete the location information for the process of bit stream transformation. That information has been kept by data owner after data transformation. As long as the location has been deleted, attacker could not recover the multimedia file. This way of deleting data is real time deletion. And can also make the data to be assured deleted. Without deletion request, the location information of data transformation will be kept by data owner forever.

4   Security Analysis and Implementation

4.1   Security Analysis

In this paper, an algorithm of bit stream transformation is created to confuse the original data. In this way, we make the cloud encrypted data neither complete nor real. What is stored in the cloud is the encrypted one of the changed data. On this condition, in order to get the real original data, the attacker has to not only get the encryption key, but also the algorithm of bit stream transformation. Or, if he only gets the encryption key, the optimal situation is that the attacker can decrypt the cloud encrypted data which is not related to the original data. I.e. the cloud data is not the real one. What is stored in the cloud is the encrypted one for the changed data. However, as for a multimedia like picture, it can not be recovery even if there is only one bit missed.

Theorem: Under the same condition of the data length, it is harder for attacker to recover the original data by using ADBST when he gets the encryption key than the traditional way when he gets the encrypted data.

Proof: From the process that is mentioned above, it is not difficult to see that the critical process is to get the function of transforming the bit stream. Compare with the scheme that the attacker gets the full encryption data without encryption key, the scheme in this paper has better security. Even though, the attacker has already had the encryption key, it is more difficult for him to guess the real original data without the function of transforming the bit stream than to guess the original data with the full encrypted data and the encryption key. The security of this scheme is determined by the security of the algorithm of transforming bit stream. Let D_t be the difficulty that how hard does the attacker guess the original data in the scenario described in this paper. Let D be the difficulty that how hard does the attacker guess the original data with the full encrypted data without the encryption key. I.e. $D = 2^p$, p is the length of the encryption key of the symmetric encryption algorithm. When the length of every data block is l bit, then $D_t = (2l)^n$, n is the number of data blocks. I.e. $p \approx l \cdot n$. Supposed, the length of encryption key equals to the length of data block, i.e. $p = n$.

$$\frac{D_t}{D} = l^n \tag{8}$$

As is shown in (8), ADBST at least has higher security than the traditional way that the attacker has the encrypted data without encryption key. Let D_s be the difficulty that how hard does the attacker guess the original data in ADCSS. I.e. $D_s = C_m^n \cdot 2^n$, m is the length of both original data and encrypted data. If the length of bits which are filled in ADBST is x, $m = l \cdot n + x$.

$$\frac{D_t}{D_s} = \frac{(2l)^n}{C_m^n \cdot 2^n} = \frac{(m-x)^n \cdot n! \cdot (m-n)!}{n^n \cdot m!} \tag{9}$$

As it is shown in (9), D_t and D_s are in the same order of magnitude for attacker to guess the original data. However, ADBST has less entities than ADCSS, which reduces more security risks. The security of ADBST is guaranteed by data owner, while the security of ADCSS is guaranteed by others. Moreover, ADBST uses logistic chaotic mapping to generate chaos sequences rather than pseudo-random sequence which is used in ADCSS. Chaotic system produces the sequence is irregular to follow, and the more times the iterations are, the stronger the chaos will be. However, the pseudorandom sequence has intrinsic regularity because of the system seed. Finally, the encryption key and encrypted data are both stolen by attacker, which only effects the current file, as long as data owner has deleted the chaos sequences. Attacker can not get any useful information about former or later file because of the chaos characteristic of logistic chaotic mapping. Thus, ADBST has guaranteed both forward secrecy and backward secrecy.

4.2   Time Costs for this System

We have implemented a prototype system of our scheme using JAVA and the experiments are conducted on a PC with Mac OS, Intel Core i5 2.7 GHz Processor and 8 GB Memory.

We have done three contractive experiments for different sizes of data block, i.e. 256 byte, 512 byte and 1024 byte. The trends of time costs for different block sizes is shown in Fig. 4. When the size of block is chosen to be 512 byte, the time cost will plunge. However, the smaller the size is, the more security we will get. So, after balancing the attractions of a high security against the prospect of little time costs, we conclude to choose 512 byte to be the size of the block. The detailed time cost with 512 byte is shown in Table 1.

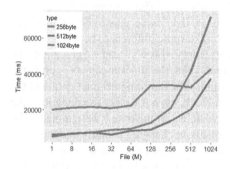

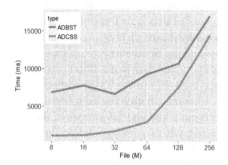

Fig. 4. Time costs with different block sizes   **Fig. 5.** Time costs comparison

Table 1. Time costs with 512 byte blocks.

File size (M)	1	8	16	32	64	128	256	512	1024
Time for transformation (ms)	6178	6729	7540	6251	8514	9181	14125	20466	37693
Time for encryption (ms)	24	102	195	380	734	1505	2912	5735	11445
Time for decryption (ms)	16	96	254	366	722	1416	2805	5919	12533
Time for combination (ms)	6216	6790	7632	6326	8620	9213	14192	20512	37137
Total time (ms)	12434	13717	15621	13323	18590	21315	34034	52632	98808

Next, we compare the two methods of time cost upon data owner: ADBST and ADCSS in [5]. As data in ADCSS is not complete, we only make six groups of experiment.

From Table 2, when the file size is not very big, the time cost of ADBST is heavier than ADCSS. However, when the file size reaches 256 M, the time cost of ADBST is only 3 ms longer than ADCSS. According the time trend in Fig. 5, it not hard to predict that when the file size is increasing, the time cost in our scheme will be nearly close to ADBST even might shorter than it. To sum up, our scheme only brings some time cost on small files, but we gain more security about the data deletion without relaying on the third party in ADCSS. When the size of file is super, this cost will be too tiny to be noticed.

Table 2. Time costs between ADBST and ADCSS

File size (M)	8	16	32	64	128	256
Time for ADBST (ms)	6831	7735	6631	9248	10686	17037
Time for ADCSS (ms)	1066	1130	1654	2880	7476	14472

5   Conclusion and Future Works

In this paper, a new scheme named ADBST to solve the problem about multimedia files assured deletion in the cloud is proposed. In this scheme, we do not need other third parties and do not store the full encrypted data in the cloud. It can realize the goal that the data will not be visited if data owner has already deleted it, even if the encryption key has been stolen by some attackers in the worst state. This scheme is based on the process of data transformation. Before encryption, data owner has to do a data transformation based on chaos sequence in order to make some differences between original data and the cloud encrypted corresponding data. Just in this way, can we guarantee that the encrypted data in the cloud is not the real one. Then, the attacker can not decrypt the encrypted data in the cloud without the algorithm of scrambling original data and the position information for each transformed data block, even if he has already gotten the encryption key and the encrypted data in the cloud. So, if the data is determined to be deleted, what we really delete is the information about changing location and the small part of the data. At last, the experimental result shows that our scheme can meet the desire that data owner can ensure the deleted data would not be visited by others. The next work is to reduce the time cost of data transformation without bring other security risks especially for small size files.

Acknowledgment.   This work was partly supported by the NSFC-Guangdong Joint Found (U1501254) and the Co-construction Program with the Beijing Municipal Commission of Education and the Ministry of Science and Technology of China (2012BAH45B01) and the Fundamental Research Funds for the Central Universities (BUPT2011RCZJ16, 2014ZD03-03) and China Information Security Special Fund (NDRC).

References

1. Perlman R.: File system design with assured deletion. In: International Security in Storage Workshop, Third IEEE International, pp. 83–88. IEEE (2005)
2. Tang, Y., Lee, P.P.C., Lui, J.C.S., Perlman, R.: FADE: secure overlay cloud storage with file assured deletion. In: Jajodia, S., Zhou, J. (eds.) SecureComm 2010. LNICST, vol. 50, pp. 380–397. Springer, Heidelberg (2010). doi:10.1007/978-3-642-16161-2_22
3. Geambasu, R., Kohno, T., Levy, A.A., Levy, H.M.: Vanish: increasing data privacy with self-destructing data. In: Conference on Usenix Security Symposium, pp. 299–316. USENIX Association (2009)
4. Wang, G., Yue, F., Liu, Q.: A secure self-destructing scheme for electronic data. J. Comput. Syst. Sci. **79**(2), 279–290 (2013)
5. Zhang, K., Yang, C., Ma, J.F., Zhang, J.W.: Novel cloud data assured deletion approach based on cipher text sample slice. J. Commun. **36**(11), 108–111 (2015)

6. Mo, Z., Qiao, Y., Chen, S.: Two-party fine-grained assured deletion of outsourced data in cloud systems. In: International Conference on Distributed Computing Systems, pp. 308–317. IEEE (2014)

7. Mo, Z., Xiao, Q., Zhou, Y., Chen, S.: On deletion of outsourced data in cloud computing. In: International Conference on Cloud Computing, pp. 344–351. IEEE (2014)

8. Reardon, J., Ritzdorf, H., Basin, D., Capkun, S.: Secure data deletion from persistent media. In: Proceedings of the 2013 ACM SIGSAC Conference on Computer & Communications Security, pp. 271–284. ACM (2013)

9. Patidar, V., Pareek, N.K., Purohit, G., Sud, K.K.: Modified substitution–diffusion image cipher using chaotic standard and logistic maps. Commun. Nonlinear Sci. Numer. Simul. **15**(10), 2755–2765 (2010)

Interval Merging Binary Tree

István Finta[1(✉)], Lóránt Farkas[1], Sándor Szénási[2], and Szabolcs Sergyán[2]

[1] Bell Labs, Nokia, Budapest 1083, Hungary
istvan.finta@nokia-bell-labs.com
[2] John von Neumann Faculty of Informatics, Óbuda University, Budapest, Hungary

Abstract. The general area of the paper is methods and data structures to efficiently avoid data duplication. In telecommunication networks operation support systems (OSS) process time series of counters related to the behaviour of network elements, such as failed location updates over the last 5 min. In general we may assume time series of key-value pairs with the key encoding the ordered sequence number of the particular counter.

In certain scenarios packets are duplicated in the course of transmission from the network element to the OSS system. In other scenarios packets arrive out of order and some of them do not arrive at all. As a result KPI-s aggregated from the individual counters held by the packets will have incorrect values potentially resulting in thresholds agreed in SLA-s being falsely exceeded. The filtering of duplicated keys and the management of missing (out of order) keys should operate fast and exhibit relatively low memory footprint. For this purpose well known data constructs like hashes or binary search trees can be used, but usually they need to store all individual keys. This implies high memory footprint and slow operation, since the time complexity of a search or insert operation is proportional to the number of stored elements in most cases. We propose a special type of binary tree that overcomes both limitations within certain constraints.

Keywords: Data structure · Tree data structure · Binary search tree · AVL tree · Red-Black tree · B tree · Interval tree · Segment tree · Streaming · Storm · Data duplication · Java collections framework · Set · Algorithm · Interval merging binary tree

1 Introduction

In a generic context of an operating support system, more specifically in relationship with the performance management of a telecommunication network, streams of performance counters need to be ingested and transformed towards higher level KPI-s in order to characterize and monitor the performance of such networks. Among several different possibilities a natural choice for such an ingestion layer and real time transformation engine is a stream processor.

Stream processors are cluster level generic processing frameworks allowing real or near real time operations over streams of data. Some of them can be

© Springer International Publishing AG 2017
S. Ibrahim et al. (Eds.): ICA3PP 2017, LNCS 10393, pp. 452–464, 2017.
DOI: 10.1007/978-3-319-65482-9_32

programmed in an SQL-like stream processing language, a construct supporting different processing primitives. Alternatively, and more widely available, it is possible to program such stream processors in high level programming languages such as C++ or Java, like in case of the actually applied Storm framework [1].

Major object-oriented programming languages support data types related to collections, like Java Collection Frameworks [2]. These contain data elements that are related to each other. Implementations range from generic collection types towards specialized ones. One collection type useful for our purposes is SET, which is not allowing the duplication of data elements within. There are three basic operations over SETs: INSERT and DELETE operations modify the number of elements in the SET, while SEARCH operation does not.

SET implementations use special data structures based on the desired trade-off between storage space and the duration of the typical operations defined on sets. When the number of involved elements is well predictable and relatively steady and there is no need for sorted iteration, hash data structure implementations are the best choice. One hash structure that can be used to implement a filter is the Bloom filter [3].

In cases when the number of elements is not well predictable, the wrongly selected capacity may led to too frequent re-hashing which makes the system slower. Additionally, Bloom filters allow for false positives. This implies that the duplication will not only be avoided, but all instances of the data item will be completely filtered out.

When sorted iteration is a must or the number of involved elements is not well predictable Binary Search Tree (BST) data structure implementations could provide better performance. The original BST was invented in 1960 [4,5] and serves as the basis of many other advanced variants. B-tree [6] has been proposed as a variant optimizing the movement of large amounts of data. Typical application areas of B-trees are file systems and databases.

The main drawback of BST is that the tree may become degenerated after certain sequences of the insert and remove operations.

To eliminate the problem of degeneration and make the BST balanced, implicitly improving the performance of the SEARCH operation, AVL Tree [7,8] has been proposed in 1962. Balancing is time demanding but only when INSERT or REMOVE operations are performed, since these operations may modify the structure of the tree. On the positive side both INSERTION and REMOVE execute embedded SEARCH operations, therefore eventually the operations required to keep the tree balanced do not appear as pure loss compared to unbalanced trees.

Red-Black Tree [9,10] combines the advantages of AVL and B-trees: it is based on a modified B-tree variant and it keeps the tree balanced. (a,b)tree [11] is a balanced tree where all the leaves reside on the same level.

There are other trees which are optimized to solve special problems faster or with less resources. Interval tree [12] and Segment tree [13] have been developed to perform a specific search operation on the number of intervals containing a particular key.

The reason behind of the so many BST variants is that all of them aiming different trade-off. However the comprehensive comparison of the variants has not been performed until 2004. [14] covers the missing gap: most of the above introduced self-balancing trees are part of the performance analysis.

It is common in the above mentioned data structures, except the last two ones, that these trees must store all the keys. In the *Problem* section we will describe why this feature might be a drawback during near real-time duplication filtering from both space and processing time point of view.

2   Problem

As stated in the 1, we assume an input stream of keys where the key is a sequence number. Keys are arriving mostly ordered respective to the sequence number. The task is to filter out those entries that arrived already once, meaning that the sequence number has had already this value in an earlier key instance. Additional boundary conditions regarding the arrival pattern apply:

1. upper unbounded range: there is no upper bound of the sequence numbers apart from the limit of the binary representation of this field,
2. lower unbounded range: at any point in time a new key can arrive to the system with a sequence number lower than any sequence number encountered so far,
3. there are long, contiguous intervals of keys with relatively few 'gaps' (missing keys) in between,
4. after a while almost all keys arrive,
5. key duplication (i.e. same key arrived at least twice) on the arrival side is possible due to some reason.

Due to condition 2., a traditional mask cannot be applied for the incoming keys that would drop all keys below a pre-defined value. Thus according to naive approach once all the previously arrived keys have to be stored and the newly arrived ones have to be compared with previously encountered keys. So as a conclusion, based on the requirements, SET abstraction could be an ideal solution for the problem, however actual implementations suffer from storage space and processing time limitations due to the two-sided unbound range, see Fig. 1. On this figure timestamps are marked by t_i, while keys are marked by n_j. Dashed arrow and striped rectangle point out to a key, which has already arrived. The storage need is linearly depending on the number of de-duplicated keys, while the search is log_2 proportional if the keys are stored in ordered fashion.

3   Methodology

We propose in the subsequent a binary tree that stores intervals of keys rather than individual values, implemented using a JSF SET-like interface. We describe the concept of the tree, then we focus on the insertion operation and the concrete data structure that can optimally implement such a tree.

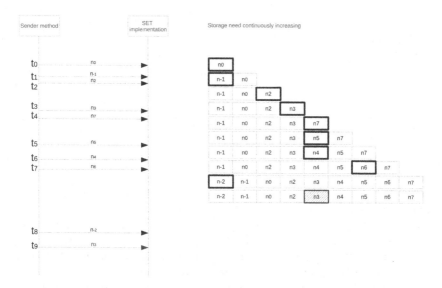

Fig. 1. Naive approach.

3.1 Concept of the Data Structure

Let's suppose that keys arrive in the following order:

$$...n_0, n_{-1}, n_2, n_3, n_7, n_5, n_4, n_6, n_{-2}, ...$$

In a naive approach all elements could be stored in a hash or in a binary search tree which is easily searchable, but still the binary search tree or the hash remains an upside-downside open system with infinite storage requirements when keys can arrive with infinite delay.

Increments are ordered, only the arrival sequence can be disordered. The first tweak to the naive approach is to represented arrived keys as pairs. So, elements will be stored like the following:

$$(n_0, n_0), (n_{-1}, n_{-1}), (n_2, n_2), (n_3, n_3), (n_7, n_7), (n_5, n_5),$$

$$(n_4, n_4), (n_6, n_6), (n_{-2}, n_{-2}).$$

At first sight it looks like that we did not win anything, but only doubled the memory footprint. The second tweak is not to automatically put newly arrived elements at the end, but rather to organize the elements in an ordered fashion, filtering at the same time duplicates found during the ordering process. This can be conceptually a sequence of 3 operations: insert at the end, order by key and a filter to skips the entry if it is already found:

$$(n_{-2}, n_{-2}), (n_{-1}, n_{-1}), (n_0, n_0), (n_2, n_2), (n_3, n_3), (n_4, n_4),$$

$$(n_5, n_5), (n_6, n_6), (n_7, n_7).$$

The third tweak is to add an operation that we call interval merging: every pair of neighbour values is checked and if the values are consecutive, the two pairs are converted into one, where the first value of the resulting pair is the first value of the first pair and the second value of the resulting pair is the second value of the second pair. Conceptually the 4th operation can be executed after the order by and filtering operations, but in a more efficient implementation these operations will be covered by a more complex variant dealing with all operations in one INSERT procedure, as described below:

1. The key for ordering is the L-value of an ordered pair and R-value is the second component.
2. If the first key/number arrives store it in the data structure as an ordered pair with the same value stored both as L- and R-values.
3. All successive keys stored according to the following: search the place for the key (remember this is the L-value of the pair) in the data structure
   (a) If it exactly matches with an element in the data structure then drop it
       ⇒ DUPLICATION (message already received)
   (b) If it is the predecessor of the first element check the distance between them (the degree of succession/predecession between them) based on the first element's L-value.
       i. In case the distance is 1 modify the R-value of the generated ordered pair to the R-value of the first element. Then delete the L-value. Insert this pair into the data structure ⇒ MERGING.
       ii. In case the distance is higher than 1, simply insert the pair into the data structure.
   (c) If it is a successor of the last element check the distance between them based on the last element's R-value.
       i. If the last element's R-value is smaller than the currently arrived one's R-value with more than 1, insert the currently arrived element into the data structure according to rule 2.
       ii. If the distance between the last element's R-value and the currently arrived one is exactly 1, then replace the last element's R-value with the currently arrived one ⇒ MERGING.
       iii. If the last element's R-value is higher or equivalent to the currently arrived one's r-value, then drop the actually arrived one ⇒ DUPLI-CATION (key already received).
   (d) If it is in the middle in the data structure both direction checking is required in the following order.
       i. Check the predecessor's value.
          A. In case the currently arrived element's distance is less than 1, drop the message ⇒ DUPLICATION.
          B. In case the currently arrived element's distance is 1 then change the R-value of the predecessor's with the current one's value. Then check the distance from the successor. If it is 1 then change again the predecessor's value (updated with the currently arrived one) to the successor's value ⇒ DOUBLE MERGING.

   ii. Else check the distance between the successor's L-value and the currently arrived element's L-value. In case of equivalence change the currently arrived element's value to the successor's L-value. Then delete the successor and insert the newly created pair $\Rightarrow$ MERGING.

   iii. Else insert the newly arrived element into the data structure according to rule 2.

In the following we describe the operation of the algorithm for our small data set:

- n_0 arrives, our data structure will store the following element:

$$(n_0, n_0)$$

- n_{-1} arrives, our data structure will store the following element:

$$(n_{-1}, n_0)$$

- n_2 arrives, our data structure will store the following element:

$$(n_{-1}, n_0), (n_2, n_2)$$

- n_3 arrives, our data structure will store the following element:

$$(n_{-1}, n_0), (n_2, n_3)$$

- n_7 arrives, our data structure will store the following element:

$$(n_{-1}, n_0), (n_2, n_3), (n_7, n_7)$$

- n_5 arrives, our data structure will store the following element:

$$(n_{-1}, n_0), (n_2, n_3), (n_5, n_5), (n_7, n_7)$$

- n_4 arrives, our data structure will store the following element:

$$(n_{-1}, n_0), (n_2, n_4), (n_5, n_5), (n_7, n_7)$$

Then

$$(n_{-1}, n_0), (n_2, n_5), (n_7, n_7)$$

- n_6 arrives, our data structure will store the following element:

$$(n_{-1}, n_0), (n_2, n_6), (n_7, n_7)$$

Then

$$(n_{-1}, n_0), (n_2, n_7)$$

- n_{-2} arrives, our data structure will store the following element:

$$(n_{-2}, n_0), (n_2, n_7)$$

So at the end storing only 4 keys, represented as 2 vectors or complex numbers, is required to represent 9 arrived elements. These two complex elements represents two intervals in which all expected keys arrived to the system, this is from where the data structure name origins.

This organization of keys can successfully fulfill the storage complexity related requirements.

3.2 Data Structure for Interval Merging

In the previous section an algorithm was introduced that performs an INSERT operation on an imaginary data structure with elements of type value pairs that represent related intervals of ranges of arrived messages without gaps. The data structure can be implemented in many ways impacting the time complexity:

1. in an array element pairs can represent L- and R-values (continuously reserved memory area for a particular type of elements),
2. in a linked list nodes can represent value pairs (not continuously reserved, but references maintained to next/previous nodes as well),
3. in potentially many other ways not listed furthermore,
4. in a newly developed binary tree that we will further elaborate on.

Examining the above mentioned implementations:

1. in case of an array with ordered value pairs the average time complexity is $T(n) = O(log(n))$. However INSERT and REMOVE can require too many movements depending on the place of the affected element in the array. INSERT cause re-indexing of all successor elements and thus moving them one step forward. REMOVE can cause the opposite direction movement.
2. SEARCH in a linked-list is not an efficient operation, however INSERT and REMOVE is very efficient.

As it is visible from the analysis of the first two data structures it seems that a tree-based approach would be effective: in case of a well balanced tree the element-related operations can be quite fast. The question is how to apply element pairs in the nodes. To solve this problem we propose the so-called Interval Merging Binary Tree (IMBT).

A node in the tree has the following signature: {*pointer_to_parent, interval_Left_Value, interval_Right_Value, pointer_to_Left_Child, pointer_to_Right_Child*}.

NULL parent pointer means that this particular element is the root node of the data structure. NULL *pointer_to_Left_Child* and *pointer_to_Right_Child* means leaf node just as in a traditional binary search tree.

A node always stores value pairs, which are the *interval_Left_Value* and the *interval_Right_Value*, despite elements to be inserted, removed, searched for being single keys.

The relation between a parent node and a *Right_Child* of the parent node is that the *interval_Left_Value* of the child node must be higher by two or more than the *interval_Right_Value* of the parent node.

The relation between a parent node and a *Left_Child* of the parent node is that the *interval_Right_Value* of the child node must be smaller by two or more than the *interval_Left_Value* of the parent node.

Additionally, pointers to parents and left or right elements are substituted by single lines. The left and right values must be indicated.

Figure 2 is the visualization of the example from previous section, based on the graphical representation of IMBT and the INSERT concept:

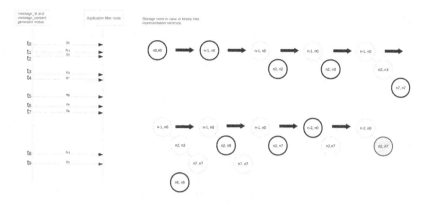

Fig. 2. The evolution in time of the IMBT based representation

4   Analysis of Interval Merging Binary Tree

At first sight IMBT behaves as an ordinary binary tree:

- It has nodes in the tree.
- Each node can have two children and one parent element.
- Special node types are the root (has no parent) and the leaf (has no child).
- Three basic operations are defined on the tree: SEARCH, INSERT, REMOVE.

If no balancing mechanisms are used, the tree - just as an ordinary binary tree - can become degenerated depending on the sequence of incoming elements. However, the nodes of the tree contain intervals and this fact highly influences the behaviour of the operations. A successful modification operation (INSERT, REMOVE) can affect 0, 1, 2 nodes in the tree. Opposed to legacy binary trees both INSERT and REMOVE operations might cause a decrease by 1, an increase by 1 or no change in the number of nodes. Because SEARCH is crucial from the above mentioned operation point of view as well it is the basis of the cost counting.

To determine the input-dependent worst-case, average and best-case scenarios it is important to highlight that nodes represent disjoint intervals therefore it requires different analysis method from that applicable to a simple BST case. In case of a legacy binary search tree the storage space complexity is $O(n)$. This means the tree occupies as much space as many elements are stored inside the tree. However, in case of IMBT, it can happen that the number of nodes in the tree is far smaller, equal, or far higher than the number stored elements.

Space complexity of IMBT is highly dependent on the input pattern. To be able to express the difference lets introduce e, which refers to the number elements represented by the tree and n referring to the number of nodes in the tree and finally N being the total number of elements. According to this the storage space complexity of IMBT can vary from $O(2)$ to $O(2e)$. This feature of IMBT influences the time complexities as well. Therefore it is not enough to check only the number of elements but their distribution is also important.

To be able to compare the difference between BST and IMBT Input Pattern Series (IPS) will be defined according to the following:

Define Input Pattern Series: IPS(ACDL, D, O, DIR) where

Average Contiguous Domain Length(ACDL) = {1...∞}; under contiguous domain we understand a countable set of keys where each member of the set except two members has a successor and one predecessor, exactly one member has only successor (first key of the domain) and exactly one member has only predecessor (last key of the domain), in simpler terms there are no 'gaps' in the set. The ACDL is in fact the element count of this set;

Distance(D) = {1, 2+}/{ACDL + 1, ACDL + 2}; this is for instance the 'distance' between the first element of a related domain and the first element of the subsequent related domain, or alternatively, the 'distance' between the last element of a related domain and the last element of the subsequent related domain. By the distance between 2 keys we mean the number of keys between them +1;

Offset(O) = {−∞, ..., 0, ..., ∞}; the ordinal number of the key associated with the very first message;

Direction(DIR) = {Left, Right, AlterWalkwithIncreasingStep(AWIS) length}.

Below we provide a set of possible IPS-es and in the next step we will assess the performance of the algorithm if keys arrive according to these patterns.

4.1 Input Pattern Series

IPS(3,4,1,R) ⇒ ACDL = 3; Distance = 4; Offset = 1; Direction = Right
  Key series: 1, 2, 3, ...
  IMBT Interval(s): (1, 2, 3), (5, 6, 7), (9, 10, 11), ...
  The formula of the series is:

$$a_n = \left\lfloor \frac{n}{d} \right\rfloor + n, n \in N, d = 3. \tag{1}$$

IPS(3,4,0,AWIS). Key series: 0, 2, −1, 3, −2, 4, −4, 6, −5, 7, −6, 8, −8....
  IMBT Interval(s): ...(−6, −5, −4), (−2, −1, 0), (2, 3, 4), (6, 7, 8), (10, ...
  The formula of the series is:

$$a_n = \left(1 + \left\lfloor \frac{n}{d} \right\rfloor + \frac{1+n}{2}\right)(n \, mod(2)) - \left(\left\lfloor \frac{n}{d} \right\rfloor + \frac{n}{2}\right)((n+1) mod(2)) \mid d = 2 \times ACDL \tag{2}$$

During all the above mentioned cases ACDL parameter was considered as a constant multiplier. However, if ACDL would be considered as a variable and as time goes by it increases, so a formula could be used like this: $ACDL = f(n)$, then it can change the growth rate from $O(n)$ to $O(c)$ or $O(1/cn)$.

Let's start with the two simplest cases when $ACDL = f(n) = n \to \infty$ (Fig. 3).

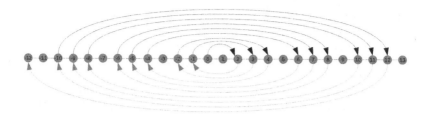

Fig. 3. IPS(3,4,0,AWIS)

IPS(n,1,1,R). Key series: $1, 2, 3, ...$
IMBT Interval(s): $(1, ..., \infty)$.
The formula of the series is:

$$a_n = n, n \in N. \tag{3}$$

IPS(1,1,0,AWIS). Key series: $0, 1, -1, 2, -2....$
IMBT Interval(s): $(-\infty, ..., \infty)$.
The formula of the series is:

$$a_n = \frac{1+n}{2}(n \bmod(2)) - \frac{n}{2}((n+1)\bmod(2)), n \in N. \tag{4}$$

The most natural function where we expect that length of intervals grows incrementally is S_n (Sum n) is the basis of $g(n)$, which is the floor function of "semi-inverse" S_n. Only the positive domain is acceptable:

$$S_n = \sum_{i=1}^{n} i = \frac{n(n+1)}{2}, \tag{5}$$

$$S_n^{-1} = \frac{-1 + \sqrt{1+8n}}{2}, \tag{6}$$

$$g(n) = \left\lfloor \frac{-1 + \sqrt{1+8n}}{2} \right\rfloor. \tag{7}$$

Declare that $ACDL = f(n) = \frac{n+1}{g(n)+1}$. Define $a_n = g(n) + n$, this will lead to the following IMBT intervals:
$(0), (2, 3), (5, 6, 7), (9, 10, 11, 12), (14, ...$
Let's examine the next pattern where:

$$g(n) = \lfloor log_d(n) \rfloor \mid n = \{1, 2, 3, ...\}, d = 2 \tag{8}$$

$$f(n) = \frac{n}{g(n)+1}. \tag{9}$$

IPS(f(n), $d^{g(n)+1}$, 1, R) Key series:
$1, 3, 4, 6, 7, 8, 9, 11, 12, 13, 14, 15, 16, 17, 18, 20,$

IMBT Interval(s): $(1), (3, 4), (6, 7, 8, 9), (11, 12, 13, 14, 15, 16, 17, 18), (20,$
The formula of the series is:

$$a_n = \lfloor log_d(n) \rfloor + n. \tag{10}$$

In this case $d = 2$, but of course this can vary to a value that fits better to our model. The most important aspect when choosing this functions is that $f(n)$ should be a slowly growing one to be able to map the result into distances via floor function.

4.2   Comparison of Balanced BST with IMBT

It is easy to recognize that IMBT degenerates into a single node in case of IPS(n,1,1,R) or IPS(1,1,0,AWIS), which is pretty good from SEARCH performance point of view. On the other hand an unbalanced BST (including IMBT) degenerates into a linked-list in case of IPS(3,4,1,R) or IPS(f(n), $d^{g(n)+1}$, 1, R), which may highly degrade the SEARCH performance. Therefore the application of one of the legacy balancing techniques (rotation strategies) is reasonable. In the following we will compare the performance of SEARCH operation against the selected IPS-es, supposing that AVL type balancing was applied for both BST and IMBT.

IPS(10,11,1,R)

a., BST - BALANCED

- $n = e = N$,
- space complexity $= O(N)$,
- time complexity $=$ worst case - $O(log(N))$, average - $O(log(N))$.

b., IMBT - BALANCED Since comparison is based on the left value this influence the result.

- $n = N/10; e = N$;
- space complexity $= O(2 * log(n))$,
- time complexity $=$ worst case - $O(2 * log(n))$, average - $O(log(n))$.

IPS($f(n) = \frac{n}{\lfloor log_d(n) \rfloor + 1}$, $d^{g(n)+1}, 0, R$)

a., BST

- $n = e = N$,
- space complexity $= O(N)$,
- time complexity $=$ worst case - $O(N)$, average - $O(N/2)$.

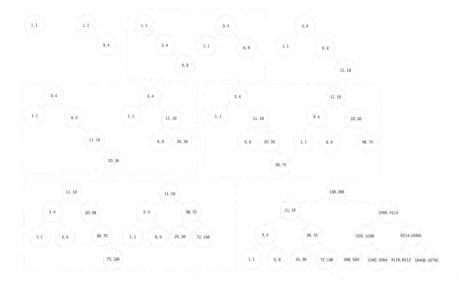

Fig. 4. IMBT with balancing

b., IMBT

- $n = log(N); e = N;$
- space complexity = $O(2log(n))$,
- time complexity = worst case - $O(2log(n)) = O(2log(log(N)))$, average $O(log(n)) = O(log(log(N)))$.

It is visible that in case of constant ACDL with a value equal or higher than 3 on average a gain can be achieved over "simple" balanced trees. However if ACDL is growing and not only constant in time the gain is significant from both time and space complexity point of view. Nevertheless IMBT structure influences the balancing effort, because the balancing should be performed on less nodes in the tree, however the key/element coverage is the same. To visualize the above mentioned, supposing that AVL was used, the last introduced IPS is visualized in Fig. 4.

5 Conclusion

In this contribution we introduced an algorithm to efficiently handle data duplicates and missing/out of order data items in a telco application, as well as a data structure that enables an efficient manipulation of missing/duplicate data that we called IMBT. We have analyzed a number of selected data arrival patterns quantifying the benefits of the proposed approach over traditional data structures used in the state of the art.

The application in a centralized environment (implemented in a Storm bolt) is straightforward. If we need distributed processing because of resource constraints, the keys may be distributed with the help of a mod function. The basis of the mod function is depending on the number of filter bolts we use in parallel. Then in a particular bolt we have to normalize the arrived key with basis of the mod function and take the floor of the given value.

Storing the lower bound along with the length of the interval in a modified IMBT is subject to future work. The space complexity might significantly decrease in case of very short ranges and many gaps, in exchange for an increase of the computational complexity.

References

1. STORM - A distributed real-time computation system. http://storm.apache.org/documentation/Home.html. Last visited 29 Mar 2017
2. Java Collections Frameworks. http://docs.oracle.com/javase/7/docs/technotes/guides/collections/overview.html. Last visited 29 Mar 2017
3. Bloom, B.H.: Space/time trade-offs in hash coding with allowable errors. Commun. ACM **13**(7), 422–426 (1970)
4. Cormen, T.H., Leiserson, C.E., Rivest, R.L., Stein, C.: Introduction to Algorithms, 3rd edn. MIT Press and McGraw-Hill (2009). ISBN: 0-262-03384-4
5. Binary Search Tree - Wiki. https://en.wikipedia.org/wiki/Binary_search_tree. Last visited 29 Mar 2017
6. Adelson-Velsky, G., Landis, E.: Organization and maintenance of large ordered indexes. Acta Informatica **1**(3), 173–189 (1972). doi:10.1007/BF00288683
7. Adelson-Velsky, G., Landis, E.: An algorithm for the organization of information. Proc. USSR Acad. Sci. **146**, 263–266 (1962)
8. AVL Tree - Wiki. https://en.wikipedia.org/wiki/AVL_tree. Last visited 29 Mar 2017
9. Bayer, R.: Symmetric binary B-Trees: data structure and maintenance algorithms. Acta Informatica **1**(4), 290–306 (1972). doi:10.1007/BF00289509
10. Red-black tree - Wiki. https://en.wikipedia.org/wiki/Red-black_tree. Last visited 29 Mar 2017
11. (a, b) Tree. https://en.wikipedia.org/wiki/(a,b)-tree. Last visited 29 Mar 2017
12. de Berg, M., van Kreveld, M., Overmars, M., Schwarzkopf, O.: Interval trees. In: Computational Geometry, 2nd revised edn., Section 10.1, pp. 212–217. Springer, Heidelberg (2000)
13. Bentley, J.L., Ottmann, T.A.: Algorithms for reporting and counting geometric intersections. IEEE Trans. Comput. **C−28**(9), 643–647 (1979). doi:10.1109/TC.1979.1675432
14. Pfaff, B.: Performance analysis of BSTs in system software. ACM SIGMETRICS 2004 **32**(1), 410–422 (2004). ISBN: 1-58113-873-3

Mining Suspicious Tax Evasion Groups in a Corporate Governance Network

Wenda Wei[1], Zheng Yan[2,3], Jianfei Ruan[1], Qinghua Zheng[1], and Bo Dong[1(✉)]

[1] SPKLSTN Lab, Xi'an Jiaotong University, Xi'an, China
dong.bo@xjtu.edu.cn
[2] State Key Lab on Integrated Services Networks, Xidian University, Xi'an, China
[3] Department of Communications and Networking, Aalto University, Espoo, Finland

Abstract. There is a new tendency for corporations to evade tax via Interest Affiliated Transactions (IAT) that are controlled by a potential "Guanxi" between the corporations' controllers. At the same time, the taxation data is a classic kind of big data. These issues challenge the effectiveness of traditional data mining-based tax evasion detection methods. To address this problem, we first coin a definition of controller interlock, which characterizes the interlocking relationship between corporations' controllers. Next, we present a colored and weighted network-based model for characterizing economic behaviors, controller interlock and other relationships, and IATs between corporations, and generate a heterogeneous information network-corporate governance network. Then, we further propose a novel Graph-based Suspicious Groups of Interlock based tax evasion Identification method, named GSG2I, which mainly consists of two steps: controller interlock pattern recognition and suspicious group identification. Experimental tests based on a real-world 7-year period tax data of one province in China, demonstrate that the GSG2I method can greatly improve the efficiency of tax evasion detection.

Keywords: Tax evasion · Controller interlock · Corporate Governance Network · Big data

1 Introduction

Tax revenue collection is considered a top priority in China. It was reported by Chinese government that the rate of tax revenue loss in China was above 22%. How to technically support tax evasion detection, especially identifying suspicious tax evasion corporations/groups, from a large scale of business transactions and related data, has become one of important and challenging issues. Meanwhile, there is a new tendency for corporations to evade tax via Interest Affiliated Transactions (IATs) that are controlled by a potential "Guanxi" between the corporations' controllers.

For dealing with these challenges, we perform an extensive literature study about potential "Guanxi" for corporations, and find that a phenomenon named

© Springer International Publishing AG 2017
S. Ibrahim et al. (Eds.): ICA3PP 2017, LNCS 10393, pp. 465–475, 2017.
DOI: 10.1007/978-3-319-65482-9_33

board interlock has been deeply researched in western economics that refers to the practice of members of a corporate board of directors serving on the boards of multiple corporations. However, scholars paid too much attention to the relationship between corporations constituted by the board interlock, but neglected the critical role of the interlocking relationship between the corporations' controllers. We believe that the ties between controllers are more important in China or other emerging economies where "Guanxi" has been rooted in the blood of the normal people. Moreover, essentially the economic behavior of a corporation is a concrete embodiment of its controllers' will. Besides, it is verified that in the process of economic transformation in China, when the corporation governance is not matured, interlocking controllers tend to find loopholes in supervision to maximize their self-interest through legal-like-transactions. Therefore, this paper coins a definition of controller interlock, which characterizes the interlocking relationship between corporations' controllers.

In order to model controller interlock and related behaviors and relationships, we propose a Colored and Weighted Network-based Model (CWNM), and generate a heterogeneous information network-Corporate Governance Network (CGN). We adopt the shareholder and management-involved role relationships between persons and corporations (such as being the corporations' executives or managers or legal persons), as well as investment and trading relationships between corporations. In CGN, persons or corporations act as nodes, and relationships between persons and/or corporations act as arcs, as well as the weight of an arc is equal to the Interest Affiliated Degree (IAD) of a direct tie.

After introducing the definition of controller interlock and CGN, this paper focuses on an important problem that is the detection of Interlock based Tax Evasion (ITE) in CGN. This problem is split into two basic questions, (i) how to recognize the controller interlock ties between corporations' controllers and (ii) how to identify suspicious groups of ITE. To solve these questions, we propose a novel Graph-based Suspicious Groups of ITE Identification method, named GSG2I, which includes (i) a graph projection algorithm to recognize the ties that meet controller interlock pattern and (ii) a component pattern matching algorithm based on the controller interlock ties to discover suspicious groups of ITE. Finally, experimental tests based on a real-world 7-year period tax data of one province in China, demonstrate that the GSG2I method can greatly improve the efficiency of ITE detection.

2   Related Work

Board interlock analysis is an emerging topic in taxation and economic field, and has received considerable attention. It has been applied to industry dynamic analysis [5,8,11,12] and corporation decision making [1,3]. Suominen et al. [12] considered board interlock as the tool of inter-organizational flows needed for innovation and growth of the companies, concentrating especially on inter-organizational flows of board networks or interlocks. Robins et al. [11] introduced a bipartite clustering coefficient to compare global structural properties of US and Australian interlocking company directors. Ma et al. [8] discovered a structurally autonomous sphere in board interlock network of Chinese non-profits associated with major political and social events in the state-society relationship. Connelly et al. [3] explored the diffusion of an emerging strategy through the interlocking directorate effected by incorporating rational actors, potentially suppressive influences, and network structural considerations, and examined a broad social network of interlocking directors in US firms.

Moreover, many researchers pointed out that there exists obviously imitation effect between interlocked companies which can improve the companies' profitability. For example, Chua et al. [2] used social network analysis to determine the relationship between interlocking directorates and corporate profitability drawn from 2010 Fortune 500 companies, and suggested that both interlocks and power asserted a positive linear relationship with companies' profitability. Peltonen et al. [10] indicated companies that have international revenue are often interlocked with each other, and interlocked boards of directors have the potential to act as important information and resource conduits.

However, negative performance effects associated with board interlocks were also analyzed in some special environment. Liu [7] studied the effect of environment dynamism to the relation between the interlocking directorates and the corporation' s performance in emerging economics such as China. He pointed that the output of the firms in the center of the social networks constituted by interlocking directorates would be negatively affected. Croci et al. [4] used measures of vertex centrality to examine interlocking directorates and their economic effects, and discovered a negative relationship between firm value and the degree and eigenvector centrality of board interlock network in Italy.

3   Definitions of Controller Interlock and Corporate Governance Network

3.1   Controller Interlock

In the literature [6,9], a board interlock was defined as sharing a common member on respective boards of directors in which a person affiliated with one corporation sits on the board of directors of another corporation.

In this paper, we extend the connotations of board interlock and develop it into a concept that fit the Chinese economic environment:

(i) The attention is changed from finding the interlocking relationship ties between corporations to mining the potential interlocking relationship ties between the corporations' controllers.

(ii) The persons concerned are extended from simple director to multiple roles of controllers: director, legal person and shareholder. The relationships concerned are extended from simple director relationship between P and C to the cover of actual control, share holding relationship between P and C, as well as investment relationship between C and C (C for Corporation, P for Person). Then, the influence from P to C is accordingly extended from direct control tie (P-C) to control trail (P-C-$\cdots$-C) covering both direct and indirect influence.

Base on the above extension, we define a controller interlock as a tie between two controllers, each of whom sits on the board or executive of or has a indirect influence on a common corporation.

3.2   Corporate Governance Network

A Corporate Governance Network (CGN) is formed to represent a kind of heterogeneous information networks built based on the CWNM. Thus, we coin the definition of CGN as follows:

Definition 1. A CGN is is formulated as a quintuple:

$$CGN = (\mathbf{V}, \mathbf{E}, \mathbf{W}, \mathbf{VColor}, \mathbf{EColor})$$

where

- $\mathbf{V} = \{v_p | p = 1, \ldots, N_V\}$ denotes a set of nodes;
- $\mathbf{E}$ denotes a set of all existing arcs, and let $\mathbf{E} = \{e_{pq}\} = \{(v_p, v_q) | 0 < p, q \leqslant N_V\}$, where $e_{pq} = (v_p, v_q)$ denotes that there exists an arc from the p-th node to the q-th node;
- $\mathbf{W} = \{w_{pq} | 0 < p, q \leqslant N_V\}$ denotes the weight (i.e., IAD) of the arc from the p-the node to the q-th node;
- $\mathbf{VColor} = \{LC, BC, CC\}$, where LC denotes the color of a legal person or director, CC denotes the color of a corporation; BC denotes the color of a shareholder; Using colors in $\mathbf{VColor}$ to classfy $\mathbf{V}$ in CGN, we can get the following conclusion $\mathbf{V} = \{L \cup C \cup B\}$, where $L = \{v_l | l = 1, \ldots, N_L, N_L < N_V\}$ denotes all legal person or director nodes marked by the color LC, $C = \{v_c | c = 1, \ldots, N_C, N_C < N_V\}$ denotes all corporation nodes marked by the color CC, $B = \{v_b | b = 1, \ldots, N_B, N_B < N_V\}$ denotes all shareholder nodes marked by the color BC, then $N_L + N_C + N_B = N_V$;
- $\mathbf{EColor} = \{CL, HR, IN, TR\}$, CL denotes the unidirectional actual controller relationship between a legal person/director v_l and a corporation v_c, and if the color of the arc e_{lc} from v_l to v_c is CL, then e_{lc} is denoted as e_{lc}^{CL}, and its weight is equal to 1, which is denoted as $w(e_{lc}^{CL}) = 1$; HR denotes the unidirectional share holding relationship between a shareholder v_b and a corporation v_c, and $w(e_{lc}^{HR}) \in (0, 1]$; IN denotes the unidirectional investment relationship between two corporations v_{c1} and v_{c2}, and $w(e_{c1c2}^{IN}) \in (0, 1]$; TR denotes the unidirectional trading relationship between two corporations v_{c1} and v_{c2}. CL, HR and IN belong to control relationship.

From the view of control relationships and trading relationship, there are two parts in a CGN: the control network and the trading network. The control network covers all relationships (actual control, investment, share holding, etc.), which have influence on transactions between *Corporation* nodes, except for the trading relationship.

4 Suspicious Groups of ITE Identification Method

We propose a novel Graph-based Suspicious Groups of ITE Identification method, named GSG2I, which consists of two parts: controller interlock pattern recognition algorithm and suspicious groups identification algorithm.

4.1 Controller Interlock Pattern Recognition Algorithm

Considering that the generated CGN is a large scale graph, the first step is to partition the CGN into a series of small weakly connected subgraphs by applying divide and conquer strategy. This step is inspired by an intuitive idea that the topology of controller interlock structure is included in one component of a control network as it belongs to a connected graph and is constructed solely by control arcs. Meanwhile, a trading relationship arc that connects two unconnected components of a control network is an unsuspicious trading relationship. Obviously, this means that there is definitely without one party (node) involved in two components at the same time behind the trading relationship arc. Therefore, the i-th maximal weakly connected subgraph of an control network and the trading relationship arcs between its corporations nodes forms the i-th interest community of a CGN, denoted as $subCGN(i)$. The control part of subCGN is denoted as subCtrlNet, and the trading part of subCGN is denoted as subTraNet.

Each suspicious Group of ITE consists of two potential control relationship trails (see Definition 2) behind an IAT with a controller interlock tie between the start nodes of each trail (controller). Therefore, it is necessary to construct a Potential Component Pattern Base (PCPB) to record all potential control relationship trails throughout the corresponding subCtrlNet in the form of *InP-OutC* walk (see Definition 3). To this end, a novel parallel label propagate-based control relationship trail traversal algorithm is then presented, which is carried out in each subCtrlNet to obtain its PCPB. The main steps of the algorithm are as follows.

Step 1: Initialization process

First, initialize each node with a unique identification label (*IdLabel*). Meanwhile, suppose that each node in a subCtrlNet carries a local trail set *LTrailSet*, which stores control relationship trails ended by the node itself. Append the unique *IdLabel* of each *Person* node (one node as a trail) to its *LTrailSet* for initialization, and define the *LTrailSet* of each *Corporation* node to a null set. Meanwhile, define a globle trail set *GTrailSet* to store all static IRR trails in the subCtrlNet and initialize it to be a null set.

Step 2: Propagation process

Let the *LTrailSet* of each node (*Person* node only for the first loop) propagate to its neighbors by tracing the directions of its adjacent edges. Then, remove the nodes which have not received any *LTrailSet* from neighbors, and break the ties to its neighbors. Next, count the number of nodes in the subCtrlNet. If the number is equal to zero, then the algorithm is terminated, and *GTrailSet* is the

PCPB that records all static IRR trails throughout this subCtrlNet; otherwise, continue.

Step 3: Updating process

Each node updates its *LTrailSet* based on the *LTrailSet* collected from its neighbors. The detailed update operation on each node consists of the following three steps: (i) pop its *LTrailSet* to the *GTrailSet*, (ii) merge the *LTrailSet* collected and remove the component trails containing the *IdLabel* of this node, and (iii) append the *IdLabel* to the rest of the component trails, and update the *LTrailSet* of this node by the set of the new trails obtained.

Steps 2 and 3 are performed iteratively until the termination condition is met. Then, all control relationship trails throughout each subCtrlNet are recorded in the corresponding PCPB, and a copy of each trail is distributed to the *LTrailSet* of the node with *IdLabel* equal to the last element of the trail.

Definition 2. *Potential control relationship trail.*

A *potential control relationship trail* is a trail, T, met the following condition:

$$T = \{(p, c_1, c_2, \ldots, c_n) | p \in P, c_1, c_2, \ldots, c_n \in C, (p, c_1), (p, c_2), \ldots, (c_n, c) \in E\}$$

Definition 3. *Person-node-start-and-corporation-node-stop walk (InP-OutC walk)*

A *Person-node-start-and corporation-node-stop walk* is a trail belongs to a set of trails in a control network and does not contain any trading arc, which is start by a *Person* node and stop by a *Corporation* node.

Finally, we propose a bipartite netwok-based model for characterizing the control relationship between persons and corporations and generating a Person-Corporation Bipartite Network (PCBN). Thus, we accomplish the task of controller interlock tie construction by map the PCBN onto a unipartite network of Person called a P-projected graph.

For each potential control relationship trails in a PCPB, in the form of *InP-OutC* walk, the first and last node (p and c) is extracted to form the *Person* node set, P, and the *Corporation* node set, C, and the edge (p, c) forms the edge set E. Then the PCBN can be represented by a bipartite graph $PCBN = \{P, C, E\}$, where P and C are two parts of the nodes in PCBN. E is the set of edges in PCBN. There is no edge between the nodes in the same set of P and C; namely, every edge $(p, c) \in E$ satisfies $p \in P$, and $c \in C$. We use $N(p) = \{c | c \in C, (p, c) \in E\}$ to denote the set of *Corporation* neighbors of *Person* node p in PCBN.

To analyze the controller interlock ties in the PCBN, we map it onto a P-projected graph (see Definition 4).

Definition 4. (P-projected graph). Given a bipartite graph $PCBN = \{P, C, E\}$, its P-projected is defined as a unipartite graph $PCBN_P = \{P, E_P\}$ where the set of edges is $E_P = \{(p_1, p_2) | p_1, p_2 \in P, \exists c \in C, c \in N(p_1) \cap N(p_2)\}$.

From the definition, we can see that if *Person* part nodes p_1 and p_2 in the bipartite network PCBN have at least one common neighbor in the *Corporation* part, then there exists a controller interlock tie (p_1, p_2) in the P-projected graph $PCBN_P$.

4.2 Suspicious Groups Identification Algorithm

According to Definition 5, a series of *FIT-OutC* walks are constructed by carrying out first-interlock-tie join (see Lemma 1) based on the PCPB and controller interlock ties. Then, the topologies pattern of ITE can be redescribed as two *FIT-OutC* walks started by a same controller interlock tie behind a transaction.

For each trading relationship arc, *tra*, in $subTraNet(i)$ $(i = 1, \ldots, L)$, extract the *LIntrlSet* of *tra*'s source vertex *src* and destination vertex *dst* from the $InPCPB$ of $subCGN(i)$. If there exist $trail_s \in LIntrlSet(src)$ and $trail_d \in LIntrlSet(dst)$, such that the combination of $trail_s$, $trail_d$ and *tra* meets the topology pattern referred above, then we say that the two trading parties of *tra* are in suspicion of being involved in ITE, that is, *tra* belongs to interest affiliated transaction, and $trail_s$ and $trail_d$ are the suspicious relationship trails.

Definition 5. *First-controller-interlock-tie-start-and-corporation-node-stop walk (FIT-OutC walk)* is a trail produced by a first-interlock-tie join (see Lemma 1), which adds a controller interlock tie to the start of a trail that belongs to the set of *InP-OutC* walks (PCPB). The newly generated local and globle *FIT-OutC* walk set is named as *LIntrlSet* and *InPCPB* corresponding to those of *InP-OutC* walk set, respectively.

Lemma 1. If a controller board tie is added to a head in a control relationship tails and it forms a new walk, *nw*, then *nw* is a trail. We can call this controller interlock tie added operation first-interlock-tie join.

5 Experimental Evaluation

5.1 Experimental Design

Data Set and Preprocess. We carried out experiments based on the real tax data of S province in China from 2009 to 2015. A series of CGNs were generated from the data monthly, average of which included 2,872,469 nodes and 2,488,982 arcs. Meanwhile, audit results of the 7 years were used as the data set. In the data set, 19,328 ITE companies and 18,209 non-ITE companies were included for each month in average.

Evaluation Technique. For each corporation, CO, in the data set, the GSG2I method was applied to detect whether it belonged to the trading parties of a suspicious tax evasion group. Then, the obtained conclusion, OC, was compared with the actual audit results (i.e., the ground truth) from the following two aspects: (i) when the identifier of t equals to 1, CO is correctly identified if OC contains any recognized suspicious group; (ii) when the identifier of CO equals to 0, OC is not falsely alarmed if OC is returned to be null.

Evaluation Criteria. To evaluate the performance of the GSG2I method, two metrics, which are *Identification Precision* and *Hit Rate*, are employed.

Identification Precision (IP) is the faction of companies which are predicted to be suspicious, and are really involved in evasion. *Hit Rate (HR)* is the fraction of companies which really carry out tax evasion behaviors, and are subsequently successfully identified. A higher *Identification Precision* and *Hit Rate* indicates a higher identification capacity.

Method for Comparison. In the experiments, we used traditional board interlock for comparison, since both board interlock and the GSG2I method refer to the practice of controllers sharing influence on multiple corporations.

For these two interlock concepts, graph-based models are employed to characterize the patterns, each of which is formed by two potential control relationship trails and one interest affiliated transaction arc. The construction of suspicious relationship trails is affected by two factors: (i) Th: the weight threshold for control arcs, and (ii) L: the max length limit for suspicious potential control relationship trails. Less control arcs will be regarded as sufficiently influential if we set a higher Th, and subsequently less trails will be constructed. Likewise, the same condition will occur if we set a smaller L. The experimental results show the influence of diversity of suspicious relationship trail construction factors (i.e., Th and L) on evaluation metrics.

5.2   Experimental Results

The Effect of Different Methods. Tables 1 and 2 show the comparisons of effects obtained by the GSG2I method and board interlock method. While the effects are of difference under different evaluation metrics, the GSG2I as a whole achieves a better performance than board interlock method. Specifically, the improvements are significant with respect to *Hit Rate*, and much smoother with respect to *Identification Precision*. As shown in Table 1 taking $L = 2$, $Th = 0.3$ as an example, the effects of the GSG2I method are described as follows: (i) its *Identification Precision* is approximately equal to board interlock method; (ii) its *Hit Rate* are much higher, with the improvements being 237%. In conclusion, the GSG2I method greatly improves the *Hit Rate* of tax evasion identification and simultaneously achieves a similar *Identification Precision*.

The Effect of Weight Threshold. Table 1 and Fig. 1(a) show the effects with respect to Th. Similarly, the effects of both method are of great difference in different settings of Th. During the increase of Th (from 0 to 0.9), *Hit Rate* decreases sharply. The reason is that as Th increases, a great number of weak control arcs are filtered and fewer potential control relationship trails will be involved in PCPBs, which means less evidence can be used to identify tax evasion behaviors. Thus, it will lead to a decrease in *Hit Rate*. Meanwhile, we find that *Identification Precision* remains stable with decreasing *Hit Rate* decreases, which means that ITE behaviors are irrelevant to the IAD of control relationship.

The Effect of Max Length. Table 2 and Fig. 1(b) show that *Identification Precision* and *Hit Rate* remain stable with increasing L; the increase is not significant when L changes from 1 to 5. Theoretically, if the max length is larger, there will be more potential control relationship trails involved in PCPBs.

Table 1. Effects with respect to Th

Th	GSG2I		Board interlock	
	IP	HR	IP	HR
0.1	0.7850	0.0331	0.8025	0.0101
0.2	0.7810	0.0316	0.7957	0.0095
0.3	0.7748	0.0283	0.7874	0.0084
0.4	0.7793	0.0258	0.7772	0.0074
0.5	0.7768	0.0225	0.7815	0.0061
0.6	0.7674	0.0188	0.7759	0.0047
0.7	0.7621	0.0162	0.7529	0.0033
0.8	0.7618	0.0151	0.7246	0.0026
0.9	0.7690	0.0131	0.7069	0.0021

Table 2. Effects with respect to L

L	GSG2I		Board interlock	
	IP	HR	IP	HR
1	0.7764	0.0282	0.7874	0.0084
2	0.7748	0.0283	0.7874	0.0084
3	0.7748	0.0283	0.7874	0.0084
4	0.7748	0.0283	0.7874	0.0084
5	0.7748	0.0283	0.7874	0.0084

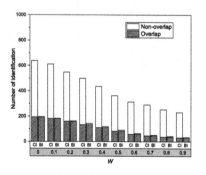

(a) Identification coverage with respect to W

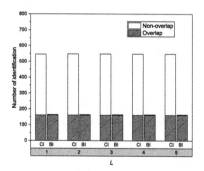

(b) Identification coverage with respect to L

Fig. 1. Identification coverage with respect to W and L (CI for GSG2I, BI for board interlock)

We analyze the reason and find that though there are many additional suspicious groups of ITE with larger lengthes of control trails when L gets larger, the extra corporations identified are quite few as most of corporations newly discovered are replicated with prior findings.

6   Conclusion

This paper focuses on the detection of corporations evading tax via IATs that are controlled by a potential interlocking relationship between the corporations' controllers. We first coin a new concept named controller interlock based on the control relationships in Chinese corporations, drawing on the deeply researched board interlock concept. Next, we present CGN to model controller interlock and related behaviors and relationships. Then, we further propose the GSG2I method to recognize controller interlock ties and discover suspicious groups of ITE. Experimental results based on a real-world big data set demonstrate that the GSG2I method can greatly improve the efficiency of ITE detection.

Acknowledgments. This work is supported by "The Fundamental Theory and Applications of Big Data with Knowledge Engineering" under the National Key Research and Development Program of China with Grant No. 2016YFB1000903, the National Science Foundation of China under Grant Nos. 61502379, 61472317, 61532015, and Project of China Knowledge Centre for Engineering Science and Technology.

References

1. Battiston, S., Bonabeau, E., Weisbuch, G.: Decision making dynamics in corporate boards. Phys. A: Stat. Mech. Appl. **322**, 567–582 (2003)
2. Chua, A.Y., Balkunje, R.S.: Interlocking directorates and profitability: a social network analysis of fortune 500 companies. In: Proceedings of the 2012 International Conference on Advances in Social Networks Analysis and Mining (ASONAM 2012), pp. 1105–1110. IEEE Computer Society (2012)
3. Connelly, B.L., Johnson, J.L., Tihanyi, L., Ellstrand, A.E.: More than adopters: competing influences in the interlocking directorate. Organ. Sci. **22**(3), 688–703 (2011)
4. Croci, E., Grassi, R.: The economic effect of interlocking directorates in Italy: new evidence using centrality measures. Comput. Math. Organ. Theory **20**(1), 89–112 (2014)
5. Elouaer, S.: A social network analysis of interlocking directorates in french firms (2006)
6. Labrinidis, A., Jagadish, H.V.: Challenges and opportunities with big data. Proc. VLDB Endow. **5**(12), 2032–2033 (2012)
7. Liu, T.: An empirical study about the effects of interlocking directorates strategy on the firm's output in the dynamic environment. In: International Joint Conference on Artificial Intelligence, JCAI 2009, pp. 818–820. IEEE (2009)
8. Ma, J., DeDeo, S.: State power and elite autonomy: The board interlock network of Chinese non-profits. arXiv preprint arXiv:1606.08103 (2016)

9. Mizruchi, M.S.: What do interlocks do? an analysis, critique, and assessment of research on interlocking directorates. Annu. Rev. Sociol. **22**(1), 271–298 (1996)

10. Peltonen, J., Rönkkö, M.: Board interlocks in high technology ventures: the relation to growth, financing, and internationalization. In: Tyrväinen, P., Jansen, S., Cusumano, M.A. (eds.) ICSOB 2010. LNBIP, vol. 51, pp. 163–168. Springer, Heidelberg (2010). doi:10.1007/978-3-642-13633-7_14

11. Robins, G., Alexander, M.: Small worlds among interlocking directors: network structure and distance in bipartite graphs. Comput. Math. Organ. Theory **10**(1), 69–94 (2004)

12. Suominen, A., Rilla, N., Oksanen, J., Still, K.: Insights from social network analysis-case board interlocks in finnish game industry. In: 2016 49th Hawaii International Conference on System Sciences (HICSS), pp. 4515–4524. IEEE (2016)

PerRec: A Permission Configuration Recommender System for Mobile Apps

Yanxiao Cheng[1] and Zheng Yan[1,2(✉)]

[1] The State Key Lab of Integrated Services Networks, School of Cyber Engineering,
Xidian University, Xi'an, China
780960172@qq.com, zyan@xidian.edu.cn
[2] Department of Communications and Networking, Aalto University, Espoo, Finland

Abstract. Android operating system uses a security mechanism based on permissions to restrict mobile apps to access sensitive device resources. However, because of such disadvantages as coarse-granularity of permission management and vague permission description, the current permission-based security mechanism of Android is not sufficiently effective in practice. In addition, only a small number of users realize the importance of permission settings and mostly they cannot make a proper decision on permission settings due to lack of runtime information and professional knowledge. In this paper, we propose PerRec, a permission configuration recommender system based on trust management, which assists the mobile users to set permissions in order to enhance user privacy and device security. It is designed based on our pre-developed reputation system named TruBeRepec [1] to get the trust and reputation values of an app and further offer recommendations on how to set permissions. Based on system implementation, we evaluate the accuracy and safety of PerRec by comparing PerRec's recommendations with the Android system default permission settings. The result shows that PerRec can provide effective permission recommendations to prevent potential security threats. We further conduct a small-scale user study to demonstrate its user acceptance.

Keywords: Android platform · Mobile application · Permission configuration · Recommender system · Trust management

1 Introduction

Android uses a unique permission mechanism to prevent a mobile app from accessing sensitive device resources without user consent. The Android system requires each app developer to explicitly request permissions by pre-specifying them in a file named Android-Manifest.xml bundled with the app. These permissions manage a set of resources required by the app for realizing its functionalities. During app installation, the Android permission system provides a user a list of permissions requested by the app. The user needs to agree with all these permission requests as a precondition of app installation (for Android API level 22 or lower) and execution (for Android API level 23) [7]. At the app runtime, the Android system allows or denies using specific resources based on its permission settings.

© Springer International Publishing AG 2017
S. Ibrahim et al. (Eds.): ICA3PP 2017, LNCS 10393, pp. 476–485, 2017.
DOI: 10.1007/978-3-319-65482-9_34

However, this permission control mechanism is ineffective to preserve user privacy and protect device security because of some disadvantages such as coarse granularity of permissions and permission over-claiming [6]. Coarse granularity of permissions results in requesting unnecessary permissions to produce over-privileged apps. Study shows that more than 70% of apps request to access data irrelevant to their main functions [7]. On the other hand, when installing a new app, only a small portion (3%) of users pay attention to and make correct decision on permission granting since they tend to rush through prompted permission requests to start app usage. In addition, current Android permission warnings cannot help most users make correct security decisions [9]. Even though users realize the importance of the permission settings, they still cannot make a correct decision on the settings due to confusion about permission descriptions and lack of runtime information and professional knowledge. Obviously, users need to be directed on permission settings. However there are few studies performed to help user in permission setting [14, 15]. This motivates our research and development.

In this paper, we propose PerRec, a permission configuration recommender system based on trust management, to assist users in permission settings. PerRec can automatically generate a recommendation on the setting of an individual permission requested by a mobile app and adjust app permission configuration based on risk evaluation. PerRec is built up based on our pre-developed reputation system TruBeRepec [1] to get the trust and reputation values of an app in the recommendation of permission settings. To the best of our knowledge, PerRec is the first permission setting recommender system based on trust management [3–5, 7, 10, 14, 15].

Differently from previous work, PerRec provides recommendations on permission configuration for mobile apps based on trust management. The contributions of this paper lie in three folds:

- We design PerRec by holistically considering the factors in the permission recommendation generation, such as the similarity between apps, the risk of granting an individual permission, the trust/reputation values of apps, and the risk of installing/ using a certain app.
- We implement PerRec based on the Android operating system;
- We evaluate the accuracy and safety of PerRec by comparing its recommendation performance with the default permission setting of customized Android system MEIZU Flyme OS 4.2.1.1.

The rest of the paper is organized as follows. Section 2 reviews related work. Section 3 introduces the design of PerRec. Section 4 describes PerRec implementation and the system performance evaluation. Finally, a conclusion is presented in the last section.

2   Related Work

Some studies aim to assist app developers to request the least amount of permissions and ensure apps can execute normally at the same time. For example, Bagheri et al. created a tool that aids the developers to assess appropriate permission requests [13]. They created one-to-many permission-API mappings by manually parsing API documentation and creating a database of functions and permissions upon which the functions depend. Bao et al. proposed an approach based on a collaborative filtering technique and the intuition that the apps with similar features usually use similar permissions [8].

Existing research also makes efforts to dynamically configure permissions in a context-aware way. Apex system [3] allows user to run an app by splitting an app's permissions to only authorize part of permissions. Dr. Android [4] and PeMo [10] can dynamically make permissions enabled and disabled. Zhang et al. [14] presented a framework to provide context-sensitive permission enforcement that regulates permission usage policies according to system-wide application contexts, which cover both intra-application context and inter-application context. TaintDroid [5] is a data flow tracking system that can track and analyze flows of permission related sensitive data and identify suspicious apps.

Wang et al. thought the malapps were basically different from benign apps on requesting different permissions and they provided a table named top 40 risky permissions. They defined a class variable that indicates the label of an app, benign or malicious. The risk of granting a permission can be evaluated by measuring the relevance between this permission/feature variable and the class variable. The top 20 most frequent permissions requested by malware referred in paper [12] is listed by Zhou et al. They compared the top permissions requested by malicious apps with the top permissions requested by benign ones. They collected 1260 Android malware samples1 in 49 different malware families, which covers the majority of existing Android malware, ranging from their debut in August 2010 to recent ones in October 2011. They find that malicious apps tends to request more permissions than benign ones.

Some mechanisms were proposed with regard to app permission settings. RecDroid [7] allows users to install apps under either a "probation" mode or a "trusted" mode. In the trusted mode, users grant all permissions to an app. In the probation mode, users can make a real-time granting decision when the app is running. RecDroid [15] relies on a small set of seed expert users that could make reliable recommendations for a limited number of apps. Due to the limitation of seed experts amount, majority of apps cannot be covered. Similar to RecDroid, LBE safety master [15] also provides a trusted mode and a probation mode. However, user sensitive information could be still stolen during the execution of benign apps. Therefore, it is risky to grant all permissions in the trust mode. In the probation mode, LBE can only provides recommendations for partial apps and the permissions that the LBE safety master can provide recommendations are limited, incomplete, less than those the app really requests. LBE safety master cannot provide complete recommendations on the whole list of app permissions to users.

We can see that the current permission recommender mechanisms are not fine-grained and accurate enough to guide users. In this paper, we aim to design and develop PerRec in order to realize fine-grained and safe recommendations for mobile app permission configuration.

3 System Design

3.1 PerRec System Structure

We design PerRec based on the TruBeRepec which is a trust-behavior-based reputation system for mobile apps [1]. It was developed based on a model of trust behavior for mobile apps explored through a large-scale user survey [16]. Our previous work showed that there are three types of trust behaviors: (1) using behavior (UB) that relates to normal application usage, which can be mainly reflected by elapsed usage time, number of usages, and usage frequency; (2) reflection behavior (RB) that concerns usage behaviors after a user confronts application problems/errors or has good/bad usage experiences; (3) correlation behavior (CB) correlated to a number of similar functioned mobile apps. TruBeRepec evaluates an individual user's trust in a mobile app based on automatically monitored trust behaviors and generates the app's reputation by aggregating individual trust.

Figure 1 shows the system structure of PerRec. In PerRec, an *app permission extractor* can extract the requested permission list of an app by analyzing Android-Manifest.xml; a *permission category risk level setting model* sets the risk level of permissions; a *similar app list and threshold calculator* can get the similar app list of a certain app and the threshold applied in the process of risk and recommendation generation; an *application installing/using risk generator* can compute the installing/using risk of an app based on its trust and reputation values and app similarities that are saved

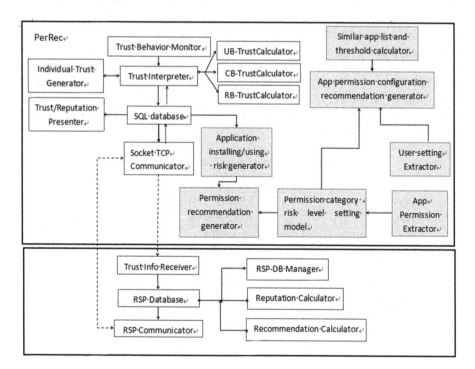

Fig. 1. Design of the permission configuration recommender system

in a *SQL database* by the TruBeRepec system; a permission recommendation generator can generate permission setting recommendations based on the installing/using application risk, the level of permission risk and a threshold; an *app permission configuration recommendation generator* can recommend permission configuration based on the permission risk level, user permission settings and a threshold.

3.2   Permission Risk Level

Android defines a set of permission categories based on functionalities. For the permissions under the same category, as long as users grant a permission to that category for an app, the app can use other permissions in the same category. So we rank the risk levels of these permissions based on their categories. It is clear that top risky permissions can help discriminating malicious apps from benign ones by checking the frequency of their appearance. We rank the permission risk based on the top 40 risky permissions requested by malicious apps [11] and the top20 most frequently used permissions requested by malware as specified in [12].

The permissions in the categories of MICROPHONE, VOICEMAIL, BLUE-TOOTH_NETWORK, and DISPLAY are not listed in [11, 12]. So we set the lowest risk level to these permission categories. The permissions under COSTMONEY category can directly cause property loss without notifying users, so we set the highest risk level to this category as 4. The resources managed by permissions in the categories of MESSAGE, SMS, SOCIAL_INFO, LOCATION, NETWORK, WIFI, PERSONAL_INFO, and STORAGE are crucial for users and have little dependence on device hardware. It is easy for malicious apps to send low-payload data packages to a remote destination without discovery by making use of these permissions. So we put these permission categories into the second risk level, marked as 3. The permissions in the categories of PHONE_CALLS, SYSTEM_TOOLS, CAMERA control device hardware and could cause device damage but their potential risk to users may not as high as that of those permissions in the risk level 3, so we set these permission categories into the third risk level as 2. The risk levels of all categories are listed in Table 1.

Table 1.   Risk level of permission categories

Category	Risk level	Category	Risk level
COSTMONEY	4	PHONE_CALLS	2
MESSAGE	3	ACCOUNTS	2
SOCIAL_INFO	3	CAMERA	2
LOCATION	3	MICROPHONE	1
NETWORK	3	DISPLAY	1
PERSONAL_INFO	3	VOICEMAIL	1
STORAGE	3	BLUETOOTH_NETWORK	1
SYSTEM_TOOLS	2		

3.3   Recommendation on Permission Configuration

By analyzing the risk of installing and using an app, the risk of granting one permission requested by an app, PerRec can analyze the risk of app permission configuration and thus provide recommendations on permission settings.

The risk of installing and using an app. The risk of installing and using an app is relevant to the reputation of the app. The lower reputation indicates the higher risk of installing and using the app. However, the category of apps should be considered because apps indifferent categories could fall into different reputation and individual trust levels. Before installing the app, we roughly filter out the app with low reputation. If the reputation value of underlying app a_o, denoted R_o is below threshold thr_0, i.e., $R_o < thr_0$, this app maybe malicious and we recommend to reject installing and using this app. In PerRec, we choose the lowest reputation of the apps installed in the user device as thr_0. Note that the user can setup thr_0 by himself/herself.

Permissions are highly related to the features that describe the functionalities of an app or its behaviors to interact with its installed device system, device data and other apps. Based on this perception, we categorize the apps based on their similarity calculated by their requested permissions. The similarity is calculated in a simple way as:
$S(a_o, a_j) = \dfrac{pn_{o,j}}{pn_o + pn_j - pn_{o,j}}$, where pn_o and pn_j stands for the number of permissions owned by app a_o and a_j respectively and $pn_{o,j}$ stands for the number of permissions both requested by a_o and a_j.

To categorize apps, we filter out the apps with lower similarity than threshold thr_1, which is set as $\dfrac{S(a_o, a_j)_{max}}{2}$, where $S(a_o, a_j)_{max}$ is the maximum similarity between a_o and its similar apps. If $S(a_o, a_j)_{max} < thr_1$, we remove app a_j from the similar app list of a_o. By comparing the reputation of app a_o and the trust value of its similar app a_j, denoted T_j, we calculate the risk impact factor $IF_{o,j}$ of a_o for referring the permission setting of similar app a_j in recommendation. Obviously, the higher the similarity $S(a_o, a_j)$ is, the lower the risk impact factor. The higher the reputation R_o and the trust T_j are, the lower the risk impact factor. Thus, we set $IF_{o,j}$ as $IF_{o,j} = (1 - S(a_o, a_j))(1 - R_o)(1 - T_j)$. We then aggregate the risk impact factors of all similar apps together by weighting $IF_{o,j}$ with T_j since T_j serves as its credibility. The purpose is to get the risk of installing and using app a_o: $Risk_o = \sum_{j=1}^{N_o} IF_{o,j} * T_j$, where N_o refers to the total number of similar apps of a_o.

The risk of granting a permission requested by an app. The risk of granting permission k for a certain app is related to the installing/using risk of this app and the risk level of permission k (denoted r_k). The risk of using an app influences user decision on its permission setting, the user prefers to grant permission to the app with low using risk. For permission k requested by app a_o, we calculate the risk of granting permission k as below by considering both $Risk_o$ and r_k: $Ris_{o,k} = f(Risk_o * r_k)$, where function $f()$ is applied to formalize the impact of $Risk_o * r_k$ on recommendation. One applicable function is $f(x) = exp\left(\frac{-x^2}{2\sigma^2}\right)$, where σ can be set based on practical demand, e.g., $\sigma = 5$.

We recommend the permission setting by measuring the risk of granting permission k requested by app a_o. We set the maximum risk $Max(Ris_{o,k})$ of the app requesting permission k in terms of all similar apps of a_o as thr_2. If $Ris_{o,k} > thr_2$, recommend rejecting the permission; else recommend granting.

The risk of application permission configuration. We further collect all permission settings and generate the risk index of app a_o permission configuration (RI_o) by aggregating $Risk_o$ and r_k of all granted permissions as below: $RI_o = \sum_{k=1}^{K}(r_k * Rec_k) * Risk_o$, where Rec_k is the user setting on permission k: if the setting is granting, $Rec_k = 1$; else $Rec\_k = 0$. r_k is the risk level of permission k. We compare RI_o with those of its similar apps. Herein, we choose $Max(RI_j)$, the maximum RI_j of similar apps of a_o as threshold thr_3. If $RI_o > thr_3$, a warning is generated to suggest user resetting.

4   System Implementation and Performance Evaluation

4.1   System Implementation

We implemented PerRec in Android phones MEIZU m1 Flyme OS 4.2.1.1 on the basis of the TruBeRepec system [2]. It has a number of functionalities: (1) Provide and display user individual trust and reputation of installed third party apps; (2) Monitor app usage statistics and record usage data; (3) Provide and display app usage statistical data, such as usage time and usage frequency; (4) Calculate app similarity and show the list of similar apps of an app and their similarity values; (5) Provide and display app permission information, such as permission category, permission risk level, permission description and setting recommendation; (6) Provide the risk levels of all permission categories or take default permission settings.

4.2   Performance Evaluation

To evaluate the recommendation performance of PerRec, we investigated the overlap proportion between the permissions actually used by the app and the permissions recommended by PerRec or set by the customized Android system MEIZU Flyme OS 4.2.1.1 by default. Note that Flyme 4.2.1.1 provides default permission settings if the users do not set permissions during app installation. Refer to Fig. 2, A + B stands for the permissions recommended by PerRec or set by Flyme 4.2.1.1 by default. B + C refers to the permissions actually used by the app. The bigger B / (A + B) is, the more accuracy of PerRec recommendations or Flyme 4.2.1.1 default settings. The bigger B / (B + C) is, the more functionalities supported by the PerRec recommendation or default settings during permission granting. In the following test, we compared the performance of

PerRec with Flyme 4.2.1.1 default permission settings in terms of B / (A + B) and B / (B + C) in order to show the accuracy and safety of PerRec.

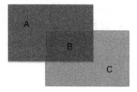

Fig. 2. The permission list corresponding area

We used 107 mobile apps falling into 11 app categories (e.g., gaming, social networking, multimedia, etc.) to perform performance evaluation on PerRec. These 107 mobile apps are come from the most popular apps ranked by Baidu MOTA, an app ranked website [19], and we download them in MEIZU official app store. We counted the number of permissions requested in app installation, the number of permissions used in app execution and calculated their average values. We got the permissions that the apps applied and used through Androguard [17] and XPrivacy [18], respectively. Androguard is a static malware analysis toolkit that can get the permissions applied by an app. XPrivacy can provide permission usage records according to the execution of app functions. We can get the permissions that an app actually uses by checking the permission usage records. We compared the proportion of A and B in terms of A + B. As shown in Fig. 3, we can see the B / (A + B) is increased from 24.68% to 69.87% after applying PerRec. Obviously, PerRec's recommendation performance is more accurate than Flyme 4.2.1.1 default permission settings. This testing result also implies that most of the permissions recommended by PerRec to be granted are used by apps. In Flyme 4.2.1.1 default permission settings, the over-claimed 75.32% permissions could cause private information leakage and potential security threats (refer to Fig. 3). From this point of view, PerRec can provide safer permission settings than the Flyme 4.2.1.1 default settings.

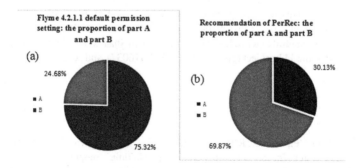

Fig. 3. The proportion of A and B based on Flyme 4.2.1.1 and PerRec

We further weighted the permissions with the permission risk levels to evaluate the risk of permissions. This risk indicates the possibility of information leakage and security threats. Comparing Figs. 3 with 4, the proportion of A based on the Android system default settings after weighting (84.03%) is much higher than that based on PerRec (28.74%). This means that the risk level of permissions that the Android system set by default but not used by apps are much higher than that based on PerRec. So it is safer to rely on PerRec than depending on the Android default settings.

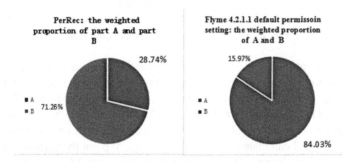

Fig. 4. The weighted proportion of A and B based on Flyme 4.2.1.1 and PerRec

5 Conclusion

In this paper, we proposed PerRec, a permission configuration recommender system for mobile apps based on trust management. It can automatically generate recommendations on permission configuration for a mobile app based on a mobile app reputation system. We presented the design and performance evaluation of PerRec. The testing result demonstrated its accuracy in permission evaluation. We are going to further improve the PerRec system by optimizing its algorithm and its user interface towards practical usage.

Acknowledgments. This work is sponsored by the National Key Research and Development Program of China (grant 2016YFB0800704), the NSFC (grants 61672410 and U1536202), the Project Supported by Natural Science Basic Research Plan in Shaanxi Province of China (Program No. 2016ZDJC-06), the 111 project (grants B08038 and B16037), and Academy of Finland (grant No. 308087).

References

1. Yan, Z., Zhang, P., Deng, R.H.: TruBeRepec: a trust-behavior-based reputation and recommender system for mobile applications. Pers. Ubiquit. Comput. **16**(5), 485–506 (2012)
2. Dang, T.L., Yan. Z., Tong. F., Zhang. W.D., Zhang. P.: Implementation of a trust-behavior based reputation system for mobile applications. In: 2014 IEEE 9th International Conference on Broadband and Wireless Computing, Communication and Applications, pp. 221–228 (2014)

3. Nauman, M., Khan, S., Zhang, X.: Apex: extending android permission model and enforcement with user_defined run time constraints. In: 5th International Symposium on ACM Symposium on Information, Computer and Communications Security, pp. 328–332 (2010)
4. Jeon, J., Micinski, K.K., Vaughan, J.A., Fogel, A., Reddy, N., et al.: Dr. Android and Mr. Hide: fine_grained permissions in android applications. In: The Second ACM Workshop on Security and Privacy in Smartphones and Mobile Devices, Raleigh, North Carolina, USA, pp. 3–14. ACM (2012)
5. Enck, W., Gilbert, P., Han, S., Tendulkar, V., Chun, B.G., Cox, L.P., et al.: TaintDroid: an information-flow tracking system for realtime privacy monitoring on smartphones. ACM Trans. Comput. Syst. **32**(2), 393–407 (2010)
6. Fang, Z., Han, W., Li, Y.: Permission based Android security: issues and countermeasures. Comput. Secur. **43**(6), 205–218 (2014)
7. Rashidi, B., Fung, C., Vu, T.: Dude, ask the experts!: Android resource access permission recommendation with RecDroid. In: IEEE International Symposium on Integrated Network Management (IM), pp. 296–304 (2015)
8. Bao, L., Lo, D., Xia, X., Li, S.: What permissions should this Android app request? In: 2016 International Conference on Software Analysis, Testing and Evolution (SATE), Kunming, pp. 36–41 (2016)
9. Felt, A.P., Ha, E., Egelman, S., Hane, A.Y., E, Chin., Wagner, D.: Android permissions: user attention, comprehension, and behavior. In: 2012 Eighth Symposium on Usable Privacy and Security(SOUPS 2012), New York, pp. 1–14 (2012)
10. Kaur, A., Upadhyay, D.: PeMo: modifying application's permissions and preventing information stealing on smartphones. In: 2014 5th International Conference - Confluence The Next Generation Information Technology Summit (Confluence), Noida, pp. 905–910 (2014)
11. Wang, W., Wang, X., Feng, D., Liu, J., Han, Z., Zhang, X.: Exploring permission-induced risk in Android applications for malicious application detection. IEEE Trans on Information Forensics and Security **9**(11), 1869–1882 (2014)
12. Wei, X., Gomez, L., Neamtiu, I., Faloutsos, M.: Permission evolution in the android ecosystem. In: ACM Computer Security Applications Conference ACSAC, pp. 31–40 (2012)
13. Bagheri, H., Sadeghi, A., Garcia, J., Malek, S.: COVERT: compositional analysis of Android inter-app permission leakage. IEEE Trans. Software Eng. **41**(9), 866–886 (2015)
14. Zhang, Y., Yang, M., Gu, G., Chen, H.: Rethinking permission enforcement mechanism on mobile systems. IEEE Trans. Inf. Forensics Secur. **11**(10), 2227–2240 (2016)
15. LBESafety Master. http://dl.pconline.com.cn/download/90435.html
16. Yan, Z., Dong, Y., Niemi, V., Yu, G.L.: Exploring trust of mobile applications based on user behaviors: an empirical study. J. Appl. Soc. Psychol. **43**(3), 638–659 (2013)
17. Feng, S.: Android software security and reverse analysis, 407 pages. Chap. 5 (2013)
18. https://forum.xda-developers.com/xposed/xposed-installer-versions-changelog-t2714053
19. http://mota.baidu.com/index.php/page/industry/apprank/use

The 5th International Workshop on Parallelism in Bioinformatics (PBio 2017)

A Resource Manager for Maximizing the Performance of Bioinformatics Workflows in Shared Clusters

Ferran Badosa[1]([⊠]) [iD], César Acevedo[1] [iD], Antonio Espinosa[1] [iD],
Gonzalo Vera[2] [iD], and Ana Ripoll[1] [iD]

[1] Universitat Autònoma de Barcelona, Bellaterra, Spain
ferran.badosa@caos.uab.cat
[2] Centre for Research in Agricultural Genomics, Bellaterra, Spain

Abstract. In order for bioinformatics workflows to achieve good performance when running on shared clusters, resources must be properly allocated, adjusting to the needs of the bioinformatics applications within.

Time-changing cluster status, caused by the dynamic workload, must also be considered. Users of bioinformatics applications are prompted with the dilemma of providing adequate job description, without prior hint of the resources used by their applications. As a result, naive approaches are taken and both platform efficiency and users' goals, such as makespan or cost, are compromised. To prevent that, we propose a Resource Manager (RM) for bioinformatics workflows running in shared clusters, capable of improving platform efficiency and reducing average makespan of queued applications.

Our RM contains a predictor that generates multiple job performance predictions, under different combinations of resources. We also included a shared-resource model, that considers the degree of multiprogramming of the nodes (DP), and determines which applications are more compatible for sharing same-node resources. With this information, we developed a scheduling algorithm capable of operating in compliance with the cluster's default manager, i.e. SLURM.

At the end, our RM is tested on a set of queued workflows, formed by multiple applications each. We prove that a 28% makespan reduction, and a 75% resource efficiency improvement, can be achieved.

Keywords: Bioinformatics workflows · Resource sharing · Multivariate regression prediction · Makespan · Scheduling

1 Introduction

Bioinformatics workflows are the main tools used by biologists to perform biological data analysis, including tasks such as genome alignment or variant calling.

Funded by the Spanish Economy ministry. Project Number: TIN2014-53234-C2-1-R.

S. Ibrahim et al. (Eds.): ICA3PP 2017, LNCS 10393, pp. 489–502, 2017.
DOI: 10.1007/978-3-319-65482-9_35

They are usually formed by various bioinformatics applications arranged in a pre-defined order. Although there are many workflows, most of them are composed of a similar subset of applications, and have a resembling structure. Applications within workflows manage large amounts of datasets that have to be analyzed by resorting to complex algorithms. Thus, workflows demand great amounts of computing resources to carry out their tasks. In this work, for simplicity, we will refer to applications and jobs indistinctly.

Shared clusters formed by heterogeneous nodes with multiple sockets and multiple cores have become a common environment to execute these workflows. However, in order to harness computing power, and meet, in so far as possible, user-defined performance criteria (ρ), such as: makespan, or execution cost, resources must be properly allocated. To do so, application's resource usage and characteristics, must be accounted for. Optimal allocation of applications to shared resources is an NP-hard issue, widely studied over the past decades. Previous knowledge of the resource requirements of jobs generated by bioinformatics workflows applications is paramount to allocate resources. In most cases, cluster-submitted HPC applications include a resource description. Implying that, prior to job submission, an estimation of the resources to be used by the job may already have been acquired by the user. In this work, as common within bioinformatics, we considered a shared-memory scenario where jobs are broken down into tasks running in same-node threads. In these cases, node descriptions should include estimation of execution time, memory, node architecture or number of processing units.

However, most bioinformatics jobs don't come along with resource descriptions. Instead, they must be provided by users themselves, without prior hint or even partial knowledge of the resources required by their application. Thus, when dealing with bioinformatics applications, mostly managed by biological data analysts, job's resource description tends to be based on their functional requirements, such as type of data processing or desired output quality. Consequently, descriptions are rarely based on the actual resources to be requested by the application.

Furthermore, bioinformatics applications show highly variable execution times or amount of resource usage, depending on: configuration *parameters*, detailing the specifics about the observed biological phenomenon, or *input datasets* characteristics, such as: file size, number or length of sequences. The same bioinformatics application may then require substantially different amount of resources depending on the case of analysis. Different underlying algorithms with different resource consumptions may be activated.

This phenomenon may be encountered in blast 2.2.27, which compares a set of query sequences versus a set of reference sequences, searches for similarities, and outputs findings. The quantity of the findings searched for on the same datasets can be adjusted with word size parameter. The blast algorithm uses the word parameter to nucleate regions of similarity and it is usually related to the query size. The lower it is, the more findings are searched for, implying more computational complexity and larger execution times, as Fig. 1 (L) shows.

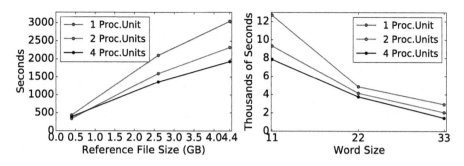

Fig. 1. Blast's performance variation caused by word size parameter and input dataset size.

In Fig. 1 (R), we can see how varying characteristics of input datasets, such as their size, also has a major impact on application's execution time, regardless of resources used. It is necessary to have a deep knowledge of the application to provide specific needed resource description. Including for instance, application scalability and memory consumption for each given combination of parameter values and input datasets characteristics. Consequently, resource reservation doesn't adjust to the needs of applications. Naive approaches are taken instead, such as over-allocation of resources, i.e. reservation of the whole node. However, most bioinformatics applications are written in programming models that don't scale well [2]. Thus, resources like processing units and memory remain practically unused as other jobs wait. As a result, cluster efficiency drops and larger waiting times arise.

Since most clusters are shared, jobs' performance is also affected by a dynamic workload, defined by the number of running jobs and their characteristics, such as the performance-bounding resource. The degree of multipgrogramming (DP) of the nodes will become greater than 1, since multiple applications will run simultaneously in the same nodes. Jobs' execution times will be extended compared with the respective exclusive cases, affecting makespan. However, execution time extension, also known as slowdown, largely depends on the characteristics and resource usage of the applications running in the same node, and can be modeled.

To improve applications' makespan and cluster efficiency, we propose a Resource Manager (RM) designed for bioinformatics workflow applications. Our RM predicts jobs' performance depending on their parameters and input datasets, so that resource description can be adjusted, preventing under or over allocation of resources. A resource-sharing model is also included in the proposed RM. It will handle the multiprogramming of resources, by determining which groups applications are more compatible to share the same node resources. Thus, the efficiency of resources will be improved and slowdown minimized. Furthermore, a resource scheduling algorithm has been developed. For each queued job, given availability of shared resources at that certain instant, we will determine the combination of resources best suiting performance criteria set by job user.

Thus, our RM will assist the user by defining resource description matching applications' needs and user criteria, in an automated, on-the-go way. As a result, cluster efficiency and applications' performance are improved. Furthermore, it has been designed to operate alongside SLURM, one of the top workload managers used in clusters. To develop our proposal, we selected a set of bioinformatics applications, as described in Sect. 3.1, and queued them up on a cluster, formed by 4 nodes containing heterogeneous resources and SLURM workload manager. Further description of cluster nodes is provided in Sect. 4.

2 Related Work

Resource Management Systems (RMS) are in charge of allocate cluster resources, monitor their status, and managing the queue of submitted jobs. Examples of these are Sun Grid Engine, MAUI or SLURM, present in 60% of world's top 500 supercomputers. SLURM is composed by several daemons, such as slurmctld (monitors resources) or slurmd, (executes work). It also includes several plug-ins. On one hand, node selection plug-ins, which determine resources to allocate. On the other, scheduling plug-ins, allowing: priority assignation, backfilling, and many other features. However, despite all functionalities included in SLURM, we haven't found any considering the dynamic characteristics of the bioinformatics applications, which prompt a single application to require substantially different resources to be executed in reasonable time.

Due to the dynamic nature of cluster status, affected by the workload: queue, variable resource availability, and the wide-range of different resource utilizations of bioinformatics applications (parameters, datasets), using previous knowledge can help predict how the system is going to behave in a near-future, and estimate resources used by bioinformatics jobs. Thanks to that knowledge and forecast, resource managers can take more enhanced scheduling decisions, adjusted to present cluster status, so that resources are more efficiently allocated to jobs. In order to improve allocation of bioinformatics applications in clusters, we considered developing a prediction-based plug-in intended for SLURM manager. The plug-in can be developed by using *slurm_spank* interface, and is able to dynamically modify SLURM's policy.

Depending on the performance issue to be predicted on clusters or grids, different prediction approaches are required. Several studies have focused on predicting jobs' execution time [14,15], queue waiting time [10,11], or slowdown caused by resource-sharing [5]. Prediction techniques can be divided into many categories, such as: benchmarking, application code analysis, simulation or parameter prediction. Benchmarking techniques are used for estimating system's performance given a reference parameter. Application code analysis techniques are employed for estimating applications' performance, however, they require thorough analysis of application code, and are not efficient when dealing with multiple applications, due to effort and cost reasons. Furthermore, they dismiss the characteristics of the system. Parameter prediction techniques estimate applications' execution times by employing estimation models. To do so, they consider applications' characteristics, such as the performance-determining parameters. Parameter prediction techniques are suitable for bioinformatics applications, due to their dynamic behavior, strongly dependent on their parameters and datasets.

Parameter prediction techniques can employ analytical or statistical models. Analytical models [12,13] can provide performance measures, such as execution time. However, they predict assuming a determined, non-dynamic, cluster status. Statistical methods include on one hand time-series modeling, which use the high over-time correlation shown by system load [7,17]. These systems can be useful for modeling workloads and queue waiting times in shared systems [4,16]. On the other hand, statistical methods include history-based learning approaches. In order to predict execution time, they not only consider the characteristics of applications to be executed, but also current system status [3]. Within statistical models, we can find two methods: categorization, accounting for applications' characteristics, and instant-based learning (IBL), also accounting for resource status. Finally, within IBL methods, correlation models can be found, such as regression models. To determine resources needed by bioinformatics applications, we base our RM on prediction. The prediction model must consider the dynamic behavior of bioinformatics applications, caused by parameters and data variables, and system resources. Thus to generate predictions, Multivariate Regression has been chosen.

Since the goal of this work is to improve resource management of bioinformatics jobs on real clusters, we develop a RM capable of operating jointly with the default RMS featuring in the cluster. In our case, SLURM. Hence, basing RMS' scheduling decisions on past events, and adjusting resource allocation to applications' needs.

3   Proposed Resource Manager

The RM proposed in this work is formed by three stages, depicted in Fig. 2, in red color: characterization, prediction and scheduling. Our RM is attached to the cluster, and features a feedback mechanism that improves its performance. Further description on proposed RM's blocks is provided below.

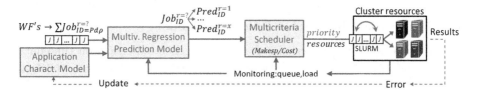

Fig. 2. Proposed RM (red blocks) attached to a SLURM cluster. (Color figure online)

3.1   Application Characterization Model

The first step consisted on building a set of popular applications to analyze. To select them, previous studies on comparative analysis of bioinformatics applications have been reviewed [6, 8, 9]. From these studies we picked different kinds of applications, with relevant performance or differential resource usage. The purpose is to build a set of applications commonly found within bioinformatics workflows and representative of many cluster queues. The resulting set is formed by memory-bound applications, performing sequence alignment or read mapping (blast 2.2.27, bwa-mem 0.7.5a, bwa-aling 0.7.5a, bowtie 2.2.6, soap 2.21, star 2.4.2a, hisat 2.0.5), and cpu-bound applications, performing phylogeny analysis (phyml 2.4.5par, mrbayes 3.1.2h, raxml 8.2.9, fasttree 2.1.3.c). From this set, we will generate a performance model that will allow us to predict the resources needed for submitted applications. The main factors determining the performance of each bioinformatics application have been reviewed, and classified in three categories: application parameters (P), IO datasets characteristics (d) and resources $(resources, \text{ or } r)$. The job execution vector is shown in Eq. 1, with ρ representing user-selected criteria: time or cost.

$$J = App^{resources}_{ID=(P),(d),\rho} = App^{node,PU,mem}_{(Par_1,..,Par_x),(data_1,..,data_y),\rho} \qquad (1)$$

Each application of the set has been given multiple (P, d) values, and executed in all cluster nodes with a wide range of PUs. For each run, performance information such as execution time or cost, has been stored in a historical database. Resource consumption metrics: CPU usage, memory or disk consumption and accesses among others, have been also thoroughly tracked and stored. A variety of Linux tools have been used to do so, including: /usr/bin/time, Perf Stat, PidStat, VmStat and Sar.

Prior to execution, job's required data sets existence in the available nodes is checked, and loaded otherwise into the local disk of the corresponding node. Applications are thread-level parallel and therefore will be executed solely in one node at a time. As customary within bioinformatics, memory consumption won't surpass node capacity. Each time an application is executed in the cluster, new performance results are stored. Hence, the database has more and more information to predict.

3.2   Multivariate Regression Prediction Model

To determine whether prediction is feasible, we generated execution time data samples and analyzed them statistically. We proved that, even when repeating same job execution, with identical conditions, little variation occurs and data is inferential. Several samples have been generated by executing all applications in the set with different parameters and IO datasets. For simplicity, and since identical conclusions have been obtained for all cases, only one case is shown. The sample used for explanation has been generated by executing 9 identical instances of blast. Makespan data is displayed within squares in Fig. 3, averaging 816 s. First, we checked whether data is parametric/Normally Distributed with *Shaphiro-Wilk Normality Test*. Obtained p-value = 0.91 (>0.05) shows data is normally distributed. Afterwards, the Confidence Interval was calculated with the *One-Sample T-Test*, which requires data to be parametric. Obtained confidence interval (UpperLim = 817 s, LowerLim = 814 s), whose width (3) equating to a tiny percentage ($3 * 100/816 = 0.36\%$) of the mean, proves data is inferential. Once data inferentiability is proven, Multivariate Regression Prediction can be carried out, based on already-obtained performance information. Although both makespan and cost are predicted, only makespan predictions are shown since from these, execution cost predictions can easily be obtained. Cost has been calculated by assigning by-the-hour fees to both CPU Model and gigabytes of memory used. Pricing has been estimated using Amazon's EC2 resource cost scale.

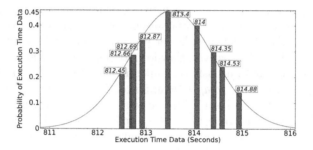

Fig. 3. Sample data values within squares, and resulting distribution.

Among existing regression prediction methods, linear regression has been chosen since data is normally distributed. Predictor variables have been picked based upon *Pearson Correlation Coefficient*, and included following *Forward Variable Selection* mechanism. To prevent over-fitting, and the consequent unwanted modeling of noise, *Adjusted R^2* coefficient has been calculated. When a user submits a job ($Job_{P,d,\rho}^{r=?}$), with unspecified resources denoted with *(r = ?)*, for any combination of cluster resources available, makespan predictions are generated. By the time multiple jobs are submitted to our varying-status cluster, we will have enough information to allocate resources best suiting average job makespan and cluster efficiency.

In Fig. 4, top, real and multivariate regression prediction results shown for bowtie and bwa-aling. Predicted variable is execution time, whereas dependent, correlated variables are PUs and the size of reads dataset file (Size). The prediction equation is:

$$PredTime = \alpha * (Size/PUs) + \beta * Size + \gamma \qquad (2)$$

Mean relative prediction errors obtained: 7.5% for bowtie and 8.7% for bwa-align, prove the accuracy of the developed prediction method.

Speedup curves, such as those shown in Fig. 4 (bottom), can be calculated from time predictions. For the displayed curves, little speed improvement is shown when employing between 12 and 16 PUs. At the end of that step, on one hand, given a job and a cluster we can determine the fastest node. On the other hand, we can determine how to properly balance the trade-off between the number of PUs and time. Not only we know the threshold beyond which time doesn't decrease ($PU_{MaxSpeed}$), but also the *time penalty* inflicted on a job, when it runs with $n° PU < PU_{MaxSpeed}$, that is $PU_{LowSpeed}$.

3.3   Resource-Sharing Model and Multicriteria Scheduler

As previously discussed, analyzed bioinformatics mappers barely scale beyond a low threshold of PUs, such as shown in Fig. 4, bottom, for bwa-align and bowtie. This downside is caused by another, performance-limiting resource. For the analyzed mappers, which have PUs and memory as predominant resources, low scalability issue is caused by poor memory management. In order to harness the idle portion of node resources, other applications can be executed in the same node (DP > 1). As a consequence, larger execution times will be obtained, that is, they are slowed down. However, slowdown of depends on which combinations of applications are simultaneously scheduled in the same node. The lesser slowdown is obtained, the more *compatible* applications are. Compatibility might be strongly influenced by the resource usage of applications, which will determine how much interference is to occur among applications sharing the node. Thus, differently-bound applications are likely to make better candidates for simultaneous execution than identically-bound applications. To minimize slowdown, and determine which applications are more compatible, analyzed applications have

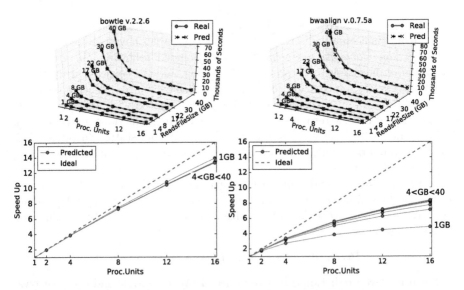

Fig. 4. Top: Real and prediction results of bowtie and bwa-align, with multiple PUs and reads sizes. Bottom: Speedups obtained from predictions, revealing $PU_{MaxSpeed}$ threshold and $PU_{LowSpeed}$ penalties.

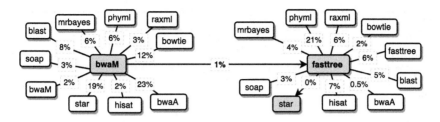

Fig. 5. Up to 22% slowdown reduction is obtained, comparing best case scenario (bwaM+fasttree = 1%), vs. worst (bwaM+fasttree = 23%).

been simultaneously executed in all cluster nodes, with n° $PU = PU_{MaxSpeed}$. Since different jobs won't have identical execution times, when the shorter ones finish, they are executed again. Slowdown have been calculated by comparing shared execution time vs. exclusive execution time of an application, in percentages. Slowdowns obtained running a top-row application alongside a left-column application are shown in Table 1. Our scheduler consults the slowdown table, and sets queued jobs' priority in such a way that slowdowns are minimized. This situation is represented in Fig. 5. Given a running application, i.e. bwaM (bwa-mem), our model prioritizes the most compatible job, over all others. Best vs. worst case scenario (1% vs. 23% slowdown), shows up to 22% slowdown reduction is be obtained. Next, we developed a scheduling algorithm capable of operating alongside one of the world's top workload manager such SLURM. Our algorithm consults applications' exclusive performance makespan predictions in function of multiple resources (*nodes, PUs*), and slowdown information at every step in order to schedule a queue of jobs. Summarized, pseudo-code description of the algorithm is provided in Algorithm 1:

Table 1. Slowdowns obtained when running top-row alongside left-column applications.

	Blast	BwaM	Bowtie	BwaA	Hisat	Star	Soap	Phyml	Mrbayes	Fasttree	Raxml
Blast	8%	%	%	%	%	%	%	%	%	%	%
BwaM	18%	2%	%	%	%	%	%	%	%	%	%
Bowtie	6%	12%	10%	%	%	%	%	%	%	%	%
BwaA	16%	23%	21%	3%	%	%	%	%	%	%	%
Hisat	18%	2%	16%	18%	8%	%	%	%	%	%	%
Star	21%	19%	30%	6%	18%	31%	%	%	%	%	%
Soap	6%	3%	15%	2%	6%	13%	10%	%	%	%	%
Phyml	2%	6%	7%	11%	3%	1%	0.2%	12%	%	%	%
Mrbayes	3%	6%	2%	3%	3%	5%	4%	27%	6%	%	%
Fasttree	5%	1%	2%	0.5%	7%	0%	0.5%	21%	4%	6%	%
Raxml	3%	3%	4%	2%	4%	7%	1%	16%	4%	6%	8%

Algorithm 1: Scheduling Pseudocode

---

    input : List of Application to Schedule (LAS), List of Predictive Time of Application Exclusive Mode
               (LPTA), List of Compatibility Slowdown Application (LCSA)
    output: List of Priority Applications

```
 1  Available Resources = Resource Status trough the Distributed Resource Management and read process log;
 2  if Available Resources == 0 then
 3      reject LAS;                                                                         // Node Full
 4  end
 5  while List of Application to Schedule (LAS) not empty do
 6      Order List of Application to Schedule (LAS) according Time ;                // Longest First
 7      Order List of Compatibility Slowdown Application (LCSA) for App; ;     // Most Compatible First
 8      App = First in List of Application to Schedule;
 9      PredResource = Max PUnits from List of Predictive Time of Application Exclusive Mode(LPTA) for
        App;
10      for i = All Applications in Resources do
11          MostCompatible = List of Compatibility Slowdown Application (LCSA) for App;
12          if MostCompotaible == i and Selected Resources != 0 then
13              List of Priority Applications = App + i;
14              if Available Resources > PredResource then
15                  Select Resources = PredResource ;                     // Maximun cores according to LPTA
16              end
17              else
18                  Select Resources = All Available Resource
19              end
20              List of Application to Schedule = Remove App ;            // App Scheduled, remove from list
21              List of Priority Applications += App + i;                // App Scheduled, Add to Priority List
22              if List of Compatibility Slowdown Application (LCSA) for App == Complete and Selected Resources != 0
                then
23                  List of Priority Applications = App;
24                  if Available Resources > PredResource then
25                      Select Resources = PredResource ;                 // Maximun cores according to LPTA
26                  end
27                  else
28                      Select Resources = All Available Resource
29                  end
30                  List of Application to Schedule = Remove App ;        // App Scheduled, remove from list
31                  List of Priority Applications += App ;               // App Scheduled, add to Priority List
32              end
33          end
34          else
35              MostCompatible = Next in List of Compatibility Slowdown Application (LCSA) for App;
36          end
37      end
38  end
39  return List of Priority Applications;
```

---

4   Experiments

In this section, we process a group of bioinformatics workflows composed by commonly used bioinformatics applications, in a shared cluster, described below. Workflow applications are executed in two different ways. On one hand, by using the proposed RM (characterization, prediction, scheduling) alongside SLURM, as in Fig. 2. On the other hand, by solely using SLURM, cluster's default manager. Among all scheduling policies included in SLURM, we discarded those requiring previous prediction of resources or execution times, such as Shortest Job First (SJF), Longest Job First (LJF) or backfilling. From 0-prior-knowledge policies, well-know First Come First Served (FCFS) has been chosen as a first approach.

The prototype cluster is shared among multiple kinds of applications, with different programming paradigms, i.e. MapReduce, MPI or multithread. First, the cluster has been properly partitioned according to the resource needs of the applications running within. Thus, for bioinformatics applications, a multithread partition has been defined, and equipped with four nodes with heterogeneous characteristics. Namely: AMD IO-6376 (2.3 GHz, 64 PU, 128 GB), Intel Xeon E5-4620 (2.2 GHz, 64 PU, 128 GB) and 2 Intel Xeon E5-2620 (2.1 GHz, 24 PU, 64 GB).

Workflows are submitted to the cluster. For each workflow applications, the predictor generates multiple makespan predictions considering: node architecture and a range of processing units. With this information, the number of PUs marking the scalability limits of each application, $PU_{MaxSpeed}$, are obtained. As well as the time penalties obtained when a application runs with: $n° PUs < PU_{MaxSpeed}$, that is: $PU_{LowSpeed}$.

The large amount of applications requests received by the cluster, and their computing requirements may overwhelm cluster's potential by far. To prevent unproportionally-long waiting times with respect to execution times, the application queue is divided into different processing batches.

To determine a proper batch size, we firstly consulted time predictions of queued applications. Secondly, we calculated the aggregated number of PUs needed in order to process them, (aggregated $n° PU_{MaxSpeed}$), and compared it with the amount of PUs of the cluster. Our criteria is based on previous studies, such as [1].

Next, we selected two batches. This amount has been chosen since allows us to recreate a real scenario, with number of requests surpassing resource availability, and show the benefits of our proposal. Each batch has 2 workflows. In turn, a list of applications is selected from each workflow. As an example, one of the workflows is shown in Fig. 6. From this workflow, 4 mappers (hisat, bowtie, bwaM, soap), and phylogeny applications (phyml, mrbayes) are selected.

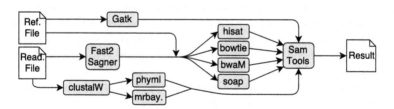

Fig. 6. Structure and applications of one of the workflows considered for the experiments.

Our experimentation starts with the processing of 4 bioinformatics workflows. The complete list of applications selected from the 4 workflows included in the two batches, can be seen in Table 2.

In order to process the workflows, their applications are scheduled for simultaneous execution in the same nodes, (DP > 1). In Fig. 7, we show that node capacity (AMD IO 64 PUs), allows for DP = 8 applications to scale in the same node, with average slowdown of 65%. However, to implement our idea, our experimentation is shown with DP = 2, since the same course of action applies, and improvements on makespan and efficiency can be shown in an easier way.

Table 2. List of workflow applications to be processed in the cluster, average predicted times with n° PU $= PU_{MaxSpeed}$ in each node (in seconds), and mean relative prediction errors.

Admited apps	Blast	BwaM	Bowt.	BwaA	Hisat	Star	Soap	Phyml	Mrbay.	Fasttr.	Raxml
WF$_1$	3640	3313	-	4136	-	-	2921	1622	3079	3000	2767
WF$_2$	-	-	2934	5688	864	-	4021	3068	3510	1985	-
WF$_3$	-	4576	3681	-	1220	1207	5362	-	-	3265	3443
WF$_4$	7021	-	5420	8346	1966	1572	-	3753	-	6508	4099
Mean.Rel.Err	4.1%	5.4%	7.5%	8.7%	7%	6.1%	11%	5.3%	7.7%	6.7%	8.1%

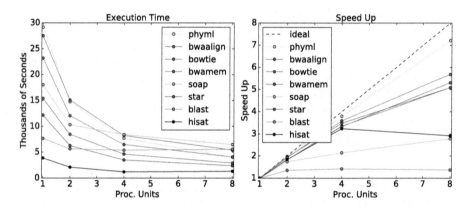

Fig. 7. Scalability with 8 applications in AMD node (DP $= 8$), containing 64 PUs. Average slowdown of all applications is 65%.

The Multicriteria Scheduler consults predictions in every node: execution times, scalability, time penalties with $PU_{LowSpeed}$, as well as the slowdown table. Thus, exclusive-mode and shared-mode application performance information is employed by our scheduler in order to determine jobs' resources and priorities, altering the course of action set by SLURM's chosen FCFS policy. At the beginning, the cluster is assumed idle. Given the queue, our scheduling algorithm, described in Sect. 3.3, performs as follows:

For idle nodes: prioritizes longest application ($bwaM_1$) containing at least one compatible job ($phyml_1$), and allocates them both to the fastest idle node (AMD), each with n° PU $= PU_{MaxSpeed}$. Minimum slowdowns and makespans are obtained for both jobs, while minimizing the amount of PUs used, and leaving for other submitted jobs. Same procedure is followed until all idle nodes have become loaded.

Once all nodes are loaded, the algorithms performs as follows:

For loaded nodes: At this point, we search for waiting jobs that are most compatible with the load of any node that still has available PUs. We also consider that since a only small number PUs per node may be available, jobs are likely to run with $PU_{LowSpeed}$. That is, less PU than $PU_{MaxSpeed}$, implying that the job will have some time penalty. Assuming the following situation: Intel

Table 3. Makespan and efficiency obtained with SLURM's FCFS, and by attaching the blocks of the proposed resource manager alongside SLURM.

Queue	SLURM (FCFS)		Proposed RM+SLURM		Comparison	
	Makespan	Efficiency	Makespan	Efficiency	Makespan reduct.	Efficien. increase
WF_1	23057 s	0.25	17959 s	0.43	22%	73%
WF_2	23589 s	0.3	18243 s	0.52	23%	74%
WF_3	25963 s	0.28	18175 s	0.51	30%	85%
WF_4	27958 s	0.31	17959 s	0.52	35%	67%
Average	*25141* s	*0.29*	*18084* s	*0.5*	*28%*	*75%*

E5-2620 (24 PU, 64 GB), is loaded with ($soap_1$) with $PU_{MaxSpeed}$. Then, the most compatible job would be: ($mrbayes_1$), which has $PU_{MaxSpeed}$. However, only 8 PUs are available, implying a time penalty for ($mrbayes$) job, since it would have to run with $PU_{LowSpeed} = 8$. In these cases, our algorithm compares whether it's fastest: to wait for the release of 12 PUs, and run with $PU_{MaxSpeed}$, or to run with $PU_{LowSpeed}$. If waiting option is chosen, then a job shorter than $mrbayes_1$'s predicted waiting time, is executed.

Once the 4 bioinformatics workflows applications are executed as described (using the proposed RM), they are also executed using solely SLURM, with FCFS policy. At the end, the average makespan and resource efficiency are calculated. Obtained workflow processing results can be seen in Table 3. Results show that a 28% makespan reduction and a 75% efficiency are obtained when attaching the proposed resource management blocks to SLURM.

5   Conclusions and Future Work

In this paper we have proposed a new RM intended for bioinformatics workflows running on shared clusters with heterogeneous resources. In order to develop our RM, we have characterized and analyzed a set of popular applications. Second, we proved data inferentiability and built a multivariate regression model, that can predict application's performance in function of multiple combinations of resources with little error. To consider the shared nature of the cluster, we also built a resource sharing method. We also proposed a scheduling algorithm that takes enhanced decisions based on available information. At the end, we tested our model. Our results show that by attaching the proposed RM alongside SLURM, our model can process bioinformatics workflows, achieving a 28% reduction of makespan by also increasing resource efficiency by 75%. Furthermore, early results shown with a higher degree of multiprogramming (8), leave the door open for higher efficiency and makespan improvement of workflow bioinformatics.

To that end, we started a new line of work, migrating our proposal into a simulated environment for workflows, such as workflowsim simulator.

References

1. Agrawal, P., Kifer, D., Olston, C.: Scheduling shared scans of large data files. Proc. VLDB Endow. **1**(1), 958–969 (2008). doi:10.1145/1453856.1453960
2. Al-Ali, R., Kathiresan, N., El Anbari, M., Schendel, E.R., Zaid, T.A.: Workflow optimization of performance and quality of service for bioinformatics application in high performance computing. J. Comput. Sci. **15**, 3–10 (2016). doi:10.1016/j.jocs.2016.03.005
3. Christopher, A., Andrew, M., Stefan, S.: Locally weighted learning. Artif. Intell. Rev. **11**(1–5), 11–73 (1997). doi:10.1023/A:1006511328852
4. Downey, A.B.: Predicting queue times on space-sharing parallel computers. In: Proceedings of the 11th International Parallel Processing Symposium, pp. 209–218. IEEE (1997) doi:10.1109/IPPS.1997.580894
5. Figueira, S.M., Berman, F.: A slowdown model for applications executing on time-shared clusters of workstations. IEEE Trans. Parallel Distrib. Syst. **12**(6), 653–670 (2001). doi:10.1109/71.932718
6. Hatem, A., Bozdağ, D., Toland, A.E., Çatalyürek, Ü.V.: Benchmarking short sequence mapping tools. BMC Bioinform. **14**(1), 184 (2013). doi:10.1109/BIBM.2011.83
7. Iosup, A., Li, H., Jan, M., Anoep, S., Dumitrescu, C., Wolters, L., Epema, D.H.: The grid workloads archive. Future Gener. Comput. Syst. **24**(7), 672–686 (2008). doi:10.1016/j.future.2008.02.003
8. Li, H., Durbin, R.: Fast and accurate short read alignment with burrows-wheeler transform. Bioinformatics **25**(14), 1754–1760 (2009). doi:10.1093/bioinformatics/btp324
9. Lord, E., Diallo, A., Makarenkov, V.: Classification of bioinformatics workflows using weighted versions of partitioning and hierarchical clustering algorithms. BMC Bioinform. **16**(1), 68 (2015). doi:10.1186/s12859-015-0508-1
10. Murali, P., Vadhiyar, S.: Qespera: an adaptive framework for prediction of queue waiting times in supercomputer systems. Concurr. Comput. Pract. Exp. **28**(9), 2685–2710 (2016). doi:10.1002/cpe.3735
11. Prodan, R.: Specification and runtime workflow support in the askalon grid environment. Sci. Program. **15**(4), 193–211 (2007). doi:10.1155/2007/734021
12. Seneviratne, S., Levy, D.: Enhanced host load prediction by division of user load signal for grid computing. J. Cluster Comput. (2005, submitted)
13. Seneviratne, S., Levy, D.C.: Task profiling model for load profile prediction. Future Gener. Comput. Syst. **27**(3), 245–255 (2011). doi:10.1016/j.future.2010.09.004
14. Seneviratne, S., Levy, D.C., Buyya, R.: A taxonomy of performance prediction systems in the parallel and distributed computing grids. arXiv preprint arXiv:1307.2380 (2013)
15. Shanthini, J., Shankarkumar, K.: Anatomy study of execution time predictions in heterogeneous systems. Int. J. Comput. Appl. **45**(7), 39–43 (2012). doi:10.5120/6795-9123
16. Song, B., Ernemann, C., Yahyapour, R.: Parallel computer workload modeling with Markov chains. In: Feitelson, D.G., Rudolph, L., Schwiegelshohn, U. (eds.) JSSPP 2004. LNCS, vol. 3277, pp. 47–62. Springer, Heidelberg (2005). doi:10.1007/11407522_3
17. Yang, L., Schopf, J.M., Foster, I.: Conservative scheduling: using predicted variance to improve scheduling decisions in dynamic environments. In: Proceedings of the 2003 ACM/IEEE conference on Supercomputing, p. 31. ACM (2003). doi:10.1109/SC.2003.10015

Massively Parallel Sequence Alignment with BLAST Through Work Distribution Implemented Using PCJ Library

Marek Nowicki[1]([⊠]), Davit Bzhalava[2], and Piotr Bała[3]([⊠])

[1] Faculty of Mathematics and Computer Science, Nicolaus Copernicus University, Chopina 12/18, 87-100 Toruń, Poland
faramir@mat.umk.pl

[2] Department of Laboratory Medicine, F46, Karolinska Institutet, 14186 Stockholm, Sweden
davit.bzhalava@ki.se

[3] Interdisciplinary Centre for Mathematical and Computational Modelling, University of Warsaw, Pawińskiego 5a, 02-106 Warsaw, Poland
bala@icm.edu.pl

Abstract. This article presents massively parallel execution of the BLAST algorithm on supercomputers and HPC clusters using thousands of processors. Our work is based on the optimal splitting up the set of queries running with the non-modified NCBI-BLAST package for sequence alignment. The work distribution and search management have been implemented in Java using a PCJ (Parallel Computing in Java) library. The PCJ-BLAST package is responsible for reading sequence for comparison, splitting it up and start multiple NCBI-BLAST executables. We also investigated a problem of parallel I/O and thanks to PCJ library we deliver high throughput execution of BLAST. The presented results show that using Java and PCJ library we achieved very good performance and efficiency. In result, we have significantly reduced time required for sequence analysis. We have also proved that PCJ library can be used as an efficient tool for fast development of the scalable applications.

Keywords: Sequence alignment · NGS · Next Generation Sequencing · Parallel programming · Java · BLAST · NCBI-BLAST · PCJ

1 Introduction

With the development of Next Generation Sequencing (NGS), there is observed continuous growth in the size of the databases storing nucleotide and protein data. In the area of computational biology, there is high demand to extract useful information from these massive data sources. In order to help researchers analyze voluminous genetic data the high-performance computing power has been developed. Different hardware such as clusters, supercomputers or even custom systems are used to solve the numerous problems originating from analysis of biological and biomolecular data.

© Springer International Publishing AG 2017
S. Ibrahim et al. (Eds.): ICA3PP 2017, LNCS 10393, pp. 503–512, 2017.
DOI: 10.1007/978-3-319-65482-9_36

Basic Local Alignment Search Tool (BLAST) [1,2] is an extensively used bioinformatics application for sequence alignment analysis. It allows for querying DNA (nucleotide) and protein sequence databases with given a query sequence. In results, the most similar sequences from a listed databases are identified. This information is then used for the description of structures and functions of unknown sequences. Another implication is understanding the evolutionary origin of particular DNA or protein sequences. Due to ultimate importance, the sequence analysis with BLAST is used in almost all bioinformatics solutions.

The success of BLAST is based on the use of heuristic methods to reduce the running time not affecting accuracy significantly. BLAST is available as an application to install on local resources or the web. The implementation from the National Center for Biotechnology Information (NCBI)[1] is the most popular one and is considered as a reference.

NCBI BLAST offers the possibility of multithreading in symmetric multi-processing (SMP) systems. Despite the parallelism in the search, NCBI can be run on only one node. NCBI BLAST keeps a regular linear speed-up behavior, but node size significantly limits overall performance.

Our parallel solution for BLAST is based on the input sequence fragmentation and efficient query load division ensuring load balancing. The database search and alignment of the parts of the input sequence are performed by the non-modified NCBI BLAST application which allows easy adoption to the improvements and further releases. This approach allows to use hundreds and thousands of processor cores and significantly reduce a time necessary to perform an analysis. What is more important, the user gets the same results as running original NCBI BLAST.

The paper is organized as follows: in the next section, we present related work on the parallelization of the BLAST. Section 3 presents PCJ library for parallelization Java applications. The following section presents an implementation of the sequence alignment using PCJ library. Section 5 presents performance and scalability benchmarks. The paper ends with the conclusions and future work sections.

2   Related Work

Since BLAST is an essential bioinformatics application and it is usage require significant computational resources, there are known attempts to run BLAST on clusters and supercomputers. Some of them [3–5] are based on the *embarrassingly parallel* approach such as the distribution of the query set across computing nodes. Each of them executes a sequential task which increases throughput, but the completion time is unchanged, despite the parallel execution of queries. Another possibility is to partition the database among computing nodes. Each node performs the search for the same query but using an assigned part of the database [6–8]. This solution was first implemented in the mpiBLAST [6] and

---

[1] http://www.ncbi.nlm.nih.gov/BLAST *[Accessed: June 8, 2017]*.

then developed further in pioBLAST [9]. In this way, one search is performed at a time; the advantage comes from the reduction of the portion of the database each thread has to look at.

Despite numerous effort in the area of parallelization of sequence alignment tools, the bioinformatics community is still lacking good and efficient tools running on the available computer architectures aligned with the recent progress of NCBI software.

Therefore, we have developed our solution, hardware independent and adjusted to the widely used HPC architectures. The compliance to the NCBI-BLAST is a key issue.

3   PCJ Library

PCJ (Parallel Computing in Java)[2] is a Java library [10] that allows performing parallel and distributed computations. The PCJ library provides users with the uniform view across nodes. It can work on the multicore systems with the various interconnects such as Ethernet or InfiniBand. The PCJ source code is available on GitHub, under Open Source license (BSD).

PCJ implements PGAS (Partitioned Global Address Space) model. The library development was inspired by the lack of such solution for the recent Java releases and by other solutions such as Co-Array Fortran [11], Unified Parallel C [12] or Titanium [13].

In the PCJ design, we ensure compliance with Java standards. In contrast to the listed above languages, the PCJ does not modify Java syntax and does not extend it. Therefore additional libraries or tools which are not part of the Java distribution are not required.

In the PCJ each PCJ thread (task) executes its own set of instructions and has its local memory. By default, instructions and variables are local to the task. Each PCJ task can access other PCJ tasks variables that have a special @Shared annotation. The library provides methods to perform basic operations such as synchronization of tasks and data transfer between PCJ threads. The data transfer operations (get and put) are executed in an one-sided asynchronous way. With the PCJ library user can also create task groups, broadcast data, and monitor variable updates.

The PCJ library completely complies with Java standards. In particular, PCJ can use Sockets Direct Protocol (SDP) which increases network performance while InfiniBand is used. The SDP is available starting from Java SE 7.

The application using PCJ library is executed as ordinary Java application. In the single node execution, it uses Java Virtual Machine (JVM). While running in the multinode setup, one (or more) JVM is started on each node. This process is performed by the PCJ library and allows a user to initiate an application on multiple nodes, running one or more threads on each node. The number of nodes and threads is set up upon a start of the application in both interactive and batch modes.

---

[2] http://pcj.icm.edu.pl *[Accessed: March 20, 2016]*.

One JVM instance is a PCJ node. Single PCJ node can hold many PCJ threads (tasks). Such design is well suited for current computer architectures containing a large number (hundreds or thousands) of nodes, each of them built on several or many cores.

Since PCJ application can be run using multiple JVMs, the communication between threads has to be realized in an appropriate manner. In particular, the Java concurrency mechanisms are used to synchronize PCJ threads and exchange information if communicating threads run within the same JVM. If data exchange is realized between different JVM's, the socket based network communication is used.

4   PCJ-BLAST

The PCJ-BLAST is implemented in Java with the help of PCJ library application which allows running multiple NCBI-BLAST instances in parallel. The parallelization is based on the distribution of the query sequence which small parts is searched against nucleotide sequence database. This approach seems to be well adjusted to the NGS data which contains a large number of short sequences searched independently against the reference database. The database contains 675 million of nucleotide sequence lines as of December 2015 and has a size of 52 GB.

4.1   Input Data

Input file for BLAST used in our processing is obtained from the NGS sequencing equipment (in this case Illumina Sequencing) and consists of about 1 million short, 100–150 character-long sequences (*reads*). The input sequence is stored in the FASTA format, and single input file can contain multiple sequences. Each sequence has the one-line description, denoted by the greater-than ("$>$") symbol. After the description, sequence data begins. Sequence data can span multiple non-blank lines. Next sequence starts with description line, which starts with the line with the greater-than symbol.

Despite the fact that the sequences included in the input file are of similar length, the processing of each sequence (i.e. search in the reference database) can take different time ranging from a couple of seconds up to thousands of seconds (see Fig. 1). The analysis time cannot be easily estimated based on the input sequence. Therefore, the workload balancing has to be performed dynamically during execution.

The large size of the input data allows us to speed-up sequence alignment based on the query-parallelized approach. Multiple query searches are distributed among different processors and can be done independently. Moreover, query parallelization can be implemented through *wrapper* to the original NCBI-BLAST. In such approach, it is important to decide which queries are assigned to which processor. The scheduling has to be performed dynamically since the time required to process the single query is not known in advance. The decision is performed based on the current state of the processor workload.

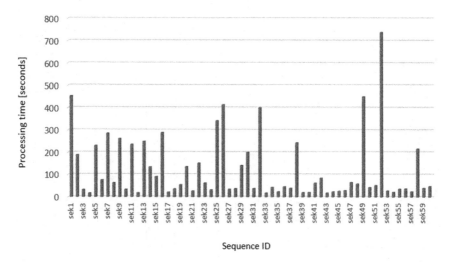

Fig. 1. Execution time for the selected reads from the input file. The execution time has been measured using single-threaded execution of the NCBI-BLAST 2.2.28.

4.2 Parallel Sequence Alignment

PCJ process sequences in parallel using multiple instances of NCBI-BLAST executed with multiple threads at a node. The number of nodes can be configured during job submission. The query string is read from the single file. Therefore, the input is not modified relate to the original NCBI-BLAST.

PCJ thread with id zero (*Scatterer*) is used for reading and distributing FASTA input file. Other PCJ threads (*Workers*) are used for run NCBI-BLAST application on sequences and process XML output into a proper format for further processing (see Fig. 2). Scatterer reads specified by the user number of sequences. Then it sends them to available workers or waits until there will be one available. The number of sequences processed by the individual worker at each round is kept low (in our case is equal to 2) to provide fine granularity and to obtain good load balancing. The sequences sent from the Scatterer to the Workers are not saved in the files.

The availability of workers is checked as follows. Workers use shared array buffer for incoming data. Scatterer uses shared array with indices of last read cell by workers (*readIndex*) in workers buffer. Initially values in this array are set to buffer size minus one. Additionally, Scatterer has local *writeIndex* array that indicates the next index in the worker's buffer to put read data. The *writeIndex* array is initialized to zeros. After sending data to the worker, Scatterer changes the value of the *writeIndex* cell associated with worker's id, to the next value.

Next read data is sent to next available workers buffer. The worker buffer is available if the value of *writeIndex* is not equal to the corresponding cell in *readIndex* array. If each worker's buffer is unavailable, Scatterer waits for a change in the *readIndex* array.

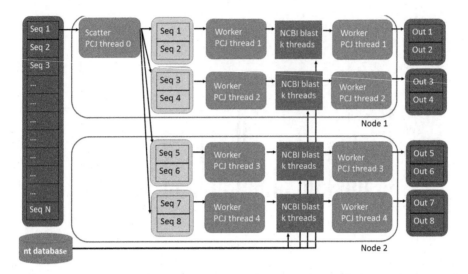

Fig. 2. Schematic view of the PCJ-BLAST. The workload is sent to the available workers based on the dynamic information sent by the workers. This information is sent using PCJ put and is not saved to the files. The input sequences can be processed in arbitrary order.

Workers wait for modification of the buffer and then read data from the first cell in the buffer. Before running NCBI-BLAST, they modify Scatterer *readIndex* array by writing the index of the cell they have just read into cell associated with their id. At that moment, a worker starts BLAST execution. After completing NCBI-BLAST execution, the Worker processes XML output into a form suitable for further processing and writes it into an output file. Each Worker uses its own output file. After completion, outputs are concatenated into one big file, as the order of sequences is not important for further processing. When there is no further data to process, Scatterer writes a null value to a proper cell in the worker's buffer, and then the workers stop their work. All communication between PCJ threads is asynchronous and does not involve saving data to the disk which allows minimizing time spent for data exchange between Scatterer and Workers.

It is worth noting that NCBI-BLAST execution time depends significantly on the query parameters described in the input. In our case we have used following query settings:

```
-word_size 11 -gapopen 0 -gapextend 2 -penalty -1 -reward 1
-max_target_seqs 10 -evalue 0.001 -show_gis -outfmt 5
```

With these settings, the output is formatted as the XML file. The parameters were tuned for the search of viruses sequences, and their optimization was performed out of this work.

4.3 Multithreaded NCBI-BLAST

The PCJ-BLAST allows for flexible configuration of many NCBI-BLAST instances run on each physical node. At the same time the number of threads used by the NCBI-BLAST can be adjusted to the efficient use of the computational node resources. To set up optimal configuration, we have run NCBI-BLAST using the different number of instances and a different threads count ensuring that a total number of threads was equal to the number of computational cores available at each node. The experiments have been performed using x86 cluster and Cray XC40 systems. In both cases, the input sequence was short (224 and 384 reads long respectively) and consisted of a copy of the same sequence (read) to ensure ideal load balancing.

5 PCJ-BLAST Performance Results

The experiments were run on the HPC x86 cluster and Cray XC40 systems.

PC cluster consisted of 223 computing nodes with the Intel Xeon E5-2697 v3 CPU (28 core each) clocked at 2.6 GHz and Infiniband FDR and Gigabit Ethernet interconnection. Every processing node has, at least, 64 GB of memory. PCJ (version 4.1.0) was run using Java JVM v. 1.8.0 from Oracle. The calculations were performed using the double precision for floating point arithmetic.

The reference database has been located at the NFS filesystem mounted at each computing node. A single instance of the reference database has been used for all NCBI-BLAST copies. The PCJ-BLAST has been run on the different number of nodes; each time nodes were allocated exclusively using all CPU cores available. The performance data presented in Fig. 3 shows good scaling up to the 64 nodes (1792 cores). The parallel efficiency calculated with respect to the single node is close to 1.0 even for a large number of cores. For example, while using 64 nodes instead of single one, the analysis time has been reduced almost 55 times (from 1453 hours to the 26.5 hours) which leads to the parallel efficiency of 91%.

Cray XT40 has 1084 nodes equipped with 2 Intel Xeon E5-2690 v3 CPUs running at 2.60 GHz. Every processing node has 128 GB of memory. Nodes are connected with Cray's Aries interconnect. PCJ (version 4.1.0) was run using JVM v. 1.8.0 from Oracle. The calculations were performed using the double precision floating point arithmetic.

The reference database has been located on the GVS filesystem mounted read only at each computing node. The PCJ-BLAST has been run on the different number of nodes under the same conditions as for x86 cluster. The performance data presented in Fig. 4 shows good scaling up to the 128 nodes (6144 cores).

The parallelization efficiency is over 90% up to 32 nodes. For 64 nodes is over 83% and than starts to decrease. The numbers presented for the PCJ-BLAST with and without XML output processing confirm parallel postprocessing of the results. The lower performance of the XML processing on the 128 nodes comes from the limits of I/O capabilities necessary for the writing analysis results to the disk.

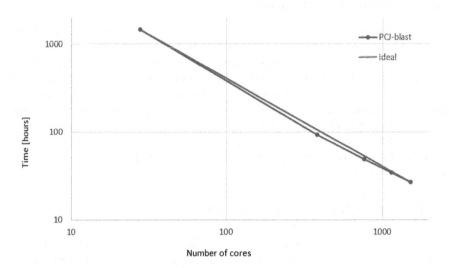

Fig. 3. Performance of the PCJ-BLAST on the HPC x86 cluster. The ideal scaling is plotted for reference. The scaling is based on the single node NCBI-BLAST execution using 28 threads. The experimental points correspond to the full nodes allocated.

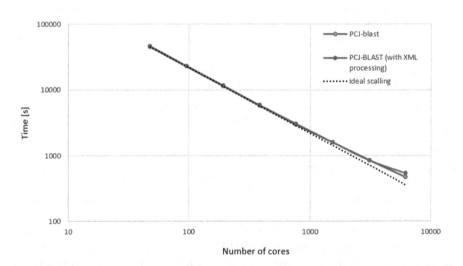

Fig. 4. Performance of the PCJ-BLAST on the Cray XC40. The ideal scaling is plotted as the dotted line for reference. The scaling is based on the single node running 4 NCBI-BLAST instances executed using 12 threads each. The results are presented for the PCJ-BLAST with and without XML output processing. The experimental points correspond to the full nodes allocated. The measurements have been performed for the 12288 sequences long input.

The performance results at Cray XC40 have been obtained for the 12288 long sequence out of 1 million reads long input. We expect that due to the larger number of sequences to process and therefore better load balancing, the parallel efficiency will be even better while processing full input file.

6   Conclusion

In this paper, we presented parallelization of the sequence search which is the key element of the processing NGS results. The parallelization is based on the work distribution based on the partitioned of the input sequence and processing using NCBI-BLAST. The parallelization schema has been implemented in Java using PCJ library and executed on the HPC cluster. The load balancing has been ensured by monitoring the execution of BLAST instances. Also, occurring I/O bottleneck while reading sequence library has been eliminated. We demonstrated that these designs allow the application to scale almost linearly (more than 90% efficiency for 32 nodes) up to 1536 cores of HPC cluster with the InfiniBand interconnect and NFS or Lustre filesystems. The performance results for Cray XC40 are similar and present at least 90% parallel efficiency for 32 nodes and 75% parallel efficiency at 128 nodes (6144 cores).

The presented work confirms the ability of PCJ library to parallelize large scale applications using Java. The design and implementation were fast and efficient and resulted in the preparation of the scalable application in short time.

The presented results show that still there is a place for the performance improvements, especially while running on a large number of nodes. This opportunity will be investigated in the future. The PCJ library is using TCP/IP protocol for intranode communication (more precisely for communication across different JVM's). This solution, especially in the case of Cray Aries interconnect, is not benefiting from all hardware advantages. The work on an extension of the PCJ library for the usage of hardware communication capabilities is in progress.

Acknowledgments. The authors would like to thank CHIST-ERA consortium for financial support under HPDCJ project (Polish part funded by NCN grant 2014/14/Z/ST6/00007) and NordForsk for the support within NIASC consortium. The performance tests have been performed using ICM University of Warsaw computational facilities.

References

1. Altschul, S.F., Gish, W., Miller, W., Myers, E.W., Lipman, D.J.: Basic local alignment search tool. J. Mol. Biol. **215**(3), 403–410 (1990)
2. Altschul, S.F., Madden, T.L., Schäffer, A.A., Zhang, J., Zhang, Z., Miller, W., Lipman, D.J.: Gapped BLAST and PSI-BLAST: a new generation of protein database search programs. Nucleic Acids Res. **25**(17), 3389–3402 (1997)
3. Braun, R.C., Pedretti, K.T., Casavant, T.L., Scheetz, T.E., Birkett, C.L., Roberts, C.A.: Parallelization of local BLAST service on workstation clusters. Future Gener. Comput. Syst. **17**(6), 745–754 (2001)

4. Cofer, H.: SGI® High Throughput Computing (HTC) Wrapper Program for Bioinformatics on SGI ICE™ and SGI UV™ Systems. Np: Silicon Graphics International (2012)
5. Chi, E.H.H., Shoop, E., Carlis, J., Retzel, E., Riedl, J.: Efficiency of shared-memory multiprocessors for a genetic sequence similarity search algorithm. Technical report, University of Minnesota, CS Department, vol. TR97-05 (1997)
6. Darling, A., Carey, L., Feng, W.C.: The design, implementation, and evaluation of mpiBLAST. In: Proceedings of ClusterWorld Conference and Expo in Conjunction with the 4th International Conference on Linux Clusters: The HPC Revolution 2003, San Jose, CA, pp. 13–15 (2003)
7. Bjornson, R.D., Sherman, A.H., Weston, S.B., Willard, N., Wing, J.: TurboBLAST(r): a parallel implementation of BLAST built on the TurboHub. In: Proceedings of the International Parallel and Distributed Processing Symposium (IPDPS), 0183. IEEE (2002)
8. Mathog, D.R.: Parallel BLAST on split databases. Bioinformatics **19**(14), 1865–1866 (2003)
9. Lin, H., Ma, X., Chandramohan, P., Geist, A., Samatova, N.: Efficient data access for parallel BLAST. In: Proceedings of the 19th IEEE International Parallel and Distributed Processing Symposium (IPDPS 2005), Washington, DC, USA. IEEE Computer Society (2005)
10. Nowicki, M., Górski, Ł., Grabrczyk, P., Bała, P.: PCJ - Java library for high performance computing in PGAS model. In: International Conference on High Performance Computing and Simulation, HPCS 2014, pp. 202–209. IEEE (2014)
11. Numrich, R.W., Reid, J.: Co-array Fortran for parallel programming. ACM SIGPLAN Fortran Forum **17**(2), 1–31 (1998). ACM
12. Carlson, W.W., Draper, J.M., Culler, D.E., Yelick, K., Brooks, E., Warren, K.: Introduction to UPC and language specification (Vol. 576). Technical report CCS-TR-99-157, IDA Center for Computing Sciences (1999)
13. Hilfinger, P., Bonachea, D., Datta, K., Gay, D., Graham, S., Liblit, B., Pike, G., Su, J., Yelick, K.: Titanium language reference manual. UC Berkeley Technical report, UCB/EECS-2005-15, Berkeley, California, USA (2005)

On the Use of Binary Trees for DNA Hydroxymethylation Analysis

César González[1], Mariano Pérez[1], Juan M. Orduña[1(✉)], Javier Chaves[2],
and Ana-Bárbara García[2]

[1] Depto. de Informática, Universidad de Valencia,
Avda. Universidad, s/n, 46100 Burjassot, Valencia, Spain
`Juan.Orduna@uv.es`
[2] INCLIVA Health Research Institute, CIBERDEM (Carlos III Health Institute),
Avda. Menéndez Pelayo 4 accesorio, 46010 Valencia, Spain

Abstract. DNA methylation (mC) and hydroxymethylation (hmC) can
have a significant effect on normal human development, health and disease status. Hydroxymethylation studies require specific treatment of
DNA, as well as software tools for their analysis. In this paper, we
propose a parallel software tool for analyzing the DNA hydroxymethylation data obtained by TAB-seq. The software is based on the use
of binary trees for searching the different occurrences of methylation
and hydroxymethylation in DNA samples. The binary trees allow to
efficiently store and access the information about the methylation of
each methylated/hydroxymethylated cytosines in the samples. Evaluation results shows that the performance of the application is only limited
by the computer input/output bandwidth, even for the case of very long
samples.

Keywords: High performance computing · DNA hydroxymethylation ·
Parallel pipeline

1 Introduction

Epigenetics (any process that alters gene activity without changing the DNA
sequence) seems to be decisive for the development of the human organism as well
as for complex diseases like Obesity, Hypertension, Cancer and Diabetes Mellitus
Type 2 (DM2) development [1,2,7]. DNA methylation (including methylation or
hydroxymethylation of cytosines (mC and hmC, respectively), seems to play a
relevant role in the genetic regulation in the medium and long term [5], although
the involved regions and mechanisms in this process are still unknown [7]. In this
sense, there are evidences indicating that DNA methylation can be modified
along the fetal and neonatal development, and it can affect the presence of

This work has been supported by Spanish MINECO and EU FEDER funds under
grants TIN2015-66972-C5-5-R, TIN2016-81850-REDC, PI14/00874 and CIBER-
DEM (Carlos III Health Institute).

© Springer International Publishing AG 2017
S. Ibrahim et al. (Eds.): ICA3PP 2017, LNCS 10393, pp. 513–522, 2017.
DOI: 10.1007/978-3-319-65482-9_37

diseases at advanced ages [7]. DNA methylation has been traditionally associated to CpG islands (DNA segments consisting of "CG" repeated sequences) present in the promoter region of many genes, but it is also present in the rest of a gene, including the codifying regions [8,10].

Therefore, the mC and hmC analysis has become an important topic in the study of human health. This analysis requires specific treatment of DNA that modifies its sequence, as well as software tools for their analysis. The methylation data can be obtained through bisulphite sequencing, which provides comprehensive DNA methylation maps at single-base pair resolution [4]. Bisulphite treatment converts unmethylated cytosines (Cs) into thymines (Ts), which gives rise to C-to-T changes in DNA sequence after sequencing, while leaving methylated cytosines (mCs) unchanged. By aligning and comparing bisulphite sequencing reads to the genomic DNA sequence, it is possible to infer DNA methylation patterns at base pair-resolution. Hydroxymethylated samples can be obtained through the Ten-eleven translocation (TET) Assisted Bisulfite Sequencing (TAB-Seq) [13,14], which produces Ts in methylated and unmetilated Cs and maintains as C the hydroxymethylated Cs. Another method is the oxidative bisulphate sequencing (oxBs-seq) [12], which produces a T from Cs and hmCs and Cs from mCs. Therefore, the analysis of DNA mCs and hmCs by next generation sequencing (NGS) requires the alignment and comparison of two datasets for the identification of each mCs and hmCs in each sequence: the samples treated with traditional bisulfite sequencing, and the samples treated with the TAB-Seq or oxBs-seq. For each base-pair, the analysis should consider three possible cases: the considered base is a mC, it is an hmC, or it is any other base different from a methylated cytosine. The detection of the first and third cases can be carried out by any of the available software tools for DNA methylation analysis like RRBSMAP [11], the widely extended tool Bismark [3], or the most recent tool HPG-Methyl [6,9]. Since these tools provide single-base information of the alignment and the methylation status of each input sequence (or read), the use of the bisulfite-treated dataset as input data for these tools can yield the alignment and methylation status of these samples. However, to the best of our knowledge, there are no software tools for the analysis of DNA hydroxymethylation based on TAB-Seq currently.

The hydroxymethylation analysis should consist in the use any of the available software tools to align and analyze the methylation status of both datasets (the bisulfite-treated and the hydroxymethylated ones). Also, it requires the comparison of the results yielded by the methylation software (usually given as file in BAM format for both datasets). The methylation information in each of the BAM files for each base pair should be compared, in order to determine the hydroxymethylation status and the proportion of each of the three possibilities. In this paper, we propose a parallel software tool, called *HPG-HMapper*, for analyzing the DNA hydroxymethylation status. This tool is based on the use of binary trees for searching the different occurrences of methylation and hydroxymethylation on each base pair in both DNA datasets. The binary tree data structure allows an efficient access, insertion and deletion of new nodes (representing methylated cytosines bases) as the samples in the dataset are processed. The performance evaluation results shows that the performance of the application is only limited by the computer input/output bandwidth, even for the case of very long samples.

The rest of the paper is organized as follows: Sect. 2 describes the implementation of the proposed tool, based on binary trees data structures. Section 3 shows the performance evaluation of the proposed tool. Finally, Sect. 4 shows some concluding remarks.

2   Binary Trees for DNA Hydroxymethylation Analysis

The objective of the proposed software tool is to find the position and the number (and rate) of each methylated and/or hydroxymethylated cytosine in a DNA sequence or read. The input data consist of two FASTQ files containing DNA samples from a human individual. One of the FASTQ files contains traditional bisulfite-treated samples, in which all the non-methylated cytosines have been transformed into thymines. The other FASTQ file contain TAB-Seq treated samples, in which both the non-methylated and the methylated cytosines have been transformed in thymines, and only the hydroxymethylated cytosines remain as cytosines.

However, it must be noted that although both datasets can come from the same individual, due to the library preparation processes for Next-Generation Sequencing the alignment of the reads contained in both datasets may overlap or not. Also, the DNA extraction process can include DNA samples from different tissues or cells, which show different methylation status. Additionally, the reads don't follow any order at all in the FASTQ file, being put as they are produced in the sequencing process. Given these conditions, the best option is the construction of one data structure per chromosome that stores information about the location of the cytosines present in the input data. Since the input sequences are not ordered within the input files and they are read and processed in a sequential manner, new methylated cytosines may appear (new nodes may have to be inserted in the data structure) at any position in the chromosome (at any position in the tree). This reason suggests that the binary tree is the most efficient data structure to insert new nodes as required.

2.1   Pipeline Design

The first step in the hydroxymethylation analysis is the alignment of all the input sequences (from both input data) against the reference genome. We have used our HPG-Methyl2 tool [6] for this step. After both files have been successfully aligned, our tool searches for methylated and hydroxymethylated cytosines, and it stores the results in the disk with the methylation and hydroxymethylation map for each chromosome. These files can be further processed using external tools.

Figure 1 depicts the different stages connected in our pipeline. The elements with dashed lines correspond to those stages out of the direct control of our software: bisulphite and/or TET treatment, sequencing the DNA and FASTQ. The elements with filled lines represent stages using our software, HPG-Methyl2 and the tool presented in this paper, denoted as *HPG-HMapper*. HPG-HMapper has been designed to be usable with any alignment software compliant with the optional tags used by Bismark [3].

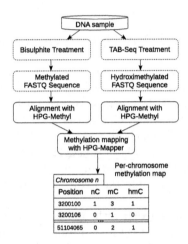

Fig. 1. Diagram of the hydroxymethylation processing pipeline.

HPG-HMapper is the new tool developed to be used as the last stage of the methylation mapping pipeline. It takes two BAM alignment files coming from the methylated and hydroxymethylated FASTQ sequences as input. Both files are processed in series, first the methylation and then the hydroxymethylation file. Those reads which have not been aligned (unmapped reads) or do not contain any methylated or hydroxymethylated cytosines are discarded. HPG-Methyl2 stores the number of methylated cytosines for each read as an optional tag. Each alignment is processed and the locations and counts of methylated and hydroxymethylated cytosines are stored in a custom binary tree structure. Finally, the locations are stored as CSV text files in the disk, one for each chromosome.

Nevertheless, the alignment process and the update of the methylation tree (including insertion operations) take longer than reading the read sequences from the BAM files and filtering unmapped sequences. This process can be accelerated by processing alignments in parallel, and in this sense HPG-HMapper fully exploits the parallel processing capacity of any multi-core CPU. In order to achieve this goal, we have developed a parallel pipeline composed of three stages, whose scheme is shown Fig. 2. The first stage consists of one producer, which reads and filters the two input BAM files. The second stage consist of a number of workers that can process in parallel the alignments found on different chromosomes. The number of workers is an input parameter that the user can change to adjust the parallelism of the pipeline to the underlying computer platform where HPG-HMapper is executed. Finally, the third stage consists of one consumer which writes the results in the CSV output file.

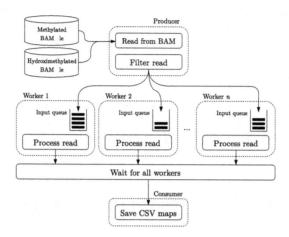

Fig. 2. Block diagram of the parallel pipeline used in HPG-HMapper

The producer stage is in charge of reading and filtering alignments from both BAM files, one at a time. The producer inserts alignments in the queue associated to the corresponding chromosome (note that the chromosome where each read is aligned is one of the informations stored in the BAM format file). The worker stage is in charge of processing the alignments and finding methylated or hydroxymethylated cytosines in the sequence. Workers are in charge of processing all alignments from one or more chromosomes. In order to avoid the use of locks and critical sections, the maximum number of workers is limited to the number of chromosomes (24 for the human genome), since the data structures for each chromosome (the input queue and the methylation binary tree) are not shared between threads. Finally, the consumer stage is in charge of storing the information of the binary trees to CSV files in the disk.

These three stages are controlled by a **scheduler**, which is in charge of creating all the threads and assigning them their data structures, as well as the chromosomes to be processed. In order to schedule an even assignment of workers, the scheduling process is done taking into account the number of methylated cytosines (mCs) in each chromosome on the input BAM file. This information is obtained from an auxiliary file created by HPG-Methyl2 after the alignment process is complete. If this information is not present, the length of each chromosome in the human genome is used as the reference. Figure 3 shows a scheduling example with four workers. The upper part of this figure, shows an array of 24 elements, one for each human chromosome, showing the number of mCs found in that chromosome by HPG-Methyl2 (or other methylation analysis tool). Below that array the figure shows the same array, sorted in descending order, according to the number of mCs found. Thus, the first chromosome in the sorted array is chromosome 2, which contains 4049 mCs, followed by chromosome 16, containing 3756 mCs, etc. In this way, the first elements show those chromosomes representing the greatest workload for the mapping software. The figure shows below how the scheduler then computes the number of chromosomes to be assigned to each worker. In this example, there are only 4 workers and therefore each worker should be assigned 6 chromosomes. Once the number is computed, then the assignment of particular chromosomes to workers is performed following a round-robin fashion, according to the sorted array of chromosomes. This strategy ensures an even workload assignment to the processing cores of the computer platform. The example in the figure assumes that only 4 workers exists, but the same procedure is to any number of workers. In this way, the software can exploit the parallelism offered by any multicore processor, regardless of the number of existing cores.

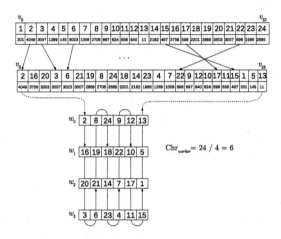

Fig. 3. Example scheduler configuration with 4 workers.

2.2 Methylation and Hydroxymethylation Mapping

HPG-HMapper uses a custom binary tree for each chromosome in the genome, in order to keep track of the count of methylated and hydroxymethylated basepairs in the sequence files. Each node of the tree stores the position in the chromosome and the number of methylated and hydroxymethylated cytosines found in a given position. Due to the presence of different phenotypes in the sequenced DNA (coming for example from different tissues), methylated, hydroxymethylated cytosines as well as non-methylated cytosines or non-cytosines can be mapped onto the same chromosome location. Nevertheless, only the methylated and hydroxymethylated cytosines should be taken into account.

For each read alignment found, a tree exploration is performed for each nucleotide containing relevant methylation data, searching the node holding the information of the current position. If a node corresponding to that chromosome position already exists, then that node is updated with the new methylation or hydroxymethylation information. If it doesn't exists, then a new node is created with the current data. Nodes are inserted taking the position in the chromosome as the key, inserting nodes with positions larger than the current position to the right, and nodes with positions smaller than the current to the left. Figure 4 shows an example showing how new nodes are inserted in the tree as the BAM files are processed. In this example, a new alignment located in the position 116516 should be inserted on the right of the existing node 116500, while a new alignment at position 116480 should be inserted pending on the right of node 116500, since position 116480 is lower than 116500 and higher than the parent node 116420.

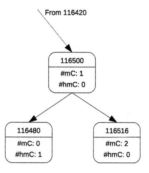

Fig. 4. Example entries of the methylation binary tree.

HPG-HMapper does not explore the binary tree following a recursive algorithm, in order to speed up the update and insertion process. Once the process has finished, the trees are traversed in order to store the methylation maps ordered by ascending position. Then, the information is stored as shown in the bottom of Fig. 1.

3 Performance Evaluation

In this section, we present the performance evaluation of HPG-HMapper. To the best of our knowledge, there is no other software available for hydroxymethylation analysis based on TAB-Seq. There is only a single existing tool for hydroxymethylation based on oxBS-Seq [12], and that tool has been evaluated only for array data, not for sequencing data. Therefore, we cannot make a fair comparison study. Instead, we have studied the execution times, speed-up and memory usage of HPG-mapper for different levels of parallelism in different synthetic datasets coming from sequencing data, in order to establish reference values for this kind of software.

We have used synthetic methylation and hydroxymethylation datasets, composed of 4 million reads. Every figure shown in this section shows plots whose points have been computed as the average value of five executions of the software tool. The performance evaluation has been performed on a computer platform based on a 12 CPU core Intel Xeon E5-2650V4 processor with 64 GB of RAM. Access to the input datasets and to the output files was performed on solid-state drives.

Figure 5 shows the elapsed execution times yielded for datasets of different read lengths (ranging from 75 nucleotides (nts) to 800 nts) when using different levels of parallelism (workers). Since current chip-array sequencing techniques do not produce sequences longer than 200 nts, we think that these lengths cover current and future read lengths.

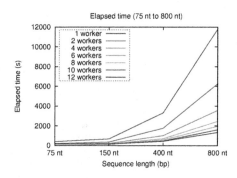

Fig. 5. Elapsed execution times for datasets of different read lengths.

Figure 5 shows how the required execution time becomes more linear to the read length as more workers are present. However, the sequential I/O tasks carried out by both the producer and the consumer stages prevent the tool performance to become fully linear. Nevertheless, an execution time of 19000 s (around 30 min) is required with six workers and a dataset of 800 nts. This time is far below other genomic software, and it has been yielded by a 8-core computer platform.

Figure 6 shows the speed-up achieved for different number of workers for datasets of different read length. This figure shows that for the dataset of 75 nts the maximum speedup of 2.4 is achieved with 4 workers, and the speedup is doubled if we use double the number of workers for a dataset whose length is double (150 nts). For the case of datasets of 400 and 800 nts, the speedup linearly increases with the number of workers. These results show that the proposed software can take advantage of any underlying computer platform, regardless of the number of existing CPU cores.

Finally, we have measured the maximum memory usage required by the software, in order to ensure that it is suitable for the usual memory size in standard computers. Figure 7 shows the peak memory usage for the different datasets and when using different number of workers.

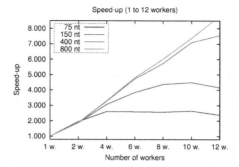

Fig. 6. Speed-up achieved with different number of workers for a given dataset.

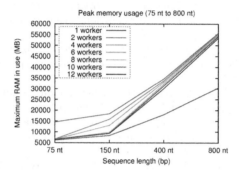

Fig. 7. Peak memory usage in the simulations for datasets of different read length.

Figure 7 shows that, as it could be expected, the size of required RAM do not change with the number of workers (except for the case of a sequential worker), but with the read length, reaching a maximum of around 55 GB of RAM for the case of 800 nts dataset and 2 workers. This memory size fits to the memory available in current workstations.

4   Conclusions

In this paper, we have proposed a software based on binary trees for DNA methylation and hydroxymethylation analysis based on TAB-Seq, called HPG-Hmapper. This tool searches the different occurrences of methylation and hidroxymethylation in DNA samples, enabling the detection and quantification of Cs, mCs and hmCs in each position of genome. The binary tree data structure allows to efficiently store and access the information about the methylation of each methylated/hydroxymethylated cytosine in the samples. The performance evaluation results show that the performance of the application is only limited by the computer input/output bandwidth, even for the case of very long sequences.

References

1. Drong, A.W., Lindgren, C.M., McCarthy, M.I.: The genetic and epigenetic basis of type 2 diabetes and obesity. Clin. Pharmacol. Ther. **92**(6), 707–715 (2012)
2. Haumaitre, C.: Epigenetic regulation of pancreatic islets. Curr. Diabetes Rep. **13**(5), 624–632 (2013)
3. Krueger, F., Andrews, S.R.: Bismark: a flexible aligner and methylation caller for Bisulfite-Seq applications. Bioinformatics **27**(11), 1571–1572 (2011)
4. Laird, P.W.: Principles and challenges of genome-wide dna methylation analysis. Nat. Rev. Genet. **11**, 191–203 (2010)
5. de Mello, V., Pulkkinen, L., Lalli, M., Kolehmainen, M., Pihlajamâmki, J., Uusitupa, M.: DNA methylation in obesity and type 2 diabetes. Ann. Med. **46**(3), 103–13 (2014)
6. Olanda, R., Pérez, M., Orduña, J.M., Tárraga, J., Dopazo, J.: A new parallel pipeline for DNA methylation analysis of long reads datasets. BMC Bioinform. **18**(1), 161 (2017)
7. Raciti, A., Nigro, C., Longo, M., Parrillo, L., Miele, C., Formisano, P., Bguino, F.: Personalized medicine and type 2 diabetes: lesson from epigenetics. Epigenomics **6**(2), 229–238 (2014)
8. Shen, L., Zhang, Y.: 5-hydroxymethylcytosine: generation, fate, and genomic distribution. Curr. Opin. Cell Biol. **25**(3), 289–296 (2013)
9. Tárraga, J., Pérez, M., Orduña, J.M., Duato, J., Medina, I., Dopazo, J.: A parallel and sensitive software tool for methylation analysis on multicore platforms. Bioinformatics **31**(19), 3130 (2015)
10. Wen, L., Li, X., Yan, L., Tan, Y., Li, R., Zhao, Y., Wang, Y., Xie, J., He, C., Li, R., Tang, F., Qiao, J.: Whole-genome analysis of 5-hydroxymethylcytosine and 5-methylcytosine at base resolution in the human brain. Genome Biol. **15**(3), R49 (2014)
11. Xi, Y., Bock, C., Muller, F., Sun, D., Meissner, A., Li, W.: RRBSMAP: a fast, accurate and user-friendly alignment tool for reduced representation bisulfite sequencing. Bioinformatics **28**(3), 430–432 (2012)
12. Xu, Z., Taylor, J.A., Leung, Y.K., Ho, S.M., Niu, L.: oxBS-MLE: an efficient method to estimate 5-methylcytosine and 5-hydroxymethylcytosine in paired bisulfite and oxidative bisulfite treated dna. Bioinformatics **32**(23), 3667–3669 (2016)
13. Yu, M., Hon, G.C., Szulwach, K.E., Song, C.X., Jin, P., Ren, B., He, C.: TET-assisted bisulfite sequencing of 5-hydroxymethylcytosine. Nat. Protoc. **7**(12), 2159–2170 (2012)
14. Yu, M., Hon, G.C., Szulwach, K.E., Song, C.X., Zhang, L., Kim, A., Li, X., Dai, Q., Park, B., Min, J.H., Jin, P., Ren, B., He, C.: Base-resolution analysis of 5-hydroxymethylcytosine in the mammalian genome. Cell **149**(6), 1368–1380 (2012)

Parallel Multi-objective Optimization for High-Order Epistasis Detection

Daniel Gallego-Sánchez[1], José M. Granado-Criado[1(✉)],
Sergio Santander-Jiménez[2], Álvaro Rubio-Largo[3],
and Miguel A. Vega-Rodríguez[1]

[1] University of Extremadura, Cáceres, Spain
dgallegos@alumnos.unex.es, {granado,mavega}@unex.es
[2] Universidade de Lisboa, Lisbon, Portugal
sesaji@unex.es
[3] Universidade NOVA de Lisboa, Lisbon, Portugal
arl@unex.es

Abstract. Many studies have shown that there is a direct relationship between Single Nucleotide Polymorphisms (SNPs) and the appearance of complex diseases, such as Alzheimer's or Parkinson's. However, recent advances in the Study of the Complete Genome Association indicate that the relationship between SNPs and these diseases goes beyond a simple one-to-one relationship, that is, the appearance of multiple SNPs (epistasis) influences the appearance of these diseases. In this sense, this work proposes the application of the NSGA-II multi-objective algorithm for the detection of epistasis of multiple loci in a database with 31,341 SNPs. Moreover, a parallel study has been performed to reduce the execution time of this problem. Our implementation not only achieves a reasonable good parallel performance and scalability, but also its biological significance overcomes other approaches published in the literature.

Keywords: Parallelism · NSGA-II · Epistasis · SNP

1 Introduction

Nowadays, several studies are demonstrating that SNPs[1] (Single Nucleotide Polymorphisms) have high influence in complex diseases like diabetes, Alzheimer's or Parkinson's [13,20]. In this way, many models used in GWAS

This work was partially funded by the AEI (State Research Agency, Spain) and the ERDF (European Regional Development Fund, EU), under the contract TIN2016-76259-P (PROTEIN project). Thanks also to the Junta de Extremadura and ERDF for the GR15011 grant provided to the group TIC015. Álvaro Rubio-Largo and Sergio Santander-Jiménez are supported by the Post-Doctoral Fellowships SFRH/BPD/100872/2014 and SFRH/BPD/119220/2016 respectively, granted by the FCT (Fundação para a Ciência e a Tecnologia), Portugal.

[1] A variation in a single nucleotide that occurs at a specific position in the genome.

S. Ibrahim et al. (Eds.): ICA3PP 2017, LNCS 10393, pp. 523–532, 2017.
DOI: 10.1007/978-3-319-65482-9_38

(Genome-Wide Association Study) to detect the genetic interaction among SNPs and diseases are based in a single interrelation, that is, there is a one-to-one relationship between a SNP and a disease. However, the importance of gen-to-gen interaction, known as epistasis, has increased in GWAS. Epistasis is defined as the phenomenon by which the effect of a gene depends on the presence of one or more modified genes. Instead of looking for a one-to-one relationship between a SNP and a disease, what are sought are the relationships among several SNPs that can cause that disease. In fact, because of the complexity of the diseases studied, single locus[2] models do not often work well, giving a high false positive rate [11]. Therefore, unlike the single locus model, the objective of the detection of many loci epistasis is to identify interactions between groups of SNPs that have a strong association with the phenotype[3].

The traditional method to perform the detection of epistasis is the exhaustive search. In this method, all possible SNP combinations are tested to identify those that cause the disease. However, due to the size of the actual databases, it is practically impossible to use exhaustive search methods due to their high computational and temporal costs. Even implementing tasks to reduce the number of possible combinations, as in [12,19]. This fact is aggravated exponentially when the number of loci is increased. In this way, several works solve three loci epistasis detection, but they use small datasets [2]. Other works use parallel programing in order to reduce the execution time, as cluster computing [7] or GPUs (Graphics Processor Units) [6], but all these solutions are not enough for a number of loci greater than three. On the other hand, in the last years, multi-objective metaheuristics have been used to solve several real problems, both in the biological field (Transcription-Factor Binding Motif [5], multiple sequence alignment [15,16]) and in other fields of engineering and telecommunications [14]. In this sense, Jing and Shen implement MACOED [10], a multi-objective metaheuristic based on the Ant Colony Algorithm (ACO) to detect two loci epistasis. Another example of this type of methodology is found in FHSA-SED [17], which is a heuristic method of detecting the relationship between two loci, based on the Harmony Search Algorithm (HSA). However, the high memory consumption of both MACOED and FHSA-SED limits their applicability to scenarios involving only two loci.

The aim of this work is to develop a parallel multi-objective implementation for the detection of 2, 5 and 8 loci epistasis employing the NSGA-II algorithm [4] (Fast Non-Dominated Sorting Genetic Algorithm) using the objective functions defined in [10].

The present article is organized as follows: Sect. 2 explains the basis of the problem; Sect. 3 describes the NSGA-II algorithm and its parallelization; following, Sect. 4 shows a detailed study of the experiments performed as well as the results obtained. Finally, Sect. 5 presents the conclusions reached.

---

[2] A locus (plural loci) is the position on a chromosome.
[3] Expression of the genetic information that owns a particular organism, or genotype.

2   Problem Definition

In order to solve the $gen-gen$ interaction (epistasis), this work uses two objective functions. The first function (y_1) is based on a logistic regression that measures the likelihood [21], defined by Eq. (1).

$$y_1 = -2 \log lik + d, \tag{1}$$

where $\log lik$ is the maximum likelihood logarithm of the model and d the number of free parameters. The lower the value of the logistic regression, the greater the relationship with the disease. Therefore, y_1 is a minimization objective function.

The second objective function (y_2) is defined by a Bayesian network (Eq. (2)). This statistical model is represented by a set of random variables and their conditional dependencies using a directed acyclic graph, where the set of nodes are formed by the genotypes and phenotypes and the set of edges are formed by their conditional dependencies. This function will be in charge of measuring the relationship between SNP nodes and disease nodes [8,9], so that the lower the value of y_2, the greater the association.

$$y_2 = \sum_{i=1}^{I} \left(\sum_{b=1}^{r_i+1} \log(b) - \sum_{j=1}^{J} \sum_{d=1}^{r_{ij}} \log(d) \right), \tag{2}$$

where I is the combinational number of SNPs with different values, J is the number of disease states for a node, r_i is the number of SNP nodes for the combination i and r_{ij} is the number of cases where the disease takes the state j and its parents have the combination i.

In this paper, the Epistasis Detection has been modeled as a Multi-objective Optimization Problem:

$$\begin{aligned} \text{minimize} \quad & F(x) = (y_1(x), y_2(x)) \\ \text{subject to} \quad & x \in \Omega \end{aligned} \tag{3}$$

where a solution x is a vector of n decision variables: $x = \{x_1, \ldots, x_n\}$. The upper and lower limits of each x component form the decision space (Ω). In our case, the objective functions y_1 and y_2 must be minimized, forming a two-dimensional space known as *objective space* (R^2): $F : \Omega \rightarrow R^2$. Thus, for each solution $x = \{x_1, \ldots, x_n\} \in \Omega$, there exists a point $z = \{z_1, z_2\}$ in the objective space.

To compare two solutions in Multi-objective Optimization, the concept of *dominance* is used: a solution $x_1 \in \Omega$ dominates $(\prec)$ another solution $x_2 \in \Omega$, if and only if: (i) $\forall i \in \{1, 2\}, y_i(x_1) \leq y_i(x_2)$, and (ii) $\exists i \in \{1, 2\}: y_i(x_1) < y_i(x_2)$.

Given a set of solutions X, a solution is considered *non-dominated* (x^*) if there is no solution in X that dominates it. The set of *non-dominated* solutions of X is known as *Pareto set* (whose graphic representation is called the Pareto front). To measure the quality of a *Pareto front* multi-objective metrics are used, the most common one is the Hypervolume (HV) [1], which measures the area/volume (in the *objective space*) covered by the *non-dominated solutions*.

Algorithm 1. NSGA-II

Input : *popSize, MaxGen, crossProb, mutProb, mutFactor*
Output: *ParetoFront* (set of non-dominated solutions)
1 $P \leftarrow \emptyset$
2 **for** $i \leftarrow 1$ *to popSize* **do**
3 $\quad$ $x_i \Leftarrow$ randomIndividual()
4 $\quad$ evaluateSolution (x_i)
5 $\quad$ $P \leftarrow P \cup x_i$
6 **end**
7 $R \leftarrow$ fastNonDominatedSort(P) $//P = (F_1, F_2, \ldots)$
8 **for** $it \leftarrow 1$ *to MaxGen* **do**
9 $\quad$ $Q \leftarrow \emptyset$
10 $\quad$ **for** $i \leftarrow 1$ *to popSize* **do**
11 $\quad\quad$ $x_{p1} \leftarrow$ Selection (P)
12 $\quad\quad$ $x_{p2} \leftarrow$ Selection (P) $//x_{p1} \neq x_{p2}$
13 $\quad\quad$ $x_i \leftarrow$ Crossover $(x_{p1}, x_{p2}, crossProb)$
14 $\quad\quad$ $x_i \leftarrow$ Mutation $(x_i, mutProb, mutFactor)$
15 $\quad\quad$ evaluateSolution(x_i)
16 $\quad\quad$ $Q \leftarrow Q \cup x_i$
17 $\quad$ **end**
18 $\quad$ $R \leftarrow P \cup Q$
19 $\quad$ $R \leftarrow$ fastNonDominatedSort(R) $//R = (F_1, F_2, \ldots)$
20 $\quad$ $P \leftarrow \emptyset$
21 $\quad$ $i \leftarrow 1$
22 $\quad$ **while** $|P + F_i| < popSize$ **do**
23 $\quad\quad$ $F_i \leftarrow$ crowdingDistanceCalculation (F_i)
24 $\quad\quad$ $P \leftarrow P \cup F_i$
25 $\quad\quad$ $i \leftarrow i + 1$
26 $\quad$ **end**
27 $\quad$ $F_i \leftarrow$ crowdingDistanceCalculation (F_i)
28 $\quad$ $P \leftarrow P \cup F_i[1 : (popSize - |P|)]$
29 $\quad$ $ParetoFront \leftarrow$ updateParetoFront(F_1)
30 **end**

The representation of the individual determines the way in which the evolutionary algorithm addresses the problem, providing the necessary knowledge to carry out the optimization process. In this paper, for each individual (solution) $x = \{x_1, \ldots, x_{popSize}\}$, each value of the chromosome (x_i) indicates the SNPs on which epistasis will be analyzed. Moreover, an individual cannot have duplicated SNPs and they must be sorted.

3   Parallelizing NSGA-II

To solve the multiple loci epistasis detection problem, we propose the use of parallelism, multi-objective optimization, and evolutionary computation jointly.

Algorithm 2. Parallel NSGA-II – Part 1, Initialization

---

1 #*pragma* omp parallel num_threads($numThreads$)
2 #*pragma* omp for schedule($schedPolicy$)
3 **for** $i \leftarrow 1$ *to popSize* **do**
4     $x_i \Leftarrow$ randomIndividual()
5   evaluateSolution (x_i)
6     $P \leftarrow P \cup x_i$
7 **end**

Algorithm 3. Parallel NSGA-II – Part 2, Offspring Generation

---

1 #*pragma* omp for schedule($schedPolicy$)
2 **for** $i \leftarrow 1$ *to popSize* **do**
3     $x_{p1} \leftarrow$ Selection (P)
4     $x_{p2} \leftarrow$ Selection $(P) \; // x_{p1} \neq x_{p2}$
5     $x_i \leftarrow$ Crossover $(x_{p1}, x_{p2}, crossProb)$
6     $x_i \leftarrow$ Mutation $(x_i, mutProb, mutFactor)$
7   evaluateSolution(x_i)
8     $Q \leftarrow Q \cup x_i$
9 **end**

The multi-objective algorithm chosen for this purpose is the standard Fast Non-Dominated Sorting Genetic Algorithm (NSGA-II), a population based algorithm created by Deb et al. [4].

Algorithm 1 shows that NSGA-II begins with the random generation and the evaluation of *popSize* solutions, which are stored in the population P (lines 2–6). This new population P is ordered in categories (*rank*) according to their dominance relations (line 7), so that $P = (F_1, F_2, \ldots)$, where F_i is the set of solutions that are found in the i category. Next, in each iteration, NSGA-II generates and evaluates a new offspring population Q by means of the parent population P and using the following genetic operators: binary tournament selection, single point crossover and mutation (one SNP is changed by another one) (lines 10–17). Then, both populations (P and Q) are mixed and sorted in categories forming a new population R (lines 18–19). After that, the best solutions of R form the next iteration population (lines 20–26). In case of a tie when selecting solutions of R for the new population, NSGA-II uses the *crowding* distance (average distance of a solution with its respective neighbors), in a way that favors the distribution of the solutions along the *Pareto front* (lines 27–28).

In order to parallelize NSGA-II, the first step is to identify its more time-consuming sections. For this purpose, we have conducted a time study in order to check the time spent by the different operations on a sequential version of the NSGA-II algorithm, concluding that the most time expensive parts of the algorithm are those that involve the new population generation, that is, lines 2–6 and 10–17 of Algorithm 1. These two code blocks have been parallelized by means

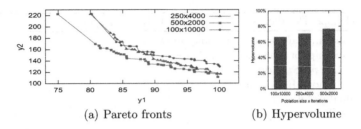

(a) Pareto fronts   (b) Hypervolume

Fig. 1. Median results of 31 executions with $k = 8$ and $100 \times 10,000$, $250 \times 4,000$ and $500 \times 2,000$ (number of individuals x number of iterations) configurations.

of OpenMP [3] (see Algorithms 2 and 3), where *numThreads* and *schedPolicy* are the number of threads and the scheduling policy used.

4   Experiments and Results

This section shows the results obtained for our implementation. In this paper, GAMETES [18] has been employed to generate the dataset to perform the experiments. Particularly, a real size data set with 31,341 SNPs with 50 controls (individuals without the disease) and 96 cases (individuals affected with the disease). The experiments have been executed over a machine with an AMD Opteron(tm) Abu Dhabi 6376 processor @2.30 GHz (32 cores) with 96 GB of RAM and compiled with g++ 4.9.3. Finally, to evaluate the quality of the non-dominated solutions, we have employed a well-known multiobjective metrics: Hypervolume (HV) with the reference points (65.85, 149.06) and (94.28, 322.24) in all the experiments of this paper.

4.1   Parametric Study

For the NSGA-II algorithm, a parametric study was carried out in order to determine the best parameter configuration: crossover probability (*crossProb*), mutation probability (*mutProb*), and mutation factor (*mutFactor*). For each parameter combination, 31 executions (on a database of size 100 SNPs and 1600 individuals) have been performed to obtain their median hypervolume value with 50 individuals and 100 iterations (same parameters as in [10]). The best configuration found is 80%, 20% and 8%, respectively.

Once these three parameters have been set, it is necessary to set the number of individuals and the number of iterations because 50 and 100 respectively are not enough for big datasets like the ones used in this paper. Under this assumption, we have tested three configurations involving 1,000,000 evaluations: $100 \times 10,000$, $250 \times 4,000$ and $500 \times 2,000$ (number of individuals x number of iterations). In addition, we have set the number of loci (k) to 8 in order to configure the algorithm for a high order epistasis detection. As we can see in Fig. 1, after 31 executions, the configuration $500 \times 2,000$ obtains the best result, so we select this configuration for our experiments.

Table 1. NSGA-II execution time (in seconds) for the static and dynamic scheduling policy, 1, 8, 16, 24, and 32 threads and k = {2, 5, 8}

k	Sched. policy	Threads				
		1	8	16	24	32
2	Static dynamic	9,237.36	1,457.05	866.66	605.66	520.47
			1,415.18	806.36	557.23	470.83
5	Static dynamic	11,256.01	1,858.73	1,131.37	928.58	834.22
			1,637.72	1,019.37	764.01	671.56
8	Static dynamic	16,835.74	2,160.77	1,599.08	1,379.49	1,279,86
			2,118.84	1,442.97	1,103.21	989.72

4.2 Parallel Study

In this section, we assess the quality of our parallel results. Using the configuration parameters described previously, we have made a pool of experiments consisting of three variations in the number of loci, particularly 2, 5 and 8, and two scheduling policies, static and dynamic. For every experiment, he have performed 11 executions.

Thanks to the parallelization of NSGA-II, the execution time for $k = 8$ has decreased from 16,835 (sequential) to 989 (dynamic parallel version) seconds. Table 1 shows the median time for every experiment. As this Table shows, in all cases, the dynamic scheduling policy behaves better than the static one. This is due to the solution generation process, which can take different times for different solutions. With regard to the scalability of our implementation, Fig. 2 shows the evolution of efficiencies and speedups reported by our implementation on increasing system and problem sizes. As it can be seen, the scalability and speed up is better in the case of dynamic scheduling, being the improvement observed over the static version more noticeable for higher problem sizes ($k > 8$). This means that the parallel solution of very complex instances of the problem benefits noticeably from the use of dynamic scheduling approaches, giving as a result a significant reduction in execution time by exploiting multicore resources more accurately.

4.3 Biological Comparison

In this section, a biological comparison with other multi-objective approach is presented. To the best of our knowledge, there are only two works that tackle the epistasis detection problem employing multi-objective algorithms: MACOED [10] and FHAS-SED [17]. Since FHAS-SED uses objective functions which are different from the ones in this paper, we will conduct our biological comparisons using MACOED as reference method. All in all, in this work, we have compared with MACOED, but only with $k = 2$, that is, only two loci epistasis. This is due to the fact that MACOED (and also FHAS-SED) uses a memory structure

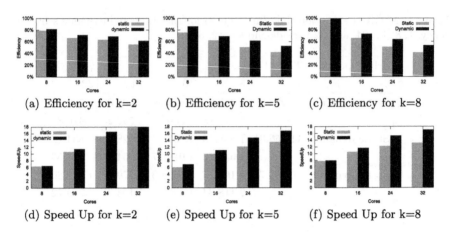

(a) Efficiency for k=2   (b) Efficiency for k=5   (c) Efficiency for k=8

(d) Speed Up for k=2   (e) Speed Up for k=5   (f) Speed Up for k=8

Fig. 2. Efficiency and speed up comparison between static and dynamic policies, $k = \{2, 5, 8\}$ and 8, 16, 24 and 32 cores

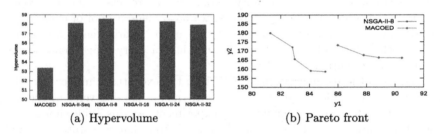

(a) Hypervolume   (b) Pareto front

Fig. 3. Comparison of the median Hypervolume (a) and Pareto front (b) of 31 executions with $k = 2$ between MACOED and sequential (*seq*) and parallel (with x threads) NSGA-II versions.

(*oracle*) that stores the values of the two objective functions of all the processing SNP pairs. By using this *oracle*, MACOED avoids to calculate the objective functions of repeated SNP pairs, speeding up the algorithm. However, MACOED has a very high memory requirement. Particularly, with the dataset used in this paper (31,341 SNPs), MACOED uses more than 43 GB of RAM memory for $k = 2$, making impossible to execute it for $k > 2$ in big datasets. With the current computing capabilities of parallel architectures, we can replace the use of memory-consuming techniques like the oracle by exploiting parallelism, thus allowing us to address satisfactorily epistasis scenarios with increasing values of k (higher than only two loci).

Figure 3(a) shows the median Hypervolume and Pareto front of 31 executions of MACOED and sequential and parallel versions of NSGA-II for $k = 2$ with the same number of evaluations. From this Figure, we can extract two conclusions: firstly, NSGA-II improves the Hypervolume value of MACOED in all cases, and secondly, the parallelization of NSGA-II does not show any negative influence over the attained solution quality. Figure 3(b) shows the median Pareto fronts obtained by MACOED and NSGA-II. As it can be observed, the Pareto front obtained by NSGA-II covers the one obtained by MACOED.

5 Conclusions

This work has proposed the use of multi-objective optimization, evolutionary computation and parallelism for the multiple loci epistasis detection problem in a real size dataset. The proposed approach, based on the standard NSGA-II, has led to an improvement in result quality over other works like MACOED, a metaheuristic based on ant colonies that has been recently proposed to address this problem. In terms of execution time, MACOED seems to be faster than the sequential version of NSGA-II, however it demands more than 43 GB to process the dataset with only two loci, making impossible to execute it with 3 loci or more. In contrast, our implementation does not only improve the MACOED execution time by using eight cores, it also can process many loci relationships.

On the other hand, a parallel study has been made with $k = \{2, 5, 8\}$ loci, with 8, 16, 24, and 32 cores, and static and dynamic scheduling policies. In this way, we can conclude that NSGA-II scales quite good from 8 to 32 cores using dynamic scheduling policy, achieving improved efficiency values in all the experiments when this policy is applied.

References

1. Auger, A., Bader, J., Brockhoff, D., Zitzler, E.: Theory of the hypervolume indicator: optimal μ-distributions and the choice of the reference point. In: Proceedings of the Tenth ACM SIGEVO Workshop on Foundations of Genetic Algorithms, pp. 87–102. ACM (2009)
2. Cattaert, T., Calle, M., Dudek, S., Hohn, J., Lishout, F., Urrea, V., Ritchie, M., Steel, K.: Model-based multifactor dimensionality reduction for detecting epistasis in case-control data in the presence of noise. Ann. Hum. Genet. **1**(75), 78–89 (2011)
3. Chapman, B., Jost, G., van der Pas, R.: Using OpenMP: Portable Shared Memory Parallel Programming. Scientific and Engineering Computation. The MIT Press, Cambridge (2007)
4. Deb, K., Pratap, A., Agarwal, S., Meyarivan, T.: A fast and elitist multiobjective genetic algorithm: NSGA-II. IEEE Tran. Evol. Comput. **6**(2), 182–197 (2002)
5. González-Álvarez, D.L., Vega-Rodríguez, M.A., Rubio-Largo, A.: Finding patterns in protein sequences by using a hybrid multiobjective teaching learning based optimization algorithm. IEEE/ACM Trans. Comput. Biol. Bioinform. **12**(3), 656–666 (2015)
6. González-Domínguez, J., Schmidt, B.: GPU-accelerated exhaustive search for third-order epistatic interactions in case-control studies. J. Comput. Sci. **8**, 93–100 (2015)
7. Goudey, B., Abedini, M., Hopper, J., Inouye, M., Makalic, E., Schmidt, D., Wagner, J., Zhou, Z., Zobel, J., Reumann, M.: High performance computing enabling exhaustive analysis of higher order single nucleotide polymorphism interaction in Genome Wide Association Studies. Health Inf. Sci. Syst. **3**(Suppl. 1), S3 (2015)

8. Han, B., Chen, X., Talebizadeh, Z., Xu, H.: Genetic studies of complex human diseases: characterizing SNP-disease associations using Bayesian networks. BMC Syst. Biol. **6**(Suppl. 3), S14 (2012)
9. Jiang, X., Neapolitan, R.E., Barmada, M.M., Visweswaran, S.: Learning genetic epistasis using bayesian network scoring criteria. BMC Bioinform. **12**(1), 89 (2011)
10. Jing, P., Shen, H.: MACOED: a multi-objective ant colony optimization algorithm for SNP epistasis detection in genome-wide association studies. Bioinformatics **31**(5), 634–641 (2015)
11. Moore, J.H., Asselbergs, F.W., Williams, S.M.: Bioinformatics challenges for genome-wide aassociation studies. Bioinformatics **26**(4), 445–455 (2010)
12. Ritchie, M.D., Hahn, L.W., Roodi, N., Bailey, L.R., Dupont, W.D., Parl, F.F., Moore, J.H.: Multifactor-dimensionality reduction reveals high-order interactions among estrogen-metabolism genes in sporadic breast cancer. Am. J. Hum. Genet. **69**, 138–147 (2001)
13. Rogus, J.J., Poznik, G.D., Pezzolesi, M.G., Smiles, A.M., Dunn, J., Walker, W., Wanic, K., Moczulski, D., Canani, L., Araki, S., Makita, Y., Warram, J.H., Krolewski, A.S.: High-density single nucleotide polymorphism genome-wide linkage scan for susceptibility genes for diabetic nephropathy in type 1 diabetes. Diabetes **57**(9), 2519–2526 (2008)
14. Rubio-Largo, A., Vega-Rodríguez, M.A.: Applying MOEAs to solve the static routing and wavelength assignment problem in optical WDM networks. Eng. Appl. Artif. Intell. **26**(5–6), 1602–1619 (2013)
15. Rubio-Largo, A., Vega-Rodríguez, M.A., González-Álvarez, D.L.: Hybrid multiobjective artificial bee colony for multiple sequence alignment. Appl. Soft Comput. **41**, 157–168 (2016)
16. Rubio-Largo, A., Vega-Rodríguez, M.A., Gonzlez-Álvarez, D.L.: A hybrid multiobjective memetic metaheuristic for multiple sequence alignment. IEEE Trans. Evol. Comput. **20**(4), 499–514 (2016)
17. Tuo, S., Zhang, J., Yuan, X., Zhang, Y., Liu, Z.: FHSA-SED: two-locus model detection for genome-wide association study with harmony search algorithm. PLOS ONE **11**(3), 1–27 (2016)
18. Urbanowicz, R.J., Kiralis, J., Sinnott-Armstrong, N.A., Heberling, T., Fisher, J.M., Moore, J.H.: GAMETES: a fast, direct algorithm for generating pure, strict, epistatic models with random rrchitectures. BioData Min. **5**(1), 16 (2012)
19. Wan, X., Yang, C., Yang, Q., Xue, H., Fan, X., Tang, N.L.S., Yu, W.: BOOST: a fast approach to detecting gene-gene interactions in genome-wide case-control studies. Am. J. Hum. Genet. **87**(3), 325–340 (2010)
20. Wanga, Y., Tanga, B., Yanga, Y., Cuia, Y., Kanga, J., Liua, Z., Lia, K., Suna, Q., Xua, Q., Yana, X., Guo, J.: Relationship between Alzheimer's disease GWAS-linked top hits and risk of Parkinson's disease with or without cognitive decline: a Chinese population-based study. Neurobiol. Aging **39**, 217.e9–217.e11 (2016)
21. Wu, T.T., Chen, Y.F., Hastie, T., Sobel, E., Lange, K.: Genome-wide association analysis by lasso penalized logistic regression. Bioinformatics **25**(6), 714–721 (2009)

Configuring Concurrent Computation of Phylogenetic Partial Likelihoods: Accelerating Analyses Using the BEAGLE Library

Daniel L. Ayres$^{(\boxtimes)}$ and Michael P. Cummings$^{(\boxtimes)}$

Center for Bioinformatics and Computational Biology,
University of Maryland, College Park, MD 20742, USA
{ayres,mike}@umiacs.umd.edu

Abstract. We describe our approach in augmenting the BEAGLE library for high-performance statistical phylogenetic inference to support concurrent computation of independent partial likelihoods arrays. Our solution involves identifying independent likelihood estimates in analyses of partitioned datasets and in proposed tree topologies, and configuring concurrent computation of these likelihoods via CUDA and OpenCL frameworks. We evaluate the effect of each increase in concurrency on throughput performance for our partial likelihoods kernel for a four-state nucleotide substitution model on a variety of parallel computing hardware, such as NVIDIA and AMD GPUs, and Intel multicore CPUs, observing up to 16-fold speedups over our previous implementation. Finally, we evaluate the effect of these gains on an domain application program, MrBayes. For a partitioned nucleotide-model analysis we observe an average speedup for the overall run time of 2.1-fold over our previous parallel implementation, and 10-fold over the native MrBayes with SSE.

Keywords: Bayes methods · Biology computing · Evolution (biology) · Phylogeny · Maximum likelihood estimation · Multicore processing · Parallel programming · High performance computing

1 Introduction

The most effective methods for inferring phylogenetic trees are based on either maximum likelihood estimation or Bayesian analysis, which share the same computational bottleneck: calculation of the likelihood of trees [7]. When profiling GARLI [11], a leading phylogenetic inference program, we have observed that, for nucleotide models, likelihood related calculations typically constitute over 94% of the overall run time. For more complex models (e.g., amino-acid or codon-based), likelihood calculation will typically incur an even greater proportion of the analysis time. Speeding the calculation of the likelihood function is key to increasing the performance of statistical inference-based phylogenetic analyses.

The core likelihood calculations apply to a subtree comprising a parent node, k, two child nodes, ℓ and m, and connecting branches of length, t_ℓ and t_m, and

© Springer International Publishing AG 2017
S. Ibrahim et al. (Eds.): ICA3PP 2017, LNCS 10393, pp. 533–547, 2017.
DOI: 10.1007/978-3-319-65482-9_39

is repeated for all such subtrees within the larger tree being considered. This partial likelihood function is as follows [7]:

$$L_k^{(i)}(z) = \left(\sum_x \Pr(x|z, t_\ell) L_\ell^{(i)}(x) \right) \times \left(\sum_y \Pr(y|z, t_m) L_m^{(i)}(y) \right) \tag{1}$$

This calculation is repeated for each character i in the data (i.e., sequence site pattern), for each state z that a character can assume, and for each internal node in the proposed tree. The computational complexity of the likelihood calculation for a given tree is $O(p \times s^2 \times n)$, where p is the number of patterns in the sequence (typically on the order of 10^2 to 10^6), s is the number of states each character in the sequence can assume (typically 4 for a nucleotide model, 20 for an amino-acid model, or 61 for a codon model), and n is the number of operational taxonomic units (e.g., species, alleles). Additionally the tree search space is very large; the number of unrooted topologies possible for n operational taxonomic units is given by the double factorial function $(2n - 5)!!$ [6]. Thus, to explore even a fraction of the total search space, a very large number of topologies are evaluated, and hence a very great number of likelihood calculations have to be performed. This leads to analyses that can take days, weeks or even months to run. Further compounding the issue, rapid advances in the collection of DNA sequence data have made the limitation for biological understanding of these data an increasingly computational problem.

1.1   The BEAGLE Library and API

The BEAGLE library and API [2] is a high-performance likelihood-calculation platform for evolutionary models. It defines a uniform application programming interface (API) and includes a collection of efficient implementations for calculating a variety of likelihood-based models on different hardware devices, such as graphics processing units (GPUs) and multicore central processing units (CPUs).

The BEAGLE library was designed to support a variety of hardware-specific implementations, each optimized for a different processor type. The library includes a set of parallel computing implementations that use the CUDA and OpenCL external computing frameworks.

The BEAGLE library has been very successful in accelerating evolutionary analyses. The library has been integrated into the most recent versions of popular phylogenetics software including BEAST [5], MrBayes [10], and PhyML [8], and has been widely used across a diverse range of evolutionary studies.

Previously, given the fine-scale parallelization of the phylogenetic likelihood function in the BEAGLE library, the problem with few sequence patterns, or one broken into small data subsets, was always *small*, and thus generally not amenable to speedups, as patterns (for a given model type and category rate count, e.g., nucleotide with four distinct rates) were the only dimension being parallelized.

In this paper we describe our recent work to configure concurrent computation of phylogenetic likelihoods by exploiting additional independent calculation opportunities. The result is that a wider variety of analyses benefit from parallel computing performance gains.

1.2 Concurrent Computation: Independent Likelihood Estimates

We have focused on the following opportunities for concurrent computation of phylogenetic likelihoods that were previously unrealized in BEAGLE.

Pattern Partitions. Evolutionary analyses benefit from increases in modeling flexibility. One clear way of improving model flexibility is to allow independent estimation of model parameters for different character data subsets (e.g., genes, codon positions). This is typically referred to as a partitioned model and is a technique available in all phylogenetic software packages that support BEAGLE. Until now partitioned analyses with BEAGLE have required the client program to create multiple instances of the library, one for each data subset defined by the partitioning scheme. When BEAGLE instances share a hardware resource they are executed in sequence, thus incurring significant performance and memory inefficiencies, specially for problems with a large number of small data subsets.

Independent Subtrees. The number of subtrees requiring calculation for any full tree is $n - 1$, where n is the number of operational taxonomic units (e.g., species, alleles), which is the number of tips (leaves) on the tree. Phylogenetic algorithms typically use a post-order traversal when calculating tree likelihood, calculating each of the $n-1$ subtrees in series. In the case of a fully pectinate tree no subtrees are independent (Fig. 1, left). However, in the case of more balanced topologies there are independent subtrees (Fig. 1, middle). The likelihoods for sets of these independent subtrees can be calculated concurrently. In order to more easily realize potential concurrency related to independent subtrees present in a given topology, partial likelihood arrays need to be processed according to a reverse level-order, or breadth-first, traversal of the tree being evaluated. In the case of a fully balanced tree the number of independent subtrees is maximized, and partial likelihood calculations can be done in sets of concurrent operations corresponding to the number of levels in the tree, $\lceil log_2 n \rceil$ (Fig. 1, right). This exploit of tree level-group concurrency is somewhat similar to a classic parallel reduction scheme.

Fig. 1. Example pectinate tree (*left*), and example of a fully balanced tree (*middle*); with sequential calculation both trees require $n - 1 = 7$ partial likelihood operations in series, corresponding to the order of the node numbers. Balanced tree (*right*) with concurrent computation requiring $\lceil log_2 n \rceil = 3$ sets of independent partial likelihood operations in the order of the shared node numbers.

2 Methods

2.1 Benchmarking and Testing

Our approach to increase concurrency in BEAGLE has been focused on the partial likelihoods kernel that is the computational bottleneck for phylogenetic analyses. To evaluate the performance of this function we used our test program (*genomictest*), which generates random synthetic datasets of arbitrary sizes. This test program is included with the BEAGLE source code and the results shown throughout this paper can be reproduced by using the default random seed, 1.

Table 1. System specifications

	System 1	*System 2*
CPU(s)	Intel Core i7-930	Dual Intel Xeon E5-2680v4
GPU(s)	AMD Radeon R9 Nano	AMD FirePro S9170
	NVIDIA Quadro P5000	
Linux kernel	4.8.13	3.10.0
GCC version	6.2.1	6.2.0
CUDA release	8.0	—
OpenCL drivers	AMD 1912.5	AMD 1800.8
	NVIDIA 375.26	Intel 1.2.0

We report a measure of throughput in terms of the effective number of floating point operations per second (GFLOPS) for computation of the partial likelihoods function (see Eq. 1). In contrast to a direct timing benchmark, throughput allows us to more easily compare performance across different problem sizes. We report benchmark results for two system configurations (Table 1). For conciseness, many results are shown only for the two best performing platforms we had available, the NVIDIA Quadro P5000 GPU under CUDA and the AMD Radeon R9 Nano GPU under OpenCL. Further comparisons across hardware platforms and frameworks are reported elsewhere [1].

2.2 Pattern Partition Concurrency

Multiple versus Single Library Instances. An initial design goal for the BEAGLE library was to make a library instance relatively light-weight, and to leave it up to the client program to manage these instances. This design objective was fitting for processors at the time, because it was easier to achieve good saturation as the number of cores and supported threads for CPUs and GPUs were modest compared to recent processors. However, we have found that this light-weight model is limited, as the client program does not have direct access to the parallel devices and cannot configure concurrent communication efficiently. Furthermore, this model of separate instances also limits us to the concurrency afforded to asynchronous kernel executions by the parallel computing framework used (i.e., CUDA or OpenCL).

Given our desire to improve concurrency for partitioned analyses, our first decision was to move away from one library instance per data subset. This gave us greater potential for concurrency, such as via single kernel launches, and more control over how computation is combined into concurrent executions. Using a single library instance also results in significant memory savings given many overhead costs become shared for all partitions.

API Changes. In order to support partitioning in a single library instance we have modified the BEAGLE API to support data subset assignment and per-subset operations. Partition assignment can be done via a pattern-count length array of integers, with support for noncontiguous assignments. These changes were done as additions to the existing BEAGLE v1 API, and the interface remains backwards compatible.

CUDA First. Our work to increase concurrency, and thus efficiency, for partitioned analyses initially focused on our parallel implementation for the CUDA framework. We have found this framework to be generally more mature than OpenCL, and to support more features. We identified two solutions to allow independent data subsets to be concurrently computed: (a) using CUDA *streams*, which would allow separate likelihood kernel launches to run concurrently; and (b) developing a *multi-operation* likelihood kernel, which would compute multiple likelihood arrays within a single kernel launch. Below we describe each approach.

Streams. This feature of the CUDA framework is described by NVIDIA as follows:

> "The CUDA programming model provides streams as a mechanism for programs to indicate dependence and independence among kernel launches. Kernels launched into the same stream are guaranteed to execute consecutively, while kernels launched into different streams are permitted to execute concurrently. Streams describe independence between work items and hence allow potentially greater efficiency through concurrency."

To achieve partition concurrency we launch our likelihood kernels on separate streams according to the data subset of the likelihood array operation. We do so in a breadth-first manner, that is, the kernel launch for the first partial likelihood array operation for data subset 1 is followed by the launch for the first operation for subset 2, and so on. This is to compensate for signal delay in each stream. We use this multi-stream approach for both partial likelihood and likelihood integration kernels. For all other kernel launches in BEAGLE we use the null stream which synchronizes with all streams.

Multi-operation Kernel. Our second solution for data subset concurrency involved modifying our partial likelihood CUDA kernel to compute multiple likelihood arrays in a single execution launch. We used pointer arithmetic to allow different input and output arrays for different execution blocks.

Figure 2 contrasts available data arrays (**nodes**, **branches**) and likelihood array index (**pattern**) for our single and multi-operation partial likelihood kernels. The first implementation is restricted to a single set of input likelihood arrays (for nodes c_1 and c_2), input branch length arrays (t_1 and t_2), and output array (d_0), for all execution blocks. Additionally the pattern computed by each execution thread is directly determined by block index n, block size $blockSize$, and thread index $threadId$.

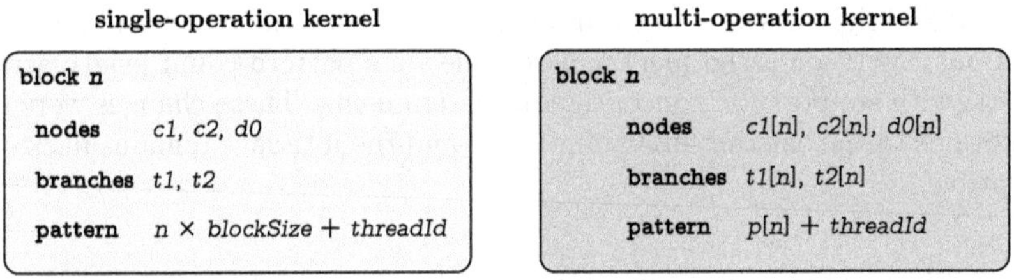

Fig. 2. Organization of data arrays and indexing for single and multi-operation kernel execution blocks for partial likelihoods computation in BEAGLE.

With the *multi-operation* approach, input and output arrays are determined based on the block index. Further, the pattern computed by each thread is only indirectly determined by n, which allows padding of data subsets when these do not fall along block-sized boundaries.

Additionally, to maximize device global memory throughput we rearrange site patterns on device memory so that data subsets are contiguous. This is done when sequence partition assignment is made by the client program and enables each execution block to operate on a single data subset more efficiently.

2.3 Independent Subtree Concurrency

As we developed the above approaches to partition concurrency, we noted we could also leverage those methods to concurrently compute partial likelihood arrays for independent subtrees. This would be specially beneficial for large trees with short sequences when running on manycore processors such as GPUs. This combination of problem size and hardware resource previously left many processing cores underutilized. Below we describe implementation details for independent subtree operations via both our *streams* and *multi-operation* solutions.

Algorithm 1. Streams and partial likelihood array operations

Data: a sequence of likelihood operations in reverse level-order traversal
Result: computation of partial likelihood arrays in concurrent streams

streamIndex $\leftarrow$ 0
foreach operation *in the operations sequence* **do**
    node $\leftarrow$ operation.parent
    if node.child1.streamIndex *is not null* **then**
        node.streamIndex $\leftarrow$ node.child1.streamIndex
        node.waitIndex $\leftarrow$ node.child2.streamIndex
    else if node.child2.streamIndex *is not null* **then**
        node.streamIndex $\leftarrow$ node.child2.streamIndex
        node.waitIndex $\leftarrow$ node.child1.streamIndex
    else
        node.streamIndex $\leftarrow$ streamIndex + 1
        streamIndex $\leftarrow$ streamIndex + 1
    end

    if node.waitIndex *is not null* **then**
        cudaStreamWaitEvent(*event* node.waitIndex, *stream* node.streamIndex)
    end
    cudaLaunchKernel(*kernel* pLikelihoods, *stream* node.streamIndex)
    cudaEventRecord(*event* node.streamIndex, *stream* node.streamIndex)
end

Streams. We further leveraged the use of CUDA streams to concurrently compute partial likelihood arrays of independent subtrees by assigning them as described by Algorithm 1. This algorithm shows how we assign a likelihood array kernel launch (**pLikelihoods**) to a stream based on an inherited index from either of the child nodes (**child1** or **child2**). Additionally, we may wait on a CUDA event that has been recorded for the other child node before launching the kernel.

Multi-operation Kernel. To implement subtree concurrency with this kernel, we process partial likelihood subtree operations according to a reverse level-order traversal of the proposed tree. We add each consecutive operation to a set until we find an operation that is dependent on the result of a previous operation in the set. We then start a new operation set, repeating the same process. Once we have processed all operations in this manner, we successively launch each operation set for concurrent computation using our *multi-operation* partial likelihoods kernel.

2.4   Extending Concurrency Gains to OpenCL

Our next step was to extend the above work, using the CUDA framework, to our OpenCL implementation.

Queues. The OpenCL equivalent to CUDA streams are concurrent execution queues. We implemented our approach in an analogous manner but found the use of concurrent queues only offered at best minimal gains in performance for the OpenCL devices we had access to (AMD Radeon R9 Nano and FirePro S9170 GPUs, and Intel Xeon E5-2680v4 CPU).

Multi-operation Kernel. For this approach, in a comparable manner to CUDA blocks, we launch OpenCL work-groups such that multiple partial likelihood operations can be performed concurrently. In contrast to CUDA, we found that the OpenCL solution was generally more performance sensitive to implementation details such as operation order and synchronization points. This was ultimately beneficial, as we iteratively refined of our likelihood kernel to optimize performance, and could then translate back some of the gains to the CUDA solution.

2.5   Memory Transfer Optimizations

For the *multi-operation* approach under either CUDA or OpenCL, we necessitate an explicit memory transfer from host to device for each tree likelihood estimation. Such memory transfers can be costly for GPU devices as they may have to go over the PCI bus. BEAGLE was designed to minimize this type of transfer and previously explicit host to device transfers only occurred at the initialization phase of an inference run.

This additional memory transfer for our *multi-operation* kernel is used to copy the address offsets for the input and output arrays each block in device memory will operate on. In order to minimize costs for this additional memory transfer, we process all subtree operations in a partial likelihoods call to the library, and perform a single transfer for multiple launches of our *multi-operation* kernel.

Table 2. GPU memory transfer optimizations; throughput in GFLOPS

Framework	GPU	Solution	*tree* A	*tree* B
CUDA	NVIDIA P5000	*write*	328.27	188.76
		pinned	**328.57**	**203.47**
OpenCL	NVIDIA P5000	*write*	320.10	183.78
		map/unmap	**321.24**	**199.58**
	AMD R9 Nano	*write*	397.92	178.04
		map/unmap	**403.72**	**210.30**

Further, we use faster methods than we had done before for host to device transfer: *pinned* host memory allocations under CUDA; and *map* and *unmap* approach with OpenCL. Table 2 shows kernel throughput performance with these approaches when compared to the performance when using the regular memory *write* transfer method under each framework. This comparison was done for two tree sizes: *tree* A has 16 tips and 100,032 sequence patterns; and *tree* B has 256 tips and 1024 patterns. We observe that the *pinned* and *map/unmap* approaches have a positive impact on overall throughput, especially for *tree* B, which has many more tips, and thus more partial likelihood operations with an ensuing larger data transfer size.

2.6   Combining Pattern Partition and Independent Subtree Concurrency

We have found that the most efficient approach (i.e., *stream/queues*, or *multi-operation*) to concurrent partial likelihood array operations depends on the number of patterns being processed per operation. In order to determine which approach to use for different problem sizes, we have benchmarked the throughput for our partial likelihood kernel when evaluating a tree with 16 tips and 100,032 patterns for an increasing number of equal-sized data subsets (Table 3) across our different parallel solutions. The CUDA implementation was tested on an NVIDIA Quadro P5000 GPU, the OpenCL-GPU implementation on an AMD Radeon R9 Nano, and the OpenCL-x86 implementation on dual Intel Xeon E5-2680v4 CPUs. Systems were as specified in Table 1.

Table 3. Concurrency solutions and partition sizes; throughput in GFLOPS with bold text indicating which concurrency approach within a parallel solution offers best performance at each problem size.

Partition		CUDA		OpenCL–GPU		OpenCL–x86	
count	size	*streams*	*multi-op*	*queues*	*multi-op*	*queues*	*multi-op*
1	100,032	**321.82**	272.61	**346.26**	335.62	**79.97**	79.43
2	50,016	**330.08**	228.21	**354.79**	341.02	**79.85**	77.85
16	6,252	**316.72**	225.64	226.77	**330.68**	70.60	**76.10**
24	4,168	**227.63**	223.40	182.71	**318.97**	65.92	**75.21**
32	3,126	164.06	**217.59**	141.50	**317.28**	54.65	**73.00**
64	1,563	87.75	**212.71**	87.98	**326.49**	24.92	**73.61**

With the CUDA implementation, we observe that for larger numbers of patterns (above 4,168) the Quadro P5000 GPU is near saturation, and the one-time overhead of the *multi-operation* approach makes it relatively inefficient (Table 3). However, for smaller problem sizes there is less work per stream, and the overhead cost for each stream makes that approach the less efficient alternative. For the OpenCL implementations we observe that the *multi-operation* approach is the most efficient or close to most efficient for any partitioned problem.

Based on these findings, and on further intermediate analyses not shown in Table 3, we set a fixed crossover point for each solution which determines which approach is used. For the CUDA implementation we have set this at 4,168 patterns, for the OpenCL-GPU it is set at 8,192 patterns, and for the OpenCL-x86 implementation the *multi-operation* approach is always used. Additionally, client programs can also explicitly request either the *streams* or *multi-operation* implementation via the library API.

2.7 Other Aspects

Although BEAGLE supports inferences with models of arbitrary state counts, the work described here has thus far only been implemented for nucleotide model inferences.

It is also worth mentioning that our implementation allows partitions to be reassigned at any point. With each new partition assignment we rearrange patterns in device memory to maintain efficient throughput. This functionality may be used by client programs in the future to enable efficient inference of partition assignments in conjunction with currently inferred parameters.

Finally, we use the `--default-stream per-thread` NVIDIA CUDA compiler (NVCC) option so that each BEAGLE instance runs on a separate default stream. This allows further concurrency gains for other independent work in addition to partitioning, such as Metropolis-coupled, Markov chain Monte Carlo chains or run replicates.

2.8 Modifications to MrBayes

In order to fully evaluate the efficacy of the concurrency improvements to the library, we have adapted MrBayes version 3.2.6 to use the new BEAGLE API partitioning extensions. This enabled MrBayes to use a single BEAGLE library instance for computing the likelihood of multiple data subsets. This modified version of MrBbayes is open-source under GPL version 3.0, and is available at https://github.com/ayresdl/mrbayes-beagle3.

2.9 Library Availability

The BEAGLE project is open source under the GPL v3.0 license. The work described here will be part of an upcoming release, and is available under a development branch of the library located at https://github.com/beagle-dev/beagle-lib/tree/kernel-concurrency.

3 Results

Here we explore the performance effect of the concurrency gains on various parallel hardware resources. System specifications are as shown in Table 1.

3.1   Pattern Partition Concurrency Gains

We observe that for both the Quadro P5000 and Radeon R9 Nano GPUs the previous approach of sequential computation of data subsets produces a sharp drop-off in throughput as we increase the number of subsets (Fig. 3). This is because as we increase the partition count the data subsets have decreasing numbers of patterns, resulting in increasingly underutilized GPU capacity.

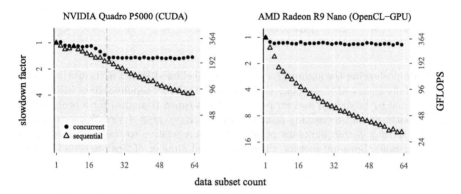

Fig. 3. Plots showing throughput for the partial likelihood kernel with data subset concurrency (black dots) and with no data subset concurrency (open triangles) for a problem with 100,032 total sequence patterns and increasing number of equal-sized data subsets for two GPU device/framework pairs. Left-axis *slowdown factor* indicates performance loss relative to the unpartitioned case. Slowdown factors and throughput in GFLOPS are on a log-scale.

For concurrent computation with the CUDA device, throughput is higher than with the sequential approach at all subset sizes. When there are fewer than 24 subsets we use the *streams* approach. Throughput with this approach starts to drop quickly after 17 subsets (corresponding to a subset size of approximately 6,000 patterns). We then note the crossover point at 24 subsets (subset size of 4,168 patterns, and indicated by a dark grey dashed line) where we switch to our *multi-operation* kernel approach. This approach exhibits consistent throughput independent of subset size.

With the OpenCL solution we use the *multi-operation* approach for all partitioned cases and note consistent and near best-case throughput, independent of the number of data subsets.

3.2   Independent Subtree Concurrency Gains

Figure 4 shows the performance improvement associated with concurrent computation of independent subtrees for a problem with 512 patterns. The pectinate case (open triangle) also represents performance for any tree topology with our previous solution of serial computation of subtree partial likelihood arrays.

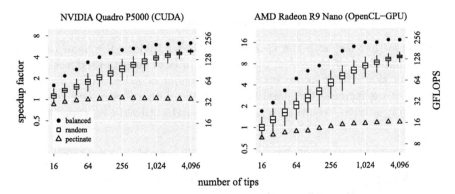

Fig. 4. Plots showing throughput for the partial likelihood kernel with subtree concurrency for fully balanced trees (black dots), for 1,000 random topology trees (distribution characterized by box plot), and for pectinate trees (open triangles) for a problem with 512 site patterns and increasing number of tips for two GPU device/framework pairs. Left-axis *speedup factor* indicates performance gain relative to the average pectinate tree throughput. Speedup factors, throughput, and number of tips are on a log-scale.

For both GPUs, we observe increasing speedups with tree size for the average random tree or for fully balanced trees. We also note that for larger trees the throughput distribution for a random tree is skewed towards the fully balanced case, which is associated with GPU saturation at these problem sizes. Finally, we note that pectinate-case performance is approximately twice as fast with the P5000 GPU under CUDA as compared to the R9 Nano GPU using our OpenCL implementation. Effective performance towards the pectinate end of the tree symmetry scale remains highly relevant as phylogenetic inference programs are optimized such that only a subtree representing the modified portion of the overall tree is recomputed for each topology change. These subtrees are often much less balanced than the full tree.

3.3   Application-Level Results

We used our adapted version of MrBayes 3.2.6 to assess application-level performance gains for our concurrency work across a variety of parallel computing devices. For these benchmarks we used a dataset with 500 taxa and 759 unique site patterns of *rbc*L, the chloroplast gene encoding the large subunit of ribulose-1,5-bisphosphate carboxylase/oxygenase, which is derived from a study of angiosperm relationships [4]. We partitioned the sequence data based on codon position, resulting in 3 subsets with 253 unique site patterns each, and inferences were run using the MrBayes default single-precision floating point format.

We chose a dataset with a high number of sequences and with few patterns, further broken into independent subsets, to best showcase the gains in concurrency described in this paper. Previously problems with these characteristics have been the most challenging for effective parallelization. BEAGLE-enabled

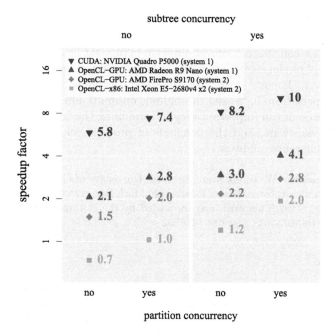

Fig. 5. Performance gains for a MrBayes nucleotide-model analysis for various hardware platforms when using the BEAGLE library, with and without partition and subtree concurrency. Speedup factors are relative to the total run time when using the standard MrBayes SSE likelihood calculator and are shown on a log-scale.

MrBayes peak performance for datasets with many more patterns and using higher state-count models are reported elsewhere [1,2].

Speedups for this challenging MrBayes analysis improve as we enable partition and subtree concurrency, across all hardware resources and corresponding frameworks (Fig. 5). We observe an average speedup gain of 1.5-fold for subtree concurrency and 1.4-fold for partition concurrency across all hardware devices. For the best performing resource (NVIDIA Quadro P5000 GPU with CUDA) we observe a 1.7-fold gain in speedup when using both concurrency improvements, ultimately resulting in a 10-fold speedup over the native MrBayes SSE run time.

We have attempted but were unable to compare our work to the most recent proposals from other authors for parallel MrBayes acceleration. For aMC^3 [3], which proposes an adaptive multi-GPU approach, we were unable to perform any analyses with the publicly available code due to execution errors. Additionally, aMC^3 is based on MrBayes 3.1.2 which lacks several features and converges more slowly than version 3.2 [10], making it unsuitable for a direct comparison to our work. For sMC^3 [9], which proposes more efficient CPU + GPU parallelism and reports speedups over previous versions of BEAGLE, neither the source code nor a binary file appear to be readily available.

4   Conclusion

Enabling further concurrency of computation in BEAGLE as described here allows a wider range of phylogenetic inferences to benefit from parallel computing hardware. Analyses with many small data subsets or with large trees but few site patterns, now benefit from increased throughput on multi and manycore resources. This work represents an important step in combining the capabilities of increasingly parallel hardware, and the demands of progressively more sophisticated phylogenetic inference analyses.

Acknowledgments. We thank Marc Suchard, University of California, Los Angeles, and Andrew Rambaut, University of Edinburgh; Mark Berger, NVIDIA; and Greg Stoner and Ben Sander, AMD. This work was supported by the National Science Foundation grant numbers DBI-0755048 and DBI-1356562.

References

1. Ayres, D.L., Cummings, M.P.: Heterogeneous hardware support in BEAGLE, a high-performance computing library for statistical phylogenetics. In: 2017 46th International Conference on Parallel Processing Workshops (ICPPW), Bristol, UK (2017, in press)
2. Ayres, D.L., Darling, A., Zwickl, D.J., Beerli, P., Holder, M.T., Lewis, P.O., Huelsenbeck, J.P., Ronquist, F., Swofford, D.L., Cummings, M.P., Rambaut, A., Suchard, M.A.: BEAGLE: an application programming interface and high-performance computing library for statistical phylogenetics. Syst. Biol. **61**(1), 170–173 (2012). doi:10.1093/sysbio/syr100
3. Bao, J., Xia, H., Zhou, J., Liu, X., Wang, G.: Efficient implementation of MrBayes on multi-GPU. Mol. Biol. Evol. **30**(6), 1471 (2013). doi:10.1093/molbev/mst043
4. Chase, M.W., Soltis, D.E., Olmstead, R.G., Morgan, D., Les, D.H., Mishler, B.D., Duvall, M.R., Price, R.A., Hills, H.G., Qiu, Y.L., Plunkett, G.M., Soltis, P.S., Swensen, S.M., Williams, S.E., Gadek, P.A., Quinn, C.J., Eguiarte, L.E., Golenberg, E., Learn Jr., G.H., Graham, S.W., Barrett, S.C.H., Dayanandan, S., Albert, V.A.: Phylogenetics of seed plants: an analysis of nucleotide sequences from the plastid gene *rbc*L. Ann. Mo. Bot. Gard. **80**(3), 528–580 (1993). doi:10.2307/2399846
5. Drummond, A.J., Suchard, M.A., Xie, D., Rambaut, A.: Bayesian phylogenetics with BEAUti and the BEAST 1.7. Mol. Biol. Evol. **29**, 1969–1973 (2012). doi:10.1093/molbev/mss075
6. Felsenstein, J.: The number of evolutionary trees. Syst. Biol. **27**(1), 27–33 (1978). doi:10.2307/2412810
7. Felsenstein, J.: Evolutionary trees from DNA sequences: a maximum likelihood approach. J. Mol. Evol. **17**(6), 368–76 (1981). doi:10.1007/BF01734359
8. Guindon, S., Dufayard, J.F., Lefort, V., Anisimova, M., Hordijk, W., Gascuel, O.: New algorithms and methods to estimate maximum-likelihood phylogenies: assessing the performance of PhyML 3.0. Syst. Biol. **59**(3), 307–321 (2010). doi:10.1093/sysbio/syq010
9. Kuan, L., Pratas, F., Sousa, L., Toms, P.: MrBayes sMC3: accelerating Bayesian inference of phylogenetic trees. Int. J. High. Perform. C. (2016). doi:10.1177/1094342016652461

10. Ronquist, F., Teslenko, M., van der Mark, P., Ayres, D.L., Darling, A., Hohna, S., Larget, B., Liu, L., Suchard, M.A., Huelsenbeck, J.P.: MrBayes 3.2: efficient Bayesian phylogenetic inference and model choice across a large model space. Syst. Biol. **61**(3), 539–542 (2012). doi:10.1093/sysbio/sys029
11. Zwickl, D.J.: Genetic algorithm approaches for the phylogenetic analysis of large biological sequence datasets under the maximum likelihood criterion. Ph.D. thesis, University of Texas, Austin, TX (2006)

Accelerating FaST-LMM for Epistasis Tests

Héctor Martínez[1(✉)], Sergio Barrachina[1], Maribel Castillo[1],
Enrique S. Quintana-Ortí[1], Jordi Rambla De Argila[2], Xavier Farré[2],
and Arcadi Navarro[2]

[1] Depto. de Ingeniería y Ciencia de los Computadores,
Universitat Jaume I, 12006 Castellón, Spain
{martineh,barrachi,castillo,quintana}@uji.es
[2] Depto. de Ciencias Experimentales y de la Salud, Universitat Pompeu Fabra,
08002 Barcelona, Spain
jordi.rambla@crg.eu, {xavier.farre,arcadi.navarro}@upf.edu

Abstract. We introduce an enhanced version of FaST-LMM that maintains the sensitivity of this software when applied to identify epistasis
interactions while delivering an acceleration factor that is close to 7.5×
on a server equipped with a state-of-the-art graphics coprocessor. This
performance boost is obtained from the combined effects of integrating
a dictionary for faster storage of the test results; a re-organization of the
original FaST-LMM Python code; and off-loading of compute-intensive
parts to the graphics accelerator.

Keywords: Epistasis · FaST-LMM · High-performance computing ·
Multithreaded parallelism · Graphics processors

1 Motivation

After years of accumulating technological improvements, we have finally
embraced the postomics era where methodological advances are quickly providing geneticists with tools to analyze massive genome-wide data sets. Recent
genomic studies illustrate that each healthy individual carries hundreds of loss-
of-function variants as well as tens of thousands of other genomic variants in
coding and regulatory regions of their genomes.

Genome-Wide Association Studies (GWAS) results are accumulating evidence at increasing pace. The aggregated study of these results is already providing medically-relevant predictions of phenotypic outcomes from genomic profiles based on Single Nucleotide Polymorphisms (SNPs) [1]. Still, part of the
problem with GWAS comes from the fact that most associated SNPs have been
detected within an additive framework that basically consists in working under
the assumption of additivity and testing each SNP separately from others. However, evidence suggests that the assumption of additivity is frequently not ful-
filled in complex organisms [6,10]. Thus, to evaluate the interplay that genetic
variants have on phenotypes, we must compare linear additivity with more complex interactions (or *epistasis*) among markers, assessing what are the sets of

© Springer International Publishing AG 2017
S. Ibrahim et al. (Eds.): ICA3PP 2017, LNCS 10393, pp. 548–557, 2017.
DOI: 10.1007/978-3-319-65482-9_40

relationships between SNPs producing the most adequate genomic risk scores to predict disease status or treatment outcome.

In this paper we contribute towards the goal of developing new high performance computing (HPC) tools for GWAS by introducing an accelerated version of the epistasis test integrated into FaST-LMM [7]. In doing so, we make the following specific contributions:

– We provide a detailed performance analysis of the current version of FaST-LMM, in the form of an experimental profile that identifies the relevant bottlenecks present in the epistasis component of this software.
– We introduce three major improvements in the epistasis component of FaST-LMM that deliver a significant acceleration:
  • A temporary data structure to store the results from each epistasis tests that delays the insertion of this information on the file with the complete results, enabling a bulk insertion operation on a database.
  • A couple of direct modifications of the code that eliminate some repeated computations that are unnecessary when FaST-LMM is specifically leveraged to perform epistasis test.
  • A module to off-load the matrix-matrix multiplications in the compute-intensive stages of FaST-LMM to a graphics processing unit (GPU).

2   Related Work on Two-Way Epistasis Software

There exist several software packages for genomic-wide epistasis analysis. These software efforts can be classified according to three criteria: the order of the interactions being inspected, where n-way applications analyze interactions between n SNPs; the method to detect the epistasis interactions; and the type of explicit parallelism (if any) they exploit.

When the target is two-way epistasis tests, BOOST [8] is an appealing choice because it combines fair sensitivity with low computational cost. On the other hand, GBOOST [9] or EpistSearch [5] can be used to reduce the execution time of BOOST while maintaining its sensitivity. For this purpose, both packages parallelize the underlying BOOST method exploiting the computational resources of a GPU (GBOOST) or multiple GPUs/FPGAs (EpistSearch).

When sensitivity is the primary goal, FaST-LMM [7] is in general the preferred option. Although it is considerably more expensive than other methods, FaST-LMM offers greater sensitivity. Furthermore, the cost of the epistasis test included in FaST-LMM can be reduced using a parallel implementation based on Hadoop that can be executed on the Microsoft Azure cloud.

Compared with previous work, in this paper we propose several techniques to speed-up epistasis tests via FaST-LMM on multicore architectures, possibly equipped with GPUs. We thus aim to accelerate the execution of this epistasis software while maintaining its sensitivity on an HPC framework.

3 Analysis of FaST-LMM Epistasis Test

We open this section with a brief description of the epistasis test module in FaST-LMM 0.2.31. Next we provide a performance evaluation of the FaST-LMM epistasis test via a profile that exposes the tasks on the critical path.

Overview. FaST-LMM is a general purpose GWAS software to perform univariate GWAS; tests for epistasis; corrections for cellular heterogeneity via the inclusion of principal components; set association tests; and heritability estimation. The package is implemented in Python[1], though, in order to avoid the performance overhead due to the use of an interpreted language, it relies on numpy, pandas, and other high-performance libraries to perform the actual computations and data processing. Therefore, the cost due to the use of Python can be expected to be negligible. FaST-LMM exploits multiprocessing by spawning multiple processes, potentially incurring higher memory and interprocess communication costs when compared with a proper multi-threaded solution.

FaST-LMM epistasis test. In order to decide whether there exists an epistatic interaction between any two SNPs, the epistasis test module integrated in FaST-LMM computes, for each possible combination of two SNPs (pair), the p-value of the chi-square test associated with the difference between the log-likelihoods of a null hypothesis and an alternative one; see [7] for details.

From the algorithmic point of view, the first stage of the epistasis test (hereafter, S1) consists of the following two consecutive operations:

S1.1 Assemble the $n \times k$ random effects matrix G, where n is the number of individuals and k denotes the number of SNPs to analyze. If $k \geq n$, compute the $n \times n$ random effects covariance matrix $K = GG^T$.

S1.2 If $k < n$, compute the singular value decomposition [4]: $G = U\Sigma V^T$, where Σ is a $k \times k$ diagonal matrix containing the singular values of G arranged in descending order of magnitude; next, set $S = \Sigma^2$. Otherwise, compute the spectral decomposition [10]: $K = USU^T$ where S is an $n \times n$ diagonal matrix containing the eigenvalues of K. In both cases, the columns of the $n \times r$ matrices U, V, with $r = \min(n, k)$, are orthonormal.

After these computations are completed, the set of all the possible SNP pairs is split into *packages* of a fixed size (by default, consisting of 1 000 SNP pairs each); a user-specified number of processes are spawned; and the packages are evenly distributed among these processes. Each process next retrieves the data corresponding to its SNP-pair packages, computes the p-value associated to each SNP pair, and stores the results to disk.

In more detail, in order to determine the p-value of an SNP pair, each process performs the following operations, grouped into two consecutive stages (hereafter, S2 and S3).

---

[1] There is also a FaST-LMM version written in C++ but, according to the authors, the Python code contains the most advanced features.

During the first of these stages, a process carries out the following operations for each package:

S2.1 Compute $M_{UX} = U^T X$, where the rows of the $r \times m$ matrix X are associated with the individuals; and the columns correspond to: (i) the covariates; (ii) the number of minor alleles of each distinct SNP present in the current SNP-pair package; and (iii) the products of the minor alleles of each SNP pair in the current SNP-pair package. As the number of distinct SNPs in a SNP-pair package can vary, the dimension m can be different from one package to another; however, it will be at most three times the number of SNP pairs of the package plus the number of covariates being considered (which in our experimentation setup was 1).

S2.2 In addition, if the number of SNPs is lower than the number of individuals (i.e., $k < n$), then compute $M_{UUX} = X - U M_{UX}$. Otherwise, M_{UUX} is void.

Once the second stage is complete, the process performs the following operations, for each SNP pair of a package, as part of stage S3:

S3.1 Compute the log-likelihood of the null hypothesis by selecting the columns of X, $U^T X$, and M_{UUX} that correspond to the covariates and each one of the two SNPs.

S3.2 Compute the log-likelihood of the alternative hypothesis by selecting the columns of X, $U^T X$, and M_{UUX} that correspond to the covariates, each one of the two SNPs, and the product of these two SNPs.

S3.3 Compute the p-value of the chi-square test for the difference of the previous log-likelihoods.

S3.4 Store the previous results as a new row into a **pandas dataframe** structure.

Experimental setup. In order to profile the execution of the epistasis test module in FaST-LMM, our tests consider a sample from the Welcome Trust Case Control Consortium (WTCCC) bipolar disorder, which provides a total of 455 086 SNPs for $n = 4\,804$ individuals. In order to reduce the execution time of our tests, we only selected a small fraction of the original SNP dataset, consisting of $k = 2\,000, 3\,000, 4\,000, 5\,000, 6\,000,$ and $7\,000$ SNPs (which involve testing from 1 998 000 to 24 493 000 SNP pairs). Note that because FaST-LMM splits the work in packages comprising 1 000 SNP pairs each, and the matrix sizes are constrained to the number of individuals, once $k \geq n$, an execution involving a dataset with a larger number of SNPs should roughly increase the execution time linearly on the number of SNP pairs included in the test ($\approx k^2/2$). Therefore, we can expect that the conclusions extracted from the following experiments with these (fragments of) datasets carry over to other cases with a larger number of SNPs. It should also be noted that the epistasis test in FaST-LMM and our modified version can be conducted on the complete collection of the SNP pairs in WTCCC (with the corresponding increases of execution time). Also, the execution time does not depend on the specific subset of SNP pairs that are selected.

The experiments were conducted on a server furnished with 2 Intel Xeon E5-2620v4 8-core processors, 32 Gbytes of memory, and an NVIDIA P100 "Pascal" GPU. The operating system was RedHat Linux 2.6.32. The following software was used for the experimentation: FaST-LMM 0.2.31, Python 2.7.13, PyCUDA 2016.1.2, Scikit-CUDA 0.5.1, Intel MKL Update 11 (icc 17.0.1), and NVIDIA CUBLAS 7.5.

Parallel execution options. The epistasis test in FaST-LMM allows the user to specify the degree of process-level parallelism by setting the number of Python processes that are spawned to execute stages S2 and S3. Thus, increasing the number of processes distributes the epistasis analysis of the SNP pairs, performed in these two stages, among more processes, with each process being then in charge of a smaller collection of packages of SNP pairs. In addition, because FaST-LMM relies on numpy for the execution of certain basic math kernels, linking in a multi-threaded instance of the BLAS (*basic linear algebra subprograms*) [2], as e.g. that provided in Intel MKL, yields a parallel execution of these kernels using multiple threads. This is the case, for example, of the matrix-matrix multiplications in S2.1, S2.2 and, to a minor extent, of the solution of the eigenproblem in S1.2. Given that the target server features a total of 16 physical cores, our experiments with FaST-LMM determined that the best combination spawns 16 processes, with a single thread per process.

Evaluation of the preset package size. As argued earlier, the SNP datasets are partitioned into packages containing a fixed number of SNP pairs, which are then evenly distributed among the processes. Furthermore, the dimension of the matrix-matrix multiplications involved in stage S2 stage are determined by the size of these packages (and the number of individuals). It is important to realize that the performance of this type of computational kernel strongly depends on the size of its matrix operands. In particular, if the dimension is too small, the costs of moving data across the memory hierarchy and the overheads of the parallel execution will deliver low performance. We ran a few independent experiments to determine the GFLOPS rate achieved by the FaST-LMM epistasis test module with the default package size configuration. Our experiments with 16 processes offered a sustained rate that is close to 92% of the theoretical peak. Therefore, we can conclude that the default SNP partitioning option embedded in FaST-LMM involves matrix operands that are large enough to obtain near optimal performance. In other words, we cannot expect a significant variation of the performance by modifying the SNP dataset partitioning to produce larger matrix-matrix multiplications.

Profile of execution time. We next analyze the distribution of costs in a parallel execution of the FaST-LMM epistasis test. Given the insights gained from the previous experiments, we utilize 16 Python processes (with a single thread per process), and employ the default package size in the following study. The target datasets evaluated in this profile consist of fragments comprising 2 000, 3 000, 4 000, 5 000, 6 000 and 7 000 SNPs of the original 4 804-individual 455 086-SNP WTCCC dataset.

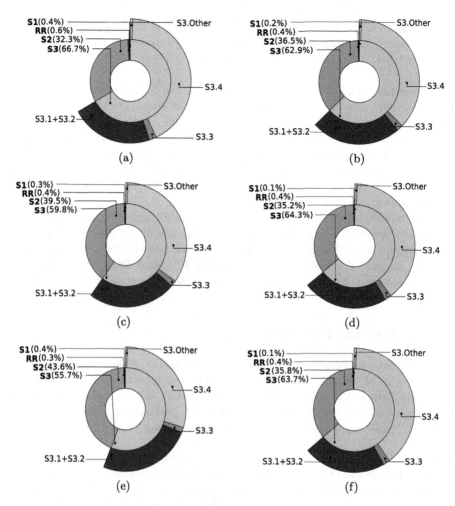

Fig. 1. Distribution of time among the stages of the FaST-LMM epistasis test (using 16 processes). The graphs on the left-hand side correspond to cases with $k \leq n$: (a) 2 000 SNPs, (c) 3 000 SNPs, and (e) 4 000 SNPs; for those on the right-hand side, $k > n$: (b) 5 000 SNPs, (d) 6 000 SNPs, and (f) 7 000 SNPs.

Figure 1 visualizes the execution time distribution of the different stages and their operations. This graphical representation clearly identifies the storage of the results (S3.4) as the major bottleneck in the FaST-LMM epistasis test module, but also ranks the relevance of the remaining operations, guiding our optimization efforts in the next section. In more detail, the figure reports the distribution of the execution time among stages S1–S3 plus an additional stage named RR, which joins the local results from every spawned process in a single dataframe structure. These results show that the costs of stages S1 and RR are negligible. Specifically, the cost of RR is below 0.6% of the total cost for any number of

SNPs, and that of S1 rapidly decays as the number of SNPs grows. In contrast, the combined execution of stages S2 and S3 always consumes more than 99% of the total time. As a result, we will exclude stages S1 and RR from the following analyses.

Figure 1 also examines the costs of stages S2 and S3 in further detail. For S2 we can observe that the execution time mainly corresponds to the matrix-matrix multiplication operations (S2.1 and S2.2). For stage S3, the operations lying on the critical path correspond to S3.1 (null hypothesis), S3.2 (alternative hypothesis), and especially S3.4 (storage of results). The remaining factors identified in this stage contribute a minor factor to the total cost, which is below 2.8% for S3.3 (compute chi-test) and around 1.0% for other operations not included in the previous groups.

In Sect. 3 we argued that, once $k \geq n$, an execution involving a dataset with a larger number of SNPs should experience an increase of the execution time that is roughly linear on the number of SNP pairs included in the test. The results in Fig. 1 support this claim, showing that, for $k \geq 5000$ SNPs, the distribution of the relative execution time among the stages tends to stabilize as the number of SNPs increases.

4   FaST-LMM Enhancements

In this section we propose and evaluate several source code optimizations and an extension of the FaST-LMM epistasis test module. Our modifications are especially designed to speed-up the operations that impose a major bottleneck on the execution of the test. As reported in the performance profile at the end of Sect. 3, these correspond to the operations in stages S2 and S3.

Dataframe. In Sect. 3 we exposed that the most expensive operation of the FaST-LMM epistasis test is S3.4, which corresponds to the insertion of the results computed for each SNP pair on a `pandas DataFrame` structure. This plays a role analogous to that of a database table. FaST-LMM inserts the result for each test on an SNP pair into this structure as soon as it is computed. Thus, each time an SNP pair result is inserted, its index is computed (in order to determine whether a previously-inserted record should be updated or a new one should be created), leading to a nonnegligible overhead as each SNP pair result is inserted just once.

In order to reduce this overhead, we created a Python dictionary to store each epistasis test result as it is computed; furthermore, we populate the `pandas DataFrame` from this dictionary only after all the epistasis tests have been performed. (This last step is analogous to a bulk insertion on a database.)

The effect of this optimization, labeled as `Dict4DataFrame` (abbreviated as D4D), is displayed in Fig. 2, showing a speed-up that is consistently around a factor of 1.85 with respect to the original implementation of FaST-LMM 0.2.31 running on 16 cores when $k \geq n = 4804$.

Last-column and log-likelihood. During stage S3, FaST-LMM computes the log-likelihood of the null and alternative hypothesis for each SNP pair. In order to

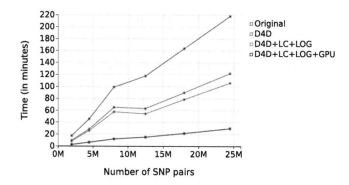

Fig. 2. Execution time of FaST-LMM and the proposed optimizations for different numbers of SNP pairs (using 16 processes).

do this, FaST-LMM assembles the matrices to compute the log-likelihood of the null hypothesis first; computes their log-likelihood; then assembles the matrices for the log-likelihood of the alternative hypothesis; and finally computes their log-likelihood.

As the matrices for the null and alternative hypotheses differ only on their last column (the alternative hypothesis matrices include an extra column with the product of the SNP pair minor alleles), by changing the order of the null and alternative computations, it is possible to first assemble the matrices for the alternative hypothesis; and to re-use those same matrices, without their last column, for the null hypothesis. Proceeding in this manner, the matrices are assembled only once. We have named this optimization as *last-column* (LC).

As part of each log-likelihood computation, an intermediate value $logdetK$ is computed as the sum of the logarithms of the elements of an array Sd of size n. For the particular case of the epistasis test module in FaST-LMM, the contents of this vector do not vary from one log-likelihood computation to another. Therefore, it is possible to compute the values of this vector once and re-use the result for the remaining log-likelihood computations. We have named this source code optimization as *log-likelihood* (LOG).

The results obtained by applying these optimizations in addition to D4D, labeled as D4D+LC+LOG, are shown in Fig. 2. For the more realistic scenarios, i.e. those with $k \geq n$, these two optimizations provide a meager acceleration factor on top of that already offered by D4D.

Matrix multiplications on the GPU. Our next optimization extends the FaST-LMM epistasis test module in order to off-load the execution of stages S2.1 and S2.2 to a graphics processing unit (GPU). Concretely, all p Python processes employ the GPU to compute the matrix multiplications in these two stages. Furthermore, to avoid overflowing the memory of the graphics accelerator, we have implemented a GPU memory manager that holds (i.e., detains) a process request until enough memory is available in the graphics device.

In order to extend the FaST-LMM software without forcing the user to recompile the source code, the GPU extension has been implemented in Python using the PyCUDA[2] library and the scikit-cuda [3] package. PyCUDA provides access to NVIDIA's CUDA parallel computation application programming interface from a Python program. Moreover, scikit-cuda provides Python interfaces to many of the CUDA device/runtime, CUBLAS, CUFFT, and CUSOLVER functions supporting, among others, high-level functions comparable to those in NumPy and Scipy.

As argued in Sect. 3, increasing the default package size did not affect the performance of FaST-LMM *when executed on a multicore processor*. However, this is not the case when the target processor is a GPU. Our experiments (omitted for brevity) revealed that, as long as there is enough memory available on the server to run all 16 processes, the execution time decreases as the package size is augmented. In consequence, the rest of the experiments using our GPU extension involve packages of 6 000 SNP pairs each. (Results with larger package sizes could not be tested due to insufficient memory on the server. However, we would like to stress here that the available memory constrains the number of SNP pairs that can be processed at the same time, but not the total number of SNP pairs that can be tested.)

The acceleration observed when using the GPU extension alongside with the aforedescribed source code optimizations, labeled as D4D+LC+LOG+GPU, is reported in Fig. 2. For those cases with $k \geq n$, we observe a speed-up factor between 7.30 and 7.92 with respect to the original implementation running on 16 cores. Here we remind the linear increase of the execution time that occurs when augmenting the number of SNP pairs involved in the test (provided $k \geq n$); see the profile analysis in Sect. 3. This linear behavior of the original and all enhanced versions of Fast-LMM can also be observed in the results corresponding to the largest three datasets (i.e., those with $k \geq n$) in Fig. 2. As a result, we can expect that the acceleration factors remain of the same order as we increase the number of SNPs beyond 7 000.

To conclude our analysis of the enhancements attained for FaST-LMM, our performance profile of the modified epistasis test with all optimizations applied show that the task on the critical path of the algorithm becomes stage S3.1 + S3.2, which now represents more than 54% of the total time.

5   Conclusions

We have explored the performance and parallel scalability of the current version of the 2-way epistasis test in FaST-LMM. In practical epistasis studies, the volume of SNPs exceeds (by far) the number of individuals and the execution time of FaST-LMM grows linearly with the number of SNP pairs involved in the test. Under these conditions, our experimental analysis of the original implementation of FaST-LMM, on a 16-core platform, identifies that the most expensive operations correspond to: (i) the matrix-matrix multiplication (S2.1); (ii) the

---

[2] PyCUDA: https://mathema.tician.de/software/pycuda/.

log-likelihood tests (S3.1 + S3.2); and (iii) the insertion of the results from the test in a Python database (S3.4). Our enhancements to FaST-LMM precisely target these three bottlenecks,

yielding a global acceleration of the FaST-LMM epistasis test in a factor that is around 7.5× with respect to the original implementation running on 16 cores. As a result, the critical path is shifted to the computations involving the log-likelihood of the null and alternative hypotheses.

References

1. Abraham, G., Tye-Din, J.A., Bhalala, O.G., Kowalczyk, A., Zobel, J., Inouye, M.: Accurate and robust genomic prediction of celiac disease using statistical learning. PLoS Genet. **10**(2), e1004137 (2014)
2. Dongarra, J.J., Croz, J.D., Hammarling, S., Duff, I.: A set of level 3 basic linear algebra subprograms. ACM Trans. Math. Softw. **16**(1), 1–17 (1990)
3. Givon, L.E., Unterthiner, T., Erichson, N.B., Chiang, D.W., Larson, E., Pfister, L., Dieleman, S., Lee, G.R., van der Walt, S., Moldovan, T.M., Bastien, F., Shi, X., Schlüter, J., Thomas, B., Capdevila, C., Rubinsteyn, A., Forbes, M.M., Frelinger, J., Klein, T., Merry, B., Pastewka, L., Taylor, S., Wang, F., Zhou, Y.: scikit-cuda 0.5.1: a Python interface to GPU-powered libraries, December 2015. http://dx.doi.org/10.5281/zenodo.40565
4. Golub, G., Loan, C.V.: Matrix Computations, 3rd edn. The Johns Hopkins University Press, Baltimore (1996)
5. Gonzalez-Dominguez, J., Wienbrandt, L., Kassens, J.C., Ellinghaus, D., Schimmler, M., Schmidt, B.: Parallelizing epistasis detection in GWAS on FPGA and GPU-accelerated computing systems. IEEE/ACM Trans. Comput. Biol. Bioinform. (TCBB) **12**(5), 982–994 (2015)
6. Hemani, G., Shakhbazov, K., Westra, H.J., Esko, T., Henders, A.K., McRae, A.F., Yang, J., Gibson, G., Martin, N.G., Metspalu, A., Franke, L., Montgomery, G.W., Visscher, P.M., Powell, J.M.: Detection and replication of epistasis influencing transcription in humans. Nature **508**(7495), 249 (2014)
7. Lippert, C., Listgarten, J., Davidson, R.I., Baxter, J., Poon, H., Kadie, C.M., Heckerman, D.: An exhaustive epistatic SNP association analysis on expanded wellcome trust data. Sci. Rep. **3**, 1099 (2013)
8. Wan, X., Yang, C., Yang, Q., Xue, H., Fan, X., Tang, N.L., Yu, W.: BOOST: a fast approach to detecting gene-gene interactions in genome-wide case-control studies. Am. J. Hum. Genet. **87**(3), 325–340 (2010)
9. Yung, L.S., Yang, C., Wan, X., Yu, W.: GBOOST: a GPU-based tool for detecting gene-gene interactions in genome-wide case control studies. Bioinformatics **27**(9), 1309–1310 (2011)
10. Zuk, O., Hechter, E., Sunyaev, S.R., Lander, E.S.: The mystery of missing heritability: genetic interactions create phantom heritability. Proc. Natl. Acad. Sci. **109**(4), 1193–1198 (2012)

Pipelined Multi-FPGA Genomic Data Clustering

Rick Wertenbroek$^{(\boxtimes)}$, Enrico Petraglio, and Yann Thoma

School of Business and Engineering Vaud HES-SO, REDS Institute at HEIG-VD,
University of Applied Sciences Western Switzerland, Yverdon-les-Bains, Switzerland
{rick.wertenbroek,enrico.petraglio,yann.thoma}@heig-vd.ch

Abstract. High throughput DNA sequencing made individual genome profiling possible and produces very large amounts of data. Today data and associated metadata are stored in FASTQ text file assemblies carrying the information of genome fragments called reads. Current techniques rely on mapping these reads to a common reference genome for compression and analysis. However, about 10% of the reads do not map to any known reference making them difficult to compress or process. These reads are of high importance because they hold information absent from any reference. Finding overlaps in these reads can help subsequent processing and compression tasks tremendously. Within this context clustering is used to find overlapping unmapped reads and sort them in groups. Clustering being an extremely time consuming task a modular multi-FPGA pipeline was designed and is the focus of this paper. A pipeline with 6 FPGAs was created and has shown a speed-up of ×5 compared to existing FPGA implementations. Resulting enriched files encoding reads and clustering results show file sizes within a 10% margin of the best DNA compressors while providing valuable extra information.

Keywords: FPGA · Acceleration · Genomic data · Clustering · Compression

1 Introduction

With the advent of high throughput sequencing, genomics has entered a new era where massive amounts of data are produced ($\sim$2–40 ExaBytes/year are to be expected in 2025 [13]). The sequencing of one human genome generates in the order of 300 GB of raw data. This data is composed of small sequences, called reads, randomly located in the genome with high redundancy (typically 30–50×). Processing data in a timely fashion as well as reducing the required storage space is imminently important for the future of genomics. Currently, many different data formats are used, and most of them are far from optimal [2,4,11]. Each format has different characteristics, and so a universal standard is required to facilitate the development of algorithms. The authors are currently working on such a new format, part of which deals with reads that do not map

© Springer International Publishing AG 2017
S. Ibrahim et al. (Eds.): ICA3PP 2017, LNCS 10393, pp. 558–568, 2017.
DOI: 10.1007/978-3-319-65482-9_41

the reference human genome[1] and are difficult to compress. Using a clustering algorithm allows to compress these reads while providing useful information with the goal of accelerating later processing such as de novo assembly.

Currently, sequencing machines, for instance from Illumina[2], cut DNA into small sequences and read them from both ends typically from 50 up to 200 base pairs (bp) the size of the unread part in the middle of the sequence is typically in the range of 100–300 bp as can be seen on the right hand side of Fig. 1. Every read is written into a text based file in the FASTQ format. Sequencing of a whole genome with ~40× coverage typically generates roughly 300 GB of data (uncompressed).

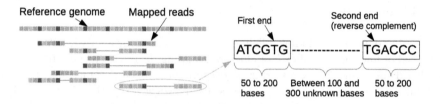

Fig. 1. Paired reads mapped onto the reference genome

Efficient compression algorithms obviously exploit data redundancy. The first step is to identify known sequences and to map them onto the reference genome as can be seen on the left hand side of Fig. 1. These sequences are easily compressed by using their position in the reference, and current compression algorithms already take advantage of this. However, not all the reads can be aligned onto the reference genome, and typically ~10% of the sequences remain unmapped [1]. This can be caused by the fact that the individual genomes differ from the reference, by errors in the sequencing or because reads are part of various other entities found in the body. Nevertheless these sequences remain important [5], as they could be sign of a mutation or genetic disease, and should therefore not be discarded. In this particular context clustering can provide extra information about the unmapped reads (i.e. similarities, interdependencies). This preprocessing step will bring useful additional information for the end user which can take advantage of the clustering results to speed up genomic data analysis such as de novo assembly or variant calling. It is in the general interest to do hard work once and use the results often. The encoding stage is the critical moment when it is possible to enrich the data at the cost of some processing time but giving an advantage for every subsequent use of the data. Adding extra information about relations between sequences with clustering will not be specially expensive in storage space since the sequences in the clusters share so many similarities, needing only to encode the differences.

---

[1] This artificial human genome was built as an average of multiple human genomes.
[2] http://www.illumina.com.

The hardware implementation presented in this paper is an improvement of the FPGA clustering architecture developed by the authors and presented in [10]. The new architecture was developed in order to implement a clustering pipeline on multiple FPGAs, resulting in a considerable speed up of the clustering process and therefore allowing the system to handle bigger FASTQ files. Furthermore, the compression strategy for the clustering results will also be presented.

The rest of this paper is organized as follows: The next section introduces the concept of clustering applied to genomic data. Section 3 presents the current hardware implementation, then Sect. 4 shows results. Finally, Sect. 5 lists conclusions and introduces future work.

2   Clustering

Clustering data is a well known field of research, and traditional algorithms have the goal of finding a number k of clusters grouping data with respect to a neighborhood function [3,8]. Clustering algorithms have been designed and tailored for different domains including genomics [12], however no specific clustering algorithm has been proven to be particularly useful for compressing genomic data. Compression will benefit more from algorithms that create a variable number of clusters with highly correlated data, rather than having a given constant number of clusters. Therefore, instead of doing k-clustering, it would be better to seek clusters regardless of a total number.

Algorithm 1 will classify sequences as members of a cluster if their distance with the cluster reference is below a threshold, and seeds new clusters when needed. The following neighborhood function is used to generate the distance:

- If two sequences overlap completely they have a distance of 0.
- If they overlap leaving out a number N of bases at the extremities the distance is N.
- If they do not overlap at all the distance considered is infinite.

Algorithm 1. Clustering algorithm

```
 1: function CLUSTERING(seqs)
 2:     clusters ← ∅
 3:     while seqs ≠ ∅ do
 4:         calcClusters ← {seed with first N non overlapping seqs};
 5:         Remove these sequences from seqs;
 6:         for all seq ∈ seqs do
 7:             for all cluster ∈ calcClusters do
 8:                 if isInCluster(seq, cluster) then
 9:                     cluster ← {cluster, seq}; Remove seq from seqs;
10:         clusters ← {clusters, calcClusters}
11:     return clusters
```

Running Algorithm 1 in a purely sequential manner is extremely time consuming, but since testing for membership is easy to parallelize at a massive scale, the cost is acceptable. An implementation of Algorithm 1 using FPGA technology will benefit from the parallelization possibilities and the on-board memory to significantly reduce processing time. To the best of our knowledge, FPGA implementations of k-clustering have been published [7,14], but nothing with a highly dynamic number of clusters.

3   Design Implementation

This section first describes the software setup, and then presents the multi-FPGA architecture implementing the clustering algorithm. The target hardware is a Micron Pico Computing EX-700 Backplane holding 6 AC-510 modules. Each module is comprised of a Xilinx Kintex Ultrascale FPGA which has access to a high bandwidth Hybrid Memory Cube (HMC) of 4 GB. All modules are connected together via a PCIe ×8 switch.

3.1   Software Setup

The interface between the data (in the form of FASTQ files) and the FPGA accelerators is represented by a C++11 software which, thanks to its multi-threaded architecture, allows for pipelined stages. The software is therefore able to read and send sequences from a FASTQ file while the FPGAs are running the clustering algorithm, and at the same time retrieve and directly encode every result coming from the FPGAs. These results are either references (center of a cluster) or sequence membership information. When a result is a reference it goes into a FASTQ file that will be compressed by a state of the art DNA compressor. All the member sequences will be encoded in relation to the reference of the cluster they belong to. This will generate a file containing all the information about the clusters, and their member sequences encoded as differences. This structured file will be compressed by a standard compressor.

3.2   Multi-FPGA Architecture

To parallelize the clustering algorithm even more compared to [10] it was decided to span a clustering pipeline on multiple FPGAs. Using a pipeline facilitates the data path and, once loaded, executes the same number of operations at a given time as a fully parallel version.

The general data flow is the following: The sequences are sent to the first FPGA for processing, they are then forwarded to the next FPGA for further processing until reaching the last FPGA of the pipeline. The last FPGA checks if the sequence is a reference, a matched sequence, or an unmatched sequence. For every reference or matched sequence a notification is sent back to the PC. In order to limit the number of transfers between the FPGAs and the PC a memory local to the FPGAs is used, a high bandwidth Hybrid Memory Cube

(HMC). To optimize the design the processing already starts when the PC begins transferring sequences, and once all the sequences are transferred the data only moves between the FPGAs and the HMC. To achieve this result the processing algorithm is split in two phases (Fig. 2):

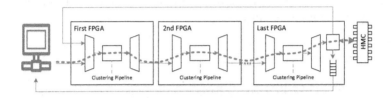

Fig. 2. Data path during phase one.

Phase one. The first FPGA receives sequences from the PC. The sequences go through its clustering pipeline and traverse the next FPGAs until they reach the last FPGA. Each stage in the clustering pipeline represents a cluster, which is initially unseeded and needs a reference sequence. This sequence cannot be a member or reference of another cluster. Seeded clusters will then compare every non reference sequence to their reference, and if a sequence can be a member of the given cluster, it will be marked as such. If a sequence was already part of another cluster it will only be updated if the distance to the new cluster reference is smaller. When reaching the last FPGA, sequences are either references, members of a cluster, or do not belong to any cluster yet. Each reference and member sequence is sent back to the PC and removed from the FPGAs. Thus only the sequences that do not belong to any cluster created so far are stored inside the HMC (Fig. 3).

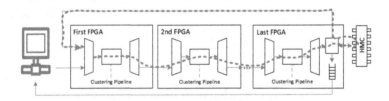

Fig. 3. Data path during phase two.

Phase two. Once all the sequences have been transferred from the PC a signal is sent to change the data flow, and sequences are now read from the HMC and sent back to the first FPGA in a loop. For each iteration of this loop the clusters are cleared to be reseeded with new sequences. All other sequences are then checked against the clusters to see if they belong to them. This is done exactly the same way as in phase one, as just the data flow has been changed. The second phase is repeated until all sequences become either a reference or member of a cluster, leaving the HMC empty.

Although phase one is executed only once, phase two is repeated a certain number of times. This high number of executions will imply a heavy utilization of the HMC memory and will generate a huge amount of communications between the FPGAs in the system. Using the maximum number of matching units (checking for membership) possible decreases the number of executions of phase two, since there will be less sequences after each run of phase two.

3.3   FPGA Internal Architecture

This section details the hardware architecture, and specifically the internal data flow. Figure 4 shows the top hierarchy of our implementation.

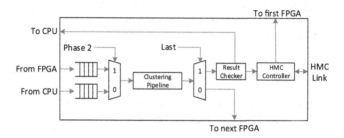

Fig. 4. Top hierarchy of the FPGA implementation.

The internal architecture of each FPGA was made to be the same on each FPGA to generate a unique and modular design. There are two main parameters that can be set from the software to change the data flow inside an FPGA. The first one is for selecting the input stream and the second one is to activate HMC storage. HMC storage can be seen as a FIFO and is only required by the last FPGA to store the huge amount of unmatched sequences between loops. If the number of sequences is so big that it exceeds the capacity of the HMC on the last FPGA any other FPGA in the chain can be set to use its HMC as a FIFO to increase the total capacity.

The data flow outside the FPGA connecting their inputs and outputs is also software programmable. This is made possible by the presence of a PCIe Switch on the backplane holding the FPGAs. Every stream coming either from an FPGA or the PC can be connected to any input. With our modular approach we are capable of chaining any number of FPGAs together, and this is reconfigurable via software. With our current setup we chained 6 FPGAs but it is possible, for instance, to make two separate chains of 3 FPGAs. Another advantage of having an on-board PCIe switch is that the communication between FPGAs never interferes with the PCIe bus of the PC. The only packets traveling on the PC's PCIe bus are the sequences being sent to the FPGAs and the results coming back.

3.4   The Clustering Pipeline

As shown in Fig. 4, the core of the FPGA design is composed of a cluster-ing pipeline. Each pipeline is encased between two FIFOs that act as a buffer when the input and output stream rates vary. Each stage of the pipeline is an autonomous machine representing a cluster. Each machine is responsible for sequence transfer, cluster management, and can communicate with the previ-ous and next stage to schedule a sequence transfer. This allows for distributed pipeline management, e.g. preventing stages from transferring data when the pipeline stalls because of back-pressure (output FIFO full). Each stage also knows when to use a sequence as a reference, check for membership using the internal matching unit, or simply transfer the sequence because it is already matched. This kind of autonomy removes the need for global management of the pipeline and allows us to span the pipeline on multiple FPGAs easily. Each stage is also responsible for updating a sequence when it becomes a reference, when it is considered to be a member of a cluster, or is updated because it fits the current cluster better.

3.5   The Matching Units

The matching unit checks the distance of a sequence in relation to the cluster center reference. It does this by aligning the sequence to the reference in several positions, from 16 bases shifted to the left up to 16 bases shifted to the right. If the overlapping parts match each other, i.e. they have the same bases (the use of wild card bases is allowed, a 'N' base being used for this), the distance is the lowest number of shifts that match. Two identical sequences would therefore match with a distance of 0. The matching unit also checks the reverse comple-ment of a sequence against the reference in all positions. Checking the reverse complement makes sense because DNA is a double helix with one side being the reverse complement of the other. If the sequence does not match within the 16 shift limit it is considered that the distance is more than the threshold and that the sequence cannot be a member of the current cluster.

Match	Match	Reverse-Compl.	No Match
ACTGATTG	TACTGATT	ACTGATTG	ACAGATTG
||||||||	///////	||||||||	||ｷ|||||
ACTGATTG	ACTGATTG	CAATCAGT	ACTGATTG

The matching unit needs seven clock cycles to check a sequence up to 126 bases long in every position from being shifted 16 bases to the left up to 16 bases to the right with reverse complement checking.

3.6   Resources Usage

The final design is implemented on an Micron Pico Computing EX-700 backplane bearing six AC-510 modules with a Xilinx Kintex Ultrascale 60 FPGA and 4 GB of HMC each. This setup realizes a global clustering pipeline composed of 420 clustering units (70 per FPGA).

Table 1. Resource usage per FPGA. Kintex Ultrascale 60 with 70 internal matching units (±16 shifts and reverse complement matching capability)

Logic utilization	Used	Avail.	Usage
Number of Slice registers	240,352	663,360	36.23%
Number of Slice LUTs	257,087	331,680	77.51%
Number of occupied Slices	41,220	41,460	99.42%
Number of BlockRAM/FIFO	323.5	1,080	29.95%

The resource utilization of the design presented in Fig. 4 for each FPGA is summarized in Table 1. Note: The pipeline runs at 125 MHz while the HMC and PCIe controllers run at 250 MHz.

4   Tests and Results

This section summarizes the performance results and shows the speed gain achieved by the new FPGA architecture compared to the old version presented in [10]. The last implementation made possible the clustering of FASTQ files composed of $\sim100 \times 10^6$ unmapped sequences that would take years in software thanks to parallelization and fast memories. With the expansion of the clustering pipeline on 6 FPGAs and the usage of direct communication links, a speed-up of 5 was measured. Moreover, this section will discuss the efficiency of the clustering compression method against one of the best state-of-the-art compression tools called SCALCE[3] [6]. In the first implementation, the matching units were grouped in a unique pipeline on a single FPGA. This limited the maximum pipeline size to 70 matching units. Furthermore the first implementation did not take the HMC controller internal read and write request reordering into account and could not guarantee a fixed order in the clustering. This made the first hardware implementation non deterministic. Memory request reordering is now taken into account, granting a total reproducibility of the algorithm. The new modular approach makes it possible to distribute the pipeline on any number of FPGAs giving high flexibility and accelerating the execution of the clustering task. To quantify the difference between the old and the new implementation, several FASTQ files were used, each composed of different amounts of reads. Figure 5 shows the performances achieved by the two FPGA designs. The sequences used during these experiments are unmapped paired reads of 126 bp. They were generated using an Illumina sequencer on a real human sample.

Figure 5 shows a measured speed-up between the old and the new design of roughly 5 times. Theoretically the expected speed-up should exceed 6 because of the number of matching units implemented and the fact that a bigger pipeline is supposed to match more reads with each pass of phase two, which will decrease the number of reads that need to be compared on all subsequent iterations of

---

[3] http://sfu-compbio.github.io/scalce/.

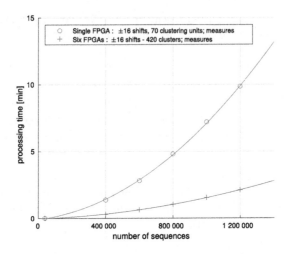

Fig. 5. New versus last implementation running datasets with up to 1,200,000 reads.

phase two. However, the huge amount of communications between the FPGAs and a more complex pipeline synchronization system are the reason the theoretical speed-up could not be achieved. Nevertheless, thanks to this speed-up the clustering of $\sim100 \times 10^6$ unmapped sequences now takes less than a day.

At the compression stage, after clustering, results are composed of two sets of reads, cluster references, and cluster members. The references are stored in a FASTQ file, while the cluster members are encoded in a new file, with for each cluster an ID linking to the reference followed by all the member sequences encoded as differences to the reference. The FASTQ file of references will be compressed by SCALCE and the encoded file will be compressed by a standard compressor such as gzip. To evaluate the cost of adding clustering information, files of $\sim16 \times 10^6$ reads (~1.58 GB of raw sequences), coming from a real human sample, were compared on average resulting file sizes using three different compression methods. First, using a standard compressor. Secondly, using SCALCE for the references and adding the clustering information using a standard compressor. Finally, with SCALCE alone. As shown in Table 2.

Table 2. Clustering compression efficiency compared to gzip and SCALCE

Original file	Compressed by gzip	Clustered and compressed	Compressed by SCALCE
1.58 GBytes	**274 MBytes**	**125 MBytes**	**114 MBytes**
100%	17.3%	7.9%	7.2%

As we can see, adding the clustering information adds a cost of less than 10% in terms of final file size compared to compressing the sequences with SCALCE. This extra information can save a lot of time for the end user. Having the reads clustered makes it possible to query the set for overlapping and related sequences in a really short time, removing the need to do an all-vs-all comparison. This could speed up processes such as de novo assembly in which a big part of processing time is comprised of finding overlapping sequences to make contigs and examining the relations between ends to make scaffolds [9]. Most of the overlaps would already be found by clustering. It is in the general interest to do hard work before encoding, if the impact on file size is reasonable, because these files need to be encoded once and will provide benefits for multiple applications.

5   Conclusions and Future Works

Using hardware accelerators made clustering possible even for big FASTQ files (over 100×10^6 sequences) and the addition of the resulting clustering information to the sequences resulted in a reasonable increase in storage cost ($\sim10\%$). The clustering results can potentially speed up consuming tasks done on unmapped reads. The encoded file makes it possible to query for overlapping reads on a given sequence almost instantaneously, helps for graph extraction, and can also speed up many statistical queries. The most time consuming part in most algorithms is an all-vs-all comparison phase and our clustering method relieves this duty from any subsequent user. The clustering information helps considerably even for applications using other all-vs-all comparisons criteria than overlaps by already creating smaller subsets with highly correlated data on which assertions are easily tested. Allowing the total number comparisons needed to be highly reduced.

Future work includes quantifying the advantages of this information in computational genomics, creating an API for ease of use of the enriched files, and refining the implementation to reduce processing time. The authors are also currently working on an algorithm creating bigger artificial internal references on which the unmapped reads could be located by position and length in order to reduce the encoded file size even more.

Acknowledgments. The research presented in this paper was funded by the Swiss PASC initiative in the framework of the PoSeNoGap (Portable Scalable Concurrency for Genomic Data Processing) project. The authors would like to thank all the participants for the fruitful discussions, namely Ioannis Xenarios, Nicolas Guex, Christian Iseli, Thierry Schüpbach and Daniel Zerzion from SIB, Marco Mattavelli, and Claudio Alberti from EPFL, Flavio Capitao, and Roberto Rigamonti from HEIG-VD.

References

1. Cox, A.J., Bauer, M.J., Jakobi, T., Rosone, G.: Large-scale compression of genomic sequence databases with the Burrows-Wheeler transform. Bioinformatics **28**, 1415–1419 (2012)
2. Deorowicz, S., Grabowski, S.: Compression of DNA sequence reads in FASTQ format. Bioinformatics **27**, 860–862 (2011)
3. Du, K.L.: Clustering: a neural network approach. Neural Networks **23**, 89–107 (2010)

4. Fritz, M.H.Y., Leinonen, R., Cochrane, G., Birney, E.: Efficient storage of high throughput DNA sequencing data using reference-based compression. Genome Res. **21**, 734–740 (2011)
5. Gouin, A., Nouhaud, P., Legeai, F., Rizk, G., Simon, J.C., Lemaitre, C.: Whole genome re-sequencing: lessons from unmapped reads. Journées Ouvertes Biologie Informatique Mathématiques (2013)
6. Guerra, A.J., Lotero, J., Isaza, S.: Performance comparison of sequential and parallel compression applications for DNA raw data. J. Supercomput. **72**, 4696–4717 (2016)
7. Hussain, H.M., Benkrid, K., Seker, H., Erdogan, A.T.: FPGA implementation of K-means algorithm for bioinformatics application: An accelerated approach to clustering Microarray data. In: Adaptive Hardware and Systems, pp. 248–255 (2011)
8. Jain, A.K.: Data clustering: 50 years beyond K-means. Pattern Recogn. Lett. **31**, 651–666 (2010)
9. Li, R., Zhu, H., Ruan, J., Qian, W., Fang, X., Shi, Z., Li, Y., Li, S., Shan, G., Kristiansen, K., Li, S., Yang, H., Wang, J., Wang, J.: De novo assembly of human genomes with massively parallel short read sequencing. Genome Res. **20**(2), 265–272 (2010)
10. Petraglio, E., Wertenbroek, R., Capitao, F., Guex, N., Iseli, C., Thoma, Y.: Genomic data clustering on FPGAs for compression. In: Wong, S., Beck, A.C., Bertels, K., Carro, L. (eds.) ARC 2017. LNCS, vol. 10216, pp. 229–240. Springer, Cham (2017). doi:10.1007/978-3-319-56258-2_20
11. Pinho, A.J., Pratas, D., Garcia, S.P.: GReEn: a tool for efficient compression of genome resequencing data. Nucleic Acids Res. **40**(4), e27 (2011)
12. Pollard, K.S., van der Laan, M.J.: Cluster analysis of genomic data. Bioinformatics and Computational Biology Solutions Using R and Bioconductor, pp. 208–228. Springer, New York (2005)
13. Stephens, Z.D., Lee, S.Y., Faghri, F., Campbell, R.H., Zhai, C., Efron, M.J., Iyer, R., Schatz, M.C., Sinha, S., Robinson, G.E.: Big data: astronomical or genomical? PLoS Biol. **13**, e1002195 (2015)
14. Winterstein, F., Bayliss, S., Constantinides, G.A.: FPGA-based K-means clustering using tree-based data structures. In: 23rd International Conference on Field Programmable Logic and Applications, pp. 1–6 (2013)

First Experiences Accelerating Smith-Waterman on Intel's Knights Landing Processor

Enzo Rucci[1], Carlos Garcia[2(✉)], Guillermo Botella[2], Armando De Giusti[1],
Marcelo Naiouf[3], and Manuel Prieto-Matias[2]

[1] III-LIDI, CONICET, Facultad de Informática,
Universidad Nacional de La Plata, 1900 La Plata, Buenos Aires, Argentina
{erucci,degiusti}@lidi.info.unlp.edu.ar
[2] Depto. Arquitectura de Computadores y Automática,
Universidad Complutense de Madrid, 28040 Madrid, Spain
{garsanca,gbotella,mpmatias}@ucm.es
[3] III-LIDI, Facultad de Informática, Universidad Nacional de La Plata,
1900 La Plata, Buenos Aires, Argentina
mnaiouf@lidi.info.unlp.edu.ar

Abstract. The well-known Smith-Waterman (SW) algorithm is the most commonly used method for local sequence alignments. However, SW is very computationally demanding for large protein databases. There are several implementations that take advantage of parallel capacities on many-cores, FPGAs or GPUs, in order to increase the alignment throughput. In this paper, we have explored SW acceleration on Intel KNL processor. The novelty of this architecture requires the revision of previous programming and optimization techniques on many-core architectures. To the best of authors knowledge, this is the first KNL architecture assessment for SW algorithm. Our evaluation, using the renowned Environmental NR database as benchmark, has shown that multi-threading and SIMD exploitation showed competitive performance (351 GCUPS) in comparison with other implementations.

Keywords: Bioinformatics · Smith-Waterman · Xeon-Phi · Intel-KNL · SIMD

1 Introduction

Nowadays the greatest challenge of Bioinformatics is no longer data generation, it is efficient information analysis and interpretation. In fact, sequencing technology [9] is currently considered one of the most successful instruments in Bioinformatics, basically solved by heuristic methods.

The key aspect of Smith-Waterman (SW) algorithm [15] is that it always finds the optimal local alignment between two sequences. This characteristic makes this method the basis of more sophisticated alignment technologies, so its study and acceleration in different platforms has motivated a great interest for the scientific community. Although many approaches, such as BLAST and

© Springer International Publishing AG 2017
S. Ibrahim et al. (Eds.): ICA3PP 2017, LNCS 10393, pp. 569–579, 2017.
DOI: 10.1007/978-3-319-65482-9_42

FASTA are more efficient in terms of execution time, they do not guarantee the optimal alignment.

SW establishes similar regions between two DNA or protein sequences. A score matrix must be built in order to determine the best alignment. Besides, matrix size depends on sequence lengths which determines the parallel scalability. From a parallel processing perspective, regarding DNA alignment with sequences up to hundreds of million nucleotide, the huge matrix created only permits performing a single sequence pair, so the low-level parallelism available in the alignment can be exploited by means of the *intra-task* scheme. Nevertheless, protein sequences which are shorter requires small matrices. This aspect permits exploiting coarse level parallelism computing multiple independent alignments simultaneously in an *inter-task* approach way.

The computational complexity of the SW algorithm has motivated a large amount of research in order to reduce execution time by means of acceleration on a great variety of architectures. In the last years, in the context of SW protein alignment, we have witnessed SIMD exploitation available on modern CPUs, highlighting the recently released *Parasail* library [2]. In the field of heterogeneous computing, the most successful solution is the *CUDASW++* software [7] for multi CUDA-enabled GPUs with concurrent CPU computing. Moreover, for Intel's co-processors based on Xeon Phi, we highlight both optimized hand-tuned SW implementations denominated as *SWAPHI* [8] and *LSBDS* [5]. Also centering on the Intel Xeon Phi alternative, Rucci et al. [13] have recently studied also energy efficiency on a hybrid implementation that exploits both CPU and co-processors simultaneously. Using FPGAs as accelerators, we can find linear systolic array implementations for Xilinx Virtex FPGAs [4], custom instructions [6] and the proposal of Rucci *et al.* [14] where the behavior of the novel paradigm of OpenCL on Altera's FPGAs is studied, whose most relevant results show that these devices are the most efficient from an energy footprint perspective.

Our paper proposes and evaluates a SW algorithm using the last generation of Intel's Xeon Phi with the Knights Landing (KNL) architecture. We would like to highlight that although there exist SW studies in old Xeon Phi with Knights Corner (KNC) architecture [5,8,13], to the best of authors knowledge there are not related works in Bioinformatics scenarios with KNL architecture due to its recent commercialization. Among the main differences of KNL regarding its predecessor, there are the incorporation of AVX-512 extensions, a remarkable number of vector units increment and new on-package high-bandwidth memory. These aspects require the revision of the previous optimization proposals for the SW algorithm.

Section 2 introduces the basic concepts of the Smith-Waterman algorithm. Section 3 briefly introduces the Intel's Xeon Phi architecture and in Sect. 4 we describe our implementation of the SW algorithm. In Sect. 5 we discuss performance results and finally, in Sect. 6, we conclude with some ideas for future research.

2   Smith-Waterman Algorithm

Given two sequences S_1 and S_2, with sizes $|S_1| = m$ and $|S_2| = n$, the recurrence relations for the SW algorithm with affine gap penalties [3] are defined below.

$$H_{i,j} = max\{0, H_{i-1,j-1} + SM(S_1[i], S_2[j]), E_{i,j}, F_{i,j}\} \tag{1}$$

$$E_{i,j} = max\{H_{i,j-1} - G_{oe}, E_{i,j-1} - G_e\} \tag{2}$$

$$F_{i,j} = max\{H_{i-1,j} - G_{oe}, F_{i-1,j} - G_e\} \tag{3}$$

$H_{i,j}$ contains the score for aligning the prefixes $S_1[1..i]$ and $S_2[1..j]$. $E_{i,j}$ and $F_{i,j}$ are the scores of prefix $S_1[1..i]$ aligned to a gap and prefix $S_2[1..j]$ aligned to a gap, respectively. SM is the *scoring matrix* which defines the substitution scores for all residue pairs. Generally, SM rewards with a positive value when q_i and d_j are identical or relatives, and punishes with a negative value otherwise. G_{oe} is the sum of gap open and gap extension penalties while G_e is the gap extension penalty. The recurrences should be calculated with $1 \leq i \leq m$ and $1 \leq j \leq n$, after initializing H, E and F with 0 when $i = 0$ or $j = 0$. The maximum value in the alignment matrix H is the optimal local alignment score.

3   Intel's Xeon Phi

With the Exascale challenge as a target in High Performance Computing (HPC), accelerators seem to be the alternative to achieve such goals due to consumption constrains in general-purpose processors. Xeon Phi (Phi) is the code brand name given by Intel to a series of massively many-core processors designed for HPC purposes. In 2012, Intel launches the first Phi generation (KNC) which mainly features up to 61×86 pentium cores with extended vector units (512-bit) and simultaneous multithreading (four hardware threads per core). While the first Phi was attached to the host processor via PCI Express bus, second generation (KNL) can operate as standalone processor.

KNL architecture corresponds up to 36 *Tiles* interconnected by 2D mesh. Each Tile includes 2 cores based on the out-of-order Intel's Atom microarchitecture (4 threads per core), 2 Vector Processing Units (VPUs) with AVX-512 support and a shared L2 cache of 1 MByte.

One of the main differences of the KNL architecture regarding its predecessor is the availability of on-package high-bandwidth memory (HBM). This particular technology permits three configuration modes: *Cache Mode*, *Flat mode* and *Hybrid mode*. In *Cache mode*, HBM is used as classical cache with lower performance rates and null source code changes. In *Flat mode*, the HBM is used as addressable memory requiring the programmer intervention to manually indicate which part of the data is allocated to this memory. It is important to note that in *Flat mode*, MCDRAM is treated as Non-Uniform-Memory-Access architectures (NUMA), thus programmers should take special care for achieving efficient memory access from the cores [1]. Finally, in the *Hybrid mode*, HBM is divided in two parts: one part in *Cache mode* and one in *Flat mode*.

KNL supports not only old Intel's multimedia extensions such as 128-bit SSEx and 256-bit AVXx, but also modern 512-bit AVX-512. In fact, Intel will unify the SIMD instruction-set on both general purpose (it announced its support on Xeon E5-26xx V5 at 2017) and KNL processors by means of AVX-512. AVX-512 performs 512-bit SIMD capabilities, 32 logical registers, vector predication via eight new mask registers and gather/scatter indirect vector accesses. Currently, modern Phi has two VPUs per core allowing SIMD parallelism which acts as 32 SIMD-lanes for single-precision (512 bits registers/32 bits in SP $\times$ 2 VPUs = 32 lanes) and 16 SIMD-lanes for double-precision [16]. Although Intel AVX-512 instructions contains several categories, Xeon Phi KNL architecture only supports four: AVX-512F (foundation instructions); AVX-512CD (conflict-detection); AVX-512ER (exponential and reciprocal); and AVX-512PF (prefetch instructions).

From a programming point of view, one of the main goals of this platform is the support of existing parallel programming models traditionally used on HPC scenario such as the OpenMP, MPI or TBB paradigms [10], which simplifies code development and improves portability over other alternatives based on accelerator-specific programming languages such as CUDA or OpenCL. In fact, although it should not be the most efficient way, KNL allows binary compatibility with Xeon families.

4   SW Implementation

In this section, we will address the optimizations performed on the Intel Xeon Phi KNL processor. Before describing them in detail, we would like to point out the algorithm flow which can be summarized in the following steps:

1. *Pre-processing stage*: database sequences are pre-processed to allow subsequent parallel computation.
2. *SW stage*: alignments are carried out.
3. *Sorting stage*: alignment scores are sorted in descending order.

The inter-task parallelism approach is performed in order to exploit the SIMD vector capabilities available on the Xeon Phi KNL processor. In that sense, database sequences are processed in groups and the size of the groups is determined by the number of SIMD vector lanes. Before grouping sequences, database sequences are sorted by their lengths in ascending order and padded with dummy symbols. This is so in order to favour memory pattern access and minimize workload imbalances.

4.1   Multiple Parallelism Levels

Our implementation exploits both data and thread parallelism levels. On the one hand, we have used SIMD instructions by means of hand-tuned intrinsic functions. In particular, we have explored the usage of SSE4.1, AVX2 and AVX-512

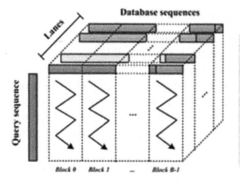

Fig. 1. Schematic representation of the inter-task matrix computation

```
vCur[j] = _mm_adds_epi8(vPrev[j-1], vSub);
vCur[j] = _mm_max_epi8(vCur[j], vF[i]);
vCur[j] = _mm_max_epi8(vCur[j], vE[j]);
vCur[j] = _mm_max_epi8(vCur[j], vZero);
vS = _mm_max_epi8(vS, vCur[j]);
vF[i] = _mm_sub_epi8(vF[i], vGe);
vE[j] = _mm_sub_epi8(vE[j], vGe);
vAux = _mm_sub_epi8(vCur[j], vGoe);
vF[i] = _mm_max_epi8(vF[i], vAux);
vE[j] = _mm_max_epi8(vE[j], vAux);
```

Fig. 2. SSE4.1 core instructions

```
vCur[j] = _mm256_adds_epi8(vPrev[j-1], vSub);
vCur[j] = _mm256_max_epi8(vCur[j], vF[i]);
vCur[j] = _mm256_max_epi8(vCur[j], vE[j]);
vCur[j] = _mm256_max_epi8(vCur[j], vZero);
vS = _mm256_max_epi8(vS, vCur[j]);
vF[i] = _mm256_sub_epi8(vF[i], vGe);
vE[j] = _mm256_sub_epi8(vE[j], vGe);
vAux = _mm256_sub_epi8(vCur[j], vGoe);
vF[i] = _mm256_max_epi8(vF[i], vAux);
vE[j] = _mm256_max_epi8(vE[j], vAux);
```

Fig. 3. AVX2 core instructions

```
vCur[j] = _mm512_add_epi32(vPrev[j-1], vSub);
vCur[j] = _mm512_max_epi32(vCur[j], vF[i]);
vCur[j] = _mm512_max_epi32(vCur[j], vE[j]);
vCur[j] = _mm512_max_epi32(vCur[j], vZero);
vS = _mm512_max_epi32(vS, vCur[j]);
vF[i] = _mm512_sub_epi32(vF[i], vGe);
vE[j] = _mm512_sub_epi32(vE[j], vGe);
vAux = _mm512_sub_epi32(vCur[j], vGoe);
vF[i] = _mm512_max_epi32(vF[i], vAux);
vE[j] = _mm512_max_epi32(vE[j], vAux);
```

Fig. 4. AVX-512 core instructions

extensions. On the other hand, we take advantage of the OpenMP programming model to express parallelism across multiple cores. The database sequences are dinamically distributed among the cores as soon as the threads become idle. Each alignment matrix is divided into vertical blocks and computed in a row-by-row manner (see Fig. 1). This blocking technique improves data locality reducing the number of cache misses. In addition, the inner loop is fully unrolled to increase performance.

Figures 2, 3 and 4 show the core instructions of SSE4.1, AVX2 and AVX-512 extensions, respectively. *vCur* is the block row being calculated while *vPrev* is the previous one. After computing the current block row, *vCur* and *vPrev* are swapped to process the next row. Besides, *vSub* represents the substitution scores for the database sequence residues against the query residue. *vE* and *vF* are the score vectors for alignments ending in a gap in the query and the database sequence, respectively. *vGoe* represents the vector for the sum of gap open and gap extension penalties while *vGe* is the vector for gap extension penalty. Last, *vS* keeps the current optimal alignment score.

4.2   Instruction Set and Integer Range Selection

Although almost all alignment scores can be represented using an 8-bit integer range in order to express as much SIMD parallelism as possible, there are some alignments that cannot be expressed with this integer range so a wider range should be used. In the context of KNL processors, the instructions sets supported are SSEx, AVXx and AVX-512. While SSE4.1 extensions allow the computation of 16 alignments in parallel, AVX2 instructions double this number. Saturated arithmetic operations are used in additions operations to detect overflow computation. When potential overflow is detected (i.e. the alignment score is equal to the maximum value of the integer representation employed), the alignment is recalculated using the next wider integer range. Overflow checking is performed to verify if the overflow occurred in the lower/upper half or in both halves of the score vector in order to avoid unnecessary recalculations. Unfortunately, Xeon Phi KNL processors do not include AVX-512BW subset (byte and word version of instructions in AVX-512F). This fact means that the narrowest integer range in these devices is 32 bit for AVX-512. So AVX-512 cannot compute more alignments simultaneously than SSE4.1 or AVX2. In contrast, operations for overflow detection are not required.

4.3   Substitution Scores

Our code also implements other well-known optimizations of the SW algorithm that have been proposed in previous works, such as the Query Profile (QP) [12] and Score Profile (SP) [11] optimisations:

- The QP strategy is based on creating an auxiliary two-dimensional array of size $|q| \times |\sum|$, where q is the query sequence and $\sum$ is the alphabet. Each row of this array contains the scores of the corresponding query residue against each possible residue in the alphabet. Since each thread compares the same query residue against different ones from the database, this optimization improves data locality at the cost of a negligible increment in memory requirements.
- The SP technique is based on constructing an auxiliary $n \times L \times \sum$ score array, where n is the length of the database sequence, L is the number of vector lanes and $\sum$ is the alphabet. This array contains the substitutions scores for each query-database residue combination and is constructed before matrix computation. SP reduces the number of operations in the innermost loop since its values can be gathered using a single vector load. However, because the score array must be re-built for each database sequence, its suitability must be evaluated, especially for short queries.

5   Experimental Results

5.1   Experimental Design

All tests have been performed on an Intel server running CentOS 7.2 equipped with a Xeon Phi 7250 processor 68-core 1.40 GHz (4 hw thread per core and

16 GB HBW memory) and 64 GB main memory. The processor was run in *Flat* memory mode and *Quadrant* cluster mode.

We have used Intel's ICC compiler (version 17.0.1.132) with the *-O3* optimization level by default. The experiments used to assess performance are similar to those in previous work [7,11,13,14]. We have evaluated our implementation by searching 20 query protein sequences against the well-known Environmental NR database (release 2016_11)[1]. This database comprises 1384686404 amino acid residues in 6962291 sequences (maximum length of 11944). The input queries come from the Swiss-Prot database[2] (accession numbers: P02232, P05013, P14942, P07327, P01008, P03435, P42357, P21177, Q38941, P27895, P07756, P04775, P19096, P28167, P0C6B8, P20930, P08519, Q7TMA5, P33450, and Q9UKN1), ranging in length from 144 to 5478. The scoring matrix selected was BLOSUM62, and gap insertion and extension penalties were set to 10 and 2, respectively.

5.2   Performance Results

GCUPS (billion cell updates per second) is commonly used as performance metric in the SW context and its value is calculated using the formula $\frac{|Q| \times |D|}{t \times 10^9}$, where $|Q|$ is the total number of residues in the query sequence, $|D|$ is the total number of residues in the database and t is the runtime in seconds [11].

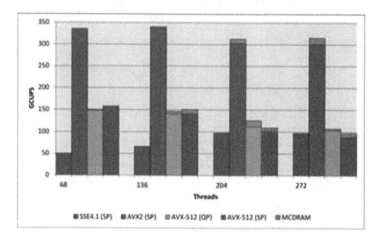

Fig. 5. Performance for the different instruction sets used varying the number of threads.

---

[1] Environmental NR: ftp://ftp.ncbi.nih.gov/blast/db/FASTA/env_nr.gz.
[2] Swiss-Prot: http://web.expasy.org/docs/swiss-prot_guideline.html.

Figure 5 shows the performance for the different instruction sets used varying the number of threads[3]. The best performances are achieved by AVX2 extensions (340.3 GCUPS) followed by AVX-512 (157.8 GCUPS) and, last, SSE4.1 (97.6 GCUPS). As mentioned before, data level exploitation is critical to achieve maximum performance in this application. Even though AVX-512 doubles vectorial width of AVX2 instructions, the lack of low-range integer operations imposes a strong limit to its performance taking into account that almost all alignment scores can be represented using 8-bit integer data. Despite the fact that the SSE4.1 version computes 16 alignments in parallel as the AVX-512 counterparts, the performance of the former is slower compared to the latter. As only one of the VPUs of each core has support for a subset of byte and word SSE instructions, codes that use these operations suffer performance losses.

In relation to the number of threads, AVX2 implementation reaches top performance using 136 threads, although performance with 68 threads is very close (just 1% slower). Similar behaviors are presented with AVX-512 and SSE4.1 intrinsics. In the AVX-512 case, performance with 68 threads is 3% higher than the corresponding to 136 threads; while SSE4.1 version is slightly better (1%) employing 204 threads compared to 272 threads.

Lastly, this figure also allows us to evaluate the performance gains obtained by HBM usage. As the entire application fits in the MCDRAM, we can get a benefit from placing all data in that memory using the *numactl* utility (without source code modification). In particular, MCDRAM exploitation achieves an average speedup of 1.04× and a maximum speedup of 1.1×.

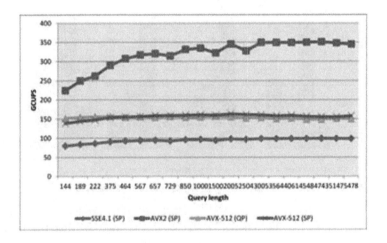

Fig. 6. Performance evolution varying query length.

---

[3] SSE4.1 and AVX2 versions using QP technique were excluded from the analysis to improve figure readability since we found that SP scheme always achieved the best performance, as in previous work [13].

Figure 6 illustrates performance evolution varying query length with the most favorable configuration for each implementation: 204, 136 and 68 threads for SSE4.1, AVX2 and AVX-512 intrinsics, respectively. Also, data is placed in MCDRAM memory. SSE4.1 and AVX-512 implementations have an almost constant performance achievement. As expected, this behavior is motivated by the exploitation of *inter-task* parallelism scheme. AVX2 version achieves an increasing performance tendency that becomes soft with larger query sequences ($m \geq 2504$). For AVX-512, the behavior of QP and SP differ, observing better performance for short sequences in QP. This aspect, also observed in previous research for the Xeon Phi KNC [8,13], is due to the additional overhead incurred by the SP construction, which does not compensate for the indexation benefits in shorter queries. As a summary, peak performances achieved are 351.2, 162.8, 157.2 and 98.9 GCUPS for AVX2, AVX-512 (SP), AVX-512 (QP) and SSE4.1 implementations.

6   Conclusions

The SW algorithm is a critical application in bioinformatics scenario and has become the base of more sophisticated alignment technologies, so its study and acceleration in different platforms has motivated a great interest for the scientific community. In this paper, we have explored SW acceleration on the last generation of Intel's Xeon Phi processors with the KNL architecture. To the best of the authors knowledge, this is the first study of this kind.

Among the main contributions of this research we can summarize:

- Exploitation of low-range integer vectors is crucial to achieve top performance in this application. Even though AVX-512 doubles vectorial width of AVX2 instructions, the latter reach the maximal performance. The lack of AVX-512BW instructions in Xeon Phi KNL processors imposes a strong limit to its performance.
- Multi-threading must be carefully evaluated. Different number of threads produced the best results for each instruction set.
- MCDRAM usage demonstrated to be an effective way to increase performance with practically null programmer intervention. In particular, it produced an average speedup of 1.04× and a maximum speedup of 1.1×.
- Peak performances are 351.2, 162.8, 157.2 and 98.9 GCUPS for AVX2, AVX-512 (SP), AVX-512 (QP) and SSE4.1 implementations.

In view of the obtained results, as future works we will consider:

- Xeon Phi KNL processors offer different cluster and memory modes. We are interested in exploring the *Flat mode* with larger genomic databases that do not fit in MCDRAM. Also, we will evaluate programming and optimization techniques in other available modes as a way to extract more performance.
- As Xeon Phi KNL processors reported competitive performance, we plan to perform a comparison with other accelerators not only from performance perspective but also from power efficiency point of view.

– Future Xeon KNL processors will include AVX-512BW set. As this characteristic enables more SIMD parallelism, we see a promising opportunity in accelerating SW database searches on these devices.

Acknowledgments. This work has been partially supported by Spanish government through research contract TIN2015-65277-R and CAPAP-H6 network (TIN2016-81840-REDT).

References

1. Asai, R.: MCDRAM as high-bandidth memory (HBM) in knights landing processors: developer's guide (2016). https://goparallel.sourceforge.net/wp-content/uploads/2016/05/Colfax_KNL_MCDRAM_Guide.pdf
2. Daily, J.: Parasail: SIMD C library for global, semi-global, and local pairwise sequence alignments. BMC Bioinform. **17**, 81 (2016)
3. Gotoh, O.: An improved algorithm for matching biological sequences. J. Mol. Biol. **162**, 705–708 (1981)
4. Isa, M., Benkrid, K., Clayton, T., Ling, C., Erdogan, A.: An FPGA-based parameterised and scalable optimal solutions for pairwise biological sequence analysis. In: 2011 NASA/ESA Conference on Adaptive Hardware and Systems (AHS), pp. 344–351, June 2011
5. Lan, H., Liu, W., Schmidt, B., Wang, B.: Accelerating large-scale biological database search on xeon phi-based neo-heterogeneous architectures. In: 2015 IEEE International Conference on Bioinformatics and Biomedicine (BIBM), pp. 503–510, November 2015
6. Li, T.I., Shum, W., Truong, K.: 160-fold acceleration of the Smith-Waterman algorithm using a field programmable gate array (FPGA). BMC Bioinform. **8**, I85 (2007)
7. Liu, Y., Wirawan, A., Schmidt, B.: CUDASW++ 3.0: accelerating Smith-Waterman protein database search by coupling CPU and GPU SIMD instructions. BMC Bioinform. **14**, 117 (2013)
8. Liu, Y., Schmidt, B.: Swaphi: Smith-waterman protein database search on xeon phi coprocessors. In: 25th IEEE International Conference on Application-Specific Systems, Architectures and Processors (ASAP 2014) (2014)
9. Mount, D.W.: Bioinformatics: Sequence and Genome Analysis. Mount Bioinformatics. Cold Spring Harbor Laboratory Press, New York (2004)
10. Reinders, J., Jeffers, J., Sodani, A.: Intel Xeon Phi Processor High Performance Programming Knights, Landing edn. Morgan Kaufmann Publishers Inc., Boston (2016)
11. Rognes, T.: Faster Smith-Waterman database searches with intersequence SIMD parallelisation. BMC Bioinform. **12**(1), 221 (2011). http://dx.doi.org/10.1186/1471-2105-12-221
12. Rognes, T., Seeberg, E.: Six-fold speed-up of Smith-Waterman sequence database searches using parallel processing on common microprocessors. Bioinformatics **16**(8), 699 (2000). http://dx.doi.org/10.1093/bioinformatics/16.8.699
13. Rucci, E., Garcia, C., Botella, G., De Giusti, A., Naiouf, M., Prieto-Matas, M.: An energy-aware performance analysis of SWIMM: Smith Waterman implementation on Intel's Multicore and Manycore architectures. Concurr. Comput. Pract. Exp. **27**(18), 5517–5537 (2015). http://dx.doi.org/10.1002/cpe.3598

14. Rucci, E., Garcia, C., Botella, G., De Giusti, A., Naiouf, M., Prieto-Matas, M.: OSWALD: OpenCL Smith-Waterman algorithm on altera FPGA for large protein databases. Int. J. High Perform. Comput. Appl. (2016). http://dx.doi.org/10.1177/1094342016654215

15. Smith, T.F., Waterman, M.S.: Identification of common molecular subsequences. J. Mol. Biol. **147**(1), 195–197 (1981)

16. Sodani, A., Gramunt, R., Corbal, J., Kim, H.S., Vinod, K., Chinthamani, S., Hutsell, S., Agarwal, R., Liu, Y.C.: Knights landing: second-generation intel xeon phi product. IEEE Micro **36**(2), 34–46 (2016)

Power-Performance Evaluation of Parallel Multi-objective EEG Feature Selection on CPU-GPU Platforms

Juan José Escobar, Julio Ortega[✉], Antonio Francisco Díaz, Jesús González, and Miguel Damas

Department of Computer Architecture and Technology, CITIC, University of Granada, Granada, Spain
{jjescobar,jortega,afdiaz,jesusgonzalez,mdamas}@ugr.es

Abstract. Heterogeneous CPU-GPU platforms include resources to benefit from different kinds of parallelism present in many data mining applications based on evolutionary algorithms that evolve solutions with time-demanding fitness evaluation. This paper describes an evolutionary parallel multi-objective feature selection procedure with subpopulations using two scheduling alternatives for evaluation of individuals according to the number of subpopulations. Evolving subpopulations usually provides good diversity properties and avoids premature convergence in evolutionary algorithms. The proposed procedure has been implemented in OpenMP to distribute dynamically either subpopulations or individuals among devices and OpenCL to evaluate the individuals taking into account the devices characteristics, providing two parallelism levels in CPU and up to three levels in GPUs. Different configurations of the proposed procedure have been evaluated and compared with a master-worker approach considering not only the runtime and achieved speedups but also the energy consumption between both scheduling models.

Keywords: Heterogeneous subpopulations scheduling · Energy-aware computing · EEG classification · Multi-objective feature selection · GPU

1 Introduction

Many data mining applications involve high-dimensional classification, clustering, feature selection and optimization problems that can take advantage of evolutionary algorithms. Although these algorithms could require big runtime in high-dimensional problems, they are amenable to be accelerated by present parallel computer architectures in several ways.

The contribution of this paper is twofold. On the one side we provide a subpopulation-based evolutionary algorithm to take advantage of parallel architectures involving multiple general-purpose superscalar multicore CPUs and GPUs for accelerating an electroencephalogram (EEG) classification problem. Precisely, EEG is a good example of the applications that can benefit from evolutionary computation as it deals with high-dimensional patterns and requires

© Springer International Publishing AG 2017
S. Ibrahim et al. (Eds.): ICA3PP 2017, LNCS 10393, pp. 580–590, 2017.
DOI: 10.1007/978-3-319-65482-9_43

feature selection techniques to remove noisy, irrelevant features or to improve the learning accuracy and result comprehensibility, especially whenever the number of features in the input patterns is higher than the number of available patterns. In our previous papers [1–3] we describe the benefits of GPUs to accelerate EEG classification for Brain Computing Interface tasks (BCI) [4], which requires solving problems with different parallelism types.

On the other side, the second contribution of the paper deals with the power-performance assessment of the here provided subpopulation-based evolutionary algorithm in comparison with a master-worker parallel implementation. Energy-saving has become an important issue in computer science and engineering for economic and environmental reasons and should be considered at par with decreasing the program running times. To the best of our knowledge, there is not any paper that compares different implementations of parallel evolutionary algorithms according to their energy consumption. For example, paper [5] deals more with the analysis of the energy consumption in different platforms of a sequential evolutionary procedure.

After this introduction, Sect. 2 describes the problem of feature selection by evolutionary multi-objective optimization and summarizes both alternatives to implement parallel evolutionary algorithms in heterogeneous CPU-GPU architectures. Section 3 gives the details of our proposed codes to implement a subpopulation-based parallel evolutionary procedure for multi-objective feature selection. Then, Sect. 4 describes and analyses the experimental results and finally, Sect. 5 summarizes the conclusions.

2 Multi-objective Feature Selection on CPU-GPU Platforms

The application here considered deals with feature selection in classification problems involving patterns with high number of features and curse of dimensionality problems. In [1], Fig. 1 describes our multi-objective approach to feature selection in unsupervised classification of EEG patterns, which can be used in data mining applications [6,7], and its benefits in both supervised and unsupervised classification have been reported elsewhere [8]. A multi-objective evolutionary procedure, in our case the well-known NSGA-II algorithm [9], evolves subpopulations of individuals that codify different feature selections.

Given a feature selection (an individual in the subpopulation), the N_P patterns included in the database, DS, will be the set of training patterns by choosing the components corresponding to the number of selected features, N_F. This way, the K-means algorithm has been applied to the N_P patterns $P_i = (p_i^1, ..., p_i^{N_F})(i = 1, ..., N_P)$ to determine the centroids $K^t(j)(j = 1, .., W)$ of the W possible clusters (W is known in our EEG classification problem, and it is equal to the number of classes). Once the clusters are built by including each pattern in its nearest centroid, the fitness of each individual in the subpopulation is evaluated by using two Clustering Validation Indices (CVIs), defined by the intraclass f_1 and the interclass f_2 distances (details given in [3]). In our codes, the evaluation of the fitness function for each individual requires between 97.36% (with 30,000 individuals) and 99.93% (for 120 individuals) of runtime.

As GPU architectures constitute the present mainstream approach to take advantage of technology improvements, their use has been described in many previous papers on parallel metaheuristics and evolutionary computation [10]. The vast majority of papers on parallel implementations of evolutionary algorithms involving CPU-GPU heterogeneous architectures deals with the acceleration rates attained by the GPUs with respect to a base parallel or even sequential implementation that only use CPU cores. As it is indicated in [11], the most direct alternative to use a GPU is to evaluate the fitness of a given individual in the subpopulation taking advantage of the data parallelism that could be present in the fitness function to be computed. The speedups achieved by this approach depend on the matching between the data parallelism of the fitness function and the characteristics of the GPU architecture and also on the time required by the data transference between the GPU and the host GPU through a bus with a limited bandwidth. The alternative of complete GPU implementation of the evolutionary algorithm [12–14] could alleviate these problems. Nevertheless, these approaches have to take into account the memory requirements of the application, as not only the individuals of the subpopulation but also the whole datasets required to compute their fitness should be located in the GPU memory.

An alternative GPU implementation of the non-dominance rank used in NSGA-II, the Archived-based Stochastic Ranking Evolutionary Algorithm (ASREA) is provided in [15]. Nevertheless, works analysing the effect in the parallel performances of heavy fitness functions requiring high-volume datasets and the parallelization on a heterogeneous platform of a whole data mining application with similar characteristics to our target application are less frequent.

In our previous papers [1–3] we propose a multi-objective feature selection scheme that implements both functional and data parallelism and can be executed either in a GPU or in multiple CPU superscalar cores. The first version of our GPU code provided in [1] has been improved by coalescing of memory accesses and minimization of memory bank conflicts optimization [2]. The relevance of taking into account the memory access patterns of the algorithms and a more detailed analysis of the use of resources to extract the data parallelism available in the codes are shown in [3]. Here we propose a subpopulation-based approach in addition to implementing two dynamic distributions of workload among the CPU and GPU according to the number of subpopulations used. The different alternatives of the procedure have been evaluated not only by the runtime but also by considering the energy consumptions.

3 A Subpopulation-Based OpenMP-OpenCL Parallel Code

In this section, we describe a new parallel multi-objective evolutionary procedure, implemented in OpenMP and OpenCL, that dynamically distributes subpopulations of individuals among both the GPU and the CPU cores. In our platform, the GPU plays the role of a coprocessor connected, through a bus, to a host including multiple superscalar CPU cores that share the main memory. In OpenCL terms, the basic computing cores of the GPU are the so-called *work-items*. Several work-items along with multiple instruction units and a register file comprise a *Streaming Multiprocessor* (SMX). A GPU can include multiple SMXs, allowing simultaneous executions of the same program on different data, i.e. Single Program Multiple Data (SPMD) model. The threads are organized within thread blocks and all threads in a block are assigned to a single SMX.

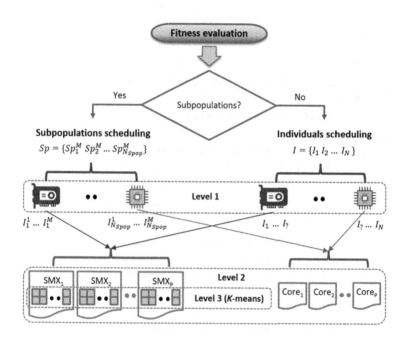

Fig. 1. Two dynamic scheduling alternatives for evaluation of individuals. The procedure schedules individuals when only one subpopulation is detected or subpopulations otherwise. Two parallelism levels can be achieved in a CPU and up to three in a GPU

Algorithm 1 describes our parallel multi-objective evolutionary algorithm based on subpopulations, named **D2S_NSGAII** (Dynamic Distribution of Subpopulations using NSGA-II), corresponding to the "*Yes*" decision shown in Fig. 1.

As many CPU threads as available OpenCL devices, N_D, are created through the corresponding OpenMP pragma to parallelise the loop which iterates over all subpopulations (lines 3–15 of Algorithm 1). This way, the subpopulations are dynamically allocated to one of these CPU threads, which implements the evolutionary operators (crossover in line 5, replacement in lines 11–13 and the migration in line 16) while the evaluation of the individuals of the corresponding subpopulation are executed either on a CPU thread (call `evaluationsCPU` in line 7) or on GPU (call `evaluationsGPU` in line 9). A migration implies to

---

Algorithm 1. Subpopulations scheduler pseudocode. The evaluation of subpopulations is distributed among all OpenCL devices, where each of them is assigned to one OpenMP thread

---

1 **Function** D2S_NSGAII($Sp, N_D, D, N_{Spop}, M, DS, K, DS^t$)

> **Input** : The initial subpopulations, $Sp_i; \forall i = 1, ..., N_{Spop}$
> **Input** : Number of available OpenCL devices, N_D
> **Input** : Object D_j containing the OpenCL devices, $\forall j = 1, ..., N_D$
> **Input** : Number of subpopulations N_{Spop} to be evolved
> **Input** : Number of individuals in each subpopulation, M
> **Input** : Dataset DS: N_P training patterns of N_F features
> **Input** : Set K of W centroids randomly chosen from DS
> **Input** : Dataset DS^t is DS in column-major order
> **Output:** S, the new solution for the problem

2   **repeat**

> // OpenMP parallel section with N_D devices
3   **repeat**

> // Start the evolution process
4   **repeat**

5   $Offspr \leftarrow$ UniformCrossover(Sp_i)
6   **if** D_j is a CPU **then**
7 | $Offspr \leftarrow$ evaluationsCPU($Offspr, M, DS, K$)
8   **else**
9 | $Offspr \leftarrow$ evaluationsGPU($Offspr, M, DS, K, DS^t$)
10 **end**

> // Replacement process
11 $Aux \leftarrow$ Join Sp_i and $Offspr$ in one array
12 $Aux \leftarrow$ nonDominatedSorting($Aux, M + N_{Offspr}$)
13 $Sp_i \leftarrow$ Copy the first M individuals from Aux

14 **until** the number of subpopulations generations is reached;

15 **until** all N_{Spop} subpopulations are evaluated;

16 $Sp \leftarrow$ migration(Sp, N_{Spop}, M)

17 **until** the number of desired migrations is reached;

> // Recombination process
18 $Sp \leftarrow$ nonDominatedSorting($Sp, N_{Spop} \times M$)
19 $S \leftarrow$ Copy the first M individuals from Sp

20 **return** S
21 **End**

---

build a new set of subpopulations. To define a new subpopulation the given set of solutions in the subpopulation receives solutions from the rest of subpopulations. More specifically, each subpopulation contributes with half of its solutions in its present Pareto front at most. Finally, the solutions obtained by the different subpopulations are recombined by the main CPU thread (lines 18–19) and returned at the end of the function (line 20). Algorithm 1 is repeated according to the required number of subpopulation generations and migrations.

4 Experimental Results

In this section, we analyse the performance of our OpenMP-OpenCL codes running on Linux CentOS 6.7 operating system, in a node with 32 GB of DDR3 memory and two Intel Xeon E5-2620 v4 processors at 2.1 GHz including eight cores per socket with Hyper-Threading, thus comprising 32 threads. The node also has a Tesla K40m with 12 GB of global memory, 288 GB/s as maximum memory bandwidth and 2880 CUDA cores at 745 MHz, distributed into 15 SMXs, thus including 192 cores per SMX. In our experiments, we have used three dataset from the BCI Laboratory at the University of Essex and described in [16]. They correspond to subjects coded as 104, 107 and 110, and each include 178 EEG patterns with 3600 features per patterns.

The implemented NSGA-II algorithm uses uniform crossover with a probability of 0.75, a mutation by inversion of the selected bit with probability of 0.025, and selection by binary tournament. The hyper volumes are obtained with (1,1) as reference point, and the minimum values of the cost functions f_1 and f_2 are respectively 0 and −1. Thus, the maximum value for the hypervolume is 2. Due to space limitations, in this paper we do not provide an analysis of the influence of the procedure characteristics in the hypervolume results. However, we have observed that the different procedures provide good enough solutions included in Pareto fronts with average hyper volumes between 1.89 and 1.97 and standard deviations among 0.001 and 0.01. Although our subpopulation algorithms are not equivalent to the sequential evolutionary algorithms with only population, they provide similar hypervolume results to those obtained by the base algorithm with one subpopulation.

Figure 2 provides the averages of the speedups obtained for the dataset of subject 110 by different platform configurations with 32 CPU threads and/or 15 GPU SMXs. The speedup characteristics for subjects 104 and 107 are similar to those shown in Fig. 2. In the Figs. 2a, b and c, populations of 480 individuals are used distributed into 2, 4, 8 and 16 subpopulations of, respectively, 240, 120, 60 and 30 individuals. Each subpopulation independently executes generations among migrations. In addition, Fig. 2 shows results for 1 to 5 migrations and, as all algorithms execute 60 generations, respectively 60, 30, 20, 15 and 12 generations of independent evolutions are executed by each subpopulation between migrations and also show improvements in the speedups as the number of individuals in the subpopulations increases, or the number of subpopulations decreases (is the same, as the number of individuals in the population is the same in all cases, i.e. 480). With respect to changes in the number of migrations, the speedups remain approximately constant. It has to be taken into account that a migration implies to send individuals and cost functions among subpopulations and thus, its cost increases with the number of individuals in the population and the number of subpopulations. Nevertheless, the communications are indeed

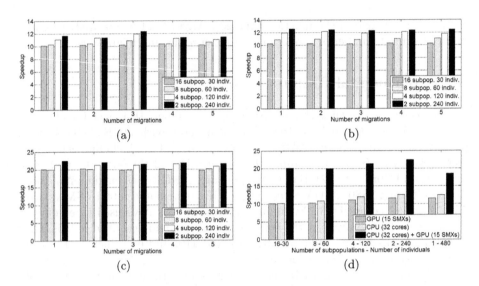

Fig. 2. Averages of speedups achieved with different platform configurations and subpopulations: (a) GPU (15 SMXs); (b) CPU (32 cores); (c) CPU + GPU; (d) Comparison of platforms for different subpopulations and individuals per subpopulation

done through the shared memory that stores the information about individuals and their fitness and their costs should not be more costly that the replacement process (lines 11–13 in Algorithm 1). The main changes shown in the speedups of Figs. 2a, b and c seems to be determined by the number of subpopulations and their size (as more subpopulations means less individuals per subpopulation). As the number of subpopulations grows, the number of calls to the GPU or CPU kernels that allocates a subpopulation to the corresponding device also grows. Moreover, as the device then distributes the individuals in the subpopulation among the corresponding GPU or CPU cores, as less individuals are included in the subpopulation more unbalanced workloads are possible.

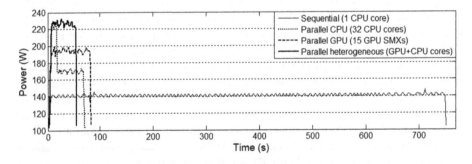

Fig. 3. Power measured along the execution of 600 generations. Four execution modes with 480 individuals, 2 subpopulations and subject 110

By comparing Figs. 2a, b and c is apparent that the speedups obtained by using only the 32 CPU cores are quite similar to those obtained by the 15 SMXs of the GPU. The two levels of parallelism provided by the GPU to accelerate the fitness computation make possible this similar performance even with respect to a much higher number of CPU cores. The effect of using both GPU and CPU cores is shown in Figs. 2c and d. As Fig. 2d shows, the speedup grows as the number of subpopulations decreases except for using only one subpopulation. In this case, the CPU kernel and the GPU kernel respectively take 32 and 15 individuals and thus, among 15 ($480/32 = 15$) and 32 ($480/15 = 32$) calls to the CPU or GPU kernels are required. Consequently, the number of calls is higher in the case of one subpopulation than in the case of multiple subpopulations.

Figure 3 provides the evolution of the instantaneous power consumed along the execution of our procedure, in four different situations: the sequential version in only one CPU core, and a parallel version with a population of 480 individuals and 2 subpopulations (240 individuals per subpopulation) executed only by the 32 CPU cores of the platform, only by the 15 SMX of the GPU, or by using both GPU and CPU cores. The power (and the energy) consumption in each node

Table 1. Running times and energy-aware measures in different computation modes, multiple number of subpopulations N_{Spop} and M individuals per subpopulation

N_{Spop}	M	Mode	Time (s)	$E(W \times h)$	% Sequential time	% Sequential energy
1	480	Seq	83.08	0.8	-	-
		Tesla	7.52	0.36	9.07	**45.66**
		Xeon	6.55	0.46	7.89	56.21
		He	4.97	0.41	**5.99**	50.34
2	240	Seq	89.36	0.91	-	-
		Tesla	7.64	0.37	8.56	40.88
		Xeon	6.53	0.42	7.31	45.88
		He	4.12	0.34	**4.62**	**40.26**
4	120	Seq	83.13	0.85	-	-
		Tesla	7.92	0.38	9.53	46.14
		Xeon	6.86	0.42	8.25	49.61
		He	4.19	0.34	**5.04**	**39.93**
8	60	Seq	82.85	0.86	-	-
		Tesla	8.51	0.42	10.27	48.74
		Xeon	7.42	0.41	8.96	47.76
		Het	4.58	0.36	**5.53**	**42.62**
16	30	Seq	79.61	0.84	-	-
		Tesla	8.59	0.43	10.78	51.74
		Xeon	8.12	0.44	10.2	52.8
		Het	4.45	0.37	**5.58**	**44.44**

has been measured by using a data acquisition system we have devised, based on *Arduino Mega*, which gives four real-time measures per second and per node of power and energy consumption. Figure 3 clearly shows the beginning and the end of each alternative. It is also clear that the highest power consumption corresponds to the "CPU+CPU" configuration, followed by the configurations including only GPU SMXs and only CPU cores. The sequential alternative presents the lowest power consumptions. Nevertheless, the energy consumption depends on the time required to complete the task, as Table 1 shows. This table provides, for different number of subpopulations and configurations and 60 generations, the running time and the energy consumed along with the percentage of running time and energy consumed by each parallel configuration, with respect to those values of the sequential execution. The energy that the node would consume in *idle* mode is not included. As can be seen, except for the case of using only one subpopulation, the best results on energy consumption correspond to the heterogeneous configuration involving CPU and GPU cores. Although the instantaneous power consumed is higher, the achieved speedup allows better consumption figures. It has to be noticed that the energy measures corresponds to the whole node including the energy consumption of buses and memories. Nevertheless, differences are still apparent for different parallel alternatives.

5   Conclusions

This paper proposes and analyses a parallel heterogeneous implementation of a multi-objective feature selection procedure based on subpopulations that takes advantage of both superscalar multicore CPU and GPU architectures. It starts OpenMP threads corresponding to the devices in the platform. Each of these threads distributes the fitness evaluation of the individuals (through a K-means algorithm) in each subpopulation either to GPU SMXs or to CPU cores by launching the corresponding OpenCL kernel (CPU or GPU [2]).

The experimental evaluation has been done in terms of speedup and energy consumption for different alternatives of subpopulations, migrations, and platform configurations. It has been shown that the heterogeneous configuration, including GPU and CPU cores, provides not only better speedups results but also lower energy consumption. Compared with a master-worker parallel implementation without subpopulations (the alternative using only one subpopulation) the heterogeneous "CPU+GPU" configuration still provides the highest speedups, although the GPU configuration provides the lowest energy consumption.

Among the alternatives that should be also explored to take advantage of both superscalar CPU and GPU cores available in present platforms, a message-passing implementation of co evolutionary subpopulations could offer new insights about the possibilities of heterogeneous parallel architectures to tackle machine learning and data mining applications that demand a high amount of heterogeneous parallelism.

Acknowledgements. Work funded by project TIN2015-67020-P (Spanish "Ministerio de Economía y Competitividad" and ERDF funds). We would also like to thank the BCI laboratory of the University of Essex, and especially prof. John Q. Gan, for allowing us to use their databases.

References

1. Escobar, J.J., Ortega, J., González, J., Damas, M.: Assessing parallel heterogeneous computer architectures for multiobjective feature selection on EEG classification. In: Ortuño, F., Rojas, I. (eds.) IWBBIO 2016. LNCS, vol. 9656, pp. 277–289. Springer, Cham (2016). doi:10.1007/978-3-319-31744-1_25
2. Escobar, J., Ortega, J., González, J., Damas, M.: Improving memory accesses for heterogeneous parallel multi-objective feature selection on EEG classification. In: Proceedings of the 4th International Workshop on Parallelism in Bioinformatics, PBIO 2016, pp. 372–383. Springer, Grenoble, August 2016
3. Escobar, J., Ortega, J., González, J., Damas, M., Prieto, B.: Issues on GPU parallel implementation of evolutionary high-dimensional multi-objective feature selection. In: Proceedings of the 20th European Conference on Applications of Evolutionary Computation, Part I, EVOSTAR 2017, pp. 773–788. Springer, Amsterdam, April 2017
4. Rupp, R., Kleih, S., Leeb, R., Millan, J., Kübler, A., Müller-Putz, G.: Brain-computer interfaces and assistive technology. In: Grübler, G., Hildt, E. (eds.) Brain-Computer-Interfaces in their Ethical, Social and Cultural Contexts. The International Library of Ethics, Law and Technology, pp. 7–38. Springer, Heidelberg (2014)
5. Vega, F.F., Chávez, F., Díaz, J., García, J.A., Castillo, P.A., Merelo, J.J., Cotta, C.: A cross-platform assessment of energy consumption in evolutionary algorithms. In: Handl, J., Hart, E., Lewis, P.R., López-Ibáñez, M., Ochoa, G., Paechter, B. (eds.) PPSN 2016. LNCS, vol. 9921, pp. 548–557. Springer, Cham (2016). doi:10.1007/978-3-319-45823-6_51
6. Mukhopadhyay, A., Maulik, U., Bandyopadhyay, S., Coello Coello, C.: A survey of multiobjective evolutionary algorithms for data mining: Part I. IEEE Trans. Evol. Comput. **18**(1), 4–19 (2014)
7. Mukhopadhyay, A., Maulik, U., Bandyopadhyay, S., Coello Coello, C.: A survey of multiobjective evolutionary algorithms for data mining: Part II. IEEE Trans. Evol. Comput. **18**(1), 20–35 (2014)
8. Handl, J., Knowles, J.: Feature subset selection in unsupervised learning via multiobjective optimization. Int. J. Comput. Intell. Res. **2**(3), 217–238 (2006)
9. Deb, K., Agrawal, S., Pratap, A., Meyarivan, T.: A Fast Elitist Non-dominated Sorting Genetic Algorithm for Multi-objective Optimization: NSGA-II. In: Schoenauer, M., Deb, K., Rudolph, G., Yao, X., Lutton, E., Merelo, J.J., Schwefel, H.-P. (eds.) PPSN 2000. LNCS, vol. 1917, pp. 849–858. Springer, Heidelberg (2000). doi:10.1007/3-540-45356-3_83
10. Collet, P.: Why GPGPUS for evolutionary computation? In: Tsutsui, S., Collet, P. (eds.) Massively Parallel Evolutionary Computation on GPGPUs. Natural Computing Series, pp. 3–14. Springer, Heidelberg (2013)
11. Jähne, P.: Overview of the current state of research on parallelisation of evolutionary algorithms on graphic cards. In: GI-Jahrestagung, INFORMATIK 2016, LNI, Bonn, Germany, pp. 2163–2174, September 2016
12. Luong, T., Melab, N., Talbi, E.G.: GPU-based island model for evolutionary algorithms. In: Proceedings of the 12th Annual Conference on Genetic and Evolutionary Computation, GECCO 2010, pp. 1089–1096. ACM, Portland, July 2010

13. Pospichal, P., Jaros, J., Schwarz, J.: Parallel genetic algorithm on the CUDA archi-tecture. In: Chio, C., Cagnoni, S., Cotta, C., Ebner, M., Ekárt, A., Esparcia-Alcazar, A.I., Goh, C.-K., Merelo, J.J., Neri, F., Preuß, M., Togelius, J., Yan-nakakis, G.N. (eds.) EvoApplications 2010. LNCS, vol. 6024, pp. 442–451. Springer, Heidelberg (2010). doi:10.1007/978-3-642-12239-2_46

14. Wong, M., Cui, G.: Data mining using parallel multi-objective evolutionary algo-rithms on graphics processing units. In: Tsutsui, S., Collet, P. (eds.) Massively Parallel Evolutionary Computation on GPGPUs. Natural Computing Series, pp. 287–307. Springer, Heidelberg (2013)

15. Sharma, D., Collet, P.: Implementation techniques for massively parallel multi-objective optimization. In: Tsutsui, S., Collet, P. (eds.) Massively Parallel Evo-lutionary Computation on GPGPUs. Natural Computing Series, pp. 267–286. Springer, Heidelberg (2013)

16. Asensio-Cubero, J., Gan, J., Palaniappan, R.: Multiresolution analysis over simple graphs for brain computer interfaces. J. Neural Eng. 10(4), 046014 (2013)

Using Spark and GraphX to Parallelize Large-Scale Simulations of Bacterial Populations over Host Contact Networks

Andreia Sofia Teixeira[1,2(✉)], Pedro T. Monteiro[1,2], João A. Carriço[3], Francisco C. Santos[1,2], and Alexandre P. Francisco[1,2]

[1] INESC-ID Lisboa, Lisboa, Portugal
[2] Instituto Superior Técnico, Universidade de Lisboa, Lisboa, Portugal
sofia.teixeira@tecnico.ulisboa.pt
[3] Faculdade de Medicina, Instituto de Microbiologia
and Instituto de Medicina Molecular, Universidade de Lisboa, Lisboa, Portugal

Abstract. Large-scale population genetics studies are fundamental for phylogenetic and epidemiology analysis of pathogens. And the validation of both evolutionary models and methods used in such studies depend on large data analysis. It is, however, unrealistic to work with large datasets as only rather small samples of the real pathogen population are available. On the other hand, given model complexity and required population sizes, large-scale simulations are the only way to address this issue. In this paper we study how to efficiently parallelize such extensive simulations on top of Apache Spark, making use of both the MapReduce programming model and the GraphX API. We propose a simulation framework for large bacterial populations, over host contact networks, implementing the Wright-Fisher model. The experimental evaluation shows that we can effectively speedup simulations. We also evaluate inherent parallelism limits, drawing conclusions on the relation between cluster computing power and simulations speedup.

Keywords: Population genetics · Large-scale simulations · Graph-parallel computations · Spark · GraphX

1 Introduction

Understanding bacterial population genetics is vital for interpreting the response of bacterial populations to selection pressures, as antibiotic treatment or vaccines targeted at only a subset of strains [15]. In this context, large-scale studies are fundamental not only for such understanding, but also for validating both models and methods, such as phylogenetic inference algorithms. But we cannot validate them with real pathogen populations as only rather small population samples are available and accessible. Hence, given model complexity and required population sizes, large-scale simulations are the only way to address this issue.

© Springer International Publishing AG 2017
S. Ibrahim et al. (Eds.): ICA3PP 2017, LNCS 10393, pp. 591–600, 2017.
DOI: 10.1007/978-3-319-65482-9_44

Previous studies have shown that observed population genetic structure of several important human pathogens, such as *Streptococcus pneumoniae* and *Neisseria meningitidis*, can be explained using a simple evolutionary model [6–9]. This model is based on neutral mutational drift and modulated by recombination, but incorporating the impact of epidemic transmission only for panmictic populations. Although this simple evolutionary model works well for local populations, at a "microepidemic" level, its predictions no longer seem to fit observed genetic relationships of large and widely distributed bacterial populations. With the increasing volume of data obtained with sequence based typing methods, namely by Multi-Locus Sequence Typing (MLST) [12], currently the gold standard for epidemiological surveillance, a much more complex pattern emerges, that cannot be explained solely by the simple "microepidemic" assumption.

The evolution of transmissible bacteria occurs by mutation and recombination, and is influenced by epidemiological as well as molecular processes. These aspects are fundamental in the process of strain diversification [16], and as a mechanism by which strains acquire virulence factors or resistance determinants [13]. On the other hand, bacterial population evolution is also influenced by the environment and by host contact networks, through which bacterial populations spread. The study of the impact of host contact network topologies, and associated transmission ratios, on bacterial population evolution and genetic diversity becomes then relevant, increasing the model complexity.

Large-scale simulations are, however, computationally demanding, in particular when model complexity increases. In this work, considering an extension of the above simple evolutionary model by incorporating the underlying host contact network, we propose a simulation framework for large bacterial populations, implementing the Wright-Fisher model [17], on top of Apache Spark [21] and making use of both MapReduce programming model and GraphX API [19]. Then we discuss how such large simulations can benefit from parallelization. We conducted several experiments on Google Cloud Platform and results show that we can effectively speedup simulations. We also evaluate inherent parallelism limits, drawing conclusions on the relation between cluster computing power and simulations speedup.

The paper is organized as follows. We describe the simulation and computational models in Sect. 2. Implementations details are discussed in Sect. 3. Finally, we present and discuss experimental evaluation results in Sect. 4.

2   Simulation and Computational Models

The simulation framework proposed in this paper allows us to observe the evolution of a bacterial population through a host contact network, while parametrizing different simulation aspects. We focus on bacterial population genetics where isolates are represented as MLST profiles. MLST is a technique in which DNA sequences are obtained for a set of housekeeping loci, and different sequences at each locus are assigned as different alleles [12]. From an abstract point of view, each isolate/pathogen is just characterized through a profile that may be subject to transformations along time, under the influence of genetic events, environment and host contact networks.

Let each strain in a bacterial population be then characterized by a MLST profile, where each sequence type (ST), or MLST profile, is defined by the combination of its alleles, a vector of labels, where different labels mean different alleles. Given an underlying host contact network, we simulate a bacterial population at each host, or vertex, with a neutral evolutionary model [5]. This model is based on a previous null model for evolutionary change, the neutral infinite alleles model (IAM) [10]. Under IAM, mutation always generates a new allele, leading to new STs. Recombination, on the other hand, introduces an existing allele randomly selected from the isolates present in the previous generation, which may lead to novel allelic profiles, or to the reappearance of existing ones. Mutation or recombination occur independently, with each event being rare and mutation taking precedence over recombination. When a new ST is produced, it is given a new ST number, and the parental ST is recorded. For recombination, the allele donor is also recorded.

We assume non-overlapping generations and, at each step of evolution, a new generation is obtained. The probability of an ST to occur in the next generation is proportional to its frequency in the current generation after migration among hosts. The interactions between hosts, over the network, takes place by allowing pathogens to migrate from one vertex to another accordingly to some frequency and edge transmission probabilities, defined by the user, followed by selection at each host through sampling with replacement from the current host generation.

The model just described, based on the IAM, is also known as the Wright-Fisher model [17]. Neutral evolution means that all individuals have the same fitness. Fitness, in population genetics, is a measure of the expected number of offspring. In the neutral Wright-Fisher model, equal fitness is implemented by equal probabilities for all individuals to be picked as a parent.

We rely on Apache Spark [21] and GraphX [19] to parallelize our simulations. Apache Spark came up with an extended MapReduce model that enables the creation of iterative programs, maintaining the scalability and fault tolerance of MapReduce, through its Resilient Distributed Datasets (RDD) [20]. MapReduce [11] is a high-level programming model originally proposed by Google [4] and it was designed to address embarrassingly parallel data processing problems using cheap commodity hardware. Apache Hadoop is probably the best well known MapReduce open source implementation, on top of which Apache Spark is built. Apache Spark provides new levels of abstraction exceeding some limitations of Apache Hadoop and a high-level API, usable through several programming languages such as Scala, Java or Python. It provides also the GraphX API [19] to address graph-parallel problems, relying also on RDDs. We will rely on both the MapReduce programming model and the GraphX API.

The MapReduce programming model has two main steps: map and reduce. The map phase processes the input as key-value pairs and applies a user defined function to each one, generating a set of intermediate key-value pairs. The reduce phase takes those intermediate key-value pairs, aggregate them by key and then apply a user defined function to the values, merging them, and generating new key-value pairs.

When thinking about applying the MapReduce programming model for solving a problem, since many mappers and reducers run in parallel, and the distributed file system is a shared global resource, special care must be taken to ensure that such operations avoid synchronization conflicts. It is then important to analyze some basic requirements. Taking a careful look into the model described above, we observe that the problem is composed by two main tasks: (1) the evolution of each population at each node where mutation and recombination take place, and (2) the exchanges between nodes and the replacement of each population taking into account the samples of the populations from the neighbourhoods.

Even with each node having its own population, and hence being able to evolve independently from one another, one must take into consideration the fact that each mutation requires the creation of a new allele, because of the IAM, demanding a unique global identifier. Thus, for the first task we find two challenges: (a) mutation process assumes that there is a central memory/database for generating/requesting new alleles; (b) recombination demands that the populations of each node must be in the same memory space—if we are to recombine an allele we must choose, randomly, other ST to provide an already existing allele, i.e., to be its parent. To avoid implementing a shared database, one solution is modifying how a new allele is generated and identified. If we guarantee that at each mutation a new allele is created and the individual gets a unique identifier, then we can have different populations evolving at the same time in independent nodes. For solving both (a) and (b) problems, we had to create a new way to identify uniquely each ST and also to make sure that after the first mapping task we group each population at the same memory space, at the cost of losing some efficiency of the MapReduce model.

For the second task, each node just has to receive a sample of the current population of its neighbours, mix with its own population, and create a new population through sampling. Besides being a simple problem when thinking about the MapReduce model, we can identify some similarities between this process and PageRank [14] or Label Propagation [22] problems. Both rely on exchanging information among neighbours to update their state, and both have already been implemented using MapReduce and, in particular, making use of GraphX. Hence we will use GraphX and a similar approach for this second task.

3   Implementation

Let $G = (V, E)$ be a connected and weighted graph, with $n = |V|$ vertices and $m = |E|$ edges, and with an edge transmission probability function $w : E \rightarrow \mathbb{R}$. Let t be the number of times that the sequence of number of evolutions followed by the number of exchanges happens.

The simulator takes eight parameters: (1) the population size of each node; (2) the file containing the populations; (3) the file containing the network;

(4) mutation rate; (5) recombination rate; (6) number of evolutions; (7) number of exchanges; (8) number of times for the cycle (6) followed by (7) to happen; (9) frequency of writing on disk. Each iteration of evolution is considered one generation.

The general workflow consists in iterating t times the following two steps: (i) perform the sequence of evolutions for each population, and (ii) perform the sequence of exchanges between nodes.

The interaction between host populations is as follows: each host copies a given proportion of its population, corresponding to the edge transmission probability $w(u, v)$, and sends it to each corresponding neighbour; each host receives the amount of population sent by the neighbours and create a pool with those bacteria mixed with its own population; a new population is built, with the same size as the previous one, but the individuals are chosen randomly from the pool.

3.1   Using MapReduce with Spark and GraphX

Adapting an algorithm into a MapReduce programming model implies some modifications in the way the input is processed and how the data is managed through the *Map* and *Reduce* phases. Frameworks based on this model, as Hadoop or Apache Spark, read the input from a file in HDFS, where each line is a pair ⟨*key, value*⟩.

We rely on Apache Spark not only because of its flexibility and easiness of use, but also because RDDs allow to develop iterative programs in a light manner. These RDDs are fault-tolerant, parallel data structures that make it possible to persist intermediate results in memory, manage how they are partitioned to optimize data placement among workers, and provide a rich set of operators to apply on data processing. Apache Spark has also an embedded API, the GraphX API, that allows the user to work with graphs in a transparent manner. With GraphX, graph-parallel and data-parallel computations are possible with a single composable API. Graphs can be viewed as collections (RDDs) without data duplication and one can attribute properties to the vertices or edges through the PropertyGraph. It also allows to access vertices, edges, or both (triplets) separately.

Let us not discuss how the two main tasks defined before can be parallelized. The first input file contains the bacterial population of all the host contact network. This file has an individual per line in which the *key* corresponds to a vertex identifier to which it belongs, and the *value* corresponds to the sequence of its alleles, and also a global unique identifier. This global unique identifier is needed to guarantee that, at each mutation event, a completely new individual is generated, as demanded in IAM. We must also modify the characterization of each allele. Although in traditional MLST data we have an array of integers, in our approach each individual is characterized by an array of strings in the form $X.Y.Z$ where X is the id of the node where the mutation occurs, Y is the generation id, and Z is the individual unique identifier. With this change we guarantee the requirements of the IAM regarding allele uniqueness on mutation events. The second input file is the network file. This file contains an edge list

Listing 1.1. Evolutionary process.

```
val nextpop = populationRDD.map{ i =>
    val idpop = i._1
    val population = i._2
    for (each indidivual in population){
        //Recombintation | //Mutation
        population.update(i, individual)}
    (idpop, population)}
populationRDD = nextpop
```

with the transmission probabilities: source, destination and the probability of transmission $w(source, destination)$. If the network is undirected the edge list must contain edges in both directions. Another requirement is that each node must have an edge to itself with a probability of transmission 1.0. The reason is explained later on. We load the input files with the *SparkContext.textFile* method, which maps the inputs into RDDs. With this method we are able to explicitly define how data should be partitioned.

Evolutions in each population and exchanges between the nodes can be implemented as independent *Map* and *Reduce* tasks as follows. For the evolution process, after loading the input into an RDD, we use the $(groupByKey)$ transformation to guarantee that each population is in the same memory space. As explained before, recombination demands elements from the same population to recombine. This transformation, when called on a dataset of (K, V) pairs, returns a dataset of $(K, Iterable\langle V \rangle)$ pairs. With this we have each population gathered in the same data structure. This is the major drawback of approach, we can not have each individual evolving independently and *groupByKey* uses shuffle operations that have some costs. After this, the approach is straightforward. Having the populations RDD, we do the *Map* transformation to make each population evolve in parallel (Listing 1.1).

In what concerns the exchange process we have an explicit notion of graph structure. For the nodes (populations) to communicate with their neighbours we use the GraphX API. By making use of the GraphX API and its PropertyGraph, we can use both the populations RDDs and the network (edge list) RDD to create the graph.

After the PropertyGraph is created, we use the *triplets* view to access all *EdgeTriplet*$[V, E]$ that contain information about the source and destination vertices, with their properties (populations), and also information about the edge and its property (transmission probability). With this we have all the information needed to generate the samples from each source node to each destination node. Regarding the fact that each node must have an edge to itself with a probability of 1.0 associated, this is necessary for the *reduceByKey* operation. After the samples are generated and emitted, the *reduceByKey* function is applied on the values with the concatenation operator $(++)$ that joins all the collections with the same key, providing a collection with all the elements to be sampled for the

Listing 1.2. Exchanging process.

```
val result = graphpopulation.triplets.map{ t =>
    //generate a collection with the proportion
    //of population to send
    (dest, fractionofpopulation)
}.reduceByKey(_ ++ _).map{ i =>
    //create the new populations by sampling
    (key, newpopulation)}
```

new population: its own population and the samples sent from the connected populations. Each new population is then generated through sampling with a *Map* transformation (Listing 1.2).

4   Results and Discussion

Apache Spark can run either in local mode or in a cluster. We relied on both for our experiments to compare how running time scales, parametrizing simulations with different population sizes and different graphs. Experiments were conducted in a cluster hosted at Google Cloud Platform[1], configured with different number of workers: 2, 4, 8 and 16. Each worker is an Intel(R) Xeon(R) CPU @ 2.50 GHz with 4 cores and 16 GB of RAM, where only 2 cores were usable by Apapche Spark. To achieve the best results possible, in each experiment we partitioned the input in as many partitions as the number of the cores available. The local setup is equivalent to a worker node.

Given the evolution model coupled with a host contact network, leading to both evolutions and interactions between populations, the operations in local mode, with each step being executed sequentially, take considerable time. And it scales reasonably well when in cluster mode. For a precise comparison, in what concerns time scale, we fixed almost all parameters of the simulator: the size of the population per node is 1000; the mutation rate is 0.001; the recombination rate is 0.01; the number of evolutions per time step is 25; the number of exchanges per time step is 1; the number of time steps is 10; the frequency for writing on disk is 10 generations; and the transmission probability is 0.01. This means that each dataset will evolve in a cycle of 25 evolutions followed by one exchange between nodes 10 times. We also write on disk every time we have exchanges to track how STs are transversing the network. This information is relevant in most biological analyses, which are however out of the scope of this paper.

The first observation is that writing on disk is the operation that takes an higher cost. We address this issue by using the *saveAsTextFile* method available in Apache Spark, exploiting the ability of parallelize write operations on HDFS.

---

[1] https://cloud.google.com/.

Table 1. Running time in seconds for different topologies and network sizes.

Topology	Size (N)	Mode				
		Local	2 workers	4 workers	8 workers	16 workers
Clique	100	170	60	53	48	43
	200	411	109	74	59	50
	500	1052	338	202	118	97
	1000	2538	796	485	267	169
Scale-free	1000	916	480	403	221	152
	2000	1807	897	519	341	292
	8000	6293	3020	1902	1300	912

We consider two different network topologies, cliques (or fully connected networks) and scale-free networks [2]. Clique topology leads to highest computational cost while performing exchanges. Scale-free networks are more realistic for host contact networks, but being very sparse lead to much less work during exchanges. We consider random scale-free networks generated with a partial duplication model, with parameter 0.5 and different number of vertices [3]. Tests were run for both topologies and different network sizes. The results averaged over 10 runs are presented in Table 1 and in Fig. 1.

We note that we used a graph partitioning schema available in GraphX designed specifically for scale-free networks. The *PartitionStrategy.EdgePartition2D* was proposed by Verma *et al.* [18] as the best for these

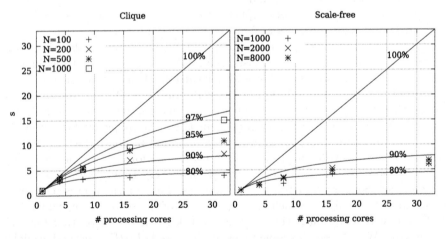

Fig. 1. Speedup as a function of the number of available cores for cliques (left) and scale-free networks (right), with different network sizes (N). The curves are provided by Amdahl's law [1], where the percentage corresponds to the fraction that is infinitely parallelizable.

networks. And we confirmed their results while running our experiments and comparing with other partitioning strategies.

We can observe that the speedup becomes more evident as networks grow in size. Running in cluster mode, and increasing the number of workers, results in a significantly boost in the running time. The fact that we can compute the population evolution at each node independently seems to be exploited as expected. The same happens with the exchange process among nodes populations.

When designing parallel algorithms, one of the analyses that should be done is to estimate the relation between achievable speedups and the number of workers. Amdahl's law is crucial here to both interpret the results and project expected speedups [1]. On one hand it points out that one should only optimize if the fraction that can be optimized constitutes a large portion of the overall time. On the other hand, if the optimization is effective the speedup we obtain is largely determined by the strictly sequential fraction, which cannot be optimized and initially constituted only a small fraction of the time. Given k workers (cores) and a program that spends a fraction f of time on operations that are infinitely parallelizable, and the remaining fraction $1 - f$ on strictly sequential operations, the overall speedup is given by $1/((1 - f) + f/m)$. In Fig. 1 we can observe that, as we increase the size of the clique networks, we obtain a higher speedup as we increase the number of workers. According to Amdahl's law, we are observing about $f = 97\%$ for a clique of 1000 nodes. For the scale-free networks, because they are much sparser than cliques, with less work performed on exchange, we observe about $f = 90\%$ and speedups are small above 16 processing cores. This seems to point out that the exchange process is highly parallelizable, independently of the network size, which is an important observation if simulations with much larger networks are desirable. We should also note that the running time grows almost linearly as we increase the number of nodes (see Table 1). This is expected as the evolution of each population can be done independently and, even not being fully parallelized due to recombinations as explained before, we can still benefit from parallelization in simulations over large networks.

As a final remark, we must note that since most real host contact networks are scale-free, according to Amdahl's law, using more than 16 processing cores does not lead to significant improvements for realistic simulations.

Acknowledgments. This work was partly supported by DEI, IST, Universidade de Lisboa, and national funds through FCT – Fundação para a Ciência e Tecnologia, under projects TUBITACK/0004/2014, LISBOA-01-0145-FEDER-016394, PTDC/EEISII/5081/2014, PTDC/MAT/STA/3358/2014, and UID/CE C/500021/2013.

References

1. Amdahl, G.M.: Validity of the single processor approach to achieving large scale computing capabilities. In: Proceedings of the Spring Joint Computer Conference, AFIPS 1967 (Spring), pp. 483–485. ACM, 18–20, April 1967
2. Barabási, A.L., Albert, R.: Emergence of scaling in random networks. Science **286**(5439), 509–512 (1999)

3. Chung, F., Lu, L., Dewey, T.G., Galas, D.J.: Duplication models for biological networks. J. Comput. Biol. **10**(5), 677–687 (2003)
4. Dean, J., Ghemawat, S.: Mapreduce: Simplified data processing on large clusters. Commun. ACM **51**(1), 107–113 (2008)
5. Fraser, C., Hanage, W., Spratt, B.: Neutral microepidemic evolution of bacterial pathogens. PNAS **102**(6), 1968–1973 (2005)
6. Fraser, C., Alm, E.J., Polz, M.F., Spratt, B.G., Hanage, W.P.: The bacterial species challenge: making sense of genetic and ecological diversity. Science **323**(5915), 741–746 (2009)
7. Fraser, C., Hanage, W.P., Spratt, B.G.: Neutral microepidemic evolution of bacterial pathogens. Proc. Natl. Acad. Sci. U.S.A. **102**(6), 1968–1973 (2005)
8. Fraser, C., Hanage, W.P., Spratt, B.G.: Recombination and the nature of bacterial speciation. Science **315**(5811), 476–480 (2007)
9. Hanage, W.P., Spratt, B.G., Turner, K.M., Fraser, C.: Modelling bacterial speciation. Philos. Trans. Roy. Soc. Lond. B: Biol. Sci. **361**(1475), 2039–2044 (2006)
10. Kimura, M.: Evolutionary rate at the molecular level. Nature **217**, 624–626 (1968)
11. Lin, J., Dyer, C.: Data-Intensive Text Processing with MapReduce. Morgan and Claypool Publishers (2010)
12. Maiden, M., Bygraves, J., Feil, E., Morelli, G., Russell, J., Urwin, R., Zhang, Q., Zhou, J., Zurth, K., Caugant, D., et al.: Multilocus sequence typing: a portable approach to the identification of clones within populations of pathogenic microorganisms. PNAS **95**(6), 3140–3145 (1998)
13. Ochman, H., Lawrence, J.G., Groisman, E.A.: Lateral gene transfer and the nature of bacterial innovation. Nature **405**, 299–304 (2000)
14. Page, L., Brin, S., Motwani, R., Winograd, T.: The PageRank Citation Ranking: Bringing Order to the Web. Technical Report 1999–66, Stanford InfoLab (1999)
15. Robinson, D.A., Falush, D., Feil, E.J.: Bacterial Population Genetics in Infectious Disease. John Wiley & Sons, Hoboken (2010)
16. Spratt, B.G., Hanage, W.P., Feil, E.J.: The relative contributions of recombination and point mutation to the diversification of bacterial clones. Curr. Opin. Microbiol. **4**(5), 602–606 (2001)
17. Tran, T.D., Hofrichter, J., Jost, J.: An introduction to the mathematical structure of the Wright-Fisher model of population genetics. Theory Biosci. **132**(2), 73–82 (2013)
18. Verma, S., Leslie, L.M., Shin, Y., Gupta, I.: An experimental comparison of partitioning strategies in distributed graph processing. Proc. VLDB Endow. **10**(5), 493–504 (2017)
19. Xin, R.S., Gonzalez, J.E., Franklin, M.J., Stoica, I.: Graphx: a resilient distributed graph system on spark. In: First International Workshop on Graph Data Management Experiences and Systems, GRADES 2013, pp. 2:1–2:6. ACM (2013)
20. Zaharia, M., Chowdhury, M., Das, T., Dave, A., Ma, J., McCauley, M., Franklin, M.J., Shenker, S., Stoica, I.: Resilient distributed datasets: a fault-tolerant abstraction for in-memory cluster computing. In: Proceedings of the 9th USENIX Conference on Networked Systems Design and Implementation, NSDI 2012, p. 2. USENIX Association (2012)
21. Zaharia, M., Chowdhury, M., Franklin, M.J., Shenker, S., Stoica, I.: Spark: cluster computing with working sets. In: Proceedings of the 2Nd USENIX Conference on Hot Topics in Cloud Computing, HotCloud 2010, p. 10. USENIX Association (2010)
22. Zhu, X., Ghahramani, Z.: Learning from labeled and unlabeled data with label propagation (2002)

PPCAS: Implementation of a Probabilistic Pairwise Model for Consistency-Based Multiple Alignment in Apache Spark

Jordi Lladós[(✉)][iD], Fernando Guirado[iD], and Fernando Cores[iD]

INSPIRES Research Center, Universitat de Lleida, Jaume II, 69, 25001 Lleida, Spain
{jordi.llados,f.guirado,fcores}@diei.udl.cat

Abstract. Large-scale data processing techniques, currently known as Big-Data, are used to manage the huge amount of data that are generated by sequencers. Although these techniques have significant advantages, few biological applications have adopted them. In the Bioinformatic scientific area, Multiple Sequence Alignment (MSA) tools are widely applied for evolution and phylogenetic analysis, homology and domain structure prediction. Highly-rated MSA tools, such as MAFFT, ProbCons and T-Coffee (TC), use the probabilistic consistency as a prior step to the progressive alignment stage in order to improve the final accuracy. In this paper, a novel approach named PPCAS (Probabilistic Pairwise model for Consistency-based multiple alignment in Apache Spark) is presented. PPCAS is based on the MapReduce processing paradigm in order to enable large datasets to be processed with the aim of improving the performance and scalability of the original algorithm.

Keywords: Multiple Sequence Alignment · Consistency · Spark · MapReduce

1 Introduction

The probabilistic pairwise model [10] is an important step in all consistency-based MSA tools. A probabilistic model can simulate a whole class of objects, assigning an associated probability to each one. In the multiple alignment field, the objects are defined as a pair of residues from the input set of sequences, and the associated weight is the probability of being aligned [14]. For any two sequences, there are many possibilities of residue matches, $Length(sequence_1) * Length(sequence_2)$. The probabilistic model assigns each residue match a score. The higher this is, the better. For a complete dataset of sequences, the collection of the all the residue matches, which implies all the pairs of sequence evaluations, is known as the Consistency Library. This library is used to guide the progressive alignment and thus improve the final pairwise accuracy. A well-known MSA tool that uses consistency is T-Coffee [3].

The computation of the consistency library evaluates $N * (N - 1)/2$ combinations, N being the number of sequences, and that may be cataloged as

© Springer International Publishing AG 2017
S. Ibrahim et al. (Eds.): ICA3PP 2017, LNCS 10393, pp. 601–610, 2017.
DOI: 10.1007/978-3-319-65482-9_45

embarrassingly parallel [3]. With the advent of the Next-Gen Sequencing, the number of sequences to align and their length have grown exponentially, with the corresponding negative impact on execution time and memory requirements. The use of massive data processing techniques can provide a solution to these limitations.

High Performance Computing (HPC) is the way to aggregate computer resources to provide parallel processing features for advanced applications. However, the fixed memory resources on each computational node and the fact that data is distributed through the interconnection network mean it is unviable for easy application to the Multiple Sequence Alignment problem. Currently, new computing technologies have been designed to manage and store huge amounts of data. These technologies, such as Hadoop [23] or Spark [17], are commonly applied to Big-Data processing and can be used to deal with this challenge. The main advantage is the ability to partition the whole data between all the nodes.

However, the increase in the number of sequences in the dataset to be treated could finally exceed the global distributed memory. The solution is the use of specialized distributed databases, such as HBase or Cassandra [1], that provide enough storage capacity to allocate any consistency library.

Thus, in the present paper, the authors present a new tool, the Probabilistic Pairwise model for Consistency-based multiple alignment in Apache Spark (PPCAS). This is able to generate the parallel probabilistic pairwise model for large datasets of proteins and can also store it in a distributed platform using the T-Coffee format.

The paper is organized as follows: Sect. 2 presents a brief state of the art of consistency-based MSA tools. In Sect. 3, we outline the development of PPCAS. In Sect. 4, the performance and accuracy evaluation are shown and finally, the main conclusions are presented in Sect. 5.

2   State of Art

Traditional aligners, like ClustalW [7], MAFFT [6] and T-Coffee [3], are based on Gotoh [5] or Myers & Miller's [11] dynamic programming techniques, using scores from two different sources (a consistency library or substitution matrices such as PAM and BLOSUM [9]) to perform the optimal alignment of two sequences.

Unfortunately, the application of dynamic programming is inefficient for alignments consisting of many (10–100) sequences. Instead, a variety of heuristic strategies have been proposed, the most popular, progressive alignment [12], builds up a final alignment by combining pairwise alignments following a guide tree (beginning with the most similar sequences to the most distantly related). However, errors in the early stages not only propagate to the final alignment but may also increase the likelihood of misalignment due to incorrect conservation signals.

To lessen these early errors, consistency-based methods, such as T-Coffee [3], MAFFT [6], ProbCons [4] or DIALIGN [21], introduce consistency as a collection of pairwise alignments obtained from computing all-against-all pairwise alignments. T-Coffee uses this via a process called library extension[1]. MAFFT uses a new objective function combining the WSP score from Gotoh and the COFFEE-like score [14] that evaluates the consistency between multiple and pairwise alignments. ProbCons improves the traditional sum-of-pairs scoring system by incorporating Hidden Markov Models to specify the probability distribution over all alignments between a pair of sequences. Furthermore, DIALIGN-T reformulates consistency by finding ungapped local alignments via segment-to-segment comparisons that determine new weights using consistency.

The main drawback of consistency-based aligners is the high computational resources (CPU and memory) required to calculate and store the consistency information. For example, the consistency library in T-Coffee has a complexity of $O(N^2 L^2)$, N being the number of sequences and L their average length. These requirements mean the method is not scalable, it being limited to aligning a few hundred sequences on a typical desktop computer. Therefore, these aligners are not feasible for large-scale alignments with thousands of sequences.

This problem of scalability is common to other tools and algorithms. Nowadays, Bioinformatics is challenged by the fact that traditional analysis tools have difficulties in processing large-scale data from high-throughput sequencing [24]. The utilization of HPC and BigData infrastructures has recently given bioinformatics researchers an opportunity to achieve scalable, efficient and reliable computing performance on Linux clusters and cloud computing services. The open-source Apache Hadoop project [23], which adopts the MapReduce framework [2] and a distributed file system, is able to store and process Petabytes of information efficiently. Moreover, Hadoop has a complete stack of services and frameworks (Spark, Cassandra, Mahout, Pig, etc.) that provides a wide range of machine-learning and data-analysis tools to process any type of workflow.

Over recent years, new tools have been developed in the bioinformatics field to improve the performance and scalability of massive data processing in current applications. In [16], a novel approach is proposed that combines the dynamic programming algorithm with the computational parallelism of Hadoop data grids to improve accuracy and accelerate Multiple Sequence Alignment. In [25], the authors developed a DNA MSA tool based on trie trees to accelerate the centre star MSA strategy. It was implemented using the MapReduce distributed framework. The use of the MapReduce paradigm and Hadoop infrastructures enabled the scalability and the alignment time to be improved.

There are more MapReduce solutions in the area of mapping short reads against a reference genome. These applications, CloudBurst [18], SEAL [15] and CloudAligner [13], implement traditional algorithms like RMAP [20] and BWA [8] using the MapReduce paradigm.

---

[1] Given a MSA containing three sequences x, y, and z, if position x_i aligns with position z_k and position z_k aligns with y_j in the projected x-z and z-y alignments, then to be consistent the x_i must align with y_j in the projected x-y alignment.

3   PPCAS Method

The programming language selected was Python with the Ctypes extension that provides C language compatibility data types and also the ability to call external shared libraries. Thus, it is possible to obtain similar performance to native compiled code in CPU-intensive applications.

The main step in the development was to adapt the probabilistic pairwise algorithm to the MapReduce paradigm used in the big data frameworks [2]. The MapReduce paradigm enables the parallel/distributed computational resources (processors, memory and disks) to be exploited in a simple and scalable way. The MapReduce paradigm breaks down the problem into multiple Map tasks that can be executed in parallel on multiple computers/processors. After this initial Map stage, all the partial results obtained are merged and then processed by several Reduce tasks, in order to finally aggregate them.

Spark is a fast engine for large-scale data processing in real-time executed over Hadoop. Spark has a master/slave architecture. It has one central coordinator (Driver) that communicates with many distributed workers (Executors). The driver is the process where the main method runs and the executors are those that process the data received.

In the implementation of PPCAS, the map stage is responsible for defining all the tasks in charge of computing the probability score for a set of pairs of sequences. In Algorithm 1, the driver generates these tasks for all the $N * (N - 1)/2$ pair combinations (line 1) and distributes them in a balanced way among all the Map tasks using a Resilient Distributed Dataset (RDD) (line 2). Then, in line 3, the map tasks are launched and scheduled for processing on the executors. As a result, each map generates a portion of the library in parallel, and this persists in the HDFS file system.

Driver
```
1: tasks_list = generate_tasks();
2: rdd_tasks = sc.parallelize(tasks_list, len(tasks_list));
3: rdd_tasks.map(executor_function).saveAsTextFile(hdfs_path);
```

Executor
```
4: for each sequence S_i ∈ task_i do
5:    for each sequence S_j ∈ task_j do
6:       _libraryC = ctypes.CDLL("./PPCAS.so")
7:       _libraryC.pair_wise(S_i, S_j)
8:    end for
9: end for
```

Algorithm 1. Spark parallel pairwise probability calculation

The executor, lines 4–9, performs a subset of the pairwise combinations. This is done in the double-nested loop in lines 4–5, which obtains the different combinations of sequences assigned to the *task*. It calculates the library for each of these combinations by calling the $pair\_wise(S_i,\ S_j)$ function of the shared library (PPCAS.so). This function calculates the probabilistic pairwise model for these two sequences and writes this portion of the library to the disk (HDFS).

4   Results and Discussion

In this section we evaluate PPCAS[2]. The experimental study is focused on (1) the use of PPCAS as the main consistency library of T-Coffee by comparing the accuracy achieved and the corresponding execution time, (2) the scalability of the PPCAS when the number of nodes increases and finally, (3) the performance behavior when the number of sequences grows.

To perform the tests, we used two different multiple alignment benchmarking suites:

- BALiBASE [22] is a database of high-quality documented and manually-refined reference alignments based on 3D structural superpositions. The accuracy of the alignments is measured using two metrics: the Sum-of-Pairs (SP) and the Total Column Score (TCS), which are obtained by comparing the user alignment against a reference alignment.
- HomFam [19]: The existing benchmark datasets are very small (150 and 50 sequences in BALiBASE and Prefab respectively). Homfam provides large datasets using Pfam families with thousands of sequences. In order to validate the results of aligning a Pfam family, the Homstrad site contains some reference alignments and the corresponding Pfam family. These references are previously de-aligned and shuffled into the dataset. After the alignment process, the reference sequences are extracted and compared with the originals in Homstrad.

HomFam contains almost one hundred sets. We selected the top five manually, sorted by size (Acetyltransf, rrm, rvp, sdr and zf-CCHH) to evaluate the method. The results for the execution time presented in this section represent the average results obtained after evaluating the corresponding family. Furthermore, each experiment corresponds to five iterations in order to show the robustness of the results. The execution environment is a distributed memory cluster made up of 20 nodes, each one characterized in Table 1.

4.1   Evaluating the PPCAS Consistency Library

To assess the correctness of PPCAS, a final alignment must be done. To this end, an MSA tool is needed. TC allows the input of an externally-generated consistency library using its $-lib$ flag, so a library was built for each set with PPCAS and introduced into TC via the parameter, which generates the alignment.

This study compares the results obtained from executing T-Coffee using its own consistency library, and the same T-Coffee using the library generated with PPCAS by processing the same dataset. The experimentation focused on the differences in accuracy and the possible execution time penalties.

---

[2] PPCAS is available on https://github.com/jllados/PPCAS.

Table 1. Hardware and software used in the experimentation

Software	Version
Apache Spark	1.6.3
Apache Hadoop	2.6
Python	2.7.13
Numpy	1.11.2
GCC	4.1.2

Hardware	Model
CPU	Intel Core 2 Quad at 2.4GHz
RAM	8GB DDR2

The BAliBASE benchmark was used for the accuracy test. The results obtained are shown in Table 2. The first column indicates the library algorithm used and the Sum-of-Pairs (SP) produced using the Bali score appears in columns 2–7. The average score over all the families is given in the last column.

Table 2. Comparison between T-Coffee and PPCAS library with BAliBASE.

Library	RV11	RV12	RV20	RV30	RV40	RV50	Total SP
T-Coffee	0.534	0.879	0.827	0.718	0.758	0.759	0.743
PPCAS	0.535	0.879	0.826	0.720	0.754	0.758	0.745

The results demonstrate that using the PPCAS library, T-Coffee is able to obtain an equivalent accuracy. The slightly differences in accuracy are due to the fact that, unlike PPCAS, T-coffee removes the smallest weighted library. This validates using the new library instead of the original one from T-Coffee.

Next, the execution time required to calculate the consistency library in T-Coffee (using the $-lib\_only$ flag) was compared with the time obtained with PPCAS, only using a single node with a quad-core processor in both cases and increasing the number of sequences. The results obtained are shown in Fig. 1.

As can be observed, PPCAS always outperforms T-Coffee for execution time. However, when the number of sequences is low (100–200), the improvement is not very large, because there is not enough parallel work to obtain the maximum infrastructure performance. Nevertheless, with a large number of sequences (over 200), the PPCAS execution time improvement increases, meaning that the code is more efficient in PPCAS than in T-Coffee.

Moreover, we verified that, with 8 GB of memory, it is only possible to calculate the consistency library for a dataset with a maximum of 1,000 sequences using T-Coffee, and this takes more than 5,000 s. Meanwhile, PPCAS takes only 3,338 s to calculate the same library, which implies a 1.62× improvement. Attempts to evaluate more sequences in TC failed because the library size did not fit into the local memory.

Both the accuracy and execution time tests demonstrate that PPCAS can be used as a new method to provide the consistency library required by TC without any penalty, and furthermore, simultaneously increasing its performance.

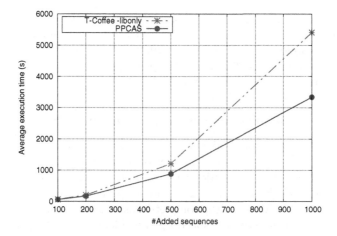

Fig. 1. Comparison of library building under a single node with HomFam sets.

4.2   Scalability Study of PPCAS

To demonstrate the real benefits of using a Big-Data infrastructure, the scalability of the method when more nodes are added must be measured. We also compare the results with the original T-Coffee to have a reference point. Thus, in this test, a fixed size of 1,000 sequences (HomFam) was used, this being the maximum number of sequences TC can handle.

Figure 2 depicts the results obtained. The left axis shows the execution time, and the right one depicts the speedup obtained. It can be seen that the PPCAS

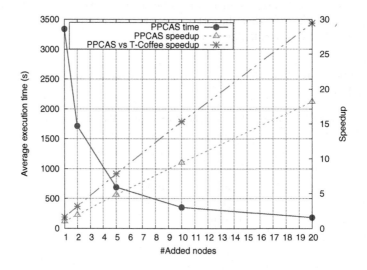

Fig. 2. Scalability of PPCAS with HomFam sets

speedup tends to be almost linear, taking 3,338 s with a single node, while it can be reduced to 183 s when using 20 nodes. This represents an 18.18× speedup over the single node execution time and 29.45× over the TC version presented in the previous section (5,409 s). These speedups are linear, denoting a good scalability as the theoretical maximum is 20×.

4.3   PPCAS Scalability Increasing the Number of Sequences

This final experimentation evaluates the behavior of PPCAS with the same computational resources when the number of sequences increases.

Table 3 compares the execution time required to calculate the library in T-Coffee using a single node with a quad-core processor, (using the *−lib_only* parameter) with PPCAS using the complete cluster infrastructure with 20 quad-core nodes. We also analyzed the speed-up and efficiency (*speedup/nodes*, which rates the improvement against cost) as the number of sequences increases.

It is important to note that it is possible to calculate bigger libraries with PPCAS because there is no limitation to the main memory of a single node. The last column shows that the library size does not fit in the memory of a single traditional computer. Thus, it was possible to calculate the library with up to 20,000 sequences, which took 64,012 s.

When the number of sequences is low (100–200), the speedup and efficiency are not good, although the lack of parallel work mitigates the infrastructure performance. However, with a large number of sequences (more than 500), both of them achieve good values. Thus, they improve as more sequences are added.

Figure 3 shows the scalability of PPCAS on a logarithmic scale for the number of sequences to be aligned. We can observe the correlation between the size of the resulting consistency library and the time required to calculate it as the number of sequences increases. It can also be seen that the growth in execution time is proportionally smaller than the increase in size, which demonstrates the efficiency of PPCAS for calculating the library.

Table 3. Library building comparison between a single TC node and PPCAS multi node with HomFam sets.

N° of seq	T-Coffee time(s)	PPCAS time(s)	Speedup	Efficiency	Library size (Mb)
100	63.06	20.79	3.03	0.15	39
200	202.73	33.90	5.98	0.30	135
500	1,206.07	63.95	18.86	0.94	760
1,000	5,409.28	183.66	29.45	1.47	2,956
2,000	—	676.83	—	—	11,702
5,000	—	4,080.02	—	—	72,357
10,000	—	16,100.69	—	—	289,006
20,000	—	64,012.79	—	—	1,151,736

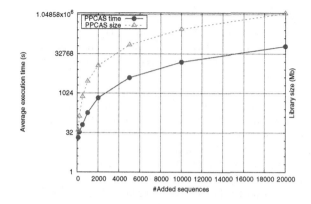

Fig. 3. Scalability of PPCAS regarding the execution time and output size.

5 Conclusions

In this paper, the authors present a scalable method to compute the probabilistic pairwise model for consistency-based multiple alignment.

We show that PPCAS is able to produce a quality library relying on a Hadoop infrastructure with Spark. In terms of execution time, the method behaves better under the same environment (single node) and benefits from almost linear speedups when more nodes are added to the ecosystem. It is also capable of computing more sequences with the same memory requirements.

In the future, we will integrate PPCAS with an aligner with a distributed database like Apache Cassandra as the interface. Storing the constraints in a high-performance database will completely eliminate the memory problems, while supplying the progressive stage with the required data. Our other aim is to reduce the execution time of the progressive itself, this being the other problematic half of an MSA with consistency.

Acknowledgments. This work was supported by the MEyC-Spain [contract TIN2014-53234-C2-2-R].

References

1. Abramova, V., Bernardino, J., Furtado, P.: Which NoSQL database? A performance overview. Open J. Databases (OJDB) **1**(2), 17–24 (2014)
2. Dean, J., Ghemawat, S.: MapReduce: a flexible data processing tool. Commun. ACM **53**(1), 72–77 (2010)
3. Di Tommaso, P., Moretti, S., Xenarios, I., Orobitg, M., Montanyola, A., Chang, J.-M., Taly, J.-F., Notredame, C.: T-Coffee: a web server for the multiple sequence alignment of protein and RNA sequences using structural information and homology extension. Nucleic Acids Res. **39**(2), 13–17 (2011)
4. Do, C.B., Mahabhashyam, M.S., Brudno, M., Batzoglou, S.: ProbCons: probabilistic consistency-based multiple sequence alignment. Genome Res. **15**(2), 330–340 (2005)

5. Gotoh, O.: Heuristic Alignment Methods. Multiple Sequence Alignment Methods, vol. 1079, pp. 29–43. Springer, Heidelberg (2014)
6. Katoh, K., Standley, D.M.: MAFFT multiple sequence alignment software version 7: improvements in performance and usability. Mol. Biol. Evol. **30**(4), 772–780 (2013)
7. Larkin, M.A., Blackshields, G., Brown, N.P., Chenna, R., McGettigan, P.A., McWilliam, H., Valentin, F., Wallace, I.M., Wilm, A., Lopez, R., Thompson, J.D., Gibson, T.J., Higgins, D.G.: Clustal W and Clustal X version 2.0. Bioinformatics **23**(21), 2947–2948 (2007)
8. Li, H., Durbin, R.: Fast and accurate short read alignment with Burrows–Wheeler transform. Bioinformatics **25**(14), 1754–1760 (2009)
9. Mount, D.W.: Comparison of the PAM and BLOSUM amino acid substitution matrices. Cold Spring Harbor Protoc. **6** (2008). doi:10.1101/pdb.ip59
10. Miyazawa, S.: A reliable sequence alignment method based on probabilities of residue correspondences. Protein Eng. Des. Sel. **8**(10), 999–1009 (1995)
11. Myers, E.W., Miller, W.: Optimal alignments in linear space. Bioinformatics **4**(1), 11–17 (1988)
12. Nguyen, K., Guo, X., Pan, Y.: Multiple sequences alignment algorithms. In: Multiple Biological Sequence Alignment Scoring Functions, Algorithms and Applications (2016)
13. Nguyen, T., Shi, W., Ruden, D.: CloudAligner: a fast and full-featured MapReduce based tool for sequence mapping. BMC Res. Notes **4**(1), 171 (2011)
14. Notredame, C., Holm, L., Higgins, D.G.: COFFEE: an objective function for multiple sequence alignments. Bioinformatics **14**(5), 407–422 (1998)
15. Pireddu, L., Leo, S., Zanetti, G.: SEAL: a distributed short read mapping and duplicate removal tool. Bioinformatics **27**(15), 2159–2160 (2011)
16. Sadasivam, G., Baktavatchalam, G.: A novel approach to Multiple Sequence Alignment using hadoop data grids. Int. J. Bioinform. Res. Appl. **6**(5), 472–483 (2010)
17. Sakr, S.: Big data processing stacks. IT Prof. **19**(1), 34–41 (2017)
18. Schatz, M.: CloudBurst: highly sensitive read mapping with MapReduce. Bioinformatics **25**(11), 1363–1369 (2009)
19. Sievers, F., Dineen, D., Wilm, A., Higgins, D.G.: Making automated multiple alignments of very large numbers of protein sequences. Bioinformatics **29**(8), 989–995 (2013)
20. Smith, A.D., Xuan, Z., Zhang, M.Q.: Using quality scores and longer reads improves accuracy of Solexa read mapping. BMC Bioinform. **9**(1), 128 (2008)
21. Subramanian, A.R., Weyer-Menkhoff, J., Kaufmann, M., Morgenstern, B.: DIALIGN-T: an improved algorithm for segment-based multiple sequence alignment. BMC Bioinform. **6**(1), 66 (2005)
22. Thompson, J.D., Koehl, P., Ripp, R., Poch, O.: BAliBASE 3.0: latest developments of the multiple sequence alignment benchmark. Proteins Struct. Funct. Bioinf. **61**(1), 127–136 (2005)
23. Zhang, Y., Cao, T., Li, S., Tian, X., Yuan, L., Jia, H., Vasilakos, A.V.: Parallel processing systems for big data: a survey. Proc. IEEE **104**(11), 2114–2136 (2016)
24. Zou, Q.: Survey of MapReduce frame operation in bioinformatics. Brief. Bioinform. **15**(4), 637–647 (2014)
25. Zou, Q., Hu, Q., Guo, M., Wang, G.: HAlign: fast multiple similar DNA/RNA sequence alignment based on the centre star strategy. Bioinformatics **31**(15), 2475–2481 (2015)

Accelerating Exhaustive Pairwise Metagenomic Comparisons

Esteban Pérez-Wohlfeil, Oscar Torreno, and Oswaldo Trelles(⊠)

Department of Computer Architecture, University of Malaga,
Boulevard Louis Pasteur 35, Malaga, Spain
{estebanpw,oscart,ortrelles}@uma.es

Abstract. In this manuscript, we present an optimized and parallel version of our previous work IMSAME, an exhaustive gapped aligner for the pairwise and accurate comparison of metagenomes. Parallelization strategies are applied to take advantage of modern multiprocessor architectures. In addition, sequential optimizations in CPU time and memory consumption are provided. These algorithmic and computational enhancements enable IMSAME to calculate near optimal alignments which are used to directly assess similarity between metagenomes without requiring reference databases. We show that the overall efficiency of the parallel implementation is superior to 80% while retaining scalability as the number of parallel cores used increases. Moreover, we also show that sequential optimizations yield up to 8× speedup for scenarios with larger data.

Keywords: High Performance Computing · Pairwise comparison · Parallel computing · Next Generation Sequencing · Metagenome comparison

1 Background

A metagenome is defined as a collection of genetic material directly recovered from the environment. In particular, a metagenome is composed of a large number of reads (DNA strings) drawn from the species present in the original population. To this day, the field of comparative metagenomics has become big-data driven [1] due to new technological improvements in high-throughput sequencing. However, the analysis of large metagenomic datasets represents a computational challenge and poses several processing bottlenecks, specially to sequence comparison algorithms.

Traditional metagenomics comparison involve intermediate pairwise (and individual) comparisons against a reference database. This procedure allows to extract a mapping distribution between reads and species, and thus enables to later on compare these distributions. A similarity measure can then be computed from the two distributions. However, due to the unknown and complex composition of metagenomes, traditional comparisons based on a reference require databases to be large, which often introduce bias and drastically increase execution

© Springer International Publishing AG 2017
S. Ibrahim et al. (Eds.): ICA3PP 2017, LNCS 10393, pp. 611–620, 2017.
DOI: 10.1007/978-3-319-65482-9_46

times. In this line, direct comparisons between metagenomes to assess overall similarity gain interest as running times can be shortened and bias avoided. Furthermore, there is yet no accepted consensus on how similarity should be assessed, and in several scenarios certainty comes at the expense of exhaustive and optimal alignments. Still, optimal alignment of large datasets is not feasible without making use of parallel infrastructure and optimization techniques.

Next Generation Sequencing platforms are generating larger amounts of data per run, of higher quality and at a lower price. However, the performance of computational approaches used to process metagenomic data suffer inversely proportional to that of the size of generated samples. High Performance Computing techniques can be applied in order to overcome the processing bottlenecks and accelerate running times.

Several parallelism strategies have been already applied to software for both comparative genomics and metagenomics, such as the multipurpose BLAST [2] family, where different types of architectures have been exploited (e.g. mpi-BLAST [3] for distributed memory or TERABLAST [4] for its use on FPGAs). Parallelization of sequence alignment algorithms have also been applied to GPUs such as GSWABE [5] or CUSHAW2-GPU [6]. FPGAs have also been employed to accelerate sequence comparisons (e.g. SWAPHI [7]). However, GPUs and FPGAs are expensive and their specificity often force the use of a reduced subset of programs due to platform dependence restrictions. Other general parallel approaches which make use of CPU multithreading such as BOWTIE [8] or PARALLEL-META3 [10] use POSIX threads [11] for UNIX-based environments in a shared memory architecture.

However, the above mentioned sequence aligners are not specifically designed to compare read to reads or contigs and particularly not to assess similarity between metagenomes. For instance, BOWTIE works best when aligning short reads to large reference genomes. Moreover, in [12] the effect of introducing intermediary agents to ultimately assess similarity between metagenomes was argued. In this line, alternative approaches that were capable of direct comparisons were discussed (e.g. MASH [13], SIMKA [14]) and when possible (BLAST, COMMET [15]), compared to IMSAME. Additionally, it was shown that coarse-grained approaches to metagenomics comparison could lead to results that were highly dependent on hyperparameters (such as the initial seed size).

To fulfill the gap, IMSAME was presented as a parallel, fine-grained, and exhaustive gapped read-to-read (including contigs and scaffolds) aligner. In this manuscript, we present an optimized version of IMSAME which is able to compute faster while using a linear and controlled amount of memory. Moreover, High Performance Computing techniques have been applied to balance the workload among threads to reduce thread synchronization.

2   Methods

IMSAME ("Incremental Multi-Stage Alignment of MEtagenomes") is intended to compare reads to reads directly, i.e. without using a reference database, and to assess similarity between them while providing a confident level of certainty. It proceeds by combining a different set of alignment-free, gapped-free and gapped alignments. Each of these procedures is intended to yield a different level of speed and sensitivity, depending on the alignment stage. For instance, the initial detection of seeds between reads (to be referred as hits) is performed using k-mers (words of length k), whereas probabilistic filtering is applied when hits are extended into High-scoring Segment Pairs (HSPs). HSPs with sufficiently small probability of belonging by chance to the underlying distribution are kept and used as anchors for a bounded Needleman-Wunsch (NW in advance) global alignment [16]. Figure 1 shows the overall architecture of IMSAME. The following sections illustrate each of the methods employed in IMSAME.

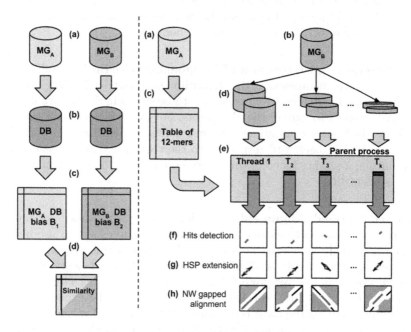

Fig. 1. Traditional metagenomics comparison (left) and overall diagram of the working procedure of IMSAME (right). Left: (a) Both metagenomes are compared individually against a chosen reference (b) Database. (c) Individual results are merged into a unified (d) result which propagates individual biases. Right: (a) and (b) Represent the input metagenomes. (c) Computation of the hash table of initial seeds. (d) Workload distribution to threads. (e) Each thread asks for a job (i.e. block of reads). (f) Each thread detects hits between reads. (g) After detection of hits, an HSP is computed by extending the hit linearly. (h) If the computed HSP has not been generated by chance, then a gapped alignment between the two reads is performed.

The computation of hits, extended fragments (HSPs) and gapped alignments will often represent more than 85% of the computation time. Therefore the parallel strategy in IMSAME is focused in these stages, whereas loading the database and workload generation and distribution is performed sequentially.

2.1   Computation of Alignments

This section depicts the internal procedure followed by IMSAME to compute pairwise alignments between the sequences contained within the inputs.

Hash Table Generation and Diagonal Filtering. A hash table is built for words of size 12 (i.e. 12-mers) for the reference metagenome. This procedure starts by linearly scanning the reference metagenome and adding an entry in the hash table for each 12-mer. The position in the file and the read number to which it belongs is stored. Each entry in the hash table will hold a linked list in order to handle collisions. Since the reference metagenome is considered as a large sequence (i.e. the coordinates of reads is global in respect to the file), then the insertion of 12-mers in the hash-table is sorted in terms of the diagonal (as in [17]) between query and reference metagenome.

Hits Detection and Extension of Fragments. Once the hash table is built for the reference metagenome, the algorithm proceeds by loading the query metagenome and matching 12-mer words to those stored in the hash table. These hits serve as seeds to extend the alignments. For every hit, a linear, ungapped extension which allows mutations -but not indels- is performed in both directions, forward and backward respective to the sequence. This extension works by optimizing a scoring function that takes into account the length and number of shared identities.

Anchored Gapped Alignment. In order to apply a bounded computation for both CPU time and memory requirements, it is necessary to use heuristic methods to explore a reduced subspace of the whole search space. Hence, the quality of the results will be directly affected by the used heuristic method. IMSAME uses a simple yet powerful anchoring procedure, which is illustrated as follows: Once a hit has been detected and extended, the expected value of the resulting extended fragment is computed. If the expected value is sufficiently small, then it is used as anchor for the alignment. A straight line is computed between the global start (0,0) of the two sequences and the anchored fragment. Another line is computed from the ending of the anchored fragment to that of the two sequences. These two lines are then discretized using Bresenhams [18] algorithm. The Bresenhams algorithm will define a discrete succession of numbers that represent the guides for the alignment procedure. A window of variable size is used to explore a subset of cells in the NW matrix to the left and to the right respective to the center of the guides (and thus conforming a window). This procedure enables a much faster computation based on the reduced search space. At the same time, high quality alignments are still produced due to the anchored computation over regions that are known to be similar.

Bounded Computation in CPU Time and Memory. Since only a subset of the search space is explored, less memory is required to store the table computed in the dynamic programming algorithm. Therefore, the size of the bounded window will determine the reduction in memory and CPU time over the algorithm. Generally, a NW algorithm will require $\mathcal{O}(n^2)$ time and space in the size of the input. In this case, for sequences of length n and m, $\mathcal{O}(nm)$ will be required, which grows quadratically. Using a bounded window in the computation reduces one of the variables to a constant. Therefore if we take n as the size of one of the inputs and k as the size of the window, we will have that $k \ll n$. Hence, the space and time complexity drops from quadratic to linear in the size of the input. However, in certain cases the difference in length between the sequences to be aligned can be considerably large. For example, consider two sequences whose length difference is of one order of magnitude. If this difference is not taken into account, the algorithm will probably explore matrix cells that are outside the boundaries of the anchoring, and thus resulting in more computation time. In this sense, we propose using the geometric mean ($\sqrt{nm}$) to produce a mapping between sequences length ratio and window size. Moreover, k is further adjusted applying a user-defined parameter. Notice that the geometric mean will not assign the same window size to two different sets of sequences s_1 and s_2 of length $10^{l+1}, 10^{l+1}$ and s_3, s_4 of length $10^{l+2}, 10^l$, although the size of the search space would be equal.

2.2 Dynamic Workload Partitioning and Distribution to Threads

IMSAME uses a modified Guided Self Scheduling (GSS) [19] to handle workload assignment. In this line, the query metagenome (the reference metagenome is only processed to generate the hash table) is separated into M partitions each of which will contain m_i subpartitions, with i ranging from 1 to M. Each of these subpartitions will hold a number of reads that will be dynamically assigned to threads using a thread-safe queue when these run out of work. Moreover, the number of partitions is user-defined, and can be adjusted depending on the size of the inputs. Each subpartition is likewise divided by the number of threads t into blocks of reads. Thus, the number of reads contained in each block is determined by the current level of partitioning i, the total number of reads R and the number of threads t. The expression to calculate the number of reads assigned to a block at partition i is as follows:

$$B_i = \frac{\frac{R}{M}}{t * i} = \frac{R}{M * t * i} \tag{1}$$

Where R is the total number of reads in the metagenome, M is the number of partitions, t is the number of available threads and i is the current partition. That is, the metagenome is firstly divided by the number of partitions, and each of these is then divided by the number of threads multiplied by the subpartition depth. Figure 2 shows how the query metagenome is decomposed per partition.

The workload distribution function belongs to the family of $1/x$ functions and shows a decay in the size of blocks in the early partitions in order to assign smaller jobs to the threads as these are consumed. Additionally, the function

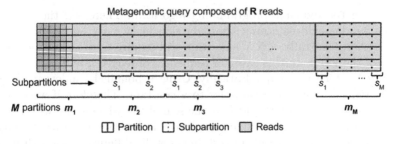

Fig. 2. Query decomposition into workload blocks. Initially, the query metagenome is divided into partitions (red solid lines). Each partition is again divided by the current partitioning level (vertical dashed lines). Finally, each subpartition is divided into blocks of equal number of reads depending of the number of threads available. (Color figure online)

shows a horizontal asymptote that guarantees blocks of reads of a minimum size despite the number of partitions chosen.

3   Results and Discussion

Two separate comparisons were carried out in order to test the two different aspects that have been improved over the original IMSAME version. All sequences used in the comparisons belong the to the Human Microbiome Project[1] (HMP), in particular to the Illumina WGS Assemblies. The run identifiers are provided at each comparison performed in order to allow reproducibility. The testing scenario is set up as follows:

1. A single comparison involving scaffolds to test sequential with optimizations.
2. A comparison involving three different datasets varying in sizes, from small to large. These comparisons will serve to account for the scalability of the parallel improvements in respect to the sequential version.

At last, the speedup from both optimization perspectives are discussed and addressed.

3.1   Infrastructure

The Picasso supercomputer located at the University of Malaga (Malaga, Spain) [20] was used to test the parallelization strategies. The computation was performed using only the fat nodes which contain 8 Intel E7-4870 processors and 2 TB of RAM each. The storage is managed by a Lustre file system supported by a DDN storage rack with five three-dimensional disk enclosures and two redundant SFA10000 controllers. The executions described in this manuscript range from 1 to 32 cores increasing by steps of powers of two. Runtime executions were measured using the *time* command from UNIX-based environments.

---

[1] http://hmpdacc.org/HMASM/.

3.2   Comparison Between the Original and Bounded IMSAME

Besides the improved parallelization strategies, IMSAME has additionally been improved with bounded CPU time and memory usage. In order to perform comparisons to measure the speedup produced by the parallelization techniques, the improvements are tested between the original IMSAME and the bounded in a sequential fashion. For this purpose, two runs composed of scaffolds, namely SRS016105 and SRS017451 were taken from the HMP database and compared using both versions. Since scaffolds are longer than reads, higher penalties were used for affine gap model (−8 for insertion of gap and −4 for extension of gap). Results remained equal for both executions, although variations can be observed if large-scale rearrangements take place (e.g. long range transpositions). The original version of IMSAME took 7 min and 29 s, whereas the bounded version took 55 s, representing a speedup of approximately 8×. This speedup is mostly produced by two facts (1) the diagonal filtering procedure reducing the number of linear extensions performed prior to a gapped alignment and (2) the bounded window applied to the NW algorithm, which substantially reduces the space search. However, it is important to note that the latter speedup is directly proportional to the size of the reads (i.e. smaller reads, smaller speedup).

3.3   Speedup Evaluation of the Parallelization Strategy

The speedup introduced by the parallelization strategy is measured by using three datasets: (1) a small-sized one, (2) a medium-sized one and (3) a large-sized one. Table 1 summarizes the three datasets. This procedure enables us to evaluate the stability of the speedup as a function of the input size.

Table 1. Summary of the dataset used for the speedup evaluation. From left to right: (1) Metagenome pairs compared, (2) Sum of reads from both metagenomes, (3) Sum of the size of both metagenomes in megabytes and (4) Average size of reads in base pairs.

Dataset (Run ID)	Number of reads	Size (MB)	Average read length (bp)
SRS017697	613,983	77	91
SRS019119			
SRS064376	3,401,514	463	100
SRS065347			
SRS018359	14,295,910	1809	99
SRS057022			

Table 2 shows the execution times for each of the datasets along with the speedup and efficiency of each execution. In the same line, Fig. 3 shows the speedup evaluation plot. The speedup is calculated as the time needed by the algorithm run using only one core divided by the time needed using more cores.

Table 2. Execution times, speedup and efficiency for the executions of IMSAME using from 1 to 32 cores. The rows indicate the number of cores whereas the columns refer to time consumption (in seconds), speedup and efficiency per each of the datasets.

Cores	Small			Medium			Large		
	Time (s)	Speedup	Efficiency	Time (s)	Speedup	Efficiency	Time (s)	Speedup	Efficiency
1	425	1.00	1.00	8,634	1.00	1.00	76,253	1.00	1.00
2	252	1.69	0.84	4,770	1.81	0.91	38,009	2.01	1.00
4	126	3.37	0.84	2,571	3.36	0.84	18,867	4.04	1.00
8	76	5.59	0.70	1,262	6.84	0.86	9,838	7.75	0.97
16	42	10.12	0.63	683	12.64	0.79	5,282	14.44	0.90
32	30	14.17	0.44	388	22.25	0.70	2,937	25.96	0.81

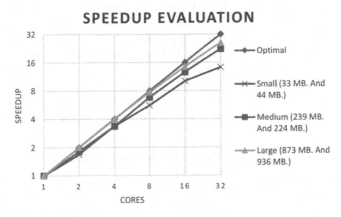

Fig. 3. The speedup is shown for the different datasets (in purple, green and red) along with the optimal speedup (in blue). The x-axis shows the number of cores used per comparison, whereas the y-axis shows the calculated speedup in respect to the number of cores used. (Color figure online)

The efficiency is calculated as the ratio between the achieved speedup and the optimal speedup (equal to the number of cores). As can be seen in Table 2 and Fig. 3, the speedup is nearly optimal in the scenario of enough data, i.e. the large dataset. However, in the case of the small and mid-sized dataset, a decay in efficiency can be observed due to the size of data not being large enough for the number of cores. Moreover:

1. Small dataset (in purple in Fig. 3): The peak of efficiency is achieved using 2 and 4 cores (reaching 84% efficiency). When using more than 4 cores, the dataset size becomes too small and some threads become inactive while others are still processing. To improve efficiency on the small dataset, a higher number of partitions should be used to remove thread balance synchronization at the end of the computation.
2. Medium dataset (in red in Fig. 3): The medium dataset represents a 143% increase in size over the small dataset, and shows a much higher efficiency,

with a peak at 86% using 8 cores. However, similarly to the smaller case, the efficiency (and thus the speedup) decays when using 32 cores.

3. Large dataset (in green in Fig. 3): The larger dataset shows the overall best efficiency and speedup, with a peak at 8 cores and slow decay up to 32 cores, where 81% efficiency is achieved. However, the fact that the speedup is optimal at 2 and 4 cores indicates that probably still more partitioning levels are required in order to avoid thread synchronization.

4 Conclusions

In this manuscript, we have shown an optimized version of IMSAME in which we applied two parallelization strategies, namely (1) a dynamic scheduler for the distribution of work and (2) an n-level parallelization in the computation of alignments using POSIX threads in a shared-memory environment. We have also applied several sequential improvements over the original version, which have improved the overall algorithm complexity and efficiency. Additionally, we have carried out two separate comparisons to prove the performance of IMSAME, that is, firstly, one to validate the sequential improvements over the original version and secondly, another one using three different datasets ranging in sizes to evaluate the achieved speedup and the parallel efficiency.

In order to keep developing IMSAME, we are currently working on:

1. Parallelization of the loading stage.
2. Improve workload distribution by building a regression model to automatically set the number of partitioning levels.
3. Use ROC curves [21] to set the optimal percentage thresholds.
4. Use genetic algorithms to determine optimal scheduling.

Acknowledgments. This work has been partially supported by the European project ELIXIR- EXCELERATE (grant no. 676559), the Spanish national projects Plataforma de Recursos Biomoleculares y Bioinformticos (ISCIII-PT13.0001.0012) and RIRAAF (ISCIII-RD12/0013/0006) and the University of Malaga.

References

1. Alyass, A., Turcotte, M., Meyre, D.: From big data analysis to personalized medicine for all: challenges and opportunities. BMC Med. Genomics **8**(1), 33 (2015)
2. Altschul, S.F., Madden, T.L., Schffer, A.A., Zhang, J., Zhang, Z., Miller, W., Lipman, D.J.: Gapped BLAST and PSI-BLAST: a new generation of protein database search programs. Nucleic Acids Res. **25**(17), 3389–3402 (1997)
3. Darling, A., Carey, L., Feng, W.C.: The design, implementation, and evaluation of mpiBLAST. In: Proceedings of ClusterWorld, pp. 13–15 (2003)
4. http://www.timelogic.com/catalog/757. Accessed 9 May 2017
5. Liu, Y., Schmidt, B.: GSWABE: faster GPU accelerated sequence alignment with optimal alignment retrieval for short DNA sequences. Concurr. Comput. Pract. Exp. **27**(4), 958–972 (2015)

6. Liu, Y., Schmidt, B.: CUSHAW2-GPU: empowering faster gapped short-read alignment using GPU computing. IEEE Design Test **31**(1), 31–39 (2014)

7. Liu, Y., Tran, T.T., Lauenroth, F., Schmidt, B.: SWAPHI-LS: Smith-Waterman algorithm on Xeon Phi coprocessors for long DNA sequences. In: Cluster Computing (CLUSTER), 2014 IEEE IC, pp. 257–265, September 2014

8. Langmead, B.: Aligning short sequencing reads with Bowtie. Curr. Protoc. Bioinform. 11–17 (2010)

9. Li, H., Durbin, R.: Fast and accurate short read alignment with Burrows Wheeler transform. Bioinformatics **25**(14), 1754–1760 (2009)

10. Jing, G., Sun, Z., Wang, H., Gong, Y., Huang, S., Ning, K., Su, X.: Parallel-META 3: comprehensive taxonomical and functional analysis platform for efficient comparison of microbial communities. Sci. Rep. **7**, 40371 (2017)

11. Nichols, B., Buttlar, D., Farrell, J.: A POSIX standard for better multiprocessing. O'Reilly Media Inc., Sebastopol (1996)

12. Perez-Wohlfeil, E., Torreno, O., Trelles, O.: Pairwise and incremental multi-stage alignment of metagenomes: a new proposal. In: International Conference on Bioinformatics and Biomedical Engineering, pp. 74–80, April 2017

13. Ondov, B.D., Treangen, T.J., Melsted, P., Mallonee, A.B., Bergman, N.H., Koren, S., Phillippy, A.M.: Mash: fast genome and metagenome distance estimation using MinHash. Genome Biol. **17**(1), 132 (2016)

14. Benoit, G., Peterlongo, P., Mariadassou, M., Drezen, E., Schbath, S., Lavenier, D., Lemaitre, C.: Multiple comparative metagenomics using multiset k-mer counting. PeerJ Comput. Sci. **2**, e94 (2016)

15. Maillet, N., Collet, G., Vannier, T., Lavenier, D., Peterlongo, P.: COMMET: comparing and combining multiple metagenomic datasets. In: Bioinformatics and Biomedicine (BIBM), 2014 IEEE IC, pp. 94–98, November 2014

16. Gotoh, O.: An improved algorithm for matching biological sequences. J. Mol. Biol. **162**(3), 705–708 (1982)

17. Torreno, O., Trelles, O.: Breaking the computational barriers of pairwise genome comparison. BMC Bioinform. **16**(1), 250 (2015)

18. Pitteway, M.L.V., Watkinson, D.J.: Bresenham's algorithm with Grey scale. Commun. ACM **23**(11), 625–626 (1980)

19. Polychronopoulos, C.D., Kuck, D.J.: Guided self-scheduling: a practical scheduling scheme for parallel supercomputers. IEEE Trans. Comput. **100**(12), 1425–1439 (1987)

20. http://www.scbi.uma.es/site/scbi/hardware. Accessed 9 May 2017

21. Hanley, J.A., McNeil, B.J.: The meaning and use of the area under a receiver operating characteristic (ROC) curve. Radiology **143**(1), 29–36 (1982)

The First International Workshop on Distributed Autonomous Computing in Smart City (DACSC 2017)

The Impact of International Inter-City Investment on Enterprises Performance: Pluralistic Interpretation of Geographical Death

Yanghao Zhan[✉], Yan Chen, and Ruirui Zhai

Beijing University of Posts and Telecommunications, Beijing, China
zhanyanghaoceline@163.com

Abstract. This paper aims to test the impact of inter-city investment on enterprises performance. By using a panel dataset of Chinese firms which have invested in 43 countries and regions over the of 2003–2009 and gravity model, we find that institutional distance is favorable to Chinas outward direct investment, which implies that the Chinese multinationals dont seem willing to enter those countries that have similar institutions with their home country, in this sense, Chinese enterprises outward direct investment can be interpreted as being driven by the motivation of institutional escape. Technology distance displays an Inversed-U shape which suggests some technical distance is the premise for ODI and may reflect the fact of simultaneous existence of both the technology utilization ODI and the technology-seeking ODI of China. Geographical distance has no significant impact on Chinas outward direct investment which supports the proposition of death of distance. These findings point to the importance of going beyond firm boundary to consider various distances between home and host countries in making investment decisions, which not only overcome the defects of the existing studies, but also propose new theoretical explanations for the phenomenon that Chinese enterprises are still capable of ODI even when the ownership advantages are missing. According to the results of this paper, Chinese enterprises should choose to invest in the countries with large institutional distance, small economic and medium technical distance from the home country, and, at the same time, they should not bother geographical distance too much.

Keywords: ODI · Enterprises performance · Geographical distance

1   Introduction

Since 2002, when China officially launched the "going out" strategy, the scale of China's outward direct investment (hereinafter referred to as ODI) has been rising rapidly. According to the "Annual Statistical Bulletin of China's Outward Direct In-vestment in 2011, 82% of China's ODI flew to developing countries (regions), while only 18% to developed economies. It is difficult to explain this kind of ODI distribution only by any single traditional theory of competitive

© Springer International Publishing AG 2017
S. Ibrahim et al. (Eds.): ICA3PP 2017, LNCS 10393, pp. 623–632, 2017.
DOI: 10.1007/978-3-319-65482-9_47

advantage or the home countrys pushing factors or the host countrys pulling factors, because these factors may play a role together [1].

As we all know, OLI paradigm argues that the premise of an enterprises foreign investment which has some specific ownership advantages, such as patents, brands, management skills, etc. Although OLI considers the importance of the host country's location factors, it doesn't take into account the relative importance of the host country's location factors in combination with home country's location factors. So it is difficult for the OLI paradigm to make valuable explanations to justify Chinese enterprises' reverse investment behaviors in the case of lacking of ownership advantages, which is the "paradox of ownership advantages". The paper goes beyond enterprises' own factors to examine the impacts of various dimensional distances between China and host countries on Chinese enterprises' ODI. Its academic contributions are mainly reflected in the following aspects. First, the probe of the impacts of various distances on ODI can provide important theoretical and practical explanations for the "ownership paradox" and, to some extent, answer the question why Chinese companies can still achieve internationalization when they are short of ownership advantages. Second, although some literature has analyzed the impacts of various dimensional gaps on China's ODI decisions, such as cultural and geographic distance, institutional differences, trade liberalization distance and financial freedom distance between the home and host countries, but from the standpoint of economic metrology, only when the impacts of other distances on ODI are put under control can we accurately single out the impact of a particular distance factor on corporate ODI. In view of the fact that there has been no literature has comprehensively analyzed the impacts of the distance dimensions on ODI, we attempt to carry out a comprehensive analysis to extend the existing work and enrich the theoretical interpretation of corporate ODI. Third, some scholars believe the development of technology and transport has made geographical distance no longer important, and put forward the proposition of "distance death" [2]. Our results provide an empirical basis for the exploration of whether the distances are already "dead" or are still affecting the strategic choice of ODI.

2   Literature Review

Traditionally, existing studies of ODI determinants mainly focus on validating OLI paradigm. Qiu and Wang [3] have analyzed the impact of domestic macroeconomic factors (export, resource requirement, wage level, etc.) on China's ODI growth. Some literature express particular concern over how ODI decisions are subject to multinational companies own advantages in configuration with various types of regional advantages [4]. In recent years, several studies have started to pay attention to the promotional or inhibition roles of the home country's institutional factors in ODI [5].

In fact, in addition to the factors of the enterprises themselves, any analysis on ODI determinants must take into account home and host country factors and the synergy. Judging from the empirical research, they have emphatically analyzed the impact of cultural and geographical distances on ODI. The research results of Flores and Aguilera [6] about U.S. multinationals show that cultural distance and ODI flow direction have a significantly negative correlation. While others have proven a significantly complicated relationship between cultural distance and ODI flow direction. For example, Yin and Lu [7] identified the S-curve relationship between cultural distance and ODI flow direction. Regarding to geographical distance, the literature has found negative effects of geographical distance on ODI [8]. Buckley et al. [1] found cultural distance and geographical distance between China and host country is an important factor to affect Chinese enterprises' ODI.

In general, the existing studies on the impact of distances on ODI are limited and fragmented, and there is no way to draw any convincing conclusions from them. The existing empirical work usually looks into one type of distance factors only, assuming that the other distance factors have no effect on ODI or the impact is a constant. This approach leads to the possibility that the impact of certain distance factors on ODI may be caused by other distance factors excluded in the models. We integrate the ODI determinants into a multivariate distance model and empirically validates the impacts of economic distance, institutional distance, cultural distance, geographic distance, technical distance, etc. on Chinas ODI, to reveal the impacts of the factors of China and the host countries' factors and the extent of their discrepancies on Chinese enterprises' ODI. Hence, we are not only to overcome the defects of the existing studies, but also propose new theoretical explanations for the phenomenon that Chinese enterprises are still capable of ODI even when the ownership advantages are missing.

3   Theories and Hypotheses

Distances include not only geographical distance, but also dimensions of culture, administration, politics, economy, etc. [9]. Due to distance types affect ODI in different way, we examine the impacts of various distances separately. Economic distance shows the differences of economic conditions between the home and host country. The convergence of the economic conditions in the market-place enables enterprises to make use of the competitive advantage developed in the home country. Jain found that the homogeneity of economic conditions reflects the convergence of income levels and lifestyles. However, given the fact that many Chinese enterprises invest in developed countries with large economic distances from China to seek strategic assets, the economic distance may also generate positive effects on ODI. As a result, we propose the following competitive hypotheses:

H1a: Economic distance has a negative effect on China's ODI.
H1b: Economic distance has a positive effect on China's ODI.

Traditional ODI theories deem host country's institution as an important location factor, emphasizing that higher quality of the institutional environment will result in higher efficiency of resource allocations and greater attractiveness to foreign investors. However, we should consider institutional quality and environmental difference between the host and home country, i.e. institutional distance.

Institutional distance is the management's subjective perception of the cost and uncertainties in its operations in the host country. Some of the home country's institutional factors (high tax rates, corruption, regulatory uncertainty, etc.) may result institution-based ODI escape [10]. Greater institutional distance between the home and host countries will bring multinationals more opportunities for institutional arbitrage, so we propose:

H2: Institutional distance has a positive effect on China's ODI.

To the Uppsala Model, enterprise ODI usually first enters countries in a shorter geographical distance, followed gradually by countries in a longer distance. Investing in a country with a shorter geographical distance will reduce uncertainty in the prospects of returns, and, simultaneously, facilitate learning experiences in the host country. Geographical distance is not merely a measure of material distance; it has an implication on transport cost as well. The geo-distance cost of bulk products such as steel and cement is significantly higher than that of other products, and the cost is exceptionally high for transporting fragile and fresh products. Therefore, geographical distance between the host and home country reduces the efficiency-seeking ODI [12]. Therefore, we propose:

H3: Geographical distance has a negative effect on China's ODI.

Traditional ODI researches are conducted mainly on the hypothesis that the home-country enterprise owns technical advantages and the premise for ODI is that there exists certain technical distance between the home and host country. Developing countries have witnessed the emergence of learning-oriented ODI and strategy-oriented ODI to seek strategic resources represented by knowledge and technology on a global scale [6]. However, in accordance with "Technological Accumulation Hypothesis" [14], when there is quite a long distance between the home and host, ODI will decrease due to the poor absorption capacity. Therefore, foreign investment occurs out of technical distance to a certain extent. However, when technical distance is too large, ODI will decrease. Thus, we propose:

H4: The effect of technology distance on China's ODI is in an inverted U-shape.

4   Research Methodology and Data

4.1   Definitions of the Variables

Dependent variable. It determined by the ODI/GDP proportion. It can eliminate the influence of home country's economic size on ODI. ODI data from Bulletin of Ministry of Commerce on China's ODI (2010) and GDP (in current US$ 100 million) from World Development Indicator Database of the World Bank (2010).

Independent variables. Economic distance (ED). We adopt the per capita GDP difference of the host and home country as an indicator to reflect the inter-state economic distance.

Institutional distance (ID). Institution can be divided into formal rule-governed institutions and normative institutions. Based on the data availability, we intend to adopt the distance of the economic system as a proxy in combination with 10 major categories of indicators from the Economic Freedom Index (EFI) released annually by the American Heritage Foundation and the Wall Street Journal. The Index of Economic Freedom is the simple mean value of the 10 categories of indicators, which will exert impacts on China's ODI. Therefore, the paper takes it to represent institutional distance.

Geographical distance (GD). We use the geographical mileage between the capital city of home country and that of host country to represent geographical distance, which automatically calculated from geographical distance on the Internet.

Technical distance (TD). We select the commonly-accepted R&D/GDP as an indicator for a country's level of technology, which from http://stats.uis.unesco.org/.

Control variables. RTG. We use the ratio of the bilateral trade flows and the GDP of the two countries as the measurement indicator to gauge economic and trade relations between China and the host country. The bilateral trade data is obtained from the website of Minis-try of Commerce of China.

Two dummy variables - the Bilateral Investment Treaty (BIP) and the Agreement on Avoidance of Double Taxation (ADT), BIP, ADT are dummy variables which obtained from "Guide to Foreign Investment" by Ministry of Commerce of China (2011).

4.2   Empirical Model

In order to use the gravity model for analysis of the relationship between distances and China's ODI, we assumed the aforementioned variables are major factors affecting the location selection of China's ODI. And in order to convert the non-linear relationship into a linear relationship, we take the log-linear conversion. The modified gravity model equation is as follows:

$$Ln\left(\text{ODI}_{ict}\right) = \alpha_t + \beta_{1t}Ln\left(\text{RTG}_{ict}\right) + \beta_{2t}Ln\left(\text{BIP}_{ict}\right) + \beta_{3t}Ln\left(\text{ADT}_{ict}\right) \\ + \beta_{4t}Ln\left(\text{VAR}_{jt}\right) + \mu_{ict}. \tag{1}$$

The following empirical model is obtained from Eq. (1):

Model 1 $Ln\left(\text{ODI}_{ict}\right) = \alpha_0 + \beta_{01}Ln\left(\text{RTG}_{ict}\right) + \beta_{02}Ln\left(\text{BIP}_{ict}\right) + \beta_{03}Ln\left(\text{ADT}_{ict}\right) + \mu_{ict}$

Model 2–4 $Ln\left(\text{ODI}_{ict}\right) = \alpha_t + \beta_{1t}Ln\left(\text{RTG}_{ict}\right) + \beta_{2t}Ln\left(\text{BIP}_{ict}\right) + \beta_{3t}Ln\left(\text{ADT}_{ict}\right) + \beta_{4t}Ln\left(\text{VAR}_{jt}\right) + \mu_{ict}$, where VAR = ED, ID, GD

Model 5 $Ln\left(\text{ODI}_{ict}\right) = \alpha_t + \beta_{1t}Ln\left(\text{RTG}_{ict}\right) + \beta_{2t}Ln\left(\text{BIP}_{ict}\right) + \beta_{3t}Ln\left(\text{ADT}_{ict}\right) + \sum \beta_{4t}Ln\left(\text{VAR}_{jt}\right) + \mu_{ict}$, where VAR = TD, TD^2

Model 6 $Ln\left(\text{ODI}_{ict}\right) = \alpha_t + \beta_{1t}Ln\left(\text{RTG}_{ict}\right) + \beta_{2t}Ln\left(\text{BIP}_{ict}\right) + \beta_{3t}Ln\left(\text{ADT}_{ict}\right) + \sum \beta_{4t}Ln\left(\text{VAR}_{jt}\right) + \mu_{ict}$, where VAR = ED, ID, GD, TD

Where α denotes the constant terms and μ residuals.

4.3 Data

In view of the availability and continuity of the data, we select 301 sample data from 43 countries over the period of 2003–2009. The basis for the sample selection interval is that China's ODI started to increase substantially on the annual basis in 2003 under the influence of China's "going out" strategy which was officially launched for implemented in 2002. Sample countries or regions are mainly the top-ranking economies in receiving of China's outward direct investments. Samples cover Asia, Europe, North America, South America and Oceania, including both developed economies and developing countries or regions which has enough representation.

5 Results

5.1 Estimation Results

As we use a panel data set, problems associated with autocorrelation may bias the estimated results. In order to avoid the problem of multicollinearity, we use the variance inflation factor method (VIF) and correlation matrix. From Table 1, we find VIF are all significantly less than 10, and there exists a slight multicollinearity among the independent variables, so, the sample data can be used for the regression analysis.

We use the generalized least square (GLS) estimator to estimate our models. Due to panel data necessitates a choice between fixed effects (FE) or random effects (RE) models, so we implemented a Hausman test which indicated that the RE model is preferred to the FE model at 1% level of significance.

Table 2 shows the results. Model 1 shows that the coefficient of ED is negative and statistically significant, corroborating H1a but leading no for support H1b. Model 2 shows the coefficient of ID is negative and statistically significant, supporting H2. Model 4 shows GD is not significant and doesn't support H3. Finally, the coefficient of TD in Model 5 is negative and highly significant, while the coefficient of TD2 is positive and significant and supports H4, indicating an

Table 1. Correlation coefficient matrix and VIF

	Mean	S.D.	BIP	ADT	RD	ID	GD	TD	VIF
RTG	−5.808	1.406	−0.089	0.204	0.485	0.435	−0.307	0.014	3.405
BIP	0.742	0.363		−0.042	0.018	0.009	−0.274	−0.011	1.3252
ADT	0.737	0.440			0.125	0.010	−0.001	−0.235	1.276
RD	7.451	1.456				0.618	−0.104	−0.003	6.054
ID	2.251	1.173					−0.138	0.051	2.397
GD	6.834	0.652						−0.357	2.194
ID	−0.226	0.723							2.935

inverted U-shaped relationship between technical distance and Chinese enterprises ODI. Regarding the results of control variables, although the BIP and the ADT variables in the model are not significant, the impact of the RTG has been significantly positive, which is consistent with interpretations of the OLI paradigm and the gravity model.

5.2 Robustness Test

We have performed certain robustness tests to examine the reliability and stability of the results in Table 2. First, we estimate the full model that includes all variables except the technical distance squared item, and the results are presented in the last column in Table 2. Model 6 shows no qualitative difference between the main results and the results in Models 1–4. Second, in theory, the inverse relationship is established between foreign investments and multiple distances. Namely, ODI shortens the distances between the home and host country (except GD). However, it is a relatively long process to shorten the distances, and ODI is just one of the factors, so it is unlikely for the distance variables to become endogenous. Despite this, we still use the instrumental variables and re-estimate the models. We select "bilateral trade volume (ST)" and "religious differences (DR)" as the instrumental variables for technical distance (TD). The bilateral trade volume between the two countries will affect the technical distance between the two countries: the greater the volume of bilateral trade between the two countries is, the smaller the technical distance will be. In addition, the "bilateral trade volume (ST)" and the "religious differences (DR)" as two

Table 2. GLS results

Independent variables	Model 1	Model 2	Model 3	Model 4	Model 5	Model 6
ED	−0.237*** (−6.162)					−0.172*** (−4.480)
ID		0.526* (1.721)				0.064*** (2.286)
GD				−0.203 (−1.441)		0.236 (1.096)
TD					−0.479*** (−2.016)	−1.121 (−1.966)
TD²					−0.326*** (−3.158)	
Control variables						
RTG	0.985*** (16.215)	0.880*** (13.130)	0.808*** (15.974)	0.891*** (11.992)	1.731*** (56.795)	0.540*** (5.526)
BIP	−0.152 (−0.681)	−0.255 (−1.194)	−0.320 (−1.001)	−0.317 (−1.281)	−0.642 (−1.627)	−0.983 (0.885)
ADT	0.065 (0.377)	−0.147 (−0.605)	0.312* (1.841)	−0.266 (−1.133)	0.614*** (2.138)	0.728*** (2.911)
R²	0.564	0.489	0.609	0.510	0.631	0.699
F	90.733	67.125	109.245	73.189	60.471	55.678
N	286	286	286	286	183	183

Table 3. IV results

Independent variables	Model 1	Model 2	Model 3	Model 4	Model 5	Model 6
ED	−0.311**					−0.721***
	(−3.021)					(−3.561)
ID		0.624*				1.812***
		(2.114)				(3.100)
GD				−0.020		0.329
				(−0.102)		(1.136)
TD					−0.301***	−0.256
					(−4.726)	(−0.412)
TD²					−0.304***	
					(−3.001)	
Control variables						
RTG	1.001***	0.745***	0.846***	0.880***	2.008***	0.981***
	(−9.216)	(−7.789)	(−10.2)	(−6.231)	(−10.232)	(−6.859)
BIP	−0.398	−0.685	−0.395	−0.425	−0.169	0.651
	(−1.319)	(−1.539)	(−1.601)	(−0.571)	(−0.368)	(−1.681)
ADT	0.270	0.051	0.563	−0.112	0.532*	0.752***
	(−0.845)	(−0.137)	(−1.643)	(−0.225)	(−1.541)	(2.984)
R²	0.501	0.51	0.514	0.41	0.54	0.56
F	45.231	40.67	52.303	40.521	56.836	35.004
N	286	286	286	286	183	183

instrumental variables do not directly affect the proportion of ODI in GDP, so these two variables are suitable as instrumental variables. Refer to Table 3 for the estimation results with the instrumental variables. We have noted that although there is some change about the significance level of some variables. Nevertheless, in general, the results in Tables 2 and 3 are highly consistent, which indicates that the estimation results of the paper are relatively stable.

6   Discussions and Conclusions

6.1   Discussions

From the results, we find that economic distance has a negative rather than positive effect on Chinas ODI, which indicates that greater economic distance leads to less ODI of Chinese enterprises. This result is consistent with that of Jain [10], who found the economic homogeneity of the home and host country conducive to ODI. Our samples capture the average effect, and the empirical results show that, in general, greater distance results in less ODI of Chinese enterprises. And we find that institutional distance has a significant role in promoting China's ODI. Geographical distance has no significant impact on China's ODI. It's generally believed that geo-graphical distance will incur the "iceberg cost". A bigger geographical distance leads to bigger iceberg costs which in turn results in greater transaction costs to generate greater impediment to investments. However, the development of modern means of transport and communication technologies, geographical distance less and less important. Our results support the proposition of "death of distance" [2]. It should be noted that, in the context of economic globalization, enterprises' international behaviors have undergone tremendous changes, which cannot be explained by the Uppsala model [15]. It is the same case with Chinese companies as well. In terms of the purpose of enterprises entering the international market, the traditional and progressive route is not the only international stage model; in terms of the enterprises' external marketing order, many Chinese enterprises dont necessarily follow the geographical distance in a step-by-step manner in their expansion. Finally, we find that technical distance between the host country and China has an inverted U-shaped impact on Chinas ODI. This suggests that some technical distance is the premise for ODI. The inverted U-shaped relation-ship may reflect the fact of simultaneous existence of both the technology utilization ODI and the technology-seeking ODI of China, which harbors very complex relation-ships between the technical distance and China's ODI. It is easy to understand the impact of technical distance on ODI may be subject to a series of corporate factors beyond the control of the models in this paper, such as industrial characteristics and other factors. Due to data limitations, there is no control over these factors in the paper.

6.2 Conclusions

Generally, the main innovation of this paper lies in its efforts to incorporate the home and host country factors into a unified framework for the purpose of analyzing the impact of the difference between the two on the location selection of China's ODI. Our results show that, when selecting locations for ODI, Chinas enterprises need to take full account of the docking and the relative levels of the home and host country factors. The empirical results are of important reference significance for potential foreign-investing enterprises. First of all, when making foreign investment decisions, managers have to consider not only their own level of competitive advantage, the home country's policy support and a variety of regional advantages of the host country, but also the various distances between the home and host country, and they must balance both the internal and external factors of the two enterprise boundaries. Second, when selecting locations by means of distance factors, managers should consider a variety of distance factors in a systematic way. According to the results of this paper, Chinese enterprises should choose to invest in the countries with large institutional distance, small economic and cultural distances and medium technical distance from the home country, and, at the same time, they should not bother geo-graphical distance too much.

References

1. Buckley, P.J., Clegg, L.J., Cross, A.R., et al.: The determinants of Chinese outward foreign direct investment. J. Int. Bus. Stud. **38**(4), 499–518 (2007)
2. Nijkamp, P.: The death of distance. In: Frey, B.S., Iselin, D. (eds.) Economic Ideas You Should Forget, pp. 93–94. Springer, Cham (2017). doi:10.1007/978-3-319-47458-8_40
3. Qiu, L.C., Wang, F.L.: Empirical study of the main macro influencing factors on China's direct investment abroad. J. Int. Trade (6), 78–80 (2008)
4. Cheng, S., Stough, R.R.: Location decisions of Japanese new manufacturing plants in China: a discrete-choice analysis. Ann. Reg. Sci. **40**(2), 369–387 (2006)
5. Luo, Y., Xue, Q., Han, B.: How emerging market governments promote out-ward FDI: experience from China. J. World Bus. **45**(1), 68–79 (2010)
6. Flores, R.G., Aguilera, R.V.: Globalization and location choice: an analysis of US multinational firms in 1980 and 2000. J. Int. Bus. Stud. **38**(7), 1187–1210 (2007)
7. Yin, H.F., Lu, M.H.: Cultural distance and foreign direct investment flows: the S-curve hypothesis. South Econ. (1), 26–38 (2011)
8. Eichengreen, B., Tong, H.: Is China's FDI coming at the expense of other countries? J. Jap. Int. Econ. **21**(2), 153–172 (2007)
9. Luostarinen, R.: Internationalization of the Firm. Helsinki School of Economics, Helsinki (1980)
10. Jain, S.C.: Standardization of international marketing strategy: some research hypotheses. J. Mark. **53**(1), 70–79 (1989)
11. Rugman, A.M., Verbeke, A.: Multinational enterprises and public policy. J. Int. Bus. Stud. **29**(1), 115–136 (1998)
12. O'Grady, S., Henry, W.L.: The psychic distance paradox. J. Int. Bus. Stud. **27**(2), 309–333 (1996)
13. Dunning, J.H.: Location and the multinational enterprise: a neglected factor? J. Int. Bus. Stud. **20**(1), 45–66 (1998)
14. Cantwell, J.: Technological Innovation and Multinational Corporations. Basil Black-well, Oxford (1989)
15. Axinn, C.N., Matthyssens, P.: Limits of Internationalization theories in an unlimited world. Int. Mark. Rev. **19**(5), 436–449 (2002)

Energy Efficient Manycast Routing, Modulation Level and Spectrum Assignment in Elastic Optical Networks for Smart City Applications

Xiao Luo$^{(\boxtimes)}$, Xue Chen, and Lei Wang

State Key Laboratory of Information Photonics and Optical Communications,
Beijing University of Posts and Telecommunications, Beijing, China
{luoxiao1218,xuechen,wang.lei}@bupt.edu.com

Abstract. As one of key technologies for supporting smart city, distributed computing provides huge networking resources for smart city applications. Manycast, as a point to multi-point communication scheme, is particularly applicable for dealing with massive data simultaneously in distributed computing. Moreover, elastic optical networks (EONs) are emerging as attractive candidates to achieve high throughput distributed computing. However, the rapid development of smart optical networks brings about substantial energy consumption which becomes a critical problem currently. In this paper, we present an energy efficient manycast routing, modulation level and spectrum assignment (EEM-RMLSA) algorithm in EONs supporting smart city applications. Firstly, a new gene encoding scheme is proposed to encapsulate incoming manycast demands in an efficient way. Then, the corresponding genetic algorithm based heuristic is proposed to solve dynamic EEM-RMLSA problem. Simulation results clearly demonstrate that the proposed heuristic achieves significant energy saving and request blocking probability reduction compared to benchmark algorithms.

Keywords: Energy efficient · Manycast · RMLSA · Elastic Optical Network · Smart city

1 Introduction

By 2050, 70% of world population which means over 6 billion people will live in urban regions [1]. To guarantee sustainable development of city, efficient management of resource and high quality of life, comprehensive information and communication infrastructure which makes critical components and services of a city more interactive should be established. With this trend, the concept of smart city [2] is proposed to achieve a seamless connection among people, education, healthcare, public safety, commercial activity and transportation, which calls for communication system and technology innovations to deal with the great emergence of high speed, heterogeneous and distributed data transmission. Specially, distributed computing technology could be applied for network

© Springer International Publishing AG 2017
S. Ibrahim et al. (Eds.): ICA3PP 2017, LNCS 10393, pp. 633–641, 2017.
DOI: 10.1007/978-3-319-65482-9_48

resources provisioning with flexible-bandwidth traffics among smart city applications, such as data-centric computing, parallel computing and transactional applications communication.

Recently, the demonstration of flexible-grid elastic optical networks (EONs) [3] realizes efficient and flexible access to vast bandwidths in optical fibers. The EONs with much finer spectrum granularity (e.g., 6.25 GHz or 12.5 GHz) dynamically provide just-enough bandwidth for arriving demands which has been considered as a promising candidate to support high-throughput and cost-effective distributed computing. Routing, modulation level and spectrum assignment (RMLSA or simply RSA) is a fundamental problem in EONs [4]. The basic constraints to RSA/RMLSA in EONs are spectrum contiguity and spectrum continuity, which states the allocated frequency slots (FSs) on one optical fiber stay contiguously on frequency axis and light path must use the same FSs in each fiber link along the entire route without wavelength conversion, respectively. Moreover, RSA/RMLSA problem is known as NP-complete [5] and massive literatures have investigated both static and dynamic RSA/RMLSA schemes in EONs [5].

In EONs, manycast [6] is a new type of point to multi-point communication framework which destination nodes are chosen from a set of candidate destination nodes (any k out of D, where $D > k$). By contrast to traditional multicast communication scheme, i.e., destination nodes are specified ahead of time, manycast has ability to dynamically determine destination nodes based on the current state of network which brings about the better network load balance. Basically, destination nodes selection criteria could depend on metrics of service needs, such as distance between source and destinations, computational power of network, and degree of traffic load on each network node. Manycast has become one of main communication schemes dealing with high bitrates and flexible traffic under big data and smart city background, particularly used in inter datacenter disaster backup, cloud computing and e-Science. Manycast routing, modulation level and spectrum assignment (MA-RMLSA) problem essentially aims to find highly efficient manycast light tree that modulation format and spectrum resources keep the same along the entire light tree, to maintain favorable network transmission performance and network resource utilization.

According to an up-to-date survey, energy consumption of global networks accounts for about 8% of total energy consumption, and the proportion will reach up to 20% by 2020 [7]. Specially, the dramatic increase of optical traffic in various bitrates and capacities leads to rapid growth of optical network energy consumption. Energy consumption of optical network has become an essential influence factor to optical network planning and management. Therefore, the energy efficient RMLSA, which can provide energy saving network provisioning approaches to serve overall traffics in light-paths with activating minimum idle equipments in networks, is the key to solve massive energy consumption problem in optical networks [8].

In this paper, we focus on energy efficiency in EONs with manycast traffic for smart city applications. To solve energy efficient manycast routing, modulation level and spectrum assignment (EEM-RMLSA) problem, we propose a new gene encoding scheme and a corresponding heuristic algorithm under genetic algorithm framework with the goal of minimizing the overall network energy consumption, called unicast requests decomposing gene encoding based genetic algorithm (URD-GA). Comparing with referenced EEM-RMLSA algorithms, URD-GA can obtain better performance in network energy efficiency and request blocking probability reduction.

The rest of the paper is organized as follows. Section 2 describes EEM-RMLSA in EONs. In Sect. 3, the gene encoding scheme is described and Sect. 4 introduces the proposed algorithm. The evaluation of proposed algorithm with numerical simulations is presented in Sect. 5. Finally, Sect. 6 summarizes the paper.

2 EEM-RMLSA in EONs

2.1 Network Model

The physical network topology of EONs is structured as a graph $G(V, E)$, where V denotes node set and E denotes fiber link set. Moreover, we assume all nodes in EONs are able to split an input optical signal to any number of output ports which is achieved by multicast-capable optical cross connect (MC-OXC) [6].

We denote a manycast request as $MaR=s, D, k, C$, where s is source node, and $D = \{d_1, d_2, , d_j\}$ is candidate destination node set and d_j represents the jth candidate destination node, k ($k < |D|$) is the number of destination nodes which must be connected to source node, C is capacity of manycast request. We assume manycast request is routed by light tree without spectrum conversion that starts from source node to all selected destination nodes.

For manycast destination node selection, the number of candidate routing light trees for each manycast request is significant rising with the increment of network scale and the number of candidate destination nodes. Different destination node combinations lead to a large number of available MA-RMLSA schemes, it is important to choose the optimum one according to the current state of network and the aim of request. For modulation level allocation, transmission adaptive modulation level allocation policy is utilized in EONs which depends on distance of the longest branch in manycast light tree. To achieve the highest spectral efficiency, we always choose the highest modulation level for manycast light tree as long as transmission distance permits [9]. There are four modulation formats, i.e., binary phase-shifted keying (BPSK), quadrature phase shift keying (QPSK), 8 quadrature amplitude modulation (8-QAM) and 16-QAM, which correspond to modulation levels from 1 to 4. Modulation format and the maximum transmission reach can be mapped with respect to the relationship shown in Table 1 [6].

For spectrum resource assignment, with the allocated modulation level and the given request capacity, we can calculate the number of continuous FSs that assigned to manycast light tree as follows.

$$N = \left\lceil \frac{C}{m \cdot C_{BPSK}} \right\rceil + n_b. \tag{1}$$

Table 1. The relationship between modulation format and transmission reach.

Modulation format	Transmission reach
BPSK	10,000 km
QPSK	5000 km
8-QAM	2500 km
16-QAM	1250 km

Where N is the number of FSs, m denotes modulation level, and C_{BPSK} is the capacity of a FS with BPSK modulation format which equals 12.5 Gbit/s. n_b represents the number of FSs used for guard band which equals 1 in this paper.

2.2   Energy Consumption Model

In this section, we model the energy consumption of EONs by considering four main energy-consuming network elements, IP router port, bandwidth variable optical transponder (BV-OPT), bandwidth variable optical cross connect (BV-OXC) and optical amplifier (OA), respectively. Furthermore, we assume that network elements can be turned off when they are idle to reach the maximum network energy efficiency.

IP router port and BV-OPT are main energy consumption elements in source and destination nodes. In this paper, we assume the energy consumption of each IP router port consists of fixed energy consumption part and traffic-variable energy consumption part, denoted as $PC_{ipFixed}$ and $PC_{ipVaria}$. The energy consumption of BV-OPT also consists of fixed energy consumption part and traffic-variable energy consumption part, denoted as $PC_{OPTFixed}$ and $PC_{OPTVaria}$. BV-OXC and OA are main energy consumption elements in intermediate nodes and transmission links, respectively. We use PC_{OXC} and PC_{OA} to represent corresponding energy consumption of them. The typical values of these four network elements that presented in [8,10] are shown in Table 2, where d indicates node degree, a indicates the number of add/drop capable ports.

Table 2. Typical energy consumption values.

Definition	Value of energy consumption
$PC_{ipFixed}$	1329.33 W
$PC_{ipVaria}$	0.465 W/Gbit/s
$PC_{OPTFixed}$	120 W
$PC_{OPTVaria}$	0.180 W/Gbit/s
PC_{OXC}	$(150 + 85d + 50a)$ W
PC_{OA}	110 W

3   Gene Encoding Scheme

In genetic algorithm, one of the most essential steps is gene encoding. An efficient gene encoding scheme named unicast requests decomposing (URD) gene encoding is proposed to constitute candidate solution set in a try to cover all way for searching possible optimal solutions. The example of URD gene encoding is shown in Fig. 1. There is an arrived manycast request, which source node is A and destination nodes should be chosen two from node B, C and D. The URD gene encoding scheme decomposes manycast request into three candidate unicast requests and selects any two of them to form a candidate unicast request combination. Then encode all candidate unicast request combinations with random selection of candidate light-path L, modulation level m and spectrum resource N to form a gene. Note that we calculate all available light-paths for each node pair in EONs ahead of time. Modulation level allocation and spectrum resource assignment are followed the rules mentioned in Sect. 2.1. We regard the set of genes as a chromosome and the set of chromosomes as a population. To keep diversity of population, we change candidate light-path of a gene to form a new one. The corresponding values of m and N may be changed along with candidate light-path changing in new gene. Finally, a large scale candidate solution set which contains various gene combinations is constituted.

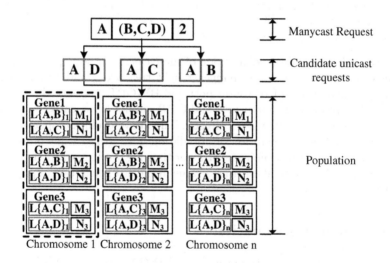

Fig. 1. The example of URD mechanism.

4   EEM-RMLSA Heuristic Algorithm

In this section, we propose a heuristic algorithm according to genetic algorithm framework based on URD gene encoding scheme, which is abbreviated to URD-GA. There are five fundamental procedures in genetic algorithm framework, gene encoding, selection, crossover, mutation and fitness value calculation, in order. For URD-GA, after gene encoding, genetic evolution operations are initiated with the first generation of population. Roulette wheel algorithm [11] is used in selection operation to get all chromosomes we need. Then crossover and mutation operations randomly happen on genes of selected chromosomes with specific rates. The fitness value of gene is calculated by fitness function at last. We assume that fitness function of URD-GA is the total energy consumption of manycast light tree, which can be expressed as follows.

$$FitVal = PC_{tree}. \tag{2}$$

Where *FitVal* and PC_{tree} denotes fitness value of a gene and energy consumption of manycast light tree, respectively. Fitness function can reflect energy consumption degree of a gene and the smaller fitness value leads to a better EEM-RMLSA solution. Moreover, the detailed energy consumption of manycast light tree can be calculated by summing energy consumption of source node, destination nodes, intermediate nodes and intermediate optical links in manycast light tree, as follows.

$$\begin{aligned}
PC_{tree} &= PC_{ip}(s) + PC_{OPT}(s) + \sum_{j=1}^{k} (PC_{ip}(d_j) + PC_{OPT}(d_j)) \\
&+ \sum_{n \in tree, n \neq s, d_j} PC_{OXC}(n) + \tau_{OA} \cdot PC_{OA} \\
&= PC_{ipFixed}(s) + PC_{ipVaria}(s) + PC_{OPTFixed}(s) + PC_{OPTVaria}(s) \\
&+ \sum_{j=1}^{k} (PC_{ipFixed}(d_j) + PC_{ipVaria}(d_j) + PC_{OPTFixed}(d_j) + PC_{OPTVaria}(d_j)) \\
&+ \sum_{n \in tree, n \neq s, d_j} PC_{OXC}(n) + \tau_{OA} \cdot PC_{OA}.
\end{aligned} \tag{3}$$

Where n denotes intermediate node of manycast request, $_{OA}$ stands for the number of optical amplifiers in manycast light tree. PC_{ip} and PC_{OPT} denote the energy consumption of IP router port and BV-OPT, respectively. The fixed energy consumption of IP router port and OPT will not be repeatedly calculated if they have been in working state already. The above evolution operations will iterate to produce new generation of population until fitness value of genes has stabilized or termination condition of algorithm has been reached. Finally, we select the gene with the smallest fitness value in the last generation of population to be EEM-RMLSA solution.

5   Performance Evaluation

We evaluate performance of the proposed URD-GA in 14-node NSFNET, with 12.5 GHz for each FS capacity. The capacity of each manycast request is randomly chosen within the range [10–100] Gbits/s. All candidate light-paths and light trees are pre-calculated. Furthermore, the multicast requests decomposing gene encoding based genetic algorithm (MRD-GA) is also proposed to be a benchmark. MRD gene encoding scheme decomposes a manycast request into a few multicast requests and encodes each multicast request with its candidate light tree, modulation level and spectrum resource to form a gene. By changing manycast light tree in a gene to form a new one, we can constitute diverse genes.

After MRD gene encoding, there are a few small scale populations corresponding to each multicast request. The total numbers of genes in all populations which are constituted by MRD gene encoding are equal to the numbers of genes in the population constituted by URD gene encoding. The genetic operations for each population in MRD-GA are the same as URD-GA. The only difference between URD-GA and MRD-GA is gene encoding scheme. Energy efficient manycast routing and spectrum algorithm (P-EEM) and the blocking aware-EEM (BA-EEM) routing and spectrum algorithm presented in [8] are also simulated as benchmarks under our network model.

Figure 2(a) shows network energy consumption with five candidate destination nodes in each manycast request, of which three should be reached ($D = 5$ and $k = 3$). Its demonstrated that URD-GA can reach the maximum network energy saving under different traffic loads. URD-GA can reduce network energy consumption in 3.5% 8.4%, 2.5% 12.9% and 13.6% 22.8% compared to MRD-GA, P-EEM and BA-EEM, respectively. This is because URD-GA searches possible optimal EEM-RMLSA solution from the larger scale candidate solution set, while MRD-GA optimizes possible multicast solutions separately in a few small scale populations and then chooses the best one from them. The P-EEM and BA-EEM choose the energy efficient manycast light tree in a number of candidate multicast shortest path spanning trees and optimize it to be the final solution, which narrows searching scope of candidate manycast light trees as well.

The comparison results of request blocking probability among four algorithms are shown in Fig. 2(b). It is observed that URD-GA has the best performance in request blocking probability reduction and the trend comes more obviously with traffic load increase. This is due to the highly efficient solution searching ability from large scale candidate solutions and reliable sub-optimal solution selection ability of URD-GA.

It is worthy to mention that simulation results of URD-GA are slightly better than MRD-GA shown in Fig. 2(a) and (b). It can be explained in two aspects, searching scale and searching diversity. The population scale in URD-GA is a few times as each population scale in MRD-GA. The larger population scale leads to

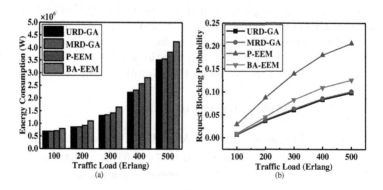

Fig. 2. (a) Energy consumption comparison and (b) blocking probability comparison.

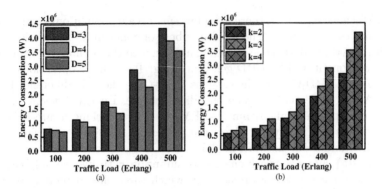

Fig. 3. (a) Energy consumption comparison of URD-GA in different D and (b) in different k.

the wider search range which further brings about a higher possibility to find the better solution. Moreover, gene crossover and mutation operations in URD-GA may change manycast routing light paths in genes which could generate different kinds of genes, while these operations in MRD-GA may change manycast light tree in genes which leads to less diversity degree of genes. The higher diversity degree of genes also makes the higher possibility to find the better solution.

Figure 3(a) shows the impact of D on total network energy consumption (let $k = 3$). It is observed that with the increase of D, network energy consumption is decreasing at each specific traffic load. This is because the freedom degree of destination node selection rising with the increase of D and more energy efficient manycast light tree may be found. In Fig. 3(b), the energy consumption under different k are shown (let $D = 5$). The similar simulation result trend can be drawn with the decrease of k. This is due to available network spectrum resource could be allocated to each manycast request increase with the decrease of k.

In Table 3, we evaluate running time of four algorithms with $k = 3$, $D = 5$ of each manycast request. Its demonstrated that P-EEM consumes the least running time due to the simplest algorithm complexity. MRD-GA has less running time than URD-GA. This is because MRD-GA encodes multicast requests as a few small scale populations leading to faster solution searching. URD-GA encodes all candidate unicast request combinations as one large scale population which needs taking more time to search the appropriate solution.

Table 3. Running time comparison.

Number of requests	URD-GA	MRD-GA	P-EEM	BA-EEM
10	0.1682 s	0.1037 s	0.0035 s	0.0039 s
20	0.3735 s	0.1988 s	0.0059 s	0.0062 s
50	0.7381 s	0.5166 s	0.0155 s	0.0178 s
100	1.6478 s	1.3024 s	0.0284 s	0.0364 s

6   Conclusion

To solve EEM-RMLSA problem in EONs for smart city applications, the unicast requests decomposing gene encoding based genetic algorithm (URD-GA) with the goal of minimizing the overall network energy consumption is proposed. URD gene encoding scheme constitutes a large scale population which tries to cover available EEM-RMLSA solutions as many as possible. Extensive candidate EEM-RMLSA solutions in population and efficient searching ability of URD-GA lead to better EEM-RMLSA solutions. Simulation results show that URD-GA achieves 22.8% energy saving at the best with the cost of acceptable algorithm complexity increase. Therefore, URD-GA is suitable for solving EEM-RMLSA problem in EONs, which has great value to smart city development.

Acknowledgments. This study is supported by National Natural Science Foundation of China (No. 61571061).

References

1. Jin, J., et al.: Network architecture and QoS issues in the internet of things for a smart city. In: Proceedings of ISCIT 2012, pp. 956–961. IEEE, Australia (2012)
2. Nam, T., Pardo, T.A.: Conceptualizing smart city with dimensions of technology, people, and institutions. In: Proceedings of the 12th Annual International Conference on Digital Government Research 2011, pp. 282–291. ACM, USA (2011)
3. Ji, Y., Zhang, J., et al.: Prospects and research issues in multi-dimensional all optical networks. Sci. China Inf. Sci. **59**(10), 101301:1–101301:14 (2016)
4. Wang, C., Shen, G., Bose, S.K.: Distance adaptive dynamic routing and spectrum allocation in elastic optical networks with shared backup path protection. J. Lightweight. Technol. **33**(14), 2955–2964 (2015)
5. Chatterjee, B.C., Sarma, N., Oki, E.: Routing and spectrum allocation in elastic optical networks: a tutorial. IEEE Commun. Surv. Tutor. **17**(3), 1776–1800 (2015)
6. Luo, X., et al.: Manycast routing, modulation level and spectrum assignment over elastic optical networks. Opt. Fiber Technol. **33**, 317–326 (2017)
7. Wu, J., Ning, Z., Guo, L.: Energy-efficient survivable grooming in software-defined. IEEE Access **5**, 6454–6463 (2017)
8. Fallahpour, A., Beyranvand, H., Salehi, J.A.: Energy-efficient manycast routing and spectrum assignment in elastic optical networks for cloud computing environment. J. Lightweight Technol. **33**(19), 4008–4018 (2015)
9. Yang, T., Liu, W., Chen, X., et al.: Modulation format independent blind polarization demultiplexing algorithms for elastic optical networks. Sci. China Inf. Sci. **60**(2), 022305:1–022305:9 (2017)
10. Zhang, S., Mukherjee, B.: Energy-efficient dynamic provisioning for spectrum elastic optical networks. In: Proceedings of IEEE International Conference on Communications 2012, pp. 3031–3035. IEEE, Canada (2012)
11. Lipowski, A., Lipowska, D.: Roulette-wheel selection via stochastic acceptance. Phys. A Stat. Mech. Appl. **391**(6), 2193–2196 (2012)

An Advanced Random Forest Algorithm Targeting the Big Data with Redundant Features

Ying Zhang, Bin Song$^{(\boxtimes)}$, Yue Zhang, and Sijia Chen

The State Key Laboratory of Integrated Services Networks,
Xidian University, Xi'an 710071, China
bsong@mail.xidian.edu.cn

Abstract. Recently, methods to big data are gaining a growing number of popularity, as we are entering the age of big data. As a result, novel methods keep emerging, among which stands random forest method. Random forest fuses multiple sub decision trees for classification and regression, with high accuracy and generalization. It, however, has unsatisfactory performance when facing data sets with more noise and redundant features. This phenomenon is mainly caused by inaccuracy from some sub decision trees, and fusing all of them directly cannot decrease their negative effect. Therefore, we proposed advanced random forest to assign less probability to those negative sub decision trees, meaning they are less likely to be chosen at fusion process. Thus, the capability of prediction is improved. Dropout and roulette method we used in the process ensures a good generalization capability, and maintains a higher accuracy simultaneously. We sample the original data set following the method of K-fold division which will increase the differences between sub decision trees, making the prediction more credible. Finally, our proposed method is validated on several data sets. Experimental results show that compared to traditional random forest method, our method has higher classification accuracy on data sets with noise and data sets with more redundant features.

Keywords: Big data · Dropout · Random forest · Redundant features

1 Introduction

Data have been accumulating at an unprecedented velocity, with the development of industry, finance, internet and other fields [1]. According to International Data Corporation (IDC), data are generated exponentially, doubling every two years, reaching 35ZB in 2020 [2]. Averagely, two million users are searching through Google every second. Facebook has over one billion users, creating over 300 TB log data every day. Meanwhile, the development of the Internet of Things, cloud computing and sensing technology facilitates the generalization and accumulation of data. Data have contained a great value, which is very necessary to be mined and applied reasonably [3].

Due to complexity, high-dimension, and variation, extracting useful patterns and knowledge from real and complicated big data requires theoretical guidance, such as

© Springer International Publishing AG 2017
S. Ibrahim et al. (Eds.): ICA3PP 2017, LNCS 10393, pp. 642–651, 2017.
DOI: 10.1007/978-3-319-65482-9_49

data mining and machine learning [4]. Currently, the most popular methods in machine learning are XGBoost [5], SVM [6], deep learning [7], and random forest [8, 9].

Random forest method has gained an increasing popularity recently. Compared to traditional machine learning methods, random forest has higher accuracy and higher generalization, and it is easier to be parallelized. Compared to deep learning, training random forest has lower requirement of time and hardware. It performs outstanding on classification and regression problems, also being suitable for data mining process.

Real data is more complicated, which may be involving a number of redundant features, reducing the performance and accuracy of random forest. Therefore, we propose advanced random forest to guide the fusion process and to improve generalization. Experimental results suggest that our proposed method exceeds traditional random forest on data sets with noise and data sets with more noise and redundant features.

The remaining of this paper is organized as follows: Sect. 2 presents some related work. Details of our method are introduced in Sect. 3 and the experimental results are shown in Sect. 4. The final section concludes the whole paper.

2 Related Work

The random forest is a common machine learning algorithm, which applies decision trees as base classifier to construct an integrated classification model. As a mature ensemble learning method, the random forest possesses such ability of classification that it has received extensive attention from the academic and industrial circles. Moreover, it is now becoming increasingly widespread application in realistic scenes of the random forest, which is a popular topic in many fields such as data mining, pattern recognition, target detection [10]. The random forest algorithm was first proposed in 2001 [8], and introduced it in detail from both theoretical and experimental aspects. Experimental results present that the random forest can overcome the problem of over-fitting better and it is easy to implement, powerful in performance and suitable for big data sets.

Due to the good performance and varies advantages, the random forest has been applied and developed in many areas. In medical science, the random forest was applied to the prediction of heart disease [11]. In industrial area, random forest was used to predict failures in the air pressure system of Scania Trucks, in order to farthest reduce overall maintenance costs of the system to a maximum extent [12]. Moreover, an article introduce a novel method combined with random forest to predict protein domain linkers and boundaries [13]. In addition, random forest was applied to 3D object recognition and achieved fairly good results [14].

It is a fact that the random forest is one of the most successful machine learning algorithms, thus theoretical research on random forest has never been stopped. An integrated method called rotation forest (RotRF) was proposed [15]. The main idea of the RotRF is to construct decision trees based on method of principle component analysis (PCA) Then, rotation forest algorithm was improved and introduced a new integrated method called RotBoost [16]. The RotBoost applied sample weighting from Adaboost to retrain sample improperly classified with re-weighting. Based on research towards different levels of contribution from features to classification, a method of weighting training samples randomly was used to produce different decision trees [17]. In a similar way, a new concept was proposed, survival trees, from the perspective of construction process of decision trees, and finally proposed the random survival forests algorithm (RSF) [18]. As the result, the RSF integrates the content of survival analysis trees and the prediction results. Later, based on consideration for applying different levels of pre-treatment to training sets for constructing decision trees, presented an improved random forest algorithm called Ensemble Feature Forest (EFF) was present [19], involving PCA and Linear Discriminant Analysis (LDA), mapping the raw data to different rotation spaces and then cascading the original features. It is also worth mentioning that random forest is easy to be parallelized, which means it can be used in processing big scale of data.

The random forest has been widely applied and has achieved remarkable results. However, it still has some limits and drawbacks while facing the realistic data sets with more noise and redundant features. Therefore, we intend to improve the flexibility and performance of random forest. Accordingly, researching on improved algorithm of random forest may have significant value for enhancing the classifying quality and more practical applications.

3   The Proposed Method

In this section, we will give a brief description of traditional random forest method. Then we will provide details of our proposed method, as a comparison.

3.1   A Subsection Sample Random Forest Algorithm

The random forest algorithm is an extended variant of bagging method, which is a combination of decision tree with the same distribution. In detail, the random forest takes n sample from raw data D using bootstrap sampling method, as $D_i \subseteq D, i = 1, 2, \ldots n$, then a sub decision tree will be constructed for every single sample set. Eventually, all decisions trees will be combined and forecast results toward the test set will be based on a vote among all results of sub trees [8]. The main structure of a random forest is shown in Fig. 1.

Data set D^{raw} will be sampled using bootstrap. Firstly, we define a function $D_i^{raw} = \mathcal{F}(D^{raw}), (i = 1, 2, \ldots n)$ that sample n times from raw data, with m samples in each, constructing n subsets, as $D_i^{raw} \subseteq D^{raw}, (i = 1, 2, \ldots n, |D_i^{raw}| = m)$. Specifically, In each sampling process, a sample set with m samples will be generated with return, meaning the same elements may occur more than once in each D_i^{raw}, and relationship $D_i^{raw} \cap D_j^{raw} = \emptyset, (i, j = 1, 2, \ldots n | i \neq j)$ does not hold.

Next, we train a decision tree for every single sample set. The general decision tree will choose the optimal division feature of the attribute domain on a particular node.

The decision trees in a random forest, however, will first take a sub-set contains d features randomly, and choose an optimal one for division. Eventually, n decision trees $\{h_1, h_2, \ldots, h_n\}$ will be constructed.

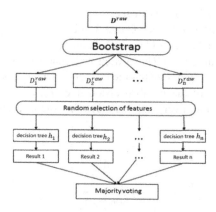

Fig. 1. The structure of random forest

The random forest model is the combination of the n sub decision trees. The final classification result is an integration of results from the n independent classifier. Therefore, a fusion algorithm is required to integrate all information and output the result. The voting method, as the simplest fusion method, is often used. The output is the majority results among all sub classifiers in a classification problem.

One drawback of traditional random forest is its limitation of the realistic data sets with more noise and redundant features. Therefore, we propose advanced random forest algorithm to increase its flexibility.

3.2 Advanced Random Forest Algorithm

The general random forest algorithm just simply combines all sub decision trees without selection, which can lead to low performance on real data sets of more redundant features and features with low correlation. In this section, we will propose an advanced random forest algorithm, which can improve RF's accuracy rate of forecast on data set with redundant features and noise while keep its high generalization capability. The main structure of the advanced random forest algorithm is shown in Fig. 2, consisting of two parts, constructing sub decision trees and selection.

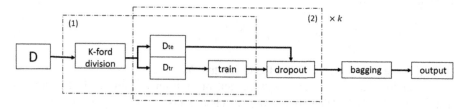

Fig. 2. Architecture of advanced random forest algorithm. (1) and (2) indicate two main processes, with detailed in this subsection.

Constructing Sub Decision Trees Process

Firstly, we divide the original data set D into K sub sets following the method of K-fold division, which is inspired by K-fold Cross Validation, as in Fig. 3. Then, $K - 1$ sets of data will be used as training set D_{tr} to train n decision trees. Normally, we can use CART or C4.5 tree in this step. Finally, the last set of data will be the test set D_{te}, which can verify the accuracy of the n sub decision trees P_t, as $P_t = \{p_1, p_2, \ldots, p_k\}$. We repeat the steps above until every sub set plays the role as a test set in one iteration.

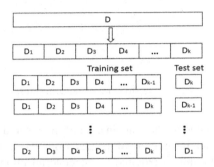

Fig. 3. The method to divide the original data set

Selection Process

After obtaining all sub decision trees, we propose selection process so that superior candidates, which may improve the performance of random forest, can be chosen with higher probability. Thus, we apply the dropout and roulette method to random forest. During the dropout process, we just let the trees with rates equal to P_d. Dropout is a generalization method from deep learning, which means that a model randomly disables some nodes in hidden layers to improve the performance and generalization ability of neural networks [20, 21]. In every iteration, we firstly calculate the weight $W_i(i = 1, 2, \ldots, n)$ of every sub decision tree, as

$$W_i = p_i - \min(P_t) \tag{1}$$

Next, we dropout some of the sub decision trees using the roulette method, and calculate the cumulative weight of every sub decision tree according to the following formula

$$q_i = \sum_{j=1}^{i} W_i \tag{2}$$

Here, q_i is the cumulative weight of decision tree h_i.

A pseudo-random number r will be generated from a uniform distribution on interval $\left[0, \sum_{i=1}^{n} W_i\right]$. Then, If $r < q_1$, we choose first decision tree, otherwise we choose the i-th tree satisfying $q_{i-1} < r < q_i$. Following the steps above, we can pick up $n \times P_d$ decision trees meanwhile dropout the others.

The last step is to merge the sub decision trees from the K iterations shown above in order to obtain an optimized random forest model. A method of weighted voting is used in the merging process.

A single detailed iteration will be shown in following pseudo-codes (Table 1):

Table 1. Pseudo-code of selection process in advanced random forest

---

Algorithm :

Input:
    D_{tr}: Training set made from K-1 sub sets of data
    D_{te}: The last set of data as test set
    P_d: reserving ratio of decision trees in dropout
    $W_i = \{W_1, W_2, ..., W_n\}$: weight of every sub decision tree
Output:
    H: Set of decision trees after dropout

for $i \leftarrow 0$ to $n \times P_d$ **do**
    Calculate the cumulative weight of decision tree h_i. $q_i = \sum_{j=1}^{i} W_j$
end for

for $i \leftarrow 0$ to $n \times P_d$ **do**
    Generate a pseudo-random number r from uniform distribution on interval $[0, \sum_{i=1}^{n} W_i]$
    if $r < q_1$ **then**
        Choose the 1st decision tree D_{tr};
    else
        Choose the i-th decision trees h_i making $q_{i-1} < r < q_i$.
    end if
end for
return H

---

4 Experiments and Results

In this section, we will evaluate our optimized model on varies data sets, and compare it with the random forest on its classification accuracy. Specifically, the data sets we apply is presented as Table 2, with detailed explanation followed.

Sparse-cnf: This data from mlcomp contains 10000 instances and 100 dimensions of features. In order to test our algorithm performance on data sets with redundant features and noise, we preprocess the data set, adding another 100 dimensions of features with random values.

Table 2. Comparison of data sets.

Data set	Number of instances	Number of dimensions
Sparse-cnf	10000	100
Madelon	2600	501
Waveform	5000	41
Fri_c0_1000_50	1000	50

Madelon: This data set is downloaded from openml, is an artificial data set, which was part of the NIPS 2003 feature selection challenge, containing 2600 instances and 501 dimensions.

Waveform: This data set is downloaded from openml, which contains 5000 instances and 41 dimensions of features. The same processed, adding another 100 dimensions of features which have random values, is executed.

Fri_c0_1000_50: This data set is downloaded from openml, which contains 1000 instances and 50 dimensions of features. The same processed, adding another 100 dimensions of features involving have random values, is executed.

Before adding another features with random values, we compare the classification accuracy of advanced random forest and traditional random forest on raw data set, as in Table 3.

Table 3. Classification accuracy on data sets without adding noise

Data set	Random forest	Advanced random forest
Sparse-cnf	91.2%	**96%**
Madelon	65.9%	**67.9%**
Waveform	**88.9%**	88.7%
Fri_c0_1000_50	85.6%	**86.7%**

Then we compare the performance of our proposed method and traditional random forest on all the data sets above, as in Tables 4 and 5. In Table 4, we conduct ten experiments on each dataset, and calculated the average and the standard deviation of accuracy. It is straightforward to find that our method exceeds traditional random forest in terms of accuracy on all four data sets. It is straightforward to find that our method exceeds traditional random forest in terms of accuracy on all four data sets with noise and redundant features. Furthermore, the gap between the two methods on data sets **Sparse-cnf** and **Fri_c0_1000_50** is large, indicating the outstanding improvement. Relatively, the improvement on data sets **Madelon** and **Waveform** is mere. The reason may be related to the performances of sub decision trees. Thus, we validate the accuracy of each of them, and calculate the dissimilarities, as the last column in Table 4.

The dissimilarities in Table 4 is calculated as the difference between the best and worst decision trees, may also indicate deviation among them. Compared to the rest two data sets, **Madelon** and **Waveform** have smaller dissimilarities, meaning all sub

Table 4. Classification accuracy on data sets (The average of accuracy ± standard deviation) and dissimilarities among sub decision trees.

Data set	Random forest	Advanced random forest	Dissimilarities
Sparse-cnf	(85.3 ± 0.79)%	**(90.4 ± 0.65)%**	0.208
Madelon	(65.9 ± 1.34)%	**(67.9 ± 0.68)%**	0.133
Waveform	(87.2 ± 0.46)%	**(88.2 ± 0.28)%**	0.102
Fri_c0_1000_50	(81.8 ± 1.57)%	**(87.1 ± 0.85)%**	0.223

Table 5. AUC on data sets

Data set	Random forest	Advanced random forest
Sparse-cnf	0.78	**0.84**
Madelon	0.66	**0.68**
Waveform	0.83	**0.84**
Fri_c0_1000_50	0.82	**0.85**

trees of them have similar performance. Therefore, even if we assign inferior trees less probability to be chosen, the remaining ones still provide similar answers. Thus, roulette selecting is not always a functional method among similar candidates. On the other hand, when all sub trees perform differently, depressing inferior trees has direct effect on the outcomes. This explains the different improvements in Table 4.

In Table 5, we calculate the AUC on each data set, and get the same conclusion as Table 4.

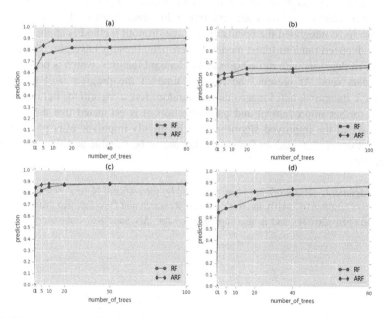

Fig. 4. The comparison of random forest (RF) and advanced random forest (ARF) on data set Sparse-cnf (a), data set Madelon (b), data set Waveform (c) and data set fri_c0_1000_50 (d).

Further, we consider the influences of number of sub decision trees on both methods. Theoretically, larger number of sub decision trees has higher probability of containing trees with high performance, less dependent on trees of low classification capability. Thus, with more trees being introduced, both methods tend to improve their accuracy until convergence, as in Fig. 4. Besides, the proportion of the dropout is usually set to 0.5. The parameter K = 9 in K-ford, as an experimental result.

From Fig. 4 we can find that with the growing number of trees, both methods tend to converge on all data sets. Meanwhile, our proposed method almost keeps higher accuracy than that of random forest, indicating its superior performance.

The results above show that our algorithm have better performance and classification ability applied to real big data sets with redundant features and noise, compared with general random forest algorithm, which means much more capable for realistic demand.

5 Conclusion

In this paper, we have proposed an advanced random forest method, to handle scenarios where realistic data sets with more noise and redundant features are involved. Firstly, we have randomly divided the original data set into K groups, according to K-fold division. For each iteration, K-1 groups of data are applied as training set, and the remaining one is as validation, in order to increase the dissimilarities among all sub decision trees. Then, we have assigned weights to each sub decision tree based on their accuracy, which further provide guidance to roulette method to select nodes in dropout method. Thus, sub decision trees with higher accuracy have a higher probability to survive, increasing their effects and improving the generalization of the whole system. At last, we have integrated the results every time dropout method is applied, obtaining the final advanced random forest model. Experimental results have proved our method is capable of data sets with more noise and redundant features, which is popular among realistic data sets. At present, the running time of the program will grow as the parameter k increases, and longer than the random forest algorithm. Future work will target on further improvement and parallelization, it is estimated that the calculation performance of the improved algorithm will be greatly improved after parallelization, which is closer to the random forest, and hoping to be suitable and flexible for larger scale of data.

Acknowledgement. This work has been supported by the National Natural Science Foundation of China (61372068, 61672410), the National Key Research and Development Program of China (grant 2016YFB0800704), and is also supported by the ISN State Key Laboratory.

References

1. Mayer-Schönberger, V., Cukier, K.: Big Data: A Revolution that will Transform How we Live, Work and Think. Eamon Dolan/Houghton Mifflin Harcourt, Boston (2013)
2. Chen, M., Mao, S., Liu, Y.: Big data: a survey. Mob. Netw. Appl. **19**(2), 171–209 (2014)
3. Tsai, C-W., Lai, C-F., Chao, H., Vasilakos, A.V.: Big data technologies and applications. In: Big Data Analytics, pp. 13–52 (2016)
4. Sowmya, R., Suneetha, K.R.: Data mining with big data. In: 2017 11th International Conference on Intelligent Systems and Control (ISCO). IEEE (2017)
5. Chen, T., Guestrin, C.: XGBoost: A Scalable Tree Boosting System. ArXiv e-prints (2016)
6. Cortes, C., Vapnik, V.: Support vector networks. Mach. Learn. **20**, 273–297 (1995)
7. LeCun, Y., Bengio, Y., Hinton, G.: Deep learning. Nature **521**, 436–444 (2015)
8. Breiman, L.: Random forests. Mach. Learn. **45**(1), 5–32 (2001)
9. Witten, I.H., Frank, E., Hall, M.A., et al.: Data Mining: Practical Machine Learning Tools and Techniques. Morgan Kaufmann, Burlington (2016)
10. Biau, G., Scornet, E.: Rejoinder on: a random forest guided tour. TEST **25**(2), 264–268 (2016)
11. Jabbar, M.A., Deekshatulu, B.L., Chandra, P.: Prediction of heart disease using random forest and feature subset selection. In: Snášel, V., Abraham, A., Krömer, P., Pant, M., Muda, A.K. (eds.) Innovations in Bio-Inspired Computing and Applications. Advances in Intelligent Systems and Computing, pp. 187–196. (2015)
12. Gondek, C., Hafner, D., Sampson, O.R.: Prediction of failures in the air pressure system of scania trucks using a random forest and feature engineering. In: Boström, H., Knobbe, A., Soares, C., Papapetrou, P. (eds.) IDA 2016. LNCS, vol. 9897, pp. 398–402. Springer, Cham (2016). doi:10.1007/978-3-319-46349-0_36
13. Shatnawi, M., Zaki, N., Yoo, P.D.: Protein inter-domain linker prediction using random forest and amino acid physiochemical properties. BMC Bioinform. **15**, S8 (2014)
14. Shotton, J., Fitzgibbon, A., Cook, M., Sharp, T., Finocchio, M., Moore, R., Kipman, A., Blake, A.: Real-time human pose recognition in parts from single depth images. In: IEEE Conference on Computer Vision and Pattern Recognition, pp. 1297–1304 (2011)
15. Rodriguez, J.J., Kuncheva, L.I., Alonso, C.J.: Rotation forest: a new classifier ensemble method. IEEE Trans. Pattern Anal. Mach. Intell. **28**, 1619–1630 (2006)
16. Zhang, C.X., Zhang, J.S.: RotBoost: a technique for combining rotation forest and adaBoost. Pattern Recogn. Lett. **29**, 1524–1536 (2008)
17. Maudes, J., Rodríguez, J.J., García-Osorio, C., et al.: Random feature weights for decision tree ensemble construction. Inf. Fusion **13**, 20–30 (2012)
18. Ishwaran, H., Kogalur, U.B., Blackstone, E.H., et al.: Random survival forests. Ann. Appl. Stat. **2**, 841–860 (2008)
19. Zhang, L., Suganthan, P.N.: Random forests with ensemble of feature spaces. Pattern Recogn. **47**, 3429–3437 (2014)
20. Hinton, G.E., Srivastava, N., Krizhevsky, A., Sutskever, I., Salakhutdinov, R.R.: Improving neural networks by preventing co-adaptation of feature detectors. arXiv preprint arXiv:1207. 0580 (2012)
21. Srivastava, N., Hinton, G., Krizhevsky, A., Sutskever, I., Salakhutdinov, R.: Dropout: a simple way to prevent neural networks from overfitting. J. Mach. Learn. Res. **15**, 1929–1958 (2014)

En-Eye: A Cooperative Video Fusion Framework for Traffic Safety in Intelligent Transportation Systems

Tianhao Wu[✉] and Lin Zhang

Beijing University of Posts and Telecommunications, No. 10 Xitucheng Road,
Beijing, Haidian District, China
wu.tianhao@bupt.edu.cn

Abstract. Limited vision is a one of the most essential cause in traffic accidents. To guarantee the safety of vehicle operating, a series of matured assistance systems choose to deploy many special sensors. These solutions, however, only emphasize the equipment on a single vehicle. In some complex environment, detecting range would be limited within 50 m by various obstacles. Exchanging data among vehicles would be useful. But most current systems transfer a small amount of data, like vehicle operating states. In this paper, a smart-terminal-based framework named En-Eye is developed to enhance the traffic safety. En-Eye is proposed as a framework use smart terminals to construct a small-scope-network to exchange video data captured by camera in real time. Furthermore, video fusion is developed inside the framework for further analysis. Finally, an Android-based implementation of En-Eye framework has been achieved and work well in real environments.

Keywords: Cooperative video network · Multicast · Shared video · Video fusion

1 Introduction

Traffic security becomes one of the crucial problems in the transportation systems. As the road is crowded with more vehicles, the drivers' vision is more easily limited by other vehicle. As a result, more traffic accidents take place in the situation that potential threat is hided in the shadow of other vehicles. According to [1], traffic accidents resulted in more than 500 thousand deaths and 14 million injures worldwide by the end of May in 2016. One of the main reasons for traffic accidents is that the drivers cannot notice the behaviors of surrounding vehicles, pedestrians and cyclists on time. To reduce the traffic accidents, it is essential to assist the drivers to have a wider vision about the surrounding environments including the coming vehicles and adjacent pedestrians and cyclists.

To enable the safety of transportations, many strategies are proposed. There are some works using the vehicle-mounted device for driving assistance system. Cameras and other sensors are used to monitor the variable environment. Although the cost of cameras and radars based safety technology is decreasing, these safety technologies have not been deployed in economy vehicles. It still needs time before the majority of vehicles are deployed with these safety technologies. Furthermore, due to lack of communication, vehicles need to make judgement by themselves.

© Springer International Publishing AG 2017
S. Ibrahim et al. (Eds.): ICA3PP 2017, LNCS 10393, pp. 652–657, 2017.
DOI: 10.1007/978-3-319-65482-9_50

In this paper, we propose En-Eye, a smart-terminal-based framework for traffic safety by sharing video streams and video fusion, which overcomes the limitations of drivers' vision to detect potential traffic threat.

En-Eye is a novel framework which only utilizes the smart terminals to improve the transportation safety. It enlarges drivers' visual range by sharing video streams produced by every vehicle. And the further video fusion improve the convenience, for drivers just need to see one video screen rather than two or more.

We highlight our main contributions as follows:

1. A driving-video shared platform is provided which can run on commodity smart terminals.
2. A video fusion mechanism is proposed to integrate the video streams on the shared platform.
3. An Android-based implementation of En-Eye has been achieved and work well in real environments.

2   Framework Overview

This section depicts the high level overview of the framework En-Eye that we proposed for traffic security. En-Eye is focused on the vehicle and pedestrian security. One of the main causes for the traffic accident is that some of vehicle and pedestrian behaviors are out of the drivers' visual range, for some vehicles might become visual obstacle to others. En-Eye considers take advantage of the smart terminal which is widespread to enlarge the vision of drivers. And finally it would help to reduce the potential threat to traffic safety.

As is shown in Fig. 1, the vision of the vehicle 0 is limited by the other three vehicles. But En-Eye allows these vehicles to deliver their video streams to others over the platform. And any one of the vehicles on the platform can obtain other vehicles' video

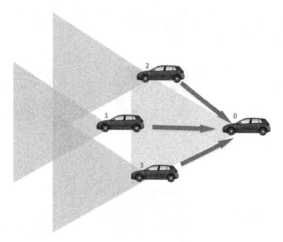

Fig. 1. Application scenarios. The forward sight of vehicle 0 is blocked by vehicle 1–3. However, vehicle 1–3 transmit their scene to vehicle 0 to help it construct a larger scene.

streams from the platform. Using the video information, the driver could get a relatively overall understanding of environment. Besides, both drivers and other systems obtain the ability of further analysis and processing on these video information.

System architecture is presented in Fig. 2, and data flow diagram is presented in Fig. 3. The framework can be divided into two parts: source and destination. The part of source takes charge of capturing video from outside, encoding the video into H.264 format and sending the H.264 streams into Multicast Network. The part of destination would receive the video streams and assign them into different decoders corresponding with specified video sources. Finally, the fusion part inside the destination device would

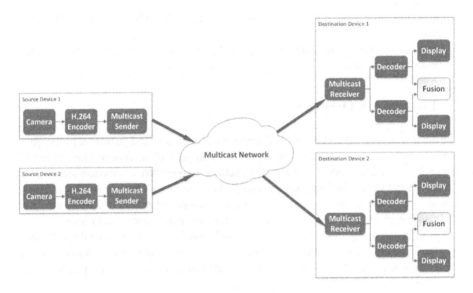

Fig. 2. System architecture. The source part captures the video, encodes it into H.264 and send it into a multicast network. The destination part gets data from the multicast network, decode them and continues the process of fusion.

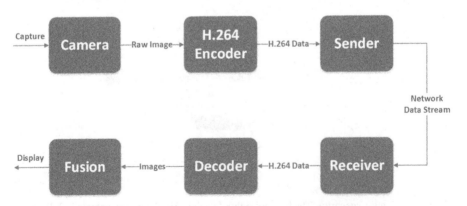

Fig. 3. Data flow diagram. The process of data change is shown clearly.

integrate the video streams from different decoders into a large one. What should be emphasized is that each terminal is equipped both source part and destination part.

2.1 Capturing Video Stream

During a vehicle operating, the terminal captures video from camera and push the raw image data into encoder to transform them into H.264 data streams. The section details the process.

The camera is composed of millions of photosensitive units. Each unit turns the optical signal into electric signal unit called pixel. Terminal store these electric units in the format of YUV, which requires big storage space to represent a pixel. It would increase the transmission pressure. To decrease the pressure, the video needs to be compressed into the format of H.264, known as a common format for transmission. We utilize the hardware codec to finish the work.

2.2 Collecting Video Streams

We use multicast for communication. Generally, there are two main protocols in transmission layer, TCP and UDP. TCP is a stable and reliable transmission protocol. However, its retransmission mechanism would not only make the video stream not playing smoothly, but also cost a period of time to let the video chase the present content. We need deliver video data from one to multiple devices. So TCP and common UDP would not be applicable in this situation. As for UDP broadcast, it could exposed all the information in the local area network, which do harm to the privacy protection. Considering the above reasons, multicast is the best choice in this transmission task.

To distinguish the different sources of video, we make an additional head at the start of each packet transmitting data streams. The head contains the information labeling the source device. Before the destination device pushes the data streams into the decoder,

Fig. 4. We can see from the picture that the four tablets are transmit the video streams among them, and the application are running well.

head would be take out to judge the target decoders where the data streams to enter. After decoding, the output can be displayed on the screen directly.

We have completed the Android application to realize the framework. The performace is shown in Fig. 4.

2.3 Video Fusion

The process of video fusion is composed of four steps: Image acquisition, Feature point extraction and matching, Image registration and Image fusion. The order is shown in Fig. 5. The feature extracting algorithm SIFT is used for feature extraction and matching. In order to improve the accuracy of matching, guided complementary matching and voting filter is used. And finally image mosaic is completed with smoothing algorithm.

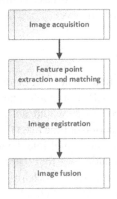

Fig. 5. The process of video fusion.

3   Conclusion

In this paper, we develop a smart-terminal-based framework for traffic safety named En-Eye, which can obtain real-time video streams to merge them into a completed scene. Firstly, a driving-video shared platform is provided which can run on commodity smart terminals. Secondly, a video fusion mechanism is proposed to integrate the video streams on the shared platform. Thirdly, we realize a real-time fusion algorithms on smart terminals. Finally, an Android-based implementation of En-Eye has been achieved and work well in real environments.

Acknowledgements. This work was supported by the National Key R&D Program of China (2016YFB0100902)

References

1. Real time traffic accidents statistics. http://www.icebike.org/real-time-traffic-accident-statistics/ Accessed 23 May 2017
2. Intelligent transportation systems-dedicated short range communications. http://www.its.dot.gov/DSRC/ Accessed 23 May 2017
3. Qin Z, Meng Z, Zhang X, et al.: Performance evaluation of 802.11 p WAVE system on embedded board. In: 2014 International Conference on. Information Networking (ICOIN), Phuket, Thailand, pp. 356–360 (2014)
4. Santa, J., Fernández, P.J., Pereñíguez, F., Bernal, F., Skarmeta, A.F.: A vehicular network mobility framework: Architecture, deployment and evaluation. In: 2015 IEEE Conference on Computer Communications Workshops (INFOCOM WKSHPS), pp. 127–132. IEEE, Hong Kong, China (2015)
5. Noguchi, S., Tsukada, M., Ernst, T., Inomata, A., Fujikawa, K.: Location-aware service discovery on IPv6 GeoNetworking for VANET. In: 2011 11th International Conference on ITS Telecommunications (ITST), pp. 224–229. IEEE, St. Petersburg, Russia (2011)
6. Vinel, A., Belyaev, E., Lamotte, O., Gabbouj, M., Koucheryavy, Y., Egiazarian, K.: Video transmission over IEEE 802.11 p: real-world measurements. In: 2013 IEEE International Conference on Communications Workshops (ICC), pp. 505–509. IEEE, Budapest, Hungary (2013)
7. Zhou, L., Zhang, Y., Song, K., Jing, W., Vasilakos, A.V.: Distributed media services in P2P-based vehicular networks. IEEE Trans. Veh. Technol. **60**(2), 692–703 (2011)
8. Gozálvez, J., Sepulcre, M., Bauza, R.: IEEE 802.11 p vehicle to infrastructure communications in urban environments. IEEE Commun. Mag. **50**(5) (2012)
9. Xie, H., Boukerche, A., Loureiro, A.A.: A multipath video streaming solution for vehicular networks with link disjoint and node-disjoint. IEEE Trans. Parallel Distrib. Syst. **26**(12), 3223–3235 (2015)
10. Seferoglu, H., Keller, L., Cici, B., Le, A., Markopoulou, A.: Cooperative video streaming on smartphones. In: 2011 49th Annual Allerton Conference on Communication, Control, and Computing, pp. 220–227. IEEE, Allerton, England (2011)

Comparing Electricity Consumer Categories Based on Load Pattern Clustering with Their Natural Types

Zigui Jiang[1]([⊠]), Rongheng Lin[1], Fangchun Yang[1], Zhihan Liu[1], and Qiqi Zhang[2]

[1] State Key Laboratory of Networking and Switching Technology,
Beijing University of Posts and Telecommunications, Beijing, China
{ziguijiang,rhlin,fcyang,zhihan}@bupt.edu.cn
[2] State Grid Shanghai Municipal Electric Power Company, Shanghai, China

Abstract. As one aspect of smart city, smart gird has similar situation such as big data issue. Data analysis of daily load data generated by smart meters can benefit both electricity suppliers and end consumers. Electricity consumer categorization based on load pattern clustering is one of research subjects. This paper aims to achieve a better understanding of electricity consumer categorization by detecting the relationships among consumer categories and their natural types. A two-stage clustering based on multi-level 1D discrete wavelet transform and K-means algorithm is applied to perform daily load curve clustering and load pattern clustering. Additionally, to obtain distinct consumer categories, method of category identification based on association rule mining and characteristic similarity is also proposed in this paper. Experiment is conducted on data set of 24-value daily load data with labels of consumer types. Based on the comparison of experimental results, both relationships and differences exist among consumer categories and consumer types but consumer types cannot determine consumer categories.

Keywords: Smart Grid · Consumer category · Consumer type · Load pattern · Clustering

1 Introduction

As information and communication technologies (ICTs) and Internet of thongs (IoT) technologies are widely applied with the development of smart cities, big data are increasingly produced in every part of the cities. Such big data Analysis is beneficial for understanding, monitoring, regulating and planing the cities [1]. This situation also exits in smart grid which is one aspect of smart city. For instance, smart meters in consumer side record power consumption of electricity consumers in a high frequency. Based on the analysis of these detailed measurements, electricity suppliers can enable their operations such as energy control, demand side management and flexible pricing schemes [2,3]. Diverse power consumption behaviors refer to distinctive characteristics of electricity consumers,

© Springer International Publishing AG 2017
S. Ibrahim et al. (Eds.): ICA3PP 2017, LNCS 10393, pp. 658–667, 2017.
DOI: 10.1007/978-3-319-65482-9_51

which drive consumer categorization based on their load pattern similarity. End consumers can choose suitable payment programs offered by electricity suppliers specifically for their categories. Furthermore, electricity consumers have their own characteristics such as natural type and location. Do these characteristics have relationships with power consumption behaviors? Thus, this paper focuses on sophisticated data analysis of daily load data generated by smart meters to detect the relationships among consumer categories and their natural types.

Every electricity consumer belongs to a type which refers to the sort that the consumer naturally is. For example, school, restaurant, hotel or normal resident. On the other hand, consumers also can be categorized into different groups based on the similarity of their electricity power consumption behaviors. Such groups are called consumer categories. Without further analysis, it cannot be ensure that electricity consumers in the same types have similar consumption behaviors or consumers in different types belong to different categories. Since consumer types are usually apparent, achieving consumer categorization is the primary task in this paper.

Following an analysis of the relevant literature dealing with consumer categorization, it is noted that there are two main research aspects, which are categorization algorithm and multi-stage categorization framework. Clustering algorithms such as self-organizing maps (SOM) and K-means are widely adopted in consumer categorization [3–7]. Moreover, consumer categorization framework generally contains a two-stage clustering [2,8–11]. The first stage is to extract load patterns for each individual consumer by daily load curves clustering. Then the next stage conducts a second clustering based on the selected representative load patterns. Panapakidis et al. [9] used K-means algorithm in the two-stage clustering. In their approach, load pattern with the largest cluster, the maximum daily energy or the peak load can be selected as the representative load pattern of each consumer for the second clustering. This simplifies consumer categorization so that the final clustering result does generate the consumer categories directly. However, those unselected load patterns lead to information loss. Mets et al. [2] adopted fast wavelet transformation and g-means algorithm for the two-stage clustering. They also mentioned the limitation of load pattern selection. Therefore, all load patterns rather than one representative are employed for the second clustering. However, this also leads to another problem which is indistinct consumer categories. The final clustering result may show that a consumer belongs to several categories.

According to this review of the literature, this paper enhance the detailed analysis of clustering results to identify the distinct consumer categories. An approach including a two-stage clustering and category identification is proposed. Power consumption characteristics of different consumer types are also be identified based on the same two-stage clustering. Additionally, this paper compares the characteristics of consumer categories and consumer types, and finds out relationships and differences among them. According to the comparison and findings, it can achieve a better understanding of power consumption characteristics which are helpful for improving consumer categorization and conducting new consumer classification.

The rest of this paper is structured as follows. Section 2 explains the proposed approach and describes the algorithms adopted in the approach. Section 3 presents the experimental results with comparison and evaluation. Finally, the paper is concluded in Sect. 4.

2   Approach

In order to compare consumer category with consumer type, it is essential to obtain the representative load patterns of every consumer category and consumer type, which present its typical electricity power consumption characteristics. As mentioned in Sect. 1, load pattern extraction and consumer categorization are based on daily load curve clustering and load pattern clustering, respectively. Thus, this section explains the main approach to achieve the two-stage clustering and consumer category identification.

The procedure of the proposed approach is described in Fig. 1. First, daily load curve clustering is applied to every individual consumer to extract load patterns. Second, another clustering is applied to the overall load patterns of all consumers to achieve fuzzy categories. Finally, consumer categories are identified based on the fuzzy categories. Characteristics are the representative load patterns of consumer categories.

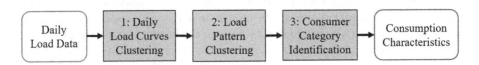

Fig. 1. The procedure of electricity consumer categorization based on a two-stage clustering and category identification.

2.1   Daily Load Curve Clustering

The load data of one day can be drawn as a curve so-called daily load curve. A daily load curve presents the power consumption of an electricity consumer in one day. It is supposed that every consumer has her/his typical consumption behaviors which can be presented by several load patterns. In general, load patterns are extracted by clustering of daily load curves in a certain period. The two-stage clustering in this paper applies a fused load curve clustering algorithm based on multi-level 1D discrete wavelet transform (DWT) and K-means. This clustering algorithm is specially designed for load curve clustering and proposed in a previous paper which is under review now. In the previous paper, it is proved that this algorithm improves curve clustering performance with less information loss of dimensionality reduction.

The curve clustering algorithm has two main steps. The first step is to reduce the dimensions of daily load curves by multi-level 1D DWT. Two types of output, approximation signals and detail signals, are produced in the first step. In the second step, two types of signals are processed separately. Taking into consideration the different properties of two signals, approximation signals are normalized with z-score to ignore the distance difference while detail signals are used directly. Then, normalized approximation signals and original detail signals are clustered separately by K-means to produce two groups of clusters, which are fused into one group of clusters finally.

Since Haar wavelet is simple and can compress a discrete signal into half, it is adopted in the multi-level 1D DWT. The mother wavelet function of Haar wavelet is described as follows:

$$\psi(t) = \begin{cases} 1 & 0 \leq t < 1/2, \\ -1 & 1/2 \leq t < 1, \\ 0 & \text{otherwise.} \end{cases} \tag{1}$$

Furthermore, the optimal Ks of K-means for two signals are determined by the Simplified Silhouette Width Criterion (SSWC) [12].

2.2   Load Pattern Clustering

After the daily load curve clustering, each consumer has several load patterns that can present her/his typical power consumption behaviors. All load patterns of consumers are employed in the load pattern clustering in order to keep as much information as possible. Since load patterns are also load curves, the clustering algorithm adopted in this stage is the same as the one adopted in daily load curve clustering.

As mentioned in the former section, the result of load pattern clustering is indistinct in terms of consumer categories. This means that several load patterns of a consumer belong to various clusters that refer to different consumer categories. Thus, the consumer categories obtained in this stage are called fuzzy consumer categories, which are required to be further analysis.

2.3   Consumer Category Identification

Based on the fuzzy consumer categories from the two-stage clustering, consumer category identification aims to obtain distinct consumer categories with diverse consumption characteristics. Generally, consumers who have several load patterns belonging to the same groups of fuzzy consumer categories are in the same consumer categories. Therefore, it is a problem of finding association rules in fuzzy consumer categories. Regarding each load pattern as an item, consumer category identification is to find all frequent itemsets using minimum support [13,14]. Apriori algorithm is adopted in this stage because it is the key algorithm for an extraction of association rules [15].

Let a couple (A, B) be an association rule, where $A \neq \emptyset$, $B \neq \emptyset$ and $A \cap B = \emptyset$, then this rule is noted as: $A \rightarrow B$. The support of an association rule $Sup(A \rightarrow B)$ is defined as the support of the itemset $A \cup B$, which refers to the percentage of transactions containing both A and B. The definition fellows the equation below:

$$Sup(A \rightarrow B) = Sup(A \cup B) = \frac{|t(A \cup B)|}{t(A)}. \tag{2}$$

For Apriori, it is to find the items with a *support* $\geq$ *minsup*. In this paper, *minsup* $= 0$ is set in order to find out all frequent itemsets of load patterns. Moreover, all frequent itemsets are then combined based on their similarity.

For electricity consumers with n-dimensional daily load curves, let $X = \{x_1, x_2, \cdots, x_m\}$ and $Y = \{y_1, y_2, \cdots, y_r\}$ be two frequent itemsets of load patterns, where $x_i = \langle x_{i1}, x_{i2}, \cdots, x_{in} \rangle$, $1 \leq i \leq m$ and $y_j = \langle y_{j1}, y_{j2}, \cdots, y_{jn} \rangle$, $1 \leq j \leq r$. The most common way to calculate similarity is based on distance measure. As Euclidean distance is the default distance measure of K-means and it is also adopted in the former clustering algorithm in the proposed approach, the similarity calculation in the stage also adopts it. However, in order to ignore the distance difference and achieve curve similarity of shape variation, z-score normalization is applied to each $x_i \in X$ and $y_j \in Y$ before the calculation. Let x_i' and y_j' be the normalized x_i and y_j, respectively. Then, the similarity of one load pattern x_i and the frequent itemset Y is calculated as follows:

$$S_{x_i, Y} = \min_{y_j \in C} \{ \mathrm{dist}(x_i', y_j') \}, \tag{3}$$

where $\mathrm{dist}(x_i, y_j)$ is the distance between x_i' and y_j'. The similarity of X and Y is calculated as the average of S_{x_i} over $i = 1, 2, \cdots, m$:

$$Sim(X, Y) = \frac{1}{m} \sum_{i=1}^{m} S_{x_i}. \tag{4}$$

A parameter *mindis* is set to determine whether combine two frequent itemsets or not. X and Y are combined into one set when $Sim(X, Y) \leq mindis$. After the combination, the remaining frequent itemsets refer to the characteristics of consumer categories.

3   Results and Evaluation

This section presents the experimental results of the proposed approach to consumer categories and consumer types with detailed comparison and discussion.

3.1   Data Set

The data set used in the experiment contains 24-value daily load data of 657 electricity consumers in a one-year period. It records the electricity power consumption at every $1\,\mathrm{h}$ so that the daily load data have 24 values from 1:00 to 24:00. Moreover, these consumers are labeled with nine consumer types which are full service restaurant, large hotel, small hotel, hospital, outpatient, midrise apartment, primary school, super market and warehouse.

3.2   Results

Experimental results include load patterns of individual consumer and the representative load patterns, also called consumption characteristics, of both consumer types and consumer categories. The characteristics of consumer categories are obtained by the proposed approach while the characteristics of consumer types are obtained by a similar two-stage clustering using the same clustering algorithm.

Load Patterns. In the first stage, daily load curve clustering is performed for every individual consumer to obtain their load patterns. Examples are shown in Fig. 2 to present the similarity and difference among consumers in the same type. The consumers are randomly selected from warehouses. In Fig. 2, each warehouse has at least one or several similar load patterns in terms of shape variation. Comparing all load patterns of 657 consumers, it is found that consumers in the same types do have similar load patterns while certain differences also exit among them.

Consumer Type. The consumption characteristics of consumer types are also obtained by a two-stage clustering. The first clustering is the same as the one in daily load curve clustering. After load pattern extraction for each consumer, the load patterns are grouped based on the labeled types of consumers. Then the second clustering is performed separately for different groups. Simply, the clustering results shown in Fig. 3 are consumption characteristics of different consumer types. Although the characteristics of the same types seems unique, part of load patterns in different characteristics also have similarity which may lead to different results of consumer categories.

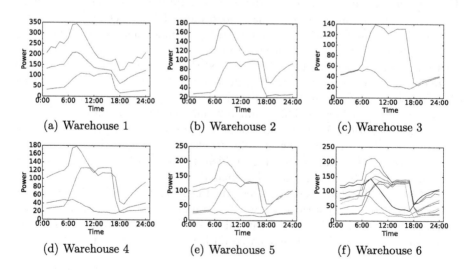

Fig. 2. Load patterns of six consumers who are randomly selected from warehouses.

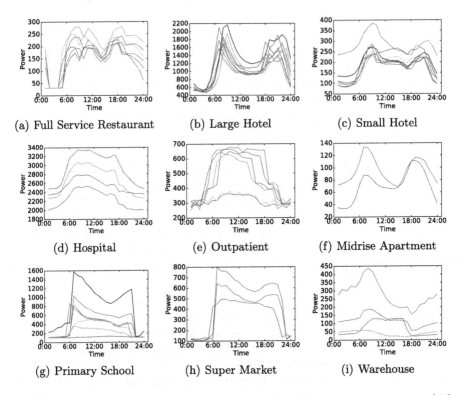

Fig. 3. Electricity power consumption characteristics of nine consumer types, which are extracted based on the load pattern clustering of consumer types.

Consumer Category. Based on the proposed approach, a group of consumer categories are identified from the daily load data of 657 electricity consumers. Figure 4 shows the consumption characteristics of nine identified consumer categories when $mindis = 2$. Each curve in Fig. 4 denotes a representative load pattern of a consumer category. It is noticed that most of characteristics show unique load patterns except for Category 4 and Category 5. Load patterns with similar shape variation but diverse power degrees are grouped in the same categories such as Category 6. This result basically meets the requirement of consumer categorization. Furthermore, these consumption characteristics can be regarded as labels and training samples to classify new electricity consumers. In that case, unsupervised clustering problem becomes supervised classification which is easier to be conducted and evaluated.

Comparing the characteristics shown in Figs. 3 and 4, some consumer types are grouped into same categories due to the similar shape variation of their load patterns. It is concluded that the natural types of electricity consumers cannot determine the categorization that based on load pattern similarity. It is highly

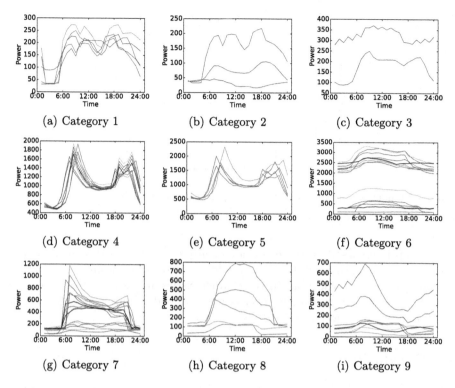

Fig. 4. Nine identified consumer categories when $mindis = 2$. Each subfigure denotes the electricity power consumption characteristic of one consumer category.

possible that grouping electricity consumers based on their natural types leads to excessively meticulous division result. On the contrary, consumer categorization can preferably describe their shared power consumption characteristics.

3.3   Parameter Estimation

Due to the normalization before similarity calculation, the value of parameter $mindis$ is small. To estimate parameter $mindis$, the experiment conducts category identification with the value of parameter $mindis$ from 0 to 5 with a step size of 0.1. Figure 5 indicates the curve of numbers of consumer categories based on parameter $mindis$. According to Fig. 5, it can be noted that the number of consumer categories decreases with the raise of parameter $mindis$ value. The decrease of the curve tends to change smoothly after around $mindis = 3$.

In the former experiment, $mindis = 2$ is set for category identification. The selection of parameter $mindis$ is based on the observation of identified categories and their characteristics. Similar load patterns should be grouped into one consumer category. On the other hand, the number of consumer categories should

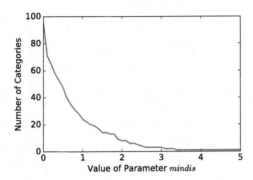

Fig. 5. Number of consumer categories vs. parameter *mindis* from 0 to 5 with a step size of 0.1.

be appropriate. Based on these two ideas, $mindis = 2$ is selected so that nine categories are identified. Actually, it would be better that parameter $mindis$ is set depending on the accuracy if the characteristics are used for new consumer classification. However, classification is not included in this paper due to the limitation of time and paper length.

4   Conclusion

This paper presents a two-stage clustering that contains daily load curve clustering and load pattern clustering, and a proposed method of distinct consumer identification based on association rule mining and characteristic similarity. The approach is implemented on the data set of 24-value daily load data of 657 electricity consumers with nine labeled consumer types. Comparing the power consumption characteristics of consumer categories with those of consumer types, the natural types of electricity consumers cannot fully determine the consumer categorization that based on load pattern similarity. Additionally, consumers can be labelled once the categorization is achieved. Thus, regarding the consumption characteristics of consumer categories as training sample, it is simple to perform new consumer classification.

Due to the limitation of time and paper length, this paper does not present a sophisticated work. As a result, the future work contains improvement of the proposed approach, experiments on various data sets and new consumer classification.

Acknowledgments. This work is supported by the National High Technology Research and Development Program (863 Program) of China (2015AA050203) and Beijing Natural Science Foundation (4174099).

References

1. Kitchin, R.: The real-time city? big data and smart urbanism. GeoJournal **79**(1), 1–14 (2014)
2. Mets, K., Depuydt, F., Develder, C.: Two-stage load pattern clustering using fast wavelet transformation. IEEE Trans. Smart Grid **7**(5), 2250–2259 (2016)
3. Kwac, J., Flora, J., Rajagopal, R.: Household energy consumption segmentation using hourly data. IEEE Trans. Smart Grid **5**(1), 420–430 (2014)
4. Figueiredo, V., Rodrigues, F., Vale, Z., Gouveia, J.B.: An electric energy consumer characterization framework based on data mining techniques. IEEE Trans. Power Syst. **20**(2), 596–602 (2005)
5. Albert, A., Rajagopal, R.: Smart meter driven segmentation: what your consumption says about you. IEEE Trans. Power Syst. **28**(4), 4019–4030 (2013)
6. Alahakoon, D., Yu, X.: Smart electricity meter data intelligence for future energy systems: a survey. IEEE Trans. Ind. Inform. **12**(1), 425–436 (2016)
7. Haben, S., Singleton, C., Grindrod, P.: Analysis and clustering of residential customers energy behavioral demand using smart meter data. IEEE Trans. Smart Grid **7**(1), 136–144 (2016)
8. Chicco, G.: Overview and performance assessment of the clustering methods for electrical load pattern grouping. Energy **42**(1), 68–80 (2012)
9. Panapakidis, I.P., Alexiadis, M.C., Papagiannis, G.K.: Electricity customer characterization based on different representative load curves. In: 2012 9th International Conference on the European Energy Market, pp. 1–8. IEEE (2012)
10. Khumchoo, K.Y., Kongprawechnon, W.: Cluster analysis for primary feeder identification using metering data. In: 2015 6th International Conference of Information and Communication Technology for Embedded Systems, pp. 1–6. IEEE (2015)
11. Wang, Y., Chen, Q., Kang, C., Zhang, M., Wang, K., Zhao, Y.: Load profiling and its application to demand response: a review. Tsinghua Sci. Technol. **20**(2), 117–129 (2015)
12. Vendramin, L., Campello, R.J., Hruschka, E.R.: On the comparison of relative clustering validity criteria. In: SDM, pp. 73–744. SIAM (2009)
13. Rohit, S.: Association rule mining algorithms: survey. Int. Res. J. Eng. Technol. **3**(10), 500–505 (2016)
14. Rathod, R.R., Garg, R.D.: Regional electricity consumption analysis for consumers using data mining techniques and consumer meter reading data. Int. J. Electr. Power Energy Syst. **78**, 368–374 (2016)
15. Addi, A.M., Tarik, A., Fatima, G.: Comparative survey of association rule mining algorithms based on multiple-criteria decision analysis approach. In: 2015 3rd International Conference on Control, Engineering & Information Technology, pp. 1–6. IEEE (2015)

When Clutter Reduction Meets Machine Learning for People Counting Using IR-UWB Radar

Xiuzhu Yang and Lin Zhang$^{(\boxtimes)}$

Beijing University of Posts and Telecommunications,
No.10 Xitucheng Road, Haidian District, Beijing, China
zhanglin@bupt.edu.cn

Abstract. People counting provides key information in sensing applications. Impulse radio ultra-wideband (IR-UWB) radar, which has strong penetration and high-range resolution, has been extensively applied to detect and count people. Current signal processing methods that rely on IR-UWB radar require to establish an environment-dependent threshold manually. Due to the high sensitivity of the IR-UWB radar, the wide diversity of scattered waveforms would bring false alarms. Clutter reduction serves a vital role in signal processing steps to obtain the signal reflected only from the target, while it may also eliminate significant information. In this paper, data-driven solutions based on two machine learning algorithms, the random forest and convolutional neural network (CNN), are proposed to address the challenge of counting people with complex changing scatters. These data-driven methods learn from selected features from radar signals or directly obtain features from radar data and analyze them to automatically produce results. A series of experiments are conducted in the Orange and Caffe platform, and the results indicate that: (i) In data-driven solutions, clutter reduction methods are harmful rather than beneficial for data analysis, verified by discussing four representative clutter reduction methods. (ii) Random forest classification for selected time-domain features in radar signals before complex clutter reduction reaches 91.5% accuracy in testing environment. (iii) CNN provides an automatic counting solution learning directly from radar data.

Keywords: People counting · IR-UWB radar · Random forest · Convolutional neural networks

1 Introduction

In intelligence systems, the number of people serves a vital role in providing statistical information and determining the status in an area of interest. People counting has a large number of applications in various areas, from energy saving to traffic control. More generally, it is also the basis of locating and tracking human presence in sensing applications. Many approaches have been proposed to

© Springer International Publishing AG 2017
S. Ibrahim et al. (Eds.): ICA3PP 2017, LNCS 10393, pp. 668–677, 2017.
DOI: 10.1007/978-3-319-65482-9_52

address challenges of people counting. Impulse radio ultra-wideband (IR-UWB) radar is an important technique, with outstanding application performance in indoor positioning, vital sign monitoring and people counting. IR-UWB radar transmits and receives a narrow impulse signal that occupies a wide bandwidth in the frequency domain, with fine resolution and excellent penetration [1]. In [1], a multi-human detection algorithm was proposed using IR-UWB radar to divide clutter-subtracted received signals into numerous coherent clusters to detect effective peaks and count people. Sample guidelines were developed to solve the problem of adjusting the threshold to select effective peaks in different environments.

Research efforts that focus on solving the problem of people counting can be categorized as sensor-based systems and vision-based systems. Vision-based methods [2–4] have excellent accuracy in people counting applications; however, improvements are needed, especially with respect to sightline obstruction and insufficient light scenes. Sensor-based systems overcome the challenge of low-light scenes. In addition to radar, sensor types include radio frequency sensors [5], infrared sensors, ultrasonic sensors and Wi-Fi sensors [6].

Due to their superior detection and localization performance, radar-based systems for people counting have been investigated. Most UWB radar researches have employed signal processing methods. Received radar signals contain target signal from moving people and unwanted clutter signals composed by the direct wave and reflected signals from static objects. So to obtain cleaner signals, clutter reduction is significantly important for further detection and counting in applications. Many clutter-reduction methods have been proposed, for example, the running average method [1], the singular value decomposition (SVD) method [7], the Kalman Filter based method [8] and the linear least-squares method [9]. After clutter removal, signal processing methods adequately distinguish traces from different people and counting; however, the clutter reduction which is vital to obtain cleaner signals also eliminates useful information from the received signals. Although sample guidelines for setting a threshold have been proposed, the normalized amplitude of clutter signals should be calculated before manually selecting the optimal threshold. In addition, complex environments would influence the performance of people counting with a manually established environment-dependent threshold.

Random forest is an ensemble of classification or regression trees [10]. Motivated by the successful application of a regression-based radar system using support vector regression to count people proposed in [11], the random forest is employed with the IR-UWB radar in this paper for people counting. To make up the drawback of the random forest, with which the features should be extracted, the convolutional neural network (CNN) method is proposed. The main contributions of this paper are based on the following three aspects:

(i) The relationship between clutter reduction methods and machine learning algorithms is discussed based on the results of a set of experiments. Four representative clutter-reduction methods are considered and discussed. They may decrease the valuable information in the radar data, and are proven to be more harmful than beneficial when using machine learning algorithms for data analysis.

(ii) The random forest is employed with the IR-UWB radar to learn from extracted time-domain features of the radar signals. It is proved to have considerably good accuracy in testing environment, without manually establishing the environment-dependent threshold.

(iii) The AlexNet is applied to provide a new solution in people counting that directly learns counting information from the radar data and automatically produces classifying results.

The remainder of this paper is organized as follows: Sect. 2 describes the structure of the solutions. The clutter reduction methods are discussed in Sect. 3, while Sect. 4 describes machine learning algorithms. Experimental settings and results are discussed in Sect. 5. The conclusions are summarized in Sect. 6.

2   Solutions Architecture

The architecture of the proposed people counting solutions is illustrated in Fig. 1. It is composed of three main elements: the IR-UWB radar acquisition module, the clutter reduction methods module and the machine learning algorithms module.

IR-UWB radar collects count information, transmits signals with narrow pulses and receives echo signals. In this paper, the radar data from a select number of people in a space is acquired by an NVA-R661 radar module with a center frequency of 6.8 GHz. The received radar samples are stored in a received

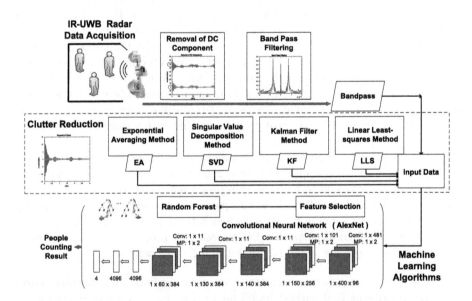

Fig. 1. Architecture of the proposed solutions, including radar acquisition, clutter reduction methods and machine learning algorithms. (Color figure online)

signal matrix by radar scans for 1280 points in each scan that represent the 5 m detection range. Several basic signal processing steps are applied to clean the raw input data. As presented in Fig. 1, the signal waves prior to each process are blue, whereas the processed signals at every step are shown in red. Before clutter reduction, the direct current (DC) component is calculated and subtracted from the raw signal. Then a Hamming window is designed as a filter to obtain the bandpass signal.

3   Clutter Reduction Methods

Clutter signals include the direct wave from radar transmitter to receiver and the signal reflected from static objects. Clutter reduction is a vital part in signal processing steps to remove all unwanted clutter signals, clean the raw input signals and obtain refined signals for additional operations to determine the number of people. In this paper, four representative methods for clutter reduction are considered to discuss the performance and relationship between clutter reduction and machine learning algorithms.

3.1   Running Average Method

Consider that the variance of the clutter signal is smaller than the signal reflected from moving people, the running average method evaluates the mean value as a clutter signal and subsequently subtracts it from the received signals [1].

$$C(t) = \alpha \cdot C(t-1) + (1-\alpha) \cdot R(t) \tag{1}$$

$$s'(t) = R(t) - C(t) \tag{2}$$

In these formulas, $C(t)$ is the modeled clutter signal. $R(t)$ is the input signal before clutter reduction, and $s'(t)$ represents the background subtracted signal. α is a designed parameter that determines the ratio of the raw received signal to the clutter signal.

3.2   Singular Value Decomposition Method

Singular Value Decomposition splits the data matrix into subspaces that correspond to clutter, target and noise, then the clutter can be rejected easily. The received signal matrix R is decomposed [7].

$$R = USV^T \tag{3}$$

Since that clutter signals consist of direct waves caused by antenna coupling and reflected signals from static objects, which change little on the same time point, the energy of clutters is usually larger than the energy from moving people. The diagonal singular values in S are arrayed with the amount of energy in descending order, so the energy of clutters is mainly distributed in the first few singular values. Based on the results of various experiments, energy contribution of the first singular value is removed, and then the data matrix is reconstructed.

3.3 Kalman Filter Method

In [8], Kalman Filter is applied to estimate points of clutter in a radar scan independently. Equations in Kalman Filter are divided into two parts, by which the clutter C is estimated and modificated respectively. Since that the clutter consists of signal reflected from static objects and direct wave, it is considered to be constant in time. Then the equations could be simplified and the clutter could be estimated and subtracted from received signals.

3.4 Linear Least-Squares Method

In [9], the means of a linear least-squares fit to estimate clutter is proposed to eliminate linear trend resulted by the amplitude instability in data acquisition in the slow-time dimension. The clutter is then subtracted from the received signal matrix R.

$$\hat{R}^T = R^T - x(x^T x)^{-1} x^T \cdot R^T \tag{4}$$

In this formula, $x = [k/K\ 1_K]$, $k = [0, ..., K-1]^T$. 1_K is a K x 1 vector containing unit values, while K is the collected radar scans.

4 Machine Learning Algorithms

Machine learning enables the computer itself to utilize and learn from existing data to establish a model, and make predictions with this model. It is a data-driven solution on handling data to contain information, which provides a different manner in people counting compared with the signal processing methods, extracting and learning directly from the data. In this section, two distinct machine learning algorithms are discussed based on people counting.

4.1 Random Forest

The random forest classifier constructs multiple decision trees to train samples and make predictions. Each tree serves as a classifier, of which the training set is a random vector sampled independently from the total training set. And each tree casts a unit vote for the most popular class to complete classification.

Design of Key Features. Different choices of features would represent different data characteristics and result in different performance. Since that in most of the signal processing methods for people counting, the threshold is used to determine the boundary for distinguishing the presence or absence of a person. It is important and meanwhile difficult to establish the value. The use of multiple features corresponding to different parameters values is of particular importance, as lower threshold would produce more active samples and higher threshold yields less active samples [11]. In the people counting system, four terms of features are selected. These selected features are defined more clearly in Table 1.

Table 1. Extracted features definitions

Terms	Definition
Global features	Mean and variance of a signal in a radar scan
thr	Threshold parameter, with domain {0.1, 0.15, 0.2, 0.25, 0.3}
Features of active samples	Number of points in a radar scan of which the amplitude > *thr*. Mean and variance of these amplitudes
Features of activity events	Number of local maximum points in a radar scan of which the amplitude > *thr* in a fixed window size. Mean and variance of these amplitudes
Event count	Amplitudes and locations of the signal peaks in each activity events

4.2 Convolutional Neural Network

CNNs have deep architectures that are divided into a convolutional module, which consists of convolutional layers and activation layers that are employed to transform the input into features, and a linear classification module, which consists of connected layers and a softmax layer to output the class probabilities [12]. In this paper, the AlexNet is investigated and discussed to obtain counting information from the gray-scale maps of the radar data of size 1×1280 and the class probabilities to determine the quantity of people. AlexNet has a deep and complex architecture with Dropout [13] layer working for preventing overfitting.

5 Experiments

IR-UWB radar data acquired by NVA-R661 are employed to validate the performance of the proposed solutions in experiments. (i) Experiments with received data from different clutter reduction methods are performed to prove that clutter reduction is not necessary, even harmful when using a machine learning solution. The performance of classification by the random forest is compared with other machine learning algorithms and the performance is validated. (ii) The effectiveness of CNN as an automatic solution is verified.

5.1 Relationship Between Clutter Reduction Methods and Machine Learning Algorithms

A set of experiments have been conducted using different inputs to machine learning algorithms to explore the relationship between clutter reduction and machine learning.

Experimental Setup. Radar data are collected from an open lobby, shown in Fig. 2. A total of 12,000 radar samples of size 1×1280 from different people are collected. Four situations are considered: space with 0, 1, 2 or 3 people, where the

Fig. 2. Experimental environment: an open lobby

testers randomly walk in the space. Shown in Fig. 1, five datasets exist for the feature selection input: the bandpass data without clutter reduction (Bandpass), the data after singular value decomposition based clutter reduction (SVD), linear least-squares based clutter reduction (LLS), running average based clutter reduction (RA) and Kalman filter based clutter reduction (KF). Then features described in Sect. 4.1 are extracted from these different datasets respectively, as the input to machine learning algorithms. 10-fold cross validation is applied to validate the accuracy of the classification. The data mining toolkit Orange is used to learn the random forest for people counting estimation. Besides the random forest, other three machine learning algorithms, the stochastic gradient descent (SGD), logistic regression (LR), and naive bayes (NB) are applied to make comparison.

Results. The detection accuracy (Ac) (i.e., the ratio of the number of correctly predicted samples and the total number of testing data points) is employed to evaluate the performance [14]. Table 2 shows the accuracies of these four machine learning algorithms applied on five different input datasets. Random forest performs the highest accuracies on all of the five datasets, compared with other three machine learning algorithms. It could be concluded that the bandpass data get the highest accuracy in all of the four machine learning algorithms.

Table 2. Accuracy (%) of the machine learning algorithms on different datasets

	Bandpass	SVD	LLS	RA	KF
Random forest	**91.5%**	**87.8%**	**87.2%**	**81.9%**	**79.9%**
SGD	89.2%	80.8%	81.1%	75.9%	74.4%
Logistic regression	81.4%	76.2%	75.8%	72.3%	71.2%
Naive bayes	84.3%	77.7%	78%	71.2%	69%

Actually, for people counting in signal processing manner, the effectiveness of clutter reduction serves a significant role in getting the counting information. To compare the four representative clutter reduction methods, the differences between amplitudes are used. On the data with given number of n people, amplitudes of peaks in n-th activity events and in $(n+1)$-th activity events are calculated. If the normalized difference between them is larger, the threshold is considered to be set more easily, then the clutter reduction performs in a better way. Several tests have been done among these four clutter reduction methods on the collected radar data, and the averaging results show that Kalman filter clutter reduction works in the best way, following is the running average method. The linear least-squares and singular value decomposition methods have similar performance.

Since that clutters composed by direct waves and reflections from static objects occupy most energy in the bandpass data, it is impossible to detect and count effective peaks caused by moving humans in the bandpass data by the threshold-based signal processing methods. While clutter reduction is crucial in signal processing methods, it results in a significant decline in the accuracy with these four machine learning algorithms. And more effective clutter reduction methods, like KF method and running average method, result in much lower accuracies. It is considered that machine learning algorithms count in a different manner with the signal processing methods. Signal processing methods aim to extract crucial signals as clean as possible, and may eliminate valuable information as well. In machine learning, the clutter signals occupy most of the energy in the signals, and the model learns the changes in the clutter signals rather than that of moving objects. However, after clutter reduction, the amount of information from which the model can learn is reduced. Therefore, the smaller amount of information included in the cleaner input signal produces worse classification results.

5.2 Performance on Convolutional Neural Network

Convolutional neural network is applied to provide another data-driven solution, directly learning from the radar data without feature selection.

Experimental Setup. Radar data collected in an open lobby are expanded to 32,000 radar samples in the CNN experiment to avoid overfitting. All samples in five datasets are converted to gray-scale images of size 1×1280, and the average value of the training set is deducted from all input pixels to centralize the dimensions of the input data to zero. The AlexNet is employed to train and learn the five datasets using the Caffe deep learning framework.

Results. Figure 3 shows a comparison of the accuracies obtained by AlexNet using different input datasets. The bandpass data without clutter reduction reaches the highest accuracy, which proves that omitting clutter reduction produces better results when using machine learning algorithm. Though CNN has strong ability to extract features automatically and learn directly from the radar

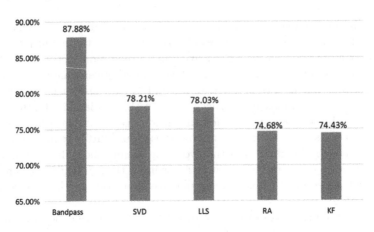

Fig. 3. Accuracy (%) of the AlexNet on different datasets.

data, the accuracy is lower than that of the random forest with feature selection. It's caused by radar data from different testers, so improving the generalization ability of CNN is important.

6   Conclusion

This paper proposes two machine learning solutions for people counting based on IR-UWB radar. By employing these data-driven algorithms, the relationship between clutter reduction and machine learning is discussed, and the results indicate that clutter reduction degrades performance of machine learning in people counting. Considerably good accuracy and stability has been achieved by random forest with selected time-domain features in radar signals. CNN provides a solution to learn and directly obtain features from radar data and analyze them to automatically produce results.

Future research will focus on improving the generalization ability of CNN to adapt this method to additional scenarios. Because radar signals are time-dependent, long short-term memory, which is a recurrent neural network model, will be applied to process radar signals.

Acknowledgments. This work was supported by the National Key R&D Program of China (2016YFB0100902).

References

1. Choi, J.W., Nam, S.S., Cho, S.H.: Multi-human detection algorithm based on an impulse radio ultra-wideband radar system. IEEE Access **PP**(99), 1 (2016)
2. Panda, D.K., Meher, S.: Detection of moving objects using fuzzy color difference histogram based background subtraction. IEEE Sig. Process. Lett. **23**(1), 45–49 (2016)

3. Zhang, C., Li, H., Wang, X., Yang, X.: Cross-scene crowd counting via deep convolutional neural networks. In: 2015 IEEE Conference on Computer Vision and Pattern Recognition (CVPR), Boston, MA, pp. 833–841 (2015)

4. Chan, A.B., Vasconcelos, N.: Counting people with low-level features and Bayesian regression. IEEE Trans. Image Process. **21**(4), 2160–2177 (2012)

5. Yuan, Y., Zhao, J., Qiu, C., Xi, W.: Estimating crowd density in an RF-based dynamic environment. IEEE Sens. J. **13**(10), 3837–3845 (2013)

6. Li, H., Chan, E.C.L., Guo, X., Xiao, J., Wu, K., Ni, L.M.: Wi-counter: smartphone-based people counter using crowdsourced wi-fi signal data. IEEE Trans. Hum. Mach. Syst. **45**(4), 442–452 (2015)

7. Rane, S.A., Gaurav, A., Sarkar, S., Clement, J.C., Sardana, H.K.: Clutter suppression techniques to detect behind the wall static human using UWB radar. In: IEEE International Conference on Proceedings of Recent Trends in Electronics, Information Communication Technology (RTEICT), May 2016

8. Nguyen, V.H., Pyun, J.Y.: Location detection and tracking of moving targets by a 2D IR-UWB radar system. Sensors **15**(3), 6740–6762 (2015)

9. Nezirovic, A., Yarovoy, A.G., Ligthart, L.P.: Signal processing for improved detection of trapped victims using UWB radar. IEEE Trans. Geosci. Remote Sens. **48**(4), 2005–2014 (2010)

10. Dapogny, A., Bailly, K., Dubuisson, S.: Dynamic pose-robust facial expression recognition by multi-view pairwise conditional random forests. IEEE Trans. Affect. Comput. **PP**(99), 1 (2017)

11. He, J., Arora, A.: A regression-based radar-mote system for people counting. In: 2014 IEEE International Conference on Pervasive Computing and Communications (PerCom), Budapest, pp. 95–102 (2014)

12. Xu, G., Wu, H.Z., Shi, Y.Q.: Structural design of convolutional neural networks for steganalysis. IEEE Sig. Process. Lett. **23**(5), 708–712 (2016)

13. Krizhevsky, A., Sutskever, I., Hinton, G.E.: ImageNet classification with deep convolutional neural networks. In: International Conference on Neural Information Processing Systems, pp. 1097–1105. Curran Associates Inc. (2012)

14. Chen, J., Kang, X., Liu, Y., Wang, Z.J.: Median filtering forensics based on convolutional neural networks. IEEE Sig. Process. Lett. **22**(11), 1849–1853 (2015)

Fine-Grained Infer $PM_{2.5}$ Using Images from Crowdsourcing

Shuai Li[✉], Teng Xi, Xirong Que, and Wendong Wang

State Key Laboratory of Networking and Switching Technology,
Beijing University of Posts and Telecommunications, Beijing, China
shli@bupt.edu.cn

Abstract. Among all air pollutants, $PM_{2.5}$, which can be inhaled into lungs, is most harmful for peoples' health. However, the number of fixed air quality measurement stations is insufficient. In order to make people be more aware of the air quality around them, this paper have proposed a method to infer fine-grained $PM_{2.5}$ concentration. We leverage different type of collected by crowdsourcing for data mining. Then, features which have strong correlation with $PM_{2.5}$ concentration are extracted. Furthermore, we train the proposed model using integrated radial basis function (rbf) kernel based ridge regression. The performance of the proposed method is evaluated thoroughly by real dataset collected by crowdsourcing. The results show that, our method can accurate infer the $PM_{2.5}$ concentration.

Keywords: Crowdsourcing · Fine-grained inference · $PM_{2.5}$ Concentration · Features extract

1 Introduction

Air pollution seriously affects people's health and social work [1]. Among all air pollutants, $PM_{2.5}$ is one of the principal contamination causing air pollution. As the diameter of $PM_{2.5}$ is less than 2.5 micron, it is easy to induce disease and haze. To monitor the fine particle concentrations, many areas in the world have established fixed air quality measurement stations. However, the number of fixed air quality measurement stations is insufficient due to the expensive cost of building and maintaining such a station [2].

Fortunately, there are different type of data that we can use to infer $PM_{2.5}$ concentration. For example, zheng et al. have proposed a method to infer real-time and fine-grained air quality based on the data of air quality, trajectory, POI and so on [2]. Similarly, Donkelaar et al. have proposed an approach to infer air pollution using the data from satellite [3]. Nowadays, as the emerge

W. Wang—This work was supported in part by the National High Technology Research and Development Program (863 Program) of China (Grant No. 2015AA016101, 2015AA015601), National Natural Science Foundation of China (Grant No. 61370197, 61402045).

© Springer International Publishing AG 2017
S. Ibrahim et al. (Eds.): ICA3PP 2017, LNCS 10393, pp. 678–686, 2017.
DOI: 10.1007/978-3-319-65482-9_53

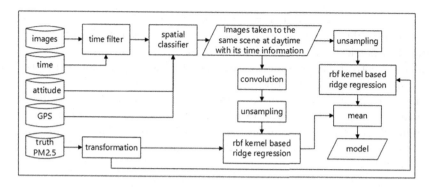

Fig. 1. $PM2.5$ inference framework

of crowdsourcing system, it is easy to collect a variety of data through mobile phones. In this paper, we propose a general framework for inferring fine-grained $PM_{2.5}$. Figure 1 shows the proposed framework. As shown in the figure, five different type of data are collected through our established crowdsourcing system. Then, we extract features of images taken at the same scene, such as pixels, taken time, magnetic sensor and gps information. Furthermore, we study the relationship between the extracted features and $PM_{2.5}$ concentration. Finally, we use the integrated rbf kernel based ridge regression to generate the inference model.

The contributions of this paper are summarized as follows:

- A general framework for inferring fine-grained $PM_{2.5}$ is proposed, which leverage different type of data collected by crowdsourcing system.
- The collected data has been mined thoroughly and features which have strong correlation with $PM_{2.5}$ concentration are extracted.
- The performance of the proposed method is evaluated thoroughly by real dataset collected by our established crowdsourcing. The results show that, the proposed approach can accurate infer the $PM_{2.5}$ concentration.

The rest of the paper is organized as follows. Section 2 presents the related work. Section 3 explains the features we extract. Section 4 describes our proposed method. Section 5 evaluates the performance of our proposed method using real dataset. Finally, Sect. 6 concludes the paper.

2 Related Works

Using the satellite remote sensing to analysis the atmospheric condition has been studied intensively in past decades. Some researchers have studied the air pollution using images taken by satellite [4,5] and have made some achievements.

Other than that, some researchers have studied the physical models of air pollutants [6,7]. For example, Rakowska [7] assumes that the concentrations of air pollutant are dispersed in a gaussian manner and wind speed equals to $1\,\mathrm{m/s}$ at certain height. Tominaga [6] have taken emission density, street width, and vertical dispersion parameters of the receptor point into consideration in their model. Recently, there are some researchers infer the air pollution using big data [2,8], and achieve better results.

Different from above approaches, we propose a general framework for inferring fine-grained $PM_{2.5}$ concentration with the dataset collected from crowdsourcing. Our proposed model leverage different type of data such as images, time, magnetic sensor and gps information, which can inference $PM_{2.5}$ concentration accurately.

3   Features

3.1   Image Features

The light will be refracted by fine particles in the air. In computer vision and computer graphics, the following model is widely used to describe the affect of the fine particles to the image [9].

$$I(p) = trans(p)R(p) + (1 - trans(p))A \qquad (1)$$

where I(.) is the luminance of image, R(.) is the scene radiation intensity, A is the global atmospheric light, p is the location of pixel and $trans(.)$ is the medium transmission describing the portion of the light that is not refracted and reaches the camera.

$PM_{2.5}$ contains all the particles whose diameter is similar to the wavelength of visible light. So it is the main cause of light scattering in the air particles. Based on this model, we extract the following features of the image.

Undersample Directly: The refracted of light reduce the brilliance of color in scene's image. We extract the image's feature directly by following equation.

$$f_{ud} = \min_{p \in \Omega(p)} \left(\min_{c \in C(p)} I^c(p) \right) \qquad (2)$$

where $\Omega(.)$ is the set of pixels in local region, F_{ud} is the features extracted in region Ω, C(.) is $\{R,G,B\}$ that is the set of channels of pixel in image, c is an channel.

Image Convolution: The refracted of light also make the image become blur, and reduce the edge of the image. We use Laplasse operator to convolute the image, then undersampling by the calculated variance in regions and get the mean of three channels. This feature can express the range of frequency spectrum.

$$Z^c = I^c * H \qquad (3)$$

$$f_{cu} = \frac{\sum\limits_{c \in C} \sum\limits_{p \in \Omega(p)} (Z^c(p) - \frac{\sum\limits_{p \in \Omega(p)} Z^c(p)}{N})^2}{3N} \qquad (4)$$

where H is the Laplasse operator $[0,-1,0;-1,4,-1;0,-1,0]$, Z is the matrix after image convolution, f_{cu} is the features extracted in region Ω, N is the numbers of pixels in region Ω.

3.2   Other Features

Taken Time. The illumination direction of the scene is different at different time of one day. We get the time of sunrise and sunset, then calculate feature using

$$f_t = \frac{(t - t_{sunrise}(t))}{(t_{sunset}(t) - t_{sunrise}(t))} \qquad (5)$$

Where f_t is the time feature we get, t is the time when image taken, $t_{sunrise}(.)$ is the sunrise time in the day when image taken, $t_{sunset}(.)$ is the sunset time in the day when image taken.

Taken Season. The color of the scene is different when there are trees or rivers in the scene in different seasons. For example, most of the trees are green in spring and summer, while are gray in autumn and winter. We use different numbers represent different seasons as feature f_s.

4   Our Method

4.1   Data Preprocessing

Our image data is collected based on crowdsourcing. Since some images may not meet the requirements, it is necessary to preprocess data.

Time Filter. Images taken at night are difficult to analysis because of the dim light. They will through an time filter when the images are uploaded. Images taken not between the time of sunrise and sunset in the day will be tagged.

Spatial Classifier. When user upload images using smart mobilephone, the images contain gps and attitude transducer information. Images taken to different scene will be classed into different categories according to their location and attitude information.

However, the images are collected by crowdsourcing, so there may be some small differences among images taken the same scene. To reduce the differences, the images will be registered. Every scene will choice the first image as the template image. We extract speeded up robust features (surf) [10] of the new images

Fig. 2. Image registration

and template image as their descriptor. Then match them, and get the homography matrix from new images to template image using the random sample consensus methods. If the translation transformation and the rotation transformation are lower than threshold according to the homography matrix, we will make transformation to the new image. As shown in Fig. 2, they are template image, new image and the new image after registered of one scene. Final, we remove black edges of the image after registered through cutting.

4.2 Features Extraction

We set the region in Sect. 3 using sliding window. In every window we extract the f_{ud} and f_{cu} features, then get an feature vectors F_{ud} and F_{cu}. To reduce the influences of season and solar incidence angle, we also use F_t and F_s features to infer the $PM_{2.5}$ concentration.

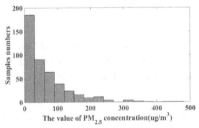

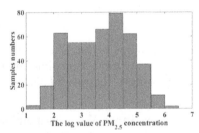

(a) The original distribution of labels   (b) The distribution of labels after transformed

Fig. 3. The effect of label transformed

4.3 Relational Model

In our statistical analysis, The distribution of $PM_{2.5}$ concentration we get as groundtruth in each scene is uneven. As shown in Fig. 3(a) is the distribution of $PM_{2.5}$ concentration in one scene. There are more small values. We transform the date by taking logarithm as $ln(y+1)$ when we training model. The distribution of $PM_{2.5}$ concentration after transformation is shown in Fig. 3(b), which is like flat gaussian distribution.

Let $x \in \mathbb{R}^D$ be the feature vector, X be the corresponding $N \times D$ features matrix, $y \in \mathbb{R}$ be the groundtruth, Y be the corresponding $N \times 1$ label matrix, and W be the weight-coefficients matrix. The loss function of the ridge regression is as following:

$$J(W) = (Y - XW)^T(Y - XW) + \lambda\|W\|^2 \tag{6}$$

Get the optimal solution:

$$W = X^T(X^TX + \lambda I_N)^{-1}Y \tag{7}$$

We solve by changing from primal to dual variables:

$$\alpha \triangleq (K + \lambda I_N)^{-1}Y \tag{8}$$

The primal variables can be rewrite as:

$$W = X^T\alpha = \sum_{i=1}^{N} \alpha_i x_i \tag{9}$$

This is just a linear sum of the N training vector. Then we use kernel function, we get:

$$\hat{f}(x) = W^TX = \sum_{i=1}^{N} \alpha_i x_i^T x = \sum_{i=1}^{N} \alpha_i \kappa(x, x_i) \tag{10}$$

where (.) is the result inferred, $\kappa(x, x_i)$ is the kernel function, and we use the rbf kernel as following:

$$\kappa(x_i, x_j) = exp(\gamma\|x_i - x_j\|^2) \tag{11}$$

where γ is an hyper parameter representing the degree of nonlinear mapping.

Finally, we get the result by simple integration method:

$$\hat{f}(x) = (\hat{f}_{ud}(x) + \hat{f}_{ud}(x))/2 \tag{12}$$

where $\hat{f}_{ud}(.)$ is the result inferred by F_{ud}, F_t and F_s, $\hat{f}_{cu}(.)$ is the result inferred by F_{cu}, F_t and F_s.

5   Experiments

5.1   Dataset

To evaluate the performance of the proposed method, we choice samples which belong to the same site as shown in Fig. 2. The samples are collected by our established crowdsourcing system from January 2016 to May 2017, which contain images, time, attitude and gps informations. There are 440 images in this site. The image resolution is 1080×1441. The sliding window is set with size of 200×200 and step of 100×100. Then, we can get two features vectors each of which has 66 parameters.

Ground Truth: The values of $PM_{2.5}$ measured at fixed air quality monitoring station in Olympic Sports Center, which is close to the site, are taken as ground truth.

5.2   Result

We evaluate the performance of the proposed method using different numbers of training set. The number of testing set is 80 and remain unchanged while the number of training range from 5 to 320. We repeat the experiment for 1000 times and randomly select the training set and testing set every time. Figure 4 shows the box plot of the independent experiments. Figure 4(a) shows the Mean absolute error (MAE). Figure 4(b) shows the fitting coefficient(R^2), which is also know as the coefficient of determination range from 0 to 1. As shown in the figure, as the number of training set increases, the inferences error decreases. When the number of training set reaches 320, the median of test MAE decreases to 19.07, and the median of R^2 increases to 0.7484.

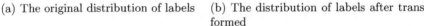
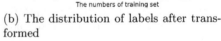

(a) The original distribution of labels   (b) The distribution of labels after transformed

Fig. 4. The results distribution when using different numbers of training set

To show the effect of the proposed approach in practical applications, we use samples collected from January 2016 to June 2016 as training set and use

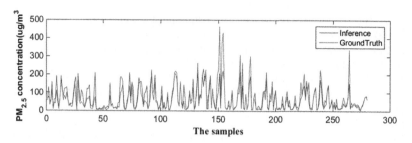

Fig. 5. The result of inferring

the samples collected after this time as testing set. Figure 5 shows the inference results. As shown in the figure, the inference values are close to the ground truth in most cases.

6 Conclusions and Future Work

In this paper, we proposed a general method to infer fine-grained $PM_{2.5}$ concentration using the images collected by crowdsourcing. The proposed method also take informations of time, gps, and the attitude of phone into consideration. We use the real dataset collected by our established crowdsourcing to evaluate the proposed method. The results show that, our proposed approach can infer fine-grained $PM_{2.5}$ concentration accurately. In the future, we will study the influence of different type of camera lens and further improve the inference accuracy.

References

1. Lim, S.S., Vos, T., Flaxman, A.D., Danaei, G., Shibuya, K., Adair-Rohani, M., Amann, M., Anderson, H.R., Andrews, K.G., Aryee, M.: A comparative risk assessment of burden of disease and injury attributable to 67 risk factors and risk factor clusters in 21 regions, 1990–2010: a systematic analysis for the global burden of disease study 2010. Lancet **380**(9859), 2224–2260 (2012)
2. Zheng, Y., Liu, F., Hsieh, H.P.: U-air: when urban air quality inference meets big data. In: Proceedings of the ACM SIGKDD International Conference on Knowledge Discovery and Data Mining (KDD), Chicago, Illinois, USA, pp. 1436–1444, 11th–14th August 2013
3. Van Donkelaar, A., Martin, R.V., Brauer, M., Boys, B.L.: Use of satellite observations for long-term exposure assessment of global concentrations of fine particulate matter. Environ. Health Perspect. **123**(2), 135 (2015)
4. Martin, R.V.: Satellite remote sensing of surface air quality. Atmos. Environ. **42**(34), 7823–7843 (2008)
5. Van Donkelaar, A., Martin, R.V., Levy, R.C., da Silva, A.M., Krzyzanowski, M., Chubarova, N.E., Semutnikova, E., Cohen, A.J.: Satellite-based estimates of ground-level fine particulate matter during extreme events: a case study of the moscow fires in 2010. Atmos. Environ. **45**(34), 6225–6232 (2011)

6. Scaar, H., Teodorov, T., Ziegler, T., Mellmann, J.: Computational fluid dynamics (CFD) analysis of air flow uniformity in a fixed-bed dryer for medicinal plants. In: Ist International Symposium on CFD Applications in Agriculture, vol. 1008, pp. 119–126 (2012)
7. Rakowska, A., Wong, K.C., Townsend, T., Chan, K.L., Westerdahl, D., Ng, S., Močnik, G., Drinovec, L., Ning, Z.: Impact of traffic volume and composition on the air quality and pedestrian exposure in urban street canyon. Atmos. Environ. **98**, 260–270 (2014)
8. Chen, L., Cai, Y., Ding, Y., Lv, M., Yuan, C., Chen, G.: Spatially fine-grained urban air quality estimation using ensemble semi-supervised learning and pruning. In: ACM International Joint Conference on Pervasive and Ubiquitous Computing, pp. 1076–1087 (2016)
9. Raanan, F.: Single image dehazing. ACM (2008)
10. Bay, H., Tuytelaars, T., Van Gool, L.: SURF: speeded up robust features. In: Leonardis, A., Bischof, H., Pinz, A. (eds.) ECCV 2006. LNCS, vol. 3951, pp. 404–417. Springer, Heidelberg (2006). doi:10.1007/11744023_32

Security/Reliability-Aware Relay Selection with Connection Duration Constraints for Vehicular Networks

Zhenyu Liu and Lin Zhang[✉]

Beijing University of Posts and Telecommunications,
Xitucheng Road. 10, Haidian District, Beijing 100876, China
zhanglin@bupt.edu.cn

Abstract. The vehicular network technology is developed to serve as a solution for traffic safety and traffic efficiency. However, if the user privacy and data security of the driver is compromised, connected vehicle cannot widely be accepted by the public. According to the security requirements of connected vehicles and the limitations of cryptographic encryption technologies, in this paper, a security/reliability-aware relay selection scheme with connection duration constraint is proposed for vehicular environments. We derive the closed-form expressions of reliable secrecy transmission probability (RSTP) for relay selection. The RSTP is proposed to serve as the performance metrics combine physical layer security with reliability. Based on the network topology and the velocity of the moving vehicles, the proposed scheme generates relay candidate sets with the connection duration constraint. Finally, based on both the RSTP and relay candidate sets, we propose a flexible route selection scheme, which enables us to select the relay according to different security and reliability requirement.

Keywords: Vehicular networks · Physical layer security · Reliability · Relay selection · Connection duration

1 Introduction

As the number of the vehicles is growing, traffic safety and traffic efficiency be-come the most serious challenges faced in the transportation systems. The connected vehicle technology is developed to serve as a solution which can provide a wide range of applications including active driving safety applications, traffic efficiency applications, location-based service applications, etc. These applications require the vehicles involved in V2V (vehicle-to-vehicle) communication, V2I (vehicle-to-infrastructure), and V2P (vehicle-to-pedestrian) to transmit necessary information which will involve the user's data security and privacy. If the user privacy and data security of the driver are compromised, connected vehicle cannot widely be accepted by the public. Therefore, it is of great necessity to protect security as well as reliability.

© Springer International Publishing AG 2017
S. Ibrahim et al. (Eds.): ICA3PP 2017, LNCS 10393, pp. 687–694, 2017.
DOI: 10.1007/978-3-319-65482-9_54

Although many communication technologies have been proposed for wireless networks, the combination of security and reliability in multi-hop vehicular networks still remains an open technical challenge. The main challenge comes from the unique feature of the vehicular networks. First, compared with other wireless net-works, the connectivity among the vehicle nodes may change frequently due to the fast movement of vehicles. Second, network security requires time efficiency and low complexity method due to the limited connection duration.

The applications of cooperative relay are studied to provide reliable end-to-end data delivery in vehicular networks [1–3].However, the openness of the wireless vehicular channels makes the transmitted data available to unauthorized users as well as the intended receiver. Thus, data security should be well-protected in the routing of vehicular networks.

Traditionally, cryptographic encryption and decryption technologies are exploited to protect the confidentiality of information [4]. The basic idea of cryptographic encryption is based on a secret key, which should be distributed secretly among the legitimate users. However, applying cryptographic encryption technologies is not suitable in vehicular communications. First, the secret key distribution and management are very vulnerable due to the dynamic topology and the open nature of the wireless medium in vehicular networks. Second, as encryption relies on the mathematical calculation complexity, it requires considerable computational resources and time, which is rigorous due to the limited connection duration of vehicular communications.

Fortunately, physical layer security approaches eliminate the key generation and distribution issues, thereby resulting in significantly lower complexity and savings in computational resources. Physical layer security approaches take consideration of the characteristic of wireless channels, and the theoretical basis of physical security is information theory.

There are some physical layer security related works, which take advantage of node cooperation to enhance data security and privacy protection. The authors explore the physical-layer security in cooperative wireless networks with multiple relays and provide optimal relay selection schemes to improve the wireless security [5]. A comprehensive investigation on the secrecy performance of opportunistic relay selection systems is proposed considering the decode-and-forward protocol over Rayleigh fading channels [6]. However, these works focus on security without reliability. Although the authors use weighted sum of the secrecy outage probability (SOP) and connection outage probability (COP) for routing selection [7], the SOP is influenced by COP and they should be considered jointly. Besides, compared with these works, vehicular network has its own characteristics, e.g., fast movement of vehicles and dynamic network topology. However, these works hardly take the characteristic of the vehicular network into consideration.

Considering the security and reliability requirements of vehicular networks, a security/reliability-aware relay selection scheme with connection duration constraint is proposed for vehicular environments. Our contributions are summarized as follow:

- The RSTP is proposed to serve as the performance metrics which combines physical layer security with reliability. The closed-form expressions of RSTP is derived for a relay selection.
- The proposed scheme generates the relay candidate set based on the network topology and the velocity of the moving vehicles to connection duration requirement.
- We propose a flexible relay selection scheme to select the optimal relay according to different security and reliability requirement. Besides, our scheme does not require instantaneous channel state information (CSI).

The rest of this paper is organized as follows. In Sect. 2, system model is provided. The secure routing design are explained in Sect. 3. Finally, this paper is concluded in Sect. 4.

2   System Model

2.1   Network Model

As is shown in Fig. 1, we consider a two-way highway scenario, which consists of several straight lanes in each direction. Within the considered rectangular area, M vehicles are uniformly distributed. As the vehicles broadcast their locations and speeds to protect their safety, we assume that each vehicle knows others' speeds and locations. There might be several vehicles having data to transmit in a

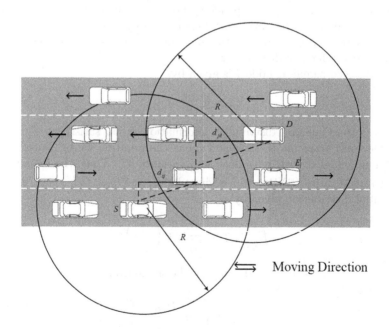

Fig. 1. An example of network model

special time. As the interference characterization depends heavily on the network behavior and related MAC protocols, we assume that this scenario happens in a network where there is a time division multiple address (TDMA) scheduler. And only one source destination pair is allowed to communicate with each other in this area, so the interference is ignorable. The transmitter and the corresponding receiver are marked as S and D, respectively. Meanwhile, there is a malicious node E existing in the area, which tries to eavesdrop the information. We assume that the direct link between S and D does not exist, i.e., the communications need the help of other vehicles serving as relays. The transmission scheme of relays is decode-and-forward (DF). To focus on the design of the relaying protocol, we also assume that the broadcast phase is secure, i.e., the direct link between S and E is not available, and corresponding scenarios have been explained in [6].

2.2 Channel Model

Considering that signals suffer from small-scale fading and large-scale path loss (power law attenuation with respect to the path distance), both the main channels and wiretap channels are assumed to undergo quasi-static independent and identically distributed (i.i.d) Rayleigh fading together with a large-scale path loss governed by exponent α. The power gain can be characterized as

$$g_{ij} = h_{ij}\sqrt{\varphi_{ij}} \tag{1}$$

where i and j denote the indexes of transmitter and receiver, h_{ij} denotes the small-scale fading gain with independent and identically distributed entries $h_{ij} \sim CN(0,1)$. φ_{ij} denotes the path loss which can be written as $\varphi_{ij} = Lr_{ij}^{-\alpha}$, where r_{ij} denotes the path distance between i and j, and L denotes the pass loss evaluated at a reference distance 1.

The received signal at node j is given by

$$y_{ij} = g_{ij}x + n_{ij}, \tag{2}$$

where x is the Gaussian distributed information signal satisfying $E[|x|^2] = P$ (P is the total transmit power), and n_{il} is the additive white Gaussian noise of the main channel with zero mean and variance σ_{ij}^2. Thus, the instantaneous signal-to-noise ratios (SNRs) at j is given by $\gamma_{ij} = P|g_{ij}|^2/\sigma_{ij}^2$, each having an exponential distribution given by

$$f_{ij}\left(\overline{\gamma}_{ij}\right) = \frac{1}{\overline{\gamma}_{ij}} \exp\left(\frac{\gamma}{\overline{\gamma}_{ij}}\right) \tag{3}$$

where is $\overline{\gamma}_{ij}$ are the average SNRs at j for the signal from i. The channel capacity can be given by

$$C_{ij} = \log\left(1 + \frac{P|g_{ij}|^2}{\sigma_{ij}^2}\right) \tag{4}$$

3   Secure Routing Design

3.1   Decode-and-Forward

During the broadcast phase, S broadcasts its message and all possible relays receive the message. The received signal at R_j, denoted by y_{sj}, is expressed as

$$y_{sj} = g_{sj}x + n_{sj}.$$ (5)

Under the DF transmission scheme, each node first decodes the signal from source node. Considering the massage can be decoded when the SNR is great than a given threshold β, we can compute the successful decoding probability at R_j as

$$p_{sj}^d = P\left(\gamma_{sj} > \beta\right) = \exp\left(-\frac{\beta}{\gamma_{sj}}\right)$$ (6)

If the decoding is successful, then the relay transmits the recoded original signal to the next hop node. Suppose that node R_j decodes the signal from S successfully, then it will transmit the original signal using the same power. Thus, the received signals at D and the corresponding eavesdropper E are given by

$$y_{jd} = g_{jd}x + n_{jd},$$ (7)

$$y_{je} = g_{je}x + n_{je}$$ (8)

and the secrecy capacity is

$$C_{jd}^s = [C_{jd} - C_{je}]^+ = [\log\left(1 + \gamma_{jd}\right) - \log\left(1 + \gamma_{je}\right)]^+$$ (9)

where $[x]^+ \triangleq \max\{0, x\}$

3.2   Relay Candidate Set Generation

As potential relays should be inside the transmission ranges of both the source and the destination, for a given SNR threshold β, we need to get the corresponding transmission range. As the successful transmission can be achieved when $\gamma_{ij} > \beta$, i.e.

$$\gamma_{ij} = P|g_{ij}|^2/\sigma_{ij}^2 = P\left|h_{ij}\sqrt{\varphi_{ij}}\right|^2/\sigma_{ij}^2 = PLr_{ij}^{-\alpha}|h_{ij}|^2/\sigma_{ij}^2 > \beta$$ (10)

Thus, the average transmission range can be formed as

$$R < \sqrt[\alpha]{\frac{PL}{\beta\sigma^2}}$$ (11)

To keep the stability of a selected routes, potential relays should be inside the transmission ranges of both the source S and the destination D for a duration which is equal or greater than a threshold T and dependent on the transmission rate size of the transmitted messages.

Define the duration of $S \to j$ link and $j \to D$ link as t_{sj} and t_{jd}, respectively. Define the projection distance of $S \to j$ link and $j \to D$ in the road direction as as d_{sj} and d_{jd}, respectively. And the projection distance can be calculated using the locations and the driving direction of corresponding vehicles. The duration t_{sj} of $S \to j$ link can be approximated as

$$t_{sj} = \begin{cases} \left(\frac{R \mp d_{sj}}{|v_s - v_j|} \right)^+, same - direction \\ \left(\frac{R \pm d_{sj}}{v_s + v_j} \right)^+, opposite - direction \end{cases} \tag{12}$$

When j is in front of S, the sign "$\mp$" becomes "-" and the sign "$\pm$" becomes "+", otherwise , "$\mp$" becomes "+" and the sign "$\pm$" becomes "$-$", respectively. Similarly, the duration t_{jd} of $j \to D$ link can be estimated by replacing s with d.

The duration of the link $S \to D$ can be expressed by $min\{t_{sj}, t_{jd}\}$, and the vehicle j belongs to the relay candidate set only if $min\{t_{sj}, t_{jd}\} > T$. Assume that the relay candidate set is Φ , and the size of the relay candidate set is N.

3.3   Route Selection

Reliability-Oriented Selection. For the reliability-oriented selection, the relay node is selected based on the connection probability of the $S \to j \to D$. Although it is an effective solution for non-eavesdropper environments, this solution does not take into account the eavesdrop-per channels. The reliability-oriented selection is written as

$$j^s = \arg \max_{j \in \Phi} p_{sd}^d \tag{13}$$

where $p_{sd}^d = p_{sj}^d p_{jd}^d = \exp\left(-\beta\left(\frac{1}{\overline{\gamma}_{sj}} + \frac{1}{\overline{\gamma}_{jd}}\right)\right)$.

Security-Oriented Selection. As a secrecy outage happens when the instantaneous secrecy capacity C_s is less than a target secrecy rate R_s, the secrecy outage probability is defined as $p^{so} = P\left(C^s < R_s\right)$ [7], the secrecy outage probability from j to D is given by

$$p_{jd}^{so} = P\left(C_{jd}^{so} < R_s\right) = \int_0^\infty \left(\int_{2^{R_s}(1+\gamma_{je})-1}^\infty f_{jd}\left(\gamma_{jd}\right) d\gamma_{jd} \right) f_{je}\left(\gamma_{je}\right) d\gamma_{je}$$
$$= 1 - \frac{\overline{\gamma}_{jd}}{\overline{\gamma}_{je} 2^{R_s} + \overline{\gamma}_{jd}} \exp\left(-\frac{2^{R_s} - 1}{\overline{\gamma}_{jd}}\right) \tag{14}$$

Thus, the secrecy transmission probability can be defined as

$$p^s = 1 - p^{so} = P\left(C^s \geq R_s\right). \tag{15}$$

The security-oriented selection scheme takes into account the relay-eavesdropper links and chooses the relay node based on the secrecy transmission probability. The optimal selection maximizes the secrecy transmission probability and is given as

$$j^s = \arg \max_{j \in \Phi} p_{jd}^s \qquad (16)$$

where $p_{jd}^s = \dfrac{\overline{\gamma}_{jd}}{\overline{\gamma}_{je} 2^{R_s} + \overline{\gamma}_{jd}} \exp\left(-\dfrac{2^{R_s}-1}{\overline{\gamma}_{jd}}\right).$

Security/Reliability-Aware Selection. However, the secrecy transmission is not enough. If the secrecy transmission message cannot be decoded, it is meaningless. As a result, we present an alternative secrecy transmission formulation, which directly measures the probability that a transmitted message can achieve perfect secrecy.

As a result, we take the security and reliability into consideration at the same time. The reliable secrecy transmission probability is defined as follow, which combines the secrecy with reliability:

$$p^{rs} = P\left(C^s \geq R_s, \gamma > \beta\right). \qquad (17)$$

Thus, the reliable secrecy transmission probability from j to D is given by

$$
\begin{aligned}
p_{jd}^{rs} &= P\left(C_{jd}^s \geq R_s, \gamma_{jd} > \beta\right) \\
&= P\left(C_{jd}^s \geq R_s | \gamma_{jd} > \beta\right) \times P\left(\gamma_{jd} > \beta\right) \\
&= \left[1 - P\left(C_{jd}^s < R_s | \gamma_{jd} > \beta\right)\right] \times P\left(\gamma_{jd} > \beta\right) \\
&= \left[1 - P\left(C_{je} > C_{jd} - R_s | \gamma_{jd} > \beta\right)\right] \times P\left(\gamma_{jd} > \beta\right) \\
&= \left[1 - P\left(\gamma_{jd} < 2^{R_s}\left(1 + \gamma_{je}\right) - 1 | \gamma_{jd} > \beta\right)\right] \times P\left(\gamma_{jd} > \beta\right) \\
&= \left[1 - \frac{P\left(\beta < \gamma_{jd} < 2^{R_s}\left(1 + \gamma_{je}\right) - 1\right)}{P\left(\gamma_{jd} > \beta\right)}\right] \times P\left(\gamma_{jd} > \beta\right) \qquad (18) \\
&= P\left(\gamma_{jd} > \beta\right) - P\left(\beta < \gamma_{jd} < 2^{R_s}\left(1 + \gamma_{je}\right) - 1\right) \\
&= P\left(\gamma_{jd} > \beta\right) - \int_{\frac{\beta+1}{2^{R_s}}-1}^{\infty} \left(\int_{\beta}^{2^{R_s}(1+\gamma_{je})-1} f_{jd}\left(\gamma_{jd}\right) d\gamma_{jd}\right) f_{je}\left(\gamma_{je}\right) d\gamma_{je} \\
&= \exp\left(-\frac{\beta}{\overline{\gamma}_{jd}}\right) \left[1 - \frac{\overline{\gamma}_{je} 2^{R_s}}{\overline{\gamma}_{je} 2^{R_s} + \overline{\gamma}_{jd}} \exp\left(-\frac{\beta + 1 - 2^{R_s}}{\overline{\gamma}_{je} 2^{R_s}}\right)\right]
\end{aligned}
$$

Thus, when the selected relay is j, the reliable secrecy transmission probability from S to D is

$$
\begin{aligned}
p_{sd}^{rs} &= p_{sj}^{rs} p_{jd}^{rs} = p_{sj}^d p_{jd}^{rs} \\
&= \exp\left(-\frac{\beta}{\overline{\gamma}_{sj}} - \frac{\beta}{\overline{\gamma}_{jd}}\right) \left[1 - \frac{\overline{\gamma}_{je} 2^{R_s}}{\overline{\gamma}_{je} 2^{R_s} + \overline{\gamma}_{jd}} \exp\left(-\frac{\beta + 1 - 2^{R_s}}{\overline{\gamma}_{je} 2^{R_s}}\right)\right] \qquad (19)
\end{aligned}
$$

where β can adapt to the reliability requirement, and R_s can be set according to the secrecy requirement. Now, we formulate the design problem of finding the relay j that maximize the reliable secrecy transmission probability

$$j^s = \arg \max_{j \in \Phi} p_{sd}^{rs}$$
$$s.t. \beta \geq 2^{R_s} - 1, R_s > 0 \tag{20}$$

4   Conclusion

In this paper, a security/reliability-aware relay selection scheme with connection duration constraint is proposed to the security requirements of vehicular environments. We propose RSTP to serve as the performance metrics combine physical layer security with reliability, and derive the closed-form expressions of reliable secrecy transmission probability (RSTP) for relay selection. The relay candidate sets with the connection duration constraint are generated based on the network topology and the velocity of the moving vehicles. Finally, based on both the RSTP and relay candidate sets, we propose a flexible route selection scheme, which enables us to select the relay according to different security and reliability requirement.

Acknowledgements. This work was supported by the National Key R&D Program of China (2016YFB0100902).

References

1. Xing, M., Cai, L.: Adaptive video streaming with inter-vehicle relay for highway VANET scenario. In: 2012 IEEE International Conference on Communications, pp. 5168–5172. IEEE Press, Ottawa (2012)
2. Smith, T.F., Waterman, M.S.: Identification of common molecular subsequences. J. Mol. Biol. **147**, 195–197 (1981)
3. Zhou, T., et al.: A novel adaptive distributed cooperative relaying MAC protocol for vehicular networks. IEEE J. Sel. Areas Commun. **29**(1), 72–82 (2011)
4. Zhang, Z., et al.: Cooperative information forwarding in vehicular networks subject to channel randomness. In: 2014 IEEE International Conference on Communications, pp. 324–329. IEEE Press, Sydney (2014)
5. Wang, H.-M., Zheng, T.-X.: Physical Layer Security in Random Cellular Networks. SpringerBriefs in computer science. Springer, Singapore (2016)
6. Zou, Y., Wang, X., Shen, W.: Optimal relay selection for physical-layer security in cooperative wireless networks. IEEE J. Sel. Areas Commun. **31**(10), 2099–2111 (2013)
7. Al-Qahtani, F.S., Zhong, C., Hussein, M.: Alnuweiri.: Opportunistic relay selection for secrecy enhancement in cooperative networks. IEEE Trans. Commun. **63**(5), 1756–1770 (2015)
8. Yang, X., et al.: Security/QoS-aware route selection in multi-hop wireless ad hoc net-works. In: 2016 IEEE International Conference on Communications, pp. 1–6. IEEE Press, Kuala Lumpur (2016)
9. Krikidis, I., Thompson, J.S., McLaughlin, S.: Relay selection for secure cooperative networks with jamming. IEEE Trans. Wirel. Commun. **8**(10), 5003–5011 (2009)

Smart City Environmental Perception from Ambient Cellular Signals

Isha Singh$^{(\boxtimes)}$ and Stephan Sigg

Aalto University, Espoo, Finland
{isha.singh,stephan.sigg}@aalto.fi

Abstract. Smart cities require perception of environmental situation and peoples activities in order to trigger smart response and interaction. A seamless, non-intrusive means of environmental perception is Radio-based recognition since it promises ubiquitous reach and does not require any on-body worn devices or any form of active collaboration from the monitored subjects. Previous work has considered high-accuracy recognition from specialized equipment as well as utilization of WiFi CSI signals. However, these solutions can only generate silos within which recognition is performed, limited to building or organization scale.

For true, city-scale environmental perception, we propose to exploit ubiquitously deployed cellular systems. In this paper, we investigate the use of cellular signals for environmental perception.

Keywords: Smart city · Device free perception · Cellular systems

1 Introduction

Recent development in Radio-vision [23] has shown remarkable progress so that location [13], presence [28], crowd [7], activities [30], gestures [1] and even breathing [34], sentiment [19,21,35] or lip movement [33] can be accurately detected from RF-fluctuation.

The signals exploited in these systems range from specialized, custom-built hardware [3], over RSSI in sensor nodes [31] or smartphones [28] and CSI in ofdm devices [18], to broadcasted FM radio [26]. From these, however, only FM-radio can provide truly city-scale coverage. However, FM radio is soon to meet is best before date and is gradually being replaced. An alternative are cellular mobile communication systems due to the dense deployment of cellular base stations and ubiquitous availability of cellular handsets. In addition and in contrast to FM radio, the cellular handsets boast significant computational and storage capabilities so that classification algorithms can be run on these devices that analyse and interpret the stimuli from environmental RF. In this paper we investigate the recognition capabilities of cellular systems for smart city environmental perception. With the introduction of 5G for IoT devices, the penetration of Smart city environments with devices operating in cellular systems will significantly increase and thus result in an environment where sensing infrastructure is ubiquitously available.

© Springer International Publishing AG 2017
S. Ibrahim et al. (Eds.): ICA3PP 2017, LNCS 10393, pp. 695–704, 2017.
DOI: 10.1007/978-3-319-65482-9_55

2   Related Work

In the following, we briefly sketch related work on smart city and RF-based environmental perception.

2.1   Smart City

The concept of a smart City has been first introduced by Gibson in 1992 [9]. Originally, the term Smart City was loosely coined to express how urban development was turning towards technology, innovation and globalisation [25]. Over defining aspects of a Smart City such as Economy, Infrastructure and Governance [25], the discussion, utilising various diverse definitions of Smart Cities [5,10,11], gradually matured to cover six main axes, namely Smart Economy, Smart Governance, Smart Mobility, Smart Environment, Smart People and Smart Living [6,14] which are woven around an omnipresent Information and Communication Technology (ICT). This ICT is seldom discussed in great detail but should generally cover sensors and real-time awareness [16]. Objects, services and people in a smart city are linked together by a networked infrastructure so that the Internet of Things (IoT), the Internet of Services (IoS) and the Internet of People (IoP) and in general the Future Internet are mere sub-topics of Smart Cities [12]. Smart City therefore needs to connect all parties in a city, in particular, objects, services, people and environmental sensors [27,29] and place the individual at the nerve center and in control of this orchestration of the enormous amount of incoming information flows and actuation and communication opportunities.

A number of frameworks and architectures has been proposed for Smart Cities [4]. A good overview and comparison is given in [32]. The authors survey 17 Smart City architectures and compare them with respect to 11 requirements identified for Smart Cities. Among others, these requirements cover *interoperability between objects, real-time monitoring, Mobility, Privacy,* and also *Social aspects.*

For these, radio-based perception from cellular systems can provide a ubiquitous, densely deployed sensing infrastructure which is also exploited to support connectivity and social interaction between smart city actors. We remark that RF-based environmental sensing, e.g. via cellular systems is among the least intrusive sensing mechanisms since it does not require people to be equipped with any hardware and naturally lowers the risk of privacy intrusion by obscuring privacy related information better than, for instance, video.

2.2   RF-based Environmental Perception

RF-based sensing of activities and gestures has been prominently studied in recent years, ranging from the recognition of gestures via Doppler fluctuation [3,17] or CSI signal envelope [2], respiration rate exploiting Fresnel zones [34] as well as emotion recognition from phase and time-domain signal strength fluctuation [20,22,35]. Recognition of environmental stimuli via radio frequency fluctuation has become undemanding, as pre-installed infrastructure can be exploited [17]. This situation will further improve with upcoming 5G communication standards as it is expected that this technology will support a significantly larger number of devices to generate RF-traffic and will partly operate at higher frequency and larger bandwidth [15]. It will add continuous activity recognition capabilities to virtually all environments.

The above mentioned systems consider point-to-point indoor installations while our work in contrast focuses on cellular systems.

Closely related studies have recently been conducted in [8,24]. The authors of [8] present a preliminary investigation of a custom-built 5G system for radio vision, while [24] present a first investigation of presence detection in the proximity of a cellular handset device. In contrast, we investigate various sensing conditions and parameters for environmental perception from cellular systems. In particular, we investigate the detection of presence, impact of distance on the recognition accuracy, and the capability of recognizing walking speed of subjects in proximity.

3   RF-based Recognition from Cellular Systems

Unlike classical RF-sensing approaches that exploit WiFi, the distance between transmit and receive components is magnitudes larger in cellular systems, where the base station is likely located outside and on top of buildings. the larger distance and necessary penetration of building walls and other obstacles results in reduced signal strength at a receiver, and consequently lower recognition accuracy. We study environmental perception in cellular systems.

3.1   System Description

The current GSM-band is expected to be occupied as part of the 5G frequency bands. Especially, the lower frequency bands are reserved for resource-restricted devices and will establish the backbone of the IoT. To investigate environmental perception in these frequency bands, we use the OsmocomBB open source GSM baseband implementation. The firmware realizes the GSM protocol stack together with device drivers for the baseband chipsets. It runs on the host machine and the connected mobile device to access the wireless interface. We used Motorola C123 mobile devices as phone hardware. In particular, the OsmocomBB network monitor is capable to capture the RSSI of overheard packages. We use this information for environmental perception.

3.2   Experimental Study

The measurements were done in a room that is approximately 10 m by 10 m (cf. Fig. 1). Two tables were used, one had height of 65 cm and the other 111 cm, on which the receiver has been placed. Firstly, the readings were taken in an

Fig. 1. Experimental setup for the three scenarios (empty, presence at a certain distance and circular motion around the device).

empty room for 5 min which were used to train the basic case. Later, we recorded another 3 min in the empty scenario for testing.

The following cases have been considered:

1. distinguishing the presence of a subject in the environment
2. distinguishing the distance from the phone in which a moving person was located
3. distinguishing different walking speeds of a person in the proximity of the receive device.

The room utilized is the study hub of Otakaari 1, Aalto University. It consists of furniture which was not moved during the observations. The test and training data were collected on different days and for different duration of time. Tables of different height were used to see the effect of height on the recognition accuracy.

To detect the presence of a person at different distances, a subject would stand at different distances from the device and conduct moderate movement with her upper body. To distinguish walking speed, a circular mat of diameter 4m was used and markers were placed around the mat at 1 m distance. Using a stopwatch, the subject then adapted her walking speed to approximately match two distinct walking speeds (60 cm per second and 130 cm per second). The receive device has been placed in the center of the table.

3.3   Results

The outcome of the experiments is described in the following, divided for the respective cases considered.

Detection of presence. Simple interaction in smart cities and smart environments can be enabled by detecting presence of subjects within a measured space. We distinguish the basic case (empty environment) from the cases where a person is standing at any distance to the receiver.

Figure 2a shows the scatterplot over Entropy and mean received signal strength (RSS) for the two presence and empty cases while the receive device

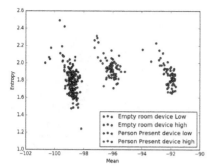

Classification		Predicted Value		Recall
		Empty	Presence	
True Value	Empty	1	0	1
	Presence	0.03	0.97	0.97
Precision		0.98	1	

(a) Scatterplot: presence and empty room for various heights of the receive device

(b) Confusion matrix for the recognition of presence of a subject.

Fig. 2. Impact of antenna height and accuracy for presence detection

is placed on tables at two different heights. We observe that, non-surprisingly, the two cases whithout presence (empty) can hardly be distinguished since no dominant activity is conducted in proximity of the receive device. On the contrary, the two presence cases, which differed in the height in which the receive device has been placed, can be well distinguished from each other. We attribute this to the different impact a person can have by blocking the transmitted signal with respect to the receive device. In particular, when the device is placed at the lower table, the mean RSS increased.

The confusion matrix, distinguishing between the two cases presence and empty room is depticted in Fig. 2b.

In particular, we grouped to gether the respective cases at 65 cm and 111 cm height so that only two distinct cases are to be distinguished between. Recall and precision values achieved are close to 100% in both cases with a slight bias towards detecting presence case as empty .

Distance of a subject to the receive device. Next, we investigated whether we are able to distinguish the distance of a subject to the receive device. This property would be useful in smart cities to localize subjects within an environment. Since the recognition accuracy has been more pronounced for this case, we placed the receiver on the lower table. Still, as visible from the scatterplot in Fig. 3a, the respective cases partly overlap, and, even more significantly, their mean RSS does not decrease linearly with distance. Consequently, under realistic conditions in a smart city, accurate detection of distance to a single receive device is unlikely. We remark that fingerprinting might result in better accuracy, but since the RSS computation differs between device vendors and might be impacted by hardware specialities, we believe that fingerprinting-based passive localization would be a very difficult and likely inaccurate undertaking. For completeness, the confusion matrix for this case is depicted in Fig. 3b.

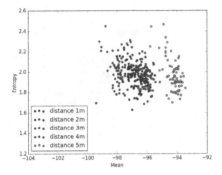 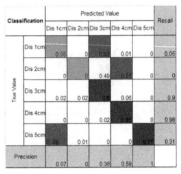

(a)Scatter plot: impact of the distance to the receive device

(b) Confusion in signal strengths at different distances.

Fig. 3. RSSI in presence of a person at different distances from the device.

While some cases have good recognition accuracy, the overall accuracy is not accpetable for practical application.

Distinction of various walking speeds. The distinction of walking speeds in smart cities and smart environments is valuable for a number of advanced interaction cases. For instance, walking speed matters in emergency cases and also in sentiment sensing e.g. to distinguish haste from relaxed mood. The speed of a walking subject effects the effects the variation of the RSS as signal paths change more drastically with higher speed. We therefore consider variance of the RSS as another feature for the recognition in this case.

We considered two different walking speeds (60 cm per second and 130 cm per second) of a moving subject that was circling the receive device at a constant distance. The slower speed corresponds to normal walking while the faster speed resembles running. In addition, we distinguished from the basic empty environment as a third case in this scenario.

As depicted in Fig. 4a, the three cases are well distinguished from each other. Consequently, the trained classification algorithm is well able to differentiate the different walking speeds and to achieve a model accuracy of 73.63%. Figure 4b depicts the confusion matrix for this case.

We observe that the recognition accuracy and precision are good in general, but the recall is low for the recognition of the empty case since this is confused with the slower walking speed. We are currently further investigating this problem and believe that tuning of the feature values and sample windows might suffice to improve the recall for the empty case.

Distinction between empty, occupied and active subjects. Finally, for smart city environments, we believe that the recognition of the activity state of the person occupying the environment is a valuable information to improve

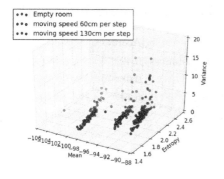

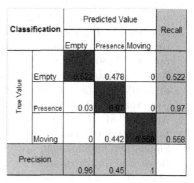

(a) Scatter plot: detection of various walking speeds   (b) Confusion matrix

Fig. 4. Detection of various walking speeds of a moving subject, respective the empty room scenario.

environmental interaction. To investicate this case, we distinguish between an empty environment, a scenario where a person is present and moving slightly but not walking and the case that a subject is walking at any speed in the proximity of the recive device. As depicted in the scatterplot in Fig. 5a, the classifier is again able to well distinguish between the respective cases, although the presence and moving cases are close.

Consequently, the classifier is able to receive a recognition accuracy of 66.1%. The confusion matrix of this case is depicted in Fig. 5b

While the overall confusion is ok, we observe a low recall and precision for the empty and presence cases respectively. As a result of the closeness of the points in the feature space, the classifier developed a bias towards the presence case.

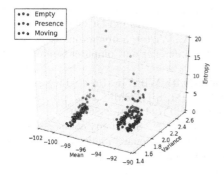

(a) Scatter plot: empty vs. occupied vs. walking.   (b) Confusion matrix

Fig. 5. Empty environment, occupied environment and subject walking at any speed.

Table 1. Accuracy achieved for different environmental situations

Cases	Accuracy
Presence at different distances	0.42
Presence test	0.98
Movement(speed) test	0.74
Environmental perception	0.67

4   Conclusion

Summarizing, we have presented a study on the feasibility of using signals from cellular systems for environmental perception. In particular, our instrumentation covered an indoor environment with thee distinct scenarios: (1) detection of presence, (2) consideration of the impact of distance on the recognition accuracy, and (3) the capability to detect walking speed. The instrumentation exploited the Osmocom-BB baseband implementation. Overall, we confirm acceptable recognition accuracy from ubiquitously deployed cellular systems as summarized in Table 1. While it was not able for us to distinguish diverse distance of a subject to the receive device, especially the presence detection was possible with high accuracy and we suggest to integrate such recognition into smart city and smart environments. For the other two, more complex cases, the recognition accuracy degraded and feasibility for a concrete case is dependent on the respective application. For smart city instrumentations, device-free recognition from cellular systems is a promising supporting technology to achieve ubiquitous environmental perception.

References

1. Abdelnasser, H., Youssef, M., Harras, K.A.: Wigest: a ubiquitous WiFi-based gesture recognition system. In: Proceedings of the 2015 INFOCOM (2015)
2. Abdelnasser, H., Youssef, M., Harras, K.A.: Wigest: a ubiquitous WiFi-based gesture recognition system. In: 2015 IEEE Conference on Computer Communications, pp. 1472–1480. IEEE (2015)
3. Adib, F., Katabi, D.: See through walls with WiFi! In: Proceedings of the ACM SIGCOMM 2013 Conference on SIGCOMM, SIGCOMM 2013, pp. 75–86. ACM, New York (2013). http://doi.acm.org/10.1145/2486001.2486039
4. Al-Hader, M., Rodzi, A., Sharif, A.R., Ahmad, N.: Smart city components architecture. In: International Conference on Computational Intelligence, Modelling and Simulation, CSSim 2009, pp. 93–97. IEEE (2009)
5. Bowerman, B., Braverman, J., Taylor, J., Todosow, H., Von Wimmersperg, U.: The vision of a smart city. In: 2nd International Life Extension Technology Workshop, Paris (2000)
6. Caragliu, A., Del Bo, C., Nijkamp, P.: Smart cities in europe. J. Urban Technol. **18**(2), 65–82 (2011)

7. Domenico, S.D., Pecoraro, G., Cianca, E., Sanctis, M.D.: Trained-once device-free crowd counting and occupancy estimation using WiFi: a doppler spectrum based approach. In: 2016 IEEE 12th International Conference on Wireless and Mobile Computing, Networking and Communications (WiMob). pp. 1–8 (2016)
8. Gholampooryazdi, B., Singh, I., Sigg, S.: 5G ubiquitous sensing: passive environmental perception in cellular systems. In: 2017 IEEE Vehicular Technology Conference (2017)
9. Gibson, D.V., Kozmetsky, G., Smilor, R.W.: The Technopolis Phenomenon: Smart Cities, Fast Systems, Global Networks. Rowman & Littlefield, New York (1992)
10. Giffinger, R., Pichler-Milanović, N.: Smart Cities: Ranking of European Medium-Sized Cities. Centre of Regional Science, Vienna University of Technology (2007)
11. Harrison, C., Eckman, B., Hamilton, R., Hartswick, P., Kalagnanam, J., Paraszczak, J., Williams, P.: Foundations for smarter cities. IBM J. Res. Dev. **54**(4), 1–16 (2010)
12. Hernández-Muñoz, J.M., Vercher, J.B., Muñoz, L., Galache, J.A., Presser, M., Gómez, L.A.H., Pettersson, J.: Smart cities at the forefront of the future internet. In: The future internet, pp. 447–462. Springer, Berlin (2011)
13. Kaltiokallio, O., Jantti, R., Patwari, N.: An adaptive radio tomographic imaging system. IEEE Trans. Veh. Technol. **99**, 1 (2017)
14. Manville, C., Cochrane, G., Cave, J., Millard, J., Pederson, J.K., Thaarup, R.K., Liebe, A., Wissner, M., Massink, R., Kotterink, B.: Mapping smart cities in the EU (2014)
15. Mogensen, P., Pajukoski, K., Tiirola, E., Lahetkangas, E., Vihriala, J., Vesterinen, S., Laitila, M., Berardinelli, G., Da Costa, G.W., Garcia, L.G., et al.: 5G small cell optimized radio design. In: Globecom Workshops, IEEE, pp. 111–116. IEEE (2013)
16. Nam, T., Pardo, T.A.: Conceptualizing smart city with dimensions of technology, people, and institutions. In: Proceedings of the 12th Annual International Digital Government Research Conference: Digital Government Innovation in Challenging Times, pp. 282–291. ACM, Berlin (2011)
17. Pu, Q., Gupta, S., Gollakota, S., Patel, S.: Whole-home gesture recognition using wireless signals. In: Proceedings of the 19th Annual International Conference on Mobile Computing & Networking, pp. 27–38. ACM, New York (2013)
18. Qian, K., Wu, C., Zhou, Z., Zheng, Y., Yang, Z., Liu, Y.: Inferring motion direction using commodity Wi-Fi for interactive exergames. In: Proceedings of the 2017 CHI Conference on Human Factors in Computing Systems, CHI2017, pp. 1961–1972 (2017). http://doi.acm.org/10.1145/3025453.3025678
19. Raja, M., Exler, A., Hemminki, S., Konomi, S., Sigg, S., Inoue, S.: Towards pervasive geospatial affect perception. Springer GeoInformatica (2017). http://dx.doi.org/10.1007/s10707-017-0294-1
20. Raja, M., Sigg, S.: Applicability of RF-based methods for emotion recognition: a survey. In: 2016 IEEE International Conference on Pervasive Computing and Communication Workshops, pp. 1–6 (2016)
21. Raja, M., Sigg, S.: RFexpress! - RF emotion recognition in the wild. In: 2017 IEEE International Conference on Pervasive Computing and Communication (WiP) (2017)
22. Raja, M., Sigg, S.: RFexpress! - exploiting the wireless network edge for RF-based emotion sensing. In: 22nd IEEE International Conference on Emerging Technologies and Factory Automation (2017)

23. Savazzi, S., Sigg, S., Nicoli, M., Rampa, V., Kianoush, S., Spagnolini, U.: Device-free radio vision for assisted living: leveraging wireless channel quality information for human sensing. IEEE Signal Proc. Mag. **33**(2), 45–58 (2016)
24. Savazzi, S., Kianoush, S., Rampa, V., Spagnolini, U.: Is someone moving around my cell-phone? tracing cellular signals for passive motion detection. In: 2017 IEEE International Conference on Pervasive Computing and Communications Workshops, pp. 10–13. IEEE (2017)
25. Schaffers, H., Komninos, N., Pallot, M., Trousse, B., Nilsson, M., Oliveira, A.: Smart cities and the future internet: towards cooperation frameworks for open innovation. In: The Future Internet, pp. 431–446. Springer, Berlin (2011)
26. Shi, S., Sigg, S., Ji, Y.: Activitune: a multi-stage system for activity recognition of passive entities from ambient FM-radio signals. In: 8th International Conference on Wireless Algorithms, Systems, and Applications (2013)
27. Sigg, S., Beigl, M.: Algorithms for closed-loop feedback based distributed adaptive beamforming in wireless sensor networks. In: Proceedings of the Fifth International Conference on Intelligent Sensors, Sensor Networks and Information Processing - Symposium on Adaptive Sensing, Control, and Optimization in Sensor Networks (2009)
28. Sigg, S., Blanke, U., Troester, G.: The telepathic phone: frictionless activity recognition from WiFi-RSSI. In: IEEE International Conference on Pervasive Computing and Communications, PerCom 2014 (2014)
29. Sigg, S., Masri, R.M.E., Beigl, M.: Feedback based closed-loop carrier synchronisation: a sharp asymptotic bound, an asymptotically optimal approach, simulations and experiments. Trans. Mob. Comput. **10**(11), 1605–1617 (2011)
30. Sigg, S., Scholz, M., Shi, S., Ji, Y., Beigl, M.: RF-sensing of activities from non-cooperative subjects in device-free recognition systems using ambient and local signals. IEEE Trans. Mob. Comput. **13**(4), 907–920 (2013)
31. Sigg, S., Shi, S., Buesching, F., Ji, Y., Wolf, L.: Leveraging RF-channel fluctuation for activity recognition. In: Proceedings of the 11th International Conference on Advances in Mobile Computing and Multimedia (2013)
32. da Silva, W.M., Alvaro, A., Tomas, G.H., Afonso, R.A., Dias, K.L., Garcia, V.C.: Smart cities software architectures: a survey. In: Proceedings of the 28th Annual ACM Symposium on Applied Computing, pp. 1722–1727. ACM, Berlin (2013)
33. Wang, G., Zou, Y., Zhou, Z., Wu, K., Ni, L.M.: We can hear you with Wi-Fi! In: Proceedings of the 20th Annual International Conference on Mobile Computing and Networking, MobiCom 2014, pp. 593–604 (2014). http://doi.acm.org/10.1145/2639108.2639112
34. Wang, H., Zhang, D., Ma, J., Wang, Y., Wang, Y., Wu, D., Gu, T., Xie, B.: Human respiration detection with commodity WiFi devices: do user location and body orientation matter? In: Proceedings of the 2016 ACM International Joint Conference on Pervasive and Ubiquitous Computing, pp. 25–36. ACM, Berlin (2016)
35. Zhao, M., Adib, F., Katabi, D.: Emotion recognition using wireless signals. In: Proceedings of the 22nd Annual International Conference on Mobile Computing and Networking, pp. 95–108. ACM, Berlin (2016)

A Multi-task Oriented Selection Strategy for Efficient Cooperation of Collocated Mobile Devices

Hui Gao[1]([envelope]), Jun Feng[2], Ruidong Wang[2], and Wendong Wang[2]

[1] School of Software Engineering,
Beijing University of Posts and Telecommunications, Beijing, China
gaohui786@bupt.edu.cn
[2] State Key Laboratory of Networking and Switching Technology,
Beijing University of Posts and Telecommunications, Beijing, China

Abstract. As the resource consumption of mobile applications continues to outweigh the hardware capacities of mobile devices, the user experience can be improved by leveraging the resources of the nearby mobile devices. In other words, a mobile device should be able to request surrounding devices to execute tasks on its behalf. By treating the resources of the devices in the vicinity collectively, one can orchestrate a distributed interaction that uses these resources efficiently, thereby improving individual user experiences. In this paper, we study the problem of allocating multiple tasks across multiple mobile devices with the goal of reducing the collective execution time, while limiting the resources consumed by each participating device. Our selection strategy uses a set of heuristics to allocate the task execution in the aforementioned type of distributed interaction scenarios. The results of our experimental evaluation indicate that this strategy can be successfully applied in Mobile Device Cloud applications.

Keywords: Mobile device · Collocated cooperation · Device selection

1 Introduction

Mobile device users are continuously increasing their expectations on the functionality and quality of service of mobile applications. Meeting these expectations requires actively engaging high accuracy sensors, large volumes of multimedia data, and complex artificial intelligence algorithms. Unfortunately, mobile applications incorporating these features consume inordinate amounts of computational power, battery budgets, high network bandwidth, and extensive sensory

This work was supported in part by the National High Technology Research and Development Program (863 Program) of China (Grant No. 2015AA016101, 2015AA015601), National Natural Science Foundation of China (Grant No. 61370197, 61402045).

© Springer International Publishing AG 2017
S. Ibrahim et al. (Eds.): ICA3PP 2017, LNCS 10393, pp. 705–714, 2017.
DOI: 10.1007/978-3-319-65482-9_56

resources. Consequently, a mobile application may rely on functionality that cannot be delivered by its host device for resource scarcity reasons [2].

Cloud-based execution has been traditionally used as a mechanism for extending the resources of mobile devices [6]. This extension of resources can not only provide additional functionality, but also improve the quality of service. Unfortunately, under certain execution scenarios, high-quality network connections may not be available to access cloud-based resources. Accessing these resources over limited networks can easily negate any potential benefits of using them. As an example, transferring data between a mobile device and the cloud server through a limited cellular network is known to consume an inordinate amount of energy [5]. As an alternative, additional resources can be obtained from collocated mobile devices [4]. Orchestrating the execution of such collocated mobile devices into distributed resource sharing scenarios is known as "*Mobile Device Clouds*" (MDC).

A major technical issue that stands on the way of effective MDCs is the problem of locating collocated devices most suitable for executing given tasks. As depicted in Fig. 1(a), multiple mobile devices are operated simultaneously in everyday environments, including restaurants, classrooms, and conference rooms. These devices differ in terms of their respective hardware, software, and runtime status, thus offering dissimilar capabilities to provide the resources required by external requests. The client requirements are not uniform either, placing different constraints on the expected latency, accuracy, and completeness. All these factors make it non-trivial to select a set of optimal target devices for a set of tasks.

In this paper, we present a solution to the above mentioned device selection problem. We present a strategy that selects a set of target devices for tasks that can provide the best collective execution time with the lowest resource consumption. Hence, we formulate the problem as a multi-objective optimal one, and use the execution time and resource consumption on target devices to evaluate the performance and cost of each task. We then propose a multi-task oriented device selection algorithm to find the sub-optimal solution for the problem. We present the effectiveness of our solution via simulation. Future work will evaluate our solution in realistic deployment environments.

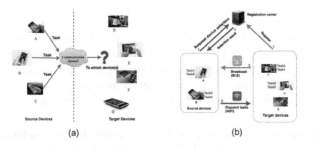

Fig. 1. (a) Target device selection problem of MDC. (b) System architecture.

2   Related Work

Popovici *et al.* and Mukhtar *et al.* presented device selection algorithms that considered user preferences and might not select the most suitable device for service composition [8]. El *et al.* proposed solutions for service selection where QoS was considered [3]. Ahmed *et al.* presented a device selection algorithm that considered the factor of Quality Of Service (QoS) and catered for user preferences [1]. They considered the device QoS, Network QoS, and user preferences, but left out dynamic device resources, which might affect device selection decisions. Xu *et al.* presented a device selection algorithm based on the consideration of device location [9]. In the area of optimal service composition, several solutions addressed the problem of matching services and devices. In mobile cloud computing, Zhou *et al.* presented a device selection method that was status- and stability-aware [10]. Parmar *et al.* took infrastructure-specific parameters into account to discover and select cloudlets [7]. Compared with these approaches, this paper studies the problem of device selection in the context of collocated mobile device cooperation with multiple tasks and multiple devices, while taking both the task execution time and resource consumption into account.

3   System Model

Figure 1(b) depicts the system architecture. It contains a set of source devices (Device A, B), a set of target devices (Device C, D and E), and a registration center (which can either be a mobile device, or be a piece of stationary network infrastructure, like a WiFi router). Because the task execution time should be short, we disregard the mobility of devices during the task execution.

We further describe the details of the task execution: (a) First, all of the target devices register with the registration center, storing their device information and getting a device id from the registration center. (b) Then, the target devices broadcast their device ids using Bluetooth Low Energy (BLE) channel. (c) Once source devices need to delegate other devices to execute their tasks, they scan for nearby devices using the BLE channel and collect the target devices' ids, uploading the collected device ids and tasks information to the registration center. (d) The registration center runs the device selection algorithm and returns the selected devices for each task of the source devices. (e) Each source device connects to the selected target devices via WiFi or BLE, and delegates the tasks to the selected target devices.

We also make the following assumptions: (a) One task can only be executed by one device. For example, if device A wants to send more than one HTTP requests, each request is treated as a single task. (b) One device can be the selected target device for multiple tasks. For simplicity, we assume that the delegated tasks are executed in sequence on each target device. So the overall time used to execute a certain task contains two parts: (1) The time needed to execute the task; (2) The time taken to wait for the task to be executed by the target device.

As Fig. 1(b) depicted, source devices A and B need to delegate four tasks to other devices. After the device discovery phase, device C, D and E comprise the collection of target devices. By sending requests to the registration center, source devices A and B get their device selection results from the registration center and delegate their tasks to device C and D accordingly. Because it will take a long time to execute the tasks on device E, or for the reason that device E has limited capabilities and resources, device E is not assigned any tasks to execute.

4   Problem Formulation

In the proposed system above, we use $\mathcal{M} = \{m = 1, 2, ...M\}$ to denote the tasks, and $\mathcal{N} = \{n = 1, 2, ...N\}$ to denote the target devices. For each device n, the available resources for task execution is $\mathcal{R} = \{R_n \mid \forall n \in \mathcal{N}\}$.

For each task $m \in \mathcal{M}$, we use $T_{m,n}, \forall n \in \mathcal{N}$ to express its estimated execution time on device n. Therefore, T is a $M \times N$ matrix. When task m is executed on device n, it will consume many kinds of resources of device n. The resources consumed by task m when being executed on device n is abstracted as $C_{m,n}, \forall m \in \mathcal{M}, \forall n \in \mathcal{N}$, therefore C is also a $M \times N$ matrix.

$$T = \begin{bmatrix} T_{1,1} & T_{1,2} & \cdots & T_{1,N} \\ T_{2,1} & T_{2,2} & \cdots & T_{2,N} \\ \vdots & \vdots & \ddots & \vdots \\ T_{M,1} & T_{M,2} & \cdots & T_{M,N} \end{bmatrix}, C = \begin{bmatrix} C_{1,1} & C_{1,2} & \cdots & C_{1,N} \\ C_{2,1} & C_{2,2} & \cdots & C_{2,N} \\ \vdots & \vdots & \ddots & \vdots \\ C_{M,1} & C_{M,2} & \cdots & C_{M,N} \end{bmatrix}.$$

Here we further define the resource impact on target devices when executing delegated tasks. The resource impact is not equal to the resource consumption on each target device, and we give an example to demonstrate this distinction: When executing an HTTP delegation task consumes 20% of the entire battery power of a device, executing this task on a device with 30% remaining battery disturbs the device owners much more than executing the task on a device with 60% remaining battery. Therefore, we define the resource impact as: $e^{\frac{C_n}{R_n \times M}} - 1, \forall n \in \mathcal{N}$, where C_n is the summed up resources consumed on device n to execute the delegated tasks. When more resources C_n are consumed on a device with limited available resources R_n, its resource impact increases rapidly. However, to prevent the ratio from increasing too fast when the overall resource consumption of delegated tasks is close to the available resources, we use $R_n \times M$ to constrain the value of $e^{\frac{C_n}{R_n \times M}}$ within $[1, e)$.

Here, we assume that the device selection matrix is A, where $A = [A_{m,n}]_{M \times N}, A_{m,n} \in \{0, 1\}$. $A_{m,n} = 1$ means that task m is delegated to device n, otherwise, $A_{m,n} = 0$. Therefore, the total task execution time of device n can be denoted as $\tau_n(A) = \sum_{m \in \mathcal{M}} A_{m,n} \times T_{m,n}$.

Similarly, the total resource impact to device n can be calculated as:

$$\phi_n(A) = e^{\frac{\sum_{m \in \mathcal{M}} A_{m,n} \times C_{m,n}}{R(n) \times M}} - 1. \tag{1}$$

The objective of our work is to find a set of target devices for all tasks, so that the overall task execution time and the overall resource impact on target devices are minimized. We compare the execution time on all devices, and use the longest time for a device to finish executing all delegated tasks as the overall task execution time, which is denoted as: $\max_{n \in \mathcal{N}} (\tau_n(A))$. For all the N devices, the overall resource impact on target devices can be further calculated as $\phi(A) = \sum_{n \in \mathcal{N}} \phi_n(A)$.

Therefore, the optimization objective of this paper can be represented as to find a device selection matrix A^* that:

$$A^* = arg \min_A \max_{n \in \mathcal{N}} (\tau_n(A)) \text{ and } arg \min_A \phi(A), \qquad (2)$$

subject to

$$A = [A_{m,n}]_{M \times N}; A_{m,n} \in \{0,1\}; \ \forall n \in \mathcal{N}, \ \forall m \in \mathcal{M}, \ \exists! n, \ let \ A_{m,n} = 1 \qquad (3)$$

5   Selection Strategy

Problem (2) is a multi-objective optimal problem, and the two optimal objectives $arg \min_A \max_{n \in \mathcal{N}} (\tau_n(A))$ and $arg \min_A \phi(A)$ are not independent. It is hard to find a set of target devices A that can provide the optimal value for both optimization objectives. To solve this multi-objective optimization problem, we need to find a Pareto solution, which cannot provide a better value for one optimal objective without providing a worse value for the other optimization objectives. Therefore, we convert the original two-objective optimization problem to a single-objective optimization problem using weight functions, and the solution of the single-objective problem is a Pareto solution of the original two-objective optimization problem. (4) shows the new optimization objective.

$$D(A) = \lambda \times \frac{\max_{n \in \mathcal{N}} \tau_n(A)}{\max_{n \in \mathcal{N}} \tau_n(A')} + (1 - \lambda) \times \frac{\sum_{n \in \mathcal{N}} \phi_n(A)}{\sum_{n \in \mathcal{N}} \phi_n(A'')}, A^* = arg \min_A (D(A)),$$
$$\qquad (4)$$

where λ is a weight function. The bigger λ is, the more concern is given to minimize the overall task execution time. A', A'' denote two devices selection matrices, that can lead to the longest overall execution time, and the biggest overall resource impact, respectively.

In (2), the two optimization objectives have different value ranges. Therefore, to be able to treat the ranges uniformly, we use the ratio between the optimization objective and its upper bound in (4). The upper bound of $\max_{n \in \mathcal{N}} \tau_n(A)$ can be reached only when all the tasks are delegated to a certain target device. Therefore, $\max_{n \in \mathcal{N}} \tau_n(A') = \max_{n \in \mathcal{N}} \sum_{m \in \mathcal{M}} T_{m,n}$. In the following discussion, $Tr(A)$ is used to reference the overall task execution time ratio, where $Tr(A) = \max_{n \in \mathcal{N}} \tau_n(A) / \max_{n \in \mathcal{N}} \tau_n(A')$.

Calculating the upper bound of $\sum_{n\in\mathcal{N}}\phi_n(A)$ is a global optimal problem, because assigning all the tasks to a certain device can not get the maximal overall resource impact. Therefore, we develop an algorithm for calculating the upper bound of $\sum_{n\in\mathcal{N}}\phi_n(A)$, which will be described later. We use $Rr(A)$ to reference the overall resource impact ratio, where $Rr(A) = \sum_{n\in\mathcal{N}}\phi_n(A)/\sum_{n\in\mathcal{N}}\phi_n(A'')$.

To verify that $Tr(A)$ and $Rr(A)$ can be added together, we randomly generate some experimental data and calculate the difference between $Tr(A)$ and $Rr(A)$. Experimental results show that the maximum and average differences between $Tr(A)$ and $Rr(A)$ are 0.98 and 0.13, respectively, which implies that $Tr(A)$ and $Rr(A)$ are in the same order of magnitude, and thus can be added together.

In summary, the final single optimization objective can be denoted as:

$$A^* = arg \min_A D(A) = arg \min_A \{\lambda \times Tr(A) + (1-\lambda) \times Rr(A)\}$$

$$= arg \min_A \{\lambda \times \frac{\max_{n\in\mathcal{N}} \tau_n(A)}{\max_{n\in\mathcal{N}} \sum_{m\in\mathcal{M}} T_{m,n}} + (1-\lambda) \times \frac{\sum_{n\in\mathcal{N}}\phi_n(A)}{\sum_{n\in\mathcal{N}}\phi_n(A'')}\} \qquad (5)$$

subject to

$$A = [A_{m,n}]_{M\times N}; A'' = [A''_{m,n}]_{M\times N}; A_{m,n} \in \{0,1\}; A''_{m,n} \in \{0,1\}$$
$$\forall m \in \mathcal{M}, \exists! n, \text{ let } A_{m,n} = 1, A''_{m,n} = 1$$

Which means that to find a device selection matrix A^* from all the possible device selection matrices, letting $D(A^*)$ get the minimum value. Obviously, the final single optimization objective can guarantee that Pareto optimality is obtained when considering with the original optimal objective in (2). Considering that the greedy algorithm can obtain a suboptimal result with greatly reduced execution time. Therefore, in this paper we proposed a solution with the mindset of greedy, which can be described as follows:

1. Let all elements in A^* equal zero, meaning that no tasks are delegated to target devices, and initiate $D(A^*)$ with ∞.
2. For all tasks $m \in \mathcal{M}$, iterate all target devices $n \in \mathcal{N}$. For each iteration, assume that task m is delegated to device n and calculate the optimization objective value according to Eq. 5. If the calculated result is less than $D(A^*)$, update the value of $D(A^*)$ and save the target device n as tar_dev.
3. Let $A^*_{m,tar\_dev} = 1$, which means that task m should be delegated to device tar_dev so $D(A^*)$ can get the minimum value.
4. When iteration is done, output the device selection matrix A^* and optimization objective value $D(A^*)$.

The device selection algorithm described above can be expressed as Algorithm 1 with ds parameter set to true.

When calculating the value of optimization objective according to (5), we need to find a device selection matrix A'' to get the upper bound of overall

---

Algorithm 1. Greedy algorithm for device selection ($\sum_{n \in \mathcal{N}} \phi_n(A'')$ in (4))

Input:

M, N - the number of task and target devices

T, C - task execution time and resource consumption matrix

$\mathcal{R}$ - available resources of target devices, λ = weight value

ds - the algorithm parameter

Output:

A^*, $D(A^*)$ - the optimal device selection matrix and upper bound

1   $A^* = \{0\}$; $D(A^*) = \infty$; $Wri = 0$;

2   **for** $i = 1; i \leq M; i + +$ **do**

3      $idx = 0$;

4   **for** $j = 1; j \leq N; j + +$ **do**

5         $A^*[i][j] = 1$;

6   **if** ds **then**

7            $t = calTargetValue(A, M, N, T, C, \lambda, \mathcal{R})$;

8   **if** $t < D(A^*)$ or $j == 1$ **then**

9               $D(A^*) = t$; $idx = j$;

10   **else**

11           $t = calRImpact(A, M, N, T, C, \mathcal{R})$;

12   **if** $t > Wri$ **then**

13              $Wri = t$; $idx = j$;

14         $A^*[i][j] = 0$;

15      $A^*[i][idx] = 1$;

16 **if** ds **then**

17   **return** $\{A^*, D(A^*)\}$;

18 **else**

19   **return** Wri;

20

---

resource impact ($\sum_{n \in \mathcal{N}} \phi_n(A'')$), which is just similar to find the optimal device selection matrix A^*, so the greedy algorithm is used and can be described as Algorithm 1 with ds parameter set to false.

6 Experimental Evaluation

6.1 Experimental Design

To illustrate the effectiveness of the proposed device selection algorithm, we simulate the process of device selection on the Linux platform by writing experimental code in C language. The steps of the simulation experiment are as follows:

(1) Let the weight value λ be 0;

(2) Randomly generate experimental data. First of all, the number of task M and target device N are generated, then the corresponding task execution time matrix, resource consumption matrix and available resources of target devices

are generated. When randomly generating the data, the maximal value of all the generated elements is constrained, so as to make the simulation closer to reality. For example, in the context of collocated mobile device collaboration, we assume the number of devices is no more than 60. More experimental configurations are listed in Table 1.

(3) When configuring the available resources of target devices, the resource consumption matrix C is generated firstly. The average resource consumption value of all the tasks, which is denoted as $AvgTskCon$, is calculated accordingly. Assuming that the max value of $C_{m,j}, m \in \mathcal{M}$ is CM_j, then the available resources of target device j is: $R_j = CM_j + rand()\%AvgNTsk \times AvgTskCon$. $AvgNTsk$ means that how many tasks device j can execute at most when average resource consumption value of tasks is $AvgTskCon$. CM_j is added to R_j so that device j has sufficient resources to execute any of the tasks, even though that $rand()\%AvgNTsk \times AvgTskCon$ is equal to zero.

Table 1. Simulation configurations

Configuration	Value
Max Device Number(N), Max Task Number(M)	60, 40
Max value of elements in T, Max value of elements in R	60, 40
Test count for one weight value, Weight value increasing interval	10000, 0.01
AvgNTsk	5

(4) Using the proposed algorithm to calculate the optimal device selection matrix A^* and the optimization objective value $D(A^*)$, overall task execution time ratio $Tr(A^*)$ and overall resource impact ratio $Rr(A^*)$. In order to compare with traditional random device selection method, we randomly delegate tasks to target devices and the device selection matrix is denoted as A^1, with which the optimization objective value $D(A^1)$, overall task execution time ratio $Tr(A^1)$ and overall resource impact ratio $Rr(A^1)$ can be calculated accordingly;

(5) Repeat steps 2, 3 for 10000 times, then calculate the average value of $D(A^*), Tr(A^*), Rr(A^*)$ and $D(A^1), Tr(A^1), Rr(A^1)$;

(6) Increase λ by 0.01 and go to step 2 when λ is less than or equal to 1.

6.2   Experimental Results

The simulation results appear in Fig. 2. The improved performance denotes the relatively decreased values of $D(A), Tr(A)$ and $Rr(A)$, when the greedy algorithm is used compared with the random device selection method. For example, the improved performance of $D(A)$ can be calculated as: $\frac{D(A^1)-D(A^*)}{D(A^1)}$. Similarly, the improved performance of $Rr(A)$ and $Tr(A)$ can be calculated as: $\frac{Rr(A^1)-Rr(A^*)}{Rr(A^1)}, \frac{Tr(A^1)-Tr(A^*)}{Tr(A^1)}$. It can be seen from Figs. 2(a) and (d) that the greedy algorithm has a great advantage over the random device selection

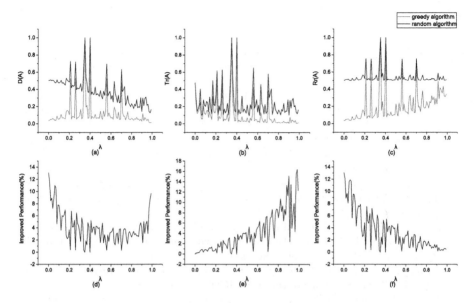

Fig. 2. $D(A)$, $Tr(A)$, $Rr(A)$ and the corresponding improved performance with different value of λ

method, with the maximum optimization factor of about 13. Figure 2(b), (e) and (c), (f) illustrate that the optimization objective of the greedy algorithm is different when different weight values are selected. For example, when the weight value is small, the greedy algorithm focuses on the optimization of the overall resource impact ratio $Rr(A)$, the improved performance of $Rr(A)$ (related to overall resource impact on target devices) is bigger than the improved performance of $Tr(A)$ (related to overall task execution time). So different weight values can be used to express the users' preference for optimizing the overall task execution time or the overall resource impact on target devices. Besides, from Fig. 2(e) and (f), we can also draw the conclusion that when using the proposed device selection algorithm in this paper, both of $Rr(A)$ and $Tr(A)$ are optimized compared with the random device selection method.

7   Conclusions

This paper presented a multi-task oriented device selection strategy for MDCs. First, we modeled the device selection problem as a multi-objective optimal problem, with the overall task execution time and the overall resource impact on mobile users as two objective targets. Then we proposed a device selection algorithm that considered the overall task execution time and the resource impact on target devices. Experimental simulation results indicated that the presented device selection algorithm in this paper could become a practical solution to selecting devices in MDC applications.

References

1. Ahmed, M.E., Mukhtar, H., Belaïd, D., Song, J.B.: Qos-aware device selection using user preferences for tasks in ubiquitous environments. In: Proceedings of the IEEE ICET'11. pp. 1–6 (2011).
2. Chun, B.G., Ihm, S., Maniatis, P., Naik, M., Patti, A.: Clonecloud: elastic execution between mobile device and cloud. In: Proceedings of the ACM Computer systems. pp. 301–314. ACM, New York (2011).
3. El Haddad, J., Manouvrier, M., Ramirez, G., Rukoz, M.: Qos-driven selection of web services for transactional composition. In: Proceedings of the IEEE ICWS'08. pp. 653–660 (2008).
4. Habak, K., Ammar, M., Harras, K.A., Zegura, E.: Femto clouds: leveraging mobile devices to provide cloud service at the edge. In: Proceedings of the IEEE Cloud-Com'15. pp. 9–16 (2015).
5. Hans, R., Burgstahler, D., Mueller, A., Zahn, M., Stingl, D.: Knowledge for a longer life: development impetus for energy-efficient smartphone applications. In: Proceedings of the IEEE Mobile Services. pp. 128–133 (2015).
6. Kwon, Y.W., Tilevich, E.: Energy-efficient and fault-tolerant distributed mobile execution. In: Proceedings of the IEEE ICDCS'12. pp. 586–595 (2012).
7. Parmar, D., Kumar, A.S., Nivangune, A., Joshi, P., Rao, U.P.: Discovery and selection mechanism of cloudlets in a decentralized MCC environment. In: Proceedings of the ACM Workshop on Mobile Software Engineering and Systems. pp. 15–16 (2016)
8. Popovici, D., Desertot, M., Lecomte, S., Peon, N.: Context-aware transportation services (cats) framework for mobile environments. Int. J. Next-Generation Comput. 2(1), 12 (2011)
9. Xu, Y., Li, S., Wu, Z., Pan, G.: An intensive location-aware framework for device-involved human tasks. In: Proceedings of the IEEE HPCC_EUC'13. pp. 2135–2142 (2013)
10. Zhou, A., Wang, S., Li, J., Sun, Q., Yang, F.: Optimal mobile device selection for mobile cloud service providing. J. Supercomput. 72, 1–14 (2016)

Research on Properties of Nodes Distribution on Internet of Vehicles

Cheng Jiujun[1], Shang Zheng[1(✉)], Mi Hao[1], Cheng Cheng[2], and Huang Zhenhua[1]

[1] Key Laboratory of Embedded, System and Service Computing of Ministry of Education,
Tongji University, Shanghai 201804, China
{chengjj,Huangzhenhua}@tongji.edu.cn, 18817871216@163.com,
18045012868@163.com
[2] Suzhou University of Science and Technology, Suzhou 215009, China
chengcheng_lcc@163.com

Abstract. In the environment of vehicle network, due to the high-speed movement of vehicle nodes, the network topology of vehicle nodes will change frequently, and the network between vehicles will be continuously connected and disconnected. All these factors lead to the instability of the whole network and cause a great impact on the network routing performance. Based on the large-scale dataset of TAPASCologne, this paper studies the node distribution characteristics in the complex form of vehicle network by simulation experiments, including: the influence of node mobility model on the vehicle node distribution characteristics, the long tail effect of node degree distribution in the network, as well as the sparseness and density of node distribution in the urban road network. These experimental results of the node distribution characteristics will be helpful for the design of routing protocol.

Keywords: Vehicle network · Node distribution characteristics · TAPASCologne dataset · Long tail effect

1 Introduction

1.1 A Subsection Sample

Vehicle network is a complex network composed of the wireless network environment and realistic road conditions. It needs to take vehicle node status, moving trajectory and moving mode into account. In the vehicle network, the highway scene can usually be regarded as a one-dimensional traffic scene, in which the vehicles can only travel along the highway. Therefore, the movement trajectory and node distribution have a certain regularity. However, due to the reasons that traffic accidents, rain and snow weather and etc., it will result in node congestion in some road sections, toll gates and service areas. The urban scene is different from the highway scene. The road traffic is more complicated and some uncertain factors like traffic accidents and rush hour will block the road, but in some remote road sections, the vehicle density will be sparse. These all factors will lead to the interconnection problems of the vehicle network.

© Springer International Publishing AG 2017
S. Ibrahim et al. (Eds.): ICA3PP 2017, LNCS 10393, pp. 715–724, 2017.
DOI: 10.1007/978-3-319-65482-9_57

In the analysis of vehicle routing protocol [1], the existing routing protocol doesn't make a systematic study of the node distribution characteristics. Based on the large-scale data set of TAPASCologne, this paper studies distribution characteristics of nodes in the complicated vehicle network through simulation experiments. It includes the influence of node mobility model on the distribution characteristics of vehicles nodes, the sparseness and density of nodes distribution in the urban road network. The experimental results are given to provide the experimental basis of node distribution for the vehicle network routing protocol.

The remainder of this paper is organized as follows. Section 2 introduces data collection methods and results of the vehicle network. Section 3 firstly discusses the influence of node mobility model on the vehicles distribution characteristics, then gives the long tail effect of network node degree distribution, and analyses the sparseness and density of node distribution in the urban scenes. Finally, Sect. 4 draws concluding remarks.

2   Vehicle Network Data Collection Methods and Results

2.1   Simulation Platform

Generally, vehicle network simulation will involve traffic simulation and network simulation. Traffic simulation is a method of simulating the real road condition by software method. It can simulate and evaluate urban planning and traffic management. However, Network simulation simulates the data transmission in a network group and the behavior of each member by software method, which can analyze network performance using statistical methods.

Commonly used traffic simulation software is: SUMO [3], VISSIM [4], Paramics [5], TransModeler [6] and so on. SUMO is an open source micro-traffic simulator. It takes a single vehicle on the road as a basic unit of simulation and simulates the relationship between vehicles, the relationship between vehicles and roads, as well as the relationship between vehicles and pedestrians.

SUMO's open source and usability make us choose SUMO and network simulation software OMNET++ as the traffic and network co-simulation. Besides, we use Veins [7] to achieve the information exchange and two-way communication, and accomplish the traffic simulation and data collection. Among them, OMNET++ is a simulation software for discrete event simulation, Veins is an open source simulation framework for the realization of vehicle communication.

Veins is a bridge between two simulators, in which SUMO as a server is responsible for traffic flow simulation and controls vehicle movement; OMNET++ as a client is responsible for network simulation, and controls message packet transmission and delivery, as shown in Fig. 1. It uses TCP connection between SUMO and OMNET++, and uses Socket to achieve the exchange of information.

At the same time, Veins uses the new IEEE 802.11p protocol and DSRC/WAVE simulation model, it can fully simulate all the features of WAVE, such as multi-channel and QoS support. Therefore, Veins meets the requirements, and the final experimental platform is composed of SUMO, Veins and OMENET++.

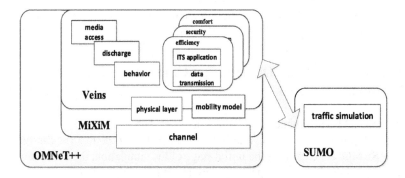

Fig. 1. Simulation experiment platform

In this paper, SUMO version is 0.21.0, OMNET++ version is 4.3.1, and Veins version is 3.0. The development environment is Eclipse integrated OMNET++ running on Windows 7.

2.2   Data Set

The data set used in this paper is the TAPASCologne large-scale dataset. This data set is the largest data set available nowadays. It collects road information and vehicle movement information within 400 km^2 of Cologne, Germany, and generates vehicle node movement in the region in 24 h. Besides, compared to other datasets, TAPASCologne data set has the larger amount of data and is closer to physical reality, thus we choose this data set. The collected data is shown in Table 1.

Table 1. SUMO simulation data.

Name	Type	Note
timestep@time	(simulation) seconds	Simulation time
timestep@id	id	Simulator id
Vtype	id	Vehicle type
vehicle@id	(vehicle) id	Vehicle id
Lane	(lane) id	Road id
Pos	m	Vehicle's location
X	m	x-coordinate of the vehicle on the road
Y	m	y-coordinate of the vehicle on the road
Lat	degrees * 100,000	Latitude
Lon	degrees * 100,000	Longitude
Speed	m/s	Speed

vehicle@id, x, y, lat, lon, speed, is the main basis for the subsequent data processing. vehicle@id is used to distinguish between different vehicles, x and y correspond to the location coordinates on the map, lat and lon are used to calculate the distance between vehicles, speed is the key data of vehicle driving.

3   The Study on Node Distribution Characteristics of Vehicle Network

Because that TAPASCologne has a huge amount of data in 24 h, we use the data from 6 am to 8 am. Figure 2 shows the number of vehicles from 6:00 to 8:00 after the simulation on SUMO. As 6 am is at the initial stage of the simulation, the simulation nodes add slowly, and don't enter the peak of work at 6 am, besides, there are not many cars on the road. This is consistent with the real situation. After 6:15, because of rush hour, the number of urban road vehicles is growing at a high speed. This high speed growing slowly at 6:30, but it would still last for about one hour. At about 7:30, the number of vehicles in the city reaches its peak, there are about 8600 cars in the city. After this time, the number of vehicles declines rapidly and the condition of urban road tends to level off steadily.

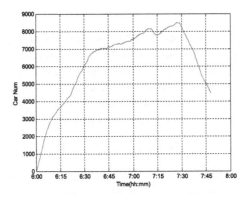

Fig. 2. Time-Car Num variation trend on TAPASCologne

3.1   The Influence of Node Moving Model on Vehicle Node Distribution

The rules of nodes movement have a great influence on the network interconnection problem in the vehicle network. It can provide the experimental basis for the research of the interconnection routing mechanism, by studying the moving rules of the vehicle network. The rules of nodes movement are called following model in the simulation platform. According to the size of the simulation scale, it can be divided into three models: Marco model, Mesoscopic model, and Micro model. The Macro model considers the overall road traffic density, the average speed, and other macro indicators. The Micro model simulates the movement of each vehicle on the road, generally assuming that the vehicle behavior depends on both the physical properties of the vehicle and the driver's control behavior [43]. The Mesoscopic model is the compromise between the Macro model and the Micro model, and its granularity is between the Micro model and the Macro model.

Because of the interconnection problem research is mainly aimed at the problem among nodes, it belongs to the category of the Micro model. The Micro-models include GM (General Motor) model, Krauss model, psychological-physiological driving behavior model, IDM (Intelligent Driving Model) and IDM evolution model. The vehicle simulation platform SUMO uses the SUMOKrauß model which is the evolution of the Krauss model. It assumes that in this model, the driver has about 1 s of reaction time and uses five parameters in Table 2.

Table 2. SUMOKrauß model parameter.

Parameter	Unit	Note
Accel	m/s^2	Maximum acceleration
Decal	m/s^2	Maximum deceleration
V_{max}	m/s	Maximum speed
L	m	Vehicle length
ϵ	$\epsilon \in (0, 1)$	Defect in the desired speed of driver

The model uses the following formula (1) [4] to calculate the safety vehicle speed.

$$v_{safe} = v_l(t) + \frac{g(t) - v_l(t) * \tau}{\dfrac{v_l(t) + v_f(t)}{2 * b} + \tau} \tag{1}$$

The safety speed is the current speed that is set to accommodate the vehicle's deceleration behavior. In this formula, $v_l(t)$ is the forward vehicle speed at time t, $v_f(t)$ is the rear vehicle speed at time t, $g(t)$ is the distance between forward the vehicle and rear vehicle, and means the reaction time of the driver.

Of course, the model used in SUMO has been improved to make it more suitable for the real situation. It can be seen from Eq. 1, in SUMO, the calculated safety vehicle speed, which is the estimated speed of the simulation. And the estimated speed is only related to the speed and distance between the front cars and the rear cars. Therefore, in the general simulation of vehicle network, the nodes mobility model could only influence the speed of the front and rear cars, so that it can affect the aggregation degree of vehicles in the local area, thus affect the entire network state.

In the highway, as the scene is single, the vehicles generally drive toward the same direction. If we need to send the message to the front vehicle, we just need to forward the message to the fast cars with same direction or the front cars. And if we want to send the message to the rear cars, we need to forward it to the vehicles in the reverse lane. Figure 3 shows the Time-Car variation trend between 6:00 and 8:00, which is simulated on the suburban road section of 400 m highway in SUMO. The number of vehicle nodes is generally maintained at 20–50, and the network state is stable.

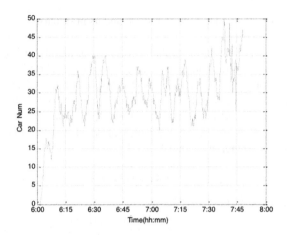

Fig. 3. Time-Car Num variation trend on highway road

3.2   The Long Tail Effect of Network Node Degree Distribution

Definition 1 network node degree D: Given a network area, the network node degree is the number of network nodes within its communication radius, for any one node i.

Using TAPASCologne data set, we collect the status information of all the vehicles at three time points: 6:03, 7:17, 7:45, and then calculate each network node degree and measure the frequency of the vehicles corresponds to the corresponding degree. It is shown in Fig. 4.

As shown from the above figure, at 6:30, although there are not enough vehicles so that it does not obey the long tail distribution, it still shows a certain long tail distribution characteristics. At 7:17 and 7:45, it clearly shows the characteristics of the long tail distribution. The nodes with a degree less than 20 occupy most of the nodes, while nodes with a degree greater than 80 occupy the small parts of the nodes at 7:17, besides, at 6:03 and 7:45, the nodes are nearly almost nonexistent. This is also consistent with the related scale-free network characteristics, which means that most of the nodes in the network connect with only few nodes, and few nodes connect with a lot of nodes.

Therefore, in the design of vehicle network routing protocol, we can screen the excellent nodes from the nodes in the network. And most of the information can be forwarded by these excellent nodes to improve the network information delivery rate. In addition, the vehicle network satisfies the local world evolution model. When a new vehicle joins in, the new vehicle communicates with local world vehicles in priority. We can choose the excellent nodes of the local world to forward the current node data, thus enhance the network interconnection.

3.3   Sparseness and Densities of Node Distribution in Urban Road Network

Modern urban road networks are becoming more and more complex. Any slight muta-tion in the network will cause the network to fluctuate in a large area. When a traffic accident occurs on a road, the number of vehicles near the accident will increase

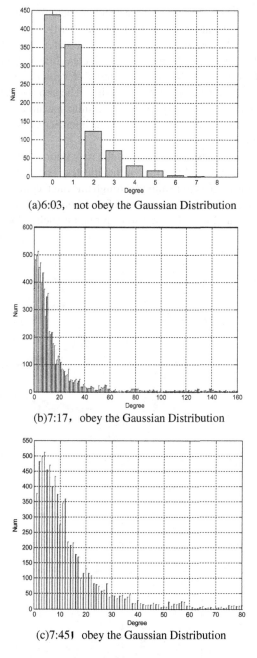

(a)6:03,   not obey the Gaussian Distribution

(b)7:17， obey the Gaussian Distribution

(c)7:45） obey the Gaussian Distribution

Fig. 4. Degree-Num distribution chart of 3 time points

dramatically, resulting in traffic congestion. At this moment, the vehicle network will show a dense state. But as the accident information is broadcast out, most drivers choose to detour and the number of vehicles near the accident increases slowly. When the traffic accident is over, the road state will return to normal slowly.

As shown in Fig. 5, the four roads are all in a sparse state. Figure 5 shows some roads the static states and Fig. 6 shows the number of vehicles collected at an intersection. We can see that from 6:00 to 8:00, the highest number of vehicles at the junction is 6:00, and the number of road vehicles is in low volatility. The above information shows that this intersection is not a traffic artery, rush hour almost has no effect on the road state. And most of the time, the number of vehicles at this intersection is 0, which will produce a communication blind spot.

Figure 7 shows some dense roads. Due to the rush hour or traffic accidents, a large number of vehicles are gathered in some traffic arteries. There are multiple relay node selections when the message is transmitted through this intersection. The general routing algorithm can maximize the transmission of information based on the map information and location information. But it will bring some problems such as loopback, and message

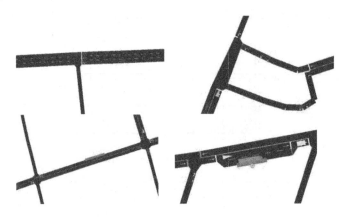

Fig. 5. Sparse network

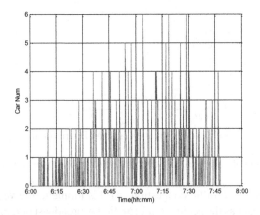

Fig. 6. Time-Car Num variation trend of intersection A

broadcasts will generate broadcast storms as well. Therefore, we need the appropriate methods to reduce the probability of these problems.

Fig. 7. Dense network

Figure 8 shows the variation trend of vehicles at an important intersection. From the figure, we can find that there are always vehicles passing through this intersection from 6:00, and the number is generally maintained at about 20–40. At about 7:20, the number of vehicles rose sharply and then fell. This may be caused by a brief traffic accident. The network state of this intersection is generally in a dense state.

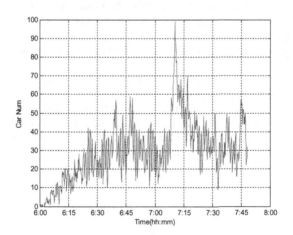

Fig. 8. Time-Car Num variation trend of intersection B

Therefore, in the design of routing vehicle network, when the car network is in a sparse state, as it cannot communicate through the vehicle nodes, messages need to be relayed via RSU, 3G/4G base station. When the vehicle network is in a dense state, the appropriate methods are required to reduce the frequency of message forwarding, as well as the probability of broadcast storms.

4   Conclusion

In this paper, we mainly study the distribution characteristics of nodes in the vehicle network. The experimental results show that, in the vehicle network which is the scale-free network, most vehicles only communicate with only a few vehicles, and these key vehicle nodes are important for the forwarding of network information. In addition, the traffic flow of the highway scene can be maintained at a stable level, while the urban road state always changes dramatically, besides, the network nodes are sometimes dense, and sometimes sparse. Therefore, in the design of routing protocols, special approaches should be taken to deal with urban road scenes.

Acknowledgments. This work was supported in part by NSFC under Grants 61472284, and the Natural Science Foundation of Shanghai under Grants 17ZR1445900.

References

1. Cheng, J., Cheng, J., Zhou, M., Liu, F., Gao, S., Liu, C.: Routing in internet of vehicles: a review. IEEE Trans. Intell. Transp. Syst. **16**(5), 2339–2352 (2015)
2. Sommer, C., German, R.: Falko Dressler.: bidirectionally coupled network and road traffic simulation for improved IVC analysis. IEEE Trans. Mob. Comput. **10**(1), 3–15 (2011)
3. Lownes, N., Machemehl, R.: Vissim: a multi-parameter sensitivity analysis. In: Proceedings of the Winter IEEE Simulation Conference, WSC 2006, pp. 1406–1413 (2006)
4. Choi S, Kim E, Oh S.: Human behavior prediction for smart homes using deep learning, pp. 173–179. IEEE, Roman (2013)
5. Paramics Microsimulation. http://www.sias.com/2013/sp/sparamicshome.htm. Accessed 16 Apr 2015
6. TransModeler Traffic Simulation Software. http://www.caliper.com/transmodeler/default.htm. Accessed 06 May 2015
7. Sumo official Websites. http://sumo.dlr.de/wiki/Simulation. Accessed 04 Mar 2014
8. Sherman, M., McNeill, K.M., Conner, K., Khuu, P., McNevin, T.: A PMP-Friendly MANET networking approach for WiMAX/IEEE 802.16TM. In: IEEE Military Communication Conference, pp. 1–7. Milcom IEEE (2006)

Application of Batch and Stream Collaborative Computing in Urban Traffic Data Processing

Tao Zhang[✉] and Shuai Zhao

State Key Laboratory of Networking and Switching Technology,
Beijing University of Posts and Telecommunications, Beijing 100876, China
{zhangtao89,zhaoshuaiby}@bupt.edu.cn

Abstract. Analysis of urban traffic data has obtained a great attention in recent years. In the study of urban traffic data processing, the batch computing based on historical data and the stream computing based on real-time data are isolated, and the two computing frameworks are not synergized. Therefore, a method of urban traffic data processing based on batch and stream collaborative computing is proposed. Batch computing has the advantage of high throughput, so it is more suitable for calculating the historical data of urban traffic and the results of stream computing deeply. Stream computing with the advantage of low delay can be used to calculate the traffic data in real time, combined with the results of batch computing, then the conclusion of urban traffic data processing are more comprehensive and accurate.

Keywords: Batch computing · Stream computing · Collaborative computing · Urban traffic data processing

1 Introduction

With the development of economy and technology, the number of urban vehicles continued to grow, followed by a large number of traffic data. The effective handling of these data allows us analyze the status of urban traffic accurately and forecast traffic conditions timely, so as to plan the traffic better. Then the city's intelligent level can be improved.

At present, in the study of urban traffic data processing, mainly related to batch computing based on the historical data and stream computing based on real-time data. The batch computing use the batch computing framework (such as Hadoop) to handle the city's historical traffic data, the main contents include analysis of vehicle trajectories, analysis of vehicle illegal grade and traffic congestion model training, the literature [1] using MapReduce framework to forecast traffic data flow. Literature [2] find the accuracy and time consuming of genetic neural network short-term traffic flow prediction algorithm based on Hadoop platform are improved significantly. The stream computing use stream computing framework (such as Storm) on the city's real-time traffic data processing, mainly involved the optimal path searching, real-time information querying and analysis of real-time traffic data, etc. Literature [3, 4] design and implement traffic data real-time processing system based on the stream computing framework Storm. At

© Springer International Publishing AG 2017
S. Ibrahim et al. (Eds.): ICA3PP 2017, LNCS 10393, pp. 725–734, 2017.
DOI: 10.1007/978-3-319-65482-9_58

the present stage, the batch computing and the stream computing are isolated, and the two computing frameworks are not combined. Therefore, this paper presents a method of urban traffic data processing based on batch and stream collaborative computing. Specifically, this paper makes the following contributions:

(1) It designs the overall architecture of collaborative computing, including technical support layer, collaborative computing layer and system application layer. Collaborative computing combines high throughput batch computing and low latency stream computing, then makes full use of historical data in the process of traffic data analysis to make the results more comprehensive.
(2) The technical framework is proposed to achieve the interaction between batch computing and stream computing. The interaction between computing frameworks is bi-directional and requires message queues, memory databases and other related technologies.
(3) It has done several simulation experiments, the results show that the interaction between the stream computing framework Storm and the batch computing framework Hadoop can be achieved by using memory database REDIS, and the conclusion of traffic data analysis is more reasonable based on collaborative computing.

This method proposed in the paper make full use of the advantages of two frameworks by realizing the interaction of data using message queue or memory database, so that the results of traffic data processing are more comprehensive and accurate.

2   Related Work

The development of batch computing and stream computing provides a theoretical basis and practical framework for the research of this paper. The batch computing framework is represented by the MapReduce processing model [5] proposed by Google. The MapReduce process uses the idea of "divide and conquer", dividing the data to be processed into multiple processing nodes, then the MapReduce summarizes the results of each processing node and continuously executes the above process until the desired result is achieved. The development of batch computing is relatively long, the relevant theory is also more mature, for example, there are Apache Hadoop [6] and Microsoft's Dryad [7] in architecture and platform area, there are Apache Mahout, Jaspersoft BI suite, Pentaho Business Analytics in data analysis and mining area, there are Tableau in visualization area. The stream computing is starting later than the batch computing, but the development speed is very fast, the corresponding processing framework has also been widely used, representative products are Storm [8], Apache Kafka [9], S4 [10, 11] and so on.

3   The Architecture of Collaborative Computing

The overall structure of this paper can be divided into three layers from bottom to top: technical support layer, collaborative computing layer and system application layer. In the technical support layer, the research contents are mainly the choice and improvement of the stream and batch computing framework, the timing control, fault-tolerant and data buffer technology in stream computing, and the data and model sharing techniques. The main content of the collaborative computing layer is the interaction between stream computing and batch computing. The main content of system application layer is based on the actual demand of smart traffic, including the illegal vehicle marking, urban traffic congestion warning, and urban traffic forecasting, as shown in Fig. 1.

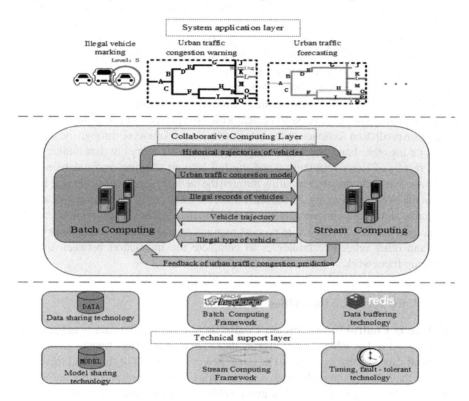

Fig. 1. The structure of collaborative computing

3.1 Batch and Stream Collaborative Computing

Batch computing has many features, for example: The amount of data processed is large; the type of data is diversified (structured data, semi-structured data, unstructured data); the processing speed is slow; the accuracy of the processing results is high. Batch computing first stores the traffic data, and then analyzes and mines the data. Therefore, the batch computing mainly involves the accumulation of the trajectories of the vehicles generated by the stream computing in real time, analysis of the historical trajectories of the vehicles, and calculation of the probability of each route the vehicle travels. According to the cumulative data of the vehicles' illegal records, the illegal grade of the vehicles can be counted. Based on the accumulated vehicle and environment data, the urban traffic congestion model can be trained by artificial neural network with feedback. The basic idea of stream computing is that the value of the data will continue to decrease over time, and the stream computing must ensure that the data is processed before the next data flow arrives. Stream computing is usually carried out memory processing on traffic data, while the data is stored in shared memory. The results of data processing can be used in real time, and obsolete data is directly discarded to save processing nodes' resources. Therefore, the stream computing include the following content: marking the vehicles whose illegal grade exceed a certain threshold; predicting the urban traffic conditions, in this process, mainly involved two parts, the first part is the real-time information (including vehicles, weather related) collected, the second part is the probability of each route the vehicle travels. These two kinds of data can be used to predict future urban traffic conditions. At the same time, according to the urban traffic congestion model, the urban traffic congestion warning can be carried out.

In the stream and batch computing frameworks, on the one hand, the stream computing framework needs to send vehicle's illegal type, real-time trajectory and traffic congestion prediction feedback to the batch computing framework through the message queue; on the other hand, the batch computing framework carry out data mining based on the results of stream computing and the full amount of urban traffic data, and the results are sent to the stream computing through the memory database to guide the further work of the stream computing. At the same time, the batch computing framework adjusts the training algorithms and parameters according to the feedback of urban traffic congestion model's prediction. The entire process requires message queues and memory databases and other related technologies to complete the interaction between the two computing framework.

3.2 Related Technical Difficulties

The Timing Control in the Stream Computing. Urban traffic data is generated in chronological order, which is time series data. Time series data streams are a set of sequential data sets that continue to be generated over a period of time, and these data arrive in the order of time attributes, so time series data is represented not only by its value but also by a certain time. But every vehicle is independent, the transmission of cars' GPS data also have different delay, so the order data arrives at the center cannot be guaranteed. And the data is valuable only with time attributes, which requires the system with a good ability of data analysis and law discovery in the process of data calculation. Timing control in stream computing is an urgent problem to be solved.

Data Buffering Technology. The generation of urban traffic data is a continuous process, and according to the actual application of the scene, we can see that the urban traffic data is prone to dynamic changes when they are collected in different time and space, resulting in the data stream has burst characteristics. The data rate at the previous time and the data rate at a later time may be very different. Therefore, the system should have good scalability and dynamic matching ability on large amount of data, and can dynamically adapt to the instream of uncertain data. In the case of burst high data flow rates, it should ensure that data is not discarded, or that unimportant data is identified and selectively cached, and important data is preferentially calculated, and in the case of low data rates, then the cached data can be re-played and calculated.

In order to improve the scalability of the buffering part of the system, a distributed caching system for time series data flow should be designed to support the efficient storage of large-scale traffic data flows, and the time series traffic data which need to persistent should be saved in time series through the caching system. In order to support the efficient storage of large-scale urban traffic flow data and to ensure that the sequential data flow can be written into disk in an orderly manner, we intend to design a distributed caching system for urban traffic times series data stream based on key-value database REDIS. All of the data in the system is based on memory storage, which can greatly reduce disk I/O and support rapid response to large-scale storage requests.

4 The Interaction Between Batch Computing and Stream Computing

The technical framework of interaction between batch computing and stream computing is shown in Fig. 2.

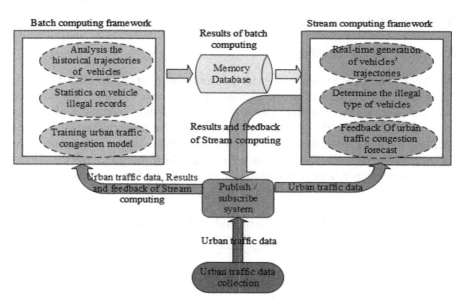

Fig. 2. Technical framework

First, the collected city traffic data is sent to the Publish/Subscribe system, the batch computing framework and the stream computing framework can subscribe to the data in the system. Batch computing uses the distributed file system to preserve the accumulated city traffic data. Batch computing, with high throughput and support of complex logical operations, can carry out deep and detailed calculation and analysis of urban traffic history data, analyze the historical trajectories of the vehicles, count the vehicles' illegal records, and train the urban traffic congestion model using the artificial neural network with feedback, the results of batch computing are stored in memory database, which is used for real-time processing. Stream computing read the city traffic data from the Publish/Subscribe system to generate the vehicle trajectory and determine the illegal type. At the same time, the stream computing framework obtain the results of batch computing about trajectories and illegal records from the memory database, and combine the vehicle's historical characteristics and real-time behavior data effectively, thus the result of traffic condition forecast can be more comprehensive and accurate. The results of stream computing also be published to the Publish/subscription system. Batch computing framework are also subscribed to the results of stream computing for deeper analysis and mining. At the same time, the stream computing part can also use the urban traffic congestion model to carry out congestion warning, and send the feedback of the effect of warning to the batch computing framework, batch computing framework adjusts the training algorithms and parameters according to the feedback. After some experiments, the simple interaction between the stream computing framework and the batch computing framework can be achieved by using REDIS as the memory database and Kafka cluster as the message queue system, so the above design is feasible.

5   Case Study

5.1   Illegal Vehicle Marking

We simulate the process of illegal vehicle marking with simulation data, batch and stream computing frameworks, and memory database. For example: The historical information of vehicles is shown in the Table 1. The real-time information of vehicles is shown in Table 2. The illegal behavior is divided into five categories, namely, normal, speeding, running a red light, retrograde motion, and other accidents, the corresponding illegal grade are 0, 1, 1.5, 2, 3. If we do not consider the historical data of the vehicle, the result is not comprehensive only to use stream computing framework to mark illegal vehicles.

Table 1.   The historical information of vehicles

The ID of vehicle	Illegal grade	Illegal time
00001	1	T1
00002	1.5	T2
00004	1	T3
00001	2	T4
00002	1.5	T5
...	...	...

We use the batch computing framework Hadoop to process the historical illegal data of vehicles. Firstly, the Map program should be written to extract vehicle ID and illegal grade from each row of data, then we write Reduce program to calculate the sum of the illegal grade of each vehicle. Finally, the results are entered into REDIS by implementing RedisOutputFormat class. The process is shown below (Fig. 3).

Table 2. The real-time information of vehicles

The ID of vehicle	Illegal grade	Illegal time
00001	1	T6
00002	1.5	T7
00003	2	T8
00004	3	T9
00006	1	T10
00007	3	T11

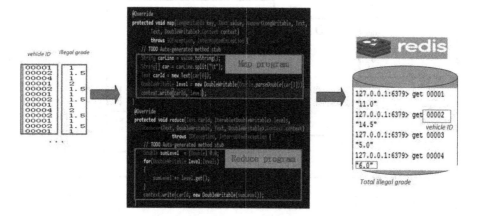

Fig. 3. Batch computing process

Stream Computing Framework Storm calculates the final illegal grade of the vehicle based on historical and real-time vehicle illegal data and updates the latest illegal grade to the REDIS database. The specific process is shown below. Obviously, the combination of vehicles' historical data to determine the illegal grade is more reasonable (Fig. 4).

Fig. 4. Stream computing process

5.2   Urban Traffic Forecast

When we predict the traffic conditions, in addition to the use of weather, vehicle speed, adjacent road conditions and other conventional factors, the probability of each route the vehicle travels based on the historical trajectories of the vehicle also should be considered. Its implementation process is similar to the illegal vehicle marking, here we only elaborate the idea. For example: a city's road path is shown in Fig. 5.

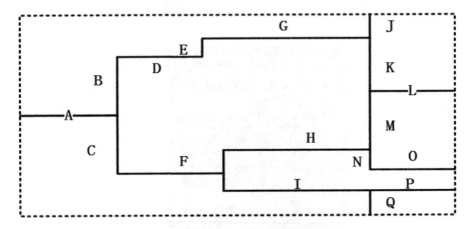

Fig. 5. City's road path

The historical vehicle trajectories of vehicle 00001 and vehicle 00002 are shown in Table 3.

Table 3. Vehicle trajectories

The ID of vehicle	Trajectories	Start time	End time
00001	BDEGJ	T1	T2
00001	BDEGKL	T3	T4
00001	ABDEGK	T5	T6
00001	BDEGKM	T7	T8
00001	CFHN	T9	T10
00002	FHNO	T11	T12
00002	FHML	T13	T14
00002	FHMKJ	T15	T16
00002	CFIP	T17	T18
00002	CFIQ	T19	T20

Therefore, when the traffic condition is predicted, the vehicle trajectories table can be used, for example, when the information collected by stream computing framework show that the vehicle 00001 is traveling on the section of G, then traverse the trajectories table, the number of vehicle 00001's paths contains G is 4, where the number of paths converted from G to K is 3 and the number of paths converted from G to J is 1. Therefore, we can think that there are 0.75 cars travel into the K section and 0.25 cars travel into the J section in the next time period. At the same time, we can also use the method with time weight to calculate, if the time of path is closer to the current time, more weight can be given.

6 Conclusion

The stream and batch computing framework, due to different design goals, respectively, are suitable for different algorithms. For logically simple algorithms with real-time requirements, such as vehicle real-time trajectory generation, vehicle real-time illegal behavior judgment, should be implemented in the stream computing framework; for complex algorithms based on large amount of data, such as urban traffic congestion model training, should be implemented in the batch computing framework. At the present stage of stream and batch collaborative computing applications, the main content is that the stream computing make use of the result of batch computing framework, the data is only one-way flow between the two frameworks. In the urban traffic data processing, the stream computing framework not only uses the results of the batch computing framework, the batch computing framework also needs the feedback and results of the stream computing framework, and the data is bi-directional flow between the two frameworks. This way makes the results of urban traffic data processing more comprehensive and accurate.

References

1. Chen, C.: Distributed modeling in a MapReduce framework for data-driven traffic stream forecasting. IEEE Trans. Intell. Transp. Syst. **14**(1), 22–33 (2013)
2. Hu, H.: Research on short-term traffic stream prediction algorithm based on hadoop platform, Master's thesis. South China University of Technology, Guangzhou, China (2016, Unpublished)
3. Situ, S.: Design and implementation of real-time traffic information processing system based on storm, Master's thesis. Sun Yat-sen University, Guangzhou, China (2015, Unpublished)
4. Nan, H.: Design and implementation of a traffic stream data real-time processing system based on STORM, Master's thesis. North China University of Technology, Beijing, China (2015, Unpublished)
5. Dean, J.: MapReduce: Simplified data processing on large clusters. Commun. ACM **51**(1), 107–113 (2008)
6. Shvachko, K.: The hadoop distributed file system. In: 2010 Proceedings of the IEEE 26th Symposium on Mass Storage Systems and Technologies (MSST), pp. 1–10. IEEE, Incline Village (2010)
7. Isard, M.: Dryad: distributed data-parallel programs from sequential building blocks. In: Proceedings of the 2nd ACM SIGOPS/EuroSys European Conference on Computer Systems, pp. 59–72. ACM, Lisbon (2007)
8. Leibiusky, J., Eisbruch, G., Simonassi, D.: Getting Started with Storm. O'Reilly, Ireland (2012)
9. Auradkar, A.: Data infrastructure at linkedin. In: 2012 IEEE 28th International Conference on Data Engineering (ICDE), pp. 1370–1381. IEEE, Washington, D.C. (2012)

10. Neumeyer, L.: S4: distributed stream computing platform. In: 2010 IEEE International Conference on Data Mining Workshops (ICDMW), pp. 170–177. IEEE, Sydney, TBD, Australia (2010)
11. Chauhan, J.: Performance evaluation of Yahoo! S4: a first look. In: 2012 Seventh International Conference on P2P, Parallel, Grid, Cloud and Internet Computing (3PGCIC), pp. 58–65. IEEE, Victoria (2012)

ESD-WSN: An Efficient SDN-Based Wireless Sensor Network Architecture for IoT Applications

Zhiwei Zhang[1], Zhiyong Zhang[1], Rui Wang[1], Zhiping Jia[1(✉)], Haijun Lei[2,3], and Xiaojun Cai[1]

[1] School of Computer Science and Technology, Shandong University, Jinan, China
jzp@sdu.edu.cn
[2] Guangdong Key Laboratory of Popular High Performance Computers, Shenzhen, China
[3] Shenzhen Key Laboratory of Service Computing and Applications, Shenzhen, China

Abstract. Wireless sensor networks (WSNs) are considered as a key enabler for the paradigm of Internet of Things (IoT). With increasing number of devices connected to the IoT environments, traditional solutions for WSNs tend to be costly in terms of network maintenance and management. Software-Defined Networking (SDN) appears as a viable alternative network architecture since it enables new services and policies to be deployed flexibly and easily. However, SDN brings excessive control overhead which significantly degrades the network performance. To relieve this problem, in this paper, we propose an Efficient Software-Defined Wireless Sensor Network (ESD-WSN) architecture to make full use of the advantages of SDN while overcoming its constraints. In the proposed architecture, the controller dynamically selects certain nodes as proxies for control traffic processing and aggregating. To this end, a Dynamic Proxy Management (DPM) strategy is presented to select the optimal subset of network nodes as proxies. Experimental results show that our scheme achieves considerable performance improvement compared with the SDN-WISE scheme [1].

Keywords: Wireless sensor networks · Internet of Things · Software Defined Network · Control overhead · Proxy management

1 Introduction

In recent years, the Internet of Things (IoT) paradigm has attracted wide attentions both in academia and in industry. In the meantime, wireless sensor networks (WSNs) are widely used as an effective medium in IoT environments to connect the physical world and the information world. However, WSNs are generally considered to be application-specific [2], thus resulting in resource under-utilization and high deployment costs. Moreover, the network policy is rigid to change, which further increases the difficulty of network management.

The above problems can be solved by making WSNs programmable. The Software Defined Networking (SDN) and OpenFlow [3] which currently is the

© Springer International Publishing AG 2017
S. Ibrahim et al. (Eds.): ICA3PP 2017, LNCS 10393, pp. 735–745, 2017.
DOI: 10.1007/978-3-319-65482-9_59

most popular southbound interface for SDN, offer the possibility of this vision. SDN is a promising network paradigm that decouples the data plane and the control plane and it allows network administrators to manage network services through abstraction of low-level network functionality.

Several works have recently investigated to extend the SDN concepts to WSNs [1,4,5]. These works make significant contributions as they provide convincing proof of the benefits of applying the SDN concept to WSNs. However, the introduction of SDN brings excessive control overhead. As pointed out in Sensor OpenFlow [4], the control overhead is a challenging issue in the software-defined wireless sensor networks since each node needs to constantly report information about its status to the controller for maintaining the network topology. Moreover, when a node has no idea about how to process an incoming packet, it will interact with the controller by the *packet-in* and *packet-out* messages. In IoT environments, this situation is exacerbated by the fact that all nodes may have the demands to communicate with each other. The excessive control overhead may lead to the energy exhausted within a short period of time, so how to build an energy-efficient network is a critical problem to be addressed.

In this paper, we propose an Efficient Software-Defined Wireless Sensor Network (ESD-WSN) architecture for IoT applications. In this architecture, we aim to establish a stable and energy-efficient control plane to reduce the control overhead. To this end, we propose the concept of *proxy* for control traffic processing and aggregating. Meanwhile, to better utilize the proxy node, a Dynamic Proxy Management (DPM) strategy is presented to select the optimal proxy-set and to balance the energy consumption of the whole network.

The remainder of this paper is organized as follows. Section 2 provides a survey of the related work. The architecture design of ESD-WSN and DPM strategy are described in Sects. 3 and 4, respectively. Section 5 analyzes the experimental results and finally, this paper is concluded in Sect. 6.

2   Related Work

Recently, WSNs have led to many studies for IoT applications [6–8]. However, WSNs are considered to be application-specific and hard to manage which tend to adversely impact the overall solution complexity and cost. Therefore, many works have been devoted to applying SDN principle to WSNs domain to simplify the network management.

Costanzo et al. [5] propose a Software Defined Wireless Network (SDWN) solution to introduce the SDN approach to wireless networks. SDWN offers a flexible specification of the rules to classify packets and supports the use of duty cycle to achieve energy efficiency. In [9], the proposed architecture consists of three types of nodes: center node, master node and sensor node. The master node acts as a controller. The center node is similar to the forwarding element of the wired network, so its location is limited. The emergence of SDN-WISE [1] can be seen as a milestone of the software-defined WSNs domain since it allows software developers to implement their network services in an intuitive and flexible way.

Meanwhile, it implements a prototype on a real platform. In order to fully exploit the resources of WSNs, Zeng et al. adopt an SDN architecture to solve the multi-task scheduling problem [10]. This study makes WSNs become versatile which promotes the development of WSNs for IoT applications.

In addition, there are still many studies that fully demonstrate the advantages of SDN, as described in [11–13]. Although these studies emphasize the benefits of SDN, they don't pay more attention to the excessive control overhead issue.

3 Architecture Design

In this section, we present the general design of the proposed architecture. First, we give the overview of our architecture, and then we describe the detailed design of the Software-Defined Sensor (SDS) node and the controller.

3.1 Overview

The proposed architecture consists of a base station, a plurality of SDS nodes and a gateway, as shown in Fig. 1. The gateway is a functional device that manages the connection of the WSNs to the Internet. Since the base station has adequate energy supply, we run an SDN controller on it.

The SDS node acts as both monitoring node and routing node. It performs sensing tasks and conducts data forwarding according to the rules installed by the controller. More specifically, the SDS nodes are divided into two categories: sensor nodes and proxy nodes. Compared with the sensor node, the proxy node takes on more functionalities such as the control message processing and aggregating. Meanwhile, all the control packets of the sensor nodes will send to its assigned proxy node. Therefore, the existence of proxy nodes effectively reduces the number of control packets. It is worth noting that when a sensor node is within one-hop distance of multiple proxy nodes, the sensor node is called an overlap member.

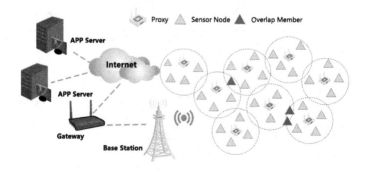

Fig. 1. A deployment scenario of ESD-WSN.

3.2 Software-Defined Sensor Node

Figure 2 shows the detailed functional design of our architecture. As a typical WSN node, the SDS node reserves the monitoring module to collect data for various sensing tasks. The topology discovery module and the flow table are necessary modules for the implementation of SDN features. In our design, the topology discovery module conducts neighbor discovery and report the topology information to the controller. The flow table contains all the rules (flow table entries) installed by the controller. When a packet matches one flow table entry, it will be processed according to *action* field of this entry. Otherwise, the SDS node will interact with the controller with *packet-in* and *packet-out* messages.

Furthermore, we add a *queue scheduling* module to avoid the control traffic being congested by the data traffic. The queue scheduling module keeps three kinds of queues for different packets: *network information queue*, *control queue* and *data queue*. The network information queue has the highest priority. It holds the topology packets which report the energy, neighbor list and other information to the controller (i.e. *report packets*). The main rationale of this assignment is that the report packets are critical to the construction of the global network topology. In addition to the report packets, the packet-in messages have the second highest priority which are placed in the control queue. Different from the control traffic, the data traffic records the application-related information, e.g. sensing packets. Therefore, we assign the lowest priority to them and cache them in the data queue.

Moreover, we adopt the finite state machine mechanism to extend the semantics of OpenFlow. The presence of the finite state machine module allows an SDS node to switch its role between the sensor node and the proxy node. The proxy node treats part of its one-hop neighbors as its member nodes and performs

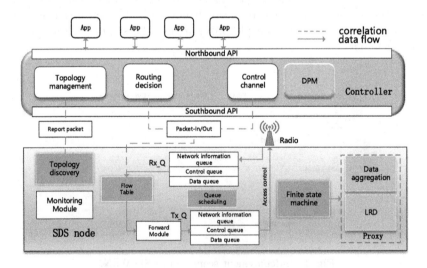

Fig. 2. The architecture design of ESD-WSN.

the control messages aggregating for these members. In addition, a local network can be built by the proxy and its members, so that some routing decisions can be made locally. The proxy node uses the LRD (Local Routing Decision) module to take over the routing selections of the local network from the controller. Therefore, the controller and the LRD module work together for the data communication among all the nodes.

3.3   Controller

The centralized controller implements the intelligence of the ESD-WSN architecture. As shown in Fig. 2, the topology management module maintains the network topology according to the received report packets. Based on the global network topology, the routing decision module and the control channel module are responsible for finding the optimal path for the data packets and the control packets, respectively.

In addition, we add the dynamic proxy management (DPM) module to reduce the control overhead. The DPM module includes proxy selection, proxy allocation and proxy rotation. The proxy selection aims to select the optimal nodes set to obtain the best effect of aggregation, while the proxy allocation is designed for the proxy allocation of the mentioned overlap members. Taking the energy balance issue into account, the proxy rotation is used to achieve balanced energy consumption, thus improving the lifetime of the whole network.

Finally, the controller provides an open programmable interface to the network administrators to make more fine-grained control policies.

4   Dynamic Proxy Management Strategy

In this section, we describe our DPM strategy for the proposed architecture. We first present the requirements of the proxy selection, followed by the notations used in this paper. Then, an ILP-based proxy selection mechanism is detailed. Finally, we discuss the proxy allocation and proxy rotation mechanism.

4.1   Requirements and Notations

In order to reduce the control overhead and prolong the network lifetime as much as possible, the proxy selection should meet the following requirements.

1. Since the proxy nodes are burdened with more tasks, the nodes selected as proxy nodes should have sufficient energy to avoid premature death.
2. The proxy selection should guarantee that all the SDS nodes in the network are under the control of the proxy nodes, which means that all the SDS nodes can find a proxy node within one-hop. By this way, all the nodes can easily communicate with the control plane of the network.
3. To achieve the best effect of aggregation, the proxy selection should minimize the control traffic overhead between the selected nodes and the other nodes under the above constraints.

For the ease of reading, Table 1 summarizes the notations to be used later.

Table 1. Notations in this paper.

Notation	Definition
C	The set of candidates
E_{tx}	Energy consumption of transmitting a 1-byte packet
E_{rx}	Energy consumption of receiving a 1-byte packet
E_i	Residual energy of node i
$nbs(i)$	Number of neighbors of node i
$Nbr(i)$	The neighbor set of node i
$queue\_load(i)$	Total bytes of the unprocessed packets in the queue of node i
Adj	The adjacency matrix of graph G
E_{DA}	Energy consumption of aggregation per byte
Agg	Aggregation coefficient
d_i	The optimal number of hops to reach the base station

4.2   Proxy Selection

Consider an ESD-WSN $G = (N, E)$ consisting of a controller and $|N| - 1$ SDS nodes. We aim to find a subset N' under the requirements mentioned above, so that the total control overhead between each node in subset N' and its neighbors is minimized.

Step 1. Suppose all the nodes are marked as $1, \ldots, n$ and the controller is node 1. We first screen out the high-energy nodes that are eligible to be the proxy nodes and put them in set C. These nodes are called candidate and should meet the following conditions:

$$E_i - E_{eec}(i) \geq \frac{\sum_{j \in Nbr(i)}(E_j - E_{eec}(j))}{nbs(i)} \tag{1}$$

Formula 1 means that the expected residual energy of node i needs to be greater than or equal to the average expected residual energy of its neighbors. $E_{eec}(i)$ represents the energy consumption of the packets to be sent in the queue, it can be calculated by $queue\_load(i)$ as follows:

$$E_{eec}(i) = queue\_load(i) \cdot E_{tx} \tag{2}$$

Step 2. After constructing the set C, a check will be performed to see whether C is a dominating set. If not, the following additional operations will be performed to find a set C' such that the union of set C and set C' is a dominating set.

1. Find the *uncovered nodes* that are not dominated by set C. Use U to represent the set of uncovered nodes and k to represent the number of uncovered nodes.

2. Find the complement M of set C. For each node in M, count the number of uncovered nodes dominated by it and remove it from M if the number is 0.
3. If there are more than one node that dominates the same uncovered nodes, only the node with highest energy is retained in M.
4. Define a binary variable m_i to indicate whether the i-th node in set M is placed in set C' or not. Use $m_{i[j]} = 1$ to represent the i-th node in set M dominates the j-th node in set U (Otherwise, $m_{i[j]} = 0$) and solve the following ILP problem:

$$m_i = \begin{cases} 1, & \text{if node } i \text{ in } M \text{ is placed in } C', \\ 0, & \text{otherwise.} \end{cases} \tag{3}$$

$$\text{min: } \sum_{i=1}^{|M|} m_i \tag{4}$$

$$\text{s.t.: } \prod_{j=1}^{k} \sum_{i=1}^{|M|} m_i \cdot m_{i[j]} \geq 1 \tag{5}$$

5. Place the obtained result in set C', then remove the nodes in set C' and the nodes in set U from graph G.
6. Update the node set N, edge set E and adjacency matrix A of graph G.

Step 3. After the above processing, we model the proxy selection problem as an ILP formulation. The binary variable v_i used in formulation is defined as follows:

$$v_i = \begin{cases} 1, & \text{if } v_i \text{ is selected as the proxy.} \\ 0, & \text{otherwise.} \end{cases} \tag{6}$$

Since only nodes in set C can become proxies and the controller must be a proxy node, the partial value of $\{v_i\}$ can be determined as follows:

$$v_i = 0, \quad \text{if } v_i \text{ is not in set } C. \tag{7}$$

$$v_1 = 1 \tag{8}$$

As discussed above, we should ensure that all the nodes either in the final solution set, or adjacent to some nodes of the final solution set, which is expressed as follows:

$$\prod_{i=1}^{|N|} (v_i + \sum_{j=1}^{|N|} v_j \cdot Adj_{j,i}) \geq 1 \tag{9}$$

We define the control overhead of the proxy nodes and the normal nodes as follows:

$$E_{\text{pro}}(i) = E_{\text{rx}} \cdot nbs(i) + (nbs(i) + 1) \cdot E_{\text{DA}} \cdot Agg + (d_i - 1) \cdot E_{\text{rx}} + d_i \cdot E_{\text{tx}} \tag{10}$$

$$E_{\text{nor}} = E_{\text{tx}} \tag{11}$$

$E_{\text{rx}} \cdot nbs(i)$ is the cost of the proxy node receiving 1-byte packets from its neighbors. $(nbs(i) + 1) \cdot E_{\text{DA}} \cdot Agg$ is the aggregation cost. Since packets are transmitted in a multi-hop way, we use $(d_i - 1) \cdot E_{\text{rx}} + d_i \cdot E_{\text{tx}}$ to represent the cost of sending the aggregated packet to the controller. It includes the transmission cost of the proxy node and the transmission and reception cost of the $d_i - 1$ relay nodes. The normal nodes only need to send control messages to the proxy nodes, so the cost of them is E_{tx}.

Finally, we get the objective function as follows:

$$\min: \sum_{i=1}^{|N|} (v_i \cdot E_{\text{pro}}(i)) + (|N| - \sum_{i=1}^{|N|} v_i) \cdot E_{\text{nor}} \tag{12}$$

Let F be the optimal solution of the ILP problem, if C is not a dominating set, the final solution N' is the union of F and C'. Otherwise, the N' is equal to F.

4.3   Proxy Allocation and Proxy Rotation

The overlap members should be assigned to an appropriate proxy node to transmit control messages correctly, i.e., the overlap member nodes exactly know which proxy node to send the control packets to, thus we build the following evaluation function. EP_i and dp_i represent the expected residual energy of the proxy node i and the distance to the proxy node i. EP_{avg} and dp_{avg} are the average of EP_i and dp_i, respectively. γ is a factor to trade off the significance of expected residual energy and distance. If an overlap member is in one-hop range of the controller, it is assigned to the controller. Otherwise, it is assigned to the proxy node that maximizes the value of the function.

$$f = \gamma \frac{EP_i}{EP_{avg}} + (1 - \gamma)(1 - \frac{dp_i}{dp_{avg}}) \tag{13}$$

Since the proxy nodes take on more tasks, they are easier to drain energy ahead of time, so the proxy rotation is essential to prolonging the network lifetime. In our strategy, the controller continuously monitors the nodes, and conducts proxy rotation if there is a proxy node that satisfies Formula 14.

$$E_i < \frac{1}{2} \cdot \frac{\sum_{j \in Nbr(i)} E_j}{nbs(i)} \tag{14}$$

In addition, since the global rotation will bring excessive computational overhead to the control plane and excessive communication overhead to the data plane, we should try to avoid the global rotation. The controller can partially update the proxy nodes. In our strategy, the controller still performs the proxy selection when the proxy rotation occurs but the search space of the ILP problem is limited to a subgraph of graph G.

5   Experiments

Due to the deployment space constraints, we conduct simulation experiments to test the performance of our solution. We implement the data plane on the Cooja platform of Contiki 2.7 and only one controller runs on a laptop to implement the control plane. In order to simulate the actual energy consumption of WSNs devices, we measured the energy consumption of Texas Instruments CC2530. The measured results together with experimental parameters are presented in Table 2.

Table 2. Simulation parameters

Parameter	Value
Initial energy	1.5 J
E_{tx}	0.0087 mJ/byte
E_{rx}	0.0072 mJ/byte
E_{DA}	40 nJ/byte
Agg	0.5
γ	0.5

We compare the performance of our scheme with SDN-WISE in terms of control overhead, end-to-end latency and network lifetime. In each measurement, we set the data packet size to 30 bytes and make the nodes send packets randomly to simulate an IoT environment. Moreover, we set the data packet generation interval to 1, 5, 10 s to test the performance of our scheme and SDN-WISE under different workloads.

Control overhead is the average energy consumption due to transmission and reception of control packets. Figures 3 and 4 show the control overhead of

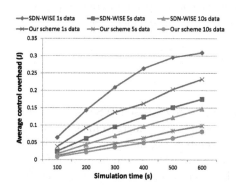

Fig. 3. Control overhead in smaller network.

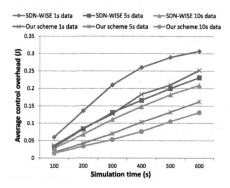

Fig. 4. Control overhead in larger network.

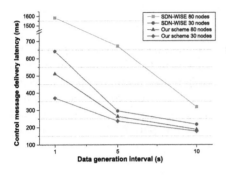

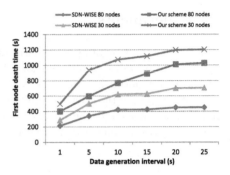

Fig. 5. End-to-end latency of control packets.   **Fig. 6.** Network lifetime.

varied network scale with 30 nodes and 80 nodes, respectively. As expected, control overhead increases as the data generation interval decreases. For the same data generation interval, the control overhead of our scheme is much less than the control overhead of SDN-WISE. This is due to the fact that our scheme aggregates most of the control traffic in the network. Meanwhile, the reduction of the control traffic can reduce the collision probability, thereby further reduce the control overhead caused by retransmission.

The average end-to-end latency of control packets is shown in Fig. 5. We can see that the latency increases as the network scale and data frequency increase. Obviously, the latency of our scheme outperforms that of SDN-WISE. The reason behind the results is that our scheme assigns the control packets a higher priority so that the control packets can be forwarded to the controller much faster. Meanwhile, the reduction of control overhead achieved by proxies further reduces the latency since collisions and queuing delays are effectively relieved.

Finally, we show the network lifetime in Fig. 6. The network lifetime is defined as the time period of the network when the first node dies. Compared with SDN-WISE, our scheme extends the network lifetime by 70.3% to 127.7%. This is because our scheme greatly reduces the energy consumption of control packets. Moreover, the proxy rotation mechanism effectively balances the traffic load among all the nodes.

6   Conclusion

In this paper we have introduced ESD-WSN, an SDN-based WSN solution for IoT applications. Aiming at establishing a stable and energy-efficient control plane, we propose a DPM strategy for our architecture, including an ILP-based proxy selection mechanism, a proxy allocation mechanism and a proxy rotation mechanism. Experimental results show that our scheme achieves considerable performance improvement.

Acknowledgement. This research is sponsored by the State Key Program of National Natural Science Foundation of China No. 61533011, Shandong Provincial Natural Science Foundation under Grant No. ZR2015FM001 and the Fundamental Research Funds of Shandong University No. 2015JC030.

References

1. Galluccio, L.A., Milardo, S., Morabito, G., et al.: SDN-WISE: design, prototyping and experimentation of a stateful SDN solution for WIreless SEnsor networks. In: 2015 IEEE Conference on Computer Communications (INFOCOM), pp. 513–521 IEEE (2015)
2. Heinzelman, W.B.: Application-Specific Protocol Architectures for Wireless Networks. Massachusetts Institute of Technology, Cambridge (2000)
3. McKeown, N., Anderson, T., Balakrishnan, H., et al.: OpenFlow: enabling innovation in campus networks. ACM SIGCOMM Comput. Commun. Rev. **38**(2), 69–74 (2008)
4. Luo, T., Tan, H.P., Quek, T.Q.S.: Sensor OpenFlow: enabling software-defined wireless sensor networks. IEEE Commun. Lett. **16**(11), 1896–1899 (2012)
5. Costanzo, S., Galluccio, L., Morabito, G., et al.: Software defined wireless networks: unbridling SDNs. In: European Workshop on Software Defined Networking (EWSDN), pp. 1–6. IEEE (2012)
6. Bellavista, P., Cardone, G., Corradi, A., et al.: Convergence of MANET and WSN in IoT urban scenarios. IEEE Sens. J. **13**(10), 3558–3567 (2013)
7. Fantacci, R., Pecorella, T., Viti, R., et al.: A network architecture solution for efficient IoT WSN backhauling: challenges and opportunities. IEEE Wirel. Commun. **21**(4), 113–119 (2014)
8. Da Xu, L., Viriyasitavat, W.: A novel architecture for requirement-oriented participation decision in service workflows. IEEE Trans. Industr. Inf. **10**(2), 1478–1485 (2014)
9. Han, Z., Ren, W.: A novel wireless sensor networks structure based on the SDN. Int. J. Distrib. Sens. Netw. **10**(3), 874047 (2014)
10. Zeng, D., Li, P., Guo, S., et al.: Energy minimization in multi-task software-defined sensor networks. IEEE Trans. Comput. **64**(11), 3128–3139 (2015)
11. De Gante, A., Aslan, M., Matrawy A.: Smart wireless sensor network management based on software-defined networking. In: 2014 27th Biennial Symposium on Communications (QBSC), pp. 71–75. IEEE (2014)
12. Wang, Y., Chen, H., Wu, X., et al.: An energy-efficient SDN based sleep scheduling algorithm for WSNs. J. Network Comput. Appl. **59**, 39–45 (2016)
13. Bera, S., Misra, S., Roy, S.K., et al.: Soft-WSN: software-defined WSN management system for IoT applications. IEEE Syst. J. (2016)

The 2nd International Workshop on Ultrascale Computing for Early Researchers (UCER 2017)

Probabilistic-Based Selection of Alternate Implementations for Heterogeneous Platforms

Javier Fernández$^{(\boxtimes)}$, Andrés Sánchez Cuadrado, David del Rio Astorga, Manuel F. Dolz, and J. Daniel García

Computer Science and Engineering Department,
University Carlos III of Madrid, 28911 Leganés, Spain
{jfmunoz,andrsanc,mdolz,jdgarcia}@inf.uc3m.es, david.rio@uc3m.es

Abstract. Over the last years, heterogeneous architectures have become a *de facto* approach for improving the performance of numerous scientific and industrial applications. However, developing for these architectures is not straightforward: each processor demands its specific programming paradigm and, often, certain applications are only well-suited to run on a particular processing unit. Therefore, a major challenge arises when programming for these platforms: to select the most suitable device and routine implementation to solve a given problem. To deal with this issue, this paper proposes a novel probabilistic-based selector that uses the problem size to automatically choose the most appropriate version of a same kernel. In order to analyze this approach, we have developed this selector within the OmpSs programming framework and evaluated its accuracy and performance gains when executing different implementations of the general matrix-matrix multiplication. Finally, we also demonstrate how this solution delivers a comparable performance with respect to a runtime approach from the state-of-the-art.

Keywords: Implementation selector · Heterogeneous platforms · Autotuning · Probabilistic modeling

1 Introduction

In the recent years, the evolution of high performance computing has moved towards heterogeneous platforms comprising multiple processing units with different features and programming models [12]. Therefore, according to the needs, application developers are able to benefit from the specific characteristics provided by these architectures, e.g., SIMD capabilities of GPUs or low power consumption of FPGAs. While the benefits of using these platforms have been clearly defined, the challenges of exploiting heterogeneity have discouraged the

J. Fernández—This work was partially supported by the EU project ICT 644235 "REPHRASE: REfactoring Parallel Heterogeneous Resource-Aware Applications" and the project TIN2013-41350-P "Scalable Data Management Techniques for High-End Computing Systems" from the *Ministerio de Economía y Competitividad*, Spain.

© Springer International Publishing AG 2017
S. Ibrahim et al. (Eds.): ICA3PP 2017, LNCS 10393, pp. 749–758, 2017.
DOI: 10.1007/978-3-319-65482-9_60

adoption of heterogeneous programming models. These challenges include the inherent difficulties of diverse programming paradigms and the fact that certain processors are only well-suited for applications with special demands. This has led to a progressive development of multiple architecture-specific implementations [5]. Thus, an additional challenge arises when programming for these platforms: to select the most convenient device and implementation to solve a given problem.

While a naive approach is to manually map tasks onto the underlying parallel processors, runtime schedulers have demonstrated to be a better solution in these scenarios [4]. Indeed, recent schedulers help in improving performance, since they learn incrementally from past executions. This mechanism allows them to self-tune applications by means of selecting the most appropriate kernel version and processor [7]. To pave the way, this paper extends the current literature with a novel probabilistic-based selector of alternate implementations for heterogeneous platforms (PRISE). In order to implement and evaluate this selector, we have leveraged the OmpSs programming framework instead of other solutions (such as StarPU [2]), given that OmpSs is more usable and allows to easily integrate new scheduling modules. Specifically, this work contributes with the following:

- We present an implementation selector that allows automatically choosing the most suitable implementation of a same kernel using a probabilistic and profile-guided approach.
- We incorporate the probabilistic selector as a scheduler into the OmpSs programming framework and detail which modifications have been required in its Mercurium compiler and Nanos++ runtime.
- We evaluate the proposed scheduler by analyzing the accuracy of the selections made and the performance gains using the general matrix-matrix multiplication as use case.
- We demonstrate how our scheduler self-tunes and delivers a comparable performance with respect to a runtime approach from the state-of-the-art.

The rest of this document is organized as follows. Section 2 reviews a few related works in the area. Section 3 describes the OmpSs programming framework along with its two major components: the Mercurium compiler and the Nanos++ runtime. Section 4 presents the probabilistic implementation selector as for the main contribution of this paper. In Sect. 5, we evaluate our approach using the general matrix-matrix multiplication and compare it with an already existing OmpSs scheduler. Finally, Sect. 6 closes this paper with a few concluding remarks and future works.

2   Related Work

Heterogeneous architectures, combining different processing units, have become a very common scenario across the scientific community. Given that these processing units have inherent advantages and drawbacks, highly-tuned implementations of a same algorithm have been developed to fully exploit them. For example, several numerical libraries comprising highly tuned kernels, from BLAS and LAPACK, are available for diverse computing architectures: clBLAS [1] has support for OpenCL processors, GSL [8] is targeted to multi-/many-core processors, etc. This fact poses the need of selecting the most suitable pair device–implementation to solve a given problem. To deal with this issue, the solutions in the state-of-the-art have generally taken two directions: *(i)* runtime schedulers, which are able to map and execute kernels from multiple libraries on the available processing units; and *(ii)* static approaches, which allow selecting at compile time the most appropriate implementation according to historical data. In the following, we review some works adopting these approaches.

Regarding the approaches making static selections, we find the work by Jun et al. [13], which proposes an automatic system based on source code analysis that maps user calls to optimized kernels. Similarly, Jie Shen et al. [11] propose an analytic system for determining which hybrid programming configuration is optimal to solve a given problem. Alternatively, the approach by Rio et al. [10] presents an adaptive implementation selector that chooses, at compile time, the tuple device-implementation that delivers the best performance.

In contrast with static approaches, dynamic solutions are also widely extended in the community. A well-known runtime selector is the *versioning* scheduler [9] from the OmpSs programming framework [7]. This scheduler chooses the most appropriate task version among those marked as implementation alternatives. Another solution is the extension for the SkePu framework [6], which leverages machine learning techniques to decide which of the available versions of a given function offers the lowest execution time. Following a similar approach, the selector presented in this paper uses a novel technique based on probabilities and problem sizes that allows determining the best implementation at runtime.

3   The OmpSs Programming Model

The OmpSs programming model [3] is an effort to complement OpenMP with new directives to support asynchronous parallelism on homogeneous and heterogeneous architectures. OmpSs extends the execution and memory models of the OpenMP programming model in two main aspects. First, it leverages a runtime based on thread-pool instead of the traditional fork-join model. Second, it is designed to handle multiple physical addresses of the available processing units of a heterogeneous platform. Therefore, the runtime takes care of where the data resides and manages data transfers as tasks consume or produce them.

One of the key features of OmpSs is its support for pragma annotations in function declarations or definitions with the well-known `task` directive. With it, each time the OmpSs runtime encounters a function annotated with this directive, a worker thread will run its associated code onto one of the available processors. Furthermore, to provide heterogeneity, the `target` directive in task declaration allows specifying the processor that must run its code.

In general, the OmpSs environment is mainly built on top of two major components: the Mercurium compiler and Nanos++ runtime system. These components are described as follows:

Mercurium is a source-to-source compilation infrastructure targeted to the C, C++ and Fortran languages. The main goal of Mercurium is to detect the OmpSs pragmas and substitute them with calls to the Nanos++ runtime. The compiling phases of Mercurium are implemented as plugins, therefore new modules can be included for supporting new features. Code modifications can be performed by introducing raw source code instead of using its internal syntactic representation.

Nanos++ has been designed to serve as runtime to deal with the OmpSs programming model. Its main goal is to manage asynchronous parallelism by means of controlling data dependencies of tasks specified in the pragma-annotated source codes. A remarkable feature of Nanos++ is the multiple scheduling policies available for deciding the order of execution of tasks and the resource where the tasks will be executed. These scheduling policies are implemented as independent modules that are dynamically loaded at runtime. An example of module supporting heterogeneity is the *versioning* scheduler [9]. This module allows selecting the most appropriate implementation of a same task depending on the target device or the execution circumstances. This is enabled via the `implements` clause, which allows marking alternate implementations of a same task targeted to different processing units in a heterogeneous platform.

All in all, thanks to the flexible design and implementation of OmpSs programming framework, it is very easy to extend any of its features, like adding new directives and clauses to the OmpSs pragma annotations in the Mercurium compiler or extending the Nanos++ runtime modules with a scheduler. In the following section, we detail how we have leveraged these features to implement PRISE within this framework.

4   The Probabilistic Implementation Selector

This section introduces the probabilistic implementation selector (PRISE) as for the main contribution of this paper. Specifically, we describe how we have integrated this selector as a scheduling module into the OmpSs programming framework and detail which modifications have been required in its Mercurium compiler and Nanos++ runtime.

Figure 1 depicts the compilation and execution framework of an OmpSs application that is executed using the Nanos++ runtime along with PRISE. In a first step, the Mercurium compiler performs a source-to-source transformation of the pragma-annotated source codes and introduces the corresponding calls to the Nanos++ runtime. Then, the resulting source code is compiled with a regular C/C++ compiler, which finally generates the binary of the OmpSs application. Afterwards, during the execution, the PRISE scheduler selects an implementation each time the task is run depending on the probabilities that are calculated using historical data. These probabilities are accordingly updated by the corresponding module at the end of the application run. Finally, the probabilities and a summary of the historical data is dumped onto disk to guide future executions.

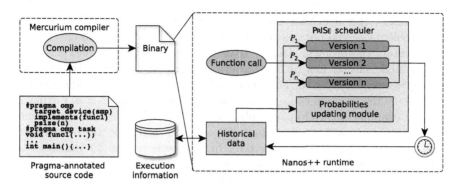

Fig. 1. Workflow from source code to execution.

In the following sections, we explain in detail the implementation selection algorithm and the probabilities updating module that have been included in the original OmpSs framework to support the new PRISE scheduler.

4.1 Implementation Selector Algorithm

The PRISE scheduler has been developed as a new module in the Nanos++ runtime. As stated in Sect. 3, the OmpSs pragmas allow specifying alternate implementations for a same task which can be selected internally by the supported scheduling modules. Specifically, this algorithm selects an alternate implementation based on the probabilities calculated for each of them. It is important to note that the weights of these probabilities depend on the version execution time and problem size. Particularly, the algorithm divides the range of problem sizes into intervals of the same length, where each might have different probabilities. With that, it uses the probabilities assigned to the interval where the input problem size belongs to.

Listing 1.1. Example of OmpSs application using different implementations.

```
1  #pragma omp target device (smp) psize (2) // The second parameter contains the problem
       size
2  #pragma omp task
3  void func(int **m, int problemSize);
4
5  #pragma omp target device (smp) implements(func)
6  #pragma omp task
7  void func_v2(int **m, int problemSize);
8
9  #pragma omp target device (smp) implements(func)
10 #pragma omp task
11 void func_v3(int **m, int problemSize);
12
13 int main() {
14   ...
15   for(int i=0; i<10; i++) {
16     func(matrix, problemSize);
17     #pragma omp taskwait
18   }
19   return 0;
20 }
```

Concretely, the algorithm takes the following steps. First, it retrieves the input problem size and obtains the probabilities of the corresponding size interval. To obtain the problem size, we have modified the Mercurium compiler in order to implement the new `psize` clause, which extends the supported clauses of the OmpSs `target` directive. This clause is basically leveraged to indicate which parameter in the function call should be used as for the problem size. Listing 1.1 shows an example of an OmpSs application where three different implementations of the function `func` are annotated as tasks using the `implements` and `psize` clauses on the `target` directive. In this code, `psize(2)` indicates the scheduler that the second parameter contains the problem size.

Next, the algorithm chooses a candidate implementation using a roulette-wheel selection approach. This approach basically divides a line segment of length $\sum_{i=0}^{N} P_i$ in subsegments whose size correspond to the probability P_i calculated for the i-th implementation. Finally, it selects an implementation depending on the location in the segment of a previously generated pseudo-random number between 0 and 1.

4.2   Probabilities Updating Module

In this section, we describe the probabilities updating module, which is in charge of recalculating, after the application run, the degree of certainty that each version provides the best performance. The computation of these probabilities is mainly based on the average execution time of the different versions. Therefore, the version having the lowest execution time will lead to a higher probability and be finally preferred by the scheduler. In order to support further explanations, Eq. 1 defines that a version A provides the best performance when its expected execution time $\mathbb{E}(A)$ is lower than any other available version in the set $\mathcal{S}$.

$$Best(A, \mathcal{S}) = \forall i \in \mathcal{S} : \mathbb{E}(A) \leq \mathbb{E}(i). \tag{1}$$

The methodology to calculate the probabilities is as follows. First of all, the confidence intervals of the available implementations are computed using the averages and standard deviations of their execution time. Next, these confidence intervals are compared among them in order to determine their probabilities. For instance, if two intervals are disjointed, the option providing the best performance has a probability of 100% of being selected. On the contrary, the probability is split between both versions. If this occurs, these versions are accordingly executed until their confidence intervals become narrow enough to avoid the overlapping. This methodology makes two general assumptions when calculating the expected execution time of a version: *(i)* it is always within the confidence interval, and *(ii)* it is distributed equally along the confidence interval, i.e., following a uniform distribution. For these reasons, the results obtained are not exact but accurate enough for our purposes.

Figure 2 shows an example of three versions (X, Y and Z) with their corresponding confidence intervals along the time axis. As observed, the three confidence intervals overlap among them in some degree. In a first step, the time

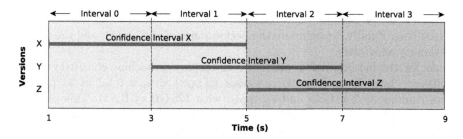

Fig. 2. Example of overlapping confidence intervals for different versions.

axis is divided into intervals that begin each time a confidence interval starts or ends. Note that in the example we obtained 4 time intervals. With this, we select those time intervals finishing at the same time or before any confidence interval, i.e., time intervals 0 and 1. This way, we can ensure that the expected execution time of the best version is within those intervals. Next, we apply the *law of total probability* in order to compute the versions probabilities by accumulating their marginal probabilities on the selected time intervals. As can be seen, the version Z does not contain any selected interval, hence, its probability is zero.

To calculate the marginal probabilities of each time interval and version, we apply again the *law of total probability* for other versions involved in the same time interval. We decompose the marginal probability into three different addends: when the expected execution time of the compared versions is lower, within or greater than the considered time interval. To illustrate the aforementioned explanation, Eqs. 2, 3, 4 calculate respectively the probability of the versions X, Y and Z, shown in Fig. 2, to be better than the rest. In these formulas, I_i denotes the i-th time interval, CI_j the confidence interval of the version j, and B_t and E_t represent the begin and the end of a given interval t. Applying these equations, we get that the highest probability is assigned to version X.

$$
\begin{aligned}
\mathbf{P}\big(Best(X, \{X, Y, Z\})\big) &= \mathbf{P}\big(Best(X, \emptyset) \mid \mathbb{E}(X) \in I_0\big)\mathbf{P}\big(\mathbb{E}(X) \in I_0\big) + \\
\mathbf{P}\big(Best(X, \{Y\}) \mid \mathbb{E}(X) \in I_1, \mathbb{E}(Y) \in I_1\big)&\mathbf{P}\big(\mathbb{E}(X) \in I_1\big)\mathbf{P}\big(\mathbb{E}(Y) \in I_1\big) + \\
\mathbf{P}\big(Best(X, \{Y\}) \mid \mathbb{E}(X) \in I_1, \mathbb{E}(Y) > I_1\big)&\mathbf{P}\big(\mathbb{E}(X) \in I_1\big)\mathbf{P}\big(\mathbb{E}(Y) > I_1\big) =
\end{aligned}
$$
$$
1 \cdot \frac{E_{I_0} - B_{I_0}}{E_{CI_X} - B_{CI_X}} + \frac{1}{2} \cdot \frac{E_{I_1} - B_{I_1}}{E_{CI_X} - B_{CI_X}} \cdot \frac{E_{I_1} - B_{I_1}}{E_{CI_Y} - B_{CI_Y}} + 1 \cdot \frac{E_{I_1} - B_{I_1}}{E_{CI_X} - B_{CI_X}} \cdot \frac{E_{CI_Y} - E_{I_1}}{E_{CI_Y} - B_{CI_Y}} = \tag{2}
$$
$$
1 \cdot \frac{3 - 1}{5 - 1} + \frac{1}{2} \cdot \frac{5 - 3}{5 - 1} \cdot \frac{5 - 3}{7 - 3} + 1 \cdot \frac{5 - 3}{5 - 1} \cdot \frac{7 - 5}{7 - 3} = \frac{28}{32} = 0.875.
$$

$$
\begin{aligned}
\mathbf{P}\big(Best(Y, \{X, Y, Z\})\big) &= \\
\mathbf{P}\big(Best(Y, \{X\}) \mid \mathbb{E}(Y) \in I_1, \mathbb{E}(X) \in I_1\big)&\mathbf{P}\big(\mathbb{E}(Y) \in I_1\big)\mathbf{P}\big(\mathbb{E}(X) \in I_1\big) = \\
\frac{1}{2} \cdot \frac{E_{I_1} - B_{I_1}}{E_{CI_Y} - B_{CI_Y}} \cdot \frac{E_{I_1} - B_{I_1}}{E_{CI_X} - B_{CI_X}} &= \frac{1}{2} \cdot \frac{5 - 3}{7 - 3} \cdot \frac{5 - 3}{5 - 1} = \frac{4}{32} = 0.125.
\end{aligned} \tag{3}
$$

$$
\mathbf{P}\big(Best(Z, \{X, Y, Z\})\big) = \mathbf{P}\big(Best(Y, \emptyset) \mid \mathbb{E}(Z) \in \emptyset\big) = 0. \tag{4}
$$

5   Evaluation

In this section, we evaluate the behavior of the PRISE scheduler using the general matrix-matrix multiplication (GEMM) as for the use case. First, we perform an evaluation of the accuracy and convergence of the selector algorithm using the GEMM case. Finally, we compare the performance of the PRISE and the OmpSs *versioning* schedulers.

As for the heterogeneous platform, we employ a machine consisting of two multi-core Intel Xeon E5-2695 processor (XEON) with a total of 24 physical cores running at 2.40 GHz and equipped with 128 GB of RAM. This platform is also equipped with two AMD Radeon GPUs, R9 290X (AMD1) and R9 285 series (AMD2), and an Intel Xeon Phi 3120 co-processor (MIC). On the other hand, the PRISE scheduler has been developed into the Mercurium compiler v2.0 and the Nanos++ runtime v0.12a, part of the OmpSs programming framework. Additionally, the source codes generated by Mercurium have been compiled with GCC 5.1 using the -O3 flag.

5.1   Analysis with the GEMM Use Case

In this section, we analyze the `dgemm` kernel performance and the selector accuracy using the implementations from the clBLAS [1] and MKL libraries on the target machine. While the clBLAS `dgemm` implementation runs on all the platform processors, the MKL implementation only runs on the XEON processor.

Figure 3 shows the accuracy progress of PRISE and the `dgemm` kernel performance rates for increasing number of training iterations. Note that the performance rates were obtained dividing the execution time of the fastest and the selected implementation. For each of these iterations, we train the system running an instance of the `dgemm` kernel using square matrices of random sizes, ranging between 64×64 and $4{,}096 \times 4{,}096$. Afterwards, we evaluate the knowledge gained by the selector performing 100 runs of the same kernel.

As can be seen in Fig. 3a, these percentages increase in a smooth curve until reaching, after 170 training iterations, roughly 99.8 % of the total accuracy. This behavior is mainly because the confidence intervals in that iteration are narrow enough, so that, on average, the selections made are already adequate. Focusing on the progress of performance rate, shown in Fig. 3b, we notice that it grows in a similar fashion than the accuracy progress. Nevertheless, each time that PRISE does not make an accurate selection, the impact in the run time is more notorious than that represented by the accuracy rate.

5.2   Comparison with an Alternative Scheduler

In this section, we compare the performance benefits of both PRISE and *versioning* OmpSs schedulers. To assess them, we developed a synthetic benchmark consisting of two consecutive 30-iteration loops that run, in each iteration, the `dgemm` kernel using square matrices of size 1,024 and random sizes, respectively.

Figure 4 depicts the execution progress of this application. As can be seen, PRISE starts from the first iteration of each loop selecting the implementations that perform best. This is because our scheduler uses an external file of historical data, which was collected during previous executions. (It is important to note

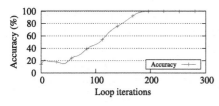
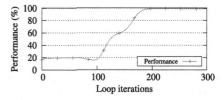

(a) Accuracy over training iterations.   (b) Performance over training iterations.

Fig. 3. Progress of the selector accuracy and performance over training iterations using the `dgemm` kernel.

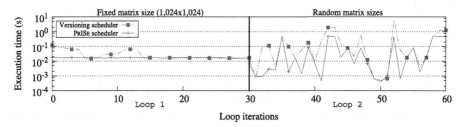

Fig. 4. Execution progress of two 30-iteration loops computing the `dgemm` kernel and using both PRISE and *versioning* schedulers.

that PRISE was previously trained performing 300 executions of the `dgemm` kernel with random matrix sizes.) On the contrary, we detect that the *versioning* scheduler does not keep any performance data among executions, so it needs a few trial runs of the different implementations until it finds the fastest one. Afterwards, the *versioning* scheduler keeps selecting the same implementation, regardless of the problem size, even if it is not the optimal. Therefore, when the matrix size varies among iterations, this scheduler is not able to self-adapt. In contrast, PRISE relies on the problem size to select the most suitable version, and thus, improves the overall performance. All in all, the presented PRISE scheduler is more adaptive and gains knowledge within application runs, while the *versioning* counterpart does not keep historical data and, therefore, needs to adapt in each execution.

6   Conclusions

In this paper, we have presented PRISE, a novel implementation selector that uses a probabilistic and profile-guided approach to choose the most appropriate implementation of a same kernel. To develop this selector we have leveraged the two main components of the OmpSs programming framework: the Mercurium compiler, to interpret a new pragma clause, and the Nanos++ runtime, to introduce a new scheduling module that implements this approach. To assess the proposed scheduler, we have evaluated its accuracy and performance using different versions of the general matrix-matrix multiplication.

Through the experimental results, we demonstrated that PRISE is able to select the fastest implementation of the `dgemm` kernel for varying square matrix sizes. We observed that the selector probabilities converges in roughly 170 training iterations and leads to sufficient accuracy and performance figures. Finally, we proved that our PRISE scheduler outperforms, in some cases, the performance delivered by the OmpSs *versioning* scheduler.

As future work, we plan to extend this approach for supporting high-level parallel patterns, such as the Pipeline and Farm constructions. Also, we intend to introduce a mechanism to update the probabilities during application run.

References

1. clBLAS, April 2015. https://github.com/clMathLibraries/clBLAS
2. Augonnet, C., Thibault, S., Namyst, R., Wacrenier, P.A.: StarPU: a unified platform for task scheduling on heterogeneous multicore architectures. Concurr. Comput.: Pract. Exper. **23**(2), 187–198 (2011)
3. Ayguadé, E., Badia, R.M., Bellens, P., Cabrera, D., Duran, A., Ferrer, R., Gonzàlez, M., Igual, F., Jiménez-González, D., Labarta, J., Martinell, L., Martorell, X., Mayo, R., Pérez, J.M., Planas, J., Quintana-Ortí, E.S.: Extending OpenMP to survive the heterogeneous multi-core era. Int. J. Parallel Prog. **38**(5), 440–459 (2010)
4. Belikov, E., Deligiannis, P., Totoo, P., Aljabri, M., Loidl, H.W.: A survey of high-level parallel programming models. Technical report, HW-MACS-TR-0103, Department of Computer Science, Heriot-Watt University, December 2013
5. Brodtkorb, A.R., Dyken, C., Hagen, T.R., Hjelmervik, J.M., Storaasli, O.O.: State-of-the-art in heterogeneous computing. Sci. Program. **18**(1), 1–33 (2010)
6. Dastgeer, U., Li, L., Kessler, C.: Adaptive implementation selection in the SkePU skeleton programming, library. In: Advanced Parallel Processing Technologies: 10th International Symposium, APPT 2013, Revised Selected Papers, Stockholm, Sweden, 27–28 August 2013, pp. 170–183 (2013)
7. Duran, A., Ayguadé, E., Badia, R.M., Labarta, J., Martinell, L., Martorell, X., Planas, J.: OmpSs: a proposal for programming heterogeneous multi-core architectures. Parallel Process. Lett. **21**, 173–193 (2011)
8. Gough, B.: GNU Scientific Library Reference Manual, 3rd edn. Network Theory Ltd., Cambridge (2009)
9. Planas, J., Badia, R.M., Ayguad, E., Labarta, J.: Self-adaptive OmpSs tasks in heterogeneous environments. In: 2013 IEEE 27th International Symposium on Parallel and Distributed Processing, pp. 138–149, May 2013
10. del Rio Astorga, D., Dolz, M.F., Sanchez, L.M., Fernández, J., García, J.D.: An adaptive offline implementation selector for heterogeneous parallel platforms. Int. J. High Perform. Comput. Appl. (2017)
11. Shen, J., Varbanescu, A., Sips, H.: Look before you leap: using the right hardware resources to accelerate applications. In: IEEE International Conference on High Performance Computing and Communications, pp. 383–391, August 2014
12. Su, L.T.: Architecting the future through heterogeneous computing. In: 2013 IEEE International Solid-State Circuits Conference Digest of Technical Papers, pp. 8–11, February 2013
13. Tan, W.J., Tang, W.T., Goh, R., Turner, S., Wong, W.F.: A code generation framework for targeting optimized library calls for multiple platforms. IEEE Trans. Parallel Distrib. Syst. **26**(7), 1789–1799 (2015)

Accelerating Processing of Scale-Free Graphs on Massively-Parallel Architectures

Mikhail Chernoskutov$^{(\boxtimes)}$

Krasovskii Institute of Mathematics and Mechanics,
Ural Federal University, Yekaterinburg, Russia
mach@imm.uran.ru

Abstract. Processing of big scale-free graphs on parallel architectures with high parallelization opportunities connected with a lot of overheads. Due to skewed degree distribution each thread receives different amount of computational workload. In this paper we present a method devoted to address this challenge by modificating CSR data structure and redistributing work across threads. The method was implemented in breadth-first search and single source shortest path algorithms for GPU architecture.

Keywords: Parallel processing · Graph algorithms · Workload balancing

1 Introduction

Graphs are a mathematical abstraction, which allows to investigate objects and links between them [9]. In particular, using the mathematical apparatus of graph theory, it is possible to explore a wide variety of systems of interrelated objects, such as neural networks in the brain [2], traffic flows in the city [7], etc. Nowadays, graph algorithms are widely used in the social networks analysis [12].

With the rapid development of computational and data storage hardware, there is also an ongoing growth in the volume of data obtained from real-world problems. At the same time, the size of graphs describing the systems of interacting objects is also growing. However, the use of parallel computations for processing large graphs involves a number of obstacles. In particular, it is known that graph algorithms are kind of "data intensive" [4] tasks. This means that the distribution of data in memory is determined by the internal structure of the data itself.

Due to the fact that real-world graphs have skewed degree distribution [1], their processing on parallel computing systems can be burdened with a large amount of overheads [10], particularly the uneven distribution of computational workload among threads (or processes). This drawback is especially acute when dealing with massively parallel computing systems, such as GPGPU accelerators. The distribution of the computational workload between thousands, and even tens of thousands of threads leads to a decrease in the amount of computations per thread. In this case, the uneven distribution of computational workload can

S. Ibrahim et al. (Eds.): ICA3PP 2017, LNCS 10393, pp. 759–765, 2017.
DOI: 10.1007/978-3-319-65482-9_61

lead to the situation when one bunch of the threads is idle, while the other works hard.

In this paper, we describe a method of workload balancing that makes it possible to accelerate the computation of graph algorithms on massively parallel computing systems (the results for the CPU and GPGPU are given). Acceleration is achieved due to the fact that the computation workload is evenly distributed between threads. The paper is organized as follows. In Sect. 2 we describe a motivating example of workload distribution during traversal of scale-free graph. In Sect. 3 we describe our method of workload balancing. We show performance results in Sect. 4 and conclude with future remarks in Sect. 5.

2   Computational Workload Distribution During Processing of Scale-Free Graphs

Parallel processing of large scale-free graphs has two key features:

- the degree of each vertex is unknown in advance and can differ significantly from one vertex to another;
- it is difficult to predict neighbors of each vertex (in comparison with, for instance, grid graphs).

Thus, relying on the two aforementioned features, it can be concluded that even in the case of uniform distribution of all the vertices among the threads, the number of all incident edges that each thread should process can be different. Moreover, with the increase in the number of threads, the relative difference in the computational workload between threads only increases. Figure 1 shows the amount of computational workload per thread during the traversal of scale-free graph with 64 threads. This graph has 8 182 vertices (2^{13}) and 18 184 edges and generated using the NetworkX system [8]. The amount of computational workload in this case is the number of edges that each thread should pass through. Even with the fact that each thread has the same number of vertices, the total number of incident edges for each thread is different in most of the cases.

In this paper, we deal with level-synchronous graph algorithms (based on bulk-synchronous model [13]). The main feature of such kind of algorithms is the fact that the iteration $N + 1$ of the algorithm can be performed if and only if the iteration N is fully complete. This computational model naturally fits into the existing parallel computing architectures, such as CPU and GPGPU.

Thus, the performance of every iteration of level-synchronous algorithms during processing of scale-free graphs depends on the processing time of the thread having the biggest number of incident edges. In the case of strong skewed degree distribution of the vertices, the performance of parallel graph algorithms may possibly be less than the performance of its sequential counterparts.

3   Method of Workload Balancing

The method presented in this section designed to balance the computational workload among threads by dissipate it between threads while processing

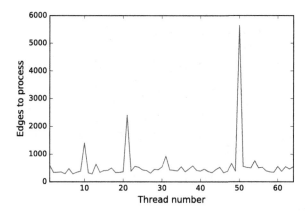

Fig. 1. Total number of incident edges for each thread for scale-free graph. Each thread has same number of vertices)

"heavyweight" vertices and, conversely, combining processing of "lightweight" vertices using a single thread.

The workload balancing method is oriented on Compress Sparse Row (CSR) graph storage format. CSR is one of the most well-known and convenient format for storing and processing *static* graphs. CSR (and its modifications) is used in various popular graph processing systems [5,6,14]. The graph representation in this format consists of several arrays:

- `row pointers` contains the offsets in the rows of the corresponding adjacency matrix;
- `column ids` contains data about the end of each edge;
- `weights` contains weights of edges.

From i to $(i+1)$ element of the `row pointers` array there are the ranges of vertex numbers in the array `column ids`, which contains outgoing edges incident to i vertex.

To avoid workload imbalance during CSR processing, we suggest a transition from "looking" through a `row pointers` array to "looking" through an `column ids` array. For this purpose, we logically divide the `column ids` array into equal pieces holding *max_edges* elements. Each thread determines the corresponding vertex for all edges in every part of the `column ids` array by using the *part_column* array, which contains the numbers of vertices incident to the first edge in the corresponding part of the `column ids` array. The pseudocode for parallel filling of the *part_column* array is presented on Fig. 2.

Pseudocode of an improved versions of breadth-first search and single source shortest path (Bellman-Ford) algorithms that uses the *part_column* array is presented on Figs. 3 and 4.

The main distinguishing feature of the modified BFS and SSSP algorithms is the limitation of the number of edges processed by single thread. As seen

```
1   parallel for each i in V.this_node
2     first := V.this_node[i]
3     last := V.this_node[i+1]
4     index := round_up(first/max_edges)
5     current := index*max_edges
6     while(current < last)
7       part_column[index] := i
8       current := current + max_edges
9       index++
```

Fig. 2. Parallel filling of *part_column* array pseudocode

```
1   // algorithm initialization ...
2   parallel for each i in part_column
3     first_edge := i*max_edges
4     last_edge := (i+1)*max_edges
5     curr_vert := part_column[i]
6     for each edge in [first_edge;last_edge)
7       if neighbors of curr_vert in [first_edge;last_edge)
8         if dist[curr_vert] = current_level
9           for each k in neighbors of curr_vert
10            if dist[k] = -1
11              dist[k] := current_level + 1
12      curr_vert++
```

Fig. 3. Parallel breadth-first search algorithm pseudocode (with workload balancing)

```
1   // preparation ...
2   for n:=1 to number_of_vertices -1
3     parallel for each i in part_column
4       first_edge := i*max_edges
5       last_edge := (i+1)*max_edges
6       curr_vert := part_column[i]
7       for each edge in [first_edge;last_edge)
8         if neighbors of curr_vert in [first_edge;last_edge)
9           for each k in neighbors of curr_vert
10            v := column_ids[k]
11            if dist[v] > dist[curr_vert] + weights[pos]
12              dist[v] := dist[curr_vert] + weights[pos]
13        curr_vert++
14  // data synchronization ...
```

Fig. 4. Parallel single source shortest path algorithm pseudocode (with workload balancing)

from line 6 in Fig. 3 and line 7 in Fig. 4, each thread processes no more than max_edges edges.

It should be noted that the use of this method in most cases results in increasing number of computational threads. However, this makes it suitable for implementation on massively parallel architectures, such as GPGPU.

4   Benchmarking

The benchmarking was carried out on a single node of the computational cluster located at the Ural Federal University (Yekaterinburg, Russia). The node is equipped with two processors Intel Xeon E5-2620 v2 and GPU accelerator Nvidia Tesla K20Xm (with 6 GB DRAM). For the development of algorithms, the ICC 16.0 compiler was used, as well as the CUDA 8.0 platform for development on GPGPU.

RMAT-graphs [3], which modeling real-world scale-free networks was used for benchmarking. RMAT-graphs can be described by two parameters (like in the Graph500 benchmark [11]):

- scale is the logarithm base 2 of the number of vertices in the graph.
- the average degree of all vertices in the graph.

Benchmarks performed for the BFS and SSSP (Bellman-Ford) algorithms with scale parameter ranging from 16 to 22 (to fit each graph into the GPGPU DRAM), and average vertex connectivity of 16 and 32 edges per vertex. As seen from the Table 1, both workload balanced implementations of algorithms demonstrate least execution time with $max\_edges = 128$. Hence, we choose $max\_edges = 128$ for subsequent computations as a best option for hardware used and as a trade-off between size of $part\_column$ array and granularity of computing.

Table 1. Execution time (in seconds) for GPGPU implementations of graph algorithms with workload balancing (for different max_edges values)

Algorithm	max_edges						
	16	32	64	128	256	512	1024
BFS	0.073	0.073	0.074	**0.064**	0.065	0.071	0.079
SSSP	2.14	2.34	1.95	**1.75**	2.48	2.38	2.59

Each of the algorithms was implemented on the CPU (using OpenMP) and on GPGPU (using CUDA). Workload balancing method was built-in in each of the algorithms on each of the architectures. The results of performance testing are shown in the Figs. 5 and 6 (each result is averaged over the five independent runs of each variation of the algorithm).

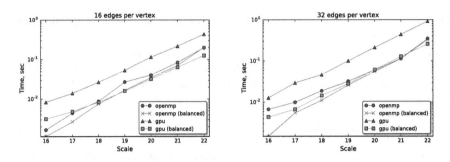

Fig. 5. Performance comparison for BFS implementations

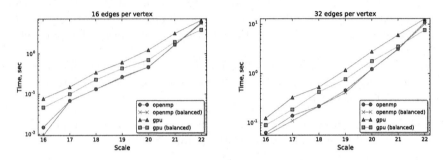

Fig. 6. Performance comparison for SSSP implementations

As seen from the figures, for both algorithms the developed method shows a steady increase in performance for the GPGPU architecture in comparison with its naive parallelization (without workload balancing). For the CPU architecture, a significant increase in performance is not observed. This is due to the fact that when using OpenMP, parallelization occurred for only 12 threads. With so few threads, the side effects of workload imbalance are not yet apparent (unlike the massively parallel GPGPU architecture). In addition, the GPGPU implementation outperforms two Intel Xeon E5-2620 v2 processors on graphs with a scale parameter equals 22 for all run configurations.

5 Conclusion

Attempts at efficient parallelization of the graph algorithms with skewed degree distribution are hampered by the workload imbalance amongst computational threads. This forms a bottleneck that makes it much more hard to make a high-performance implementation for such algorithms.

In this paper, we suggest a methods for workload balancing, which allows to increase the performance of the parallel level-synchronous breadth-first search and single-source shortest path by efficient utilization of GPGPU architecture.

In our future work, we intend to focus on the research in scalability of the suggested algorithms and testing it on RMAT graphs with bigger and graphs obtained from real-world applications. Another important task is to modify our custom implementation to use other computational architectures such as Intel MIC.

Acknowledgments. The research was supported by the Ministry of Education and Science of the Russian Federation Agreement no. 02.A03.21.0006.

References

1. Barabási, A.L., Albert, R.: Emergence of scaling in random networks. Science **286**(5439), 509–512 (1999). http://science.sciencemag.org/content/286/5439/509
2. Bullmore, E., Sporns, O.: Complex brain networks: graph theoretical analysis of structural and functional systems. Nat. Rev. Neurosci. **10**(3), 186–198 (2009)
3. Chakrabarti, D., Zhan, Y., Faloutsos, C.: R-mat: a recursive model for graph mining. In: Proceedings of the 2004 SIAM International Conference on Data Mining, pp. 442–446. SIAM (2004)
4. Chen, C.P., Zhang, C.Y.: Data-intensive applications, challenges, techniques and technologies: a survey on big data. Inf. Sci. **275**, 314–347 (2014). http://www.sciencedirect.com/science/article/pii/S0020025514000346
5. Ediger, D., Jiang, K., Riedy, E.J., Bader, D.A.: Graphct: multithreaded algorithms for massive graph analysis. IEEE Trans. Parallel Distrib. Syst. **24**(11), 2220–2229 (2013)
6. Gregor, D., Lumsdaine, A.: The parallel BGL: a generic library for distributed graph computations
7. Guimera, R., Mossa, S., Turtschi, A., Amaral, L.N.: The worldwide air transportation network: anomalous centrality, community structure, and cities' global roles. Proc. Nat. Acad. Sci. **102**(22), 7794–7799 (2005)
8. Hagberg, A.A., Schult, D.A., Swart, P.J.: Exploring network structure, dynamics, and function using networkx. In: Varoquaux, G., Vaught, T., Millman, J. (eds.) Proceedings of the 7th Python in Science Conference, Pasadena, CA USA, pp. 11–15 (2008)
9. Kepner, J., Gilbert, J.: Graph Algorithms in the Language of Linear Algebra. Society for Industrial and Applied Mathematics (2011). http://epubs.siam.org/doi/abs/10.1137/1.9780898719918
10. Lumsdaine, A., Gregor, D., Hendrickson, B., Berry, J.: Challenges in parallel graph processing. Parallel Process. Lett. **17**(01), 5–20 (2007). http://www.worldscientific.com/doi/abs/10.1142/S0129626407002843
11. Murphy, R.C., Wheeler, K.B., Barrett, B.W., Ang, J.A.: Introducing the graph 500. Cray Users Group (CUG) (2010)
12. Otte, E., Rousseau, R.: Social network analysis: a powerful strategy, also for the information sciences. J. Inf. Sci. **28**(6), 441–453 (2002). http://dx.doi.org/10.1177/016555150202800601
13. Valiant, L.G.: A bridging model for parallel computation. Commun. ACM **33**(8), 103–111 (1990). http://doi.acm.org/10.1145/79173.79181
14. Wang, Y., Davidson, A., Pan, Y., Wu, Y., Riffel, A., Owens, J.D.: Gunrock: a high-performance graph processing library on the GPU. In: Proceedings of the 21st ACM SIGPLAN Symposium on Principles and Practice of Parallel Programming, PPoPP 2016, pp. 11:1–11:12. ACM, New York (2016). http://doi.acm.org/10.1145/2851141.2851145

A Hybrid Parallel Search Algorithm for Solving Combinatorial Optimization Problems on Multicore Clusters

Victoria Sanz[1,2(✉)], Armando De Giusti[1,3], and Marcelo Naiouf[1]

[1] School of Computer Sciences, III-LIDI, National University of La Plata,
La Plata, Argentina
{vsanz,degiusti,mnaiouf}@lidi.info.unlp.edu.ar
[2] CIC, Buenos Aires, Argentina
[3] CONICET, Buenos Aires, Argentina

Abstract. Multicore clusters are widely used to solve combinatorial optimization problems, which require high computing power and a large amount of memory. In this sense, Hash Distributed A* (HDA*) parallelizes A*, a combinatorial optimization algorithm, using the MPI library. HDA* scales well on multicore clusters and on multicore machines. Additionally, there exist several versions of HDA* that were adapted for multicore machines, using the Pthreads library. In this paper, we present Hybrid HDA* (HHDA*), a hybrid parallel search algorithm based on HDA* that combines message-passing (MPI) with shared-memory programming (Pthreads) to better exploit the computing power and memory of multicore clusters. We evaluate the performance and memory consumption of HHDA* on a multicore cluster, using the 15-puzzle as a case study. The results reveal that HHDA* achieves a slightly higher average performance and uses considerably less memory than HDA*. These improvements allowed HHDA* to solve one of the hardest 15-Puzzle instances.

Keywords: Parallel search algorithms · Hybrid programming · Multicore cluster · Combinatorial optimization problems · Hash Distributed A*

1 Introduction

Several search algorithms require high computing power and a large amount of memory, thus, different parallel approaches have been proposed in order to take advantage of the resources of multicore clusters. This is the case of the A* algorithm, a variant of Best-First Search, which is used for solving combinatorial optimization problems. These problems require finding a sequence of actions that minimizes a goal function and allows transforming an initial configuration (i.e., the problem to be solved) into a final configuration (i.e., the solution).

A* [1,2] explores the graph that represents the state space of the problem using a cost function $\hat{f}$ to value the nodes, which is defined as follows: $\hat{f}(n) = g(n) + \hat{h}(n)$, where $g(n)$ is the known cost of the path from the initial

© Springer International Publishing AG 2017
S. Ibrahim et al. (Eds.): ICA3PP 2017, LNCS 10393, pp. 766–775, 2017.
DOI: 10.1007/978-3-319-65482-9_62

node to the current node n and $h(\hat{n})$ is a heuristic estimate that represents the unknown cost of the path from the current node n to the solution node. In this algorithm the search tree is generated as the search progresses. During the process, it keeps two data structures: one for the unexplored nodes sorted by $\hat{f}$ (open list), and another for the already explored nodes (closed list) used to avoid processing the same state multiple times. In each iteration, the most promising node (according to $\hat{f}$) available on the open list is removed, it is added to the closed list, and legal actions are applied to it to generate successor nodes, that will be added to the open list under certain conditions (verification known as duplicate detection). The search process continues until the node that represents the solution is removed from the open list.

Hash Distributed A* (HDA*) [3,4] is a parallel A* algorithm in which each processor has its own open/closed lists and performs a quasi-independent search. It uses a standard hash function to assign each state of the problem to a single processor. This hash-based node distribution scheme allows balancing the load and pruning duplicate nodes (i.e., nodes representing the same state) in an absolute way, as they are always sent to the same processor. This version of HDA* was implemented using the MPI library, thus, it can be run on distributed-memory, shared-memory, or hybrid systems.

Other authors [5–7] adapted HDA* for multicore machines, using the Pthreads library. In this way, it is possible to eliminate some inefficiencies that arise when the original HDA* algorithm is run on a shared-memory machine.

Since current clusters are composed of shared-memory nodes, some applications may benefit from hybrid programming, i.e. by combining message-passing (MPI) with shared-memory programming (Pthreads or OpenMP) [8,9]. To our best knowledge, no hybrid version of HDA* has been proposed until now, to better exploit the computing power and memory of multicore clusters.

In this paper, we present Hybrid HDA* (HHDA*), a hybrid MPI/Pthreads parallel search algorithm based on HDA*. We evaluate the performance and memory consumption of HHDA* on a multicore cluster, using the 15-puzzle as a case study. The results reveal that HHDA* achieves a slightly higher average performance and uses considerably less memory than HDA*. These improvements allowed HHDA* to solve one of the hardest 15-Puzzle instances.

The rest of the paper is organized as follows. Section 2 discusses background and related work. Section 3 introduces HDA* (HDA* MPI) and HDA* for shared-memory architectures (HDA* Pthreads). Section 4 describes the Hybrid HDA* algorithm. Section 5 shows our experimental evaluation. Finally, Sect. 6 presents the main conclusions and some ideas for future research.

2   Related Work

Today, many commodity clusters are composed of shared-memory machines. Applications to be run on these systems can be developed by using only message-passing or by combining message-passing with shared-memory programming (hybrid programming). While the former approach requires less programming effort, the latter may improve performance and reduce the memory used [10].

The most common and efficient way to parallelize A* is to use a decentralized strategy [11]: each process/thread (processor) is equipped with its own local open and closed lists and performs a quasi-independent search. This strategy is suitable both for shared-memory and distributed-memory architectures. However, communication among the processors is needed due to the following reasons: the workload should be distributed dynamically; duplicate nodes can be generated by different processors and should be pruned in order to prevent processors from performing duplicated work; the termination criterion should be modified because if the search is ended when the first solution is found, there will be no guarantee that such solution is the best one; the costs of the partial solutions found so far should be communicated in order to use them to prune the paths that lead to suboptimal cost solutions.

Hash Distributed A* (HDA*) [3] parallelizes A* by applying a decentralized strategy. It was implemented using only MPI and asynchronous communication. It uses a standard hash function to assign states to processors. This hash-based node distribution scheme allows balancing the load and pruning duplicate nodes in an absolute way, as the nodes representing the same state are always sent to the same processor, which performs the duplicate detection procedure. The algorithm works as follows. Periodically, each process P performs the following steps until a global optimal solution is reached: (1) P checks if a message with nodes has arrived. (2) If so, for each node, P determines if the node must be added to the open list or if it should be discarded. (3) If no messages were received, P selects a node from its open list (the one with the lowest $\hat{f}$-value). Then, P expands the node and, for each successor, it calculates the hash value to identify the owner process. If the node belongs to another process Q, P sends a message with the node to Q. To reduce the communication overhead, a given number of nodes whose recipient is the same are packed into a single message.

On the other hand, in [5] the authors adapted HDA* for multicore machines. This version does not have the extra overhead of message-passing between processors (threads) on a shared-memory architecture. Also, it uses less memory as threads share common data structures. The algorithm works as follows. Each thread is given an input queue, where the rest of the threads will deposit nodes that must be processed by this thread, and a local output queue for each peer thread. When a thread t_i generates a node that belongs to another thread t_j, t_i tries to acquire the lock associated with t_j's input queue. If the lock is obtained immediately, the node is transferred and the lock is released. Otherwise, the node is added to the local output queue for t_j. After t_i carries out a certain number of node expansions from its open list: (1) It tries to communicate the nodes stored in each non-empty output queue to the respective thread, but it is never forced to wait on a lock (2) It tries to consume nodes from its input queue (it is only forced to wait when its open list is empty).

We developed our own versions of HDA* (HDA* MPI) and HDA* for multicore machines (HDA* Pthreads), which are summarized in Sect. 3. Implementation details can be found in [4,6] respectively. The former differs from the original version in that it includes a parameter which indicates the maximum number of nodes to be processed per algorithm iteration. We noted that performance does not improve by processing one node per algorithm iteration, as done in the original version. The latter includes a technique to group several nodes before transferring them to the corresponding thread. We observed that this technique reduces the amount of node transfers and mitigates communication and contention.

From the above it can be concluded that significant efforts were made to parallelize the A* algorithm on different parallel architectures. However, neither of the known algorithms considers hybrid programming to better utilize the resources of multicore clusters. It should be noted that, although in [12] a hybrid parallel algorithm is presented for solving combinatorial problems, the parallelization is based on the Weighted A* algorithm (a suboptimal version of A* that trades-off solution quality for search time). However, Hybrid HDA* is based on the A* algorithm and it aims to find optimal solutions.

3   Implementation of the HDA* Algorithms

3.1   HDA* (HDA* MPI)

Each process carries out an A* search locally and communicates with its peers for sending/receiving messages containing nodes, the costs of solutions found and messages that allow detecting termination.

Each process maintains its own open/closed lists, the cost of the best global solution known so far (*best_solution_cost*), the best solution found by the process (*best_solution*), among others. In order to pack several nodes into a single message, the process is equipped with a buffer (*send_buffer*) for each peer process.

Each process P performs the following stages until a global optimal solution is reached:

1. Work message reception stage: P checks if *work messages* containing nodes have arrived. If so, P receives each message and, for each node with $\hat{f} < best\_solution\_cost$, it performs the duplicate detection and adds the node to the open list as appropriate.
2. Cost message reception stage: P checks if *cost messages* containing the cost of a solution have arrived. If so, P receives the messages and updates *best_solution_cost* as appropriate.
3. Processing stage: P extracts nodes from its open list, discarding those with $\hat{f} >= best\_solution\_cost$. When the extracted node represents a solution, P updates *best_solution* and *best_solution_cost* and sends the solution cost to the other processes. Otherwise, P adds the node to its closed list and expands the node. Then, for each successor, P calculates the hash value to determine the owner process. When the successor belongs to P, it adds the node to its open list as appropriate. Otherwise, P adds the node to the *send_buffer* for the destination process and, if the buffer became full, it sends the *work message* asynchronously.

4. Idle stage: P enters this stage when its open list is empty. Firstly, it sends *work messages* to those destination processes whose *send_buffer* is non-empty. Then, it remains waiting for: (1) work messages, (2) cost messages, (3) messages that allow detecting termination. P ends this stage when its open list is non-empty, as a result of having received a *work message*, or when it receives the *termination notification message*. Messages of types (1) and (2) are processed in a similar way as described above; messages of type (3) are processed based on Dijkstra's termination detection algorithm [13].

When computation ends, the optimal solution (i.e. the sequence of actions that allows transforming the initial state into the final state) is retrieved in a distributed manner.

3.2 HDA* for Multicore Machines (HDA* Pthreads)

Each thread has its own open/closed lists. The node communication strategy is based on the use of input/output queues. All threads share the best global solution found so far (*best_solution*), its cost (*best_solution_cost*), among others.

Each thread t_i performs the following stages until a global optimal solution is reached:

1. Work reception stage: t_i tries to consume nodes from its input queue. If it obtains the lock immediately, it takes all the nodes stored in the queue, releases the lock, and then for each node with $\hat{f} < best\_solution\_cost$, t_i performs the duplicate detection procedure adding the node to the open list as appropriate.
2. Processing stage: the main difference with HDA* MPI is the way in which nodes are communicated between threads. When t_i generates a node that belongs to another thread t_j, it stores the node in the local output queue for t_j; when the amount of stored nodes reaches a certain limit, t_i tries to acquire the lock associated with t_j's input queue and, if it obtains the lock immediately, it transfers the stored nodes.
3. Idle stage: t_i enters this stage when its open list is empty. Firstly, it transfers the nodes stored in each non-empty output queue. Then, it remains waiting until it receives work or it receives a termination notification from the master thread (to this end, we adapted Dijkstra's termination detection algorithm for shared-memory machines [6]).

When computation ends, the optimal solution is retrieved by the master thread.

4   Hybrid HDA* (HHDA*)

Hybrid HDA* (HHDA*) is based on the HDA* algorithm and its version for multicore machines. HHDA* assigns only one process per machine. Each process (master thread) creates threads that will perform the search procedure, along with the master thread. The proposed algorithm uses communication via shared-variables, among threads on the same machine, and communication via message-passing, among processes on different machines.

All threads on the same machine share the best solution found locally by these threads (*best_solution*), the cost of the best global solution known so far (*best_solution_cost*), among others.

Each thread has: its own open/closed lists, a global input queue, an output queue for each peer thread on the machine, message buffers for inter-process communication, among others.

Each thread t_i performs the following stages until a global optimal solution is reached:

1. Message reception stage: any thread on the machine can receive messages addressed to its process, containing either (1) nodes or (2) the cost of a solution found. In the first case, for each received node, t_i identifies the owner thread and, depending on whether the node belongs to t_i or not (a) it carries out the duplicate detection and adds the node to its open list (as appropriate) or (b) it stores the node in the local output queue for the destination thread. In the second case, t_i updates *best_solution_cost*, as appropriate.
2. Work reception stage (from the input queue): the thread checks the state of its input queue, in order to consume the nodes left by other threads, as in HDA* Pthreads.
3. Processing stage: the main difference with HDA* MPI and HDA* Pthreads is the way in which nodes are communicated among threads. When a generated node belongs to another thread on the same machine, the node is communicated via shared-memory, using input/output queues, as in HDA* Pthreads. When a generated node belongs to a thread running on a different machine, the node is communicated via message-passing. In the last case, each thread has a send buffer for each process in the system, where nodes that must be communicated are stored, as in HDA* MPI.
4. Idle stage: t_i enters this stage when its open list is empty. Firstly, it transfers the nodes stored in each non-empty output queue and each non-empty send buffer to its owner thread/process, via shared-memory or message-passing, respectively. Then, t_i remains waiting until it receives nodes in its input queue or it receives a termination notification from the master thread. The master thread behaves differently: when it detects local termination (i.e., on the machine, using Dijkstra's termination detection algorithm for shared-memory machines [6]), it will wait for: (1) work messages (2) cost messages (3) messages that allow detecting global termination. Messages of types (1) and (2) are processed in a similar way as described above; messages of type (3) are processed based on Dijkstra's termination detection algorithm [13].

When computation ends, the master thread on each machine remains active. Together, they will retrieve the optimal solution in a distributed manner.

5   Experimental Results

Experimental tests were carried out on a cluster composed of 7 machines connected through 1 GB Ethernet. Each machine has two Intel Xeon E5620 processors and 32 GB RAM. Each processor has four 2.4 Ghz physical cores.

The tests considered sixteen 15-Puzzle instances presented in [14] (numbered 3, 15, 17, 21, 26, 32, 33, 49, 53, 56, 59, 60, 66, 82, 88, 100) and six of the 10 configurations proposed by [15] (numbered 101–106 in this paper). These configurations present different levels of complexity.

A* was run on a single machine of the previous cluster. HDA* MPI and HHDA* were run on the cluster, varying the number of machines used between 2 and 7. In HDA* MPI, 4 processes/workers were assigned to each machine. In HHDA*, 1 process (master thread) was assigned to each machine, each one will create 3 threads (4 threads/workers per machine).

In this section, we compare the performance achieved (speedup and efficiency[1]) and the amount of memory consumed by HDA* MPI and HHDA*.

5.1   Performance Analysis

Figures 1a and b illustrate the average Speedup and the average Efficiency achieved by HDA* MPI and HHDA*, for different number of workers. The results reveal that, on average, the speedup of HHDA* is similar for 8 and 12 workers, and slightly better for 16, 20, 24 and 28 workers, compared to HDA* MPI. Also, HHDA* exhibits an almost constant average Efficiency, which ranges between 0.71 and 0.73, whereas HDA* MPI shows a decreasing average Efficiency, with values ranging between 0.64 and 0.74.

To clarify the improvement in the performance of HHDA*, Figs. 2a and b show the average Search Overhead (SO) and the average Load Balance (LB)

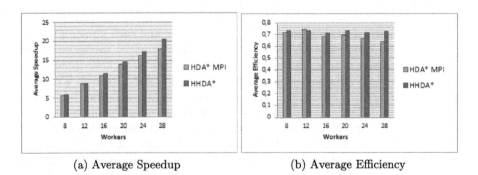

(a) Average Speedup   (b) Average Efficiency

Fig. 1. Performance of HDA* MPI and HHDA*

---

[1] Efficiency is defined as Sp/N, where Sp is the speedup of the parallel algorithm over the sequential algorithm and N is the number of workers/cores used.

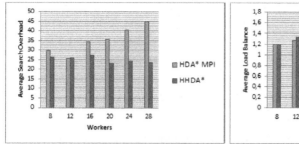

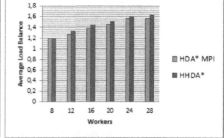

(a) Average Search Overhead   (b) Average Load Balance

Fig. 2. Search Overhead and Load Balance of HDA* MPI and HHDA*

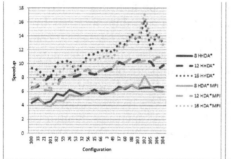

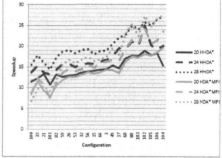

(a) Speedup for 8, 12 and 16 workers   (b) Speedup for 20, 24 and 28 workers

Fig. 3. Speedup of HDA* MPI and HHDA*, sorted by problem complexity

achieved by HDA* MPI and HHDA*, for different number of workers. The definitions of SO and LB can be found in [3]. In general, the results show that HDA* MPI exhibits a higher average SO, compared to HHDA*, which augments as the number of workers increases, and ranges between 29% and 44%. However, HHDA* presents an almost constant average SO, which varies between 23% and 27%. SO arises as a side effect of using multiple inconsistent open lists in a parallel A* algorithm. Since each worker performs a local A*, the nodes expanded by a worker do not necessary represent a global best selection. This occurs because the access to global knowledge is restricted. This, however, has less impact on HHDA*, because threads on the same machine share *best_solution_cost*. When a thread finds a solution or receives a cost message, it updates *best_solution_cost*, so threads on the same machine immediately know this information and use it to prune nodes. Consequently, in HHDA*, the last iterations of the search explore less nodes, compared to HDA* MPI. On the other hand, the average LB is similar for both algorithms.

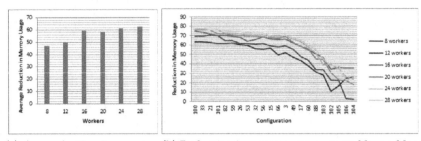

(a) Avg reduction in memory   (b) Reduction in memory usage, sorted by problem
usage   complexity

Fig. 4. Reduction in memory consumption: HHDA* vs HDA* MPI

In order to determine the improvement in the performance of HHDA* by
problem complexity, Figs. 3a and b illustrate the Speedup obtained by both
algorithms, for different number of workers and instances (sorted by complexity). As it can be observed, when the problem scales up and the number of
workers remains constant, similar values of speedup are obtained for 8 and 12
workers. However, for 16, 20, 24, and 28 workers, HHDA* performs better for
some instances. Furthermore, as the number of workers increases, the number of
instances which are solved more efficiently by HHDA* increases. Similar conclusions for Efficiency were reached. We observed that a lower SO is obtained by
HHDA* for these instances and workers.

5.2 Memory Consumption Analysis

Figure 4a shows the average reduction in memory usage for HHDA*, with respect
to HDA* MPI. We observe that the average reduction ranges between 46% and
62%, and it augments as the number of workers increases. Figure 4b illustrates
the reduction in memory usage for each instance (sorted by complexity). As it can
be seen, when the number of workers is constant, a higher reduction is achieved
for the easier instances, and the reduction decreases as the problem scales up.
In general, for hard instances, the reduction ranges between 20% and 40%.

The reduction in memory requirements for HHDA* over HDA* MPI allowed
solving one of the hardest 15-Puzzle instances[2], presented in [16]. HHDA* solved
this instance using 7 machines (224 GB RAM) and 28 workers. A* (1 machine,
32 GB RAM) and HDA* MPI (7 machines, 224 GB RAM, 28 workers) did not
solve this instance since both algorithms ran out of memory.

6 Conclusions and Future Work

In this paper we presented HHDA*, a hybrid MPI/Pthread version of the HDA*
algorithm for solving combinatorial problems. We compared the performance

---

[2] 15 14 13 12 10 11 8 9 2 6 5 1 3 7 4 0.

achieved and the amount of memory consumed by HDA* (pure MPI) and HHDA* (MPI/Pthreads). The results revealed that HHDA* achieves a slightly higher performance and consumes less memory, compared to HDA* (pure MPI). These improvements allowed HHDA* to solve one of the hardest 15-Puzzle instances.

As for future work, we plan to parallelize suboptimal search algorithms using our hybrid parallelization strategy.

References

1. Hart, P., et al.: A formal basis for the heuristic determination of minimum cost paths. IEEE Trans. Syst. Sci. Cybern. **4**(2), 100–107 (1968)
2. Russel, S., Norvig, P.: Artificial Intelligence: A Modern Approach, 2nd edn. Prentice Hall, Upper Saddle River (2003)
3. Kishimoto, A., et al.: Evaluation of a simple, scalable, parallel best-first search strategy. Artif. Intell. **195**, 222–248 (2013)
4. Sanz, V., et al.: Scalability analysis of Hash Distributed A* on commodity cluster: results on the 15-puzzle problem. In: Proceedings of PDPTA 2016, 221–230. CSREA Press, Georgia (2016)
5. Burns, E., et al.: Best-first heuristic search for multicore machines. J. Artif. Intell. Res. **39**(1), 689–743 (2010)
6. Sanz, V., et al.: On the optimization of HDA* for multicore machines. Performance analysis. In: Proceedings of PDPTA 2014, pp. 625–631. CSREA Press, Georgia (2014)
7. Sanz, V., et al.: Performance tuning of the HDA* algorithm for multicore machines. In: Computer Science and Technology Series 2015. EDULP, La Plata (2015)
8. Chow, E., et al.: Assessing performance of hybrid MPI/OpenMP programs on SMP clusters. Technical report, UCRL-JC-143957. Lawrence Livermore National Laboratory, California (2001)
9. Rabenseifner, R., et al.: Hybrid MPI, OpenMP parallel programming on clusters of multi-core SMP nodes. In: Proceedings of PDP 2009, pp. 427–436. IEEE Computer Society, Washington, D.C. (2009)
10. Hager, G., et al.: Introduction to High Performance Computing for Scientists and Engineers, 1st edn. CRC Press, Boca Raton (2010)
11. Kumar, V., et al.: Parallel best-first search of state-space graphs: a summary of results. In: Proceedings of AAAI 1988, pp. 122–127. AAAI Press, California (1988)
12. Vidal, V., et al.: Parallel AI planning on the SCC. In: 4th Many-Core Applications Research Community (MARC) Symposium, pp. 15–20. Postdam University Press (2011)
13. Dijkstra, E.W.: Shmuel Safra's version of termination detection. EWD-Note 998. Department of Computer Sciences, University of Texas, Austin (1987)
14. Korf, R.: Depth-first iterative-deepening: an optimal admissible tree search. Artif. Intell. **27**(1), 97–109 (1985)
15. Brüngger, A.: Solving hard combinatorial optimization problems in parallel: two cases studies. Ph.D. thesis, ETH Zurich, Dissertation ETH No. 12358 (1998)
16. Brüngger, A., et al.: The parallel search bench ZRAM and its applications. Ann. Oper. Res. **90**, 45–63 (1999)

Concurrent Treaps

Praveen Alapati$^{(\boxtimes)}$, Swamy Saranam, and Madhu Mutyam

Indian Institute of Technology Madras, Chennai, Tamil Nadu, India
{praveena,srswamy,madhu}@cse.iitm.ac.in

Abstract. We propose algorithms to perform operations concurrently on treaps in a shared memory multi-core and multi-processor environment. Concurrent treaps hold the advantage of nodes' priority for maintaining height of treaps. Concurrent treaps make use of logical ordering and physical ordering of nodes' keys, and pessimistic locking mechanism to achieve synchronization. We observe that our concurrent treap implementations scale well as compared to the state-of-the-art implementations. We also study the impact of different locking objects on throughput of concurrent treaps. Our experimental results show that the concurrent treap implementation that uses *AtomicInteger* locking object provides better throughput and utilizes less memory footprint.

Keywords: Concurrent data structures · Trees · Treaps

1 Introduction and Related Work

Importance of scalable and efficient concurrent data structures is increasing with growth in the area of multi-core and multi-processors [20]. The ease of performing concurrent operations is heavily dependent on the type of data structure. For example, concurrent operations on data structures like linked lists and hash tables are easier than performing them on structures like binary search trees (BSTs) and AVL trees. Most frequently used data structures in sequential context are BSTs and its variations. Simple and efficient algorithms to perform basic operations, such as *insert()*, *delete()*, and *contains()*, on concurrent binary search trees are useful for developers, that require a concurrent tree-like structure.

The lock based AVL-tree implementation of a BST, proposed by Drachsler et al. [10], maintains strict height balancing. Though the update operation (*insert()* or *delete()*) is local to a few nodes, balancing the height is global. Strict height balancing condition on each update operation creates contention on the tree. A contention friendly tree proposed in [9] is a partially external concurrent binary search tree (CBST). It runs an explicit thread to remove the logically deleted nodes and balance the height of the tree. This method is not always effective, for example, for sorted input distributions, height of the tree increases linearly with the number of nodes, leading to performance degradation. The search operation on CBST suggested by Bronson et al. [8] needs a hand-over-hand optimistic validation, which impacts performance as the size of the

© Springer International Publishing AG 2017
S. Ibrahim et al. (Eds.): ICA3PP 2017, LNCS 10393, pp. 776–790, 2017.
DOI: 10.1007/978-3-319-65482-9_63

tree increases. Afek et al. [5] explained a counting based self adjusting binary search tree, that is built using Bronson et al. [8] implementation. Though concurrency is often managed through locks, few lock-free implementations of binary search trees are also available in the literature [11,17,18].

Ellen et al. [11] proposed an external unbalanced CBST. External trees consume more storage space as compared to that of internal trees and also have a high average access path length in successful searches, leading to further impact on performance for large trees. A fast CBST suggested by Natarajan and Mittal [17] is also an external CBST and it does not maintain height balance. An alternative to lock-free implementations of BSTs is a lock-free skiplist [18]. Even though an update operation on the skiplist is performed in logarithmic time, a thread has to update nodes at different levels, which results in performance degradation.

From the literature we observe that: (i) for high contention workloads, the strict height balancing condition of AVL trees affects concurrency negatively. Because while performing an update operation, the number of rotations is proportional to the height of a tree [21], this causes for a change in the structure of the tree and affects all the other threads working in that vicinity; (ii) Unbalanced CBST implementations suffer with skewness for sorted inputs. To overcome the problems of the existing implementations, a treap data structure can be a better candidate of interest.

Treap [6] is a collection of nodes and each node contains a key and a priority. Treap satisfies two properties: (i) binary search tree (BST) property, and (ii) heap order property. BST property states that for every node X, the key of X is greater than all the keys in the left subtree of X, and it is less than all the keys in the right subtree of X. Heap order property states that for every node X, the priority of X is maximal (minimal) of its children. The priority of nodes' is used for maintaining the height balance in a treap and no need to maintain strict height balancing condition at each internal node. Treap height is $\mathcal{O}(\log n)$ (with high probability), where n is the number of nodes in a treap. In the expected case, an update operation on a treap requires less than two rotations [6]. For treaps, the expected time complexity of the basic operations such as *insert()*, *delete()*, and *contains()* is $\mathcal{O}(\log n)$, where n is the number of nodes in a treap. In this paper, we propose algorithms to perform the basic operations concurrently on treaps.

In concurrent implementations, synchronization provides a solution to update the shared data using multiple threads without any data races [13]. Synchronization objects for the state-of-the-art concurrent data structure implementations

Table 1. Synchronization objects for different state-of-the-art implementations.

Synchronization object	Implementations
ReentrantLock	CVM tree [9], DVY tree [10]
synchronized keyword	BCCO tree [8]
AtomicReferenceFieldUpdater	EFRB tree [11], Skiplist [15]

are shown in Table 1. Lock-free skiplist [15] and EFRB tree [11] are implemented using *AtomicReferenceFieldUpdater*. Lock based CBSTs [8–10] are implemented using either *ReentrantLock* or *synchronized* keyword. *ReentrantLock* is a kind of lock using that a thread can lock a particular node any number of times [3]. In [9,10], concurrent binary search trees are implemented using *ReentrantLocks*. Drachsler et al. [10] use two *ReentrantLock* objects per node: (i) to acquire a lock on a node using tree ordering, and (ii) to acquire a lock on a node using logical ordering. Bronson et al. [8] use a *synchronized* keyword to provide synchronization among multiple threads while executing a code block [1].

In this paper, we first discuss algorithms for concurrent implementation of treaps using two *ReentrantLock* objects per node (2-RL). Result analysis shows that, our 2-RL based concurrent treap implementation provides better throughput as compared to that of the state-of-the-art implementations. The 2-RL implementation achieves average speedup of 1.25×, 1.31×, 1.4×, 3.5×, and 1.31×, respectively, as compared to the state-of-the-art implementations, DVY tree [10], BCCO tree [8], CVM tree [9], Skiplist [15], and EFRB tree [11]. Further, we explore two other implementations of concurrent treaps: (i) using one *ReentrantLock* object per node (1-RL), and (ii) using one *AtomicInteger* object per node (1-AI). We observe that the 1-AI implementation provides better throughput and has smaller memory footprint as compared to the remaining concurrent treap implementations.

Note that Blelloch et al. [7] discussed concurrent treaps to perform *union*, *join* and *intersection* operations, whereas our work considers *insert*, *delete*, and *contains* on treaps.

2   Background

Treap [6] is a kind of search tree that satisfies both the BST property and the heap order property. Treap for the set of (key, priority) pairs: {(D, 31), (E, 15), (M, 55), (N, 45), (T, 65), (V, 41), (Z, 54)} is shown in Fig. 1(a). An *insert* operation on a treap is performed in two steps: (i) a node is inserted into the treap using the BST property, and (ii) the newly inserted node checks for heap order property, if the heap order property is not satisfied, single rotations are performed until the property is satisfied. To insert a node: (W, 60), into a treap as shown in Fig. 1(a), first the node is inserted using the BST property, shown in Fig. 1(b). Now the newly inserted node results in violation of the heap order property. To satisfy the property, first a left rotation is applied on this node followed by a right rotation, shown in Fig. 1(c) and (d), respectively. In Fig. 1(d), all the nodes satisfy both the properties of a treap.

To remove a node: (M, 55), first the node that has the key value M is searched using the BST property. If the node exists, it is deleted logically, shown in Fig. 1(e). If the logically deleted node has two children, the maximum priority child is pushed as the root of the subtree by performing appropriate single rotations. The above step is repeated until the logically deleted node has only one child. If the logically deleted node has only one child, it is deleted physically by updating its child. The resultant treap is shown in Fig. 1(f).

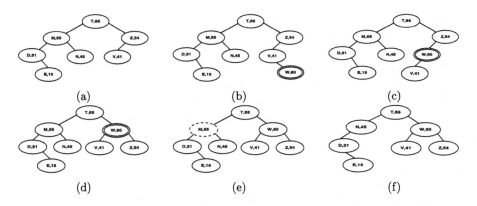

Fig. 1. Operations on treaps: an insert (b, c, d) followed by a delete (e, f).

While implementing the algorithms for concurrent treaps, we use the concept of logical ordering, as discussed in [10]. In the logical ordering, the nodes are ordered based on respective keys. For example, the logical ordering of the nodes of the treap (i.e., in-order traversal of the treap), shown in Fig. 1(f) is: (D, 31), (E, 15), (N, 45), (T, 65), (V, 41), (W, 60), (Z, 54). Every node in the logical ordering has a unique predecessor and a unique successor. The predecessor and successor relationships among the nodes are useful when multiple threads are performing operations on the nodes of a treap concurrently.

3   Concurrent Treaps

In this section we present fields of a concurrent treap node, sketch on synchronization, and algorithms to perform the basic operations on a concurrent treap.

Fields of a typical concurrent treap node are shown in Table 2. The **key** is immutable and it is used to store an item in a node. The **priority** field is used to assign priority to a node. The fields **transit1** and **transit2** are used to identify the nodes that are in transit phase of insertion and deletion, respectively. If a node is in the transit phase, the corresponding boolean value is set to **true**. The **mark** field of a node is set to **true** just before the node is going to be deleted physically from the tree. The fields **left**, **right**, and **parent** contain the addresses

Table 2. Fields of a concurrent treap node.

```
class TreapNode {
final K key
final int priority
volatile boolean transit1, transit2, mark
volatile TreapNode  left, right, parent, pred, succ
ReentrantLock succLock, treeLock
}
```

of left subtree, right subtree, and parent of a node, respectively. The fields `pred` and `succ` contain the addresses of predecessor and successor nodes, respectively. The fields `succLock` and `treeLock` are ReentrantLocks. ReentrantLock is a kind of lock that enables a thread to lock a particular node any number of times [3]. A `succLock` is used to protect the `pred` and `succ` fields of a node. A `treeLock` is used to modify `left`, `right`, and `parent` fields of a node. As two reentrant locks are used, we consider the implementation as 2-reentrant lock (2-RL) based concurrent treap implementation.

3.1   Sketch on Synchronization

While performing update operations on a treap, threads achieve synchronization by applying locks at node level. During locking phase, the threads make use of two layouts: (i) logical ordering layout, and (ii) treap physical layout. Logical ordering layout is achieved using the `pred` and `succ` fields of the TreapNode class. Treap physical layout is formed using the `left`, `right`, and `parent` fields of the TreapNode class. A thread performs an update operation using four steps: (i) acquire locks using the logical ordering, (ii) acquire locks using a treap physical structure, (iii) update the logical ordering layout and release the locks acquired using the logical ordering, and (iv) update the physical structure and release the locks acquired using the physical layout.

   To find a required treap node using lookup operation, first a thread traverses using a physical layout of a treap. During this process it may stray from its path due to concurrent updates of other threads. Later, the thread uses the logical ordering layout to identify the required node. Because different physical layouts for a set of treap nodes will have one logical ordering layout [10] and if a thread traverses using the logical ordering, it does not stray from its path due to the mutations from other threads. So, a lookup operation can proceed along with other operations without need for acquiring any locks.

3.2   Operations on a Concurrent Treap

The following subsections deal with algorithms to perform basic operations on a concurrent treap using 2-RL implementation.

3.2.1   Contains( ) Operation

Algorithm 1 explains *contains(x)* operation and returns `true` if x is found in a treap and `false`, otherwise. Initially, a thread calls *search(x)* method to identify a treap node that consists of key x with the help of a treap physical layout. If the required treap node exists, the *search(x)* returns that node otherwise returns a treap node (*tnode*) where it is terminated. If *tnode.key* is not equal to x, the thread uses the logical ordering layout (i.e., lines 3–8) to find a treap node with the required `key`. Finally, if *tnode.key* is equal to x and *tnode.transit2* is `false`, the thread returns `true`.

Algorithm 1. contains(x)

```
1: tnode ← search(x)
2: if (tnode.key ! = x) then
3:     while tnode.key > x do
4:         tnode ← tnode.pred
5:     end while
```

```
6:     while tnode.key < x do
7:         tnode ← tnode.succ
8:     end while
9: end if
10: return ((tnode.key=x) and
        !(tnode.transit2))
```

3.2.2   Insert( ) Operation

Algorithm 2 explains *insert()* operation on a treap and returns `true` on successful insert and `false`, otherwise. To insert a new node with (`key`, `priority`): (x, pri) into a treap, first a thread calls *search(x)*, that returns a treap node (*tnode*). The thread identifies a predecessor (p) of x using *tnode* and locks p using `succLock`. The thread identifies whether the treap consists of x or not. If x does not exist in the treap, the thread locks *tnode* using `treeLock` and inserts a new treap node (x, *pri*) using Algorithm 3, otherwise the thread releases the lock on the predecessor and returns `false`.

Algorithm 3: *insertIntoTreap(p, tnode, x, pri)* returns `true` on successful insertion and `false`, otherwise. A thread inserts a new treap node (x, *pri*) by updating the logical ordering layout followed by the physical ordering layout of the treap. If no other concurrent thread is inserting a new node either as a left child of *tnode* or a right child of *tnode* (i.e. satisfies condition at line 2 of Algorithm 3), the thread inserts the new treap node. Finally, the thread calls Algorithm 4: *adjustHeap(tnode)*, to push the newly inserted treap node to the appropriate level with the help of left or right single rotations to

Algorithm 2. insert(x, pri)

```
1: while (true) do
2:     tnode ← search(x)
3:     parent ← tnode.parent
4:     if tnode.key ≥ x then
5:         p ← tnode.pred
6:     else
7:         p ← tnode
8:     end if
9:     if (!p.trySuccLock()) then
10:         repeat //starts from the while loop
11:     end if
12:     s←p.succ
13:     if (p.transit2) or (s.mark) then
14:         unLock(p)
15:         repeat
16:     end if
17:     if ((x > p.key) and (x ≤ s.key)) then
18:         if (x = s.key) then
19:             unLock(p)
20:             return false
21:         end if
```

```
22:         if (!tnode.tryTreeLock()) then
23:             unLock(p)
24:             repeat
25:         end if
26:         if (tnode.transit1) or (tnode.transit2)
            or (parent! =tnode.parent) then
27:             unLock(p,tnode)
28:             repeat
29:         end if
30:         flag ← insertIntoTreap(p,tnode, x,pri)
31:         if (flag = true) then
32:             return true
33:         else
34:             unLock(p, tnode)
35:         end if
36:     end if
37:     unLock(p)
38:     repeat
39: end while
```

Algorithm 3. insertIntoTreap(p, tnode, x, pri)

1: s ← p.succ	9: **if** (x < tnode.key) **then**
2: **if** ((x < tnode.key **and** tnode.left = null)	10: tnode.left ← newTNode
or (x > tnode.key **and** tnode.right = null))	11: **else**
then	12: tnode.right ← newTNode
3: newTNode ← new Node(x,pri)	13: **end if**
4: newTNode.parent ← tnode	14: unLock(p, tnode)
5: newTNode.succ ← s	15: adjustHeap(newTNode)
6: newTNode.pred ← p	16: **return true**
7: s.pred ← newTNode	17: **end if**
8: p.succ ← newTNode	18: **return false**

Algorithm 4. adjustHeap(tnode)

1: **while** (true) **do**	25: **if** !tnRight.tryTreeLock() **then**
2: tnParentParent ← tnode.parent.parent	26: unLock(tnParentParent,
3: **if** (!tnParentParent.tryTreeLock()) **then**	tnParent, tnode)
4: repeat //starts from the while loop	27: repeat
5: **end if**	28: **end if**
6: tnParent ← tnode.parent	29: **if** (tnRight ≠ tnode.right) **or**
7: **if** (tnParentParent.mark **or**	(tnRight.mark) **or**
!tnParent.tryTreeLock()) **then**	(tnRightParent ≠ tnode) **then**
8: unLock(tnParentParent)	30: unLock(tnParentParent,
9: repeat	tnParent, tnode, tnRight)
10: **end if**	31: repeat
11: **if** (tnParent.transit1 **or** tnParent.transit2	32: **end if**
or !tnode.tryTreeLock()) **then**	33: flag=true
12: unLock(nParentParent, nParent)	34: **end if**
13: repeat	35: singleRotateRight(tnParent,tnode)
14: **end if**	36: **if** (flag=true) **then**
15: **if** (tnParentParent≠tnode.parent.parent) **or**	37: unLock(tnParent.left)
(tnParent≠tnode.parent) **then**	38: **end if**
16: unLock(tnParentParent, tnParent, tnode)	39: **else**
	40: Symmetric to tnode.right
17: repeat	41: **end if**
18: **end if**	42: unLock(tnParentParent, tnParent, tnode)
19: **if** (tnParent.pri ≤ tnode.pri) **then**	43: **else**
20: boolean flag ← false	44: tnode.transit1 ← false
21: **if** (tnParent.left = tnode) **then**	45: unLock(tnParentParent, tnParent, tnode)
22: **if** tnode.right ≠ null **then**	46: break
23: tnRight ← tnode.right	47: **end if**
24: tnRightParent ← tnode.	48: **end while**
right.parent	

---

satisfy the heap order property. Using Algorithm 4, a thread acquires locks on few treap nodes while performing rotations to prevent concurrent updates on **left**, **right**, and **parent** fields of treap nodes. To perform a rotation between a treap node (*tnode*) and it's parent (*tnode.parent*), the thread has to acquire locks on *tnode.parent.parent*, *tnode.parent*, and *tnode*, respectively. If a thread acquires locks on required treap nodes, it performs an appropriate single rotation. In the lock acquisition process, if a thread fails to acquire any lock, it releases all the acquired locks and repeats the lock acquisition process.

Algorithm 5. delete(x)

```
1: while (true) do                             33:     else if (child = tnode.right) and
2:     tnode ← search(x)                                (child.left ≠ null) then
3:     if tnode.key = x then                   34:         tnodeChild ← child.left
4:         p ← tnode.pred                       35:     end if
5:     else                                     36:     if (child = tnode.left) then
6:         p ← tnode                            37:         singleRotateRight(tnode,
7:     end if                                            tnode.left)
8:     if (!p.trySuccLock()) then              38:     else
9:         repeat  //starts from the while loop  39:         singleRotateLeft(tnode,
10:    end if                                            tnode.right)
11:    if (p.mark) then                        40:     end if
12:        unLock(p)                            41:     if (tnodeChild ≠ null) then
13:        repeat                               42:         unLock(tnodeChild)
14:    end if                                   43:     end if
15:    s ← p.succ                               44:     unLock(tnode.parent.parent,
16:    if ((x > p.key) and (x ≤ s.key)) then            tnode.parent, tnode)
17:        if (s.key > x) then                  45:     flag ← acquireTreeLocks(tnode)
18:            unLock(p)                         46: else
19:            return false                      47:     tnode.mark ← true
20:        end if                                48:     sSucc ← s.succ
21:        if (!s.trySuccLock()) then           49:     sSucc.pred ← p
22:            unLock(p)                         50:     p.succ ← sSucc
23:            repeat                            51:     unLock(p, s)
24:        end if                                52:     removeFromTreap(tnode)
25:        s.transit2 ← true                    53:     return true
26:        tnode ← s                            54: end if
27:        boolean flag←acquireTreeLocks(tnode) 55:     end while
28:        while (flag) do                      56:     if !flag then
29:            if (tnode.left ≠ null) and       57:         unLock(p,s)
               (tnode.right ≠ null) then        58:         repeat
30:                child ← maxPriorityNode(     59:     end if
                   tnode.left, tnode.right)     60: end if
31:                if (child = tnode.left) and  61: unLock(p)
                   (child.right ≠ null) then    62: end while
32:                    tnodeChild ← child.right;
```

3.2.3   Delete( ) Operation

Algorithm 5 explains *delete()* operation on a concurrent treap. It returns **true**
on successful delete and **false**, otherwise. In successful delete, first, a thread
logically deletes a treap node (*tnode*) by acquiring necessary **succLocks** on the
required treap nodes. Further, the thread acquires the necessary **treeLocks** on
the treap nodes and updates the logical ordering layout followed by the physical
layout of a treap. A thread uses *acquireTreeLocks(tnode)* to acquire **treeLocks**
returns **true**, if it acquires the locks successfully and **false**, otherwise. First,
the thread locks the parent of *tnode* (*tnode.parent*). Further, the thread acquires
the necessary locks based on the number of children the *tnode* contains. It is
classified into two cases: (i) if the *tnode* has at most one child, the thread locks
the child; (ii) if the *tnode* has two children, the thread locks the child node that
has the maximum priority. If the maximum priority child is left (right) child of
its parent, the thread locks right (left) child of the maximum priority child, if
exists.

If the node to be deleted (*tnode*) has two children, the thread pushes the *tnode* towards leaf nodes by performing single left/right rotations until it has a single child. Suppose the *tnode* has a single child, it sets the mark field of the *tnode* to `true` (i.e., *tnode* is just going to be deleted physically from the treap), and updates the logical ordering. Finally, the thread calls *removeFromTreap()* to remove the *tnode* from the treap and updates the physical layout.

4   Correctness

To show that our concurrent implementation of treaps is correct, we provide a sketch of proof. It shows that our implementation is deadlock free and it generates linearizable executions.

4.1   Safety Property

In our implementation, update operations (*insert()* and *delete()*) need locks to achieve synchronization among multiple threads. While performing update operations, threads acquire locks on the nodes of a treap in a specific order to avoid deadlock. First, threads get locks on the nodes of a treap using the treap logical ordering layout with smallest key first. If more than one thread is contending for the same predecessor, only one thread gets a lock and the remaining threads spin in a while loop without holding a lock on any treap node. Later, threads acquire locks using the treap physical layout, following the level order from root to leaves (lock the node closer to the root first). In the locking process, if a thread is unable to acquire a lock either in the logical ordering layout or in the treap physical layout, it releases all the locks that it is currently holding and restarts the locking process. Hence threads working on update operations do not create any deadlock.

4.2   Linearizability

Linearizability is a correctness condition for concurrent objects [14]. To show linearizability, we provide linearization points (LPs) for each operation.

The LP of successful *insert(x, pri)* operation depends on where the new treap node is added to its parent. If the new treap node is added as a left child of its parent, the LP is line 7 of Algorithm 3, where the predecessor field of the successor, *s.pred*, is updated with new treap node. Otherwise if the new treap node is added as a right child of its parent, the LP is line 8 of Algorithm 3, where the successor field of the predecessor, *p.succ*, is updated with new treap node. The LP of unsuccessful *insert(x, pri)* is where it returns `false`, i.e., line 20 of Algorithm 2. The LP of successful *delete(x)* operation is line 25 of Algorithm 5, where *s*'s `transit2` field is set to `true`. The LP of unsuccessful *delete(x)* is where it returns `false`, i.e., line 19 of Algorithm 5.

The LP of successful *contains(x)* is when the `transit2` field of the treap node is observed to be `false` (i.e., at line 10 of Algorithm 1). The LP of unsuccessful *contains(x)* is upon observing bigger key in line 6 or when the `transit2` of the treap node is observed to be `true`. However, it is possible that other concurrent threads may insert new nodes with key x and these updates may not be observed at line 6. In such cases, the LP of unsuccessful *contains(x)* is just before the LP of new insert.

4.3   Progress Guarantee

The *contains()* operation is lock-free and it has two phases: (i) traverse using a treap physical layout; (ii) traverse using the logical ordering of a treap. In the first phase, a thread may stray from its path due to concurrent *insert()* or *delete()* operations of other threads. So at least one of the other threads makes progress by updating the structure of a treap. In the second phase, the thread traverses using the logical ordering of keys in the treap. This operation either will be completed in finite number of steps if there are no concurrent updates or it may be delayed due to other concurrent updates, but other concurrent threads update the treap. Hence progress is guaranteed.

5   Experimental Evaluation

5.1   Experimental Setup

To evaluate performance of our implementations, we conduct experiments on an AMD Opteron processor 6376 with frequency 2.3 GHz, 64 GB RAM, and 64 cores spread across 8 NUMA nodes. Each NUMA node has 8 cores: 16KB L1 D-cache is local to each core, 64KB L1 I-cache and 2MB L2 cache are shared by two consecutive cores, and 6MB L3 cache is shared by all the cores in a NUMA node. The AMD 6376 has CentOS release 6.4 and OpenJDK Runtime version 1.7.0_09 using 64-bit Server VM (build 23.03 -b09, mixed mode). We focus on three types of workloads:

- Low contention: 70%Contains - 20%Insert - 10%Delete (70C-20I-10D)
- Medium contention: 50%Contains - 25%Insert - 25%Delete (50C-25I-25D)
- High contention: 30%Contains - 35%Insert - 35%Delete (30C-35I-35D)

For our experimental analysis, we consider **keys** from three different range sizes $(2 \times 10^5, 2 \times 10^6, \text{and } 2 \times 10^7)$ and **priorities** are randomly generated from a large discrete set (range of 32-bit integers) using uniform distribution. Before each trial, we prefill the data structure to the size of half of its keys range and set the trial duration for hundred seconds. We vary the number of threads in powers of 2 (from 1 to 64) and calculate the sum of operations performed by all the threads together. The average of 10 trials is considered. For our analysis, we use the source code provided by *Synchrobench* [4] and compare throughput of our implementation with the following state-of-the-art implementations:

- DVY tree – Lock-based AVL tree via logical ordering by Drachsler et al. [10].
- BCCO tree – Lock-based relaxed AVL tree by Bronson et al. [8].
- Skiplist – Lea's lock-free skipslist [15] implemented using the work of Fraser [12].
- CVM tree – Lock-based partially external relaxed AVL tree by Crain et al. [9].
- EFRB tree – A non-blocking, external BST by Ellen et al. [11].

5.2   Results Analysis

Table 3 shows average speedup of concurrent treaps as compared to the sequential implementation for different workloads when the number of threads is 64. Speedup of concurrent treaps increases with the increase in keys range because the probability of overlapping operations decreases with the increase in keys range. It increases as we move from high contention workload to low contention workload because the *contains* operation is lock-free.

Table 3. Average speedup of concurrent treaps as compared to sequential implementation for different workloads when the number of threads is 64.

Keys range	Average speedup		
	30C-35I-35D	50C-25I-25D	70C-20I-10D
2×10^5	6.42	7.50	11.56
2×10^6	15.14	16.55	19.88
2×10^7	21.69	22.38	23.75

Figure 2 shows throughput of different tree implementations with varying number of threads under different workloads. From the figure we observe that for larger keys range (2×10^7) and for all the workloads, concurrent treap implementation provides better throughput. Because concurrent treap implementation does not maintain strict height balance condition on every non-leaf node and on expectation it maintains $\mathcal{O}(\log n)$ height [16], contention reduces as the number of threads increases. In concurrent treaps while deleting a treap node, a thread moves the logically deleted node from top (root) to bottom (leaves) until the node has at most one child. In DVY tree, a thread replaces the logically deleted node with the smallest key in the right subtree and adjusts the height of BST by performing rotations on the access path from bottom to top, to satisfy AVL tree property. While performing operations on a treap, the probability of overlapping nodes on concurrent treap is less as compared to that of DVY tree. As a result, concurrent treaps provide better throughput as compared to DVY tree. BCCO tree needs hand-over-hand optimistic validation while performing a search operation and that impacts performance as the tree size increases. EFRB tree is an external BST and its average access path length is more as compared to that of the internal BSTs, which causes degradation in performance for large keys range. For high contention workloads (30C-35I-35D) and smaller keys range (2×10^5), CVM and EFRB trees provide better throughput because their update operations do not need any rotations, which results in less contention.

Figure 3 shows throughput of different tree implementations when keys are inserted in sorted order. For all the workloads, our concurrent treap implementation provides better throughput because heap property of a treap keeps the height of a concurrent treap to be $\mathcal{O}(\log n)$ on expectation [16]. CVM tree and EFRB tree implementations provide very less throughput as the implementations create skewed trees if the input is in sorted order.

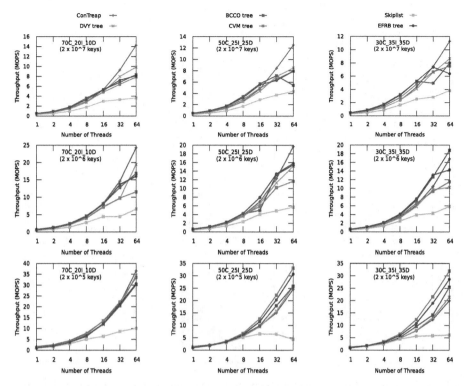

Fig. 2. Throughput of different tree implementations with varying number of threads under different workloads. Higher is better.

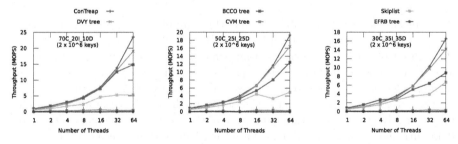

Fig. 3. Throughput of different tree implementations for sorted keys with varying number of threads under different workloads and for 2×10^6 keys. Higher is better.

5.3 Impact of Different Locking Objects

Thus far we consider a concurrent treap implementation using two Reentrant-Lock objects per node (2-RL). We now explore the impact of different locking objects used in concurrent treap implementation on throughput. We implement concurrent treaps using two other synchronization mechanisms: (i) One ReentrantLock object per node (1-RL), and (ii) One AtomicInteger object per node (1-AI). Figure 4 shows throughput of different concurrent treap implementa-

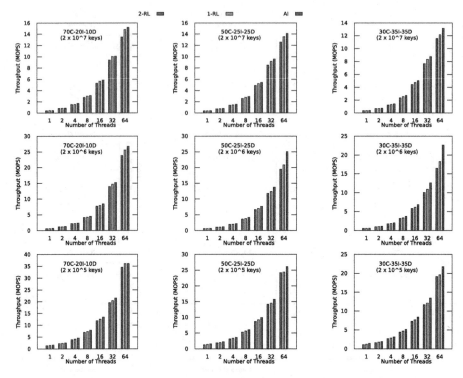

Fig. 4. Throughput of concurrent treap implementation with locking objects for varying number of threads under different workloads. Higher is better.

tions. From the figure, we observe that throughput of 2-RL based concurrent treap implementation is less than that of 1-RL based implementation. Note that throughput of 1-RL is in turn less than that of 1-AI based implementation. To identify the reasons behind these variations in throughput, first we calculate cache-misses per operation (cache-misses) using perf tool [2], shown in Fig. 5.

From Fig. 5, we observe that in majority of the cases the number of cache-misses of 2-RL implementation is more than that of 1-RL implementation; 1-RL is in turn more than that of 1-AI based implementation. Because 2-RL based implementation consumes more memory than 1-RL based implementation, it

Table 4. Footprint (in MB) of different treap implementations. Lower is better.

Number of keys	Average memory footprint (in MB)		
	2-RL	1-RL	1-AI
10^5	22	17	14
10^6	155	107	74
10^7	1522	1044	724

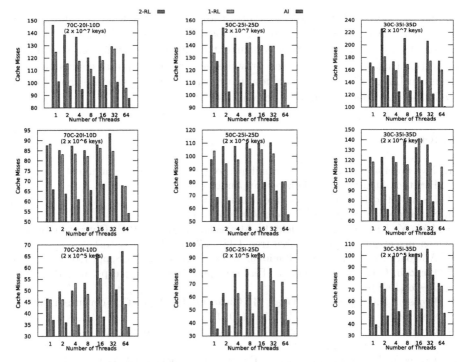

Fig. 5. Cache Misses of concurrent treap implementation with locking objects for varying number of threads under different workloads. Lower is better.

incurs more cache misses than 1-RL. Similarly, 1-AI based implementation has fewer cache misses because it consumes less memory than ReentrantLock implementations (refer Table 4). That is, footprint per node of 2-RL, 1-RL, and 1-AI implementations is in the decreasing order and hence, their cache misses. As a result the number of cache-line evictions of 2-RL, 1-RL, and 1-AI implementations also is in the decreasing order and it helps to improve the throughput. Reduced memory footprint helps in decreasing the memory response time and increasing the stability of the implementation [19]. Later we calculate the time taken by a thread (i.e., average over one billion times) to acquire and release a lock on a node. We observe that a thread takes 33.7 ns and 26.3 ns using ReentrantLock and AtomicInteger, respectively. Hence concurrent treap implementation with AtomicInteger locking object is a good choice to get better throughput.

6   Conclusion

In this work, we proposed algorithms for concurrent treap implementation. We observed that for large tree sizes and different workloads, our concurrent treap implementation provides better throughput as compared with the state-of-the-art implementations. For small tree sizes and high contention workloads, existing implementations EFRB and CVM trees yield better throughput. For sorted inputs, our concurrent treap implementation scales well with the number of threads. We also observed the impact of locking objects on throughput of concurrent treaps. Among different concurrent treap implementations, the implementation that uses AtomicInteger provides better throughput as compared with ReentrantLocks. Finally, we conclude that our concurrent treap implementations are better candidates of interest for end users.

References

1. Java programming. https://en.wikibooks.org/wiki/Java_Programming
2. Perf tool. https://perf.wiki.kernel.org/index.php
3. Reentrant locks. http://docs.oracle.com/java7/api/
4. Synchrobench. https://github.com/gramoli/synchrobench
5. Afek, Y., Kaplan, H., Korenfeld, B., Morrison, A., Tarjan, R.E.: Cbtree: a practical concurrent self-adjusting search tree. DISC **27**(6), 393–417 (2014)
6. Aragon, C.R., Seidel, R.G.: Randomized search trees. In: FOCS, pp. 450–454 (1989)
7. Blelloch, G.E., Reid-Miller, M.: Fast set operations using treaps. In: SPAA, pp. 16–26 (1998)
8. Bronson, N.G., Casper, J., Chafi, H., Olukotun, K.: A practical concurrent binary search tree. In: PPoPP, pp. 257–268 (2010)
9. Crain, T., Gramoli, V., Raynal, M.: A contention-friendly binary search tree. In: ICPP, pp. 229–240 (2013)
10. Drachsler, D., Vechev, M., Yahav, E.: Practical concurrent binary search trees via logical ordering. In: PPoPP, pp. 343–356 (2014)
11. Ellen, F., Fatourou, P., Ruppert, E., van Breugel, F.: Non-blocking binary search trees. In: PODC, pp. 131–140 (2010)
12. Fraser: Practical lock freedom. Ph.D. thesis, University of Cambridge (2003)
13. Herlihy, M.P., Shavit, N.: The Art of Multiprocessor Programming. Morgan Kaufmann Publishers, San Francisco (2008)
14. Herlihy, M.P., Wing, J.M.: Linearizability: a correctness condition for concurrent objects. TOPLAS **12**(3), 463–492 (1990)
15. Lea, D.: Concurrent skip list (2005)
16. Martínez, C., Roura, S.: Randomized binary search trees. JACM **45**(2), 288–323 (1998)
17. Natarajan, A., Mittal, N.: Fast concurrent lock-free binary search trees. In: PPoPP, pp. 317–328 (2014)
18. Pugh, W.: Skip lists: a probabilistic alternative to balanced trees. CACM **33**(6), 668–676 (1990)
19. Reitbauer, A.: Java Enterprise Performance. entwickler Press, Frankfurt (2011)
20. Shavit, N.: Data structures in the multicore age. CACM **54**(3), 76–84 (2011)
21. Weiss, M.A.: Data Structures and Algorithm Analysis in C++, 3rd edn. Pearson Press, Boston (2009)

Survey on Energy-Saving Technologies for Disk-Based Storage Systems

Ce Yu$^{(\boxtimes)}$, Jianmei Wang, Chao Sun, Xiaoxiao Lu, Jian Xiao, and Jizhou Sun

School of Computer Science and Technology,
Tianjin University, Tianjin 300350, China
{yuce,wangjianmei,sch,mldssr,xiaojian,jzsun}@tju.edu.cn

Abstract. The explosive growth of data from various research fields has led to increasing requirement and serious energy consumption of data storage in big data era. As a component of a data center, the storage system consumes almost 27% of the total energy. Therefore, increasing attention has been drawn to the research on energy conservation. In this paper, existing energy-saving methods for disk drives are summarized, which include disk power management, cache management, workload skew and RAID configuration. We find that power management is the basic strategy widely used in other models. Workload skew is efficient for energy saving although it could cause response delay due to the load concentration. Multiple models based on RAID are also developed for energy conservation. In the end, this paper forecasts the development of energy-saving technologies and come to the conclusion that a co-design scheme of hardware and software is necessary for the application-oriented system.

Keywords: Big data · Disk array · Energy saving · Power-aware · Storage system

1 Introduction

Nowadays the explosive growth of data has led to the increasing requirement of data storage. The storage form varies from single disk to massive disk storage system. The amount of energy consumed by a data center can be equivalent to a medium-sized town. Among varieties of components in data center, the energy consumption of storage system is nonnegligible - the energy consumption of the storage system is close to 27%. How to reduce the energy consumption of the storage system has become a significant issue and hot topic in the field of computer science and technology. Consequently, the research in this field has important academic value and practical significance to promote the development and application of energy-saving technologies of storage system.

Research on data accessing to different data centers shows that the total accessed data is less than 5% of the total storage data in most of the storage systems in any given day, which indicates that the average workload of disk is low,

© Springer International Publishing AG 2017
S. Ibrahim et al. (Eds.): ICA3PP 2017, LNCS 10393, pp. 791–800, 2017.
DOI: 10.1007/978-3-319-65482-9_64

and there is plenty of idle time able to be used for energy savings. Accordingly, the energy-saving principle of disk storage system is as follows: the disk without data access can enter low power state to save energy and when a new request arrives will be woken up to serve it. Relevant survey has been conducted before [6], and we expand the content in this paper. According to the different energy-saving ways, energy-saving techniques are divided into power management, cache management, workload skew and RAID configuration.

2   Disk Power Management

In order to reduce the energy consumption of the storage system, kinds of energy-saving schemes are proposed. Among these, disk power management is frequently used as an approach to saving energy. The related research is mainly divided into two types: one is the traditional power management, the other is dynamic power management.

2.1   Traditional Power Management (TPM)

A disk is roughly consist of disc, magnetic head, magnetic head arm, motor and electronic control circuit etc. Motor and electronic control circuit are the two main energy components of the disk drive. Power management is the basic technique for energy saving based on disk storage system. Traditional power management can save energy by switching disk between the states of spinning down and up. There are generally three states of a disk: active state, idle state and standby state. The energy consumption is the largest in the active state and the smallest in the standby state. The usual energy-efficient idea is to transform the disk in the long idle state to a lower power state. Traditional power management is limited to desktop, laptop and mobile devices.

2.2   DRPM

Multi-speed disk system is proposed in order to adapt to the various workload of the real environment and each disk has a plurality of rotation speeds. DRPM is an energy-efficient strategy which uses multi-speed disks [8]. The disk in DRPM rotates at a low speed in light load and high speed in heavy load, instead of completely spinning down disks which can incur significant time and power costs. The main value of DRPM is that it breaks the disk model with single speed. DRPM dynamically select a suitable disk speed according to the current workload, even the short idle interval can save energy by reducing speed. Besides, DRPM also provides the option of serving the request at a lower RPM (revolutions per minute) if performance is not very important to gain additional energy savings. The deficiency of DRPM is the great difficulty to implement the multi-speed disks. There are only a few disk manufactures to launch a two-speed disk, while the large scale applications in the actual storage system need to wait.

3   Cache Management and Workload Skew

A great many technologies conserve energy by cache management and workload skew. Specifically, the workload is concentrated on a few disks, so that other disks can be in the low power state to save energy. Relocating data and redirecting request are two main research directions for workload skew.

3.1   Caching and Buffering Across Disks

An available idea for energy savings is to divide the disks into the cache disks which store the copied of frequently accessed data and data disks which have opportunities to get into a low power state.

MAID. MAID (Massive Arrays of Idle Disks) is a typical representative of this kind of energy-saving technology [4]. The disk array is divided into one or a plurality of active drives which are served as read/write cache and the others are passive drives. Read requests have a priority to search the data in the cache. Similarly, write requests are served by cache if the target disk is in the standby state. MAID is suitable for archiving storage systems, namely, massive storage system with a large number of disks. MAID has both advantages and disadvantages: the advantage is the obvious energy-saving effect because of the concentration of workload; the disadvantage is the response delay resulted from the high frequency of request towards active drives. There are a number of related research on MAID, such as DT-MAID [27], MCS-SSD [30], Eco-storage [1].

WO. Write off-loading (WO) is proposed on the idea of buffering writes across disk to avoid disk spin-ups, which writes from a logical volume in standby mode to an active volume [17]. It believes that buffering writes is more important than caching data for the data-center workload. WO is suitable for write-dominated workload, which means write is dominant for a relatively long period of time. Other buffering schemes are as follows: [20, 28].

3.2   Caching and Buffering in Memory

Caching and buffering in memory is another cache policy.

Power-Aware Cache Replacement Policies. Power-Aware LRU(PA-LRU) is an on-line caching algorithm which is proposed to improve the energy efficiency of storage systems based on the observation that different disks have different workload characteristics such as time interval distribution of request arrival [32]. Its main idea is to dynamically keep track of workload characteristics for each disk, including the percentage of cold misses and the cumulative distribution of interval lengths.

Partition-Based LRU(PB-LRU) is a new power-aware on-line algorithm that requires little parameter tuning [33]. PB-LRU partitions the total system cache according to the characteristics of each disk.

Energy-Efficient Cache Write Policies. Two cache write policies based on memory are presented to save energy: write-back with eager update (WBEU) and write-through with deferred update (WTDU) [34]. WBEU writes all modified data blocks to disk whenever the target disk is active, which reduces the number of disk spin-ups. In WTDU, modified data blocks are written to a log temporarily if the target disk is in the standby state. Logs could reside in any persistent storage device, such as NVRAM or dedicated log disks.

Power-Aware Prefetching. Based on spatial locality – data close to access data have a high probability to be accessed soon after, adjacent data blocks are prefetched to memory in advance to improve performance. Moreover, energy could be saved due to the change of access time. EEFS (energy-efficient file system) is a typical representative which applies power-aware prefetching at the file rather than block level [14].

3.3   Data Migration

PDC(Popular Data Concentration) is another technique to shape workload [19], the core idea of which is to concentrate the popular data which are accessed frequently to a subset of the disk system. PDC migrates data according to their priorities, the most popular data are migrated to the first disk, then to the second and so on, such that other disks have more opportunities to spin down. PDC is suitable for the application with high access frequency, such as Web applications. The advantage is the same as MAID. The disadvantage is computational complexity and heavy workload due to the regular data migration. Besides, response delay is also a disadvantage because of load concentration. There are many improved algorithms: PDC-NH [12], other schemes:[3,18].

3.4   Hibernator

Hibernator is an energy management system of disk array [31]. The storage system is consist of multiple RAID which have different rotation speeds. Hibernator provides better energy savings while guaranteeing performance. Several techniques are used to support Hibernator: the use of multi-speed disks; a coarse-grained approach called CR to dynamically deciding rotation speed for each disk; an efficient data migration strategy to select the proper data and an appropriate-speed disk; automatic performance boosts while there is a risk that performance may not be met because of disk energy management.

4   RAID Configuration

RAID is mostly used to improve performance and reliability in the storage system. There are also some studies on RAID from the point of energy conservation. The energy-saving strategy of the software and the architecture of hardware based on RAID are both introduced in this paper, such as eRAID, PARAID, EERAID.

4.1 eRAID

The eRAID (energy-efficient RAID) model makes full use of the redundant characteristic of RAID1 to redirect the I/O request [23]. The main idea of eRAID is to spin down partial or entire mirror groups to low power state to save energy while guaranteeing acceptable performance. Read requests towards the standby disks are redirected to data copies in the primary disks, while write requests are buffered to controller cache and served after the standby disks are spun up.

4.2 PARAID

Weddle *et al.* proposed PARAID (Power-Aware RAID) model based on the characteristics of periodic fluctuation of specific workload using the experience of car shift principle [24]. Each RAID in PARAID contains a different number of disks and is similar to a gear of a car, different RAID provide different degrees of parallelism, that is, different read and write performance. Reliability can be guaranteed by the constraint of disk power cycles as well as the application of various RAID coding methods.

4.3 RAIS

SSD (Solid State Driver) has great potential for energy saving based on RAID group. Compared to HDD (Hard Disk Driver), SSD possess multiple advantages, such as lower power consumption, lighter weight, and smaller I/O access times. Replacing some HDD with SSD can improve the performance while reduce energy consumption. Therefore, RAIS (Redundant Array of Independent Solid-State Drivers) is proposed for energy conservation [9]. Besides, studies related to RAIS have been enriched and developed recently, such as CGC-RAIS [10], CD-RAIS [5], MC-RAIS [25].

4.4 EERAID

Cache structure is a common way to save energy. D. Li *et al.* made full use of the redundant information in the disk array, combined the redundant information with the I/O scheduling policy and cache management strategy, and put forward the high efficiency disk array called EERAID (Energy-Efficient RAID) [13]. EERAID adopts non-volatile cache for write back policy to optimize the write request.

4.5 RIMAC

On the basis of EERAID, a redundancy-based, two-level I/O cache architecture called RIMAC is proposed [29]. RIMAC combines memory cache and NVRAM of RAID 5 to store data block information and parity block information respectively. The idea of RIMAC is to enable data on the standby disk to be recovered by accessing data in the two-level I/O cache or on currently active/idle disks.

Except these, there are other types of models based on RAID, such as S-RAID (Semi-RAID) [26], ThinRAID [22], GRAID [15].

5   Power-Proportional Distributed File System

In this section, two power-proportional strategies based on Distributed File System (DFS) will be presented. Instead of saving energy across disk, DFS save energy across node.

5.1   Rabbit

Rabbit is a power-proportional distributed file system (PPDFS), based on Hadoop distributed file system (HDFS) [2]. Rabbit explicates the idea of a covering set (CS) – at least one replica of a data block must be stored in the subset of nodes. Rabbit alleviates the node failure rates through data layouts, which minimize the number of nodes that need to be spin-up after a failure. For a shared infrastructure, Rabbit also allows different datasets to use different subsets of nodes as a building block to avoid interference.

5.2   Sierra

Sierra is also a power-proportional DFS [21]. While Rabbit is focused on read-only workloads, Sierra is targeted at general workloads, including read and write. Sierra uses redundant data to divert accesses and serves write request by integrating write off-loading, as described above. Sierra allows spinning down a substantial part of servers during light loads without data migration and extra capacity requirements.

6   Research Prospect

In the above, many techniques for energy conservation are introduced that mainly include the improvements of hardware device and the use of software strategy. The major research direction in future is also considered from the two aspects. For the strategy of software, it is potential to make a breakthrough from multiple aspects, such as disk power management, dynamic workload, data placement etc. Besides, the combination of some energy-efficient strategies is able to get a better effect. From a hardware perspective, energy can be saved by using more energy-efficient storage devices to replace previously ordinary devices. Therefore it is workable to adopt novel storage architectures or apply new energy-efficient devices, like NVMs (non-volatile memories) [7], such as STT-RAM (spin transfer torque RAM) [11], PCM (phase change memory) [16]. Considering the improvement of disk drive, Ultrastar He disk is a new technique proposed by HGST, which is filled with helium inside instead of ordinary air such that the distance between the discs is shortened and the capacity of disk is expanded. Hardware and software co-design is the developing trend in future. It is essential to combine effective or novel algorithms and new hardware device, such as PCM, Ultrastar He.

Table 1. Classification of power-reduction techniques according to the storage-stack layer to which they are applied

Storage-stack layer	Techniques
Storage-server cluster	WO, Rabbit, Sierra
RAID	Hibernator, eRAID, PARAID, S-RAID, RAIS, EERAID, RIMAC
JBOD (non-RAID)	DRPM, MAID, PDC, PA/PB-LRU
Single disk	TPM, Cache, PA prefetch, PA buffer, EEFS

Table 2. Power-reduction techniques classified according to targeted workload

Targeted workload	Techniques
Read-many/write-many	PARAID, PDC, Hibernator, EERAID, RIMAC, eRAID, DPRM, Sierra
Read-dominated	cache, PA/PB-LRU, PA prefetch, EEFS, Rabbit
Write-once/read-maybe	MAID, TPM
Write-dominated	PA buffer, WO

Table 3. Comparison of typical energy saving technologies

Energy-saving strategy	Redundancy	Multi-speed	Cache	Workload skew	Comprehensive performance
TPM	NO	NO	NO	NO	General
DRPM	NO	YES	NO	NO	High
MAID	NO	NO	YES	YES(Relocating Data)	General
PA/PB-LRU	NO	YES	YES	NO	High
WO	NO	NO	YES	NO	High
PDC	NO	NO	NO	YES(Relocating data)	Low
Hibernator	NO	YES	NO	YES(Relocating data)	High
eRAID	YES	NO	NO	NO	High
PARAID	YES	NO	NO	YES	High
S-RAID	YES	NO	NO	NO	High
EERAID	YES	YES	YES	NO	High
RIMAC	YES	NO	YES	YES(Redirecting request)	High
RAIS	YES	NO	NO	NO	High

7 Conclusions

Modern storage systems vary from single disk to large scale many-disk systems because of the fast-growing data, and the energy consumption of data storage has increased rapidly. Studies have shown that the energy consumption of a data center could be equivalent to a medium-sized town, and the storage system accounts for 27% which can not be ignored. Therefore, an increasing number of research concerning energy conservation emerged. In this paper, we make a survey on energy-saving methods for disk drives and classify them into power management, cache management and workload skew and RAID configuration, and analyze the advantages and disadvantages of these methods as well as their possible applications. Besides, we discuss the prospects for future studies from both hardware and software aspects, and provide insights to future research possibilities.

In Table 1, all of the existing energy-saving techniques for data-center storage are classified according to the storage-stack layer they were originally targeted at. The more specific a technique, the more it is tied to a specific layer of the storage stack. Many existing techniques target a specific type of workload. Table 2 maps every technique into one of four quadrants according to the targeted read and write request arrival rate. In view of the energy-saving techniques mentioned above, the comparison and summary are given in Table 3.

All in all, we can draw the following conclusions. Firstly, improvements in the storage device and system architecture are useful to save energy for universal storage system. A variety of energy-efficient storage media have been used for energy conservation, such as SSD, multi-speed disks, PCM, RM, Ultrastar He. Caching and tiering are also effective approaches for energy savings, such as MAID, PA/PB-LRU, EERAID and RIMAC. Secondly, software strategy is also an available option for universal storage system, such as algorithms used in DRPM, PDC, PARAID, Hibernator. Thirdly, hardware and software co-design is a better alternative for application-oriented storage systems. Different application scenarios have different requirements. For instance, astronomical data and financial data make different demands on storage system. Combination of customized storage device and the special file system is a better alternative for these special applications.

Acknowledgments. This work is supported by the National Natural Science Foundation of China (11573019, 61602336), the Joint Research Fund in Astronomy (U1531111) under cooperative agreement between the National Natural Science Foundation of China (NSFC) and Chinese Academy of Sciences (CAS).

References

1. Al Assaf, M.M., Jiang, X., Abid, M.R., Qin, X.: Eco-storage: A hybrid storage system with energy-efficient informed prefetching. J. Signal Process. Syst. **72**(3), 165–180 (2013)
2. Amur, H., Cipar, J., Gupta, V., Ganger, G.R., Kozuch, M.A., Schwan, K.: Robust and flexible power-proportional storage. In: Proceedings of the 1st ACM symposium on Cloud computing, pp. 217–228. ACM (2010)
3. Chai, Y., Du, Z., Bader, D.A., Qin, X.: Efficient data migration to conserve energy in streaming media storage systems. IEEE Trans. Parallel and Distrib. Syst. **23**(11), 2081–2093 (2012)

4. Colarelli, D., Grunwald, D.: Massive arrays of idle disks for storage archives. In: Proceedings of the 2002 ACM/IEEE conference on Supercomputing, pp. 1–11. IEEE Computer Society Press (2002)

5. Du, Y., Zhang, Y., Xiao, N., Liu, F.: Cd-rais: Constrained dynamic striping in redundant array of independent SSDS. In: 2014 IEEE International Conference on Cluster Computing (CLUSTER), pp. 212–220. IEEE (2014)

6. Jian, S., Zhanhuai, L., Xiao, Z., Huifeng, W., Qinlu, H.: Review in power consumption of disk based storage systems. In: 2013 8th International Conference on Computer Science and Education (ICCSE), pp. 47–50. IEEE (2013)

7. Kim, H., Seshadri, S., Dickey, C.L., Chiu, L.: Evaluating phase change memory for enterprise storage systems: a study of caching and tiering approaches. In: Proceedings of the 12th USENIX Conference on File and Storage Technologies (FAST 14), pp. 33–45 (2014)

8. Kim, M., Song, M.: Saving energy in video servers by the use of multispeed disks. IEEE Trans. Circuits Syst. Video Technol. 22(4), 567–580 (2012)

9. Kim, Y.: An empirical study of redundant array of independent solid-state drives (rais). Cluster Comput. 18(2), 963–977 (2015)

10. Kim, Y., Oral, S., Shipman, G.M., Lee, J., Dillow, D.A., Wang, F.: Harmonia: A globally coordinated garbage collector for arrays of solid-state drives. In: 2011 IEEE 27th Symposium on Mass Storage Systems and Technologies (MSST), pp. 1–12. IEEE (2011)

11. Lee, B.C., Ipek, E., Mutlu, O., Burger, D.: Architecting phase change memory as a scalable dram alternative. In: ACM SIGARCH Computer Architecture News, vol. 37, pp. 2–13. ACM (2009)

12. Lee, D., Koh, K.: PDC-NH: Popular data concentration on nand flash and hard disk drive. In: 2009 10th IEEE/ACM International Conference on Grid Computing, pp. 196–200. IEEE (2009)

13. Li, D., Wang, J.: Eeraid: energy efficient redundant and inexpensive disk array. In: Proceedings of the 11th workshop on ACM SIGOPS European workshop, p. 29. ACM (2004)

14. Li, D., Wang, J.: A performance-oriented energy efficient file system. In: Proceedings of the international workshop on Storage network architecture and parallel I/Os, pp. 58–65. ACM (2004)

15. Mao, B., Feng, D., Jiang, H., Wu, S., Chen, J., Zeng, L.: Graid: A green raid storage architecture with improved energy efficiency and reliability. In: 2008 IEEE International Symposium on Modeling, Analysis and Simulation of Computers and Telecommunication Systems, pp. 1–8. IEEE (2008)

16. Mao, W., Liu, J.N., Tong, W., Feng, D., Li, Z., Zhou, W., Zhang, S.W.: A review of storage technology research based on phase change memory. Jisuanji Xuebao/Chin. J. Comput. 38(5), 944–960 (2015)

17. Narayanan, D., Donnelly, A., Rowstron, A.: Write off-loading: Practical power management for enterprise storage. ACM Trans. Storage 4(3), 10 (2008)

18. Ou, J., Shu, J., Lu, Y., Yi, L., Wang, W.: Edm: An endurance-aware data migration scheme for load balancing in ssd storage clusters. In: 2014 IEEE 28th International Parallel and Distributed Processing Symposium, pp. 787–796. IEEE (2014)

19. Pinheiro, E., Bianchini, R.: Energy conservation techniques for disk array-based servers. In: Proceedings of the International Conference on Supercomputing (2004)

20. Tarihi, M., Asadi, H., Haghdoost, A., Arjomand, M., Sarbazi-Azad, H.: A hybrid non-volatile cache design for solid-state drives using comprehensive i/o characterization. IEEE Trans. Comput. 65(6), 1678–1691 (2016)

21. Thereska, E., Donnelly, A., Narayanan, D.: Sierra: practical power-proportionality for data center storage. In: Proceedings of the sixth conference on Computer systems, pp. 169–182. ACM (2011)
22. Wan, J., Qu, X., Zhao, N., Wang, J., Xie, C.: Thinraid: Thinning down raid array for energy conservation. IEEE Trans. Parallel Distrib. Syst. **26**(10), 2903–2915 (2015)
23. Wang, J., Zhu, H., Li, D.: eraid: Conserving energy in conventional disk-based raid system. IEEE Trans. Comput. **57**(3), 359–374 (2008)
24. Weddle, C., Oldham, M., Qian, J., Wang, A.I.A., Reiher, P., Kuenning, G.: Paraid: a gear-shifting power-aware raid. ACM Trans. Storage **3**(3), 13 (2007)
25. Wu, S., Yang, W., Mao, B., Lin, Y.: MC-RAIS: multi-chunk redundant array of independent ssds with improved performance. In: Wang, G., Zomaya, A., Perez, G.M., Li, K. (eds.) ICA3PP 2015. LNCS, vol. 9531, pp. 18–32. Springer, Cham (2015). doi:10.1007/978-3-319-27140-8_2
26. Xiao, L., Yu-An, T., Zhizhuo, S.: Semi-raid: A reliable energy-aware raid data layout for sequential data access. In: 2011 IEEE 27th Symposium on Mass Storage Systems and Technologies (MSST), pp. 1–11. IEEE (2011)
27. Xie, X., Zhao, Y., Zhu, W., Long, S.: Design of a novel energy-aware storage system named dt-maid. J. Converg. Inf. Technol. **7**(2), 293–301 (2012)
28. Yang, L.H., Zhou, J., Gong, W., Zhao, J., Chen, L.: Lifetime and Qos-aware energy-saving buffering schemes. J. Syst. Softw. **86**(5), 1408–1425 (2013)
29. Yao, X., Wang, J.: Rimac: a novel redundancy-based hierarchical cache architecture for energy efficient, high performance storage systems. In: ACM SIGOPS Operating Systems Review, vol. 40, pp. 249–262. ACM (2006)
30. Yuan, Z., Yu, C., Sun, J., Xiao, J., Wang, J., Shang, Z., Hu, Y.: An energy efficient storage system for astronomical observation data on dome A. In: Wang, G., Zomaya, A., Perez, G.M., Li, K. (eds.) ICA3PP 2015. LNCS, vol. 9531, pp. 33–46. Springer, Cham (2015). doi:10.1007/978-3-319-27140-8_3
31. Zhu, Q., Chen, Z., Tan, L., Zhou, Y., Keeton, K., Wilkes, J.: Hibernator: helping disk arrays sleep through the winter. ACM SIGOPS Oper. Syst. Rev. **39**(5), 177–190 (2005)
32. Zhu, Q., David, F.M., Devaraj, C.F., Li, Z., Zhou, Y., Cao, P.: Reducing energy consumption of disk storage using power-aware cache management. In: Software, IEEE Proceedings, p. 118. IEEE (2004)
33. Zhu, Q., Shankar, A., Zhou, Y.: Pb-lru: a self-tuning power aware storage cache replacement algorithm for conserving disk energy. In: Proceedings of the 18th annual international conference on Supercomputing, pp. 79–88. ACM (2004)
34. Zhu, Q., Zhou, Y.: Power-aware storage cache management. IEEE Trans. Comput. **54**(5), 587–602 (2005)

The Open Community Runtime on the Intel Knights Landing Architecture

Jiri Dokulil[1]([✉]), Siegfried Benkner[1], and Jakub Yaghob[2]

[1] Faculty of Computer Science, University of Vienna, Vienna, Austria
{jiri.dokulil,siegfried.benkner}@univie.ac.at
[2] Department of Software Engineering, Charles University, Prague, Czech Republic
yaghob@ksi.mff.cuni.cz

Abstract. The Intel Xeon Phi Knights Landing manycore processor comes with new interesting features: on-chip high-bandwidth memory and several user-selectable NUMA configurations. In this paper, we look into how these affect applications that target the Open Community Runtime (OCR), an asynchronous tasked-based runtime system for future parallel architectures. We have extended our OCR runtime to make it NUMA aware and to allow it to use the high-bandwidth memory. We have conducted a range of experiments, comparing OpenMP, TBB, our OCR implementation, and the reference OCR implementation on different machine configurations using a memory intensive seismic simulation.

Keywords: Open Community Runtime · Knights Landing · Intel Xeon Phi · High-bandwidth memory · Parallel runtime systems · NUMA

1 Introduction

Given the ever increasing complexity and architectural variety of parallel systems, asynchronous task-based programming systems have gained a lot of momentum since they facilitate decoupling the specification of parallelism from its actual implementation. With a task-based programming model the user exposes the potential parallelism by decomposing a problem into tasks with well-defined inputs and outputs and delegates to the runtime system how tasks are scheduled for parallel execution to the available hardware resources. Such an approach not only allows a program to be dynamically adapted to a specific architecture, but also to reorganize parallel execution in case of changing workloads or varying hardware performance characteristics.

The Open Community Runtime (OCR) [11] is an open specification of a low-level runtime system for future extreme-scale architectures. OCR has been developed in the context of the US X-Stack program in order to provide a common foundation for research on runtime systems and higher-level parallel programming models. OCR relies on an event-driven, asynchronous task-based model where the potential parallelism available in an application is expressed by a large number of tasks (referred to as event driven tasks) with explicit dependences. All data is organized in data blocks, which are relocatable, contiguous

© Springer International Publishing AG 2017
S. Ibrahim et al. (Eds.): ICA3PP 2017, LNCS 10393, pp. 801–813, 2017.
DOI: 10.1007/978-3-319-65482-9_65

chunks of memory managed by the OCR runtime. Coordination and synchronization is expressed by means of events, which are used to establish control and data dependences.

A task can only access data in a data block if the data block was explicitly passed to it or if it created the data block. As a result, the runtime is aware of all the data a task can possibly access. Once all data blocks a task depends on are available and all events are satisfied, a task becomes *runnable* and will eventually be executed on some execution unit and run to completion regardless of the behavior of other tasks.

At runtime an OCR program forms a dynamically created directed acyclic graph (DAG) of tasks, with explicit information about which data blocks are used (consumed and produced) by which tasks. This gives the runtime system the ability to relocate tasks and data blocks to achieve a better load balance, to optimize memory and energy consumption, and to deal with failures.

In this paper, we report on the extensions of OCR-Vx (our implementation of the OCR specification [6]) for the new Intel Xeon Phi Knights Landing processor (KNL). Our contributions are: First, a NUMA-aware task scheduler for OCR-Vx, which is also beneficial on other NUMA machines, not just the KNL. Second, enabling OCR-Vx to use the on-chip high-bandwidth MCDRAM of the KNL. Finally, we have evaluated the performance of the runtime on six different configurations of the KNL, using a seismic simulation code. To provide a wider context, the same code was tested with the reference OCR implementation [10] and rewritten in OpenMP. We also compare our OCR and OpenMP codes to the original native TBB application. In total, five application variants were tested.

This paper is organized as follows: Sect. 2 briefly presents the new features of the KNL architecture. Section 3 describes relevant components of our OCR implementation and the extensions to support NUMA systems and high-bandwidth memory. Experimental results are provided in Sect. 4. Section 5 discusses related work followed by a conclusion and discussion of future work.

2   Knights Landing Architecture

Knights Landing is the latest release in the Intel Xeon Phi product range. Formerly known as MIC (Many Integrated Cores), Xeon Phi is a family of high-performance many-core architectures. Unlike the previous architecture, the Knights Corner (KNC), which was available as a coprocessor PCIe card, the KNL is a "full" CPU, which is used as the only processor of a server. In our experiments, we use a machine with one Intel Xeon Phi Processor 7230, which has 64 cores, four way hyperthreading (256 threads), it runs at 1.30 GHz, and it has 16 GB of on-chip high-bandwidth MCDRAM. The main memory (DDR4) is 96 GB. Each core has 32 KB data cache and 32 KB instruction cache and there are two vector processing units with AVX-512 support attached to each core. The cores are arranged into tiles, with each tile containing two cores and 1 MB L2 cache shared by the two cores. The tiles are laid out as a 2D mesh. Since 64 cores occupy 32 tiles, there is 32 MB of L2 cache in total.

The whole processor is fully cache coherent. To maintain cache coherency, it has a distributed tag directory, organized as a set of per-tile tag directories (TDs), which identify the state and the location on the chip of any cache line. For any memory address, the hardware can identify (using a hash function) the TD responsible for that address. If there is a cache miss, the tile where the cache miss occurred must send a message to the tile with the TD corresponding to the accessed memory address. Depending on whether the cache line is cached somewhere (this is determined from the TD), the message is forwarded to the tile with the cached data or to the memory. To support different workloads, the KNL chip can be configured (in BIOS) to use different ways of organizing the tag directories. These are called *clustering modes*.

With the *all-to-all* clustering mode, memory addresses are uniformly distributed across all TDs on the chip. As a result, there is a high probability that when a tag directory needs to be used (e.g., a cache miss), the corresponding tag directory may be far away from the core that needs it, causing a high latency of the cache operation. In the *quadrant* clustering mode, the tiles are divided into four parts called quadrants, which are spatially local to four groups of memory controllers. Memory addresses served by a memory controller in a quadrant are guaranteed to be mapped only to TDs contained in that quadrant. On average, this provides a much lower latency than in the all-to-all mode. In *hemisphere* mode, two groups are used instead of four. The division of the cores is hidden from the operating system and the whole system is presented as a single NUMA node, except for the MCDRAM, which is shown as one separate NUMA node. The *SNC-4* (Sub-NUMA Clustering) mode uses the same tile partitioning as the quadrant mode, but each quadrant is exposed as a separate NUMA node. The MCDRAM is also split into four NUMA nodes. The *SNC-2* mode is the same as SNC-4, except that only two groups of cores are used. If cache traffic crosses the boundary between two NUMA nodes in SNC-2/4, it is more expensive than in the corresponding hemisphere/quadrant mode.

In our experiments, we only use the quadrant and SNC-4 modes. The all-to-all mode should only be used as a failsafe and not in production. We did some tests with the hemisphere and SNC-2 modes, but they did not bring any new interesting results, so we will only present the numbers for quadrant and SNC-4.

Another configuration option is the usage model of the MCDRAM. There are three options, independent of the clustering modes. First, the MCDRAM can be used in the *flat* mode, where it is available as a separate NUMA node (or nodes, depending on the clustering mode), which can be used by the application to allocate memory. MCDRAM and the machine's main memory (DDR) share the same physical address space. Aside from possibly different memory allocation calls, both memory types can be used by the application in exactly the same way. Another mode for the MCDRAM is the *cache* mode. In that case, the MCDRAM is used as a last level cache for the main memory. This cache is completely transparent to software. The last available mode is the *hybrid* mode, where part of the MCDRAM is available in the flat mode and the rest is used as cache. The core organization and NUMA nodes for the flat MCDRAM mode

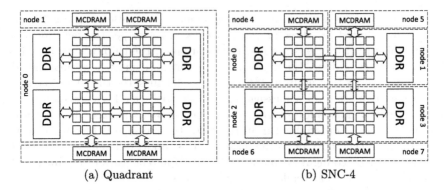

(a) Quadrant   (b) SNC-4

Fig. 1. KNL clustering modes. Displayed are cores, memory (MCDRAM and DDR), and NUMA nodes. Both configurations are shown with MCDRAM switched to flat mode. In cache modes, the NUMA nodes with the MCDRAM (node 1 in quadrant mode and nodes 4–7 in SNC-4 mode) would not be present.

with quadrant and SNC-4 clustering modes are shown in Fig. 1. Note that the MCDRAM NUMA nodes don't contain any cores, only memory.

In the flat mode, the MCDRAM can be allocated using the `hbw_malloc` call, which is part of the *memkind* library. Since the MCDRAM is available as one or more separate NUMA nodes (node 1 in quadrant, nodes 4–7 in SNC-4), it is also possible to use `numa_alloc_onnode`, which is part of *libnuma*. In SNC-4 mode, `numa_alloc_onnode` can be used to directly specify which of the four MCDRAM nodes to use, giving the application more control. This is not possible with `hbw_malloc`.

3   OCR-Vx

OCR-Vx is a collection of open source[1] OCR implementations that we created at the University of Vienna [6]. For this paper, the relevant implementation is OCR-Vsm, which is a shared-memory implementation. Originally, it was built on top of the task scheduler from Intel Threading Building Blocks (TBB). The latest version can be configured to use different schedulers (see Sect. 3.1 for details). OCR-Vsm is similar to OCR-Vdm, the distributed-memory implementation, but it uses several optimizations, which are much easier to do in a shared memory environment and we have yet not implemented them in the distributed runtime.

Eventually, the optimized shared-memory runtime will be used within the distributed runtime, to control a single node. This approach is already being used by the XSOCR runtime [10], which was created by Intel and Rice University as part of the XStack project (hence the "XS" in the name) as a reference implementation of the OCR specification.

---

[1] Stable releases of the runtime are available at http://www.univie.ac.at/ocr-vx/.

3.1 NUMA Support

Most of today's high performance computing systems can be characterized as Non-Uniform Memory Architectures (NUMA). In NUMA systems, the different CPU cores don't have uniform access to the system memory. Usually, different parts of memory are "closer" to certain cores, giving them faster access compared to the rest of the memory. Overall, a NUMA machine consists of several NUMA nodes. A NUMA node contains zero or more CPU cores and some portion of the total system memory. In a typical four socket NUMA server, there are four NUMA nodes, each containing cores from one of the four CPUs and a quarter of the main memory. The KNL configured as SNC-4 with MCDRAM as cache looks the same way.

In OCR, task and data placement is handled by the runtime. The OCR API provides a way to influence the placement using affinities. An affinity is an OCR abstraction which represents the hardware architecture. The OCR specification leaves the actual organization of affinities to the runtime implementation. It only provides a way to list all affinities, to get the affinity of the current task, and to set an affinity for data blocks and tasks. The runtime is also allowed to ignore any affinity specified by the application. A common solution is to make the affinities correspond to machines in a cluster. This way, if a task has the same affinity as a data block, it should have direct access to the data block's data. If two tasks share an affinity, they should be able to efficiently share data. The data and task placement within the affinity (the machine) is completely handled by the runtime.

An alternative is to use finer grained affinities. We have modified our runtime to provide one affinity per NUMA node, making the application more involved in data and task placement even within a node. Even a single machine may now have multiple affinities, making it look more like a distributed-memory system from the application's point of view. The OCR runtime uses the hwloc library to explore the hardware architecture and determine the number of affinities to provide.

However, the TBB task scheduler which we used within our OCR implementation cannot be used to execute tasks on a specified NUMA node. Thus, we have created our own NUMA-aware scheduler, which uses the same task-stealing principles as the TBB scheduler, but the threads are split into several groups corresponding to NUMA nodes. For example, in a four socket server capable of supporting 16 threads per core, the runtime uses 64 threads split into four groups with 16 threads per group. Each group is pinned (using OS thread affinities) to a different NUMA node. Task stealing is only done within a NUMA node, not across the boundaries. Therefore, if a task is spawned to a NUMA node, it is guaranteed to be executed by that NUMA node.

The same approach applies also to the KNL. If 128 worker threads are used on KNL configured as SNC-4, there will be four groups with 32 threads each. Naturally, only the four NUMA nodes that contain the cores are used, not the NUMA nodes with MCDRAM and zero cores.

3.2 High-Bandwidth Memory Support

Another issue is the high-bandwidth MCDRAM memory of the KNL. If it's con-figured as cache, no changes to the code are necessary. But to use the MCDRAM in flat mode, it is necessary to change the way memory is allocated by the application if the memory needs to be placed in the MCDRAM. Two options are available in that case. First, the `hbw_malloc` call can be used instead of the normal `malloc` function to allocate data in the MCDRAM. The way this data is placed in the MCDRAM (in which of the four MCDRAM nodes) is determined by the OS. The second alternative is to use `numa_alloc_onnode` and specify one of the NUMA nodes that correspond to the MCDRAM. In SNC-4 mode, this allows the application to specify which of the four nodes to use, giving it more control. Note that `numa_alloc_onnode` could also be used as an alternative to `malloc` to allocate data in a specific part of the DDR memory. In SNC-4 mode, allocating data on nodes 0 to 3 results in the data being placed in DDR, while allocating on nodes 4 to 7 places it in MCDRAM.

The modified OCR-Vsm runtime can be configured in four different ways: to use `malloc`, to use `hbw_malloc`, to use `numa_alloc_onnode` to place data in DDR, and to use to use `numa_alloc_onnode` to place data in MCDRAM. If the NUMA allocator is used to target DDR, the data is placed to the NUMA node that corresponds to the affinity provided by the user when the data block is created. If no affinity is given, it's placed in the NUMA node local to the task that created the data block. If the NUMA allocator targets MCDRAM, the placement algorithm is the same, except it places the data in the adjacent MCDRAM. For example, in SNC-4 mode, it uses NUMA node 4 instead of 0, 5 instead of 1, etc.

4   Experimental Evaluation

We have used the Seismic application, which was also used in our earlier work evaluating OCR on KNC, the previous Xeon Phi architecture [5]. However, the application was substantially updated, to better reflect the task nature of OCR.

4.1 Seismic Application

The original Seismic application is distributed as an example with the TBB library. It simulates propagation of seismic waves through 2D terrain. There are several properties associated with each grid point (stress, velocity, dampening, etc.). All values are stored as double precision floating point numbers and they are always processed in double precision. For our earlier experiments on the KNC, we modified the code to make it more computationally intense. No such modification was used this time. The code performs a comparable number of arithmetic operations and memory (load/store) operations. This makes the performance of the memory subsystem much more important. At the same time, the smaller amount of computation performed by each iteration makes any runtime overhead more pronounced.

Seismic runs in several iterations and each iteration comprises two phases. First, horizontal and vertical stress is updated for each grid point based on values of properties (other than the stresses) of the point and its neighbors to the right and below. Second, the seismic wave velocity is updated for each point based on properties (not including the velocity) of the point and its neighbors to the left and above. There are no dependences within a phase, just between phases. These dependences are limited only to dependences between neighbors. We have created three implementation variants of the Seismic code: using TBB, OpenMP, and OCR.

The TBB version is the code distributed as an example with the TBB library, with minimal modifications required to make it usable as a benchmark. The original Seismic is an interactive graphical application, with fixed problem size. We have removed the GUI code and put the simulation iterations into a simple for loop. We also modified the data structures to make the problem size configurable at runtime.

The OpenMP variant is very similar to the TBB code. The two phases of the simulation are performed by a parallel for loop. Although a different OpenMP parallelization strategy might be more efficient on the KNL, especially in the SNC-4 mode, we decided to use parallel for loops, because our goal is to investigate how common parallelization techniques compare to their OCR alternative.

In both codes, there are three levels of nested for loops. The outermost loop advances the iterations of the simulation. The middle loop iterates over the y-dimension. It is repeated two times, one after the other, doing the two phases in sequence. These two middle loops are the ones being parallelized using TBB parallel algorithms and OpenMP parallel for. The innermost loop (present in both middle loops) iterates over the x-dimension. Hints are provided for compiler auto-vectorization, so that the innermost loop is vectorized, i.e., SIMD instructions are used to perform several consecutive iterations of the loop together.

Due to the nature of the OCR programming model, the OCR code needs to be structured differently. To allow for distributed execution, the data is split into smaller blocks, each containing the same number of (consecutive) rows. These are distributed evenly across the available OCR affinities. Initially, one task is created for each block. This task is responsible for generating all tasks that are needed to perform one iteration step on the data block. If it is not the last iteration, another copy of this generator task is added at the end of the iteration. All tasks that process a certain block of data are bound (using OCR affinities) to the compute node where the data is located. The tasks that process neighboring blocks are synchronized using channel events, a new experimental extension of the OCR specification, which simplifies implementation of synchronization where the same pattern is repeated multiple times.

An example of the tasks and their dependences for one iteration is shown in Fig. 2. In the example, the data is split into two blocks. The tasks are labeled with their type, which corresponds to the C function they execute as their body. There are two phases per iteration and two worker tasks are used per block in each phase. The number of blocks and the number of tasks per block is configurable.

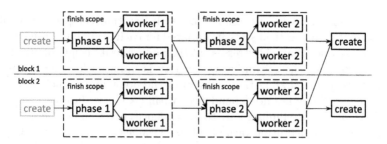

Fig. 2. An example of tasks (boxes) and their dependences (arrows) within one iteration of the Seismic on OCR, with data split into two blocks and with two tasks working on each block in every phase in parallel.

The `create` task creates all of the following tasks, up to (and including) the next `create`. A task called `phase 1` creates two worker tasks (of the `worker 1` type) to process the data block in parallel. The `phase 1` task is a *finish* task, which means that any further tasks it creates (denoted by the *finish scope* boxes) have to finish before the original finish task considered to be finished. Therefore, the `phase 2` task, which depends on the `phase 1` task, cannot start before both worker tasks finish. For this reason, the dependence is drawn going from the finish scope to the `phase 2` task. The dependences going across the block boundary (the vertical line in the middle of the picture) are used to exchange data and synchronize tasks that process neighboring blocks.

In the TBB and OpenMP codes, there is an (implicit) barrier at the end of each phase. There is no such barrier in the OCR code, except for the very end of the computation. This allows some tasks from the next phase to start before all of the tasks from the current phase have finished, which is not the case with the more coarsely synchronized TBB and OpenMP codes. Of course, the fine-grain synchronization could also be used with the TBB and OpenMP codes. While this style of programming is a natural fit for the OCR code, the high-level parallel for (`pragma` in OpenMP, parallel algorithm in TBB) is the first choice in OpenMP and TBB.

4.2   Application and Runtime Configuration

The applications provide several configuration options, depending on the implementation variant. The size of the data and number of iterations can be configured in all cases. We have used 8192 × 8192 as the data size, which translates to memory footprint of around 3 GB. With 1000 iterations, this provides a good reasonably long execution times (tens of seconds), but the data still easily fits into the MCDRAM, which we needed for some of the experiments. All source codes were compiled with GCC 6.3, with AVX-512 instruction set enabled.

The OpenMP runtime used in the OpenMP variant can be configured using environment variables. We have experimented with different thread placement, but the default option turned out to be the most efficient, so only the number of threads is adjusted by setting `OMP_NUM_THREADS`. Using 128 threads provided the fastest execution times. The task-based runtimes (TBB and all OCR variants) also performed best with 128 threads, except for the XSOCR, which performed best with 256 threads.

The TBB variant uses automatic task granularity selection provided by the `parallel_for` construct. The task granularity of the OCR Seismic code can be configured using command line parameters. For OCR-Vsm, the data was split into 128 equally-sized horizontal blocks and there was one task per block in each phase. In total, there are worker 128 tasks per phase. For XSOCR, we used 256 tasks per phase and 256 blocks. The task and block counts were obtained by manual tuning, where the relevant search space was exhaustively searched. The 128 and 256 tasks provided the best performance on the respective runtimes. Other configurations consistently resulted in a significant performance degradation (>30%).

The OpenMP and TBB applications can be configured to either use `malloc` or `hbw_malloc`. `malloc` is used in cache mode and in flat mode to avoid using the MCDRAM. `hbw_malloc` is used only in flat mode, to allocate application data in MCDRAM. The OCR-Vsm runtime can be configured in several ways. It's possible to either use the TBB scheduler or the new NUMA scheduler. The internal structures of the runtime are always allocated using `malloc`, but the data blocks (the application data) can be allocated using `malloc`, `hbw_malloc`, or `numa_alloc_onnode`.

The fastest options turned out to be `malloc` and `hbw_malloc` (i.e., the same allocators as the ones used in OpenMP and native TBB) when combined with the TBB scheduler. In quadrant mode, this was also the best option for the NUMA scheduler. The only exception is the NUMA scheduler on SNC-4, where `numa_alloc_onnode` was used with all MCDRAM modes. In flat mode, it can either be used to allocate data in the nearest DDR NUMA node or nearest MCDRAM node. In cache mode, it always targets the nearest DDR NUMA node, but the data is also automatically cached in the nearest MCDRAM.

4.3 Results

An overview of the results obtained by executing 1000 iterations of the different variants of the Seismic application is shown in Table 1. Note that in all cases, only the actual computation is timed. The measurements exclude application setup, where the runtimes are started, memory for application data is allocated and the data is filled with initial values. However, it does include task creation in the task-based variants. This is not only fair, it is also unavoidable since the tasks are created on the fly, not upfront (which was the case with our earlier Seismic OCR code [5]).

As you can see, the fastest version is either the native TBB application on a KNL configured in quadrant cluster mode and explicitly using the MCDRAM to store the data, or the OpenMP code on a KNL in quadrant mode with the MCDRAM serving as an automatic cache. The difference is too small to declare a clear winner.

Table 1. The execution time in seconds for 1000 iterations of the Seismic application, using different clustering modes (quadrant and SNC-4) and MCDRAM usage models (none, flat, cache). Mode *none* means that the machine was switched to flat (explicit) MCDRAM mode, but the data was allocated in DDR, not MCDRAM.

	Quadrant			SNC-4		
	None	Flat	Cache	None	Flat	Cache
OpenMP	92.44	20.69	17.38	100.01	80.94	25.56
TBB	92.72	17.32	18.53	110.23	78.80	40.24
OCR-Vsm TBB	93.83	20.93	19.33	95.29	34.04	25.48
OCR-Vsm NUMA	93.56	20.76	19.42	92.27	19.53	20.75
XSOCR	98.66	20.68	19.19	99.08	20.66	31.66

Table 2. The difference (in percent) between the slowest and fastest run. Each configuration was executed 10 times. A value of 0 would mean that every run had exactly the same execution time. A value of 100 would indicate that the longest run took double the time needed by the fastest run.

	Quadrant			SNC-4		
	None	Flat	Cache	None	Flat	Cache
OpenMP	0.13	2.38	2.09	5.28	2.82	10.46
TBB	0.43	1.35	2.72	3.16	10.56	7.84
OCR-Vsm TBB	0.34	1.08	1.56	2.36	38.02	10.93
OCR-Vsm NUMA	0.37	0.68	2.07	0.34	2.13	2.71
XSOCR	0.51	3.75	4.79	4.78	3.39	7.53

The results clearly show that it's essential to use the MCDRAM in codes like Seismic, which require high memory bandwidth. This is an expected result, but it's interesting to note the scale of the potential performance benefit. For example, the TBB variant is over 5.3x faster when `hbw_malloc` is used on the quadrant/flat configuration instead of plain `malloc`.

Using MCDRAM either directly or as a cache always provided some performance improvement. In most cases, the cache was more efficient than manual allocation, although there were several cases where it is the other way round (TBB on quadrant, OCR-Vsm NUMA on SNC-4, and XSOCR on SNC-4). The automatic and explicit MCDRAM management is not the only difference between the two modes. If the MCDRAM is used as cache, all memory accesses are cached, including data used by the runtime, like the memory used to store the tasks. In flat mode, OpenMP, TBB, and both OCR-Vsm variants only store the application data in MCDRAM. To make the XSOCR use the MCDRAM, we've changed the runtime source codes to make all allocations using `hbw_malloc`. This moves both application data and runtime data into the MCDRAM.

All application variants that use the MCDRAM run reasonably fast in the quadrant mode of the KNL. If we switch the KNL to SNC-4, this is no longer the case. It's important to note at this point that in SNC-4, the cost for memory accesses that cross the boundaries between the four core groups is significantly higher than in the quadrant mode. As a result, the codes that are not NUMA aware (all except for OCR-Vsm NUMA) suffer from a significant performance penalty. For example, the native TBB application is 2.2x slower in cache mode and 4.5x slower if `hbw_malloc` is used. OCR-Vsm NUMA provides similar results on quadrant and SNC-4, running even slightly faster on SNC-4 if MCDRAM is not used as cache. It's interesting to compare the performance of native TBB and OCR TBB on SNC-4/flat. The OCR-based code is 2.3x faster, despite using the same task scheduler. This shows that even a small change to the way data is allocated and the way tasks are created and submitted for execution can cause a significant difference in performance.

Each software/hardware configuration was executed 10 times. Table 2 shows the difference (in percent) between the slowest and fastest runs. If you look at the values for the TBB and OCR-Vsm TBB codes on SNC-4/flat, you can see a significant performance fluctuation (10.56% and 38.02%, respectively). This suggests that a necessary condition for a good result in these cases is that the TBB scheduler and `numad` manage to line up correctly. In quadrant mode, no automatic memory movement is performed (all MCDRAM is just one NUMA node), and the results are stable. The differences are just 1.35% and 1.08%.

5   Related Work

In the following, we briefly discuss a few related task-based runtimes and programming systems. We are not yet aware of any such system that would be tuned specifically for the KNL. However, of the three main optimization directions (vectorization, NUMA-aware parallelism, and MCDRAM) two were already relevant on existing systems. Vectorization is usually relevant inside of the tasks, so the runtimes are mostly concerned with efficient NUMA-aware task scheduling.

StarPU [1] was among the first task-based runtime systems that specifically targeted single-node heterogeneous architectures comprised of CPUs and GPUs. StarPU uses the `hwloc` library to explore the machine architecture and it creates combined workers based on this topology. The workers are then used by different schedulers provided by StarPU. Since StarPU is already used with architectures that combine different memories (e.g., local memory of a GPU), it should be possible to extend it to also deal with the MCDRAM. The schedulers could then also explicitly move data from DDR to MCDRAM.

OmpSs [4] extends the OpenMP shared-memory programming model with directives for task-parallel programming. The underlying runtime (Nanos++) also relies on the `hwloc` library. The socket-aware scheduler uses this information to keep tasks local (inside a NUMA node). It can be configured not to steal tasks from other NUMA nodes (like our scheduler) or to steal from neighboring nodes.

ParalleX [8] is a parallel and distributed programming model around the concept of message-driven work-queues supporting fine-grained parallel execution through cooperative lightweight threads within a global address space.

The HPX runtime system [9] is a C++-based implementation of ParalleX within an active global address space, which supports migration of objects between the nodes of clusters. HPX provides different schedulers and some of the schedulers can be configured to be *NUMA sensitive*, in which case they first try to steal work from the local NUMA node, before going to other nodes.

Legion [2] is a data-centric, task-based programming system that supports dynamic hierarchical data partitioning based on the concept of logical regions. Tasks are bound to regions and may access regions with different privileges and subject to different coherence modes. Legion provides a mapping interface that enables programmers to control the mapping of tasks and data regions to a specific parallel architecture. This mapping allows processors to be combined into *processor groups* and let the whole group serve a single work-queue. Processor groups can be created to mirror the NUMA nodes. An implementation of Legion on top of OCR is being realized within the US X-Stack program.

PaRSEC [3] is a generic framework for task-scheduling on heterogeneous many-core architectures. PaRSEC relies on a symbolic representations of task graphs that can be enhanced with user-provided priorities and data/task mappings that can take into account the NUMA characteristics of an architecture.

The Bobox system [7] is also a parallel and distributed programming model, but it is focused on applications that are close to database query evaluation. Yet it also successfully employs a task-based runtime. Its task scheduler is also NUMA-aware and, like most of the other systems, it first tries to steal tasks locally, before stealing across NUMA node boundaries.

6   Conclusion and Future Work

We have evaluated different implementations of the Seismic application on the KNL. We managed to extract very good performance from the KNL, using all of the programming models and runtimes. Native TBB and OpenMP variants were the fastest, but they were followed closely by the three OCR variants. This is a good result for the OCR, since the Seismic application is almost a textbook example of an application which can be parallelized with OpenMP.

For most variants, we achieved better performance on the non-NUMA quadrant clustering mode. The NUMA-aware OCR-Vsm runtime was slightly faster on SNC-4 (except when MCDRAM was used as cache), but the other variants, which are NUMA-oblivious, suffered a significant performance penalty. In our experience, mapping the four NUMA nodes of the KNL to four OCR affinities and treating it like a distributed system with four nodes is a reasonable solution. Overall, it seems the non-NUMA clustering mode is a better choice, except for very well-tuned NUMA-aware codes.

For a memory intensive application like Seismic, the MCDRAM is critical for achieving good performance. However, that may not always be the case. In our case, the application data is way too large to fit into L1 and L2 caches, but small enough to fit into the MCDRAM. Using the MCDRAM as cache worked very well as a result. However, if the data is very small (and mostly fits into L1 and L2 caches) or larger than the available MCDRAM, the application could suffer from the higher latency of cache misses caused by the extra cache level.

In the future, we plan to extend our NUMA-aware scheduler for the distributed-memory OCR implementation and to investigate hierarchical scheduling approaches and automatic means for utilizing the MCDRAM.

Acknowledgments. The work was supported in part by the Austrian Science Fund (FWF) project P 29783 Dynamic Runtime System for Future Parallel Architectures and by Charles University project PROGRES Q48.

References

1. Augonnet, C., Thibault, S., Namyst, R., Wacrenier, P.A.: StarPU: a unified platform for task scheduling on heterogeneous multicore architectures. Concurrency Comput. Pract. Exp. Euro-Par **2009**(23), 187–198 (2011)
2. Bauer, M., Treichler, S., Slaughter, E., Aiken, A.: Legion: expressing locality and independence with logical regions. In: Proceedings of the International Conference on High Performance Computing, Networking, Storage and Analysis, SC 2012, pp. 66:1–66:11. IEEE Computer Society Press, Los Alamitos (2012)
3. Bosilca, G., Bouteiller, A., Danalis, A., Faverge, M., Herault, T., Lemariner, P., Dongarra, J.: PaRSEC: exploiting heterogeneity to enhance scalability. IEEE Comput. Sci. Eng. **15**(6), 36–45 (2013)
4. Bueno, J., Planas, J., Duran, A., Badia, R., Martorell, X., Ayguade, E., Labarta, J.: Productive programming of GPU clusters with OmpSs. In: IPDPS 2012 Parallel Distributed Processing Symposium (2012)
5. Dokulil, J., Benkner, S.: Retargeting of the open community runtime to intel xeon phi. In: International Conference On Computational Science, ICCS 2015, pp. 1453–1462. Procedia Computer Science (2015)
6. Dokulil, J., Sandrieser, M., Benkner, S.: OCR-Vx - an alternative implementation of the open community runtime. In: International Workshop on Runtime Systems for Extreme Scale Programming Models and Architectures, in Conjunction with SC 2015, Austin, Texas (2015)
7. Falt, Z., Krulis, M., Bednarek, D., Yaghob, J., Zavoral, F.: Towards efficient locality aware parallel data stream processing. J. Univ. Comput. Sci. **21**(6), 816–841 (2015)
8. Hartmut, K., Brodowicz, M., Sterling, T.: Parallex an advanced parallel execution model for scaling-impaired applications. In: Proceedings of the 2009 International Conference on Parallel Processing Workshops (ICPPW 2009), pp. 94–401 (2009)
9. Kaiser, H., Heller, T., Adelstein-Lelbach, B., Serio, A., Fey, D.: HPX - a task based programming model in a global address space. In: The 8th International Conference on Partitioned Global Address Space Programming Models (PGAS) (2014)
10. Mattson, T.G., et al.: The open community runtime: a runtime system for extreme scale computing. In: 2016 IEEE High Performance Extreme Computing Conference (HPEC), pp. 1–7 (2016)
11. Mattson, T., Cledat, R. (eds.): The Open Community Runtime Interface, April 2016. https://xstack.exascale-tech.com/git/public?p=ocr.git;a=blob;f=ocr/spec/ocr-1.1.0.pdf

High-Performance Graphics in Racket with DirectX

Antoine Bossard[(✉)]

Graduate School of Science, Kanagawa University,
2946 Tsuchiya, Hiratsuka, Kanagawa 259-1293, Japan
abossard@kanagawa-u.ac.jp

Abstract. Nowadays, modern computer systems rely heavily on parallel processing, and not only because of the multicore CPUs bundled with any machine, even mobile devices, but more and more thanks to the parallel processing capacities of graphics processing units (GPU), general-purpose computing on graphics processing units (GPGPU) being one example. In this paper, relying on the DirectX 12 framework, we propose an innovative approach to enable parallel processing for graphical rendering on both the CPU and GPU for the popular Racket functional programming language (formerly PLT Scheme), and importantly without compromising Racket's usability and programmer-friendliness. Our performance evaluations show significant improvements with respect to execution time ($\times 3$ speed-up in some cases), CPU utilisation time (reduced by as much as 80% in some scenarios) and the frame rate when using moving graphics.

Keywords: GPU · Parallel processing · Functional · Programming · Scheme

1 Introduction

Advances in semiconductors enable to embed numerous processing cores onto graphics processing units (GPU), and the optimized parallel structures of GPUs make them suitable for parallel processing [1]. From a computer system point of view, this results in more parallel processing by offloading tasks from the CPU to the graphics hardware, recent GPUs embodying thousands of cores (e.g. 2560 for the Nvidia GTX 1080 [1]), compared with a few only for CPUs. In order to fully benefit from such hardware capacities, system vendors provide APIs to programmatically interact with the GPU, and in user mode (i.e. indirect but secured access to hardware). For instance, Nvidia has the CUDA parallel computing platform, and Microsoft provides the DirectX framework.

Direct2D is built on top of Direct3D in order to benefit from graphics hardware acceleration, Direct3D (from Direct3D 10) being itself built on top of the DirectX Graphics Infrastructure (DXGI). DXGI is the lowest layer of the user mode and is in charge of communicating with the kernel mode (drivers) [2]. In addition, Direct2D provides fallback to software rendering in case hardware

© Springer International Publishing AG 2017
S. Ibrahim et al. (Eds.): ICA3PP 2017, LNCS 10393, pp. 814–825, 2017.
DOI: 10.1007/978-3-319-65482-9_66

acceleration is unavailable. It is important to note that the software rasterizer provided by Direct2D performs significantly better than the legacy Graphics Device Interface (GDI, GDI+) software rendering solutions.

In this paper, our objective is to provide such parallel processing capacity for graphics on both the CPU and GPU to the popular Racket (previously PLT Scheme) functional programming language and development environment [3] with DirectX. More precisely, we shall propose for the first time an implementation of Direct2D into Racket and evaluate the induced performance. In addition, we aim at showing the high usability of such approach, compared to existing solutions. By focusing on DirectX, this research is obviously applicable to the Microsoft Windows implementation of Racket.

Racket provides the <dc%> interface to realise 2D graphics via a device context. The merit of this approach is its simplicity. Technically, it relies on the legacy GDI software renderer. In addition, Racket provides minimal support for 3D graphics with OpenGL. However, OpenGL's usability in Racket is very low: the function bindings are merely declared, thus inducing low usability due to complexity, especially for users targeting 2D graphics. Hence, currently, the Racket user is given the choice of either relying on the easy-to-use <dc%> interface which has poor performances, or switching to the overpowered OpenGL bindings which are not well suited for 2D graphics. And this is precisely to solve this dilemma for Windows native applications that Microsoft introduced Direct2D: it was too cumbersome to use Direct3D to "only" do 2D graphics. Hence, Direct2D, similarly to Racket's <dc%> interface, works in *immediate mode*, that is without handling graphics through a scene, as OpenGL and Direct3D do.

2   Preliminaries: The <dc%> Interface

Let us briefly recall the conventional method to render graphics inside a Racket window: canvas painting. This method relies on the legacy GDI software renderer. A frame (a.k.a. window) is first created, then a canvas is added onto it. The canvas object has a paint callback function which is called when its parent window requests repaint. Canvas drawing is conducted via the drawing context <dc%> interface, an instance of which is given as second parameter of the paint callback. Drawing commands such as **draw-rectangle** and **set-brush** are methods of the <dc%> interface; see Listing 1.1.

Listing 1.1. Conventional window painting with the <dc%> interface.

```
1  (define (dc-paint canvas dc) ; paint callback
2    (send dc set-pen"" 0 'transparent)
3    (send dc set-brush "blue" 'solid)
4    (send dc draw-rectangle 40 40 260 160))
5  (define classic-frame (new frame% [label "Classic"] [width 320] [height 240]))
6  (define classic-canvas (new canvas% [parent classic-frame] [paint-callback dc-paint]))
7  (send classic-canvas set-canvas-background (make-object color%))
8  (send classic-frame show #t) ; display window
```

3   Direct2D from Within Racket

3.1   Foreign Function Interface and COM

Racket enables the programmer to call foreign functions through the Foreign Function Interface (FFI). Amongst others, this library allows for easy external library loading, and makes data types that are originally absent from Racket, such as pointers, available. C structures are also accessible with the define-cstruct function; a structure of type A is then initialized with the main-A function which returns a pointer to the newly created structure.

The DirectX subsystem is accessible through the Component Object Model (COM) [4]. Yet, DirectX allows to abbreviate COM's CoCreate-Instance and QueryInterface calls to instantiate Direct2D interfaces by conveniently providing the D2D1CreateFactory function. Indeed, directly from the interface identifier of the ID2D1Factory interface (IID, here {06152247-6f50-465a-9245-118bfd3b6007}), this function will provide us with a pointer to a ID2D1Factory instance, the gate to Direct2D interfacing. Before being accessible from within Racket, the D2D1CreateFactory function needs to be loaded from the dynamic-linked library (DLL) d2d1.dll, which is done with the two functions of Listing 1.2.

Listing 1.2. Retrieving an instance of the ID2D1Factory COM interface.

```
1  (define-ffi-definer define-d2d1 (ffi-lib "d2d1.dll")) ; load library
2  (define-d2d1 D2D1CreateFactory ; import library function
3    (_hfun _int
4          (_ptr i _GUID) ; pointer to IID's value
5          _D2D1_FACTORY_OPTIONS-pointer/null
6          (pIFactory : (_ptr o _ID2D1Factory-pointer))
7          -> D2D1CreateFactory pIFactory)) ; return ID2D1Factory*
```

The FFI library also provides helper functions for COM. They are used in our implementation to manipulate interface's instances, like declaring and calling interface methods. For example, the previously retrieved ID2D1Factory instance requires to first declare the corresponding interface. Because interface methods are function pointers, the method declaration order within an interface has to be strictly reproduced. To obtain such information, it is required to investigate the Windows SDK header files. ID2D1Factory interface declaration is shown as example in Listing 1.3.

Interface methods that are not called in our program are simply declared as _fpointer. The only method we will call from this interface is CreateHwndRenderTarget, which is explained below. The #:release-with-function statement (l.10) indicates that the FFI library Release method is automatically called on the resulting instance (ID2D1HwndRenderTarget).

The next step is to use the factory instance to bind a Direct2D render target to a window. This is done by calling the CreateHwndRenderTarget method of the ID2D1Factory interface, specifying amongst others the handle (HWND) of

Listing 1.3. Declaring the ID2D1Factory COM interface.

```
1  (define-com-interface (_ID2D1Factory _IUnknown)
2    ([ReloadSystemMetrics _fpointer]
3     [GetDesktopDpi _fpointer]
4     ... ; the declaration of the other methods is abbreviated
5     [CreateHwndRenderTarget ; return ID2D1HwndRenderTarget*
6      (_hmfun _D2D1_RENDER_TARGET_PROPERTIES-pointer
7              _D2D1_HWND_RENDER_TARGET_PROPERTIES-pointer
8         (pHwndRenderTarget : (_ptr o _ID2D1HwndRenderTarget-pointer))
9         -> CreateHwndRenderTarget pHwndRenderTarget)
10      #:release-with-function Release]
11     [CreateDxgiSurfaceRenderTarget _fpointer]
12     [CreateDCRenderTarget _fpointer]))
```

the window to be bound. Window creation in Racket has been overviewed in Sect. 2; calling the window method `get-handle` returns the desired HWND. The other parameters are setting structures, which include the window dimensions. The first member of the D2D1_RENDER_TARGET_PROPERTIES structure is an important setting: it specifies whether to use hardware, software, or default rendering, the latter letting DirectX decide: hardware rendering if available, software rendering otherwise. The main result of the CreateHwndRenderTarget method is a pointer to a render target, in this case a pointer to an instance of the ID2D1HwndRenderTarget interface, which inherits from ID2D1RenderTarget. Henceforth, all Direct2D drawing primitives called on our render target instance shall be reflected in the window. This is illustrated in the next section.

3.2   Sample Application Implementation

In Listing 1.4 is a sample Racket application relying on Direct2D graphics. COM source code as introduced earlier is abbreviated. Line 8 shows that the first member of the D2D1_RENDER_TARGET_PROPERTIES structure is set to default rendering, hence letting DirectX choose between hardware and software rendering. Lines 10–12 correspond to Direct2D resources creation, like a blue brush.

Listing 1.4. Sample racket application relying on Direct2D graphics.

```
1  (define d2d-frame (new frame% [label "Direct2D"] [width 320] [height 240]))
2  (define d2d-hwnd (send d2d-frame get-handle))
3  (define-values (client-w client-h) (send d2d-frame get-client-size))
4  (define pDirect2dFactory (D2D1CreateFactory 0 IID_ID2D1Factory #f))
5  (define pRenderTarget
6    (CreateHwndRenderTarget
7     pDirect2dFactory
8     (make-D2D1_RENDER_TARGET_PROPERTIES 0 (make-D2D1_PIXEL_FORMAT 0 0) 0.0 0.0 0 0)
9     (make-D2D1_HWND_RENDER_TARGET_PROPERTIES d2d-hwnd (make-D2D_SIZE_U client-w client-h)
         0)))
10 (define pBlueColor (make-D3DCOLORVALUE 0.0 0.0 1.0 1.0))
11 (define pSolidColorBrush (CreateSolidColorBrush pRenderTarget pBlueColor #f))
12 (define pIdentityMatrix (make-D2D_MATRIX_3X2_F 1.0 0.0 0.0 1.0 0.0 0.0))
13 (send d2d-frame show #t) ; make the window visible
```

Listing 1.5. Function executing Direct2D actual drawing operations.

```
1 (define (d2d-paint)
2   (BeginDraw pRenderTarget)
3   (SetTransform pRenderTarget pIdentityMatrix)
4   (Clear pRenderTarget #f) ; black by default
5   (FillRectangle pRenderTarget (make-D2D_RECT_F 40.0 40.0 260.0 160.0) pSolidColorBrush)
6   (EndDraw pRenderTarget))
```

In addition, we define the **d2d-paint** function to conduct Direct2D actual operations such as drawing (see Listing 1.5). Direct2D enforces immediate mode rendering; its operations are delimited by the BeginDraw and EndDraw methods of the ID2D1RenderTarget interface. Once the window created and displayed, evaluating in the Racket REPL the **d2d-paint** function updates the window.

3.3   Window Interaction Improvement

In the previous section, we have shown with a sample application that once the window created by Racket, it is possible to emit Direct2D commands which will update and render graphics inside the window. Yet, the common approach is to render graphics at window creation time, that is, not first displaying a blank window. The conventional approach is to execute drawing commands when the application receives the WM_PAINT message. In Racket, as illustrated in Sect. 2, this is done by adding a canvas to the window (for drawing operations), and by providing a paint callback to the canvas, the callback providing access to the <dc%> for drawing. This callback function would be called each time the system needs to update the window content.

If we follow the same approach of adding a canvas to the window and conducting Direct2D graphical operations onto this canvas (through the canvas' HWND handle, a canvas being a child window), we run into the following issue. Since a canvas is double-buffered [5], any change made inside canvas' paint callback function by Direct2D, that is directly through the canvas' HWND handle, and not through its <dc%>, is ineffective as the very last operation once the paint callback function completed is the buffer swap between the back buffer and the front buffer (this buffer swap operation is an implicit finalisation operation by a canvas). So, we *have to* use the window's HWND handle directly as we unfortunately can not rely on a canvas' HWND handle.

This is indeed unfortunate as, unlike for a canvas object, there is no easy way to catch the painting event for a window created in Racket. One solution to catch the WM_PAINT message for our Racket window is to subclass the window. This can be done by using the comctl32.dll library function SetWindowSubclass to install a new layer of WindowProc callback for message catching and processing. Messages not handled by the newly installed WindowProc are directly forwarded to the next WindowProc callback with a call to DefSubclassProc. See Listing 1.6. Even though we successfully subclassed the Racket window to catch messages, it was at the cost of application stability and responsiveness.

Listing 1.6. Subclassing a racket window to catch repaint events.

```
1  (define-comctl32 SetWindowSubclass ; import library function
2    (_wfun _pointer
3      (_wfun _pointer _uint _long _long _intptr _intptr -> _long)
4      _intptr _intptr -> _int))
5  (define-comctl32 DefSubclassProc ; import library function
6    (_wfun _pointer _uint _long _long -> _long))
7  (define (my-proc hWnd uMsg wParam lParam uIdSubClass dwRefData)
8    (if (= uMsg 15) ; WM_PAINT message
9      (begin (d2d-paint) 0) ; message processed, return 0
10     (DefSubclassProc hWnd uMsg wParam lParam))) ; forward other messages
11 (SetWindowSubclass d2d-hwnd my-proc 0 0) ; subclass the window
```

As the subclassing approach was not satisfactory, we considered to instead rely on a canvas for its paint callback which catches repaint messages, but forcing the canvas to stay transparent so that the double-buffering issue does not erase Direct2D renderings made on the canvas' underlying window (see Fig. 1). This can be achieved by specifying the 'no-autoclear canvas style when instantiating the canvas% class. Yet, at window display time the canvas would still erase underlying window graphics. To address this remaining issue, one trick is to use the 'gl canvas style in addition to 'no-autoclear, this time completely preventing canvas underlying content erasing. Eventually, the window is created as in Listing 1.7.

Listing 1.7. Window creation for repaint event catching with DirectX rendering.

```
1  (define d2d-frame (new frame% [label "Direct2D"] [width 320] [height 240]))
2  (new canvas% [parent d2d-frame] [style '(no-autoclear gl)]
3    [paint-callback (lambda (cv dc) (d2d-paint))])
```

Another satisfactory approach is to use a canvas with the 'no-autoclear style only and with the same paint callback, and make a trade-off to catch repaint messages with the on-superwindow-show message which is triggered upon window visibility changes, including the window creation event. Still, visibility change events are not identical to repaint events, hence the trade-off. The merit here is clarity (no 'gl canvas style trick). This is done by deriving the frame% class and calling the refresh method to trigger the canvas paint callback (see Listing 1.8).

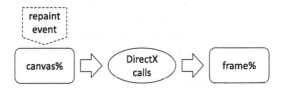

Fig. 1. Catching repaint events with a canvas but directly drawing onto the window.

Listing 1.8. Deriving the `frame%` class to catch visibility change events.

```
1  (define d2d-frame%
2    (class frame% ; base class
3      (define/override (on-superwindow-show shown?) ; catch visibility changes
4        (when shown? (send this refresh))) ; request a repaint
5      (super-new))) ; base class constructor
```

As a result, we solved all the repainting issues so that our DirectX-enabled window behaves fully as a normal Racket window, and as a normal window in general. Now, the COM interfacing, COM interface method calls and other various technical issues of the proposed Direct2D Racket system must induce computational overhead. It is thus important to evaluate the performance that can be achieved with this system. This is the purpose of the next section.

4 Performance Evaluation

We quantitatively measure the performance of our DirectX implementation and the gains made compared to the conventional `<dc%>` approach with several experiments. The results were obtained with the `time` Racket function and reported as *CPU time* (i.e. actual CPU time taken to run the program), *real time* (i.e. actual execution time of the program) and *garbage collection time*. We conducted experiments with both hardware and software Direct2D rendering modes.

The experiments were conducted on a computer equipped with a 4-core (8-thread) Intel Core i7-4510U CPU (mobile processors) and its embedded GPU Intel HD 4400 (GT2) which includes 20 cores. Importantly as our implementation relies on DirectX 12, hardware acceleration is available and this GPU supports the Direct3D device driver interface (DDI) 12 and has feature levels up to 11_1.

4.1 Experiment 1 - Simple Shapes

The first performance evaluation experiment focused on drawing simple shapes, precisely a large amount of rectangles (10,000) inside a 640×480 pixels window, measuring the time required for rendering. The drawing function `d2d-paint` for our Direct2D approach, and `dc-paint` for the conventional `<dc%>` one are given in Listing 1.9. Each of the two programs was run 3 times consecutively.

Both interpreted (i.e. run from within the Racket development environment DrRacket) and compiled (i.e. run from an executable file) versions of these experiment programs were tested. First, the results obtained with the conventional `<dc%>` approach and the Direct2D software rendering mode are given in Table 1.

Next, the results obtained with the Direct2D hardware rendering mode are given in Table 2. In this table, the results obtained with the conventional `<dc%>` approach are those from Table 1 as they are indeed not impacted by the software/hardware rendering modes of Direct2D.

Listing 1.9. Drawing functions for Experiment 1.

```
1  (define (d2d-paint)
2    (BeginDraw pRenderTarget)
3    (SetTransform pRenderTarget pIdentityMatrix)
4    (Clear pRenderTarget #f)
5    (for ([i (in-range 1 10000)]) ; 1 <= i < 10000 (integers)
6      (FillRectangle pRenderTarget (make-D2D_RECT_F 0.0 0.0 (exact->inexact i)
           (exact->inexact i)) pSolidColorBrush))
7    (EndDraw pRenderTarget))
8  (define (dc-paint canvas dc)
9    (send dc set-pen "" 0 'transparent)
10   (send dc set-brush "blue" 'solid)
11   (for ([i (in-range 1 10000)]) (send dc draw-rectangle 0 0 i i)))
```

Table 1. Performance comparison of the conventional `<dc%>` approach and the Direct2D software rendering mode (Experiment 1). Units: milliseconds.

	Conventional (`<dc%>`)			Direct2D (software)		
	CPU	real	gc	CPU	real	gc
interpret.	766	770	31	735	216	0
	750	748	16	782	201	0
	718	717	0	766	201	0
compiled	688	718	0	750	216	0
	718	720	0	750	200	0
	703	702	0	812	201	0

Table 2. Performance comparison of the conventional `<dc%>` approach and the Direct2D hardware rendering mode (Experiment 1). Units: milliseconds.

	Conventional (`<dc%>`)			Direct2D (hardware)		
	CPU	real	gc	CPU	real	gc
interpret.	766	770	31	125	804	0
	750	748	16	172	782	0
	718	717	0	172	788	0
compiled	688	718	0	172	760	0
	718	720	0	110	776	0
	703	702	0	94	808	0

4.2   Experiment 2 - Animation

While Experiment 1 focused on the rendering of still simple shapes, in this second experiment, we measure the performance of our approach in the case of animations. Concretely, using the same machine as in Experiment 1, we render numerous small shapes in a grid fashion, and the animation consists in rotating the whole by 0.1 radian at each frame. The performance is quantitatively measured with the frame per second (FPS, a.k.a. frame rate) metric which is commonly used by various graphics benchmarks.

More precisely, the animation involved 8×8 pixels circles, filled according to a linear gradient brush horizontal and 100 pixels wide, with three stops: red at 0.0, green at 0.5 and blue at 1.0. Anti-aliasing was used (default anti-aliasing for Direct2D, and set-smoothing set to 'smoothed for the device context of the conventional <dc%> approach). The drawing functions used in the <dc%> and Direct2D cases are shown in Listing 1.10. It can be observed that the two functions are as similar as possible for fair evaluation. In the <dc%> case, the translation transformation is already applied as preprocessing, hence not appearing in the drawing function (this can thus be seen as a slight performance disadvantage for our approach; we will see that our approach anyway beats clearly the conventional one).

Listing 1.10. Drawing functions for Experiment 2.

```
 1 (define (dc-paint canvas dc)
 2   (send dc clear)
 3   (send dc rotate 0.1)
 4   (for* ([x (in-range -320 320 10)] [y (in-range -240 240 10)])
 5     (send dc draw-ellipse x y 8 8)))
 6
 7 (define (d2d-paint)
 8   (BeginDraw pRenderTarget)
 9   (Clear pRenderTarget #f)
10   (mat32-multiply! pMatrix pRotMatrix) ; rotation
11   (SetTransform pRenderTarget (mat32-multiply pMatrix pTranslateMatrix)) ; translation
12   (for* ([x (in-range -320 320 10)] [y (in-range -240 240 10)])
13     (FillEllipse pRenderTarget (make-D2D1_ELLIPSE (make-D2D_POINT_2F (exact->inexact x)
              (exact->inexact y)) 4.0 4.0) pGradientBrush))
14   (EndDraw pRenderTarget))
```

The animation loop in the <dc%> case is given in Listing 1.11. It is exactly the same for the Direct2D case, except that d2d-paint is called instead of dc-paint, and d2d-frame instead of classic-frame. See Fig. 2 for a screenshot of the animation. The frame rates for the first 50 frames of the animation are given in Table 3.

Listing 1.11. Animation loop for Experiment 2.

```
 1 (define (run-classic)
 2   (send classic-frame show #t)
 3   (let run ([t (current-milliseconds)])
 4     (yield)
 5     (dc-paint classic-canvas dc)
 6     (let ([t2 (current-milliseconds)])
 7       (displayln (/ 1 (* 0.001 (- t2 t)))) ; FPS value
 8       (run t2))))
```

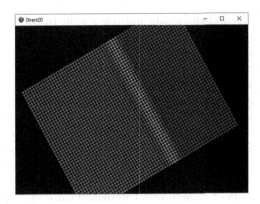

Fig. 2. Screenshot of the rotating animation in Experiment 2.

Table 3. Performance comparison of the conventional `<dc%>` approach and the Direct2D one with animation (Experiment 2). Units: FPS (the higher the better).

	`<dc%>`	D2D (software)	D2D (hardware)
FPS	6	38	61
Flickering	severe	none	none

5   Results Discussion

First, we notice from Experiment 1 results that there is no significant performance difference between interpreted and compiled versions of the programs. Then, it is important to observe that the conventional approach induces longest (or near-longest) times in both CPU time and real time. Now, when using Direct2D in software mode, the CPU time stays similar to that of the conventional approach (an average time increase of +6% for the Direct2D approach with respect to the `<dc%>` approach) while the real time is reduced by about 70% (an average time decrease of 72% for the Direct2D approach with respect to the `<dc%>` approach), which is a first significant positive result. That the CPU time is not improved is no surprise since the rendering, even though using Direct2D, is done in software-mode, that is without any support by GPU hardware. Hence the time taken by the CPU in total is similar to the `<dc%>` approach. The execution time (real time) significant improvement can be explained by the multicore architecture of the CPU used for the experiment.

Regarding the hardware rendering experiment, this is the reversed situation. Effectively, while the execution time (real time) remains similar to that of the conventional approach (an average time increase of +8% for the Direct2D approach with respect to the `<dc%>` approach), the CPU time taken in total by the hardware-accelerated Direct2D program is reduced by about 80% (an average time decrease of 81% for the Direct2D approach with respect to the `<dc%>`

approach), which a second significant positive result. In Direct2D hardware rendering mode, graphics-related processing is mainly conducted on the GPU, so the total CPU time taken stays very low. Yet, the execution time remains high since the GPU used in this experiment is low-end (CPU embedded), and the graphics involved are simple. Still, being able to achieve such a CPU usage reduction (balanced with GPU usage obviously) is an important achievement for at least two reasons: (1) CPU time is made available for other system applications, especially those that do not rely on the GPU (they are a majority), and (2) CPUs have a much lower GFLOP/Watt ratio than GPUs [7], especially when considering the GFLOP per second per processing element (core) ratio [6], and are thus much less environment-friendly (see Green 500 [8]) than GPUs.

The positive results of Experiment 1 were confirmed by Experiment 2. Effectively, from the frame rate measurements obtained in the second experiment, it is easy to assess the large performance increase when using our Direct2D approach compared to the conventional `<dc%>` approach. We would observe a jump from an average 6 FPS for the `<dc%>` approach to full animation fluidity with Direct2D. Also, when measuring the average frame rate of the first 50 frames, we noticed a 40% FPS increase when using the hardware mode of Direct2D compared to its software mode. Qualitatively, it is also important to mention that the conventional `<dc%>` approach produced severe ickering during the animation.

6   Conclusions

Parallel processing is ubiquitous nowadays. Furthermore, with advances in GPU multicore technologies, parallel processing has become essential for graphical rendering. In this paper, we have proposed an innovative approach to enable parallel processing for graphical rendering inside the Racket development environment. We showed (1) that it is possible to use DirectX within a Racket program, even interpreted; (2) that it is easy: we proposed an elegant implementation; and (3) that it gives excellent results thanks to parallel processing capacities of the CPU and GPU chips. Precisely, we managed to reduce the CPU time for graphics by more than 80% in average with the Direct2D hardware rendering mode compared to the legacy approach. Also, by using the Direct2D software rendering mode instead of the legacy `<dc%>` approach of Racket, we were able to achieve in average a ×3 execution speed-up. Eventually, we confirmed that the animation frame rate was significantly higher when using Direct2D instead of `<dc%>`. Regarding future work, accessing Nvidia's CUDA from within Racket is meaningful.

References

1. Nvidia, GeForce GTX 1080 user guide (2016)
2. Luna, F.: 3D game programming with DirectX 12 (Chapter 4). Mercury Learning and Information, Dulles (2016)
3. Flatt, M.: Creating languages in Racket. Comm. ACM **55**(1), 48–56 (2012)

4. Box, D.: Essential COM. Addison-Wesley Professional, Boston (1998)
5. Sheeparamatti, R.B., Sheeparamatti, B.G., Bharamagoudar, M., Ambali, N.: Simulink model for double buffering. In: Proceedings of the 32nd Conference on IEEE Industrial Electronics, pp. 4593–4597. Paris (2006)
6. Rupp, K.: CPU, GPU and MIC Hardware Characteristics over Time (2013–2016). https://www.karlrupp.net/2013/06/cpu-gpu-and-mic-hardware-characteristics-over-time/. Accessed 29 June 2017
7. Hindriksen, V.: Processors that can do 20+ GFLOPS per Watt (2012). https://streamcomputing.eu/blog/2012-08-27/processors-that-can-do-20-gflops-watt/. Accessed 29 June 2017
8. Feng, W.-C., Cameron, K.: The green500 list: Encouraging sustainable supercomputing. Computer **40**(12), 50–55 (2007)

Author Index

Acevedo, César 489
Acosta, Alejandro 81
Afonso, Sergio 81
Alapati, Praveen 776
Almeida, Francisco 81
An, Hong 18
Ayres, Daniel L. 533

Badosa, Ferran 489
Bała, Piotr 503
Barrachina, Sergio 548
Benkner, Siegfried 801
Bossard, Antoine 814
Botella, Guillermo 569
Bzhalava, Davit 503

Cai, Xiaojun 115, 735
Cao, Liang 165
Cao, Pengfei 387, 420
Carriço, João A. 591
Castillo, Maribel 548
Chai, Zhilei 65
Challal, Yacine 149
Chaves, Javier 513
Chen, Hanhua 180
Chen, Jing 285
Chen, Junshi 18
Chen, Mingsong 65
Chen, Sijia 642
Chen, Wenjie 65
Chen, Wenzhi 51
Chen, Xin 345
Chen, Xue 633
Chen, Yan 623
Chen, Yijie 441
Chen, Yong 18, 180
Cheng, Cheng 715
Cheng, Yanxiao 476
Chernoskutov, Mikhail 759
Cores, Fernando 601
Crockett, Keeley 407
Cuadrado, Andrés Sánchez 749
Cummings, Michael P. 533

Damas, Miguel 580
Daniel García, J. 749
De Argila, Jordi Rambla 548
De Giusti, Armando 569, 766
del Rio Astorga, David 749
Deng, Robert H. 297
Díaz Redondo, Rebeca P. 407
Díaz, Antonio Francisco 580
Ding, Wenxiu 297
Dokulil, Jiri 801
Dolz, Manuel F. 749
Dong, Bo 465

E, Haihong 359, 372
Escobar, Juan José 580
Espinosa, Antonio 489
Evans, Lewis 407

Fang, Binxing 313
Farkas, Lóránt 452
Farré, Xavier 548
Feng, Jinghua 431
Feng, Jun 705
Feng, Yongquan 268
Fernández, Javier 749
Fernández-Vilas, Ana 407
Finta, István 452
Fonal, Krzysztof 211
Francisco, Alexandre P. 591
Fu, Hao 239

Gallego-Sánchez, Daniel 523
Gao, Hui 705
García, Ana-Bárbara 513
Garcia, Carlos 569
Gheid, Zakaria 149
González, César 513
González, Jesús 580
Granado-Criado, José M. 523
Guirado, Fernando 601
Guo, Yunchuan 313

Hagihara, Kenichi 254
Hao, Mi 715

Haudebourg, Timothée   132
He, Chunjiang   180
He, Daojing   65
Holmbacka, Simon   3
Hu, Xiaoteng   239
Hu, Yi   431
Hu, Yingxi   372
Huang, Haibing   225
Huang, Kai   33
Huang, Yanyan   239

Ino, Fumihiko   254

Ji, Ke   397
Jia, Zhiping   115, 735
Jiang, Zigui   658
Jin, Hai   180
Jiujun, Cheng   715

Keller, Jörg   3
Knoll, Alois   33

Lei, Haijun   735
Li, Chen   239
Li, Fenghua   313
Li, Guoxi   51
Li, Kun   239
Li, Shuai   678
Li, Xiaole   99
Liang, Weihao   18
Liao, Chung-Yu   197
Lin, Changwei   359
Lin, Cheng-Hung   197
Lin, Rongheng   658
Liu, Linlin   33
Liu, Luning   345
Liu, Weiyu   345
Liu, Xiaoguang   225
Liu, Zhenyu   687
Liu, Zhihan   658
Lladós, Jordi   601
Lu, Xiaoxiao   791
Lu, Zhaoming   345
Lu, Zhongyong   51
Luo, Xiao   633

Ma, Kun   397
Ma, Yangyang   65
Martínez, Héctor   548

Meng, Jia   165
Monteiro, Pedro T.   591
Mutyam, Madhu   776

Naiouf, Marcelo   569, 766
Navarro, Arcadi   548
Niu, Xiangyang   331
Nowicki, Marek   503

Orduña, Juan M.   513
Orgerie, Anne-Cécile   132
Ortega, Julio   580
Ou, Zhonghong   359, 372
Owda, Majdi   407

Pérez, Mariano   513
Pérez-Wohlfeil, Esteban   611
Petraglio, Enrico   558
Prieto-Matias, Manuel   569

Qin, Hao   115
Que, Xirong   678
Quintana-Ortí, Enrique S.   548

Ren, Mingming   225
Ripoll, Ana   489
Ruan, Jianfei   465
Ruan, Ou   285
Rubio-Largo, Álvaro   523
Rucci, Enzo   569

Santander-Jiménez, Sergio   523
Santos, Francisco C.   591
Sanz, Victoria   766
Saranam, Swamy   776
Sergyán, Szabolcs   452
Shang, Zhaohui   431
Shen, Jingcheng   254
Shigeoka, Kentaro   254
Sigg, Stephan   695
Singh, Isha   695
Song, Bin   642
Song, Meina   359, 372
Stones, Rebecca J.   225
Su, Kui   51
Sun, Chao   431, 791
Sun, Jizhou   431, 791
Sun, Yanwei   313
Szénási, Sándor   452

Tang, Yuhua 268
Tao, Jing 387, 420
Teixeira, Andreia Sofia 591
Thoma, Yann 558
Torreno, Oscar 611
Trelles, Oswaldo 611

Vega-Rodríguez, Miguel A. 523
Vera, Gonzalo 489

Wang, Dongbin 441
Wang, Gang 225
Wang, Hua 99
Wang, Jianmei 791
Wang, Lei 633
Wang, Rui 115, 735
Wang, Ruidong 705
Wang, Wendong 678, 705
Wang, XianChao 331
Wang, Xiebing 33
Wang, Xinrui 372
Wang, Zheng 387, 420
Wang, Zonghui 51
Wei, Wenda 465
Wen, Xiangming 345
Wertenbroek, Rick 558
Wu, Tianhao 652

Xi, Teng 678
Xiao, Jian 239, 431, 791
Xu, Liyang 268
Xu, Qingqing 18
Xu, Xinhai 268

Yaghob, Jakub 801
Yan, Jie 431
Yan, Zheng 297, 465, 476
Yang, Bo 397

Yang, Fangchun 658
Yang, Xiuzhu 668
Yao, Juncheng 180
Yao, Wenbin 441
Yao, Xibo 99
Yi, Shanwen 99
Yin, Lihua 313
Yu, Ce 239, 431, 791
Yu, Huashan 165
Yu, Yang 18
Yu, Ziqiang 397

Zdunek, Rafał 211
Zhai, Linbo 99
Zhai, Ruirui 623
Zhan, Yanghao 623
Zhang, Lin 652, 668, 687
Zhang, Mian 331
Zhang, Mingwu 285
Zhang, Qiqi 658
Zhang, Rui 225
Zhang, Sulan 331
Zhang, Tao 725
Zhang, Yan 387, 420
Zhang, Ying 642
Zhang, Yongjun 268
Zhang, Yue 642
Zhang, Zhiwei 735
Zhang, Zhiyong 115, 735
Zhao, Jia 331
Zhao, Qiqi 387, 420
Zhao, Shuai 725
Zhao, Yue 225
Zheng, Qinghua 465
Zheng, Shang 715
Zhenhua, Huang 715
Zhu, Fangjin 99